RICHMOND CROOM BEATTY
Vanderbilt University

FLOYD C. WATKINS
Emory University

THOMAS DANIEL YOUNG
Mississippi Southern College

RANDALL STEWART
General Editor
Brown University

Scott, Foresman and Company · Chicago, Atlanta, Dallas, New York

The Literature of **THE SOUTH**

Design by Catherine Hinkle

Illustrations by Franz Altschuler

part **1**

THE EARLY SOUTH
to 1815

CONTENTS

part 2

THE RISE OF THE CONFEDERATE SOUTH
1815–1865

Poe

Kennedy

The Charleston School

Humorists of the Old Southwest

Spirituals

Civil War Songs

part **3**

THE NEW SOUTH

1865–1918

x

Defenders of the Ante-Bellum Society

Spokesmen for the New South

Lanier

Local Colorists

part 4

THE MODERN RENAISSANCE
1918 to the present

xii

Folk Trends

Poets and Critics

xiii

xiv

I

In the literary history of the United States, certain regions have in one period or another taken a position of distinct leadership. In the 1820's and 1830's, for example, New York City—with writers like Bryant, Irving, and Cooper—was our literary capital, but before the middle of the century, leadership had passed to New England, with Boston the chief literary center. New England's primacy lasted for several decades, not only during the great Flowering of Emerson, Thoreau, and Hawthorne, but well into the Indian Summer of Emily Dickinson and Henry Adams; for as late as the end of the century no region had challenged the New England hegemony, despite the isolated brilliance of such figures as Walt Whitman and Mark Twain. In the twentieth century our literary center has already shifted twice, dramatically: first to the Middle West, where during the first quarter of the century Dreiser, Lindsay, Anderson, Sandburg, and others provided a brilliant literary leadership; and subsequently to the South. As yet, the Southern literary movement shows no sign of falling off.

The South's leadership during the last twenty-five or thirty years is now generally recognized, and it has become accepted usage to speak of the "Southern literary renaissance." This renaissance—like all great, vital movements—is far-reaching and widespread. It takes in not only the well-known names (Faulkner, Wolfe, Caldwell, Young, Ransom, Tate, Warren, and the like), but many lesser names as well. The literary activity is widely diffused. The *furor scribendi* has taken possession of many breasts; writers, manuscripts spring up everywhere. It is scarcely an exaggeration to say that the South of today recalls the England of Elizabeth, if not in the literary products themselves, at least in the contagion of its fine frenzy. Like Elizabethan England, it has become a nest of singing birds.

No one knows what brought this renaissance about, but a few observations may be ventured on the movement itself. One is that it was long deferred. The older South was politically minded, and the best Southern talents went into politics. Writing might be a gentleman's avocation, the adornment of his idle hours, and an amusement to his private friends, but hardly a profession or a means of livelihood. Poe and Simms, it is true, were hard-working professionals, but neither was in very good "standing" in the South during his lifetime, or for a considerable time thereafter. These explanations, however, do not really account for the unconscionable delay in the South's literary

FOREWORD

xvi

flowering, but merely put the real explanation at one remove further. It is perhaps sufficient here to say that the Southern renaissance was by an inscrutable
wisdom deferred until (in the words of Saint Paul) "the fulness of the time was
come." For its copiousness and force are surely owing in part to the fact that the
creative energies had been so long pent up.

A second observation is that the renaissance has coincided in time with the
industrial transformation of the South. Before 1918, industrial change moved at
a snail's pace, comparatively speaking; since that date, it has gone by leaps and
bounds. A Southern exile returns today to find, to his surprise and perhaps his
grief, that the tempo of Atlanta or Birmingham, of Richmond or Nashville even,
is not much slower than that of the great Northern cities. Southern writers have
dealt seriously with the change. Some have praised the old order, or have pointed
out ancestral virtues which men would do well to emulate in any age. Others have
shown the impact of the new order—the disintegration of the old under the impact, the dislocations and deracinations, the gains in science and democracy, the
losses in stability and tone. It might be said that the grand subject of the modern
Southern writers is "The South in Transition." More than once in the world's
history, a sharp social transition seems to have provided the most favorable creative situation. The important literary movements and the great writers—Dante,
Shakespeare, and the rest—have appeared when the world, or a particular part of
it, was moving into a new phase. The South of our time has been moving
out of a kind of feudalism into something more progressive but possibly less
interesting.

A third observation is that while from one point of view modern Southern literature dwarfs the earlier literary achievements of the South (about forty per
cent of the present volume belongs to the modern period), from another, it
throws light upon and actually enhances all that has gone before, very much as
a distinguished man awakens an interest in, and gives a new value to, his ancestry. For there are ancestral ties which bind the modern writers to the older
writers of the South, and it should be one of the occupations of the student of
Southern literature to discover what these ties are. As these connections are explored, backward and forward, it will become clear that the literary importance
of the South dates not from 1918, but from the very beginning; that the present
mighty stream (though often fed by tributaries from outside the South) had its
origins in the Southern literary past. The present volume, accordingly, serves
several useful aims: it applauds the achievements of the moderns, while claiming
for the older literature an importance scarcely accorded it hitherto; it shows the
continuity of Southern letters. The older literature, indeed, becomes more dear
both for its own sake and for its connections with what was to follow.

II

What is a Southern writer? Is there a Southern literary tradition? What are
the distinguishing marks of the Southern mind and the Southern way of life, and
consequently of the literature in which the mind and the way of life are reflected?
To what extent is Southern literature provincial, and to what extent is the provincialism modified by world influences? There are no categorical answers to these
questions, but the student of Southern literature ought to address himself to such
questions and speculate freely upon them.

xvii

The genuinely Southern writer is usually recognizable as such. He almost necessarily grew up in the South. He shows an awareness of Southern ties and cannot throw them off if he would. Consciously or unconsciously, he is likely to exhibit Southern "prejudices" (in much the same way in which people of other regions are likely to exhibit theirs). Although he may live in later years outside the South, he will continue to draw upon a fund of Southern materials for his writing. Most of the writers in the present volume fit such a description, at least approximately, and some writers with certain claims to eligibility have been excluded because they do not fit it sufficiently. Mark Twain, for example, whose dominant milieu was the West, hardly belongs in this collection despite the rich Southern matter in a book like *Huckleberry Finn;* nor does Woodrow Wilson, the greatest statesman to come out of the South since the Civil War, belong, because his Southern relationships too soon became tenuous and his writings took little color from his Southern experience.

The South not being everywhere the same, the Southern experience has been richly varied, and this variety is reflected in the literature. One cannot speak, therefore, of *"the* Southern literary tradition," for there have been several traditions, and oftentimes two or more are mingled in the work of a single author.

There is, for example, the courtly, sophisticated (or "tidewater") tradition which is first exemplified in William Byrd and reappears in later writers as different from each other as Ellen Glasgow, Stark Young, and John Crowe Ransom. There is, in sharp contrast to this, the frontier tradition, with more than a touch of the uncouth and wild, which is best displayed in Longstreet's *Georgia Scenes* and G. W. Harris' *Sut Lovingood's Yarns*, and which in the modern period dominates a good deal of the writing of Thomas Wolfe. The courtly and frontier strains are sometimes found combined, as in the work of Mary Noailles Murfree and Robert Penn Warren, masters of both traditions.

A literary, rather than a social and geographic, approach to the question of tradition yields the well-worn yet useful categories of "classic" and "romantic." Many Southern writers have followed the classical tradition, if by that term is meant restraint and a nice attention to form. The classical tradition, indeed, was dominant in the South until well into the nineteenth century—witness the Charleston of the 1830's. Perhaps—despite the romantic lushness of a Lanier, or the romantic extravagance of a Simms or a G. W. Harris or a Wolfe—it has never ceased to be dominant, in somewhat the same way in which the classical has prevailed over the romantic in the long history of French literature. It might well be asked if there is a correspondence between the two pairs of categories, courtly-frontier and classic-romantic, and the answer would seem to be that there is one. The writers whose roots are in the old centers of culture (witness the writers of Charleston, Richmond, Nashville) are likely to follow the classical tradition of form and decorum, while those belonging to the frontier or hill country are likely to display the vagaries of the romantic, though exceptions must be allowed for in each case (Simms himself was an exception in the older Charleston). The correspondence, at all events, should not be pushed too hard, and the truth is perhaps to be found in what Edd Winfield Parks has called "the duality of Southern intellect," the intermingling of classic and romantic, of tidewater and frontier.

There are still other traditions. There is, for example, the patriotic tradition, which has been unusually strong in Southern literature. Southern writers have in general displayed an extraordinary love of the South; most of them would agree with Timrod when he said,

> No fairer land hath fired a poet's lays,
> Or given a home to man.

Modern Southern writers (writing in an age when so much American literature can be classified under the cold dissection of a Dos Passos or the iconoclastic indictment of a Farrell) are likely to reveal a profound and loyal affection for their region, even while they display with complete candor its imperfections. Faulkner, for example, writes almost in Timrod's strain when his subject—as in the following passage from "The Bear"—is the natural blessings which God has bestowed upon the South:

> . . . this land for which He has done so much with woods for game and streams for fish and deep rich soil for seed and lush springs to sprout it and long summers to mature it and serene falls to harvest it and short mild winters for men and animals.

Wolfe's South is in many respects unlovely and hateful even to Wolfe himself; but underneath the surface repulsion is a passionate devotion to "Old Catawba, there in the hills of home." The complex attitude here suggested is sometimes misunderstood by readers in other regions, where traditional ties have been weakened, to a greater extent, by migration and modern change.

There is, to cite only one other approach—for the purpose of these remarks is merely to suggest a few possible lines of inquiry—the philosophical distinction between the humanistic and the naturalistic, and it is worth noting that the naturalistic view, which has been so prominent elsewhere for three-quarters of a century, has never taken hold in the South, where Protestant orthodoxy has been remarkably persistent. Southern literature has been prevailingly humanistic: it has been informed, not by the amorality of science, but by the responsibility of an ethical system. To put it another way, man does not appear in these pages as an automaton or an irresponsible puppet. He may not act ethically, but there is no doubt of his power and responsibility. If he behaves like a devil, his deviltry is not cloaked in an amoral disguise, but is seen for what it is. Such a view of the world might have been regarded a few decades ago as an instance of Southern "backwardness"; it is likely to be taken today as an example of the persistence of truth in an age of error.

One of the greatest of modern Southern writers, William Faulkner, for example, who has been mistakenly called a naturalist, is in reality a humanist of the deepest dye. The conflict between the Sartorises and the Snopeses, which runs through so much of Faulkner's work, is (his best commentator, George Marion O'Donnell, has pointed out) "fundamentally a struggle between humanism and naturalism"; the Sartorises "act always with an ethically responsible will"; the Snopeses "acknowledge no ethical duty." The author's sympathies are with the Sartorises even though their action is often misguided, for an archaic code is better than the ruthless self-seeking of those who have no code at all. Faulkner's world—like the Southern world generally—is one in which sin is still to be reckoned with, and the distinction between right and wrong is still unblurred by the extenuations of modern science. His speech at Stockholm in 1950, delivered on the occasion of his receipt of the Nobel Prize, had a fine humanistic (and even religious) tone. Man, he said, "is immortal . . . because he has a soul, a spirit capable of compassion and sacrifice and endurance." The purpose of literature is "to help man endure by lifting up his heart."

The separateness of the South, despite the rapid changes of recent years, continues to be a fact, and the student is constantly searching for the distinguishing marks of Southern life and culture. Some of these have already been suggested. Others are set forth by Allen Tate in his essay "The Profession of Letters in the South" (1935):

> The South was settled by the same European strains as originally settled in the North. Yet, in spite of war, reconstruction, and industrialism, the South to this day finds its most perfect contrast in the North. In religious and social feeling I should stake everything on the greater resemblance to France. The South clings blindly to forms of European feeling and conduct that were crushed by the French Revolution and that, in England at any rate, are barely memories. How many Englishmen have told us that we still have the eighteenth-century amiability and consideration of manners, supplanted in their country by middle-class reticence and suspicion? And where, outside the South, is there a society that believes even covertly in the Code of Honor? . . . Where else in the modern world is the patriarchal family still innocent of the rise and power of other forms of society? Possibly in France; probably in the peasant countries of the Balkans and of Central Europe. Yet . . . the rise of new Southern points of view, even now in the towns, is tied still to the image of the family on the land. Where else does so much of the reality of the ancient land-society endure, along with the infatuated avowal of beliefs that are hostile to it? . . . The anomalous structure of the South is, I think, finally witnessed by its religion. . . . Only in the South does one find a convinced supernaturalism: it is nearer to Aquinas than to Calvin, Wesley, or Knox. . . . Nor, moreover, should we allow ourselves to forget that philosophers of the State, from Sir Thomas More to John C. Calhoun, were political defenders of the older religious community.

Mr. Tate's list of distinguishing marks is impressive: manners, a code of honor, the importance of the family, an agrarian society, religious supernaturalism, the political defense of the religious community. Few people are so well qualified (by study, experience, and insight) as Mr. Tate to make pronouncements about the South, and one must take his list seriously. The things he mentions undoubtedly were real, to a greater or lesser degree, in the South of the past. They embodied great virtues which the world can ill afford to let die. They embodied also serious defects—inequalities of various kinds, for example—which modern democracy has sought, and is still seeking, to remedy. The impending changes may or may not compensate, or may more than compensate, for the

losses—depending upon one's point of view; for with the modern gains there
seems to have been a weakening of some of the ancient virtues. But quite apart
from the view one takes, one must go to the literature to find the truest and most
valuable account of all these matters.

The foregoing observations have stressed the separateness, and by implication
the provincialism, of the South and its literature. Provincialism is often a source
of strength: a provincial writer is likely to have roots that strike deep in his
native soil. But Southern literature is more than a provincial record. One of the
best of the Southern writers, Ellen Glasgow, wisely said: "I would write not of
Southern characteristics, but of human nature." And she went on to say of her
fine novel *Barren Ground* and its heroine, Dorinda Oakley: "Though she had
been close to me for ten years before I began her story, Dorinda is universal. She
exists wherever a human being has learned to live without joy, wherever the spirit
of fortitude has triumphed over the sense of futility. The book is hers, and all
minor themes, episodes, and impressions are blended with the one dominant
meaning that character is fate." Important literature, that is to say, has meanings
which transcend its local origins.

Most Southern writers, too, have drawn stimulus and nutriment from sources
outside the South: Byrd from Restoration London; Jefferson from the philosophers
of France and England; Poe from the European Gothic writers; Simms from Scott
and Cooper; Lanier from Keats and Emerson; Wolfe and Jesse Stuart from Walt
Whitman; the modern poets from the English metaphysicals and the French
symbolists; the sophisticated modern fictionists from Flaubert, Henry James, and
Virginia Woolf; and most, if not all, of the modern fictionists from James Joyce
(who must have been an important agent of "release"). Southern literature, despite its frequently provincial preoccupations and tone, is no exception to Mr.
Tate's fine dictum (found also in "The Profession of Letters in the South") that
"the arts everywhere spring from a mysterious union of indigenous materials
and foreign influences: there is no great art or literature that does not bear the
marks of this fusion."

The view that Southern literature is provincial, therefore, must be modified by
the fact that outside influences have played upon it. It must be modified also by
the fact that important influences have been exerted from time to time by Southern writers upon writers and movements outside the South: by Jefferson upon
the political and social thought of the Western world, by Poe upon Baudelaire
and symbolism in modern French poetry, by the Southwestern humorists upon
Mark Twain, by Joel Chandler Harris upon national amity and upon the writers
of dialect everywhere in the nation, by O. Henry upon the popular short story,
by Paul Green upon regional drama and pageantry throughout the country, by
John Crowe Ransom and his associates upon modern procedures in literary criticism, by William Faulkner and Robert Penn Warren upon the techniques of
modern fiction. Such a list—though incomplete and intended only to be suggestive—gives a national and a world importance to a body of literature which is at
the same time rightly thought of as belonging in a special sense to its own region.

xxi

Randall Stewart
Brown University
Providence, Rhode Island

This book undertakes to represent Southern literature from its colonial beginnings to the present. Critical commentary has been held to a minimum in order that we might offer the broadest representation of Southern literature possible and because we believe that the selections should, mainly, tell their own story. An effort has been made to supply the reader with enough editorial comment to indicate important tendencies in Southern letters and to suggest the correlation of the literature with its changing political and social background.

The selections chosen have been divided into four periods. The authors represented have, in so far as was practicable, been arranged within each period by "type" and, within these smaller groupings, chronologically by date of birth. Exceptions have been made when they were dictated by logic: for example, the works of political authors are arranged according to the chronology of the selections themselves so that they trace a continuous development in political and social thought. The dates which appear at the end of the selections are those of publication; a second date indicates a revision unless otherwise noted.

Footnotes have been supplied only where they seemed necessary. The authors' own footnotes have nearly always been included and are indicated as such. We have added notes only for such references and expressions as might actually impede the reader's progress. For example, foreign phrases are translated if they do not appear in *Webster's Collegiate Dictionary*.

The illustrations have been designed to add a decorative element to the format. They were drawn by Franz Altschuler and represent the artist's imaginative interpretation of each author's work.

We wish to thank the many scholars whose work has helped to make this volume possible. Specifically, we are grateful to George Boswell for his suggestions about folk music; to John Welsh for his assistance with the material on William Gilmore Simms; and to Donald Davidson, Thomas H. English, Edwin T. Martin, Rob Roy Purdy, H. Blair Rouse, Hewitt B. Vinnedge, John Donald Wade, and Robert Penn Warren. Their generous help and encouragement proved invaluable. We are further indebted to the following members of the 1950 seminar in English 535 at Vanderbilt University: Aaron Book, Hatton Burke, Joseph Cohen, Kenneth England, Robert Gilbert, Robert C. Grayson, Kelsie B. Harder, John Holland, Lewis Maiden, Eunice Smith, and Robert Snyder. Their close

PREFACE

xxii

critical reading and suggestions were, in many cases, of great assistance in deciding what selections to use. We wish also to acknowledge our debt to the pioneering labors in the field of Southern literature of J. B. Hubbell, Gregory Paine, Edd Winfield Parks, and the late Vernon L. Parrington.

Finally, we want to express our personal gratitude to Edwin Mims, who has been for a full half-century an outstanding interpreter of Southern literature. His *Sidney Lanier*, published in 1905, did much to awaken the South and the nation to an appreciation not only of Lanier but of Southern writers generally. Through his enthusiastic efforts as author, teacher, and lecturer, he has had a stimulating effect upon many people—even upon those who could not be regarded as disciples or followers—and has quickened their awareness of the South and its problems. A great many people, both in our own country and abroad, owe to him their first introduction to some of the older literature in this book.

Richmond Croom Beatty
Floyd C. Watkins
Thomas Daniel Young

part **1**

THE EARLY SOUTH

to 1815

The Early South

Historical background

Southern literature properly begins with that period when the South became distinct in politics and culture from both Europe and the Northern and Middle Colonies. In some respects the South for a long time gave allegiance to things English, but cultural differences between the sections themselves came early, basically because of the origins of populations. A large number of New Englanders came from east England, from regions settled by the Danes; early Southerners were quite frequently from the ranks of the Cavaliers or from that part of England still predominantly Celtic. Thus differences in origin and background to some extent brought about differences in sectional temperaments.

The first century of life in the South following the settlement of Jamestown in 1607 was nothing like the dreams told by the more recent Southern romancers. The floodgates of the Negro slave trade were not opened until the beginning of the eighteenth century, and the tobacco, rice, indigo, and naval stores sent to England and sold at home in small quantities were grown mostly on small farms cultivated by the owners. North Carolina was a frontier for many years after Virginia was well colonized and the city-state of Charleston was flourishing. In 1709 there was only one town in North Carolina, and it had a total of twelve houses. Georgia remained an unsettled territory claimed by Spain until the first group of colonists pushed up the Savannah River in 1733.

In spite of the unsettled character of the colonial South, there was an opulence that early in the eighteenth century created the leisure of the planters in Virginia and the indolence of the inhabitants of Byrd's Lubberland. From the beginning, Southerners on the whole were less troubled by the necessity for hard work than were their contemporaries in New England. Even in the seventeenth century an outsider would have recognized the beginnings of a Southern mode of life in the structure of houses, the plans of farms, and the crops grown. Southerners were also less fanatic about religion than were the strict New Englanders. Settled by members of many denominations—Catholics, Methodists, Baptists, Scotch Presbyterians, and deists—the South consequently became a region of comparative religious tolerance.

During the first years of the eighteenth century, too, the slave trade increased in Virginia until a single man was able to supervise the cultivation of huge areas of land. Unable to stand the competition of slave labor, many a yeoman farmer degenerated into "poor white trash," or moved his family westward, or bought one or two slaves and tried to become self-sustaining. The growth of the institution of slavery brought to the planter aristocracy a greater degree of leisure, with the resulting opportunity both for entertainment and the serious study of such subjects as literature and philosophy. The fruits of this study were to be reflected in the significant role played by many Southern planters in molding the policies of the new nation.

The normal pattern of development in the South was dramatically altered at the beginning of the next century. In 1803, before the territory in the east was thoroughly populated or even well explored, Jefferson bought from France the Louisiana Territory, consisting of enough land to double the territory of the original thirteen colonies. A great part of that land lay adjacent to the South, openly inviting exploration by the courageous or unfortunate. The results of Jefferson's bargain were tremendous both over a long period of time and immediately. The Northeast, fearful of the increasing political power of the South, threatened secession, and sectional bickerings over slavery in new territories grew more violent as more land was added. There was, furthermore, a great migration to the new territory after the War of 1812, and many of the older communities decreased in population. Some counties in South Carolina lost half of their people. It became increasingly apparent that the Louisiana Purchase had added more than size to the United States: it had added local and sectional problems. There could hardly have been a Civil War had the Louisiana Territory not been acquired.

Early Southern culture

A colonial historian, Thomas J. Wertenbaker, has described the aristocratic life of eighteenth-century Virginia as follows:

> The eighteenth century was the golden age of the Virginia slave holders. It was then that they built the handsome homes once so numerous in the older counties, many of which still remain as interesting monuments of former days; it was then that they surrounded themselves with graceful furniture and costly silverware, in large part imported from Great Britain; it was then that they collected paintings and filled their libraries with the works of standard writers; it was then that they purchased coaches and berlins; it was then that men and women alike wore rich and expensive clothing.[1]

Many early plantation owners of the South were as much concerned with science, philosophy, and literary culture as they were with gracious living. When they were in England, they visited Oxford and Cambridge, and many attended the Inns of Court. Tastes ran generally in the direction of drama and the classics. The young American Cavaliers in Europe attended dramatic performances, and toward the latter part of the eighteenth century advertisements of dramatic productions frequently were printed in newspapers of several Southern cities. Approximately one-sixth of the books in William Byrd's library of 3675 volumes were drama collections. Many planters knew the classic languages, Latin and Greek, and many of them were accomplished linguists. Richard Lee owned books in five languages. Byrd read English, Hebrew, Greek, Latin, French, and Italian. Usually the planters owned enough books for their own use. They were readers as well as collectors, and their broad knowledge of the humanistic past helped them to solve the problems of the Revolution and the young republic.

[1] *Thomas J. Wertenbaker*, The Planters of Colonial Virginia (*Princeton University Press,* 1922), pp. 158–159.

There are many phases of early Southern cultural history which are of interest to the student of the period. It is known that a printing press was set up in Maryland as early as 1685, but from 1729 to the Revolutionary War there was only one printing press in Virginia, and it was controlled by the government. The first Southern newspaper, *The Maryland Gazette*, was founded at Baltimore in 1727, twenty-three years after the founding of *The Boston News-Letter*, the first newspaper in America. *The Virginia Gazette* was first published in 1736 at Williamsburg. Those Southern newspapers in the Mississippi Valley that were to serve as organs for the first native American humor were not founded until after 1800.

Unrestricted by Puritan bans on drama, Williamsburg in 1716 built the first theater in America, and Addison's *Cato* was presented at the College of William and Mary in 1736. Plays were produced in South Carolina as early as the 1730's, and a playhouse in Annapolis, Maryland, was giving frequent performances by 1752. It is unlikely that any original plays were produced before the last half of the century, but in 1776 Hugh Henry Brackenridge wrote for his pupils in Baltimore a drama which he entitled *The Battle of Bunkers-Hill*, and Colonel Robert Munford wrote *The Candidates; or, The Humours of a Virginia Election* in Petersburg in 1798.

Education and libraries in the South were mainly for the aristocracy, though of course there were exceptions to the rule. The College of William and Mary, the second American college and the only one in the South before the Revolution, was chartered in 1693 with a primary purpose of training Anglican ministers. Yet after its establishment, the increasing income from tobacco sent many young Southerners to England for their education. Southern libraries, though relatively few, were not poor by colonial standards. Many of the wealthy planters maintained extensive libraries for their own use. William Byrd's collection of books was the largest in early America with the possible exception of Cotton Mather's. Congress founded the Library of Congress by buying more than half of Jefferson's library of ten thousand volumes. Although the greatest number of libraries were privately owned, in early Maryland, Virginia, and North and South Carolina there were a good many church libraries, as well as a few operated by local governments.

Belles-lettres

Only by a great stretch of the imagination can the first writing in the South be designated as Southern literature. The process of rowing ashore from the ships at Roanoke and Jamestown did not make Elizabethans into Southerners nor transform accounts of Elizabethan travelers into Southern literature. John Smith and other ranging Englishmen of early colonial times were neither Southerners nor Americans; they were the sojourners and adventurers of an expanding empire. Things traditionally Southern, for example, are almost nonexistent in "Newes from Virginia," by "R. Rich, Gent.," who published the poem in 1610 after a stay of a year or less in Virginia. George Sandys' translation of Ovid's *Metamorphoses* (1626) was an interesting event in Southern culture, but not a part of Southern literature. What should mainly concern the student of this

5

early literature is the representation of life as set down by those authors who belong to the region by birth and temperament and who attempt to reflect the facets of its complex society in their writings.

Belles-lettres enjoyed little prominence in the South before the nineteenth century. Most potential authors could ill afford to relax from the tasks involved in settling a new country. William Byrd and other gentlemen from settled areas—seeing no machinery for publication and a busy, mostly illiterate audience if their writings were published—recorded their observations primarily for the amusement of friends or wrote for self-satisfaction. With the single exception of Byrd, every author in the years before 1815 represented in this book wrote from a political or economic motive. They were men of action, not dilettantes.

Though the Southerner probably read more novels and felt less moral disapproval of them than did the Northerner, fiction and narrative were seldom written. Folk tales about Daniel Boone circulated early in the South, and in 1794 John Filson wrote a narrative about the adventures of Boone. The vogue of the sentimental novel in the eighteenth century resulted in probably only one such work by a Southern author: *The Stepmother*, published in 1799 by Helena Wells, an American Loyalist, who left Charleston for London during the Revolution. The scene of the novel, however, is English, and consequently consideration of it as Southern is misleading. In 1805 John Davis, probably only a traveler in Virginia, wrote *The First Settlers of Virginia*, which was described in the subtitle as a historical novel about Jamestown and the Indians. Gilbert Imlay, living for a time in Kentucky, wrote what has been termed the first Kentucky novel, *The Emigrants, or The History of an Expatriated Family, being a Delineation of English Manners drawn from Real Characters* (London, 1793).

Poetry of esthetic value was even rarer in the South than in the North, where only Freneau and Edward Taylor wrote with anything like superior craftsmanship before 1800. S. M. Tucker found less than one thousand lines written by authors in the Southern colonies during the seventeenth century; and those few lines include such performances as "Bacon's Epitaph, Made by His Man" (probably by John and Ann Cotton), and Richard Rich's "Ballad on the Settlement of Jamestown." [2] By severe strain on the definition of both *poetry* and *Southern*, Carl Holliday in *Three Centuries of Southern Poetry* managed to collect twenty-two poems for the period before 1815. Edd Winfield Parks in *Southern Poets* included only eight poems written before Francis Scott Key's "The Star-Spangled Banner," and of these, one of the poems is by John Smith and one a version of an English ballad. There are in the group a few good poems. "Song," by John Shaw, a physician of Baltimore, might well be a seventeenth-century English lyric:

> Who has robbed the ocean cave,
> To tinge thy lips with coral hue?
> Who from India's distant wave,

[2] *"The Beginnings of Verse, 1610–1808,"* The Cambridge History of American Literature (*New York, 1947*), I, 150–184.

For thee those pearly treasures drew?
   Who, from yonder orient sky,
   Stole the morning of thine eye?

Thousand charms, thy form to deck,
   From sea, and earth, and air are torn;
Roses bloom upon thy cheek,
   On thy breath their fragrance borne.
   Guard thy bosom from the day,
   Lest thy snows should melt away.

But one charm remains behind,
   Which mute earth can ne'er impart;
Nor in ocean wilt thou find,
   Nor in the circling air a heart.
   Fairest! would'st thou perfect be,
   Take, oh take that heart from me.

A poem from Byrd's *History of the Dividing Line* is interesting because it is one of the earliest American statements in verse about the Indian. Except for the ballad "The Battle of King's Mountain" and "Bacon's Epitaph," it is the only one of Parks' early selections that is based on an American scene:

Long Has the Furious Priest

Long has the furious priest assay'd in vain
With sword and fagot infidels to gain;
But now the milder soldier wisely tries,
By gentler methods, to unveil their eyes.
Wonders apart, he knew 'twere vain t'engage
The fixed perversions of misguided age:
With fairer hopes, he forms the Indian youth
To early manners, probity, and truth.
The lion's whelp, thus, on the Libyan shore,
Is tamed and gentled by the artful Moor,
Not the grim sire inured to blood before.[3]

Almost all anthologists have excluded the work of Thomas Johnson, Jr., "the first Kentucky poet," author of *The Kentucky Miscellany* (1796). However, John Wilson Townsend, editor of *Kentucky in American Letters*, had the courage to include in his selections verses by Johnson beginning

I hate Kentucky, curse the place,
And all her vile and miscreant race![4]

[3] William Byrd's Histories of the Dividing Line Betwixt Virginia and North Carolina, *edited by W. K. Boyd (The North Carolina Historical Commission, 1929).*
[4] Kentucky in American Letters, 1784–1912, *edited by John Wilson Townsend (The Torch Press, 1913). By permission of Mr. Townsend.*

7

Perhaps some of the spirit of the frontier may be found in "The Poet's Epitaph,"
by Johnson:

> Underneath this marble tomb,
> In endless shades lies drunken Tom;
> Here safely moored, dead as a log,
> Who got his death by drinking grog.
> By whiskey grog he lost his breath—
> Who would not die so sweet a death?

In the early Southern colonies a great part of the literature was oral, and
therefore is largely inaccessible. Variants of the Old English and Scottish
ballads exist in every state in the South today. These old ballads were doubtless
sung in colonial times, but the study of them in the South by scholars and by
entertainers like Burl Ives has been a comparatively recent phenomenon.[5]
Probably no effort was made before the nineteenth century to preserve oral literature. That early Southern writers did not greatly bother to set this material
down for printing means that they must have regarded it as part of a living
and unconsciously accepted tradition.

Political and economic thought

At a time when the South was still mostly a wilderness and when the
Southern way of life was only coming into existence, a group of Southern
statesmen, most of them young Virginians, became spokesmen for the needs
of independence for the nation and cultural identity for the section. The intellect
of the planters was well supported by the brawn and independence of the
frontiersmen and yeoman farmers who explored, cleared, and cultivated the
land. Though the population was far from homogeneous and political views
were far from identical in different areas of the South, the differing classes
gradually worked out an identity which defined itself in ultimate terms in 1861.

A unique spokesman of the early period was Patrick Henry, who stood in rude
contrast to his frequent political ally, the polished Thomas Jefferson. A personifi-
cation of the early frontier, Henry is the only pre-Revolutionary figure represented in this volume from outside the pale of the Virginia aristocracy. He was
an exception in his own time, for the American frontier was almost inarticulate
before 1800, and its cultural impact on the South, though present from the beginning, made little appearance in the writings of the eighteenth century. The
aristocrats of the Tidewater region in Virginia and the stable coastal regions of
the rest of the South remained in control of Southern politics and social life until the frontier found a champion in Andrew Jackson.

The economic thought predominant in the South found expression in the
philosophy of agrarianism. This resembled somewhat the economic principles
of the French Physiocrats, but it is evident that an agrarian way of life existed

8

[5] *A section on Southern folklore is included in Part Four, "The Modern Renaissance."*

in the South before the Physiocratic philosophy was transplanted to the New World. The mild climate, the fertile soil, and the hungry demands of Europe for Southern products made the economy of the region predominantly agricultural. The philosophy of agrarianism simply interpreted conditions that already existed. Jefferson's apostleship for agrarianism was preceded not only by Franklin's formal introduction of the philosophy into America but also by the establishment of conditions that demanded articulation. Furthermore—though Jefferson was familiar with the Physiocrats, Voltaire, Diderot, and (disputably) Rousseau—most recent scholars maintain that such English philosophers as Bolingbroke and Locke had a greater influence upon his thinking than did these French writers.

In his *Notes on Virginia* Jefferson acclaimed the agricultural workers "the chosen people of God." Among the farm laborers, he said, God is able to keep alive "that sacred fire which otherwise might escape the face of the earth." Following the example of the Physiocrats, he insisted that evil and corruption were the results of commercial cities. "I have no fear of a people . . . dispersed over their farms," he wrote; "I say *over their farms,* because they constitute the body of our citizens; the inhabitants of towns are but zero on the scales." In the early nineteenth century Jeffersonian agrarianism was generally accepted in the South. The necessity for industrial development in the War of 1812, however, led to changes in some of Jefferson's beliefs. For example, he, along with Madison and the young Calhoun, came to favor a protective tariff designed to help bring about economic independence and self-sufficiency.

John Taylor of Caroline expanded and elaborated Jefferson's principles in his *Arator* and other writings. The happy life, as Taylor conceived it, embraced contented farmers living on their holdings far removed from the degrading influences of the city. Taylor was not only the most philosophical of the liberal agrarians; in many respects he was also the most practical. He argued that the entire economic and social system should be directed toward improving America's most important asset—agriculture. The farmers and small tradesmen, he felt, were being exploited by nonproductive capitalists because the latter group had political strength. The fact that a majority of the American people were engaged in agriculture obligated the farmers, he believed, to become politically strong so that they could demand what justly belonged to them and at the same time give to society the service which they owed it. The protective tariff, Taylor said—taking up an issue long paramount in Southern politics— is nothing more than a weapon by which the capitalists are legally able to rob the farmers. The long persistence of Jefferson's and Taylor's agrarian ideas in the South is seen in Professor Edd Winfield Parks' suggestion in *Segments of Southern Thought* that the Southerners fought the Civil War for agrarianism rather than for slavery.

But the South of the early days was by no means exclusively agrarian. When the plantations expanded in the eighteenth century and the plantation owners ceased to deal solely with agents in England, colonial merchants became an important group, located mainly in such cities as Norfolk and Charleston. Not tied to the soil, the merchants became Tories more frequently than did other Southerners. They felt closer to George Washington after he appointed Hamilton

9

to his cabinet, because Hamilton supported a financial policy beneficial to merchants and capitalists. The division of classes in the South is evident in the attacks of Jefferson and Madison on Hamilton's proposal for a Bank of the United States and in Washington's reluctant decision in favor of Hamilton. The Hamiltonians in the North and South felt the Bank was necessary to make the country sound economically. Jefferson, Madison, and the small farmers saw it as an instrument to give unfair support to commerce and manufactures and as the creator of an economic aristocracy.

Conflicts between the Southern colonies and the crown, frequent from the very beginning and typified by the independence of the Virginia House of Burgesses, were forerunners of the final conflict with Britain. For a time, eagerness to further a common cause swept aside sectional conflicts. The literature of protest against wrongs by the English was not sectional. All colonies except Georgia were represented in the First Continental Congress. George Washington was nominated commander-in-chief by John Adams. Richard Henry Lee made the motion for independence in Congress, and Franklin from Pennsylvania and Adams from Massachusetts suggested minor changes in Jefferson's first draft of the Declaration of Independence.

Though the writings in the South from the Revolutionary period until the close of the century do not fall into the category of belles-lettres, they are literature in a broad sense. Southerners played an important role in creating a body of political literature that has not been surpassed in eloquence or in importance in the history of man; their pens were not still from the time of Patrick Henry's early and determined opposition to the Stamp Act in 1765 until the final adoption of the Constitution. In the Declaration of Independence, the culmination of the literature of protest against Great Britain, Jefferson with assistance wrote what is perhaps the greatest rhetorical achievement of the age. Later, after the Constitutional Convention unanimously elected Washington as its president, Madison's Virginia Plan, presented by Edmund Randolph of Virginia, became an important foundation for the Constitution of the United States. Madison's recording of the Convention has survived as the most complete and intelligent political reporting of the time. Finally, Madison was the Southerner who, through his contributions to the *Federalist,* helped to gain support for the Constitution in the separate states. By 1815 the South, through the writings and actions of its humanists and statesmen, had established its own patterns of life and had helped to stabilize a democratic government for all the country.

10

WILLIAM BYRD

1674–1744

William Byrd was born March 28, 1674, at the falls of the James River near the present city of Richmond, Virginia, which he established and named. He received his education abroad, studying law at the Middle Temple in London and qualifying for membership in the Royal Society. Byrd spent much of his life in England, where he twice served as a colonial agent; exactly half of his seventy years were spent abroad. A prominent Virginia planter active in public life, Byrd served at various times as a representative in the House of Burgesses, as receiver-general of Virginia, and for many years as a member of the Supreme Council. He also played a prominent role in the controversy that arose between the large Virginia planters and Governor Spotswood, who was endeavoring to reduce the power of the Council. After his return from England in 1726, Byrd spent the remaining eighteen years of his life "exiled" to the colony, where he found himself saddled with an eccentric second wife half his own age and harassed by debts incurred mainly in the building of his fine Georgian mansion, "Westover." In 1728 he was appointed a member of a commission to establish the boundary line between Virginia and North Carolina; his records of this expedition form the basis of the *History of the Dividing Line* and *Secret History of the Line*. In Virginia, Byrd lived the active life of a country gentleman and was an avid reader and self-disciplined scholar. At the time of his death his holdings in land approximated 180,000 acres. His library, numbering over 3600 volumes, was one of the most sizable private collections of books in America before the Revolution.

Byrd's significance as a writer and recorder of colonial Southern plantation and backwoods society has increased remarkably in recent years, chiefly through the decoding of his diaries. He kept these manuscripts in a system of shorthand which went out of general use in the eighteenth century. It is a reasonable conjecture that he kept them religiously, day by day, throughout his adult life. The diaries establish him beyond question as a profoundly learned and vigorous man; he has long been recognized as a wit. Two segments of this work are available. A third, covering the years 1717–1721, is in the possession of the Virginia Historical Society, which so far has refused to sanction its publication. (Byrd's first wife had died by this date; he was footloose, in his early forties, and rather free in his attentions to ladies of both high and low degree.)

11

During his own lifetime Byrd allowed only scattered pieces to be printed, though the *Newly Discovered Eden* [Virginia], which appeared in 1737, in German, was based upon information which he himself supplied. Edmund Ruffin first brought out the better-known of his writings (under title of *The Westover Manuscripts*) in the *Virginia Farmers Register* for 1841. Byrd at this date had been dead for ninety-seven years.

Byrd has become recognized as one of the major figures in our colonial literature. Writing with a lively and engaging style that continues to appeal to modern readers, he has supplied the social historian with a wealth of information about early Southern life. Collectively considered, his manuscripts seem to challenge gravely the generalization that the aristocrats of the early South were idle men concerned merely with high living, heavy drinking, and fox hunting.

from The Secret Diary

September 1710

1. I rose at 5 o'clock and read a chapter in Hebrew and some Greek in Lucian. I said my prayers and ate boiled milk for breakfast. I danced my dance.[1] My wife and I had a quarrel because she neglected to give the child the bitter drink. I settled some accounts. About 11 o'clock Captain Burbydge came and he and I played at billiards. I had a letter from Joe Wilkinson which told me he was sick. I ate roast pigeon for dinner. In the afternoon Captain Burbydge went away to my cousin Harrison's. Colonel Randolph and Captain Bolling were chosen burgesses for the upper county. My wife and I took a long walk about the plantation. In the evening I read a sermon of Dr. Sacheverell, and had good health, good thoughts, and good humor, thank God Almighty.

2. I rose at 5 o'clock and found it extremely cold. I read a chapter in Hebrew and some Greek in Lucian. I said my prayers and ate boiled milk for breakfast. I danced my dance. I settled some accounts and read some Latin. Several of my people were sick and Indian Ned among the rest. It was exceedingly cold. I ate fish for dinner. In the afternoon Mr. C——s came from above and brought me an English letter, and Colonel Eppes came and gave me two other English letters, but no news. I sent Captain Llewellyn a dose of physic. Colonel Eppes stayed about [an hour]. In the evening we took a walk and Jimmy from Falling Creek brought me word that Mr. G——r——l was very ill of the gripes. All the people were well. In the evening I read some English and had good health, good thoughts, and good humor, thank God Almighty.

24. I rose at 6 o'clock and shaved myself and said a short prayer. The Governor's horses got away but Colonel Hill sent men after them and got them again. We had chocolate for breakfast and about 10 o'clock rode home to my house, where we refreshed ourselves and then the Governor and I went to church in the coach and my wife was terribly out of humor because she could

From The Secret Diary of William Byrd of Westover, 1709–1712, *The Dietz Press, 1941. Used with the permission of Louis B. Wright and Marion Tinling.*
[1] *Obviously some form of "setting-up" exercise which Byrd practiced throughout his life.*

not go likewise. Mr. Anderson preached very well and pleased the Governor. After church I invited abundance of gentlemen home where we had a good dinner. My wife after much persuasion came to dinner with us. The company went away in the evening and the Governor and I took a walk on the river side. The Governor was very willing to favor the iron works. We sat up till 9 o'clock. I neglected to say my prayers but had good health, good thoughts, and good humor, thank God Almighty.

October 1710

9. I rose about 5 o'clock and got myself ready for my journey, and about 6 o'clock [I] recommended my wife and my family to God's protection, and after my people had set me over the creek, I got on horseback about 7 and proceeded to Williamsburg where I arrived about 12. About one I went to wait on the Governor, where I found Colonel Digges and several other gentlemen. My wife sent a present of blue wing which were kindly accepted. I ate some roast beef for dinner. In the afternoon we drank a bottle of claret and then we took leave of the Governor and went to the coffeehouse[2] where after we had settled some accounts of the naval officers we played at cards till 11 o'clock. Then I went to my lodgings but my man was gone to bed and I was shut out. However I called him and beat him for it. I neglected to say my prayers but had good thoughts, good health, and good humor, thank God Almighty.

10. I rose about 6 o'clock and read nothing because I prepared my matters against the Council. I neglected to say my prayers but ate boiled milk for breakfast. I settled accounts with several people and then went to the Governor's where several of the Council were. Here I drank chocolate and then we all went to Council, where several matters were debated, and particularly we had the journal of the commissioners for settling the bounds between this colony and Carolina, which made the business much in our favor. About 4 o'clock we went to dine with the Governor and I ate boiled beef and several other things. After dinner we went to cards and I won half a crown. About 9 o'clock we went home. I neglected to say my prayers but had good thoughts, good health, and good humor, thank God Almighty.

27. I rose at 6 o'clock and read a chapter in Hebrew and 200 verses in Homer. I neglected to say my prayers and ate boiled milk for breakfast. I wrote letters to England and settled all my business. Mr. Bland came over this morning. About 10 o'clock I went to court, where we sat till 4 o'clock; then we went to Council for half an hour. I went to dine at the Governor's where I ate roast mutton for dinner. After dinner we drank a bottle of wine and then took our leave. I went to the coffeehouse where I found several of the Council playing at dice and I played with them and won 40 shillings. Then I went home, where I wrote 2 letters to my overseers. I said my prayers and had good health, good thoughts, and good humor, thank God Almighty.

November 1710

10. I rose at 7 o'clock and read two chapters in Hebrew and 250 verses in Homer. I neglected to say my prayers and ate boiled milk for breakfast. Major

[2] *The Raleigh Tavern.*

Harrison and Will Randolph came to see me. About 10 o'clock I went to see the Governor and drank tea with him and discoursed with him concerning several matters. About 12 o'clock we came to the capitol and went into the Council, where two bills were read of no consequence. Colonel Lewis was very drunk with drinking canary. About 4 o'clock we went to dinner and I ate boiled beef. Then we went to the coffeehouse where I lost 40 shillings at cards and dice. Mrs. Russell was indisposed again. I said my prayers and had good health, good thoughts, and good humor, thank God Almighty.

from *Secret History of the Line*

Byrd was one of the three Virginia commissioners appointed by George II to settle the boundary dispute between Virginia and North Carolina. Soon after their appointment, the commissioners for Virginia wrote the following letter to the commissioners of North Carolina.

Gentlemen:

We are Sorry we can't have the Pleasure of meeting you in January next as is desired by Your Governour. The Season of the Year in which that is proposed to be done, & the distance of our Habitation from your Frontier, we hope will make our Excuse reasonable. Besides his Majesty's Order marks out our Business so plainly, that we are perswaded that there can be no difficulty in the Construction of it. After this, what imaginable Dispute can arise amongst Gentlemen who meet together with minds averse to Chicane, and Inclinations to do equal Justice both to his Majesty and the Lords Proprietors, in which disposition we make no doubt the Commissioners on both Sides will find each other.

We shall have full powers to agree at our first meeting on what Preliminarys shall be thought necessary, which we hope you will likewise be, that an affair of so great Consequence may have no Delay or Disappointment.

It is very proper to acquaint You in what manner we intend to come provided, that so you, Gentlemen who are appointed in the same Station, may if you please do the same Honour to Your Government. We shall bring with us about 20 men furnish't with Provisions for 40 days. We shall have a Tent with us & a Marquis for the convenience of ourselves & Servants. We shall be provided with [as] much Wine & Rum as [shall] just enable us, and our men to drink every Night to the Success of the following Day, and because we understand there are many Gentiles on your Frontier, who never had an opportunity of being Baptized, we shall have a chaplain with us to make them Christians. For this Purpose we intend to rest in our Camp every Sunday that there may be leizure for so good a work. And whoever of your Province shall be desirous of novelty may repair on Sundays to our Camp, & hear a Sermon. Of this you may please to give publick notice that the Charitable Intentions of this Government may meet with the happier Success.

14

From William Byrd's Histories of the Dividing Line Betwixt Virginia and North Carolina, *edited by W. K. Boyd. The North Carolina Historical Commission, 1929.*

Thus much Gentlemen we thought it necessary to acquaint you with and to make use of this first Opportunity of Signifying with how much Satisfaction we receiv'd the News that such able Commissioners are appointed for the Government, with whom we promise our selves we shall converse with prodigious Pleasure, & Execute our Commissions to the full content of those by whom we have the Honour to be employ'd, We are

Gentlemen   Your most humble Servants

FIREBRAND   MEANWELL   STEDDY [1]

March 12 [1728]

Complaint was made to Me this Morning, that the Men belonging to the Periauga, had stole our People's Meat while they Slept. This provoked me to treat them a la Dragon, that is to swear at them furiously; & by the good Grace of my Oaths, I might have past for an Officer in his Majesty's Guards. I was the more out of Humour, because it disappointed us in our early March, it being a standing Order to boil the Pot over Night, that we might not be hinder'd in the Morning. This Accident, & Necessity of drying our Bed-Cloaths kept us from decamping til near 12 a Clock. By this delay the Surveyors found time to plot off their Work, and to observe the Course of the River. Then they past it over against Northern's Creek, the Mouth of which was very near our Line. But the Commissioners made the best of their way to the Bridge, and going ashoar walkt to Mr. Ballance's Plantation. I retir'd early to our Camp at some distance from the House, while my Collegues tarry'd within Doors, & refresh't themselves with a Cheerful Bowl. In the Gaiety of their Hearts, they invited a Tallow-faced Wench that had sprain'd her Wrist to drink with them, and when they had rais'd her in good Humour, they examined all her hidden Charms, and play'd a great many gay Pranks. While Firebrand who had the most Curiosity, was ranging over her sweet Person, he pick't off several Scabs as big as Nipples, the Consequence of eating too much Pork. The poor Damsel was disabled from making any resistance by the Lameness of her Hand; all she cou'd do, was, to sit stil, & make the Fashionable Exclamation of the Country, Flesh a live & tear it, & by what I can understand she never spake so properly in her Life. One of the Representatives of N. Carolina made a Midnight Visit to our Camp, & his Curiosity was so very clamorous that it waked Me, for which I wish't his Nose as flat as any of his Porcivorous Countrymen. [2]

from History of the Dividing Line

March 6 [1728]

After both Commissions were considered, the first Question was, where the Dividing Line was to begin. This begat a Warm debate; the Virginia Commis-

15

[1] *Richard Fitzwilliam, William Dandridge, and William Byrd.*
[2] *Byrd entertained a theory that constant eating of pork "undermined the foundation" of the nose.*
From William Byrd's Histories of the Dividing Line Betwixt Virginia and North Carolina, *edited by* W. K. Boyd. *The North Carolina Historical Commission, 1929.*

sioners contending, with a great deal of Reason, to begin at the End of the Spitt of Sand, which was undoubtedly the North Shore of Corautck Inlet. But those of Carolina insisted Strenuously, that the Point of High Land ought rather to be the Place of Beginning, because that was fixt and certain, whereas the Spitt of Sand was ever Shifting, and did actually run out farther now than formerly. The Contest lasted some Hours, with great Vehemence, neither Party receding from their Opinion that Night. But next Morning, Mr. M . . . . . , to convince us he was not that Obstinate Person he had been represented, yielded to our Reasons, and found Means to bring over his Collegues.

Here we began already to reap the Benefit of those Peremptory Words in our Commission, which in truth added some Weight to our Reasons. Nevertheless, because positive proof was made by the Oaths of two Credible Witnesses, that the Spitt of Sand had advanced 200 Yards towards the Inlet since the Controversy first began, we were willing for Peace-sake to make them that allowance. Accordingly we fixed our Beginning about that Distance North of the Inlet, and there Ordered a Cedar-Post to be driven deep into the Sand for our beginning. While we continued here, we were told that on the South Shore, not far from the Inlet, dwelt a Marooner, that Modestly call'd himself a Hermit, tho' he forfeited that Name by Suffering a wanton Female to cohabit with Him.

His Habitation was a Bower, cover'd with Bark after the Indian Fashion, which in that mild Situation protected him pretty well from the Weather. Like the Ravens, he neither plow'd nor sow'd, but Subsisted chiefly upon Oysters, which his Handmaid made a Shift to gather from the Adjacent Rocks. Sometimes, too, for Change of Dyet, he sent her to drive up the Neighbour's Cows, to moisten their Mouths with a little Milk. But as for raiment, he depended mostly upon his Length of Beard, and She upon her Length of Hair, part of which she brought decently forward, and the rest dangled behind quite down to her Rump, like one of Herodotus's East Indian Pigmies.

Thus did these Wretches live in a dirty State of Nature, and were mere Adamites, Innocence only excepted.

March 25

The air was chill'd this Morning with a Smart North-west Wind, which favour'd the Dismalites [1] in their Dirty March. They return'd by the Path they had made in coming out, and with great Industry arriv'd in the Evening at the Spot where the Line had been discontinued.

After so long and laborious a Journey, they were glad to repose themselves on their couches of Cypress-bark, where their sleep was as sweet as it wou'd have been on a Bed of Finland Down.

In the mean time, we who stay'd behind had nothing to do, but to make the best observations we cou'd upon that Part of the Country. The Soil of our Landlord's Plantation, tho' none of the best, seem'd more fertile than any thereabouts, where the Ground is near as Sandy as the Desarts of Affrica, and consequently barren. The Road leading from thence to Edenton, being in distance about 27 Miles, lies upon a Ridge call'd Sandy-Ridge, which is so wretchedly Poor that it will not bring Potatoes.

The Pines in this Part of the country are of a different Species from those

16

[1] *It was necessary to run the survey through the Dismal Swamp.*

that grow in Virginia: their bearded Leaves are much longer and their Cones much larger. Each Cell contains a Seed of the Size and Figure of a black-ey'd Pea, which, Shedding in November, is very good Mast for Hogs, and fattens them in a Short time.

The Smallest of these Pines are full of Cones, which are 8 or 9 Inches long, and each affords commonly 60 or 70 Seeds. This Kind of Mast has the Advantage of all other, by being more constant, and less liable to be nippt by the Frost, or Eaten by the Caterpillars. The Trees also abound more with Turpentine, and consequently yield more Tarr, than either the Yellow or the White Pine; And for the same reason make more durable Timber for building. The Inhabitants hereabouts pick up Knots of Lightwood in Abundance, which they burn into tar, and then carry it to Norfolk or Nansimond for a Market. The Tar made in this method is the less Valuable, because it is said to burn the Cordage, tho' it is full as good for all other uses, as that made in Sweden and Muscovy.

Surely there is no place in the World where the Inhabitants live with less Labour than in N Carolina. It approaches nearer to the Description of Lubberland than any other, by the great felicity of the Climate, the easiness of raising Provisions, and the Slothfulness of the People.

Indian Corn is of so great increase, that a little Pains will Subsist a very large Family with Bread, and then they may have meat without any pains at all, by the Help of the Low Grounds, and the great Variety of Mast that grows on the High-land. The Men, for their Parts, just like the Indians, impose all the Work upon the poor Women. They make their Wives rise out of their Beds early in the Morning, at the same time that they lye and Snore, till the Sun has run one third of his course, and disperst all the unwholesome Damps. Then, after Stretching and Yawning for half an Hour, they light their Pipes, and, under the Protection of a cloud of Smoak, venture out into the open Air; tho', if it happens to be never so little cold, they quickly return Shivering into the Chimney corner. When the weather is mild, they stand leaning with both their arms upon the corn-field fence, and gravely consider whether they had best go and take a Small Heat at the Hough: but generally find reasons to put it off till another time.

Thus they loiter away their Lives, like Solomon's Sluggard, with their Arms across, and at the Winding up of the Year Scarcely have Bread to Eat.

To speak the Truth, tis a thorough Aversion to Labor that makes People file off to N Carolina, where Plenty and a Warm Sun confirm them in their Disposition to Laziness for their whole Lives.

March 26

Since we were like to be confin'd to this place, till the People return'd out of the Dismal, twas agreed that our Chaplain might Safely take a turn to Edenton, to preach the Gospel to the Infidels there, and Christen their Children. He was accompany'd thither by Mr. Little, One of the Carolina Commissioners, who, to shew his regard for the Church, offer'd to treat Him on the Road with a Fricassee of Rum. They fry'd half a Dozen Rashers of very fat Bacon in a Pint of Rum, both which being disht up together, serv'd the Company at once for meat and Drink.

17

Most of the Rum they get in this Country comes from New England, and is so bad and unwholesome, that it is not improperly call'd "Kill-Devil." It is distill'd there from forreign molosses, which, if Skilfully manag'd yields near Gallon for Gallon. Their molasses comes from the same country, and has the name of "Long Sugar" in Carolina, I suppose from the Ropiness of it, and Serves all the purposes of Sugar, both in their Eating and Drinking.

When they entertain their Friends bountifully, they fail not to set before them a Capacious Bowl of Bombo, so call'd from the Admiral of that name. This is a Compound of Rum and Water in Equal Parts, made palatable with the said long Sugar. As good Humour begins to flow, and the Bowl to Ebb, they take care to replinish it with Shear Rum, of which there always is a Reserve under the Table. But such Generous doings happen only when that Balsam of life is plenty; for they have often such Melancholy times, that neither Land-graves nor Cassicks can procure one drop for their Wives, when they ly in, or are troubled with the Colick or Vapours. Very few in this Country have the Industry to plant Orchards, which, in a Dearth of Rum, might supply them with much better Liquor.

The Truth is, there is one Inconvenience that easily discourages lazy People from making This improvement: very often, in Autumn, when the Apples begin to ripen, they are visited with Numerous Flights of paraqueets, that bite all the Fruit to Pieces in a moment, for the sake of the Kernels. The Havock they make is Sometimes so great, that whole Orchards are laid waste in Spite of all the Noises that can be made, or Mawkins that can be dresst up, to fright 'em away. These Ravenous Birds visit North Carolina only during the warm Season, and so soon as the Cold begins to come on, retire back towards the Sun. They rarely Venture so far North as Virginia, except in a very hot Summer, when they visit the most Southern Parts of it. They are very Beautiful; but like some other pretty Creatures, are apt to be loud and mischievous.

October 13

This being Sunday, we rested from our Fatigue, and had leisure to reflect on the signal Mercies of Providence.

The great Plenty of Meat herewith Bearskin[2] furnisht us in these lonely Woods made us once more Shorten the men's allowance of Bread, from 5 to 4 Pounds of bisket a week. This was the more necessary, because we knew not yet how long our Business might require us to be out.

In the Afternoon our Hunters went forth, and return'd triumphantly with three brace of wild Turkeys. They told us they cou'd see the Mountains distinctly from every Eminence, tho' the Atmosphere was so thick with Smoak that they appear'd at a greater Distance than they really were.

In the Evening we examin'd our Friend Bearskin, concerning the Religion of his Country and he explain'd it to us, without any of that Reserve to which his Nation is Subject.

He told us he believ'd there was one Supreme God, who had Several Sub-altern Deities under Him. And that this Master-God made the World a long time ago. That he told the Sun, the Moon, and Stars, their Business in the

[2] An Indian guide and hunter whom the party had taken along.

Beginning, which they, with good looking after, have faithfully perform'd ever Since.

That the same Power that made all things at first has taken care to keep them in the same Method and Motion ever since.

He believ'd God had form'd many Worlds before he form'd this, that those Worlds either grew old and ruinous, or were destroyed for the Dishonesty of the Inhabitants.

That God is very just and very good—ever well pleas'd with those men who possess those God-like Qualities. That he takes good People into his safe Protection, makes them very rich, fills their Bellies plentifully, preserves them from sickness, and from being surpriz'd or Overcome by their Enemies.

But all such as tell Lies, and Cheat those they have Dealings with, he never fails to punish with Sickness, Poverty and Hunger, and, after all that, Suffers them to be knockt on the Head and scalpt by those that fight against them.

He believ'd that after Death both good and bad People are conducted by a strong Guard into a great Road, in which departed Souls travel together for some time, till at a certain Distance this Road forks into two Paths, the one extremely Levil, and the other Stony and Mountainous.

Here the good are parted from the Bad by a flash of Lightening, the first being hurry'd away to the Right, the other to the Left. The Right hand Road leads to a charming warm Country, where the Spring is everlasting, and every Month is May; and as the year is always in its Youth, so are the People, and particularly the Women are bright as Stars, and never Scold.

That in this happy Climate there are Deer, Turkeys, Elks, and Buffaloes innumerable, perpetually fat and gentle, while the Trees are loaded with delicious Fruit quite throughout the four Seasons.

That the Soil brings forth Corn Spontaneously, without the Curse of Labour, and so very wholesome, that None who have the happiness to eat of it are ever Sick, grow old, or dy.

Near the Entrance into this Blessed Land Sits a Venerable Old Man on a Mat richly woven, who examins Strictly all that are brought before Him, and if they have behav'd well, the Guards are order'd to open the Crystal Gate, and let them enter into the Land of Delights.

The left Hand Path is very rugged and uneaven, leading to a dark and barren Country, where it is always Winter. The Ground is the whole year round cover'd with Snow, and nothing is to be seen upon the Trees but Icicles.

All the People are hungry, yet have not a Morsel of any thing to eat, except a bitter kind of Potato, that gives them the Dry-Gripes, and fills their whole Body with loathsome Ulcers, that Stink, and are unsupportably painfull.

Here all the Women are old and ugly, having Claws like a Panther, with which they fly upon the Men that Slight their Passion. For it seems these haggard old Furies are intolerably fond, and expect a vast deal of Cherishing. They talk much and exceedingly Shrill, giving exquisite Pain to the Drum of the Ear, which in that Place of the Torment is so tender, that every Sharp Note wounds it to the Quick.

At the End of this Path sits a dreadful old Woman on a monstrous Toad-Stool, whose head is cover'd with Rattle-Snakes instead of Tresses, with glaring white Eyes, that strike a Terror unspeakable into all that behold her.

19

This Hag pronounces Sentence of Woe upon all the miserable Wretches that hold up their hands at her Tribunal. After this they are deliver'd over to huge Turkey-Buzzards, like harpys, that fly away with them to the Place above mentioned.

Here, after they have been tormented a certain Number of years, according to their several Degrees of Guilt, they are again driven back into this World, to try if they will mend their Manners, and merit a place the next time in the Regions of Bliss.

This was the Substances of Bearskin's Religion, and was as much to the purpose as cou'd be expected from a meer State of Nature, without one Glimpse of Revelation or Philosophy.

It contain'd, however, the three Great Articles of Natural Religion: The Belief of a God; The Moral Distinction betwixt Good and Evil; and the Expectation of Rewards and Punishments in Another World.

Indeed, the Indian Notion of a Future Happiness is a little Gross and Sensual, like Mahomet's Paradise. But how can it be otherwise, in a People that are contented with Nature as they find Her, and have no other Lights but what they receive from purblind Tradition?

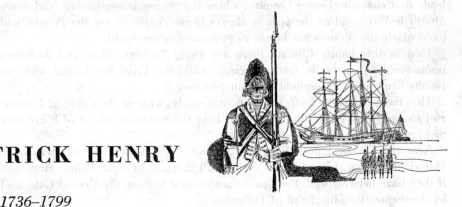

PATRICK HENRY

1736–1799

Patrick Henry, celebrated orator and champion of the rights of the common people, was one of the most famous trial lawyers of his day. He was born in Hanover County, Virginia. After attending several typical frontier grammar schools, he withdrew at the age of fifteen to enter business. However, he met with little success either as a storekeeper or as a farmer, and soon turned his attention to the law. A born talker, he was immediately successful in this profession, collecting 1185 fees during his first three years of practice. In 1774 he was sent to the first Continental Congress and the next year was appointed to represent his county at the Virginia Convention of Delegates. It was before this latter body that, on March 23, 1775, he delivered his most quoted address. Memorized by school boys and repeated at patriotic functions in the eloquent manner characteristic of nineteenth-century oratory, it came to be considered a superb statement of man's desire for freedom. The text of the speech appears in this volume as it was reconstructed by William Wirt in his *Sketches of the Life and Character of Patrick Henry* (1817). Although the authenticity of this text has not been established, the point of view it represents is invaluable to the student of our later colonial literature.

Speech in the Virginia Convention of Delegates

No man thinks more highly than I do of the patriotism, as well as abilities, of the very worthy gentlemen who have just addressed the house. But different men often see the same subjects in different lights; and, therefore, I hope it will not be thought disrespectful to those gentlemen, if, entertaining as I do, opinions of a character very opposite to theirs, I shall speak forth my sentiments freely, and without reserve. This is no time for ceremony. The question before the house is one of awful moment to this country. For my own part, I consider it as nothing less than a question of freedom or slavery. And in proportion to the magnitude of the subject, ought to be the freedom of the debate. It is only in this way that we can hope to arrive at truth, and fulfil the great responsibility which we hold to God and our country. Should I keep back my opinions at such a time, through fear of giving offence, I should consider myself as guilty of treason towards my country, and of an act of disloyalty toward the majesty of Heaven, which I revere above all earthly kings.

Mr. President, it is natural to man to indulge in the illusions of hope. We are apt to shut our eyes against a painful truth and listen to the song of that syren, till she transforms us into beasts. Is this the part of wise men, engaged in a great and arduous struggle for liberty? Are we disposed to be of the number of those, who having eyes, see not, and having ears, hear not, the things which so nearly concern their temporal salvation? For my part, whatever anguish of spirit it may cost, I am willing to know the whole truth; to know the worst, and to provide for it.

I have but one lamp by which my feet are guided; and that is the lamp of experience. I know of no way of judging of the future but by the past. And judging by the past, I wish to know what there has been in the conduct of the British ministry for the last ten years, to justify those hopes with which gentlemen have been pleased to solace themselves and the house? Is it that insidious smile with which our petition has been lately received? Trust it not, sir; it will prove a snare to your feet. Suffer not yourselves to be betrayed with a kiss. Ask yourselves how this gracious reception of our petition comports with those warlike preparations which cover our waters and darken our land. Are fleets and armies necessary to a work of love and reconciliation? Have we shown ourselves so unwilling to be reconciled, that force must be called in to win back our love? Let us not deceive ourselves, sir. These are the implements of war and subjugation, the last arguments to which kings resort.

I ask gentlemen, sir, what means this martial array, if its purpose be not to

21

force us to submission? Can gentlemen assign any other possible motive for it? Has Great Britain any enemy in this quarter of the world, to call for all this accumulation of navies and armies? No, sir, she has none. They are meant for us; they can be meant for no other. They are sent over to bind and rivet upon us those chains, which the British ministry have been so long forging. And what have we to oppose to them? Shall we try argument? Sir, we have been trying that for the last ten years. Have we any thing new to offer upon the subject? Nothing. We have held the subject up in every light of which it is capable; but it has been all in vain. Shall we resort to entreaty and humble supplication? What terms shall we find, which have not been already exhausted? Let us not, I beseech you, sir, deceive ourselves longer. Sir, we have done every thing that could be done, to avert the storm which is now coming on. We have petitioned, we have remonstrated, we have supplicated, we have prostrated ourselves before the throne, and have implored its interposition to arrest the tyrannical hands of the ministry and parliament. Our petitions have been slighted; our remonstrances have produced additional violence and insult; our supplications have been disregarded; and we have been spurned, with contempt, from the foot of the throne. In vain, after these things, may we indulge the fond hope of peace and reconciliation. There is no longer any room for hope. If we wish to be free, if we mean to preserve inviolate those inestimable privileges for which we have been so long contending, if we mean not basely to abandon the noble struggle in which we have been so long engaged, and which we have pledged ourselves never to abandon, until the glorious object of our contest shall be obtained, we must fight!—I repeat it, sir, we must fight!! An appeal to arms and to the God of Hosts is all that is left us!

They tell us, sir, that we are weak, unable to cope with so formidable an adversary. But when shall we be stronger? Will it be the next week or the next year? Will it be when we are totally disarmed, and when a British guard shall be stationed in every house? Shall we gather strength by irresolution and inaction? Shall we acquire the means of effectual resistance by lying supinely on our backs, and hugging the delusive phantom of hope, until our enemies shall have bound us hand and foot? Sir, we are not weak, if we make a proper use of those means which the God of nature hath placed in our power. Three millions of people, armed in the holy cause of liberty, and in such a country as that which we possess, are invincible by any force which our enemy can send against us. Besides, sir, we shall not fight our battles alone. There is a just God who presides over the destinies of nations, and who will raise up friends to fight our battles for us. The battle, sir, is not to the strong alone; it is to the vigilant, the active, the brave. Besides, sir, we have no election. If we were base enough to desire it, it is now too late to retire from the contest. There is no retreat, but in submission and slavery! Our chains are forged. Their clanking may be heard on the plains of Boston! The war is inevitable—and let it come!! I repeat it, sir, let it come!!!

It is in vain, sir, to extenuate the matter. Gentlemen may cry, peace, peace—but there is no peace. The war is actually begun! The next gale that sweeps from the north will bring to our ears the clash of resounding arms! Our brethren are already in the field! Why stand we here idle? What is it that

22

gentlemen wish? What would they have? Is life so dear, or peace so sweet, as to be purchased at the price of chains and slavery? Forbid it, Almighty God! I know not what course others may take; but as for me, give me liberty, or give me death! (*1775*)

GEORGE MASON

1725–1792

George Mason was born in Virginia in 1725, the fourth Mason of that name in America. His father died when George was ten, but the prosperity of the family was such that he inherited five thousand acres. He was educated by tutors and by reading in the 1500-volume library belonging to his uncle, John Mercer.

Always desiring to remain a private citizen and a plantation owner, George Mason refused to consider himself a public servant, despite the many offices he actually held. Late in life, this temperament even led him to refuse to become a United States Senator. In local government, however, Mason was trustee of the town of Alexandria, justice of his county court, and vestryman of Truro Parish. His experience as a member of the Ohio Company led to *Extracts from the Virginia Charters, with Some Remarks upon Them* (1773), which supported Virginia's boundary claims in the West and after the Revolution influenced the location of the boundaries of the United States.

Mason's part in the protests against England was important, though, because of his retiring disposition, usually unofficial. He prepared a paper against the Townshend Acts for Washington's use in the House of Burgesses. Without assistance he wrote the Fairfax Resolves, a review of the dispute between Great Britain and the colonies. When Washington resigned from the House of Burgesses to become commander-in-chief, Mason took his place. As a member of the Committee of Safety, he wrote the Declaration of Rights and most of the Constitution of Virginia. The former of these documents, says his biographer, Helen Hill, "was drawn upon by Jefferson in the first part of the Declaration of Independence, was widely copied in the other colonies, became the basis for the first ten amendments to the Constitution of the United States, and had a considerable influence in France at the time of the French Revolution."

23

In the early 1780's Mason retired from public life, but in 1786 he returned to the Virginia Assembly to fight against inflation and to advocate a stronger federal bond than the Articles of Confederation. As a delegate to the Constitutional Convention, he spoke more often than any other except Madison, Morris, and Wilson. Displeased with the sectional compromises on slavery and the tariff and with the lack of a Bill of Rights, Mason, like Patrick Henry, campaigned against the adoption of the Constitution in Virginia. Along with many other early Virginians, he opposed the slave trade on economic and moral grounds.

Declaration of Rights[1]

A Declaration of Rights made by the representatives of the good people of Virginia, assembled in full and free Convention; which rights do pertain to them, and their posterity, as the basis and foundation of government.

I. That all men are by nature equally free and independent, and have certain inherent rights, of which, when they enter into a state of society, they cannot, by any compact, deprive or divest their posterity; namely, the enjoyment of life and liberty, with the means of acquiring and possessing property, and pursuing and obtaining happiness and safety.

II. That all power is vested in, and consequently derived from the people; that Magistrates are their trustees and servants, and at all times amenable to them.

III. That government is or ought to be, instituted for the common benefit, protection, and security of the people, nation, or community; of all the various modes and forms of government, that is best, which is capable of producing the greatest degree of happiness and safety, and is most effectually secured against the danger of mal-administration; and that when any government shall be found inadequate or contrary to these purposes, a majority of the community hath an indubitable, unalienable, and indefeasible right, to reform, alter, or abolish it, in such manner as shall be judged most conducive to the public weal.

IV. That no man, or set of men, are entitled to exclusive or separate emoluments or privileges from the community, but in consideration of public services; which not being descendible, neither ought the offices of Magistrate, Legislator, or Judge to be hereditary.

V. That the Legislative and Executive powers of the State should be separate and distinct from the Judiciary; and that the members of the two first may be restrained from oppression, by feeling and participating the burthens of the people, they should, at fixed periods, be reduced to a private station, return into that body from which they were originally taken, and the vacancies be supplied by frequent, certain, and regular elections, in which all, or any part of

24

---

[1] *The text is almost entirely the work of George Mason, though it was slightly altered and expanded by the Virginia Convention.*

the former members, to be again eligible, or ineligible, as the laws shall direct.

VI. That elections of members to serve as representatives of the people, in Assembly, ought to be free; and that all men having sufficient evidence of permanent common interest with and attachment to, the community, have the right of suffrage, and cannot be taxed or deprived of their property for public uses without their own consent, or that of their representatives so elected, nor bound by any law to which they have not, in like manner, assented for the public good.

VII. That all power of suspending laws, or the execution of laws, by any authority without consent of the representatives of the people, is injurious to their rights and ought not to be exercised.

VIII. That in all capital or criminal prosecutions a man hath a right to demand the cause and nature of his accusation, to be confronted with the accusers and witnesses, to call for evidence in his favor, and to a speedy trial by an impartial jury of his vicinage, without whose unanimous consent he cannot be found guilty, nor can he be compelled to give evidence against himself; that no man be deprived of his liberty except by the law of the land, or the judgment of his peers.

IX. That excessive bail ought not to be required, nor excessive fines imposed, nor cruel and unusual punishments inflicted.

X. That general warrants, whereby an officer or messenger may be commanded to search suspected places without evidence of a fact committed, or to seize any person or persons not named, or whose offence is not particularly described and supported by evidence, are grievous and oppressive, and ought not to be granted.

XI. That in controversies respecting property, and in suits between man and man, the ancient trial by jury is preferable to any other and ought to be held sacred.

XII. That the freedom of the press is one of the great bulwarks of liberty, and can never be restrained but by despotic governments.

XIII. That a well regulated militia, composed of the body of the people, trained to arms, is the proper, natural, and safe defence of a free state; that standing armies, in time of peace, should be avoided, as dangerous to liberty; and in all cases, the military should be under strict subordination to, and governed by, the civil power.

XIV. That the people have a right to uniform government; and therefore, that no government separate from, or independent of, the government of Virginia, ought to be erected or established within the limits thereof.

XV. That no free government, or the blessing of liberty, can be preserved to any people but by a firm adherence to justice, moderation, temperance, frugality, and virtue, and by frequent recurrence to fundamental principles.

XVI. That religion, or the duty which we owe to our Creator, and the manner of discharging it, can be directed only by reason and conviction, not by force or violence, and therefore all men are equally entitled to the free exercise of religion, according to the dictates of conscience; and that it is the mutual duty of all to practise Christian forbearance, love, and charity towards each other. (*1776*)

25

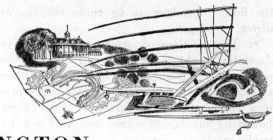

GEORGE WASHINGTON

1732–1799

From the time of his birth until his death in 1799, George Washington spent his private life in Virginia. Like the typical Virginia planter, he was interested in his plantation more than in anything else. As a young surveyor, he saved his wages to invest them in land, and in his will he indicated that he owned 41,136 acres, in addition to his large holdings at Mount Vernon. Washington was an exact, scientific, and learned farmer, and kept a daily account of minute details about the activities on his plantation and even about the weather. He frequently corresponded with English agronomists. After importing asses from Europe, he succeeded in making the mule a reliable American farm animal, and from Europe he also brought the Woburn breed of hogs. On the slavery issue, Washington supported the Virginia liberal aristocrats who desired to see the institution abolished, and in his will he left instructions that his slaves were to be freed after his wife's death.

In 1783 Washington sent a letter to the governors of the states urging a central government with greater power. From that time until the adoption of the Constitution, he worked for the establishment of a stronger federal government to replace the inadequate Articles of Confederation. His success as commander-in-chief of the revolutionary armies, his desire for a more authoritative government, and his ability to command the faith of the people led to his unanimous election as president of the Constitutional Convention. Following the adoption of the Constitution, Washington served two terms as President, receiving the unanimous vote of the electors in both 1788 and 1792. Refusing offers for a third term, he was happy to retire to his Mount Vernon estate.

Letters

To George Mason

26

Mount Vernon, April 5, 1769

Dear Sir: Herewith you will receive a letter and Sundry papers which were forwarded to me a day or two ago by Doctor Ross of Bladensburg. I transmit

From Basic Writings of George Washington, *edited by Saxe Commins. Random House, 1948.*

them with the greater pleasure, as my own desire of knowing your sentiments upon a matter of this importance exactly coincides with the Doctors inclinations.

At a time when our lordly Masters in Great Britain will be satisfied with nothing less than the deprication of American freedom, it seems highly necessary that some thing shou'd be done to avert the stroke and maintain the liberty which we have derived from our Ancestors; but the manner of doing it to answer the purpose effectually is the point in question.

That no man shou'd scruple, or hesitate a moment to use a——ms in defence of so valuable a blessing, on which all the good and evil of life depends, is clearly my opinion; yet A——ms I wou'd beg leave to add, should be the last resource; the denier resort. Addresses to the Throne, and remonstrances to parliament, we have already, it is said, proved the inefficacy of; how far then their attention to our rights and priviledges is to be awakened or alarmed by starving their Trade and manufactures, remains to be tryed.

The northern Colonies, it appears, are endeavouring to adopt this scheme. In my opinion it is a good one, and must be attended with salutary effects, provided it can be carried pretty generally into execution; but how far it is practicable to do so, I will not take upon me to determine. That there will be difficulties attending the execution of it every where, from clashing interests, and selfish designing men (ever attentive to their own gain, and watchful of every turn that can assist their lucrative views, in preference to any other consideration) cannot be denied; but in the Tobacco Colonies where the Trade is so diffused, and in a manner wholly conducted by Factors for their principals at home, these difficulties are certainly enhanced, but I think not insurmountably increased, if the Gentlemen in their several Counties wou'd be at some pains to explain matters to the people, and stimulate them to a cordial agreement to purchase none but certain innumerated Articles out of any of the Stores after such a period, not import nor purchase any themselves. This, if it did not effectually withdraw the Factors from their Importations, wou'd at least make them extremely cautious in doing it, as the prohibited Goods could be vended to none but the non-associator, or those who wou'd pay no regard to their association; both of whom ought to be stigmatized, and made the objects of publick reproach.

The more I consider a Scheme of this sort, the more ardently I wish success to it, because I think there are private, as well as public advantages to result from it; the former certain, however precarious the other may prove; for in respect to the latter I have always thought that by virtue of the same power (for here alone the authority derives) which assume's the right of Taxation, they may attempt at least to restrain our manufactories; especially those of a public nature; the same equity and justice prevailing in the one case as the other, it being no greater hardship to forbid my manufacturing, than it is to order me to buy Goods of them loaded with Duties, for the express purpose of raising a revenue. But as a measure of this sort will be an additional exertion of arbitrary power, we cannot be worsted I think in putting it to the Test. On the other hand, that the Colonies are considerably indebted to Great Britain, is a truth universally acknowledged. That many families are reduced, almost, if not quite, to penury and want, from the low ebb of their fortunes, and Estates daily selling for the discharge of Debts, the public papers furnish but too many melancholy proofs

27

of. And that a scheme of this sort will contribute more effectually than any other I can devise to immerge the Country from the distress it at present labours under, I do most firmly believe, if it can be generally adopted. And I can see but one set of people (the Merchants excepted) who will not, or ought not, to wish well to the Scheme; and that is those who live genteely and hospitably, on clear Estates. Such as these were they, not to consider the valuable object in view, and the good of others, might think it hard to be curtail'd in their living and enjoyments; for as to the penurious Man, he saves his money, and he saves his credit, having the best plea for doing that, which before perhaps he had the most violent struggles to refrain from doing. The extravagant and expensive man has the same good plea to retrench his Expences. He is thereby furnished with a pretext to live within bounds, and embraces it, prudence dictated œconomy to him before, but his resolution was too weak to put in practice; for how can I, says he, who have lived in such and such a manner change my method? I am ashamed to do it; and besides such an alteration in the system of my living, will create suspicions of a decay in my fortune, and such a thought the World must not harbour; I will e'en continue my course: till at last the course discontinues the Estate, a sale of it being the consequence of his perseverance in error. This I am satisfied is the way that many who have set out in the wrong tract, have reasoned, till ruin stares them in the face. And in respect to the poor and needy man, he is only left in the same situation he was found; better I might say, because as he judges from comparison his condition is amended in proportion as it approaches nearer to those above him.

Upon the whole therefore, I think the Scheme a good one, and that it ought to be tryed here, with such alterations as the exigency of our circumstances render absolutely necessary; but how, and in what manner to begin the work, is a matter worthy of consideration, and whether it can be attempted with propriety, or efficacy (further than a communication of sentiments to one another) before May, when the Court and Assembly will meet together in Williamsburg, and a uniform plan can be concerted, and sent into the different counties to operate at the same time, and in the same manner every where, is a thing I am somewhat in doubt upon, and shou'd be glad to know your opinion of. I am Dr. Sir, etc.

To William Pearce

Philadelphia 18t Decemr 1793

Mr. Pearce,[1]

The paper enclosed with this letter will give you my ideas, generally, of the course of Crops I wish to pursue.—I am sensible more might be made from the farms for a year or two—but my object is to recover the fields from the exhausted state into which they have fallen, by oppressive crops, and to restore them (if possible by any means in my power) to health and vigour.—But two ways will enable me to accomplish this.—The first is to cover them with as

28

From Letters and Recollections of George Washington, *edited by Jared Sparks. Doubleday & Company, Inc.*
[1] *Manager of Washington's estate.*

much manure as possible (winter and summer).—The 2d a judicious succession of Crops.

Manure can not be had in the abundance the fields require; for this reason, and to open the land which is hard bound by frequent cultivation and want of proper dressings, I have introduced Buck Wheat in the plentiful manner you will perceive by the Table, both as a manure, and as a substitute for Indian Corn for horses &ct; it being a great ameliorator of the soil.—How far the insufferable conduct of my Overseers, or the difficulty of getting Buck Wheat and Oats for seed, will enable me to carry my plan into effect, I am unable at this moment to decide.—You possibly, will be better able to inform me sometime hence.—Colo. Ball of Leesburgh has promised to use his endeavours to procure and send the first to Mount Vernon; but where to get as much of the latter as will answer my purposes (unless I send them from this city) I know not; but before I can decide on the quantity it may be necessary for me to purchase, it is essential I should know the quantity grown on my own estate; and which after I went to Virginia in September last I directed should no longer be fed away.—The common Oats which are brought from the Eastern Shore to Alexandria for sale, I would not sow—first, because they are not of a good quality—and 2dly because they are rarely, if ever, free from Garlick and wild Onions: with which, unfortunately, many of my fields are already but too plentifully stocked from the source already mentioned; and that too before I was aware of the evil.

I have already said that the insufferable conduct of my Overseers may be one mean of frustrating my plan for the next year.—I will now explain myself.— You will readily perceive by the rotation of Crops I have adopted, that a great deal of Fall plowing is indispensable.—Of this I informed every one of them, and pointed out the fields which were to be plowed at this season.—So anxious was I, that this work should be set about early, that I made an attempt soon after you were at Mount Vernon in September, to begin it; and at several times afterwards repeated the operation in different fields at Dogue-run farm;—but the ground being excessively hard and dry, I found that to persevere would only destroy my horses without effecting the object in the manner it ought to be, and therefore I quit it; but left positive directions that it should recommence at every farm as soon as ever there should come rain to moysten the earth—and to stick constantly at it, except when the horses were employed in treading out Wheat (which was a work I also desired might be accomplished as soon as possible).—Instead of doing either of these, as I ordered, I find by the reports, that McKoy has, now and then, plowed a few days only as if it were for amusement.—That Stuart has but just begun to do it.—And that neither Crow nor Davy [at] Muddy-hole had put a plow into the ground so late as the 7th. of this month.—Can it be expected then, that frosts, Snow and Rain will permit me to do much of this kind of work before March or April? When Corn planting, Oats sowing, and Buck Wht for manure, ought to be going into the grd, in a well prepared state, instead of having it to flush up at that season—and when a good deal of Wheat is to be got out with the same horses.—Crow having got out none of his that was stacked in the field, nor Stuart and McKoy much of theirs, which is in the same predicament;—the excuse being, as far as it is communicated to me, that their whole time and force since the month of October

29

has been employed in securing their Corn—When God knows how little enough of that article will be made.

I am the more particular on this head for two reasons—first to let you see how little dependence there is on such men when left to themselves (for under Mr. Lewis it was very little better)—and 2dly to show you the necessity of keeping these Overseers strictly to their duty—that is—to keep them from running about, and to oblige them to remain constantly with their people;—and moreover, to see at what time they turn out of a morning—for I have strong suspicions that this, with some of them, is at a late hour, the consequence of which to the Negroes is not difficult to foretell.—All these Overseers as you will perceive by their agreements, which I herewith send, are on standing wages; and this with men who are not actuated by the principles of honor or honesty, and not very regardful of their characters, leads naturally to endulgences—as *their* profits, whatever may be *mine,* are the same whether they are at a horse race or on the farm—whether they are entertaining company (which I believe is too much the case) in their own houses, or are in the field with the Negroes.

Having given you these ideas, I shall now add, that if you find any one of them inattentive to the duties which by the articles of agreement they are bound to perform, or such others as may be reasonably enjoined,—Admonish them in a calm, but firm manner of the consequences.—If this proves ineffectual, discharge them, at any season of the year without scruple or hesitation, and do not pay them a copper;—putting the non-compliance with their agreemt in bar.

To treat them civilly is no more than what all men are entitled to, but, my advice to you is, to keep them at a proper distance; for they will grow upon familiarity, in proportion as you will sink in authority, if you do not.—Pass by no faults or neglects (especially at first) for overlooking one only serves to generate another, and it is more than probable that some of them (one in particular) will try, at first, what lengths he may go.—A steady and firm conduct, with an inquisitive inspection into, and a proper arrangement of everything on your part, will though it may give, trouble at first, save a great deal in the end—and you may rest assured that in everything that is just, and proper to be done ib your part, [you] shall meet with the fullest support ib mine.—Nothing will contribute more to effect these desirable purposes than a good example—unhappily this was not set (from what I have learnt lately) by Mr. Whiting, who, it is said, drank freely—kept bad company in my house in Alexandria—and was a very debauched person—wherever this is the case it is not easy for a man to throw the first stone for fear of having it returned to him; —and this I take to be the true cause why Mr. Whiting did not look more scrupulously into the conduct of the Overseers, and more minutely into the smaller matters belonging to the Farms—which, though individually [they] may be trifling, are not found so in the agregate; for there is no addage more true than an old Scotch one, that "many mickles make a muckle."

I have had but little opportunity of forming a correct opinion of my white Overseers, but such observations as I have made I will give.

Stuart appears to me to understand the business of a farm very well, and seems attentive to it.—He is I believe a sober man, and according to his own account a very honest one.—As I never found him (at the hours I usually visited the farm) absent from some part or another of his people, I presume he is

30

industrious and seldom from home.—He is talkative, has a high opinion of his own skill and management—and seems to live in peace and harmony with the Negros who are confided to his care.—He speaks extremely well of them, and I have never heard any complaint of him.—His work however, has been behind hand all the year, owing he says, and as I believe, to his having too much plowing to do—and the last omission, of not plowing when he knew my motives for wishing it, has been extremely repre[he]nsible.—But upon the whole, if he stirs early, and works late, I have no other fault to find than the one I have just mentioned—His talkativeness and vanity may be humoured.

Crow is an active man, and not deficient in judgment.—If kept strictly to his duty would, in many respects, make a good Overseer.—But I am much mistaken in his character, if he is not fond of visiting, and receiving visits.—This, of course, withdraws his attention from his business, and leaves his people too much to themselves; which produces idleness, or slight work on one side, and flogging on the other—the last of which besides the dissatisfactions which it creates, has, in one or two instances been productive of serious consequences— I am not clear either, that he gives due attention to his Plow horses and other stock which is necessary, although he is very fond of riding the former—not only to Alexandria &ct but about the farm, which I did not forbid as his house was very inconvenient to the scene of his business.

McKoy appears to me to be a sickly, slothful and stupid fellow.—He had many more hands than were necessary merely for his Crop, and though not 70 acres of Corn to cultivate, did nothing else.—In short to level a little dirt that was taken out of the meadow ditch below his house seems to have composed the principal part of his Fall work; altho' no finer season could have happened for preparing the second lot of the Mill swamp for the purpose of laying it to grass.—If more exertion does not appear in him when he gets into better health he will be found an unfit person to overlook so important a farm, especially as I have my doubts also of his care and attention to the horses &ct.

As to Butler, you will soon be a judge whether he will be of use to you or not.—He may mean well, and for ought I know to the contrary may, in some things have judgment; but I am persuaded he has no more authority over the Negros he is placed, than an old woman would have; and is as unable to get a proper day's Work done by them as she would, unless led to it by their own inclination wch I know is not the case.

Davy at Muddy-hole carries on his business as well as the White Overseers, and with more quietness than any of them.—With proper directions he will do very well; and probably give you less trouble than any of them, except in attending to his care of the stock, of which I fear he is negligent; as there are deaths too frequent among them.—

Thomas Green [2] will, I am persuaded, require your closest attention, without which I believe it will be impossible to get any work done by my Negro Carpenters—in the first place, because, it has not been in my power, when I am away from home, to keep either him, or them in any settled work; but they will be flying from one trifling thing to another, with no other design, I believe, than to have the better opportunity to be idle, or to be employed on their own

31

[2] *Foreman of the carpenters.*

business—and in the next place, because,—although authority is given to him— he is too much upon a level with the Negros to exert it; from which cause, if no other every one works, or not, as they please and carve out such jobs as they like.—I had no doubt when I left home the 28th of Oct. but that the house intended for Crow wd have been nearly finished by this time, as in order to facilitate the execution I bought Scantling, Plank and S[h]ingles for the building: instead of this I do not perceive by his weekly report that a tool has yet been employed in it—nor can I find out by the said report that the barn at Dogue-run is in much greater forwardness than when I left it.

To correct the abuses which have crept into all parts of my business—to arrange it properly, and to reduce things to system; will require, I am sensible, a good deal of time and your utmost exertions;—of the last, from the character you bear, I entertain no doubt; the other, I am willing to allow, because I had rather you should probe things to the bottom, whatever time it may require to do it, than to decide hastily upon the first view of them; as to establish good rules, and a regular system, is the life, and the soul of every kind of business. These [rest of letter missing].

from *Last Will and Testament*

Recorded in Fairfax County, Virginia,
July 9, 1799

In the name of God, amen.

I George Washington of Mount Vernon, a citizen of the United States, and lately President of the same, do make, ordain and declare this Instrument; which is written with my own hand and every page thereof subscribed with my name, to be my last Will and Testament, revoking all others.

Imprimus. All my debts, of which there are but few, and none of magnitude, are to be punctually and speedily paid; and the Legacies hereinafter bequeathed, are to be discharged as soon as circumstances will permit, and in the manner directed.

Item. To my dearly beloved wife Martha Washington I give and bequeath the use, profit and benefit of my whole Estate, real and personal, for the term of her natural life; except such parts thereof as are specifically disposed of hereafter: My improved lot in the Town of Alexandria, situated on Pitt and Cameron Streets, I give to her and her heirs forever, as I also do my household and Kitchen furniture of every sort and kind, with the liquors and groceries which may be on hand at the time of my decease; to be used and disposed of as she may think proper.

Item. Upon the decease of my wife, it is my Will and desire that all the Slaves which I hold in my own right, shall receive their freedom. To emancipate them during her life, would, tho' earnestly wished by me, be attended with such insuperable difficulties on account of their intermixture by Marriages with the Dower Negroes, as to excite the most painful sensations, if not disagreeable

32

From Basic Writings of George Washington, *edited by Saxe Commins. Random House,* 1948.

consequences from the latter, while both descriptions are in the occupancy of the same Proprietor; it not being in my power, under the tenure by which the Dower Negroes are held, to manumit them. And whereas among those who will receive freedom according to this devise, there may be some, who from old age or bodily infirmities, and others who on account of their infancy, that will be unable to support themselves; it is my Will and desire that all who come under the first and second description shall be comfortably cloathed and fed by my heirs while they live; and that such of the latter description as have no parents living, or if living are unable, or unwilling to provide for them, shall be bound by the Court until they shall arrive at the age of twenty five years; and in cases where no record can be produced, whereby their ages can be ascertained, the judgment of the Court upon its own view of the subject, shall be adequate and final. The Negroes thus bound, are (by their Masters or Mistresses) to be taught to read and write; and to be brought up to some useful occupation, agreeably to the Laws of the Commonwealth of Virginia, providing for the support of Orphan and other poor Children. And I do hereby expressly forbid the Sale, or transportation out of the said Commonwealth, of any Slave I may die possessed of, under any pretence whatsoever. And I do moreover most pointedly, and most solemnly enjoin it upon my Executors hereafter named, or the Survivors of them, to see that *this* clause respecting Slaves, and every part thereof be religiously fulfilled at the Epoch at which it is directed to take place; without evasion, neglect or delay, after the Crops which may then be on the ground are harvested, particularly as it respects the aged and infirm; Seeing that a regular and permanent fund be established for their Support so long as there are subjects requiring it; not trusting to the uncertain provision to be made by individuals. And to my Mulatto man William (calling himself William Lee) I give immediate freedom; or if he should prefer it (on account of the accidents which have befallen him, and which have rendered him incapable of walking or of any active employment) to remain in the situation he now is, it shall be optional in him to do so: In either case however, I allow him an annuity of thirty dollars during his natural life, which shall be independent of the victuals and cloaths he has been accustomed to receive, if he chuses the last alternative; but in full, with his freedom, if he prefers the first; and this I give him as a testimony of my sense of his attachment to me, and for his faithful services during the Revolutionary War. . . .

That as it has always been a source of serious regret with me, to see the youth of these United States sent to foreign Countries for the purpose of Education, often before their minds were formed, or they had imbibed any adequate ideas of the happiness of their own; contracting, too frequently, not only habits of dissipation and extravagence, but principles unfriendly to Republican Governmt. and to the true and genuine liberties of mankind; which, thereafter are rarely overcome. For these reasons, it has been my ardent wish to see a plan devised on a liberal scale which would have a tendency to sprd. systematic ideas through all parts of this rising Empire, thereby to do away local attachments and State prejudices, as far as the nature of things would, or indeed ought to admit, from our National Councils. Looking anxiously forward to the accomplishment of so desirable an object as this is (in my estimation) my mind has not been able to contemplate any plan more likely to effect the measure

33

than the establishment of a UNIVERSITY in a central part of the United States, to which the youth of fortune and talents from all parts thereof might be sent for the completion of their Education in all the branches of polite literature; in arts and Sciences, in acquiring knowledge in the principles of Politics and good Government; and (as a matter of infinite Importance in my judgment) by associating with each other, and forming friendships in Juvenile years, be enabled to free themselves in a proper degree from those local prejudices and habitual jealousies which have just been mentioned; and which, when carried to excess, are never failing sources of disquietude to the Public mind, and pregnant of mischievous consequences to this Country: Under these impressions, so fully dilated,

Item. I give and bequeath in perpetuity the fifty shares which I hold in the Potomac Company (under the aforesaid Acts of the Legislature of Virginia) towards the endowment of a UNIVERSITY to be established within the limits of the District of Columbia, under the auspices of the General Government, if that government should incline to extend a fostering hand towards it; and until such Seminary is established, and the funds arising on these shares shall be required for its support, my further WILL and desire is that the profit accruing therefrom shall, whenever the dividends are made, be laid out in purchasing Stock in the Bank of Columbia, or some other Bank, at the discretion of my Executors; or by the Treasurer of the United States for the time being under the direction of Congress; provided that Honourable body should Patronize the measure, and the Dividends proceeding from the purchase of such Stock is to be vested in more stock, and so on, until a sum adequate to the accomplishment of the object is obtained, of which I have not the smallest doubt, before many years passes away; even if no aid or encouraged is given by Legislative authority, or from any other source. . . .

THOMAS JEFFERSON

1743–1826

34   The third child of a father of Welsh descent and a mother from the family of the Virginia Randolphs, Thomas Jefferson was born on "Shadwell" estate near the frontier of Virginia on April 13, 1743. After attending an "English school" and later studying Latin, Greek, and French under the Reverend William Douglas, he enrolled in the College of William and Mary and was graduated in 1762. From 1767 until shortly before the Revolution he practiced law. When

he married the widow Martha Skelton in 1772, his own inheritance of 2750 acres was supplemented by an estate almost as large (though heavily encumbered by debt). Thereafter Jefferson always endeavored to put his agricultural theories into practice on his plantation, which at one time consisted of about ten thousand acres and over one hundred slaves.

Public life began for him when he became a member of the House of Burgesses in 1769. He served in this body until 1775, usually siding with Patrick Henry against the Tidewater aristocrats. No one was more active than Jefferson in the defense of the rights of the colonies; in *A Summary View of the Rights of British America* (1774) he gives a clear statement of his opinions. While in the House of Burgesses he also served at different times as county lieutenant, county surveyor, a member of the Virginia Committee of Correspondence, and an alternate for Peyton Randolph in the Continental Congress. He was the main author of the Declaration of Independence.

In 1776 Jefferson returned to the Virginia House of Delegates. As governor for two terms, beginning in 1779, he opposed primogeniture, entail, and hereditary aristocracy in favor of an aristocracy of ability and talent. In the formation of the state he was so active that he has been called the "architect of Virginia government."

Jefferson began his career in the new federal government as a delegate to Congress in 1783. In 1785 he succeeded Franklin as minister to France, returning to the United States four years later and accepting the appointment as Secretary of State. At this time Jefferson and Hamilton—both members of Washington's cabinet—began the long struggle which grew out of their conflicting philosophies of government. Jefferson's service as Vice-President under John Adams was followed by election to the presidency in 1800. During two terms as President, he tried to establish a republican simplicity in government and sponsored, among other things, the Louisiana Purchase, the Lewis and Clark expedition, and the Embargo Act of 1807. Retiring from a long public career in 1809, he returned to his home, Monticello, to face a neglected plantation and tremendous debts. The sale of the greater part of his library of ten thousand volumes to Congress (to form the nucleus of the Library of Congress) alleviated his difficulties only temporarily. Despite gifts received just before his death, his heirs lost all claims to his property.

Jefferson stands out as perhaps the most versatile of our early American statesmen. His interests and accomplishments extended into almost every field of human activity; he was an author, philologist, philosopher, agriculturist, inventor, architect, and practical and theoretical scientist. Firmly convinced of the importance of education in a democracy, he was largely responsible for the establishment of the University of Virginia and state-supported education in Virginia.

In political theory, Jefferson was a strict-constructionist who believed that the powers of the federal government should be strictly limited in order to protect the rights and well-being of the individual and of the state. Influenced mainly by temperament and environment, but to some extent also by the theories of the French Physiocrats, he founded the agrarian school of thought in the South. The early Jefferson excluded large industries and cities from his ideal state, but during the War of 1812 he modified his opinions to include some in-

35

dustry. Though the issues have been changed by many additional complications since his lifetime, the tenets of his beliefs are still basic in much Southern thought. "He understood," wrote Vernon Louis Parrington, "how the movement from simplicity to complexity—from freedom to regimentation—creates a psychology and an institutionalism that conducts straight to the Leviathan state, controlled by a ruling caste, serving the demands of exploitation, heedless of the well-being of the regimented mass."

The Declaration of Independence

When in the Course of human events, it becomes necessary for one people to dissolve the political bands which have connected them with another, and to assume among the powers of the earth, the separate and equal station to which the Laws of Nature and of Nature's God entitle them, a decent respect to the opinions of mankind requires that they should declare the causes which impel them to the separation.

We hold these truths to be self-evident, that all men are created equal, that they are endowed by their Creator with certain inalienable Rights, that among these are Life, Liberty and the pursuit of Happiness. That to secure these rights, Governments are instituted among Men, deriving their just powers from the consent of the governed. That whenever any Form of Government becomes destructive of these ends, it is the Right of the People to alter or to abolish it, and to institute new Government, laying its foundation on such principles and organizing its powers in such form, as to them shall seem most likely to effect their Safety and Happiness. Prudence, indeed, will dictate that Governments long established should not be changed for light and transient causes; and accordingly all experience hath shewn, that mankind are more disposed to suffer, while evils are sufferable, than to right themselves by abolishing the forms to which they are accustomed. But when a long train of abuses and usurpations, pursuing invariably the same Object evinces a design to reduce them under absolute Despotism, it is their right, it is their duty, to throw off such Government, and to provide new Guards for their future security. Such has been the patient sufferance of these Colonies; and such is now the necessity which constrains them to alter their former Systems of Government. The history of the present King of Great Britain is a history of repeated injuries and usurpations, all having in direct object the establishment of an absolute Tyranny over these States. To prove this, let Facts be submitted to a candid world.

He has refused his Assent to Laws, the most wholesome and necessary for the public good.

He has forbidden his Governors to pass Laws of immediate and pressing importance, unless suspended in their operation till his Assent should be obtained; and when so suspended, he has utterly neglected to attend to them.

He has refused to pass other Laws for the accommodation of large districts of people, unless those people would relinquish the right of Representation in the Legislature, a right inestimable to them and formidable to tyrants only.

He has called together legislative bodies at places unusual, uncomfortable, and distant from the depository of their public Records, for the sole purpose of fatiguing them into compliance with his measures.

He has dissolved Representative Houses repeatedly, for opposing with manly firmness his invasions on the rights of the people.

He has refused for a long time, after such dissolutions, to cause others to be elected; whereby the Legislative powers, incapable of Annihilation, have returned to the People at large for their exercise; the State remaining in the mean time exposed to all the dangers of invasion from without, and convulsions within.

He has endeavoured to prevent the population of these States; for that purpose obstructing the Laws for Naturalization of Foreigners; refusing to pass others to encourage their migrations hither, and raising the conditions of new Appropriations of Lands.

He has obstructed the Administration of Justice, by refusing his Assent to Laws for establishing Judiciary powers.

He has made Judges dependent on his Will alone, for the tenure of their offices, and the amount and payment of their salaries.

He has erected a multitude of New Offices, and sent hither swarms of Officers to harrass our people, and eat out their substance.

He has kept among us, in times of peace, standing Armies without the Consent of our legislatures.

He has affected to render the Military independent of and superior to the Civil power.

He has combined with others to subject us to a jurisdiction foreign to our constitution, and unacknowledged by our laws; giving his Assent to their Acts of pretended Legislation: For Quartering large bodies of armed troops among us: For protecting them, by a mock Trial, from punishment for any Murders which they should commit on the Inhabitants of these States: For cutting off our Trade with all parts of the world: For imposing Taxes on us without our Consent: For depriving us in many cases of the benefits of Trial by Jury: For transporting us beyond Seas to be tried for pretended offences: For abolishing the free System of English Laws in a neighbouring Province, establishing therein an Arbitrary government, and enlarging its Boundaries so as to render it at once an example and fit instrument for introducing the same absolute rule into these Colonies: For taking away our Charters, abolishing our most valuable Laws, and altering fundamentally the Forms of our Governments: For suspending our own Legislatures, and declaring themselves invested with power to legislate for us in all cases whatsoever.

He has abdicated Government here, by declaring us out of his Protection and waging War against us.

He has plundered our seas, ravaged our Coasts, burnt our towns, and destroyed the Lives of our people.

He is at this time transporting large Armies of foreign Mercenaries to compleat the works of death, desolation, and tyranny, already begun with circumstances of Cruelty & perfidy scarcely paralleled in the most barbarous ages, and totally unworthy the Head of a civilized nation.

He has constrained our fellow Citizens taken Captive on the high Seas to bear Arms against their Country, to become the executioners of their friends and Brethren, or to fall themselves by their Hands.

37

He has excited domestic insurrections amongst us, and has endeavoured to bring on the inhabitants of our frontiers, the merciless Indian Savages, whose known rule of warfare, is an undistinguished destruction of all ages, sexes and conditions.

In every stage of these Oppressions We have Petitioned for Redress in the most humble terms: Our repeated Petitions have been answered only by repeated injury.

A Prince, whose character is thus marked by every act which may define a Tyrant, is unfit to be the ruler of a free people.

Nor have We been wanting in attentions to our British brethren. We have warned them from time to time of attempts by their legislature to extend an unwarrantable jurisdiction over us. We have reminded them of the circumstance of our emigration and settlement here. We have appealed to their native justice and magnanimity, and we have conjured them by the ties of our common kindred to disavow these usurpations, which would inevitably interrupt our connections and correspondence. They too have been deaf to the voice of justice and of consanguinity. We must, therefore, acquiesce in the necessity, which denounces our Separation, and hold them, as we hold the rest of mankind, Enemies in War, in Peace Friends.

We, therefore, the Representatives of the United States of America, in General Congress, Assembled, appealing to the Supreme Judge of the world for the rectitude of our intentions, do, in the Name, and by Authority of the good People of these Colonies, solemnly publish and declare, That these United Colonies are, and of Right ought to be Free and Independent States; that they are Absolved from all Allegiance to the British Crown, and that all political connection between them and the State of Great Britain, is and ought to be totally dissolved; and that as Free and Independent States, they have full Power to levy War, conclude Peace, contract Alliances, establish Commerce, and to do all other Acts and Things which Independent States may of right do.

And for the support of this Declaration, with a firm reliance on the protection of divine Providence, we mutually pledge to each other our Lives, our Fortunes and our sacred Honor. (*1776*)

from Notes on Virginia[1]

Query 6. A notice of the mines and other subterraneous riches; its trees, plants, fruits, etc.

Our quadrupeds have been mostly described by Linnæus and Mons. de Buffon. Of these the mammoth, or big buffalo, as called by the Indians, must certainly have been the largest. Their tradition is, that he was carnivorous, and still exists in the northern parts of America. A delegation of warriors from the Delaware tribe having visited the Governor of Virginia, during the revolution,

38

From The Writings of Thomas Jefferson, *edited by Andrew A. Lipscomb, The Thomas Jefferson Memorial Association.*
[1] *Jefferson's footnotes to the* Notes on Virginia *are omitted in the following text.*

on matters of business, after these had been discussed and settled in council, the Governor asked them some questions relative to their country, and among others, what they knew or had heard of the animal whose bones were found at the Saltlicks on the Ohio. Their chief speaker immediately put himself into an attitude of oratory, and with a pomp suited to what he conceived the elevation of his subject, informed him that it was a tradition handed down from their fathers, "That in ancient times a herd of these tremendous animals came to the Big-bone licks, and began an universal destruction of the bear, deer, elks, buffaloes, and other animals which had been created for the use of the Indians; that the Great Man above, looking down and seeing this, was so enraged that he seized his lightning, descended on the earth, seated himself on a neighboring mountain, on a rock of which his seat and the print of his feet are still to be seen, and hurled his bolts among them till the whole were slaughtered, except the big bull, who presenting his forehead to the shafts, shook them off as they fell; but missing one at length, it wounded him in the side; whereon, springing round, he bounded over the Ohio, over the Wabash, the Illinois, and finally over the great lakes, where he is living at this day." It is well known, that on the Ohio, and in many parts of America further north, tusks, grinders, and skeletons of unparalleled magnitude, are found in great numbers, some lying on the surface of the earth, and some a little below it. A Mr. Stanley, taken prisoner near the mouth of the Tennessee, relates, that after being transferred through several tribes, from one to another, he was at length carried over the mountains west of the Missouri to a river which runs westwardly; that these bones abounded there, and that the natives described to him the animal to which they belonged as still existing in the northern parts of their country; from which description he judged it to be an elephant. Bones of the same kind have been lately found, some feet below the surface of the earth, in salines opened on the North Holston, a branch of the Tennessee, about the latitude of $36\frac{1}{2}°$ north. From the accounts published in Europe, I suppose it to be decided that these are of the same kind with those found in Siberia. Instances are mentioned of like animal remains found in the more southern climates of both hemispheres; but they are either so loosely mentioned as to leave a doubt of the fact, so inaccurately described as not to authorize the classing them with the great northern bones, or so rare as to found a suspicion that they have been carried thither as curiosities from the northern regions. So that, on the whole, there seem to be no certain vestiges of the existence of this animal farther south than the salines just mentioned. It is remarkable that the tusks and skeletons have been ascribed by the naturalists of Europe to the elephant, while the grinders have been given to the hippopotamus, or river horse. Yet it is acknowledged, that the tusks and skeletons are much larger than those of the elephant, and the grinders many times greater than those of the hippopotamus, and essentially different in form. Wherever these grinders are found, there also we find the tusks and skeleton; but no skeleton of the hippopotamus nor grinders of the elephant. It will not be said that the hippopotamus and elephant came always to the same spot, the former to deposit his grinders, and the latter his tusks and skeleton. For what became of the parts not deposited there? We must agree then, that these remains belong to each other, that they are of one and the same animal, that this was not a hippopotamus, because the hippopota-

39

mus had no tusks, nor such a frame, and because the grinders differ in their size as well as in the number and form of their points. That this was not an elephant, I think ascertained by proofs equally decisive. I will not avail myself of the authority of the celebrated anatomist, who, from an examination of the form and structure of the tusks, has declared they were essentially different from those of the elephant; because another anatomist, equally celebrated, has declared, on a like examination, that they are precisely the same. Between two such authorities I will suppose this circumstance equivocal. But, 1. The skeleton of the mammoth (for so the incognitum has been called) bespeaks an animal of five or six times the cubic volume of the elephant, as Mons. de Buffon has admitted. 2. The grinders are five times as large, are square, and the grinding surface studded with four or five rows of blunt points; whereas those of the elephant are broad and thin, and their grinding surface flat. 3. I have never heard an instance, and suppose there has been none, of the grinder of an elephant being found in America. 4. From the known temperature and constitution of the elephant, he could never have existed in those regions where the remains of the mammoth have been found. The elephant is a native only of the torrid zone and its vicinities; if, with the assistance of warm apartments and warm clothing, he has been preserved in the temperate climates of Europe, it has only been for a small portion of what would have been his natural period, and no instance of his multiplication in them has ever been known. But no bones of the mammoth, as I have before observed, have been ever found further south than the salines of Holston, and they have been found as far north as the Arctic circle. Those, therefore, who are of opinion that the elephant and mammoth are the same, must believe, 1. That the elephant known to us can exist and multiply in the frozen zone; or, 2. That an eternal fire may once have warmed those regions, and since abandoned them, of which, however, the globe exhibits no unequivocal indications; or, 3. That the obliquity of the ecliptic, when these elephants lived, was so great as to include within the tropics all those regions in which the bones are found; the tropics being, as is before observed, the natural limits of habitation for the elephant. But if it be admitted that this obliquity has really decreased, and we adopt the highest rate of decrease yet pretended, that is, of one minute in a century, to transfer the northern tropic to the Arctic circle, would carry the existence of these supposed elephants two hundred and fifty thousand years back; a period far beyond our conception of the duration of animal bones less exposed to the open air than these are in many instances. Besides, though these regions would then be supposed within the tropics, yet their winters would have been too severe for the sensibility of the elephant. They would have had, too, but one day and one night in the year, a circumstance to which we have no reason to suppose the nature of the elephant fitted. However, it has been demonstrated, that, if a variation of obliquity in the ecliptic takes place at all, it is vibratory, and never exceeds the limits of nine degrees, which is not sufficient to bring these bones within the tropics. One of these hypotheses, or some other equally voluntary and inadmissible to cautious philosophy, must be adopted to support the opinion that these are the bones of the elephant. For my own part, I find it easier to believe that an animal may have existed, resembling the elephant in his tusks, and general anatomy, while his nature was in other respects extremely different. From the 30th degree of

40

south latitude to the 30th degree of north, are nearly the limits which nature has fixed for the existence and multiplication of the elephant known to us. Proceeding thence northwardly to 36½ degrees, we enter those assigned to the mammoth. The farther we advance north, the more their vestiges multiply as far as the earth has been explored in that direction; and it is as probable as otherwise, that this progression continues to the pole itself, if land extends so far. The centre of the frozen zone, then, may be acmé of their vigor, as that of the torrid is of the elephant. Thus nature seems to have drawn a belt of separation between these two tremendous animals, whose breadth, indeed, is not precisely known, though at present we may suppose it about 6½ degrees of latitude; to have assigned to the elephant the region south of these confines, and those north to the mammoth, founding the constitution of the one in her extreme of heat, and that of the other in the extreme of cold. When the Creator has therefore separated their nature as far as the extent of the scale of animal life allowed to this planet would permit, it seems perverse to declare it the same, from a partial resemblance of their tusks and bones. But to whatever animal we ascribe these remains, it is certain such a one has existed in America, and that it has been the largest of all terrestrial beings. It should have sufficed to have rescued the earth it inhabited, and the atmosphere it breathed, from the imputation of impotence in the conception and nourishment of animal life on a large scale; to have stifled, in its birth, the opinion of a writer, the most learned, too, of all others in the science of animal history, that in the new world, "La nature vivante est beaucoup moins agissante, beaucoup moins forte:" that nature is less active, less energetic on one side of the globe than she is on the other. As if both sides were not warmed by the same genial sun; as if a soil of the same chemical composition was less capable of elaborations into animal nutriment; as if the fruits and grains from that soil and sun yielded a less rich chyle, gave less extension to the solids and fluids of the body, or produced sooner in the cartilages, membranes, and fibres, that rigidity which restrains all further extension, and terminates animal growth. The truth is, that a pigmy and a Patagonian, a mouse and a mammoth, derive their dimensions from the same nutritive juices. The difference of increment depends on circumstances unsearchable to beings with our capacities. Every race of animals seems to have received from their Maker certain laws of extension at the time of their formation. Their elaborate organs were formed to produce this, while proper obstacles were opposed to its further progress. Below these limits they cannot fall, nor rise above them. What intermediate station they shall take may depend on soil, on climate, on food, on a careful choice of breeders. But all the manna of heaven would never raise the mouse to the bulk of the mammoth.

The opinion advanced by the Count de Buffon, is 1. That the animals common both to the old and new world are smaller in the latter. 2. That those peculiar to the new are on a smaller scale. 3. That those which have been domesticated in both have degenerated in America; and 4. That on the whole it exhibits fewer species. And the reason he thinks is, that the heats of America are less; that more waters are spread over its surface by nature, and fewer of these drained off by the hand of man. In other words, that *heat* is friendly, and *moisture* adverse to the production and development of large quadrupeds. I will not meet this hypothesis on its first doubtful ground, whether the climate of America be

41

comparatively more humid? Because we are not furnished with observations sufficient to decide this question. And though, till it be decided, we are as free to deny as others are to affirm the fact, yet for a moment let it be supposed. The hypothesis, after this supposition, proceeds to another; that *moisture* is unfriendly to animal growth. The truth of this is inscrutable to us by reasonings *a priori*. Nature has hidden from us her *modus agendi*. Our only appeal on such questions is to experience; and I think that experience is against the supposition. It is by the assistance of *heat* and *moisture* that vegetables are elaborated from the elements of earth, air, water, and fire. We accordingly see the more humid climates produce the greater quantity of vegetables. Vegetables are mediately or immediately the food of every animal; and in proportion to the quantity of food, we see animals not only multiplied in their numbers, but improved in their bulk, as far as the laws of their nature will admit. Of this opinion is the Count de Buffon himself in another part of his work; "en general il paroit que les pays un peu *froids* conviennent mieux à nos bœufs que les pays chauds, et qu'ils sont d'autant plus gros et plus grands que le climat est plus *humide* et plus abondans en pâturages. Les bœufs de Danemarck, de la Podolie, de l'Ukraine et de la Tartarie qu'habitent les Calmouques sont les plus grands de tous." [2] Here then a race of animals, and one of the largest too, has been increased in its dimensions by *cold* and *moisture,* in direct opposition to the hypothesis, which supposes that these two circumstances diminish animal bulk, and that it is their contraries *heat* and *dryness* which enlarge it. But when we appeal to experience we are not to rest satisfied with a single fact. Let us, therefore, try our question on more general ground. Let us take two portions of the earth, Europe and America for instance, sufficiently extensive to give operation to general causes; let us consider the circumstances peculiar to each, and observe their effect on animal nature. America, running through the torrid as well as temperate zone, has more *heat* collectively taken, than Europe. But Europe, according to our hypothesis, is the *dryest.* They are equally adapted then to animal productions; each being endowed with one of those causes which befriends animal growth, and with one which opposes it. If it be thought unequal to compare Europe with America, which is so much larger, I answer, not more so than to compare America with the whole world. Besides, the purpose of the comparison is to try an hypothesis, which makes the size of animals depend on the *heat* and *moisture* of climate. If, therefore, we take a region, so extensive as to comprehend a sensible distinction of climate, and so extensive, too, as that local accidents, or the intercourse of animals on its borders, may not materially affect the size of those in its interior parts, we shall comply with those conditions which the hypothesis may reasonably demand. The objection would be the weaker in the present case, because any intercourse of animals which may take place on the confines of Europe and Asia, is to the advantage of the former, Asia producing certainly larger animals than Europe. Let us then take a comparative view of the quadrupeds of Europe and America, presenting them to the eye in three different tables, in one of which shall be enumerated those found in both countries; in a second, those found in

42

---

[2] *In general it seems that rather cold countries are better suited to our cattle than hot countries, and that cattle are fatter and taller in proportion to the humidity of the climate and to the abundance of pasturage. Cattle from Denmark, from Podolia, from the Ukraine and from that part of Turkestan inhabited by the Kalmucks are the largest of all.*

one only; in a third, those which have been domesticated in both. To facilitate the comparison, let those of each table be arranged in gradation according to their sizes, from the greatest to the smallest, so far as their sizes can be conjectured. The weights of the large animals shall be expressed in the English avoirdupoise pound and its decimals; those of the smaller, in the same ounce and its decimals. Those which are marked thus *, are actual weights of particular subjects, deemed among the largest of their species. Those marked thus †, are furnished by judicious persons, well acquainted with the species, and saying, from conjecture only, what the largest individual they had seen would probably have weighed. The other weights are taken from Messrs. Buffon and D'Aubenton, and are of such subjects as came casually to their hands for dissection. This circumstance must be remembered where their weights and mine stand opposed; the latter being stated not to produce a conclusion in favor of the American species, but to justify a suspension of opinion until we are better informed, and a suspicion, in the meantime, that there is no uniform difference in favor of either; which is all I pretend.

A Comparative View of the Quadrupeds of Europe and of America

I. ABORIGINALS OF BOTH

	Europe lb.	America lb.
Mammoth		
Buffalo, Bison		*1800
White Bear. Ours blanc		
Carribou. Renne		
Bear. Ours	153.7	*410
Elk. Elan. Original palmated . . .		
Red deer. Cerf	288.8	*273
Fallow deer. Daim	167.8	
Wolf. Loup	69.8	
Roe. Chevreuil	56.7	
Glutton. Glouton. Carcajou . . .		
Wild Cat. Chat sauvage		†30
Lynx. Loup cervier	25.	
Beaver. Castor	18.5	*45

. . . Hitherto I have considered this hypothesis as applied to brute animals only, and not in its extension to the man of America, whether aboriginal or transplanted. It is the opinion of Mons. de Buffon that the former furnishes no exception to it. [*Here Jefferson quotes a long passage by de Buffon on the American Indian.*]

An afflicting picture, indeed, which for the honor of human nature, I am glad to believe has no original. Of the Indian of South America I know nothing; for I would not honor with the appellation of knowledge, what I derive from the

43

fables published of them. These I believe to be just as true as the fables of Æsop. This belief is founded on what I have seen of man, white, red, and black, and what has been written of him by authors, enlightened themselves, and writing among an enlightened people. The Indian of North America being more within our reach, I can speak of him somewhat from my own knowledge, but more from the information of others better acquainted with him, and on whose truth and judgment I can rely. From these sources I am able to say, in contradiction to this representation, that he is neither more defective in ardor, nor more impotent with his female, than the white reduced to the same diet and exercise; that he is brave, when an enterprise depends on bravery; education with him making the point of honor consist in the destruction of an enemy by strategem, and in the preservation of his own person free from injury; or, perhaps, this is nature, while it is education which teaches us to honor force more than finesse; that he will defend himself against a host of enemies, always choosing to be killed, rather than to surrender, though it be to the whites, who he knows will treat him well; that in other situations, also, he meets death with more deliberation, and endures tortures with a firmness unknown almost to religious enthusiasm with us; that he is affectionate to his children, careful of them, and indulgent in the extreme; that his affections comprehend his other connections, weakening, as with us, from circle to circle, as they recede from the centre; that his friendships are strong and faithful to the uttermost extremity; that his sensibility is keen, even the warriors weeping most bitterly on the loss of their children, though in general they endeavor to appear superior to human events; that his vivacity and activity of mind is equal to ours in the same situation; hence his eagerness for hunting, and for games of chance. The women are submitted to unjust drudgery. This I believe is the case with every barbarous people. With such, force is law. The stronger sex imposes on the weaker. It is civilization alone which replaces women in the enjoyment of their natural equality. That first teaches us to subdue the selfish passions, and to respect those rights in others which we value in ourselves. Were we in equal barbarism, our females would be equal drudges. The man with them is less strong than with us, but their woman stronger than ours; and both for the same obvious reason; because our man and their woman is habituated to labor, and formed by it. With both races the sex which is indulged with ease is the least athletic. An Indian man is small in the hand and wrist, for the same reason for which a sailor is large and strong in the arms and shoulders, and a porter in the legs and thighs. They raise fewer children than we do. The causes of this are to be found, not in a difference of nature, but of circumstance. The women very frequently attending the men in their parties of war and of hunting, child-bearing becomes extremely inconvenient to them. It is said, therefore, that they have learned the practice of procuring abortion by the use of some vegetable; and that it even extends to prevent conception for a considerable time after. During these parties they are exposed to numerous hazards, to excessive exertions, to the greatest extremities of hunger. Even at their homes the nation depends for food, through a certain part of every year, on the gleanings of the forest; that is, they experience a famine once in every year. With all animals, if the female be badly fed, or not fed at all, her young perish; and if both male and female be reduced to like want,

44

generation becomes less active, less productive. To the obstacles, then, of want and hazard, which nature has opposed to the multiplication of wild animals, for the purpose of restraining their numbers within certain bounds, those of labor and of voluntary abortion are added with the Indian. No wonder, then, if they multiply less than we do. Where food is regularly supplied, a single farm will show more of cattle, than a whole country of forests can of buffalos. The same Indian women, when married to white traders, who feed them and their children plentifully and regularly, who exempt them from excessive drudgery, who keep them stationary and unexposed to accident, produce and raise as many children as the white women. Instances are known, under these circumstances, of their rearing a dozen children. An inhuman practice once prevailed in this country, of making slaves of the Indians. It is a fact well known with us, that the Indian women so enslaved produced and raised as numerous families as either the whites or blacks among whom they lived. It has been said that Indians have less hair than the whites, except on the head. But this is a fact of which fair proof can scarcely be had. With them it is disgraceful to be hairy on the body. They say it likens them to hogs. They therefore pluck the hair as fast as it appears. But the traders who marry their women, and prevail on them to discontinue this practice, say, that nature is the same with them as with the whites. Nor, if the fact be true, is the consequence necessary which has been drawn from it. Negroes have notoriously less hair than the whites; yet they are more ardent. But if cold and moisture be the agents of nature for diminishing the races of animals, how comes she all at once to suspend their operation as to the physical man of the new world, whom the Count acknowledges to be "à peu près de même stature que l'homme de notre monde,"[3] and to let loose their influence on his moral faculties? How has this "combination of the elements and other physical causes, so contrary to the enlargement of animal nature in this new world, these obstacles to the development and formation of great germs," been arrested and suspended, so as to permit the human body to acquire its just dimensions, and by what inconceivable process has their action been directed on his mind alone? To judge of the truth of this, to form a just estimate of their genius and mental powers, more facts are wanting, and great allowance to be made for those circumstances of their situation which call for a display of particular talents only. This done, we shall probably find that they are formed in mind as well as body, on the same module with the "Homo sapiens Europæus." The principles of their society forbidding all compulsion, they are to be led to duty and to enterprise by personal influence and persuasion. Hence eloquence in council, bravery and address in war, become the foundations of all consequence with them. To these acquirements all their faculties are directed. Of their bravery and address in war we have multiplied proofs, because we have been the subjects on which they were exercised. Of their eminence in oratory we have fewer examples, because it is displayed chiefly in their own councils. Some, however, we have, of very superior lustre. I may challenge the whole orations of Demosthenes and Cicero, and of any more eminent orator, if Europe has furnished any more eminent, to produce a single passage, superior to the speech

[3] *Of about the same stature as a man of our world.*

of Logan, a Mingo chief, to Lord Dunmore, when governor of this state. And as a testimony of their talents in this line, I beg leave to introduce it, first stating the incidents necessary for understanding it.

In the spring of the year 1774, a robbery was committed by some Indians on certain land-adventurers on the river Ohio. The whites in that quarter, according to their custom, undertook to punish this outrage in a summary way. Captain Michael Cresap, and a certain Daniel Greathouse, leading on these parties, surprised, at different times, travelling and hunting parties of the Indians, having their women and children with them, and murdered many. Among these were unfortunately the family of Logan, a chief celebrated in peace and war, and long distinguished as the friend of the whites. This unworthy return provoked his vengeance. He accordingly signalized himself in the war which ensued. In the autumn of the same year a decisive battle was fought at the mouth of the Great Kanhaway, between the collected forces of the Shawanese, Mingoes and Delawares, and a detachment of the Virginia militia. The Indians were defeated and sued for peace. Logan, however, disdained to be seen among the suppliants. But lest the sincerity of a treaty should be distrusted, from which so distinguished a chief absented himself, he sent, by a messenger, the following speech, to be delivered to Lord Dunmore:

> "I appeal to any white man to say, if ever he entered Logan's cabin hungry, and he gave him not meat; if ever he came cold and naked, and he cloathed him not. During the course of the last long and bloody war Logan remained idle in his cabin an advocate for peace. Such was my love for the whites, that my countrymen pointed as they passed, and said, 'Logan is the friend of white men.' I had even thought to have lived with you, but for the injuries of one man. Colonel Cresap, the last spring in cold blood, and unprovoked, murdered all the relations of Logan, not sparing even my women and children. There runs not a drop of my blood in the veins of any living creature. This called on me for revenge. I have sought it: I have killed many: I have fully glutted my vengeance: for my country I rejoice at the beams of peace. But do not harbour a thought that mine is the joy of fear. Logan never felt fear. He will not turn on his heel to save his life. Who is there to mourn for Logan?—Not one."

Before we condemn the Indians of this continent as wanting genius, we must consider that letters have not yet been introduced among them. Were we to compare them in their present state with the Europeans North of the Alps, when the Roman arms and arts first crossed those mountains, the comparison would be unequal, because, at that time, those parts of Europe were swarming with numbers: because numbers produce emulation and multiply the chances of improvement, and one improvement begets another. Yet I may safely ask, how many good poets, how many able mathematicians, how many great inventors, in arts or sciences, had Europe, North of the Alps, then produced? And it was sixteen centuries after this before a Newton could be formed. I do not mean to deny that there are varieties in the race of man, distinguished by their powers both of body and mind. I believe there are, as I see to be the case in the races

46

of other animals. I only mean to suggest a doubt, whether the bulk and faculties of animals depend on the side of the Atlantic on which their food happens to grow, or which furnishes the elements of which they are compounded? Whether nature has enlisted herself as a Cis- or Trans-Atlantic partisan? I am induced to suspect there has been more eloquence than sound reasoning displayed in support of this theory; that it is one of those cases where the judgment has been seduced by a glowing pen; and whilst I render every tribute of honor and esteem to the celebrated Zoologist, who has added, and is still adding, so many precious things to the treasures of science, I must doubt whether in this instance he has not cherished error also by lending her for a moment his vivid imagination and bewitching language.

So far the Count de Buffon has carried this new theory of the tendency of nature to belittle her productions on this side the Atlantic. Its application to the race of whites transplanted from Europe, remained for the Abbè Raynal. "On doit etre etonné (he says) que l'Amerique n'ait pas encore produit un bon poëte, un habile mathematicien, un homme de genie dans un seul art, ou seule science." [4] Hist. Philos. pa. 92, edn. Maestricht, 1774. "America has not yet produced one good poet." When we shall have existed as a people as long as the Greeks did before they produced a Homer, the Romans a Virgil, the French a Racine and Voltaire, the English a Shakespeare and Milton, should this reproach be still true, we will inquire from what unfriendly causes it has proceeded, that the other countries of Europe and quarters of the earth shall not have inscribed any name in the roll of poets. But neither has America produced "one able mathematician, one man of genius in a single art or a single science." In war we have produced a Washington, whose memory will be adored while liberty shall have votaries, whose name will triumph over time, and will in future ages assume its just station among the most celebrated worthies of the world, when that wretched philosophy shall be forgotten which would have arranged him among the degeneracies of nature. In physics we have produced a Franklin, than whom no one of the present age has made more important discoveries, nor has enriched philosophy with more, or more ingenious solutions of the phenomena of nature. We have supposed Mr. Rittenhouse second to no astronomer living; that in genius he must be the first, because he is self taught. As an artist he has exhibited as great a proof of mechanical genius as the world has ever produced. He has not indeed made a world; but he has by imitation approached nearer its Maker than any man who has lived from the creation to this day. As in philosophy and war, so in government, in oratory, in painting, in the plastic art, we might show that America, though but a child of yesterday, has already given hopeful proofs of genius, as well as of the nobler kinds, which arouse the best feelings of man, which call him into action, which substantiate his freedom, and conduct him to happiness, as of the subordinate, which serve to amuse him only. We therefore suppose, that this reproach is as unjust as it is unkind: and that, of the geniuses which adorn the present age, America contributes its full share. For comparing it with those countries where genius is most cultivated, where are the most excellent models for art, and scaffoldings for

47

[4] *One is surprised that America has not yet produced a good poet, a capable mathematician, a man of genius in a single art or in a single science.*

the attainment of science, as France and England for instance, we calculate thus: The United States contains three millions of inhabitants; France twenty millions; and the British islands ten. We produce a Washington, a Franklin, a Rittenhouse. France then should have half a dozen in each of these lines, and Great Britain half that number, equally eminent. It may be true that France has: we are but just becoming acquainted with her, and our acquaintance so far gives us high ideas of the genius of her inhabitants. It would be injuring too many of them to name particularly a Voltaire, a Buffon, the constellation of Encyclopedists, the Abbè Raynal himself, etc., etc. We, therefore, have reason to believe she can produce her full quota of genius. The present war having so long cut off all communication with Great Britain, we are not able to make a fair estimate of the state of science in that country. The spirit in which she wages war, is the only sample before our eyes, and that does not seem the legitimate offspring either of science or of civilization. The sun of her glory is fast descending to the horizon. Her philosophy has crossed the channel, her freedom the Atlantic, and herself seems passing to that awful dissolution whose issue is not given human foresight to scan.

Query 18. The particular customs and manners that may happen to be received in that State?

It is difficult to determine on the standard by which the manners of a nation may be tried, whether *catholic* or *particular*. It is more difficult for a native to bring to that standard the manners of his own nation, familiarized to him by habit. There must doubtless be an unhappy influence on the manners of our people produced by the existence of slavery among us. The whole commerce between master and slave is a perpetual exercise of the most boisterous passions, the most unremitting despotism on the one part, and degrading submissions on the other. Our children see this, and learn to imitate it; for man is an imitative animal. This quality is the germ of all education in him. From his cradle to his grave he is learning to do what he sees others do. If a parent could find no motive either in his philanthropy or his self-love, for restraining the intemperance of passion towards his slave, it should always be a sufficient one that his child is present. But generally it is not sufficient. The parent storms, the child looks on, catches the lineaments of wrath, puts on the same airs in the circle of smaller slaves, gives a loose to the worst of passions, and thus nursed, educated, and daily exercised in tyranny, cannot but be stamped by it with odious peculiarities. The man must be a prodigy who can retain his manners and morals undepraved by such circumstances. And with what execration should the statesman be loaded, who, permitting one half the citizens thus to trample on the rights of the other, transforms those into despots, and these into enemies, destroys the morals of the one part, and the *amor patriae* of the other. For if a slave can have a country in this world, it must be any other in preference to that in which he is born to live and labor for another; in which he must lock up the faculties of his nature, contribute as far as depends on his individual endeavors to the evanishment of the human race, or entail his own miserable condition on

48

the endless generations proceeding from him. With the morals of the people, their industry also is destroyed. For in a warm climate, no man will labor for himself who can make another labor for him. This is so true, that of the proprietors of slaves a very small proportion indeed are ever seen to labor. And can the liberties of a nation be thought secure when we have removed their only firm basis, a conviction in the minds of the people that these liberties are of the gift of God? That they are not to be violated but with His wrath? Indeed I tremble for my country when I reflect that God is just; that his justice cannot sleep forever; that considering numbers, nature and natural means only, a revolution of the wheel of fortune, an exchange of situation is among possible events; that it may become probable by supernatural interference! The Almighty has no attribute which can take side with us in such a contest. But it is impossible to be temperate and to pursue this subject through the various considerations of policy, of morals, of history natural and civil. We must be contented to hope they will force their way into every one's mind. I think a change already perceptible, since the origin of the present revolution. The spirit of the master is abating, that of the slave rising from the dust, his condition mollifying, the way I hope preparing, under the auspices of heaven, for a total emancipation, and that this is disposed, in the order of events, to be with the consent of the masters, rather than by their extirpation.

Query 19. The present state of manufactures, commerce, interior and exterior trade?

We never had an interior trade of any importance. Our exterior commerce has suffered very much from the beginning of the present contest. During this time we have manufactured within our families the most necessary articles of clothing. Those of cotton will bear some comparison with the same kinds of manufacture in Europe; but those of wool, flax and hemp are very coarse, unsightly, and unpleasant; and such is our attachment to agriculture, and such our preference for foreign manufactures, that be it wise or unwise, our people will certainly return as soon as they can, to the raising raw materials, and exchanging them for finer manufactures than they are able to execute themselves.

The political economists of Europe have established it as a principle, that every State should endeavor to manufacture for itself; and this principle, like many others, we transfer to America, without calculating the difference of circumstance which should often produce a difference of result. In Europe the lands are either cultivated, or locked up against the cultivator. Manufacture must therefore be resorted to of necessity not of choice, to support the surplus of their people. But we have an immensity of land courting the industry of the husbandman. Is it best then that all our citizens should be employed in its improvement, or that one half should be called off from that to exercise manufactures and handicraft arts for the other? Those who labor in the earth are the chosen people of God, if ever He had chosen people, whose breasts He has made His peculiar deposit for substantial and genuine virtue. It is the focus in which he keeps alive that sacred fire, which otherwise might escape from the

49

face of the earth. Corruption of morals in the mass of cultivators is a phenomenon of which no age nor nation has furnished an example. It is the mark set on those, who, not looking up to heaven, to their own soil and industry, as does the husbandman, for their subsistence, depend for it on casualties and caprice of customers. Dependence begets subservience and venality, suffocates the germ of virtue, and prepares fit tools for the designs of ambition. This, the natural progress and consequence of the arts, has sometimes perhaps been retarded by accidental circumstances; but, generally speaking, the proportion which the aggregate of the other classes of citizens bears in any State to that of its husbandmen, is the proportion of its unsound to its healthy parts, and is a good enough barometer whereby to measure its degree of corruption. While we have land to labor then, let us never wish to see our citizens occupied at a workbench, or twirling a distaff. Carpenters, masons, smiths, are wanting in husbandry; but, for the general operations of manufacture, let our workshops remain in Europe. It is better to carry provisions and materials to workmen there, than bring them to the provisions and materials, and with them their manners and principles. The loss by the transportation of commodities across the Atlantic will be made up in happiness and permanence of government. The mobs of great cities add just so much to the support of pure government, as sores do to the strength of the human body. It is the manners and spirit of a people which preserve a republic in vigor. A degeneracy in these is a canker which soon eats to the heart of its laws and constitution.

Query 22. The public Income and Expense?

. . . To this estimate of our abilities, let me add a word as to the application of them. If, when cleared of the present contest, and of the debts with which that will charge us, we come to measure force hereafter with any European power. Such events are devoutly to be deprecated. Young as we are, and with such a country before us to fill with people and with happiness, we should point in that direction the whole generative force of nature, wasting none of it in efforts of mutual destruction. It should be our endeavor to cultivate the peace and friendship of every nation, even of that which has injured us most, when we shall have carried our point against her. Our interest will be to throw open the doors of commerce, and to knock off all its shackles, giving perfect freedom to all persons for the vent of whatever they may choose to bring into our ports, and asking the same in theirs. Never was so much false arithmetic employed on any subject, as that which has been employed to persuade nations that it is their interest to go to war. Were the money which it has cost to gain, at the close of a long war, a little town, or a little territory, the right to cut wood here, or to catch fish there, expended in improving what they already possess, in making roads, opening rivers, building ports, improving the arts, and finding employment for their idle poor, it would render them much stronger, much wealthier and happier. This I hope will be our wisdom. And, perhaps, to remove as much as possible the occasions of making war, it might be better for us to abandon the ocean

altogether, that being the element whereon we shall be principally exposed to
jostle with other nations; to leave to others to bring what we shall want, and to
carry what we can spare. This would make us invulnerable to Europe, by offering none of our property to their prize, and would turn all our citizens to the
cultivation of the earth; and, I repeat it again, cultivators of the earth are the
most virtuous and independent citizens. It might be time enough to seek employment for them at sea, when the land no longer offers it. But the actual habits of
our countrymen attach them to commerce. They will exercise it for themselves.
Wars then must sometimes be our lot; and all the wise can do, will be to avoid
that half of them which would be produced by our own follies and our own
acts of injustice; and to make for the other half the best preparations we can.
Of what nature should these be? A land army would be useless for offence, and
not the best nor safest instrument of defence. For either of these purposes, the
sea is the field on which we should meet an European enemy. On that element
it is necessary we should possess some power. To aim at such a navy as the
greater nations of Europe possess, would be a foolish and wicked waste of the
energies of our countrymen. It would be to pull on our own heads the load of
military expense which makes the European laborer go supperless to bed, and
moistens his bread with the sweat of his brows. It will be enough if we enable
ourselves to prevent insults from those nations of Europe which are weak on
the sea, because circumstances exist, which render even the stronger ones weak
as to us. Providence has placed their richest and most defenceless possessions
at our door; has obliged their most precious commerce to pass, as it were, in
review before us. To protect this, or to assail, a small part only of their naval
force will ever be risked across the Atlantic. The dangers to which the elements
expose them here are too well known, and the greater dangers to which they
would be exposed at home were any general calamity to involve their whole
fleet. They can attack us by detachment only; and it will suffice to make ourselves equal to what they may detach. Even a smaller force than they may detach
will be rendered equal or superior by the quickness with which any check may
be repaired with us, while losses with them will be irreparable till too late. A
small naval force then is sufficient for us, and a small one is necessary. What
this should be, I will not undertake to say. I will only say, it should by no means
be so great as we are able to make it. Suppose the million of dollars, or three hundred thousand pounds, which Virginia could annually spare without distress, to
be applied to the creating a navy. A single year's contribution would build,
equip, man, and send to sea a force which should carry three hundred guns.
The rest of the confederacy, exerting themselves in the same proportion, would
equip in the same time fifteen hundred guns more. So that one year's contributions would set up a navy of eighteen hundred guns. The British ships of the
line average seventy-six guns; their frigates thirty-eight. Eighteen hundred guns
then would form a fleet of thirty ships, eighteen of which might be of the line,
and twelve frigates. Allowing eight men, the British average, for every gun, their
annual expense, including subsistence, clothing, pay, and ordinary repairs,
would be about $1,280 for every gun, or $2,304,000 for the whole. I state this
only as one year's possible exertion, without deciding whether more or less than
a year's exertion should be thus applied. . . . (1785)

51

Second Inaugural Address

Proceeding, fellow citizens, to that qualification which the constitution requires, before my entrance on the charge again conferred upon me, it is my duty to express the deep sense I entertain of this new proof of confidence from my fellow citizens at large, and the zeal with which it inspires me, so to conduct myself as may best satisfy their just expectations.

On taking this station on a former occasion, I declared the principles on which I believed it my duty to administer the affairs of our commonwealth. My conscience tells me that I have, on every occasion, acted up to that declaration, according to its obvious import, and to the understanding of every candid mind.

In the transaction of your foreign affairs, we have endeavored to cultivate the friendship of all nations, and especially of those with which we have the most important relations. We have done them justice on all occasions, favored where favor was lawful, and cherished mutual interests and intercourse on fair and equal terms. We are firmly convinced, and we act on that conviction, that with nations, as with individuals, our interests soundly calculated, will ever be found inseparable from our moral duties; and history bears witness to the fact, that a just nation is taken on its word, when recourse is had to armaments and wars to bridle others.

At home, fellow citizens, you best know whether we have done well or ill. The suppression of unnecessary offices, of useless establishments and expenses, enabled us to discontinue our internal taxes. These covering our land with officers, and opening our doors to their intrusions, had already begun that process of domiciliary vexation which, once entered, is scarcely to be restrained from reaching successively every article of produce and property. If among these taxes some minor ones fell which had not been inconvenient, it was because their amount would not have paid the officers who collected them, and because, if they had any merit, the state authorities might adopt them, instead of others less approved.

The remaining revenue on the consumption of foreign articles, is paid cheerfully by those who can afford to add foreign luxuries to domestic comforts, being collected on our seaboards and frontiers only, and incorporated with the transactions of our mercantile citizens, it may be the pleasure and pride of an American to ask, what farmer, what mechanic, what laborer, ever sees a tax-gatherer of the United States? These contributions enable us to support the current expenses of the government, to fulfil contracts with foreign nations, to extinguish the native right of soil within our limits, to extend those limits, and to apply such a surplus to our public debts, as places at a short day their final redemption, and that redemption once effected, the revenue thereby liberated may, by a just repartition among the states, and a corresponding amendment of the constitution, be applied, *in time of peace*, to rivers, canals, roads, arts, manufactures, education, and other great objects within each state. *In time of war*, if injustice, by ourselves or others, must sometimes produce war, increased as the same revenue will be increased by population and consumption,

52

From The Writings of Thomas Jefferson, *edited by Paul L. Ford, G. P. Putnam's Sons.*

and aided by other resources reserved for that crisis, it may meet within the year all the expenses of the year, without encroaching on the rights of future generations, by burdening them with the debts of the past. War will then be but a suspension of useful works, and a return to a state of peace, a return to the progress of improvement.

I have said, fellow citizens, that the income reserved had enabled us to extend our limits; but that extension may possibly pay for itself before we are called on, and in the meantime, may keep down the accruing interest; in all events, it will repay the advances we have made. I know that the acquisition of Louisiana has been disapproved by some, from a candid apprehension that the enlargement of our territory would endanger its union. But who can limit the extent to which the federative principle may operate effectively? The larger our association, the less will it be shaken by local passions; and in any view, is it not better that the opposite bank of the Mississippi should be settled by our own brethren and children, than by strangers of another family? With which shall we be most likely to live in harmony and friendly intercourse?

In matters of religion, I have considered that its free exercise is placed by the constitution independent of the powers of the general government. I have therefore undertaken, on no occasion, to prescribe the religious exercises suited to it; but have left them, as the constitution found them, under the direction and discipline of state or church authorities acknowledged by the several religious societies.

The aboriginal inhabitants of these countries I have regarded with the commiseration their history inspires. Endowed with the faculties and the rights of men, breathing an ardent love of liberty and independence, and occupying a country which left them no desire but to be undisturbed, the stream of overflowing population from other regions directed itself on these shores; without power to divert, or habits to contend against, they have been overwhelmed by the current, or driven before it; now reduced within limits too narrow for the hunter's state, humanity enjoins us to teach them agriculture and the domestic arts; to encourage them to that industry which alone can enable them to maintain their place in existence, and to prepare them in time for that state of society, which to bodily comforts adds the improvement of the mind and morals. We have therefore liberally furnished them with the implements of husbandry and household use; we have placed among them instructors in the arts of first necessity; and they are covered with the ægis of the law against aggressors from among ourselves.

But the endeavors to enlighten them on the fate which awaits their present course of life, to induce them to exercise their reason, follow its dictates, and change their pursuits with the change of circumstances, have powerful obstacles to encounter; they are combated by the habits of their bodies, prejudice of their minds, ignorance, pride, and the influence of interested and crafty individuals among them, who feel themselves something in the present order of things, and fear to become nothing in any other. These persons inculcate a sanctimonious reverence for the customs of their ancestors; that whatsoever they did, must be done through all time; that reason is a false guide, and to advance under its counsel, in their physical, moral, or political condition, is perilous innovation; that their duty is to remain as their Creator made them,

53

ignorance being safety, and knowledge full of danger; in short, my friends, among them is seen the action and counter-action of good sense and bigotry; they, too, have their anti-philosophers, who find an interest in keeping things in their present state, who dread reformation, and exert all their faculties to maintain the ascendency of habit over the duty of improving our reason, and obeying its mandates.

In giving these outlines, I do not mean, fellow citizens, to arrogate to myself the merit of the measures; that is due, in the first place, to the reflecting character of our citizens at large, who, by the weight of public opinion, influence and strengthen the public measures; it is due to the sound discretion with which they select from among themselves those to whom they confide the legislative duties; it is due to the zeal and wisdom of the characters thus selected, who lay the foundations of public happiness in wholesome laws, the execution of which alone remains for others; and it is due to the able and faithful auxiliaries, whose patriotism has associated with me in the executive functions.

During this course of administration, and in order to disturb it, the artillery of the press has been levelled against us, charged with whatsoever its licentiousness could devise or dare. These abuses of an institution so important to freedom and science, are deeply to be regretted, inasmuch as they tend to lessen its usefulness, and to sap its safety; they might, indeed, have been corrected by the wholesome punishments reserved and provided by the laws of the several States against falsehood and defamation; but public duties more urgent press on the time of public servants, and the offenders have therefore been left to find their punishment in the public indignation.

Nor was it uninteresting to the world, that an experiment should be fairly and fully made, whether freedom of discussion, unaided by power, is not sufficient for the propagation and protection of truth—whether a government, conducting itself in the true spirit of its constitution, with zeal and purity, and doing no act which it would be unwilling the whole world should witness, can be written down by falsehood and defamation. The experiment has been tried; you have witnessed the scene; our fellow citizens have looked on, cool and collected; they saw the latent source from which these outrages proceeded; they gathered around their public functionaries, and when the constitution called them to the decision by suffrage, they pronounced their verdict, honorable to those who had served them, and consolatory to the friend of man, who believes he may be intrusted with his own affairs.

No inference is here intended, that the laws, provided by the State against false and defamatory publications, should not be enforced; he who has time, renders a service to public morals and public tranquillity, in reforming these abuses by the salutary coercions of the law; but the experiment is noted, to prove that, since truth and reason have maintained their ground against false opinions in league with false facts, the press, confined to truth, needs no other legal restraint; the public judgment will correct false reasonings and opinions, on a full hearing of all parties; and no other definite line can be drawn between the inestimable liberty of the press and its demoralizing licentiousness. If there be still improprieties which this rule would not restrain, its supplement must be sought in the censorship of public opinion.

Contemplating the union of sentiment now manifested so generally, as auguring harmony and happiness to our future course, I offer to our country sincere congratulations. With those, too, not yet rallied to the same point, the disposition to do so is gaining strength; facts are piercing through the veil drawn over them; and our doubting brethren will at length see, that the mass of their fellow citizens, with whom they cannot yet resolve to act, as to principles and measures, think as they think, and desire what they desire; that our wish, as well as theirs, is, that the public efforts may be directed honestly to the public good, that peace be cultivated, civil and religious liberty unassailed, law and order preserved; equality of rights maintained, and that state of property, equal or unequal, which results to every man from his own industry, or that of his fathers. When satisfied of these views, it is not in human nature that they should not approve and support them; in the meantime, let us cherish them with patient affection; let us do them justice, and more than justice, in all competitions of interest; and we need not doubt that truth, reason, and their own interests, will at length prevail, will gather them into the fold of their country, and will complete their entire union of opinion, which gives to a nation the blessing of harmony, and the benefit of all its strength.

I shall now enter on the duties to which my fellow citizens have again called me, and shall proceed in the spirit of those principles which they have approved. I fear not that any motives of interest may lead me astray; I am sensible of no passion which could seduce me knowingly from the path of justice; but the weakness of human nature, and the limits of my own understanding, will produce errors of judgment sometimes injurious to your interests. I shall need, therefore, all the indulgence I have heretofore experienced—the want of it will certainly not lessen with increasing years. I shall need, too, the favor of that Being in whose hands we are, who led our forefathers, as Israel of old, from their native land, and planted them in a country flowing with all the necessaries and comforts of life; who has covered our infancy with his providence, and our riper years with his wisdom and power; and to whose goodness I ask you to join with me in supplications, that he will so enlighten the minds of your servants, guide their councils, and prosper their measures, that whatsoever they do, shall result in your good, and shall secure to you the peace, friendship, and approbation of all nations. (*1805*)

Letters

To Robert Skipwith

Monticello, Aug. 3, 1771

I sat down with a design of executing your request to form a catalogue of books to the amount of about 50 lib. sterling.[1] But could by no means satisfy myself with any partial choice I could make. Thinking, therefore, it might be

Jefferson's letters from The Writings of Thomas Jefferson, *edited by Andrew A. Lipscomb, The Thomas Jefferson Memorial Association.*
[1] *Robert Skipwith, husband of the half sister of the future Mrs. Jefferson, had asked Jefferson for advice on reading.*

as agreeable to you I have framed such a general collection as I think you would wish and might in time find convenient to procure. Out of this you will choose for yourself to the amount you mentioned for the present year and may hereafter as shall be convenient proceed in completing the whole. A view of the second column in this catalogue would I suppose extort a smile from the face of gravity. Peace to its wisdom! Let me not awaken it. A little attention however to the nature of the human mind evinces that the entertainments of fiction are useful as well as pleasant. That they are pleasant when well written every person feels who reads. But wherein is its utility asks the reverend sage, big with the notion that nothing can be useful but the learned lumber of Greek and Roman reading with which his head is stored?

I answer, everything is useful which contributes to fix in the principles and practices of virtue. When any original act of charity or of gratitude, for instance, is presented either to our sight or imagination, we are deeply impressed with its beauty and feel a strong desire in ourselves of doing charitable and grateful acts also. On the contrary when we see or read of any atrocious deed, we are disgusted with its deformity, and conceive an abhorrence of vice. Now every emotion of this kind is an exercise of our virtuous dispositions, and dispositions of the mind, like limbs of the body acquire strength by exercise. But exercise produces habit, and in the instance of which we speak the exercise being of the moral feelings produces a habit of thinking and acting virtuously. We never reflect whether the story we read be truth or fiction. If the painting be lively, and a tolerable picture of nature, we are thrown into a reverie, from which if we awaken it is the fault of the writer. I appeal to every reader of feeling and sentiment whether the fictitious murder of Duncan by Macbeth in Shakespeare does not excite in him as great a horror of villany, as the real one of Henry IV. by Ravaillac as related by Davila? And whether the fidelity of Nelson and generosity of Blandford in Marmontel do not dilate his breast and elevate his sentiments as much as any similar incident which real history can furnish? Does he not in fact feel himself a better man while reading them, and privately covenant to copy the fair example? We neither know nor care whether Lawrence Sterne really went to France, whether he was there accosted by the Franciscan, at first rebuked him unkindly, and then gave him a peace offering: or whether the whole be not fiction. In either case we equally are sorrowful at the rebuke, and secretly resolve *we* will never do so: we are pleased with the subsequent atonement, and view with emulation a soul candidly acknowledging its fault and making a just reparation. Considering history as a moral exercise, her lessons would be too infrequent if confined to real life. Of those recorded by historians few incidents have been attended with such circumstances as to excite in any high degree this sympathetic emotion of virtue. We are, therefore, wisely framed to be as warmly interested for a fictitious as for a real personage. The field of imagination is thus laid open to our use and lessons may be formed to illustrate and carry home to the heart every moral rule of life. Thus a lively and lasting sense of filial duty is more effectually impressed on the mind of a son or daughter by reading King Lear, than by all the dry volumes of ethics, and divinity that ever were written. This is my idea of well written Romance, of Tragedy, Comedy and Epic poetry.—If you are fond of speculation the books under the

56

head of Criticism will afford you much pleasure. Of Politics and Trade I have given you a few only of the best books, as you would probably choose to be not unacquainted with those commercial principles which bring wealth into our country, and the constitutional security we have for the enjoyment of that wealth. In Law I mention a few systematical books, as a knowledge of the minutiae of that science is not necessary for a private gentleman. In Religion, History, Natural philosophy, I have followed the same plan in general.—But whence the necessity of this collection? Come to the new Rowanty, from which you may reach your hand to a library formed on a more extensive plan. Separated from each other but a few paces the possessions of each would be open to the other. A spring centrically situated might be the scene of every evening's joy. There we should talk over the lessons of the day, or lose them in music, chess or the merriments of our family companions. The heart thus lightened our pillows would be soft, and health and long life would attend the happy scene. Come then and bring our dear Tibby with you, the first in your affections, and second in mine. Offer prayers for me, too, at that shrine to which though absent I pray continual devotions. In every scheme of happiness she is placed in the foreground of the picture, as the principal figure. Take that away, and it is no picture for me. Bear my affections to Wintipock clothed in the warmest expressions of sincerity; and to yourself be every human felicity. Adieu.

To John Adams

Monticello, October 28, 1813

Dear Sir,—According to the reservation between us, of taking up one of the subjects of our correspondence at a time, I turn to your letters of August the 16th and September the 2nd. The passage you quote from Theognis, I think has an ethical rather than a political object. The whole piece is a moral *exhortation* . . . and this passage particularly seems to be a reproof to man, who, while with his domestic animals he is curious to improve the race, by employing always the finest male, pays no attention to the improvement of his own race, but intermarries with the vicious, the ugly, or the old, for considerations of wealth or ambition. It is in conformity with the principle adopted afterwards by the Pythagoreans, and expressed by Ocellus in another form . . . which, as literally as intelligibility will admit, may be thus translated: "concerning the interprocreation of men, how, and of whom it shall be, in a perfect manner, and according to the laws of modesty and sanctity, conjointly, this is what I think right. First to lay it down that we do not commix for the sake of pleasure, but of the procreation of children. For the powers, the organs and desires for coition have not been given by God to man for the sake of pleasure, but for the procreation of the race. For as it were incongruous, for a mortal born to partake of divine life, the immortality of the race being taken away, God fulfilled the purpose by making the generations uninterrupted and continuous. This, therefore, we are especially to lay down as a principle, that coition is not for the sake of pleasure." But nature, not trusting to this moral and abstract motive, seems to have provided more securely for the perpetuation of the species,

57

by making it the effect of the *œstrum* implanted in the constitution of both sexes. And not only has the commerce of love been indulged on this unhallowed impulse, but made subservient also to wealth and ambition by marriage, without regard to the beauty, the healthiness, the understanding, or virtue of the subject from which we are to breed. The selecting the best male for a Harem of well chosen females also, which Theognis seems to recommend from the example of our sheep and asses, would doubtless improve the human, as it does the brute animal, and produce a race of veritable ἄριστοι.[1] For experience proves, that the moral and physical qualities of man, whether good or evil, are transmissible in a certain degree from father to son. But I suspect that the equal rights of men will rise up against this privileged Solomon and his Harem, and oblige us to continue acquiescence under the "Αμαύρωσις γένεος ἀστῶν"[2] which Theognis complains of, and to content ourselves with the accidental aristoi produced by the fortuitous concourse of breeders. For I agree with you that there is a natural aristocracy among men. The grounds of this are virtue and talents. Formerly, bodily powers gave place among the aristoi. But since the invention of gunpowder has armed the weak as well as the strong with missile death, bodily strength, like beauty, good humor, politeness and other accomplishments, has become but an auxiliary ground of distinction. There is also an artificial aristocracy, founded on wealth and birth, without either virtue or talents; for with these it would belong to the first class. The natural aristocracy I consider as the most precious gift of nature, for the instruction, the trusts, and government of society. And indeed, it would have been inconsistent in creation to have formed man for the social state, and not to have provided virtue and wisdom enough to manage the concerns of the society. May we not even say, that that form of government is the best, which provides the most effectually for a pure selection of these natural aristoi into the offices of government? The artificial aristocracy is a mischievous ingredient in government, and provision should be made to prevent its ascendency. On the question, what is the best provision, you and I differ; but we differ as rational friends, using the free exercise of our own reason, and mutually indulging its errors. You think it best to put the pseudo-aristoi into a separate chamber of legislation, where they may be hindered from doing mischief by their co-ordinate branches, and where, also, they may be a protection to wealth against the Agrarian and plundering enterprises of the majority of the people. I think that to give them power in order to prevent them from doing mischief, is arming them for it, and increasing instead of remedying the evil. For if the co-ordinate branches can arrest their action, so may they that of the co-ordinates. Mischief may be done negatively as well as positively. Of this, a cabal in the Senate of the United States has furnished many proofs. Nor do I believe them necessary to protect the wealthy; because enough of these will find their way into every branch of the legislation, to protect themselves. From fifteen to twenty legislatures of our own, in action for thirty years past, have proved that no fears of an equalization of property are to be apprehended from them. I think the best remedy is exactly that provided by all our constitutions, to leave to the citizens the free election and separation of the aristoi from the pseudo-aristoi,

58

[1] *The best* [people].
[2] *Weakening of the breed of citizens.*

of the wheat from the chaff. In general they will elect the really good and wise. In some instances, wealth may corrupt, and birth blind them; but not in sufficient degree to endanger the society.

It is probable that our difference of opinion may, in some measure, be produced by a difference of character in those among whom we live. From what I have seen of Massachusetts and Connecticut myself, and still more from what I have heard, and the character given of the former by yourself, who know them so much better, there seems to be in those two States a tradionary reverence for certain families, which has rendered the offices of the government nearly hereditary in those families. I presume that from an early period of your history, members of those families happening to possess virtue and talents, have honestly exercised them for the good of the people, and by their services have endeared their names to them. In coupling Connecticut with you, I mean it politically only, not morally. For having made the Bible the common law of their land, they seem to have modeled their morality on the story of Jacob and Laban. But although this hereditary succession to office with you, may, in some degree, be founded in real family merit, yet in a much higher degree, it has proceeded from your strict alliance of Church and State. These families are canonised in the eyes of the people on common principles, "you tickle me, and I will tickle you." In Virginia we have nothing of this. Our clergy, before the revolution, having been secured against rivalship by fixed salaries, did not give themselves the trouble of acquiring influence over the people. Of wealth, there were great accumulations in particular families, handed down from generation to generation, under the English law of entails. But the only object of ambition for the wealthy was a seat in the King's Council. All their court then was paid to the crown and its creatures; and they Philipised in all collisions between the King and the people. Hence they were unpopular; and that unpopularity continues attached to their names. A Randolph, a Carter, or a Burwell must have great personal superiority over a common competitor to be elected by the people even at this day. At the first session of our legislature after the Declaration of Independence, we passed a law abolishing entails. And this was followed by one abolishing the privilege of primogeniture, and dividing the lands of intestates equally among all their children, or other representatives. These laws, drawn by myself, laid the axe to the foot of pseudo-aristocracy. And had another which I prepared been adopted by the legislature, our work would have been complete. It was a bill for the more general diffusion of learning. This proposed to divide every county into wards of five or six miles square, like your townships; to establish in each ward a free school for reading, writing and common arithmetic; to provide for the annual selection of the best subjects from these schools, who might receive, at the public expense, a higher degree of education at a district school; and from these district schools to select a certain number of the most promising subjects, to be completed at an University, where all the useful sciences should be taught. Worth and genius would thus have been sought out from every condition of life, and completely prepared by education for defeating the competition of wealth and birth for public trusts. My proposition had, for a further object, to impart to these wards those portions of self-government for which they are best qualified, by confiding to them the care of their poor, their roads, police, elections, the nomina-

59

tion of jurors, administration of justice in small cases, elementary exercises of militia; in short, to have made them little republics, with a warden at the head of each, for all those concerns which, being under their eye, they would better manage than the larger republics of the county or State. A general call of ward meetings by their wardens on the same day through the State, would at any time produce the genuine sense of the people on any required point, and would enable the State to act in mass, as your people have so often done, and with so much effect by their town meetings. The law for religious freedom, which made a part of this system, having put down the aristocracy of the clergy, and restored to the citizen the freedom of the mind, and those of entails and descents nurturing an equality of condition among them, this on education would have raised the mass of the people to the high ground of moral respectability necessary to their own safety, and to orderly government; and would have completed the great object of qualifying them to select the veritable aristoi, for the trusts of government, to the exclusion of the pseudalists. . . . Although this law has not yet been acted on but in a small and inefficient degree, it is still considered as before the legislature, with other bills of the revised code, not yet taken up, and I have great hope that some patriotic spirit will, at a favorable moment, call it up, and make it the keystone of the arch of our government.

With respect to aristocracy, we should further consider, that before the establishment of the American States, nothing was known to history but the man of the old world, crowded within limits either small or overcharged, and steeped in the vices which that situation generates. A government adapted to such men would be one thing; but a very different one, that for the man of these States. Here every one may have land to labor for himself, if he chooses; or, preferring the exercise of any other industry, may exact for it such compensation as not only to afford a comfortable subsistence, but wherewith to provide for a cessation from labor in old age. Every one, by his property, or by his satisfactory situation, is interested in the support of law and order. And such men may safely and advantageously reserve to themselves a wholesome control over their public affairs, and a degree of freedom, which, in the hands of the *canaille* of the cities of Europe, would be instantly perverted to the demolition and destruction of everything public and private. The history of the last twenty-five years of France, and of the last forty years in America, nay of its last two hundred years, proves the truth of both parts of this observation.

But even in Europe a change has sensibly taken place in the mind of man. Science had liberated the ideas of those who read and reflect, and the American example had kindled feelings of right in the people. An insurrection has consequently begun, of science, talents, and courage, against rank and birth, which have fallen into contempt. It has failed in its first effort, because the mobs of the cities, the instrument used for its accomplishment, debased by ignorance, poverty, and vice, could not be restrained to rational action. But the world will recover from the panic of this first catastrophe. Science is progressive, and talents and enterprise on the alert. Resort may be had to the people of the country, a more governable power from their principles and subordination; and rank, and birth, and tinsel-aristocracy will finally shrink into insignificance,

60

even there. This, however, we have no right to meddle with. It suffices for us, if the moral and physical condition of our own citizens qualifies them to select the able and good for the direction of their government, with a recurrance of elections at such short periods as will enable them to displace an unfaithful servant, before the mischief he meditates may be irremediable.

I have thus stated my opinion on a point on which we differ, not with a view to controversy, for we are both too old to change opinions which are the result of a long life of inquiry and reflection; but on the suggestions of a former letter of yours, that we ought not to die before we have explained ourselves to each other. We acted in perfect harmony, through a long and perilous contest for our liberty and independence. A constitution has been acquired, which, though neither of us thinks perfect, yet both consider as competent to render our fellow citizens the happiest and the securest on whom the sun has ever shone. If we do not think exactly alike as to its imperfections, it matters little to our country, which, after devoting to it long lives of disinterested labor, we have delivered over to our successors in life, who will be able to take care of it and of themselves. . . .

To General James Breckinridge

Monticello, February 15, 1821

Dear Sir,[1]—I learn, with deep affliction, that nothing is likely to be done for our University this year. So near as it is to the shore that one shove more would land it there, I had hoped that would be given; and that we should open with the next year an institution on which the fortunes of our country may depend more than may meet the general eye. The reflections that the boys of this age are to be the men of the next; that they should be prepared to receive the holy charge which we are cherishing to deliver over to them; that in establishing an institution of wisdom for them, we secure it to all our future generations; that in fulfilling this duty, we bring home to our own bosoms the sweet consolation of seeing our sons rising under a luminous tuition, to destinies of high promise; these are considerations which will occur to all; but all, I fear, do not see the speck in our horizon which is to burst on us as a tornado, sooner or later. The line of division lately marked out between different portions of our confederacy, is such as will never, I fear, be obliterated, and we are now trusting to those who are against us in position and principle, to fashion to their own form the minds and affections of our youth. If, as has been estimated, we send three hundred thousand dollars a year to the Northern seminaries, for the instruction of our own sons, then we must have there five hundred of our sons, imbibing opinions and principles in discord with those of their own country. This canker is eating on the vitals of our existence, and if not arrested at once, will be beyond remedy. We are now certainly furnishing recruits to their school. If it be asked what are we to do, or said we cannot give the last lift to the University without stopping our primary schools, and

61

[1] *Breckinridge was the chief exponent in the legislature of Jefferson's plans for the University of Virginia.*

these we think most important; I answer, I know their importance. Nobody can doubt my zeal for the general instruction of the people. Who first started that idea? I may surely say, myself. Turn to the bill in the revised code, which I drew more than forty years ago, and before which the idea of a plan for the education of the people, generally, had never been suggested in this State. There you will see developed the first rudiments of the whole system of general education we are now urging and acting on; and it is well known to those with whom I have acted on this subject, that I never have proposed a sacrifice of the primary to the ultimate grade of instruction. Let us keep our eye steadily on the whole system. If we cannot do everything at once, let us do one at a time. The primary schools need no preliminary expense; the ultimate grade requires a considerable expenditure in advance. A suspension of proceeding for a year or two on the primary schools, and an application of the whole income, during that time, to the completion of the buildings necessary for the University, would enable us then to start both institutions at the same time. The intermediate branch, of colleges, academies and private classical schools, for the middle grade, may herafter receive any necessary aids when the funds shall become competent. In the meantime, they are going on sufficiently, as they have ever yet gone on, at the private expense of those who use them, and who in numbers and means are competent to their own exigencies. The experience of three years has, I presume, left no doubt that the present plan of primary schools, of putting money into the hands of twelve hundred persons acting for nothing, and under no responsibility, is entirely inefficient. Some other must be thought of; and during this pause, if it be only for a year, the whole revenue of that year, with that of the last three years which has not been already thrown away, would place our University in readiness to start with a better organization of primary schools, and both may then go on, hand in hand, forever. No diminution of the capital will in this way have been incurred; a principle which ought to be deemed sacred. A relinquishment of interest on the late loan of sixty thousand dollars, would so far, also, forward the University without lessening the capital.

But what may be best done I leave with entire confidence to yourself and your colleagues in legislation, who know better than I do the conditions of the literary fund and its wisest application; and I shall acquiesce with perfect resignation to their will. I have brooded, perhaps with fondness, over this establishment, as it held up to me the hope of continuing to be useful while I continued to live. I had believed that the course and circumstances of my life had placed within my power some services favorable to the outset of the institution. But this may be egotism; pardonable, perhaps, when I express a consciousness that my colleagues and successors will do as well, whatever the legislature shall enable them to do.

I have thus, my dear Sir, opened my bosom, with all its anxieties, freely to you. I blame nobody for seeing things in a different light. I am sure that all act conscientiously, and that all will be done honestly and wisely which can be done. I yield the concerns of the world with cheerfulness to those who are appointed in the order of nature to succeed to them; and for yourself, for our colleagues, and for all in charge of our country's future fame and fortune, I offer up sincere prayers.

62

To Jared Sparks

Monticello, February 4, 1824

Dear Sir,[1]—I duly received your favor of the 13th, and with it, the last number of the North American Review. This has anticipated the one I should receive in course, but have not yet received, under my subscription to the new series. The article on the African colonization of the people of color, to which you invite my attention, I have read with great consideration. It is, indeed, a fine one, and will do much good. I learn from it more, too, than I had before known, of the degree of success and promise of that colony.

In the disposition of these unfortunate people, there are two rational objects to be distinctly kept in view. First. The establishment of a colony on the coast of Africa, which may introduce among the aborigines the arts of cultivated life, and the blessings of civilization and science. By doing this, we may make to them some retribution for the long course of injuries we have been committing on their population. And considering that these blessings will descend to the *"nati natorum, et qui nascentur ab illis,"* [2] we shall in the long run have rendered them perhaps more good than evil. To fulfil this object, the colony of Sierra Leone promises well, and that of Mesurado adds to our prospect of success. Under this view, the colonization society is to be considered as a missionary society, having in view, however, objects more humane, more justifiable, and less aggressive on the peace of other nations, than the others of that appellation.

The second object, and the most interesting to us, as coming home to our physical and moral characters, to our happiness and safety, is to provide an asylum to which we can, by degrees, send the whole of that population from among us, and establish them under our patronage and protection, as a separate, free and independent people, in some country and climate friendly to human life and happiness. That any place on the coast of Africa should answer the latter purpose, I have ever deemed entirely impossible. And without repeating the other arguments which have been urged by others, I will appeal to figures only, which admit no controversy. I shall speak in round numbers, not absolutely accurate, yet not so wide from truth as to vary the result materially. There are in the United States a million and a half of people of color in slavery. To send off the whole of these at once, nobody conceives to be practicable for us, or expedient for them. Let us take twenty-five years for its accomplishment, within which time they will be doubled. Their estimated value as property, in the first place, (for actual property has been lawfully vested in that form, and who can lawfully take it from the possessors?) at an average of two hundred dollars each, young and old, would amount to six hundred millions of dollars, which must be paid or lost by somebody. To this, add the cost of their transportation by land and sea to Mesurado, a year's provision of food and clothing, implements of husbandry and of their trades, which will amount to three hundred millions more, making thirty-six millions of dollars a year for twenty-five years, with insurance of peace all that time, and

63

---

[1] *Sparks was at this time owner and editor of* The North American Review.
[2] *Children's children, and those who are born of them.*

it is impossible to look at the question a second time. I am aware that at the end of about sixteen years, a gradual detraction from this sum will commence, from the gradual diminution of breeders, and go on during the remaining nine years. Calculate this deduction, and it is still impossible to look at the enterprise a second time. I do not say this to induce an inference that the getting rid of them is forever impossible. For that is neither my opinion nor my hope. But only that it cannot be done in this way. There is, I think, a way in which it can be done; that is, by emancipating the afterborn, leaving them, on due compensation with their mothers, until their services are worth their maintenance, and then putting them to industrious occupations, until a proper age for deportation. This was the result of my reflections on the subject five and forty years ago, and I have never yet been able to conceive any other practicable plan. It was sketched in the Notes on Virginia, under the fourteenth query. The estimated value of the new-born infant is so low, (say twelve dollars and fifty cents,) that it would probably be yielded by the owner gratis, and would thus reduce the six hundred millions of dollars, the first head of expense, to thirty-seven millions and a half; leaving only the expenses of nourishment while with the mother, and of transportation. And from what fund are these expenses to be furnished? Why not from that of the lands which have been ceded by the very States now needing this relief? And ceded on no consideration, for the most part, but that of the general good of the whole. These cessions already constitute one-fourth of the States of the Union. It may be said that these lands have been sold; are now the property of the citizens composing those States; and the money long ago received and expended. But an equivalent of lands in the territories since acquired, may be appropriated to that object, or so much, at least, as may be sufficient; and the object, although more important to the slave States, is highly so to the others also, if they were serious in their arguments on the Missouri question. The slave States, too, if more interested, would also contribute more by their gratuitous liberation, thus taking on themselves alone the first and heaviest item of expense.

In the plan sketched in the Notes on Virginia, no particular place of asylum was specified; because it was thought possible, that in the revolutionary state of America, then commenced, events might open to us some one within practicable distance. This has now happened. St. Domingo has become independent, and with a population of that color only; and if the public papers are to be credited, their Chief offers to pay their passage, to receive them as free citizens, and to provide them employment. This leaves, then, for the general confederacy, no expense but of nurture with the mother a few years, and would call, of course, for a very moderate appropriation of the vacant lands. Suppose the whole annual increase to be of sixty thousand effective births, fifty vessels, of four hundred tons burden each, constantly employed in that short run, would carry off the increase of every year, and the old stock would die off in the ordinary course of nature, lessening from the commencement until its final disappearance. In this way no violation of private right is proposed. Voluntary surrenders would probably come in as fast as the means to be provided for their care would be competent to it. Looking at my own State only, and I presume not to speak for the others, I verily believe that this surrender of

64

property would not amount to more, annually, than half our present direct taxes, to be continued fully about twenty or twenty-five years, and then gradually diminishing for as many more until their final extinction; and even this half tax would not be paid in cash, but by the delivery of an object which they have never yet known or counted as part of their property; and those not possessing the object will be called on for nothing. I do not go into all the details of the burdens and benefits of this operation. And who could estimate its blessed effects? I leave this to those who will live to see their accomplishment, and to enjoy a beatitude forbidden to my age. But I leave it with this admonition, to rise and be doing. A million and a half are within their control; but six millions, (which a majority of those now living will see them attain,) and one million of these fighting men, will say, "we will not go."

I am aware that this subject involves some constitutional scruples. But a liberal construction, justified by the object, may go far, and an amendment of the Constitution, the whole length necessary. The separation of infants from their mothers, too, would produce some scruples of humanity. But this would be straining at a gnat, and swallowing a camel.

I am much pleased to see that you have taken up the subject of the duty on imported books. I hope a crusade will be kept up against it, until those in power shall become sensible of this stain on our legislation, and shall wipe it from their code, and from the remembrance of man, if possible.

I salute you with assurances of high respect and esteem.

JAMES MADISON

1751–1836

James Madison was born in Port Conway, Virginia. He received his early education from tutors and at the famous academy of Donald Robertson. At Princeton, where he enrolled in 1769, he excelled particularly in history and government. Contemplating a career in the church, he remained in school for a year beyond graduation in order to study Hebrew and ethics. However, his ministerial ambitions were apparently forgotten soon after his return to Virginia in 1772, for he enthusiastically joined the group which was agitating for political and religious freedom. In 1776 he was a member of the Virginia Convention and helped to draw up the constitution and Declaration of Rights for that state.

Madison was one of the most conscientious of the many prominent statesmen in the new republic, serving in the Virginia House of Delegates, in the Congress

65

of the United States, and as a member of the Philadelphia Constitutional Convention. In 1809 he became fourth President of the United States.

It was the fight over the adoption of the Constitution that gave rise to Madison's most important literary effort. In cooperation with Hamilton and Jay he wrote a series of articles explaining the Constitution and urging its adoption. These eighty-five essays, first published in several New York newspapers under the name of Publius, became widely publicized throughout the states and were eventually collected as *The Federalist* (1788). At the time of their appearance, the papers were extremely influential in winning general ratification of the Constitution, and they soon became a major source of constitutional interpretation. They have been widely regarded as our country's most important contribution to the field of political science.

In the framing of the Constitution, Madison argued that the larger states deserved a greater number of representatives in Congress and, consequently, bitterly opposed equal distribution of senatorial seats. He advocated a legislature of two houses whose members would have different terms of office; a strong federal government, composed of executive, judicial, and legislative branches; popular election of members of both houses of the legislature; and immediate abolition of the slave trade. Although many of his proposals were not adopted, his influence was so great that he has been called "the master builder of the Constitution."

from *The Federalist*

No. 10. The Union a Check on Faction

Among the numerous advantages promised by a well-constructed union, none deserves to be more accurately developed than its tendency to break and control the violence of faction. The friend of popular governments never finds himself so much alarmed for their character and fate as when he contemplates their propensity to this dangerous vice. He will not fail, therefore, to set a due value on any plan which, without violating the principles to which he is attached, provides a proper cure for it. The instability, injustice, and confusion introduced into the public councils have, in truth, been the mortal diseases under which popular governments have everywhere perished; as they continue to be the favorite and fruitful topics from which the adversaries to liberty derive their most specious declamations. The valuable improvements made by the American constitutions on the popular models, both ancient and modern, cannot certainly be too much admired; but it would be an unwarrantable partiality, to contend that they have as effectually obviated the danger on this side as was wished and expected. Complaints are everywhere heard from our most considerate and virtuous citizens, equally the friends of public and private faith and of public and personal liberty, that our governments are too unstable; that the public good is disregarded in the conflicts of rival parties; and that measures are too often decided, not according to the rules of justice, and the rights of

66

the minor party, but by the superior force of an interested and overbearing majority. However anxiously we may wish that these complaints had no foundation, the evidence of known facts will not permit us to deny that they are in some degree true. It will be found, indeed, on a candid review of our situation, that some of the distresses under which we labor have been erroneously charged on the operation of our governments; but it will be found, at the same time, that other causes will not alone account for many of our heaviest misfortunes; and, particularly, for that prevailing and increasing distrust of public engagements, and alarm for private rights, which are echoed from one end of the continent to the other. These must be chiefly, if not wholly, effects of the unsteadiness and injustice with which a factious spirit has tainted our public administrations.

By a faction, I understand a number of citizens, whether amounting to a majority or minority of the whole, who are united and actuated by some common impulse of passion, or of interest, adverse to the rights of other citizens or to the permanent and aggregate interests of the community.

There are two methods of curing the mischiefs of faction: the one, by removing its causes; the other, by controlling its effects.

There are again two methods of removing the causes of faction: the one, by destroying the liberty which is essential to its existence; the other, by giving to every citizen the same opinions, the same passions, and the same interests.

It could never be more truly said than of the first remedy, that it was worse than the disease. Liberty is to faction what air is to fire, an aliment without which it instantly expires. But it could not be less folly to abolish liberty, which is essential to political life, because it nourishes faction, than it would be to wish the annihilation of air, which is essential to animal life, because it imparts to fire its destructive agency.

The second expedient is as impracticable as the first would be unwise. As long as the reason of man continues fallible, and he is at liberty to exercise it, different opinions will be formed. As long as the connection subsists between his reason and his self-love, his opinions and his passions will have a reciprocal influence on each other; and the former will be objects to which the latter will attach themselves. The diversity in the faculties of men, from which the rights of property originate, is not less an insuperable obstacle to a uniformity of interests. The protection of these faculties is the first object of government. From the protection of different and unequal faculties of acquiring property, the possession of different degrees and kinds of property immediately results; and from the influence of these on the sentiments and views of the respective proprietors ensues a division of the society into different interests and parties.

The latent causes of faction are thus sown in the nature of man; and we see them everywhere brought into different degrees of activity, according to the different circumstances of civil society. A zeal for different opinions concerning religion, concerning government and many other points, as well of speculation as of practice; an attachment to different leaders ambitiously contending for pre-eminence and power, or to persons of other descriptions whose fortunes have been interesting to the human passions, have, in turn, divided mankind into parties, inflamed them with mutual animosity, and rendered them much more disposed to vex and oppress each other, than to co-operate for their common

67

good. So strong is this propensity of mankind to fall into mutual animosities, that where no substantial occasion presents itself, the most frivolous and fanciful distinctions have been sufficient to kindle their unfriendly passions and excite their most violent conflicts. But the most common and durable source of factions has been the various and unequal distribution of property. Those who hold and those who are without property have ever formed distinct interests in society. Those who are creditors and those who are debtors fall under a like discrimination. A landed interest, a manufacturing interest, a mercantile interest, a moneyed interest, with many lesser interests, grow up of necessity in civilized nations, and divide them into different classes, actuated by different sentiments and views. The regulation of these various and interfering interests forms the principal task of modern legislation, and involves the spirit of party and faction in the necessary and ordinary operations of the government.

No man is allowed to be a judge in his own cause; because his interest would certainly bias his judgment and, not improbably, corrupt his integrity. With equal, nay, with greater reason, a body of men are unfit to be both judges and parties at the same time; yet what are many of the most important acts of legislation, but so many judicial determinations, not indeed concerning the rights of single persons, but concerning the rights of large bodies of citizens? and what are the different classes of legislators, but advocates and parties to the causes which they determine? Is a law proposed concerning private debts? —it is a question to which the creditors are parties on one side, and the debtors on the other. Justice ought to hold the balance between them. Yet the parties are, and must be, themselves the judges; and the most numerous party, or, in other words, the most powerful faction, must be expected to prevail. Shall domestic manufactures be encouraged, and in what degree by restrictions on foreign manufactures? are questions which would be differently decided by the landed and the manufacturing classes, and probably by neither with a sole regard to justice and the public good. The apportionment of taxes on the various descriptions of property is an act which seems to require the most exact impartiality; yet there is, perhaps, no legislative act in which greater opportunity and temptation are given to a predominant party, to trample on the rules of justice. Every shilling with which they overburden the inferior number is a shilling saved to their own pockets.

It is in vain to say that enlightened statesmen will be able to adjust these clashing interests and render them all subservient to the public good. Enlightened statesmen will not always be at the helm; nor, in many cases, can such an adjustment be made at all, without taking into view indirect and remote considerations, which will rarely prevail over the immediate interest which one party may find in disregarding the rights of another or the good of the whole.

The inference to which we are brought is that the causes of faction cannot be removed, and that relief is only to be sought in the means of controlling its effects.

If a faction consists of less than a majority, relief is supplied by the republican principle, which enables the majority to defeat its sinister views by regular vote. It may clog the administration, it may convulse the society; but it will be unable to execute and mask its violence under the forms of the Constitution.

68

When a majority is included in a faction, the form of popular government, on the other hand, enables it to sacrifice to its ruling passion or interest both the public good and the rights of other citizens. To secure the public good, and private rights, against the danger of such a faction, and at the same time to preserve the spirit and the form of popular government, is then the great object to which our inquiries are directed. Let me add that it is the great *desideratum*, by which alone this form of government can be rescued from the opprobrium under which it has so long labored, and be recommended to the esteem and adoption of mankind.

By what means is this object attainable? Evidently by one of two only. Either the existence of the same passion or interest in a majority, at the same time, must be prevented; or the majority, having such coexistent passion or interest, must be rendered, by their number and local situation, unable to concert and carry into effect schemes of oppression. If the impulse and the opportunity be suffered to coincide, we well know that neither moral nor religious motives can be relied on as an adequate control. They are not found to be such on the injustice and violence of individuals, and lose their efficacy in proportion to the number combined together; that is, in proportion as their efficacy becomes needful.

From this view of the subject it may be concluded that a pure democracy, by which I mean a society consisting of a small number of citizens, who assemble and administer the government in person, can admit of no cure for the mischiefs of faction. A common passion or interest will, in almost every case, be felt by a majority of the whole; a communication and concert results from the form of government itself; and there is nothing to check the inducements to sacrifice the weaker party or an obnoxious individual. Hence it is that such democracies have ever been spectacles of turbulence and contention; have ever been found incompatible with personal security, or the rights of property, and have in general been as short in their lives as they have been violent in their deaths. Theoretic politicians, who have patronized this species of government, have erroneously supposed that by reducing mankind to a perfect equality in their political rights, they would at the same time be perfectly equalized and assimilated in their possessions, their opinions, and their passions.

A republic, by which I mean a government in which the scheme of representation takes place, opens a different prospect, and promises the cure for which we are seeking. Let us examine the points in which it varies from pure democracy, and we shall comprehend both the nature of the cure and the efficacy which it must derive from the union.

The two great points of difference between a democracy and a republic are: First, the delegation of the government, in the latter, to a small number of citizens elected by the rest; secondly, the greater number of citizens, and greater sphere of country, over which the latter may be extended.

The effect of the first difference is, on the one hand, to refine and enlarge the public views, by passing them through the medium of a chosen body of citizens, whose wisdom may best discern the true interest of their country, and whose patriotism and love of justice will be least likely to sacrifice it to temporary or partial considerations. Under such a regulation, it may well happen that the public voice, pronounced by the representatives of the people, will be more consonant to the public good than if pronounced by the people themselves, convened for the purpose. On the other hand, the effect may be inverted. Men of factious tempers, of local prejudices, or of sinister designs, may by intrigue, by corruption, or by other means, first obtain the suffrages, and then betray the interests of the people. The question resulting is, whether small or extensive republics are most favorable to the election of proper guardians of the public weal; and it is clearly decided in favor of the latter by two obvious considerations.

In the first place, it is to be remarked that, however small the republic may be, the representatives must be raised to a certain number, in order to guard against the cabals of a few; and that, however large it may be, they must be limited to a certain number, in order to guard against the confusion of a multitude. Hence, the number of representatives in the two cases not being in proportion to that of the constituents, and being proportionally greatest in the small republic, it follows that if the proportion of fit characters be not less in the large than in the small republic, the former will present a greater option, and consequently a greater probability of a fit choice.

In the next place, as each representative will be chosen by a greater number of citizens in the large than in the small republic, it will be more difficult for unworthy candidates to practise with success the vicious arts, by which elections are too often carried; and the suffrages of the people, being more free, will be more likely to centre in men who possess the most attractive merit and the most diffusive and established characters.

It must be confessed that in this as in most other cases, there is a mean, on both sides of which inconveniences will be found to lie. By enlarging too much the number of electors, you render the representative too little acquainted with all their local circumstances and lesser interests; as by reducing it too much, you render him unduly attached to these, and too little fit to comprehend and pursue great and national objects. The federal Constitution forms a happy combination in this respect; the great and aggregate interests being referred to the national, the local and particular to the State, legislatures.

The other point of difference is, the greater number of citizens and extent of territory which may be brought within the compass of republican than of democratic government; and it is this circumstance principally which renders factious combinations less to be dreaded in the former, than in the latter. The smaller the society, the fewer probably will be the distinct parties and interests composing it; the fewer the distinct parties and interests, the more frequently will a majority be found of the same party; and the smaller the number of individuals composing a majority, and the smaller the compass within which they are placed, the more easily will they concert and execute their plans of oppression. Extend the sphere, and you take in a greater variety of parties and interests; you make it less probable that a majority of the whole will have a common motive to invade the rights of other citizens; or if such a common motive exists, it will be more difficult for all who feel it to discover their own strength, and to act in unison with each other. Besides other impediments, it may be remarked that where there is a consciousness of unjust or dishonorable purposes, communication is always checked by distrust, in proportion to the number whose concurrence is necessary.

Hence it clearly appears that the same advantage which a republic has over a democracy, in controlling the effects of faction, is enjoyed by a large over a small republic—is enjoyed by the Union over the States composing it. Does the advantage consist in the substitution of representatives, whose enlightened views and virtuous sentiments render them superior to local prejudices, and to schemes of injustice? It will not be denied that the representation of the Union will be most likely to possess these requisite endowments. Does it consist in the greater security afforded by a greater variety of parties, against the event of any one party being able to outnumber and oppress the rest? In an equal degree does the increased variety of parties, comprised within the Union, increase this security? Does it, in fine, consist in the greater obstacles opposed to the concert and accomplishment of the secret wishes of an unjust and interested majority? Here, again, the extent of the Union gives it the most palpable advantage.

The influence of factious leaders may kindle a flame within their particular States, but will be unable to spread a general conflagration through the other States. A religious sect may degenerate into a political faction in a part of the confederacy; but the variety of sects dispersed over the entire face of it must secure the national councils against any danger from that source. A rage for paper money, for an abolition of debts, for an equal division of property, or for any other improper and wicked project will be less apt to pervade the whole body of the Union than a particular member of it; in the same proportion as such a malady is more likely to taint a particular county or district than an entire State.

In the extent and proper structure of the Union, therefore, we behold a republican remedy for the diseases most incident to republican government. And according to the degree of pleasure and pride we feel in being republicans, ought to be our zeal in cherishing the spirit and supporting the character of federalists. (*1787*)

No. 14. *Extent of the Country No Objection to Union*

We have seen the necessity of the Union, as our bulwark against foreign danger, as the conservator of peace among ourselves, as the guardian of our commerce and other common interests, as the only substitute for those military establishments which have subverted the liberties of the Old World, and as the proper antidote for the diseases of faction, which have proved fatal to other popular governments, and of which alarming symptoms have been betrayed by our own. All that remains, within this branch of our inquiries, is to take notice of an objection that may be drawn from the great extent of country which the Union embraces. A few observations on this subject will be the more proper, as it is perceived that the adversaries of the new Constitution are availing themselves of the prevailing prejudice with regard to the practicable sphere of republican administration, in order to supply, by imaginary difficulties, the want of those solid objections which they endeavor in vain to find.

The error which limits republican government to a narrow district has been unfolded and refuted in preceding papers. I remark here only that it seems to owe its rise and prevalence chiefly to the confounding of a republic with a democracy, applying to the former reasonings drawn from the nature of the latter. The true distinction between these forms was also adverted to on a former occasion. It is, that in a democracy, the people meet and exercise the government in person; in a republic, they assemble and administer it by their representatives and agents. A democracy, consequently, will be confined to a small spot. A republic may be extended over a large region.

To this accidental source of the error may be added the artifice of some celebrated authors, whose writings have had a great share in forming the modern standard of political opinions. Being subjects either of an absolute or limited monarchy, they have endeavored to heighten the advantages, or palliate the evils, of those forms, by placing in comparison the vices and defects of the republican, and by citing as specimens of the latter the turbulent democracies of ancient Greece and modern Italy. Under the confusion of names, it has been an easy task to transfer to a republic observations applicable to a democracy only; and among others, the observation that it can never be established but among a small number of people, living within a small compass of territory.

Such a fallacy may have been the less perceived, as most of the popular governments of antiquity were of the democratic species; and even in modern Europe, to which we owe the great principle of representation, no example is seen of a government wholly popular, and founded, at the same time, wholly on that principle. If Europe has the merit of discovering this great mechanical power in government, by the simple agency of which the will of the largest political body may be concentred, and its force directed to any object which the public good requires, America can claim the merit of making the discovery the basis of unmixed and extensive republics. It is only to be lamented that any of her citizens should wish to deprive her of the additional merit of displaying its full efficacy in the establishment of the comprehensive system now under her consideration.

As the natural limit of a democracy is that distance from the central point which will just permit the most remote citizens to assemble as often as their public functions demand, and will include no greater number than can join in those functions; so the natural limit of a republic is that distance from the centre which will barely allow the representatives to meet as often as may be necessary for the administration of public affairs. Can it be said that the limits of the United States exceed this distance? It will not be said by those who recollect that the Atlantic coast is the longest side of the Union, that during the term of thirteen years, the representatives of the States have been almost continually assembled, and that the members from the most distant States are not chargeable with greater intermissions of attendance than those from the States in the neighborhood of Congress.

That we may form a juster estimate with regard to this interesting subject, let us resort to the actual dimensions of the Union. The limits, as fixed by the treaty of peace, are: on the east the Atlantic, on the south the latitude of thirty-one degrees, on the west the Mississippi, and on the north an irregular line running in some instances beyond the forty-fifth degree, in others falling as low as the forty-second. The southern shore of Lake Erie lies below that latitude. Computing the distance between the thirty-first and forty-fifth degrees, it amounts to nine hundred and sixty-four miles and a half. Taking the mean for the distance, the amount will be eight hundred and sixty-eight miles and three fourths. The mean distance from the Atlantic to the Mississippi does not probably exceed seven hundred and fifty miles. On a comparison of this extent with that of several countries in Europe, the practicability of rendering our system commensurate to it appears to be demonstrable. It is not a great deal larger than Germany, where a diet representing the whole empire is continually assembled; or than Poland before the late dismemberment, where another national diet was the depositary of the supreme power. Passing by France and Spain, we find that in Great Britain, inferior as it may be in size, the representatives of the northern extremity of the island have as far to travel to the national council as will be required of those of the most remote parts of the Union.

Favorable as this view of the subject may be, some observations remain which will place it in a light still more satisfactory.

In the first place it is to be remembered that the general government is not to be charged with the whole power of making and administering laws. Its jurisdiction is limited to certain enumerated objects, which concern all the members of the republic, but which are not to be attained by the separate provisions of any. The subordinate governments, which can extend their care to all those other objects which can be separately provided for, will retain their due authority and activity. Were it proposed by the plan of the convention to abolish the governments of the particular States, its adversaries would have some ground for their objection; though it would not be difficult to show that if they were abolished the general government would be compelled, by the principle of self-preservation, to reinstate them in their proper jurisdiction.

A second observation to be made is that the immediate object of the Federal Constitution is to secure the union of the thirteen primitive States, which we know to be practicable; and to add to them such other States as may arise in their own bosoms, or in their neighborhoods, which we cannot doubt to be equally practicable. The arrangements that may be necessary for those angles and fractions of our territory which lie on our northwestern frontier, must be left to those whom further discoveries and experience will render more equal to the task.

Let it be remarked, in the third place, that the intercourse throughout the Union will be facilitated by new improvements. Roads will everywhere be shortened, and kept in better order; accommodations for travellers will be multiplied and meliorated; an interior navigation on our eastern side will be opened throughout, or nearly throughout, the whole extent of the thirteen States. The communication between the Western and Atlantic districts, and between different parts of each, will be rendered more and more easy by those numerous canals with which the beneficence of nature has intersected our country, and which art finds it so little difficult to connect and complete.

A fourth and still more important consideration is, that as almost every State will, on one side or other, be a frontier, and will thus find, in a regard to its

73

safety, an inducement to make some sacrifices for the sake of the general protection; so the States which lie at the greatest distance from the heart of the
Union, and which, of course, may partake least of the ordinary circulation of
its benefits, will be at the same time immediately contiguous to foreign nations,
and will consequently stand, on particular occasions, in greatest need of its
strength and resources. It may be inconvenient for Georgia, or the States forming our western or northeastern borders, to send their representatives to the
seat of government; but they would find it more so to struggle alone against an
invading enemy, or even to support alone the whole expense of those precautions
which may be dictated by the neighborhood of continual danger. If they should
derive less benefit, therefore, from the Union in some respects than the less
distant States, they will derive greater benefit from it in other respects, and thus
the proper equilibrium will be maintained throughout.

I submit to you, my fellow-citizens, these considerations, in full confidence
that the good sense which has so often marked your decisions will allow them
their due weight and effect; and that you will never suffer difficulties, however
formidable in appearance, or however fashionable the error on which they may
be founded, to drive you into the gloomy and perilous scene into which the
advocates for disunion would conduct you. Hearken not to the unnatural voice
which tells you that the people of America, knit together as they are by so many
cords of affection, can no longer live together as members of the same family;
can no longer continue the mutual guardians of their mutual happiness; can no
longer be fellow-citizens of one great, respectable, and flourishing empire.
Hearken not to the voice which petulantly tells you that the form of government
recommended for your adoption is a novelty in the political world; that it has
never yet had a place in the theories of the wildest projectors; that it rashly
attempts what it is impossible to accomplish. No, my countrymen, shut your
ears against this unhallowed language. Shut your hearts against the poison
which it conveys; the kindred blood which flows in the veins of American
citizens, the mingled blood which they have shed in defence of their sacred
rights, consecrate their Union, and excite horror at the idea of their becoming
aliens, rivals, enemies. And if novelties are to be shunned, believe me, the most
alarming of all novelties, the most wild of all projects, the most rash of all
attempts, is that of rending us in pieces, in order to preserve our liberties and
promote our happiness. But why is the experiment of an extended republic to be
rejected, merely because it may comprise what is new? Is it not the glory of the
people of America, that, whilst they have paid a decent regard to the opinions of
former times and other nations, they have not suffered a blind veneration for
antiquity, for custom, or for names, to overrule the suggestions of their own
good sense, the knowledge of their own situation, and the lessons of their own
experience? To this manly spirit, posterity will be indebted for the possession,
and the world for the example, of the numerous innovations displayed on the
American theatre, in favor of private rights and public happiness. Had no important step been taken by the leaders of the Revolution for which a precedent
could not be discovered, no government established of which an exact model did
not present itself, the people of the United States might, at this moment, have
been numbered among the melancholy victims of misguided councils, must at

74

best have been laboring under the weight of some of those forms which have crushed the liberties of the rest of mankind. Happily for America, happily, we trust, for the whole human race, they pursued a new and more noble course. They accomplished a revolution which has no parallel in the annals of human society. They reared the fabrics of governments which have no model on the face of the globe. They formed the design of a great Confederacy, which it is incumbent on their successors to improve and perpetuate. If their works betray imperfections, we wonder at the fewness of them. If they erred most in the structure of the Union, this was the work most difficult to be executed; this is the work which has been new modelled by the act of your convention, and it is that act on which you are now to deliberate and to decide. (*1787*)

JOHN TAYLOR

1753–1824

John Taylor, philosopher and statesman of agrarianism, was, according to V. L. Parrington, "the most original economist of his generation." He was born in either Orange or Caroline County, Virginia, and died at "Hazelwood," one of his several plantations. Having received his earliest education from private tutors, he later attended the academy of Donald Robertson (who also taught James Madison) and William and Mary College. He read law in the office of Edmund Pendleton and was admitted to the bar in 1774, but before his practice was fairly established, war was declared. Taylor immediately volunteered and saw combat in New York and Pennsylvania, attaining the rank of major before resigning in 1779. He resumed his military career two years later as a lieutenant colonel in the Virginia militia, which fought under the command of Lafayette in the campaign against the Hessians.

Taylor was a famous lawyer and a successful farmer. From 1783 to 1793 he practiced law in Virginia and amassed a fortune, although competing with such illustrious men as John Marshall, Patrick Henry, and Alexander Campbell. In 1783 he married Lucy Penn, a wealthy cousin, whose dowry helped to set him up as one of the most prosperous planters of his day.

Taylor was first of all a farmer. Always intent upon improving agricultural methods, he began publishing in 1803 a series of newspaper articles explaining his ideas. In these essays, which were collected as *The Arator*, he advocated "inclosing" and crop rotation as means of restoring fertility to the soil. Like Jefferson, he rejected slavery, although not for moral reasons, but because he thought the overseer system was unprofitable. He also urged the farmers to assert their political rights and not to allow the "paper aristocracy" to gain control of the country. Since the agrarian way of life was, in his view, the best life, he insisted that the farmers fight to retain it.

Like Calhoun and Legaré in later years, Taylor spent much of his life in public office. He was active in the Virginia legislature from 1796 to 1800. He also served several years in the United States Senate. In politics Taylor is usually regarded as a Jeffersonian democrat. While a member of the legislature he supported complete religious freedom, a wider franchise, and a system of equal representation. He opposed the federal Constitution, arguing that under it the rights of individuals and of the states were not sufficiently protected. Later, upon the establishment of the federal government, he insisted upon a strict interpretation of the Constitution. His states' rights beliefs were advanced in their most obvious form in 1798, when he introduced in the Virginia legislature resolutions supporting delegated powers and the right of states to protest in cases of "deliberate, palpable, and dangerous exercise of other powers."

Even in his own time most of Taylor's prestige came from his writings. The best known of these today are *The Arator* (1803) and *An Inquiry into the Principles and Policy of the Government of the United States* (1814). Of the latter, Charles A. Beard has remarked that, despite its stylistic defects, it "deserves to rank among the two or three really historic contributions to political science which have been produced in the United States." In this scholarly treatise Taylor opposed both the natural-aristocracy theory of John Adams and the capitalistic-aristocratic theory of Hamilton. He sought to explode these hypotheses by pointing out that social classes are caused, not by biological inequality, but by chance, unscrupulousness, and force. The United States, he said, because of the availability of free land, was in no peril of a feudal aristocracy, but the most dangerous of all monopolies—one based on money and credit, or, in his words, a "paper aristocracy"—was an imminent, serious threat to the American democratic system.

The principal points in Taylor's argument have been summarized by Beard substantially as follows: The masses have always been exploited by some dominant class in society—royal, ecclesiastical, or feudal. This ruling faction, furthermore, has retained its power by the use of such devices as "loyalty to the throne or altar." Now a new class has emerged—the capitalists, who exploit the public by the use of inflated paper and the protective tariff. These vultures prosper on wealth taken from productive laborers, particularly agricultural workers. Herein, he concluded, lies the essential conflict between agrarianism and capitalism, which has fostered the development of the party system in our government. Seemingly the only remedy for this situation is to destroy special privilege without compensation.

Scholars have become increasingly aware of Taylor's significance as a social and political philosopher. He is now recognized as one of the most important intellectual leaders of the agrarian movement.

from *The Arator*

No. 3. The Political State of Agriculture

In collecting the causes which have contributed to the miserable agricultural state of the country, as it is a national calamity of the highest magnitude, we should be careful not to be blinded by partiality for our customs or institutions, nor corrupted by a disposition to flatter ourselves or others. I shall begin with those of a political nature. These are a secondary providence, which govern unseen the great interests of society; and if agriculture is bad and languishing in a country and climate, where it may be good and prosperous, no doubt remains with me, that political institutions have chiefly perpetrated the evil; just as they decide the fate of commerce.

The device of subjecting it to the payment of bounties to manufacturing, is an institution of this kind. This device is one item in every system for rendering governments too strong for nations. Such an object never was and never can be effected, except by factions legally created at the publick expense. The wealth transferred from the nation to such factions, devotes them to the will of the government, by which it is bestowed. They must render the service for which it was given, or it would be taken away. It is unexceptionably given to support a government against a nation, or one faction against another. Armies, loaning, banking, and an intricate treasury system, endowing a government with the absolute power of applying publick money, under the cover of nominal checks, are other devices of this kind. Whatever strength or wealth a government and its legal factions acquire by law, is taken from a nation; and whatever is taken from a nation, weakens and impoverishes that interest, which composes the majority. There, political oppression in every form must finally fall, however it may oscillate during the period of transit from a good to a bad government, so as sometimes to scratch factions. Agriculture being the interest covering a great majority of the people of the United States, every device for getting money or power, hatched by a fellow-feeling or common interest, between a government and its legal creatures, must of course weaken and impoverish it.—Desertion, for the sake of reaping without labour, a share in the harvest of wealth and power, bestowed by laws at its expense, thins its ranks; an annual tribute to these legal factions, empties its purse; and poverty debilitates both its soil and understanding.

The device of protecting duties, under the pretext of encouraging manufactures, operates like its kindred, by creating a capitalist interest, which instantly seizes upon the bounty taken by law from agriculture; and instead of doing any good to the actual workers in wood, metals, cotton or other substances, it helps to rear up an aristocratical order, at the expense of the workers in earth, to unite with governments in oppressing every species of useful industry.

The products of agriculture and manufacturing, unshackled by law, would seek each for themselves, the best markets through commercial channels, but these markets would hardly ever be the same; protecting duties tie travellers together, whose business and interest lie in different directions. This ligature upon nature, will, like all unnatural ligatures, weaken or kill. The best markets of our agriculture lie in foreign countries, whilst the best markets of our manufactures are at home.—Our agriculture has to cross the ocean, and encounter a competition with foreign agriculture on its own ground. Our manufactures meet at home a competition with foreign manufactures. The disadvantages of the first competition, suffice to excite all the efforts of agriculture to save her life; the advantages of the second suffice gradually to bestow a sound constitution on manufacturing. But the manufacture of an aristocratical interest, under the pretext of encouraging work of a very different nature, may reduce both manufacturers and husbandmen, as Strickland says, is already effected in the case of the latter, to the "lowest state of degradation."

This degradation could never have been seen by a friend to either, who could afterwards approve of protecting duties. Let us take the article of wheat to unfold an idea of the disadvantages which have produced it. If wheat is worth 16s. sterling in England the 70 lb. the farmers sell it here at about 6s. sterling.—American agriculture then meets English agriculture in a competition, compelling her to sell at little more than one third of the price obtained by her rival. But American manufactures take the field against English on very different terms. These competitors meet in the United States. The American manufactures receive first, a bounty equal to the freight, commission and English taxes, upon their English rivals; and secondly, a bounty equal to our own necessary imposts. Without protecting duties, therefore, the American manufacturer gets for the same article, about 25 per cent. more, and the American agriculturalist about 180 per cent. less, than their English rivals. Protecting duties added to these inequalities, may raise up an order of masters for actual manufacturers, to intercept advantages too enormous to escape the vigilance of capital, impoverish husbandmen, and aid in changing a fair to a fraudulent government; but they will never make either of these intrinsically valuable classes richer, wiser or freer.

No. 60. The Rights of Agriculture

It is lamentable to confess, that this, to be a true, must be almost a negative number.—This most useful and virtuous interest, enjoys no rights, except in the United States; and there it enjoys no exclusive rights, whilst the few in which it shares are daily contracted by the various arts of ambition and avarice. Every where else, agriculture is a slave; here she is only a dupe. Abroad she is condemned by avowed force to feed voluptuousness, avarice and ambition; here, she is deluded by flattery and craft, during fits of joy or of fury, to squander her property, to mortgage her labourers, and to shackle her freedom. Abroad, she suffers contempt, and is sensible of her degradation; here, she is a blind Quixote, mounted on a wooden horse, and persuaded by the acclamations of her foes, that she is soaring to the stars, whilst she is ready to tumble into the dust.

Privileges are rearing by laws all around at her expense, and whilst she is taught to believe that they will only take from her a few inconsiderable slips,

78

they will at length draw a spacious circumvallation, within which will gradually grow up a power, beyond her control. Tricks, as well as inventions, are daily fortified with legal bulwarks, called charters, to transfer her wealth, and to secure frauds against her efforts. Capital in every form, save that of agriculture, is fed by taxes and by bounties, which she must pay; whilst not a single bounty is paid to her by capital in any form; and instead of being favoured with some prizes in the lottery of society, she pays most, and is rewarded herself by the blanks of underwriting the projects of statesmen, and bearing the burdens of government.

The use of society, is to secure the fruits of his own industry and talents to each associator. Its abuse consists in artifice or force, for transferring those fruits from some partners to others. Of this abuse, that interest covering the majority of partners is the victim. And the difficulty of discriminating laws, transferring such fruits for the benefit of society, from those having in view the gratification of avarice and ambition, produces a sympathy and combination between these distinct kinds of law. As the members of the government, and members of legal frauds, both extract power and income from the majority, they are apt to coalesce; and each party to favour the designs of its ally, in their operations upon the common enemy. Hence governments love to create exclusive rights, and exclusive rights cling to governments. The ligament of parent and child, binds them together, and the power creating these abuses, must make them props for its support, or instruments for its subversion. Its election between these alternatives is certain, and society is thus unavoidably thrown into two divisions. One containing all those who pay, and the other those who receive contributions, required either for publick use, or to foster private avarice or ambition. Good government is graduated by this latter kind of contribution thus unfortunately allied to the former. The highest amount constitutes the worst, and the lowest, the best possible species of government. But as both are drawn from the majority of every society, whenever the agricultural interest covers that majority, this interest is the victim of the coalition; and as it almost universally does cover this majority, the agricultural interest is almost universally its slaves.

The consequences to agriculture will be demonstrated by converting this coalition between government and its creatures, or of all who receive tolls given by law, into a political pope, and placing in his mouth an address to agriculture, in a parody of Ernulphus's form of excommunication.

"May you be taxed in your land, your slaves, your houses, your carriages, your horses, your clothing, your liquors, your coffee, your tea, and your salt. May you be taxed by banks, by protecting duties, by embargoes, and by charters of a thousand different forms. May the exemption of your exports from taxation be removed, and may you then be taxed through your wheat, your corn, your tobacco, your cotton, your rice, your indigo, your sugar, your hemp, your live stock, your beef, your pork, your tar, pitch and turpentine, your onions, your cheese, and your potatoes. May you be taxed for the support of government, or to enrich exclusive or chartered interests, through every article you import, and through every article you export, by duties called protecting, but intended to take away your constitutional protection against taxation for the benefit of capitalists. May you be taxed through every article produced by your labour or

79

necessary to your subsistence, comfort and pleasure, by exercises [excises]. And whilst every species of your products, and of your consumptions are thus taxed, may your capital, being visible, be moreover taxed in various modes. May all these taxes whether plain or intricate, (after deducting the small sum necessary to produce the genuine end of society) be employed in enriching capitalists, and buying soldiers, placemen and contractors, to make you submissive to usurpations, and as quiet under your burthens, as a martyr tied to the stake, under the flames. After you have been taxed as far as you can pay, may you by the bounty of God Almighty be moreover mortgaged up to your value or credit, for the benefit of the said coalition of capitalists. And finally, may none of this good and useful coalition, to whom is given the wealth of this world, as the kingdom of heaven is to the pope and his clergy, be taxed in their stock or principal held under any law or charter whatsoever; nor in their capital employed in any manufacture or speculation, nor in any profit drawn from such principal stock or capital; nor thro' any of their sinecures, salaries, contracts or incomes; but on the contrary, may such stock, principal, capital, profits, salaries, contracts, and sinecures, be constantly fostered by bounties in various injurious forms, to be paid by you, you damned dirty working, productive bitch, agriculture." Throughout the world, agriculture, like one of Ernulphus's contrite excommunicants, responds, amen, to this pious invocation.

Throughout the world, agriculture has enjoyed, and in England, continues to enjoy, one of the rights in which she has a share in the United States; that of a voice in elections.—And throughout the world, this right has been unable to shield her against an anathema, which prescribes for her as perfect a hell, as the formula of Ernulphus prescribes for his heretick. Let the agricultural interest of the United States, pause here and look around. Is a blind confidence in a right so universally ineffectual, a sufficient safeguard for its freedom and happiness? To me it seems, that an interest can never be long free, which blindly confides in a coalition, whose object it is to draw from that interest, power and wealth. That the major interest must be as cunning, as wise and as watchful, as the minor, or that the minor interest will enslave it. And that agriculture must as attentively keep her eyes upon the coalition, to avoid its operations upon her, as the coalition does upon agriculture, for the purpose of transfering to its members portions of her power and wealth, whenever she slumbers.

Hence have arisen the political suggestions to be found in these essays. I cannot discern much good in an improvement of agriculture, to get luxury, voluptuousness and tyranny for a few, and wretchedness for a multitude.—The best cultivated country in the world, abounds most in paupers and thieves. Agriculture must be a politician to avoid this fate; and those who ridicule her pretensions to knowledge in this science, intend by persuading her to repose in a blind confidence, built upon the frail right of election, to expose her to it. How can she even judiciously elect, if she cannot or will not judge of publick measures, by the light of her own interest?

80   The moral consequence of this supineness or ignorance, is, that social happiness gradually becomes the dependant of a minority, and of course it is provided for, by continually subtracting from the happiness of a majority. The visible immorality of this, demonstrates the virtue, as well as wisdom of suggestions designed to obstruct it.

The remaining right in which agriculture participates, in common with all other interests, having any thing to export, is bestowed by the constitutional prohibition of duties upon exports. This right originated in state jealousies, and not from a disposition to favour agriculture, but yet it is her best security, for the preservation of that portion of our government, which will longest be sensible of her elective influence; and its relinquishment will be the most fatal wound which can be inflicted on her. The coalition I have described will try every art in her most unguarded moments, to snatch it from her, and it will be the last relinquishment it will need. To determine whether her elective influence can bear further wounds, let agriculture re-survey the legislation of our whole term of independence, and compare the catalogues she may select, of laws for creating or fostering privileges and exclusive interests, with those for fostering herself; and let this comparison form the criterion for ascertaining her legislative influence. Thus only can she judiciously increase this influence, if it has settled too low, or diminish it, if it has raised too high. There is no fair mode of judging, except by these legislative acts. To infer, that the agricultural interest influences legislatures, because it chiefly elects them, would be like inferring, that the French nation influences the tribunate, because they wholly elect it. Let agriculture therefore hold fast the solitary security she enjoys in common with her industrious associates, against the ambitions of usurpers, and the avarice of capitalists, nor be deluded into the absurd notion, that it is wise to relinquish the only peculium of industry, for the sake of some temporary operation upon foreign nations, inevitably resulting upon herself in the form of retaliation, whilst the protection of exports against taxation, will be gone forever.

A Note: Political Morality

Society is unavoidably made up of two interests only, in one of which all special and particular modifications of interest are included; namely, one subsisting by industry; the other, by law. Government is instituted for the happiness of the first interest, but belonging itself to the second, it is perpetually drawn towards that by the strongest cords. Therefore, unless the first is able very accurately to distinguish between laws calculated to do it a benefit or an injury, it must be gradually sacrificed to the appetites of the second, because government, a member of the second, legislates. All men enjoying honour, power or wealth by law, or striving to acquire either through that channel, are like coin struck with the same dies. The engravers, avarice and ambition, constantly mark the same etching, and the aqua fortis, self-interest, indeliably [indelibly] imprints it on the human mind. From this fact, the preference of a republican government is deduced, as being calculated for checking the natural disposition of legislatures or the government, to favour the minor class, composed of legal or factitious interests, at the expense of the major class, composed of natural interests; including all who subsist, not by means of legal donations, but by useful talents in every form, such as those employed in agriculture, manufacturing, tuition, physick, and all trades and scientifick professions. The propensity of law to sacrifice the great or natural interest of nations, to the class of little or factitious interests, arises from two causes; one, the government being

81

the matrix of the latter, views her progeny with the eyes of an owl, and considers them as beautiful; the other, that although law can enable the small class to live on the great one, it cannot enable the great class to live upon the small one; uniting to produce this propensity in a degree so violent, that mankind have pronounced it irresistible, except by a countervailing union between strong republican fetters upon government, and a degree of political knowledge in the major class, sufficient to prevent these fetters from being broken by laws. The remedy is so rare, that many honest men doubt of its existence; and have concluded in despair, that the major class or general interest of a nation, must inevitably become the slave of the minor or factitious interest in some mode. Others believe, that by exciting the general interest to watch, to think, and to judge for itself, its intellect will be brightened, and its rights preserved. But all agree that neither any individual nor any interest dictated to by another, can prosper; and that political ignorance universally implies political slavery. Election has no power beyond a charter or a commission, to prevent the elected from being transferred by his election from the great class of general interest, to the little class of factitious or legal interest; on the contrary, the structure of republican government is raised upon the principle, that it necessarily transfers him from one to the other, at least in most instances. This is unanimously admitted by the elected themselves. They separate into two parties, called inns and outs. The inns say that the outs are influenced by a desire to get in, and the outs, that the inns are influenced by a desire to keep in. Agreeing that both belong to the minor class, and neither to the major class, which can neither get in nor keep in; these two members of the minor class vote in constant opposition, because they stand in each other's way, which could not possibly happen if they were genuine members of the general interest class. How then can the major class expect happiness from this species of political gambling for a rich stake which it pays, and the gamblers alternately win, if it has no skill in the game?

Agriculture is the most powerful member of the class constituting the general interest, but if her sons are too ignorant to use this power with discretion (like a body of elephants thrown into confusion in a battle) they rush in every direction, trampling down friends and foes for a short time, and inevitably become an easy prey to their enemies. As the most powerful individual constituting the major class of general interest, the political ignorance of agriculture, would of course destroy the rights of the whole class. If she divides herself between any of the members of the inferiour class, each of her moieties enlist under an aristocratical or monarchical power, whether it be called executive, legislative, credit or charter, and the member obtaining the victory by her aid, becomes her master. Just as in a division of her forces between a king and a nobility, the king or the nobility and not agriculture, gains a victory, both over her, and over all her weaker associates in the class of the general interest.

As there are two classes of interest only in society, there are also only two political codes, each appropriated by nature to one class. The code of the minor class is constituted of intrigues and stratagems to beguile the major class, and to advance the separate interests of the individuals, parties and legal combinations, of which the minor class is compounded.—The code of the major class consists of good moral principles, by which the national rights and happiness

82

can only be preserved. The guilt of offensive war, and the virtue of defensive, are the essential qualities of the respective codes. One is compounded of the best, and the other of the worst qualities of human nature; and the members of the general or natural interest of society, can never avoid oppression nor sustain a just and free government unless they are skilled in both.

As the extension of comfort and happiness is the only good motive for writing an agricultural book, whatever would defeat the end belongs to the subject; and as a legal profusion in overstocking a nation with members of the minor class, is the solitary process for enslaving it, unless the major class understands the sublime branch of ethicks, namely, political morality, it cannot counteract this process. Thus only can it distinguish between laws and projects calculated for benefitting or injuring the nation. This science only can prevent the liberty, the virtue, the happiness, the bravery and the talents of the nation from being extinguished. The treasury of the United States has been cited as a proper subject for its application. If the agricultural and other members of the major class should discern that the president had become a king of the treasury, surrounded with nominal checks and balances appointed by himself; if they should discern that the representatives of the people were convinced of a great waste of publick money, and yet ignorant of the modes by which it was effected; if they should recollect the consequences of such an errour in the English form of government; and if they knew that nations were enslaved by a corrupting application of their own treasure, would not the correction of the evil be founded in genuine political morality, and be plainly adverse to the erroneous and flagitious political code of the minor class. . . . (*1813*)

from An Inquiry into the Principles and Policy of the Government of the United States

Chapter 1. Aristocracy

. . . Whether the human mind is able to circumscribe its own powers, is a question, between the two modern political parties. One (of which Mr. Adams [1] is a disciple) asserts that man can ascertain his own moral capacity, deduces consequences from this postulate, and erects thereon schemes of government—right, say they, because natural. The other, observing that those who affirm the doctrine, have never been able to agree upon this natural form of government; and that human nature has been perpetually escaping from all forms; considers government as capable of unascertained modification and improvement, from moral causes.

To illustrate this question; let us confront Mr. Adams's opinion "that aristocracy is natural and therefore unavoidable," with one "that it is artificial and factitious, and therefore avoidable." He seems to use the term "natural" to convey an idea distinct from moral, by coupling it with the idea of fatality. But moral causes, being capable of human modification, events flowing from them,

[1] *Taylor is referring to John Adams. The* Inquiry *was written in reply to Adams'* A Defense of the Constitutions of Government of the United States of America Against the Attacks of Mr. Turgot *(1787).*

83

possess the quality of freedom or evitation. . . . If, therefore, by the term "natural" Mr. Adams intended to include "moral," the idea of "fatality" is inaccurately coupled with it; if he resigns this idea, the infallibility of his system, as being natural, must also be resigned.

That he must resign his political predestination, and all its consequences, I shall attempt to prove, by shewing, that aristocracies, both ancient and modern, have been variable and artificial; that they have all proceeded from moral, not from natural causes; and they are evitable and not inevitable.

. . . It will be an effort of this essay to prove, that the United States have refuted the ancient axiom, "that monarchy, aristocracy and democracy, are the only elements of government," by planting theirs in moral principles, without any reference to those elements; and that by demolishing the barrier hitherto obstructing the progress of political science, they have cleared the way for improvement.

Mr. Adams's system promises nothing. It tells us that human nature is always the same: that the art of government can never change; that it is contracted into three simple principles; as at Athens, Venice, or Constantinople; or those of the same principles compounded, as at London, Rome, or Lacedemon. And it gravely counts up several victims of democratic rage, as proofs, that democracy is more pernicious than monarchy or aristocracy. Such a computation is a spectre, calculated to arrest our efforts, and appal our hopes, in pursuit of political good. If it be correct, what motives of preference between forms of government remain? On one hand, Mr. Adams calls our attention to hundreds of wise and virtuous patricians, mangled and bleeding victims of popular fury; on the other, he might have exhibited millions of plebeians, sacrificed to the pride, folly and ambition of monarchy and aristocracy; and, to complete the picture, he ought to have placed right before us, the effects of these three principles commixed, in the wars, rebellions, persecutions and oppressions of the English form, celebrated by Mr. Adams as the most perfect of the mixed class of governments. Is it possible to convince us, that we are compelled to elect one of these evils? After having discovered principles of government, distinct from monarchy, aristocracy or democracy, in the experience of their efficacy, and the enjoyment of their benefits; can we be persuaded to renounce the discovery, to restore the old principles of political navigation, and to steer the commonwealth into the disasters, against which all past ages have pathetically warned us? It is admitted, that man, physically, is "always the same"; but denied that he is so, morally. Upon the truth or error of this distinction, the truth or error of Mr. Adams's mode of reasoning and of this essay, will somewhat depend. If it is untrue, then the cloud of authorities collected by him from all ages, are irrefutable evidence, to establish the fact, that political misery is unavoidable; because man is always the same. But if the moral qualities of human nature are not always the same, but are different both in nations and individuals; and if government ought to be constructed in relation to these moral qualities, and not in relation to factitious orders; the authorities do not produce a conclusion so deplorable. . . .

84

Having apprized the reader, by these general remarks, of the political principles to be vindicated or assailed in this essay; and that an effort will be made to prove, that the policy of the United States is rooted in moral or intellectual principles, and not in orders, class or caste, natural or factitious; this effort must be postponed, until the way is opened to it, by a more particular review of Mr. Adams's system. To this, therefore, I return.

He supposes "that every society must *naturally* produce an aristocratical order of men, which it will be impossible to confine to an equality of rights with other men." To determine the truth of this position, an inquiry must be made into the mode by which these orders have been produced in those countries, placed before us by Mr. Adams, as objects of terror or imitation.

. . . The position first presenting itself is, "that an aristocracy is the work of nature." A position equivalent to the antiquated doctrine, "that a king is the work of God." A particular attention will now be paid to this point, because Mr. Adams's theory is entirely founded upon it.

Superior abilities constitutes one among the enumerated causes of a natural aristocracy. This cause is evidently as fluctuating as knowledge and ignorance; and its capacity to produce aristocracy, must depend upon this fluctuation. The aristocracy of superior abilities will be regulated by the extent of the space, between knowledge and ignorance. As the space contracts or widens, it will be diminished or increased; and if aristocracy may be thus diminished, it follows that it may be thus destroyed.

No certain state of knowledge, is a natural or unavoidable quality of man. As an intellectual or moral quality, it may be created, destroyed and modified by human power. Can that which may be created, destroyed and modified by human power, be a natural and inevitable cause of aristocracy?

It has been modified in an extent, which Mr. Adams does not even compute, by the art of printing, discovered subsequently to almost the whole of the authorities which have convinced Mr. Adams, that knowledge, or as he might have more correctly asserted, ignorance, was a cause of aristocracy.

The peerage of knowledge or abilities, in consequence of its enlargement by the effects of printing, can no longer be collected and controlled in the shape of a noble order or a legislative department. The great body of this peerage must remain scattered throughout every nation, by the enjoyment of the benefit of the press. By endowing a small portion of it with exclusive rights and privileges, the indignation of this main body is excited. If this endowment should enable a nation to watch and control an inconsiderable number of that species of peerage produced by knowledge, it would also purchase the dissatisfaction of its numberless members unjustly excluded; and would be a system for defending a nation against imbecility, and inviting aggression from strength, equivalent to a project for defeating an army, by feasting its vanguard.

If this reasoning is correct, the collection of that species of natural aristocracy (as Mr. Adams calls it) produced by superior abilities, into a legislative department, for the purpose of watching and controlling it, is now rendered impracticable, however useful it might have been, at an era when the proportion between ignorance was essentially different; and this impracticability is a strong indication of the radical inaccuracy of considering aristocracy as an inevitable natural law. The wisdom of uniting exclusive knowledge by exclusive privileges, that it may be controlled by disunited ignorance, is not considered as being an hypothetical question, since this aristocratical knowledge cannot now exist.

Similar reasoning applies still more forcibly to the idea of nature's consti-

85

tuting aristocracy, by means of exclusive virtue. Knowledge and virtue both fluctuate. A steady effect, from fluctuating causes, is morally and physically impossible. And yet Mr. Adams infers a natural aristocracy, from the error, that virtue and knowledge are in an uniform relation to vice and ignorance; sweeps away by it every human faculty, for the attainment of temporal or eternal happiness; and overturns the efficacy of law, to produce private or public moral rectitude.

Had it been true, that knowledge and virtue were natural causes of aristocracy, no fact could more clearly have exploded Mr. Adams's system, or more unequivocally have dissented from the eulogy he bestows on the English form of government. Until knowledge and virtue shall become genealogical they cannot be the causes of an inheritable aristocracy; and its existence, without the aid of superior knowledge and virtue, is a positive refutation of the idea, that nature creates aristocracy with these tools.

. . . Alienation is the remedy for an aristocracy founded on landed wealth; inhibitions upon monopoly and incorporation, for one founded on paper wealth. Knowledge, enlisted by Mr. Adams under the banner of aristocracy, deserted her associate by the invention of alienation, and became its natural enemy. Discovering its hostility to human happiness, like Brutus, she has applied the axe to the neck of what Mr. Adams calls her progeny; and instead of maintaining the exclusiveness of wealth, contributes to its division by inciting competition, and assailing perpetuities. How successfully, let England illustrate. She, no longer relying upon nature for an aristocracy, is perpetually obliged to repair the devastations it sustains from alienation; the weapon invented by knowledge; by resorting to the funds of paper systems, pillage, patronage and hierarchy, for fresh supplies.

. . . In order to illustrate the opinion, that the aristocracy exhibited to us by Mr. Adams, as creating a necessity for his system, is only a ghost, let us turn our eyes for a moment towards its successor.

As the aristocracies of priestcraft and conquest decayed, that of patronage and paper stock grew; not the rival, but the instrument of a king; without rank or title; regardless of honor; of insatiable avarice; and neither conspicuous for virtue and knowledge, or capable of being collected into a legislative chamber. Differing in all its qualities from Mr. Adams's natural aristocracy, and defying his remedy, it is condensed and combined by an interest, exclusive, and inimical to public good.

Why has Mr. Adams written volumes to instruct us how to manage an order of nobles, sons of the Gods, of exclusive virtue, talents, and wealth, and attended by the pomp and fraud of superstition; or one of feudal barons, holding great districts of unalienable country, warlike, high spirited, turbulent and dangerous; now that these orders are no more? Whilst he passes over in silence the aristocracy of paper and patronage, more numerous, more burdensome, unexposed to public jealousy by the badge of title, and not too honorable or high spirited to use and serve executive power, for the sake of pillaging the people. Are these odious vices, to be concealed under apprehensions of ancient aristocracies, which, however natural, are supplanted by this modern one?

. . . For the sake of perspicuity, I shall call the ancient aristocracy, chiefly created and supported by superstition, "the aristocracy of the first age"; that

86

produced by conquest, known by the title of the feudal system, "the aristocracy of the second age"; and that erected on paper and patronage, "the aristocracy of the third or present age." If aristocracy is the work of nature, by deserting her accustomed constancy, and slily changing the shape of her work, she has cunningly perplexed our defensive operations: to create the aristocracy of the first age, she used Jupiter; of the second, Mars; and of the third, Mercury. Jupiter is dethroned by knowledge; the usurpations of Mars are scattered by commerce and alienation; and it only remains to detect the impostures of Mercury.

. . . Plebian ignorance was both the cause and justification of the Roman aristocracy. That might have been a worse magistrate, than patrician knowledge; and the magic circle drawn by superstition around the conscript fathers, might have been necessary to restrain the excesses of a rude nation inclosed within a single city. But this supplies no argument in favor of an aristocracy in societies not of national aggregation, but of national dispersion; not of national ignorance, but of national intelligence; not sustained by superstition, but by a common interest.

Similar causes produced the feudal aristocracy. The conquering tribes were moving cities and colonizing armies; and hereditary privileges were preferred to national annihilation. The feudal commanders, compared with their ignorant vassals, possessed that superiority in renown, talents and wealth, which might have produced the feudal system as the moral effect of these moral causes. Such a form of government might have been the best which these moving cities, these tribes or these armies could bear, and yet execrable for a nation, not in the same moral state.

Having thus conceded to Mr. Adams, that wherever a few possess the mass of the renown, virtue, talents and wealth of a nation, that they will become an aristocracy, and probably ought to do so; it would be a concession, strictly reciprocal, to admit, that wherever no such body is to be found, an aristocracy ought not to be created by legal assignments of wealth and poverty. As the first species of minority will govern, because of the power arising from such monopolies only, so no other species can, without these sources of power. Where its sources are, power will be found; and hence the great mass of wealth, created by the system of paper and patronage, has annihilated the power of the didactick and titled peerage of England; because it has not a sufficient mass of virtue, renown, talents or wealth, to oppose against stock and patronage.

The aristocracies of the first and second ages were indebted for their power to ignorance, fraud and superstition; now reason, sincerity and truth, are demanded by the human mind. It disdains to worship a pageant or fear a phantom, and is only to be guided by views of interest or happiness. This change in the human character indicates an impossibility of reviving the principles which sustained the aristocracies of the first and second age, when mankind believed in the Gods of a pantheon, and in the prophetic powers of convulsed women.

Talents and virtue are now so widely distributed, as to have rendered a monopoly of either, equivalent to that of antiquity, impracticable; and if an aristocracy ought to have existed, whilst it possessed such a monopoly, it ought not also to exist, because this monopoly is irretrievably lost. The distribution of wealth produced by commerce and alienation, is equal to that of knowledge

87

and virtue, produced by printing; but as the first distribution might be artificially counteracted, with a better prospect of success than the latter, aristocracy has abandoned a reliance on a monopoly of virtue, renown and abilities, and resorted wholly to a monopoly of wealth, by the system of paper and patronage. Modern taxes and frauds to collect money, and not ancient authors, will therefore afford the best evidence of its present character.

. . . When the principles and practice of the American policy come to be considered, one subject of inquiry will be, whether public opinion, or the declaration of the mass of national virtue, talents and wealth, will be able to exercise this its just sovereignty, in union with the system of paper and patronage. If not, it is very remarkable, that this system, denominated the aristocracy of the third age, is equally inimical to Mr. Adams's principles and to mine. We both assign political power to the mass of virtue, talents and wealth in a nation. He only contends for an aristocracy from a supposition that it must possess this mass, and be the only organ of its will; I acknowledge the sovereignty of these qualities, deny their residence in a minority compressible into an aristocracy, and contend for a different organ. In order to discover whether the aristocracy of paper and patronage, is a good organ for expressing the will of the sovereign we have agreed upon, let us return to England, and consider, whether the revolution, which finally destroyed the aristocracy of the second age, and established that of the third, has placed the government in the hands of the wealth, virtue and talents of the nation, or subjected it to the influence of public opinion.

If you had seen the vulture preying upon the entrails of the agonized Prometheus, would you have believed, though Pluto himself had sworn it, that the vulture was under the control of Prometheus? If you could not have believed this, neither can you believe, that the concubinage between a government, and the system of paper and patronage, is an organ of national opinion, or of the wealth, virtue and talents of the nation, and not a conspiracy between avarice and ambition; because, it is as impossible that a nation should derive pleasure from a government founded in the principle of voraciousness, as the man from the laceration of his bowels.

It has been said, that paper and office are property; and as by their means, a minority may bring into its coffers, the whole profit of national labour, so it ought to be considered as the nation. Had Prometheus fattened by being fed upon by the vulture, it would have given some colour to this ingenious deception.

Again it has been said, that the system of paper and patronage encourages commerce, agriculture, manufactures and conquest; it aggravated the misery of Prometheus, that his liver was made to grow for the gratification of a harpy, without appeasing its voracity.

The difficulty of producing a correct opinion of the cause and consequences of the new-born aristocracy of paper and patronage, surpasses the same difficulty in relation to the aristocracies of the first and second ages, as far as its superior importance. The two last being substantially dead, their bodies may be cut up, the articulation of their bones exposed, and the convolution of their fibres unravelled; but whenever the intricate structure of the system of paper and patronage is attempted to be dissected, we moderns surrender our intellects to yells uttered by the living monster, similar to those with which its predecessors astonished, deluded, and oppressed the world for three thousand years. The aristocracy of superstition defended itself by exclaiming, the Gods! the temples! the sacred oracles! divine vengeance! and Elysian fields!—and that of paper and patronage exclaims, national faith! sacred charters! disorganization! and security of property!

Let us moderns cease to boast of our victory over superstition and the feudal system, and our advancement in knowledge. Let us neither pity, ridicule or despise the ancients, as dupes of frauds and tricks, which we can so easily discern; lest some ancient sage should rise from his grave, and answer, "You moderns are duped by arts more obviously fraudulent, than those which deceived us. The agency of the Gods was less discernable, than the effects of paper and patronage. We could not see, that the temporal and eternal pains and pleasures, threatened and promised by our aristocracy, could not be inflicted or bestowed by it; you see throughout Europe the effects of your aristocracy. Without your light, oracles were necessary to deceive us; with the help of printing, and two detections, you are deceived by aristocracy in a third form, although it pretends neither to the divinity nor heroism claimed by its two first forms. And under these disadvantages, the impositions of our aristocracy were restrained within narrower bounds than those of yours. Did any aristocracy of the first age, extend its annual spoliation from one to thirty-five millions of pounds sterling, in less than a century?"

. . . We discern but two kinds of aristocracy; that which is the tyrant itself, and that which is the instrument of the tyrant. The ancient feudal and hierarchical aristocracies of England were tyrants themselves. The modern nobles and bishops; the patronage and stock interests; the generals and titulars of Bonaparte, and the mandarins of China, are instruments of tyranny. The same reasons inducing the people to unite with kings against aristocracies, which were themselves tyrants, ought to determine them to assail such as are instruments of kings. Independent of kings, they are universally the first kind of evil; dependent on them, the second. . . . .

The effect of opposite interests, one enriched by and governing the other, correctly follows its cause. One interest is a tyrant, the other its slave. In Britain, one of these interests owes to the other above ten hundred millions of pounds sterling, which would require twelve millions of slaves to discharge, at eighty pounds sterling each. If the debtor interest amounts to ten millions of souls, and would be worth forty pounds sterling round, sold for slaves, it pays twelve and an half per centum on its capitation value, to the creditor interest, for the exclusive items of debt and bank stock. This profit for their masters, made by those who are called freemen, greatly exceeds what is generally made by those who are called slaves. But as nothing is calculated except two items, by including the payments for useless offices, excessive salaries, and fat sinecures, it is evident that one interest makes out of the other, a far greater profit than if it had sold this other, and placed the money in the most productive state of usance.

Such is the freeman of paper and patronage. Had Diogenes lived until this day, he would have unfledged a cock once more, and exhibited him as an emblem, not of Plato's man, but of a freeborn Englishman. Had Sancho known of a paper stock system, he would not have wished for the government of an island inhabited by negroes. Has Providence used this system to avenge the Africans, upon the Europeans and Americans?

89

Whatever destroys an unity of interest between a government and a nation, infallibly produces oppression and hatred. Human conception is unable to invent a scheme, more capable of afflicting mankind with these evils, than that of paper and patronage. It divides a nation into two groups, creditors and debtors; the first supplying its want of physical strength, by alliances with fleets and armies, and practising the most unblushing corruption. A consciousness of inflicting or suffering injuries, fills each with malignity towards the other. This malignity first begets a multitude of penalties, punishments and executions, and then vengeance.

A legislature, in a nation where the system of paper and patronage prevails, will be governed by that interest, and legislate in its favour. It is impossible to do this, without legislating to the injury of the other interest, that is, the great mass of the nation. Such a legislature will create unnecessary offices, that themselves or their relations may be endowed with them. They will lavish the revenue, to enrich themselves. They will borrow for the nation, that they may lend. They will offer lenders great profits, that they may share in them. As grievances gradually excite national discontent, they will fix the yoke more securely, by making it gradually heavier. And they will finally avow and maintain their corruption, by establishing an irresistible standing army, not to defend the nation, but to defend a system for plundering the nation.

An uniform deception resorted to by a funding system, through legislative bodies, unites with experience in testifying to its uniform corruption of legislatures. It professes that its object is to pay debts. A government must either be the fraudulent instrument of the system, or the system a fraudulent instrument of a government; or it would not utter this falsehood to deceive the people.

This promise is similar to that of protecting property. It promises to diminish, and accumulates; it promises to protect, and invades. All political oppressors deceive, in order to succeed. When did an aristocracy avow its purpose? Sincerity demanded of that of the third age, the following confession: "Our purpose is to settle wealth and power upon a minority. It will be accomplished by national debt, paper corporations, and offices, civil and military. These will condense king, lords and commons, a monied faction, and an armed faction, in one interest. This interest must subsist upon another, or perish. The other interest is national, to govern and pilfer which, is our object; and its accomplishment consists in getting the utmost a nation can pay. Such a state of success can only be maintained by armies, to be paid by the nation, and commanded by this minority; by corrupting talents and courage; by terrifying timidity; by inflicting penalties on the weak and friendless, and by distracting the majority with deceitful professions. That with which our project commences, is invariably a promise to get a nation out of debt; but the invariable effect of it is, to plunge it irretrievably into debt."

The English system of paper and patronage, has made these confessions by the whole current of its actions for a century, and laboured to hide them by its words. That guilt should eternally endeavour to beguile, is natural. Is it also natural, that innocence should eternally be its dupe? Is it the character of virtue, in spite of common sense, to shut her eyes upon truth, and open her ears to falsehood?

. . . The only two modes extant of enslaving nations, are those of armies and the system of paper and patronage. The European nations are subjected by both, so that their chains are doubly riveted. The Americans devoted their effectual precautions to the obsolete modes of title and hierarchy, erected several barriers against the army mode, and utterly disregarded the mode of paper and patronage. The army mode was thought so formidable, that military men are excluded from legislatures, and limited to charters or commissions at will; and the paper mode so harmless, that it is allowed to break the principle of keeping legislative, executive and judicative powers separate and distinct, to infuse itself into all these departments, to unite them in one conspiracy, and to obtain charters or commissions for unrestricted terms, entrenched behind publick faith, and out of the reach, it is said, of national will; which it may assail, wound and destroy, with impunity. This jealousy of armies, and confidence in paper systems, can only be justified, if the following argument in its defence is correct.

"An army of soldiers have a separate interest from the nation, because they draw their subsistence from it, and therefore they will combine for their own interest against the national interest; but an army of stockjobbers have no such separate interest, and will not combine. Soldiers admitted into the legislature, would legislate in favour of soldiers; but stockjobbers will not legislate in favour of stockjobbers. Soldiers may use our arms to take our money; but stockjobbers cannot use our money to take our arms. Soldiers may adhere to a chief in preference to the nation, as an instrument for gratifying their avarice and ambition upon the nation; but stockjobbers have no avarice nor ambition to be gratified, and will not therefore adhere to a chief for that purpose. Soldiers are dangerous, because they assail the liberty of a nation by open force; stockjobbers harmless, because they do it by secret fraud. All are jealous of soldiers, and therefore they will not be watched; few are jealous of stockjobbers, and therefore they will be watched. Many instances have occurred of the oppressions by the army system; one instance only of a perfect capacity in the paper system for oppression can be adduced; and as that has lasted only a single century, it would be precipitate to detect and destroy the aristocracy of paper and patronage, in less time than was requisite to detect and destroy those of superstition and the feudal system."

Alas! is it true, that ages are necessary to understand, whilst a moment will suffice to invent, an imposture? Is it true, that the example of their venerable ancestor, groaning for a century under the oppressions of this modern system of aristocracy, is incapable of awakening the Americans; and that they themselves must also become a beacon for the benefit of a more enlightened era? Caesar profited by the failure of Marius, in the art of enslaving his country; will no nation ever profit by the failure of another in the art of preserving its liberty?

. . . Thus whilst a paper system pretends to make a nation rich and potent, it only makes a minority of that nation rich and potent, at the expense of the majority, which it makes poor and impotent. Wealth makes a nation, a faction or an individual, powerful; and therefore if paper systems extracted the wealth they accumulate from the winds, and not from property and labour, they would still be inimical to the principles of every constitution, founded in the idea of national will; because the subjection of a nation to the will of individuals or factions, is an invariable effect of great accumulation of wealth; but when the accumulation of a minority, impoverishes a majority, a double operation rivets this subjection.

The delusion of all paper projects is at once detected by turning upon them their own doctrine. All boast of doing good to a nation. Suppose a nation was to decline this beneficence, and propose to reward it, by doing good to paper projects, exactly in the same way they propose to benefit the nation; that is, by taking from the owners of stock, their income, and consigning over to them the taxes and the credit attached to the debtor, with the blessing of a paper circulation; the credulity which believes, that these institutions do really impose upon nations debt and taxes, direct and indirect, from motives of public good, would be presently cured by the faltering tongues, the wan faces, and the distressing lamentations, which a proposition for this exchange would produce. These paper projects which pretend to be blessings to nations, would be deprecated as curses by themselves, if the case was thus altered.

It is said that paper systems being open to all, are not monopolies. He who has money, may buy stock. All then is fair, as every man (meaning however only every monied man) may share in the plunder.

Every man may enlist in an army, yet an army may enslave a nation. A monopoly may be open to a great number, yet those who do engage in it, may imbibe the spirit of faction; but it cannot be open to all, because no interest, which must subsist upon a nation, can consist of that nation; as I cannot fatten myself by eating myself. If every citizen should go into an army, it would transform that army into the nation itself, and its pay and subsistence would cease; in like manner the profits of paper, were they generally or universally distributed, would cease; because each citizen would be his own paymaster. Had the objection been as true in practice as it is plausible in theory, these answers suffice to prove, that it would have converted paper aristocracies into paper democracies.

The reason, however, for this apparent common power of becoming a stock-jobber, consists in the constant necessity felt for recruits by every species of aristocracy. The Mamalukes of Egypt have sufficient penetration to discover this. No individual, nor an inconsiderable number of individuals, can enslave a nation. A despot raises soldiers by bounties. This system is also recruited by bounties. The soldier sometimes deserts, or takes part with the nation, after his bounty is spent; but the bounty of paper systems is so contrived, that it is perpetually going on, and annually repeated; so that the aristocracy of an oppressive system, never deserts or takes part with the nation, as the army of an oppressive prince has sometimes done.

Where avarice and ambition beat up for recruits, too many are prone to enlist. Kings, ministers, lords and commons will be obliged to command the army, and share in the plunder, or submit to be cashiered. The makers and managers of aristocracy, gamble with a certainty of winning, for a stake extorted and increased by themselves. If they deposit their penny, they draw a pound, and augment their power. The system of paper and patronage, freights annual gallions for a government and a faction, at a national mine called industry; and bestows on the people such blessings, as those enjoy who dig up the ores of Peru and Mexico. The receivers of the profit drawn from this mine, reap wealth and power; the earners reap armies, wars, taxes, monopolies, faction, poverty and ten hundred millions of debt. This is an English picture. America hopes that her governors and citizens are neither ambitious nor avaricious, and upon this solid hope, is committing the custody of her liberty to the same system. Oh! America, America, thou art the truly begotten of John Bull! It is not proposed to follow this system throughout its deleterious effects upon the morals of private citizens. But if it is capable of corrupting publick officers, or government itself, a remark to exhibit its superior malignity over the aristocracies of the first and second ages, cannot be suppressed. The manners and principles of government, are objects of imitation, and influence national character. The aristocracy of the first age, exhibited sanctity, veneration for the Gods, and moral virtues, to the publick view; not unuseful in their operation, and particularly so in times of ignorance; that of the second, the virtues of generosity, honour and bravery, not unuseful in softening barbarism into civilization, by the magnanimity and even the folly of chivalry; but what virtues for imitation appear in the aristocracy of the present age? Avarice and ambition being its whole soul, what private morals will it infuse, and what national character will it create? A consciousness of fraud, impels it towards perpetration. By ever affecting, and never practising sincerity, it teaches a perpetual fear of treachery, and a perpetual effort to insnare. Its end is distrust and fraud, which convert the earth into a scene of ambuscade, man against man. Its acquisitions inflict misery, without bestowing happiness; because they can only feed a rapacity which can never be satisfied, and a luxury which cannot suppress remorse. In relation to private people, this system may only encourage idleness, teach swindling, ruin individuals, and destroy morals; but allied to a government, it presents a policy of such unrivalled malignity, as only to be expressed by saying, "the government is a speculator upon the liberty and property of the nation."

. . . It is universally agreed that power is attracted by wealth. Ten hundred millions of pounds sterling, being a great sum of wealth, must therefore attract some share of power to the paper interest of England. Whatever it attracts was not bestowed by the English form of government, and is of course an unconstitutional and revolutionary acquisition. This must be admitted, or it must be proved, that great wealth acquired by a particular interest, does not attract power. If the system of paper and patronage, will destroy the principles of limited monarchy without changing its form, either by amalgamating king, lords and commons, or by creating a new power, may it not also destroy the principles of a republican government, and leave its form also standing?

. . . Hereafter, when our constitution is considered, the competency of its security against the aristocracy of paper and patronage, or that of the present age, will be computed; and then it is not meant to shrink from the consideration of this species of aristocracy, in reference to the United States; on the contrary, an effort will be made to place it in several points of view, inadmissible, whilst considering it in relation to England.

At present, supposing that the paper and patronage system of England, is a modern political power of vast force; that it has corrupted or supplanted the old English form of government; that its oppressions overspread the land; that its principles are vicious, and its designs fraudulent; we will proceed to inquire what ought to be done.

93

Superstition and noble orders were defended by the strongest sanctions within the scope of human inventions. Penalties, temporal and eternal; splendour, pomp and honour; united to terrify, to dazzle, to awe and to flatter the human mind; and the real or external virtues of charity and meekness, hospitality and nobleness of mind, induced some to love that, which most hated, and all feared. Yet the intellect of the last age pierced through the delusions, behind which the oppressions of hierarchy and nobility had taken shelter.

We pity the ancients for their dullness in discovering oppressions, so clearly seen by ourselves now that they are exploded. We moderns; we enlightened Americans; we who have abolished hierarchy and title; and we who are submitting to be taxed and enslaved by patronage and paper, without being deluded or terrified by the promise of heaven, the denunciation of hell, the penalties of law, the brilliancy and generosity of nobility, or the pageantry and charity of superstition.

A spell is put upon our understandings by the words "publick faith and national credit," which fascinates us into an opinion, that fraud, corruption and oppression, constitute national credit; and debt and slavery, publick faith. This delusion of the aristocracy of the present age, is not less apparent, than the ancient divinity of kings, and yet it required the labours of Locke and Sidney to detect that ridiculous imposture.

Publick faith is made with great solemnity to mount the rostrum, and to pronounce the following lecture:

"Law enacted for the benefit of a nation, is repealable; but law enacted for the benefit of individuals, though oppressive to a nation, is a charter, and irrepealable. The existing generation is under the tutelage of all past generations, and must rely upon the responsibility of the grave for the preservation of its liberty. Posterity, being bound by the contracts of its ancestry, in every case which diminishes its rights, man is daily growing less free by a doctrine which never increases them. A government intrusted with the administration of publick affairs for the good of a nation, has a right to deed away that nation for the good of itself or its partisans, by law charters for monopolies or sinecures; and posterity is bound by these deeds. But although an existing generation can never reassume the liberty or property held by its ancestor, it may recompense itself by abridging or abolishing the rights of its descendant."

Such is the doctrine which has prevented the eye of investigation from penetrating the recesses of the aristocracy of the present age. It simply offers the consolation of softening injuries to ourselves by adding to the wretchedness of our descendants. By this artifice, (the offspring of interest and cunning,) whenever men cut off their shackles with the sword, they are riveted on again by the pen. A successful war, to avenge a small and temporary injury, is made to gain a great and lasting calamity. Victory over enemies is followed by defeat from friends. And an enemy destroyed abroad, is only the head of an hydra, which produces two at home. This is not exaggeration, if the idea of the aristocracy of paper and patronage is not chimerical. And thence occur these curious questions: Can the United States kill one Englishman or Frenchman, without converting two at least of their own citizens, into members of this aristocracy? Which would be most dangerous and burdensome to the union, one of these foreigners abroad, or two of these aristocrats at home?

94

The best argument in favour of the mortgage of a nation to a faction, is, that it is a purchase; an argument however, which does not extend to the family of law charters in general. A few of a nation, have bought the nation. Caesar by plunder and rapine, amassed the means of buying or corrupting the Roman government; was his title to despotism over the Roman people therefore sound? If Jugurtha had been rich enough to buy Rome, ought the nation to have submitted to the sale, because the bargain was made with the government? If a freeman has no right to enslave his child by selling him, can one generation sell another? And if one generation has no right to sell another, can a government which exercises the double character of seller and buyer, in erecting the aristocracy of the present age, transform the most atrocious iniquity into political or moral rectitude, by writing in its forehead "publick faith?" Then let us acquit every thief, who assumes for his motto the words "honest man."

This kind of faith and honesty, have invented the opinion "that policy and justice require a law, beneficial to individuals at the expense of a nation, to exist for the period prescribed;" to sustain which, it is necessary to reverse the elemental political maxim "that the good of the whole, ought to be preferred to the good of a few." Government is erected for the purpose of carrying this maxim into execution, by passing laws for the benefit of a nation; and shall a violation of the purpose of its institution, by passing laws injurious to a nation, in creating or fostering the aristocracy of paper and patronage, be cleansed of its guiltiness, because individuals have become the accomplices of the government?

A law or a contract, prescribing an immoral action, is void. No sanction can justify murder, perjury or theft. Yet the murder of national liberty, the perjury of a traitorous government, and the theft of national wealth, by the gradual introduction of the aristocracy of the third age, are varnished into a gloss by a cunning dogma, capable even of dazzling men, so excessively honest as to put other men to death for petty thefts, committed to appease hunger or cover nakedness.

The same mouth will solemnly assert, that the principles of equity annul every contract, which defrauds an individual; and that justice or policy requires a catalogue of law charters which defraud a nation, to exist and have their effect.

This is owing to the artful conversion of good words, into knavish dogmas. It is not new, to see errour take refuge under the garb of truth. Superstition has in all ages called itself religion. Thus law charters, with the faithless design of enslaving a nation by the introduction of the aristocracy of the present age, crouch behind the good and honest words "publick faith and national credit," to prevent a nation from destroying that, which is destroying it. And they succeed; because we are as unsuspicious that a false and fraudulent dogma, is hidden under fair language, as that a well dressed gentleman indicates a thief.

To come at truth, we ought not to stop at a verbal investigation. We must consider whether the effects of every law and every measure, by whatever names the law or measure are called, are on the side of virtue or vice.

An irrepealable law charter is a standing temptation to governments to do evil, and an invitation to individuals to become their accessaries; by its help, a predominant party may use temporary power, to enact corporate or individual emoluments for itself, at the national expense. Successive parties will repeat the same iniquity; and even the outs or opposition will be corrupted, to do obeisance at the shrine of the dogma, that they also may reap of the fruit it bestows, when a nation shall fall into their hands; which upon every change of administration, will have its hopes of reform gratified, by new pillages under the sanction of publick faith and national credit.

This modern system of law charters is founded in the same design, with the ancient system of a social compact. Under the sanction of social compact, governments have formerly tyrannised over nations. Under the sanction of law charters, governments now buy a faction, rob nations of enormous wealth, and soar beyond responsibility. The inviolability of a social compact was the old dogma; the inviolability of law charters is the new; for effecting the same end. The last is however an engine in the hands of avarice and ambition, of power far superior to the first. It is able to corrupt and pillage a nation without limit. The first was an opinion unable to purchase partisans; the last offers every thing to its disciples, which can gratify pernicious passions, and meets arguments with bribes. Thus a nation, which won self-government by exploding the doctrine of the antiquated compact dogma, may lose it again in the modern law charter dogma, and thus a nation, which thought it morally wrong to suffer slavery from troops hired by clothes, pay and rations, may be persuaded that it is morally right to suffer slavery from troops hired by dividends, interests upon stock, and protecting duty bounties.

As the English began to emerge from Gothic ignorance, the idea of liberty by compact, and not of natural right, led them to extort charters from their princes; but wofully is the doctrine of deriving a right to liberty from charters, turned upon this gallant nation. By allowing them to bestow, it was discovered that they could destroy. Such as diminish, and not those which enlarge national freedom, have become the sacred charters. The errour of parchment liberty, has made liberty the creature of parchment. A government, good or bad, can easily take away that liberty by charters, which was created by charters. Before the idea of deriving liberty from charter or compact became fashionable, the evils produced by bad governments were temporary; now, slavery, as liberty condescended to be, is created by charters, so as to perpetuate these evils, and to hem in the efforts of patriotism so narrowly, as to destroy the effect of virtue in office.

By admitting that donations of publick property by a government to individuals, should irrevocably transform it into private property, it is obvious that the stock of publick rights will be continually whittled away. Tyranny is only a partial disposition of publick rights, in favour of one or a few. The system of paper and patronage, bottomed upon charters and commissions, enables avarice and ambition to draw more extensively upon the national stock, than any system hitherto invented. It can convert publick property into private, with unexampled rapidity, or transfer wealth and power from the mass of a nation to a few. Its guilt is made its sanction. Neither "private nor publick property" is allowed to be a sanction against the frauds and invasions of paper and patronage, until the fraud or invasion is committed; and then "private property" (good words, as are "publick faith and national credit") is converted into a dogma for the protection of this fraud and invasion. Titles, tythes, feudal services, monasteries, South

Sea and Mississippi projects, funding and banking systems, sinecure offices, and every species of fraud, monopoly and usurpation, call the pillages of private property, private property, and generally contrive to make it so by laws or armies.

But in the eye of justice, property, publick or private, cannot be transferred by fraud. A nation erects a government for the publick benefit, and does not empower it to bring about the aggrandisement of itself, and its faction, to the publick detriment. If this is effected by a transfer of property, publick or private, the transfer is fraudulent, and void; because the nation never empowered the government, by that or any other mode, to injure its liberty or happiness. The principles of moral rectitude, do not forbid a nation to resume power, usurped by a government; nor property, chartered away to individuals, by fraudulent laws; because otherwise they could not resume just rights, since power and law are the vehicles in which these rights are constantly taken away.

. . . Publick faith is the moral principle, called upon to defend monopoly and law charter, under the name of private property. Let us consider what this sanction is in a free government. If the government should solemnly, by law, enter into a contract with a number of individuals, the object of which was to diminish the liberty and wealth of the people, by increasing the power and wealth of the government and these individuals, does publick faith require from the nation a fulfilment of this contract? If the question is answered in the negative, a correct definition of publick faith, must comprise both a faithfulness to the publick good, and also a faithfulness in contracts with individuals; nor can these two duties be made inconsistent with each other by publick faith, without admitting it to be a principle of a double character, sometimes good and sometimes bad. Because, if it compels the performance of one duty, by the breach of another; and if the duty required to be fulfilled, is trivial, compared with that required to be infringed; it would bestow on publick faith a mixed character, and even a prevalence of evil. Publick faith then, considered as a good moral principle, must either include and reconcile, a loyalty both to the publick good and to contracts with individuals; or if the former is not a duty imposed by publick faith, it must be a duty of superior and superseding obligation.

The construction of publick faith by monopoly, avarice and ambition, is precisely the reverse of this. They confine it to a fulfilment of every species of contract made by a government with individuals, especially if entered into for the purpose of gratifying themselves at the expense of a nation; and thus limited, consider it as the most sacred of all duties. And so far are these glossographers from considering publick faith as a good moral principle, that they make it enforce contracts, entered into for every conceivable vicious purpose; from those of betraying nations, armies, cities and forts, down to those of perjury, theft and assassination. Under this construction, whenever the publick good and a contract with an individual come in conflict, publick faith is made to decide, that the contract shall prevail; and thus its definition will come out, "national duty to suffer oppression, and lose its liberty, by laws, charters or contracts, made by a government for that purpose, provided they convey an interest to individuals." So soon as it is thus changed from a good to a vicious principle, its effects change also. From being a pledge of publick good, it becomes the protector of political fraud; it compels a nation to be an accomplice in its own ruin;

97

it takes from it the right of self-preservation; and it becomes the modern sub-
terfuge of the modern aristocracy.

Hitherto, in comparing the duty of a government to a nation, and to a law
charter, the comparison has been exhibited in the most favourable light for the
latter, by forbearing to insist upon any degree of criminality in a faction, which
accepts of a charter from a government, injurious to a nation. It is, however,
questionable, whether the priesthood were innocent, which executed the evil of
hierarchy; or the barons, who sustained that of the feudal aristocracy; or the
solicitors and holders of sinecure offices; or those who pilfer a nation by means
of a law charter. If their accomplices are not guilty, tyrants themselves must be
innocent.

Individuals may be aiders and abettors in projects replete with publick evil,
without discerning their tendency; but the rarity of this case is evinced, by the
tacit compact and union produced by such projects. This compact and union,
disclose a thorough knowledge of the interest on one side, and the injury on
the other, because it is the plain effect of profit; and a fear of losing profit can
only be inspired by a conviction of committing an injury in its acquisition. This
fear makes every individual who is conscious of drawing wealth from a nation
unjustly, the friend and encomiast of the strongest power he can find; because
power is the only protector of injustice. And if he cannot find a power strong
enough to protect injustice, he will exert himself to erect one. When such a
power exists, the more unfaithful it is to the publick good, the more its publick
faith will be celebrated by those who receive the benefit of its unfaithfulness.
Lewis the fourteenth, an ignorant, fanatical and tyrannical prince, was celebrated
even by philosophers, because he robbed the French nation, to give them
pensions.

Individuals, who do not derive their acquisitions from projects replete with
publick evil, are never formed into a tacit compact or union, because, being
unconscious of drawing gain from a nation unjustly, they have nothing to fear.
Being unconscious of injustice, they are not naturally the friends and encomiasts
of a power, strong enough to protect injustice. And deriving no benefit from the
unfaithfulness of a government to the publick good, they will not celebrate a
government for it. In order to see the force of this comparison, it is only necessary to conceive a society consisting of two classes, one made up of agricultur-
ists, professions, trades and commerce, all unconnected with banking, funding
and patronage; the other, of a funding system, bank charters, pensions and
patronage. Which class would be the disciple and parasite of despotism? If this
is discernible, the consequence of erecting this modern species of aristocracy is
also discernible.

The exact similarity in nature and principle, between laws or charters establishing funding systems, banks, or sinecure profit of any kind; and laws or
charters establishing privileged orders or endowed hierarchies; appears in their
common union with, and devotion to, a power capable of protecting injustice.

98   It is still objected "that unless laws, beneficial to individuals, though injurious
to a nation, are supported, confidence in government will be destroyed, and national credit, lost." The doctrine amounts to this: "that it is good policy in a
nation, to make a few individuals its masters or owners, to excite an inclination

in these few individuals to lend it money, for a handsome premium and high interest." And this policy is literally pursued, by establishing a certain number of paper systems and charters, for drawing money from the nation directly or indirectly, in order to enable a few to lend a part of this money to the nation.

To this item of the value of a confidence "that laws and charters, injurious to a nation, but beneficial to individuals, will be maintained," must be added a corruption of manners, arising from the traffick between a government and a faction, for the objects of gratifying the ambition of one dealer, and the avarice of the other; and the customary violent and wretched parties, between the commencement of this confidence and its catastrophe.

On the other hand, a confidence that laws and charters injurious to a nation, will be repealed, whenever their pernicious tendency is discovered, will prevent the destructive evils generated by a contrary opinion; will enable honest governments to correct the frauds of knavish; and will check or even cure the malevolence of factions. And one effect of inestimable value flowing from this latter confidence, would be the detection and overthrow of an insidious sanction, under cover of which the modern aristocracy of paper and patronage, is fast fettering modern nations.

The analysis of aristocracy, by the first, the second, and the third ages, has been used for the purpose of a distinct arrangement of the arguments adduced to explain the superstitious, feudal, and fiscal modes of enslaving nations, by placing the powers in the hands of a minority; an effect, however produced, denominated aristocracy, throughout this essay. But it is not intended to insinuate, that the causes of aristocracy have generally acted singly; on the contrary, they more frequently unite.

It was necessary thoroughly to understand the most prominent causes of aristocracy, before we proceeded to a closer examination of our civil policy, and Mr. Adams's principles; in order to keep in mind that we have never seen a venerated and wealthy hierarchy, an army stronger than the nation, an endowed, titled and privileged order of men, or an incorporated, enriched or united faction, without having at the same time seen the aristocracy of the first, the second, or the third age. By recollecting this testimony, derived from universal experience, an inference, equivalent to mathematical certainty, "that such ends will eternally flow from such means," will unavoidably present itself.

Few would deny these premises or the inference, if it was proposed to revive oracles or feudal services. These causes of aristocracy are distinctly seen, because they do not exist. They have no counsel in court. They are, therefore, better understood than when they flourished. But both the premises and the inference are denied, when they implicate the aristocracy of paper and patronage. This cause of aristocracy is not seen, because it does not exist; and the more oppressive it shall become, the greater will be the difficulty of discovering its existence. The two first are exposed naked to our view; and the third, disguised in the garb of republicanism, and uttering patriotick words, joins the mob in kicking them about, by way of diverting the publick attention from itself. An opinion that aristocracy can only exist in the form of a hereditary order, or a hierarchy, is equivalent to an opinion, that the science of geometry can only be illustrated by a square or a triangle. (*1814*)

99

part **2**

THE RISE OF THE
CONFEDERATE SOUTH

1815-1865

The Rise of the Confederate South

Changes in economic and political thought

During the War of 1812, much capital which previously had been invested in farming and commerce was directed toward the development of industrial enterprise, particularly in the North. Thus the conflict between agrarianism and commercial capitalism—which had had its beginnings in the time of Jefferson and Hamilton—was given new impetus. There arose, too, a new manner of looking at Southern problems. Before 1812 the Physiocratic agrarianism of Jefferson and Taylor had been the dominant system of thought in the South. Although this agrarianism was never abandoned, by 1820 drastic changes had occurred in Southern political and social thinking—changes which were in large part the result of an economic revolution. The mechanical improvements in the methods of spinning and weaving that gave impetus to the textile industry in England and the invention of the cotton gin in America had resulted in corresponding changes in Southern agriculture. A tremendous demand for American raw cotton quickly developed, and in the decade between 1815 and 1825 an increasing amount of Southern land was devoted to the raising of cotton, creating a new economy in the South—an economy which became increasingly dependent for its existence upon the continuance and expansion of slavery.

As it became apparent to Southerners that the institution of slavery must be maintained and permitted to spread, political and economic leadership in the South passed from Virginia to South Carolina—particularly Charleston—and other areas of the Black Belt. The new group of leaders no longer felt the need to apologize for slavery; instead they attempted to defend it—indeed, to praise it. Since there is no moral wrong in slavery, they argued, the institution should flourish wherever it is profitable, not only in the South, but also in Texas, the Midwestern territories, and California.

A new political philosophy was created in the South to meet the changing needs of the new economy. From the older theory of states' rights was evolved the doctrine of Nullification, by which the Southern states asserted their right to veto any federal measure which threatened the continuance of slavery or the prosperity and independence of the South. The enunciation of this doctrine created a tremendous stir, but as V. L. Parrington points out, "it was little more than a warning gesture" on the part of the South.

> The deeper purpose that lay behind the gesture of Nullification was the purpose of erecting in the slave states a civilization founded on a landed aristocracy that should serve as a sufficient counterweight to the mercantile and industrial civilization of the North; and in the event that the institution of slavery were not assured of peaceful extension through the new West, to secede and establish a southern Confederacy wherein a generous civilization might develop, modeled after the Greek democracy. Such at least was the dream of the noblest minds of the South.[1]

103

[1] *Vernon L. Parrington*, Main Currents in American Thought (*Harcourt, Brace and Company*, 1930), II, 68.

During the 1830's and 1840's, the increasing necessity to defend itself against attacks from without made the South a politically unified section, as it had not been during the colonial period. Nat Turner's slave insurrection in Virginia (1831) and the demands of the militant abolitionists contributed to a growing fear of the Negro, and Southerners began an even more passionate defense of slavery, which seemed the surest means of safeguarding the supremacy and security of the whites. Journalists, professors, and politicians attempted to vindicate the "peculiar institution." One such effort was "The Hireling and the Slave" (1854) by William Grayson, a long poem composed of over 800 heroic couplets. It emphasized the thesis that chattel slavery is far more humane than the wage slavery existing in the North, an idea expressed also by George Fitzhugh in his *Cannibals All! or Slaves Without Masters* (1857). Grayson's poem is divided into two parts. The first gives a vividly realistic picture of the Northern wage slave; the second contrasts the sordidness of this portrait with a romanticized picture of the idyllic existence of the Southern bondslave. Grayson concluded that the slave in the South gets a larger return from his labor than the wage slave in the North. Slavery, to Grayson, was not an evil, and therefore needed no defense; it was actually a blessing.

Slavery has become in the minds of many people the fundamental cause of the Civil War, but it should not be supposed that the Southern cause was confined to this alone. The Southern position was bound up with a political, economic, and social philosophy as well as with the specific issue of slavery. Conscious of its agrarian heritage, the South favored free trade and states' rights as opposed to the encroachments of an all-powerful federal government. Many historians now hold the opinion, expressed by Edd W. Parks in his *Segments of Southern Thought* (1938), that Southerners, forced to defend slavery, developed a theory of government upon it. But the basic principles upon which their theory was based and for which, in the final analysis, the South fought were those of agrarianism and local sovereignty.

The statesmen

The shift from Jeffersonianism to the Greek idea of democracy was chiefly the work of two men, John C. Calhoun and Alexander H. Stephens. Calhoun, perhaps the foremost economic philosopher of the time, was convinced that slavery was a permanent institution. He justified the South's position by referring to the idea of democracy which prevailed among the ancient Greeks. "Liberty," he argued, "is a reward to be earned, not a blessing to be gratuitously lavished on all alike." The Greek ideal of democracy was a society in which *inequality*, rather than *equality*, was recognized as the fundamental condition of nature. The most competent and worthy individuals in the society, acting in the best interest of all, voluntarily assumed the care and direction of the incompetent. Thus Calhoun denied the validity of Jefferson's natural-rights theory. He also contradicted the idea that government should be a contract between the governed and the governor, asserting that men are essentially selfish and that the government must, therefore, be given sufficient power to control individual lusts and passions in order to protect the other members of society. Calhoun advocated the idea of a "concurrent majority," which would enable one section to protect its interests even though another possessed a numerical majority. In his *Disquisition on Government* (1851), Calhoun explained "concurrent majority" in this manner:

> . . . there are two different modes in which the sense of the community may be taken: one, simply, by the right of suffrage, unaided; the other by the right through a proper organism. Each collects the sense of the majority. But one regards numbers only and considers the whole community one unit, having but one common interest throughout; and collects the sense of the greater number of the whole, as that of the community. The other, on the contrary, regards interests as well as numbers;—considering the community as made up of different and conflicting interests as far as the action of the government is concerned; and takes the sense of each, through its majority or appropriate organ, and the united sense of all, as the sense of the entire community. The former of these I call the numerical, or absolute majority; and the latter, the concurrent, or constitutional majority.

A practical application of this hypothesis, in his view, was that the South should be able to veto high protective tariffs and unfavorable slave laws. The checking power of the individual states, he believed, should supplement the system of checks and balances established within the framework of the federal government. It was on this basis that he supported Nullification.

Alexander H. Stephens—United States Senator, Governor of Georgia, and Vice-President of the Confederacy—was, like Calhoun, an active political figure. Our interest here, however, is not in Stephens' political career, but in the attitudes expressed in his monumental study, *Constitutional View of the Late War Between the States* (1868–1870). This work contains the ablest defense ever made for secession. Unlike Calhoun, Stephens was not a political philosopher concerned with principle and theory; instead he was a constitutional historian who endeavored to plot the course that the fundamental laws of America had taken in their development. Always a serious student of the United States Constitution and of American history generally, he was well prepared to deal with the problems presented by his approach to the Civil War. His particular contribution to the thinking of the time was in attacking the highly controversial issue of secession from an entirely new angle. Working at a time when the cause was already lost and when the fortunes of the South were at ebb tide, he attempted to prove that state sovereignty was a cherished belief of the makers of the Constitution and that the Southern states were justified by the Constitution in their attempt to protect their rights. He established, to the satisfaction of many, both the constitutionality of secession and its corollary, Northern responsibility for the war.

Southern thought during the Civil War era was influenced to a considerable extent by a group of more radical pro-slavery thinkers, who came to be known as the "Fire-Eaters." Led by such men as Edmund Ruffin, Robert B. Rhett, and William L. Yancey, these extremists were the first to start a movement for Southern secession. Ruffin stands out as one of the leading (and most radical) anti-

105

abolitionists and secessionists of the South. So extreme were his views that he opposed Jefferson because he thought him too democratic and "an abolitionist, covertly and cunningly." Like Alexander Hamilton, Ruffin despised universal suffrage and mob tyranny. No sense of humor tempered his severity. His *Anticipations of the Future,* written in 1860 to advocate secession, takes the form of a prophecy about the years 1864–1869. Ruffin shows the South deprived by the North of all its power and privileges, and then describes an imaginary war that breaks out between the two sections. The conflict ends, of course, with the military and economic triumph of the South.

Like Ruffin, Albert Taylor Bledsoe was one of the most avid defenders of the Southern cause. In the numerous articles which he contributed to periodicals in the decade following the Civil War, he repeatedly insisted that slavery was neither constitutionally illegal nor morally wrong. Though the South had been defeated on the battle field, he said, loyal Southerners should continue to "cherish the principle of freedom for which [they] fought" and take care to preserve their sectional heritage from the Northern invaders.

The course of Southern letters

The South produced many talented writers during this period of sectional controversy and bitterness, yet it took little part in the American literary renaissance that had its center in New England. Put increasingly upon the defensive, the South tended more and more to withdraw from intellectual contact with the North. With the drift toward a separate nationality in the South came a movement for a distinctly Southern literature which would present the Southern point of view and justify the Southern way of life.

This movement, however, was attended by many difficulties and its results fell short of what they might have been under different circumstances. For one thing, the great publishing centers of the country were in the North, where what might be termed a "literary monopoly" had been created. If Southern authors wrote for a Southern audience—or for a Northern audience from the Southern viewpoint— they had difficulty in getting their work published or, once published, in finding a market for it. Then too, much of the South was still in its early stages of settlement. Alabama, Mississippi, Louisiana, and Arkansas were just beginning their statehood, and Texas was not then so much a state as a desperate adventure. There was little time to contemplate new scenes, except on the part of writers who had been reared in more settled communities. And when he could afford to relax at all from the tasks of pioneering, the potential Southern author tended to regard himself as an heir to the Renaissance tradition; that is, he was a gentleman first, and only incidentally an author, as Sir Philip Sidney and Sir Walter Raleigh had been in Elizabethan days. It must be confessed, too, that the serious Southern writer often failed to cultivate literature as a profession because of the general indifference his works were almost certain to meet within his own region. Timrod defined the situation in 1859:

106

We think that at no time, and in no country, has the position of an author been beset with such peculiar difficulties as the Southern writer is compelled to struggle with from the beginning to the end of his career. In no country in which literature has ever flourished has an author obtained so limited an audience. In no country, and at no period that we can recall, has an author been constrained with the indifference of the public amid which he lived, to publish with a people who were prejudiced against him. It would scarcely be too extravagant to entitle the Southern author the Pariah of modern literature.[2]

Meeting indifference in their own region and forced to publish in the North, Southern writers tended to go their separate ways. The only Southern literary center of any importance was Charleston, South Carolina. The members of the "Charleston School," in addition to doing an impressive amount of writing, met (usually at Russell's Bookstore) and discussed the literary questions of their day. They did so, apparently, in an informal fashion and with a courtesy that precluded any sharp criticism of one another's essays, novels, or poems—criticism which all of them would ultimately have found profitable.

Hugh Swinton Legaré was certainly a leader in this school during its early phase, although his importance has been overshadowed by a more prolific and more able contemporary, William Gilmore Simms. Legaré was the most frequent contributor to the *Southern Review* (organized in Charleston in 1828 and published over a period of four years), and for a time served as its editor. In 1857 another notable Charleston publication, *Russell's Magazine*, was founded. Its best-known contributors were Henry Timrod, Paul Hamilton Hayne, Simms, and William John Grayson (author of "The Hireling and the Slave"). The magazine existed for three years, collapsing on the eve of the Civil War. With the coming of war, the virtual extinction of the Charleston School was inevitable.

The narrative as an art form in and for itself was a relatively late development in Southern literature. Southern writers did not contribute greatly to the gift books and annuals which enjoyed a vogue in the United States from the 1820's to the Civil War. When the vogue for this kind of representation was in its incipient state, much of the South was still in the process of being molded into a civilized society. It was almost inevitable, therefore, that the early figures in Southern narrative literature should express themselves in terms of caricature (as William Byrd had done in the colonial era) or that they should become recounters of tall tales (as did Longstreet, Baldwin, and the other frontier humorists).

Except for Poe, Simms, and the Old Southwest humorists, the greatest writer of fiction in the ante-bellum South was John Pendleton Kennedy, who, avoiding Poe's set patterns, wrote in the more leisurely tradition of Irving. Poe was too much in earnest for him. One might think of Kennedy primarily as a man of affairs in the Elizabethan sense—politician, educator, and sometime lawyer—to whom literature was simply a pleasant avocation, an incidental accomplishment which, like music, any gentleman should cultivate. He produced mostly sketches, of which those in *Swallow Barn* afford a pleasant example.

William Gilmore Simms—novelist, short-story writer, critic, journalist, and editor—was the most versatile man of letters in the South before the Civil War. Much of the narrative and humorous poetry which flowed from his facile pen is

107

[2] The Essays of Henry Timrod, *edited by Edd Winfield Parks* (*University of Georgia Press, 1942*), *p. 83.*

in the present day neglected. His reputation rests upon his novels and short stories, though a few of his lyrics about the Carolina woodlands are still widely read. Attempting to refute the idea, current at the time, that American life and manners were not fit subjects for fiction, Simms produced a large number of historical narratives, which many critics believe are unsurpassed in American literature. Perhaps his best-known novels are *The Yemassee* (1835), the story of an Indian uprising in South Carolina in 1715, and *The Forayers* (1855), one of a series of novels the American Revolution. In some of his short stories Simms achieves a place of eminence beside Thomas Nelson Page and Joel Chandler Harris for his authentic and artistic use of Southern dialect.

Like the fiction, the poetry produced in the South before 1860, with a few notable exceptions, was not of highest merit, but it nevertheless rewards our attention. Studying the early Southern lyrists, one finds Richard Henry Wilde registering his praise of the "Mocking Bird" and of Lord Byron—that "Tacitus of Song." Edward Coote Pinkney breaks the glass, like his heart, to an image "chambered in his brain." These poets reflected very little of their Southern background. Pinkney, in particular, turned his back on American literary tradition and followed instead the pattern set by the Cavalier and metaphysical poets of seventeenth-century England. Poe and Thomas Holley Chivers, however, controvert any argument that the poetry of the section was wholly derivative. Chivers, like Poe, believed that poetry should exist for its own sake, never as an instrument of instruction. The themes of the two poets are so similar that each has been accused of plagiarizing from the other, but the differences between the poetry of the two make these charges seem without real justification.

Two later Southern poets of importance were Henry Timrod and Paul Hamilton Hayne, leading figures in the Charleston School. When the Civil War began, both men were still very young and really just beginning their literary careers— Timrod was but thirty-two and Hayne thirty-one. Of the two, Timrod seems to have been more grimly aware of the eventualities of the conflict, and a tragic sense of the inevitable reinforces the solemn metrics of his best performances. Both young poets were poverty-stricken and sick. As Hayne wrote to John Esten Cooke in 1866: "To be brief, I am a beggar." Eight years later, he could declare to the comfortably situated Longfellow: "Great Heavens! What a clinging *curse* is poverty! It killed my friend *Timrod* before his time, and many a dark hour and sleepless night of bitterness and bewildered fear, has it brought upon me." At one time Hayne decided to demand some payment for his poems, if nothing more than the pens and paper for his work. But he was never paid in any way that could decently keep him alive. He was as surely a victim of the war as were Stonewall Jackson and the thousands of his forgotten contemporaries who lie in unmarked graves.

Edgar Allan Poe

108

The ever-present and somewhat false idea of Edgar Allan Poe as an artist apart from time and place—a sort of spirit voluntarily living in a mortal limbo—has made him far less a Southerner than he wanted to be. Poe added to the impression that he was cosmopolitan by spending his last years in the middle states, the publishing center of American letters to which he was compelled to turn after his separation from the *Southern Literary Messenger*. In spite of the impression that Poe was non-regional, however, he was—or wanted to be—a conservative Southerner, and consequently he opposed the New England group, at least partly because they were New Englanders. The inhabitants of Boston were "Frogpondians" to Poe.

The works of Poe are more non-Southern than he was, but some of his stories, most notably "The Gold Bug," have settings near Charleston or in Virginia. Furthermore, Poe appreciated the use of Southern materials in the writings of others. Though Longstreet's *Georgia Scenes* was totally unlike Poe's own works or the type of literature defined in his critical writings, Poe greatly enjoyed the humor of the Georgian. In his review of the *Scenes* the usually melancholy Poe wrote, "Seldom—perhaps never in our lives—have we laughed as immoderately over any book as over the one now before us." William Gilmore Simms and John Pendleton Kennedy were also highly praised in Poe's reviews. At one time Poe thought of Simms as America's greatest novelist, but later he came to believe the works of Kennedy surpassed even those of Simms. Moreover, Poe went beyond support of artistic works from the South; he praised books written in defense of slavery, and he himself used conventional Southern arguments for the institution.

It is possible to trace some of Poe's critical tenets to his Southern heritage, though in such a venture the grounds must necessarily be somewhat tenuous. His opposition to didacticism ("a didactic poem, in our opinion, being precisely no poem at all") was characteristic of the nineteenth-century Cavalier poets in general. Richard Henry Wilde, Edward Coote Pinkney, Thomas Holley Chivers, Simms, and Poe himself looked with disfavor on the moral tags in poems by New England authors. Poe was like his fellow Southerners, too, in writing short poems. Wilde was the only early Southern poet of any prominence who wrote a book-length poem.

In any final estimate, however, Poe cannot be treated as fundamentally a Southerner. Perhaps more than any man of his age he was concerned with the art of writing for its own sake. No other man has maintained more consistently that literature exists primarily and perhaps solely to entertain. This approach may be found in his criticism, his poetry, and his short stories.

His central theories about literature deserve brief recapitulation in their own right, for they are the work of a pioneer. The short story began to fall into a general pattern of fiction only after Poe had described the way in which he thought it should be written. Poe worked in the light—or darkness—of a clearly defined formula, one that was to become definitive, if not consciously copied, for more than half a century. In his review of Hawthorne's *Twice-Told Tales* he explained his theory in the following manner:

> A skillful literary artist has constructed a tale. If wise, he has not fashioned his thoughts to accommodate his incidents: but having conceived, with deliberate care, a certain unique or single *effect* to be wrought out, he then invents such incidents—he then combines such events as may best aid him in establishing this pre-conceived effect. If

109

his very initial sentence tend not to the outbringing of this effect, then he has failed in his first step. In the whole composition there should be no word written, of which the tendency, direct or indirect, is not to the one pre-established design. And by such means, with such care and skill, a picture is at length painted which leaves in the mind of him who contemplates it with a kindred art, a sense of the fullest satisfaction. The idea of the tale has been presented unblemished because undisturbed.

Cleanth Brooks and Robert Penn Warren (in their *Understanding Fiction*) assert that Poe failed, specifically in "The Fall of the House of Usher," because of his creation of horror for horror's sake. Opposing this evalution, however, are Poe's own critical theories and the demonstrations of man's love for unadulterated horror in folk tales, Gothic romances, and the Frankenstein myths. Once the reader accepts Poe's premises, it must be admitted that he does achieve the single effect. In the first sentence of "The Cask of Amontillado," for example, the tone of the entire story is established: "The thousand injuries of Fortunato I had borne as best I could; but when he ventured upon insult, I vowed revenge."

The detective story, Poe said in his review of Dickens' *Barnaby Rudge,* is based upon curiosity. For Poe, *Barnaby Rudge* was a failure as a detective story since he discovered the secret on page seven of the novel and published the solution to the novel while it was still in the process of publication in serial form. Success or failure of a detective story is to be determined by the author's ability to conceal the identity of the criminal, to tell only the truth when speaking in his own person, and to let the characters be as confused as they would be by a mystery in real life. The author is guilty of no violation of art or truth so long as he does not in his own person assert a falsehood.

Poe was inclined to fit other forms of expression into similarly neat categories. The ideal length of a poem was one hundred lines, or at any rate, it should be of a length possible for the reader, in a state of intense excitement, to finish at one sitting. In poetry even more than in prose Poe conceived of a perfect unity, so perfect as to be attainable only in a short poem. More broadly, a poem to him

. . . is opposed to a work of science by having for its immediate object, pleasure, not truth; to romance by having for its object an *indefinite* instead of a definite pleasure . . . to which end music is an *essential*, since the comprehension of sweet sound is our most indefinite conception. Music, when combined with a pleasurable idea, is poetry; music without the idea is simply music; the idea without the music is prose from its very definitiveness.

He was, then, primarily interested in the sound, or in T. S. Eliot's word, the "incantation," of poetry; and when he could not reconcile sound and sense, sound often triumphed. When he blended rhythm and tone coloring with meaning, as he did in a few of his best poems, he produced memorable poetry.

To summarize, Poe was a major American innovator. He was the first professional author in the country deliberately to set about freeing poetry from what he called the "heresy of the didactic." Poe thus anticipated the art-for-art's-

110

sake theory of literature by several decades. His significance has always been held in higher estimation by French critics and authors than by those of America and England. T. S. Eliot points out (in an article in the *Hudson Review*, Autumn 1949) that Poe influenced three literary generations in France, represented by Baudelaire, Mallarmé, and Paul Valéry. Some reactions to Poe's critical tenet and practice that poetry is the "rhythmical creation of beauty" have been far less sympathetic than the opinions of the French poets or of the reading public. Aldous Huxley, for example, criticized the "ready-made" music and the "too musical meter."

Edgar Allan Poe formulated the most succinct if arbitrary set of theories that nineteenth-century American literature can claim. He wrote with uncompromising conviction about the nature of poetry and about the fault of the novel and the epic. He defined the short story in terms that until recently have proved classic, and he virtually invented the technique of modern detective fiction.

Humorists of the Old Southwest

In all the history of American letters, no literature has been more a product of its time and place than the writings of the Southern humorists from around 1830 until the Civil War. Georgia, Alabama, Mississippi, Tennessee, Louisiana, and Arkansas—the states close to the lower Mississippi or the Gulf of Mexico—produced the men who created this peculiar brand of humor. Three of these states were admitted to the Union between 1812 and 1821, and Arkansas became a state in 1836. All of them were at least partly new territory in the first half of the century. Of the four states in the South that were among the original thirteen, only Georgia was reckless enough to participate wholeheartedly in the swash-buckling laughter of frontier life.

It is a fallacy to speak of this humor as a product of the virgin frontier; rather, it is representative of that stage when the frontier was being molded into a civilized society. Perhaps, too, there were in some of the people described elements of the backwash of the frontier and the beginning of the isolation which made possible the later writings of the early local colorists. Some of the humorists, like Davy Crockett and T. B. Thorpe, found their tall tales in exploits like those of Daniel Boone; but Ransy Sniffle and Sut Lovingood, created by Augustus Baldwin Longstreet and George Washington Harris, were forerunners of the degenerates portrayed a century later by Erskine Caldwell and William Faulkner.

Vigorous and witty men by their very natures delight in the tall tale. The humorists of the Old Southwest were no frustrated Shelleys, depressed by the bleakness of their literary environment; they enjoyed the belly laughs they found around them and improved upon them. The authors of these wild yarns were a curious group, heterogeneous in every way except as men who liked to laugh. Among the first was Davy Crockett, professional frontiersman, politician, and soldier of fortune, the subject of so many almanacs, biographies, and autobiographies that he has become almost inextricably tangled with legend. Early, too, in the writing of the genre was Augustus Baldwin Longstreet, just plain Gus in his youth. When his *Georgia Scenes* were appearing in small Georgia papers,

111

from 1832 to 1835, he was a newspaper editor and an enterprising young lawyer. Later, when he became judge and college president, he regretted and disowned his earlier literary indiscretions. Perhaps the most completely professional of the humorists was William Tappan Thompson, early colleague of Longstreet, author of *Major Jones' Courtship,* and editor of the *Savannah News* (in which capacity he was employer of Joel Chandler Harris). Another outstanding Southern humorist was Joseph Glover Baldwin, author of *The Flush Times in Alabama and Mississippi.* Baldwin was a prosperous young lawyer in Alabama and Mississippi and later Chief Justice of the State Supreme Court of California. Johnson J. Hooper, the creator of Simon Suggs, was also a lawyer, and during the period of the Confederacy was Secretary of the Confederate Senate. George Washington Harris, literary father of that "natural born dern fool," Sut Lovingood, was more versatile, though perhaps less dignified, than his contemporaries. His list of professions runs to nearly a dozen. These men, most of them prominent citizens, were the outstanding observers of the humorous life of their times.

For every one of the major figures mentioned above there were ten minor spinners of yarns publishing tall tales in the numberless small-town newspapers, and possibly for every publishing liar there were several talking and whittling and playing checkers on the village bench. It was a literary movement springing from the folk, but reaching every facet of society. The vein was inexhaustible, and the material can never be gathered completely, though in recent years it has been well anthologized. Besides twenty-five selections from the works of the men named above, Franklin J. Meine in *Tall Tales of the Southwest* included twenty-three other tales by less well-known men. Hamilton C. Jones, C. F. M. Noland, Oliver H. Prince, William P. Brannan, John S. Robb, Sol Smith, George W. Bagby (Mozis Addums), Charles H. Smith (Bill Arp), Richard M. Johnston (Philemon Perch)—these men and hundreds more of their kind were filling newspapers, periodicals, and books with tall tales about the South.

Times were flush in the South in many ways, and in any village there could be found manners to serve as worthy subjects for humorous social satire. In a sense, the literature of the Old Southwest was a comedy of manners, though the life here described was far different from the polished societies that gave rise to that term. The Southern recreations were repugnant to those of delicate tastes. The writings and the life had spilled over the brim of polished convention. There were "quiltin's" and "courtin's," "coon" and bear and "possum" hunts, eye-gougings and gander pullings, camp meetings and militia drills. Always there was a country store in which to "loafer" around.

The activities at these entertainments were too boisterous for young ladies of cultivated or squeamish sensibilities. There had to be a willing suspension of morality, which for the moment resulted in unbridled pleasure and humor. "One holesum quiltin," Sut Lovingood says, "am wuth three old pray'r-meetins on the poperlashum pint. . . ." Even in modern fiction there is seldom found more suggestive and bawdy writing than in Harris' "Rare Ripe Garden Seed," a story that, like many others of the time, belongs to the medieval or oral genre of the fabliaux. One of Harris' ruffians "hates a circuit rider, a nigger, and a shot gun —loves a woman, old sledge, and sin in eny shape." Nor was Harris alone in ribaldry; it was typical of the time and the writing. In "Georgia Theatrics"

112

Longstreet wrote: "If any man can name a trick or sin which had not been committed at the time of which I am speaking, in the very focus of the county's illumination (Lincolnton), he must himself be the most inventive of the tricky and the very Judas of sinners."

Comic sin was not the only element in this humor offensive to those of less hearty constitutions. Cruelty, trickery, and knavery were ever-recurrent themes. The leading figures of Old Southwest humor were picaresque heroes, close relatives to the swindlers, adventurers, and rogues described in Elizabethan prose. It is an essential requirement of humor that the victim be either laughed at or forgotten. One must not waste sympathy on the Reverend Bela Bugg when Simon Suggs walks off with the collection plate from a camp meeting; he must laugh and share in Simon's triumph. This was the spirit of frontier humor. Sut Lovingood's "conshuns felt clar es a mountin spring" after he started a practical joke that ended in the death of two of the revelers at a quilting party, and after the joke was over the kissing went on with hardly an interruption. There is great merriment in Longstreet's "The Horse-Swap" when a sharp trader discovers that he has swapped a blind and deaf horse for a horse with a hideous sore on his back. And Joseph Glover Baldwin objected only to the *methods* used in Ovid Bolus' swindling of $1,600—"A child could have done it." Swindling, he complained, had been lowered "to a beggarly process of mean deception. . . . It was like catching a cow with a lariat, or setting a steel trap for a pet pig."

It is small wonder that the humor of the Old Southwest did not appeal to the parents of the Puritan damsels who had to read surreptitiously the popular sentimental novels still frowned upon as unwholesome fare. The humorists had adapted a literature to their type of life, rather than writing to civilize their neighbors and to make them subscribe to the romanticisms and sentimentalities of other literatures in the early nineteenth century. They were some of America's first realists, the first writers to describe Southern life with the veneer of civilization stripped off and with all pretenses to respectability neglected. Their stories are primarily narratives of situation, based on the comic crudities of the most ludicrous and desperate incidents of the society around them. They were no more solicitous for prudery than any folk; and if they were not always retelling folk fabliaux, they retained the masculine and folkish qualities. They professed no desire to appeal to the tastes of those who were readers of Lamb or Tennyson, or of Holmes and his New England contemporaries.

The humor of the Old Southwest was not unprecedented, but it was unusual in that it consistently found its exaggerations and characters at home rather than in the strange lands and times of Munchausen, Eulenspiegel, and Sinbad the Sailor. For the first time there was a truly American character, shown in the guffaws of men of action rather than in the worship of legendary heroisms.

With the passing of the half-century mark, the last of the frontiersmen began to move on from the South. Longstreet became judge and college president, Baldwin went to the West, tastes changed, and frontier humor to a degree lost favor. It became tinged with the romantic—and sometimes sterile—quaintness and sentimentality of the local colorists. The inhibitions of the American Victorians replaced the realism and gusto of a time that was uninhibited. The Civil War gave the old humorists their last fling at political satire.

The last humorist of the Old Southwest was Mark Twain, but a great deal of his work, like that of Bill Nye and Artemus Ward, sprang from the popular lecture platform of the nineteenth century. Twain in his later years was, furthermore, more Westerner and New Englander than Southerner, so that his work does not properly belong to this volume. His first literary publication, "The Dandy Frightening a Squatter," printed in B. P. Shillaber's *Carpet-Bag* in May 1852, belongs to the lore of the South, and the rudiments of "The Celebrated Jumping Frog" were reputedly imported from Tennessee by John Quarles, an uncle of Twain who owned the slave characterized as "Nigger Jim" in *Huckleberry Finn*. But although the South molded Twain and gave him his literary background, it did not retain him.

The importance of the Southern humorists should not be underestimated. Longstreet and his followers set a pattern for the writers of prose fiction in the South. They were among the first Southern authors to break with the Old World tradition, to look at the life around them, and to record it as they saw it.

Spirituals

It has been argued that the spirituals are not original creations, but that they are imitations of other folksongs and religious hymns or that their original inspiration came from the snatches of French opera which the whites brought back from their frequent visits to New Orleans. James Weldon Johnson and certain other authorities, however, not only believe that the spirituals were original with the Negroes,[3] but regard them as America's only folk music and the finest distinctive artistic contribution America has made to the world.

Scholars have also debated the question whether the spirituals were the spontaneous expressions of a group or were composed primarily by individuals. This question of composition will probably remain a vexing one, in relation to both the spirituals and folk literature in general. The most satisfactory explanation, seemingly, is that the spirituals were originally of individual inspiration, but were gradually modified by many group responses until they assumed the form in which we know them today.

The spirituals are religious songs which, in most cases, translate Biblical episodes into the idiom of the Negro race; they are, above all, attempts by the Negro to express his feelings and experiences in terms of religious sentiment. Most of their effect is obtained through their harmonies as rendered by a large number of voices. The fact that they must be sung in this way to be fully appreciated is the characteristic which distinguishes them from other forms of folk music. Despite the triteness of the words and the monotonous repetition of lines, the spirituals contain fine poetic qualities: suggestiveness, graphic description, and, in many cases, dramatic presentation of incident.

For years the artistic beauty of the spirituals was overlooked, but in recent years, the researches of scholars and poets and the excellent presentations by

114

[3] *Scholars like George Pullen Jackson* (White Spirituals in the Southern Uplands, *Chapel Hill, 1933*) *should be consulted before an opinion is reached on this question.*

many choral groups have aroused considerable interest. Performances by such groups as the Jubilee Singers of Fisk University, who have given numerous concerts both here and abroad, have done much to create an appreciative audience for this distinctive type of American folk literature.

Civil War ballads and poems

In popular literature, the Civil War produced a greater quantity of contemporary verse, good and bad, than any other major incident in our national and sectional lives. The Civil War was the heyday of the soldier-singer in America, and its songs have enjoyed a continued popularity that has been rivaled only by "Yankee Doodle" and "Hinky-Dinky Parlez-Vous." Besides the stimulus provided by the war itself, there was inevitably in the South a feeling that secession had established cultural independence. As one manifestation of this, publishing houses of Confederate music sprang up in over a dozen Southern cities—such as New Orleans, Augusta, Richmond, and Macon.

During the early part of the war, lofty and frequently sentimental verses of high polish were composed and printed in abundance. The popularity of these sophisticated songs remained unabated, but as the conflict progressed and Southern soldiers saw the true reality of war, they began to compose and adapt songs more appropriate to their own feelings. The improvised and realistic chants, comic songs, and satirical verses which came out of the Confederate ranks have the merit of being grounded on actuality. Many of them were too crude to be hummed in the patriotic gatherings on the home front.

The songs of the Civil War were inspired by innumerable occasions and they came from wide sources. There were ballads composed especially for victories and defeats, and for the deaths of heroes and prominent generals. On the whole, the Confederate paid little attention to the origins of his music. He sang old and new songs from all sources. During and after the war, the South sang "My Darling Nellie Gray" without bothering to change the abolitionist lyrics; but, perhaps because of the concrete images evoked, uncompromising hatred was aroused whenever Southerners heard "Marching Through Georgia." "Dixie," the most enduring song of the era, was composed by Daniel Decatur Emmett, an actor in a Northern minstrel show. Though his words have been the ones to remain in use, there have been many attempts to make popular more partisan versions. Abram Joseph Ryan's war experiences (the smallpox epidemic at New Orleans; the death of his brother, a Confederate soldier; and the catastrophes of the latter years of the conflict) inspired some of the most famous verses of the war. Two of Ryan's poems, "The Conquered Banner" and "The Sword of Robert Lee," were so popular after Appomattox that Ryan came to be recognized as "the poet of the Confederacy."

Seldom has any literature been more expressive of a harassed people than the popular literature of the Civil War era. Song books were carried about by the armies, and some military units even organized glee clubs. No other recreation was so well able to relieve the deep emotions of the soldier or to provide escape from those harrowing times.

115

ANDREW JACKSON

1767–1845

Born March 15, 1767, in the backwoods of South Carolina, Andrew Jackson was from the beginning a product of the frontier that in later years chose him for its champion. Jackson learned to face hardship in his early childhood, for his father died a few days before he was born, and he lost his two brothers in the American Revolution. Jackson himself as a mere child fought in the Battle of Hanging Rock, following which he was taken prisoner and contracted small-pox. When he was only fourteen, his mother died, leaving him without close relatives.

Jackson tried teaching school for a time but soon went to North Carolina to read law. Moving to Tennessee to practice, he eventually settled in Nashville. His experience as a lawyer and then as a solicitor was followed by gradual advancement in both civilian and military professions. He became delegate to the Tennessee Constitutional Convention, first congressman from Tennessee, major general of the Tennessee militia, senator, and circuit judge.

It was Jackson's success as a general that first led to his tremendous popularity in the West. After his victory over the Creek Indians at Horseshoe Bend in 1814, he was made a major general in the United States Army, and he commanded the American forces in the victory over the British at New Orleans. Later, called upon to settle the Seminole war, he invaded Spanish Florida without authorization, captured a town, and hanged two British subjects. Although diplomatic and political troubles ensued, Jackson became a still greater hero in the eyes of the people.

Having been elected as a senator for the second time in 1823, Jackson ran for the presidency the following year but was defeated despite a popular majority. In 1828, however, he was elected by an overwhelming majority and the Jacksonian era began. Few stronger personalities ever sat in the White House. During his administration Jackson consistently opposed internal improvements, over-ruled Vice-President Calhoun in the famous Nullification controversy, and vetoed a bill for continuing the Bank of the United States.

116

Jackson was no philosopher, theorist, or man of letters. One legend is that he once said in exasperation, "Damn the man that knows how to spell a word in just one way." His political theories were motivated by justice and expediency rather than by system. Yet Jacksonianism was a practical manifestation of the economics of Jefferson and John Taylor. His attack on the Bank was an out-growth of agrarianism and hatred of an economic aristocracy; his general atti-tude toward banking was a stand for stability as opposed to speculation. Jackson was the champion of the producers against the handlers, buyers, and speculators. He represented the emerging frontier West.

Letters

To Brigadier-General John Coffee

Washington, March 22, 1829

My D'r Genl [1]: I have Just received your letter of the 1st instant, enclosing me one from Doctor Lindsley to you, convaying the unpleasant information of my little ward Hutchings having been suspended from college, and having gone to the Hermitage where he now is. This is information, of the most distressing kind to me, but upon the best reflection I can give the subject I have determined to send him to Mr. Otte at Franklin who, if any man can, will controle and pre-serve him, and carefully attend to his morales. I have just written a short letter to Mr. Wm. Donelson, requesting him to have Hutchings immediately, on the receipt of my letter, sent to Mr. Otte and advise you of it, and I beseech you to address Mr. Otte, requesting his particular attention to him, and to his morales, enquiring of him the amount of tuition, and board, and transmit Mr. Otte the amount—and dealing to Hutchings but little funds.

I wish him taught penmanship, arithmetic, and Book keeping, algebra, and some other branches of mathematics, moral philosophy, belles letters, and such other branches that may be profitable to him as a farmer, and private gentle-man. I have lost all hope of making him a classic scholar, and do not wish him to touch the languages, except to review those Books of latin and Greek that he has read, but wish him to understand his grammar well. These are only useful to him as a farmer, or a politician, and should he ever form a taste for reading and improvement, being well versed in the branches named, he has it in his power to become useful to himself and country. If Mr. Ote cannot control him, then Sir I know not what to do with him, as I have determined never, whilst I hold my present office, to place one of my young relatives, either in the military school, or the navy. I hope and trust Mr. Ote will be able to controle him. I shall leave him to your direction under the observations made. I shall write him under cover to William.

I shall refer you to the papers and other channels of information for news of this place, since the 4th I have been crowded with thousand of applicants for office, and if I had a tit for every applicant to suck the Treasury pap, all would go away well satisfied, but as their are not office for more than one out of five hundred who applies, many must go away dissatisfied. all I can do is, to select

117

Jackson's letters from Correspondence of Andrew Jackson, *edited by John Spencer Bassett. Carnegie Institution of Washington, 1926–1935.*
[1] *Coffee was an Indian fighter and, at one time, a business partner of Jackson. He was al-ways one of Jackson's close friends.*

honest and competant men. this I will do, as far as I can be informed, and reform and retrenchment will be made, as far as sound principle will warrant it.

Much pains was taken to prevent me from taking Mr. Eaton into the Cabinet, his wife was assailed secretly, in the most shameful manner, and every plan that Clay and his minions could invent to deter me, in hopes I would be intimidated and drop Eaton, which would have been destruction to him. Under those circumstances I could not, nay I would not, abandon an old and tried friend. I sustained him, and I have no doubt he will become the most popular of the heads of the Departments and the War office will be well directed.

My labours have been great, my health is not good, but if my constitution will bear me up for one year I have no fear but I will make such an expose to the nation that will be satisfactory to the people. The late administration has left everything in such a state as to embarrass me but you know when I am excited all my energies come forth. . . .

To Captain John Donelson

Washington, June 7, 1829

My D'r Sir,[1] Your letter of the 29th ult is just received. What satisfaction to me to be informed that you and Mr Hume had visited the Hermitage and Tomb of my dear departed wife. how distressing it has been to me to have been drawn by public duty from that interesting spot, where my thoughts delight to dwell, so soon after this heavy bereavement to mingle with all the bustle, labour, and care of public life, when my age, my enfeebled health and constitution forwarned me, that my time cannot be long here upon earth, and admonished me that it was time I should place my earthly house in order and prepare for another, and I hope a better world. My dear wife had your future state, much at heart, she often spoke to me on this interesting subject in the dead hours of the night, and has shed many tears on the occasion. your reflection upon the sincere interest your dear sister took in your future happiness are such as sound reason dictates. yes, my friend it is time that you should withdraw from the turmoils of this world, and prepare for another and better. you have well provided for your household, you have educated your children and have furnished them with an outfit into life sufficient, with good management and oeconomy, to build an independence upon. you have sufficient around you to make you and your old lady independent and comfortable during life, and when gone hence, perhaps as much as will be prudently managed, and if it should be imprudently managed, then it will be a curse, rather than a blessing to your children. I therefore join in the sentiments of my dear departed and beloved wife, in admonishing you to withdraw from the busy cares of this world, and put your house in order for the next, by laying hold "of the one thing needful." go read the Scriptures, the joyful promises it contains, will be a balsome to all your troubles, and create for you a kind of heaven here on earth, a consolation to your troubled mind that is not to be found in the hurry and bustle of this world.

Could I but withdraw from the scenes that surround me, to the private walks

118

---

[1] *Donelson was the brother of Jackson's wife.*

of the Hermitage, how soon would I be found in the solitary shades of my garden, at the tomb of my wife, there to spend my days in silent sorrow and in
peace from the toils and strife of this world, with which I have been long since
surfeited. but this is denied me. I cannot retire with propriety. when my friends
draged me before the public, contrary to my wishes, and that of my dear wife,
I foresaw all this evil but I was obliged to bend to the wishes of my friends, as
it was believed, it was necessary to perpetuate the blessings of liberty to our
country, and to put down misrule. My political creed, compelled me to yield to
the call, and I consoled myself with the idea of having the council and society
of my dear wife, and one term would soon run round, when we could retire to
the Hermitage and spend our days in the service of our god. But, O, how fluctuating are all earthly things. at the time I least expected it and could least spare
her, she was snatched from me, and I left here a solitary monument of grief,
without the least hope of any happiness here below, surrounded with all the turmoil of public life and no time for recreation, or for friendship. from this busy
scene I would to god I could retire, and live in solitude. . . .

P. s. Mr Steel has written me but one letter, say to him to write me how much
crop he has in, how many coalts, lambs and calves, and how my last years coalts
are, and of the health of my negroes. I learn old Ned and Jack are both dead.
Jack was a fine boy, but if he was well attended to, I lament not. he has gone
the way of all the earth.

To Andrew Jackson, Jr.

Washington, July 4, 1829
Dear Andrew,[1] I have Just returned from my visit to Fortress Monroe, the
Navy yard at gossport etc and recd a letter from Colo. Charles J. Love of the
27th ult. advising me of the death of my negroman Jim, and the manner of it.
I pray you my son to examine minutely into this matter, and if the death was
produced by the cruelty of Mr. Steel, have him forthwith discharged. But as you
are young, advise with Col Love upon this matter. My negroes shall be treated
humanely. When I employed Mr Steel, I charged him upon this subject, and
had expressed in our agreement that he was to treat them with great humanity,
feed and cloath them well, and work them in moderation. if he has deviated
from this rule, he must be discharged.

Since I left home I have lost three of my family. Old Ned, I expected to die,
but I am fearful the death of Jack, and Jim, has been produced by exposure and
bad treatment. Your Uncle John Donelson writes, that *Steel has ruled with a
rod of iron.* This is so inconsistent to what I expected, that I cannot bear the
inhumanity that he has exercised towards my poor negroes, contrary to his
promise and has impaired my confidence in him. Unless he changes his conduct,
dismiss him, and employ another.

I write in haste that it may go by to nights mail and meet you at Nashville.
Consult with Colo. Love and Doctor Hogg about Mr Steel and whether he ought
to be discharged. I am your affectionate father.

119

[1] *Jackson's adopted son.*

To Martin Van Buren

Private

Washington, January 13, 1833

My D'r sir, . . . I have recd. several letters from you which remain unanswered, you know I am a bad correspondent at any time, lately I have been indisposed by cold, and surrounded with the nullifiers of the south, and the Indians in the south, and west; that has occupied all my time, not leaving me a moment for private friendship, or political discussion with a friend.

I beg of you not to be disturbed by any thing you hear from the alarmists at this place. many nullifiers are here under disguise, working hard to save calhoun and would disgrace their country and the Executive to do it. Be assured that I have and will act with all the forbearence [I possess] to do my duty, and extend that protection to our good citizens and the officers of our Government in the south who are charged with the execution of the laws; but it would destroy all confidence in our government, both at home and abroad, was I to sit with my arms folded and permit our good citizens in So Carolina who are standing forth in aid of the laws to be imprisoned, fined, and perhaps hung, under the ordinance of South Carolina and the laws to carry it into effect, all which, are palbable violations of the constitution and subversive of every right of our citizens. Was this to be permitted the Government would loose the confidence of its citizens and it would induce disunion every where.

No my friend, the crisis must be now met with firmness, our citizens protected, and the modern doctrine of nullification and secession put down forever —for we have yet to learn, whether some of the eastern states may not secede or nullify, if the tariff is reduced. I have to look at both ends of the union to preserve it. I have only time to add, that So Carolina, has by her replevin, and other laws, closed our courts, and authorised the Governor to raise 12,000 men to keep them closed, giving all power to the sheriffs to use this army as the *posse comitatus*. I must appeal to congress to cloath our officers and marshall with the same power to aid them in executing the laws, and apprehending those who may commit treasonable acts. This call upon congress must be made as long before the 1rst. of Feby next as will give congress time to act before that day, or I would be chargeable with neglect of my duty, and as congress are in session, and as I have said in my message, which was before the So. C. ordinance reached me, if other powers were wanted I would appeal to congress. was I therefore to act without the aid of congress, or without communicating to it, I would be branded with the epithet, *tyrant*. from these remarks you will at once see the propriety of my course, and be prepared to see the communication I will make to congress on the 17th instant, which will leave congress ten days to act upon it before the 1rst of February after it is printed. The parties in So. C. are arming on both sides, and drilling in the night, and I expect soon to hear that a civil war of extermination has commenced. I will meet all things with deliberate firmness and forbearance, but wo, to those nullifiers who shed the first blood. The moment I am prepared with proof I will direct prosecutions for treason to be instituted against the leaders, and if they are surrounded with 12,000 bayo-

120

nets our marshall shall be aided by 24,000 and arrest them in the midst thereof
—nothing must be permitted to weaken our government at home or abroad.

Virginia except a few nullifiers and politicians, is true to the core; I could
march from that state 40,000 men in forty days—nay, they are ready in N. C.
in Tennessee, in all the western states, and from good old democratic Pennsylvania I have a tender of upwards of 50,000, and from the borders of So. C. in
No. C. I have a tender of one entire Reggt. The union *shall be* preserved.

In haste yr friend

P.S. I will be happy to hear from you often, and see you as early as a just sense
of delicacy will permit. My whole houshold salute thee affectionately. A J

Opinion on the Bank[1]

The great point to be steadily kept in view is the establishment of the general
Govt. and the sovereign powers granted to it by the people and the states. 1st,
all sovereign power was in the people and the states. 2d, where sovereignity is
vested it cannot be divested but by express grant, therefore as the general Government is based upon the confederation of sovereign states, you must look into
the constitution for the grants of sovereignity made by the people inhabiting
those sovereign states to find what portion of sovereign power has been granted
to the general government for no sovereign power not expressly granted can be
exercised, by implication.

Is the sovereign power to grant corporations expressly given to the general
Government to be found in the constitution, I answer no. Therefore as all powers granted are general and national, not local, or for local objects, and all
powers not delegated etc. are retained to the states and to the people, a corporation or monoply cannot be granted by congress beyond the limits of the ten
miles square, and it is fair to advert to the journals of the convention to prove
that the power to grant corporations in various ways was attempted to be introduced in the constitution and was rejected in every form presented by the
convention who formed it. It is therefore worse than idle to contend that congress can have this sovereign power by implication when it was rejected in the
convention, and when sovereign power can only be convayed from one power
to another by express grant—If it be true that necessity gives the power to create
Banks and corporations. It is true necessity creates its own law, but it must be
a positive necessity not a fained one. The powers of the Government are general
and national, not local. it must follow then that if necessity creates the power,
that the Bank must be exclusively national having no concern with corporations. it must be an appendage of the Treasury, a Bank merely of deposit and
exchange.

Within the 10 miles square, Congress has the sole sovereign power, can therein

121

From *Correspondence of Andrew Jackson, edited by John Spencer Bassett. Carnegie Institution of Washington, 1926–1935.*
[1] *Written by Jackson as a memorandum, this selection was a reply to a speech made by
Erastus Root in the House of Representatives.*

grant a corporation, and exercise all the Legislative powers as a state can, but neither state or general Government can create or grant a monoply. It is inconsistant with any of the powers granted that our Gov. should form a corporation and become a member of it. The framers were too well aware of the corrupting influence of a great monied monopoly upon government to legalise such a corrupting monster by any grant either express or implied in the constitution. Bank corporations says Mr A. is brokers on a large scale, and could it be really urged that the framers of the constitution intended that our Govert. should become a government of brokers? if so, then the profits of this national brokers shop must anure to the benefit of the whole and not to a few privileged monied capitalist, to the utter rejection of the many.

But it is said (by mr Root in debate) that their is as much power vested in congress to establish a Bank by the constitution as to establish a custom House or a post office—could either of these be established by creating a corporation. Admit his doctrine and it clearly shews the unconsti[tu]tionality of the present bank charter, for if it is for the safe deposit of the Revenue it must appurtain like the custom Houses to the Treasury Dept, all its profits if any accrue to the nation as the Taxes collected do, its only power to deposit and the power of exchange by which it can transmit the funds of the Govt. to any place wanted, and as part of the Dept. its whole transaction exposed to the congress and the nation annually.

A Bank might be established in the District and by the consent of the states and in compact with it it might be branched into the states, but the Genl Government cannot consistant with any power granted, become a member of any corporation congress may create. *(1832)*

JOHN C. CALHOUN

1782–1850

Born and reared in South Carolina, John C. Calhoun spent most of his adult life in Washington, representing his state in the House of Representatives and the Senate, and serving as Secretary of War, Secretary of State, and Vice-President.

After receiving his early training at the famous academy of his brother-in-law, Dr. Moses Waddell, Calhoun entered Yale College, graduating in 1804. He studied law in the Tapping Reeve School at Litchfield, Connecticut, and in the offices of a Charleston attorney, before being admitted to the bar in 1807. Shortly after opening his office at Abbeville, South Carolina, however, he decided that politics would be more congenial to his temperament and announced his candi-

122

dacy for the state legislature. Elected by a sizable majority, he served without particular distinction for two terms.

In 1811 Calhoun married his distant cousin, Floride Calhoun, from whom the struggling young politician obtained money enough to free himself from the immediate necessity of earning a living; he could now concentrate all his efforts toward a successful political career. Calhoun used the modest fortune wisely, and by 1825 he had acquired enough property to establish the plantation-homestead "Fort Hill," which still stands on the campus of Clemson College.

Upon his election to Congress in 1810, Calhoun immediately became identified with the "War Hawks," who were anxious for the United States to enter war against England. Once war had been declared, he prosecuted the American cause so diligently that A. J. Dallas, Secretary of the Treasury under Madison, called him "the young Hercules who carried the war on his shoulders." After the Treaty of Ghent, he turned his attention to domestic issues, supporting measures which favored a program of internal improvements, the establishment of a national bank, and the encouragement of manufacturing by means of a protective tariff.

Before the end of his third term in Congress, Calhoun was appointed Secretary of War by President Monroe. Primarily because of the exemplary manner in which he discharged the duties of this office, he was elected Vice-President and served two terms. During his vice-presidency, Calhoun altered his views on many important matters. The turning point in his career, perhaps, came in 1828 when he helped to write the "South Carolina Exposition," the document which has become famous as expounding the doctrine of Nullification. For political reasons, however, his part in this project was not revealed until 1831, when he formally announced his acceptance of its principles in a letter to Governor Hamilton. Overruled by President Jackson on the Nullification issue, he resigned the vice-presidency in 1832 to become a member of the Senate, where he served until his death (except for the period 1844–1845, when he was Secretary of State under Tyler).

With his entrance into the Senate, Calhoun's career entered its final phase. He fought for states' rights and for the expansion of slavery into the West, as well as for its retention in the South. Before he died his name became synonymous with the Southern cause. He expended his declining energies in an attempt to promote Southern prosperity and to frame a new system of government based upon his theory of the concurrent majority. These ideas are expressed in his *Discourses on the Constitution and Government of the United States* and *A Disquisition on Government*, both published posthumously. Summarizing Calhoun's achievements, V. L. Parrington says: "He was the one outstanding political thinker in a period singularly barren and uncertain. . . . Long before his death he expanded a political philosophy into a school of thought."

Speech on the Slavery Question   123

I have, Senators, believed from the first that the agitation of the subject of slavery would, if not prevented by some timely and effective measure, end in disunion. Entertaining this opinion, I have, on all proper occasions, endeavored to call the attention of both the two great parties which divide the country to adopt some measure to prevent so great a disaster, but without success. The agitation has been permitted to proceed, with almost no attempt to resist it, until it has reached a point when it can no longer be disguised or denied that the Union is in danger. You have thus had forced upon you the greatest and the gravest question that can ever come under your consideration—How can the Union be preserved?

To give a satisfactory answer to this mighty question, it is indispensable to have an accurate and thorough knowledge of the nature and the character of the cause by which the Union is endangered. Without such knowledge it is impossible to pronounce, with any certainty, by what measure it can be saved; just as it would be impossible for a physician to pronounce, in the case of some dangerous disease, with any certainty, by what remedy the patient could be saved, without similar knowledge of the nature and character of the cause which produced it. The first question, then, presented for consideration, in the investigation I propose to make, in order to obtain such knowledge, is—What is it that has endangered the Union?

To this question there can be but one answer,—that the immediate cause is the almost universal discontent which pervades all the States composing the Southern section of the Union. This widely-extended discontent is not of recent origin. It commenced with the agitation of the slavery question, and has been increasing ever since. The next question, going one step further back, is—What has caused this widely diffused and almost universal discontent?

It is a great mistake to suppose, as is by some, that it originated with demagogues, who excited the discontent with the intention of aiding their personal advancement, or with the disappointed ambition of certain politicians, who resorted to it as the means of retrieving their fortunes. On the contrary, all the great political influences of the section were arrayed against excitement, and exerted to the utmost to keep the people quiet. The great mass of the people of the South were divided, as in the other section, into Whigs and Democrats. The leaders and the presses of both parties in the South were very solicitous to prevent excitement and to preserve quiet; because it was seen that the effects of the former would necessarily tend to weaken, if not destroy, the political ties which united them with their respective parties in the other section. Those who know the strength of party ties will readily appreciate the immense force which this cause exerted against agitation, and in favor of preserving quiet. But, great as it was, it was not sufficient to prevent the widespread discontent which now pervades the section. No; some cause, far deeper and more powerful than the one supposed, must exist, to account for discontent so wide and deep. The question then recurs—What is the cause of this discontent? It will be found in the belief of the people of the Southern States, as prevalent as the discontent itself, that they cannot remain, as things now are, consistently with honor and safety, in the Union. The next question to be considered, is—What has caused this belief?

One of the causes is, undoubtedly, to be traced to the long-continued agitation of the slave question on the part of the North, and the many aggressions which they have made on the rights of the South during the time. I will not enumerate them at present, as it will be done hereafter in its proper place.

124

There is another lying back of it—with which this is intimately connected—that may be regarded as the great and primary cause. This is to be found in the fact that the equilibrium between the two sections, in the Government as it stood when the constitution was ratified and the Government put in action, has been destroyed. At that time there was nearly a perfect equilibrium between the two, which afforded ample means to each to protect itself against the aggression of the other; but, as it now stands, one section has the exclusive power of controlling the Government, which leaves the other without any adequate means of protecting itself against its encroachment and oppression. To place this subject distinctly before you, I have, Senators, prepared a brief statistical statement, showing the relative weight of the two sections in the Government under the first census of 1790 and the last census of 1840.

According to the former, the population of the United States, including Vermont, Kentucky, and Tennessee, which then were in their incipient condition of becoming States, but were not actually admitted, amounted to 3,929,827. Of this number the Northern States had 1,997,899, and the Southern 1,952,072, making a difference of only 45,827 in favor of the former States. The number of States, including Vermont, Kentucky, and Tennessee, were sixteen; of which eight, including Vermont, belonged to the Northern section, and eight, including Kentucky and Tennessee, to the Southern,—making an equal division of the States between the two sections under the first census. There was a small preponderance in the House of Representatives, and in the electoral college, in favor of the Northern, owing to the fact that, according to the provisions of the constitution, in estimating federal numbers five slaves count but three; but it was too small to affect sensibly the perfect equilibrium which, with that exception, existed at the time. Such was the equality of the two sections when the States composing them agreed to enter into a Federal Union. Since then the equilibrium between them has been greatly disturbed.

According to the last census the aggregate population of the United States amounted to 17,063,357, of which the Northern section contained 9,728,920, and the Southern 7,334,437, making a difference, in round numbers, of 2,400,-000. The number of States had increased from sixteen to twenty-six, making an addition of ten States. In the mean time the position of Delaware had become doubtful as to which section she properly belonged. Considering her as neutral, the Northern States will have thirteen and the Southern States twelve, making a difference in the Senate of two Senators in favor of the former. According to the apportionment under the census of 1840, there were two hundred and twenty-three members of the House of Representatives, of which the Northern States had one hundred and thirty-five, and the Southern States (considering Delaware as neutral) eighty-seven, making a difference in favor of the former in the House of Representatives of forty-eight. The difference in the Senate of two members, added to this, gives to the North in the electoral college, a majority of fifty. Since the census of 1840, four States have been added to the Union—Iowa, Wisconsin, Florida, and Texas. They leave the difference in the Senate as it stood when the census was taken; but add two to the side of the North in the House, making the present majority in the House in its favor fifty, and in the electoral college fifty-two.

The result of the whole is to give the Northern section a predominance in

every department of the Government, and thereby concentrate in it the two elements which constitute the Federal Government—majority of States, and a majority of their population, estimated in federal numbers. Whatever section con-
centrates the two in itself possesses the control of the entire Government.

But we are just at the close of the sixth decade, and the commencement of the
seventh. The census is to be taken this year, which must add greatly to the decided preponderance of the North in the House of Representatives and in the
electoral college. The prospect is, also, that a great increase will be added to its
present preponderance in the Senate, during the period of the decade, by the
addition of new States. Two territories, Oregon and Minnesota, are already in
progress, and strenuous efforts are making to bring in three additional States
from the territory recently conquered from Mexico; which, if successful, will
add three other States in a short time to the Northern section, making five
States; and increasing the present number of its States from fifteen to twenty,
and of its Senators from thirty to forty. On the contrary, there is not a single
territory in progress in the Southern section, and no certainty that any additional State will be added to it during the decade. The prospect then is, that the
two sections in the Senate, should the efforts now made to exclude the South
from the newly acquired territories succeed, will stand, before the end of the
decade, twenty Northern States to fourteen Southern (considering Delaware as
neutral), and forty Northern Senators to twenty-eight Southern. This great increase of Senators, added to the great increase of members of the House of
Representatives and the electoral college on the part of the North, which must
take place under the next decade, will effectually and irretrievably destroy the
equilibrium which existed when the Government commenced.

Had this destruction been the operation of time, without the interference of
Government, the South would have had no reason to complain; but such was
not the fact. It was caused by the legislation of this Government, which was appointed, as the common agent of all, and charged with the protection of the interests and security of all. The legislation by which it has been effected, may be
classed under three heads. The first, is that series of acts by which the South
has been excluded from the common territory belonging to all the States as
members of the Federal Union—which have had the effect of extending vastly
the portion allotted to the Northern section, and restricting within narrow limits
the portion left the South. The next consists in adopting a system of revenue
and disbursements, by which an undue proportion of the burden of taxation has
been imposed upon the South, and an undue proportion of its proceeds appropriated to the North; and the last is a system of political measures, by which
the original character of the Government has been radically changed. I propose
to bestow upon each of these, in the order they stand, a few remarks, with the
view of showing that it is owing to the action of this Government, that the equilibrium between the two sections has been destroyed, and the whole powers of
the system centered in a sectional majority.

126 The first of the series of acts by which the South was deprived of its due share
of the territories, originated with the confederacy which preceded the existence
of this Government. It is to be found in the provision of the ordinance of 1787.
Its effect was to exclude the South entirely from that vast and fertile region which

lies between the Ohio and the Mississippi rivers, now embracing five States and one territory. The next of the series is the Missouri compromise, which excluded the South from that large portion of Louisiana which lies north of 36° 30', excepting what is included in the State of Missouri. The last of the series excluded the South from the whole of the Oregon Territory. All these, in the slang of the day, were what are called slave territories, and not free soil; that is, territories belonging to slaveholding powers and open to the emigration of masters with their slaves. By these several acts, the South was excluded from 1,238,-025 square miles—an extent of country considerably exceeding the entire valley of the Mississippi. To the South was left the portion of the Territory of Louisiana lying south of 36° 30', and the portion north of it included in the State of Missouri, with the portion lying south of 36° 30', including the States of Louisiana and Arkansas, and the territory lying west of the latter, and south of 36° 30', called the Indian country. These, with the Territory of Florida, now the State, make, in the whole, 283,503 square miles. To this must be added the territory acquired with Texas. If the whole should be added to the Southern section, it would make an increase of 325,520, which would make the whole left to the South, 609,023. But a large part of Texas is still in contest between the two sections, which leaves it uncertain what will be the real extent of the portion of territory that may be left to the South.

I have not included the territory recently acquired by the treaty with Mexico. The North is making the most strenuous efforts to appropriate the whole to herself, by excluding the South from every foot of it. If she should succeed, it will add to that from which the South has already been excluded 526,078 square miles, and would increase the whole which the North has appropriated to herself, to 1,764,023, not including the portion that she may succeed in excluding us from in Texas. To sum up the whole, the United States, since they declared their independence, have acquired 2,373,046 square miles of territory, from which the North will have excluded the South, if she should succeed in monopolizing the newly acquired territories, about three-fourths of the whole, leaving to the South but about one-fourth.

Such is the first and great cause that has destroyed the equilibrium between the two sections in the Government.

The next is the system of revenue and disbursements which has been adopted by the Government. It is well known that the Government has derived its revenue mainly from duties on imports. I shall not undertake to show that such duties must necessarily fall mainly on the exporting States, and that the South, as the great exporting portion of the Union, has in reality paid vastly more than her due proportion of the revenue; because I deem it unnecessary, as the subject has on so many occasions been fully discussed. Nor shall I, for the same reason, undertake to show that a far greater portion of the revenue has been disbursed at the North, than its due share; and that the joint effect of these causes has been, to transfer a vast amount from South to North, which, under an equal system of revenue and disbursements, would not have been lost to her. If to this be added, that many of the duties were imposed, not for revenue, but for protection—that is, intended to put money, not in the treasury, but directly into the pocket of the manufacturers—some conception may be formed of the immense

127

amount which, in the long course of sixty years, has been transferred from South to North. There are no data by which it can be estimated with any certainty; but it is safe to say, that it amounts to hundreds of millions of dollars. Under the most moderate estimate, it would be sufficient to add greatly to the wealth of the North, and thus greatly increase her population by attracting emigration from all quarters to that section.

This, combined with the great primary cause, amply explains why the North has acquired a preponderance in every department of the Government by its disproportionate increase of population and States. The former, as has been shown, has increased, in fifty years, 2,400,000 over that of the South. This increase of population, during so long a period, is satisfactorily accounted for, by the number of emigrants, and the increase of their descendants, which have been attracted to the Northern section from Europe and the South, in consequence of the advantages derived from the causes assigned. If they had not existed—if the South had retained all the capital which has been extracted from her by the fiscal action of the Government; and, if it had not been excluded by the ordinance of 1787 and the Missouri compromise, from the region lying between the Ohio and the Mississippi rivers, and between the Mississippi and the Rocky Mountains north of 36° 30′—it scarcely admits of a doubt, that it would have divided the imigration with the North, and by retaining her own people, would have at least equalled the North in population under the census of 1840, and probably under that about to be taken. She would also, if she had retained her equal rights in those territories, have maintained an equality in the number of States with the North, and have preserved the equilibrium between the two sections that existed at the commencement of the Government. The loss, then, of the equilibrium is to be attributed to the action of this Government.

But while these measures were destroying the equilibrium between the two sections, the action of the Government was leading to a radical change in its character, by concentrating all the power of the system in itself. The occasion will not permit me to trace the measures by which this great change has been consummated. If it did, it would not be difficult to show that the process commenced at an early period of the Government; and that it proceeded, almost without interruption, step by step, until it absorbed virtually its entire powers; but without going through the whole process to establish the fact, it may be done satisfactorily by a very short statement.

That the Government claims, and practically maintains the right to decide in the last resort, as to the extent of its powers, will scarcely be denied by any one conversant with the political history of the country. That it also claims the right to resort to force to maintain whatever power it claims, against all opposition, is equally certain. Indeed it is apparent, from what we daily hear, that this has become the prevailing and fixed opinion of a great majority of the community. Now, I ask, what limitation can possibly be placed upon the powers of a government claiming and exercising such rights? And, if none can be, how can the separate governments of the States maintain and protect the powers reserved to them by the Constitution—or the people of the several States maintain those which are reserved to them, and among others, the sovereign powers by which they ordained and established, not only their separate State Constitutions and

128

Governments, but also the Constitution and Government of the United States? But, if they have no constitutional means of maintaining them against the right claimed by this Government, it necessarily follows, that they hold them at its pleasure and discretion, and that all the powers of the system are in reality concentrated in it. It also follows, that the character of the Government has been changed in consequence, from a federal republic, as it originally came from the hands of its framers, into a great national consolidated democracy. It has indeed, at present, all the characteristics of the latter, and not one of the former, although it still retains its outward form.

The result of the whole of these causes combined is—that the North has acquired a decided ascendency over every department of this Government, and through it a control over all the powers of the system. A single section governed by the will of the numerical majority, has now, in fact, the control of the Government and the entire powers of the system. What was once a constitutional federal republic, is now converted, in reality, into one as absolute as that of the Autocrat of Russia, and as despotic in its tendency as any absolute government that ever existed.

As, then, the North has the absolute control over the Government, it is manifest, that on all questions between it and the South, where there is a diversity of interests, the interest of the latter will be sacrificed to the former, however oppressive the effects may be; as the South possesses no means by which it can resist, through the action of the Government. But if there was no question of vital importance to the South, in reference to which there was a diversity of views between the two sections, this state of things might be endured, without the hazard of destruction to the South. But such is not the fact. There is a question of vital importance to the Southern section, in reference to which the views and feelings of the two sections are as opposite and hostile as they can possibly be.

I refer to the relation between the two races in the Southern section, which constitutes a vital portion of her social organization. Every portion of the North entertains views and feelings more or less hostile to it. Those most opposed and hostile regard it as a sin, and consider themselves under the most sacred obligation to use every effort to destroy it. Indeed, to the extent that they conceive that they have power, they regard themselves as implicated in the sin, and responsible for not suppressing it by the use of all and every means. Those less opposed and hostile, regard it as a crime—an offence against humanity, as they call it; and although not so fanatical, feel themselves bound to use all efforts to effect the same object; while those who are least opposed and hostile, regard it as a blot and a stain on the character of what they call the Nation, and feel themselves accordingly bound to give it no countenance or support. On the contrary, the Southern section regards the relation as one which cannot be destroyed without subjecting the two races to the greatest calamity, and the section to poverty, desolation, and wretchedness; and accordingly they feel bound, by every consideration of interest and safety, to defend it.

This hostile feeling on the part of the North towards the social organization of the South long lay dormant, but it only required some cause to act on those who felt most intensely that they were responsible for its continuance, to call it

129

into action. The increasing power of this Government, and of the control of the Northern section over all its departments, furnished the cause. It was this which made an impression on the minds of many, that there was little or no restraint to prevent the Government from doing whatever it might choose to do. This was sufficient of itself to put the most fanatical portion of the North in action, for the purpose of destroying the existing relation between the two races in the South.

The first organized movement towards it commenced in 1835. Then, for the first time, societies were organized, presses established, lecturers sent forth to excite the people of the North, and incendiary publications scattered over the whole South, through the mail. The South was thoroughly aroused. Meetings were held everywhere, and resolutions adopted, calling upon the North to apply a remedy to arrest the threatened evil, and pledging themselves to adopt measures for their own protection, if it was not arrested. At the meeting of Congress, petitions poured in from the North, calling upon Congress to abolish slavery in the District of Columbia, and to prohibit, what they called, the internal slave trade between the States—announcing at the same time, that their ultimate object was to abolish slavery, not only in the District, but in the States and throughout the Union. At this period, the number engaged in the agitation was small, and possessed little or no personal influence.

Neither party in Congress had, at that time, any sympathy with them or their cause. The members of each party presented their petitions with great reluctance. Nevertheless, small and contemptible as the party then was, both of the great parties of the North dreaded them. They felt, that though small, they were organized in reference to a subject which had a great and a commanding influence over the Northern mind. Each party, on that account, feared to oppose their petitions, lest the opposite party should take advantage of the one who might do so, by favoring them. The effect was, that both united in insisting that the petitions should be received, and that Congress should take jurisdiction over the subject. To justify their course, they took the extraordinary ground, that Congress was bound to receive petitions on every subject, however objectionable they might be, and whether they had, or had not, jurisdiction over the subject. These views prevailed in the House of Representatives, and partially in the Senate; and thus the party succeeded in their first movements, in gaining what they proposed—a position in Congress from which agitation could be extended over the whole Union. This was the commencement of the agitation, which has ever since continued, and which, as is now acknowledged, has endangered the Union itself.

As for myself, I believed at that early period, if the party who got up the petitions should succeed in getting Congress to take jurisdiction, that agitation would follow, and that it would in the end, if not arrested, destroy the Union. I then so expressed myself in debate, and called upon both parties to take grounds against assuming jurisdiction; but in vain. Had my voice been heeded, and had Congress refused to take jurisdiction, by the united votes of all parties, the agitation which followed would have been prevented, and the fanatical zeal that gives impulse to the agitation, and which has brought us to our present perilous condition, would have become extinguished, from the want of fuel to feed the flame. *That* was the time for the North to have shown her devotion to the Union;

but, unfortunately, both of the great parties of that section were so intent on obtaining or retaining party ascendency, that all other considerations were overlooked or forgotten.

What has since followed are but natural consequences. With the success of their first movement, this small fanatical party began to acquire strength; and with that, to become an object of courtship to both the great parties. The necessary consequence was, a further increase of power, and a gradual tainting of the opinions of both of the other parties with their doctrines, until the infection has extended over both; and the great mass of the population of the North, who, whatever may be their opinion of the original abolition party, which still preserves its distinctive organization, hardly ever fail, when it comes to acting, to co-operate in carrying out their measures. With the increase of their influence, they extended the sphere of their action. In a short time after the commencement of their first movement, they had acquired sufficient influence to induce the legislatures of most of the Northern States to pass acts, which in effect abrogated the clause of the constitution that provides for the delivery up of fugitive slaves. Not long after, petitions followed to abolish slavery in forts, magazines, and dock-yards, and all other places where Congress had exclusive power of legislation. This was followed by petitions and resolutions of legislatures of the Northern States, and popular meetings, to exclude the Southern States from all territories acquired, or to be acquired, and to prevent the admission of any State hereafter into the Union, which, by its constitution, does not prohibit slavery. And Congress is invoked to do all this, expressly with the view to the final abolition of slavery in the States. That has been avowed to be the ultimate object from the beginning of the agitation until the present time; and yet the great body of both parties of the North, with the full knowledge of the fact, although disavowing the abolitionists, have co-operated with them in almost all their measures.

Such is a brief history of the agitation, as far as it has yet advanced. Now I ask, Senators, what is there to prevent its further progress, until it fulfils the ultimate end proposed, unless some decisive measure should be adopted to prevent it? Has any one of the causes, which has added to its increase from its original small and contemptible beginning until it has attained its present magnitude, diminished in force? Is the original cause of the movement—that slavery is a sin, and ought to be suppressed—weaker now than at the commencement? Or is the abolition party less numerous or influential, or have they less influence with, or control over the two great parties of the North in elections? Or has the South greater means of influencing or controlling the movements of this Government now, than it had when the agitation commenced? To all these questions but one answer can be given: No—no—no. The very reverse is true. Instead of being weaker, all the elements in favor of agitation are stronger now than they were in 1835, when it first commenced, while all the elements of influence on the part of the South are weaker. Unless something decisive is done, I again ask, what is to stop this agitation, before the great and final object at which it aims —the abolition of slavery in the States—is consummated? Is it, then, not certain, that if something is not done to arrest it, the South will be forced to choose between abolition and secession? Indeed, as events are now moving, it will not require the South to secede, in order to dissolve the Union. Agitation will of

131

itself effect it, of which its past history furnishes abundant proof—as I shall next proceed to show.

It is a great mistake to suppose that disunion can be effected by a single blow. The cords which bound these States together in one common Union, are far too numerous and powerful for that. Disunion must be the work of time. It is only through a long process, and successively, that the cords can be snapped, until the whole fabric falls asunder. Already the agitation of the slavery question has snapped some of the most important, and has greatly weakened all the others, as I shall proceed to show.

The cords that bind the States together are not only many, but various in character. Some are spiritual or ecclesiastical; some political; others social. Some appertain to the benefit conferred by the Union, and others to the feeling of duty and obligation.

The strongest of those of a spiritual and ecclesiastical nature, consisted in the unity of the great religious denominations, all of which originally embraced the whole Union. All these denominations, with the exception, perhaps, of the Catholics, were organized very much upon the principle of our political institutions. Beginning with smaller meetings, corresponding with the political divisions of the country, their organization terminated in one great central assemblage, corresponding very much with the character of Congress. At these meetings the principal clergymen and lay members of the respective denominations, from all parts of the Union, met to transact business relating to their common concerns. It was not confined to what appertained to the doctrines and discipline of the respective denominations, but extended to plans for disseminating the Bible—establishing missions, distributing tracts—and of establishing presses for the publication of tracts, newspapers, and periodicals, with a view of diffusing religious information—and for the support of their respective doctrines and creeds. All this combined contributed greatly to strengthen the bonds of the Union. The ties which held each denomination together formed a strong cord to hold the whole Union together; but, powerful as they were, they have not been able to resist the explosive effect of slavery agitation.

The first of these cords which snapped, under its explosive force, was that of the powerful Methodist Episcopal Church. The numerous and strong ties which held it together, are all broken, and its unity gone. They now form separate churches; and, instead of that feeling of attachment and devotion to the interests of the whole church which was formerly felt, they are now arrayed into two hostile bodies, engaged in litigation about what was formerly their common property.

The next cord that snapped was that of the Baptists—one of the largest and most respectable of the denominations. That of the Presbyterian is not entirely snapped, but some of its strands have given way. That of the Episcopal Church is the only one of the four great Protestant denominations which remains unbroken and entire.

132   The strongest cord, of a political character, consists of the many and powerful ties that have held together the two great parties which have, with some modifications, existed from the beginning of the Government. They both extended to every portion of the Union, and strongly contributed to hold all its parts together. But this powerful cord has fared no better than the spiritual. It resisted, for a long time, the explosive tendency of the agitation, but has finally snapped under its force—if not entirely, in a great measure. Nor is there one of the remaining cords which has not been greatly weakened. To this extent the Union has already been destroyed by agitation, in the only way it can be, by sundering and weakening the cords which bind it together.

If the agitation goes on, the same force, acting with increased intensity, as has been shown, will finally snap every cord, when nothing will be left to hold the States together except force. But, surely, that can, with no propriety of language, be called a Union, when the only means by which the weaker is held connected with the stronger portion is *force*. It may, indeed, keep them connected; but the connection will partake much more of the character of subjugation, on the part of the weaker to the stronger, than the union of free, independent, and sovereign States, in one confederation, as they stood in the early stages of the Government, and which only is worthy of the sacred name of Union.

Having now, Senators, explained what it is that endangers the Union, and traced it to its cause, and explained its nature and character, the question again recurs—How can the Union be saved? To this I answer, there is but one way by which it can be—and that is—by adopting such measures as will satisfy the States belonging to the Southern section, that they can remain in the Union consistently with their honor and their safety. There is, again, only one way by which this can be effected, and that is—by removing the causes by which this belief has been produced. *Do this*, and discontent will cease—harmony and kind feelings between the sections be restored—and every apprehension of danger to the Union removed. The question, then, is—How can this be done? But, before I undertake to answer this question, I propose to show by what the Union cannot be saved.

It cannot, then, be saved by eulogies on the Union, however splendid or numerous. The cry of "Union, Union—the glorious Union!" can no more prevent disunion than the cry of "Health, health—glorious health!" on the part of the physician, can save a patient lying dangerously ill. So long as the Union, instead of being regarded as a protector, is regarded in the opposite character, by not much less than a majority of the States, it will be in vain to attempt to conciliate them by pronouncing eulogies on it.

Besides this cry of Union comes commonly from those whom we cannot believe to be sincere. It usually comes from our assailants. But we cannot believe them to be sincere; for, if they loved the Union, they would necessarily be devoted to the constitution. It made the Union—and to destroy the constitution would be to destroy the Union. But the only reliable and certain evidence of devotion to the constitution is, to abstain, on the one hand, from violating it, and to repel, on the other, all attempts to violate it. It is only by faithfully performing these high duties that the constitution can be preserved, and with it the Union.

But how stands the profession of devotion to the Union by our assailants, when brought to this test? Have they abstained from violating the constitution? Let the many acts passed by the Northern States to set aside and annul the clause of the constitution providing for the delivery up of fugitive slaves

133

answer. I cite this, not that it is the only instance (for there are many others), but because the violation in this particular is too notorious and palpable to be denied. Again: have they stood forth faithfully to repel violations of the constitution? Let their course in reference to the agitation of the slavery question, which was commenced and has been carried on for fifteen years, avowedly for the purpose of abolishing slavery in the States—an object all acknowledged to be unconstitutional—answer. Let them show a single instance, during this long period, in which they have denounced the agitators or their attempts to effect what is admitted to be unconstitutional, or a single measure which they have brought forward for that purpose. How can we, with all these facts before us, believe that they are sincere in their profession of devotion to the Union, or avoid believing their profession is but intended to increase the vigor of their assaults and to weaken the force of our resistance?

Nor can we regard the profession of devotion to the Union, on the part of those who are not our assailants, as sincere, when they pronounce eulogies upon the Union, evidently with the intent of charging us with disunion, without uttering one word of denunciation against our assailants. If friends of the Union, their course should be to unite with us in repelling these assaults, and denouncing the authors as enemies of the Union. Why they avoid this, and pursue the course they do, it is for them to explain.

Nor can the Union be saved by invoking the name of the illustrious Southerner whose mortal remains repose on the western bank of the Potomac. He was one of us—a slaveholder and a planter. We have studied his history, and find nothing in it to justify submission to wrong. On the contrary, his great fame rests on the solid foundation, that, while he was careful to avoid doing wrong to others, he was prompt and decided in repelling wrong. I trust that, in this respect, we profited by his example.

Nor can we find any thing in his history to deter us from seceding from the Union, should it fail to fulfil the objects for which it was instituted, by being permanently and hopelessly converted into the means of oppressing instead of protecting us. On the contrary, we find much in his example to encourage us, should we be forced to the extremity of deciding between submission and disunion.

There existed then, as well as now, a union—that between the parent country and her then colonies. It was a union that had much to endear it to the people of the colonies. Under its protecting and superintending care, the colonies were planted and grew up and prospered, through a long course of years, until they became populous and wealthy. Its benefits were not limited to them. Their extensive agricultural and other productions, gave birth to a flourishing commerce, which richly rewarded the parent country for the trouble and expense of establishing and protecting them. Washington was born and grew up to manhood under that union. He acquired his early distinction in its service, and there is every reason to believe that he was devotedly attached to it. But this devotion was a rational one. He was attached to it, not as an end, but as a means to an end. When it failed to fulfil its end, and, instead of affording protection, was converted into the means of oppressing the colonies, he did not hesitate to draw his sword, and head the great movement by which that union was for ever severed, and the independence of these States established. This was the great and crowning glory of his life, which has spread his fame over the whole globe, and will transmit it to the latest posterity.

Nor can the plan proposed by the distinguished Senator from Kentucky, nor that of the administration save the Union. I shall pass by, without remark, the plan proposed by the Senator, and proceed directly to the consideration of that of the administration. I however assure the distinguished and able Senator, that, in taking this course, no disrespect whatever is intended to him or his plan. I have adopted it, because so many Senators of distinguished abilities, who were present when he delivered his speech, and explained his plan, and who were fully capable to do justice to the side they support, have replied to him.

The plan of the administration cannot save the Union, because it can have no effect whatever, towards satisfying the States composing the Southern section of the Union, that they can, consistently with safety and honor, remain in the Union. It is, in fact, but a modification of the Wilmot Proviso. It proposes to effect the same object—to exclude the South from all territory acquired by the Mexican treaty. It is well known that the South is united against the Wilmot Proviso, and has committed itself by solemn resolutions, to resist, should it be adopted. Its opposition *is not to the name*, but that which it *proposes to effect*. That, the Southern States hold to be unconstitutional, unjust, inconsistent with their equality as members of the common Union, and calculated to destroy irretrievably the equilibrium between the two sections. These objections equally apply to what, for brevity, I will call the Executive Proviso. There is no difference between it and the Wilmot, except in the mode of effecting the object; and in that respect, I must say, that the latter is much the least objectionable. It goes to its object openly, boldly, and distinctly. It claims for Congress unlimited power over the territories and proposes to assert it over the territories, acquired from Mexico, by a positive prohibition of slavery. Not so the Executive Proviso. It takes an indirect course, and in order to elude the Wilmot Proviso, and thereby avoid encountering the united and determined resistance of the South, it denies, by implication, the authority of Congress to legislate for the territories, and claims the right as belonging exclusively to the inhabitants of the territories. But to effect the object of excluding the South, it takes care, in the mean time, to let in emigrants freely from the Northern States and all other quarters, except from the South, which it takes special care to exclude by holding up to them the danger of having their slaves liberated under the Mexican laws. The necessary consequence is to exclude the South from the territory, just as effectually as would the Wilmot Proviso. The only difference in this respect is, that what one proposes to effect directly and openly, the other proposes to effect indirectly and covertly.

But the Executive Proviso is more objectionable than the Wilmot, in another and more important particular. The latter, to effect its object, inflicts a dangerous wound upon the constitution, by depriving the Southern States, as joint partners and owners of the territories, of their rights in them; but it inflicts no greater wound than is absolutely necessary to effect its object. The former, on the contrary, while it inflicts the same wound, inflicts others equally great, and, if possible, greater, as I shall next proceed to explain.

135

In claiming the right for the inhabitants, instead of Congress, to legislate for the territories, the Executive Proviso assumes that the sovereignty over the territories is vested in the former: or to express it in the language used in a resolution offered by one of the Senators from Texas (General Houston, now absent), they have "the same inherent right of self-government as the people in the States." The assumption is utterly unfounded, unconstitutional, without example, and contrary to the entire practice of the Government, from its commencement to the present time. . . .

Having now shown what cannot save the Union, I return to the question with which I commenced, How can the Union be saved? There is but one way by which it can with any certainty; and that is, by a full and final settlement, on the principle of justice, of all the questions at issue between the two sections. The South asks for justice, simple justice, and less she ought not to take. She has no compromise to offer, but the constitution; and no concession or surrender to make. She has already surrendered so much that she has little left to surrender. Such a settlement would go to the root of the evil, and remove all cause of discontent, by satisfying the South, that she could remain honorably and safely in the Union, and thereby restore the harmony and fraternal feelings between the sections, which existed anterior to the Missouri agitation. Nothing else can, with any certainty, finally and for ever settle the questions at issue, terminate agitation, and save the Union.

But can this be done? Yes, easily; not by the weaker party, for it can of itself do nothing—not even protect itself—but by the stronger. The North has only to will it to accomplish it—to do justice by conceding to the South an equal right in the acquired territory, and to do her duty by causing the stipulations relative to fugitive slaves to be faithfully fulfilled—to cease the agitation of the slave question, and to provide for the insertion of a provision in the constitution, by an amendment, which will restore to the South, in substance, the power she possessed of protecting herself, before the equilibrium between the sections was destroyed by the action of this Government. There will be no difficulty in devising such a provision—one that will protect the South, and which, at the same time, will improve and strengthen the Government, instead of impairing and weakening it.

But will the North agree to this? It is for her to answer the question. But, I will say, she cannot refuse, if she has half the love of the Union which she professes to have, or without justly exposing herself to the charge that her love of power and aggrandizement is far greater than her love of the Union. At all events, the responsibility of saving the Union rests on the North, and not on the South. The South cannot save it by any act of hers, and the North may save it without any sacrifice whatever, unless to do justice, and to perform her duties under the constitution, should be regarded by her as a sacrifice.

It is time, Senators, that there should be an open and manly avowal on all sides, as to what is intended to be done. If the question is not now settled, it is uncertain whether it ever can hereafter be; and we, as the representatives of the States of this Union, regarded as governments, should come to a distinct understanding as to our respective views, in order to ascertain whether the great questions at issue can be settled or not. If you, who represent the stronger portion, cannot agree to settle them on the broad principle of justice and duty, say so; and let the States we both represent agree to separate and part in peace. If you are unwilling we should part in peace, tell us so; and we shall know what to do, when you reduce the question to submission or resistance. If you remain silent, you will compel us to infer by your acts what you intend. In that case, California will become the test question. If you admit her, under all the difficulties that oppose her admission, you compel us to infer that you intend to exclude us from the whole of the acquired territories, with the intention of destroying, irretrievably, the equilibrium between the two sections. We would be blind not to perceive in that case, that your real objects are power and aggrandizement, and infatuated not to act accordingly.

I have now, Senators, done my duty in expressing my opinions fully, freely, and candidly, on this solemn occasion. In doing so, I have been governed by the motives which have governed me in all the stages of the agitation of the slavery question since its commencement. I have exerted myself, during the whole period, to arrest it, with the intention of saving the Union, if it could be done; and if it could not, to save the section where it has pleased Providence to cast my lot, and which I sincerely believe has justice and the constitution on its side. Having faithfully done my duty to the best of my ability, both to the Union and my section, throughout this agitation, I shall have the consolation, let what will come, that I am free from all responsibility. (*1850*)

from *A Disquisition on Government*

. . . To perfect society, it is necessary to develope the faculties, intellectual and moral, with which man is endowed. But the main spring to their development, and, through this, to progress, improvement and civilization, with all their blessings, is the desire of individuals to better their condition. For this purpose, liberty and security are indispensable. Liberty leaves each free to pursue the course he may deem best to promote his interest and happiness, as far as it may be compatible with the primary end for which government is ordained;—while security gives assurance to each, that he shall not be deprived of the fruits of his exertions to better his condition. These combined, give to this desire the strongest impulse of which it is susceptible. For, to extend liberty beyond the limits assigned, would be to weaken the government and to render it incompetent to fulfil its primary end—the protection of society against dangers, internal and external. The effect of this would be, insecurity; and, of insecurity—to weaken the impulse of individuals to better their condition, and thereby retard progress and improvement. On the other hand, to extend the powers of the government, so as to contract the sphere assigned to liberty, would have the same effect, by disabling individuals in their efforts to better their condition.

Herein is to be found the principle which assigns to power and liberty their proper spheres, and reconciles each to the other under all circumstances. For, if power be necessary to secure to liberty the fruits of its exertions, liberty, in

137

turn, repays power with interest, by increasing population, wealth, and other advantages, which progress and improvement bestow on the community. By thus assigning to each its appropriate sphere, all conflicts between them cease; and each is made to co-operate with and assist the other, in fulfilling the great ends for which government is ordained.

But the principle, applied to different communities, will assign to them different limits. It will assign a larger sphere to power and a more contracted one to liberty, or the reverse, according to circumstances. To the former, there must ever be allotted, under all circumstances, a sphere sufficiently large to protect the community against danger from without and violence and anarchy within. The residuum belongs to liberty. More cannot be safely or rightly allotted to it.

But some communities require a far greater amount of power than others to protect them against anarchy and external dangers; and, of course, the sphere of liberty in such, must be proportionally contracted. The causes calculated to enlarge the one and contract the other, are numerous and various. Some are physical—such as open and exposed frontiers, surrounded by powerful and hostile neighbors. Others are moral—such as the different degrees of intelligence, patriotism, and virtue among the mass of the community, and their experience and proficiency in the art of self-government. Of these, the moral are, by far, the most influential. A community may possess all the necessary moral qualifications, in so high a degree, as to be capable of self-government under the most adverse circumstances; while, on the other hand, another may be so sunk in ignorance and vice, as to be incapable of forming a conception of liberty, or of living, even when most favored by circumstances, under any other than an absolute and despotic government.

The principle, in all communities, according to these numerous and various causes, assigns to power and liberty their proper spheres. To allow to liberty, in any case, a sphere of action more extended than this assigns, would lead to anarchy; and this, probably, in the end, to a contraction instead of an enlargement of its sphere. Liberty, then, when forced on a people unfit for it, would, instead of a blessing, be a curse; as it would, in its reaction, lead directly to anarchy—the greatest of all curses. No people, indeed, can long enjoy more liberty than that to which their situation and advanced intelligence and morals fairly entitle them. If more than this be allowed, they must soon fall into confusion and disorder—to be followed, if not by anarchy and despotism, by a change to a form of government more simple and absolute; and, therefore, better suited to their condition. And hence, although it may be true, that a people may not have as much liberty as they are fairly entitled to, and are capable of enjoying—yet the reverse is unquestionably true—that no people can long possess more than they are fairly entitled to.

Liberty, indeed, though among the greatest of blessings, is not so great as that of protection; inasmuch, as the end of the former is the progress and improvement of the race—while that of the latter is its preservation and perpetuation. And hence, when the two come into conflict, liberty must, and ever ought, to yield to protection; as the existence of the race is of greater moment than its improvement.

138

It follows, from what has been stated, that it is a great and dangerous error to suppose that all people are equally entitled to liberty. It is a reward to be earned, not a blessing to be gratuitously lavished on all alike—a reward reserved for the intelligent, the patriotic, the virtuous and deserving—and not a boon to be bestowed on a people too ignorant, degraded and vicious, to be capable either of appreciating or of enjoying it. Nor is it any disparagement to liberty, that such is, and ought to be the case. On the contrary, its greatest praise—its proudest distinction is, that an all-wise Providence has reserved it, as the noblest and highest reward for the development of our faculties, moral and intellectual. A reward more appropriate than liberty could not be conferred on the deserving—nor a punishment inflicted on the undeserving more just, than to be subject to lawless and despotic rule. This dispensation seems to be the result of some fixed law—and every effort to disturb or defeat it, by attempting to elevate a people in the scale of liberty, above the point to which they are entitled to rise, must ever prove abortive, and end in disappointment. The progress of a people rising from a lower to a higher point in the scale of liberty, is necessarily slow—and by attempting to precipitate, we either retard, or permanently defeat it.

There is another error, not less great and dangerous, usually associated with the one which has just been considered. I refer to the opinion, that liberty and equality are so intimately united, that liberty cannot be perfect without perfect equality.

That they are united to a certain extent—and that equality of citizens, in the eyes of the law, is essential to liberty in a popular government, is conceded. But to go further, and make equality of *condition* essential to liberty, would be to destroy both liberty and progress. The reason is, that inequality of condition, while it is a necessary consequence of liberty is, at the same time, indispensable to progress. In order to understand why this is so, it is necessary to bear in mind, that the main spring to progress is, the desire of individuals to better their condition; and that the strongest impulse which can be given to it is, to leave individuals free to exert themselves in the manner they may deem best for that purpose, as far at least as it can be done consistently with the ends for which government is ordained—and to secure to all the fruits of their exertions. Now, as individuals differ greatly from each other, in intelligence, sagacity, energy, perseverance, skill, habits of industry and economy, physical power, position and opportunity—the necessary effect of leaving all free to exert themselves to better their condition, must be a corresponding inequality between those who may possess these qualities and advantages in a high degree, and those who may be deficient in them. The only means by which this result can be prevented are, either to impose such restrictions on the exertions of those who may possess them in a high degree, as will place them on a level with those who do not; or to deprive them of the fruits of their exertions. But to impose such restrictions on them would be destructive of liberty—while, to deprive them of the fruits of their exertions, would be to destroy the desire of bettering their condition. It is, indeed, this inequality of condition between the front and rear ranks, in the march of progress, which gives so strong an impulse to the former to maintain their position, and to the latter to press forward into their

139

files. This gives to progress its greatest impulse. To force the front rank back to the rear, or attempt to push forward the rear into line with the front, by the interposition of the government, would put an end to the impulse, and effectually arrest the march of progress.

These great and dangerous errors have their origin in the prevalent opinion that all men are born free and equal—than which nothing can be more un- founded and false. It rests upon the assumption of a fact, which is contrary to universal observation, in whatever light it may be regarded. It is, indeed, difficult to explain how an opinion so destitute of all sound reason, ever could have been so extensively entertained, unless we regard it as being confounded with another, which has some semblance of truth—but which, when properly understood, is not less false and dangerous. I refer to the assertion, that all men are equal in the state of nature; meaning, by a state of nature, a state of individuality, supposed to have existed prior to the social and political state; and in which men lived apart and independent of each other. If such a state ever did exist, all men would have been, indeed, free and equal in it; that is, free to do as they pleased, and exempt from the authority or control of others— as, by supposition, it existed anterior to society and government. But such a state is purely hypothetical. It never did, nor can exist; as it is inconsistent with the preservation and perpetuation of the race. It is, therefore, a great misnomer to call it *the state of nature.* Instead of being the natural state of man, it is, of all conceivable states, the most opposed to his nature—most repugnant to his feelings, and most incompatible with his wants. His natural state is, the social and political—the one for which his Creator made him, and the only one in which he can preserve and perfect his race. As, then, there never was such a state as the, so called, state of nature, and never can be, it follows, that men, in- stead of being born in it, are born in the social and political state; and of course, instead of being born free and equal, are born subject, not only to parental authority, but to the laws and institutions of the country where born, and under whose protection they draw their first breath. With these remarks, I return from this digression, to resume the thread of the discourse.

It follows, from all that has been said, that the more perfectly a government combines power and liberty—that is, the greater its power and the more en- larged and secure the liberty of individuals, the more perfectly it fulfils the ends for which government is ordained. To show, then, that the government of the concurrent majority is better calculated to fulfil them than that of the numerical, it is only necessary to explain why the former is better suited to combine a higher degree of power, and a wider scope of liberty than the latter. I shall begin with the former.

The concurrent majority, then, is better suited to enlarge and secure the bounds of liberty, because it is better suited to prevent government from passing beyond its proper limits, and to restrict it to its primary end—the protection of the community. But in doing this, it leaves, necessarily, all beyond it open and free to individual exertions; and thus enlarges and secures the sphere of liberty to the greatest extent which the condition of the community will admit, as has been explained. The tendency of government to pass beyond its proper limits is what exposes liberty to danger, and renders it insecure; and it is the strong counteraction of governments of the concurrent majority to this tendency which makes them so favorable to liberty. On the contrary, those of the numerical, instead of opposing and counteracting this tendency, add to it increased strength, in consequence of the violent party struggles incident to them, as has been fully explained. And hence their encroachments on liberty, and the danger to which it is exposed under such governments.

So great, indeed, is the difference between the two in this respect, that liberty is little more than a name under all governments of the absolute form, including that of the numerical majority; and can only have a secure and durable existence under those of the concurrent or constitutional form. The latter, by giving to each portion of the community which may be unequally affected by its action, a negative on the others, prevents all partial or local legislation, and restricts its action to such measures as are designed for the protection and the good of the whole. In doing this, it secures, at the same time, the rights and liberty of the people, regarded individually; as each portion consists of those who, whatever may be the diversity of interests among themselves, have the same interest in reference to the action of the government.

Such being the case, the interest of each individual may be safely confided to the majority, or voice of his portion, against that of all others, and, of course, the government itself. It is only through an organism which vests each with a negative, in some one form or another, that those who have like interests in preventing the government from passing beyond its proper sphere, and encroaching on the rights and liberty of individuals, can co-operate peaceably and effectually in resisting the encroachments of power, and thereby preserve their rights and liberty. Individual resistance is too feeble, and the difficulty of concert and co-operation too great unaided by such an organism, to oppose, successfully, the organized power of government, with all the means of the community at its disposal; especially in populous countries of great extent; where concert and co-operation are almost impossible. Even when the oppression of the government comes to be too great to be borne, and force is resorted to in order to overthrow it, the result is rarely ever followed by the establishment of liberty. The force sufficient to overthrow an oppressive government is usually sufficient to establish one equally, or more, oppressive in its place. And hence, in no governments, except those that rest on the principle of the concurrent or constitutional majority, can the people guard their liberty against power; and hence, also, when lost, the great difficulty and uncertainty of regaining it by force.

It may be further affirmed that, being more favorable to the enlargement and security of liberty, governments of the concurrent, must necessarily be more favorable to progress, development, improvement, and civilization—and, of course, to the increase of power which results from, and depends on these, than those of the numerical majority. That it is liberty which gives to them their greatest impulse, has already been shown; and it now remains to show, that these, in turn, contribute greatly to the increase of power.

In the earlier stages of society, numbers and individual prowess constituted the principal elements of power. In a more advanced stage, when communities had passed from the barbarous to the civilized state, discipline, strategy,

141

weapons of increased power, and money—as the means of meeting increased expense—became additional and important elements. In this stage, the effects of progress and improvement on the increase of power, began to be disclosed; but still numbers and personal prowess were sufficient, for a long period, to enable barbarous nations to contend successfully with the civilized—and, in the end, to overpower them—as the pages of history abundantly testify. But a more advanced progress, with its numerous inventions and improvements, has furnished new and far more powerful and destructive implements of offence and defence, and greatly increased the intelligence and wealth, necessary to engage the skill and meet the increased expense required for their construction and application to purposes of war. The discovery of gunpowder, and the use of steam as an impelling force, and their application to military purposes, have for ever settled the question of ascendency between civilized and barbarous communities, in favor of the former. Indeed, these, with other improvements, belonging to the present state of progress, have given to communities the most advanced, a superiority over those the least so, almost as great as that of the latter over the brute creation. And among the civilized, the same causes have decided the question of superiority, where other circumstances are nearly equal, in favor of those whose governments have given the greatest impulse to development, progress, and improvement; that is, to those whose liberty is the largest and best secured. Among these, England and the United States afford striking examples, not only of the effects of liberty in increasing power, but of the more perfect adaptation of governments founded on the principle of the concurrent, or constitutional majority, to enlarge and secure liberty. They are both governments of this description, as will be shown hereafter.

But in estimating the power of a community, moral, as well as physical causes, must be taken into the calculation; and in estimating the effects of liberty on power, it must not be overlooked, that it is, in itself, an important agent in augmenting the force of moral, as well as of physical power. It bestows on a people elevation, self-reliance, energy, and enthusiasm; and these combined, give to physical power a vastly augmented and almost irresistible impetus.

These, however, are not the only elements of moral power. There are others, and among them harmony, unanimity, devotion to country, and a disposition to elevate to places of trust and power, those who are distinguished for wisdom and experience. These, when the occasion requires it, will, without compulsion, and from their very nature, unite and put forth the entire force of the community in the most efficient manner, without hazard to its institutions or its liberty.

All these causes combined, give to a community its maximum of power. Either of them, without the other, would leave it comparatively feeble. But it cannot be necessary, after what has been stated, to enter into any further explanation or argument in order to establish the superiority of governments of the concurrent majority over the numerical, in developing the great elements of moral power. So vast is this superiority, that the one, by its operation, necessarily leads to their development, while the other as necessarily prevents it—as has been fully shown. . . . (1851)

142

ALBERT TAYLOR BLEDSOE

1809–1877

Albert Taylor Bledsoe—soldier, lawyer, college professor, author, editor, and "Fire-Eater"—spent his early youth in his native Kentucky. In 1826 he entered West Point, where he was a schoolmate of Robert E. Lee and Jefferson Davis. After graduating, he served briefly in the Indian wars in the West, but soon resigned his commission to study law, theology, and philosophy at Kenyon College. His studies completed, he taught for three years—first at Kenyon and then at Miami University in Ohio—before starting his law practice. From 1838 to 1848 he lived in Springfield, Illinois, where he worked in the same courts as Lincoln and Douglas. It was during this period that he published his first important work, *Examination of President Edwards' "Inquiry into the Freedom of the Will"* (1845).

Returning to teaching in 1848, Bledsoe served as professor of mathematics at the University of Mississippi until 1854, and in the same capacity at the University of Virginia from 1854 until 1861. While he was at Virginia he published the treatise for which he is primarily remembered today, *Essay on Liberty and Slavery* (1856). At the beginning of the Civil War, Bledsoe entered the Confederate Army with the rank of colonel. He later served briefly as assistant Secretary of War under President Davis, and was ultimately sent on a special assignment to London, where he remained until the close of the war.

In 1867, Bledsoe founded *The Southern Review* in Baltimore, and for the next ten years wrote innumerable articles in defense of the "Lost Cause." He regarded the South's defeat as the best modern example of the overthrow of exemplary principles by brute force. Bledsoe repeatedly attempted to prove that secession was not a violation of the Constitution and that slavery was sanctioned by the Bible. Harking back to the tradition of Jefferson and Taylor —as writers like John Esten Cooke, Thomas Nelson Page, and the twentieth-century agrarians were to do—he argued that much in Southern life worth preserving was being destroyed by industrialism and science. He died in Alexandria, Virginia, exhausted by ten years of controversy and embittered by the lack of Southern support for his views.

143

from *Liberty and Slavery*

Chapter 3. The Argument from the Scriptures [1]

In discussing the arguments of the abolitionists, it was scarcely possible to avoid intimating, to a certain extent, the grounds on which we intend to vindicate the institution of slavery, as it exists among us at the South. But these grounds are entitled to a more distinct enunciation and to a more ample illustration. In the prosecution of this object we shall first advert to the argument from revelation; and, if we mistake not, it will be found that in the foregoing discussion we have been vindicating against aspersion not only the peculiar institution of the Southern States, but also the very legislation of Heaven itself.

I. The argument from the Old Testament.

The ground is taken by Dr. Wayland and other abolitionists, that slavery is always and everywhere, *semper et ubique*, morally wrong, and should, therefore, be instantly and universally swept away. We point to slavery among the Hebrews, and say, There is an instance in which it was not wrong, because there it received the sanction of the Almighty. Dr. Wayland chooses to overlook or evade the bearing of that case upon his fundamental position; and the means by which he seeks to evade its force is one of the grossest fallacies ever invented by the brain of man.

Let the reader examine and judge for himself. Here it is: "Let us reduce this argument to a syllogism, and it will stand thus: Whatever God sanctioned among the Hebrews he sanctions for all men and at all times. God sanctioned slavery among the Hebrews; therefore God sanctions slavery for all men at all times."

Now I venture to affirm that no man at the South has ever put forth so absurd an argument in favor of slavery—not only in favor of slavery for the negro race so long as they may remain unfit for freedom, but in favor of slavery for all men and for all times. If such an argument proved any thing, it would, indeed, prove that the white man of the South, no less than the black, might be subjected to bondage. But no one here argues in favor of the subjection of the white man, either South or North, to a state of servitude. No one here contends for the subjection to slavery of any portion of the civilized world. We only contend for slavery in certain cases; in opposition to the thesis of the abolitionist, we assert that it is not always and everywhere wrong. For the truth of this assertion we rely upon the express authority of God himself. We affirm that since slavery has been ordained by him, it cannot be always and everywhere wrong. And how does the abolitionist attempt to meet this reply? Why, by a little legerdemain, he converts this reply from an argument against his position, that slavery is always and everywhere wrong, into an argument in favor of the monstrous dogma that it is always and everywhere right! If we should contend that, in some cases, it is right to take the life of a man, he might just as fairly insist that we are in favor of having every man on earth put to death! Was any fallacy ever more glaring? was any misrepresentation ever more flagrant?

Indeed we should have supposed that Dr. Wayland might have seen that his

144

---

[1] *Bledsoe divided this chapter into two parts: "The argument from the Old Testament" and "The argument from the New Testament." Only the first section is reprinted here.*

representation is not a fair one, if he had not assured us of the contrary. We should have supposed that he might have distinguished between an argument in favor of slavery for the lowest grade of the ignorant and debased, and an argument in favor of slavery for all men and all times, if he had not assured us that he possesses no capacity to make it. For after having twisted the plea of the most enlightened statesmen of the South into an argument in favor of the universal subjection of mankind to slavery, he coolly adds, "I believe that in these words I express the argument correctly. If I do not, it is solely because I do not know how to state it more correctly." Is it possible Dr. Wayland could not distinguish between the principle of slavery for some men and the principle of slavery for all men? between the proposition that the ignorant, the idle, and the debased may be subjected to servitude, and the idea that all men, even the most enlightened and free, may be reduced to bondage? If he had not positively declared that he possessed no such capacity, we should most certainly have entertained a different opinion.

It will not be denied, we presume, that the very best men, whose lives are recorded in the Old Testament, were the owners and holders of slaves. "I grant at once," says Dr. Wayland, "that the Hebrews held slaves from the time of the conquest of Canaan, and that Abraham and the patriarchs held them many centuries before. I grant also that Moses enacted laws with special reference to that relation . . . I wonder that any should have had the hardihood to deny so plain a matter of record. I should almost as soon deny the delivery of the ten commandments to Moses."

Now, is it not wonderful that directly in the face of "so plain a matter of record," a pious Presbyterian pastor should have been arraigned by abolitionists, not for holding slaves, but for daring to be so far a freeman as to express his convictions on the subject of slavery? Most abolitionists must have found themselves a little embarrassed in such a proceeding. For *there* was the fact, staring them in the face, that Abraham himself, "the friend of God" and the "Father of the faithful," was the owner and holder of more than a thousand slaves. How, then, could these professing Christians proceed to condemn and excommunicate a poor brother for having merely approved what Abraham had practiced? Of all the good men of old, Abraham was the most eminent. The sublimity of his faith and the fervor of his piety has, by the unerring voice of inspiration itself, been held up as a model for the imitation of all future ages. How, then, could a parcel of poor common saints presume, without blushing, to cry and condemn one of their number because he was no better than "Father Abraham"? This was the difficulty; and, but for a very happy discovery, it must have been an exceedingly perplexing one. But "Necessity is the mother of invention." On this trying occasion she conceived the happy thought that the plain matter of record "was all a mistake"; that Abraham never owned a slave; that, on the contrary, he was "a prince," and the "men whom he bought with his money" were "his subjects" merely! If, then, we poor sinners of the South should be driven to the utmost extremity—all honest arguments and pleas failing us—may we not escape the unutterable horrors of civil war, by calling our masters princes, and our slaves subjects?

We shall conclude this topic with the pointed and powerful words of Dr. Fuller, in his reply to Dr. Wayland: "Abraham," says he, "was 'the friend of

145

God,' and walked with God in the closest and most endearing intercourse; nor can any thing be more exquisitely touching than those words, 'Shall I hide from Abraham that thing which I do?' It is the language of a friend who feels that concealment would wrong the confidential intimacy existing. The love of this venerable servant of God in his promptness to immolate his son has been the theme of apostles and preachers for ages; and such was his faith, that all who believe are called 'the children of faithful Abraham.' This Abraham, you admit, held slaves. Who is surprised that Whitefield, with this single fact before him, could not believe slavery to be a sin? Yet if your definition of slavery be correct, holy Abraham lived all his life in the commission of one of the most aggravated crimes against God and man which can be conceived. His life was spent in outraging the rights of hundreds of human beings, as moral, intellectual, immortal, fallen creatures, and in violating their relations as parents and children, and husbands and wives. And God not only connived at this appalling iniquity, but, in the covenant of circumcision made with Abraham, expressly mentions it, and confirms the patriarch in it, speaking of those 'bought with his money,' and requiring him to circumcise them. Why, at the very first blush, every Christian will cry out against this statement. To this, however, you must come, or yield your position; and this is only the first utterly incredible and monstrous corollary involved in the assertion that slavery is essentially and always 'a sin of appalling magnitude.'"

Slavery among the Hebrews, however, was not left merely to a tacit or implied sanction. It was thus sanctioned by the express legislation of the Most High: "Both thy bondmen and thy bondmaids, which thou shalt have, shall be of the heathen that are round about you; of them shall ye buy bondmen and bondmaids. Moreover, of the children of the strangers that do sojourn among you, of them shall ye buy, and of their families that are with you, which they begat in your land; and they shall be your possession. And ye shall take them as an inheritance for your children after you, to inherit them for a possession; they shall be your bondmen forever." [2] Now these words are so perfectly explicit, that there is no getting around them. Even Dr. Wayland, as we have seen, admits that the authority to take slaves *seems* to be a part of "this original, peculiar," and perhaps "anomalous grant." No wonder it appeared *peculiar* and *anomalous*. The only wonder is, that it did not appear impious and absurd. So it has appeared to some of his co-agitators, who, because they could not agree with Moses, have denied his mission as an inspired teacher, and joined the ranks of infidelity.

Dr. Channing makes very light of this and other passages of Scripture. He sets aside this whole argument from revelation with a few bold strokes of the pen. "In this age of the world," says he, "and amid the light which has been thrown on the true interpretation of the Scriptures, such reasoning hardly deserves notice." Now, even if not for our benefit, we think there are two reasons why such passages as the above were worthy of Dr. Channing's notice. In the first place, if he had condescended to throw the light in his possession on such passages, he might have saved Dr. Wayland, as well as other of his admirers, from the necessity of making the very awkward admission that the Almighty had authorized his chosen people to buy slaves, and hold them as

146

2 *Lev. xxv. 44, 45,* [46]. (*Bledsoe's note.*)

"bondmen forever." He might have enabled them to see through the great difficulty, that God has authorized his people to commit "a sin of appalling magnitude," to perpetrate as "great a crime as can be conceived"; which seems so clearly to be the case, if their views of slavery be correct. Secondly, he might have enabled his followers to espouse the cause of abolition without deserting, as so many of them have openly done, the armies of the living God. For these two reasons, if for no other, we think Dr. Channing owed it to the honor of his cause to notice the passages of Scripture bearing on the subject of slavery.

The Mosaic Institutes not only recognize slavery as lawful; they contain a multitude of minute directions for its regulation. We need not refer to all of them; it will be sufficient for our purpose if we only notice those which establish some of the leading characteristics of slavery among the people of God.

1. Slaves were regarded as property. They were, as we have seen, called a "possession" and an "inheritance." [3] They were even called the "money" of the master. Thus, it is said, "if a man smite his servant or his maid with a rod, and he die under his hand, he shall surely be punished. Notwithstanding, if he continue a day or two, he shall be punished, for he is his money." [4] In one of the ten commandments this right of property is recognized: "Thou shalt not covet thy neighbor's house, thou shalt not covet thy neighbor's wife, nor *his* man-servant, nor *his* maid-servant, nor his ox, nor his ass, nor any thing that is thy neighbor's."

2. They might be sold. This is taken for granted in all those passages in which, for particular reasons, the master is forbidden to sell his slaves. Thus it is declared: "Thou shalt not make merchandise of her, because thou hast humbled her." And still more explicitly: "If a man sell his daughter to be a maid-servant, she shall not go out as the men-servants do. If she please not her master who hath betrothed her to himself, then shall he let her be redeemed: to sell her to a strange nation, he shall have no power, seeing he hath dealt deceitfully with her." [5]

3. The slavery thus expressly sanctioned was hereditary and perpetual: "Ye shall take them as an inheritance for your children after you, to inherit them for a possession; they shall be your bondmen forever." Even the Hebrew servant might, by his own consent, become in certain cases a slave for life: "If thou buy a Hebrew servant, six years shall he serve; and in the seventh shall he go out free for nothing. If he came in by himself, he shall go out by himself: if he were married, then his wife shall go out with him. If his master have given him a wife, and she have borne him sons or daughters, the wife and the children shall be her master's, and he shall go out by himself. And if the servant shall plainly say, I love my master, my wife, and my children; I will not go out free: then his master shall bring him unto the judges: he shall also bring him to the door or unto the door-post, and his master shall bore his ear through with an awl, and *he shall serve him forever.*"

Now it is evident, we think, that the legislator of the Hebrews was not inspired with the sentiments of an abolitionist. The principles of his legislation are, indeed, so diametrically opposed to the political notions of the abolitionist,

147

[3] *Lev. xxv. 44, 45, 46. (Bledsoe's note.)*
[4] *Exod. xxi. 20, 21. (Bledsoe's note.)*
[5] *Exod. xxi. 7, 8. (Bledsoe's note.)*

that the latter is sadly perplexed to dispose of them. While some deny the authority of these principles altogether, and of the very book which contains them, others are content to evade their force by certain ingenious devices of their own. We shall now proceed to examine some of the more remarkable of these cunningly-devised fables.

It is admitted by the inventors of these devices, that God expressly permitted his chosen people to buy and hold slaves. Yet Dr. Wayland, by whom this admission is made, has endeavored to weaken the force of it by alleging that God has been pleased to enlighten our race progressively. If, he argues, the institution of slavery among His people appears so very "peculiar and anomalous," this is because He did not choose to make known His whole mind on the subject. He withheld a portion of it from His people, and allowed them, by express grant, to hold slaves until the fuller revelation of His will should blaze upon the world. Such is, perhaps, the most plausible defense which an abolitionist could possibly set up against the light of revelation.

But to what does it amount? If the views of Dr. Wayland and his followers, respecting slavery, be correct, it amounts to this: The Almighty has said to his people, you may commit "a sin of appalling magnitude"; you may perpetrate "as great an evil as can be conceived"; you may persist in a practice which consists in "outraging the rights" of your fellow-men, and in "crushing their intellectual and moral" nature. They have a natural, inherent, and inalienable right to liberty as well as yourselves, but yet you may make slaves of them, and they may be your bondmen forever. In one word, *you*, my chosen people, may degrade "rational, accountable, and immortal beings" to the "rank of brutes." Such, if we may believe Dr. Wayland, is the first stage in the divine enlightenment of the human race! It consists in making known a part of God's mind, not against the monstrous iniquity of slavery, but in its favor! It is the utterance, not of a partial truth, but of a monstrous falsehood! It is the revelation of his will, not against sin, but in favor of as great a sin "as can be conceived." Now, we may fearlessly ask if the cause which is reduced to the necessity of resorting to such a defense may not be pronounced desperate indeed, and unspeakably forlorn?

It is alleged that polygamy and divorce, as well as slavery, are permitted and regulated in the Old Testament. This, we reply, proves, in regard to polygamy and divorce, exactly what it proves in regard to slavery—namely, that neither is in itself sinful, that neither is *always* and *everywhere* sinful. In other words, it proves that neither polygamy nor divorce, as permitted in the Old Testament, is *"malum in se,"* is inconsistent with the eternal and unchangeable principles of right. They are forbidden in the New Testament, not because they are in themselves absolutely and immutably wrong, but because they are inconsistent with the best interests of society; especially in civilized and Christian communities. If they had been wrong in themselves, they never could have been permitted by a holy God, who is of purer eyes than to behold iniquity, except with infinite abhorrence.

148

Again, it is contended by Dr. Wayland that "Moses intended to abolish slavery," because he forbade the Jews "to deliver up a fugitive slave." The words are these: "Thou shalt not deliver unto his master the servant that is escaped from his master unto thee: He shall dwell with thee, even among you, in that place which he shall choose in one of the gates where it liketh him best: thou shalt not oppress him." [6] "This precept, I think," says Dr. Wayland, "clearly shows that Moses intended to abolish slavery. How could slavery long continue in a country where every one was forbidden to deliver up a fugitive slave? How different would be the condition of slaves, and how soon would slavery itself cease, were this the law of compulsory bondage among us!"

The above passage of Scripture is a precious morsel with those who are opposed to a fugitive slave law. A petition from Albany, New York, from the enlightened seat of empire of the Empire State itself, signed, if we recollect right, by one hundred and fifty persons, was presented to the United States Senate by Mr. Seward, praying that no bill in relation to fugitive slaves might be passed, which should not contain that passage. Whether Mr. Seward was enlightened by his constituents, or whether he made the discovery for himself, it is certain that he holds an act for the reclamation of fugitive slaves to be "contrary to the divine law." It is certain that he agrees with his constituents, who, in the petition referred to, pronounced every such act "immoral," and contrary to the law of God. But let us look at this passage a little, and see if these abolitionists, who thus plant themselves so confidently upon "a higher law," even upon "the divine law" itself, be not as hasty and rash in their interpretation of this law as they are accustomed to be in their judgment respecting the most universal and long-established institutions of human society.

In the first place, if their interpretation be correct, we are at once met by a very serious difficulty. For we are required to believe that one passage of Scripture grants an "authority to take slaves," while another passage is designed to annul this authority. We are required to believe that, in one portion of the divine law, the right of the master to hold his slaves as "bondmen" is recognized, while another part of the same law denies the existence of such right. In fine, we are required to believe that the legislator of the Jews intended, in one and the same code, both to establish and to abolish slavery; that with one hand he struck down the very right and institution which he had set up with the other. How Dr. Channing and Mr. Sumner would have disposed of this difficulty we know full well, for they carry within their own bosoms a higher law than this higher law itself. But how Dr. Wayland, as an enlightened member of the good old orthodox Baptist Church, with whom the Scripture is really and in truth the inspired word of God, would have disposed of it, we are at some loss to conceive.

We labor under no such difficulty. The words in question do not relate to slaves owned by Hebrew masters. They relate to those slaves only who should escape from heathen masters, and seek an asylum among the people of God. "The first inquiry of course is," says a learned divine,[7] "in regard to those very words, 'Where does his master live?' Among the Hebrews, or among foreigners? The language of the passage fully develops this and answers the question. 'He has escaped from his master unto the Hebrews; (the text says—*thee, i.e. Israel;*) *he shall dwell with thee, even among you . . . in one of thy gates.*' Of course, then, he is an *immigrant*, and did *not dwell among them* before his flight. If he

149

---

[6] *Deut. xxiii. 15, 16. (Bledsoe's note.)*
[7] *Moses Stewart, a divine of Massachusetts, who had devoted a long and laborious life to the interpretation of Scripture, and who was by no means a friend to the institution of slavery. (Bledsoe's note.)*

had been a Hebrew servant, belonging to a Hebrew, the whole face of the thing would be changed. Restoration, or restitution, if we may judge by the tenor of other property-laws among the Hebrews, would have surely been enjoined. But, be that as it may, the language of the text puts it beyond a doubt that the serv-ant is a *foreigner*, and has fled from a *heathen master*. This entirely changes the complexion of the case. The Hebrews were God's chosen people, and were the only nation on earth which worshipped the only living and true God . . . In case a slave escaped from them (the heathen) and came to the Hebrews, two things were to be taken into consideration, according to the views of the Jewish legislator. The first was that the treatment of slaves among the heathen was far more severe and rigorous than it could lawfully be under the Mosaic law. The heathen master possessed the power of life and death, of scourging or imprison-ing, or putting to excessive toil, even to any extent that he pleased. Not so among the Hebrews. *Humanity* pleaded there for the protection of the fugitive. The second and most important consideration was, that only among the Hebrews could the fugitive slave come to the knowledge and worship of the only living and true God."

Now this view of the passage in question harmonizes one portion of Scrip-ture with another, and removes every difficulty. It shows, too, how greatly the abolitionists have deceived themselves in their rash and blind appeal to "the divine law" in question. "The reason of the law," says my Lord Coke, "is the law." It is applicable to those cases, and to those cases only, which come within the reason of the law. Hence, if it be a fact, and if our Northern brethren really believe that we are sunk in the darkness of heathen idolatry, while the light of the true religion is with them alone, why, then, we admit that the reason and principle of the divine law in question is in their favor. Then we admit that the return of our fugitive slaves is "contrary to the divine law." But if we are not heathen idolaters, if the God of the Hebrews be also the God of Southern mas-ters, then the Northern States do not violate the precept in question—they only discharge a solemn constitutional obligation—in delivering up our "fugitives from labor.". . . (*1856*)

GEORGE FITZHUGH

1806–1881

150

George Fitzhugh was born in Prince William County, Virginia, on November 4, 1806. When he was six years old, his family moved to a home near Alex-andria, where he attended a "field school." He later studied law for a brief period, married in 1829, and finally settled in Port Royal. Sometime between

1854 and 1856, he traveled through the Northern states, where he probably met Harriet Beecher Stowe; his visit to the North tended to reconfirm his pro-slavery views. Fitzhugh began his career as author with the publication of *Sociology for the South; or, the Failure of Free Society* (1854). In 1856 he challenged the abolitionist William Lloyd Garrison to a public debate on the slavery issue. His *Cannibals All! or, Slaves Without Masters* appeared during the following year.

As a leader of the Southern school of pro-slavery writers, Fitzhugh is distinguished mainly by his attacks upon the ideologies of Northern industrialists and abolitionists. It was his belief that the patriarchal system of economy in the South was a solution to the evils of a capitalistic society based upon the principles of laissez faire. He saw the Southern planter class as the best possible source of leaders for the country. Slavery was a necessary universal principle, he argued; and primogeniture and entail, by setting up a more powerful benevolent aristocracy, could best bring about the greatest good for the greatest number. Fitzhugh also argued that, in order to follow out his principles, all free Negroes in the South should be made slaves again. The cannibals in his second book were the Northern Capitalists, the cruel masters of so-called free laborers.

During the period of Reconstruction following the war, Fitzhugh urged Southern tolerance, together with the continuance of a paternalistic economy in the South. He died at the home of one of his children in Huntsville, Texas, on July 29, 1881.

from *Cannibals All! or, Slaves Without Masters*

Chapter 1. The Universal Trade

We are all, North and South, engaged in the White Slave Trade, and he who succeeds best, is esteemed most respectable. It is far more cruel than the Black Slave Trade, because it exacts more of its slaves, and neither protects nor governs them. We boast, that it exacts more, when we say, "that the *profits* made from employing free labor are greater than those from slave labor." The profits, made from free labor, are the amount of the products of such labor, which the employer, by means of the command which capital or skill gives him, takes away, exacts or "exploitates" from the free laborer. The profits of slave labor are that portion of the products of such labor which the power of the master enables him to appropriate. These profits are less, because the master allows the slave to retain a larger share of the results of his own labor, than do the employers of free labor. But we not only boast that the White Slave Trade is more exacting and fraudulent (in fact, though not in intention) than Black Slavery; but we also boast, that it is more cruel, in leaving the laborer to take care of himself and family out of the pittance which skill or capital have allowed him to retain. When the day's labor is ended, he is free, but is overburdened with the cares of family and household, which make his freedom an empty and delusive mockery. But his employer is really free, and may enjoy the profits made by others' labor, without a care, or a trouble, as to their well-

151

being. The negro slave is free, too, when the labors of the day are over, and free in mind as well as body; for the master provides food, raiment, house, fuel, and everything else necessary to the physical well-being of himself and family. The master's labors commence just when the slave's end. No wonder men should prefer white slavery to capital, to negro slavery, since it is more profitable, and is free from all the cares and labors of black slave-holding.

Now, reader, if you wish to know yourself—to "descant on your own deformity"—read on. But if you would cherish self-conceit, self-esteem, or self-appreciation, throw down our book; for we will dispel illusions which have promoted your happiness, and shew you that what you have considered and practiced as virtue, is little better than moral Cannibalism. But you will find yourself in numerous and respectable company; for all good and respectable people are "Cannibals all," who do not labor, or who are successfully trying to live without labor, on the unrequited labor of other people:—Whilst low, bad, and disreputable people, are those who labor to support themselves, and to support said respectable people besides. Throwing the negro slaves out of the account, and society is divided in Christendom into four classes: The rich, or independent respectable people, who live well and labor not at all; the professional and skillful respectable people, who do a little light work, for enormous wages; the poor hard-working people, who support every body, and starve themselves; and the poor thieves, swindlers and sturdy beggars, who live like gentlemen, without labor, on the labor of other people. The gentlemen exploitate, which being done on a large scale, and requiring a great many victims, is highly respectable—whilst the rogues and beggars take so little from others, that they fare little better than those who labor.

But, reader, we do not wish to fire into the flock. "Thou art the man!" You are a Cannibal! and if a successful one, pride yourself on the number of your victims, quite as much as any Feejee chieftain, who breakfasts, dines and sups on human flesh.—And your conscience smites you, if you have failed to succeed, quite as much as his, when he returns from an unsuccessful foray.

Probably, you are a lawyer, or a merchant, or a doctor, who have made by your business fifty thousand dollars, and retired to live on your capital. But, mark! not to spend your capital. That would be vulgar, disreputable, criminal. That would be, to live by your own labor; for your capital is your amassed labor. That would be, to do as common working men do; for they take the pittance which their employers leave them, to live on. They live by labor; for they exchange the results of their own labor for the products of other people's labor. It is, no doubt, an honest, vulgar way of living; but not at all a respectable way. The respectable way of living is, to make other people work for you, and to pay them nothing for so doing—and to have no concern about them after their work is done. Hence, white slave-holding is much more respectable than negro slavery—for the master works nearly as hard for the negro, as he for the master. But you, my virtuous, respectable reader, exact three thousand dollars per annum from white labor, (for your income is the product of white labor) and make not one cent of return in any form. You retain your capital, and never labor, and yet live in luxury on the labor of others. Capital commands labor, as the master does the slave. Neither pays for labor; but the master permits the slave to retain a larger allowance from the proceeds of his own labor,

152

and hence "free labor is cheaper than slave labor." You, with the command over labor which your capital gives you, are a slave owner—a master, without the obligations of a master. They who work for you, who create your income, are slaves, without the rights of slaves. Slaves without a master! Whilst you were engaged in amassing your capital, in seeking to become independent, you were in the White Slave Trade. To become independent, is to be able to make other people support you, without being obliged to labor for *them*. Now, what man in society is not seeking to attain this situation? He who attains it, is a slave owner, in the worst sense. He who is in pursuit of it, is engaged in the slave trade. You, reader, belong to the one or other class. The men without property, in free society, are theoretically in a worse condition than slaves. Practically, their condition corresponds with this theory, as history and statistics every where demonstrate. The capitalists, in free society, live in ten times the luxury and show that Southern masters do, because the slaves to capital work harder and cost less, than negro slaves.

The negro slaves of the South are the happiest, and, in some sense, the freest people in the world. The children and the aged and infirm work not at all, and yet have all the comforts and necessaries of life provided for them. They enjoy liberty, because they are oppressed neither by care nor labor. The women do little hard work, and are protected from the despotism of their husbands by their masters. The negro men and stout boys work, on the average, in good weather, not more than nine hours a day. The balance of their time is spent in perfect abandon. Besides, they have their Sabbaths and holidays. White men, with so much of license and liberty, would die of ennui; but negroes luxuriate in corporeal and mental repose. With their faces upturned to the sun, they can sleep at any hour; and quiet sleep is the greatest of human enjoyments. "Blessed be the man who invented sleep." 'Tis happiness in itself—and results from contentment with the present, and confident assurance of the future. We do not know whether free laborers ever sleep. They are fools to do so; for whilst they sleep, the wily and watchful capitalist is devising means to ensnare and exploitate them. The free laborer must work or starve. He is more of a slave than the negro, because he works longer and harder for less allowance than the slave, and has no holiday, because the cares of life with him begin when its labors end. He has no liberty, and not a single right. We know, 'tis often said, air and water, are common property, which all have equal right to participate and enjoy; but this is utterly false. The appropriation of the lands carries with it the appropriation of all on or above the lands, *usque ad cœlum, aut ad inferos.*[1] A man cannot breathe the air, without a place to breathe it from, and all places are appropriated. All water is private property "to the middle of the stream," except the ocean, and that is not fit to drink.

Free laborers have not a thousandth part of the rights and liberties of negro slaves. Indeed, they have not a single right or a single liberty, unless it be the right or liberty to die. But the reader may think that he and other capitalists and employers are freer than negro slaves. Your capital would soon vanish, if you dared indulge in the liberty and abandon of negroes. You hold your wealth and position by the tenure of constant watchfulness, care and circumspection. You never labor; but you are never free.

[1] *Even unto heaven, or unto hell.*

153

Where a few own the soil, they have unlimited power over the balance of society, until domestic slavery comes in, to compel them to permit this balance of society to draw a sufficient and comfortable living from "terra mater." Free society, asserts the right of a few to the earth—slavery, maintains that it belongs, in different degrees, to all.

But, reader, well may you follow the slave trade. It is the only trade worth following, and slaves the only property worth owning. All other is worthless, a mere *caput mortuum*,[2] except in so far as it vests the owner with the power to command the labors of others—to enslave them. Give you a palace, ten thousand acres of land, sumptuous clothes, equipage and every other luxury; and with your artificial wants, you are poorer than Robinson Crusoe, or the lowest working man, if you have no slaves to capital, or domestic slaves. Your capital will not bring you an income of a cent, nor supply one of your wants, without labor. Labor is indispensable to give value to property, and if you owned every thing else, and did not own labor, you would be poor. But fifty thousand dollars means, and is, fifty thousand dollars worth of slaves. You can command, without touching on that capital, three thousand dollars' worth of labor per annum. You could do no more were you to buy slaves with it, and then you would be cumbered with the cares of governing and providing for them. You are a slaveholder now, to the amount of fifty thousand dollars, with all the advantages, and none of the cares and responsibilities of a master.

"Property in man" is what all are struggling to obtain. Why should they not be obliged to take care of man, their property, as they do of their horses and their hounds, their cattle and their sheep. Now, under the delusive name of liberty, you work him, "from morn to dewy eve"—from infancy to old age— then turn him out to starve. You treat your horses and hounds better. Capital is a cruel master. The free slave trade, the commonest, yet the cruellest of trades.

Chapter 21. Negro Slavery

Until the lands of America are appropriated by a few, population becomes dense, competition among laborers active, employment uncertain, and wages low, the personal liberty of all the whites will continue to be a blessing. We have vast unsettled territories; population may cease to increase, or increase slowly, as in most countries, and many centuries may elapse before the question will be practically suggested, whether slavery to capital be preferable to slavery to human masters. But the negro has neither energy nor enterprise, and, even in our sparser population, finds, with his improvident habits, that his liberty is a curse to himself, and a greater curse to the society around him. These considerations, and others equally obvious, have induced the South to attempt to defend negro slavery as an exceptional institution, admitting, nay asserting, that slavery, in the general or in the abstract, is morally wrong, and against common right. With singular inconsistency, after making this admission, which admits away the authority of the Bible, of profane history, and of the almost universal practice of mankind—they turn round and attempt to bolster up the cause of negro slavery by these very exploded authorities. If we mean not to repudiate

154

[2] *Death's head; skull.*

all divine, and almost all human authority in favor of slavery, we must vindicate that institution in the abstract.

To insist that a status of society, which has been almost universal, and which is expressly and continually justified by Holy Writ, is its natural, normal, and necessary status, under the ordinary circumstances, is on its face a plausible and probable proposition. To insist on less, is to yield our cause, and to give up our religion; for if white slavery be morally wrong, be a violation of natural rights, the Bible cannot be true. Human and divine authority do seem in the general to concur, in establishing the expediency of having masters and slaves of different races. The nominal servitude of the Jews to each other, in its temporary character, and no doubt in its mild character, more nearly resembled our wardship and apprenticeship, than ordinary domestic slavery. In very many nations of antiquity, and in some of modern times, the law has permitted the native citizens to become slaves to each other. But few take advantage of such laws; and the infrequency of the practice, establishes the general truth that master and slave should be of different national descent. In some respects, the wider the difference the better, as the slave will feel less mortified by his position. In other respects, it may be that too wide a difference hardens the hearts and brutalizes the feelings of both master and slave. The civilized man hates the savage, and the savage returns the hatred with interest. Hence, West India slavery, of newly caught negroes, is not a very humane, affectionate or civilizing institution. Virginia negroes have become moral and intelligent. They love their master and his family, and the attachment is reciprocated. Still, we like the idle, but intelligent house-servants, better than the hard-used, but stupid out-hands; and we like the mulatto better than the negro; yet the negro is generally more affectionate, contented and faithful.

The world at large looks on negro slavery as much the worst form of slavery; because it is only acquainted with West India slavery. Abolition never arose till negro slavery was instituted; and now abolition is only directed against negro slavery. There is no philanthropic crusade attempting to set free the white slaves of Eastern Europe and of Asia. The world, then, is prepared for the defense of slavery in the abstract—it is prejudiced only against negro slavery. These prejudices were in their origin well founded. The Slave Trade, the horrors of the Middle Passage, and West India slavery, were enough to rouse the most torpid philanthropy.

But our Southern slavery has become a benign and protective institution, and our negroes are confessedly better off than any free laboring population in the world.

How can we contend that white slavery is wrong, whilst all the great body of free laborers are starving; and slaves, white or black, throughout the world, are enjoying comfort?

We write in the cause of Truth and Humanity, and will not play the advocate for master or for slave.

The aversion to negroes, the antipathy of race, is much greater at the North than at the South; and it is very probable that this antipathy to the person of the negro, is confounded with or generates hatred of the institution with which he is usually connected. Hatred of slavery is very generally little more than hatred of negroes.

155

There is one strong argument in favor of negro slavery over all other slavery: that he, being unfitted for the mechanic arts, for trade, and all skillful pursuits, leaves those pursuits to be carried on by the whites; and does not bring all industry into disrepute, as in Greece and Rome, where the slaves were not only the artists and mechanics, but also the merchants.

Whilst, as a general and abstract question, negro slavery has no other claims over other forms of slavery, except that from inferiority, or rather peculiarity, of race, almost all negroes require masters, whilst only the children, the women, the very weak, poor, and ignorant, &c., among the whites, need some protective and governing relation of this kind; yet as a subject of temporary, but world-wide importance, negro slavery has become the most necessary of all human institutions.

The African slave trade to America commenced three centuries and a half since.[3] By the time of the American Revolution, the supply of slaves had exceeded the demand for slave labor, and the slave-holders, to get rid of a burden, and to prevent the increase of a nuisance, became violent opponents of the slave trade, and many of them abolitionists. New England, Bristol, and Liverpool, who reaped the profits of the trade, without suffering from the nuisance, stood out for a long time against its abolition. Finally, laws and treaties were made, and fleets fitted out to abolish it; and after a while, the slaves of most of South America, of the West Indies, and of Mexico were liberated. In the meantime, cotton, rice, sugar, coffee, tobacco, and other products of slave labor, came into universal use as necessaries of life. The population of Western Europe, sustained and stimulated by those products, was trebled, and that of the North increased ten-fold. The products of slave labor became scarce and dear, and famines frequent. Now, it is obvious, that to emancipate all the negroes would be to starve Western Europe and our North. Not to extend and increase negro slavery, *pari passu*, with the extension and multiplication of free society, will produce much suffering. If all South America, Mexico, the West Indies, and our Union south of Mason and Dixon's line, of the Ohio and Missouri, were slave-holding, slave products would be abundant and cheap in free society; and their market for their merchandise, manufactures, commerce, &c., illimitable. Free white laborers might live in comfort and luxury on light work, but for the exacting and greedy landlords, bosses and other capitalists.

We must confess, that overstock the world as you will with comforts and with luxuries, we do not see how to make capital relax its monopoly—how to do aught but tantalize the hireling. Capital, irresponsible capital, begets, and ever will beget, the "immedicabile vulnus" [4] of so-called Free Society. It invades every recess of domestic life, infects its food, its clothing, its drink, its very atmosphere, and pursues the hireling, from the hovel to the poor-house, the prison and the grave. Do what he will, go where he will, capital pursues and persecutes him. "Hæret lateri lethalis arundo!" [5]

Capital supports and protects the domestic slave; taxes, oppresses and persecutes the free laborer.

156

[3] *An error in fact. Slaves were first brought to Virginia in 1619, about two centuries and a half before Fitzhugh wrote this selection.*
[4] *Immedicable wound.*
[5] *The deadly shaft sticks in his side.*

Chapter 27. Slavery—Its Effects on the Free

Beaten at every other quarter, we learn that a distinguished writer at the North, is about to be put forward by the Abolitionists, to prove that the influence of slavery is deleterious on the whites who own no slaves.

Now, at first view it elevates those whites; for it makes them not the bottom of society, as at the North—not the menials, the hired day laborer, the work scavengers and scullions—but privileged citizens, like Greek and Roman citizens, with a numerous class far beneath them. In slave society, one white man does not lord it over another; for all are equal in privilege, if not in wealth; and the poorest would not become a menial—hold your horse, and then extend his hand or his hat for a gratuity, were you to proffer him the wealth of the Indies. The menial, the exposed and laborious, and the disgraceful occupations, are all filled by slaves. But filled they must be by some one, and in free society, half of its members are employed in occupations that are not considered or treated as respectable. Our slaves till the land, do the coarse and hard labor on our roads and canals, sweep our streets, cook our food, brush our boots, wait on our tables, hold our horses, do all hard work, and fill all menial offices. Your freemen at the North do the same work and fill the same offices. The only difference is, we love our slaves, and we are ready to defend, assist and protect them; you hate and fear your white servants, and never fail, as a moral duty, to screw down their wages to the lowest, and to starve their families, if possible, as evidence of your thrift, economy and management—the only English and Yankee virtues.

In free society, miscalled freemen fulfill all the offices of slaves for less wages than slaves, and are infinitely less liked and cared for by their superiors than slaves. Does this elevate them and render them happy?

The trades, the professions, the occupations that pay well, and whose work is light, is reserved for freemen in slave society. Does this depress them?

The doctor, the lawyer, the mechanic, the dentist, the merchant, the overseer, every trade and profession, in fact, live from the proceeds of slave labor at the South. They divide the profits with the owner of the slaves. He has nothing to pay them except what his slaves make. But you Yankees and Englishmen more than divide the profits—you take the lion's share. You make more money from our cotton, and tobacco, and sugar, and indigo, and wheat, and corn, and rice, than we make ourselves. You live by slave labor—would perish without it—yet you abuse it. Cut off England and New England from the South American, East and West India and our markets, from which to buy their food, and in which to sell their manufactures, and they would starve at once. You live by our slave labor. It elevates your whites as well as ours, by confining them, in a great degree, to skillful, well-paying, light and intellectual employments—and it feeds and clothes them. Abolish slavery, and you will suffer vastly more than we, because we have all the lands of the South, and can *command* labor as you do, and a genial soil and climate, that require less labor. But while in the absence of slavery, we could support ourselves, we should cease to support you. We would neither send you food and clothing, nor buy your worse than useless notions. (*1857*)

157

ROBERT E. LEE

1807–1870

Robert Edward Lee, the third son of the celebrated Revolutionary hero, "Light-Horse Harry" Lee, was born in Westmoreland County, Virginia. Because of a series of unsuccessful financial speculations, "Light-Horse Harry" was forced in 1811 to give up "Stratford," the family estate, and move his family to Alexandria, Virginia. It was in the public schools here that Robert received his early education. A diligent student, young Lee was always near the head of his class, excelling particularly in mathematics. Inspired by his father's brilliant military career and faced with the necessity of getting his higher education without expense to the family, he entered West Point in 1825.

The seventeen years following his graduation were uneventful. He served in various parts of the country as a junior officer in the Engineering Corps, but failed to distinguish himself until the outbreak of the war with Mexico. Then, as an officer under General Winfield Scott in the Vera Cruz expedition, he was decorated and raised in rank for gallantry in action. From 1848 until 1852 Lee served as superintendent at West Point; three years later he was relieved of his duties as staff officer and reassigned to the Second Cavalry. Although he liked the activity of a line command, for a time he considered resigning from the army because of the long absences from home and the ill health of his wife.

Chancing to be in Washington in 1859, Lee was sent to Harpers Ferry to put down the insurrection led by John Brown and was commended for handling the situation with little loss of life or property. Although he was little interested in, or even aware of, the many ramifications of the secessionist controversy, he was unsympathetic toward the general movement. However, when he learned that his state had voted to secede, in April 1861, he resigned from the United States Army (having attained the rank of colonel) and accepted command of the Virginia forces. On May 31, 1862, Lee was assigned the leadership of the body of troops which he named "The Army of Northern Virginia." It was at the age of fifty-five, then, and after more than thirty years in the service, that Lee's career as a field general began. For the next thirty-four months, faced by one crisis after another, he demonstrated his military genius to the world. Finally, rather than subject his troops to further privation and needless slaughter, he surrendered to General Grant on April 9, 1865.

From September of that year until his death, Lee served as president of Washington College in Lexington, Virginia. During the bleak days of Recon-

158

struction and "Black Republicanism," he advised all who sought his counsel to submit to authority and become law-abiding citizens of the United States. Though Lee's career as an educator was in every respect meritorious, he is mainly remembered today as a great soldier who lived to the letter the life of a Christian gentleman.

General Order No. 9—
Farewell Address to the Troops

Headquarters Army of Northern Virginia
10th April 1865

After four years of arduous service marked by unsurpassed courage and fortitude the Army of Northern Virginia has been compelled to yield to overwhelming numbers and resources.

I need not tell the survivors of so many hard fought battles, who have remained steadfast to the last, that I have consented to this result from no distrust of them. But feeling that valor and devotion could accomplish nothing that could compensate for the loss that would have accompanied the continuance of the contest, I determined to avoid the useless sacrifice of those whose past services have endeared them to their country.

By the terms of the agreement Officers and men can return to their homes and remain there until exchanged. You will take with you the satisfaction that proceeds from the consciousness of duty faithfully performed and I earnestly pray that a merciful God will extend to you his blessing and protection.

With an unceasing admiration of your constancy and devotion to your country and a grateful remembrance of your kind and generous consideration of myself, I bid you all an affectionate farewell.

R. E. Lee
General

Letters

To Matthew Fontaine Maury

Near Cartersville, Va.
September 8, 1865

My dear Captain: [1] I have just received your letter of the 8th ult. We have certainly not found our form of government all that was anticipated by its original

159

---

[1] *Disgusted with the corruption which characterized the Reconstruction period in the South, many of Lee's former soldiers seriously considered leaving the South and attempting to mend their broken fortunes elsewhere. Whenever possible, Lee exerted his influence to prevent such action, believing that the section needed the assistance and loyalty of her faithful sons now more than ever before. Matthew Fontaine Maury was a great scientist and a former captain in the Confederate Army.*

founders, but that may be partly our effect in expecting too much and partly in the absence of virtue in the people. As long as virtue was dominant in the republic so long was the happiness of the people secure. I can not, however, despair of it yet. I look forward to better days and trust that time and experience, the great teachers of men, under the guidance of an ever-merciful God, may save us from destruction and restore to us the bright hopes and prospects of the past.

The thought of abandoning the country and all that must be left in it is abhorrent to my feelings, and I prefer to struggle for its restoration and share its fate rather than to give up all as lost. I have a great admiration for Mexico. The salubrity of its climate, the fertility of its soil and the magnificence of its scenery possess for me great charms; but I still look with delight upon the mountains of my native state. To remove our people with their domestics to a portion of Mexico which would be favorable to them would be a work of much difficulty. Did they possess the means and could the system of apprenticeship you suggest be established, the United States Government I think would interpose obstacles; and under the circumstances there would be difficulty in persuading the freedmen to emigrate.

Those citizens who can leave the country and others who may be compelled to do so will reap the fruits of your considerate labor; but I shall be very sorry if your presence be lost to Virginia. She has now need for all her sons and can ill afford to spare you. I am very much obliged to you for all you have done for us, and hope your labors in the future may be as efficacious as in the past and that your separation from us may not be permanent.

To G. T. Beauregard

Lexington, Va.
October 3, 1865

My dear General: [1] I have received your letter of the 1st ult. and am very sorry to learn that the papers of yourself and Johnston are lost, or at least beyond your reach, and I hope they may be recovered. Mine never can be, though some may be replaced. . . . I hope both you and Johnston will write the history of your campaigns. Every one should do all in his power to collect and disseminate the truth, in the hope that it may find a place in history and descend to posterity.

I am glad to see no indication in your letter of an intention to leave the country. I think the South requires the aid of her sons now more than at any period of her history. As you ask my purpose, I will state that I have no thought of abandoning her unless compelled to do so.

After the surrender of the Southern armies in April, the revolution in the opinions and feelings of the people seemed so complete and the return of the Southern States into the Union of all the states so inevitable, that it became in my opinion the duty of every citizen, the contest being virtually ended, to cease opposition and place himself in a position to serve the country . . . I need not tell you that true patriotism sometimes requires of men to act exactly contrary

160

[1] *Beauregard was a distinguished Southern general.*

at one period to that which it does at another, and the motive that impels them—the desire to do right—is precisely the same. The circumstances which govern their actions change and their conduct must conform to the new order of things. History is full of illustrations of this. Washington himself is an example: at one time he fought against the French, under Braddock in the service of the King of Great Britain; at another he fought with the French at Yorktown, under the orders of the Continental Congress of America, against the King. He has not been branded by the world with reproach for this, but his course has been applauded.

RICHARD HENRY WILDE

1789–1846

Born in Dublin, Ireland, September 24, 1789, Richard Henry Wilde emigrated with his family to Baltimore in 1797. Following the death of his father several years later, he and his mother moved to Augusta, Georgia, where they ran a general store. At the age of eighteen, Wilde began the study of law; he was admitted to the bar two years later, and became attorney-general of Georgia in 1811. He was elected to Congress five different times and appointed to fill vacancies twice, but after his defeat by the Jacksonian Whigs in 1834, he permanently retired from politics.

Traveling in Europe for five years following 1835, Wilde developed an interest in Italy and soon became an accomplished Italian scholar. This interest is reflected in his *Conjectures and Researches Concerning the Love, Madness, and Imprisonment of Torquato Tasso.* In addition, the Library of Congress has the manuscripts of two other works, both unfinished—"The Life and Writings of Dante" and "Italian Lyric Poets." Wilde was also responsible for discovering a lost portrait of Dante done by Giotto.

About 1842 Wilde moved to New Orleans and became professor of constitutional law at the University of Louisiana, now Tulane University. He died of yellow fever four years later.

Wilde's most famous poem is "The Lament of the Captive," which became the center of a long dispute about plagiarism. Patrick O'Kelly, a vagabond poet of Ireland, claimed that he had written it; and after Anthony Barclay translated the poem into Greek, it was argued that the Greek was authentic and that Wilde had merely done a translation. Wilde's other well-known work, *Hesperia*, existed

161

only in manuscript until 1867, when it was published by his son. A Byronic description of travels in Europe and America written under the pseudonym of Fitzhugh de Lancey, the poem is divided into four cantos: "Florida," "Virginia," "Acadia," and "Louisiana." It is one of the few book-length poems written by a Southern author.

The Lament of the Captive

My life is like the summer rose,
　That opens to the morning sky,
But, ere the shades of evening close,
　Is scattered on the ground—to die!
Yet on the rose's humble bed
The sweetest dews of night are shed,
As if she wept the waste to see—
But none shall weep a tear for me!

My life is like the autumn leaf
　That trembles in the moon's pale ray:
Its hold is frail—its date is brief,
　Restless—and soon to pass away!
Yet, ere that leaf shall fall and fade,
The parent tree will mourn its shade,
The winds bewail the leafless tree—
But none shall breathe a sigh for me!

My life is like the prints which feet
　Have left on Tampa's desert strand;
Soon as the rising tide shall beat,
　All trace will vanish from the sand;
Yet, as if grieving to efface
All vestige of the human race,
On that lone shore loud moans the sea—
But none, alas! shall mourn for me!

(1814? 1815?)

To the Mocking-Bird

Winged mimic of the woods! thou motley fool!
　Who shall thy gay buffoonery describe?
Thine ever-ready notes of ridicule
　Pursue thy fellows still with jest and gibe.
　Wit, sophist, songster, Yorick of thy tribe,

Thou sportive satirist of Nature's school,
　　To thee the palm of scoffing we ascribe.
Arch-mocker and mad Abbot of Misrule!
　　For such thou art by day—but all night long
Thou pourest a soft, sweet, pensive, solemn strain,
　　As if thou didst in this thy moonlight song
Like to the melancholy Jacques complain,
　　Musing on falsehood, folly, vice, and wrong,
And sighing for thy motley coat again.

(Date unknown.)

To Lord Byron

Byron! 'tis thine alone on eagles' pinions,
　　In solitary strength and grandeur soaring,
　　To dazzle and delight all eyes; outpouring
The electric blaze on tyrants and their minions;
Earth, sea, and air, and powers and dominions,
　　Nature, man, time, the universe exploring;
And from the wreck of worlds, thrones, creeds, opinions,
　　Thought, beauty, eloquence, and wisdom storing:
O! how I love and envy thee thy glory,
　　To every age and clime alike belonging;
Link'd by all tongues with every nation's glory,
　　Thou Tacitus of song! whose echoes, thronging
O'er the Atlantic, fill the mountains hoary
　　And forests with the name my verse is wronging.

(1834)

from *Hesperia*

ALLA NOBILLISSIMA DAMA,
LA SIGNORA MARCHESA MANFREDINA DI COSENZA.[1]

It were useless to ask your pardon for these lines, since before you read them the writer will be past the reach of love or anger.

You once advised me to attempt a poem of some length, in hopes that an occupation suitable to my inclinations might divert my inexplicable weariness of life and spirit.

You may remember my telling you some of the difficulties of such an undertaking. Few write well, except from personal experience,—from what they have seen and felt,—and modern life, in America especially, is utterly commonplace.

163

[1] *Apparently nothing is known about this lady except what Wilde says in the poem. Perhaps she was an Italian whom he first met in Washington.*

It wants the objects and events which are essential to poetry,—excludes all romance, and admits but one enthusiasm.

In addition to these inherent obstacles came my own want of invention, and the impossibility of adopting a foreign story, because the scenes and manners to be painted were unknown to me.

You urged me no further. Years have intervened. Perhaps you have forgotten the subject, and supposed it forgotten. It was treasured up, however, like every wish of yours, and though it could not be literally fulfilled, has given birth to the rhymes I send you.

> "Utinam modo dicere possem
> Carmina digna Deæ." [2]

They were written in different lands at distant times; some of them so long since that they are obsolete. They do not constitute a poem, for they have no plan. The charm they had for me will be felt by no one else,—that of recalling the scenes we visited together, or those otherwise associated in my memory with you.

To some of the minor pieces in the notes, I pretend no claim. You will readily guess the places or persons that connect them with yourself. Others, like portions of the text, written before my task assumed the character that changed its destiny, were meant to relieve the monotony of mere description, and supply the want of incident and adventure.

Adopting a somewhat loose and general geographical division of the immense country over which we wandered, my recollections of our travels naturally assumed a fourfold distribution,—FLORIDA, VIRGINIA, ACADIA, and LOUISIANA,— each one being supposed to include a large part of its ancient boundaries.

I have called the whole HESPERIA, for want of a better title. You must not suppose, however, that I mean any invasion of the classical prerogatives of your native, and my adopted country. The word, as you well know, comes from *Hesperus*, a name given to Venus when the star of evening, and signifies a setting, or the West.

The Greeks, therefore, who lived to the eastward of Italy, naturally called it Hesperia. But inasmuch as, since that time, the West has moved westward, the appellation may now without violence be applied to America, especially as an Italian discovered it. Hesperia Maxima might be more precise, to distinguish it from Spain as well as Italy; but the term is equivocal, and might savor of national vanity. We will call it Hesperia Nova if you like.

Ausonia and Italia will still be left to your native land, names beautiful enough for any country on earth, even her who bears them, and whose love and fame (another excuse for my temerity) I have endeavored to blend with America's and yours. If you are still dissatisfied, call my verses what you please. To the "ten thousand rents in her imperial garment," I would not add one more to save all I have ever written from the flames.

164

Intended at first merely to sketch scenes and objects, my rhymes insensibly and involuntarily became the depositary of thoughts inseparable from them in my mind, though always buried in my own bosom:—

[2] *Would that I were able to sing songs worthy of the goddess.*

"Per suo amor m' er io messo
A faticosa impresa assai per tempo,
Tal che s'i' arrivo al desiato porto,
Spero per lei gran tempo
Viver, quand' altri mi terra per morto." [3]

Considering the time and manner of their utterance, my words surely cannot wound the most scrupulous delicacy, since the sentiment they indicate reaches you only from the dust. If I err, however, you are mistress of my verses' destiny. There is no other copy in existence. They were written for you alone. When you have read them, their office is fulfilled, and my offence may be expiated by their sacrifice. I have often been on the point of destroying them myself; but the patient labor of so many solitary hours, the only confidant of so many cherished thoughts, had become dear to a distempered fancy, and could not be parted from, while life remained.

Farewell! Forgive my madness, and think of me sometimes as your friend.

F. de L.[4]

Palermo, 18—.

Canto First. Florida

LVII.

Once in the front of empire doomed to feel
The scourge of border war, which o'er thy brow
Flashed its destroying torch and angry steel,
Could thy great founder but behold thee now,
Offspring of Oglethorpe! his generous zeal
Were well repaid: save from the gentle plough,
There is no mark of ravage on thy soil,
Whose riches well reward thy children's toil.

LVIII.

And Georgia! here upon St. Mary's banks
I greet thine ever hospitable shore,
Paying my homage to his name which ranks
Among thy household gods for evermore;
Well did he win a nation's praise and thanks,
Who would not stain his hands with kindred gore,—
They were as children of his heart's desire,
And still they hold him as their country's sire!

LIX.

Thy silver source, St. Mary's stream, is near,—
Those vast morasses which man's foot defy,

165

[3] *For love of you I was put for a long time to an arduous task, so that if I arrive at the desired haven, I hope for your sake that I live a long time, when others consider me dead.*
[4] *Fitzhugh de Lancey, Wilde's pseudonym.*

A labyrinth of sweets, that all the year
Blooms inaccessible save to the eye;
Wherein the enchanted lake and isle appear,
Whose sights, sounds, scents, intoxicate the sky,
And they the loveliest daughters of the sun,
Beauteous and kind, but never to be won!

LX.

Wert thou indeed the refuge of a tribe,
Where all beside were savage,—mild and fair?
Or doth thy witching fable but describe
Man's love, imagination, and despair?
Vain dreams, the sober sage's jest and gibe,
Created by fantastic brains from air!
Or in thy tale might Wisdom's eye discern
The lesson man's vain hope has yet to learn?

LXI.

Into what new Atlantis had been wrought
By Grecian poetry thy thrilling tale,
Of beauties yet unfound, though often sought,
Dangers at which the stoutest heart might quail,
The bright elysium of desiring thought,
The burning wish to win—the fear to fail;
And all that Fancy, with the Muses' aid,
From such a legend might have well portrayed.

LXII.

Lo! the pine forest's endless evergreen,
Whose level waste presents for miles and miles,
Vista on vista, the same sombre scene,
Image of old religion's gloomy piles,
Where slender shaft with pointed arch between,
Nature's dim cloisters and long Gothic aisles,
Speak to the heart in that mysterious voice
Wherewith the spirits of the earth rejoice.

LXIII.

In the deep shadow of this mighty wood,
Where the winds match the ocean with their roar,
There is a sense profound of solitude,
Such as the pathless desert, or sea-shore,
Or island desolate, where ne'er intrude
The steps of man, produces;—it comes o'er
The fancy with a strange, vague dread of ill,
A sad, sublime, cold, soul-subduing thrill.

Canto Fourth. Louisiana

LXXXI.

Where dost thou lie, great Nimrod of the West!
Lord of the wilderness! unhouséd BOONE?
Upon what mountain dost thou take thy rest,
The starry sky thy tent, thy lamp the Moon?
Thou wouldst not sleep with so profound a zest
If thy prophetic dreams could tell how soon
Man and his arts thy forest haunts will spoil
With farms, roads, houses, cities, strife, and toil!

LXXXII.

And where is he, the noble savage,—one
Who, had his nation annals, should not die,—
The native orator that called the Sun
"Father of Colors," blending Newton's eye
With Tully's pictured words?—His goal is won,
And now in hunting-grounds beyond the sky
The "Little Turtle" deer and elk pursues,
Nor dreams his fame inspires the white man's muse.

(*1867*)

EDWARD COOTE PINKNEY

1802–1828

The brief life of Edward Coote Pinkney began in England, where his father, serving on a diplomatic mission, was stationed. Until 1811, when the family returned to Baltimore, young Pinkney attended school in London. His formal education was completed at Baltimore College and St. Mary's College, Maryland.

Pinkney enlisted in the Navy when he was only fourteen and remained in the service for ten years. He spent nearly three years in and around Italy, traveled extensively in American waters, and assisted in a number of campaigns against pirates in the Caribbean. After getting his discharge from the Navy, Pinkney became a lawyer, but scanty records seem to indicate that clients rarely required his attentions. In 1827 he assumed the editorship of *The Marylander,* in which

167

position he asserted himself as a strong supporter of John Quincy Adams and, consequently, as an opponent of Jacksonianism.

In all three of his professions, Pinkney revealed a colorful, impetuous personality. Indeed, he seems almost a caricature of the dueling young Southerner of the pre-Civil War South. There is a legend that when Pinkney was in Mexico seeking a position in Commodore Porter's Mexican Navy, he was forced to leave the country after having killed an officer in a duel. In another instance, he posted the non-dueling John Neal as a coward because the latter had allegedly insulted his father. And as an editor, he is said to have journeyed to Philadelphia to pursue in person a duel that he had been conducting through the press. In spite of the aura which has surrounded Pinkney, however, it is unlikely (owing to legal intervention and refusals) that he ever fought an actual duel. He died on April 11, 1828, as a result of what his obituary called "an affection of the liver."

Extremely little of the American or Southern scene is to be found in Pinkney's poems. His aristocratic environment and temperament were determining factors that led him to ignore the New England Puritan tradition and to write, instead, love lyrics reminiscent of seventeenth-century English poetry. Byronic and other romantic influences are discernible in many of his poems, but his European romanticism went little further than phraseology. His lyrics are distinguished by words chosen from the romantics, by conceits and elaborate figures in the fashion of Donne and the metaphysical poets, and by love songs in the manner of Lovelace and Carew. Like the Cavaliers, Pinkney published no complete, sustained work (he always thought of the Byronic love poem, *Rodolph* [1825], as a fragment), but the beauty of his short lyrics was sufficient to draw the comment from the admiring Edgar Allan Poe that Pinkney was "the first of American lyrists."

Serenade

Look out upon the stars, my love,
And shame them with thine eyes,
On which, than on the lights above,
There hang more destinies.
Night's beauty is the harmony
Of blending shades and light;
Then, Lady, up,—look out, and be
A sister to the night!—

Sleep not!—thine image wakes for aye,
Within my watching breast:
Sleep not!—from her soft sleep should fly,
Who robs all hearts of rest.
Nay, Lady, from thy slumbers break,
And make this darkness gay,
With looks whose brightness well might make
Of darker nights a day.

(*1823–1825*)

168

On Parting

Alas! our pleasant moments fly
  On rapid wings away,
While those recorded with a sigh,
  Mock us by long delay.

Time,—envious time,—loves not to be
  In company with mirth,
But makes malignant pause to see
  The work of pain on earth.

(1823–1825)

A Health

I fill this cup to one made up of loveliness alone,
A woman, of her gentle sex the seeming paragon;
To whom the better elements and kindly stars have given
A form so fair, that, like the air, 'tis less of earth than heaven.

Her every tone is music's own, like those of morning birds,
And something more than melody dwells ever in her words;
The coinage of her heart are they, and from her lips each flows
As one may see the burthened bee forth issue from the rose.

Affections are as thoughts to her, the measures of her hours;
Her feelings have the fragrancy, the freshness, of young flowers;
And lovely passions, changing oft, so fill her, she appears
The image of themselves by turns,—the idol of past years!

Of her bright face one glance will trace a picture on the brain,
And of her voice in echoing hearts a sound must long remain,
But memory such as mine of her so very much endears,
When death is nigh my latest sigh will not be life's but hers.

I fill this cup to one made up of loveliness alone,
A woman, of her gentle sex the seeming paragon—
Her health! and would on earth there stood some more of such a frame,
That life might be all poetry, and weariness a name.

(1824–1825)

The Widow's Song

I burn no incense, hang no wreath,
  On this, thine early tomb;
Such cannot cheer the place of death,
  But only mock its gloom.
Here odorous smoke and breathing flower
  No grateful influence shed;

169

They lose their perfume and their power,
  When offered to the dead.

And if, as is the Afghaun's creed,
  The spirit may return,
A disembodied sense to feed,
  On fragrance, near its urn—
It is enough, that she, whom thou
  Did'st love in living years,
Sits desolate beside it now,
  And falls these heavy tears.

(1825)

The Voyager's Song

"A tradition prevailed among the natives of Puerto Rico, that in the Isle of Bimini, one of the Lucayos, there was a fountain of such wonderful virtue, as to renew the youth and recall the vigor of every person who bathed in its salutary waters. In hopes of finding this grand restorative, Ponce de Leon and his followers, ranged through the islands, searching with fruitless solicitude for the fountain, which was the chief object of the expedition."

Robertson's History of America

I.

Sound trumpets, ho!—weigh anchor—loosen sail—
The seaward flying banners chide delay;
As if 'twere heaven that breathes this kindly gale,
Our life-like bark beneath it speeds away.
Flit we, a gliding dream, with troublous motion,
Across the slumbers of uneasy ocean;
And furl our canvass by a happier land,
So fraught with emanations from the sun,
That potable gold streams through the sand
  Where element should run.

II.

Onward, my friends, to that bright, florid isle,
The jewel of a smooth and silver sea,
With springs on which perennial summers smile
A power of causing immortality.
For Bimini;—in its enchanted ground,
The hallowed fountains we would seek, are found;
Bathed in the waters of those mystic wells,
The frame starts up in renovated truth,
And, freed from Time's deforming spells,
  Resumes its proper youth.

170

III.

Hail, better birth!—once more my feelings all
A graven image to themselves shall make,
And, placed upon my heart for pedestal,
That glorious idol long will keep awake
Their natural religion, nor be cast
To earth by Age, the great Iconoclast.
As from Gadara's founts they once could come,
Charm-called, from these Love's genii shall arise,
And build their perdurable home,
    Miranda, in thine eyes.

IV.

By Nature wisely gifted, not destroyed
With golden presents, like the Roman maid,—
A sublunary paradise enjoyed,
Shall teach thee bliss incapable of shade;—
An Eden ours, nor angry gods, nor men,
Nor star-clad Fates, can take from us again.
Superior to animal decay,
Sun of that perfect heaven, thou'lt calmly see
Stag, raven, phenix, drop away
    With *human* transiency.

V.

Thus rich in being,—beautiful,—adored,
Fear not exhausting pleasure's precious mine;
The wondrous waters we approach, when poured
On passion's lees, supply the wasted wine:
Then be thy bosom's tenant prodigal,
And confident of termless carnival.
Like idle yellow leaves afloat on time,
Let others lapse to death's pacific sea,—
We'll fade nor fall, but sport sublime
    In green eternity.

VI.

The envious years, which steal our pleasures, thou
May'st call at once, like magic memory, back,
And, as they pass o'er thine unwithering brow,
Efface their footsteps ere they form a track.
Thy bloom with wilful weeping never stain,
Perpetual life must not belong to pain.
For me,—this world hath not yet been a place
Conscious of joys so great as will be mine,
Because the light has kissed no face
    Forever fair as thine.

(1825)

171

Song

We break the glass, whose sacred wine
  To some beloved health we drain,
Lest future pledges, less divine,
  Should e'er the hallowed toy profane;
And thus I broke a heart, that poured
  Its tide of feelings out to thee,
In draughts, by after-times deplored,
  Yet dear to memory.

But still the old empassioned ways
  And habits of my mind remain,
And still unhappy light displays
  Thine image chambered in my brain,
And still it looks as when the hours
  Went by like flights of singing birds,
Or that soft chain of spoken flowers,
  And airy gems, thy words.

                  (1825)

A Picture Song

How may this little tablet feign the features of a face,
Which o'er-informs with loveliness its proper share of space;
Or human hands on ivory enable us to see
The charms, that all must wonder at, thou work of Gods, in thee!

But yet, methinks, that sunny smile familiar stories tells,
And I should know those placid eyes, two shaded crystal wells;
Nor can my soul, the limner's art attesting with a sigh,
Forget the blood, that decked thy cheek, as rosy clouds the sky.

They could not semble what thou art, more excellent than fair,
As soft as sleep or pity is, and pure as mountain-air;
But here are common, earthly hues, to such an aspect wrought,
That none, save thine, can seem so like the beautiful of thought.

The song I sing, thy likeness like, is painful mimicry
Of something better, which is now a memory to me,
Who have upon life's frozen sea arrived the icy spot,
Where men's magnetic feelings show their guiding task forgot.

The sportive hopes, that used to chase their shifting shadows on,
Like children playing in the sun, are gone—forever gone;

172

And on a careless, sullen peace, my double-fronted mind,
Like Janus when his gates were shut, looks forward and behind.

Apollo placed his harp, of old, awhile upon a stone,
Which has resounded since, when struck, a breaking harp-string's tone;
And thus my heart, though wholly now from early softness free,
If touched, will yield the music yet, it first received of thee.

(1825)

Evergreens

To ———

When Summer's sunny hues adorn
   Sky, forest, hill and meadow,
The foliage of the evergreens,
   In contrast, seems a shadow.

But when the tints of Autumn have
   Their sober reign asserted,
The landscape that cold shadow shows,
   Into a light converted.

Thus thoughts that frown upon our mirth
   Will smile upon our sorrow,
And many dark fears of to-day
   May be bright hopes to-morrow.

And thine unfading image thus
   Shall often cheer my sadness,
Though now its constant looks reprove
   A momentary gladness.

(1825)

Song

Those starry eyes, those starry eyes,
   Those eyes that used to be
Unto my heart, as beacon-lights
   To pilgrims of the sea!—

I see them yet, I see them yet,
   Though long since quenched and gone—
I could not live enlumined by
   The common sun alone.

173

> Could they seem thus, could they seem thus,
>   If but a memory?—
>   Ah, yes! upon this wintry earth,
>   They burn no more for me.
>
> (1825)

THOMAS HOLLEY CHIVERS

1809–1858

The son of a plantation owner, Thomas Holley Chivers was born in Washington, Georgia. Before he was twenty, he entered into a marriage of which little is known. It has been proved only by the contents of his poems and by his will, in which he disinherited his first wife and daughter. Apparently Chivers' wife left him after he had been slandered by her friends; in any case, the marriage ended in divorce. Disillusioned, Chivers fled to Transylvania University at Lexington, Kentucky, where in 1830 he received an M.D. degree with distinction. In 1832 he published an autobiographical collection of eighteen poems, mostly about his unfortunate marriage—*The Path of Sorrow, or the Lament of Youth: A Poem.* This was followed in 1834 by *Conrad and Eudora; or, the Death of Alonzo,* a drama based upon the famous Sharpe-Beauchamp murder in Kentucky.

Between the years 1832 and 1855, Chivers spent most of his time in New York, though he made occasional trips to the South and twice returned to Washington, Georgia, to spend several years. His second marriage, to sixteen-year-old Harriet Hunt of Massachusetts, occurred on November 21, 1837. Chivers' pro-slavery views were not well received in the North during the fifties, and in 1855 he changed his residence permanently to the South. His strange life and personality made him seem mad to conservative Washingtonians, and in 1856 he moved to Decatur, Georgia, where he remained until his death in 1858.

During his lifetime Chivers published a total of twelve volumes of drama and verse. The most notable of these are *The Lost Pleiad* (1845), a group of poems concerned almost solely with death; *Search After Truth* (1848), an exploration into mysticism and occultism in the fashion of the mid-nineteenth century; *Eonchs of Ruby* (1851), an uneven experiment in poetic technique and sound; and *Virginalia* (1853), the most unusual, interesting, and experimental of his volumes.

The publication of *Eonchs of Ruby* projected Chivers into a controversy

174

about plagiarism (which has lasted nearly a hundred years), centering around his work and that of Poe. Chivers was a friend of Poe, and like most of Poe's friends he had had his difficulties in the relationship. Poe wanted loans and support for magazines, was often a severe critic of his friend, and was heavily given to drinking. On the other hand, he also had praise for Chivers, and the Georgian poet at one time felt kindly enough disposed toward Poe to start a biography of him in refutation of the slurs made by Rufus Wilmot Griswold. Nevertheless, when Chivers was accused by his critics of being the plagiarist, he retorted with the accusation that all the thieving had been done by Poe. No proof has ever been advanced to clear or convict either poet. Most of the problem, if not all, is to be explained by the strong influence each man had on the other, the similarity of their artistic tastes, and the lengthy correspondence conducted between the two.

The two important characteristics of Chivers stressed by S. Foster Damon in his biography, *Thomas Holley Chivers: Friend of Poe* (New York, 1930), reveal the similarity between his poetic temperament and that of Poe: "He endeavored to express subtle states of mind by a series of words (often his own invention) and of images, the surface meanings of which are subordinate to the general hypnotic effect. . . . Chivers also tried to build poems out of pure sound, with results that are surprisingly modern."

To Allegra Florence in Heaven [1]

When thy soft round form was lying
On the bed where thou wert sighing,
I could not believe thee dying,
   Till thy angel-soul had fled;
For no sickness gave me warning,
Rosy health thy cheeks adorning—
Till that hope-destroying morning,
   When my precious child lay dead!

Now, thy white shroud covers slightly
Thy pale limbs, which were so sprightly,
While thy snow-white arms lie lightly
   On thy soul-abandoned breast;
As the dark blood faintly lingers
In thy pale, cold, lily fingers,
Thou, the sweetest of Heaven's singers!
   Just above thy heart at rest!

Yes, thy sprightly form is crowded
In thy coffin, all enshrouded,
Like the young Moon, half enclouded,
   On the first night of her birth;

[1] *An elegy to Chivers' daughter, who died on October 18, 1842.*

175

And, as down she sinks when westing,
Of her smiles the Night divesting—
In my fond arms gently resting,
   Shall thy beauty to the earth!

Like some snow-white cloud just under
Heaven, some breeze has torn asunder,
Which discloses, to our wonder,
   Far beyond, the tranquil skies;
Lay thy pale, cold lids, half closing,
(While in death's cold arms reposing,
Thy dear seraph form seemed dozing—)
   On thy violet-colored eyes.

For thy soft blue eyes were tender
As an angel's, full of splendor,
And, like skies to earth, did render
   Unto me divine delight;
Like two violets in the morning
Bathed in sunny dews, adorning
One white lily-bed, while scorning
   All the rest, however bright.

Some fair Flower, which loves to flourish
As the Earth desires to nourish
On her breast, while it doth perish,
   And will barren look when gone;
So, my soul did joy in giving
Thee what thine was glad receiving
From me, ever more left grieving
   In this dark, cold world alone!

Holy angels now are bending
To receive thy soul ascending
Up to Heaven to joys unending,
   And to bliss which is divine;
While thy pale, cold form is fading
Under death's dark wings now shading
Thee with gloom which is pervading
   This poor, broken heart of mine!

For, as birds of the same feather
On the earth will flock together,
So, around thy Heavenly Father,
   They now gather there with thee—
Ever joyful to behold thee—
In their soft arms to enfold thee,
And to whisper words oft told thee,
   In this trying world by me!

With my bowed head thus reclining
On my hand, my heart repining,
Shall my salt tears, ever shining,
  On my pale cheeks, flow for thee—
Bitter soul-drops ever stealing
From the fount of holy feeling,
Deepest anguish now revealing,
  For thy loss, dear child! to me!

As an egg, when broken, never
Can be mended, but must ever
Be the same crushed egg forever—
  So shall this dark heart of mine!
Which, though broken, is still breaking,
And shall never more cease aching
For the sleep which has no waking—
  For the sleep which now is thine!

And as God doth lift thy spirit
Up to Heaven, there to inherit
Those rewards which it doth merit
  Such as none have reaped before;
Thy dear father will, tomorrow,
Lay thy body with deep sorrow,
In the grave which is so narrow—
  There to rest forevermore!

                                        (1845)

The Shell

  "It seems in truth the fairest shell of ocean."—*Shelley*.

I.
What is it makes thy sound unto my ear
  So mournful, Angel of the mighty Sea?
Is it the soul of her who once was here,
  Speaking affection, through thy lips, to me?

II.
Oh! from my childhood this has been to me
  A mystery which no one could solve!—It sounds
And sorrows for the Sea incessantly—
  Telling the grief with which my soul abounds!

III.
Here, in its labyrinthine curve, it leaves
  The foot-prints of its song in many dyes;

177

And here, incessantly, it ever weaves
The rainbow-tissue of its melodies.

IV.

When any harsher sound disturbs me here,
In my lamentings in this world for thee,
I will apply it to my listening ear,
And think it is thy soul come down to me.

(1851)

Isadore

"I approach thee—I look dauntless into thine eyes. The soul that loves can dare
all things. Shadow, I defy thee, and compel."—*Zanoni.*

I.

While the world lay round me
sleeping,
I, alone, for *Isadore*,
Patient Vigils lonely keeping—
Some one said to me while
weeping,
"Why this grief forever more?"
And I answered, "I am weeping
For my blessed *Isadore!*"

II.

Then the Voice again said, "Never
Shall thy soul see *Isadore!*
God from thee thy love did sever—
He has damned thy soul forever!
Wherefore then her loss deplore?
Thou shalt live in Hell forever!
Heaven now holds thine *Isadore!*"

III.

"She is dead—the world benighted—
Dark for want of *Isadore!*
Have not all your hopes been
blighted?
How can you be reunited?
Can mere words the dead restore?
Have not all your hopes been
blighted?
Why then hope for *Isadore?*"

IV.

"Back to Hell, thou ghostly Horror!"
Thus I cried, dear *Isadore!*
"Phantom of remorseless Sorrow!
Death might from thee pallor borrow—
Borrow leanness ever more!
Back to Hell again!—tomorrow
I will go to *Isadore!*"

V.

"When my soul to Heaven is taken,"
Were thy words, dear *Isadore!*
"Let no other one awaken
In thy heart, because forsaken,
What was felt for me before!
When my soul to Heaven is taken,
Oh! forget not *Isadore!*"

VI.

"Oh! remember this, Politian!"
Said my dying *Isadore!*
"Till from out this clayey prison
In the flowery *Fields Elysian*
We unite forever more!
Oh! remember this, Politian!
And forget not *Isadore!*"

VII.

Then before my raptured vision
Came sweet *Hope,* dear *Isadore!*

178

From the flowery *Fields Elysian*
Crying out to me, "Politian!
 Rise—rejoice forever more!
Angels wait for thee, Politian!
 Up to Heaven to *Isadore!*"

VIII.

Then from out my soul departed
 Deepest grief, dear *Isadore!*
Bliss, that never me deserted,
Entered in the broken-hearted—
 Giving life forever more—
Bliss that never me deserted,
 Like thy love, dear *Isadore!*

IX.

Myriad *Voices* still are crying,
 Day and night, dear *Isadore!*
"Come, come to the *Pure Land* [2]
 lying
Far up in the sky undying—
 There to rest forever more!
Purified, redeemed, undying—
 Come to Heaven to *Isadore!*

X.

"Blest Companion of th' Eternal!
 Come away to *Isadore!*
From the griefs that are diurnal
To the joys that are supernal—
 Sempiternal on Heaven's shore!
Bliss supernal, joys eternal
 Up in Heaven with *Isadore.*

XI.

"Cast away thy garb of mourning,
 Worn so long for *Isadore!*
For those glory-garments burning
In the *Bright Isles of the Morning*,
 Like the stars forever more.

Golden Days are now returning—
 Up to Heaven to *Isadore!*

XII.

"Lay aside thy load of sorrow,
 Borne so long for *Isadore!*
Pilgrim, pierced by Death's cold
 arrow,
Thou shalt see thy love tomorrow
 Up in Heaven forever more!
Lay aside thy load of sorrow—
 Come to Heaven to *Isadore!*

XIII.

"Come away, Oh! mournful mortal!
 Come to Heaven to *Isadore!*
Through Death's ebon, iron Portal
To the joys that are immortal
 On Helusion's happy shore!
"Come away, Oh! mournful mortal!
 Into Heaven to *Isadore!*

XIV.

"Up to God who will befriend you!
 Up to Heaven to *Isadore!*
Angels waiting to attend you—
Every aid you wish to lend you—
 Singing, shouting on Heaven's
 shore!
Angels waiting to attend you
 To your blessed *Isadore!*"

XV.

From the griefs that are diurnal—
 Bitter griefs, dear *Isadore!*
To the joys that are eternal—
To the bliss that is supernal—
 Sempiternal on Heaven's shore—
Thou art gone through years eternal
 There to rest, dear *Isadore!*

---

[2] *Plato speaks of the "Pure Earth" above,* (την γην χαθαραν εν χαθαρω χεισθαι ουρανο) *the abode of Divinity, of innocence, and life. It is an immemorial tradition. It was a revelation to the Hebrews. This "Pure Earth" above, is, no doubt, the primeval Paradise of Love—the antetype of that which Adam lost. Aristotle in his* Hymn to Virtue, *speaks of the "Blessed Isles" above. The* Νησοι Μακάρων, *or Isles of the Blest, were the* Elysium *of the departed Heroes who were considered immortal—the same as the* Manitoline *of the Indians, where they say the souls of the deathless Chieftains of the world dance in hormonian choirs around the throne of Ataensic to the most delightful music. They believe that the future felicity of the departed of this world consists in rejoining, in the flower-gemmed Savannahs of the Fields of Immortality, the long lost objects of their affections in the joyful festivities of the Chase. (Chivers' note.)*

XVI.

There thy comates shall be Angels—
    White-robed Angels, *Isadore!*
Singing Heaven's *Divine Evangels*
Through the Eternal Years, all
        change else,
    Changeless there forever more!
Thou, *Astarte of the Angels!*
    Knowest this so, dear *Isadore!*

XVII.

From the Paradise now wasted
    Of thy form, dear *Isadore!*
Lilly-bell that Death has blasted!
Purest Pleasures have I tasted
    In the Edenic days of Yore.
Joys celestial have I tasted
    From thy flower, dear *Isadore!*

XVIII.

Like two spirits in one being,
    Were our souls, dear *Isadore!*
Every object singly seeing—

In all things, like one, agreeing
    In those *Halcyon Days of Yore.*
We shall live so in our being
    Up in Heaven, dear *Isadore!*

XIX.

Myriad Voices still are crying
    Day and night, dear *Isadore!*
"Come, come to the *Pure Land*
        lying
Far up in the sky undying—
    There to rest forever more!
Purified, redeemed, undying—
    Come to Heaven to *Isadore!*"

XX.

Adon-Ai! God of Glory!
    Who dost love mine *Isadore!*
Who didst hear her prayerful story
In this world when she was sorry—
    Gone to Heaven forever more!
Adon-Ai! God of Glory!
    Take me home to *Isadore!*

(1851)

Lily Adair

I.

The Apollo Belvidere was adorning [3]
    The Chamber where Eulalie lay,
While Aurora, the Rose of the Morning,
    Smiled full in the face of the Day.
All around stood the beautiful Graces
    Bathing Venus—some combing her hair—
While she lay in her husband's embraces
    A-moulding my Lily Adair—
    Of my fawn-like Lily Adair—
    Of my dove-like Lily Adair—
    Of my beautiful, dutiful Lily Adair.

II.

180

Where the Oreads played in the Highlands,
    And the Water-Nymphs bathed in the streams,

[3] *It was a beautiful idea of the Greeks that the procreation of beautiful children might be promoted by keeping in their sleeping apartments an Apollo or Hyacinthus. In this way they not only patronized Art, but begat a likeness of their own love. (Chivers' note.)*

In the tall Jasper Reeds of the Islands—
   She wandered in life's early dreams.
For the Wood-Nymphs then brought from the Wildwood
   The turtle-doves Venus kept there,
Which the Dryades tamed, in his childhood,
    For Cupid, to Lily Adair—
    To my dove-like Lily Adair—
    To my lamb-like Lily Adair—
    To my beautiful, dutiful Lily Adair.

III.

Where the Opaline Swan circled, singing,
   With her eider-down Cygnets at noon,
In the tall Jasper Reeds that were springing
   From the marge of the crystal Lagoon—
Rich Canticles, clarion-like, golden,
   Such as only true love can declare,
Like an Archangel's voice in times olden—
    I went with my Lily Adair—
    With my lamb-like Lily Adair—
    With my saint-like Lily Adair—
    With my beautiful, dutiful Lily Adair.

IV.

Her eyes, lily-lidded, were azure,
   Cerulian, celestial, divine—
Suffused with the soul-light of pleasure,
   Which drew all the soul out of mine.
She had all the rich grace of the Graces,
   And all that they had not to spare;
For it took all their beautiful faces
    To make one for Lily Adair—
    For my Christ-like Lily Adair—
    For my Heaven-born Lily Adair—
    For my beautiful, dutiful Lily Adair.

V.

She was fairer by far than that Maiden,
   The star-bright Cassiope,
Who was taken by Angels to Aiden,
   And crowned with eternity.
For her beauty the Sea-Nymphs offended,
   Because so surpassingly fair;
And so death then the precious life ended
    Of my beautiful Lily Adair—
    Of my Heaven-born Lily Adair—
    Of my star-crowned Lily Adair—
    Of my beautiful, dutiful Lily Adair.

181

VI.

From her Paradise-Isles in the ocean,
  To the beautiful City of On,
By the mellifluent rivers of Goshen,
    My beautiful Lily is gone!
In her Chariot of Fire translated,
    Like Elijah, she passed through the air,
To the City of God golden-gated—
    The Home of my Lily Adair—
    Of my star-crowned Lily Adair—
    Of my God-loved Lily Adair—
    Of my beautiful, dutiful Lily Adair.

VII.

On the vista-path made by the Angels,
    In her Chariot of Fire, she rode,
While the Cherubim sang their Evangels—
    To the Gates of the City of God.
For the Cherubim-band that went with her,
    I saw them pass out of the air—
I saw them go up through the ether
    Into Heaven with my Lily Adair—
    With my Christ-like Lily Adair—
    With my God-like Lily Adair—
    With my beautiful, dutiful Lily Adair.

                                    (1851)

Apollo

What are stars, but hieroglyphics of God's glory writ in lightning
    On the wide-unfolded pages of the azure scroll above?
But the quenchless apotheoses of thoughts forever brightening
    In the mighty Mind immortal of the God, whose name is Love?
Diamond letters sculptured, rising, on the azure ether pages,
    That now sing to one another—unto one another shine—
God's eternal Scripture talking, through the midnight, to the Ages,
    Of the life that is immortal, of the life that is divine—
    Life that *cannot* be immortal, but the life that is divine.

Like some deep, impetuous river from the fountains everlasting,
    Down the serpentine soft valley of the vistas of all Time,
Over cataracts of adamant uplifted into mountains,
    Soared his soul to God in thunder on the wings of thought sublime,
With the rising golden glory of the sun in ministrations,
    Making oceans metropolitan of splendor for the dawn—

182

Piling pyramid on pyramid of music for the nations—
    Sings the Angel who sits shining everlasting in the sun,
For the stars, which are the echoes of the shining of the sun.

Like the lightnings piled on lightnings, ever rising, never reaching,
    In one monument of glory towards the golden gates of God—
Voicing out themselves in thunder upon thunder in their preaching,
    Piled this Cyclop up his Epic where the Angels never trod.
Like the fountains everlasting that forever more are flowing
    From the throne within the centre of the City built on high,
With their genial irrigation life forever more bestowing—
    Flows his lucid, liquid river through the gardens of the sky,
    For the stars forever blooming in the gardens of the sky.

                         (*1853*)

Rosalie Lee

"Les Anges ne sont plus pures que le cœur d'un jeune homme qui aime en verite." [4]—*Madame Dudevant.*

    On the banks of the yellow lilies,
      Where the cool wave wanders by,
    All bedamasked with Daffodillies,
      And the bee-beset Crowtie;
    More mild than the Paphian Luna
      To her nude Nymphs on the Sea,
    There dwelt, with her milk-white Una,
        My beautiful Rosalie Lee—
        My high-born Rosalie Lee—
        My child-like Rosalie Lee—
    My beautiful, dutiful Rosalie Lee.

    More coy than the wild Goldfinches,
      When they hunt for the Butterfly,
    Which the dew of the morning quenches,
      In the psychical month July;
    Like an opaline Dove's neck chiming
      Cherubic beauty for me,
    Were her ovaline arms in their rhyming,
        Of my beautiful Rosalie Lee—
        Of my lamb-like Rosalie Lee—
        Of my Heaven-born Rosalie Lee—
    Of my beautiful, dutiful Rosalie Lee.

183

[4] *The angels are no more pure than the heart of a young man who truly loves.*

Many mellow Cydonian Suckets,
  Sweet apples, anthosmial, divine,
From the Ruby-rimmed Beryline buckets,
  Star-gemmed, lily-shaped, hyaline—
Like that sweet golden goblet found growing
  On the wild emerald Cucumber-tree—
Rich, brilliant, like Chrysopraz blowing—
    I then brought to my Rosalie Lee—
    To my lamb-like Rosalie Lee—
    To my Dove-like Rosalie Lee—
To my beautiful, dutiful Rosalie Lee.

Warbling her wood-notes wild, she wended
  Her way with the turtle Doves,
And the Wood-nymphs weird that attended
  Her steps through the flowery groves.
In the light of her eyes of azure,
  My soul seemed on earth to see
All that Heaven could give me of pleasure,
    With my beautiful Rosalie Lee—
    With my Heaven-born Rosalie Lee—
    With my Christ-like Rosalie Lee—
With my beautiful, dutiful Rosalie Lee.

But my darling Ulpsyche sighing
  Her soul out to give me delight,
Went away with the great Undying
  To the Courts of the Heavenly Light.
Through an arc made in the azure
  Of God's azimuth, Heaven to see,
There to dwell with the Angels in pleasure—
    Went my beautiful Rosalie Lee—
    Went my fair-browed Rosalie Lee—
    Went my much loved Rosalie Lee—
Went my beautiful, dutiful Rosalie Lee.

Through the Valley of Avalon lonely,
  By the light of the argentine Moon,
From the presence that lived for her only
  On the banks of the Rivers of Rune;
Through the Star-Islands studding the Ether,
  With the Angels that took her from me—
(Though my soul in its sorrow went with her—)
    Soared my beautiful Rosalie Lee—
    Soared my Christ-like Rosalie Lee—
    Soared my God-loved Rosalie Lee—
Soared my beautiful, dutiful Rosalie Lee.

                                    (1853)

184

PHILIP PENDLETON COOKE

1816–1850

Philip Pendleton Cooke, older brother of the novelist John Esten Cooke, is known today primarily for one poem, "Florence Vane," published in *Burton's Magazine* in 1840, while that journal was edited by Edgar Allan Poe. Some modern commentators, however, have chosen him as the best example of "unfulfilled renown" among men of letters in the ante-bellum South. When the variety of his interests is considered, the reasons for his limited achievement in literature become obvious. John Donald Wade, for example, says: "The Southern world of the Cooke brothers was so very full of a number of enthralling things, including weather and natural prospects and field sports, that both of them found it hard to remain indoors, inactive and contemplative." The active outdoor life so dominated the thinking of Philip Pendleton Cooke that he is said to have written narrative verse because it was best for reading aloud to his hunting companions after dinner.

Cooke received his early education from tutors and at fifteen entered Princeton, where he had trouble with the authorities because he spent more time reading English poetry than studying the required courses. During this period, too, he was writing verse, some of which appeared in the *Knickerbocker Magazine* as early as 1833.

After graduating from college in 1834, he returned to Charles Town, Virginia, where he studied law in his father's office. But his interest in literature, though never the dominant force in his life, was never completely forgotten. From 1835 until his death he sent occasional pieces to the *Southern Literary Messenger*, his first contribution being a series of articles on early English poetry. The same magazine later published several of Cooke's prose romances: *The Crime of Andrew Blair, John Carper, The Hunter of Lost River,* and *Chevalier Merlin* (which was appearing serially at the time of Cooke's death). His only volume of poetry, *Froissart Ballads and Other Poems* (1847), was issued upon the suggestion of his cousin, John Pendleton Kennedy. This volume shows a genuine but immature talent which he was never to develop further. He died three years later as a result of exposure caused by swimming the Shenandoah in mid-winter while on a hunting expedition.

185

Florence Vane

I love thee long and dearly
  Florence Vane;
My life's bright dream and early
  Hath come again;
I renew, in my fond vision,
  My heart's dear pain,
My hopes, and thy derision,
  Florence Vane.

The ruin lone and hoary,
  The ruin old,
Where thou didst hark my story,
  At even told,—
That spot—the hues Elysian
  Of sky and plain—
I treasure in my vision,
  Florence Vane.

Thou wast lovelier than the roses
  In their prime;
Thy voice excelled the closes
  Of sweetest rhyme;

Thy heart was as a river
  Without a main;
Would I had loved thee never,
  Florence Vane.

But fairest, coldest wonder!
  Thy glorious clay
Lieth the green sod under—
  Alas the day!
And it boots not to remember
  Thy disdain—
To quicken love's pale ember,
  Florence Vane.

The lilies of the valley
  By young graves weep,
The pansies love to dally
  Where maidens sleep;
May their bloom, in beauty vieing,
  Never wane
Where thine earthly part is lying,
  Florence Vane!

(1840)

Life in the Autumn Woods

Summer has gone,
And fruitful Autumn has advanced so far
That there is warmth, not heat, in the broad sun,
And you may look, with naked eye, upon
  The ardors of his car;
The stealthy frosts, whom his spent looks embolden,
  Are making the green leaves golden.

What a brave splendor
Is in the October air! how rich, and clear,
And bracing, and all-joyous! We must render
Love to the Spring-time, with its sproutings tender,
  As to a child quite dear;
But Autumn is a thing of perfect glory,
  A manhood not yet hoary.

I love the woods,
In this good season of the liberal year;

186

I love to seek their leafy solitudes,
And give myself to melancholy moods,
 With no intruder near,
And find strange lessons, as I sit and ponder,
 In every natural wonder.

 But not alone,
As Shakespeare's melancholy courtier loved Ardennes,
Love I the browning forest; and I own
I would not oft have mused, as he, but flown
 To hunt with Amiens—
And little thought, as up the bold deer bounded,
 Of the sad creature wounded.

 A brave and good,
But world-worn knight—soul-wearied with his part
In this vexed life—gave man for solitude,
And built a lodge, and lived in Wantley wood,
 To hear the belling hart.
It was a gentle taste, but its sweet sadness
 Yields to the hunter's madness.

 What passionate
And keen delight is in the proud swift chase!
Go out what time the lark at heaven's red gate
Soars joyously singing—quite infuriate
 With the high pride of his place;
What time the unrisen sun arrays the morning
 In its first bright adorning.

 Hark! the quick horn—
As sweet to hear as any clarion—
Piercing with silver call the ear of morn;
And mark the steeds, stout Curtal and Topthorne,
 And Greysteil and the Don—
Each one of them his fiery mood displaying
 With pawing and with neighing.

 Urge your swift horse
After the crying hounds in this fresh hour;
Vanquish high hills, stem perilous streams perforce,
On the free plain give free wings to your course,
 And you will know the power
Of the brave chase,—and how of griefs the sorest
 A cure is in the forest.

        187

 Or stalk the deer;
The same red lip of dawn has kissed the hills,
The gladdest sounds are crowding on your ear,

There is a life in all the atmosphere:—
    Your very nature fills
With the fresh hour, as up the hills aspiring
    You climb with limbs untiring.

    It is a fair
And goodly sight to see the antlered stag
With the long sweep of his swift walk repair
To join his brothers; of the plethoric bear
    Lying in some high crag,
With pinky eyes half closed, but broad head shaking,
    As gadflies keep him waking.

    And these you see,
And, seeing them, you travel to their death
With a slow, stealthy step, from tree to tree,
Noting the wind, however faint it be.
    The hunter draws a breath
In times like these, which, he will say, repays him
    For all care that waylays him.

    A strong joy fills
(A joy beyond the tongue's expressive power)
My heart in Autumn weather—fills and thrills!
And I would rather stalk the breezy hills
    Descending to my bower
Nightly, by the sweet spirit of Peace attended,
    Than pine where life is splendid.

                                        (1843)

THEODORE O'HARA

1820–1867

188   Theodore O'Hara, the son of an Irish schoolteacher, was born in either Danville or Frankfort, Kentucky, February 11, 1820. After graduating from St. Joseph's College, Bardstown, Kentucky, he taught Greek at that institution for a time, but soon resigned to study law. O'Hara spent most of his maturity in military service and journalism. At various times he edited the *Mobile Register*, the *Louisville Times,* and the *Frankfort Yeoman.* He served two years in the Mexican War; fought and was wounded in the Lopez expedition for Cuban Independence in 1850; took part in expeditions against the Indians in 1855–1856, as captain of a cavalry regiment; and served in the Confederate Army as a captain and a temporary colonel (he was disappointed in his rank). For two years following the Civil War, he owned a cotton business in Columbus, Georgia, but retired after suffering heavy losses in a disastrous fire. He died in 1867.

Only two poems can definitely be attributed to the pen of O'Hara. "The Old Pioneer" (1845) is an elegy on the reburial of Daniel Boone. His more famous poem, "The Bivouac of the Dead" (1847), commemorates the burial, in the State Cemetery at Frankfort, of Kentucky soldiers who had died at the Battle of Buena Vista in the Mexican War. There is no record that O'Hara fought in the battle, and it is certain that he was still in Mexico at the time of the mass burial. The admirers of "The Bivouac of the Dead" have called it "the greatest martial elegy in existence." Such praise is indicative of the tremendous popularity which the poem has enjoyed; part of it, for example, was inscribed on a monument in the Crimea. Its popularity has led it to be construed erroneously as a tribute to the Civil War soldiers of both North and South.

The Bivouac of the Dead

The muffled drum's sad roll has beat
   The soldier's last tattoo;
No more on Life's parade shall meet
   The brave and daring few.
On Fame's eternal camping-ground
   Their silent tents are spread,
And Glory guards with solemn round
   The bivouac of the dead.

No answer of the foe's advance
   Now swells upon the wind;
No troubled thought at midnight haunts
   Of loved ones left behind;
No vision of the morrow's strife
   The warrior's dream alarms;
No braying horn nor screaming fife
   At dawn shall call to arms.

Their shivered swords are red with rust;
   Their plumèd heads are bowed;
Their haughty banner, trailed in dust,
   Is now their martial shroud;
And plenteous funeral-tears have washed
   The red stains from each brow,
And their proud forms, in battle gashed,
   Are free from anguish now.

189

The neighing steed, the flashing blade,
  The trumpet's stirring blast,
The charge, the dreadful cannonade,
  The din and shout, are past;
No war's wild note, nor glory's peal,
  Shall thrill with fierce delight
Those breasts that nevermore shall feel
  The rapture of the fight.

Like the dread northern hurricane
  That sweeps his broad plateau,
Flushed with the triumph yet to gain,
  Came down the serried foe.
Our heroes felt the shock, and leapt
  To meet them on the plain;
And long the pitying sky hath wept
  Above our gallant slain.

Sons of our consecrated ground,
  Ye must not slumber there,
Where stranger steps and tongues resound
  Along the heedless air.
Your own proud land's heroic soil
  Shall be your fitter grave:
She claims from war his richest spoil—
  The ashes of her brave.

So 'neath their parent turf they rest,
  Far from the gory field;
Borne to a Spartan mother's breast
  On many a bloody shield.
The sunshine of their native sky
  Smiles sadly on them here,
And kindred hearts and eyes watch by
  The heroes' sepulcher.

Rest on, embalmed and sainted dead!
  Dear as the blood you gave,
No impious footsteps here shall tread
  The herbage of your grave;
Nor shall your glory be forgot
  While fame her record keeps,
Or honor points the hallowed spot
  Where valor proudly sleeps.

190

Yon marble minstrel's voiceless tone
  In deathless songs shall tell,

When many a vanquished age hath flown,
    The story how ye fell.
Nor wreck, nor change, nor winter's blight,
    Nor time's remorseless doom,
Shall dim one ray of holy light
    That gilds your glorious tomb.

(*1847*)

EDGAR ALLAN POE

1809–1849

Edgar Poe—the Allan he added later—was born January 19, 1809, in Boston, where his parents were playing in a stock company. By the time he reached his third year, both his father and mother were dead, and he was adopted—though never legally—by John Allan and his wife, of Richmond, Virginia. Poe spent the years from 1815 to 1820 in or near London, where Mr. Allan, a prosperous tobacco merchant, had gone in the interests of his expanding business. Returning to Richmond, he attended a private academy before entering Jefferson's newly founded University of Virginia. He stayed in college for only one year, 1826; denied adequate expense money by his foster father, he turned to gambling and left the school owing some $2000 in "debts of honor." His relationship with his father was never again truly amicable.

Poe left his home, such as it was, and went to Boston, where—at the age of eighteen—he published *Tamerlane and Other Poems*. When the volume failed to attract attention, he enlisted in the army under the name of Edgar A. Perry and, before obtaining his release in 1829, achieved the rank of sergeant major. *Al Aaraaf, Tamerlane, and Minor Poems* appeared the year of his discharge. On July 1, 1830, Poe entered West Point, but realizing at last that Mr. Allan was through with him, he deliberately neglected his classes and drills and was dismissed from the academy the following winter.

During the eighteen years left to him, both his progress and disintegration as a writer were meteoric. In 1833 he won a prize of a hundred dollars offered by the *Baltimore Saturday Visitor*, and in 1835 became an associate editor of the *Southern Literary Messenger*. The following year he married his cousin, Virginia Clemm, who was not quite fourteen years old at the time. He was

191

discharged from the *Messenger* at the end of that year, mainly because of alcoholism. The years from 1838 to 1843 were spent in Philadelphia, where Poe was editor, associate editor, and contributor to several periodicals, notably *Graham's* and *Burton's Gentleman's Magazine*. He left Philadelphia for New York, and, except for various excursions, lived there or at Fordham for the remainder of his life. After his wife's death early in 1847, whatever stability Poe may have possessed deteriorated rapidly, although he did manage to compose a number of memorable poems and an ambitiously conceived pseudo-philosophical essay, "Eureka."

Poe's position as a pioneer in the writing of short stories and in the field of analytical criticism is still unquestioned. As a poet, he has enjoyed widespread popularity both in this country and abroad, proving especially influential in France, through the attention given his work by Baudelaire and his followers.

Sonnet—To Science [1]

Science! true daughter of Old Time thou art!
Who alterest all things with thy peering eyes,
Why preyest thou thus upon the poet's heart,
Vulture, whose wings are dull realities?
How should he love thee? or how deem thee wise,
Who wouldst not leave him in his wandering
To seek for treasure in the jewelled skies,
Albeit he soared with an undaunted wing?
Hast thou not dragged Diana from her car?
And driven the Hamadryad from the wood
To seek a shelter in some happier star?
Hast thou not torn the Naiad from her flood,
The Elfin from the green grass, and from me
The summer dream beneath the tamarind tree?

(1829)

To Helen

Helen, thy beauty is to me
Like those Nicean barks of yore,
That gently, o'er a perfumed sea,
The weary, wayworn wanderer bore
To his own native shore.

192

[1] *Poe prefaced the 1829 edition of poems, in which this sonnet appeared, with the following remark: "Private reasons—some of which have reference to the sin of plagiarism, and others to the date of Tennyson's first poems—have induced me, after some hesitation, to re-publish these, the crude compositions of my earliest boyhood. They are printed* verbatim—*without alteration from the original edition—the date of which is too remote to be judiciously acknowledged. E. A. P."*

On desperate seas long wont to roam,
    Thy hyacinth hair, thy classic face,
Thy Naiad airs, have brought me home
    To the Glory that was Greece
And the grandeur that was Rome.

Lo! in yon brilliant window-niche
    How statue-like I see thee stand,
    The agate lamp within thy hand!
Ah, Psyche, from the regions which
    Are Holy Land!

(1831)

The City in the Sea [2]

Lo! Death has reared himself a throne
In a strange city lying alone
Far down within the dim West,
Where the good and the bad and the worst
    and the best
Have gone to their eternal rest.
There shrines and palaces and towers
(Time-eaten towers that tremble not)
Resemble nothing that is ours.
Around, by lifting winds forgot,
Resignedly beneath the sky
The melancholy waters lie.

No rays from the holy heaven come down
On the long night-time of that town;
But light from out the lurid sea
Streams up the turrets silently,
Gleams up the pinnacles far and free:
Up domes, up spires, up kingly halls;
Up fanes, up Babylon-like walls,
Up shadowy long-forgotten bowers
Of sculptured ivy and stone flowers,
Up many and many a marvelous shrine
Whose wreathed friezes intertwine
The viol, the violet, and the vine.

Resignedly beneath the sky
The melancholy waters lie.
So blend the turrets and shadows there
That all seem pendulous in air,

193

[2] *This poem appeared as "The Doomed City" in the 1831 edition of Poe's poems.*

While from a proud tower in the town
Death looks gigantically down.

There open fanes and gaping graves
Yawn level with the luminous waves;
But not the riches there that lie
In each idol's diamond eye,—
Not the gayly-jewelled dead,
Tempt the waters from their bed;
For no ripples curl, alas,
Along that wilderness of glass;
No swellings tell that winds may be
Upon some far-off happier sea;
No heavings hint that winds have been
On seas less hideously serene!

But lo, a stir is in the air!
The wave—there is a movement there!
As if the towers had thrust aside,
In slightly sinking, the dull tide;
As if their tops had feebly given
A void within the filmy Heaven!
The waves have now a redder glow,
The hours are breathing faint and low;
And when, amid no earthly moans,
Down, down that town shall settle hence,
Hell, rising from a thousand thrones,
Shall do it reverence.

(*1831, 1845*)

The Raven

Once upon a midnight dreary, while I pondered, weak and weary,
Over many a quaint and curious volume of forgotten lore—
While I nodded, nearly napping, suddenly there came a tapping,
As of some one gently rapping, rapping at my chamber door.
" 'Tis some visitor," I muttered, "tapping at my chamber door—
Only this and nothing more."

Ah, distinctly I remember it was in the bleak December;
And each separate dying ember wrought its ghost upon the floor.
Eagerly I wished the morrow;—vainly I had sought to borrow
From my books surcease of sorrow—sorrow for the lost Lenore—
For the rare and radiant maiden whom the angels named Lenore—
Nameless *here* for evermore.

194

And the silken, sad, uncertain rustling of each purple curtain
Thrilled me—filled me with fantastic terrors never felt before;
So that now, to still the beating of my heart, I stood repeating
" 'Tis some visitor entreating entrance at my chamber door,
Some late visitor entreating entrance at my chamber door:
   This it is and nothing more."

Presently my soul grew stronger, hesitating then no longer,
"Sir," said I, "or Madam, truly your forgiveness I implore:
But the fact is I was napping, and so gently you came rapping,
And so faintly you came tapping, tapping at my chamber door,
That I scarce was sure I heard you"—here I opened wide the door;—
   Darkness there and nothing more.

Deep into that darkness peering, long I stood there wondering, fearing,
Doubting, dreaming dreams no mortals ever dared to dream before:
But the silence was unbroken, and the stillness gave no token,
And the only word there spoken was the whispered word, "Lenore?"
This I whispered, and an echo murmured back the word, "Lenore!"
   Merely this and nothing more.

Back into the chamber turning, all my soul within me burning,
Soon again I heard a tapping somewhat louder than before.
"Surely," said I, "surely that is something at my window lattice;
Let me see, then, what thereat is, and this mystery explore;
Let my heart be still a moment and this mystery explore:
   'Tis the wind and nothing more!"

Open here I flung the shutter, when, with many a flirt and flutter,
In there stepped a stately Raven of the saintly days of yore;
Not the least obeisance made he; not a minute stopped or stayed he;
But with mien of lord or lady, perched above my chamber door,
Perched upon a bust of Pallas just above my chamber door:
   Perched, and sat, and nothing more.

Then this ebon bird beguiling all my fancy into smiling
By the grave and stern decorum of the countenance it wore,
"Though thy crest be shorn and shaven, thou," I said, "art sure no craven,
Ghastly grim and ancient Raven wandering from the Nightly shore—
Tell me what thy lordly name is on the Night's Plutonian shore!"
   Quoth the Raven "Nevermore."

Much I marveled this ungainly fowl to hear discourse so plainly,
Though its answer little meaning—little relevancy bore;
For we cannot help agreeing that no living human being
Ever yet was blessed with seeing bird above his chamber door,
Bird or beast upon the sculptured bust above his chamber door,
   With such name as "Nevermore."

195

But the Raven, sitting lonely on the placid bust, spoke only
That one word, as if his soul in that one word he did outpour,
Nothing further then he uttered, not a feather then he fluttered,
Till I scarcely more than muttered,—"Other friends have flown before;
On the morrow *he* will leave me, as my Hopes have flown before."
    Then the bird said "Nevermore."

Startled at the stillness broken by reply so aptly spoken,
"Doubtless," said I, "what it utters is its only stock and store,
Caught from some unhappy master whom unmerciful Disaster
Followed fast and followed faster till his songs one burden bore—
Till the dirges of his Hope that melancholy burden bore
    Of 'Never—nevermore.' "

But the Raven still beguiling all my fancy into smiling,
Straight I wheeled a cushioned seat in front of bird and bust and door;
Then, upon the velvet sinking, I betook myself to linking
Fancy unto fancy, thinking what this ominous bird of yore,
What this grim, ungainly, ghastly, gaunt, and ominous bird of yore
    Meant in croaking "Nevermore."

This I sat engaged in guessing, but no syllable expressing
To the fowl whose fiery eyes now burned into my bosom's core;
This and more I sat divining, with my head at ease reclining
On the cushion's velvet lining that the lamp-light gloated o'er,
But whose velvet violet lining with the lamp-light gloating o'er
    She shall press, ah, nevermore!

Then, methought, the air grew denser, perfumed from an unseen censer
Swung by Seraphim whose foot-falls tinkled on the tufted floor.
"Wretch," I cried, "thy God hath lent thee—by these angels he hath
    sent thee
Respite—respite and nepenthe, from thy memories of Lenore;
Quaff, oh quaff this kind nepenthe and forget this lost Lenore!"
    Quoth the Raven "Nevermore."

"Prophet!" said I, "thing of evil! prophet still, if bird or devil!
Whether Tempter sent, or whether tempest tossed thee here ashore,
Desolate yet all undaunted, on this desert land enchanted—
On this home by Horror haunted—tell me truly, I implore:
Is there—*is* there balm in Gilead?—tell me—tell me, I implore!"
    Quoth the Raven "Nevermore."

"Prophet!" said I, "thing of evil—prophet still, if bird or devil!
By that Heaven that bends above us, by that God we both adore,
Tell this soul with sorrow laden if, within the distant Aidenn,
It shall clasp a sainted maiden whom the angels name Lenore—
Clasp a rare and radiant maiden whom the angels name Lenore!"
    Quoth the Raven "Nevermore."

196

"Be that word our sign of parting, bird or fiend!" I shrieked, up-
    starting:
"Get thee back into the tempest and the Night's Plutonian shore!
Leave no black plume as a token of that lie thy soul hath spoken!
Leave my loneliness unbroken! quit the bust above my door!
Take thy beak from out my heart, and take thy form from off my door!"
    Quoth the Raven "Nevermore."

And the Raven, never flitting, still is sitting, *still* is sitting
On the pallid bust of Pallas just above my chamber door;
And his eyes have all the seeming of a demon's that is dreaming,
And the lamplight o'er him streaming throws his shadow on the floor;
And my soul from out that shadow that lies floating on the floor
    Shall be lifted—nevermore!

(1845)

To Helen

I saw thee once—once only—years ago:
I must not say *how* many—but *not* many.
It was a July midnight; and from out
A full-orbed moon, that like thine own soul soaring,
Sought a precipitate pathway up through heaven,
There fell a silvery-silken veil of light,
With quietude, and sultriness and slumber,
Upon the upturn'd faces of a thousand
Roses that grew in an enchanted garden,
Where no wind dared to stir, unless on tiptoe—
Fell on the upturn'd faces of these roses
That gave out, in return for the love-light,
Their odorous souls in an ecstatic death—
Fell on the upturn'd faces of these roses
That smiled and died in this parterre, enchanted
By thee, and by the poetry of thy presence.

Clad all in white, upon a violet bank
I saw thee half-reclining; while the moon
Fell on the upturn'd faces of the roses,
And on thine own, upturn'd—alas, in sorrow!
Was it not Fate, that, on this July midnight—
Was it not Fate (whose name is also Sorrow),
That bade me pause before that garden-gate,
To breathe the incense of those slumbering roses?
No footstep stirred: the hated world all slept,
Save only thee and me. I paused—I looked—
And in an instant all things disappeared.
(Ah, bear in mind this garden was enchanted!)

197

The pearly lustre of the moon went out:
The mossy banks and the meandering paths,
The happy flowers and the repining trees,
Were seen no more: the very roses' odours
Died in the arms of the adoring airs.
All—all expired save thee—save less than thou:
Save only the divine light in thine eyes—
Save but the soul in thine uplifted eyes.
I saw but them—they were the world to me.
I saw but them—saw only them for hours—
Saw only them until the moon went down.
What wild heart-histories seemed to lie enwritten
Upon those crystalline, celestial spheres!
How dark a woe! yet how sublime a hope!
How silently serene a sea of pride!
How daring an ambition! yet how deep—
How fathomless a capacity for love!

But now, at length, dear Dian sank from sight,
Into a western couch of thunder-cloud;
And thou, a ghost, amid the entombing trees
Didst glide away. *Only thine eyes remained.*
They *would not* go—they never yet have gone.
Lighting my lonely pathway home that night,
They have not left me (as my hopes have) since.
They follow me—they lead me through the years.
They are my ministers—yet I their slave.
Their office is to illumine and enkindle—
My duty, *to be saved* by their bright light
And purified in their electric fire,
And sanctified in their elysian fire.
They fill my soul with Beauty (which is Hope),
And are far up in Heaven—the stars I kneel to
In the sad, silent watches of my night;
While even in the meridian glare of day
I see them still—two sweetly scintillant
Venuses, unextinguished by the sun!   (*1848*)

Ulalume[3]

The skies they were ashen and sober;
  The leaves they were crisped and sere—
  The leaves they were withering and sere;
It was night in the lonesome October
  Of my most immemorial year;

[3] *This poem was published in* Colton's American Review *for December 1847, under the signature of N. P. Willis.*

In the misty mid region of Weir—
It was down by the dank tarn of Auber;
It was hard by the dim lake of Auber,
    In the ghoul-haunted woodland of Weir.

Here once, through an alley Titanic,
    Of cypress, I roamed with my Soul—
    Of cypress, with Psyche, my Soul.
These were days when my heart was volcanic
    As the scoriac rivers that roll—
    As the lavas that restlessly roll
Their sulphurous currents down Yaanek
    In the ultimate climes of the pole—
That groan as they roll down Mount Yaanek
    In the realms of the boreal pole.

Our talk had been serious and sober,
    But our thoughts they were palsied and sere—
    Our memories were treacherous and sere—
For we knew not the month was October,
    And we marked not the night of the year—
    (Ah, night of all nights in the year!)
We noted not the dim lake of Auber—
    (Though once we had journeyed down here)—
Remembered not the dank tarn of Auber,
    Nor the ghoul-haunted woodland of Weir.

And now, as the night was senescent
    And star-dials pointed to morn—
    As the star-dials hinted of morn—
At the end of our path a liquescent
    And nebulous lustre was born,
Out of which a miraculous crescent
    Arose with a duplicate horn—
Astarte's bediamonded crescent
    Distinct with its duplicate horn.

And I said—"She is warmer than Dian:
    She rolls through an ether of sighs—
    She revels in a region of sighs:
She has seen that the tears are not dry on
    These cheeks, where the worm never dies
And has come past the stars of the Lion
    To point us the path to the skies—
    To the Lethean peace of the skies—
Come up, in despite of the Lion,
    To shine on us with her bright eyes—
Come up through the lair of the Lion,
    With love in her luminous eyes."

199

But Psyche, uplifting her finger,
　　Said—"Sadly this star I mistrust—
　　Her pallor I strangely mistrust:—
Oh, hasten!—oh, let us not linger!
　　Oh, fly!—let us fly!—for we must."
In terror she spoke, letting sink her
　　Wings till they trailed in the dust—
In agony sobbed, letting sink her
　　Plumes till they trailed in the dust—
　　Till they sorrowfully trailed in the dust.

I replied—"This is nothing but dreaming:
　　Let us on by this tremulous light!
　　Let us bathe in this crystalline light!
Its Sibyllic splendour is beaming
　　With Hope and in Beauty to-night:—
　　See!—it flickers up the sky through the night!
Ah, we safely may trust to its gleaming,
　　And be sure it will lead us aright—
We safely may trust to a gleaming
　　That cannot but guide us aright,
Since it flickers up to Heaven through the night."

Thus I pacified Psyche and kissed her,
　　And tempted her out of her gloom—
　　And conquered her scruples and gloom,
And we passed to the end of the vista,
　　But were stopped by the door of a tomb—
　　By the door of a legended tomb:
And I said—"What is written, sweet sister,
　　On the door of this legended tomb?"
　　She replied—"Ulalume—Ulalume—
　　'Tis the vault of thy lost Ulalume!"

Then my heart it grew ashen and sober
　　As the leaves that were crisped and sere—
　　As the leaves that were withering and sere;
And I cried—"It was surely October
　　On *this* very night of last year
　　That I journeyed—I journeyed down here—
　　That I brought a dread burden down here!
　　On this night of all nights in the year,
　　Ah, what demon has tempted me here?
Well I know, now, this dim lake of Auber—
　　This misty mid region of Weir—
Well I know, now, this dank tarn of Auber,
　　This ghoul-haunted woodland of Weir."

200

(1847)

The Bells

I.

Hear the sledges with the bells—
　　　Silver bells!
What a world of merriment their melody foretells!
　　How they tinkle, tinkle, tinkle,
　　　In the icy air of night!
　　While the stars, that oversprinkle
　　All the heavens, seem to twinkle
　　　　With a crystalline delight;
　　　Keeping time, time, time,
　　　In a sort of Runic rhyme,
To the tintinnabulation that so musically wells
　　From the bells, bells, bells, bells,
　　　Bells, bells, bells—
From the jingling and the tinkling of the bells.

II.

　　Hear the mellow wedding bells,
　　　Golden bells!
What a world of happiness their harmony foretells!
　　Through the balmy air of night
　　How they ring out their delight!
　　　From the molten golden-notes,
　　　　And all in tune,
　　　What a liquid ditty floats
To the turtle-dove that listens, while she gloats
　　　On the moon!
　　Oh, from out the sounding cells,
What a gush of euphony voluminously wells!
　　　How it swells!
　　　How it dwells
　　　On the future! how it tells
　　　Of the rapture that impels
　　To the swinging and the ringing
　　　Of the bells, bells, bells,
　Of the bells, bells, bells, bells,
　　　Bells, bells, bells—
To the rhyming and the chiming of the bells!

III.

　　Hear the loud alarum bells—
　　　Brazen bells!
What a tale of terror now their turbulency tells!
　　In the startled ear of night
　　How they scream out their affright!

Too much horrified to speak,
They can only shriek, shriek,
Out of tune,
In a clamorous appealing to the mercy of the fire,
In a mad expostulation with the deaf and frantic fire
Leaping higher, higher, higher,
With a desperate desire,
And a resolute endeavour
Now—now to sit or never,
By the side of the pale-faced moon.
Oh, the bells, bells, bells!
What a tale their terror tells
Of Despair!
How they clang, and clash, and roar!
What a horror they outpour
On the bosom of the palpitating air!
Yet the ear it fully knows,
By the twanging
And the clanging.
How the danger ebbs and flows;
Yet the ear distinctly tells,
In the jangling,
And the wrangling,
How the danger sinks and swells,
By the sinking or the swelling in the anger of the bells—
Of the bells—
Of the bells, bells, bells, bells,
Bells, bells, bells—
In the clamour and the clangour of the bells!

IV.

Hear the tolling of the bells—
Iron bells!
What a world of solemn thought their monody compels!
In the silence of the night,
How we shiver with affright
At the melancholy menace of their tone!
For every sound that floats
From the rust within their throats
Is a groan.
And the people—ah, the people—
They that dwell up in the steeple,
All alone,
And who tolling, tolling, tolling,
In that muffled monotone,
Feel a glory in so rolling
On the human heart a stone—
They are neither man nor woman—

They are neither brute nor human—
　　They are Ghouls:
And their king it is who tolls;
And he rolls, rolls, rolls,
　　　Rolls
　　A pæan from the bells!
　And his merry bosom swells
　　With the pæan of the bells!
　And he dances and he yells;
　Keeping time, time, time,
　In a sort of Runic rhyme,
　　To the pæan of the bells—
　　　Of the bells:
　Keeping time, time, time,
　In a sort of Runic rhyme,
　　To the throbbing of the bells—
Of the bells, bells, bells—
　To the sobbing of the bells;
Keeping time, time, time,
　As he knells, knells, knells,
In a happy Runic rhyme,
　To the rolling of the bells—
Of the bells, bells, bells—
　To the tolling of the bells,
Of the bells, bells, bells, bells,
　　Bells, bells, bells—
To the moaning and the groaning of the bells.

(1849)

Annabel Lee [4]

It was many and many a year ago,
　In a kingdom by the sea,
That a maiden there lived whom you may know
　By the name of Annabel Lee;
And this maiden she lived with no other thought
　Than to love and be loved by me.

I was a child and *she* was a child,
　In this kingdom by the sea:
But we loved with a love that was more than love—
　I and my Annabel Lee;
With a love that the winged seraphs of heaven
　Coveted her and me.

[4] *It is generally believed that Poe wrote this poem in memory of his wife, Virginia Clemm.*

203

And this was the reason that, long ago,
   In this kingdom by the sea,
A wind blew out of a cloud, chilling
   My beautiful Annabel Lee;
So that her highborn kinsman came
   And bore her away from me,
To shut her up in a sepulchre
   In this kingdom by the sea.

The angels, not half so happy in heaven,
   Went envying her and me—
Yes!—that was the reason (as all men know,
   In this kingdom by the sea)
That the wind came out of the cloud by night,
   Chilling and killing my Annabel Lee.

But our love it was stronger by far than the love
   Of those who were older than we—
   Of many far wiser than we—
And neither the angels in heaven above,
   Nor the demons down under the sea,
Can ever dissever my soul from the soul
   Of the beautiful Annabel Lee:—

For the moon never beams without bringing me dreams
   Of the beautiful Annabel Lee;
And the stars never rise but I see the bright eyes
   Of the beautiful Annabel Lee;
And so, all the night-tide, I lie down by the side
Of my darling, my darling, my life and my bride,
   In her sepulchre there by the sea—
   In her tomb by the side of the sea.

                                       (1849)

The Fall of the House of Usher

"Son cœur est un luth suspendu;
Sitot qu'on le touche il resonne." [1]—De Beranger.

During the whole of a dull, dark, and resoundless day in the autumn of the year, when the clouds hung oppressively low in the heavens, I had been passing alone, on horseback, through a singularly dreary tract of country, and at length found myself, as the shades of evening drew on, within view of the melancholy House of Usher. I know not how it was—but, with the first glimpse of the building, a sense of insufferable gloom pervaded my spirit. I say insufferable; for the

204

[1] *His heart is a lute suspended; whenever it is touched it sounds.*

feeling was unrelieved by any of that half-pleasurable, because poetic, sentiment, with which the mind usually receives even the sternest natural images of the desolate or terrible. I looked upon the scene before me—upon the mere house, and the simple landscape features of the domain—upon the bleak walls—upon the vacant eye-like windows—upon a few rank sedges—and upon a few white trunks of decayed trees—with an utter depression of soul, which I can compare to no earthly sensation more properly than to the after-dream of the reveller upon opium—the bitter lapse into every-day life—the hideous dropping of the veil.

There was an iciness, a sinking, a sickening of the heart—an unredeemed dreariness of thought which no goading of the imagination could torture into aught of the sublime. What was it—I paused to think—what was it that so unnerved me in the contemplation of the House of Usher? It was a mystery all insoluble; nor could I grapple with the shadowy fancies that crowded upon me as I pondered. I was forced to fall back upon the unsatisfactory conclusion, that while, beyond doubt, there *are* combinations of very simple natural objects which have the power of thus affecting us, still the analysis of this power lies among considerations beyond our depth. It was possible, I reflected, that a mere different arrangement of the particulars of the scene, of the details of the picture, would be sufficient to modify, or perhaps to annihilate its capacity for sorrowful impression; and, acting upon this idea, I reined my horse to the precipitous brink of a black and lurid tarn that lay in unruffled lustre by the dwelling, and gazed down—but with a shudder even more thrilling than before—upon the remodelled and inverted images of the gray sedge, and the ghastly tree-stems, and the vacant and eye-like windows.

Nevertheless, in this mansion of gloom I now proposed to myself a sojourn of some weeks. Its proprietor, Roderick Usher, had been one of my boon companions in boyhood; but many years had elapsed since our last meeting. A letter, however, had lately reached me in a distant part of the country—a letter from him—which, in its wildly importunate nature, had admitted of no other than a personal reply. The MS. gave evidence of nervous agitation. The writer spoke of acute bodily illness—of a mental disorder which oppressed him—and of an earnest desire to see me, as his best and indeed his only personal friend, with a view of attempting, by the cheerfulness of my society, some alleviation of his malady. It was the manner in which all this, and much more, was said—it was the apparent *heart* that went with his request—which allowed me no room for hesitation; and I accordingly obeyed forthwith what I still considered a very singular summons.

Although, as boys, we had been even intimate associates, yet I really knew little of my friend. His reserve had been always excessive and habitual. I was aware, however, that his very ancient family had been noted, time out of mind, for a peculiar sensibility of temperament, displaying itself, through long ages, in many works of exalted art, and manifested, of late, in repeated deeds of munificent yet unobtrusive charity, as well as in a passionate devotion to the intricacies, perhaps even more than to the orthodox and easily recognizable beauties, of musical science. I had learned, too, the very remarkable fact, that the stem of the Usher race, all time-honored as it was, had put forth, at no period, any enduring branch; in other words, that the entire family lay in the direct line of descent, and had always, with very trifling and very temporary

205

variations, so lain. It was this deficiency, I considered, while running over in thought the perfect keeping of the character of the premises with the accredited character of the people, and while speculating upon the possible influence which the one, in the long lapse of centuries, might have exercised upon the other— it was this deficiency, perhaps of collateral issue, and the consequent undeviating transmission, from sire to son, of the patrimony with the name, which had, at length, so identified the two as to merge the original title of the estate in the quaint and equivocal appellation of the "House of Usher"—an appellation which seemed to include, in the minds of the peasantry who used it, both the family and the family mansion.

I have said that the sole effect of my somewhat childish experiment—that of looking down within the tarn—had been to deepen the first singular impression. There can be no doubt that the consciousness of the rapid increase of my super-stition—for why should I not so term it?—served mainly to accelerate the in-crease itself. Such, I have long known, is the paradoxical law of all sentiments having terror as a basis. And it might have been for this reason only, that, when I again uplifted my eyes to the house itself, from its image in the pool, there grew in my mind a strange fancy—a fancy so ridiculous, indeed, that I but men-tion it to show the vivid force of the sensations which oppressed me. I had so worked upon my imagination as really to believe that about the whole mansion and domain there hung an atmosphere peculiar to themselves and their imme-diate vicinity—an atmosphere which had no affinity with the air of heaven, but which had reeked up from the decayed trees, and the gray wall, and the silent tarn—a pestilent and mystic vapor, dull, sluggish, faintly discernible and leaden-hued.

Shaking off from my spirit what *must* have been a dream, I scanned more narrowly the real aspect of the building. Its principal feature seemed to be that of an excessive antiquity. The discoloration of ages had been great. Minute fungi overspread the whole exterior, hanging in a fine tangled web-work from the eaves. Yet all this was apart from any extraordinary dilapidation. No portion of the masonry had fallen; and there appeared to be a wild inconsistency between its still perfect adaptation of parts, and the crumbling condition of the individual stones. In this there was much that reminded me of the specious totality of old woodwork which has rotted for long years in some neglected vault, with no disturbance from the breath of the external air. Beyond this indication of exten-sive decay, however, the fabric gave little token of instability. Perhaps the eye of a scrutinizing observer might have discovered a barely perceptible fissure, which, extending from the roof of the building in front, made its way down the wall in a zigzag direction, until it became lost in the sullen waters of the tarn.

Noticing these things, I rode over a short causeway to the house. A servant in waiting took my horse, and I entered the Gothic archway of the hall. A valet, of stealthy step, then conducted me, in silence, through many dark and intricate passages in my progress to the *studio* of his master. Much that I encountered on the way contributed, I know not how, to heighten the vague sentiments of which I have already spoken. While the objects around me—while the carvings of the ceilings, the sombre tapestries of the walls, the ebon blackness of the floors, and the phantasmagoric armorial trophies which rattled as I strode, were but matters to which, or to such as which, I had been accustomed from my infancy—while

206

I hesitated not to acknowledge how familiar was all this—I still wondered to find how unfamiliar were the fancies which ordinary images were stirring up. On one of the staircases, I met the physician of the family. His countenance, I thought, wore a mingled expression of low cunning and perplexity. He accosted me with trepidation and passed on. The valet now threw open a door and ushered me into the presence of his master.

The room in which I found myself was very large and lofty. The windows were long, narrow, and pointed, and at so vast a distance from the black oaken floor as to be altogether inaccessible from within. Feeble gleams of encrimsoned light made their way through the trellised panes, and served to render sufficiently distinct the more prominent objects around; the eye, however, struggled in vain to reach the remoter angles of the chamber, or the recesses of the vaulted and fretted ceiling. Dark draperies hung upon the walls. The general furniture was profuse, comfortless, antique, and tattered. Many books and musical instruments lay scattered about, but failed to give any vitality to the scene. I felt that I breathed an atmosphere of sorrow. An air of stern, deep, and irredeemable gloom hung over and pervaded all.

Upon my entrance, Usher arose from a sofa on which he had been lying at full length, and greeted me with a vivacious warmth which had much in it, I at first thought, of an overdone cordiality—of the constrained effort of the *ennuyé* man of the world. A glance, however, at his countenance convinced me of his perfect sincerity. We sat down; and for some moments, while he spoke not, I gazed upon him with a feeling half of pity, half of awe. Surely, man had never before so terribly altered, in so brief a period, as had Roderick Usher! It was with difficulty that I could bring myself to admit the identity of the wan being before me with the companion of my early boyhood. Yet the character of his face had been at all times remarkable. A cadaverousness of complexion; an eye large, liquid, and luminous beyond comparison; lips somewhat thin and very pallid, but of a surpassingly beautiful curve; a nose of a delicate Hebrew model, but with a breadth of nostril unusual in similar formations; a finely moulded chin, speaking, in its want of prominence, of a want of moral energy; hair of a more than web-like softness and tenuity—these features, with an inordinate expansion above the regions of the temple, made up altogether a countenance not easily to be forgotten. And now in the mere exaggeration of the prevailing character of these features, and of the expression they were wont to convey, lay so much of change that I doubted to whom I spoke. The now ghastly pallor of the skin, and the now miraculous lustre of the eye, above all things startled and even awed me. The silken hair, too, had been suffered to grow all unheeded, and as, in its wild gossamer texture, it floated rather than fell about the face, I could not, even with effort, connect its Arabesque expression with any idea of simple humanity.

In the manner of my friend I was at once struck with an incoherence—an inconsistency; and I soon found this to arise from a series of feeble and futile struggles to overcome an habitual trepidancy—an excessive nervous agitation. For something of this nature I had indeed been prepared, no less by his letter than by reminiscences of certain boyish traits, and by conclusions deduced from his peculiar physical conformation and temperament. His action was alternately vivacious and sullen. His voice varied rapidly from a tremulous indecision

207

(when the animal spirits seemed utterly in abeyance) to that species of energetic concision—that abrupt, weighty, un-hurried, and hollow-sounding enunciation—that leaden, self-balanced, and perfectly modulated guttural utterance, which may be observed in the lost drunkard, or the irreclaimable eater of opium, during the periods of his most intense excitement.

It was thus that he spoke of the object of my visit, of his earnest desire to see me, and of the solace he expected me to afford him. He entered, at some length, into what he conceived to be the nature of his malady. It was, he said, a constitutional and a family evil and one for which he despaired to find a remedy— a mere nervous affection, he immediately added, which would undoubtedly soon pass off. It displayed itself in a host of unnatural sensations. Some of these, as he detailed them, interested and bewildered me; although, perhaps, the terms and the general manner of their narration had their weight. He suffered much from a morbid acuteness of the senses; the most insipid food was alone endurable; he could wear only garments of certain texture; the odors of all flowers were oppressive; his eyes were tortured by even a faint light; and there were but peculiar sounds, and these from stringed instruments, which did not inspire him with horror.

To an anomalous species of terror I found him a bounden slave. "I shall perish," said he, "I *must* perish in this deplorable folly. Thus, thus, and not otherwise, shall I be lost. I dread the events of the future, not in themselves, but in their results. I shudder at the thought of any, even the most trivial, incident, which may operate upon this intolerable agitation of soul. I have, indeed, no abhorrence of danger, except in its absolute effect—in terror. In this unnerved, in this pitiable, condition I feel that the period will sooner or later arrive when I must abandon life and reason together, in some struggle with the grim phantasm, FEAR."

I learned, moreover, at intervals, and through broken and equivocal hints, another singular feature of his mental condition. He was enchained by certain superstitious impressions in regard to the dwelling which he tenanted, and whence, for many years, he had never ventured forth—in regard to an influence whose supposititious force was conveyed in terms too shadowy here to be restated—an influence which some peculiarities in the mere form and substance of his family mansion had, by dint of long sufferance, he said, obtained over his spirit—an effect which the *physique* of the gray walls and turrets, and of the dim tarn into which they all looked down, had at length, brought about upon the *morale* of his existence.

He admitted, however, although with hesitation, that much of the peculiar gloom which thus afflicted him could be traced to a more natural and far more capable origin—to the severe and long-continued illness—indeed to the evidently approaching dissolution—of a tenderly beloved sister, his sole companion for long years, his last and only relative on earth. "Her decease," he said, with a bitterness which I can never forget, "would leave him (him, the hopeless and the frail) the last of the ancient race of the Ushers." While he spoke, the lady Madeline (for so was she called) passed through a remote portion of the apartment, and, without having noticed my presence, disappeared. I regarded her with an utter astonishment not unmingled with dread; and yet I found it impossible to account for such feelings. A sensation of stupor oppressed me as my eyes followed her retreating steps. When a door, at length, closed upon her, my glance sought instinctively and eagerly the countenance of the brother; but he had buried his face in his hands, and I could only perceive that a far more than ordinary wanness had overspread the emaciated fingers through which trickled many passionate tears.

The disease of the lady Madeline had long baffled the skill of her physicians. A settled apathy, a gradual wasting away of the person, and frequent although transient affections of a partially cataleptical character were the unusual diagnosis. Hitherto she had steadily borne up against the pressure of her malady, and had not betaken herself finally to bed; but on the closing in of the evening of my arrival at the house, she succumbed (as her brother told me at night with inexpressible agitation) to the prostrating power of the destroyer; and I learned that the glimpse I had obtained of her person would thus probably be the last I should obtain—that the lady, at least while living, would be seen by me no more.

For several days ensuing, her name was unmentioned by either Usher or myself; and during this period I was busied in earnest endeavors to alleviate the melancholy of my friend. We painted and read together, or I listened, as if in a dream, to the wild improvisations of his speaking guitar. And thus, as a closer and still closer intimacy admitted me more unreservedly into the recesses of his spirit, the more bitterly did I perceive the futility of all attempt at cheering a mind from which darkness, as if an inherent positive quality, poured forth upon all objects of the moral and physical universe in one unceasing radiation of gloom.

I shall ever bear about me a memory of the many solemn hours I thus spent alone with the master of the House of Usher. Yet I should fail in any attempt to convey an idea of the exact character of the studies, or of the occupations, in which he involved me, or led me the way. An excited and highly distempered ideality threw a sulphureous lustre over all. His long improvised dirges will ring forever in my ears. Among other things, I hold painfully in mind a certain singular perversion and amplification of the wild air of the last waltz of Von Weber. From the paintings over which his elaborate fancy brooded, and which grew, touch by touch, into vaguenesses at which I shuddered the more thrillingly, because I shuddered knowing not why—from these paintings (vivid as their images now are before me) I would in vain endeavor to educe more than a small portion which should lie within the compass of merely written words. By the utter simplicity, by the nakedness of his designs, he arrested and overawed attention. If ever mortal painted an idea, that mortal was Roderick Usher. For me at least, in the circumstances then surrounding me, there arose out of the pure abstractions which the hypochondriac contrived to throw upon his canvas, an intensity of intolerable awe, no shadow of which felt I ever yet in the contemplation of the certainly glowing yet too concrete reveries of Fuseli.

One of the phantasmagoric conceptions of my friend, partaking not so rigidly of the spirit of abstraction, may be shadowed forth, although feebly, in words. A small picture presented the interior of an immensely long and rectangular vault or tunnel, with low walls, smooth, white and without interruption or device. Certain accessory points of the design served well to convey the idea that this excavation lay at an exceeding depth below the surface of the earth. No out-

209

let was observed in any portion of its vast extent, and no torch or other artificial source of light was discernible; yet a flood of intense rays rolled throughout, and bathed the whole in a ghastly and inappropriate splendor.

I have just spoken of that morbid condition of the auditory nerve which rendered all music intolerable to the sufferer, with the exception of certain effects of stringed instruments. It was, perhaps, the narrow limits to which he thus confined himself upon the guitar which gave birth, in great measure, to the fantastic character of his performances. But the fervid *facility* of his *impromptus* could not be so accounted for. They must have been, and were, in the notes, as well as in the words of his wild fantasias (for he not unfrequently accompanied himself with rhymed verbal improvisations), the result of that intense mental collectedness and concentration to which I have previously alluded as observable only in particular moments of the highest artificial excitement. The words of one of these rhapsodies I have easily remembered. I was, perhaps, the more forcibly impressed with it as he gave it, because, in the under or mystic current of its meaning, I fancied that I perceived, and for the first time, a full consciousness on the part of Usher of the tottering of his lofty reason upon her throne. The verses, which were entitled "The Haunted Palace," ran very nearly, if not accurately, thus:—

I.

In the greenest of our valleys,
    By good angels tenanted,
Once a fair and stately palace—
    Radiant palace—reared its head.
In the monarch Thought's dominion—
    It stood there!
Never seraph spread a pinion
    Over fabric half so fair.

II.

Banners yellow, glorious, golden,
    On its roof did float and flow
(This—all this—was in the olden
    Time long ago);
And every gentle air that dallied,
    In that sweet day,
Along the ramparts plumed and pallid,
    A winged odor went away.

III.

Wanderers in that happy valley
    Through two luminous windows saw
Spirits moving musically
    To a lute's well-tuned law;
Round about a throne, where sitting
    (Porphyrogene!)
In state his glory well befitting,
    The ruler of the realm was seen.

210

IV.

And all with pearl and ruby glowing
  Was the fair palace door,
Through which came flowing, flowing, flowing
  And sparkling evermore,
A troop of Echoes whose sweet duty
  Was but to sing,
In voices of surpassing beauty,
  The wit and wisdom of their king.

V.

But evil things, in robes of sorrow,
  Assailed the monarch's high estate;
(Ah, let us mourn, for never morrow
  Shall dawn upon him, desolate!)
And, round about his home, the glory
  That blushed and bloomed
Is but a dim-remembered story
  Of the old time entombed.

VI.

And travellers now within that valley,
  Through the red-litten windows see
Vast forms that move fantastically
  To a discordant melody;
While, like a rapid ghastly river,
  Through the pale door,
A hideous throng rush out forever,
  And laugh—but smile no more.

I well remember that suggestions arising from this ballad led us into a train of thought wherein there became manifest an opinion of Usher's which I mention not so much on account of its novelty (for other men have thought thus), as on account of the pertinacity with which he maintained it. This opinion, in its general form, was that of the sentience of all vegetable things. But, in his disordered fancy the idea had assumed a more daring character, and trespassed, under certain conditions, upon the kingdom of inorganization. I lack words to express the full extent, or the earnest *abandon* of his persuasion. The belief, however, was connected (as I have previously hinted) with the gray stones of the home of his forefathers. The conditions of the sentence had been here, he imagined, fulfilled in the method of collocation of these stones—in the order of their arrangement, as well as in that of the many *fungi* which overspread them, and of the decayed trees which stood around—above all, in the long undisturbed endurance of this arrangement, and in its reduplication in the still waters of the tarn. Its evidence—the evidence of the sentience—was to be seen, he said (and I here started as he spoke), in the gradual yet uncertain condensation of an atmosphere of their own about the waters and the walls. The result was discoverable, he added, in that silent yet importunate and terrible influence which for centuries had moulded the destinies of his family, and which made *him* what I

211

now saw him—what he was. Such opinions need no comment, and I will make none.

Our books—the books which, for years, had formed no small portion of the mental existence of the invalid—were, as might be supposed, in strict keeping with this character of phantasm. We pored together over such works as the "Belphegor" of Machiavelli; the "Heaven and Hell" of Swedenborg; the "Subterranean Voyage of Nicholas Klimm" by Holberg; the "Chiromancy" of Robert Flud, of Jean D'Indaginé and of De la Chambre; the "Journey into the Blue Distance" of Tieck; and the "City of the Sun" of Campanella. One favorite volume was a small octavo edition of the "Directorium Inquisitorium," by the Dominican Eymeric de Gironne; and there were passages in Pomponius Mela, about the old African Satyrs and Œgipans, over which Usher would sit dreaming for hours. His chief delight, however, was found in the perusal of an exceedingly rare and curious book in quarto Gothic—the manual of a forgotten church—the *Vigiliæ Mortuorum secundum Chorum Ecclesiæ Maguntinæ*.[2]

I could not help thinking of the wild ritual of this work, and of its probable influence upon the hypochondriac, when, one evening, having informed me abruptly that the lady Madeline was no more, he stated his intention of preserving her corpse for a fortnight (previously to its final interment), in one of the numerous vaults within the main walls of the building. The worldly reason, however, assigned for this singular proceeding, was one which I did not feel at liberty to dispute. The brother had been led to his resolution (so he told me) by consideration of the unusual character of the malady of the deceased, of certain obtrusive and eager inquiries on the part of her medical men, and of the remote and exposed situation of the burial-ground of the family. I will not deny that when I called to mind the sinister countenance of the person whom I met upon the staircase, on the day of my arrival at the house, I had no desire to oppose what I regarded as at best but a harmless, and by no means an unnatural precaution.

At the request of Usher, I personally aided in the arrangements for the temporary entombment. The body having been encoffined, we two alone bore it to its rest. The vault in which we placed it (and which had been so long unopened that our torches, half smothered in its oppressive atmosphere, gave us little opportunity for investigation) was small, damp, and entirely without means of admission for light; lying, at great depth, immediately beneath that portion of the building in which was my own sleeping apartment. It had been used, apparently, in remote feudal times, for the worst purposes of a donjon-keep, and, in later days, as a place of deposit for powder, or some other highly combustible substance, as a portion of its floor, and the whole interior of a long archway through which we reached it, were carefully sheathed with copper. The door, of massive iron, had been, also, similarly protected. Its immense weight caused an unusually sharp, grating sound, as it moved upon its hinges.

Having deposited our mournful burden upon tressels within this region of horror, we partially turned aside the yet unscrewed lid of the coffin, and looked upon the face of the tenant. A striking similitude between the brother and sister now first arrested my attention; and Usher, divining, perhaps, my thoughts,

212

---

[2] *Vigils for the Dead According to the Choir of the Church of Mayence.*

murmured out some few words from which I learned that the deceased and himself had been twins, and that sympathies of a scarcely intelligible nature had always existed between them. Our glances, however, rested not long upon the dead—for we could not regard her unawed. The disease which had thus entombed the lady in the maturity of youth, had left, as usual in all maladies of a strictly cataleptical character, the mockery of a faint blush upon the bosom and the face, and that suspiciously lingering smile upon the lip which is so terrible in death. We replaced and screwed down the lid, and, having secured the door of iron, made our way, with toil, into the scarcely less gloomy apartments of the upper portion of the house.

And now, some days of bitter grief having elapsed, an observable change came over the features of the mental disorder of my friend. His ordinary manner had vanished. His ordinary occupations were neglected or forgotten. He roamed from chamber to chamber with hurried, unequal, and objectless step. The pallor of his countenance had assumed, if possible, a more ghastly hue—but the luminousness of his eye had utterly gone out. The once occasional huskiness of his tone was heard no more; and a tremulous quaver, as if of extreme terror, habitually characterized his utterance. There were times, indeed, when I thought his unceasingly agitated mind was laboring with some oppressive secret, to divulge which he struggled for the necessary courage. At times, again, I was obliged to resolve all into the mere inexplicable vagaries of madness, for I beheld him gazing upon vacancy for long hours, in an attitude of the profoundest attention, as if listening to some imaginary sound. It was no wonder that his condition terrified—that it infected me. I felt creeping upon me, by slow yet uncertain degrees, the wild influences of his own fantastic yet impressive superstitions.

It was, especially, upon retiring to bed late in the night of the seventh or eighth day after the placing of the lady Madeline within the donjon, that I experienced the full power of such feelings. Sleep came not near my couch—while the hours waned and waned away. I struggled to reason off the nervousness which had dominion over me. I endeavored to believe that much, if not all of what I felt, was due to the bewildering influence of the gloomy furniture of the room—of the dark and tattered draperies, which, tortured into motion by the breath of a rising tempest, swayed fitfully to and fro upon the walls, and rustled uneasily about the decorations of the bed. But my efforts were fruitless. An irrepressible tremor gradually pervaded my frame; and, at length, there sat upon my very heart an incubus of utterly causeless alarm. Shaking this off with a gasp and a struggle, I uplifted myself upon the pillows, and, peering earnestly within the intense darkness of the chamber, hearkened—I know not why, except that an instinctive spirit prompted me—to certain low and indefinite sounds which came, through the pauses of the storm, at long intervals, I knew not whence. Overpowered by an intense sentiment of horror, unaccountable yet unendurable, I threw on my clothes with haste (for I felt that I should sleep no more during the night), and endeavored to arouse myself from the pitiable condition into which I had fallen by pacing rapidly to and fro through the apartment.

I had taken but few turns in this manner, when a light step on an adjoining staircase arrested my attention. I presently recognized it as that of Usher. In an

213

instant afterward he rapped, with a gentle touch, at my door, and entered, bearing a lamp. His countenance was, as usual, cadaverously wan—but, moreover, there was a species of mad hilarity in his eyes—an evidently restrained *hysteria* in his whole demeanor. His air appalled me—but any thing was preferable to the solitude which I had so long endured, and I even welcomed his presence as a relief.

"And you have not seen it?" he said abruptly, after having stared about him for some moments in silence—"you have not then seen it?—but, stay! you shall." Thus speaking, and having carefully shaded his lamp, he hurried to one of the casements, and threw it freely open to the storm.

The impetuous fury of the entering gust nearly lifted us from our feet. It was, indeed, a tempestuous yet sternly beautiful night, and one wildly singular in its terror and its beauty. A whirlwind had apparently collected its force in our vicinity; for there were frequent and violent alterations in the direction of the wind; and the exceeding density of the clouds (which hung so low as to press upon the turrets of the house) did not prevent our perceiving the life-like velocity with which they flew careering from all points against each other, without passing away into the distance. I say that even their exceeding density did not prevent our perceiving this—yet we had no glimpse of the moon or stars, nor was there any flashing forth of the lightning. But the under surfaces of the huge masses of agitated vapor, as well as all terrestrial objects immediately around us, were glowing in the unnatural light of a faintly luminous and distinctly visible gaseous exhalation which hung about and enshrouded the mansion.

"You must not—you shall not behold this!" said I, shuddering, to Usher, as I led him, with a gentle violence, from the window to a seat. "These appearances, which bewilder you, are merely electrical phenomena not uncommon—or it may be that they have their ghastly origin in the rank miasma of the tarn. Let us close this casement;—the air is chilling and dangerous to your frame. Here is one of your favorite romances. I will read, and you shall listen:—and so we will pass away this terrible night together."

The antique volume which I had taken up was the "Mad Trist" of Sir Launcelot Canning; but I had called it a favorite of Usher's more in sad jest than in earnest; for, in truth, there is little in its uncouth and unimaginative prolixity which could have had interest for the lofty and spiritual ideality of my friend. It was, however, the only book immediately at hand; and I indulged a vague hope that the excitement which now agitated the hypochondriac, might find relief (for the history of mental disorder is full of similar anomalies) even in the extremeness of the folly which I should read. Could I have judged, indeed, by the wild overstrained air of vivacity with which he hearkened, or apparently hearkened, to the words of the tale, I might well have congratulated myself upon the success of my design.

I had arrived at that well-known portion of the story where Ethelred, the hero of the Trist, having sought in vain for peaceable admission into the dwelling of the hermit, proceeds to make good an entrance by force. Here, it will be remembered, the words of the narrative run thus:

"And Ethelred, who was by nature of a doughty heart, and who was now mighty withal, on account of the powerfulness of the wine which he had drunken, waited no longer to hold parley with the hermit, who, in sooth, was of an obstinate and maliceful turn, but feeling the rain upon his shoulders, and fearing the rising of the tempest, uplifted his mace outright, and, with blows, made quickly room in the plankings of the door for his gauntleted hand; and now pulling therewith sturdily, he so cracked, and ripped, and tore all asunder, that the noise of the dry and hollow-sounding wood alarumed and reverberated throughout the forest."

At the termination of this sentence I started and, for a moment, paused; for it appeared to me (although I at once concluded that my excited fancy had deceived me)—it appeared to me that, from some very remote portion of the mansion, there came, indistinctly to my ears, what might have been, in its exact similarity of character, the echo (but a stifled and dull one certainly) of the very cracking and ripping sound which Sir Launcelot had so particularly described. It was, beyond doubt, the coincidence alone which had arrested my attention; for, amid the rattling of the sashes of the casements, and the ordinary commingled noises of the still increasing storm, the sound, in itself, had nothing, surely, which should have interested or disturbed me. I continued the story:

"But the good champion Ethelred, now entering within the door, was sore enraged and amazed to perceive no signal of the maliceful hermit; but, in the stead thereof, a dragon of a scaly and prodigious demeanor, and of a fiery tongue, which sate in guard before a palace of gold, with a floor of silver; and upon the wall there hung a shield of shining brass with this legend enwritten—

> Who entereth herein, a conqueror hath bin;
> Who slayeth the dragon, the shield he shall win.

And Ethelred uplifted his mace, and struck upon the head of the dragon, which fell before him, and gave up his pesty breath, with a shriek so horrid and harsh, and withal so piercing, that Ethelred had fain to close his ears with his hands against the dreadful noise of it, the like whereof was never before heard."

Here again I paused abruptly, and now with a feeling of wild amazement —for there could be no doubt whatever that, in this instance, I did actually hear (although from what direction it proceeded I found it impossible to say) a low and apparently distant, but harsh, protracted, and most unusual screaming or grating sound—the exact counterpart of what my fancy had already conjured up for the dragon's unnatural shriek as described by the romancer.

Oppressed, as I certainly was, upon the extraordinary coincidence, by a thousand conflicting sensations, in which wonder and extreme terror was predominant, I still retained sufficient presence of mind to avoid exciting, by an observation, the sensitive nervousness of my companion. I was by no means certain that he had noticed the sounds in question; although, assuredly, a strange alteration had, during the last few minutes, taken place in his demeanor. From a position fronting my own, he had gradually brought round his chair, so as to sit with his face to the door of the chamber; and thus I could but partially perceive his features, although I saw that his lips trembled as if he were murmuring inaudibly. His head had dropped upon his breast—yet I knew that he was not asleep, from the wide and rigid opening of the eye as I caught a glance of it in profile. The motion of his body, too, was at variance with this idea— for he rocked from side to side with a gentle yet constant and uniform sway.

215

Having rapidly taken notice of all this, I resumed the narrative of Sir Launce-lot, which thus proceeded:

"And now, the champion, having escaped from the terrible fury of the dragon, bethinking himself of the brazen shield, and of the breaking up of the enchantment which was upon it, removed the carcass from out of the way before him, and approached valorously over the silver pavement of the castle to where the shield was upon the wall; which in sooth tarried not for his full coming, but fell down at his feet upon the silver floor, with a mighty great and terrible ringing sound."

No sooner had these syllables passed my lips, than—as if a shield of brass had indeed, at the moment, fallen heavily upon a floor of silver—I became aware of a distinct, hollow, metallic, and clangorous, yet apparently muffled, reverberation. Completely unnerved, I leaped to my feet; but the measured rocking movement of Usher was undisturbed. I rushed to the chair in which he sat. His eyes were bent fixedly before him, and throughout his whole counte-nance there reigned a stony rigidity. But, as I placed my hand upon his shoulder, there came a strong shudder over his whole person; a sickly smile quivered about his lips; and I saw that he spoke in a low, hurried and gibbering mur-mur, as if unconscious of my presence. Bending closely over him I at length drank in the hideous import of his words.

"Not hear it?—yes, I hear it, and *have* heard it. Long—long—long—many minutes, many hours, many days, have I heard it—yet I dared not—oh, pity me, miserable wretch that I am!—I dared not—I *dared* not speak! *We have put her living in the tomb!* Said I not that my senses were acute? I *now* tell you that I heard her first feeble movement in the hollow coffin. I heard them—many, many days ago—yet I dared not—*I dared not speak!* And now—to-night—Ethelred—ha! ha!—the breaking of the hermit's door, and the death-cry of the dragon, and the clangor of the shield—say, rather, the rending of her coffin, and the grating of the iron hinges of her prison, and her struggles within the coppered archway of the vault! Oh! whither shall I fly? Will she not be here anon? Is she not hurrying to upbraid me for my haste? Have I not heard her footstep on the stair? Do I not distinguish that heavy and horrible beating of her heart? Madman!"—here he sprang furiously to his feet, and shrieked out his syllables, as if in the effort he were giving up his soul—"*Madman! I tell you that she now stands without the door!*"

As if in the superhuman energy of his utterance there had been found the potency of a spell, the huge antique panels to which the speaker pointed threw slowly back, upon the instant, their ponderous and ebony jaws. It was the work of the rushing gust—but then without those doors there *did* stand the lofty and enshrouded figure of the lady Madeline of Usher. There was blood upon her white robes, and the evidence of some bitter struggle upon every portion of her emaciated frame. For a moment she remained trembling and reeling to and fro upon the threshold—then, with a low moaning cry, fell heavily inward upon the person of her brother, and in her violent and now final death-agonies, bore him to the floor a corpse, and a victim to the terrors he had anticipated.

216

From that chamber, and from that mansion, I fled aghast. The storm was still abroad in all its wrath as I found myself crossing the old causeway. Suddenly there shot along the path a wild light, and I turned to see whence a gleam so unusual could have issued; for the vast house and its shadows were alone behind me. The radiance was that of the full, setting and blood-red moon which now shone vividly through that once barely-discernible fissure of which I have before spoken as extending from the roof of the building, in a zigzag direction, to the base. While I gazed, this fissure rapidly widened—there came a fierce breath of the whirlwind—the entire orb of the satellite burst at once upon my sight—my brain reeled as I saw the mighty walls rushing asunder— there was a long tumultuous shouting sound like the voice of a thousand waters —and the deep and dank tarn at my feet closed sullenly and silently over the fragments of the "HOUSE OF USHER." (*1839*)

The Purloined Letter

At Paris, just after dark one gusty evening in the autumn of 18—, I was enjoying the twofold luxury of meditation and a meerschaum, in company with my friend, C. Auguste Dupin, in his little back library, or book-closet, *au troisième*, No. 33 *Rue Dunot, Faubourg St. Germain*. For one hour at least we had maintained a profound silence; while each, to any casual observer, might have seemed intently and exclusively occupied with the curling eddies of smoke that oppressed the atmosphere of the chamber. For myself, however, I was mentally discussing certain topics which had formed matter for conversation between us at an earlier period of the evening; I mean the affair of the Rue Morgue, and the mystery attending the murder of Marie Roget. I looked upon it, therefore, as something of a coincidence, when the door of our apartment was thrown open and admitted our old acquaintance, Monsieur G——, the Prefect of the Parisian police.

We gave him a hearty welcome; for there was nearly half as much of the entertaining as of the contemptible about the man, and we had not seen him for several years. We had been sitting in the dark, and Dupin now arose for the purpose of lighting a lamp, but sat down again, without doing so, upon G.'s saying that he had called to consult us, or rather to ask the opinion of my friend, about some official business which had occasioned a great deal of trouble.

"If it is any point requiring reflection," observed Dupin, as he forebore to enkindle the wick, "we shall examine it to better purpose in the dark."

"That is another of your odd notions," said the Prefect, who had the fashion of calling every thing "odd" that was beyond his comprehension, and thus lived amid an absolute legion of "oddities."

"Very true," said Dupin, as he supplied his visitor with a pipe, and rolled toward him a comfortable chair.

"And what is the difficulty now?" I asked. "Nothing more in the assassination way I hope?"

"Oh, no; nothing of that nature. The fact is, the business is *very* simple indeed, and I make no doubt that we can manage it sufficiently well ourselves; but then I thought Dupin would like to hear the details of it, because it is so excessively *odd*."

"Simple and odd," said Dupin.

"Why, yes; and not exactly that either. The fact is, we have all been a good deal puzzled because the affair *is* so simple, and yet baffles us altogether."

"Perhaps it is the very simplicity of the thing which puts you at fault," said my friend.

"What nonsense you *do* talk!" replied the Prefect, laughing heartily.

"Perhaps the mystery is a little *too* plain," said Dupin.

"Oh, good heavens! who ever heard of such an idea?"

"A little *too* self-evident."

"Ha! ha! ha!—ha! ha! ha!—ho! ho! ho!" roared our visitor, profoundly amused, "oh, Dupin, you will be the death of me yet!"

"And what, after all, *is* the matter on hand?" I asked.

"Why, I will tell you," replied the Prefect, as he gave a long, steady, and contemplative puff, and settled himself in his chair. "I will tell you in a few words; but, before I begin, let me caution you that this is an affair demanding the greatest secrecy, and that I should most probably lose the position I now hold, were it known that I confided it to any one."

"Proceed," said I.

"Or not," said Dupin.

"Well, then; I have received personal information, from a very high quarter, that a certain document of the last importance has been purloined from the royal apartments. The individual who purloined it is known; this beyond a doubt; he was seen to take it. It is known, also, that it still remains in his possession."

"How is this known?" asked Dupin.

"It is clearly inferred," replied the Prefect, "from the nature of the document, and from the non-appearance of certain results which would at once arise from its passing *out* of the robber's possession—that is to say, from his employing it as he must design in the end to employ it."

"Be a little more explicit," I said.

"Well, I may venture so far as to say that the paper gives its holder a certain power in a certain quarter where such power is immensely valuable." The Prefect was fond of the cant of diplomacy.

"Still I do not quite understand," said Dupin.

"No? Well; the disclosure of the document to a third person, who shall be nameless, would bring in question the honor of a personage of most exalted station; and this fact gives the holder of the document an ascendancy over the illustrious personage whose honor and peace are so jeopardized."

"But this ascendancy," I interposed, "would depend upon the robber's knowledge of the loser's knowledge of the robber. Who would dare—"

"The thief," said G., "is the Minister D——, who dares all things, those unbecoming as well as those becoming a man. The method of the theft was not less ingenious than bold. The document in question—a letter, to be frank—had been received by the personage robbed while alone in the royal *boudoir*. During its perusal she was suddenly interrupted by the entrance of the other exalted personage from whom especially it was her wish to conceal it. After a hurried and vain endeavor to thrust it in a drawer, she was forced to place it, open as it was, upon a table. The address, however, was uppermost, and, the contents

218

thus unexposed, the letter escaped notice. At this juncture enters the Minister D——. His lynx eye immediately perceives the paper, recognizes the handwriting of the address, observes the confusion of the personage addressed, and fathoms her secret. After some business transactions, hurried through in his ordinary manner, he produces a letter somewhat similar to the one in question, opens it, pretends to read it, and then places it in close juxtaposition to the other. Again he converses, for some fifteen minutes, upon the public affairs. At length, in taking leave, he takes also from the table the letter to which he had no claim. Its rightful owner saw, but, of course, dared not call attention to the act, in the presence of the third personage who stood at her elbow. The Minister decamped; leaving his own letter—one of no importance—upon the table."

"Here, then," said Dupin to me, "you have precisely what you demand to make the ascendancy complete—the robber's knowledge of the loser's knowledge of the robber."

"Yes," replied the Prefect; "and the power thus attained has, for some months past, been wielded, for political purposes, to a very dangerous extent. The personage robbed is more thoroughly convinced, every day, of the necessity of reclaiming her letter. But this, of course, cannot be done openly. In fine, driven to despair, she has committed the matter to me."

"Than whom," said Dupin, amid a perfect whirlwind of smoke, "no more sagacious agent could, I suppose, be desired, or even imagined."

"You flatter me," replied the Prefect; "but it is possible that some such opinion may have been entertained."

"It is clear," said I, "as you observe, that the letter is still in the possession of the Minister; since it is this possession, and not any employment of the letter, which bestows the power. With the employment the power departs."

"True," said G.; "and upon this conviction I proceeded. My first care was to make thorough search of the Minister's hotel; and here my chief embarrassment lay in the necessity of searching without his knowledge. Beyond all things, I have been warned of the danger which would result from giving him reason to suspect our design."

"But," said I, "you are quite *au fait* in these investigations. The Parisian police have done this thing often before."

"Oh, yes; and for this reason I did not despair. The habits of the Minister gave me, too, a great advantage. He is frequently absent from home all night. His servants are by no means numerous. They sleep at a distance from their master's apartment, and, being chiefly Neapolitans, are readily made drunk. I have keys, as you know, with which I can open any chamber or cabinet in Paris. For three months a night has not passed, during the greater part of which I have not been engaged, personally, in ransacking the D—— Hotel. My honor is interested, and, to mention a great secret, the reward is enormous. So I did not abandon the search until I had become fully satisfied that the thief is a more astute man than myself. I fancy that I have investigated every nook and corner of the premises in which it is possible that the paper can be concealed."

219

"But is it not possible," I suggested, "that although the letter may be in possession of the Minister, as it unquestionably is, he may have concealed it elsewhere than upon his own premises?"

"This is barely possible," said Dupin. "The present peculiar condition of affairs at court, and especially of those intrigues in which D—— is known to be involved, would render the instant availability of the document—its susceptibility of being produced at a moment's notice—a point of nearly equal importance with its possession."

"Its susceptibility of being produced?" said I.

"That is to say, of being *destroyed*," said Dupin.

"True," I observed; "the paper is clearly then upon the premises. As for its being upon the person of the Minister, we may consider that as out of the question."

"Entirely," said the Prefect. "He has been twice waylaid, as if by footpads, and his person rigidly searched under my own inspection."

"You might have spared yourself this trouble," said Dupin. "D——, I presume, is not altogether a fool, and, if not, must have anticipated these waylayings, as a matter of course."

"Not *altogether* a fool," said G., "but then he is a poet, which I take to be only one remove from a fool."

"True," said Dupin, after a long and thoughtful whiff from his meerschaum, "although I have been guilty of certain doggerel myself."

"Suppose you detail," said I, "the particulars of your search."

"Why, the fact is, we took our time, and we searched *everywhere*. I have had long experience in these affairs. I took the entire building, room by room; devoting the nights of a whole week to each. We examined, first, the furniture of each apartment. We opened every possible drawer; and I presume you know that, to a properly trained police-agent, such a thing as a 'secret' drawer is impossible. Any man is a dolt who permits a 'secret' drawer to escape him in a search of this kind. The thing is *so* plain. There is a certain amount of bulk—of space—to be accounted for in every cabinet. Then we have accurate rules. The fiftieth part of a line could not escape us. After the cabinets we took the chairs. The cushions we probed with the fine long needles you have seen me employ. From the tables we removed the tops."

"Why so?"

"Sometimes the top of a table, or other similarly arranged piece of furniture, is removed by the person wishing to conceal an article; then the leg is excavated, the article deposited within the cavity, and the top replaced. The bottoms and tops of bedposts are employed in the same way."

"But could not the cavity be detected by sounding?" I asked.

"By no means, if, when the article is deposited, a sufficient wadding of cotton be placed around it. Besides, in our case, we were obliged to proceed without noise."

"But you could not have removed—you could not have taken to pieces *all* articles of furniture in which it would have been possible to make a deposit in the manner you mention. A letter may be compressed into a thin spiral roll, not differing much in shape or bulk from a large knitting-needle, and in this form it might be inserted into the rung of a chair, for example. You did not take to pieces all the chairs?"

"Certainly not; but we did better—we examined the rungs of every chair in the hotel, and, indeed, the jointings of every description of furniture, by the

220

aid of a most powerful microscope. Had there been any trace of recent disturbance we should not have failed to detect it instantly. A single grain of gimlet-dust, for example, would have been as obvious as an apple. Any disorder in the gluing—any unusual gaping in the joints—would have sufficed to insure detection."

"I presume you looked to the mirrors, between the boards and the plates, and you probed the beds and the bedclothes, as well as the curtains and carpets."

"That of course; and when we had absolutely completed every particle of the furniture in this way, then we examined the house itself. We divided its entire surface into compartments, which we numbered, so that none might be missed; then we scrutinized each individual square inch throughout the premises, including the two houses immediately adjoining, with the microscope, as before."

"The two houses adjoining!" I exclaimed; "you must have had a great deal of trouble."

"We had; but the reward offered is prodigious."

"You include the *grounds* about the houses?"

"All the grounds are paved with brick. They gave us comparatively little trouble. We examined the moss between the bricks, and found it undisturbed."

"You looked among D——'s papers, of course, and into the books of the library?"

"Certainly; we opened every package and parcel; we not only opened every book, but we turned over every leaf in each volume, not contenting ourselves with a mere shake, according to the fashion of some of our police officers. We also measured the thickness of every book-*cover*, with the most accurate admeasurement, and applied to each the most jealous scrutiny of the microscope. Had any of the bindings been recently meddled with, it would have been utterly impossible that the fact should have escaped observation. Some five or six volumes, just from the hands of the binder, we carefully probed, longitudinally, with the needles."

"You explored the floors beneath the carpets?"

"Beyond doubt. We removed every carpet, and examined the boards with the microscope."

"And the paper on the walls?"

"Yes."

"You looked into the cellars?"

"We did."

"Then," I said, "you have been making a miscalculation, and the letter is *not* upon the premises, as you suppose."

"I fear you are right there," said the Prefect. "And now, Dupin, what would you advise me to do?"

"To make a thorough research of the premises."

"That is absolutely needless," replied G——. "I am not more sure that I breathe than I am that the letter is not at the hotel."

"I have no better advice to give you," said Dupin. "You have, of course, an accurate description of the letter?"

"Oh, yes!"—And here the Prefect, producing a memorandum-book, proceeded to read aloud a minute account of the internal, and especially of the external appearance of the missing document. Soon after finishing the perusal of this description, he took his departure, more entirely depressed in spirits than I had ever known the good gentleman before.

In about a month afterward he paid us another visit, and found us occupied very nearly as before. He took a pipe and a chair and entered into some ordinary conversation. At length I said:

"Well, but G——, what of the purloined letter? I presume you have at last made up your mind that there is no such thing as over-reaching the Minister?"

"Confound him, say I—yes; I made the re-examination, however, as Dupin suggested—but it was all labor lost, as I knew it would be."

"How much was the reward offered, did you say?" asked Dupin.

"Why, a very great deal—a *very* liberal reward—I don't like to say how much, precisely; but one thing I *will* say, that I wouldn't mind giving my individual check for fifty thousand francs to any one who could obtain me that letter. The fact is, it is becoming of more and more importance every day; and the reward has been lately doubled. If it were trebled, however, I could do no more than I have done."

"Why, yes," said Dupin, drawlingly between the whiffs of his meerschaum, "I really—think, G——, you have not exerted yourself—to the utmost in this matter. You might—do a little more, I think, eh?"

"How?—in what way?"

"Why—puff, puff—you might—puff, puff—employ counsel in the matter, eh? —puff, puff, puff. Do you remember the story they tell of Abernethy?"

"No; hang Abernethy!"

"To be sure! hang him and welcome. But, once upon a time, a certain rich miser conceived the design of sponging upon this Abernethy for a medical opinion. Getting up, for this purpose, an ordinary conversation in a private company, he insinuated his case to the physician, as that of an imaginary individual.

" 'We will suppose,' said the miser, 'that his symptoms are such and such; now, doctor, what would *you* have directed him to take?'

" 'Take!' said Abernethy, 'why, take *advice*, to be sure.' "

"But," said the Prefect, a little discomposed, "*I* am *perfectly* willing to take advice, and to pay for it. I would *really* give fifty thousand francs to any one who would aid me in the matter."

"In that case," replied Dupin, opening a drawer, and producing a checkbook, "you may as well fill me up a check for the amount mentioned. When you have signed it, I will hand you the letter."

I was astounded. The Prefect appeared absolutely thunder-stricken. For some minutes he remained speechless and motionless, looking incredulously at my friend with open mouth, and eyes that seemed starting from their sockets; then apparently recovering himself in some measure, he seized a pen, and after several pauses and vacant stares, finally filled up and signed a check for fifty thousand francs, and handed it across the table to Dupin. The latter examined it carefully and deposited it in his pocket-book; then, unlocking an *escritoire*, took thence a letter and gave it to the Prefect. This functionary grasped it in a perfect agony of joy, opened it with a trembling hand, cast a rapid glance at its contents, and then scrambling and struggling to the door, rushed at length unceremoniously from the room and from the house, without having uttered a syllable since Dupin had requested him to fill up the check.

When he had gone, my friend entered into some explanations.

"The Parisian police," he said, "are exceedingly able in their way. They are persevering, ingenious, cunning, and thoroughly versed in the knowledge which their duties seem chiefly to demand. Thus, when G—— detailed to us his mode of searching the premises at the Hotel D——, I felt entire confidence in his having made a satisfactory investigation—so far as his labors extended."

"So far as his labors extended?" said I.

"Yes," said Dupin. "The measures adopted were not only the best of their kind, but carried out to absolute perfection. Had the letter been deposited within the range of their search, these fellows would, beyond a question, have found it."

I merely laughed—but he seemed quite serious in all that he said.

"The measures then," he continued, "were good in their kind, and well executed; their defect lay in their being inapplicable to the case and to the man. A certain set of highly ingenious resources are, with the Prefect, a sort of Procrustean bed, to which he forcibly adapts his designs. But he perpetually errs by being too deep or too shallow for the matter in hand; and many a schoolboy is a better reasoner than he. I knew one about eight years of age, whose success at guessing in the game of 'even and odd' attracted universal admiration. This game is simple, and is played with marbles. One player holds in his hand a number of these toys, and demands of another whether that number is even or odd. If the guess is right, the guesser wins one; if wrong, he loses one. The boy to whom I allude won all the marbles of the school. Of course he had some principle of guessing; and this lay in mere observation and admeasurement of the astuteness of his opponents. For example, an arrant simpleton is his opponent, and, holding up his closed hand, asks, 'Are they even or odd?' Our school-boy replies, 'Odd,' and loses; but upon the second trial he wins, for he then says to himself: 'The simpleton had them even upon the first trial, and his amount of cunning is just sufficient to make him have them odd upon the second; I will therefore guess odd';—he guesses odd, and wins. Now, with a simpleton a degree above the first, he would have reasoned thus: 'This fellow finds that in the first instance I guessed odd, and, in the second, he will propose to himself, upon the first impulse, a simple variation from even to odd, as did the first simpleton; but then a second thought will suggest that this is too simple a variation, and finally he will decide upon putting it even as before. I will therefore guess even';—he guesses even, and wins. Now this mode of reasoning in the school-boy, whom his fellows termed 'lucky,'—what, in its last analysis, is it?"

"It is merely," I said, "an identification of the reasoner's intellect with that of his opponent."

"It is," said Dupin; "and, upon inquiring of the boy by what means he effected the *thorough* identification in which his success consisted, I received answer as follows: 'When I wish to find out how wise, or how stupid, or how

223

good, or how wicked is any one, or what are his thoughts at the moment, I fashion the expression of my face, as accurately as possible, in accordance with the expression of his, and then wait to see what thoughts or sentiments arise in my mind or heart, as if to match or correspond with the expression.' This response of the school-boy lies at the bottom of all the spurious profundity which has been attributed to Rochefoucault, to La Bougive, to Machiavelli, and to Campanella."

"And the identification," I said, "of the reasoner's intellect with that of his opponent, depends, if I understand you aright, upon the accuracy with which the opponent's intellect is admeasured."

"For its practical value it depends upon this," replied Dupin; "and the Prefect and his cohort fail so frequently, first by default of this identification, and, secondly, by ill-admeasurement, or rather through non-admeasurement, of the intellect with which they are engaged. They consider only their *own* ideas of ingenuity; and, in searching for anything hidden advert only to the modes in which *they* would have hidden it. They are right in this much—that their own ingenuity is a faithful representative of that of *the mass*; but when the cunning of the individual felon is diverse in character from their own, the felon foils them, of course. This always happens when it is above their own, and very usually when it is below. They have no variation of principle in their investigations; at best, when urged by some unusual emergency—by some extraordinary reward—they extend or exaggerate their old modes of *practice*, without touching their principles. What, for example, in this case of D——, has been done to vary the principle of action? What is all this boring, and probing, and sounding, and scrutinizing with the microscope, and dividing the surface of the building into registered square inches—what is it all but an exaggeration *of the application* of the one principle or set of principles of search, which are based upon the one set of notions regarding human ingenuity, to which the Prefect, in the long routine of his duty, has been accustomed? Do you not see he has taken it for granted that *all* men proceed to conceal a letter, not exactly in a gimlet-hole bored in a chair-leg, but, at least, in *some* out-of-the-way hole or corner suggested by the same tenor of thought which would urge a man to secrete a letter in a gimlet-hole bored in a chair-leg? And do you not see also that such *recherches* nooks for concealment are adapted only for ordinary occasions, and would be adopted only by ordinary intellects; for, in all cases of concealment, a disposal of the article concealed—a disposal of it in this *recherche* manner,—is in the very first instance, presumable and presumed; and thus its discovery depends, not at all upon the acumen, but altogether upon the mere care, patience, and determination of the seekers; and where the case is of importance—or, what amounts to the same thing in the political eyes, when the reward is of magnitude,—the qualities in question have *never* been known to fail. You will now understand what I meant in suggesting that, had the purloined letter been hidden anywhere within the limits of the Prefect's examination—in other words, had the principle of its concealment been comprehended within the principles of the Prefect—its discovery would have been a matter altogether beyond question. This functionary, however, has been thoroughly mystified; and the remote source of his defeat lies in the supposition that the Minister is a fool, because he has acquired renown as a poet. All fools are poets; this the Prefect feels; and he is

224

merely guilty of a *non distributio medii* [1] in thence inferring that all poets are fools."

"But is this really the poet?" I asked. "There are two brothers, I know; and both have attained reputation in letters. The Minister I believe has written learnedly on the Differential Calculus. He is a mathematician, and no poet."

"You are mistaken; I know him well; he is both. As poet *and* mathematician, he would reason well; as mere mathematician, he could not have reasoned at all, and thus would have been at the mercy of the Prefect."

"You surprise me," I said, "by these opinions, which have been contradicted by the voice of the world. You do not mean to set at naught the well-digested idea of centuries. The mathematical reason has long been regarded as *the* reason *par excellence.*"

"'*Il y a parier,*'" replied Dupin, quoting from Chamfort, "'*que toute idee publique, toute convention reçue, est une sottise, car elle a convenue au plus grand nombre.*' [2] The mathematicians, I grant you, have done their best to promulgate the popular error to which you allude, and which is none the less an error for its promulgation as truth. With an art worthy a better cause, for example, they have insinuated the term 'analysis' into application to algebra. The French are the originators of this particular deception; but if a term is of any importance—if words derive any value from applicability—then 'analysis' conveys 'algebra' about as much as, in Latin '*ambitus*' implies 'ambition,' '*religio*' 'religion,' or '*homines honesti*' a set of *honorable* men."

"You have a quarrel on hand, I see," said I, "with some of the algebraists of Paris; but proceed."

"I dispute the availability, and thus the value, of that reason which is cultivated in any especial form other than the abstractly logical. I dispute, in particular, the reason educed by mathematical study. The mathematics are the science of form and quantity; mathematical reasoning is merely logic applied to observation upon form and quantity. The great error lies in supposing that even the truths of what is called *pure* algebra are abstract or general truths. And this error is so egregious that I am confounded at the universality with which it has been received. Mathematical axioms are *not* axioms of general truth. What is true of *relation*—of form and quantity—is often grossly false in regard to morals, for example. In this latter science it is very usually *un*true that the aggregated parts are equal to the whole. In chemistry also the axiom fails. In the consideration of motive it fails; for two motives, each of a given value, have not necessarily, a value when united, equal to the sum of their values apart. There are numerous other mathematical truths which are only truths within the limits of *relation*. But the mathematician argues from his *finite truths*, through habit, as if they were of an absolutely general applicability—as the world indeed imagines them to be. Bryant, in his very learned 'Mythology,' mentions an analogous source of error, when he says that 'although the pagan fables are not believed, yet we forget ourselves continually, and make inferences from them as existing realities.' With the algebraists, however, who are pagans themselves, the 'pagan fables' *are* believed, and the in-

225

---

[1] *Undistributed middle (logic).*
[2] *I'll wager that every idea which is generally held, every set convention, is a stupidity; for it has suited the majority.*

ferences are made, not so much through lapse of memory as through an unaccountable addling of the brains. In short, I never yet encountered the mere mathematician who could be trusted out of equal roots, or one who did not clandestinely hold it as a point of his faith that $x^2 + px$ was absolutely and unconditionally equal to q. Say to one of these gentlemen, by way of experiment, if you please, that you believe occasions may occur where $x^2 + px$ is not altogether equal to q, and, having made him understand what you mean, get out of his reach as speedily as convenient, for, beyond doubt, he will endeavor to knock you down.

"I mean to say," continued Dupin, while I merely laughed at his last observations, "that if the Minister had been no more than a mathematician, the Prefect would have been under no necessity of giving me this check. I knew him, however, as both mathematician and poet, and my measures were adapted to his capacity, with reference to the circumstances by which he was surrounded. I knew him as a courtier, too, and as a bold *intriguant*. Such a man, I considered, could not fail to be aware of the ordinary political modes of action. He could not have failed to anticipate—and events have proved that he did not fail to anticipate—the waylayings to which he was subjected. He must have foreseen, I reflected, the secret investigations of his premises. His frequent absences from home at night, which were hailed by the Prefect as certain aids to his success, I regarded only as *ruses*, to afford opportunity for thorough search to the police, and thus the sooner to impress them with the conviction to which G——, in fact, did finally arrive—the conviction that the letter was not upon the premises. I felt, also, that the whole train of thought, which I was at some pains in detailing to you just now, concerning the invariable principle of political action in searches for articles concealed—I felt that this whole train of thought would necessarily pass through the mind of the Minister. It would imperatively lead him to despise all the ordinary *nooks* of concealment. *He* could not, I reflected, be so weak as not to see that the most intricate and remote recess of his hotel would be as open as his commonest closets to the eyes, to the probes, to the gimlets, and to the microscopes of the Prefect. I saw, in fine, that he would be driven, as a matter of course, to *simplicity*, if not deliberately induced to it as a matter of choice. You will remember, perhaps, how desperately the Prefect laughed when I suggested, upon our first interview, that it was just possible this mystery troubled him so much on account of its being so *very* self-evident."

"Yes," said I, "I remember his merriment well. I really thought he would have fallen into convulsions."

"The material world," continued Dupin, "abounds with very strict analogies to the immaterial; and thus some color of truth has been given to the rhetorical dogma, that metaphor, or simile, may be made to strengthen an argument as well as to embellish a description. The principle of the *vis inertiæ*,[3] for example, seems to be identical in physics and metaphysics. It is not more true in the former, that a large body is with more difficulty set in motion than a smaller one, and that its subsequent *momentum* is commensurate with this difficulty, than it is, in the latter, that intellects of the vaster capacity, while more forcible, more constant, and more eventful in their movements than those of inferior

226

[3] *Force of inertia.*

grade, are yet the less readily moved, and more embarrassed, and full of hesitation in the first few steps of their progress. Again: have you ever noticed which of the street signs, over the shop doors, are the most attractive of attention?"

"I have never given the matter a thought," I said.

"There is a game of puzzles," he resumed, "which is played upon a map. One party playing requires another to find a given word—the name of town, river, state, or empire—any word, in short, upon the motley and perplexed surface of the chart. A novice in the game generally seeks to embarrass his opponents by giving them the most minutely lettered names; but the adept selects such words as stretch, in large characters, from one end of the chart to the other. These, like the overlargely lettered signs and placards of the street, escape observation by dint of being excessively obvious; and here the physical oversight is precisely analogous with the moral inapprehension by which the intellect suffers to pass unnoticed those considerations which are too obtrusively and too palpably self-evident. But this is a point, it appears, somewhat above or beneath the understanding of the Prefect. He never once thought it probable, or possible, that the minister had deposited the letter immediately beneath the nose of the whole world by way of best preventing any portion of that world from perceiving it.

"But the more I reflected upon the daring, dashing, and discriminating ingenuity of D——; upon the fact that the document must always have been *at hand*, if he intended to use it to good purpose; and upon the decisive evidence, obtained by the Prefect, that it was not hidden within the limits of that dignitary's ordinary search—the more satisfied I became that, to conceal this letter, the Minister had resorted to the comprehensive and sagacious expedient of not attempting to conceal it at all.

"Full of these ideas, I prepared myself with a pair of green spectacles, and called one fine morning quite by accident, at the Ministerial hotel. I found D—— at home, yawning, lounging, and dawdling, as usual, and pretending to be in the last extremity of *ennui*. He is, perhaps, the most really energetic human being now alive—but that is only when nobody sees him.

"To be even with him, I complained of my weak eyes, and lamented the necessity of the spectacles, under cover of which I cautiously and thoroughly surveyed the whole apartment, while seemingly intent only upon the conversation of my host.

"I paid especial attention to a large writing-table near which he sat, and upon which lay, confusedly, some miscellaneous letters and other papers, with one or two musical instruments and a few books. Here, however, after a long and very deliberate scrutiny, I saw nothing to excite particular suspicion.

"At length my eyes, in going the circuit of the room, fell upon a trumpery filigree card-rack of pasteboard, that hung dangling by a dirty blue ribbon, from a little brass knob just beneath the middle of the mantel-piece. In this rack, which had three or four compartments, were five or six visiting cards and a solitary letter. This last was much soiled and crumpled. It was torn nearly in two, across the middle—as if a design, in the first instance, to tear it entirely up as worthless, had been altered or stayed in the second. It had a large black seal, bearing the D—— cipher *very* conspicuously, and was addressed, in a diminutive female hand, to D——, the minister, himself. It was thrust care-

227

lessly, and even, as it seemed, contemptuously, into one of the uppermost divisions of the rack.

"No sooner had I glanced at this letter than I concluded it to be that of which I was in search. To be sure, it was, to all appearance, radically different from the one of which the Prefect had read us so minute a description. Here the seal was large and black, with the D—— cipher; there it was small and red, with the ducal arms of the S—— family. Here, the address, to the minister, was diminutive and feminine; there the superscription, to a certain royal personage, was markedly bold and decided; the size alone formed a point of correspondence. But, then, the *radicalness* of these differences, which was excessive; the dirt; the soiled and torn condition of the paper, so inconsistent with the *true* methodical habits of D——, and so suggestive of a design to delude the beholder into an idea of the worthlessness of the document;—these things, together with the hyperobtrusive situation of this document, full in the view of every visitor, and thus exactly in accordance with the conclusions to which I had previously arrived; these things, I say, were strongly corroborative of suspicion, in one who came with the intention to suspect.

"I protracted my visit as long as possible, and, while I maintained a most animated discussion with the Minister, upon a topic which I knew well had never failed to interest and excite him, I kept my attention really riveted upon the letter. In this examination, I committed to memory its external appearance and arrangement in the rack; and also fell, at length, upon a discovery which set at rest whatever trivial doubt I might have entertained. In scrutinizing the edges of the paper, I observed them to be more *chafed* than seemed necessary. They presented the *broken* appearance which is manifested when a stiff paper, having been once folded and pressed with a folder, is refolded in a reversed direction, in the same creases or edges which had formed the original fold. This discovery was sufficient. It was clear to me that the letter had been turned as a glove, inside out, redirected and resealed. I bade the Minister good-morning, and took my departure at once, leaving a gold snuff-box upon the table.

"The next morning I called for the snuff-box, when we resumed, quite eagerly, the conversation of the preceding day. While thus engaged, however, a loud report, as if of a pistol, was heard immediately beneath the windows of the hotel, and was succeeded by a series of fearful screams, and the shoutings of a terrified mob. D—— rushed to a casement, threw it open, and looked out. In the meantime I stepped to the card-rack, took the letter, put it in my pocket, and replaced it by a *fac-simile*, (so far as regards externals) which I had carefully prepared at my lodgings—imitating the D—— cipher, very readily, by means of a seal formed of bread.

"The disturbance in the street had been occasioned by the frantic behavior of a man with a musket. He had fired it among a crowd of women and children. It proved, however, to have been without ball, and the fellow was suffered to go his way as a lunatic or a drunkard. When he had gone, D—— came from the window, whither I had followed him immediately upon securing the object in view. Soon afterward I bade him farewell. The pretended lunatic was a man in my own pay."

"But what purpose had you," I asked, "in replacing the letter by a *fac-simile?*

Would it not have been better at the first visit, to have seized it openly, and departed?"

"D——," replied Dupin, "is a desperate man, and a man of nerve. His hotel, too, is not without attendants devoted to his interests. Had I made the wild attempt you suggest, I might never have left the Ministerial presence alive. The good people of Paris might have heard of me no more. But I had an object apart from these considerations. You know my political prepossessions. In this matter, I act as a partisan of the lady concerned. For eighteen months the Minister has had her in his power. She has now him in hers—since, being unaware that the letter is not in his possession, he will proceed with his exactions as if it was. Thus will he inevitably commit himself, at once, to his political destruction. His downfall, too, will not be more precipitate than awkward. It is all very well to talk about the *facilis descensus Averni;* but in all kinds of climbing, as Catalani said of singing, it is far more easy to get up than to come down. In the present instance I have no sympathy—at least no pity—for him who descends. He is that *monstrum horrendum,*[4] an unprincipled man of genius. I confess, however, that I should like very well to know the precise character of his thoughts, when, being defied by her whom the Prefect terms 'a certain personage,' he is reduced to opening the letter which I left for him in the card-rack."

"How? did you put any thing particular in it?"

"Why—it did not seem altogether right to leave the interior blank—that would have been insulting. D——, at Vienna once, did me an evil turn, which I told him, quite good-humoredly, that I should remember. So, as I knew he would feel some curiosity in regard to the identity of the person who had outwitted him, I thought it a pity not to give him a clew. He is well acquainted with my MS., and I just copied into the middle of the blank sheet the words—

'—Un dessein si funeste,
S'il n'est digne d'Atrée, est digne de Thyeste.'[5]

They are to be found in Crébillon's 'Atrée.' " *(1845)*

The Cask of Amontillado

The thousand injuries of Fortunato I had borne as I best could, but when he ventured upon insult, I vowed revenge. You, who so well know the nature of my soul, will not suppose, however, that I gave utterance to a threat. *At length* I would be avenged; this was a point definitively settled—but the very definitiveness with which it was resolved, precluded the idea of risk. I must not only punish, but punish with impunity. A wrong is unredressed when retribution overtakes its redresser. It is equally unredressed when the avenger fails to make himself felt as such to him who has done the wrong.

It must be understood that neither by word nor deed had I given Fortunato cause to doubt my good will. I continued as was my wont, to smile in his face, and he did not perceive that my smile *now* was at the thought of his immolation.

229

[4] *Horrible monster.*
[5] *"So deadly a scheme, if it is not worthy of Atreus, is at least worthy of Thyestes."*

He had a weak point—this Fortunato—although in other regards he was a man to be respected and even feared. He prided himself on his connoisseurship in wine. Few Italians have the true virtuoso spirit. For the most part their enthusiasm is adapted to suit the time and opportunity—to practice imposture upon the British and Austrian *millionaires*. In painting and gemmary Fortunato, like his country men, was a quack—but in the matter of old wines he was sincere. In this respect I did not differ from him materially: I was skilful in the Italian vintages myself, and bought largely whenever I could.

It was about dusk, one evening during the supreme madness of the carnival season, that I encountered my friend. He accosted me with excessive warmth, for he had been drinking much. The man wore motley. He had on a tight-fitting parti-striped dress, and his head was surmounted by the conical cap and bells. I was so pleased to see him, that I thought I should never have done wringing his hand.

I said to him: "My dear Fortunato, you are luckily met. How remarkably well you are looking to-day! But I have received a pipe of what passes for Amontillado, and I have my doubts."

"How?" said he. "Amontillado? A pipe? Impossible! And in the middle of the carnival!"

"I have my doubts," I replied; "and I was silly enough to pay the full Amontillado price without consulting you in the matter. You were not to be found, and I was fearful of losing a bargain."

"Amontillado!"

"I have my doubts."

"Amontillado!"

"And I must satisfy them."

"Amontillado!"

"As you are engaged, I am on my way to Luchesi. If any one has a critical turn, it is he. He will tell me——"

"Luchesi cannot tell Amontillado from Sherry."

"And yet some fools will have it that his taste is a match for your own."

"Come, let us go."

"Whither?"

"To your vaults."

"My friend, no; I will not impose upon your good nature. I perceive you have an engagement. Luchesi——"

"I have no engagement—come."

"My friend, no. It is not the engagement, but the severe cold with which I perceive you are afflicted. The vaults are insufferably damp. They are encrusted with nitre."

"Let us go, nevertheless. The cold is merely nothing. Amontillado! You have been imposed upon. And as for Luchesi, he cannot distinguish Sherry from Amontillado."

230 Thus speaking, Fortunato possessed himself of my arm. Putting on a mask of black silk, and drawing a *roquelaire* closely about my person, I suffered him to hurry me to my palazzo.

There were no attendants at home; they had absconded to make merry in honor of the time. I had told them that I should not return until the morning, and had given them explicit orders not to stir from the house. These orders were sufficient, I well knew, to insure their immediate disappearance, one and all, as soon as my back was turned.

I took from their sconces two flambeaux, and giving one to Fortunato, bowed him through several suites of rooms to the archway that led into the vaults. I passed down a long and winding staircase, requesting him to be cautious as he followed. We came at length to the foot of the descent, and stood together on the damp ground of the catacombs of the Montresors.

The gait of my friend was unsteady, and the bells upon his cap jingled as he strode.

"The pipe?" said he.

"It is farther on," said I; "but observe the white webwork which gleams from these cavern walls."

He turned toward me, and looked into my eyes with two filmy orbs that distilled the rheum of intoxication.

"Nitre?" he asked, at length.

"Nitre," I replied. "How long have you had that cough?"

"Ugh! ugh! ugh!—ugh! ugh! ugh!—ugh! ugh! ugh!—ugh! ugh! ugh!—ugh! ugh! ugh!"

My poor friend found it impossible to reply for many minutes.

"It is nothing," he said, at last.

"Come," I said, with decision, "we will go back; your health is precious. You are rich, respected, admired, beloved; you are happy, as once I was. You are a man to be missed. For me it is no matter. We will go back; you will be ill, and I cannot be responsible. Besides, there is Luchesi——"

"Enough," he said; "the cough is a mere nothing; it will not kill me. I shall not die of a cough."

"True—true," I replied; "and, indeed, I had no intention of alarming you unnecessarily; but you should use all proper caution. A draught of this Medoc will defend us from the damps."

Here I knocked off the neck of a bottle which I drew from a long row of its fellows that lay upon the mould.

"Drink," I said, presenting him the wine.

He raised it to his lips with a leer. He paused and nodded to me familiarly, while his bells jingled.

"I drink," he said, "to the buried that repose around us."

"And I to your long life."

He again took my arm, and we proceeded.

"These vaults," he said, "are extensive."

"The Montresors," I replied, "were a great and numerous family."

"I forget your arms."

"A huge human foot d'or, in a field azure; the foot crushes a serpent rampant whose fangs are imbedded in the heel."

"And the motto?"

Nemo me impune lacessit." [1]

"Good!" he said.

231

---

[1] *No one attacks me with impunity.*

The wine sparkled in his eyes and the bells jingled. My own fancy grew warm with the Medoc. We had passed through walls of piled bones, with casks and puncheons intermingling, into the inmost recesses of the catacombs. I paused again, and this time I made bold to seize Fortunato by an arm above the elbow.

"The nitre!" I said; "see, it increases. It hangs like moss upon the vaults. We are below the river's bed. The drops of moisture trickle among the bones. Come, we will go back ere it is too late. Your cough——"

"It is nothing," he said; "let us go on. But first, another draught of the Medoc."

I broke and reached him a flagon of De Grave. He emptied it at a breath. His eyes flashed with a fierce light. He laughed and threw the bottle upward with a gesticulation I did not understand.

I looked at him in surprise. He repeated the movement—a grotesque one.

"You do not comprehend?" he said.

"Not I," I replied.

"Then you are not of the brotherhood."

"How?"

"You are not of the masons."

"Yes, yes," I said; "yes, yes."

"You? Impossible! A mason?"

"A mason," I replied.

"A sign," he said.

"It is this," I answered, producing a trowel from beneath the folds of my *roquelaire*.

"You jest," he exclaimed, recoiling a few paces. "But let us proceed to the Amontillado."

"Be it so," I said, replacing the tool beneath the cloak, and again offering him my arm. He leaned upon it heavily. We continued our route in search of the Amontillado. We passed through a range of low arches, descended, passed on, and descending again, arrived at a deep crypt, in which the foulness of the air caused our flambeaux rather to glow than flame.

At the most remote end of the crypt there appeared another less spacious. Its walls had been lined with human remains, piled to the vault overhead, in the fashion of the great catacombs of Paris. Three sides of this interior crypt were still ornamented in this manner. From the fourth the bones had been thrown down, and lay promiscuously upon the earth, forming at one point a mound of some size. Within the wall thus exposed by the displacing of the bones, we perceived a still interior recess, in depth about four feet, in width three, in height six or seven. It seemed to have been constructed for no especial use within itself, but formed merely the interval between two of the colossal supports of the roof of the catacombs, and was backed by one of their circumscribing walls of solid granite.

232

It was in vain that Fortunato, uplifting his dull torch, endeavored to pry into the depth of the recess. Its termination the feeble light did not enable us to see.

"Proceed," I said; "herein is the Amontillado. As for Luchesi——"

"He is an ignoramus," interrupted my friend, as he stepped unsteadily forward, while I followed immediately at his heels. In an instant he had reached the extremity of the niche, and finding his progress arrested by the rock, stood stupidly bewildered. A moment more and I had fettered him to the granite. In its surface were two iron staples, distant from each other about two feet, horizontally. From one of these depended a short chain, from the other a padlock. Throwing the links about his waist, it was but the work of a few seconds to secure it. He was too much astounded to resist. Withdrawing the key I stepped back from the recess.

"Pass your hand," I said, "over the wall; you cannot help feeling the nitre. Indeed it is *very* damp. Once more let me *implore* you to return. No? Then I must positively leave you. But I must first render you all the little attentions in my power."

"The Amontillado!" ejaculated my friend, not yet recovered from his astonishment.

"True," I replied; "the Amontillado."

As I said these words I busied myself among the pile of bones of which I have before spoken. Throwing them aside, I soon uncovered a quantity of building stone and mortar. With these materials and with the aid of my trowel, I began vigorously to wall up the entrance of the niche.

I had scarcely laid the first tier of the masonry when I discovered that the intoxication of Fortunato had in a great measure worn off. The earliest indication I had of this was a low moaning cry from the depth of the recess. It was *not* the cry of a drunken man. There was then a long and obstinate silence. I laid the second tier, and the third, and the fourth; and then I heard the furious vibrations of the chain. The noise lasted for several minutes, during which, that I might hearken to it with the more satisfaction, I ceased my labors and sat down upon the bones. When at last the clanking subsided, I resumed the trowel, and finished without interruption the fifth, the sixth, and the seventh tier. The wall was now nearly upon a level with my breast. I again paused, and holding the flambeaux over the mason work, threw a few feeble rays upon the figure within.

A succession of loud and shrill screams, bursting suddenly from the throat of the chained form, seemed to thrust me violently back. For a brief moment I hesitated—I trembled. Unsheathing my rapier, I began to grope with it about the recess; but the thought of an instant reassured me. I placed my hand upon the solid fabric of the catacombs, and felt satisfied. I reapproached the wall. I replied to the yells of him who clamored. I re-echoed—I aided—I surpassed them in volume and in strength. I did this, and the clamorer grew still.

It was now midnight, and my task was drawing to a close. I had completed the eighth, the ninth, and the tenth tier. I had finished a portion of the last and the eleventh; there remained but a single stone to be fitted and plastered in. I struggled with its weight; I placed it partially in its destined position. But now there came from out the niche a low laugh that erected the hairs upon my head. It was succeeded by a sad voice, which I had difficulty in recognizing as that of the noble Fortunato. The voice said—

"Ha! ha! ha!—he! he!—a very good joke indeed—an excellent jest. We will

233

have many a rich laugh about it at the palazzo—he! he! he!—over our wine—he! he! he!"

"The Amontillado!" I said.

"He! he! he!—he! he! he!—yes, the Amontillado. But is it not getting late? Will not they be awaiting us at the palazzo, the Lady Fortunato and the rest? Let us be gone."

"Yes," I said, "let us be gone."

"For the love of God, Montresor!"

"Yes," I said, "for the love of God!"

But to these words I hearkened in vain for a reply. I grew impatient. I called aloud:

"Fortunato!"

No answer. I called again:

"Fortunato!"

No answer still. I thrust a torch through the remaining aperture and let it fall within. There came forth in return only a jingling of the bells. My heart grew sick—on account of the dampness of the catacombs. I hastened to make an end of my labor. I forced the last stone into its position; I plastered it up. Against the new masonry I re-erected the old rampart of bones. For the half of a century no mortal has disturbed them. *In pace requiescat!* [2] (1846)

from Letter to Mr. B—— [1]

West Point, 1831

. . . You are aware of the great barrier in the path of an American writer. He is read, if at all, in preference to the combined and established wit of the world. I say established; for it is with literature as with law or empire—an established name is an estate in tenure, or a throne in possession. Besides, one might suppose that books, like their authors, improve by travel—their having crossed the sea is, with us, so great a distinction. Our antiquaries abandon time for distance; our very fops glance from the binding to the bottom of the title-page, where the mystic characters which spell London, Paris, or Genoa, are precisely so many letters of recommendation.

I mentioned just now a vulgar error as regards criticism. I think the notion that no poet can form a correct estimate of his own writings is another. I re-marked before that in proportion to the poetical talent would be the justice of a critique upon poetry. Therefore a bad poet would, I grant, make a false critique, and his self-love would infallibly bias his little judgment in his favour; but a poet, who is indeed a poet, could not, I think, fail of making a just critique; whatever should be deducted on the score of self-love might be replaced on account of his intimate acquaintance with the subject; in short, we have more instances of false criticism than of just where one's own writings are the test, simply because we have more bad poets than good. There are, of course,

234

[2] *May he rest in peace!*
[1] *Poe's publisher, Elam Bliss. The letter prefaced the 1831 edition of Poe's poems.*

many objections to what I say: Milton is a great example of the contrary; but his opinion with respect to the "Paradise Regained" is by no means fairly ascertained. By what trivial circumstances men are often led to assert what they do not really believe! Perhaps an inadvertent word has descended to posterity. But, in fact, the "Paradise Regained" is little, if at all, inferior to the "Paradise Lost," and is only supposed so to be because men do not like epics, whatever they may say to the contrary, and reading those of Milton in their natural order, are too much wearied with the first to derive any pleasure from the second.

I dare say Milton preferred "Comus" to either—if so—justly.

As I am speaking of poetry, it will not be amiss to touch slightly upon the most singular heresy in its modern history—the heresy of what is called, very foolishly, the Lake School. Some years ago I might have been induced, by an occasion like the present, to attempt a formal refutation of their doctrine; at present it would be a work of supererogation. The wise must bow to the wisdom of such men as Coleridge and Southey, but being wise, have laughed at poetical theories so prosaically exemplified.

Aristotle, with singular assurance, has declared poetry the most philosophical of all writings—but it required a Wordsworth to pronounce it the most metaphysical. He seems to think that the end of poetry is, or should be, instruction; yet it is a truism that the end of our existence is happiness; if so, the end of every separate part of our existence, everything connected with our existence, should be still happiness. Therefore the end of instruction should be happiness; and happiness is another name for pleasure;—therefore the end of instruction should be pleasure; yet we see the above-mentioned opinion implies precisely the reverse.

To proceed: *ceteris paribus,* he who pleases is of more importance to his fellow-men than he who instructs, since utility is happiness, and pleasure is the end already obtained while instruction is merely the means of obtaining. . . .

What is poetry?—Poetry! that Proteus-like idea, with as many appellations as the nine-titled Corcyra! "Give me," I demanded of a scholar some time ago, "give me a definition of poetry." *"Tres-volontiers"* [2]; and he proceeded to his library, brought me a Dr. Johnson, and overwhelmed me with a definition. Shade of the immortal Shakespeare! I imagine to myself the scowl of your spiritual eye upon the profanity of that scurrilous Ursa Major. Think of poetry, dear B——, think of poetry, and then think of Dr. Samuel Johnson! Think of all that is airy and fairy-like, and then of all that is hideous and unwieldy; think of his huge bulk, the Elephant! and then—and then think of the "Tempest"—the "Midsummer Night's Dream"—Prospero—Oberon—and Titania!

A poem, in my opinion, is opposed to a work of science by having, for its *immediate* object, pleasure, not truth; to romance, by having, for its object, an *indefinite* instead of a *definite* pleasure, being a poem only so far as this object is attained; romance presenting perceptible images with definite, poetry with *in*definite sensations, to which end music is an *essential,* since the comprehension of sweet sound is our most indefinite conception. Music, when combined with a pleasurable idea, is poetry; music, without the idea, is simply music; the idea, without the music, is prose, from its very definitiveness. . . .

[2] *Very willingly.*

235

The Philosophy of Composition

Charles Dickens, in a note now lying before me, alluding to an examination I once made of the mechanism of "Barnaby Rudge," says—"By the way, are you aware that Godwin wrote his Caleb Williams backwards? He first involved his hero in a web of difficulties, forming the second volume, and then, for the first, cast about him for some mode of accounting for what had been done."

I cannot think this the *precise* mode of procedure on the part of Godwin—and indeed what he himself acknowledges is not altogether in accordance with Mr. Dickens's idea—but the author of "Caleb Williams" was too good an artist not to perceive the advantage derivable from at least a somewhat similar process. Nothing is more clear than that every plot, worth the name, must be elaborated to its *denouement* before anything be attempted with the pen. It is only with the *denouement* constantly in view that we can give a plot its indispensable air of consequence, or causation, by making the incidents, and especially the tone, at all points, tend to the development of the intention.

There is a radical error, I think, in the usual mode of constructing a story. Either history affords a thesis—or one is suggested by an incident of the day—or, at best, the author sets himself to work in the combination of striking events to form merely the basis of his narrative—designing, generally, to fill in with description, dialogue, or authorial comment, whatever crevices of fact or action may, from page to page, render themselves apparent.

I prefer commencing with the consideration of an *effect*. Keeping originality *always* in view—for he is false to himself who ventures to dispense with so obvious and so easily attainable a source of interest—I say to myself, in the first place, "Of the innumerable effects or impressions of which the heart, the intellect, or (more generally) the soul is susceptible, what one shall I, on the present occasion, select?" Having chosen a novel first, and secondly, a vivid effect, I consider whether it can be best wrought by incident or tone—whether by ordinary incidents and peculiar tone, or the converse, or by peculiarity both of incident and tone—afterwards looking about me (or rather within) for such combinations of event or tone as shall best aid me in the construction of the effect.

I have often thought how interesting a magazine paper might be written by any author who would—that is to say, who could—detail, step by step, the processes by which any one of his compositions attained its ultimate point of completion. Why such a paper has never been given to the world, I am much at a loss to say—but perhaps the authorial vanity has had more to do with the omission than any one other cause. Most writers—poets in especial—prefer having it understood that they compose by a species of fine frenzy—an ecstatic intuition—and would positively shudder at letting the public take a peep behind the scenes, at the elaborate and vacillating crudities of thought—at the true purposes seized only at the last moment—at the innumerable glimpses of idea that arrived not at the maturity of full view—at the fully-matured fancies discarded in despair as unmanageable—at the cautious selections and rejections—at the painful erasures and interpolations—in a word, at the wheels and pinions—the tackle for scene-shifting—the step-ladders, and demon-traps—the cock's feathers, the red paint and the black patches, which, in ninety-nine cases out of the hundred, constitute the properties of the literary *histrio*.

I am aware, on the other hand, that the case is by no means common, in which an author is at all in condition to retrace the steps by which his conclusions have been attained. In general, suggestions, having arisen pell-mell, are pursued and forgotten in a similar manner.

For my own part, I have neither sympathy with the repugnance alluded to, nor, at any time, the least difficulty in recalling to mind the progressive steps of any of my compositions, and, since the interest of an analysis, or reconstruction, such as I have considered a *desideratum,* is quite independent of any real or fancied interest in the thing analysed, it will not be regarded as a breach of decorum on my part to show the *modus operandi* by which some one of my own works was put together. I select "The Raven" as most generally known. It is my design to render it manifest that no one point in its composition is referable either to accident or intuition—that the work proceeded step by step, to its completion, with the precision and rigid consequence of a mathematical problem.

Let us dismiss, as irrelevant to the poem, *per se,* the circumstance—or say the necessity—which, in the first place, gave rise to the intention of composing *a* poem that should suit at once the popular and the critical taste.

We commence, then, with this intention.

The initial consideration was that of extent. If any literary work is too long to be read at one sitting, we must be content to dispense with the immensely important effect derivable from unity of impression—for, if two sittings be required, the affairs of the world interfere, and everything like totality is at once destroyed. But since, *ceteris paribus,* no poet can afford to dispense with *any-thing* that may advance his design, it but remains to be seen whether there is, in extent, any advantage to counterbalance the loss of unity which attends it. Here I say no, at once. What we term a long poem is, in fact, merely a succession of brief ones—that is to say, of brief poetical effects. It is needless to demonstrate that a poem is such only inasmuch as it intensely excites, by elevating the soul; and all intense excitements are, through a psychal necessity, brief. For this reason, at least, one-half of the "Paradise Lost" is essentially prose—a succession of poetical excitements interspersed, *inevitably,* with corresponding depressions—the whole being deprived, through the extremeness of its length, of the vastly important artistic element, totality, or unity of effect.

It appears evident, then, that there is a distinct limit, as regards length, to all works of literary art—the limit of a single sitting—and that, although in certain classes of prose composition, such as "Robinson Crusoe" (demanding no unity), this limit may be advantageously overpressed, it can never properly be over-passed in a poem. Within this limit, the extent of a poem may be made to bear mathematical relation to its merit—in other words, to the excitement or elevation —again, in other words, to the degree of the true poetical effect which it is capable of inducing; for it is clear that the brevity must be in direct ratio of the intensity of the intended effect—this, with one proviso—that a certain degree of duration is absolutely requisite for the production of any effect at all.

237

Holding in view these considerations, as well as that degree of excitement which I deemed not above the popular, while not below the critical taste, I reached at once what I conceived the proper *length* for my intended poem—a length of about one hundred lines. It is, in fact, a hundred and eight.

My next thought concerned the choice of an impression, or effect, to be conveyed: and here I may as well observe that, throughout the construction, I kept steadily in view the design of rendering the work *universally* appreciable. I should be carried too far out of my immediate topic were I to demonstrate a point upon which I have repeatedly insisted, and which, with the poetical, stands not in the slightest need of demonstration—the point, I mean, that Beauty is the sole legitimate province of the poem. A few words, however, in elucidation of my real meaning, which some of my friends have evinced a disposition to misrepresent. That pleasure which is at once the most intense, the most elevating, and the most pure is, I believe, found in the contemplation of the beautiful. When, indeed, men speak of Beauty, they mean, precisely, not a quality, as is supposed, but an effect—they refer, in short, just to that intense and pure elevation of *soul*—*not* of intellect, or of heart—upon which I have commented, and which is experienced in consequence of contemplating the "beautiful." Now I designate Beauty as the province of the poem, merely because it is an obvious rule of Art that effects should be made to spring from direct causes—that objects should be attained through means best adapted for their attainment—no one as yet having been weak enough to deny that the peculiar elevation alluded to is *most readily* attained in the poem. Now the object Truth, or the satisfaction of the intellect, and the object Passion, or the excitement of the heart, are, although attainable to a certain extent in poetry, far more readily attainable in prose. Truth, in fact, demands a precision, and Passion, a *homeliness* (the truly passionate will comprehend me), which are absolutely antagonistic to that Beauty which, I maintain, is the excitement, or pleasurable elevation of the soul. It by no means follows, from anything here said, that passion, or even truth, may not be introduced, and even profitably introduced, into a poem for they may serve in elucidation, or aid the general effect, as do discords in music, by contrast— but the true artist will always contrive, first, to tone them into proper subservience to the predominant aim, and, secondly, to enveil them, as far as possible, in that Beauty which is the atmosphere and the essence of the poem.

Regarding, then, Beauty as my province, my next question referred to the *tone* of its highest manifestation—and all experience has shown that this tone is one of *sadness.* Beauty of whatever kind, in its supreme development, invariably excites the sensitive soul to tears. Melancholy is thus the most legitimate of all the poetical tones.

The length, the province, and the tone, being thus determined, I betook myself to ordinary induction, with the view of obtaining some artistic piquancy which might serve me as a key-note in the construction of the poem—some pivot upon which the whole structure might turn. In carefully thinking over all the usual artistic effects—or more properly *points*, in the theatrical sense—I did not fail to perceive immediately that no one had been so universally employed as that of the *refrain*. The universality of its employment sufficed to assure me of its intrinsic value, and spared me the necessity of submitting it to analysis. I considered it, however, with regard to its susceptibility of improvement, and soon saw it to be in a primitive condition. As commonly used, the *refrain*, or burden, not only is limited to lyric verse, but depends for its impression upon the force of monotone—both in sound and thought. The pleasure is deduced solely from the sense of identity—of repetition. I resolved to diversify, and so heighten the effect, by adhering in general to the monotone of sound, while I continually varied that of thought: that is to say, I determined to produce continuously novel effects, by the variation *of the application* of the *refrain*—the *refrain* itself remaining, for the most part, unvaried.

These points being settled, I next bethought me of the *nature* of my *refrain*. Since its application was to be repeatedly varied it was clear that the *refrain* itself must be brief, for there would have been an insurmountable difficulty in frequent variations of application in any sentence of length. In proportion to the brevity of the sentence would, of course, be the facility of the variation. This led me at once to a single word as the best *refrain*.

The question now arose as to the character of the word. Having made up my mind to a *refrain*, the division of the poem into stanzas was of course a corollary, the *refrain* forming the close to each stanza. That such a close, to have force, must be sonorous and susceptible of protracted emphasis, admitted no doubt, and these considerations inevitably led me to the long *o* as the most sonorous vowel in connection with *r* as the most producible consonant.

The sound of the *refrain* being thus determined, it became necessary to select a word embodying this sound, and at the same time in the fullest possible keeping with that melancholy which I had pre-determined as the tone of the poem. In such a search it would have been absolutely impossible to overlook the word "Nevermore." In fact it was the very first which presented itself.

The next *desideratum* was a pretext for the continuous use of the one word "nevermore." In observing the difficulty which I had at once found in inventing a sufficiently plausible reason for its continuous repetition, I did not fail to perceive that this difficulty arose solely from the preassumption that the word was to be so continuously or monotonously spoken by a *human* being—I did not fail to perceive, in short, that the difficulty lay in the reconciliation of this monotony with the exercise of reason on the part of the creature repeating the word. Here, then, immediately arose the idea of a *non*-reasoning creature capable of speech, and very naturally, a parrot, in the first instance, suggested itself, but was superseded forthwith by a Raven as equally capable of speech, and infinitely more in keeping with the intended *tone*.

I had now gone so far as the conception of a Raven, the bird of ill-omen, monotonously repeating the one word "Nevermore" at the conclusion of each stanza in a poem of melancholy tone, and in length about one hundred lines. Now, never losing sight of the object—*supremeness* or perfection at all points, I asked myself—"Of all melancholy topics what, according to the *universal* understanding of mankind, is the *most* melancholy?" Death, was the obvious reply. "And when," I said, "is this most melancholy of topics most poetical?" From what I have already explained at some length the answer here also is obvious—"When it most closely allies itself to *Beauty*: the death then of a beautiful woman is unquestionably the most poetical topic in the world, and equally is it beyond doubt that the lips best suited for such topic are those of a bereaved lover."

I had now to combine the two ideas of a lover lamenting his deceased mistress and a Raven continuously repeating the word "Nevermore." I had to combine these, bearing in mind my design of varying at every turn the *application* of the

239

word repeated, but the only intelligible mode of such combination is that of imagining the Raven employing the word in answer to the queries of the lover. And here it was that I saw at once the opportunity afforded for the effect on which I had been depending, that is to say, the effect of the *variation of application.* I saw that I could make the first query propounded by the lover—the first query to which the Raven should reply "Nevermore"—that I could make this first query a commonplace one, the second less so, the third still less, and so on, until at length the lover, startled from his original *nonchalance* by the melancholy character of the word itself, by its frequent repetition, and by a consideration of the ominous reputation of the fowl that uttered it, is at length excited to superstition, and wildly propounds queries of a far different character—queries whose solution he has passionately at heart—propounds them half in superstition and half in that species of despair which delights in self-torture—propounds them not altogether because he believes in the prophetic or demoniac character of the bird (which reason assures him is merely repeating a lesson learned by rote), but because he experiences a frenzied pleasure in so modelling his questions as to receive from the *expected* "Nevermore" the most delicious because the most intolerable of sorrows. Perceiving the opportunity thus afforded me, or, more strictly, thus forced upon me in the progress of the construction, I first established in my mind the climax or concluding query—that query to which "Nevermore" should be in the last place an answer—that query in reply to which this word "Nevermore" should involve the utmost conceivable amount of sorrow and despair.

Here then the poem may be said to have had its beginning, at the end where all works of art should begin, for it was here at this point of my preconsiderations that I first put pen to paper in the composition of the stanza:

"Prophet!" said I, "thing of evil! prophet still if bird or devil!
By that Heaven that bends above us—by that God we both adore,
Tell this soul with sorrow laden, if, within the distant Aidenn,
It shall clasp a sainted maiden whom the angels name Lenore—
Clasp a rare and radiant maiden whom the angels name Lenore."
        Quoth the Raven—"Nevermore."

I composed this stanza, at this point, first, that, by establishing the climax, I might the better vary and graduate, as regards seriousness and importance, the preceding queries of the lover, and secondly, that I might definitely settle the rhythm, the metre, and the length and general arrangement of the stanza, as well as graduate the stanzas which were to precede, so that none of them might surpass this in rhythmical effect. Had I been able in the subsequent composition to construct more vigorous stanzas I should without scruple have purposely enfeebled them so as not to interfere with the climacteric effect.

And here I may as well say a few words of the versification. My first object (as usual) was originality. The extent to which this has been neglected in versification is one of the most unaccountable things in the world. Admitting that there is little possibility of variety in mere *rhythm,* it is still clear that the possible varieties of metre and stanza are absolutely infinite, and yet, *for centuries, no man, in verse, has ever done, or ever seemed to think of doing, an original*

240

thing. The fact is that originality (unless in minds of very unusual force) is by no means a matter, as some suppose, of impulse or intuition. In general, to be found, it must be elaborately sought, and although a positive merit of the highest class, demands in its attainment less of invention than negation.

Of course I pretend to no originality in either the rhythm or metre of the "Raven." The former is trochaic—the latter is octametre acatalectic, alternating with heptametre catalectic repeated in the *refrain* of the fifth verse, and terminating with tetrametre catalectic. Less pedantically—the feet employed throughout (trochees) consist of a long syllable followed by a short; the first line of the stanza consists of eight of these feet, the second of seven and a half (in effect two-thirds), the third of eight, the fourth of seven and a half, the fifth the same, the sixth three and a half. Now, each of these lines taken individually has been employed before, and what originality the "Raven" has, is in their *combination into stanza*—nothing even remotely approaching this combination has ever been attempted. The effect of this originality of combination is aided by other unusual and some altogether novel effects, arising from an extension of the application of the principles of rhyme and alliteration.

The next point to be considered was the mode of bringing together the lover and the Raven—and the first branch of this consideration was the *locale.* For this the most natural suggestion might seem to be a forest, or the fields—but it has always appeared to me that a close *circumscription of space* is absolutely necessary to the effect of insulated incident—it has the force of a frame to a picture. It has an indisputable moral power in keeping concentrated the attention, and, of course, must not be confounded with mere unity of place.

I determined, then, to place the lover in his chamber—in a chamber rendered sacred to him by memories of her who had frequented it. The room is represented as richly furnished—this in mere pursuance of the ideas I have already explained on the subject of Beauty, as the sole true poetical thesis.

The *locale* being thus determined, I had now to introduce the bird—and the thought of introducing him through the window was inevitable. The idea of making the lover suppose, in the first instance, that the flapping of the wings of the bird against the shutter, is a "tapping" at the door, originated in a wish to increase, by prolonging, the reader's curiosity, and in a desire to admit the incidental effect arising from the lover's throwing open the door, finding all dark, and thence adopting the half-fancy that it was the spirit of his mistress that knocked.

I made the night tempestuous, first to account for the Raven's seeking admission, and secondly, for the effect of contrast with the (physical) serenity within the chamber.

I made the bird alight on the bust of Pallas, also for the effect of contrast between the marble and the plumage—it being understood that the bust was absolutely *suggested* by the bird—the bust of *Pallas* being chosen, first, as most in keeping with the scholarship of the lover, and secondly, for the sonorousness of the word, Pallas, itself.

About the middle of the poem, also, I have availed myself of the force of contrast, with a view of deepening the ultimate impression. For example, an air of the fantastic—approaching as nearly to the ludicrous as was admissible—is given to the Raven's entrance. He comes in "with many a flirt and flutter."

241

Not the *least obeisance made he*—not a moment stopped or stayed he,
But with mien of lord or lady, perched above my chamber door.

In the two stanzas which follow, the design is more obviously carried out:—

Then this ebony bird, beguiling my sad fancy into smiling
By the *grave and stern decorum of the countenance it wore*,
"Though thy *crest be shorn and shaven*, thou," I said, "art sure no craven,
Ghastly grim and ancient Raven wandering from the Nightly shore—
Tell me what thy lordly name is on the Night's Plutonian shore?"
    Quoth the Raven—"Nevermore."

Much I marvelled *this ungainly fowl* to hear discourse so plainly,
Though its answer little meaning—little relevancy bore;
For we cannot help agreeing that no living human being
Ever yet was blessed with seeing bird above his chamber door—
Bird or beast upon the sculptured bust above his chamber door,
    With such name as "Nevermore."

The effect of the *denouement* being thus provided for, I immediately drop the fantastic for a tone of the most profound seriousness—this tone commencing in the stanza directly following the one last quoted, with the line,

But the Raven, sitting lonely on that placid bust, spoke only, etc.

From this epoch the lover no longer jests—no longer sees anything even of the fantastic in the Raven's demeanour. He speaks of him as a "grim, ungainly, ghastly, gaunt, and ominous bird of yore," and feels the "fiery eyes" burning into his "bosom's core." This revolution of thought, or fancy, on the lover's part, is intended to induce a similar one on the part of the reader—to bring the mind into a proper frame for the *denouement*—which is now brought about as rapidly and as *directly* as possible.

With the *denouement* proper—with the Raven's reply, "Nevermore," to the lover's final demand if he shall meet his mistress in another world—the poem, in its obvious phase, that of a simple narrative, may be said to have its completion. So far, everything is within the limits of the accountable—of the real. A raven, having learned by rote the single word "Nevermore," and having escaped from the custody of its owner, is driven at midnight, through the violence of a storm, to seek admission at a window from which a light still gleams—the chamber-window of a student, occupied half in poring over a volume, half in dreaming of a beloved mistress deceased. The casement being thrown open at the fluttering of the bird's wings, the bird itself perches on the most convenient seat out of the immediate reach of the student, who amused by the incident and the oddity of the visitor's demeanour, demands of it, in jest and without looking for a reply, its name. The raven addressed, answers with its customary word, "Nevermore"—a word which finds immediate echo in the melancholy heart of the student, who, giving utterance aloud to certain thoughts suggested by the occasion, is again startled by the fowl's repetition of "Nevermore." The student now guesses the state of the case, but is impelled, as I have before explained, by the human thirst for self-torture, and in part by superstition, to propound such queries to the bird as will bring him, the lover, the most of the luxury of sorrow, through the anticipated answer, "Nevermore." With the indulgence, to the extreme, of this self-torture, the narration, in what I have termed its first or obvious phase, has a natural termination, and so far there has been no overstepping of the limits of the real.

But in subjects so handled, however skillfully, or with however vivid an array of incident, there is always a certain hardness or nakedness which repels the artistical eye. Two things are invariably required—first, some amount of complexity, or more properly, adaptation; and, secondly, some amount of suggestiveness—some under-current, however indefinite, of meaning. It is this latter, in especial, which imparts to a work of art so much of that *richness* (to borrow from colloquy a forcible term), which we are too fond of confounding with *the ideal*. It is the *excess* of the suggested meaning—it is the rendering this the upper instead of the under-current of the theme—which turns into prose (and that of the very flattest kind), the so-called poetry of the so-called transcendentalists.

Holding these opinions, I added the two concluding stanzas of the poem—their suggestiveness being thus made to pervade all the narrative which has preceded them. The under-current of meaning is rendered first apparent in the line—

"Take thy beak from out *my heart,* and take thy form from off my door!"
  Quoth the Raven "Nevermore!"

It will be observed that the words, "from out my heart," involve the first metaphorical expression in the poem. They, with the answer, "Nevermore," dispose the mind to seek a moral in all that has been previously narrated. The reader begins now to regard the Raven as emblematical—but it is not until the very last line of the very last stanza that the intention of making him emblematical of *Mournful and never ending Remembrance* is permitted distinctly to be seen:

And the Raven, never flitting, still is sitting, still is sitting,
On the pallid bust of Pallas just above my chamber door;
And his eyes have all the seeming of a demon that is dreaming,
And the lamplight o'er him streaming throws his shadow on the floor;
And my soul *from out that shadow* that lies floating on the floor
  Shall be lifted—nevermore. *(1846)*

from *The Poetic Principle*

In speaking of the Poetic Principle, I have no design to be either thorough or profound. While discussing very much at random the essentiality of what we call Poetry, my principal purpose will be to cite for consideration some few of those minor English or American poems which best suit my own taste, or which, upon my own fancy, have left the most definite impression. By "minor poems" I mean, of course, poems of little length. And here, in the beginning, permit me to say a few words in regard to a somewhat peculiar principle, which, whether rightfully or wrongfully, has always had its influence in my own critical estimate of the poem. I hold that a long poem does not exist. I maintain that the phrase, "a long poem," is simply a flat contradiction in terms.

I need scarcely observe that a poem deserves its title only inasmuch as it excites, by elevating the soul. The value of the poem is in the ratio of this elevating excitement. But all excitements are, through a psychal necessity, transient. That degree of excitement which would entitle a poem to be so called at all, cannot be sustained throughout a composition of any great length. After the lapse of half an hour, at the very utmost, it flags—fails—a revulsion ensues—and then the poem is, in effect, and in fact, no longer such.

There are, no doubt, many who have found difficulty in reconciling the critical dictum that the "Paradise Lost" is to be devoutly admired throughout, with the absolute impossibility of maintaining for it, during perusal, the amount of enthusiasm which that critical dictum would demand. This great work, in fact, is to be regarded as poetical only when, losing sight of that vital requisite in all works of Art, Unity, we view it merely as a series of minor poems. If, to preserve its Unity—its totality of effect or impression—we read it (as would be necessary) at a single sitting, the result is but a constant alternation of excitement and depression. After a passage of what we feel to be true poetry, there follows, inevitably, a passage of platitude which no critical pre-judgment can force us to admire; but if, upon completing the work, we read it again, omitting the first book—that is to say, commencing with the second—we shall be surprised at now finding that admirable which we before condemned—that damnable which we had previously so much admired. It follows from all this that the ultimate, aggregate, or absolute effect of even the best epic under the sun, is a nullity—and this is precisely the fact.

In regard to the "Iliad," we have, if not positive proof, at least very good reason, for believing it intended as a series of lyrics; but, granting the epic intention, I can say only that the work is based in an imperfect sense of Art. The modern epic is, of the supposititious ancient model, but an inconsiderate and blindfold imitation. But the day of these artistic anomalies is over. If, at any time, any very long poem *were* popular in reality—which I doubt—it is at least clear that no very long poem will ever be popular again.

That the extent of a poetical work is, *ceteris paribus,* the measure of its merit, seems undoubtedly, when we thus state it, a proposition sufficiently absurd—yet we are indebted for it to the Quarterly Reviews. Surely there can be nothing in mere *size,* abstractly considered—there can be nothing in mere *bulk,* so far as a volume is concerned, which has so continuously elicited admiration from these saturnine pamphlets! A mountain, to be sure, by the mere sentiment of physical magnitude which it conveys, *does* impress us with a sense of the sublime—but no man is impressed after *this* fashion by the material grandeur of even "The Columbiad." Even the Quarterlies have not instructed us to be so impressed by it. *As yet,* they have not *insisted* on our estimating Lamartine by the cubic foot, or Pollock by the pound—but what else are we to *infer* from their continual prating about "sustained effort"? If, by "sustained effort," any little gentleman has accomplished an epic, let us frankly commend him for the effort—if this indeed be a thing commendable—but let us forbear praising the epic on the effort's account. It is to be hoped that common sense, in the time to come, will prefer deciding upon a work of Art rather by the impression it makes—by the effect it produces—than by the time it took to impress the effect, or by the amount of "sustained effort" which had been found necessary in effecting the impression. The fact is, that perseverance is one thing and genius quite another—nor can all the Quarterlies in Christendom confound them. By and by, this proposition, with many which I have been just urging, will be received as self-evident. In the meantime, by being generally condemned as falsities, they will not be essentially damaged as truths.

On the other hand, it is clear that a poem may be improperly brief. Undue brevity degenerates into mere epigrammatism. A *very* short poem, while now and then producing a brilliant or vivid, never produces a profound or enduring effect. There must be the steady pressing down of the stamp upon the wax. De Beranger has wrought innumerable things, pungent and spirit-stirring, but in general they have been too imponderous to stamp themselves deeply into the public attention, and thus, as so many feathers of fancy, have been blown aloft only to be whistled down the wind.

A remarkable instance of the effect of undue brevity in depressing a poem, in keeping it out of the popular view, is afforded by the following exquisite little Serenade—

> I arise from dreams of thee
>   In the first sweet sleep of night,
> When the winds are breathing low,
>   And the stars are shining bright.
> I arise from dreams of thee,
>   And a spirit in my feet
> Has led me—who knows how?—
>   To thy chamber-window, sweet!
>
> The wandering airs they faint
>   On the dark, the silent stream—
> The champak odors fail
>   Like sweet thoughts in a dream;
> The nightingale's complaint,
>   It dies upon her heart,
> As I must die on thine,
>   O, beloved as thou art!
>
> O, lift me from the grass!
>   I die, I faint, I fail!
> Let thy love in kisses rain
>   On my lips and eyelids pale.
> My cheek is cold and white, alas!
>   My heart beats loud and fast:
> O, press it close to thine again,
>   Where it will break at last.

245

Very few perhaps are familiar with these lines, yet no less a poet than Shelley is their author. Their warm, yet delicate and ethereal imagination will be appreciated by all, but by none so thoroughly as by him who has himself arisen from sweet dreams of one beloved to bathe in the aromatic air of a southern midsummer night. . . .

While the epic mania, while the idea that to merit in poetry prolixity is indispensable, has for some years past been gradually dying out of the public mind, by mere dint of its own absurdity, we find it succeeded by a heresy too palpably false to be long tolerated, but one which, in the brief period it has already endured, may be said to have accomplished more in the corruption of our Poetical Literature than all its other enemies combined. I allude to the heresy of *The Didactic*. It has been assumed, tacitly and avowedly, directly and indirectly, that the ultimate object of all Poetry is Truth. Every poem, it is said, should inculcate a moral, and by this moral is the poetical merit of the work to be adjudged. We Americans especially have patronized this happy idea, and we Bostonians very especially have developed it in full. We have taken it into our heads that to write a poem simply for the poem's sake, and to acknowledge such to have been our design, would be to confess ourselves radically wanting in the true poetic dignity and force:—but the simple fact is that would we but permit ourselves to look into our own souls we should immediately there discover that under the sun there neither exists nor *can* exist any work more thoroughly dignified, more supremely noble, than this very poem, this poem *per se*, this poem which is a poem and nothing more, this poem written solely for the poem's sake.

With as deep a reverence for the True as ever inspired the bosom of man, I would nevertheless limit, in some measure, its modes of inculcation. I would limit to enforce them. I would not enfeeble them by dissipation. The demands of Truth are severe. She has no sympathy with the myrtles. All *that* which is so indispensable in Song is precisely all *that* with which *she* has nothing whatever to do. It is but making her a flaunting paradox to wreathe her in gems and flowers. In enforcing a truth we need severity rather than efflorescence of language. We must be simple, precise, terse. We must be cool, calm, unimpassioned. In a word, we must be in that mood which, as nearly as possible, is the exact converse of the poetical. *He* must be blind indeed who does not perceive the radical and chasmal difference between the truthful and the poetical modes of inculcation. He must be theory-mad beyond redemption who, in spite of these differences, shall still persist in attempting to reconcile the obstinate oils and waters of Poetry and Truth.

Dividing the world of mind into its three most immediately obvious distinctions, we have the Pure Intellect, Taste, and the Moral Sense. I place Taste in the middle, because it is just this position which in the mind it occupies. It holds intimate relations with either extreme; but from the Moral Sense is separated by so faint a difference that Aristotle has not hesitated to place some of its operations among the virtues themselves. Nevertheless we find the *offices* of the trio marked with a sufficient distinction. Just as the Intellect concerns itself with Truth, so Taste informs us of the Beautiful, while the Moral Sense is regardful of Duty. Of this latter, while Conscience teaches the obligation, and Reason the expediency, Taste contents herself with displaying the charms, waging war upon Vice solely on the ground of her deformity, her disproportion, her animosity to the fitting, to the appropriate, to the harmonious, in a word, to Beauty.

246

An immortal instinct deep within the spirit of man is thus plainly a sense of the beautiful. This it is which administers to his delight in the manifold forms, and sounds, and odors and sentiments amid which he exists. And just as the lily is repeated in the lake, or the eyes of Amaryllis in the mirror, so is the mere oral or written repetition of these forms, and sounds, and colors, and odors, and sentiments a duplicate source of delight. But this mere repetition is not poetry. He who shall simply sing, with however glowing enthusiasm, or with however vivid a truth of description, of the sights, and sounds, and odors, and colors, and sentiments which greet *him* in common with all mankind—he, I say, has yet failed to prove his divine title. There is still a something in the distance which he has been unable to attain. We have still a thirst unquenchable, to allay which he has not shown us the crystal springs. This thirst belongs to the immortality of Man. It is at once a consequence and an indication of his perennial existence. It is the desire of the moth for the star. It is no mere appreciation of the Beauty before us, but a wild effort to reach the Beauty above. Inspired by an ecstatic prescience of the glories beyond the grave, we struggle by multiform combinations among the things and thoughts of Time to attain a portion of that Loveliness whose very elements perhaps appertain to eternity alone. And thus when by Poetry, or when by Music, the most entrancing of the poetic moods, we find ourselves melted into tears, we weep then, not as the Abbate Gravina [1] supposes, through excess of pleasure, but through a certain petulant, impatient sorrow at our inability to grasp *now*, wholly, here on earth, at once and for ever, those divine and rapturous joys of which *through* the poem, or *through* the music, we attain to but brief and indeterminate glimpses.

The struggle to apprehend the supernal Loveliness—this struggle, on the part of souls fittingly constituted—has given to the world all *that* which it (the world) has ever been enabled at once to understand and *to feel* as poetic.

The Poetic Sentiment, of course, may develop itself in various modes—in Painting, in Sculpture, in Architecture, in the Dance—very especially in Music —and very peculiarly, and with a wide field, in the composition of the Landscape Garden. Our present theme, however, has regard only to its manifestation in words. And here let me speak briefly on the topic of rhythm. Contenting myself with the certainty that Music, in its various modes of metre, rhythm, and rhyme, is of so vast a moment in Poetry as never to be wisely rejected—is so vitally important an adjunct, that he is simply silly who declines its assistance, I will not now pause to maintain its absolute essentiality. It is in Music perhaps that the soul most nearly attains the great end for which, when inspired by the Poetic Sentiment, it struggles—the creation of supernal Beauty. It *may* be, indeed, that here this sublime end is, now and then, attained in *fact*. We are often made to feel, with a shivering delight, that from an earthly harp are stricken notes which *cannot* have been unfamiliar to the angels. And thus there can be little doubt that in the union of Poetry with Music in its popular sense, we shall find the widest field for the Poetic development. The old Bards and Minnesingers had advantages which we do not possess—and Thomas Moore, singing his own songs, was, in the most legitimate manner, perfecting them as poems.

247

[1] *Giovanni Vincenzio Gravina (1664–1718), a critic of poetry and author of several tragedies.*

To recapitulate then:—I would define, in brief, the Poetry of words as *The Rhythmical Creation of Beauty*. Its sole arbiter is Taste. With the Intellect or with the Conscience it has only collateral relations. Unless incidentally, it has no concern whatever either with Duty or with Truth.

A few words, however, in explanation. *That* pleasure which is at once the most pure, the most elevating, and the most intense, is derived, I maintain, from the contemplation of the Beautiful. In the contemplation of Beauty we alone find it possible to attain that pleasurable elevation, or excitement *of the soul*, which we recognise as the Poetic Sentiment, and which is so easily distinguished from Truth, which is the satisfaction of the Reason, or from Passion, which is the excitement of the heart. I make Beauty, therefore—using the word as inclusive of the sublime—I make Beauty the province of the poem, simply because it is an obvious rule of Art that effects should be made to spring as directly as possible from their causes:—no one as yet having been weak enough to deny that the peculiar elevation in question is at least *most readily* attainable in the poem. It by no means follows, however, that the incitements of Passion, or the precepts of Duty, or even the lessons of Truth, may not be introduced into a poem, and with advantage; for they may subserve incidentally, in various ways, the general purposes of the work: but the true artist will always contrive to tone them down in proper subjection to that *Beauty* which is the atmosphere and the real essence of the poem. . . . *(1850)*

JOHN PENDLETON KENNEDY

1795–1870

The first child of aristocratic parents, John Pendleton Kennedy was born in Baltimore on October 25, 1795. After attending a private school and Priestly's and Sinclair's Academies, he enrolled in Baltimore College, from which he received his B.A. degree at the age of eighteen. Though Kennedy was strongly attracted to both literature and a military career, he followed the common practice of aristocratic young Southerners and studied law. His legal training was interrupted briefly for service in the War of 1812, but after the war he completed his studies and soon became a successful lawyer and a leading figure in Baltimore society.

248

During the 1820's, Kennedy was elected to four successive terms as a member of the Maryland legislature. At this time, he was a mild abolitionist and a supporter of tariffs for the protection of manufacturers. Kennedy's first wife died within a year of his marriage, and in 1829 he married Elizabeth Gray, the daughter of a wealthy cotton-spinner. His connection with the Gray family greatly strengthened his capitalistic views. He supported the administration of John Quincy Adams and opposed the extension of slavery. Elected in 1838 to the first of three successive terms in Congress, Kennedy advocated the colonization of free Negroes in Liberia and served as chairman of the Committee on Commerce. After being defeated in a race for Congress in 1844, he was elected in 1846 to the Maryland House of Delegates. He also served briefly as Secretary of the Navy under President Fillmore. Although Kennedy fought secession in 1860 and was a Unionist throughout the Civil War, with the coming of peace he advocated a mild reconstruction for the South. His last political activity was to preside over a meeting of the Republican Party in Baltimore in 1868, two years before his death.

The first of Kennedy's notable literary activities came in 1818, when he and Peter Hoffman became the anonymous editors of *The Red Book*, a short-lived periodical similar in type to *Salmagundi*. In 1833 he was one of three judges who awarded a prize in a short-story contest to Poe's "A MS. Found in a Bottle." Thereafter, he was almost a patron to Poe, introducing him to T. W. White of *The Southern Literary Messenger* and giving him ample advice and "loans."

Kennedy's literary career really began in 1832 with the publication, under the pseudonym of "Mark Littleton," of *Swallow Barn*, an Irvingesque series of sketches noteworthy mainly for the establishment of the plantation tradition, which lasted in literature at least until the publication of *Gone with the Wind*. *Swallow Barn* is a portrayal of plantation atmosphere, setting, and social arrangements—there are no poor whites involved. V. L. Parrington has said, "Nowhere else does the plantation life of the Old Dominion in the days before its decline appear so vividly as in these discursive pages."

Horse Shoe Robinson (1835) combines elements of the historical romance with limited realism. The conventional adventure and love are given a Revolutionary background accurate in costume, setting, and military strategy, though William Gilmore Simms objected to the number of Tories that Kennedy found in South Carolina. Horse Shoe Robinson himself is a study in rustic natural goodness. The portrayal of his character and the accurate picture of the war that was almost a civil war in the South save the novel from the weaknesses of the sentimental historical romance.

Another novel, *Rob of the Bowl*, followed in 1838. Although it has not been one of Kennedy's most popular works, some modern critics have called it his best. It is a story of cavalier love and piratical adventure during a war between Protestants and Catholics in the colony of Maryland under Charles Calvert, the third Lord Baltimore.

It is chiefly on these works that Kennedy's literary reputation must rest, though his publications include several lesser items: *Quodlibet* (1840), a keen and amusing satire on Jacksonian democracy; *Defence of the Whigs* (1844), a criticism of Tyler for deserting the Whigs; *Memoirs of the Life of William*

249

Wirt (1849); a number of pamphlets published before the Civil War; and *Letters of Mr. Ambrose,* written during the war to reconcile the differences between the sections. In estimating Kennedy's importance, Parrington says: "Few Americans of his day were so generously gifted; none possessed a lighter touch. He has been somewhat carelessly forgotten even by our literary historians who can plead no excuse for so grave a blunder."

from Swallow Barn, or, A Sojourn in the Old Dominion

Chapter 1. Swallow Barn

Swallow Barn is an aristocratic old edifice which sits, like a brooding hen, on the southern bank of the James River. It looks down upon a shady pocket or nook, formed by an indentation of the shore, from a gentle acclivity thinly sprinkled with oaks whose magnificent branches afford habitation to sundry friendly colonies of squirrels and woodpeckers.

This time-honored mansion was the residence of the family of Hazards. But in the present generation, the spells of love and mortgage have translated the possession to Frank Meriwether, who having married Lucretia, the eldest daughter of my late Uncle Walter Hazard, and lifted some gentlemanlike incumbrances which had been sleeping for years upon the domain, was thus inducted into the proprietary rights. The adjacency of his own estate gave a territorial feature to this alliance, of which the fruits were no less discernible in the multiplication of negroes, cattle, and poultry, than in a flourishing clan of Meriwethers.

The main building is more than a century old. It is built with thick brick walls, but one story in height, and surmounted by a double-faced or hipped roof, which gives the idea of a ship bottom upwards. Later buildings have been added to this, as the wants or ambition of the family have expanded. These are all constructed of wood, and seem to have been built in defiance of all laws of congruity, just as convenience required. But they form altogether an agreeable picture of habitation, suggesting the idea of comfort in the ample space they fill, and in their conspicuous adaptation to domestic uses.

The hall door is an ancient piece of walnut, which has grown too heavy for its hinges, and by its daily travel has furrowed the floor in a quadrant, over which it has an uneasy journey. It is shaded by a narrow porch, with a carved pediment upheld by massive columns of wood, somewhat split by the sun. An ample court-yard, inclosed by a semi-circular paling, extends in front of the whole pile, and is traversed by a gravel road leading from a rather ostentatious iron gate, which is swung between two pillars of brick surmounted by globes of cut stone. Between the gate and the house a large willow spreads its arched and pendent drapery over the grass. A bridle rack stands within the inclosure, and near it a ragged horse-nibbled plum-tree—the current belief being that a plum-tree thrives on ill usage—casts its skeleton shadow on the dust.

250

Some Lombardy poplars, springing above a mass of shrubbery, partially screen various supernumerary buildings at a short distance in the rear of the mansion. Amongst these is to be seen the gable end of a stable, with the date of its erection stiffly emblazoned in black bricks near the upper angle, in figures set in after the fashion of the work on a girl's sampler. In the same quarter a pigeon-box, reared on a post and resembling a huge tee-totum, is visible, and about its several doors and windows a family of pragmatical pigeons are generally strutting, bridling, and bragging at each other from sunrise until dark.

Appendant to this homestead is an extensive tract of land which stretches some three or four miles along the river, presenting alternately abrupt promontories mantled with pine and dwarf oak, and small inlets terminating in swamps. Some sparse portions of forest vary the landscape, which, for the most part, exhibits a succession of fields clothed with Indian corn, some small patches of cotton or tobacco plants, with the usual variety of stubble and fallow grounds. These are inclosed by worm fences of shrunken chestnut, where lizards and ground-squirrels are perpetually running races along the rails.

A few hundred steps from the mansion, a brook glides at a snail's pace towards the river, holding its course through a wilderness of laurel and alder, and creeping around islets covered with green mosses. Across this stream is thrown a rough bridge, which it would delight a painter to see; and not far below it an aged sycamore twists its roots into a grotesque framework to the pure mirror of a spring, which wells up its cool waters from a bed of gravel and runs gurgling to the brook. There it aids in furnishing a cruising ground to a squadron of ducks who, in defiance of all nautical propriety, are incessantly turning up their sterns to the skies. On the grass which skirts the margin of the spring, I observe the family linen is usually spread out by some three or four negro women, who chant shrill music over their wash-tubs, and seem to live in ceaseless warfare with sundry little besmirched and bowlegged blacks, who are never tired of making somersets, and mischievously pushing each other on the clothes laid down to dry.

Beyond the bridge, at some distance, stands a prominent object in the perspective of this picture—the most venerable appendage to the establishment—a huge barn with an immense roof hanging almost to the ground, and thatched a foot thick with sunburnt straw, which reaches below the eaves in ragged flakes. It has a singularly drowsy and decrepit aspect. The yard around it is strewed knee-deep with litter, from the midst of which arises a long rack resembling a chevaux de frise, which is ordinarily filled with fodder. This is the customary lounge of half a score of oxen and as many cows, who sustain an imperturbable companionship with a sickly wagon, whose parched tongue and drooping swingle-trees, as it stands in the sun, give it a most forlorn and invalid character; whilst some sociable carts under the sheds, with their shafts perched against the walls, suggest the idea of a set of gossiping cronies taking their ease in a tavern porch. Now and then a clownish hobble-de-hoy colt, with long fetlocks and disordered mane, and a thousand burs in his tail, stalks through this company. But as it is forbidden ground to all his tribe, he is likely very soon to encounter a shower of corn-cobs from some of the negro men; upon which contingency he makes a rapid retreat across the bars which imperfectly guard the entrance to the yard, and with an uncouth display of his heels bounds away

251

towards the brook, where he stops and looks back with a saucy defiance; and after affecting to drink for a moment, gallops away with a braggart whinny to the fields.

Chapter 2. A Country Gentleman

The master of this lordly domain is Frank Meriwether. He is now in the meridian of life—somewhere about forty-five. Good cheer and an easy temper tell well upon him. The first has given him a comfortable, portly figure, and the latter a contemplative turn of mind, which inclines him to be lazy and philosophical.

He has some right to pride himself on his personal appearance, for he has a handsome face, with a dark blue eye and a fine intellectual brow. His head is growing scant of hair on the crown, which induces him to be somewhat particular in the management of his locks in that locality, and these are assuming a decided silvery hue.

It is pleasant to see him when he is going to ride to the Court House on business occasions. He is then apt to make his appearance in a coat of blue broadcloth, astonishingly glossy, and with an unusual amount of plaited ruffle strutting through the folds of a Marseilles waistcoat. A worshipful finish is given to this costume by a large straw hat, lined with green silk. There is a magisterial fulness in his garments which betokens condition in the world, and a heavy bunch of seals, suspended by a chain of gold, jingles as he moves, pronouncing him a man of superfluities.

It is considered rather extraordinary that he has never set up for Congress: but the truth is, he is an unambitious man, and has a great dislike to currying favor—as he calls it. And, besides, he is thoroughly convinced that there will always be men enough in Virginia willing to serve the people, and therefore does not see why he should trouble his head about it. Some years ago, however, there was really an impression that he meant to come out. By some sudden whim, he took it into his head to visit Washington during the session of Congress, and returned, after a fortnight, very seriously distempered with politics. He told curious anecdotes of certain secret intrigues which had been discovered in the affairs of the capital, gave a clear insight into the views of some deep-laid combinations, and became, all at once, painfully florid in his discourse, and dogmatical to a degree that made his wife stare. Fortunately, this orgasm soon subsided, and Frank relapsed into an indolent gentleman of the opposition; but it had the effect to give a much more decided cast to his studies, for he forthwith discarded the "Richmond Whig" from his newspaper subscription, and took to "The Enquirer," like a man who was not to be disturbed by doubts. And as it was morally impossible to believe all that was written on both sides, to prevent his mind from being abused, he from this time forward took a stand against the re-election of Mr. Adams to the Presidency, and resolved to give an implicit faith to all alleged facts which set against his administration. The consequence of this straight-forward and confiding deportment was an unexpected complimentary notice of him by the Executive of the State. He was put into the commission of the peace, and having thus become a public man

252

against his will, his opinions were observed to undergo some essential changes.
He now thinks that a good citizen ought neither to solicit nor decline office;
that the magistracy of Virginia is the sturdiest pillar which supports the fabric
of the Constitution; and that the people, "though in their opinions they may
be mistaken, in their sentiments they are never wrong;"—with some such other
dogmas as, a few years ago, he did not hold in very good repute. In this temper,
he has of late embarked on the millpond of county affairs, and notwithstanding
his amiable character and his doctrinary republicanism, I am told he keeps the
peace as if he commanded a garrison, and administers justice like a Cadi.

He has some claim to supremacy in this last department; for during three
years he smoked segars in a lawyer's office in Richmond, which enabled him
to obtain a bird's-eye view of Blackstone and the Revised Code. Besides this,
he was a member of a Law Debating Society, which ate oysters once a week
in a cellar; and he wore, in accordance with the usage of the most promising
law students of that day, six cravats, one over the other, and yellow-topped
boots, by which he was recognized as a blood of the metropolis. Having in this
way qualified himself to assert and maintain his rights, he came to his estate,
upon his arrival at age, a very model of landed gentlemen. Since that time his
avocations have had a certain literary tincture; for having settled himself down
as a married man, and got rid of his superfluous foppery, he rambled with
wonderful assiduity through a wilderness of romances, poems, and dissertations,
which are now collected in his library, and, with their battered blue covers,
present a lively type of an army of continentals at the close of the war, or a
hospital of invalids. These have all, at last, given way to the newspapers—a
miscellaneous study very attractive and engrossing to country gentlemen. This
line of study has rendered Meriwether a most perilous antagonist in the matter
of legislative proceedings.

A landed proprietor, with a good house and a host of servants, is naturally
a hospitable man. A guest is one of his daily wants. A friendly face is a necessary of life, without which the heart is apt to starve, or a luxury without which
it grows parsimonious. Men who are isolated from society by distance, feel
these wants by an instinct, and are grateful for the opportunity to relieve them.
In Meriwether, the sentiment goes beyond this. It has, besides, something
dialectic in it. His house is open to every body, as freely almost as an inn. But
to see him when he has had the good fortune to pick up an intelligent, educated
gentleman—and particularly one who listens well!—a respectable, assentatious
stranger!—All the better if he has been in the Legislature, or better still, if in
Congress. Such a person caught within the purlieus of Swallow Barn, may set
down one week's entertainment as certain—inevitable, and as many more as
he likes—the more the merrier. He will know something of the quality of
Meriwether's rhetoric before he is gone.

Then again, it is very pleasant to see Frank's kind and considerate bearing
towards his servants and dependents. His slaves appreciate this, and hold him
in most affectionate reverence, and, therefore, are not only contented, but happy
under his dominion.

Meriwether is not much of a traveller. He has never been in New England, and
very seldom beyond the confines of Virginia. He makes now and then a winter
excursion to Richmond, which, I rather think, he considers as the centre of

253

civilization; and towards autumn, it is his custom to journey over the mountain to the Springs, which he is obliged to do to avoid the unhealthy season in the tide-water region. But the upper country is not much to his taste, and would not be endured by him if it were not for the crowds that resort there for the same reason which operates upon him; and I may add—though he would not confess it—for the opportunity this concourse affords him for discussion of opinions.

He thinks lightly of the mercantile interest, and, in fact, undervalues the manners of the large cities generally. He believes that those who live in them are hollow-hearted and insincere, and wanting in that substantial intelligence and virtue, which he affirms to be characteristic of the country. He is an ardent admirer of the genius of Virginia, and is frequent in his commendation of a toast in which the state is compared to the mother of the Gracchi:—indeed, it is a familiar thing with him to speak of the aristocracy of talent as only inferior to that of the landed interest—the idea of a freeholder inferring to his mind a certain constitutional pre-eminence in all the virtues of citizenship, as a matter of course.

The solitary elevation of a country gentleman, well to do in the world, begets some magnificent motions. He becomes as infallible as the Pope; gradually acquires a habit of making long speeches; is apt to be impatient of contradiction, and is always very touchy on the point of honor. There is nothing more conclusive than a rich man's logic any where, but in the country, amongst his dependents, it flows with the smooth and unresisted course of a full stream irrigating a meadow, and depositing its mud in fertilizing luxuriance. Meriwether's sayings, about Swallow Barn, import absolute verity. But I have discovered that they are not so current out of his jurisdiction. Indeed, every now and then, we have quite obstinate discussions when some of the neighboring potentates, who stand in the same sphere with Frank, come to the house; for these worthies have opinions of their own, and nothing can be more dogged than the conflict between them. They sometimes fire away at each other with a most amiable and unconvinceable hardihood for a whole evening, bandying interjections, and making bows, and saying shrewd things with all the courtesy imaginable. But for unextinguishable pertinacity in argument, and utter impregnability of belief, there is no disputant like your country gentleman who reads the newspapers. When one of these discussions fairly gets under weigh, it never comes to an anchor again of its own accord;—it is either blown out so far to sea as to be given up for lost, or puts into port in distress for want of documents—or is upset by a call for the boot-jack and slippers—which is something like the previous question in Congress.

If my worthy cousin be somewhat over-argumentative as a politician, he restores the equilibrium of his character by a considerate coolness in religious matters. He piques himself upon being a high-churchman, but is not the most diligent frequenter of places of worship, and very seldom permits himself to get into a dispute upon points of faith. If Mr. Chub, the Presbyterian tutor in the family, ever succeeds in drawing him into this field, as he occasionally has the address to do, Meriwether is sure to fly the course; he gets puzzled with scripture names, and makes some odd mistakes between Peter and Paul, and

254

then generally turns the parson over to his wife, who, he says, has an astonishing memory.

He is somewhat distinguished as a breeder of blooded horses; and, ever since the celebrated race between Eclipse and Henry, has taken to this occupation with a renewed zeal, as a matter affecting the reputation of the state. It is delightful to hear him expatiate upon the value, importance, and patriotic bearing of this employment, and to listen to all his technical lore touching the mystery of horse-craft. He has some fine colts in training, which are committed to the care of a pragmatical old negro, named Carey, who, in his reverence for the occupation, is the perfect shadow of his master. He and Frank hold grave and momentous consultations upon the affairs of the stable, in such a sagacious strain of equal debate, that it would puzzle a spectator to tell which was the leading member in the council. Carey thinks he knows a great deal more upon the subject than his master, and their frequent intercourse has begot a familiarity in the old negro which is almost fatal to Meriwether's supremacy. The old man feels himself authorized to maintain his positions according to the freest parliamentary form, and sometimes with a violence of asseveration that compels his master to abandon his ground, purely out of faint-heartedness. Meriwether gets a little nettled by Carey's doggedness, but generally turns it off in a laugh. I was in the stable with him, a few mornings after my arrival, when he ventured to expostulate with the venerable groom upon a professional point, but the controversy terminated in its customary way. "Who sot you up, Master Frank, to tell me how to fodder that 'ere cretur, when I as good as nursed you on my knee?"

"Well, tie up your tongue, you old mastiff," replied Frank, as he walked out of the stable, "and cease growling, since you will have it your own way;"— and then, as we left the old man's presence, he added, with an affectionate chuckle—"a faithful old cur, too, that snaps at me out of pure honesty; he has not many years left, and it does no harm to humor him!"

Chapter 46. The Quarter

Having despatched these important matters at the stable, we left our horses in charge of the servants, and walked towards the cabins, which were not more than a few hundred paces distant. These hovels, with their appurtenances, formed an exceedingly picturesque landscape. They were scattered, without order, over the slope of a gentle hill; and many of them were embowered under old and majestic trees. The rudeness of their construction rather enhanced the attractiveness of the scene. Some few were built after the fashion of the better sort of cottages; but age had stamped its heavy traces upon their exterior: the green moss had gathered upon the roofs, and the coarse weatherboarding had broken, here and there, into chinks. But the more lowly of these structures, and the most numerous, were nothing more than plain log-cabins, compacted pretty much on the model by which boys build partridge-traps; being composed of the trunks of trees, still clothed with their bark, and knit together at the corners

255

with so little regard to neatness that the timbers, being of unequal lengths, jutted beyond each other, sometimes to the length of a foot. Perhaps, none of these latter sort were more than twelve feet square, and not above seven in height. A door swung upon wooden hinges, and a small window of two narrow panes of glass were, in general, the only openings in the front. The intervals between the logs were filled with clay; and the roof, which was constructed of smaller timbers, laid lengthwise along it and projecting two or three feet beyond the side or gable walls, heightened, in a very marked degree, the rustic effect. The chimneys communicated even a droll expression to these habitations. They were, oddly enough, built of billets of wood, having a broad foundation of stone, and growing narrower as they rose, each receding gradually from the house to which it was attached, until it reached the height of the roof. These combustible materials were saved from the access of the fire by a thick coating of mud; and the whole structure, from its tapering form, might be said to bear some resemblance to the spout of a tea kettle; indeed, this domestic implement would furnish no unapt type of the complete cabin.

From this description, which may serve to illustrate a whole species of habitations very common in Virginia, it will be seen, that on the score of accommodation, the inmates of these dwellings were furnished according to a very primitive notion of comfort. Still, however, there were little garden-patches attached to each, where cymblings, cucumbers, sweet potatoes, water-melons and cabbages flourished in unrestrained luxuriance. Add to this, that there were abundance of poultry domesticated about the premises, and it may be perceived that, whatever might be the inconveniences of shelter, there was no want of what, in all countries, would be considered a reasonable supply of luxuries.

Nothing more attracted my observation than the swarms of little negroes that basked on the sunny sides of these cabins, and congregated to gaze at us as we surveyed their haunts. They were nearly all in that costume of the golden age which I have heretofore described; and showed their slim shanks and long heels in all varieties of their grotesque natures. Their predominant love of sunshine, and their lazy, listless postures, and apparent content to be silently looking abroad, might well afford a comparison to a set of terrapins luxuriating in the genial warmth of summer, on the logs of a mill-pond.

And there, too, were the prolific mothers of this redundant brood—a number of stout negro-women who thronged the doors of the huts, full of idle curiosity to see us. And, when to these are added a few reverend, wrinkled, decrepit old men, with faces shortened as if with drawing-strings, noses that seemed to have run all to nostril, and with feet of the configuration of a mattock, my reader will have a tolerably correct idea of this negro-quarter, its population, buildings, external appearance, situation and extent.

Meriwether, I have said before, is a kind and considerate master. It is his custom frequently to visit his slaves, in order to inspect their condition, and, where it may be necessary, to add to their comforts or relieve their wants. His coming amongst them, therefore, is always hailed with pleasure. He has constituted himself into a high court of appeal, and makes it a rule to give all their petitions a patient hearing, and to do justice in the premises. This, he tells me, he considers as indispensably necessary;—he says, that no overseer is entirely to be trusted; that there are few men who have the temper to administer whole-

256

some laws to any population, however small, without some omissions or ir-regularities; and that this is more emphatically true of those who administer them entirely at their own will. On the present occasion, in almost every house where Frank entered, there was some boon to be asked; and I observed, that in every case, the petitioner was either gratified or refused in such a tone as left no occasion or disposition to murmur. Most of the women had some bargains to offer, of fowls or eggs or other commodities of household use, and Meriwether generally referred them to his wife, who, I found, relied almost entirely on this resource, for the supply of such commodities; the negroes being regularly paid for whatever was offered in this way.

One old fellow had a special favour to ask—a little money to get a new padding for his saddle, which, he said, "galled his cretur's back." Frank, after a few jocular passages with the veteran, gave him what he desired, and sent him off rejoicing.

"That, sir," said Meriwether, "is no less a personage than Jupiter. He is an old bachelor, and has his cabin here on the hill. He is now near seventy, and is a kind of King of the Quarter. He has a horse, which he extorted from me last Christmas; and I seldom come here without finding myself involved in some new demand, as a consequence of my donation. Now he wants a pair of spurs which, I suppose, I must give him. He is a preposterous coxcomb, and Ned has administered to his vanity by a present of a *chapeau de bras*—a relic of my military era, which he wears on Sundays with a conceit that has brought upon him as much envy as admiration—the usual condition of greatness."

The air of contentment and good humor and kind family attachment, which was apparent throughout this little community, and the familiar relations exist-ing between them and the proprietor struck me very pleasantly. I came here a stranger, in great degree, to the negro character, knowing but little of the domestic history of these people, their duties, habits or temper, and somewhat disposed, indeed, from prepossessions, to look upon them as severely dealt with, and expecting to have my sympathies excited towards them as objects of com-miseration. I have had, therefore, rather a special interest in observing them. The contrast between my preconceptions of their condition and the reality which I have witnessed, has brought me a most agreeable surprise. I will not say that, in a high state of cultivation and of such self-dependence as they might possibly attain in a separate national existence, they might not become a more respect-able people; but I am quite sure they never could become a happier people than I find them here. Perhaps they are destined, ultimately, to that national existence, in the clime from which they derive their origin—that this is a transition state in which we see them in Virginia. If it be so, no tribe of people have ever passed from barbarism to civilization whose middle stage of progress has been more secure from harm, more genial to their character, or better sup-plied with mild and beneficent guardianship, adapted to the actual state of their intellectual feebleness, than the negroes of Swallow Barn. And, from what I can gather, it is pretty much the same on the other estates in this region. I hear of an unpleasant exception to this remark now and then; but under such condi-tions as warrant the opinion that the unfavorable case is not more common than that which may be found in a survey of any other department of society. The oppression of apprentices, of seamen, of soldiers, of subordinates, indeed,

257

in every relation, may furnish elements for a bead-roll of social grievances quite as striking, if they were diligently noted and brought to view.

What the negro is finally capable of, in the way of civilization, I am not philosopher enough to determine. In the present stage of his existence, he presents himself to my mind as essentially parasitical in his nature. I mean that he is, in his moral constitution, a dependant upon the white race; dependant for guidance and direction even to the procurement of his most indispensable necessaries. Apart from this protection he has the helplessness of a child— without foresight, without faculty of contrivance, without thrift of any kind. We have instances, in the neighborhood of this estate, of individuals of the tribe falling into the most deplorable destitution from the want of that constant supervision which the race seems to require. This helplessness may be the due and natural impression which two centuries of servitude have stamped upon the tribe. But it is not the less a present and insurmountable impediment to that most cruel of all projects—the direct, broad emancipation of these people;— an act of legislation in comparison with which the revocation of the edict of Nantes would be entitled to be ranked among political benefactions. Taking instruction from history, all organized slavery is inevitably but a temporary phase of human condition. Interest, necessity and instinct, all work to give progression to the relations of mankind, and finally to elevate each tribe or race to its maximum of refinement and power. We have no reason to suppose that the negro will be an exception to this law.

At present, I have said, he is parasitical. He grows upward, only as the vine to which nature has supplied the sturdy tree as a support. He is extravagantly imitative. The older negroes here have—with some spice of comic mixture in it —that formal, grave and ostentatious style of manners, which belonged to the gentlemen of former days; they are profuse of bows and compliments, and very aristocratic in their way. The younger ones are equally to be remarked for aping the style of the present time, and especially for such tags of dandyism in dress as come within their reach. Their fondness for music and dancing is a predominant passion. I never meet a negro man—unless he is quite old—that he is not whistling; and the women sing from morning till night. And as to dancing, the hardest day's work does not restrain their desire to indulge in such pastime. During the harvest, when their toil is pushed to its utmost—the time being one of recognized privileges—they dance almost the whole night. They are great sportsmen, too. They angle and haul the seine, and hunt and tend their traps, with a zest that never grows weary. Their gayety of heart is constitutional and perennial, and when they are together they are as voluble and noisy as so many blackbirds. In short, I think them the most good-natured, careless, light-hearted, and happily-constructed human beings I have ever seen. Having but few and simple wants, they seem to me to be provided with every comfort which falls within the ordinary compass of their wishes; and, I might say, that they find even more enjoyment—as that word may be applied to express positive pleasures scattered through the course of daily occupation—than any other laboring people I am acquainted with.

I took occasion to express these opinions to Meriwether, and to tell him how much I was struck by the mild and kindly aspect of this society at the Quarter.

258

This, as I expected, brought him into a discourse.

"The world," said he, "has begun very seriously to discuss the evils of slavery, and the debate has sometimes, unfortunately, been levelled to the comprehension of our negroes, and pains have even been taken that it should reach them. I believe there are but few men who may not be persuaded that they suffer some wrong in the organization of society—for society has many wrongs, both accidental and contrived, in its structure. Extreme poverty is, perhaps, always a wrong done to the individual upon whom it is cast. Society can have no honest excuse for starving a human being. I dare say you can follow out that train of thought and find numerous evils to complain of. Ingenious men, some of them not very honest, have found in these topics themes for agitation and popular appeal in all ages. How likely are they to find, in this question of slavery, a theme for the highest excitement; and, especially, how easy is it to inflame the passions of these untutored and unreckoning people, our black population, with this subject! For slavery, as an original question, is wholly without justification or defence. It is theoretically and morally wrong —and fanatical and one-sided thinkers will call its continuance, even for a day, a wrong, under any modification of it. But, surely, if these people are consigned to our care by the accident, or, what is worse, the premeditated policy which has put them upon our commonwealth, the great duty that is left to us is, to shape our conduct, in reference to them, by a wise and beneficent consideration of the case as it exists, and to administer wholesome laws for their government, making their servitude as tolerable to them as we can consistently with our own safety and their ultimate good. We should not be justified in taking the hazard of internal convulsions to get rid of them; nor have we a right, in the desire to free ourselves, to whelm them in greater evils than their present bondage. A violent removal of them, or a general emancipation, would assuredly produce one or the other of these calamities. Has any sensible man, who takes a different view of this subject, ever reflected upon the consequences of committing two or three millions of persons, born and bred in a state so completely dependent as that of slavery—so unfurnished, so unintellectual, so utterly helpless, I may say—to all the responsibilities, cares and labors of a state of freedom? Must he not acknowledge, that the utmost we could give them would be but a nominal freedom, in doing which we should be guilty of a cruel desertion of our trust—inevitably leading them to progressive debasement, penury, oppression, and finally to extermination? I would not argue with that man whose bigotry to a sentiment was so blind and so fatal as to insist on this expedient. When the time comes, as I apprehend it will come—and all the sooner, if it be not delayed by these efforts to arouse something like a vindictive feeling between the disputants on both sides—in which the roots of slavery will begin to lose their hold in our soil; and when we shall have the means for providing these people a proper asylum, I shall be glad to see the State devote her thoughts to that enterprise, and, if I am alive, will cheerfully and gratefully assist in it. In the mean time, we owe it to justice and humanity to treat these people with the most considerate kindness. As to what are ordinarily imagined to be the evils or sufferings of their condition, I do not believe in them. The evil is generally felt on the side of the master. Less work is exacted of them than volun-

259

tary laborers choose to perform: they have as many privileges as are compatible with the nature of their occupations: they are subsisted, in general, as comfortably—nay, in their estimation of comforts, more comfortably, than the rural population of other countries. And as to the severities that are alleged to be practised upon them, there is much more malice or invention than truth in the accusation. The slaveholders in this region are, in the main, men of kind and humane tempers—as pliant to the touch of compassion, and as sensible of its duties, as the best men in any community, and as little disposed to inflict injury upon their dependents. Indeed, the owner of slaves is less apt to be harsh in his requisitions of labor than those who toil much themselves. I suspect it is invariably characteristic of those who are in the habit of severely tasking themselves, that they are inclined to regulate their demands upon others by their own standard. Our slaves are punished for misdemeanors, pretty much as disorderly persons are punished in all societies; and I am quite of opinion that our statistics of crime and punishment will compare favorably with those of any other population. But the punishment, on our side, is remarked as the personal act of the master; whilst, elsewhere, it goes free of ill-natured comment, because it is set down to the course of justice. We, therefore, suffer a reproach which other polities escape, and the conclusion is made an item of complaint against slavery.

"It has not escaped the attention of our legislation to provide against the ill-treatment of our negro population. I heartily concur in all effective laws to punish cruelty in masters. Public opinion on that subject, however, is even stronger than law, and no man can hold up his head in this community who is chargeable with mal-treatment of his slaves.

"One thing I desire you specially to note: the question of emancipation is exclusively our own, and every intermeddling with it from abroad will but mar its chance of success. We cannot but regard such interference as an unwarrantable and mischievous design to do us injury, and, therefore, we resent it—sometimes, I am sorry to say, even to the point of involving the innocent negro in the rigor which it provokes. We think, and, indeed, we know, that we alone are able to deal properly with the subject; all others are misled by the feeling which the natural sentiment against slavery, in the abstract, excites. They act under imperfect knowledge and impulsive prejudices which are totally incompatible with wise action on any subject. We, on the contrary, have every motive to calm and prudent counsel. Our lives, fortunes, families—our commonwealth itself, are put at the hazard of this resolve. You gentlemen of the North greatly misapprehend us, if you suppose that we are in love with this slave institution—or that, for the most part, we even deem it profitable to us. There are amongst us, it is true, some persons who are inclined to be fanatical on this side of the question, and who bring themselves to adopt some bold dogmas tending to these extreme views—and it is not out of the course of events that the violence of the agitations against us may lead ultimately to a wide adoption of these dogmas amongst the slaveholding States. It is in the nature of men to recalcitrate against continual assault, and, through the zeal of such opposition, to run into ultraisms which cannot be defended. But at present, I am sure the Southern sentiment on this question is temperate and wise, and that we neither regard slavery as a good, nor account it, except in some favorable conditions, as profitable. The most we can say of it is that, as matters stand, it is the best auxiliary within our reach.

"Without troubling you with further reflections upon a dull subject, my conclusion is that the real friends of humanity should conspire to allay the ferments on this question, and, even at some cost, to endeavor to encourage the natural contentment of the slave himself, by arguments to reconcile him to a present destiny, which is, in fact, more free from sorrow and want than that of almost any other class of men occupying the same field of labor."

Meriwether was about to finish his discourse at this point, when a new vein of thought struck him:

"It has sometimes occurred to me," he continued, "that we might elevate our slave population, very advantageously to them and to us, by some reforms in our code. I think we are justly liable to reproach, for the neglect or omission of our laws to recognize and regulate marriages, and the relation of family amongst the negroes. We owe it to humanity and to the sacred obligation of Christian ordinances, to respect and secure the bonds of husband and wife, and parent and child. I am ashamed to acknowledge that I have no answer to make, in the way of justification of this neglect. We have no right to put man and wife asunder. The law should declare this, and forbid the separation under any contingency, except of crime. It should be equally peremptory in forbidding the coercive separation of children from the mother—at least during that period when the one requires the care of the other. A disregard of these attachments has brought more odium upon the conditions of servitude than all the rest of its imputed hardships; and a suitable provision for them would tend greatly to gratify the feelings of benevolent and conscientious slaveholders, whilst it would disarm all considerate and fairminded men, of what they deem the strongest objection to the existing relations of master and slave.

"I have also another reform to propose," said Meriwether, smiling. "It is, to establish by law, an upper or privileged class of slaves—selecting them from the most deserving, above the age of forty-five years. These I would endue with something of a feudal character. They should be entitled to hold small tracts of land under their masters, rendering for it a certain rent, payable either in personal service or money. They should be elevated into this class through some order of court, founded on certificates of good conduct, and showing the assent of the master. And I think I would create legal jurisdictions, giving the masters or stewards civil and criminal judicial authority. I have some dream of a project of this kind in my head," he continued, "which I have not fully matured as yet. You will think, Mr. Littleton, that I am a man of schemes, if I go on much longer—but there is something in this notion which may be improved to advantage, and I should like, myself, to begin the experiment. Jupiter, here, shall be my first feudatory—my tenant in socage—my old villain!"

"I suspect," said I, "Jupiter considers that his dignity is not to be enhanced by any enlargement of privilege, as long as he is allowed to walk about in his military hat as King of the Quarter."

"Perhaps not," replied Meriwether, laughing; "then I shall be forced to make my commencement upon Carey."

"Carey," interrupted Hazard, "would think it small promotion to be allowed to hold land under you!"

"Faith! I shall be without a feudatory to begin with," said Meriwether. "But come with me; I have a visit to make to the cabin of old Lucy."   (*1832–1851*)

from *Horse Shoe Robinson*

Horse Shoe Robinson, Mildred Lindsay, her brother Henry, and the colored gardener Isaac are traveling to see Lord Cornwallis in the hope that an exposure of villainies against Major Butler, Mildred's betrothed, will gain Cornwallis' promise that "no harm shall befall Arthur Butler beyond the necessary durance of a prisoner of war."

Chapter 40

From Tarborough our travellers continued their route towards the Pedee, by the main road which led through Cross creek, a small hamlet on Cape Fear river, near the site of the present town of Fayetteville. The general features of the country were even more forbidding than those I have already described as characteristic of this portion of North Carolina. Even to the present day, cultivation has done but little to cheer up the natural desolation of those tracts of wilderness which lie between the rivers. But at the early period to which the events I have been detailing have reference, the journey undertaken by our little caravan might be compared to that which is now frequently made through the more southern extremity of the Union, from the Atlantic to the Gulf of Mexico, an attempt seldom essayed by a female, and sufficiently trying to the hardihood of the stoutest travellers. The forethought and attention of Horse Shoe Robinson, however, contributed to alleviate the pains of the enterprise, and to enable Mildred to overcome its difficulties.

In the present alarmed and excited state of this province, the party were less liable to interruption in this secluded and destitute section of the country, than they might have been, had they chosen a lower and more populous district; and the consciousness that every day's perseverance brought them nearer to the ultimate term of their journey, gave new vigor, at least, to Mildred's capacity to endure the privations to which she was exposed. But few vestiges of the war yet occurred to their view. The great wilderness, like the great ocean, retains no traces of the passage of hostile bodies. Sometimes, indeed, the signs of a woodland encampment were visible in the midst of the forest, on the margin of some sluggish brook or around a sylvan fountain, where the impression of recent hoof-prints, the scattered fragments of brushwood cut for temporary shelter, and the still smouldering ashes of camp fires, showed that masses of men had been in motion. The deer fled, too, with a more frightened bound towards their coverts, as if lately alarmed by the pursuit of the huntsman; but the images of devastation, which are associated with the horrid front of war in the mind of all familiar with its ravage, were absent. The eternal, leafy shade high arching over the heads of the wayfarers, furnished no object for human

262

vengeance; and it still sighed in the fanning of the breeze, as of old it sighed before man claimed dominion in the soil it sheltered. A far different scene was shortly to be looked upon by our venturesome friends.

Several days had again passed by, for the journey through the wilderness had been slowly prosecuted, when Robinson, towards the approach of evening, announced to Mildred his conjecture that they were not far off the Pedee. The banks of this river had been the scene of frequent hostilities, and the war that had been carried on here was of the most ruthless kind. The river is characterized by a broad, deep, and quiet stream, begirt with a vegetation of exceeding luxuriance. Its periodical overflow seems to have poured out upon its margin a soil of inexhaustible richness, that, for a mile or two on either side, forms a striking contrast with the low, barren sand-hills that hem in the river plain. Along this tract of level border, all the way to the Atlantic, are found, as is usually the case throughout the Carolinas, the large plantations of opulent gentlemen, who, by the cultivation of rice and cotton, turn the fertility of the soil to the best account. These possessions, presenting the most assailable points to an enemy, and, indeed, almost the only ones in which the great interests of the province might be wounded, were, during the whole of that bloody struggle which distinguished the days of the "Tory Ascendency," the constant objects of attack; and here the war was waged with a vindictive malignity, on the part of the British and Tory partisans, that is scarcely surpassed in the history of civil broils. The finest estates were sacked, the dwellings burnt, and the property destroyed with unsparing rage. The men were dragged from their houses and hung, the women and children turned without food or raiment into the wilderness, and political vengeance seemed to gorge itself to gluttony upon its own rapine.

The thoughts of Robinson had been, for some days past, running upon the probable difficulties that might attend the guise in which he was now about to return to his native province. This was a subject of some concern, since he ran a risk of being compelled either to desert his charge, or to bring his companions into jeopardy, amongst the many persons of both armies who were, at least by report, acquainted with his name and his military connexions. He had explained to Mildred the necessity of his appearing in some definite character, associated with the object of her journey, and of which, upon emergency, he might claim the benefit to retain his post near her. This matter was summarily settled by Henry.

"In general, Mr. Horse Shoe, you can call yourself Stephen Foster; you know Steve; and you can say that you are Mr. Philip Lindsay's gardener. Isaac, here, can let you enough into the craft to pass muster, if any of them should take it into their heads to examine you. Mind that, Isaac: and recollect, old fellow, you are only sister Mildred's waiting man."

"Sartainly, master," replied Isaac.

"And sergeant, I'll tell you all about Steve; so that you can get your lesson by heart. You have a wife and five children—remember that. I'll give you all their names by-and-by."

"Thanks to the marcies of God, that ar'n't my misfortune yet," said Horse Shoe, laughing; "but, Mr. Henry, I have got conscience enough now for any lie that can be invented. The major and me talked that thing over, and he's of

263

opinion that lying, in an enemy's country, is not forbidden in the scriptures. And I have hearn the preacher say that Rahab, who was not a woman of good fame no how, yet she was excused by the Lord for telling the king of Jericho a most thumping lie, consarning her not knowing what had become of the two men that Joshua, the judge of Israel, who was a general besides, had sent into the town to reconnoitre; which was a strong case, Mister Henry, seeing that Rahab, the harlot, was a taking of sides against her own people. So, I like your plan and I'll stick by it."

This being agreed upon, it became one of the amusements of the road-side to put the sergeant through his catechism, which was designed to make him familiar with the traits of private history relating to the Dove Cote and its appurtenances, that he might thereby maintain his identity, in the event of a close investigation. Horse Shoe was but an awkward scholar in this school of disguise, and gave Henry sufficient employment to keep him in the path of probability; and, indeed, the young teacher himself found it difficult to maintain an exact verisimilitude in the part which it was his own province to play in this deception.

On the evening to which we have alluded, the sergeant, finding himself within a short distance of the district of country in which he was almost certain to encounter parties of both friends and foes, adopted a greater degree of circumspection than he had hitherto deemed it necessary to observe. His purpose was to halt upon the borders of the forest, and endeavor to obtain accurate information of the state of affairs along the river, before he entered upon this dangerous ground. Like a soldier who had a rich treasure to guard, he was determined to run no hazard that might be avoided, in the safe conduct of the lady in whose service he was enlisted. In accordance with this caution, he directed the cavalcade to move onward at a moderate walk, in order that they might not reach the limit of the woodland before the dusk of the evening; and also in the hope of finding there some habitation where they might pass the night. They had not advanced far in this manner before the sergeant descried, at some distance ahead, a small log hut standing by the road side, which, by the smoke that issued from the chimney, he perceived to be inhabited. Upon this discovery, he ordered the party to stop and await his return. Then giving spurs to his horse he galloped forward, and, after a short interval of absence, returned, made a favorable report of his reconnaissance, and conducted his companions to the house.

The little cabin to which Mildred was thus introduced was the homestead of an honest Whig soldier, by the name of Wingate, who was now in service, under the command of one of the most gallant partisans that any country ever produced, Francis Marion, then recently promoted to the rank of a brigadier. The inmates were the soldier's family, consisting of a young woman and a number of small children, all demonstrating by their appearance a condition of exceedingly limited comfort. The hut contained no more than two rooms, which exhibited but a scanty supply of the meanest furniture. The forest had been cleared for the space of a few acres around the dwelling, and these were occupied by a small garden or vegetable patch, meagerly stocked with scattered and half parched plants; and by a cornfield, along the skirts of which some lean

264

hogs were seen groping with a felonious stealthiness. A shed, in the same inclosure, formed a rendezvous for a few half-starved cattle, that probably obtained their principal but slender support from the neighboring wood. Add to
these a troop of fowls, that were now at roost upon one of the trees hard by,
and we have, probably, a tolerably correct inventory of the worldly goods of
this little family.

The woman of the house was kind and hospitable, and her attentions were
in no small degree quickened by the application of a few pieces of money
which Mildred insisted upon her receiving—much to the discomfiture of the
dame's self-possession—the boon consisting of hard coin, to an amount of
which, perhaps, she had never before been mistress.

Mildred was exceedingly fatigued, and it was an object of early consideration to furnish her the means of rest. Our hostess, assisted by old Isaac, and
officiously but awkwardly superintended by Horse Shoe, began her preparations for supper, to the abundance of which the provident sergeant was enabled
to contribute some useful elements from his wallet. In one of the apartments
of the hut, a shock-bed was spread for the lady, and by the assistance of her
cloak and some other commodities which had been provided as part of her
travelling gear, she was supplied with a couch that formed no ill exchange for
the weariness of her long-inhabited saddle. Use and necessity are kind nursing-
mothers to our nature, and do not often fail to endow us with the qualities
proper to the fortune they shape out for us. This was not Mildred's first experience of a homely lodging since she left the Dove Cote; and, as privation
and toil have a faculty to convert the rough pallet of the peasant into a bed of
down, she hailed the present prospect of rest with a contented and grateful
spirit.

The supper being dispatched, our lady was left alone with her hostess, to
seek the repose of which she stood so much in need.

The sergeant now set about making provision for the rest of his party. This
was done by erecting a shelter beneath one of the trees of the forest, opposite
to the door of the cabin. It was composed of a few boughs stacked against the
trunk of the tree, sufficiently covered with leaves to turn aside any rain that
might happen to fall. Under this cover Horse Shoe appointed that he and his
comrades should pass the night, enjoining them to keep a regular watch for
the security of the lady, whose welfare was now the object of his most sedulous
attention. All these preparations were made with the exactness of military rule,
and with a skill that greatly delighted Henry.

The long summer twilight had faded away. Mildred had been, from an early
period, in the enjoyment of a profound slumber, and Henry and his negro
ally were seated at the front of their sylvan tent. The sergeant had lighted his
pipe, and now, taking his seat upon a log that lay near his post, he began to
smoke in good earnest, with a mind as free from anxiety as if universal peace
prevailed. In the sedate enjoyment of this luxury, he fell into a descant on
matters and things, interlarded with long and strange stories of his own singular adventures, which he told to the no small edification and amusement of
Henry and the negro.

The habits of the experienced soldier were curiously illustrated in the thought-

265

ful and sober foresight with which Robinson adapted his plans to the exigencies of his condition, and then in the imperturbable light-heartedness with which, after his measures of safety were taken, he waited the progress of events. His watchfulness seemed to be an instinct, engendered by a familiarity with danger, whilst the steady and mirthful tone of his mind was an attribute that never gave way to the inroads of care. He was the same composed and self-possessed being in a besieged garrison, in the moment of a threatened escalade, as amongst his cronies by a winter fireside.

"In this here starlight, Mister Henry," he said, after he had puffed out two or three charges of his pipe, "I can't see your eyes, but by your yawning, I judge you are a little sleepy. Take my advice and turn in. A sodger ought to snatch his rest when he can get it. I'll keep guard over our young lady; the Lord protect her, for a most an elegant and oncommon precious young creature! Fling your great coat upon the leaves, and go at it, my lad, like a good fellow."

"If I was at home, Mr. Horse Shoe, at the Dove Cote, I could sit up all night listening to your stories; but I believe I am bewitched to-night, for my eyelids, this hour past, have been snapping like rat traps. So, I'll just stretch out for an hour or so, and then get up and take my turn at the guard."

"Don't trouble your head about watching," replied Horse Shoe, "you are not old enough for that yet. At your time of life, Mr. Lindsay, a good night's rest is the best part of a ration. And to-morrow, if I'm not mistaken, you will have need of all the strength you can muster to-night. As for me, it isn't much account whether I'm asleep or awake."

"Not so fast, sergeant," rejoined the youth, "I'm an older soldier than you take me for; Stephen and I have watched many a night for raccoons. No, no, I'll have my turn towards morning. So, you and Isaac take the first part of the night between you, and if anything should happen, call me; I'm one of your minute men. So good night. My horse trots harder than I thought he did."

It was not long before our boasted minute man was locked up in a spell apparently as profound as that which the legend affirms assailed the seven sleepers: and Isaac, not even waiting for the good example of his master, had already sunk upon the ground, with that facility which distinguishes his race, the most uncaring and happiest of mortals.

Chapter 41

> Our fortress is the good green wood,
>   Our tent the cypress tree,
> We know the forest round us
>   As seamen know the sea.
>
> We know its walls of thorny vines,
>   Its glades of reedy grass,
> Its safe and silent islands
>   Within the dark morass.—*Bryant.*

266

The faithful Horse Shoe being thus left to himself, replenished his pipe, and, taking his rifle in his hand, paced to and fro upon the border of the road, holding communion with his own thoughts, carefully weighing the probabilities connected with his present singular expedition, and revolving, after his own fashion, the fortunes of Arthur Butler and Mildred Lindsay.

It was within an hour of midnight, when the sergeant's meditations were interrupted by the tramp of a horse approaching the hut at a gallop. But a few moments elapsed before a traveller, who, in the starlight, Horse Shoe could discern to be armed, drew up his rein immediately at the door of the dwelling, against which he struck several blows with his weapon, calling out loudly at the same time—

"Mistress Wingate—for God's sake, open your door quickly! I have news to tell you, good woman."

"In the name of mercy! who are you?" exclaimed the voice of the dame within, whilst a note of alarm was also heard from her fellow-lodger.

"What do you mean by this racket and clatter?" demanded Horse Shoe, in the midst of the uproar, at the same time laying his hand upon the stranger's bridle rein. "What brings you here, sir?—stand back; the women in that house are under my charge, and I won't have them disturbed."

"If you are a friend to Mistress Wingate," said the horseman, sternly, "speak the word; if an enemy, I will shiver your skull with the butt of my musket."

"Don't be rash, good fellow," replied Horse Shoe; "I take it you and me are on the same side. What's afoot that you stir in such a hurry?"

"The Tories are afoot—the devil's afoot! Open, Mistress Wingate—open to Dick Peyton!"

"The Lord preserve us!" ejaculated the mistress of the hovel, as she opened the door; "Bloody Spur, is it you? What ill luck brings you here to-night?"

"A gang of Tories, Mistress Wingate, from the Black River, under that cutthroat Fanning, crossed Pedee this morning at Lowder's Lake. They have been thieving and burning as far as Waggamaw, and are now on the road home by the upper ferry. They will be along here in less than half an hour. Your husband, Bob Wingate, and myself, were sent out by General Marion this morning, to reconnoitre the roads. We fell in with the ruffians, after sun-set, below Lumberton, and have tracked them up here. Bob has got a pistol-shot through his arm. He was lucky enough, however, to escape their clutches; but believing they had a spite against him, and would ride past his house to-night, he told me to call and give you warning, and to help you to drive the cattle back into the swamp."

"How many mought there be, friend?" asked Horse Shoe, calmly.

"Between two and three hundred, at least," said the trooper; "we counted fifty in the vanguard—those that followed made a long column of march. They have stolen a good many horses and cattle, all of which are with them, and several prisoners."

"What, ho!—Isaac, Henry Lindsay; fall to, and saddle, boys," shouted Horse Shoe. "Miss Mildred, it will not do to stand. I am sorry to break in upon your rest, but you must be ready to move in a few minutes."

Everything about the hut was now in confusion. Henry and the sergeant

267

were equipping the horses, whilst Isaac was gathering up the baggage. Bloody Spur—to adopt the rider's *nom de guerre*—had dismounted, and was busy in removing the few articles of value from the hut; the mother and children, meanwhile, were pouring forth loud lamentations.

Mildred, in the midst of this scene of uproar, hurriedly made her preparations for departure; and whilst she was yet engaged in this care, a confused murmur was heard, at some distance up the road—and the rattle of sabres, as well as the hoarse voice and abrupt laughter of men, announced that the freebooters were at no great distance from the dwelling.

"Merciful heaven!" exclaimed Mildred, giving way for the first time to her fears; "they are fast approaching, and we shall be captured."

"Sister," said Henry, with scarcely less alarm, "I will die by your side, before they shall hurt a hair of your head."

Horse Shoe, who at this moment was tightening the girths of Mildred's saddle, paused for an instant to listen, and then said:

"The wind is north-east, young lady, and the voice sounds far to-night. One could hardly expect you to be cool when one of these night-frays is coming on, but there's no occasion to be frightened. Now, ma'am, if you please, I'll heave you into your seat. There," continued the sergeant, setting Mildred upon her horse, "you have got four good legs under you, and by a fair use of them will be as safe as a crowned king. Mister Henry, mount, and ride with your sister slowly down the road, till I overtake you."

Henry obeyed the order.

"Is the portmanteau and the rest of the baggage all safe, Isaac? Don't be flurried, you old sinner, but look about you, before you start off."

"All safe," replied the negro.

"Up and follow your master, then. Hark you, Mr. Bloody Spur," said Horse Shoe, as Isaac rode off, to the trooper, who was still actively employed in turning the cattle loose from the inclosure, "what is the best road hereabouts for my squad to keep out of the way of these bullies?"

"About a mile from here, take a road that strikes into the woods, upon your right hand," answered the trooper hastily, "it will lead you up the river to the falls of Pedee. If you should meet any of Marion's men, tell them what you have seen; and say Dick Peyton will be along close after you."

"Where is Marion?" asked the sergeant, mounting his horse.

"What man that knows Frank Marion could ever answer that question?" said the trooper. "He is everywhere, friend. But you have no time to lose: be off."

As Bloody Spur said this, he disappeared, driving the cattle before him; whilst the mother, laden with an infant and as many pieces of furniture as she could carry, and followed by her terrified children, fled towards the neighboring thicket.

Horse Shoe in a few moments overtook his companions, and, urging them forward at a rapid flight, soon reached the diverging road, along which they journeyed with unabated speed for upwards of a mile.

"How do you bear it, sister?" asked Henry, with concern.

"Ah, brother, with a sore heart to be made so painfully acquainted with these frightful scenes. I lose all thought of my own annoyance, in seeing the calamities that are heaped upon the unoffending family of a man who dares to draw his sword for his country."

"Yes, ma'am," said Horse Shoe, gravely, "these incarnivorous devils have broken the rest of many a good woman in the Carolinas, before they routed you out to-night, ma'am. But it is one of God's marcies to see how you keep up under it."

"Mine's a trifling grievance, good sergeant: I lose but a little repose: that poor mother flies to save her children, uncertain, perhaps, of to-morrow's subsistence; and her husband's life is in daily peril. It is a sad lot. Yet truly," added Mildred with a sigh, "mine is scarcely better. Gracious heaven!" she exclaimed, looking behind her, "they have set fire to the dwelling!"

In the quarter to which she directed her eyes, the horizon was already illuminated with the blaze of Wingate's hut. The light grew brighter for a short interval, and brought into bold relief upon the sky, the tall, dark forms of the stately pines of which the forest was composed.

"They are fools as well as villains," said Horse Shoe, with an angry vehemence; "they have had liquor to-night, or they would hardly kindle up a blaze which should rouse every Whig on Pedee to track them like hounds. It would be sport worth riding to look at, if Marion should get a glimpse of that fire. But these wolves have grown obstropolous ever since Horatio Gates made his fox-paw at Camden."

"Oh, it is a most savage war," said Mildred, "that roots up the humble hearth, and fires the lowly roof, where none but defenceless women and children abide. I shudder to think of such wanton barbarity."

"There's the thing, Miss Lindsay, that turns all our blood bitter. Man to man is fair game, all the world over: but this ere stealing of cattle, and burning of houses, and even cutting up by the roots the plants of the 'arth, and turning of women and children naked into the swamps, in the dead of night! it's a sorry business to tell of a Christian people, and a cowardly business for a nation that's a boasting of its bravery."

The light of the conflagration had soon died away, and our wanderers pursued their solitary road in darkness, ignorant of the country through which they passed, and uncertain of the point to which they tended. A full hour had gone by in this state of suspense, and Robinson had once more resolved to make a halt, and encamp his party in the wood. Before, however, he could put his design into execution, he was unexpectedly challenged, from the road-side, with the military demand of—"Who goes there?"

"Travellers," was the reply.

"Where do you come from, and where are you going?"

"The first question I can answer," said Horse Shoe, "and that is, from Old Virginny, a fortnight ago, but, to-night, from a tolerable snug lodging, where some onmannerly fellows troubled our sleep. But as to where we're going, it's more likely you can tell that for us."

"You are saucy, sir."

"It's more than I meant to be," replied the sergeant. "Mayhap you mought have hearn of a man they call Bloody Spur?"

269

"He has pricked your pillows for you—has he? Dick Peyton is good at that," said a second questioner.

"Aha, comrades, I understand you now," said Horse Shoe, with alacrity. "Dick Peyton and Bob Wingate both belong to your party. Am I right? We are friends to Marion."

"And therefore friends to us," said the patrole. "Your name, sir, and the number you have in company?"

"Take us to the general, and we will answer that," replied Horse Shoe. "The Tories have set upon Wingate's house and burnt it to the ground. It's like we may be able to tell something worth hearing at head-quarters. Your man Bloody Spur gave us in charge to report him, and to say that he would soon follow upon our track. I wonder that he isn't here before now."

"I will remain," said one of the soldiers to his companion; "you shall take charge of the travellers."

The trooper accordingly turned his horse's head and commanded Horse Shoe and his party to follow.

The scout conducted our adventurers along a by-road that led round the head of a marsh, and through several thickets which, in the darkness of the night, were penetrated with great difficulty; during this ride he interrogated Horse Shoe as to the events of the late inroad of the Tories. He and his comrade had been stationed upon the path where the sergeant encountered them, to direct the out-riding parties of his corps to the spot of Marion's encampment, the policy of this wary officer being to shift his station so frequently as almost equally to defy the search of friend and foe. Peyton and Wingate were both expected; and the trooper who remained behind only waited to conduct them to the commanding officer, who had, since the disappearance of daylight, formed a bivouac in this neighborhood. Marion's custom was to order his reconnoitring parties to return to him by designated roads, where videttes were directed to repair in order to inform them of his position—a fact which, as his movements were accomplished with wonderful celerity and secrecy, they were generally unable to ascertain in any other way.

At length, emerging from the thicket, and crossing what seemed, by the plash of the horse's feet, a morass, the party, under the guidance of the scout, came upon a piece of thinly-timbered woodland, which, rising by a gentle slope, furnished what might be called an island of dry ground, that seemed to be only accessible by crossing the circumjacent swamp. Upon this spot were encamped, in the rudest form of the bivouac, a party of cavalry, which might have amounted to two hundred men. Several fires, whose ruddy glare had been discerned for the last half mile of the journey, were blazing forth from different quarters of the wood, and threw a bold and sharp light upon the figures of men and horses, imparting a feature of lively, picturesque beauty to the scene. The greater portion of the soldiers were stretched beneath the trees, with no other covering than the leafy bowers above them. The horses were picketed in the neighborhood of their riders; and the confused array of saddles, sabres, muskets, rifles and other warlike instruments, that were hung upon projecting boughs, or leant against the trunks, as they caught the flashes of frequent fires, seemed to be magnified in number equal to the furniture of thrice the force. Sentinels were seen pacing their limits on the outskirts of this

270

company, and small bodies of patroles on horseback moved across the encampment with the regularity of military discipline. Here and there, as if regardless
of rest, or awaiting some soon-expected tour of duty, small knots of men sat
together amusing themselves, by torchlight, at cards; and, more appropriately,
others had extended their torpid frames in sleep upon their grassy pallets and
knapsack pillows.

"We have seen war in its horrors," exclaimed Mildred, with an involuntary
vivacity; "and here it is in all its romance!"

"Sister, I wish you were at home," said Henry, eagerly, "and Steve and I
had the Rangers on this field to-night. I would undertake to command a picket
with any man here!"

To Horse Shoe these were familiar scenes, and he could not comprehend
the source of that sudden interest which had so vividly aroused the admiration
of his companions; but asking the guide to conduct them immediately to General Marion, he followed the soldier across the whole extent of the bivouac,
until they halted beneath a large tree, near which a few officers were assembled.
One of this group was seated on the ground; and close by him, planted in the
soil, a blazing pine-faggot flung a broad light upon a saddle, the flap of which
the officer had converted, for the occasion, into a writing-desk.

"Make way for a squad of travellers picked up on the road to-night," said
the scout in a loud voice. "They wish to see General Marion."

In a moment our party was surrounded by the officers; and Horse Shoe, unceremoniously dismounting, addressed the person nearest to him:—

"A lady, sir, from Virginia, that I started with from her father's house, to
fetch to Carolina; but who has been most audaciously unhoused and unbedded
in the very middle of the night by a hellish pack of Tories."

"My name is Lindsay, sir," said Henry, riding to the front; "my sister and
myself were travelling south, and have been obliged to fly, to-night, before a
detachment of horse-stealers."

"From Bob Wingate's," said Horse Shoe, "as I should judge, some six miles
back. I want to report to General Marion: the lady, likewise, is tired, as she
has good right to be."

The officer to whom this was addressed, directed a soldier to seek General
Marion, and then approaching Mildred said:

"Madam, we can promise little accommodation suitable to a lady: the green-
wood tree is but an uncouth resting-place: but what we can supply shall be
heartily at your service."

"I feel sufficiently thankful," replied Mildred, "to know that I am in the
hands of friends."

"Sister, alight," said Henry, who now stood beside her stirrup, and offered
his hand: and in a moment Mildred was on her feet.

The officer then conducted her to a bank, upon which a few blankets were
thrown by some of the soldiers in attendance. "If this strange place does not
alarm you," he said, "you may perhaps find needful repose upon a couch even
as rough as this."

271

"You are very kind," replied Mildred, seating herself. "Brother, do not quit
my side," she added, in a low voice: "I feel foolishly afraid."

But a few moments elapsed before the light of the torches, gleaming upon his figure, disclosed to Mildred the approach of a person of short stature and delicate frame, in whose step there was a singular alertness and rapidity. He wore the blue and buff uniform of the staff, with a pair of epaulets, a buckskin belt, and broadsword. A three-cornered cocked-hat, ornamented with a bucktail, gave a peculiar sharpness to his naturally sharp and decided features; and a pair of small, dark eyes twinkled in the firelight, from a countenance originally sallow, but now swarthy from sun and wind. There was a conspicuous alacrity and courtesy in the gay and chivalrous tone in which he accosted Mildred:

"General Marion, madam, is too happy to have his poor camp honored by the visit of a lady. They tell me that the Tories were so uncivil as to break in upon your slumbers to-night. It adds greatly to my grudge against them."

"I have ventured," said Mildred, "into the field of war, and it does not become me to complain that I have met its vicissitudes."

"Gallantly spoken, madam! May I be allowed to know to whom I am indebted for the honor of this visit?"

"My name is Lindsay, my father resides at the Dove Cote in Virginia: under the protection of my brother and a friend, I left home to travel into Carolina."

"A long journey, madam," interrupted Marion; "and you have been sadly vexed to-night, I learn. We have a rude and unquiet country."

"My sister and myself," said Henry, "counted the chances before we set out."

"I would call you but an inexperienced guide, sir," said the General, addressing Henry, and smiling.

"Oh, as to that," replied the youth, "we have an old soldier with us—Horse Shoe Robinson—hem—Stephen Foster, I meant to say."

"Horse Shoe Robinson!" exclaimed Marion, "where is he?"

"Mr. Henry Lindsay, General, and me," said the sergeant, bluntly, "have been practising a lie to tell the Tories, in case they should take us unawares; but it sticks, you see, in both of our throats. It's the true fact that I'm Horse Shoe himself. This calling me Stephen Foster is only a hanging out of false colors for the benefit of the red-coats and Tories, upon occasion."

"Horse Shoe, good fellow, your hand," said Marion, with vivacity, "I have heard of you before. Miss Lindsay, excuse me, if you please; I have business to-night which is apt impertinently to thrust itself between us and our duty to the ladies. Richards," he continued, addressing a young officer who stood near him, "see if you can find some refreshment that would be acceptable to the lady and her brother. Horse Shoe, this way: I would speak with you."

Marion now retired towards the place where the writing materials were first noticed, and entered into an examination of the sergeant, as to the particulars of the recent attack upon Wingate's cabin.

Before Robinson had finished his narrative of the events of the night, a horseman dashed up almost at full speed to the spot where Marion stood, and, flinging himself from his saddle, whilst his horse stood panting beside him, asked for the General.

"How now, Bloody Spur! What's the news?" demanded Marion.

"The Black River hawks are flying," said the soldier.

"I have heard that already," interrupted the chieftain. "Tell me what else."

"I stayed long enough to secure Wingate's cattle, and then set out for the river to cut loose the boats at the Ferry. I did it in good time. Four files followed close upon my heels, who had been sent ahead to make sure of the means of crossing. The fellows found me after my work was done, and chased me good three miles. They will hardly venture, General, to swim the river to-night, with all the thievery they have in their hands; and I rather take it they will halt at the ferry till daylight."

"Then that's a lucky cast, Dick Peyton," exclaimed Marion. "Ho, there! Peters, wake up that snoring trumpeter. Tell him to sound 'to saddle.' Come lads, up, up. Gentlemen, to your duties!"

Forthwith the trumpet sounded, and with its notes everything asleep started erect. Troopers were seen hurrying across the ground in rapid motion: some hastily buckling on broadswords and slinging their muskets; others equipping the horses; and everywhere torches were seen passing to and fro in all the agitation of a sudden muster. As soon as Marion had set this mass in action, he repaired to Mildred, and in a manner that betokened no excitement from the general stir around him, he said—

"I owe you an apology, Miss Lindsay, for this desertion, which I am sure you will excuse when you know that it is caused by my desire to punish the varlets who were so ill-mannered as to intrude upon your slumbers. I hope, however, you will not be a loser by the withdrawal of our people, as I will take measures to put you under the protection of a good friend of mine, the widow of a worthy soldier, Mistress Rachel Markham, who lives but two miles from this, and whose hospitable mansion will afford you a shelter more congenial to your wishes than this broad canopy of ours. A guide shall be ready to conduct you."

"Your kindness, general," said Mildred, "puts me under many obligations."

"Horse Shoe shall take a line of explanation to my friend," added Marion. "And now, madam, farewell," he said, offering his hand. "And you, Master or Mister Henry, I don't know which—you seem entitled to both—good night, my brave lad: I hope, before long, to hear of your figuring as a gallant soldier of independence."

"I hope as much myself," replied Henry.

Marion withdrew, and by the time that he had prepared the letter and put it into Horse Shoe's hands, his troops were in line, waiting their order to march. The general mounted a spirited charger, and galloping to the front of his men, wheeled them into column, and, by a rapid movement, soon left Horse Shoe and his little party, attended by one trooper who had been left as a guide, the only tenants of this lately so busy scene. The change seemed almost like enchantment. The fires and many torches were yet burning, but all was still, except the distant murmur of the receding troops, which grew less and less, until, at last, there reigned the silence of the native forest.

Our travellers waited, almost without exchanging a word, absorbed in the contemplation of an incident so novel to Mildred and her brother, until the distant tramp of the cavalry could be no longer heard: then, under the direction of the guide, they set out for the residence of Mrs. Markham. (1835, 1852)

273

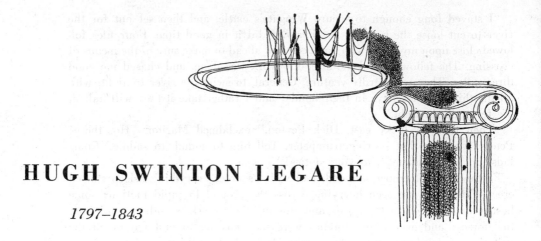

HUGH SWINTON LEGARÉ

1797–1843

Hugh Swinton Legaré's reputation today rests upon his varied political activities, his contributions to the periodical literature of the Old South, and his career as a diplomat. This "Charleston Intellectual," as V. L. Parrington calls him, spent most of his life in public office, though he was by temperament a recluse and by training a scholar. His literary criticism, which is our primary concern here, was definitely an avocation.

Legaré was born near Charleston, South Carolina. When he was two years old, his father died, leaving the responsibility of rearing the family in the hands of Hugh's mother, an unusually capable and resourceful woman. Permanently crippled before he was five by a smallpox inoculation, the boy was unable to participate in active childhood games and therefore spent much of his time reading and studying. After a few years of tutoring by his mother, Legaré attended several private schools and in 1807 enrolled in Charleston High School. At the age of fourteen he entered South Carolina College as a sophomore, and graduated from that institution in 1814, at the head of his class. In order to continue the study of law, which had occupied his attention for three years, and "to see something of the world," he went to Europe in 1818, where for two years he studied French, natural philosophy, mathematics, and chemistry.

Returning to South Carolina, Legaré was elected to the state legislature for the first of nine one-year terms. In 1822 he began practicing law in Charleston, but met with little success. He was next appointed Attorney General of South Carolina (1830) and Chargé d'Affaires in Belgium (1832). Upon his return to the United States in 1835, he was elected to Congress. Failing to be re-elected after one term, he resumed private practice in Charleston, this time with marked success. In 1841 he was appointed Attorney General of the United States by his close personal friend, John Tyler. Throughout his long public career Legaré strongly advocated states' rights and bitterly opposed the protective tariff. Like Simms, however, he aroused much antagonism in his native state because he did not support Calhoun's stand on Nullification.

274

The majority of Legaré's reviews and critical articles were written while he was editor of Stephen Elliott's *Southern Review* (1828–1832), a journal patterned after the great quarterlies of England. Despite its short life (and primarily because of Legaré's contributions), the *Southern Review* is regarded as one of the most influential of the many periodicals which flourished and died in the Old South. Legaré's numerous essays reveal erudition, a thorough classical background, keen critical perception, and cultivated taste. His most important articles on purely classical subjects are "On Classical Learning" and "Roman Literature." He is also remembered for his thorough studies of Byron, Scott, and Sir Philip Sidney in English literature, Jeremy Bentham in economics, and Cooper and Bryant in American literature. His reviews indicate that he made a serious attempt to read and evaluate contemporary American literature, although, unfortunately, his editorship came too early for him to write estimates of Simms, Baldwin, Longstreet, Poe, and the great writers of the New England renaissance. Legaré's most recent biographer, Linda Rhea, says of his literary criticism: "He had the wide range of reading necessary for the critic and went into his subjects with exhaustive thoroughness. He wrote with the spirit of one who had a mission to perform, or a real duty to point out the best, and to lead readers away from the mediocre. Legaré, like Matthew Arnold . . . held up high standards and applied severe tests, and, as was true of Arnold, the classics had much to do with determining these standards."

from Byron's Letters and Journals

[The Classical and Romantic Styles]

. . . This last allusion leads us to remark upon that distinction between the "classical" and "romantic" styles, which Byron . . . alludes to as a novel and condemns as an absurd one.[1] We are glad to hear an opinion, which we ventured to advance in our first number,[2] confirmed by so high an authority—for if any writer has a claim to a high place in the new school, it is undoubtedly Byron. The distinction, now alluded to, originated in Germany. It was seized by Madame de Staël with avidity, as well adapted to her purposes of metaphysical, mystical, and ambitious declamation, and it has since been entertained, with more respect than we conceive it deserves, in the literary circles of Europe. A. W. Schlegel, in his valuable *Lectures upon Dramatic Poetry*, makes it the basis of all his comparisons between the ancients and the moderns in that art. His main object is to account for the simplicity of the Greek drama, and its close adherence to the three unities, as well as the rigid exclusion from it of every thing comic and incongruous, on principles which shall explain the difference between that style and the complicated and irregular plots and tragi-comic mixtures of Calderon and Shakespeare, without supposing any inferiority in the latter. It was not enough for him to say, that ancient taste was too fastidious; or that ancient criticism was more severe, as the modern is more indulgent— that the former exacted of genius more than it can perform, at least without a sacrifice of much of its power and enthusiasm—while the latter unshackles the

275

[1] *In the preceding paragraph Legaré notes that certain passages in Byron's poetry "contribute nothing either to the distinctness or vividness" of his poetic images. "Is this," he asks, "good 'romantic' writing?"*
[2] *Legaré is referring to an article of his, "Classical Learning," which had appeared in the first issue of the* Southern Review *(1828).*

"muse of fire" and gives it full scope and boundless regions to soar in—and that this is the reason, in short, why *Macbeth* and *Othello* are so much better (as *we* say they are) than the *Orestiad* or the *Œdipus*. This did not suit with Schlegel's way of thinking, first, because he was a good scholar, and knew better; and, next and principally, because he was a German philosopher, and therefore bound to explain the phenomenon by some subtle process of reasoning of his own invention. This he has attempted to do, and the result (as we understand it) is that, in all the arts of taste, the genius of modern times is *essentially* different from that of the Greeks, and *requires*, for its gratification, works of a structure totally distinct from those which he admits to have been the best imaginable models of the classic style.

The principle, by which it is attempted to account for this mighty revolution in art and criticism, is *religion*. That of the Greeks, we are told, was "the deification of the powers of nature and of earthly life." Under a Southern sky, amidst the sweets of a genial and radiant climate, genius naturally dreams of joy and beauty, and the forms, with which a poetical fancy peopled heaven, were fashioned upon those with which it was familiar on earth. A gay, sensual and elegant mythology grew up under its plastic hands—its visions of ideal perfection were embodied in the idols of superstitious worship—and Venus, Apollo, Minerva, Hercules, etc., have been individualized as images of certain attributes, and identified with the conception of all mankind, by the master-pieces which they may be said to have patronized, since they were created to adorn their temples or to grace their festivals. But this system of religious adoration was confined to the present life, addressed itself exclusively to the *senses*, exacted of the worshipper only forms and oblations, and confirmed him in the tranquil self-complacency or the joyous spirit which the face of nature and the circumstances of his own condition inspired. Christianity was, in all these particulars, the very opposite of Paganism. It added to the material world, a mysterious world of spirits—it substituted the infinite for the finite, and endless future for the transitory present—at the end of every vista in life, it presents the grave, and it has shrouded the grave itself in a deeper gloom, and made death emphatically the King of Terrors. But Schlegel has expressed himself so well upon this subject, that we are tempted to quote a long passage from him:

"Among the Greeks, human nature was in itself all sufficient; they were conscious of no wants, and aspired of no higher perfection than that which they could actually attain by the exercise of their own faculties. We, however, are taught by superior wisdom that man, through a high offense, forfeited the place for which he was originally destined: and that the whole object of his earthly existence is to strive to regain that situation which, if left to his own strength, he could never accomplish. The religion of the senses had only in view the possession of outward and perishable blessings; and immortality, in so far as it was believed, appeared in an obscure distance like a shadow, a faint dream of this bright and vivid futurity. The very reverse of all this is the case with the Christian: every thing finite and mortal is lost in the contemplation of infinity; life has become shadow and darkness, and the first dawning of our real existence is beyond the grave. Such a religion must awaken the foreboding, which slumbers in every feeling heart, to the most thorough consciousness that the happiness after which we strive we can never here obtain: that no external

276

object can ever entirely fill our souls, and that every mortal enjoyment is but a fleeting and momentary deception. When the soul resting, as it were, under the willows of exile, breathes out its longing for its distant home, the prevailing character of its song must be melancholy. Hence the poetry of the ancients was the poetry of enjoyment, and ours is that of desire; the former had its foundation in the scene which is present, while the latter hovers between recollection and hope. Let us not be understood to affirm that every thing flows in one strain of wailing and complaint, and that the voice of melancholy must always be loudly heard. As the austerity of tragedy was not incompatible with the joyous views of the Greeks, so the romantic poetry can assume every tone, even that of the most lively gladness; but still it will always, in some shape or other, bear traces of the source from which it originated. *The feeling of the moderns is, upon the whole, more intense, their fancy more incorporeal, and their thoughts more contemplative."* [3]

Now, we are disposed to assent, in general, to the justness of these observations. We think that modern literature does differ from that of the Greeks in its *complexion and spirit*—that it is more pensive, sombre and melancholy, perhaps we may add, more abstract, and metaphysical—and it has, no doubt, been "sicklied o'er" with this sad hue, by the influence of a religious faith which connects morality with worship, and teaches men to consider every thought, word and action of their lives as involving, in some degree, the tremendous issues of eternity. Machiavelli has a similar theory of his own. He refers the existence of democratic governments among the ancients, and the almost total absence of it in his time, to the same cause. The spirit of polytheism he conceives to have been bold, hardy and masculine; that of Christianity to be so meek, lowly and self-abasing, as to fit its professors for any sort of imposition or contumely.[4] This notion has been signally refuted by the history of the last three centuries—especially by the exploits of our Puritan and Huguenot ancestors—but the theory of the Florentine secretary is, in practical matters, very much what Schlegel's is, in literature. Certainly we are more given to *spiritualizing* than the Greeks were—sensible objects suggest moral reflections more readily—the external world is treated as if it were the symbol of the invisible, and the superiority of the mind to matter, of the soul to the body, is almost as much admitted by the figures of rhetoric and poetry, as in the dogmas of philosophy. There were no Herveys and Dr. Youngs at Athens. The *spirit*, we repeat it, is changed—the associations, which natural objects suggest, are different, of course—but does this alter, in any essential degree, the *forms* of beauty? Does it affect the *proportions* which the parts of a work of art ought to bear to each other and to the whole? Does it so far modify the relations of things that what would be fit and proper in a poem, an oration, a colonnade, a picture, if it were ancient, is misplaced and incongruous now? In short, has the philosophy of literature and the arts, the reason, the logic—which controls their execution and results as much as it does the conclusions of science, though in a less palpable manner—undergone any serious revolution? Schlegel and the rest of the same school affirm that such a revolution has taken place. Their favorite illustration of it is, as we have already remarked, the drama and the unities; Shakespeare

277

---

[3] *Dram. Lit.—Lect. vi. p. 15. (Legaré's note.)*
[4] *Discorsi. (Legaré's note.)*

and Sophocles are the great representatives of the "romantic" and the "classical"—and they compare the former to painting which is various, the latter to sculpture, which is of course characterized by singleness and simplicity. "Why," say they, "are the Greek and romantic poets so different in their practice, with respect to place and time." The question is an interesting one. Many solutions may be offered; and the very last we should adopt would be the following: which, indeed, so far as it is intelligible, is only a different way of asserting the same thing; in other words, a very palpable *petitio principii*.[5] "The principal cause of the difference is the *plastic* spirit of the antique and the *picturesque* spirit of the romantic poetry. *Sculpture* directs our attention exclusively to the group exhibited to us, it disentangles it as far as possible from all external accompaniments, and where they can [not] be altogether dispensed with, they are indicated as lightly as possible. *Painting*, on the other hand, delights in exhibiting in a minute manner, along with the principal figures, the surrounding locality and all the secondary objects, and to open to us in the background, a prospect into a boundless distance; light and perspective are its peculiar charms. Hence the dramatic, and especially the tragic art of the ancients annihilates in some measure, the external circumstances of space and time; while the romantic drama adorns by their changes its more diversified pictures. Or to express myself in other terms, the principle of antique poetry is ideal, that of the romantic mystical: the former subjects, space and time, to the internal free activity of the mind; the latter adores these inconceivable essences as supernatural powers, in whom something of the divinity has its abode."[6]

We are willing to impute the transcendent, or, if the epithet be preferred, the truly *romantic* nonsense of the last sentence to the translator; but we may conjecture from the context, and from the other parts of his works, what was the drift of the author. M. Schlegel means to say (as he does affirm elsewhere) that this difference between ancient and modern genius, which is thus illustrated by sculpture and painting, or the *plastic* and the *picturesque*, pervades all the departments of literature and art, without exception. In music, for instance, the ancients are said to have preferred melody, the moderns harmony—in architecture, compare the Parthenon or the Pantheon with Westminster Abbey, or the Church of St. Stephen at Vienna—even the sculpture of the moderns, according to the opinion of Hemster Husius, is too much like painting, as the painting of the ancients was probably too much like sculpture. Now, in the first place, we deny the fact that the taste of the moderns *is* different from that of the Greeks in these particulars. As for the drama, *we* have no tragedies but Shakespeare's, and, if we had, his incomparable genius has settled that part of the controversy irreversibly, so far as popular opinion is concerned. But do not all scholars, without exception, admire and delight in the Greek tragedy? As for music, we suspect that melody is as much preferred now to harmony, as it ever was at Athens; but if it were not, it would be for time to decide, whether the taste of the day were not a transitory and false one. We know too little of the state of that art among the Greeks to enable us to draw any sure inferences from it. Besides the proper comparison would be not between melody and harmony, but between romantic melody or harmony, and classical melody or harmony,

---

[5] *Questioning of principles.*
[6] *Dramatic Lit.—Lect. ix. p. 348. (Legaré's note.)*

since both existed at each of the two great periods, and there can be no fair comparison but between things of the same kind. So with architecture. A Gothic cathedral has its beauties—it has its own peculiar proportions—it has fitness to the solemn purpose for which it was designed—it has gorgeous ornament, imposing massiveness, striking altitude, immense extent—its long-drawn aisle and fretted vault—its storied windows—the choir, the altar, the crucifixes, the confessional of the penitent, the stones of the pavement worn by the knees of pilgrims and crusaders, the air of venerable antiquity and religious gloom pervading the whole interior—a thousand interesting associations of the past and of the future, of history and the church, conspire to make it one of the most impressive objects that can be presented to the imagination of man. The origin of the style was in a dark age; but it has taken root, nor is it at all probable that, so long as Christianity shall endure, the modern world will ever be brought to think as meanly of these huge piles, as a Greek architect (if one were suddenly revived) possibly might. Still, there are very few builders of the present age who do not prefer the orders of Greece—and, even if they did not, how would that prove that future ages would not? "Time will show," as Byron says, which taste is the more natural and reasonable: and time only, and the voice of the majority, can show it conclusively.

Meanwhile, let us descend to details: suppose a particular object proposed to be painted or described in the strict sense of those words? Are there two ways of doing that perfectly, and yet as different from each as the styles in question are supposed to be? A portrait, for instance—is a classical likeness, a different thing from a romantic one, and yet both are good likenesses of the same thing. Suppose the object described to be twilight. If the pictures were confined to the *sensible phenomena*, it is obvious there *could not be* any variety in them, as anyone who doubts what is obvious to reason, may convince himself by comparing parallel passages in the ancient and modern classics—e.g., Milton's lines, "Now came still evening on, and twilight gray," Virgil's beautiful verses on midnight in the fourth *Æneid*, Homer's on moonlight in the eighth *Iliad*. The exquisite sketches of these objects, executed by the great masters just mentioned, are all in precisely the same style, and, if they were in the same language, might easily be ascribed to the same age of poetry. To be sure, if without, or besides describing the object, some striking association of ideas be suggested, that may make a very material difference, because such things are essentially accidental and mutable. For instance, Dante's famous lines on the evening describe it, not as the period of the day when nature exhibits such or such phenomena, which must always be the same while her everlasting order be maintained, but by certain casual circumstances which may or may not accompany that hour—the vesper bell, tolling the knell of the dying day, the lonely traveller looking back, with a heart oppressed with fond regrets, to the home which he has just left—very touching circumstances no doubt to those who have a home or have lived in Catholic countries, but still extraneous, and it may be, transitory circumstances.

The same thing may be affirmed of any other particular object, either in the moral or the material world. A picture of conjugal love, for instance, as in Hector and Andromache—of maternal despair, as in Shakespeare's Blanche—of filial devotedness as in the Antigone. We do not comprehend how it is possible

279

to exhibit such objects in more than one style that shall be perfect—and that the *natural*, the universal, the unchangeable—*quod semper, quod ubique, quod ab omnibus*.[7] And what is clearly true of the details we take to be equally true of the combinations. The *spirit* may vary, the *associations*, the colouring or complexions; but, substantially, there can be but one form of ideal beauty, with which human nature, that never changes, will rest forever satisfied.

We will borrow an illustration, on this subject, from the learned Michaelis. If any two systems of religion and poetry differ in their spirit, in the associations with which they surround the objects of their adoration and praise, and the effect they produce upon the mind of the votary, it is the Jewish and the Pagan —the one dwelling forever, in its prophetic raptures, upon the sublime unity of the Godhead filling immensity, whose invisible glory it was the guiltiest audacity to degrade by attempting to represent it in any sensible image; the other crowding all space with a mob of thirty thousand deities of every rank and shape. The sacred poetry of the Hebrews, besides, is the great fountain of modern inspiration, strictly so called. Yet, differing as widely as it is possible in the very element of thought and character from which Schlegel deduces such important results, there is no essential difference in the *forms* of Hebrew and Classical poetry. The illustration we shall borrow from the learned author referred to is the following. He remarks that, as the Heathen assigned to Jupiter a chariot and horses of thunder, so the Hebrews have a similar fable, and the Cherubim are expressly the horses of Jehovah's chariot. He is frequently described as sitting upon the Cherubim. He thunders so that the earth shakes— or as Horace might have expressed it,

> "Jehovah per cœlum tonantes
> Egit equos, volucremque currum;
> Quo bruta tellus, et vaga flumina
> Quo Styx et invisi horrida Toenari
> Sedes, Atlanteusque finis
> Concutitur." [8]

The same observation holds, in the strictest manner true, of Milton and Dante, the two most sublime poets of modern times, the most Christian in spirit, and the most classical and severe in style.

After all, this classification of styles may only be a more artificial and scholastic way of confessing that those irregular works of modern genius, which are designated as romantic, *par excellence*, in fact, deviate very materially from the Greek standard. Of this no one who has studied criticism in the works of the ancients, can have any doubt at all. Three things were considered as essential to all excellence, in a composition of genius, perfect unity of purpose, simplicity of style, and ease of execution—and it is in these things that the literature and art of Greece exhibit their matchless perfection. Other nations have produced works indicating as rare and fertile invention, as much depth of thought, as much vigor of conception, as much intensity of feeling—but no body of literature

280

---

[7] *At all times, at all places, and by all persons.*
[8] *Jehovah drives onward the horses, thundering through Heaven, and the flying chariot; while the barren earth and the wandering rivers, the Styx and the dreadful citadel of unseen Toenarres, and the boundaries of Atlas are mightily shaken.*

or of art can be compared to the *antique* for the severe *reason*, the close, unsparing *logic* of its criticism. Unity of design, especially, which is more immediately connected with the subject at hand, they rigorously exacted. They considered a work of art always as a *whole*—a sort of organized body—to the very structure of which certain parts and proportions, and none others, were essential, and in which the least violation of this fitness and harmony was a deformity, more or less uncouth and monstrous.[9] The details were sacrificed without mercy to the general effect. In an oration, for instance, they looked to the end which the speaker had in view, and whatever was not calculated to further that, however brilliant and impressive in itself, was rejected without reserve. The notion of Pythagoras that the sublime order of the universe was maintained by the secret power of *proportion*, by the magic of mathematical relations, probably sprang out of this truly Greek idea of the perfection of art, applied by analogy to works of the creation.[10] . . . This unity of thought, this harmony in composition, this ἀνάγκη λόγογραφικη as Plato calls it, a sort of necessary connection, like that of cause and effect, between the parts, everything being in its right place, following logically from what goes before it, leading inevitably to what comes after it, pervades all the monuments of genius which that wonderful race has left behind it. The superiority in their exquisite *logic* of literature and the arts—a logic not a jot less exact and elegant than the demonstrations of their own unrivalled geometry—is, we fear, a lamentable truth, nor will it help us much to call our deformities, peculiarities, and to dignify what is only *not* art with the specious title of the 'romantic.'

This severe study of unity naturally led, it seems to us, to the two other prominent excellencies of Greek style, simplicity and ease or grace. Their genius was most enthusiastic—their sensibilities were even acute and lively to excess. Let any one read those passages of their best authors wherein they treat of poetry, and he will not fail to be struck with the force of their expressions. They speak of it as a heavenly inspiration, a divine fury, the revelry and intoxication of the soul—they compare it to the madness of the Pythoness, the rage of the bacchanal, the convulsive *improvisations* of the Corybantes awakened by the peculiar μελος of their God.[11] But their taste was as refined as their temperament was ardent, and hence the severity of the restraints which they laid upon their own genius. They seem to have been conscious of their tendency to exceed, rather than be wanting, in energy and warmth, and to overstep the modesty of nature by indulging her impulses too freely. They studied perpetually how to speak the language of soberness and truth. The smallest appearance of effort or exaggeration was particularly disagreeable to them, as leading to the vice they most avoided. The intense love of beauty which possessed them, the influence of a happy climate and still happier organization, the native inspiration of genius, were common advantages, and those were enough, they thought, to insure all the *power* necessary, (with sufficient discipline) to attain a high degree of excellence. The artist was supposed to possess *this* qualification

[9] *Plato, Phaed. p. 244. Socrates says, . . . "I think you ought to say that every composition is, as it were, an animal having a body of its own: so that it should be neither without a head or feet, but should have its various parts, suitable to one another, and composing one perfect whole." (Legaré's note.)*
[10] *Here Legaré refers to a passage from Cicero.*
[11] *See the truly Dithyrambic effusion of Socrates in Plato's Io. (Legaré's note.)*

as [a matter] of course. His aim, therefore, was not to show that he possessed it, by an affected or ostentatious and unseasonable display of it, but to manage it with a wise economy, to turn it to the greatest account in creating, in whatever might be his province, some perfect form of beauty. His study of the ideal led him to think, as we have shown, of the compositions of a *whole*; for details, however brilliant, were still mere fragments, and as such were unworthy of his ambition. Any body could accomplish them, and abundance always creates fastidiousness. But to do all that can be done by the greatest effort of genius, yet to be free from all the faults into which genius, when it exerts itself most, is so apt to be betrayed—to put forth his whole power, yet never to transcend the limits of reason, and to embody the visions of an excited imagination in a form so perfect as to defy the most fastidious criticism of his country, and to challenge a place among the imperishable monuments of his art—this was indeed to be a '*maker*', ποιητης—this was to be truly Attic and classical. Accordingly, what is most admirable in that matchless literature is this simplicity and ease, produced by the study of unity and the severe reasoning on which we have been dwelling. It is, we conceive, impossible not to be struck with the difference, in this respect, between its master-pieces, and those of any other language—for Shakespeare himself frequently falls into bombast and conceit. In short, the strength of Greek genius is never discovered in monstrous contortions of laborious struggles —it wields the mightiest subjects, apparently, without an effort, and with all the grace of conscious superiority. Its beauty is not confined to a single feature, "to a lip or eye," but is emphatically "the joint force and full result of all"— it is not the hectic glow of disease, or the meretricious lustre of a painted cheek, but the *lumen juventae purpureum*, the bloom of youth, the proper hue, as the natural effect of a vigorous and robust constitution. . . . (*1831*)

WILLIAM GILMORE SIMMS

1806–1870

282 William Gilmore Simms, one of the most talented men of letters in the Old South, was born in Charleston, South Carolina, where he spent most of his life. Young Simms was virtually orphaned at the age of two when his father, disheartened by the death of his wife and the failure of his mercantile business, went to Mississippi and became a member of Andrew Jackson's volunteers, leaving William Gilmore in the care of his maternal grandmother. Simms

attended the public schools of South Carolina (which he later said were useless),
served for a short time as a druggist's apprentice, and then decided to study
law. At the age of eighteen Simms visited his father in Mississippi and, for a
time, considered remaining there permanently. For undetermined reasons he
returned to Charleston, but his sojourn had given him valuable firsthand information about the frontier which he later incorporated in his border novels.

When he was twenty years old, Simms married Anna Malcolm Giles. The
following year was highlighted by his admittance to the bar and the publication
of his first volume of verse. He then became associated for a few months in the
publication of the Charleston *City Gazette*, but the paper met with little success,
and following the death of his wife in 1832, the discouraged Simms left the
South. Determined to win fame and recognition as a writer, he felt that he
should be in the East, the great publishing center of the country. He settled
for a while in New Haven, where he cultivated the better-known literary figures
of the time (particularly William Cullen Bryant), and began to write furiously.

By 1836 Simms had returned to his native Charleston, married Chevilette
Roach, and set himself up as a gentleman farmer on her "Woodlands" estate.
Here began the period of Simms' greatest influence. He became the guiding
spirit behind one of the most productive literary groups in the ante-bellum
South. Both benefactor and critic to Hayne, Timrod, and other lesser-known
members of the coterie which gathered in Russell's bookshop, he came to be
known as the "Dr. Johnson of Charleston."

Although Simms was a prolific writer (he produced nearly seventy volumes of
poetry, novels, short stories, biography, and history), he is remembered today
primarily for his "epic of the Revolution." This series consists of seven novels:
The Partisan (1835); *Mellichampe* (1836); *The Kinsman* (1841), revised and
renamed *The Scout*; *Katharine Walton* (1851); *The Sword and the Distaff*
(1852), later published as *Woodcraft*; *The Forayers* (1855); and *Eutaw*
(1856). Well known also is his romantic tale of conflict between the English
settlers and the Indians, *The Yemassee: A Romance of Carolina* (1835). His
"border novels," based upon colonial and nineteenth-century frontier life in
the South, include *Guy Rivers* (1834), *Richard Hurdis: A Tale of Alabama*
(1838), *Border Beagles: A Tale of Mississippi* (1840), *Beauchampe, or the
Kentucky Tragedy* (1842), and *Charlemont* (1856).

Simms' poetry—with the exception of a few much-anthologized pieces such
as "The Swamp Fox"—apparently is of little interest to the twentieth-century
reader, but his *Atalantis*, a long poem relating the story of a sea fairy in love
with a sea demon, merits the consideration of any serious student of Southern
literature. Many of his best stories and novelettes are collected in the following
volumes: *The Book of My Lady* (1833), *Martin Faber and Other Tales* (1838),
Carl Werner (1838), *The Wigwam and the Cabin: Life in America* (1848), *The
Lily and the Totem* (1850), and *Southward Ho!* (1854).

In addition to his creative efforts, Simms did a prodigious amount of work
on the nine newspapers and magazines with which he was connected. His
Southern Literary Gazette was, for its brief duration, a serious challenge to
Hugh Swinton Legaré's *Southern Review*, one of the most important periodicals
published in the South. In his reviews and critical articles, as well as in his
novels and short stories, Simms argued for regionalism in literature. In politics

and economics he held, along with Calhoun and others, what has been called the "Greek idea of Democracy."

One of the most outspoken defenders of slavery and secession, Simms wrote incessantly in support of the Southern cause. After the outbreak of the Civil War, he followed the course of events with enthusiasm, and his optimism, fostered by Southern victories during the early part of the war, was undimmed even by the burning of "Woodlands" in 1862. He later became extremely disillusioned by the South's defeat and by the events of Reconstruction, with the result that he wrote little of importance during the last years of his life.

The Swamp Fox

We follow where the Swamp Fox guides,
    His friends and merry men are we;
And when the troop of Tarleton rides,
    We burrow in the cypress tree.
The turfy hammock is our bed,
    Our home is in the red deer's den,
Our roof, the tree-top overhead,
    For we are wild and hunted men.

We fly by day and shun its light,
    But prompt to strike the sudden blow,
We mount and start with early night,
    And through the forest track our foe,
And soon he hears our chargers leap,
    The flashing saber blinds his eyes,
And ere he drives away his sleep,
    And rushes from his camp, he dies.

Free bridle-bit, good gallant steed,
    That will not ask a kind caress
To swim the Santee at our need,
    When on his heels the foemen press—
The true heart and the ready hand,
    The spirit stubborn to be free,
The twisted bore, the smiting brand—
    And we are Marion's men, you see.

Now light the fire and cook the meal,
    The last, perhaps, that we shall taste;
I hear the Swamp Fox round us steal,
    And that's a sign we move in haste.
He whistles to the scouts, and hark!
    You hear his order calm and low.

Come, wave your torch across the dark,
　And let us see the boys that go.

We may not see their forms again,
　God help 'em, should they find the strife!
For they are strong and fearless men,
　And make no coward terms for life;
They'll fight as long as Marion bids,
　And when he speaks the word to shy,
Then, not till then, they turn their steeds,
　Through thickening shade and swamp to fly.

Now stir the fire and lie at ease—
　The scouts are gone, and on the brush
I see the Colonel bend his knees,
　To take his slumbers too. But hush!
He's praying, comrades; 'tis not strange;
　The man that's fighting day by day
May well, when night comes, take a change,
　And down upon his knees to pray.

Break up that hoecake, boys, and hand
　The sly and silent jug that's there;
I love not it should idly stand
　When Marion's men have need of cheer.
'Tis seldom that our luck affords
　A stuff like this we just have quaffed,
And dry potatoes on our boards
　May always call for such a draught.

Now pile the brush and roll the log;
　Hard pillow, but a soldier's head
That's half the time in brake and bog
　Must never think of softer bed.
The owl is hooting to the night,
　The cooter crawling o'er the bank,
And in that pond the flashing light
　Tells where the alligator sank.

What! 'tis the signal! start so soon,
　And through the Santee swamp so deep,
Without the aid of friendly moon,
　And we, Heaven help us! half asleep!
But courage, comrades! Marion leads;
　The Swamp Fox takes us out tonight;
So clear your swords and spur your steeds,
　There's goodly chance, I think, of fight.

285

We follow where the Swamp Fox guides,
    We leave the swamp and cypress tree,
Our spurs are in our coursers' sides,
    And ready for the strife are we.
The Tory camp is now in sight,
    And there he cowers within his den;
He hears our shouts, he dreads the fight,
    He fears, and flies from Marion's men.

(1832)

The Edge of the Swamp

'Tis a wild spot, and even in summer hours,
With wondrous wealth of beauty and a charm
For the sad fancy, hath the gloomiest look,
That awes with strange repulsion. There, the bird
Sings never merrily in the sombre trees,
That seem to have never known a term of youth,
Their young leaves all being blighted. A rank growth
Spreads venomously round, with power to taint;
And blistering dews await the thoughtless hand
That rudely parts the thicket. Cypresses,
Each a great ghastly giant, eld and gray,
Stride o'er the dusk, dank tract,—with buttresses
Spread round, apart, not seeming to sustain,
Yet link'd by secret twines, that underneath,
Blend with each arching trunk. Fantastic vines,
That swing like monstrous serpents in the sun,
Bind top to top, until the encircling trees
Group all in close embrace. Vast skeletons
Of forests, that have perish'd ages gone,
Moulder, in mighty masses, on the plain;
Now buried in some dark and mystic tarn,
Or sprawl'd above it, resting on great arms,
And making, for the opossum and the fox,
Bridges, that help them as they roam by night.
Alternate stream and lake, between the banks,
Glimmer in doubtful light: smooth, silent, dark,
They tell not what they harbor; but, beware!
Lest, rising to the tree on which you stand,
You sudden see the moccasin snake heave up
His yellow shining belly and flat head
Of burnish'd copper. Stretch'd at length, behold
Where yonder Cayman, in his natural home,
The mammoth lizard, all his armor on,
Slumbers half-buried in the sedgy grass,

286

Beside the green ooze where he shelters him.
The place, so like the gloomiest realm of death,
Is yet the abode of thousand forms of life,—
The terrible, the beautiful, the strange,—
Wingéd and creeping creatures, such as make
The instinctive flesh with apprehension crawl,
When sudden we behold. Hark! at our voice
The whooping crane, gaunt fisher in these realms,
Erects his skeleton form and shrieks in flight,
On great white wings. A pair of summer ducks,
Most princely in their plumage, as they hear
His cry, with senses quickening all to fear,
Dash up from the lagoon with marvellous haste,
Following his guidance. See! aroused by these,
And startled by our progress o'er the stream,
The steel-jaw'd Cayman, from his grassy slope,
Slides silent to the slimy green abode,
Which is his province. You behold him now,
His bristling back uprising as he speeds
To safety, in the centre of the lake,
Whence his head peers alone,—a shapeless knot,
That shows no sign of life; the hooded eye,
Nathless, being ever vigilant and sharp,
Measuring the victim. See! a butterfly,
That, travelling all the day, has counted climes
Only by flowers, to rest himself a while,
And, as a wanderer in a foreign land,
To pause and look around him ere he goes,
Lights on the monster's brow. The surly mute
Straightway goes down; so suddenly, that he,
The dandy of the summer flowers and woods,
Dips his light wings, and soils his golden coat,
With the rank waters of the turbid lake.
Wondering and vex'd, the pluméd citizen
Flies with an eager terror to the banks,
Seeking more genial natures,—but in vain.
Here are no gardens such as he desires,
No innocent flowers of beauty, no delights
Of sweetness free from taint. The genial growth
He loves, finds here no harbor. Fetid shrubs,
That scent the gloomy atmosphere, offend
His pure patrician fancies. On the trees,
That look like felon spectres, he beholds
No blossoming beauties; and for smiling heavens,
That flutter his wings with breezes of pure balm,
He nothing sees but sadness—aspects dread,
That gather frowning, cloud and fiend in one,
As if in combat, fiercely to defend

287

Their empire from the intrusive wing and beam.
The example of the butterfly be ours.
He spreads his lacquer'd wings above the trees,
And speeds with free flight, warning us to seek
For a more genial home, and couch more sweet
Than these drear borders offer us tonight.

(1853)

from *The Forayers*

The Forayers, *set in South Carolina in 1781, depicts conditions in that colony during the Revolutionary War. The episode presented here is almost entirely removed from the central action of the novel (Marion's harassing forays against the British). It introduces Captain Porgy, who to many readers is Simms' most memorable character. Taking advantage of a brief lull in the fighting, Captain Porgy entertains a group of celebrated Americans, among whom are "Light-Horse Harry" Lee and General Francis Marion, Porgy's commanding officer.*

Chapter 43. The Frog Concert and Campaign

The army of Greene were taking rest for the first time for several days, at the close of that which witnessed their insulting demonstrations before the garrison of Orangeburg. We have seen that their camp lay only four miles from that village:—a mellow sunset overspread the scene, and gentle breezes from the west cooled off sweetly the heat of a day, the ardency of which had severely tried all parties. The utmost languor for a while pervaded the encampment. The troops lay about upon the grass, under the trees, with half-shut eyes, enjoying that dreamy sensation which supervenes after fatigue, and before recuperation —mind and body in concert, as it were, for mutual restoration. But few of the groups visible in our foreground, were capable of exertion, and but few, indeed, of those whom we do not see, were any more equal to it than those immediately before our eyes. Here and there, some important adjutant, ensign, or corporal, might be found, restlessly employed, giving orders about the use of moonshine. Troopers who had thrown their chief burdens on the loins of their horses, were, perhaps, the most lively; and groups of these were to be seen, busy in consuming the last drops of sunshine and Jamaica at command, while flirting the cards at "old sledge" from well-thumbed and greasy packs of "pictures," pitching quoits, or grooming horses. We confess that Marion's men were the chief sinners after this fashion; his boys of Santee, Pedee, Waccamaw, and the parish country generally, having a sort of natural calling for the fine arts, were busy with cards and coppers at every rest: Cards and dice constituted so many fine arts in their hands. It was the boast of some of them that they could extract all sorts of music, fun, and philosophy, from the four aces.

288

To this general rest and languor of the army, there were, however, some striking exceptions. The command of Marion stretched toward the Caw-caw. In the woods of this region, an hour before sunset, there might be seen a squad of twenty troopers, dark, bronzed, half-naked young savages, following with some interest, the speech and movements of a large, broad-shouldered, and great-bellied personage, wearing the uniform—somewhat doubtful, indeed, because of rents, stains, and deficiencies—of a captain of dragoons. He was on foot, and by no means active of movement, though taking his steps with the confidence of a war-horse, and the solid firmness of an elephant. He was a fine-looking fellow, in spite of the too great obtrusion upon the sight of his abdominal territory, a region which he, nevertheless, endeavored to circumscribe within reasonable bounds by a girthing of leather, only half covered with a crimson sash, which no doubt had the desired effect in some degree, though at some sacrifice of the wearer's comforts. His face was full almost as the moon at full, of a ruddy brown, his head massive, chin large and prominent eyes, bright but small, and mouth eager with animation. His nose was decidedly intellectual. At his elbow stood a Negro, jacket off, and arms akimbo, who followed the motions of his superior with a mixed air of deference and assurance. Around these two the troopers were gathered. Before the group, slaughtered and skinned, hanging from a tree, was one of the lean beeves of the country—a poor skinny beast, weighing some two hundred pounds, gross, bone, meat, skin, offal! Near at hand stood a small, rickety, covered wagon, the contents of which we may conjecture. It was one of Marion's recent captures from the convoy of Stewart; and contained, no doubt, some resources, the value of which may be guessed from the mysterious looks which were, every now and then, cast upon it by passing groups of thirsty dragoons, the very glances of whom are apt to burst locks, and consume stores.

Our captain was busy with the commissariat of the brigade—not as the head of it, by no means, but as premier—head-counsellor, and legal and moral adviser.

"I tell you, Fickling, it will never do. Tell me there were no better beeves to be had! You have just taken what they please to give you. You are too modest. It is the infirmity of your family, whenever the interest is not absolutely and directly your own. We do this business of foraging for all the army, yet it seems that the meanest share is always to fall to us. Tell me nothing of Colonel Lee. He has an independent legion; let him pick up his own beeves. As for the field-officers, I do not see that their official position confers upon them any right to better tastes and appetites than a poor captain of partisan cavalry. I thank my stars that I have tastes which are as well cultivated as any brigadier or colonel in the army. And shall my tastes be defrauded, because these epauletted buffalos are greedy, and you are mealy-mouthed? Why the devil don't you assert yourself, man, and assist us, as you should, when the distribution of the beef takes place? You are a fool, Fickling, for your submission! Colonel Lee's man steps before you, and says, 'Colonel Lee;' and Colonel Washington's man starts up, and says, 'Colonel Washington'—and these, and a score of others, even while they speak, clap hands on the best pieces, and choose the fattest flanks; and when all are served, you steal up, with finger in your mouth, and

289

murmur, 'Is anything left for General Marion?' Is that the way to do business? I tell you, 'No, sir!' Your true way is to take the best that offers—lay bold hands on it—nay, thrust it through with your naked sabre, and say, 'Marion's brand!' Do the thing as you should, with the proper look and manner, and not a rapscallion in the army, representing no matter what division, dare lay hands on it after that! If they do, let me be at your elbow next time, with two or three fellows of my choosing!"

"But, Captain Porgy—"

"But me no buts, Mr. Fickling. I'll have you out of your office, if you do not but against this sort of distribution. You are to provide us; and, if you do not comprehend that our soldiers are just as deserving of good food as any continentals in the service, you are not fit for our service, and I'll have you out of it. General Marion himself submits quite too much to this sort of treatment. If there is a fine horse in the brigade, it is immediately wanted for some one of Lee's dragoon's—some d———d henchman or bugleman—and off the colonel goes to Greene and tells him that his legion wants horses, and that Marion has enough and to spare, and we are called upon to dismount, and provide other people. Yet are we kept day and night on the trot—off to-day for the Pon-pon and Savannah, to-morrow for the Pedee—now running down tories, now cattle; seeking information, scouting, spying, called out at all hours; and how is this to be done, if we are to give up our horses. The brigade has covered all this low country, from the Pedee to the Savannah, for three years and more, and the best that is got in the forays that we alone make, are served out to these hungry feeders. I won't submit to it. They shall neither have my horses nor my cattle; and if you take any more such beef as this, Fickling, when better is to be had, we'll turn you, neck and heels, out of your department."

"But, Captain Porgy—"

"See to it!"

"But—"

"See to it! That's all! I say no more—to you!—Tom!"

"Sah!"

"Get our share of that carrion! See what you can do with it. We must have soup, I suppose. Make a pilaw. We have plenty of pepper now. You can hardly get a decent steak from the beast. But do what you can. I must see after something more. We are to have company to-night. I have asked the great men, the big-wigs, the governor, Generals Marion and Sumter, the colonels of the brigade, Maham, Singleton, and a few others. Have everything ready by ten o'clock. Did you succeed in getting any melons?"

"I empty one patch, maussa."

"Whose?"

"I dunn know quite 'zackly, but he's a fiel' jes' yer on de back ob de village. De melons is quite 'spectable."

"Ripe?"

"As de sunshine kin make 'em."

"Good! Do as much stealing in an honest way as you can! D———n the patriotism that can't eat stolen fruits!"

"Wha' else you guine hab, maussa."

290

"Who knows what I can get? I must look. There ought to be frogs here in abundance, and of good size. Not such as we can find in a rice reserve, Tom, but passable in war-time, and delicate enough for hot weather. I shall look out for a young alligator or two."

"Dat'll do! Gi' me two young alligator tail, and de frog, and I gi' you fus' rate tuttle soup and ball, and steak."

"Must have a ragout, Tom. Have you seen no pigs about, Tom?"

"Nebber yer de fus' squeak, maussa."

"Well"—with a grunt—"we must do as we can. Come, boys, are you ready?"

"Ay, ay, captain!" from a score of voices; and a dozen active young fellows presented themselves, armed with wooden spears and knives.

"Where's George Dennison?"

A voice answered from the foot of a tree.

"Come along, George; don't be lazy. What you shall see this evening will enable you to beat Homer in a new epic, in which cranes and frogs shall figure to posterity."

And, following the corpulent captain, the whole party pushed down to the swamp.

"There's a battalion for you, George Dennison. Not a rascal under six feet— half a dozen nearer seven. I chose them specially for the expedition. They are our cranes, and are all eager for the war."

"And the frogs are sounding for the conflict. Hear their tongues, already. The concert for the evening is begun. Hear the chirruping overture:—

> " 'Fry bacon—tea-table!
> Coyong! coyong! coyong!
> Supper on table—supper on table,
> Eat if you're able!
> Blood an' 'ounds—blood an' 'ounds.'

"By the way, captain, a frog concert would not be a bad speculation in the great cities of Europe. How a score or two of musical fellows, who had once or twice slept in our swamps, or lingered after sunset along our rice-fields, would make capital out of it! And such a sensation. What a hurly-burly, sub-dued to order, they could make of it."

"No doubt! The notes and tones occupy every note of the *gamut!* It is a rare original music. But the secret would lie in making the music tributary to satire. The frogs should furnish a running commentary on the follies and vices of society as in Aristophanes, only adapted to our times. It would task art admirably to work out of it an opera—the Loves of the Frogs! Little Squeaka, the dreaming sentimental damsel, just emerging into society—coming out; in her train some half a dozen Jockos—minnows of fashion, that sing in a love-lisp always—Therubina! ah! Therubina! Oh the rich fun of such a farcical! Of what a delightful variety would the affair admit! The lover, the villain, the priest, the mother—all the usual varieties, not forgetting Arlecchino. Of course, the frogs are not less fortunate than their betters. They have a Jack Pudding among them. The squirrels have I know."

291

"Don't forget the duenna! Hear her falsetto, squeaking through a score of crevices in her broken teeth:—

> " 'On your knees, O,
>   Not a sneeze, O,
> Don't you hear your mother coming?'
>   'To be kissed, O,
>   By the priest, O,
> Is the saintliest sort of mumming.'
>
> " 'O, alack, O,
>   Such a smack, O,
> Makes the very echoes jealous;'
>   'But it proves, O,
>   Holy loves, O,
> Most particularly zealous.'
>
> " 'Hark that drumming!'
>   'Mother coming!'
>   'And that pother?'
>   " 'Tis your father!'
>   'Awful sounds, O!'
>   'Blood and 'ounds, O!'—
>
> "In full fresco swells the chorus,
> From the motley group before us;
>   Sighing, swelling,
>   Barking, belling—
> Such a moaning, such intoning,
> So much groaning, honing, droning,
> Calling, falling, bawling, drawling,
> Speaking, shrieking, squeezing, squeaking,
>
> "All subsiding to a quiver,
>   And a shiver,
> Only to ascend, in thunder,
> Rolling up and roaring under—
> Blood and 'ounds, O! blood and 'ounds, O!
> Awful sounds, breaking bounds,
> Setting all the woods a-shaking,
> Setting all the bog a-quaking,
> All the swampy empire waking,
>   With the eternal blood and 'ounds, O!
>
> "Rending, raging,
>   Battle waging,
> 'Yond all musical assuaging—
> O'er all mortal sounds uproarious,
> O'er all mortal sense victorious,

292

Like the diapason glorious,—
That through pipes and stops,
Shrieks, and bounds, and hops,
Foams, and frisks, and frolics,
Rolls and rages, rocks and rollicks,
Feeding every mortal stopper, ah!
Of the grand Italian opera!"

Thus it was that the rustic poet of the partisans, gave forth extempore an embodiment of the music of the frog-pondians.

"Hurrah!" cried Porgy, "hurrah, Geordie—why, man, you are native, to frog manor born, with all the pipes and bellows of the swamp in your own wind-bags; or to requite you in your own coin:—

"Worthy venison,
Geordie Dennison,
You will soon require a stopper, O,
Scaring off with greater clamor,
Every leap-frog from his armour,
Turning every mother's son of 'em
Making fun of 'em,—
To a hopper off, from a hopper, O!"

And thus doggrelizing as they went, the two led their laughing cohort down into the swamp.

The Caw-caw was in full concert. Bull and bell, squeak and shriek, moan and groan. All the artistes were in exercise, engaged, no doubt, in some rehearsal, preparatory to some great ceremonial—the bridal, possibly, of the young princess of the pondians.

Porgy and his corps, with their pointed spears of wood, wooden forks, baskets, and knives, stole down into the lagunes. What a picture for the stage! What an action for the burlesque drama! But the matter was a serious one enough for one of the parties. Long will the frogs of that ilk remember with wailing the raid of the cranes of that day. Could you have seen those long, gaunt backwoodsmen, each with shaft, prong, or trident, striding hither and thither in the bog, and lake, striding right and left, poised above their great-eyed enemies, and plunging forward to grapple the wounded and squalling victim before he should sheer off, or, as George Dennison said afterward, describing the affair in sonorous heroics:—

"Could you have seen that theatre of frogs,
As each in due delight and bog immersed,
Sprawled out, at length, in slime and sandy bed;
Great legs of green or brown outstretching wide;
Great arms thrown out as if embracing heaven;
With eyes dilating, big as Bullace grapes,
Upturned, and gloating as with rapturous rage;
Great flattened jaws, that, ever and anon,

293

> Distending with voluminous harmonies,
> Sent forth their correspondences of sound,
> In due obedience to the choragus,
> Who still, at proper intervals, pour'd out
> The grand refrain—sonorous, swelling still,
> Till, at the last, the apex diapason
> Was caught, was won, in glorious 'Blood and 'ounds!' "

It was a war of shallow waters. Habitual croakers are only justified when they perish. They have nothing to complain of. They always seem to anticipate their fate, and this seems to prove it only just execution after judgment—which, of course, is legal and becoming. Our partisans had grown expert in this sort of warfare. The Caw-caw swamp was a region in which the frogs held populous communities and cities, and—you know the proverb—"Thick grass is easier cut than thin." It was a massacre! Every spearman could count his score or two of slain, and, really, a very pretty spectacle they made when, emerging from the swamp, each carried his victims aloft, transfixed upon a sharp and slender rod, run through at the neck, eyes wider than ever, and legs and arms spread about in all directions. Nor was this all. No less than three young alligators and three times as many terrapins were surprised and captured, almost without a struggle, and borne off in triumph to the camp! The wailing in the Caw-caw that night was not greatly lessened by the loss of so many sonorous voices, since we may reasonably suppose that maternal suffering sent up such extra clamors for the absence of precious young ones, as more than atoned for the diminished forces of the community.

"On your lives, boys, not a word of what we have been doing," said Captain Porgy. They all swore to keep faith.

"There are thousands of clever people in the world," he added, "who require to be surprised into happiness. Some of my guests, to-night, are probably of this description. I shall teach them a new pleasure—nay, a new moral in a new pleasure—teach them how absurd it is to despise any of the gifts of Providence."

And, following out this policy, it was with great secrecy that the spoils of the frog campaign were conveyed to his quarters, and delivered over to the custody of Tom, his cook. Tom, we may add, like every sensible cook, made a sufficient mystery of his art to keep prying curiosity away from the kitchen whenever he was engaged in any of his culinary combinations. Let us leave these for other parties, and for proceedings of more imposing consequence if less attractive performance. We shall seek to be present when supper is on the table.

Chapter 45. Doings in the Apollo Chamber

294

Our partisan division of the army, with their horses, occupied no small extent of territory. Our Captain Porgy, himself, with his little personal equipage, demanded considerable space. He was the person always to secure that "ample room and verge enough," which, as he himself said, were essential to his individual girth. "My breadth of belt," he was wont to say, "implies a fair field; and, having that, I ask no favors." Besides being of social habits, his mess was always a large one. Among his immediate associates, retainers rather, he kept not only his cook, but his poet; the one almost as necessary as the other. Then, he never was without a guest, and whenever his commissariat was particularly well supplied, he was sure to have a full table. Such an idea as a good table, without an adequate number of guests to enjoy it, seemed to him a thing vile, unreasonable, inhuman, and utterly unchristian. We have seen that, particularly fortunate in his foray among the green-jacketed denizens of the Caw-caw, he had made arrangements for a larger circle than usual. His own tastes and purposes requiring it, Captain Porgy usually chose his own ground whenever tents were to be pitched. He had a great eye to proper localities.

"The open woods, on the south and west," was his rule. "Let the swamp and thicket cover my back on the east. That east wind has been of evil tendency from the earliest periods of time. The Bible speaks of it. A bad-tempered person, soured and surly, growing always, and insufferable from bile and conceit, is said to fill his bowels with the east wind. It has a bad effect on the best bowels. Give me just opening enough on the east for the purposes of draught, but let your tent be open to the full pressure of the winds from south and west. You need, in our climate, an eastern opening at the dinner-hour, dining at three, or thereabout; but beware of it after the sun has set. Don't sleep with the east wind blowing upon you. If you do, face it—let your feet receive it first. Every wind that blows has a specific quality. The east, northeast, and southeast, are all more or less pernicious, muddy, insidious, hateful. Our natural winds in midsummer are from the south and west. The south persuades you to languor, pleasantly relaxes, discourages the exertion which would be too exhaustive for the season. The west is the agitator, the thunder-storm wind, that purges and purifies; the northwest is the cleaning wind, that sweeps up the sky, and brushes off all its cobwebs. Each wind having thus a specific mission, it is wonderful that men who build know so little of the means of ventilation. Now, you see, I choose my ground with an open pine-forest in front, that is south and west and northwest. I take care that the land slopes down from me in all these directions. If there be hill, swamp, or dense thicket, I put them, with the devil, behind me. I have here chosen the very pleasantest spot in the whole encampment. There is not one of these continental officers who knows anything of the subject. Yet, to the health of an army, a difference of fifty yards in the location of a camp, is very frequently all the difference between life and death!"

And, in that broad, terrace-like spread of wood and thicket, he had chosen the most agreeable region. The pine-woods opened at his feet, and spread away almost interminably, giving the necessary degree of shade, yet leaving free passage for the wind.

"Free circulation, Geordie Dennison," said he, as with hands outspread he seemed to welcome the gentle play of the breezes reeking up from the southwest—"that is the secret of health—free circulation for the winds, the waters, and the blood. It is stagnation that is death. This is the reason why a pine-forest is more healthy than any other. It is the only forest that suffers free play to the winds. Hence you hear the music in a pine-forest which you hear in no

295

other. The breezes pour through, and swell up, until all the tree-tops become so many organ-pipes. The vulgar notion is that there is some virtue in the odor of the pines to neutralize malaria. But this is all nonsense. Pine-woods that have a dense undergrowth, are not more healthy than any other. It is the shape of the tree, a tall column, without lateral branches, naked a hundred feet high, and arching above, umbrella fashion, into a grand ceiling, which shuts out the intense heat of the sun, and suffers free exercise to the breeze. Here it plays with delight and impunity. In the dense thickets it trickles only, and finally stagnates; and hence the fevers of uncleared lands. Bays, swamps, ponds, are unhealthy, not because of the water which they contain, but because of the dense thickets which they nurture. The hottest place in the world in mid-summer, is a deep forest or thicket, with a close undergrowth. Fools talk of decaying vegetation as the secret of disease; yet when our fevers are raging most, vegetation has not begun to decay. Gardens, fields, forests, are never more fresh and beautiful, never more vigorous and verdant, than when death seems lurking under every flower, like some venomous reptile watching for and creeping to the ear of the unconscious sleeper. But, Geordie Dennison, boy, once suppose that the air is stagnant in any locality, and you need not suppose the necessity for its impregnation by any deleterious agent. A stagnant atmosphere is, *per se,* malaria. And that fact that we can assign a distinct locality for the disease—that we can say with confidence, to sleep here is death, while you may sleep with safety within half a mile—establishes the fact conclusively that the atmosphere is localized—no matter by what cause—though even that is a matter which I have considered also—and once let the atmosphere be fixed, and it is only in degree that it differs from that of an old sink or well. It is putrid, and to inhale it is a danger. You can not impregnate with miasma any region, where the winds are allowed to penetrate freely from three points of the com-pass, and where they do penetrate. When we are very sickly, you will always find a pressure of winds, daily from a single quarter, for a long-continued pe-riod of time. The atmosphere loses its equilibrium, as it were; the winds lack their *balance;* and running one course only, they run into a *cul de sac,* as water that can not escape, rises to a level with its source, becomes a pond, and stag-nates. A thunder-storm purifies, not from its electricity, as some contend, but because it is a storm. All storms purify because they agitate. They disperse the local atmosphere over a thousand miles of space, and restore its equilibrium."

"But, Captain Porgy, were it not better that you should be thinking of your supper and company, instead of philosophizing here about the atmosphere?"

"It is because I am thinking of my company and supper, Master Geordie, that I do philosophize about the atmosphere. A wholesome atmosphere is half of a good supper. We can eschew the water. We need not drink that, if we can find any other liquor; but make what wry faces we will, the atmosphere we must drink, even though we know it to be impregnated with poison. Better drink the vilest ditch-water a thousand times. That may disorder the stomach, but the other must vitiate the lungs and so directly disease the blood and the heart. I am trying to teach you, sir, that in giving a good supper or dinner to your friends, you are to serve it up in properly-ventilated apartments."

"Well, we have it airy enough here."

"True; but had it been left to anybody else, ten to one you would have had our tents pitched in a villanous thicket where we never could have got a breath of air. Look, now, at the Legion encamped on the left; they are in a bottom, the breeze passing clean over their heads. Their camp-master had no idea of what was the duty to be done, beyond the simply getting room enough for the horses and wagons of some three hundred men. Sir, the partisan cavalry have never been so healthy as when I have been permitted to select the ground for their bivouac."

"That's true!"

"To be sure it's true; and you see the fruits of it in the pleasant sleeps that we enjoy, and the hardy elasticity with which we travel. There never was any people so exposed as ours have been, night and day, in all weathers, and the most wearisome marches, that have ever enjoyed such admirable health. And they owe it to me, sir—to me, Geordie Dennison—yet, d—— 'em, they are not half so grateful for this blessing as for my soups and suppers. They would readily compound to drink any quantity of malaria, if they could swallow a pint of my rum-punch after it."

"Ah, they regard the rum-punch as the antidote, and there is nothing unreasonable, therefore, in their practice. But, captain, the hour latens."

"*Latens!* By what right do you use that word?"

"It's a good word, captain."

"So it is; but I never heard it used before."

"Very likely; but would you permit that argument to be used against any new dish that Tom should put on the table to-night!"

"No, sir; no, Geordie, you are right. You could not have answered me better if you had argued a thousand years. And I will remember the word;—so, as the hour *latens*, Geordie, get up and help me with these tables. I must summon Frampton and Millhouse. We shall need their knives and hatchets. I have invited thirty-one guests, Geordie, not counting you and Lance; we three will make the number thirty-four. There's no such table to be spread in camp to-night. Think of it;—a simple captain of militia giving a supper to thirty guests, and upon such short commons as are allowed us. Half of the poor devils in camp think it monstrous impudent of me to give a supper at all—and to thirty persons——"

"They can't guess how it's to be done."

"No! indeed! the blockheads! But their vexation increases when they find my guests all outranking myself. The envious rascals! Beware of envy, Geordie —it is the dirtiest, sneakingest, meanest little passion in the world, the younger brother of vanity, furnishing all the venom to its sleek-skinned and painted senior."

"And you are to have the governor, captain?"

"Ay, he accepts. John Rutledge is a great fellow, without affectation, Geordie —no pretender—one of the few men who really do *think*. The greater number, even when they greatly rank, only repeat each other—they do not think. Thought, George Dennison, is really confined to a very few. Men, as a race, are not thinking animals. They are gregarious and imitative. They go in droves and follow a leader, whom they contrive after a while to mimic after a monkey fashion.

297

Thought is always an individual. But—where is that boy Frampton? Sound your whistle, George."

The whistle was sounded.

"Now help me with these poles. There are forty cut. We must have crotch-sticks—two, four, six, eight, ten, twelve—it will require twenty-four; we must make our tables solid."

Lance Frampton now appeared, followed by half a dozen young troopers, bearing slim green poles upon their shoulders, forked sticks, and all the appliances necessary to the construction of the rustic tables and seats of the company. Long practice had made all of them familiar with the rude sort of manufacture which was required. The crotch-sticks were soon driven upright into the ground, in frequent parallels; cross pieces were laid in the crotchets of these, and the poles were stretched along, forming a crossed table with four ends, for so many dignitaries, and capable to accommodate forty guests with ease. Of a similar, but stouter fashion, were the seats for the guests. It was surprising how soon the area was filled—how soon the mechanical preparations for the feast were fashioned. The amphitheatre beneath the pines was ample. Porgy, as he boasted, had the proper eye for locality. When reared and steadied, stanchioned and strengthened, the tables were covered with great oak-leaves, green, looking very clean, nice, and fresh—a verdant tablecloth.

"Now, see that you have torches, Lance; for, though we have a glorious moon, we need torches for the dark corners. Many of the guests will bring their Negroes to wait. But we shall need some waiters besides. Engage some of these young chaps. They shall sweep the platters clean. Forget nothing, boy. We are to have big wigs to supper, remember. Geordie, come with me to *our* wagon. I think we shall astonish these epauletted gentry to-night."

And the two turned off to another part of the wood where stood the little wagon already described—a sort of covered box—a thing which one man might have rolled, but to which a couple of stout hackneys were harnessed, when taken.

"Little," said Porgy, as he unlocked the cover of the vehicle, "little did stuttering Pete dream what he lost and we gained when we cut off the four wagons of Stewart. His eyes opened only upon the big wagons. He never gave a look at the one little one upon which I fastened—as if the most precious commodities were not always packed in the smallest compass! Yet, look there, Geordie."

The poet looked in:—

"Lemons, captain."

"Ay, lemons and white sugar, and nutmegs, and cloves, and spices of all sorts, and an anchor of Geneva, and a box of cocoa, and a bag of coffee, and a good supply of old Jamaica, and, see you that keg?—tongues, beef-tongues, English beef-tongues. Now please you to read the name on the cover; ay! Lord Rawdon's own prog, by the pipers, specially selected for his table and palate. We shall astonish these wooden-headed continentals to-night, Geordie! won't we? You thought me mad, didn't you, when I invited so many? But I knew what I was about. They shall stare, they shall sup, though they lament for ever, after the acquisition of such a taste as their vulgar fortunes can never hereafter satisfy. But mum! Not a word in anticipation."

298

And Porgy closed the wagon with haste and locked it, as half a dozen troopers lounged carelessly by, looking, with some curiosity as they passed, to the proceedings of the two.

"Stay here, Geordie, and keep watch till I return. I must put Millhouse on duty over this wagon, or there will be a Flemish account of its contents when supper's called. The morals of the dragoon service, imply theft as a necessity. A good scout has all the capabilities of a good pickpocket."

And, moralizing as he went, Porgy hurried off for succor. Dennison was relieved by Millhouse, a one-armed trooper of iron aspect, and as stubborn of purpose as a mule. The wagon was safe in his keeping as long as his left arm could lift sabre or pistol—and he was duly armed with both.

The next visit of our host was to Tom, the cook, who had a precinct of his own, some twenty-five yards from the spot where the tables had been spread. The terrapin soup was discussed, the *ragout*; the stew; the boiled tongues; nothing escaped attention. Then, a survey was taken of the crockery; the bowls, plates, dishes; the knives and forks; the spoons of iron, the drinking vessels of delph, tin, or calabash. These commodities were too frail of character, not to need the greatest care and attention; and every feast given by our captain, mortified him with the slenderness of his resources. But there was no remedy. If half a dozen good bowls of delph, and platters of tin, could be provided for the more distinguished guests, the rest might surely be satisfied with clean calabashes. We will suppose our captain satisfied in respect to these things. He was in the midst of the examination, however, venting his annoyances at his limited resources, in uneasy exclamations, when a messenger from Rutledge brought him the note from that personage apprizing him that Greene and Lee would appear among his guests. The governor wrote:—

"I shall take the liberty, my dear Captain Porgy, of bringing with me a couple of additional guests, in General Greene and Colonel Lee, knowing that your provision will not only be ample, but that the taste which usually presides over your banquets will give to our friends from Rhode Island and Virginia such a notion of the tastes of Apicius and Lucullus, as certainly never yet dawned upon them in their own half-civilized regions. Your own courtesy will do the rest and will, I trust, sufficiently justify the confidence with which I have insisted upon their coming.   "Yours,
                    "JOHN RUTLEDGE."

"Humph!" exclaimed Porgy, "I should not have ventured to ask General Greene, not that I stand in awe of his epaulettes, but it is so rare to find a *parvenu* who would not hold such an invitation from a poor captain of militia, to be a piece of impertinence and presumption. Our own folks know me too well to exhibit any such *gaucherie*. As for Lee, he is a popinjay! I should never ask him myself; but have no objection that he should occasionally appear among gentlemen who can teach him, by example, how gentlemen can be good fellows without any loss of dignity.—Geordie—your pen and a scrap of paper. I hope I diminish none of your verses by consuming your foolscap."

299

The pen and paper were had, and our captain wrote:—

"Governor Rutledge can take no liberty for the propriety of which his name is not a sufficient guaranty. Captain Porgy will be most happy to welcome any guests whom he may think proper to bring."

This written, he handed it to the messenger. It was then that Greene's cook uncovered a small tumbril or box in a wheelbarrow, containing the uncooked provisions which had been destined for his own table. Porgy looked at the bloody and livid meats with unqualified disgust.

"But," said he *sotto voce*, "we can't reject them. Here, Tom."

The cook appeared, apron in front and knife in hand.

"Tom, take charge of these provisions. They are sent by the general—General Greene, do you hear? Use them. Cook them. Turn them into soup, hash, steak, what you will!" then, as the messengers of Rutledge and Greene disappeared— "but d——m you, boy, don't let them show themselves upon my table. The meat is villanously butchered. That alone should condemn it. Make it up for some of these young fellows that have been working for us. And—Tom—"

"Well, maussa—talk quick."

"Don't forget the balls. Let there be a plenty in the soup."

"Psho, maussa, enty I know."

"Enough! Begone!"

The active mind of our corpulent captain began to grow restless. He had seen to everything that he could think of, and grew peevish from nothing to do. Suddenly he stuck his fingers into his hair.

"No! the vessels for the punch; Geordie. By heavens, I had almost forgotten. Let us after the punchbowls, and then for the manufacture. *You* are good at that; a poet should be. Curious problem, Geordie—the affinity between poetry and the bottle."

"Not at all. It only implies the ardency of the poet. It is so with the orator. You never saw poet or orator yet, that was not ardent and fond of the juices of the grape."

"Not the didactic orders, surely. But how is it, then, that Bacchus is not your deity instead of Apollo?"

"Because Apollo, with virtues of his own, includes those of Bacchus. He is a ripener of Bacchus, and loves not the wine less, nor is less the true god of it, because he employs a vintner. I see no difficulty in the matter."

"And, perhaps, there is none. Yet what would Apollo say, or Bacchus even, to such a punchbowl as ours."

And he pointed to an enormous calabash, holding a couple of gallons at the least, that, duly valued and taken care of, had survived all the vicissitudes of the campaign.

"They would, either of them, feel that there was wholesome propriety in the vessel. It is one which Ceres has presented for the occasion, to a kindred deity. Boon nature has provided where vulgar art has failed. It would be much more staggering to either of the ancient gods to try them with the Jamaica, instead of the blood of Tuscany."

"Ah! they never got such liquor on Olympus. Their nectar was a poor wishy-washy sort of stuff, of not more body than some of those thin vaporing French and German liquors, of which we have had a taste occasionally. Their wine of Tuscany, nay, the Falernian of Horace, would not take rank now-a-days with

300

the juices of the common corn, prepared according to our process. Drinking whiskey or Jamaica, Nero might have been a fool, a wretch, a murderer—might fire his city or butcher his mother—might have committed any crime, but cowardice! Whiskey or Jamaica might have saved Rome from Gaul and Vandal. The barbarians, be sure, drank the most potent beverages."

"A notion deserving of study. We drink deep now-a-days. Will our descendants beat us? Will they laugh at our potations, which rarely leave a gentleman on his legs after midnight?"

"Ah! say nothing of our progeny. Do not build upon the degenerates. It may be that the milksops will fancy it bad taste, nay, even immoral, on the part of their ancestors, to have swallowed Jamaica or whiskey at all. In proportion as their heads are weak, will they pronounce ours vicious; and just because we have a certain amount of strength in our virtue—a certain quality of brawn and blood and muscle, to keep our sentiment from etherealizing—growing into mere thin air—will they presume to stroke their beards in self-complaisant satisfaction, thanking God that such poor *publicans,* have given way to a more saintly race of sinners. I am half inclined to thank my stars that, when I disappear, the race of Porgy will not be continued in the person of one who prides himself upon having no head—for a bottle!"

"Yes! save us from all degenerate children. But, captain, will this *one* calabash of punch suffice for forty? Impossible! Two gallons among forty! Never in the world! Why, sir, there are three generals, and one governor, a score of colonels, and others of inferior rank, who are emulous of great men's virtues. Two gallons to forty such persons."

"Oh! don't stop to calculate. Luckily there are two calabashes."

And the little wagon yielded up the desired article.

"Make it rich, Geordie."

"Captain Porgy, when they drink of this liquor, each man will feel that his will has been made. He will feel that he has no more care in life—will fold his robes about him for flight."

"Or fall! Well, give us a taste. I profess to be a very competent judge of what a good Jamaica punch should be."

Smacks his lips.

"The proportions are good: the acid has yielded to the embrace of the sugar with the recognition of a perfect faith, and both succumb to the spirit, as with the recognition of a perfect deity. Next to poetry, Geordie, you are an adept at punch."

Geordie somewhat proudly:—

"Yes, captain, on this score I feel safe. I am not always certain of my verses. I sometimes feel that they lack the sweet and the ardent—but I am never doubtful of the perfect harmony that prevails among all the elements when I manufacture punch."

Porgy quaffs off the contents of the *dipper.*

"Geordie, you are a benefactor. When this war ceases, you shall partake my fortunes. You shall live with me; and, between punch and poetry, we will make the latter end of life a felicitous *finale* to a very exciting drama. By the way, Geordie, talking of poetry and punch reminds me. You must be prepared with

301

something good to-night. I shall have you out. You shall give us some heroic ballad. I know you have not been drowsing in that thicket for nothing. Have you got anything ready?"

"I *have* been doing a trifle, but—"

"None of your buts. Get aside, and memorize it. These two vessels of punch, meanwhile, we will put under lock and key, and yield to the guardianship of Sergeant Millhouse."

Chapter 46. How Porgy Feasted the Captains

With vulgar people, a dinner party is the occasion of much fuss and fidgeting. The vulgar egotism is always on the *qui vive* lest something should go wrong—lest something should be wanting to the proper effect—lest, in brief, some luckless excess or deficiency should certainly convey to the guest the secret of those deficiencies, in taste, manners, experiences, and resources, which would, if known, be fatal to the claims of good breeding and high tone which the host is most anxious to establish. Those, on the contrary, who feel assured on such points are apt to take the events of a dinner-table coolly and with comparative indifference. A blunder or a deficiency of steward or servant, occasions little or no concern; is never allowed to disturb the equilibrium of the master, who takes for granted that such small matters will be ascribed, by every sensible guest, to the right cause; and for the opinion of all other persons he cares not a button.

The result of this equanimity is to enable him to keep *his mind "in hand"* for the entertainment of his company. He is able to observe and to minister with promptness and full resource, as his wits are not disordered by any feverish workings of his *amour propre.* He sees what is wanting at a glance; supplies the deficiency with a nod; his servants are duly taught in the value of his nod and glance; and the skill of the host, by which the guests are diverted, enables Jack and Gill to wipe up the water which they have spilt so awkwardly, in their up-hill progress, without attracting any notice—without filling the scene with most admired disorder.

Our host *knows* his company, and conjures up the special topic which appeals directly to the tastes or the fancies of each. He is vigilant even while he seems most at ease; when his indifference is most apparent, it is made to cover a becoming solicitude for the comfort of the humblest person present. He provides himself with the proper cue to all your prejudices and affections, as by a divine instinct, so that he steers clear of the one, and shapes his course directly for the other; and when the waters are unluckily ruffled, by some bull-headed companion, who treads on his neighbor's toes without even suspecting that he has corns, our host is at hand to pour oil upon the troubled waters, and soothe to calm the temper which is ruffled. He contrives, at the same time, that the offender shall be taught the nature of his offence, without being brought up to the halberds and set in pillory, *"Pour encourager les autres."* [1]

302

[1] *Simms here uses a portion of a famous quotation from Voltaire's* Candide *(1759): "Dans ce pays-ci il est bon de tuer de temps en temps un amiral pour encourager les autres." (In this country it is well to kill an admiral from time to time in order to encourage the others.)*

There was nothing doubtful about the *aplomb* of Captain Porgy. Having prepared his feast according to the full extent of his resources; drilled his awkward squad to the utmost of his capacity and their susceptibilities; seen that they were in sufficient numbers for proper attendance; and made, in brief, all his preparations, he gave himself no further concern, but prepared to receive his guests, with the easy good nature, the frank politeness, the smiling grace, of an old-school gentleman. And it is quite an error to talk, as we are apt to do, of the formality of the old-school gentleman. The gentleman of two hundred or one hundred years ago, differed very slightly in his bearing from the same class at the present day. In due degree as his ceremonials ran into formalities, did he lose the character of the gentleman. In no period was mere form and buckram ever confounded, by sensible people, with politeness and refinement.

Never was gentleman more perfectly at ease in crowded assembly, yet more solicitous of the claims of all about him, than our corpulent captain. His shrewd good sense, nice tastes, playful humors, and frank spirit, all harmonizing happily, enabled him to play the host generally to the equal satisfaction of all his company. He had the proper welcome for each as he drew nigh; the proper word, which set each person at his ease, and prepared him for the development of all his conversational resources.

Among the first of his guests to appear were Governor Rutledge and General Greene. "The really great," said Porgy to Lance Frampton who stood behind him, "never keep the table waiting."

The approach to the scene was through a great natural avenue of lofty green pines, through which the moon was peeping curiously with a bright smile, a disinterested spectator of the proceedings. Music timed the approaches of the guests, the army band having been secured for the evening. Porgy welcomed his guests at the entrance of the area in which his tables had been spread.

"General Greene, Captain Porgy," said Rutledge. Greene took the outstretched hand of the host, saying:—

"What I have heard of you, Captain Porgy, makes me trespass without fear of the consequences."

"And what I know of General Greene enables me to welcome him with every hope of the consequences. I am very grateful to Governor Rutledge for doing that which, as a poor captain of militia, I should scarcely have ventured to do myself."

"I knew my customers both, my dear captain," said Rutledge, "and knew how little was necessary to render the regular and volunteer service grateful to each other."

"Be seated, gentlemen," said Porgy, "while I put myself on duty for a while;" and he resumed his place at the opening of the avenue, while Sumter, Marion, and the rest severally presented themselves, were welcomed and conducted to the interior by young Frampton, who did the duties of an aide. Colonel Lee was among the latest to appear.

"My dear Porgy," said he condescendingly—"I am late; but the cavalry of the legion is on vigilant duty to-night, and a good officer you know—eh!"

And he left it to our host to conceive the rest.

"Col. Lee may be forgiven, if late among his friends, when we know that his enemies rarely reproach him for a like remissness."

303

The grace of Porgy's manner happily blended with the grave dignity of his address. Lee smiled at the compliment:—

"Always ready, Porgy—never to be outdone in the play of compliment, or the retort courteous;" and while speaking he was ushered in with other visitors.

The company was at length assembled. The music ceased. A single bugle sounded from the amphitheatre, and the guests disposed themselves without confusion under the whispered suggestions of Lieutenant Frampton. Porgy took his place at the head of the table, standing, till all were seated.

"Gentlemen," said he, "be pleased to find places at the board. Colonel Singleton, you are my *vis-a-vis*. Governor Rutledge will you honor me by sitting at my right. General Greene, I have presumed to assign you the seat at my left."

Right and left of Singleton, Marion and Sumter were placed. At one end of the table crossing the centre of the board, Colonel Lee was seated, Colonel Maham occupied the other. Carrington, Horry, Mellichampe, St. Julien, and others found places between these several termini. Scarcely had they been seated when four great calabash tureens were placed severally at the extremities, the odorous vapors from which appealed gratefully to every nostril in company.

"Turtle soup!" was the delighted murmur.

"And lemons!"

And as the smoking vessels were set before the governor and General Greene, the former exclaimed:—

"Faith, Captain Porgy, your last voyage to the West Indies seems to have been a highly prosperous adventure."

"In truth," said Greene, "I am half inclined to think that there must have been some such enterprise, of which General Marion has forgotten to apprize me."

"I begin seriously to suspect him," said Rutledge. "The fact is that General Marion is so fond of secret enterprises, and audacious ones—does things with so much despatch, and thinks it so easy to do the impossible, that I half believe he has made a three nights' run for the Havana, or sent off a favorite squad on a sortie in that direction. Say, general, is it not so? Let us know the truth of it. You found, among your captures at Georgetown, some ready-rigged sloop or schooner, and sent her out on a cruise in anticipation of this very occasion."

"Nay, governor, the merits of the enterprise, such as it was and the fruits thereof, are due entirely to our host. It was his adventure wholly, though we share the spoils."

"But, where—where—where—" began Peter Horry, stuttering, "where the devil did he—did he—get 'em—turtles and lemons! I don't—don't—understand it—at all."

"Better not press the inquiry, Horry," said Singleton with a sly smile upon the company—"the discovery will hardly add to your own laurels."

"How—my laurels! What—what—I want to—to know—have my laurels—to do—to do—with the matter?"

"Let's have it, Colonel Singleton," said Rutledge eagerly. "Out with the story. Colonel Horry is so seldom to be caught napping that I shall rejoice to have one story at his expense."

"Ay, ay, the story, Singleton," from a dozen voices around the board.

"Tell—tell—tell, if you will," stuttered Horry—"only be sure, and tell—the—the—truth, and shame—you know who."

"The adventure illustrates the military character of the two gentlemen most admirably," said Singleton. "Colonel Horry is a gentleman of large eyes and grapples with objects of magnitude always. It is Captain Porgy's pleasure to be discriminating and select. The lemons and a variety of other edibles are furnished, unwillingly, I grant you, by Lord Rawdon himself. They form a part of the supplies brought up by Colonel Stewart. In dashing at Stewart's convoy, Horry passed a mean little wagon in the rear, as quite unworthy his regards. He swept off as you know three or four others of considerable value to the army. But the very littleness of this wagon which Horry had despised, fixed the regards of our host. He quietly possessed himself of it, and was rewarded with the private stores designed for Lord Rawdon himself." The story produced a laugh at the expense of Horry.

"Who—who—who—the devil," said he, "would have thought—of—of—anything good in—that rickety concern? I'd like to know, Captain Porgy, what you got besides the lemons?"

"White sugars, coffee, tea, spices, Spanish sweetmeats, preserved ginger, three kegs of Jamaica, and a goodly variety besides!"

"The d——l!—and—and—I to miss 'em all."

"But you got loads of bacon and flour, Horry."

"Several bales of blankets."

"Ay, and a bathing-tub and complete set of chamber crockery!"

"What," said Rutledge, "was there a bathing-tub and chamber crockery?"

"Yes, indeed."

"Who could have wanted that, I wonder?"

"Some young ensign of the buffs or blues," said Porgy, "whose mother was duly considerate of the young man's skin in a warm climate. You should have discovered Colonel Horry's visage when that wagon was burst open and the contents revealed. The bathing-tub and furniture filled the wagon."

"What did he say, Porgy? Tell us that!"

"Say! Ah! What was it, colonel? Deliver it yourself: nobody can repeat it half so well."

"Re—re—peat it yourself, if you can!" said Horry stuttering and dipping up his soup with increased rapidity.

"Out with it, Captain Porgy. Horry's speech."

Porgy nodded to Singleton, who answered:—

"I heard it, and as Horry permits will deliver it. He said, stamping his feet in a rage: 'Throw out the d——d basins, and break up the blasted tub. Who would have thought of any fellow being such a bloody booby as to bring a bathing-tub and chamber crockery into a pond and bush country?'"

And slightly imitating the stammer of Horry so as to give a lively idea of his manner, Singleton set the table in a roar. When the laugh had subsided:—

"But did he break up the crockery, Porgy?"

"Every bowl and basin. He was merciless. You never saw such havoc. His broadsword played elephant in the crockery shop to perfection, and the dragoons, delighted with the humors of their colonel, went into the work of demolition with a rush."

305

"I had—no—no—no use for the d——d—d—d——d—d——d things," said Horry; "and I was—de—de—de—termined to give the d——d puppy that owned them a lesson."

"Ha! ha! ha!"

"But where did the turtles come from?"

"From the genius of my cook, Tom," said Porgy. "The turtle are terrapin from the Caw-caw."

"Not the alligator terrapin, captain, I hope," said Sumter. "I could never bring myself to eat any of that order."

"You have done it on this occasion," said Porgy.

"And very effectually too, general," said Singleton, "since I have helped you to a second supply, and you seem in a fair way to need a third."

Sumter looked a little blank.

"Do not be discomfited, general," said Porgy, "since I took the precaution to have all their tails cut off before they were hashed up for the soup."

"But what did you do with the tails?"

"Ah! they were made into balls, with a due proportion of beef and bacon."

"You have caught me beyond escape, captain, since I confess to have done as much execution on the balls as on the soup."

"And you are surprised into a wisdom, general, that has cured you of the prejudices of twenty years! What we call the alligator terrapin is the best of the tribe—the fattest, richest, best flavored. It requires only that skill in the dressing which my man Tom supplies."

The bugle sounded. Sergeant Millhouse marshalled the waiters to their stations, and the emptied vessels were removed. With another blast of the bugle, new dishes were set on the table.

"A noble-looking fish," said Greene. "What fish is this, Captain Porgy?"

"The greatest delicacy of a fresh-water river, this is the Edisto blue cat—for very nice people a most discouraging name.—Gentlemen, look to yourselves. Here is boiled fish, such as George the Third can not procure; dressed in a style which would not discredit the table of our great ally, the king of France. Men of *goût* will of course prefer the boiled—for the undeveloped taste, the fry is abundant. There are perch and trout in those several dishes. They are all fresh from the Edisto within five hours."

"Your troopers have been busy, captain."

"Ay, sir, and my cook. He was fortunate in his search along the river this morning, to come upon three or four fish-traps, which he emptied without leave. Governor, the melted butter is beside you. By-the-way, those naval biscuit are also from the stores of my Lord Rawdon.—General, do not dream of defiling that fish with vinegar. It is an abomination in this case. The fish only entreats the butter, and the dressing is complete."

The eye of Porgy swept the table. The guests discussed [2] the fish with the relish of starving men. There was a cessation. The finger of Porgy was lifted. Millhouse's bugle gave tongue, and the fish was superseded with a variety of dishes.

306

---

[2] *Tested the quality of, by consuming.*

"General Greene—Governor Rutledge—suffer me to persuade you both to the ragout which is before me."

"What is it, captain?"

"Try it, general. It is the alerta—the green alerta—a sort of chicken you will find it, but far superior. The stew is of the *lagarta*, according to the Spaniards, and a dish quite as rare as exquisite on table. Gentlemen, interspersed with these dishes you will find more familiar, but inferior ones. There are hams and tongues, both from the stores of Lord Rawdon, and, in fact, most of this course will be found of foreign character. You will please ask me for no more revelations touching my mode of procuring supplies, as I have no wish to expose the breaking of any more crockery. It is not every one of our partisans who can bear, with so much equanimity as Colonel Horry, the story of his own acquisitions, and how made."

"This—what do you call it?" said Greene.

"Alerta!"

"Is delicious!"

"And nothing could be more savory than this stew, Captain Porgy."

"Yes, indeed, governor—the Spaniards have the merit of the discovery. But gentlemen, with this course, it is time to spiritualize the feast."

The speaker's finger was uplifted, and two enormous bowls of punch were set down at the two ends of the table.

"Gentlemen, we owe a great deal to the providence of Lord Rawdon."

"And the improvidence of Horry," whispered Rutledge, "for, of a verity, had he captured these spoils, he would never have made the same use of them as our host has done."

"Sir," said Porgy with solemnity, "he would have wasted them—naked, upon his dragoons.—Gentlemen, you will please fill for a sentiment. Colonel Singleton, see that your end of the table charges duly."

"We are ready, captain."

Porgy rising:—

"Gentlemen, our first regular sentiment: 'The cause of Liberty—the cause of the American continent—the cause of all continents wherever man has a living soul!' "

"Music." And the bands struck up.

"Captain Porgy," said Lee, "send me, if you please, a second supply of that dish which you call the alerta. I don't know what sort of bird it is, but the savor is that of young pigeons. It is wonderfully nice."

"I agree with you, Lee," said Colonel Williams, "though I have no more idea what the bird is than of the mansions of the moon. Let me trouble you also, Captain Porgy."

"I must also trespass, captain," said Carrington. "Ordinarily, I seldom suffer myself to eat of dishes of which I know nothing; but these foreign meats come to us under good guaranties, though half the time without a name at all."

"Unless French, which is so much Greek to me," said Maham. "Captain, that *lagarta* stew is princely."

"No crowned head in Europe enjoys the like. Shall I help you, Colonel Maham?"

307

"Thank you, yes. But I thought you called it foreign."

"So it is—in one sense; but this is not imported. It is wholly domestic."

"Well, foreign or domestic, it is first rate," said Greene. "I will try a little more of it, Captain Porgy."

"Ah! general,"—with a smile—"suffer me to say that it is only in the militia service, after all, that the taste properly refines. Governor, shall I serve you?"

"Thank you, I will mince a little of your *lagarta*, captain," and a sly glance of Rutledge apprized the captain of his suspicions. But the face of Porgy made no revelations.

"Gentlemen," said Singleton, at the other end of the table, "fill your glasses."

"Ready, all," said Porgy.

Singleton rose, and gave:—

"South Carolina—almost freed from the footsteps of the foreign tyrant, and rising to the full assertion of her own sovereignty!"

A brilliant burst from John Rutledge, brief, but like a fiery tongue speaking to the soul, followed this sentiment; and the music rose into a triumphant peal as his voice died away upon the echoes. Other sentiments succeeded other speeches; Rutledge, Greene, Marion, Sumter, Lee, were all duly honored with toasts, and all responded, each after his own fashion, all unaffectedly, simply, and with the proper earnestness of soldiers. And the punch flowed anew into fresh goblets, and the merriment grew high, and some of the grave barons began to sing in snatches, and the volunteer toasts filled up the pauses in the conversation. Meanwhile, a score of melons were placed upon the board, and the preserved fruits from the West Indies, guava and ginger, were crowded upon the board, and provoked new merriment at the expense of Rawdon, who lost, and Horry who refused to find the prize.

And while they gashed deeply the purple centres of the melons, Rutledge suddenly said to Porgy:—

"And now, captain, that you have had your triumph, that all present have borne testimony in the least equivocal manner to the merits of your feast, I would fain know of what those foreign dishes were compounded, of which, knowing nothing, all have partaken so freely. Hams and tongues, fresh from Britain, designed for my Lord Rawdon's own table, have been sent away from yours uncut—proof of homage, the most profound, to yet preferable meats. Pray tell us, then, what were the elements of your *lagarta* and your *alerta*—your *ragouts* and stews."

"Ay, ay," seconded the company, "let us know. What were the birds?"

"I should really be pleased to know, Captain Porgy," said General Greene, bowing, "touching those birds."

"There need be no mystery in it now, general, since, as Governor Rutledge says, the feast has triumphed. But I am afraid I shall too greatly confound you, when I state that the dishes contained no birds at all. The stew of *alerta* was compounded chiefly of the race which helped Homer in the construction of an epic—a race which Milton describes as the—

" 'Small infantry
Warred on by cranes.' "

308

"You surely do not mean *frogs*, Captain Porgy?" cried Lee, with affected horror in his accents.

"Your guess is a sagacious one, and worthy of the legion, Colonel Lee."

"Good heavens! and is it come to this, that the soldiers of liberty should be reduced to the necessity of frog-eating?"

"Necessity, Colonel Lee!" exclaimed Rutledge. "By heavens, sir, it should be matter of taste and preference, sir, if only in due deference to our great Gallic ally; but, of a truth, sir, after to-day's feast, it should be a new argument in behalf of liberty, that she has brought us to such rare fine feeding and such improved tastes."

"And the other dish, Captain Porgy," demanded Sumter, "the stew with the Spanish name?"

"The name speaks for itself—*lagarta*. It is of the great lizard family—the cayman—in vulgar speech, the alligator. But the specimens employed, gentlemen, were mere juveniles; young vagabonds, whose affectionate parents had hardly suffered them out of sight before. They had probably never fed on larger prey than their neighbors of the alerta family."

"One question, Captain Porgy," said Carrington; "be so good as to inform me, if, among your several unfamiliar dishes, I have had the happiness to eat of the rattlesnake, the viper, the moccasin, or the boa-constrictor?"

"Alas! colonel, I grieve to say that you have not. I should have been pleased to have got a couple of young chicken-snakes, but I was not fortunate in the search. We got glimpse of a few runners [black-snakes],[3] but they were quite too swift of foot for the hunters. The chicken-snake is of unexceptionable tenderness; the runner is a little too muscular, if not previously well sodden; but, unless near a hencoop, or a corncrib, it is not easy to find the chicken-snake. I repeat my regrets that I could not secure this delicacy for my table. But another time, Colonel Carrington, should you sup with me, I will make a special effort in your behalf."

"I thank you, sir; do not suffer your regrets to disturb you. For that matter, I am half doubtful whether your *alerta* and *lagarta*, of which I have, in my ignorance, partaken somewhat too freely, will continue to lie lightly on my soul or stomach."

"Have no fears, sir; and the better to secure their repose, do me the honor, sir, of a bowl of punch with me. Gentlemen, I entreat the whole table to our companionship."

And the vessels were filled and emptied.

"And now, gentlemen," continued the host, "I give you—The poets, who minister at once to Apollo, to Bacchus, and to Mars, and beg to introduce you to the only representative of the faculty in our squadron, Mr. George Dennison, my ensign. If I mistake not, he has been this day as busy with the muse, as I with my cook; and, if we will suffer him, he will bring us gifts from Parnassus not unworthy of those which we have enjoyed from the provision-wagon of Lord Rawdon."

"In which Horry, going from Dan to Beersheba, could see nothing."

"Having a taste for baths, warming-pans, and chamber-furniture."

[3] *Simms' brackets.*

" 'Nough of that—that—Singleton! I—I—I'm a sinner be—be—beyond salvation, if I ever pass a little mean-looking wagon again, without seeing what's in it."

"But—Mr. Dennison," said Rutledge.

"George! Geordie!" said Porgy, good-humoredly. The poet, hitherto the only silent person at table, now rose—a tall, slender person, of bright, lively eye, mouth full of expression, Grecian nose, and great forehead rising up like a tower. His cheeks were flushed, his frame trembled, and there was an evident quivering of the lip which was discernible to every eye about him. Dennison sang the verses, which he wrote, in a clear, military voice, shrill like a clarion. There was, perhaps, no great deal of music in his composition, but enough for the present purpose, and of the kind best suited, perhaps, for a military gathering—bold, free, eager and full of animation. His ballad had been the work of that very afternoon.

He had no prefaces. But, waiting till the music hushed, and the voices, he then began:—

The Battle Feast

To the dark and bloody feast,
   Haste ye battle vultures, haste;
There is banquet, man and beast,
   For your savage taste:
Never on such costly wassail
   Did ye flesh your beaks before;
Come, ye slaves of Hesse Cassel,[4]
   To be sold no more!

Small your cost to George of Britain,
   One and sixpences sterling down[5]
Yet for this, ye sorry chapmen,
   Each will lose his crown;
Freedom knows no price for valor,
   Yours is measured by the groat,
Britain pays in gold and silver,
   We in steel and shot.

Recreants, ye from Scottish Highlands,[6]
   Lately rebels to the throne
Of that brutal foreign despot,

---

[4] *The Hessians, hired at so much per head to the crown of Britain, for the war in America, formed no small portion of the British army. (Simms' note.)*

[5] *We are not sure that Master George Dennison is altogether right in this statement of the hire of the Hessian per head, but the difference is immaterial, whether in poetry or history. (Simms' note.)*

[6] *The exiled rebels of '45, when settled in America, almost wholly proved adherents of that monarch whom, as followers of the Stuarts, they opposed to the knife. The disasters of '45 cured them of all propensity to rebellion. Even the Macdonalds, the famous Hector—Flora who saved the Pretender—all became loyal to George the Third in America, and fought against the patriots. (Simms' note.)*

310

Now, whose sway ye own;
Ye are welcome to the banquet,
　Which is spread for all who come,
Where the eater is the eaten,
　And the deathsman goes to doom.

And ye braggart sons of Erin,
　Loathing still the sway ye bear,
Groaning in the very fetters,
　Ye would make us wear;
Ever writhing, ever raging,
　'Neath the bonds ye can not break—
Here the bloody banquet woos ye,
　Gather and partake!

Stoop, ye vultures, to the issue,
　It will be ere set of sun!
Mark whose valor bides the longest,
　Blood of price or blood of none.
Comes the Tartan of Glenorchy,
　Comes the sullen Saxon boor,
Comes the light-heeled German yager
　Crowding to the shore!

Who shall meet them by the water
　On the mountain, in the vale,
Meet them with the stroke of slaughter
　Till the right arm fail?
Wherefore ask? Yon pealing summons
　Finds fit answer, sharp and soon,
Answer fit for peers and commons,
　Yager and dragoon.

Lo! the soul that makes a nation,
　Which, from out the ranks of toil,
Upward springs in day of peril,
　Soul to save the soil!
Comes a high and mighty aspect,
　From the shores of Powhatan;—
Lo! in him the nation's hero,
　Glorious perfect man!

Follows, rugged as his mountains,
　Daring man from Bennington;
Blacksmith stout from Narraganset,
　Good where deeds are done:
Comes the keen-eyed Santee rifle,
　Sleepless still and swift as flame,

Rowel rashing, bullet winging
  Man of deadly aim.

Stoop, ye vultures, to the issue,
  Stoop, and scour the bloody plain
Flesh your beaks where fat the carnage,
  Mountains up the slain:
Whose the skull your talon rendeth
  Eye, within your dripping beak,
Speechless tongue that loosely lolleth
  On divided cheek!

In the tartan of Glenorchy,
  Scarlet of the Saxon boor,
Gray frock of the Hessian yager
  Strewn from mount to shore,
Read the fate of hireling valor,
  Read the doom of foreign foe,
Know that he who smites for freedom,
  Ever strikes the deadly blow!

It was in the midst of the compliments of the party to the poet, that Willie Sinclair [7] stole in to the table, and plucked the sleeve of Marion, who rose quickly and quietly, and went out with him in silence. The company sat at the table some time longer.

"Why your poet seems a genuine Birserker, Captain Porgy. This chant was worthy to be sung in the hall of Odin. Does he fight as bravely as he sings?"

"Every bit, sir, and he goes into battle with the same convulsive sort of tremor with which he begins to sing or to recite. But that passes off in a few moments, and then he fairly rages. In fact, sir, it is not easy for him to arrest himself, and he sometimes shows himself rather too savage in strife—with rather too great an appetite for blood."

"You are as fortunate, Captain Porgy, in your poet as your cook; I would I could persuade them from you!—Who?—Do you say?"

These last words were spoken to Lieutenant Frampton, who had whispered something into Rutledge's ear.

"Colonel Sinclair, your excellency. He waits you without, along with General Marion."

"Instantly"—and, watching his opportunity, while beakers were filling, Rutledge stole away. Greene followed his example, so did Sumter and the elder officers; the young ones remained, and soon Captain Porgy, his veneration no longer active, was in full flight, keeping the table in a roar, with merry jest, jibe, and story, till the hours grew something smaller than the stars, and the moon had a hooded, downcast looking visage, as if she had seen or heard something to shock her modesty. Let us leave the revellers while they make a final onslaught upon the punchbowls. (*1855*)

312

---

[7] *A major in Marion's troop, Sinclair is the hero of* The Forayers.

Letters

To James H. Hammond

Woodlands, May 1, 1847

My dear Hammond.[1]

I am really quite sorry that you could not meet me at the village. There was so much to be said and letter writing is such an inadequate substitute to good speech. There is no reason, however, why we should not meet in N. Y. I shall go to Charleston on Monday & leave in the Wilmington boat on Tuesday or Wednesday,—remain in Phil. & Balt. a few days, then proceed to N. Y. where I shall probably continue till the middle of July. Enquire for me at Harper & Brothers or Bartlett & Welford's or Wiley & Putnam's. But in the meantime write me to that city, and let me know whether I may hope to see you there or not. Our interviews there would then be untrammelled and *unsuspected.* Some of our friends, I fancy, have been *sounded.* Aldrich tells me that Elmore charged upon us hostilities—was apprised of the contemplated paper, and either had heard or had assumed that the principle by which we were bound together was hostility to him. I am very sure that all of us have been very forbearing and very friendly to him. I don't know any arrangement that could better please me than to put him & yourself in the Senate together. I confess to a really friendly feeling for Elmore, and don't know, indeed, but that this feeling has somewhat modified that hostility to the Bank which has been growing upon me regularly from the moment when you first drew my regard to the subject. I told E. myself, that I should be opposed to a Charter, that I looked on the Bank as unconstitutional, and my only question was that of expediency—in other words how shall we avoid doing mischief. Perhaps, I should have arrived at my conclusions without your aid, if I had not, after my repudiation 20 years ago as a Union man, dismissed as much as possible from my mind the consideration of subjects over which it appeared to me I was destined to have no control. It was then that I first appreciated Mr. Calhoun's powers for evil as well as good. It was then that I first became conscious of the intense passion for the Presidency that has ever since warped his better mind, and baffled his own purposes, realizing for him the description of that vaulting ambition, which Shakespeare tells us "falls on tother side." You, perhaps, will not agree with me, but my notion is that, but for the fact that Jackson showed him that V. B. was the heir apparent & said to him in the language of Othello to M. Cassio, "never more be officer of mine"—you never would have heard *from him* of the doctrines of the veto. He has been *nullifying* ever since, and precisely under the same provocation. I have no doubt that Taylor will be elected by acclamation, if nothing untoward should happen. His fortune has been very curious. Chosen, with an *inferior force*—he himself but a Col. to tempt the Mexicans to a commencement of hostilities, he was used in the first instance as a foil to Scott. His successes were fatal to Scott and dangerous to the administration. Scott being no longer to be feared,

313

From "Letters of William Gilmore Simms to James H. Hammond, 1847–1850," edited by Alfred T. Odell, The Furman Bulletin, XXVI.
[1] *James H. Hammond was an agricultural reformer and political leader in South Carolina. He was one of the most avid defenders of slavery in the ante-bellum South.*

it was necessary that he should be used against Taylor, and a brilliant affair against San Juan de Ulloa & the Villa Rica was to obscure the impression of Taylor's victories. But the affair of San Juan, though of great & necessary importance, was anything but a brilliant one, and Scott's subsequent penetration of the country, even to the halls of Montezuma will avail nothing against the man, who, at the very moment when Scott & the administration together, had withdrawn from [him] all his regulars & favorite troops, leaving him in front of a very subtle & powerful foe, achieves his greatest victory. There is a fate in it which works against the administration—against the existing organization of parties, and for a new organization—in other words *for us*. Scott will not be permitted to bring the war to a close. This was the reason for putting Benton forward. Scott & Taylor were to win the victories, compel the subjection of the Mexicans, and Benton, at the moment of their humiliation, was to interpose and make a Brilliant Bentonian treaty in which the New England and Middle States were to be benefitted by peculiar commercial & trading facilities, and the West by lands, all of which were to be bought, if necessary, out of the common purse. Benton's vanity, as a military man, probably defeated the scheme. He was not content simply to be a civilian, and, except as Lt. Gen., he could not have controlled the military operations which were as necessary to his self esteem as his negotiations were supposed to be to his hopes. So far, fate favors Taylor. We should not hesitate to support him. He is our instrument no less than Fate's. He will assist in breaking down the System, and in laying a host of selfish graybeards upon the shelf forever. I confess to you that I greatly regret that such is to be the fate of Mr. Calhoun. He would have made a first rate President, with a bold foreign policy which is what we want. Our foreign policy, derived from Washington's time & notions, has always been feeble & purposeless. Jackson did more for it than all the Presidents. As for Taylor's Whiggism that's all in my eye. The Whigs don't believe him. Besides, what are the substantials? He is a Southron—a slave holder—a man who has good sense, and if he does not write his own dispatches himself has very judiciously chosen the person who does. As was said of Queen Elizabeth, a fool never chooses wise counsellors. He could not if he would forego the free trade policy. He might as a western man, recognize the new definition of the Mississippi Valley—might approve of large appropriations for national roads, bridges & ferries. But, on this subject of the inland sea something may be said. Sometime ago, more than five or six years, I thought I saw in the erection of the town of Natchez into a port of entry the surrender of the Mississippi to this point at least to the care of the general govt. The discovery of Atlantic steam navagation may give Silver Bluff & Augusta new privileges at the expense of Savannah, and change the political relations between these regions & the gov. at Washington. Eh? Quien Sabe? But to return. Nothing could be more fatal in the suggestions of Mr. Calhoun, than that the South should take him at his word & organize a party on the slavery question. This would at once force the North to do the same & then, according to Mr. C's. own showing where would we be, with the *free* states growing with such rapidity. As for the idea that there is a considerable body at the North with us on this question of Slavery, this is the absurdest of all. There is not a man, woman or child, who is not against us. The farmers & mechanics are everywhere so—it is only the commercial men engaged in Southern trade who are willing to

314

avoid the subject, but even their opinions are uniform, certainly against us. Force them to take sides in any organization upon this subject & they side against us to a man, however reluctantly. The truth is, the organization of the Democratic party is truly valuable *to us only as a mask for them.* Under this cover they find an excuse for their inactivity on the slavery question. Deprive them of this excuse, and they are as rabid against us as any of the rest.—But if not democrats, we certainly are not *Whigs*. But if I mistake not the signs of the times, this is to be the *parole* with Mr. Calhoun's followers. The occasion for the first decisive demonstration will probably be made on the advent of Mr. Webster. *Nous verrons.* Now, it is better that Taylor should be elected by acclamation than by the Whigs & the Calhoun Wing in alliance. Such an alliance would only bind us in subjection for at least two years to a Whig dynasty.— But I don't know that we have any need to talk on this subject. We can do nothing & prevent nothing. Will Elmore commit himself in this business? I think not. It will be the process by which to cut Mr. Calhoun off very effectually from any future but that of Fort Hill, but will E. commit such suicide? The close of Taylor's term of four years, will give signal of requisition for new men, and who has sown so heedfully or so judiciously with regard to this very exigency as Elmore?—I tire you however, and will postpone the topic to your wiser consideration & our better leisure.—I suspect that Judge Tucker's volume is only printed by Carey & Hart, and not *published* in the usual business sense of the word, except among the immediate pupils of the professor. I have never seen them. You have done right in representing me as willing to do what I can in procuring new editions of his writings. You may repeat the assurance authoritatively, and if the Judge will write me in New York, and find means to send me in that city, the copy of anything he particularly desires to put forth, I will serve him with as much diligence as I would yourself. Let me repeat the counsel, however, which I have already given. Let all the writings be *classed,* and such as are of a sort to permit of this mode of publication, ought to be put forth anonymously. "George Balcombe" by the Judge, was thus published, but his secret was badly kept. I knew it before the work was out of the press.—I don't exactly recollect what I told you touching certain books. Very probably my suggestion was that you should possess yourself by subscribing (they can be got no other way) to the several *serials* of ancient English Literature, now in course of publication in England, under the titles of the Camden Society Publications, The Shakspeare Society & the Percy Society. The subscription is £1. Per Ann. to each. $6.50 will probably cover the expense of each year, and the publication runs back five or six years. Say $100 for all, already published, & then £3.12 for the annual subs. to the three. There is a copy of Shakspeare in N. Y. (or was) for $20 or $25 which was unique, being one of the best folio editions & containing all the *imputed* plays viz: Locrine, The London Prodigal, Sir Thomas Cromwell, Widow of Watling Street, Sir John Oldcastle &c. which Shakspeare was at one time supposed to have written & which he may have written when a boy. In some of them he certainly had a hand. If you come on to N. Y. I can easily show you these things, or can have them procured & sent you if you desire it.—The letter of W. C. P. does not surprise me. I never did give him the credit of prompting the Columbia movement, for the simple reason that I always thought him too old a stager to commit so rank a folly. Whatever his

315

errors & faults, *he is in position,* and would not be so blind as to peril himself where he could gain nothing in any event and might lose much in your triumph. Perhaps his letter, (which I assume to have been intended for your eye) indicates something of the political wind at home. It is certain that *your strength* is acknowledged and fully understood; whether he tells the truth or not, his letter, *being intended for your eye,* indicates a strong *desire that you should suppose he told the truth.* This in other words exhibits a consciousness that you are able to exert a local influence, to do mischief, to make yourself felt by an enemy who provokes beyond his limit. One thing strikes me as a matter for your consideration. You are disposed, naturally enough, to acquit the tender gender of all participation in this crusade against you. It may be so; yet the report is that H. is engaged to J. M., and these alliances breed strange antipathies as well as sympathies. Besides, duty requires that they should denounce and hate you, if they would be consistent with themselves. It is highly probable that *disappointed* that you should be the first to show signs of relucting & repenting they feel equally the goadings of mortified self esteem as well as passion. But—God bless and make a good man of you.

Yours &c.
W. G. S.

Woodlands, Nov. 24, 1848

dear Hammond.

I am in receipt of your letter & greatly regret its tone of despondency. Doubtless the day at present is dark, but this is only, I trust, the forerunner of the dawn. I am in hopes that the fanatics in Congress will goad the Southern men out of the propriety, or into it this very session. What you suggest, touching the sources of our difficulty, is no doubt perfectly true; with this exception, that Calhoun, with all his selfish aspirations, has, through these, been made the instrument of other men. This particular instance—that of casting the vote of the state for Cass, is, I am sure, directly in hostility with his real desires; and has this advantage, that, if he be not utterly demented, he must see that the proceedings goes farther, & absolutely lays him on the shelf. The thing was worked through the Mercury & Carolinian, which are vulgarly supposed to be his organs but which have really been the organs of Mr. Rhett. He has been the mover of the wires in this instance, seconded by Elmore, Bailey & others below, and by Pickens & others above. The latter being governed directly by the wish to throw Calhoun aside, or give him a mortal stab. Their failure stabs themselves; since neither Rhett nor Pickens can possibly now realize their 30 pieces of silver. You must not despond. Above all you must not deceive yourself with the idea that you are no longer of use. I *know* that you are looked to, *as the future man* of S. C. if not of the South. Be true to yourself & you must be so. You have the faculties for a *public* leader. Your deficiencies are all *private.* I will explain this when we meet. You are in error, I think, about Virginia. She *cannot* lead & will not. She is already bought & sold through her politicians. The true state to lead, & to which we must address ourselves is *Louisiana.* She has the deepest interest (slavery &c. considered) of all of us in the contest. Her interest in slavery cannot decline for the next 300 years. In Virginia, N. C. &, I may add,

316

S. C. it is visibly on the decline. In 15 years Va. will be a free soil state, and will be instantly followed by N. C.; S. C. will be a frontier & where? Now *Louisiana* exports alone 85 millions. She holds the key of all the Valley of the West. *She* can control Kentucky, Tennessee, &c. when we can't. Carry her with us, at the head, and she closes the door upon Western Exports measurably. She has great talent, and a great ambition, & has been too much neglected & oversloughed. We should put her in the lead. We shall never be able to do so with Va. while her sons are all in the market. Think of this. Touching Conner [2] & the Bank, I am doubtful. It may be true of Boyce.[3] *He* is *jealous* of *Conner's influence* in the city. A day or two before I left Charleston, I had a talk with Conner. Among other things he told me this curious story. The city of Charleston wanting money, sent a circular last summer to all the Banks to know upon what terms it might be got. It held out the lure of doing business with the leading Bank, making its tax deposits &c. The Bank of the State agreed to let it have what was wanted at any time for 3 per ct! The contract was made. But just as I was leaving, the City wanted $6000, which the Bank *could not* provide! This, I fancy, accounts for the peremptory sale of the Victoria & Charleston Hotels, otherwise the City must have stopt payments! Rich,—eh? Conner chuckles at all this, and, I am thinking, has come to feel that he *must* wrestle with Elmore for life or death. I presume the chief matter which has made him reluctant is the fact that both Banks are to be rechartered during the same year. This afflicts some others in the same category.—I will think of what you suggest, touching your literary experiments. Without invention, as you say, the drama is the last thing to be attempted; but you are the very man for the subject you once suggested to me —viz. The political History of the Country. Think of it.—For me, if possible, the mission to Naples or Turin. There is this difficulty. Holmes [4] has seen that he can scarcely hope again to be reelected from Charleston. But for the Taylor movement, he would have been defeated. He must look out for employment. He will be in the way, and Gadsden [5] will support him. But, at all events, it is worth a trial & I will thank you to bestir yourself in it. Holmes may get a Secretaryship. I need the mission. Literature is in a wretched condition. I have a work ready which the publishers dare not publish. They tell me it would be sacrificed to do so now. And just now, my expenses are greatly increased. My wife is as women wish to be &c, and proposes to go [to] the city to be confined. The thing could take place in the country just as well as in the city & would save me considerable expense; but she thinks differently, and the case is one which admits of no discussion. It will take some $300 surplus out of my pocket, and greatly abridge my chicken money. I think the Italian mission could be got. It would save me, and place me free of the world. The argument in my favor, ought to be of weight with Taylor. I am almost the only professional author of the South, and have done service. You could better show how than myself. I have some claims to such a court as that of Naples, where my literary reputation might be felt. I once had a little Italian, which I shall set myself to recover & improve. I should

317

[2] *Conner, Henry Workman, successful banker of Charleston. (Odell's note.)*
[3] *Boyce, Ker, wealthy cotton merchant of Charleston. (Odell's note.)*
[4] *Holmes, for many years represented district in Congress; known as inflammatory Southerner, close friend of J. Q. Adams and Webster. (Odell's note.)*
[5] *Gadsden, James, for ten years President of Luisville, Cincinnati & Charleston Railway; as minister to Mexico negotiated Gadsden Purchase. (Odell's note.)*

endeavor to go [to] that court, speaking its dialect. But a truce to this. You know all. How & through whom you will work I know not, but, as you say, the sooner we move the better. I propose to go to the city by the 7th or 10 Decr. Is it possible for you to send or meet me at Aiken or Hamburg, between this & then? I have none but the carriage horses, which I cannot take from my wife. My only horses have gone the way of all flesh. If you can meet me at either place, so as to let me return by the 10th Decr.—I would run up & spend a couple or three days with you. Let me know in season, if the thing is possible. I scribble this hour in which I have read your letter. I send you a pamphlet of which you will give me your opinion. There is a sequel to it. But I am weary—half desponding like yourself. But I go to work when I am dull & expend my stupidity upon the public or my friends. God bless you. Yours,

Simms

To E. A. Duyckinck

Columbia, S. C., Oct. 1, 1865

My dear Duyckinck.[1]

Thanks for your several letters and your attention to my petty commissions. I know not whether my letters reach you regularly or not, & doubting, I may have to repeat something already expressed. As yet we have no regular mails, and need to employ chance travellers to some city or town, whither the mails go. Thanks, by the way, for your supply of poststamps. Please hold me your debtor for them. We could, & even now, can get none here, there being no post office, & but a nominal post master. This day, I resign the Editorial Chair of the Phoenix Newspaper. I created it, & have already made it the best organ of opinion in the State. In the end, it will be a fortune to its publisher. At present, it gives too little compensation to justify me in bestowing any further care upon it. It has answered my purpose in giving me employment during the summer, & bread & meat. That is all. In the course of the week, I propose to go down to the plantation, where I shall stay some week or 10 days, return, & proceed from Columbia to the North. I hope to be in N. Y. & to see you somewhere about the 20th or 25th inst. I told you in previous letters that I had been appointed by the Masonic bodies of this place, the Chairman of a Commission to represent them in the Northern cities in the hope to procure some assistance. I prepared their memorial, a copy of which I will send or bring you. They are to raise the necessary funds for the Commission—not so easy a matter in a place so utterly stript of resources. Lawson authorizes me to draw on him for $100—the amt. of a dft. from Widdleton. Wretched as this return is, the money enables me to send off by wagon, all the little luggage, clothing, bedding & furniture which I have here, to my children on the plantation. Of 16 Bedsteads, I have 1 left; so, in proportion of mattresses & feather beds. We have not a chair or a table. Not a knife or fork; hardly a cup or plate or tumbler.

318

From "Letters of William Gilmore Simms in the Post-War Years," edited by Alfred T. Odell, The Furman Bulletin, XXIX.
[1] Duyckinck was editor of the Cyclopaedia of American Literature, to which Simms contributed.

And such things we cannot buy. Our basins for washing are of tin, made out of tin, saved amid the ruins of Columbia. We have literally nothing left us but our lands, & how to dispossess the negroes is the problem. They will no longer work. They steal. We can scarcely keep a horse or mule, unless in a lodge directly beneath your chamber, under the muzzle of a gun. They are perishing by thousands of exposure, drunkeness, starvation & all brutal practices. The old are deserted by the young. Sons abandon their fathers, mothers their infants, all to crowd to the cities where they quarter themselves for rations on the government. They are daily convicted of robbery, & murders are frequent. But I will tell you all when we meet. I will endeavour, before I leave Columbia for the plantation to correct & copy out for you a few favorite pieces of verse, written during the last year, which I think well of, & for which, if possible, I wish you to procure me as much compensation as you can. If you knew my straits, you would find much merit in the pieces. At all events, they will I think neither discredit me nor any publisher. I saw a number of Scribner's Magazine yesterday. He needs some help from other hands than those which he has employed. After four, nearly five dreadful years, it will give me the greatest pleasure to meet with you again. But say as little as possible to me about the War, and my miserable Country. Did I say to you that the portrait of your brother is admirable? Poor Boy! Alas! Alas! We are mere cherry stones in the hands of fate who delights in flinging! God bless you. Yours as Ever,

W. G. S.

Charleston, 4 Nov. 1866

My dear Duyckinck.

Your letter came to me while I was on a visit to my plantation. I found everything very miserable there; no crop; a terrible drouth, and no work to be got out of the negroes, when work is essential to the safety of the crops. The efforts of my son, & all my expenditure of money, for the last 9 months, in vain. I shall probably continue to work here in Charleston where I am tolerably comfortable, until you see me again in New York. I have paid 2 visits to the plantation, of a few days each, yet have been sufficiently laborious, while here, to write some 250 pp. M. S. on a new revolutionary romance called "Joscelyn." [2] This is to be put forth serially. I have received a letter from Widdleton. Please say to him that I will write him in a few days. In the meantime request him to send me a copy of my "Yemassee" which I find wanting to my collection; and should he be in a liberal vein, tell him that I will be grateful to him for copies—his old editions will answer—of Poe's works; of the Noctes Ambrosianae, and of the Maquia papers, for all of which I am prepared to say a good word in one or other of our Newspapers. I enclose you a notice of Freneau, which was printed in the Courier during my absence in N. Y. I had left it, when I went North, & its publication was delayed till some weeks after. I take for granted that you or Widdleton have received the several notices which I printed of his & your several publications (as I received them) either in the Courier or the Carolinian. Shall I remind you here not to forget to send me

319

---

[2] Joscelyn *was published in* The Old Guard, *a pro-Southern magazine. (Odell's note.)*

the photographs promised me of yourself & brother; as also copies of his several little volumes. May I beg also that you will procure the publications of Mr. Johnson which he was so good as to promise me. These, if sent to Richardson & Co. will reach me in safety. They have now on hand sundry packages for me, & will soon be forwarding. I enclose you an autograph—a pair of them—of Brig. Gen. Isaac Huger, of the Continental Army. They are very scarce. These you will please deliver, with my regards, to *our* friend, Mr. Moreau, with a request from me that he will accept & place the sheet in his collection. Did you not, on the morning of my departure, receive at an early hour a note from me apprising you of my inability to come and begging you to meet me at the boat. I sent the note by one of Richardson's Clerks, somewhere between 10 & 11 A.M. & saw him depart with it. Had you been able to meet me at the boat you would have encountered Professor Bruns,[3] fresh from Europe, who became my *compagnon de voyage* home. He was quite anxious to see you again. He has gone to take his Professor's chair at New Orleans, & should you need or desire any relationship in that section, aside from Gayarré, write to him. He will respond with whole heart, & a good head. I was doubly & trebly unfortunate in missing Halleck & Verplanck on two occasions. I should have rejoiced at a shake of the hand, once more, with two of those men, who never sunk the Gentlemen in the author—a thing quite rare, as you & I have so frequently found in our experience. Halleck was always a true man, & by nature, an aristocrat! But I must hope for better luck hereafter. Meanwhile, should you see him again, give him a goodby gripe of the fist on my account & believe me

Ever truly yours
W. Gilmore Simms

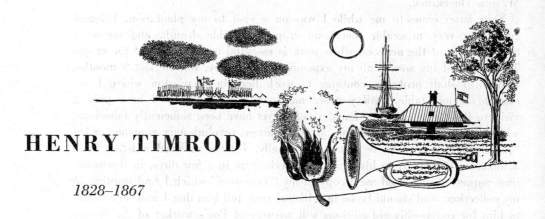

HENRY TIMROD

1828–1867

Born December 8, 1828, Timrod was a native of Charleston, South Carolina. He was educated in the private schools of this city and later became a student at Franklin College (the University of Georgia), but a temporary illness and chronic poverty compelled him to withdraw after only two years.

320

Back in Charleston, Timrod read law for a while but soon found himself unhappy in his choice of a profession. He became intimate with a group of

[3] *Dickson Bruns, a former professor in the medical college at Charleston, had been a member of the group which met at Russell's bookstore. (Odell's note.)*

Charleston writers, of whom William Gilmore Simms was the leader, and determined to become an author. In 1857 he helped found the short-lived publication known as *Russell's Magazine.* A collection of his poems, published three years later, was well received by critics in both North and South, but was soon lost sight of in the desperate emergencies of the Civil War. Ill health kept Timrod out of this conflict until March 1862, when he joined the Confederate Army in the West as a war correspondent for *The Charleston Mercury.* He was sent home in December of the same year, however, suffering from incipient tuberculosis.

In 1864 Timrod moved to Columbia as part owner and associate editor of the *South Carolinian,* but this project ended disastrously when the city was burned by Sherman's forces. Writing his friend Paul Hamilton Hayne in 1866, he epitomized his life during the preceding year. It had meant for him, he said, "beggary, starvation, death [of a son and other relatives], bitter grief, utter want of hope." He avoided starvation for himself and his crowded household by selling what tangible goods the enemy had ignored: "We have eaten two silver pitchers, one or two dozen silver forks, several sofas, innumerable chairs, and a huge bedstead." He remarked that he was willing to consign every line of verse he had written "to eternal oblivion, for *one hundred dollars in hand.*" Shortly after the war, in October 1867, Timrod died of tuberculosis.

Two of Timrod's most esteemed essays are "A Theory of Poetry" and "The Character and Scope of the Sonnet," both of which received general attention only in the twentieth century. His greatest recognition was for his poetry. As the writer of a limited number of sensitive and moving poems about the Civil War, his status remains unquestioned. The title "Laureate of the Confederacy" —a term his contemporaries seemed to impose upon him—is generally recognized as appropriate almost a century after he began his desperate struggle to establish himself as an author.

Ethnogenesis [1]

I.

Hath not the morning dawned with added light?
And shall not evening call another star
Out of the infinite regions of the night,
To mark this day in Heaven? At last, we are
A nation among nations; and the world
Shall soon behold in many a distant port
    Another flag unfurled!
Now, come what may, whose favor need we court?
And, under God, whose thunder need we fear?
    Thank Him who placed us here
Beneath so kind a sky—the very sun
Takes part with us; and on our errands run
All breezes of the ocean; dew and rain
Do noiseless battle for us; and the Year,

321

[1] *Timrod attempts to express here the hopes of the South at the beginning of the Civil War.*

And all the gentle daughters in her train,
March in our ranks, and in our service wield
　　Long spears of golden grain!
A yellow blossom as her fairy shield,
June flings her azure banner to the wind,
　　While in the order of their birth
Her sisters pass, and many an ample field
Grows white beneath their steps, till now, behold,
　　Its endless sheets unfold
THE SNOW OF SOUTHERN SUMMERS! Let the earth
Rejoice! beneath those fleeces soft and warm
　　Our happy land shall sleep
　　In a repose as deep
　As if we lay intrenched behind
Whole leagues of Russian ice and Arctic storm!

II.

And what if, mad with wrongs themselves have wrought,
　　In their own treachery caught,
　　By their own fears made bold,
　　And leagued with him of old,
Who long since in the limits of the North
Set up his evil throne, and warred with God—
What if, both mad and blinded in their rage,
Our foes should fling us down their mortal gage,
And with a hostile step profane our sod!
We shall not shrink, my brothers, but go forth
To meet them, marshaled by the Lord of Hosts,
And overshadowed by the mighty ghosts
Of Moultrie and of Eutaw—who shall foil
Auxiliars such as these? Nor these alone,
　　But every stock and stone
　　Shall help us; but the very soil,
And all the generous wealth it gives to toil,
And all for which we love our noble land,
Shall fight beside, and through us; sea and strand,
　　The heart of woman, and her hand,
Tree, fruit, and flower, and every influence,
　　Gentle, or grave, or grand;
　　The winds in our defence
Shall seem to blow; to us the hills shall lend
　　Their firmness and their calm;
And in our stiffened sinews we shall blend
　　The strength of pine and palm!

322

III.

Nor would we shun the battle-ground,
　　Though weak as we are strong;

Call up the clashing elements around,
    And test the right and wrong!
On one side, creeds that dare to teach
What Christ and Paul refrained to preach;
Codes built upon a broken pledge,
And Charity that whets a poniard's edge;
Fair schemes that leave the neighboring poor
To starve and shiver at the schemer's door,
While in the world's most liberal ranks enrolled,
He turns some vast philanthropy to gold;
Religion, taking every mortal form
But that a pure and Christian faith makes warm,
Where not to vile fanatic passion urged,
Or not in vague philosophies submerged,
Repulsive with all Pharisaic leaven,
And making laws to stay the laws of Heaven!
And on the other, scorn of sorted gain,
Unblemished honor, truth without a stain,
Faith, justice, reverence, charitable wealth,
And, for the poor and humble, laws which give,
Not the mean right to buy the right to live,
    But life, and home, and health!
To doubt the end were want of trust in God,
    Who, if he has decreed
  That we must pass a redder sea
Than that which rang to Miriam's holy glee,
    Will surely raise at need
    A Moses with his rod!

IV.

But let our fears—if fears we have—be still,
And turn us to the future! Could we climb
Some mighty Alp, and view the coming time,
The rapturous sight would fill
    Our eyes with happy tears!
Not only for the glories which the years
Shall bring us; not for lands from sea to sea,
And wealth, and power, and peace, though these shall be;
But for the distant peoples we shall bless,
And the hushed murmurs of a world's distress:
For, to give labor to the poor,
    The whole sad planet o'er,
And save from want and crime the humblest door,
Is one among the many ends for which
    God makes us great and rich!
The hour perchance is not yet wholly ripe
When all shall own it, but the type
Whereby we shall be known in every land

323

Is that vast gulf which lips our Southern strand,
And through the cold, untempered ocean pours
Its genial streams, that far off Arctic shores
May sometimes catch upon the softened breeze
Strange tropic warmth and hints of summer seas.

(1861)

The Cotton Boll

While I recline
At ease beneath
This immemorial pine,
Small sphere!
(By dusky fingers brought this morning here
And shown with boastful smiles),
I turn thy cloven sheath,
Through which the soft white fibres peer,
That, with their gossamer bands,
Unite, like love, the sea-divided lands,
And slowly, thread by thread,
Draw forth the folded strands,
Than which the trembling line,
By whose frail help yon startled spider fled
Down the tall spear-grass from his swinging bed,
Is scarce more fine;
And as the tangled skein
Unravels in my hands,
Betwixt me and the noonday light,
A veil seems lifted, and for miles and miles
The landscape broadens on my sight,
As, in the little boll, there lurked a spell
Like that which, in the ocean shell,
With mystic sound,
Breaks down the narrow walls that hem us round,
And turns some city lane
Into the restless main,
With all his capes and isles!

Yonder bird,
Which floats, as if at rest,
In those blue tracts above the thunder, where
No vapors cloud the stainless air,
And never sound is heard,
Unless at such rare time
When, from the City of the Blest,
Rings down some golden chime,

324

Sees not from his high place
So vast a cirque of summer space
As widens round me in one mighty field,
Which, rimmed by seas and sands,
Doth hail its earliest daylight in the beams
Of gray Atlantic dawns;
And, broad as realms made up of many lands,
Is lost afar
Behind the crimson hills and purple lawns
Of sunset, among plains which roll their streams
Against the Evening Star!
And lo!
To the remotest point of sight,
Although I gaze upon no waste of snow,
The endless field is white;
And the whole landscape glows,
For many a shining league away,
With such accumulated light
As Polar lands would flash beneath a tropic day!
Nor lack there (for the vision grows,
And the small charm within my hands—
More potent even than the fabled one,
Which oped whatever golden mystery
Lay hid in fairy wood or magic vale,
The curious ointment of the Arabian tale—
Beyond all mortal sense
Doth stretch my sight's horizon, and I see,
Beneath its simple influence,
As if with Uriel's crown,
I stood in some great temple of the Sun,
And looked, as Uriel, down!)
Nor lack there pastures rich and fields all green
With all the common gifts of God,
For temperate airs and torrid sheen
Weave Edens of the sod;
Through lands which look one sea of billowy gold
Broad rivers wind their devious ways;
A hundred isles in their embraces fold
A hundred luminous bays;
And through yon purple haze
Vast mountains lift their plumèd peaks cloud-crowned;
And, save where up their sides the ploughman creeps,
An unhewn forest girds them grandly round,
In whose dark shades a future navy sleeps!
Ye Stars, which, though unseen, yet with me gaze
Upon this loveliest fragment of the earth!
Thou Sun, that kindlest all thy gentlest rays

325

Above it, as to light a favorite hearth!
Ye Clouds, that in your temples in the West
See nothing brighter than its humblest flowers!
And you, ye Winds, that on the ocean's breast
Are kissed to coolness ere ye reach its bowers!
Bear witness with me in my song of praise,
And tell the world that, since the world began,
No fairer land hath fired a poet's lays,
Or given a home to man!

But these are charms already widely blown!
His be the meed whose pencil's trace
Hath touched our very swamps with grace,
And round whose tuneful way
All Southern laurels bloom;
The Poet of "The Woodlands," unto whom
Alike are known
The flute's low breathing and the trumpet's tone,
And the soft west wind's sighs;
But who shall utter all the debt,
O Land wherein all powers are met
That bind a people's heart,
The world doth owe thee at this day,
And which it never can repay,
Yet scarcely deigns to own!
Where sleeps the poet who shall fitly sing
The source wherefrom doth spring
That mighty commerce which, confined
To the mean channels of no selfish mart,
Goes out to every shore
Of this broad earth, and throngs the sea with ships
That bear no thunders; hushes hungry lips
In alien lands;
Joins with a delicate web remotest strands;
And gladdening rich and poor,
Doth gild Parisian domes,
Or feed the cottage-smoke of English homes,
And only bounds its blessings by mankind!
In offices like these, thy mission lies,
My Country! and it shall not end
As long as rain shall fall and Heaven bend
In blue above thee; though thy foes be hard
And cruel as their weapons, it shall guard
Thy hearth-stones as a bulwark; make thee great
In white and bloodless state;
And haply, as the years increase—
Still working through its humbler reach

With that large wisdom which the ages teach—
Revive the half-dead dream of universal peace!
As men who labor in that mine
Of Cornwall, hollowed out beneath the bed
Of ocean, when a storm rolls overhead,
Hear the dull booming of the world of brine
Above them, and a mighty muffled roar
Of winds and waters, yet toil calmly on,
And split the rock, and pile the massive ore,
Or carve a niche, or shape the archèd roof;
So I, as calmly, weave my woof
Of song, chanting the days to come,
Unsilenced, though the quiet summer air
Stirs with the bruit of battles, and each dawn
Wakes from its starry silence to the hum
Of many gathering armies. Still,
In that we sometimes hear,
Upon the Northern winds, the voice of woe
Not wholly drowned in triumph, though I know
The end must crown us, and a few brief years
Dry all our tears,
I may not sing too gladly. To Thy will
Resigned, O Lord! we cannot all forget
That there is much even Victory must regret.
And, therefore, not too long
From the great burthen of our country's wrong
Delay our just release!
And, if it may be, save
These sacred fields of peace
From stain of patriot or of hostile blood!
Oh, help us, Lord! to roll the crimson flood
Back on its course, and, while our banners wing
Northward, strike with us! till the Goth shall cling
To his own blasted altar-stones, and crave
Mercy; and we shall grant it, and dictate
The lenient future of his fate
There, where some rotting ships and crumbling quays
Shall one day mark the Port which ruled the Western seas.

(*1861*)

Carolina

327

I.

The despot treads thy sacred sands,
Thy pines give shelter to his bands,

Thy sons stand by with idle hands,
Carolina!
He breathes at ease thy airs of balm,
He scorns the lances of thy palm;
Oh! who shall break thy craven calm,
Carolina!
Thy ancient fame is growing dim,
A spot is on thy garment's rim;
Give to the winds thy battle hymn,
Carolina!

II.

Call on thy children of the hill,
Wake swamp and river, coast and rill,
Rouse all thy strength and all thy skill,
Carolina!
Cite wealth and science, trade and art,
Touch with thy fire the cautious mart,
And pour thee through the people's heart,
Carolina!
Till even the coward spurns his fears,
And all thy fields and fens and meres
Shall bristle like thy palm with spears,
Carolina!

III.

Hold up the glories of thy dead;
Say how thy elder children bled,
And point to Eutaw's battle-bed,
Carolina!
Tell how the patriot's soul was tried,
And what his dauntless breast defied;
How Rutledge ruled and Laurens died,
Carolina!
Cry! till thy summons, heard at last,
Shall fall like Marion's bugle-blast
Re-echoed from the haunted Past,
Carolina!

IV.

I hear a murmur as of waves
That grope their way through sunless caves,
Like bodies struggling in their graves,
Carolina!
And now it deepens; slow and grand
It swells, as, rolling to the land,
An ocean broke upon thy strand,
Carolina!

328

Shout! let it reach the startled Huns!
And roar with all thy festal guns!
It is the answer of thy sons,
   Carolina!

V.

They will not wait to hear thee call;
From Sachem's Head to Sumter's wall
Resounds the voice of hut and hall,
   Carolina!
No! thou hast not a stain, they say,
Or none save what the battle-day
Shall wash in seas of blood away,
   Carolina!
Thy skirts indeed the foe may part,
Thy robe be pierced with sword and dart,
They shall not touch thy noble heart,
   Carolina!

VI.

Ere thou shalt own the tyrant's thrall
Ten times ten thousand men must fall;
Thy corpse may hearken to his call,
   Carolina!
When, by thy bier, in mournful throngs
The women chant thy mortal wrongs,
'Twill be their own funereal songs,
   Carolina!
From thy dead breast by ruffians trod
No helpless child shall look to God;
All shall be safe beneath thy sod,
   Carolina!

VII.

Girt with such wills to do and bear,
Assured in right, and mailed in prayer,
Thou wilt not bow thee to despair,
   Carolina!
Throw thy bold banner to the breeze!
Front with thy ranks the threatening seas
Like thine own proud armorial trees,
   Carolina!
Fling down thy gauntlet to the Huns,
And roar the challenge from thy guns;
Then leave the future to thy sons,
   Carolina!

                  329

        (1862)

Charleston

Calm as that second summer which precedes
  The first fall of the snow,
In the broad sunlight of heroic deeds,
  The City bides the foe.

As yet, behind their ramparts stern and proud,
  Her bolted thunders sleep—
Dark Sumter, like a battlemented cloud,
  Looms o'er the solemn deep.

No Calpe frowns from lofty cliff or scar
  To guard the holy strand;
But Moultrie holds in leash her dogs of war
  Above the level sand.

And down the dunes a thousand guns lie couched,
  Unseen, beside the flood—
Like tigers in some Orient jungle crouched
  That wait and watch for blood.

Meanwhile, through streets still echoing with trade,
  Walk grave and thoughtful men,
Whose hands may one day wield the patriot's blade
  As lightly as the pen.

And maidens, with such eyes as would grow dim
  Over a bleeding hound,
Seem each one to have caught the strength of him
  Whose sword she sadly bound.

Thus girt without and garrisoned at home,
  Day patient following day,
Old Charleston looks from roof, and spire, and dome,
  Across her tranquil bay.

Ships, through a hundred foes, from Saxon lands
  And spicy Indian ports,
Bring Saxon steel and iron to her hands,
  And Summer to her courts.

330

But still, along yon dim Atlantic line,
  The only hostile smoke
Creeps like a harmless mist above the brine,
  From some frail, floating oak.

Shall the Spring dawn, and she still clad in smiles,
    And with an unscathed brow,
Rest in the strong arms of her palm-crowned isles,
    As fair and free as now?

We know not; in the temple of the Fates
    God has inscribed her doom;
And, all untroubled in her faith, she waits
    The triumph or the tomb.

(1862)

Ode²

I.

Sleep sweetly in your humble graves,
    Sleep, martyrs of a fallen cause;
Though yet no marble column craves
    The pilgrim here to pause.

II.

In seeds of laurel in the earth
    The blossom of your fame is blown,
And somewhere, waiting for its birth,
    The shaft is in the stone!

III.

Meanwhile, behalf the tardy years
    Which keep in trust your storied tombs,
Behold! your sisters bring their tears,
    And these memorial blooms.

IV.

Small tributes! but your shades will smile
    More proudly on these wreaths today,
Than when some cannon-moulded pile
    Shall overlook this bay.

V.

Stoop, angels, hither from the skies!
    There is no holier spot of ground
Than where defeated valor lies,
    By mourning beauty crowned!

(1866)

331

---

² *The "Ode" was sung at memorial exercises for decorating the graves of the Confederate dead at Magnolia Cemetery, Charleston, South Carolina.*

PAUL HAMILTON HAYNE

1830–1886

Paul Hamilton Hayne was born January 1, 1830, in Charleston, South Carolina, where his family had lived for more than a century. While a student at Mr. Coate's school he met Henry Timrod, and the two formed a lasting friendship. He was graduated from Charleston College in 1850 and practiced law briefly, but soon decided to give it up for writing.

Until the Civil War, Hayne was occupied both as a journalist and a poet. Writing for the *Southern Literary Messenger* and the Charleston *Evening News*, he nevertheless managed to issue three volumes of verse during the decade before the war. They were *Poems* (1855), *Sonnets and Other Poems* (1857), and *Avolio, a Legend of the Island of Cos* (1860). His poetry received the enthusiastic approval of Holmes, Bryant, Bayard Taylor, and Longfellow in America, and of Tennyson and Swinburne in England. During this period Hayne also served on the short-lived *Russell's Magazine* (1857–1860) as co-editor, an occupation which he afterwards described as "one of the most difficult, exacting, and thankless tasks imaginable."

Unfit for active military service, Hayne became an aide to Governor Pickens during the Civil War. He lost practically all of his possessions in the war; his home and library were burned by Sherman's soldiers and the family silver stolen. After peace was declared, he moved to Groveton, Georgia—near Augusta—and built with his own hands "a little apology for a dwelling," which he named "Copse Hill." He furnished it, he declared, with three mattresses and a cot, and had, by way of supplies, "a box of hard tack, two sides of bacon, and four score smoked herring." Letters to prosperous literary friends, whom he was constantly imploring to visit him, always contained the assurance that ample stores of corn whiskey were on hand.

Under these outwardly depressing circumstances Hayne lived out his days, with courage and an irrepressible enthusiasm for literature. In 1872 he published perhaps his best single volume, *Legends and Lyrics*, to be followed three years later by *The Mountain of the Lovers*. His collected *Poems* appeared in 1882.

332

Critics are in general agreement that Hayne wrote too much and revised his first drafts too infrequently. And all too often the voices of Tennyson and Keats seem to echo in his verse. Yet, in spite of his shortcomings, he was recognized as one of the prominent literary leaders of the South.

Aspects of the Pines

Tall, sombre, grim, against the morning sky
   They rise, scarce touched by melancholy airs,
Which stir the fadeless foliage dreamfully,
   As if from realms of mystical despairs.

Tall, sombre, grim, they stand with dusky gleams
   Brightening to gold within the woodland's core,
Beneath the gracious noontide's tranquil beams—
   But the weird winds of morning sigh no more.

A stillness, strange, divine, ineffable,
   Broods round and o'er them in the wind's surcease,
And on each tinted copse and shimmering dell
   Rests the mute rapture of deep hearted peace.

Last, sunset comes—the solemn joy and might
   Borne from the West when cloudless day declines—
Low, flutelike breezes sweep the waves of light,
   And lifting dark green tresses of the pines,

Till every lock is luminous—gently float,
   Fraught with hale odors up the heavens afar
To faint when twilight on her virginal throat
   Wears for a gem the tremulous vesper star.

                           (1882)

Shelley

Because they thought his doctrines were not just,
Mankind assumed for him the chastening rod,
And tyrants reared in pride, and strong in lust,
Wounded the noblest of the sons of God;
The heart's most cherished benefactions riven,
Basely they strove to humble and malign
A soul whose charities were wide as heaven,
Whose *deeds*, if not his *doctrines*, were divine;
And in the name of Him, whose sunshine warms
The evil as the righteous, deemed it good
To wreak their bigotry's relentless storms
On one whose nature was not understood.
Ah, well! God's ways are wondrous; it may be
His seal hath not been set to man's decree.

                           (1882)

333

Vicksburg

A BALLAD

For sixty days and upwards,
  A storm of shell and shot
Rained round us in a flaming shower,
  But still we faltered not.
"If the noble city perish,"
  Our grand young leader said,
"Let the only walls the foe shall scale
  Be ramparts of the dead!"

For sixty days and upwards,
  The eye of heaven waxed dim;
And e'en throughout God's holy morn,
  O'er Christian prayer and hymn,
Arose a hissing tumult,
  As if the fiends in air
Strove to engulf the voice of faith
  In the shrieks of their despair.

There was wailing in the houses,
  There was trembling on the marts,
While the tempest raged and thundered,
  'Mid the silent thrill of hearts;
But the Lord, our shield, was with us,
  And ere a month had sped,
Our very women walked the streets
  With scarce one throb of dread.

And the little children gambolled,
  Their faces purely raised,
Just for a wondering moment,
  As the huge bombs whirled and blazed,
Then turned with silvery laughter
  To the sports which children love,
Thrice-mailed in the sweet, instinctive thought
  That the good God watched above.

Yet the hailing bolts fell faster,
  From scores of flame-clad ships,
And about us, denser, darker,
  Grew the conflict's wild eclipse,
Till a solid cloud closed o'er us,
  Like a type of doom and ire,
Whence shot a thousand quivering tongues
  Of forked and vengeful fire.

But the unseen hands of angels
    Those death-shafts warned aside,
And the dove of heavenly mercy
    Ruled o'er the battle tide;
In the houses ceased the wailing,
    And through the war-scarred marts
The people strode, with step of hope,
    To the music in their hearts.

(1882)

To Longfellow

(ON HEARING HE WAS ILL)

O thou, whose potent genius (like the sun
    Tenderly mellowed by a rippling haze)
    Hast gained thee all men's homage, love and praise,
Surely thy web of life is not outspun,
Thy glory rounded, thy last guerdon won!
    Nay, poet, nay!—from thought's calm sunset ways
May new-born notes of undegenerate lays
Charm back the twilight gloom ere day be done!

But past the poet crowned I see the friend—
    Frank, courteous, true—about whose locks of gray,
Like golden bees, some glints of summer stray;
    Clear-eyed, with lips half poised 'twixt smile and sigh;
A brow in whose soul-mirroring manhood blend
    Grace, sweetness, power and magnanimity!

(1882)

Letters

To William Gilmore Simms

"Copse Hill"
Dec 28th 1869

Dear Friend;

    Notwithstanding all the cares, anxieties, troubles, doubts, & misfortunes, physical and mental, which your last letter records, I have read it with a species of exhilaration. Your brave words embodying braver thoughts, your expressions of gallant resolution under circumstances the most trying, affect one's moral

335

Hayne's letters from Collection of Hayne Letters, *edited by Daniel M. McKeithan, University of Texas Press, 1944. Used with the kind permission of Elise Frost Hayne, Alice P. Hayne, and Henrietta Hayne Gadsden.*

sense as with the ring of great spiritual trumpets, the blare of silver clarions from some unseen region far above our heads!

It is impossible for me to express in words my profound admiration of your moral *pluck*, of the true Anglo-Saxon, I ought rather to say, Anglo-*Norman grit*, and steel-like endurance, (which may be made to *bend*, but refuses to *break*,) that characterise your nature, and make you in misfortune simply *great!*

You indulge neither in a whine, nor a *snarl*, but accepting the *Inevitable*, with a mental *"Kismet," "it is written,"* you reserve your forces to battle with enemies whom mortal skill & courage *may* overcome!

I confess to the greatest astonishment at what you tell me of your literary labors during portions of this year, and the preceding. Such uninterrupted work, (*imaginative* toil too, which is the most exhausting of all), was eno', & *more than* eno' to *kill* you, or worse, consign you to that lamentable condition of mental wreck of which the concluding years of Walter Scott's life furnish us with so sad an example. It seems to me that no necessity short of *absolute starvation*, or its direct approach, could have justified you in undertaking such *suicidal* tasks.

But the mischief has been done, & I can only trust 'tis not irremediable.

All the symptoms of ill-health you describe I clearly recognize at once.

Every one of these pains and aches has at some one period or another, been mine own familiar——fiend! *Dyspepsia!!*, bless your soul!, I've shaken hands with that particular devil ten thousand times at least;—he has taken up his abode in every conceivable corner of my poor brain, and poorer stomach! has twisted my back, clutched savagely at my bowels; cut my breath off as sharply, & neatly as if my Breath had aristocratic pretentions, & must be decapitated by an invisible Guillotine;—has *now*, loosened my *liver*, until I thought my whole being would melt away in liquid abominations, and then, plugged me up so tightly, that (I'm *not* joking!!) every operation became a sort of bastard *accouchement* which caused me to yell like twenty regiments of monkeys afflicted *ad eadem tempore*,[1] with Asiatic cholera!!

And as for *nerves!* I have been, and often *am* one huge bundle thereof!! Fancy a conglomeration of sensitive cords, inextricably tangled together, & each one going off into *St* Vitus' dance, and *there* you have a *faint* picture of my frequent condition of—the Lord only knows *what* to call it!

Who then, on this broad earth, can comprehend, and sympathise with, your sicknesses more sincerely than myself?

And what in *your* case makes the matter worse, is the fact that all your life until these recent years—, health and strength have been always with you!

After all, a constitution like yours, even *after* 60, may revive, with proper rest, and *regimen!* The resilient powers of the human frame are wonderful.

Tho when thinking of *you*, I feel like an idle dog, yet I *have* tried to "perform my devoirs" bravely during the year about to close. Almost the entire field of periodical literature, North & South, I have at least *hurried* over! That is to say, I have written for all styles of magazine, weekly paper, and quarterly Review. Indeed, in Literature, I am little better than a *lanskneight* [*landsknecht?*], or "free rider," gathering all the plunder I can from North, South, East & West.

336

---

[1] *At the same time.*

Long ago I made up my mind never, (upon *principle*), to write *gratis*. *Something,*—if only pens, paper, & ink—, I peremptorily demand for my work. When the Blacksmith is paid, & the carpenter, when the very Scavenger, collecting refuse, has his annual salary—, I don't see why the Poet—however humble—, should be expected to sing for *love* not *money!!* At all events, *I* invariably refuse to do so!

Some trifling reputation as a verse-monger, has helped me so far, that "Appleton's Journal" (for example) pays me on an average, $15.00 for each poem of 6 or 8 stanzas, and I get the same from *"Hearth & Home,"* Edited by *Donald Mitchell.*

Bledsoe's Review I'm now writing for likewise.

In the Jan issue you will find a long article on H. Legaré. That is mine. And a *story* (in verse) called *"Daphles,"* occupying about 10 pp of the Review, and embracing nearly 600 lines, *that* also is mine.

The *two* contributions will probably bring me from 80 to 100 dollars, but this is an unusual haul!!

Did Jno Bruns, in writing, send you his photograph? I have it on my mantle-piece, as large, or rather *larger* than life;——you would scarcely recognize our friend in his present condition of superfluous fat. His abdomen sticks out a couple of feet, and shakes like a huge jelly whenever he moves. His cheeks are dew-lappy, and his chin is not a *double*, but a *treble* one! When last summer I went as John's *second* to W. Point (in that desperate quarrel of Dick Michel's), and we expected him to *fight* the very *next morning*, I could not but look on his abdomen with melancholy anticipations. I suggested a *brace* of some kind around it—, but no, the obstinate fellow swore it was *only fat*, and said, that a bullet thro that quarter would do no harm, but could be plugged up with —bread, & cheese!!

Those "old boys" at Montgomery were amazed at Bruns' manners, his hilarity in the most trying circumstances, his *bonhommie*, rich humor, and never failing sources of fun, anecdote, and wit! They regarded him with open eyes, and mouths, as

> "A man in all the world's new fashion planted,
> That had a mint of phrases in his brain,"

without I am sure, completing the couplet even in thought, or fancying that he could under any conditions be one,

> "one whom the music of his own vain tongue
> Doth ravish like enchanting harmony."

I am glad to hear that *Govan*, (whom I recollect as a chubby little chap, with *Dutchified* legs) goes to the same school with my son & heir——(to *nil!*), Willie. The news that the latter "promises to be a Poet," has seriously *shocked* me.

Mon Dieu! *Can* it be possible that the poor little devil has inherited this dreadful *virus* from his unlucky papa? Let us trust that the report is exaggerated!!

To be in earnest, my boy *is* doubtless, quite intelligent, tho very *backward* in his studies! I kept [him] by me in the Country to the last possible moment,

337

for the purpose of developing his *physique*—naturally feeble—, and I've succeeded so far at least, that I believe *Willie* will grow up into a moderately vigorous man, and never be tormented by the constant ill-health which more than aught else, has dogged his father's progress thro life. *Morally;* he is pure as any youthful Sir Galahad;—and I have never known him *hint a lie,* or outline deliberately or carelessly even the shadow of falsehood!!

[*Written in the margin of—and partly across—the last page of the letter:*]

The evening shades warn me to close. Mary (my wife) sends her *best love* and wishes for your speedy recovery.

Write soon, if possible, & Believe me

Always Faithfully
Paul H. Hayne

[*Written at the top of the first page of the preceding letter:* "*Please* return the Poem I enclose. 'Tis my only copy."]

To Henry Wadsworth Longfellow

Augusta Geo.
Jan 24th 1872

My Dear Sir;

I venture to send you, (thro my *Publishers*) a copy of a little vol, *one* Poem in which, ("*Daphles*") met with your kind approval some years ago, when issued in one of the magazines.

Perhaps a few other pieces, as they now appear, will interest you likewise.

At least, allow me to *hope* so.

A political "ode" on the Bravery of *So* soldiers &c, will be pardoned by you, (I mean in reference to some undue bitterness of expression), when you look at the *date* of its composition. In 1866, we, of the *South*, were *heartbroken,* and *desperate!* A generous foe will remember *that!*

From the obscure lower regions of *Parnassus,* I send greeting to *you,* whom a beneficent *Fate* has placed so near the glorious *summit!*

Long may you continue to live, & delight the world with music as full of *perfect art,* as of a divine *hope,* & a faith in all things good, pure, and noble! *Your* poetry elevates the spirit, and makes strong the heart, instead of merely charming the *fancy,* and then leaving one in the twilight of scepticism, as to the existence even of a *Hereafter!* Recent poetry is the poetry of *Doubt;*—Look at Morris, Rossetti, Swinburne!

But I must close.

Ever Most Faithfully
Paul H. Hayne

338

P O Box 635
Augusta Geo.

Augusta
Jan 6th 1874

My Dear Mr Longfellow;

Since I saw you last—forgive my egotism; it is necessary to the clearness of certain explanations—; since I saw you last—, I have suffered from illness so *severe*, that *twice* I confidently expected a removal from this strange world to the mysterious *Beyond*. *Partially* recovering, I hastened South, and my native air has somewhat restored the strength which seemed gone forever. Believe me, I take the *first* opportunity of thanking you for the generous kindness shown me during the summer; and had I only been able to *work* as usual,—or, had not that terrible autumn "Panic," struck *me* down—pecuniarily—with so many others—I would long since have cancelled my obligation, in a *material sence* [sic], tho in far *higher* respects, it never *can* be cancelled, nor would I *desire* it!

As matters *now* stand, I am *forced*, literally forced, to solicit your indulgence & generous construction of my conduct. *"Who of us is stronger than destiny?"*—

Need I observe, that *as soon as* possible, I will refund that most kindly loan?

Great Heaven! what a clinging *curse* is Poverty! It *killed* my friend *Timrod*, long before his time; and many a dark hour, & sleepless night of bitterness & bewildered fear, has it brought upon me!

Pardon such an outburst;—I don't mean to complain, or whine against Fate. One must endure one's own burdens manfully.

More than a year ago, the idea occurred to me of composing *three* brief Poems upon our chief American Poets; *namely, yourself, Bryant, & Whittier. Two* of these have been completed; and *now* I venture to enclose for examination, the verses dedicated to your honored *self*. They can claim *one* merit—a profound *sincerity*.

Had you lived in Ancient Greece, Mr Longfellow,—I think they would have called you a favorite of the Gods!

What a splendid career you can now look back upon! And ah! how much better than all splendors of mortal fame must be the conviction that you have penned no line,—no solitary line, which,

"Dying, you could wish to blot!"

Now-a-days, there are many writers, and as many readers, who sneer at what they choose to term *"moral* verse," confounding *such*, wilfully, with a dull didacticism; but for my part, I can perceive no valid reason why a *Poet*, however passionately intense his genius, & and [sic] temperament—, should not be a Christian, and a gentleman! In default of the *latter*, Swinburne's sonorous stanzas are likely to become *"vox, et praterea nihil"*, (always excepting his *"Atalanta in Calydon"*), and as for this new "Light", *Miller*, he seems fated to illustrate the common saying of "going up like a *Rocket*, and descending like a *stick!"* You meet Dr Holmes, occasionally, I presume?—Will you courteously give him my *best regards*, and say, I shall write him soon?

Farewell, *my Dear Sir*, and may the year—'74 bring you *many blessings*.

339

And please believe that in this quarter of the World, you have no more earnest Admirer, or truer friend,

than Yours Always Faithfully
Paul Hayne

P. O. Box 635, Augusta Ga.

P. S. I formed the acquaintance, last summer, of your quaint old *Gardener;* and your *former* housekeeper, who despite her affliction, seemed intelligent still. I would like much to be remembered to them, *both*.

DAVID CROCKETT

1786–1836

Davy Crockett has existed both as a man and as a legend. The man Crockett was born in Tennessee in 1786. Having "completed" his formal schooling in six months or less, he always prided himself on his illiteracy and common sense. Crockett fought against the Creek Indians for two years under General Andrew Jackson and then served two terms in the state legislature. He was twice elected to Congress, but after being defeated in an attempt for reëlection, he became disgusted with political life. He led a group of Tennesseans into the war for the independence of Texas and was killed in the Battle of the Alamo in 1836. His heroic death made an appropriate ending for the life of a frontiersman.

Crockett's frontier background, colorful character, and political attitudes made him a fit subject for exploitation by both humorists and politicians. Because he disagreed with the political opinions of President Jackson, the Whigs found him a ready-made opponent to use in offsetting Jackson's popularity in the West. Crockett did not oppose the mythmakers; indeed, he helped them, so that the legend which developed around him began with some authentic biography. The legend reached such huge proportions that approximately fifty Crockett almanacs were published in the twenty years following his death.

340   *Sketches and Eccentricities of Col. David Crockett,* an anonymous work, was published in 1833. The most authentic of the Crockett books, for which he supplied most of the information himself, is the autobiography, *A Narrative of the Life of David Crockett of the State of Tennessee, Written by Himself* (1834). This was followed in 1835 by *An Account of Col. Crockett's Tour to*

the North and Down East and *The Life of Martin Van Buren,* both of which were
frankly political in purpose, written to offset the President's popularity on
the frontier. Their authorship has never been determined, but it is quite certain
that they were done with Crockett's sanction, if not under his direct supervision. In 1836, the year of Crockett's death, there appeared *Col. Crockett's
Exploits and Adventures in Texas,* another anonymous work, which had little, if
any, basis in fact.

from *A Narrative of the Life of David Crockett*

Bear Hunting in Tennessee

But the reader, I expect, would have no objection to know a little about my
employment during the two years while my competitor was in Congress. In
this space I had some pretty tuff times, and will relate some few things that
happened to me. So here goes, as the boy said when he run by himself.

In the fall of 1825, I concluded I would build two large boats, and load them
with pipe staves for market. So I went down to the lake, which was about
twenty-five miles from where I lived, and hired some hands to assist me, and
went to work; some at boat building, and others to getting staves. I worked on
with my hands till the bears got fat, and then I turned out to hunting, to lay
in a supply of meat. I soon killed and salted down as many as were necessary for
my family; but about this time one of my old neighbours, who had settled down
on the lake about twenty-five miles from me, came to my house and told me he
wanted me to go down and kill some bears about in his parts. He said they
were extremely fat, and very plenty. I know'd that when they were fat, they
were easily taken, for a fat bear can't run fast or long. But I asked a bear no
favours, no way, further than civility, for I now had *eight* large dogs, and as
fierce as painters; so that a bear stood no chance at all to get away from them.
So I went home with him, and then went on down towards the Mississippi, and
commenced hunting.

We were out two weeks, and in that time killed fifteen bears. Having now
supplied my friend with plenty of meat, I engaged occasionally again with my
hands in our boat building, and getting staves. But I at length couldn't stand
it any longer without another hunt. So I concluded to take my little son, and
cross over the lake, and take a hunt there. We got over, and that evening
turned out and killed three bears, in little or no time. The next morning we
drove up four forks, and made a sort of scaffold, on which we salted up our
meat, so as to have it out of the reach of the wolves, for as soon as we would
leave our camp, they would take possession. We had just eat our breakfast,
when a company of hunters came to our camp, who had fourteen dogs, but all
so poor, that when they would bark they would almost have to lean up against
a tree and take a rest. I told them their dogs couldn't run in smell of a bear,
and they had better stay at my camp, and feed them on the bones I had cut
out of my meat. I left them there, and cut out; but I hadn't gone far, when my
dogs took a first-rate start after a very large fat old *he-bear,* which run right

341

plump towards my camp. I pursued on, but my other hunters had heard my dogs coming, and met them, and killed the bear before I got up with him. I gave him to them, and cut out again for a creek called Big Clover, which wa'n't very far off. Just as I got there, and was entering a cane brake, my dogs all broke and went ahead, and, in a little time, they raised a fuss in the cane, and seemed to be going every way. I listened a while, and found my dogs was in two companies, and that both was in a snorting fight. I sent my little son to one, and I broke for t'other. I got to mine first, and found my dogs had a two-year-old bear down, a-wooling away on him; so I just took out my big butcher, and went up and slap'd it into him, and killed him without shooting. There was five of the dogs in my company. In a short time, I heard my little son fire at his bear; when I went to him he had killed it too. He had two dogs in his team. Just at this moment we heard my other dog barking a short distance off, and all the rest immediately broke to him. We pushed on too, and when we got there, we found he had still a larger bear than either of them we had killed, treed by himself. We killed that one also, which made three we had killed in less than half an hour. We turned in and butchered them, and then started to hunt for water, and a good place to camp. But we had no sooner started, than our dogs took a start after another one, and away they went like a thundergust, and was out of hearing in a minute. We followed the way they had gone for some time, but at length we gave up the hope of finding them, and turned back. As we were going back, I came to where a poor fellow was grubbing, and he looked like the very picture of hard times. I asked him what he was doing away there in the woods by himself? He said he was grubbing for a man who intended to settle there; and the reason why he did it was, that he had no meat for his family, and he was working for a little.

I was mighty sorry for the poor fellow, for it was not only a hard, but a very slow way to get meat for a hungry family; so I told him if he would go with me, I would give him more meat than he could get by grubbing in a month. I intended to supply him with meat, and also to get him to assist my little boy in packing in and salting up my bears. He had never seen a bear killed in his life. I told him I had six killed then, and my dogs were hard after another. He went off to his little cabin, which was a short distance in the brush, and his wife was very anxious he should go with me. So we started and went to where I had left my three bears, and made a camp. We then gathered my meat and salted, and scaffled it, as I had done the other. Night now came on, but no word from my dogs yet. I afterwards found they had treed the bear about five miles off, near to a man's house, and had barked at it the whole enduring night. Poor fellows! many a time they looked for me, and wondered why I didn't come, for they knowed there was no mistake in me, and I know'd they were as good as ever fluttered. In the morning, as soon as it was light enough to see, the man took his gun and went to them, and shot the bear, and killed it. My dogs, however, wouldn't have any thing to say to this stranger; so they

342   left him, and came early in the morning back to me.

We got our breakfast, and cut out again; and we killed four large and very fat bears that day. We hunted out the week, and in that time we killed seventeen, all of them first-rate. When we closed our hunt, I gave the man over a thousand weight of fine fat bear-meat, which pleased him mightily, and made him feel as rich as a Jew. I saw him the next fall, and he told me he had plenty of meat to do him the whole year from his week's hunt. My son and me now went home. This was the week between Christmass and New-year that we made this hunt.

When I got home, one of my neighbours was out of meat and wanted me to go back, and let him go with me, to take another hunt. I couldn't refuse; but I told him I was afraid the bear had taken to house by that time, for after they get very fat in the fall and early part of the winter, they go into their holes, in large hollow trees, or into hollow logs, or their cane-houses, or the harricanes; and lie there till spring, like frozen snakes. And one thing about this will seem mighty strange to many people. From about the first of January to about the last of April, these varments lie in their holes altogether. In all that time they have no food to eat; and yet when they come out, they are not an ounce lighter than when they went to house. I don't know the cause of this, and still I know it is a fact; and I leave it for others who have more learning than myself to account for it. They have not a particle of food with them, but they just lie and suck the bottom of their paw all the time. I have killed many of them in their trees, which enables me to speak positively on this subject. However, my neighbour, whose name was McDaniel, and my little son and me, went on down to the lake to my second camp, where I had killed my seventeen bears the week before, and turned out to hunting. But we hunted hard all day without getting a single start. We had carried but little provisions with us, and the next morning was entirely out of meat. I sent my son about three miles off, to the house of an old friend, to get some. The old gentleman was much pleased to hear I was hunting in those parts, for the year before the bears had killed a great many of his hogs. He was that day killing his bacon hogs, and so he gave my son some meat, and sent word to me that I must come in to his house that evening, that he would have plenty of feed for my dogs, and some accommodations for ourselves; but before my son got back, we had gone out hunting, and in a large cane brake my dogs found a big bear in a cane-house, which he had fixed for his winter-quarters, as they sometimes do.

When my lead dog found him, and raised the yell, all the rest broke to him, but none of them entered his house until we got up. I encouraged my dogs, and they knowed me so well, that I could have made them seize the old serpent himself, with all his horns and heads, and cloven foot and ugliness into the bargain, if he would only have come to light, so that they could have seen him. They bulged in, and in an instant the bear followed them out, and I told my friend to shoot him, as he was mighty wrathy to kill a bear. He did so, and killed him prime. We carried him to our camp, by which time my son had returned; and after we got our dinners we packed up, and cut for the house of my old friend, whose name was Davidson.

We got there, and staid with him that night; and the next morning, having salted up our meat, we left it with him, and started to take a hunt between the Obion lake and the Red-foot lake; as there had been a dreadful harricane, which passed between them, and I was sure there must be a heap of bears in the fallen timber. We had gone about five miles without seeing any sign at all; but at length we got on some high cany ridges, and, as we rode along, I saw a hole in a large black oak, and on examining more closely, I discovered that

343

a bear had clomb the tree. I could see his tracks going up, but none coming down, and so I was sure he was in there. A person who is acquainted with bear-hunting, can tell easy enough when the varment is in the hollow; for as they go up they don't slip a bit, but as they come down they make long scratches with their nails.

My friend was a little ahead of me, but I called him back, and told him there was a bear in that tree, and I must have him out. So we lit from our horses, and I found a small tree which I thought I could fall so as to lodge against my bear tree, and we fell to work chopping it with our tomahawks. I intended, when we lodged the tree against the other, to let my little son go up, and look into the hole, for he could climb like a squirrel. We had chop'd on a little time and stop'd to rest, when I heard my dogs barking mighty severe at some distance from us, and I told my friend I knowed they had a bear; for it is the nature of a dog, when he finds you are hunting bears, to hunt for nothing else; he becomes fond of the meat, and considers other game as "not worth a notice," as old Johnson said of the devil.

We concluded to leave our tree a bit, and went to my dogs, and when we got there, sure enough they had an eternal great big fat bear up a tree, just ready for shooting. My friend again petitioned me for liberty to shoot this one also. I had a little rather not, as the bear was so big, but I couldn't refuse; and so he blazed away, and down came the old fellow like some great log had fell. I now missed one of my dogs, the same that I before spoke of as having treed the bear by himself sometime before, when I had started the three in the cane brake. I told my friend that my missing dog had a bear somewhere, just as sure as fate; so I left them to butcher the one we had just killed, and I went up on a piece of high ground to listen for my dog. I heard him barking with all his might some distance off, and I pushed ahead for him. My other dogs hearing him broke to him, and when I got there, sure enough again he had another bear ready treed; if he hadn't, I wish I may be shot. I fired on him, and brought him down; and then went back, and help'd finish butchering the one at which I had left my friend. We then packed both to our tree where we had left my boy. By this time, the little fellow had cut the tree down that we intended to lodge, but it fell the wrong way; he had then feather'd in on the big tree, to cut that, and had found that it was nothing but a shell on the outside, and all doted in the middle, as too many of our big men are in these days, having only an outside appearance. My friend and my son cut away on it, and I went off about a hundred yards with my dogs to keep them from running under the tree when it should fall. On looking back at the hole, I saw the bear's head out of it, looking down at them as they were cutting. I hollered to them to look up, and they did so; and McDaniel catched up his gun, but by this time the bear was out, and coming down the tree. He fired at it, and as soon as it touch'd ground the dogs were all round it, and they had a roll-and-tumble fight to the foot of the hill, where they stop'd him. I ran up, and putting my gun against the bear, fired and killed him. We now had three, and so we made our scaffold and salted them up.

In the morning I left my son at the camp, and we started on towards the harricane; and when we had went about a mile, we started a very large bear, but we got along mighty slow on account of the cracks in the earth occasioned by the earthquakes. We, however, made out to keep in hearing of the dogs for about three miles, and then we come to the harricane. Here we had to quit our horses, as old Nick himself couldn't have got through it without sneaking it along in the form that he put on, to make a fool of our old grandmother Eve. By this time several of my dogs had got tired and come back; but we went ahead on foot for some little time in the harricane, when we met a bear coming straight to us, and not more than twenty or thirty yards off. I started my tired dogs after him, and McDaniel pursued them, and I went on to where my other dogs were. I had seen the track of the bear they were after, and I knowed he was a screamer. I followed on to about the middle of the harricane, but my dogs pursued him so close, that they made him climb an old stump about twenty feet high. I got in shooting distance of him and fired, but I was all over in such a flutter from fatigue and running, that I couldn't hold steady; but, however, I broke his shoulder, and he fell. I run up and loaded my gun as quick as possible, and shot him again and killed him. When I went to take out my knife to butcher him, I found I had lost it in coming through the harricane. The vines and briers was so thick that I would sometimes have to get down and crawl like a varment to get through at all; and a vine had, as I supposed, caught in the handle and pulled it out. While I was standing and studying what to do, my friend came to me. He had followed my trail through the harricane, and had found my knife, which was mighty good news to me; as a hunter hates the worst in the world to lose a good dog, or any part of his hunting-tools. I now left McDaniel to butcher the bear, and I went after our horses, and brought them as near as the nature of case would allow. I then took our bags, and went back to where he was; and when we had skin'd the bear, we fleeced off the fat and carried it to our horses at several loads. We then packed it up on our horses, and had a heavy pack of it on each one. We now started and went on till about sunset, when I concluded we must be near our camp; so I hollered and my son answered me, and we moved on in the direction to the camp. We had gone but a little way when I heard my dogs make a warm start again; and I jumped down from my horse and gave him up to my friend, and told him I would follow them. He went on to the camp, and I went ahead after my dogs with all my might for a considerable distance, till at last night came on. The woods were very rough and hilly, and all covered over with cane.

I now was compel'd to move on more slowly; and was frequently falling over logs, and into the cracks made by the earthquakes, so that I was very much afraid I would break my gun. However I went on about three miles, when I came to a good big creek, which I waded. It was very cold, and the creek was about knee-deep; but I felt no great inconvenience from it just then, as I was all over wet with sweat from running, and I felt hot enough. After I got over the creek and out of the cane, which was very thick on all our creeks, I listened for my dogs. I found they had either treed or brought the bear to a stop, as they continued barking in the same place. I pushed on as near in the direction to the noise as I could, till I found the hill was too steep for me to climb, and so I backed and went down the creek some distance till I came to a hollow, and then took up that, till I come to a place where I could climb up the hill. It was mighty dark, and was difficult to see my way or any thing else. When I got up the hill, I found I had passed the dogs; and so I turned and went to them. I found, when I got there, they had treed the bear in a large forked poplar, and it was setting in the fork.

345

THE CONFEDERATE SOUTH

I could see the lump, but not plain enough to shoot with any certainty, as there was no moonlight; and so I set in to hunting for some dry brush to make me a light; but I could find none, though I could find that the ground was torn mightily to pieces by the cracks.

At last I thought I could shoot by guess, and kill him; so I pointed as near the lump as I could, and fired away. But the bear didn't come; he only clomb up higher, and got out on a limb, which helped me to see him better. I now loaded up again and fired, but this time he didn't move at all. I commenced loading for a third fire, but the first thing I knowed, the bear was down among my dogs, and they were fighting all around me. I had my big butcher in my belt, and I had a pair of dressed buckskin breeches on. So I took out my knife, and stood, determined, if he should get hold of me, to defend myself in the best way I could. I stood there for some time, and could now and then see a white dog I had, but the rest of them, and the bear, which were dark coloured, I couldn't see at all, it was so miserable dark. They still fought around me, and sometimes within three feet of me; but, at last, the bear got down into one of the cracks, that the earthquakes had made in the ground, about four feet deep, and I could tell the biting end of him by the hollering of my dogs. So I took my gun and pushed the muzzle of it about, till I thought I had it against the main part of his body, and fired; but it happened to be only the fleshy part of his foreleg. With this, he jumped out of the crack, and he and the dogs had another hard fight around me, as before. At last, however, they forced him back into the crack again, as he was when I had shot.

I had laid down my gun in the dark, and I now began to hunt for it; and, while hunting, I got hold of a pole, and I concluded I would punch him awhile with that. I did so, and when I would punch him, the dogs would jump in on him, when he would bite them badly, and they would jump out again. I concluded, as he would take punching so patiently, it might be that he would lie still enough for me to get down in the crack, and feel slowly along till I could find the right place to give him a dig with my butcher. So I got down, and my dogs got in before him and kept his head towards them, till I got along easily up to him; and placing my hand on his rump, felt for his shoulder, just behind which I intended to stick him. I made a lunge with my long knife, and fortunately stuck him right through the heart; at which he just sank down, and I crawled out in a hurry. In a little time my dogs all come out too, and seemed satisfied, which was the way they always had of telling me that they had finished him.

I suffered very much that night with cold, as my leather breeches, and every thing else I had on, was wet and frozen. But I managed to get my bear out of this crack after several hard trials, and so I butchered him, and laid down to try to sleep. But my fire was very bad, and I couldn't find any thing that would burn well to make it any better; and I concluded I should freeze, if I didn't warm myself in some way by exercise. So I got up, and hollered a while, and then I would just jump up and down with all my might, and throw myself into all sorts of motions. But all this wouldn't do; for my blood was now getting cold, and the chills coming all over me. I was so tired, too, that I could hardly walk; but I thought I would do the best I could to save my life, and then, if I died, nobody would be to blame. So I went to a tree about two feet through, and not a limb on it for thirty

346

feet, and I would climb up it to the limbs, and then lock my arms together around it, and slide down to the bottom again. This would make the insides of my legs and arms feel mighty warm and good. I continued this till daylight in the morning, and how often I clomb up my tree and slid down I don't know, but I reckon at least a hundred times.

In the morning I got my bear hung up so as to be safe, and then set out to hunt for my camp. I found it after a while, and McDaniel and my son were very much rejoiced to see me get back, for they were about to give me up for lost. We got our breakfasts, and then secured our meat by building a high scaffold, and covering it over. We had no fear of its spoiling, for the weather was so cold that it couldn't.

We now started after my other bear, which had caused me so much trouble and suffering; and before we got him, we got a start after another, and took him also. We went on to the creek I had crossed the night before and camped, and then went to where my bear was, that I had killed in the crack. When we examined the place, McDaniel said he wouldn't have gone into it, as I did, for all the bears in the woods.

We took the meat down to our camp and salted it, and also the last one we had killed; intending, in the morning, to make a hunt in the harricane again.

We prepared for resting that night, and I can assure the reader I was in need of it. We had laid down by our fire, and about ten o'clock there came a most terrible earthquake, which shook the earth so, that we were rocked about like we had been in a cradle. We were very much alarmed; for though we were accustomed to feel earthquakes, we were now right in the region which had been torn to pieces by them in 1812, and we thought it might take a notion and swallow us up, like the big fish did Jonah.

In the morning we packed up and moved to the harricane, where we made another camp, and turned out that evening and killed a very large bear, which made *eight* we had now killed in this hunt.

The next morning we entered the harricane again, and in little or no time my dogs were in full cry. We pursued them, and soon came to a thick cane-brake, in which they had stop'd their bear. We got up close to him, as the cane was so thick that we couldn't see more than a few feet. Here I made my friend hold the cane a little open with his gun till I shot the bear, which was a mighty large one. I killed him dead in his tracks. We got him out and butchered him, and in a little time started another and killed him, which now made *ten* we had killed; and we know'd we couldn't pack any more home, as we had only five horses along; therefore we returned to the camp and salted up all our meat, to be ready for a start homeward next morning.

The morning came, and we packed our horses with the meat, and had as much as they could possibly carry, and sure enough cut out for home. It was about thirty miles, and we reached home the second day. I had now accommodated my neighbour with meat enough to do him, and had killed in all, up to that time, fifty-eight bears, during the fall and winter.

As soon as the time come for them to quit their houses and come out again in the spring, I took a notion to hunt a little more, and in about one month I killed forty-seven more, which made one hundred and five bears I had killed in less than one year from that time. (*1834*)

347

A Useful Coon-Skin

While on the subject of election matters, I will relate a little anecdote about myself, which will show the people to the East how we manage these things on the frontiers. It was when I first run for Congress; I was then in favor of the Hero, (Andrew Jackson), for he had chalked out his course so sleek in his letter to the Tennessee legislature that, like Sam Patch, says I, "There can be no mistake in him," and so I went ahead. No one dreamt about the monster and the deposits at that time, and so, as I afterward found, many like myself were taken in by these fair promises, which were worth about as much as a flash in the pan when you have a fair shot at a fat bear.

But I am losing sight of my story. Well, I started off to the Cross Roads dressed in my hunting shirt, and my rifle on my shoulder. Many of our constituents had assembled there to get a taste of the quality of the candidates at orating. Job Snelling, a gander-shanked Yankee, who had been caught somewhere about Plymouth Bay, and been shipped to the West with a cargo of codfish and rum, erected a large shantee, and set up shop for the occasion. A large posse of the voters had assembled before I arrived, and my opponent had already made considerable headway with his speechifying and his treating, when they spied me about a rifle shot from camp, sauntering along as if I was not a party in business. "There comes Crockett," cried one. "Let us hear the colonel," cried another; and so I mounted the stump that had been cut down for the occasion, and began to bushwhack in the most approved style.

I had not been up long before there was such an uproar in the crowd that I could not hear my own voice, and some of my constituents let me know that they could not listen to me on such a dry subject as the welfare of the nation until they had something to drink, and that I must treat them. Accordingly I jumped down from the rostrum, and led the way to the shantee, followed by my constituents, shouting, "Huzza for Crockett!" and "Crockett forever!"

When we entered the shantee Job was busy dealing out his rum in a style that showed he was making a good day's work of it, and I called for a quart of the best; but the crooked crittur returned no other answer than by pointing to a board over the bar, on which he had chalked in large letters, *"Pay to-day and trust to-morrow."* Now that idea brought me up all standing; it was a sort of cornering in which there was no back-out, for ready money in the West, in those times, was the shyest thing in all natur, and it was most particularly shy with me on that occasion.

The voters, seeing my predicament, fell off to the other side, and I was left deserted and alone, as the Government will be, when he no longer has any offices to bestow. I saw as plain as day that the tide of popular opinion was against me, and that unless I got some rum speedily I should lose my election as sure as there are snakes in Virginny; and it must be done soon, or even burnt brandy wouldn't save me. So I walked away from the shantee, but in another manner from the way I entered it, for on this occasion I had no train after me, and not a voice shouted, "Huzza for Crockett!" Popularity sometimes depends on a very

348

From Henry Watterson, Oddities in Southern Life and Character (Boston, 1882). There apparently is no record of the original source of this story, but Watterson regarded it as an authentic Crockett anecdote, and it has been generally accepted as such.

small matter indeed; in this particular it was worth a quart of New England rum, and no more.

Well, knowing that a crisis was at hand, I struck into the woods, with my rifle on my shoulder, my best friend in time of need; and, as good fortune would have it, I had not been out more than a quarter of an hour before I treed a fat coon, and in the pulling of a trigger he lay dead at the foot of the tree. I soon whipped his hairy jacket off his back, and again bent my steps towards the shantee, and walked up to the bar, but not alone, for this time I had half a dozen of my constituents at my heels. I threw down the coon-skin upon the counter, and called for a quart, and Job, though busy dealing out rum, forgot to point at his chalked rules and regulations; for he knew that a coon was as good a legal tender for a quart in the West as a New York shilling any day in the year.

My constituents now flocked about me, and cried, "Huzza for Crockett!" "Crockett forever!" and finding the tide had taken a turn, I told them several yarns to get them in a good humour; and having soon dispatched the value of the coon, I went out and mounted the stump without opposition, and a clear majority of the voters followed me to hear what I had to offer for the good of the nation. Before I was half through one of my constituents moved that they would hear the balance of my speech after they had washed down the first part with some more of Job Snelling's extract of cornstalk and molasses, and the question being put, it was carried unanimously. It wasn't considered necessary to tell the yeas and nays, so we adjourned to the shantee, and on the way I began to reckon that the fate of the nation pretty much depended upon my shooting another coon.

While standing at the bar, feeling sort of bashful while Job's rules and regulations stared me in the face, I cast down my eyes, and discovered one end of the coon-skin sticking between the logs that supported the bar. Job had slung it there in the hurry of business. I gave it a sort of quick jerk, and it followed my hand as natural as if I had been the rightful owner. I slapped it on the counter, and Job, little dreaming that he was barking up the wrong tree, shoved along another bottle, which my constituents quickly disposed of with great good humour, for some of them saw the trick; and then we withdrew to the rostrum to discuss the affairs of the nation.

I don't know how it was, but the voters soon became dry again, and nothing would do but we must adjourn to the shantee; and as luck would have it, the coon-skin was still sticking between the logs, as if Job had flung it there on purpose to tempt me. I was not slow in raising it to the counter, the rum followed, of course, and I wish I may be shot if I didn't, before the day was over, get ten quarts for the same identical skin, and from a fellow, too, who in those parts was considered as sharp as a steel trap and as bright as a pewter button.

This joke secured me my election, for it soon circulated like smoke among my constituents, and they allowed, with one accord, that the man who could get the whip hand of Job Snelling in fair trade, could outwit Old Nick himself, and was the real grit for them in Congress. Job was by no means popular; he boasted of always being wide awake, and that any one who could take him in was free to do so, for he came from a stock that, sleeping or waking, had always one eye open, and the other not more than half closed. The whole family were geniuses. His father was the inventor of wooden nutmegs, by which Job said he might have made a fortune, if he had only taken out a patent and kept the business in his

349

own hands; his mother, Patience, manufactured the first white oak pumpkin seeds of the mammoth kind, and turned a pretty penny the first season; and his aunt Prudence was the first to discover that corn husks, steeped into tobacco water, would make as handsome Spanish wrappers as ever came from Havana, and that oak leaves would answer all the purpose of filling, for no one could discover the difference except the man who smoked them, and then it would be too late to make a stir about it. Job himself bragged of having made some useful discoveries, the most profitable of which was the art of converting mahogany sawdust into cayenne pepper, which he said was a profitable and safe business; for the people have been so long accustomed to having dust thrown in their eyes that there wasn't much danger of being found out.

The way I got to the blind side of the Yankee merchant was pretty generally known before election day, and the result was that my opponent might as well have whistled jigs to a milestone as attempt to beat up for votes in that district. I beat him out and out, quite back into the old year, and there was scarce enough left of him, after the canvass was over, to make a small grease spot. He disappeared without even leaving a mark behind; and such will be the fate of Adam Huntsman, if there is a fair fight and no gouging.

After the election was over, I sent Snelling the price of the rum, but took good care to keep the fact from the knowledge of my constituents. Job refused the money, and sent me word that it did him good to be taken in occasionally, as it served to brighten his ideas; but I afterwards learnt when he found out the trick that had been played upon him, he put all the rum I had ordered in his bill against my opponent, who, being elated with the speeches he had made on the affairs of the nation, could not descend to examine into the particulars of a bill of a vender of rum in the small way. (*1882*)

AUGUSTUS BALDWIN LONGSTREET

1790–1870

350 "Judge Longstreet," as he was later to be called, was born in Augusta, Georgia. His interest in books was slow in developing, but at the age of eighteen he entered an academy in Willington, South Carolina, where he studied for two years. In 1813, influenced by his friend John C. Calhoun, he entered Yale, and upon completing his course of study there, attended the Law School at Litchfield, Connecticut. He returned to Georgia in 1814.

As a practicing attorney, Longstreet was very successful and soon won many friends. He was elected to the legislature, and from 1822 to 1825 served as judge of the superior court in his state. He also became a devout Methodist at this time and in 1838 was ordained a minister. From 1839 to 1861, Longstreet served successively as president of four different colleges: Emory; Centenary, in Jackson, Louisiana; the University of Mississippi; and the University of South Carolina. Despite his many fields of activity, however, his political interests never waned. He was known as an outspoken advocate of Nullification.

Longstreet's numerous political and religious pronouncements are rewarding to the social historian, but his primary value in any representation of Southern letters is as a pioneer in the field of native humor. As early as 1827 he began publishing his *Georgia Scenes*, a series of sketches which purported to represent life in his state as it had been half a century before. First appearing in the *Southern Recorder*, the sketches proved amazingly popular, and in 1835 were collected and published in book form.

In a sense, Longstreet's role was that of an outsider—that is, of a formally educated person—describing, after the manner of Byrd, the antics of relative illiterates. Without his precedent, the work of his followers, including Mark Twain and the local colorists, might have taken a different and less rewarding course.

from Georgia Scenes

The Fight

In the younger days of the Republic there lived in the county of ———— two men, who were admitted on all hands to be the very *best men* in the county; which, in the Georgia vocabulary, means they could flog any other two men in the county. Each, through many a hard-fought battle, had acquired the mastery of his own battalion; but they lived on opposite sides of the Courthouse, and in different battalions: consequently, they were but seldom thrown together. When they met, however, they were always very friendly; indeed, at their first interview, they seemed to conceive a wonderful attachment to each other, which rather increased than diminished as they became better acquainted; so that, but for the circumstance which I am about to mention, the question, which had been a thousand times asked, "Which is the best man, Billy Stallions (Stallings) or Bob Durham?" would probably never have been answered.

Billy ruled the upper battalion, and Bob the lower. The former measured six feet and an inch in his stockings, and, without a single pound of cumbrous flesh about him, weighed a hundred and eighty. The latter was an inch shorter than his rival, and ten pounds lighter; but he was much the most active of the two. In running and jumping he had but few equals in the county; and in wrestling, not one. In other respects they were nearly equal. Both were admirable specimens of human nature in its finest form. Billy's victories had generally been achieved by the tremendous power of his blows, one of which had often proved decisive of his battles; Bob's, by his adroitness in bringing his adversary to the ground. This advantage he had never failed to gain at the onset, and, when gained, he never

351

failed to improve it to the defeat of his adversary. These points of difference have involved the reader in a doubt as to the probable issue of a contest between them. It was not so, however, with the two battalions. Neither had the least difficulty in determining the point by the most natural and irresistible deductions *a priori;* and though, by the same course of reasoning, they arrived at directly opposite conclusions, neither felt its confidence in the least shaken by this circumstance. The upper battalion swore "that Billy only wanted one lick at him to knock his heart, liver, and lights out of him; and if he got two at him, he'd knock him into a cocked hat." The lower battalion retorted, "that he wouldn't have time to double his fist before Bob would put his head where his feet ought to be; and that, by the time he hit the ground, the meat would fly off his face so quick, that people would think it was shook off by the fall." These disputes often led to the *argumentum ad hominem*,[1] but with such equality of success on both sides as to leave the main question just where they found it. They usually ended, however, in the common way, with a bet; and many a quart of old Jamaica (whiskey had not then supplanted rum) were staked upon the issue. Still, greatly to the annoyance of the curious, Billy and Bob continued to be good friends.

Now there happened to reside in the county just alluded to a little fellow by the name of Ransy Sniffle: a sprout of Richmond, who, in his earlier days, had fed copiously upon red clay and blackberries. This diet had given to Ransy a complexion that a corpse would have disdained to own, and an abdominal rotundity that was quite unprepossessing. Long spells of the fever and ague, too, in Ransy's youth, had conspired with clay and blackberries to throw him quite out of the order of nature. His shoulders were fleshless and elevated; his head large and flat; his neck slim and translucent; and his arms, hands, fingers, and feet were lengthened out of all proportion to the rest of his frame. His joints were large and his limbs small; and as for flesh, he could not, with propriety, be said to have any. Those parts which nature usually supplies with the most of this article—the calves of the legs, for example—presented in him the appearance of so many well-drawn blisters. His height was just five feet nothing; and his average weight in blackberry season, ninety-five. I have been thus particular in describing him, for the purpose of showing what a great matter a little fire sometimes kindleth. There was nothing on this earth which delighted Ransy so much as a fight. He never seemed fairly alive except when he was witnessing, fomenting, or talking about a fight. Then, indeed, his deep-sunken gray eye assumed something of a living fire, and his tongue acquired a volubility that bordered upon eloquence. Ransy had been kept for more than a year in the most torturing suspense as to the comparative manhood of Billy Stallings and Bob Durham. He had resorted to all his usual expedients to bring them in collision, and had entirely failed. He had faithfully reported to Bob all that had been said by the people in the upper battalion "agin him," and "he was sure Billy Stallings started it. He heard Billy say himself to Jim Brown, that he could whip him, *or any other man in his battalion;*" and this he told to Bob; adding, "Dod darn his soul, if he was a little bigger, if he'd let any man *put upon* his battalion in such a way." Bob replied, "If he (Stallings) thought so, he'd better come and try it." This Ransy carried to Billy, and delivered it with a spirit becoming his own dignity and the character of his battalion, and with a colouring well calculated to give it effect.

---

[1] *Argument using an opponent's own words or acts in support of one's views.*

These, and many other schemes which Ransy laid for the gratification of his curiosity, entirely failed of their object. Billy and Bob continued friends, and Ransy had begun to lapse into the most tantalizing and hopeless despair, when a circumstance occurred which led to a settlement of the long-disputed question.

It is said that a hundred gamecocks will live in perfect harmony together if you do not put a hen with them; and so it would have been with Billy and Bob, had there been no women in the world. But there were women in the world, and from them each of our heroes had taken to himself a wife. The good ladies were no strangers to the prowess of their husbands, and, strange as it may seem, they presumed a little upon it.

The two battalions had met at the Courthouse upon a regimental parade. The two champions were there, and their wives had accompanied them. Neither knew the other's lady, nor were the ladies known to each other. The exercises of the day were just over, when Mrs. Stallings and Mrs. Durham stepped simultaneously into the store of Zephaniah Atwater, from "down east."

"Have you any Turkey-red?" said Mrs. S.

"Have you any curtain calico?" said Mrs. D. at the same moment.

"Yes, ladies," said Mr. Atwater, "I have both."

"Then help me first," said Mrs. D., "for I'm in a hurry."

"I'm in as great a hurry as she is," said Mrs. S., "and I'll thank you to help me first."

"And, pray, who are you, madam?" continued the other.

"Your better, madam," was the reply.

At this moment Billy Stallings stepped in. "Come," said he, "Nancy, let's be going; it's getting late."

"I'd a been gone half an hour ago," she replied, "if it hadn't a' been for that impudent huzzy."

"Who do you call an impudent huzzy, you nasty, good-for-nothing, snaggle-toothed gaub of fat, you?" returned Mrs. D.

"Look here, woman," said Billy, "have you got a husband here? If you have, I'll *lick* him till he learns to teach you better manners, you *sassy* heifer you." At this moment something was seen to rush out of the store as if ten thousand hornets were stinging it; crying, "Take care—let me go—don't hold me—where's Bob Durham?" It was Ransy Sniffle, who had been listening in breathless delight to all that had passed.

"Yonder's Bob, setting on the Courthouse steps," cried one. "What's the matter?"

"Don't talk to me!" said Ransy. "Bob Durham, you'd better go long yonder, and take care of your wife. They're playing h——l with her there, in Zeph Atwater's store. Dod eternally darn my soul, if any man was to talk to my wife as Bill Stallions is talking to yours, if I wouldn't drive blue blazes through him in less than no time."

Bob sprang to the store in a minute, followed by a hundred friends; for the bully of a county never wants friends.

"Bill Stallions," said Bob, as he entered, "what have you been saying to my wife?"

"Is that your wife?" inquired Billy, obviously much surprised and a little disconcerted.

353

"Yes, she is, and no man shall abuse her, I don't care who he is."

"Well," rejoined Billy, "it an't worth while to go over it; I've said enough for a fight: and, if you'll step out, we'll settle it!"

"Billy," said Bob, "are you for a fair fight?"

"I am," said Billy. "I've heard much of your manhood, and I believe I'm a better man than you are. If you will go into a ring with me, we can soon settle the dispute."

"Choose your friends," said Bob; "make your ring, and I'll be in with mine as soon as you will."

They both stepped out, and began to strip very deliberately, each battalion gathering round its champion, except Ransy, who kept himself busy in a most honest endeavour to hear and see all that transpired in both groups at the same time. He ran from one to the other in quick succession; peeped here and listened there; talked to this one, then to that one, and then to himself; squatted under one's legs and another's arms and, in the short interval between stripping and stepping into the ring, managed to get himself trod on by half of both battalions. But Ransy was not the only one interested upon this occasion; the most intense interest prevailed everywhere. Many were the conjectures, doubts, oaths, and imprecations uttered while the parties were preparing for the combat. All the knowing ones were consulted as to the issue, and they all agreed, to a man, in one of two opinions: either that Bob would flog Billy, or Billy would flog Bob. We must be permitted, however, to dwell for a moment upon the opinion of Squire Thomas Loggins; a man who, it was said, had never failed to predict the issue of a fight in all his life. Indeed, so unerring had he always proved in this regard, that it would have been counted the most obstinate infidelity to doubt for a moment after he had delivered himself. Squire Loggins was a man who said but little, but that little was always delivered with the most imposing solemnity of look and cadence. He always wore the aspect of profound thought, and you could not look at him without coming to the conclusion that he was elaborating truth from its most intricate combinations.

"Uncle Tommy," said Sam Reynolds, "you can tell us all about it if you will; how will the fight go?"

The question immediately drew an anxious group around the squire. He raised his teeth slowly from the head of his walking cane, on which they had been resting; pressed his lips closely and thoughtfully together; threw down his eyebrows, dropped his chin, raised his eyes to an angle of twenty-three degrees, paused about half a minute, and replied, "Sammy, watch Robert Durham close in the beginning of the fight; take care of William Stallions in the middle of it; and see who has the wind at the end." As he uttered the last member of the sentence, he looked slyly at Bob's friends, and winked very significantly; whereupon they rushed, with one accord, to tell Bob what Uncle Tommy had said. As they retired, the squire turned to Billy's friends, and said, with a smile, "Them boys think I mean that Bob will whip."

354

Here the other party kindled into joy, and hastened to inform Billy how Bob's friends had deceived themselves as to Uncle Tommy's opinion. In the meantime the principals and seconds were busily employed in preparing themselves for the combat. The plan of attack and defence, the manner of improving the various turns of the conflict, "the best mode of saving wind," &c., &c., were all discussed and settled. At length Billy announced himself ready, and his crowd were seen moving to the centre of the Courthouse Square; he and his five seconds in the rear. At the same time, Bob's party moved to the same point, and in the same order. The ring was now formed, and for a moment the silence of death reigned through both battalions. It was soon interrupted, however, by the cry of "Clear the way!" from Billy's seconds; when the ring opened in the centre of the upper battalion (for the order of march had arranged the centre of the two battalions on opposite sides of the circle), and Billy stepped into the ring from the east, followed by his friends. He was stripped to the trousers, and exhibited an arm, breast, and shoulders of the most tremendous portent. His step was firm, daring, and martial; and as he bore his fine form a little in advance of his friends, an involuntary burst of triumph broke from his side of the ring; and, at the same moment, an uncontrollable thrill of awe ran along the whole curve of the lower battalion.

"Look at him!" was heard from his friends; "just look at him."

"Ben, how much you ask to stand before that man two seconds?"

"Pshaw, don't talk about it! Just thinkin' about it's broke three o' my ribs a'ready!"

"What's Bob Durham going to do when Billy lets that arm loose upon him?"

"God bless your soul, he'll think thunder and lightning a mint-julep to it."

"Oh, look here, men, go take Bill Stallions out o' that ring, and bring in Phil Johnson's stud horse, so that Durham may have some chance! I don't want to see the man killed right away."

These and many other like expressions, interspersed thickly with oaths of the most modern coinage, were coming from all points of the upper battalion, while Bob was adjusting the girth of his pantaloons, which walking had discovered not to be exactly right. It was just fixed to his mind, his foes becoming a little noisy, and his friends a little uneasy at his delay, when Billy called out, with a smile of some meaning, "Where's the bully of the lower battalion? I'm getting tired of waiting."

"Here he is," said Bob, lighting, as it seemed, from the clouds into the ring, for he had actually bounded clear of the head of Ransy Sniffle into the circle. His descent was quite as imposing as Billy's entry, and excited the same feelings, but in opposite bosoms.

Voices of exultation now rose on his side.

"Where did he come from?"

"Why," said one of his seconds (all having just entered), "we were girting him up, about a hundred yards out yonder, when he heard Billy ask for the bully; and he fetched a leap over the Courthouse, and went out of sight; but I told them to come on, they'd find him here."

Here the lower battalion burst into a peal of laughter, mingled with a look of admiration, which seemed to denote their entire belief of what they had heard.

"Boys, widen the ring, so as to give him room to jump."

"Oh, my little flying wild-cat, hold him if you can! and, when you get him fast, holding lightning next."

"Ned, what do you think he's made of?"

355

"Steel springs and chicken-hawk, God bless you!"

"Gentlemen," said one of Bob's seconds, "I understand it is to be a fair fight; catch as catch can, rough and tumble: no man touch till one or the other halloos."

"That's the rule," was the reply from the other side.

"Are you ready?"

"We are ready."

"Then blaze away, my game cocks!"

At the word, Bob dashed at his antagonist at full speed; and Bill squared himself to receive him with one of his most fatal blows. Making his calculation, from Bob's velocity, of the time when he would come within striking distance, he let drive with tremendous force. But Bob's onset was obviously planned to avoid this blow; for, contrary to all expectations, he stopped short just out of arm's reach, and, before Billy could recover his balance, Bob had him "all under-hold." The next second, sure enough, "Found Billy's head where his feet ought to be." How it was done no one could tell; but, as if by supernatural power, both Billy's feet were thrown full half his own height in the air, and he came down with a force that seemed to shake the earth. As he struck the ground, commingled shouts, screams, and yells burst from the lower battalion, loud enough to be heard for miles. "Hurra, my little hornet!" "Save him!" "Feed him!" "Give him the Durham physic till his stomach turns!" Billy was no sooner down than Bob was on him, and lending him awful blows about the face and breast. Billy made two efforts to rise by main strength, but failed. "Lord bless you, man, don't try to get up! *Lay* still and take it! you *bleege* to have it!"

Billy now turned his face suddenly to the ground, and rose upon his hands and knees. Bob jerked up both his hands and threw him on his face. He again recovered his late position, of which Bob endeavoured to deprive him as before; but, missing one arm, he failed, and Billy rose. But he had scarcely resumed his feet before they flew up as before, and he came again to the ground. "No fight, gentlemen!" cried Bob's friends; "the man can't stand up! Bouncing feet are bad things to fight in." His fall, however, was this time comparatively light; for, having thrown his right arm round Bob's neck, he carried his head down with him. This grasp, which was obstinately maintained, prevented Bob from getting on him, and they lay head to head, seeming, for a time, to do nothing. Presently they rose, as if by mutual consent; and, as they rose, a shout burst from both battalions. "Oh, my lark!" cried the east, "has he foxed you? Do you begin to feel him? He's only beginning to fight; he ain't got warm yet."

"Look yonder!" cried the west; "didn't I tell you so! He hit the ground so hard it jarred his nose off. Now ain't he a pretty man as he stands? He shall have my sister Sal just for his pretty looks. I want to get in the breed of them sort o' men, to drive ugly out of my kinfolks."

I looked, and saw that Bob had entirely lost his left ear, and a large piece from his left cheek. His right eye was a little discoloured, and the blood flowed profusely from his wounds.

356 Bill presented a hideous spectacle. About a third of his nose, at the lower extremity, was bit off, and his face so swelled and bruised that it was difficult to discover in it anything of the human visage, much more the fine features which he carried into the ring.

They were up only long enough for me to make the foregoing discoveries, when down they went again, precisely as before. They no sooner touched the ground than Bill relinquished his hold upon Bob's neck. In this he seemed to all to have forfeited the only advantage which put him upon an equality with his adversary. But the movement was soon explained. Bill wanted this arm for other purposes than defence; and he had made arrangements whereby he knew that he could make it answer these purposes; for, when they rose again, he had the middle finger of Bob's left hand in his mouth. He was now secure from Bob's annoying trips; and he began to lend his adversary tremendous blows, every one of which was hailed by a shout from his friends. "Bullets!" "*Hoss*-kicking!" "Thunder!" "That'll do for his face; now feel his short ribs, Billy!"

I now considered the contest settled. I deemed it impossible for any human being to withstand for five seconds the loss of blood which issued from Bob's ear, cheek, nose, and finger, accompanied with such blows as he was receiving. Still he maintained the conflict, and gave blow for blow with considerable effect. But the blows of each became slower and weaker after the first three or four; and it became obvious that Billy wanted the room which Bob's finger occupied for breathing. He would therefore, probably, in a short time, have let it go, had not Bob anticipated his politeness by jerking away his hand, and making him a present of the finger. He now seized Bill again, and brought him to his knees, but he recovered. He again brought him to his knees, and he again recovered. A third effort, however, brought him down, and Bob on top of him. These efforts seemed to exhaust the little remaining strength of both; and they lay, Bill undermost and Bob across his breast, motionless, and panting for breath. After a short pause, Bob gathered his hand full of dirt and sand, and was in the act of grinding it in his adversary's eyes, when Bill cried "ENOUGH!" Language cannot describe the scene that followed; the shouts, oaths, frantic gestures, taunts, replies, and little fights, and therefore I shall not attempt it. The champions were borne off by their seconds and washed; when many a bleeding wound and ugly bruise was discovered on each which no eye had seen before.

Many had gathered round Bob, and were in various ways congratulating and applauding him, when a voice from the centre of the circle cried out, "Boys, hush and listen to me!" It proceeded from Squire Loggins, who had made his way to Bob's side, and had gathered his face up into one of its most flattering and intelligible expressions. All were obedient to the squire's command. "Gentlemen," continued he, with a most knowing smile, "is—Sammy—Reynold—in—this—company—of—gentlemen?"

"Yes," said Sam, "here I am."

"Sammy," said the squire, winking to the company and drawing the head of his cane to his mouth with an arch smile as he closed, "I—wish—you—to tell—cousin—Bobby—and—these—gentlemen here present—what—your—Uncle—Tommy—said—before—the—fight—began?"

"Oh! get away, Uncle Tom," said Sam, smiling (the squire winked), "you don't know nothing about *fighting*." (The squire winked again.) "All you know about it is how it'll begin, how it'll go on, how it'll end; that's all. Cousin Bob, when you going to fight again, just go to the old man, and let him tell you all about it. If he can't, don't ask nobody else nothing about it, I tell you."

The squire's foresight was complimented in many ways by the by-standers; and he retired, advising "the boys to be at peace, as fighting was a bad business."

357

Durham and Stallings kept their beds for several weeks, and did not meet again for two months. When they met, Billy stepped up to Bob and offered his hand, saying, "Bobby, you've *licked* me a fair fight; but you wouldn't have done it if I hadn't been in the wrong. I oughtn't to have treated your wife as I did; and I felt so through the whole fight; and it sort o' cowed me."

"Well, Billy," said Bob, "let's be friends. Once in the fight, when you had my finger in your mouth, and was pealing me in the face and breast, I was going to halloo; but I thought of Petsy, and knew the house would be too hot for me if I got whipped when fighting for her, after always whipping when I fought for myself."

"Now that's what I always love to see," said a by-stander. "It's true I brought about the fight, but I wouldn't have done it if it hadn't o' been on account of *Miss* (Mrs.) Durham. But dod etarnally darn my soul, if I ever could stand by and see any woman put upon, much less *Miss* Durham. If Bobby hadn't been there, I'd o' took it up myself, be darned if I wouldn't, even if I'd o' got whipped for it. But we're all friends now." The reader need hardly be told that this was Ransy Sniffle.

Thanks to the Christian religion, to schools, colleges, and benevolent associations, such scenes of barbarism and cruelty as that which I have been just describing are now of rare occurrence, though they may still be occasionally met with in some of the new counties. Wherever they prevail, they are a disgrace to that community. The peace-officers who countenance them deserve a place in the Penitentiary. (*1835*)

The Gander Pulling

In the year 1798 I resided in the city of Augusta, and, upon visiting the market-house one morning in that year, my attention was called to the following notice, stuck upon one of the pillars of the building.

"*advurtysement.*

"Thos woo wish To be inform heareof, is heareof notyfide that edwd. Prator will giv a gander pullin, jis this side of harisburg, on Satterday of thes pressents munth to All woo mout wish to partak tharof.

"e Prator, thos wishin to purtak
will cum yearly, as the pullin will begin soon.
"e. p."

If I am asked why "jis this side of harisburg" was selected for the promised feat instead of the city of Augusta, I answer from conjecture, but with some confidence, because the ground chosen was near the central point between four rival towns, the citizens of all which "*mout wish to partak tharof;*" namely, Augusta, Springfield, Harrisburg, and Campbellton. Not that each was the rival of all the others, but that the first and the last were competitors, and each of the others backed the pretensions of its nearest neighbour. Harrisburg sided with Campbellton, *not because she had any interest in seeing the business of the two*

358

states centre upon the bank of the river, nearly opposite to her, but because, like the "Union Democratic Republican Party of Georgia," she thought, after the adoption of the Federal Constitution, that the several towns of the confederacy should no longer be "separated" by the distinction of local party; but that, laying down all former prejudices and jealousies as a sacrifice on the altar of their country, they should become united in a *single body,* for the maintenance of those principles which they deemed essential to the *public welfare.*

Springfield, on the other hand, espoused the State Rights' creed. She admitted that, under the Federal Compact, she ought to love the sister states very much; but that, under the *Social Compact,* she ought to love her own state a little more; and she thought the two compacts perfectly reconcilable to each other. Instead of the towns of the several states getting into *single bodies* to preserve the *public welfare,* her doctrine was, that they should be kept in *separate bodies* to preserve the *private welfare.* She admitted frankly, that, living, as she always had lived, right amid gullies, vapours, fogs, creeks, and lagoons, she was wholly incapable of comprehending that expansive kind of benevolence, which taught her to love people whom she knew nothing about, as much as her next-door neighbours and friends. Until, therefore, she should learn it from the practical operation of the Federal Compact, she would stick to the oldfashioned Scotch love, which she understood perfectly, and "go in" for Augusta, live or die, hit or miss, right or wrong. As in the days of Mr. Jefferson, the Springfield doctrines prevailed, Campbellton was literally *nullified;* insomuch that, ten years ago, there was not a house left to mark the spot where once flourished this active, busy little village. Those who are curious to know where Springfield stood at the time of which I am speaking, have only to take their position at the intersection of Broad and Marbury streets, in the city of Augusta, and they will be in the very heart of old Springfield. Sixty steps west, and as many east of this position, will measure the whole length of this Jeffersonian republican village, which never boasted of more than four dwelling-houses; and Broad-street measures its width, if we exclude kitchens and stables. And, while upon this subject, since it has been predicted by a man for whose opinions I entertain the profoundest respect [1] (especially since the prediction), that my writings will be read with increased interest a hundred years to come; and as I can see no good reason, if this be true, why they should not be read a thousand years hence with more interest, I will take the liberty of dropping a word here to the curious reader of the year 1933. He will certainly wish to know the site of Harrisburg (seeing it is doomed, at no distant period, to share the fate of Springfield) and of Campbellton.

Supposing, then, that if the great fire in Augusta, on the 3d of April, 1829, did not destroy that city, nothing will; I select this as a permanent object.

In 1798, Campbell-street was the western verge of Augusta, a limit to which it had advanced but a few years before, from Jackson-street. Thence to Springfield led a large road, now built up on either side, and forming a continuation of Broad-street. This road was cut across obliquely by a deep gully, the bed of which was an almost impassable bog, which entered the road about one hundred yards below Collock-street on the south, and left it about thirty yards below Collock-street on the north side of now Broad-street. It was called Campbell's Gully, from the name of the gentleman through whose possessions and near whose

359

[1] *The Editor of the "Hickory Nut." (Longstreet's note.)*

dwelling it wound its way to the river. Following the direction of Broad-street from Springfield westward, 1347 yards, will bring you to Harrisburg, which had nothing to boast of over Springfield but a warehouse for the storage of tobacco, then the staple of Georgia. Continue the same direction 700 yards, then face to your right hand, and follow your nose directly across Savannah river, and, upon ascending the opposite bank, you will be in the busiest part of Campbellton in 1798. Between Harrisburg and Springfield, and 1143 yards from the latter, there runs a stream which may be perpetual. At the time just mentioned, it flowed between banks twelve or fourteen feet high, and was then called, as it still is, "Hawk's Gully." [2]

Now Mr. Prator, like the most successful politician of the present day, was on all sides in a doubtful contest; and, accordingly, he laid off his gander-pulling ground on the nearest suitable unappropriated spot to the centre point between Springfield and Harrisburg. This was between Harrisburg and Hawk's Gully, to the south of the road, and embraced part of the road, but within 100 yards of Harrisburg.

When "*Satterday of thes pressents munth*" rolled round, I determined to go to the gander-pulling. When I reached the spot, a considerable number of persons, of different ages, sexes, sizes, and complexions, had collected from the rival towns and the country around. But few females were there, however; and those few were from the lowest walks of life.

A circular path of about forty yards diameter had already been laid out; over which, from two posts about ten feet apart, stretched a rope, the middle of which was directly over the path. The rope hung loosely, so as to allow it, with the weight of a gander attached to it, to vibrate in an arc of four or five feet span, and so as to bring the breast of the gander within barely easy reach of a man of middle stature upon a horse of common size.

A hat was now handed to such as wished to enter the list; and they threw into it twenty-five cents each; this sum was the victor's prize.

The devoted gander was now produced; and Mr. Prator, having first tied his feet together with a strong cord, proceeded to the *neck-greasing*. Abhorrent as it may be to all who respect the tenderer relations of life, *Mrs.* Prator had actually prepared a gourd of *goose*-grease for this very purpose. For myself, when I saw Ned dip his hands into the grease, and commence stroking down the feathers from breast to head, my thoughts took a melancholy turn. They dwelt in sadness upon the many conjugal felicities which had probably been shared between the *greasess* and the *greasee*. I could see him as he stood by her side, through many a chilly day and cheerless night, when she was warming into life the offspring of their mutual loves, and repelled, with chivalrous spirit, every invasion of the consecrated spot which she had selected for her incubation. I could see him moving with patriarchal dignity by the side of his loved one, at the head of a smiling, prattling group, the rich reward of their mutual care, to the luxuries of the meadow or to the recreations of the pool. And now, alas! an extract from the smoking sacrifice of his bosom friend was desecrated to the unholy purpose of making his neck "a fit object" for Cruelty to reach "her quick, unerring fingers

360

[2] *It took its name from an old man by the name of Hawk, who lived in a log hut on a small knoll on the eastern side of the gully and about 100 yards south of the Harrisburg road.* (*Longstreet's note.*)

at." Ye friends of the sacred tie! judge what were my feelings when, in the midst of these reflections, the voice of James Prator thundered on mine ear, "Darn his old dodging soul; brother Ned! grease his neck till a fly can't light on it!"

Ned, having fulfilled his brother Jim's request as well as he could, attached the victim of his cruelty to the rope, directly over the path. On each side of the gander was stationed a man, whose office it was to lash forward any horse which might linger there for a moment; for, by the rules of the ring, all pulling was to be done at a brisk canter.

The word was now given for the competitors to mount and take their places on the ring. Eight appeared: Tall Zubley Zin, mounted upon Sally Spitfire; Arch Odum, mounted on Bull and Ingons (onions); Nathan Perdew, on Hellcat; James Dickson, on Nigger; David Williams, on Gridiron; Fat John Fulger, on Slouch; Gorham Bostwick, on Gimlet; and Turner Hammond, on 'Possum.

"Come, *gentlemen*," said Commandant Prator, "fall in. All of you git behind one another, sort o' in a row."

All came into the track very kindly but Sally Spitfire and Gridiron. The former, as soon as she saw a general movement of horses, took it for granted there was mischief brewing, and, because she could not tell where it lay, she concluded it lay everywhere, and therefore took fright at everything.

Gridiron was a grave horse; but a suspicious eye which he cast to the right and left, wherever he moved, showed that "he was wide awake," and that "no-body better not go fooling with him," as his owner sometimes used to say. He took a sober but rather intense view of things; insomuch that, in his contempla-tions, he passed over the track three times before he could be prevailed upon to stop in it. He stopped at last, however; and when he was made to understand that this was all that was required of him for the present, he surrendered his suspi-cions at once, with a countenance which seemed plainly to say, "Oh, if this is all you want, I've no objection to it."

It was long before Miss Spitfire could be prevailed upon to do the like.

"Get another horse, Zube," said one; "Sal will never do for a gander pullin."

"I won't," said Zube. "If she won't do, I'll make her do. I want a nag that goes off with a spring; so that, when I get a hold, she'll cut the neck in two like a steel-trap."

At length Sally was rather flung than coaxed into the track, directly ahead of Gridiron.

"Now, gentlemen," said the master of the ceremonies, "no man's to make a grab till all's been once round; and when the first man *are* got round, then the whole twist and tucking of you grab away as you come under ("Look here, Jim Fulger! you better not stand too close to that gander, I tell you"), one after an-other. Now blaze away!" (the command for an onset of every kind with people of this order).

Off they went, Miss Sally delighted; for she now thought the whole parade would end in nothing more nor less than her favourite amusement, a race. But Gridiron's visage pronounced this the most nonsensical business that ever a horse of sense was engaged in since the world began.

For the first three rounds Zubley was wholly occupied in restraining Sally to her place; but he lost nothing by this, for the gander had escaped unhurt. On com-pleting his third round, Zube reached forth his long arm, grabbed the gander by

361

the neck with a firmness which seemed likely to defy *goose-grease*, and, at the same instant, he involuntarily gave Sally a sudden check. She raised her head, which before had been kept nearly touching her leader's hocks, and for the first time saw the gander in the act of descending upon her; at the same moment she received two pealing lashes from the whippers. The way she now broke for Springfield "is nothing to nobody." As Zube dashed down the road, the whole Circus raised a whoop after him. This started about twenty dogs, hounds, curs, and pointers, in full chase of him (for no one moved without his dog in those days). The dogs alarmed some belled cattle, which were grazing on Zube's path, just as he reached them; these joined him, with tails up and a tremendous rattling. Just beyond these went three tobacco-rollers, at distances of fifty and a hundred yards apart; each of whom gave Zube a terrific whoop, scream, or yell as he passed.

He went in and out of Hawk's Gully like a trapball, and was in Springfield "in less than no time." Here he was encouraged onward by a new recruit of dogs; but they gave up the chase as hopeless before they cleared the village. Just beyond Springfield, what should Sally encounter but a flock of geese! the tribe to which she owed all her misfortunes. She stopped suddenly, and Zube went over her head with the last acquired velocity. He was up in a moment, and the activity with which he pursued Sally satisfied every spectator that he was unhurt.

Gridiron, who had witnessed Miss Sally's treatment with astonishment and indignation, resolved not to pass between the posts until the whole matter should be explained to his satisfaction. He therefore stopped short, and, by very intelligible looks, demanded of the whippers whether, if he passed between them, he was to be treated as Miss Spitfire had been? The whippers gave him no satisfaction, and his rider signified, by reiterated thumps of the heel, that he should go through whether he would or not. Of these, however, Gridiron seemed to know nothing. In the midst of the conference, Gridiron's eye lit upon the oscillating gander, and every moment's survey of it begat in him a growing interest, as his slowly rising head, suppressed breath, and projected ears plainly evinced. After a short examination, he heaved a sigh, and looked behind him to see if the way was clear. It was plain that his mind was now made up; but, to satisfy the world that he would do nothing rashly, he took another view, and then wheeled and went for Harrisburg as if he had set in for a year's running. Nobody whooped at Gridiron, for all saw that his running was purely the result of philosophic deduction. The reader will not suppose all this consumed half the time which has been consumed in telling it, though it might have been so without interrupting the amusement; for Miss Spitfire's flight had completely suspended it for a time.

The remaining competitors now went on with the sport. A few rounds showed plainly that Odum or Bostwick would be the victor; but which, no one could tell. Whenever either of them came round, the gander's neck was sure of a severe wrench. Many a half pint of Jamaica was staked upon them, besides other things. The poor gander withstood many a strong pull before his wailings ceased. At length, however, they were hushed by Odum. Then came Bostwick, and broke the neck. The next grasp of Odum, it was thought, would bear away the head; but it did not. Then Bostwick was sure of it; but he missed it. Now Odum must surely have it. All is interest and animation; the horses sweep round with redoubled speed; every eye is upon Odum; his backers smiling, Bostwick's trembling. To the rope he comes; lifts his hand; when, lo! Fat John Fulger had borne it away the second before. All were astonished, all disappointed, and some were vexed a little; for it was now clear that, "if it hadn't o' been for his great, fat, greasy paw," to use their own language, "Odum would have gained the victory." Others cursed "that long-legged Zube Zin, who was so high he didn't know when his feet were cold, for bringing such a nag as Sal Spitfire to a gander pullin; for if he'd o' been in his place, it would o' flung Bostwick right where that *gourd* o' hog's *lard* (Fulger) was."

Fulger's conduct was little calculated to reconcile them to their disappointment.

"Come here, Neddy Prator," said he, with a triumphant smile; "let your Uncle Johnny put his potato stealer (hand) into that hat, and tickle the chins of them *are* shiners a little! Oh you little shining sons o' bitches! walk into your Mas' Johnny's pocket, and jingle so as Arch Odum and Gory Bostwick may hear you! You hear 'em, Gory? *Boys*, don't pull with *men* any more. I've jist got my hand in; I wish I had a pond full o' ganders here now, jist to show how I could make their heads fly. Bet all I've won, you may hang three upon that rope, and I'll set Slouch at full speed, and take off the heads of all three the first grab; two with my hands and one with my teeth."

Thus he went on, but really there was no boasting in all this; it was all fun; for John knew, and all were convinced that he knew, that his success was entirely the result of accident. John was really "a good-natured fellow," and his *cavorting* had an effect directly opposite to that which the reader would suppose it had; it reconciled all to their disappointment save one. I except little Billy Mixen, of Spirit Creek; who had staked the net proceeds of six quarts of huckleberries [3] upon Odum, which he had been long keeping for a safe bet. *He* could not be reconciled until he fretted himself into a pretty little *piney*-woods fight, in which he got whipped; and then he went home perfectly satisfied. Fulger spent all his winnings with Prator in treats to the company; made most of them drunk, and thereby produced four Georgia *rotations;* [4] after which all parted good friends. (*1835*)

The Horse-Swap

During the session of the Supreme Court, in the village of ———, about three weeks ago, when a number of people were collected in the principal street of the village, I observed a young man riding up and down the street, as I supposed, in a violent passion. He galloped this way, then that, and then the other; spurred his horse to one group of citizens, then to another, then dashed off at half speed, as if fleeing from danger; and, suddenly checking his horse, returned first in a pace, then in a trot, and then in a canter. While he was performing these various evolutions, he cursed, swore, whooped, screamed, and tossed himself in every attitude which man could assume on horseback. In short, he *cavorted* most magnanimously (a term which, in our tongue, expresses all that I have described, and

363

[3] *I give them their Georgia name. I should hardly be understood if I called them* whortleberries. (*Longstreet's note.*)
[4] *I borrowed the term from Jim Inman at the time. "Why Jim," said I to him, just as he rose from a fight, "what have you been doing?" "Oh," said he, "nothing but taking a little* rotation *with Bob M'Manus." (Longstreet's note.*)

a little more), and seemed to be setting all creation at defiance. As I like to see all that is passing, I determined to take a position a little nearer to him, and to ascertain, if possible, what it was that affected him so sensibly. Accordingly, I approached a crowd before which he had stopped for a moment, and examined it with the strictest scrutiny. But I could see nothing in it that seemed to have anything to do with the cavorter. Every man appeared to be in good humour, and all minding their own business. Not one so much as noticed the principal figure. Still he went on. After a semicolon pause, which my appearance seemed to produce (for he eyed me closely as I approached), he fetched a whoop, and swore that he "could out-swap any live man, woman, or child that ever walked these hills, or that ever straddled horseflesh since the days of old daddy Adam. Stranger," said he to me, "did you ever see the *Yellow* Blossom from Jasper?"

"No," said I, "but I have often heard of him."

"I'm the boy," continued he; "perhaps a *leetle*, jist a *leetle*, of the best man at a horse-swap that ever trod shoe-leather."

I began to feel my situation a little awkward, when I was relieved by a man somewhat advanced in years, who stepped up and began to survey the "*Yellow* Blossom's" horse with much apparent interest. This drew the rider's attention, and he turned the conversation from me to the stranger.

"Well, my old coon," said he, "do you want to swap *hosses?*"

"Why, I don't know," replied the stranger; "I believe I've got a beast I'd trade with you for that one, if you like him."

"Well, fetch up your nag, my old cock; you're jist the lark I wanted to get hold of. I am perhaps a *leetle*, jist a *leetle*, of the best man at a horse-swap that ever stole *cracklins* out of his mammy's fat gourd. Where's your *hoss?*"

"I'll bring him presently; but I want to examine your horse a little."

"Oh! look at him," said the Blossom, alighting and hitting him a cut; "look at him. He's the best piece of *hoss*flesh in the thirteen united universal worlds. There's no sort o' mistake in little Bullet. He can pick up miles on his feet, and fling 'em behind him as fast as the next man's *hoss*, I don't care where he comes from. And he can keep at it as long as the sun can shine without resting."

During this harangue, little Bullet looked as if he understood it all, believed it, and was ready at any moment to verify it. He was a horse of goodly countenance, rather expressive of vigilance than fire; though an unnatural appearance of fierceness was thrown into it by the loss of his ears, which had been cropped pretty close to his head. Nature had done but little for Bullet's head and neck; but he managed, in a great measure, to hide their defects by bowing perpetually. He had obviously suffered severely for corn; but if his ribs and hip bones had not disclosed the fact, *he* never would have done it; for he was in all respects as cheerful and happy as if he commanded all the corn-cribs and fodder-stacks in Georgia. His height was about twelve hands; but as his shape partook somewhat of that of the giraffe, his haunches stood much lower. They were short, strait, peaked, and concave. Bullet's tail, however, made amends for all his defects. All that the artist could do to beautify it had been done; and all that horse could do to compliment the artist, Bullet did. His tail was nicked in superior style, and exhibited the line of beauty in so many directions, that it could not fail to hit the most fastidious taste in some of them. From the root it dropped into a graceful festoon; then rose in a handsome curve; then resumed its first direction; and

364

then mounted suddenly upward like a cypress knee to a perpendicular of about two and a half inches. The whole had a careless and bewitching inclination to the right. Bullet obviously knew where his beauty lay, and took all occasions to display it to the best advantage. If a stick cracked, or if any one moved suddenly about him, or coughed, or hawked, or spoke a little louder than common, up went Bullet's tail like lightning; and if the *going up* did not please, the *coming down* must of necessity, for it was as different from the other movement as was its direction. The first was a bold and rapid flight upward, usually to an angle of forty-five degrees. In this position he kept his interesting appendage until he satisfied himself that nothing in particular was to be done; when he commenced dropping it by half inches, in second beats, then in triple time, then faster and shorter, and faster and shorter still, until it finally died away imperceptibly into its natural position. If I might compare sights to sounds, I should say its *settling* was more like the note of a locust than anything else in nature.

Either from native sprightliness of disposition, from uncontrollable activity, or from an unconquerable habit of removing flies by the stamping of the feet, Bullet never stood still; but always kept up a gentle fly-scaring movement of his limbs, which was peculiarly interesting.

"I tell you, man," proceeded the Yellow Blossom, "he's the best live hoss that ever trod the grit of Georgia. Bob Smart knows the hoss. Come here, Bob, and mount this hoss, and show Bullet's motions." Here Bullet bristled up, and looked as if he had been hunting for Bob all day long, and had just found him. Bob sprang on his back. "Boo-oo-oo!" said Bob, with a fluttering noise of the lips; and away went Bullet, as if in a quarter race, with all his beauties spread in handsome style.

"Now fetch him back," said Blossom. Bullet turned and came in pretty much as he went out.

"Now trot him by." Bullet reduced his tail to "*customary;*" sidled to the right and left airily, and exhibited at least three varieties of trot in the short space of fifty yards.

"Make him pace!" Bob commenced twitching the bridle and kicking at the same time. These inconsistent movements obviously (and most naturally) disconcerted Bullet; for it was impossible for him to learn, from them, whether he was to proceed or stand still. He started to trot, and was told that wouldn't do. He attempted a canter, and was checked again. He stopped, and was urged to go on. Bullet now rushed into the wide field of experiment, and struck out a gait of his own, that completely turned the tables upon his rider, and certainly deserved a patent. It seemed to have derived its elements from the jig, the minuet, and the cotillion. If it was not a pace, it certainly had *pace* in it, and no man would venture to call it anything else; so it passed off to the satisfaction of the owner.

"Walk him!" Bullet was now at home again; and he walked as if money was staked on him.

The stranger, whose name, I afterward learned, was Peter Ketch, having examined Bullet to his heart's content, ordered his son Neddy to go and bring up Kit. Neddy soon appeared upon Kit; a well-formed sorrel of the middle size, and in good order. His *tout ensemble* threw Bullet entirely in the shade, though a glance was sufficient to satisfy any one that Bullet had the decided advantage of him in point of intellect.

365

"Why, man," said Blossom, "do you bring such a hoss as that to trade for Bullet? Oh, I see you're no notion of trading."

"Ride him off, Neddy!" said Peter. Kit put off at a handsome lope.

"Trot him back!" Kit came in at a long, sweeping trot, and stopped suddenly at the crowd.

"Well," said Blossom, "let me look at him; maybe he'll do to plough."

"Examine him!" said Peter, taking hold of the bridle close to the mouth; "he's nothing but a tacky. He an't as *pretty* a horse as Bullet, I know; but he'll do. Start 'em together for a hundred and fifty *mile;* and if Kit an't twenty mile ahead of him at the coming out, any man may take Kit for nothing. But he's a mon-strous mean horse, gentlemen; any man may see that. He's the scariest horse, too, you ever saw. He won't do to hunt on, no how. Stranger, will you let Neddy have your rifle to shoot off him? Lay the rifle between his ears, Neddy, and shoot at the blaze in that stump. Tell me when his head is high enough."

Ned fired, and hit the blaze; and Kit did not move a hair's breadth.

"Neddy, take a couple of sticks, and beat on that hogshead at Kit's tail."

Ned made a tremendous rattling, at which Bullet took fright, broke his bridle, and dashed off in grand style; and would have stopped all farther negotiations by going home in disgust, had not a traveller arrested him and brought him back; but Kit did not move.

"I tell you, gentlemen," continued Peter, "he's the scariest horse you ever saw. He an't as gentle as Bullet, but he won't do any harm if you watch him. Shall I put him in a cart, gig, or wagon for you, stranger? He'll cut the same capers there he does here. He's a monstrous mean horse."

During all this time Blossom was examining him with the nicest scrutiny. Having examined his frame and limbs, he now looked at his eyes.

"He's got a curious look out of his eyes," said Blossom.

"Oh, yes, sir," said Peter, "just as blind as a bat. Blind horses always have clear eyes. Make a motion at his eyes, if you please, sir."

Blossom did so, and Kit threw up his head rather as if something pricked him under the chin than as if fearing a blow. Blossom repeated the experiment, and Kit jerked back in considerable astonishment.

"Stone blind, you see, gentlemen," proceeded Peter; "but he's just as good to travel of a dark night as if he had eyes."

"Blame my buttons," said Blossom, "if I like them eyes."

"No," said Peter, "nor I neither. I'd rather have 'em made of diamonds; but they'll do—if they don't show as much white as Bullet's."

"Well," said Blossom, "make a pass at me."

"No," said Peter; "you made the banter, now make your pass."

"Well, I'm never afraid to price my hosses. You must give me twenty-five dollars boot."

"Oh, certainly; say fifty, and my saddle and bridle in. Here, Neddy, my son, take away daddy's horse."

"Well," said Blossom, "I've made my pass, now you make yours."

"I'm for short talk in a horse-swap, and therefore always tell a gentleman at once what I mean to do. You must give me ten dollars."

Blossom swore absolutely, roundly, and profanely that he never would give boot.

366

"Well," said Peter, "I didn't care about trading; but you cut such high shines that I thought I'd like to back you out, and I've done it. Gentlemen, you see I've brought him to a hack."

"Come, old man," said Blossom, "I've been joking with you. I begin to think you do want to trade; therefore, give me five dollars and take Bullet. I'd rather lose ten dollars any time than not make a trade, though I hate to fling away a good hoss."

"Well," said Peter, "I'll be as clever as you are. Just put the five dollars on Bullet's back, and hand him over; it's a trade."

Blossom swore again, as roundly as before, that he would not give boot; and, said he, "Bullet wouldn't hold five dollars on his back, no how. But, as I bantered you, if you say an even swap, here's at you."

"I told you," said Peter, "I'd be as clever as you, therefore, here goes two dollars more, just for trade sake. Give me three dollars, and it's a bargain."

Blossom repeated his former assertion; and here the parties stood for a long time, and the by-standers (for many were now collected) began to taunt both parties. After some time, however, it was pretty unanimously decided that the old man had backed Blossom out.

At length Blossom swore he "never would be backed out for three dollars after bantering a man"; and, accordingly, they closed the trade.

"Now," said Blossom, as he handed Peter the three dollars, "I'm a man that, when he makes a bad trade, makes the most of it until he can make a better. I'm for no rues and after-claps."

"That's just my way," said Peter; "I never goes to law to mend my bargains."

"Ah, you're the kind of boy I love to trade with. Here's your hoss, old man. Take the saddle and bridle off him, and I'll strip yours; but lift up the blanket easy from Bullet's back, for he's a mighty tender-backed hoss."

The old man removed the saddle, but the blanket stuck fast. He attempted to raise it, and Bullet bowed himself, switched his tail, danced a little, and gave signs of biting.

"Don't hurt him, old man," said Blossom, archly; "take it off easy. I am, perhaps, a leetle of the best man at a horse-swap that ever catched a coon."

Peter continued to pull at the blanket more and more roughly, and Bullet became more and more *cavortish:* insomuch that, when the blanket came off, he had reached the *kicking* point in good earnest.

The removal of the blanket disclosed a sore on Bullet's back-bone that seemed to have defied all medical skill. It measured six full inches in length and four in breadth, and had as many features as Bullet had motions. My heart sickened at the sight; and I felt that the brute who had been riding him in that situation deserved the halter.

The prevailing feeling, however, was that of mirth. The laugh became loud and general at the old man's expense, and rustic witticisms were liberally bestowed upon him and his late purchase. These Blossom continued to provoke by various remarks. He asked the old man "if he thought Bullet would let five dollars lie on his back." He declared most seriously that he had owned that horse three months, and had never discovered before that he had a sore back, "or he never should have thought of trading him," &c., &c.

The old man bore it all with the most philosophic composure. He evinced no

367

astonishment at his late discovery, and made no replies. But his son Neddy had not disciplined his feelings quite so well. His eyes opened wider and wider from the first to the last pull of the blanket; and, when the whole sore burst upon his view, astonishment and fright seemed to contend for the mastery of his countenance. As the blanket disappeared, he stuck his hands in his breeches pockets, heaved a deep sigh, and lapsed into a profound revery, from which he was only roused by the cuts at his father. He bore them as long as he could; and, when he could contain himself no longer, he began, with a certain wildness of expression which gave a peculiar interest to what he uttered: "His back's mighty bad off; but dod drot my soul if he's put it to daddy as bad as he thinks he has, for old Kit's both blind and *deef*, I'll be dod drot if he eint."

"The devil he is," said Blossom.

"Yes, dod drot my soul if he *eint*. You walk him, and see if he *eint*. His eyes don't look like it; but he'd *jist as leve go agin* the house with you, or in a ditch, as any how. Now you go try him." The laugh was now turned on Blossom; and many rushed to test the fidelity of the little boy's report. A few experiments established its truth beyond controversy.

"Neddy," said the old man, "you oughtn't to try and make people discontented with their things. Stranger, don't mind what the little boy says. If you can only get Kit rid of them little failings, you'll find him all sorts of a horse. You are a *leetle* the best man at a horse-swap that ever I got hold of; but don't fool away Kit. Come, Neddy, my son, let's be moving; the stranger seems to be getting snappish." (*1835*)

JOHNSON JONES HOOPER

1815–1862

Johnson Jones Hooper was born in Wilmington, North Carolina. His formal schooling, never very regular, was stopped abruptly in 1830, when he began working for a newspaper in Charleston. Tiring of his routine assignments after five years, he gave up his position and went on an extended vagabond tour of the deep South and the Gulf Coast region. He settled in 1840 at Lafayette, Alabama, where he studied law in the office of his brother. The legal profession, however, had no special appeal for him, and a short while later he returned to journalism, serving in varying capacities on several Alabama newspapers within the next few years.

During this period the humorous exploits of Hooper's backwoods creation, Simon Suggs, were attracting considerable attention. Hooper's national reputation was established by the publication between 1842 and 1846 of many of his sketches in *Spirit of the Times*, the New York humor magazine which flourished from 1831 to 1856. In the latter year, a Philadelphia publisher issued a collection of the tales as *Some Adventures of Captain Simon Suggs, Late of the Tallapoosa Volunteers*. This volume and *The Widow Rugby's Husband, A Night at the Ugly Man's and Other Tales of Alabama* (1851) give Hooper a secure place among the humorists of the Old Southwest.

Simon Suggs, the principal figure in many of Hooper's tales, is a picaresque character whose every action is motivated by one principle: "It is good to be shifty in a new country." He puts his dictum into practice by duping everyone he meets, including the gamblers at the Faro table, the congregation at the camp meeting, and his own father. According to Professor Harold W. Thompson, Simon is the "best example of the genus rogue in Southwestern humor and the most spirited before Mark Twain and H. T. Lewis."

from *Adventures of Captain Simon Suggs*

Chapter 8. A Masterpiece in the Ludicrous

Great was the commotion at Fort Suggs on the morning next after the occurrence of the events related in the last chapter. At Fort Suggs we say—for so had the Captain christened "Taylor's store" and the enclosure thereof. Nor let anyone reprehend him for so doing. It was but an exhibition of a vanity, which, if not laudable, at least finds its sufficient excuse in a custom that has prevailed, "time out of mind." Had not Romulus his Rome? Did not the pugnacious son of Philip call his Egyptian military settlement Alexandria? And—to descend to later times and to cases more directly in point—is there not a Fort Gaines in Georgia, and a Fort Jessup in Florida? Who then shall carp, when we say that Captain Simon Suggs bestowed *his* name upon the spot strengthened by his wisdom, and protected by his valor!

Great then, we repeat, was the commotion at Fort Suggs on the morning in question. The fact had become generally known—how could it be otherwise with thirty women in the immediate vicinity!—that Mrs. Haycock was to be "court-martialed" on that morning; and the commotion was the consequence. The widow herself was suffering great mental disquietude on this subject, in addition to considerable physical discomfort occasioned by the fall and rough handling of the previous night. Under such circumstances, it could hardly be expected that her woes would fail to find utterance. And it would have been equally unreasonable to suppose that her fellow gossips would restrain the natural propensity of the sex. Let the reader, then, imagine—if he be not nervous—all the uproar and din which three dozen women can make under the most exciting circumstances, and he will have some faint conception of the commotion at Fort Suggs on the morning of the trial.

369

It was at an early hour; in fact—speaking according to the chronometrical standard in use at Fort Suggs—not more than "fust-drink time," when Captain Suggs took Lieutenant Snipes aside to consult with him in regard to some of the details of preparation for the court-martial.

"Snipes," said the Captain, as he seated himself a-straddle of the fence, and saw his lieutenant safely adjusted in a like position—"Snipes, as sure's you're born, thar's a diffikilty about this here court-martial. Now I want you to tell me *how* we're to hold a *drum-head* court-martial *when we ain't got a drum!*"

Lieutenant Snipes looked very much puzzled, and in fact he *was* exceedingly puzzled, and he considered the matter for several moments, but could see no way by which the "diffikilty" might be surmounted. At length he remarked,

"It *does* look aukerd, Capting!"

"Yes. You see when these here court-martials is jumped up all of a sudden, like this, they're *ableeged* to be of the drum-head sort—that's what I've *allers* hearn. Well now, supposin' we was to hold one *without the drum*, and heng or shoot that everlastin' old she-devil; *would* the law jestify us in doin' so? Sometimes I sorter think it would, and then again it looks sorter jubous. What's *your* apinion, Lewtenant?"

"That's it—what you jist said," replies Lieutenant Snipes, deferentially.

"Good!" said the Captain—"lewtenants ought allers to think jist as ther captings do. It's a good sign."

"It's what *I've* allers done, and what I allers *expects* to do," replied Snipes.

"Well, well!" remarked Suggs, whose chief object was to impress Snipes with the idea that the widow's life was in actual danger—and through his lieutenant, create that impression upon Mrs. Haycock herself, and all the rest—"well, well, *don't* you believe that ef I was to git a bar'l, or somethin' else pretty nigh *like* a drum, and hold the court-martial by that—don't you believe *that* would jestify us ef any thing was brought up here-arter, supposin' we was to condemn the old woman to deth?"

"Belikes it would," said Snipes.

"I *know* it would!" said Suggs emphatically.

"*I* know so too!" remarked the lieutenant, with increased confidence.

"Well, now, all *that's* settled," said the Captain, with an air of satisfaction—"the next thing is, how are we agwine to put her to death?"

"Why, we ain't *tried* her yit!" said Snipes.

"To be sure! to be sure! I'd forgot that!—but you know thar's no way to git round condemnin' of her—is thar?"

"No way as *I* see!"

"It's a painful duty, Lewtenant! a very painful duty, Lewtenant Snipes; and very distressin'. But the rules of war is very strict, you know!"

"*Very* strict," said Snipes.

"And officers must do ther duty, come what may!"

"They're *ableeged* to," said the lieutenant.

370 "Ah! well!" remarked Captain Suggs with considerable emotion, "it'll be time enough to fix how we shall execute the old critter at the trial. You think the bar'l will do?"

"Jist as good as any thing," replied Snipes—"a bar'l and a drum's sorter alike, any way."

"Well, you'd better go and fix up as well as you kin, and the natur' of the case will admit. Officers oughter dress as well as they kin at sich times, ef no other. I must go and bresh up, myself." And with that, the consultation between Captain Suggs and Lieutenant Snipes ended; the former going off to put himself in a little more military trim; while the latter industriously employed himself in disseminating the result of the conference.

It was with extreme difficulty that the Captain arranged his costume to his own satisfaction, and made it befitting so solemn and impressive an occasion. After a great deal of trouble, however, he did contrive to cut a somewhat military figure. With a sword he was already "indifferently well" provided; having found one—rusty and without a scabbard—some where about the premises. This he buckled, or rather tied, to his side with buckskin strings. He wore at the time, the identical blue jeanes frockcoat which has since become so familiar to the people of Talla-poosa—it was then new, but on this there were, of course, no epaulettes. Long time did Captain Suggs employ himself in devising expedients to supply the deficiency. At length he hit it. His wife had a large crimson pin-cushion, and this he fastened upon his left shoulder, having first caused some white cotton fringe to be attached to the outward edge. In lieu of crimson sash, he fastened around his waist a bright-red silk handkerchief, with only a few white spots on it. And this was an admirable substitute, except that it was almost too short to tie before, and exhibited no inconsiderable portion of itself in a depending triangle behind. The chapeau now alone remained to be managed. This was easily done. Two sides of the brim of his capacious beaver were stitched to the body of the hat, and at the fastening on the left side, Mrs. Suggs sewed a cockade of red ferreting, nearly as big as the bottom of a saucer. Thus imposingly habited—and having first stuffed the legs of his pantaloons into the tops of a very antique pair of boots—Captain Simon Suggs went forth.

At the upper end of the enclosure, and standing near an empty whiskey barrel, was Lieutenant Snipes. He had not been so successful as the Captain in the matter of his toilette. Around his black wool hat was pasted, or stitched, a piece of deep purple gilt paper, such as is often found upon bolts of linen. Upon this was represented a battle between a lion and a unicorn; and in a scroll above were certain letters, which as Lieutenant Snipes himself remarked, "didn't spell nothing"—at least, nothing that he could comprehend. In his hand was the handle of a hoe, armed at one extremity with a rusty bayonet—the only weapon of its kind, at that moment, to be found in the whole garrison at Fort Suggs. Equipped thus, and provided with a dirty sheet of paper, a portable inkstand (containing poke-berry juice), and the stump of a pen—all of which were upon the head of the barrel—the doughty Lieutenant awaited the moment when it should please Captain Suggs to arraign the prisoner and proceed with the trial.

"Tallapoosy Vollantares, parade here!" thundered Captain Suggs, as he walked up to the barrel.

Very soon the "component parts" of the "Vollantares" were grouped about their Captain.

"Form in a straight line!" squealed Lieutenant Snipes.

The company took the form of a half-moon!

Captain Suggs now ordered Mrs. Haycock to be brought out; whereupon Snipes went into the back-room of the store, and directly appeared again, leading

371

the widow—who limped considerably, and howled like a full pack of wolves—by the hand. The Captain, however, by a judicious threat of instant decapitation, reduced the noise to a series of mere sobbings.

"Hadn't we better fix some way to have some music," said Suggs, "and march round the house once, before we perceed with the trial?"

Lieutenant Snipes suggested that there was no drum or fife, as the Captain knew, on the premises, but that "uncle Billy Allen" was an excellent drummer, and Joe Nalls a first-rate performer on the fife, and that perhaps those individuals might, for the nonce, be induced to make vocal imitations of their respective instruments, and with their hands "go through the motions" indispensable to their proper effect. Captain Suggs immediately spoke to those gentlemen, and they "kindly consented" to serve, on the very equitable condition of receiving a "drink" each, as soon as the affair was over.

The "vollantares" were now formed in double files, and between the two columns Mrs. Haycock, supported by a female friend on each side, was placed.

"Music to the front!" shouted Suggs; and the order was promptly obeyed.

"Company! March!"

"Dub—dub—dub-a-dub-a-dub," went "uncle Billy Allen," inclining dangerously from the perpendicular, in order to support properly, a non-existent drum!

"Phee-ee-phee-fee," whistled Mr. Nalls, as his fingers played rapidly upon the holes of his imaginary fife!

And the company marched, as it was ordered. Suggs, of course, headed the array, walking backwards in order to inspect its movements; while Snipes, with his bayonet, walked alongside and kept a sharp eye on the prisoner. Thus they marched slowly around the enclosure, and returned to the spot whence they started.

"Halt! Form a round ring all round the drum!" ordered the Captain, pointing to the barrel.

The "vollantares" arranged themselves so as to describe, not exactly a mathematical circle, but a figure slightly approximating thereto, with the Captain, Lieutenant Snipes, and the widow, in the centre.

"Betsy Haycock," said Captain Suggs, "you're fotch up here accordin' to the rigelations of drum-head court-martial, for infringin' on the rules of war, by crossin' of the lines agin orders; and that too, when the fort was under martial law. Ef you've got any thing to say agin havin' your life tuk, less hear it."

Poor Mrs. Haycock became livid; her eyes dilated, and all her features assumed that sudden sharpness which mortal terror often produces. Trembling in all her joints, and with pallid lips, she gasped,

"Mercy! mercy! Captain Suggs! For God's sake don't kill me—oh don't ef you please! I only went for my tobakker—for the love of the Lord *don't* murder me! Have mercy—I'll never—no never—as long——"

"It aint *me*," said the Captain interrupting her; "it aint *me* that's a-gwine to kill you; it's the *Rules of War*. The rules of war is mighty strict—aint they, Lewtenant Snipes?"

372

"*Powerful* strict!" said Snipes.

"You've 'fessed the crime," continued Suggs, "and ef me and the Lewtenant wanted to let you off ever so bad, the rules of war would lay us liable ef we was to. But come, Lewtenant Snipes," he added, addressing that person; "the prisoner has made her acknowledgements; take your pen and ink, and let's go and see what's to be done about it."

The Lieutenant took up his writing materials, and the couple retired to a corner of the fence, where they seated themselves upon the ground. Directly Snipes was seen to write; and then he picked up his pen and ink again, and they returned.

"What—what—what's it?" chokingly inquired the widow, as they reassumed their positions at the barrel.

"Read out the judg*ment*," said Suggs with immense solemnity.

Snipes read what he had written in the fence-corner, as follows:

"Whares, Betsy Haycock were brought up afore us, bein' charged with in-fringin' the rules of war by crossin' of the lines agin orders, and Fort Suggs bein' under martial law at the time, and likewise ecknowlidged she was gilty, Tharfore we have tried her eccordin to said rules of war, and condemns her to be baggonet-ted to deth in one hour from this time, witness our hands and seals."

A paleness more ghastly than that of death, came over the widow's face as she heard the sentence. Falling to the earth, she grovelled at the feet of Captain Suggs.

"Save me—pity—help! for God's sake! Oh don't kill me Captain Suggs!—beg for me, Mr. Snipes. Oh, you won't—I know you won't murder me! You're jest in fun!—aint you? You couldn't have the *heart* to kill a poor woman creetur like me!"—and then she added in a hoarse whisper—"I'll humble myself to you, Cap-tain Suggs! I'll git down on my very knees, and kiss your shoe! Don't take my life away with that—" she didn't finish the sentence, but shuddered all over, as she thought of Snipes' rusty bayonet.

"Oh! Jimminny Crimminny! what a cussed old fool!" exclaimed a voice from the fence-corner, outside, which was instantly recognized as belonging to Yellow-legs—"he darsent no more kill you, 'an he dare to fight an Injun!"

The widow looked up, but took no comfort from the words. Captain Suggs, highly indignant, seized a large stone and projected it with Titan-like force, at the dirt-eater; but it struck the fence. Yellow-legs, not at all alarmed, turned his back to Suggs, and made a gesture expressive of the highest degree of contempt, and then bounded off.

"Lewtenant, prepar' for execution!" said the Captain, as he returned to the barrel.

Mrs. Haycock renewed her lamentations and entreaties.

"I wish," said Suggs, in a fit of mental abstraction, but soliloquizing *aloud*; "thar *was* some way to save her. But ef I was to let her off with a *fine*, I might be layin' myself liable to be tried for my own life."

"Oh yes! Captain Suggs, I'll pay any fine you'll put on me—I'll give up all the money I've got, ef you'll jest let me off—do now, dear Captain——"

"Hey? What? Have *I* been talkin' out loud?" inquired Suggs, starting with a disconcerted look from his reverie.

"Yes, yes!" answered the widow with great earnestness; "you said ef I'd pay a fine, you'd spar my life—didn't you now, *dear, good* Captain Suggs?"

"Ef I did, I oughtent to 'a done it. I don't think I'd be jestified ef I was to let

373

you off. The rules of war would hold *me* 'countable ef I did—don't you think they would, Lewtenant?"

"*Mighty* apt!" said Snipes, as he sharpened the end of his rusty bayonet on a fragment of rock, by way of preparing for the execution of the widow.

Mrs. Haycock adjured Captain Suggs by his affection for his own offspring, to impose a fine, instead of "makin' her poor fatherless children, orfins!" Tears came into Suggs' eyes at this appeal, and the sternness of the officer was lost in the sensibility of the man.

"Don't you think, Lewtenant," he asked, "bein' as it's a *woman*—a *widder* woman too—the rules of war wouldn't be as severe on us for lettin' her off, *purvidin'* she paid a reasonable fine?"

"They wouldn't be severe at all!" replied Snipes.

"Well, well, widder! Bein' as it's you—a perticlar friend and close neighbour— and bein' *as* you're a widder, and on the 'count of my feelins for Billy Haycock, which was your husband afore he died, I s'pose I'll have to run the resk. But it's a orful 'sponsibility I'm takin, jist for friend*ship*, widder——"

Mrs. Haycock interrupted him with a torrent of thanks and benedictions.

"Thar aint *many*," continued Suggs, "I'd take sich a 'sponsibility for: I may be a-runnin of *my own neck* into a halter!"

"The Lord in Heaven purvent your ever sufferin' bekase yu've tuk pity on a poor widder like me!" was the grateful woman's ejaculation.

"Hows'ever," added Suggs, "to shorten the matter, jist pay down twenty-five dollars, and I'll pardon you if I *do* git into a scrape about it—I never *could* bar to see a woman suffer! it strikes me right *here!*" and the Captain placed his hand upon his breast in a most impressive manner.

The joyful Mrs. Haycock immediately untied a key from her girdle, and handing it to one of her friends, sent her into the store, with directions to "sarch low down, in the left hand corner before of her chist," and bring a certain stocking she would find there filled with coin. This was speedily done, and the amount of the fine handed to Captain Suggs.

"This here money," he remarked as he received it, "I want you all to onderstand, ain't *my* money. No! no! I have to keep it here"—sliding it into his pockets —"ontwell I get *my* orders about it. It's the *government's* money, and *I* darsent spend a cent of it—do I, Lewtenant?"

"No more'n you dar to put your head in a blazin' log-pile!" answered the Lieutenant.

A whistling—just such as always implied that somebody, in the immediate neighbourhood of the whistler, *lies tremendously*—was heard at this moment, and Suggs looking round, saw Yellow-legs in his old corner, dealing a supposititious hand of cards to an imaginary antagonist—as if he would thereby intimate that Captain Simon Suggs would embezzle the public money, or at any rate, hazard its loss at cards.

"Charge baggonets on that cussed, pumpkin-faced whelp of the devil!" roared the Captain in the frenzy of the moment; and Lieutenant Snipes dashed at Yellow-legs with his rusty weapon, which he plunged through a crack of the fence. Before the gallant Snipes, however, could recover from the impetus of his attack and withdraw the bayonet, the dirt-eater had pulled it off the hoe-handle, and fixing it on a dry corn-stalk, bore it aloft upon his shoulder most contumaciously, under the very nose of Captain Suggs!

*   *   *   *   *   *   *   *   *   *   *   *   *

The reader will please suppose fifteen minutes to have elapsed, and Captain Suggs and his Lieutenant to be behind the store chimney, in private conversation.

"Lewtenant Snipes!" said Suggs, "I look upon you as a high-minded, honubble officer, and a honor to the Tallapoosy Vollantares. I like to see a man do his duty like you done *yourn!* Here, take *that!*"—handing him one of Mrs. Haycock's dollars—"Simon Suggs never forgits his friends—NEVER! His motter is allers, *Fust* his *country*, and *then* his friends!"

"Captain Suggs"—was the Lieutenant's reply, as he made a minute examination of the Mexican coin in his hand—"I've said it *behind your back*, and I'll say it *to your face;* you're a *gentleman* from the top of your head to the end of your bigtoe nail! Less go in and liquor; damn expenses!"

Chapter 10. Simon Suggs Attends a Camp Meeting

Captain Suggs found himself as poor at the conclusion of the Creek war, as he had been at its commencement. Although no "arbitrary," "despotic," "corrupt," and "unprincipled" judge had fined him a thousand dollars for his proclamation of martial law at Fort Suggs, or the enforcement of its rules in the case of Mrs. Haycock; yet somehow—the thing is alike inexplicable to him and to us—the money which he had contrived, by various shifts, to obtain, melted away and was gone forever. To a man like the Captain, of intense domestic affections, this state of destitution was most distressing. "He could stand it himself—didn't care a d——n for it, no way," he observed, "but the old woman and the children; *that* bothered him!"

As he sat one day, ruminating upon the unpleasant condition of his "financial concerns," Mrs. Suggs informed him that "the sugar and coffee was nigh about out," and that there were not "a dozen j'ints and middlins, *all put together*, in the smoke-house." Suggs bounced up on the instant, exclaiming, "D——n it! *somebody* must suffer!" But whether this remark was intended to convey the idea that he and his family were about to experience the want of the necessaries of life; or that some other, and as yet unknown, individual should "suffer" to prevent that prospective exigency, must be left to the commentators, if perchance any of that ingenious class of persons should hereafter see proper to write notes for this history. It is enough for us that we give all the facts in this connection, so that ignorance of the subsequent conduct of Captain Suggs may not lead to an erroneous judgment in respect to his words.

Having uttered the exclamation we have repeated—and perhaps, hurriedly walked once or twice across the room—Captain Suggs drew on his famous old green-blanket overcoat, and ordered his horse, and within five minutes was on his way to a camp-meeting, then in full blast on Sandy Creek, twenty miles distant, where he hoped to find amusement, at least. When he arrived there, he found the hollow square of the encampment filled with people, listening to the mid-day

375

sermon, and its dozen accompanying "exhortations." A half-dozen preachers were dispensing the word; the one in the pulpit, a meek-faced old man, of great simplicity and benevolence. His voice was weak and cracked, notwithstanding which, however, he contrived to make himself heard occasionally, above the din of the exhorting, the singing, and the shouting which were going on around him. The rest were walking to and fro, (engaged in the other exercises we have indicated), among the "mourners"—a host of whom occupied the seat set apart for their especial use—or made personal appeals to the mere spectators. The excitement was intense. Men and women rolled about on the ground, or lay sobbing or shouting in promiscuous heaps. More than all, the negroes sang and screamed and prayed. Several, under the influence of what is technically called "the jerks," were plunging and pitching about with convulsive energy. The great object of all seemed to be, to see who could make the greatest noise——

> "And each—for madness ruled the hour—
> Would try his own expressive power."

"Bless my poor old soul!" screamed the preacher in the pulpit; "ef yonder aint a squad in that corner that we aint got one outen yet! It'll never do"—raising his voice—"you must come outen that! Brother Fant, fetch up that youngster in the blue coat! I see the Lord's a-workin' upon him! Fetch him along—glory—yes!—hold to him!"

"Keep the thing warm!" roared a sensual seeming man, of stout mould and florid countenance, who was exhorting among a bevy of young women, upon whom he was lavishing caresses. "Keep the thing warm, breethring!—come to the Lord, honey!" he added, as he vigorously hugged one of the damsels he sought to save.

"Oh, I've got him!" said another in exulting tones, as he led up a gawky youth among the mourners—"I've got him—he tried to git off, but—ha! Lord!"—shaking his head as much as to say, it took a smart fellow to escape him—"ha! Lord!"—and he wiped the perspiration from his face with one hand, and with the other, patted his neophyte on the shoulder—"he couldn't do it! No! Then he tried to argy wi' me—but bless the Lord!—he couldn't do that nother! Ha! Lord! I tuk him, fust in the Old Testament—bless the Lord!—and I argyed him all thro' Kings —then I throwed him into Proverbs,—and from that, here we had it up and down, kleer down to the New Testament, and then I begun to see it work him!—then we got into Matthy, and from Matthy right straight along to Acts; and *thar* I throwed him! Y-e-s—L-o-r-d!"—assuming the nasal twang and high pitch which are, in some parts, considered the perfection of rhetorical art—"Y-e-s—L-o-r-d! and h-e-r-e he is! Now g-i-t down thar," addressing the subject, "and s-e-e ef the L-o-r-d won't do somethin' f-o-r you!" Having thus deposited his charge among the mourners, he started out, summarily to convert another soul!

"Gl-o-*ree!*" yelled a huge, greasy negro woman, as in a fit of the jerks, she threw herself convulsively from her feet, and fell "like a thousand of brick," across a diminutive old man in a little round hat, who was speaking consolation to one of the mourners.

"Good Lord, have mercy!" ejaculated the little man earnestly and unaffectedly, as he strove to crawl from under the sable mass which was crushing him.

In another part of the square a dozen old women were singing. They were in a state of absolute ecstasy, as their shrill pipes gave forth.

"I rode on the sky,
Quite ondestified I,
And the moon it was under my feet!"

Near these last, stood a delicate woman in that hysterical condition in which the nerves are incontrollable, and which is vulgarly—and almost blasphemously —termed the "holy laugh." A hideous grin distorted her mouth, and was accompanied with a maniac's chuckle; while every muscle and nerve of her face twitched and jerked in horrible spasms.[1]

Amid all this confusion and excitement Suggs stood unmoved. He viewed the whole affair as a grand deception—a sort of "opposition line" running against his own, and looked on with a sort of professional jealousy. Sometimes he would mutter running comments upon what passed before him.

"Well now," said he, as he observed the full-faced brother who was "officiating" among the women, "that ere feller takes *my* eye!—thar he's been this half-hour, a-figurin amongst them galls, and's never said the fust word to nobody else. Wonder what's the reason these here preachers never hugs up the old, ugly women? Never seed one do it in my life—the sperrit never moves 'em that way! It's nater tho'; and the women, *they* never flocks round one o' the old dried-up breethring—bet two to one old splinter-legs thar,"—nodding at one of the ministers—"won't git a chance to say turkey to a good-lookin gall to-day! Well! who blames 'em? Nater will be nater, all the world over; and I judge ef I was a preacher, I should save the purtiest souls fust, myself!"

While the Captain was in the middle of this conversation with himself, he caught the attention of the preacher in the pulpit, who inferring from an indescribable something about his appearance that he was a person of some consequence, immediately determined to add him at once to the church if it could be done; and to that end began a vigorous, direct personal attack.

"Breethring," he exclaimed, "I see yonder a man that's a sinner; I *know* he's a sinner! Thar he stands," pointing at Simon, "a missubble old crittur, with his head a-blossomin for the grave! A few more short years, and d-o-w-n he'll go to perdition, lessen the Lord have mer-cy on him! Come up here, you old hoary-headed sinner, a-n-d git down upon your knees, a-n-d put up your cry for the Lord to snatch you from the bottomless pit! You're ripe for the devil—you're b-o-u-n-d for hell, and the Lord only knows what'll become on you!"

"D——n it," thought Suggs, "ef I only had you down in the krick swamp for a minit or so, *I'd* show you who's *old!* I'd alter your tune *mighty* sudden, you sassy, 'saitfull old rascal!" But he judiciously held his tongue and gave no utterance to the thought.

---

[1] *The reader is requested to bear in mind, that the scenes described in this story are not now to be witnessed. Eight or ten years ago, all classes of population of the Creek country were very different from what they now are. Of course no disrespect is intended to any denomination of Christians. We believe that camp-meetings are not peculiar to any church, though most usual in the Methodist—a denomination whose respectability in Alabama is attested by the fact, that very many of its worthy clergymen and lay members, hold honourable and profitable offices in the gift of the state legislature; of which, indeed, almost a controlling portion are themselves Methodists. (Hooper's note.)*

377

The attention of many having been directed to the Captain by the preacher's remarks, he was soon surrounded by numerous well-meaning, and doubtless very pious persons, each one of whom seemed bent on the application of his own particular recipe for the salvation of souls. For a long time the Captain stood silent, or answered the incessant stream of exhortations only with a sneer; but at length, his countenance began to give token of inward emotion. First his eye-lids twitched —then his upper lip quivered—next a transparent drop formed on one of his eye-lashes, and a similar one on the tip of his nose—and, at last, a sudden bursting of air from nose and mouth, told that Captain Suggs was overpowered by his emotions. At the moment of the explosion, he made a feint as if to rush from the crowd, but he was in experienced hands, who well knew that the battle was more than half won.

"Hold to him!" said one—"It's a-workin in him as strong as a Dick horse!"

"Pour it into him," said another, "it'll all come right directly!"

"That's the way I love to see 'em do," observed a third; "when you begin to draw the water from their eyes, taint gwine to be long afore you'll have 'em on their knees!"

And so they clung to the Captain manfully, and half dragged, half led him to the mourner's bench; by which he threw himself down, altogether unmanned, and bathed in tears. Great was the rejoicing of the brethren, as they sang, shouted, and prayed around him—for by this time it had come to be generally known that the "convicted" old man was Captain Simon Suggs, the very "chief of sinners" in all that region.

The Captain remained grovelling in the dust during the usual time, and gave vent to even more than the requisite number of sobs, and groans, and heart-piercing cries. At length, when the proper time had arrived, he bounced up, and with a face radiant with joy, commenced a series of vaultings and tumblings, which "laid in the shade" all previous performances of the sort at that camp-meeting. The brethren were in ecstasies at this demonstrative evidence of completion of the work; and whenever Suggs shouted "Gloree!" at the top of his lungs, every one of them shouted it back, until the woods rang with echoes.

The effervescence having partially subdivided, Suggs was put upon his pins to relate his experience, which he did somewhat in this style—first brushing the tear-drops from his eyes, and giving the end of his nose a preparatory wring with his fingers, to free it of the superabundant moisture:

"Friends," he said, "it don't take long to curry a short horse, accordin' to the old sayin', and I'll give you the perticklers of the way I was 'brought to a knowl-edge' "—here the Captain wiped his eyes, brushed the tip of his nose and snuffled a little—"in less'n no time."

"Praise the Lord!" ejaculated a bystander.

"You see I come here full o' romancin' and devilment, and jist to make game of all the purceedins. Well, sure enough, I done so for some time, and was a-thinkin how I should play some trick——"

"Dear soul alive! *don't* he talk sweet!" cried an old lady in black silk—"Whar's John Dobbs? You Sukey!" screaming at a negro woman on the other side of the square—"ef you don't hunt up your mass John in a minute, and have him here to listen to this 'sperience, I'll tuck you up when I git home and give you a hundred

378

and fifty lashes, madam!—see ef I don't! Blessed Lord!"—referring again to the Captain's relation—"aint it a *precious* 'scource!"

"I was jist a-thinkin' how I should play some trick to turn it all into redecule, when they began to come round me and talk. Long at fust I didn't mind it, but arter a little that brother"—pointing to the reverend gentleman who had so successfully carried the unbeliever through the Old and New Testaments, and who Simon was convinced was the "big dog of the tanyard"—"that brother spoke a word that struck me kleen to the heart, and run all over me, like fire in dry grass——"

"*I—I—I* can bring 'em!" cried the preacher alluded to, in a tone of exultation—"Lord thou knows ef thy servant can't stir 'em up, nobody else needn't try—but the glory aint mine! I'm a poor worrum of the dust," he added, with ill-managed affectation.

"And so from that I felt somethin' a-pullin' me inside——"

"Grace! grace! nothin' but grace!" exclaimed one; meaning that "grace" had been operating in the Captain's gastric region.

"And then," continued Suggs, "I wanted to git off, but they hilt me, and bimeby I felt so missuble, I had to go yonder"—pointing to the mourner's seat—"and when I lay down thar it got wuss and wuss, and 'speared like somethin' was a-mashin' down on my back——"

"That was his load o' sin," said one of the brethren—"never mind, it'll tumble off presently, see ef it don't!" and he shook his head professionally and knowingly.

"And it kept a-gittin heavier and heavier, ontwell it looked like it might be a four year old steer, or a big pine log, or somethin' of that sort——"

"Glory to my soul," shouted Mrs. Dobbs, "it's the sweetest talk I *ever* hearn! You Sukey! aint you got John yit? never mind, my lady, *I'll* settle wi' you!" Sukey quailed before the finger which her mistress shook at her.

"And arter awhile," Suggs went on, " 'peared like I fell into a trance, like, and I seed——"

"Now we'll git the good on it!" cried one of the sanctified.

"And I seed the biggest, longest, rip-roarenest, blackest, scaliest—" Captain Suggs paused, wiped his brow, and ejaculated "Ah, L-o-r-d!" so as to give full time for curiosity to become impatience to know what he saw.

"*Sarpent!* warn't it?" asked one of the preachers.

"No, not a sarpent," replied Suggs, blowing his nose.

"Do tell us *what* it war, soul alive!—whar *is* John?" said Mrs. Dobbs.

"Allegator!" said the Captain.

"Alligator!" repeated every woman present, and screamed for very life.

Mrs. Dobbs' nerves were so shaken by the announcement, that after repeating the horrible word, she screamed to Sukey, "You Sukey, I say, you Su-u-ke-e-y! ef you let John come a-nigh this way, whar the dreadful alliga—shaw! what am I thinkin' 'bout? 'Twarn't nothin' but a vishin!"

"Well," said the Captain in continuation, "the allegator kept a-comin' and a-comin' to'ards me, with his great long jaws a-gapin' open like a ten-foot pair o' tailor's shears——"

"Oh! oh! oh! Lord! gracious above!" cried the women.

379

"Satan!" was the laconic ejaculation of the oldest preacher present, who thus informed the congregation that it was the devil which had attacked Suggs in the shape of an alligator.

"And then I concluded the jig was up, 'thout I could block his game some way; for I seed his idee was to snap off my head——"

The women screamed again.

"So I fixed myself jist like I was purfectly willin' for him to take my head, and rather he'd do it as not"—here the women shuddered perceptibly—"and so I hilt my head straight out"—the Captain illustrated by elongating his neck—"and when he come up and was a gwine to *shet down* on it, I jist pitched in a big rock which choked him to death, and that minit I felt the weight slide off, and I had the best feelin—sorter like you'll have from *good* sperrits—any body ever had!"

"Didn't I *tell* you so? Didn't I *tell* you so?" asked the brother who had predicted the off-tumbling of the load of sin. "Ha, Lord! fool *who!* I've been *all* along thar!—yes, *all along thar!* and I know every inch of the way jist as good as I do the road home!"—and then he turned round and round, and looked at all, to receive a silent tribute to his superior penetration.

Captain Suggs was now the "lion of the day." Nobody could pray so well, or exhort so movingly, as "brother Suggs." Nor did his natural modesty prevent the proper performance of appropriate exercises. With the reverend Bela Bugg (him to whom, under providence, he ascribed his conversion) he was a most especial favorite. They walked, sang, and prayed together for hours.

"Come, come up; thar's room for all!" cried brother Bugg, in his evening exhortation. "Come to the 'seat,' and ef you won't pray yourselves, let *me* pray for you!"

"Yes!" said Simon, by way of assisting his friend; "it's a game that all can win at! Ante up! ante up, boys—friends I mean—don't back out!"

"Thar aint a sinner here," said Bugg, "no matter ef his soul's black as a nigger, but what thar's room for him!"

"No matter what sort of a hand you've got," added Simon in the fulness of his benevolence; "take stock! Here am *I*, the wickedest and blindest of sinners—has spent my whole life in the sarvice of the devil—has now come in on *narry pair* and won a *pile!*" and the Captain's face beamed with holy pleasure.

"D-o-n-'t be afeard!" cried the preacher; "come along! the meanest won't be turned away! humble your selves and come!"

"No!" said Simon, still indulging in his favourite style of metaphor; "the bluff game aint played here! No runnin' of a body off! Every body holds four aces, and when you bet, you win!"

And thus the Captain continued, until the services were concluded, to assist in adding to the number at the mourners' seat; and up to the hour of retiring, he exhibited such enthusiasm in the cause, that he was unanimously voted to be the most efficient addition the church had made during that meeting.

The next morning, when the preacher of the day first entered the pulpit, he announced that "brother Simon Suggs," mourning over his past iniquities, and desirous of going to work in the cause as speedily as possible, would take up a collection to found a church in his own neighbourhood, at which he hoped to make himself useful as soon as he could prepare himself for the ministry, which the preacher didn't doubt, would be in a very few weeks, as brother Suggs was "a

380

man of mighty good judgement, and of a great discorse." The funds were to be collected by "brother Suggs," and held in trust by brother Bela Bugg, who was the financial officer of the circuit, until some arrangement could be made to build a suitable house.

"Yes, breethring," said the Captain, rising to his feet; "I want to start a little 'sociation close to me, and I want you all to help. I'm mighty poor myself, as poor as any of you—don't leave, breethring"—observing that several of the well-to-do were about to go off—"don't leave; ef you aint able to afford any thing, jist give us your blessin' and it'll be all the same!"

This insinuation did the business, and the sensitive individuals reseated themselves.

"It's mighty little of this world's goods I've got," resumed Suggs, pulling off his hat and holding it before him; "but I'll bury *that* in the cause any how," and he deposited his last five-dollar bill in the hat.

There was a murmur of approbation at the Captain's liberality throughout the assembly.

Suggs now commenced collecting, and very prudently attacked first the gentlemen who had shown a disposition to escape. These, to exculpate themselves from anything like poverty, contributed handsomely.

"Look here, breethring," said the Captain, displaying the bank-notes thus received, "brother Snooks has drapt a five wi' me, and brother Snodgrass a ten! In course 'taint expected that you *that aint as well off as them,* will give *as much;* let every one give *accordin'* to ther means."

This was another chain-shot that raked as it went! "Who so low" as not to be able to contribute as much as Snooks and Snodgrass?

"Here's all the *small* money I've got about me," said a burly old fellow, ostentatiously handing to Suggs, over the heads of a half dozen, a ten dollar bill.

"That's what I call maganimus!" exclaimed the Captain; "that's the way *every* rich man ought to do!"

These examples were followed, more or less closely, by almost all present, for Simon had excited the pride of purse of the congregation, and a very handsome sum was collected in a very short time.

The reverend Mr. Bugg, as soon as he observed that our hero had obtained all that was to be had at that time, went to him and inquired what amount had been collected. The Captain replied that it was still uncounted, but that it couldn't be much under a hundred.

"Well, brother Suggs, you'd better count it and turn it over to me now. I'm goin' to leave presently."

"No!" said Suggs—"can't do it!"

"Why?—what's the matter?" inquired Bugg.

"It's got to be *prayed over,* fust!" said Simon, a heavenly smile illuminating his whole face.

"Well," replied Bugg, "les go one side and do it!"

"No!" said Simon, solemnly.

Mr. Bugg gave a look of inquiry.

"You see that krick swamp?" asked Suggs—"I'm gwine down in *thar,* and I'm gwine to lay this money down *so*"—showing how he would place it on the ground—"and I'm gwine to git on these here knees"—slapping the right one—

381

"and I'm *n-e-v-e-r* gwine to quit the grit ontwell I feel it's got the blessin! And nobody aint got to be thar but me!"

Mr. Bugg greatly admired the Captain's fervent piety, and bidding him Godspeed, turned off.

Captain Suggs "struck for" the swamp sure enough, where his horse was already hitched. "Ef them fellers aint done to a cracklin," he muttered to himself as he mounted, "I'll never bet on two pair agin! They're peart at the snap game, theyselves; but they're badly lewed this hitch! Well! Live and let live is a good old motter, and it's my sentiments adzactly!" And giving the spur to his horse, off he cantered. (*1845*)

JOSEPH GLOVER BALDWIN

1815–1864

Joseph Glover Baldwin was born near Winchester, Virginia, January 21, 1815. In his sketches of life in frontier Alabama and Mississippi he was—somewhat like William Byrd—a product of an older society, looking at the beginnings of another civilization from the perspective of a sophisticate.

Baldwin's formal education ended when he was fourteen, at which time he became a deputy clerk for his county court. His primary duty was recording legal proceedings. Gaining experience from this job, he also read law under the guidance of his uncle, and soon qualified for admittance to the bar. In April 1836, he hung out his shingle in De Kalb, Mississippi, where, as he phrased it, "all the floodgates of civilization were rampant and the pent-up tide let loose upon the [new] country."

Baldwin moved around the legal circuit regularly, and, in August 1843, became a member of the Alabama legislature. Out of his experiences emerged his best known book, *The Flush Times of Alabama and Mississippi* (1853). The purpose motivating these sketches, he said, was "to illustrate the periods, the characters, and the phases of society" in the two states. He considered himself no narrator of tall tales, but, rather, an amateur social historian. The book was dedicated to "the old folks at home."

In a sense, Baldwin may be described as a restless follower of the frontier. He chased it—indeed, outstripped it—all the way to San Francisco, where "the people talked and thought of money by the twenty dollar gold piece as they thought of a

382

five in Alabama." This was in 1854. Four years later he was elected a judge of the California Supreme Court, a position he held until 1862, when business affairs called him to New York and, a bit later, to Washington. While in the capital, he was granted an interview with President Lincoln. "Abe and I," he wrote a friend, "grew very pleasant and spent an hour in the White House very cosily. He was very kind and affable and knew all about me and more about *Flush Times* (which seemed to be one of his classics) than I knew myself. He says he is always quoting me when he gets facetious (probably to restore gravity to his guests)."

In addition to *The Flush Times of Alabama and Mississippi*, Baldwin published *Party Leaders* (1855). His "Flush Times in California" is still in manuscript. Baldwin died of tetanus on September 30, 1864.

from The Flush Times of Alabama and Mississippi

How the Times Served the Virginians. Virginians in a New Country. The Rise, Decline, and Fall of the Rag Empire.

The disposition to be proud and vain of one's country, and to boast of it, is a natural feeling, indulged or not in respect to the pride, vanity, and boasting, according to the character of the native: but, with a Virginian, it is a passion. It inheres in him even as the flavor of a York river oyster in that bivalve, and no distance of deportation, and no trimmings of a gracious prosperity, and no pickling in the sharp acids of adversity, can destroy it. It is a part of the Virginia character—just as the flavor is a distinctive part of the oyster—"which cannot, save by annihilating, die." It is no use talking about it—the thing may be right, or wrong:—like Falstaff's victims at Gadshill, it is past praying for: it is a sort of cocoa grass that has *got* into the soil, and has so matted over it, and so *fibred* through it, as to have become a part of it; at least, there is no telling which is the grass and which is the soil; and certainly it is useless labor to try to root it out. You may destroy the soil, but you can't root out the grass.

Patriotism with a Virginian is a noun personal. It is the Virginian himself and something over. He loves Virginia *per se* and *propter se:* he loves her for herself and for himself—because *she is* Virginia and—every thing else beside. He loves to talk about her: out of the abundance of the heart the mouth speaketh. It makes no odds where he goes, he carries Virginia with him; not in the entirety always— but the little spot he came from is Virginia—as Swedenborg says the smallest part of the brain is an abridgment of all of it. *"Caelum non animum mutant qui trans mare currunt,"* [1] was made for a Virginian. He never gets acclimated elsewhere; he never loses citizenship to the old Home. The right of expatriation is a pure abstraction to him. He may breathe in Alabama, but he lives in Virginia. His treasure is there, and his heart also. If he looks at the Delta of the Mississippi, it reminds him of James River "low grounds"; if he sees the vast prairies of

383

---

[1] *The heavens do not change the mind of him who passes across the sea.*

Texas, it is a memorial of the meadows of the Valley. Richmond is the centre of attraction, the *depot* of all that is grand, great, good and glorious. "It is the Kentucky of a place," which the preacher described Heaven to be to the Kentucky congregation.

Those who came many years ago from the borough towns, especially from the vicinity of Williamsburg, exceed, in attachment to their birthplace, if possible, the *emigrés* from the metropolis. It is refreshing in these costermonger times, to hear them speak of it:—they remember it when the old burg was the seat of fashion, taste, refinement, hospitality, wealth, wit, and all social graces; when genius threw its spell over the public assemblages and illumined the halls of justice, and when beauty brightened the social hour with her unmatched and matchless brilliancy.

Then the spirited and gifted youths of the College of old William and Mary, some of them just giving out the first scintillations of the genius that afterwards shone refulgent in the forum and the senate, added to the attractions of a society gay, cultivated and refined beyond example—*even in* the Old Dominion. A hallowed charm seems to rest upon the venerable city, clothing its very dilapidation in a drapery of romance and of serene and classic interest: as if all the sweet and softened splendor which invests the "Midsummer Night's Dream" were poured in a flood of mellow and poetic radiance over the now quiet and half "deserted village." There is something in the shadow from the old college walls, cast by the moon upon the grass and sleeping on the sward, that throws a like shadow soft, sad and melancholy upon the heart of the returning pilgrim who saunters out to view again, by moonlight, his old *Alma Mater*—the nursing mother of such a list and such a line of statesmen and heroes.

There is nothing presumptuously froward in this Virginianism. The Virginian does not make broad his phylacteries and crow over the poor Carolinian and Tennesseean. He does not reproach him with his misfortune of birthplace. No, he thinks the affliction is enough without the triumph. The franchise of having been born in Virginia, and the prerogative founded thereon, are too patent of honor and distinction to be arrogantly pretended. The bare mention is enough. He finds occasion to let the fact be known, and then the fact is fully able to protect and take care of itself. Like a ducal title, there is no need of saying more than to name it: modesty then is a becoming and expected virtue; forbearance to boast is true dignity.

The Virginian is a magnanimous man. He never throws up to a Yankee the fact of his birthplace. He feels on the subject as a man of delicacy feels in alluding to a rope in the presence of a person, one of whose brothers "stood upon nothing and kicked at the U. S.," or to a female indiscretion, where there had been scandal concerning the family. So far do they carry this refinement, that I have known one of my countrymen, on occasion of a Bostonian owning where he was born, generously protest that he had never heard of it before. As if honest confession half obliterated the shame of the fact. Yet he does not lack the grace to acknowledge worth or merit in another, wherever the native place of that other: for it is a common thing to hear them say of a neighbor, "he is a clever fellow, *though* he *did* come from New Jersey or even Connecticut."

In politics the Virginian is learned much beyond what is written—for they have heard a great deal of speaking on that prolific subject, especially by one or two

384

Randolphs and any number of Barbours. They read the same papers here they read in Virginia—the *Richmond Enquirer* and the *Richmond Whig*. The democrat stoutly asseverates a fact, and gives *the Enquirer* as his authority with an air that means to say, *that* settles it: while the whig quoted Hampden Pleasants with the same confidence. But the faculty of personalizing every thing which the exceeding social turn of a Virginian gives him, rarely allowed a reference to the paper, *eo nomine;* but made him refer to the editor: as "Ritchie said" so and so, or "Hampden Pleasants said" this or that. When two of opposite politics got together, it was amusing, if you had nothing else to do that day, to hear the discussion. I never knew a debate that did not start *ab urbe condita.*[2] They not only went back to first principles, but also to first times; nor did I ever hear a discussion in which old John Adams and Thomas Jefferson did not figure—as if an interminable dispute had been going on for so many generations between those disputatious personages; as if the quarrel had begun before time, but was not to end with it. But the strangest part of it to me was, that the dispute seemed to be going on without poor Adams having any defence or champion; and never waxed hotter than when both parties agreed in denouncing the man of Braintree as the worst of public sinners and the vilest of political heretics. They both agreed on one thing, and that was to refer the matter to the Resolutions of 1798–99; which said Resolutions, like Goldsmith's "Good Natured Man," arbitrating between Mr. and Mrs. Croaker, seemed so impartial that they agreed with both parties on every occasion.

Nor do I recollect of hearing any question debated that did not resolve itself into a question of constitution—strict construction, &c.,—the constitution being a thing of that curious virtue that its chief excellency consisted in not allowing the government to do any thing; or in being a regular prize fighter that knocked all laws and legislators into a cocked hat, except those of the objector's party.

Frequent reference was reciprocally made to "gorgons, hydras, and chimeras dire," to black cockades, blue lights, Essex juntos, the Reign of Terror, and some other mystic entities—but who or what these monsters were, I never could distinctly learn; and was surprised, on looking into the history of the country, to find that, by some strange oversight, no allusion was made to them.

Great is the Virginian's reverence of great men, that is to say, of great Virginians. This reverence is not Unitarian. He is a Polytheist. He believes in a multitude of Virginia Gods. As the Romans of every province and village had their tutelary or other divinities, besides having divers national gods, so the Virginian of every county has his great man, the like of whom cannot be found in the new country he has exiled himself to. This sentiment of veneration for talent, especially for speaking talent,—this amiable propensity to lionize men, is not peculiar to any class of Virginians among us: it abides in all. I was amused to hear "old Cul pepper," as we call him (by nickname derived from the county he came from), declaiming in favor of the Union. "What, gentlemen," said the old man, with a sonorous swell—"what, burst up this glorious Union! and who, if *this* Union is torn up, could write another? Nobody except Henry Clay and J—— S. B——, of Culpepper—and may be *they* wouldn't—and what then would you do for another?"

385

---

[2] *From the founding of the city.*

The greatest compliment a Virginian can ever pay to a speaker, is to say that he reminds him of a Col. Broadhorn or a Captain Smith, who represented some royal-named county some forty years or less in the Virginia House of Delegates; and of whom, the auditor, of course, has heard, as he made several speeches in the capitol at Richmond. But the force of the compliment is somewhat broken, by a long narrative, in which the personal reminiscences of the speaker go back to sundry sketches of the Virginia statesman's efforts, and recapitulations of his sayings, interspersed *par parenthèse*, with many valuable notes illustrative of his pedigree and performances; the whole of which, given with great historical fidelity of detail, leaves nothing to be wished for except the point, or rather, two points, the gist and the period.

It is not to be denied that Virginia is the land of orators, heroes and statesmen; and that, directly or indirectly, she has exerted an influence upon the national councils nearly as great as all the rest of the States combined. It is wonderful that a State of its size and population should have turned out such an unprecedented quantum of talent, and of talent as various in kind as prodigious in amount. She has reason to be proud; and the other States so largely in her debt (for, from Cape May to Puget's Sound she has colonized the other States and the territories with her surplus talent,) ought to allow her the harmless privilege of a little bragging. In the showy talent of oratory has she especially shone. To accomplish her in this art the State has been turned into a debating society, and while she has been *talking* for the benefit of the nation, as she thought, the other, and, by nature, less favored States, have been *doing* for their own. Consequently, what she has gained in reputation, she has lost in wealth and *material aids*. Certainly the Virginia character has been less distinguished for its practical than its ornamental traits, and for its business qualities than for its speculative temper. *Cui bono* and utilitarianism, at least until latterly, were not favorite or congenial inquiries and subjects of attention to the Virginia politician. What the Virginian was upon his native soil, that he was abroad; indeed, it may be said that the *amor patriae*, strengthened by absence, made him more of a conservative abroad than he would have been if he had staid at home; for most of them here would not, had they been consulted, have changed either of the old constitutions.

It is far, however, from my purpose to treat of such themes. I only glance at them to show their influence on the character as it was developed on a new theatre.

Eminently social and hospitable, kind, humane and generous is a Virginian, at home or abroad. They are so by nature and habit. These qualities and their exercise develop and strengthen other virtues. By reason of these social traits, they necessarily become well mannered, honorable, spirited, and careful of reputation, desirous of pleasing, and skilled in the accomplishments which please. Their insular position and sparse population, mostly rural, and easy but not affluent fortunes kept them from the artificial refinements and the strong temptations which corrupt so much of the society of the old world and some portions of the new. There was no character more attractive than that of a young Virginian, fifteen years ago, of intelligence, of good family, education and breeding.

It was of the instinct of a Virginian to seek society: he belongs to the gregarious, not to the solitary division of animals; and society can only be kept up

386

by grub and gab—something to eat, and, if not something to talk about, talk. Accordingly they came accomplished already in the knowledge and the talent for these important duties.

A Virginian could always get up a good dinner. He could also do his share—a full hand's work—in disposing of one after it was got up. The qualifications for hostmanship were signal—the old Udaller himself, assisted by Claud Halrco, could not do up the thing in better style, or with a heartier relish, or a more cordial hospitality. In *petite* manners—the little attentions of the table, the filling up of the chinks of the conversation with small fugitive observations, the supplying the hooks and eyes that *kept* the discourse together, the genial good humor, which, like that of the family of the good Vicar, made up in laughter what was wanting in wit—in these, and in the science of getting up and in getting through a picnic or chowder party, or fish fry the Virginian, like Eclipse, was first, and there was no second. Great was he too at mixing an apple toddy, or mint julep, where ice could be got for love or money; and not deficient, by any means, when it came to his turn to do honor to his own fabrics. It was in this department, that he not only shone but *out*shone, not merely all others but himself. Here he was at home indeed. His elocution, his manner, his learning, his education, were of the first order. He could discourse of every thing around him with an accuracy and a fulness which would have put Coleridge's or Mrs. Ellis's table talk to the blush. Every dish was a text, horticulture, hunting, poultry, fishing—(Izaak Walton or Daniel Webster would have been charmed and instructed to hear him discourse piscatory-wise,)—a slight divergence in favor of fox-chasing and a detour towards a horse-race now and then, and continual parentheses of recommendation of particular dishes or glasses—Oh! I tell you if ever there was an interesting man it was he. Others might be agreeable, but he was fascinating, irresistible, not-to-be-done-without.

In the fulness of time the new era had set in—the era of the second great experiment of independence: the experiment, namely, of credit without capital, and enterprise without honesty. The Age of Brass had succeeded the Arcadian period when men got rich by saving a part of their earnings, and lived at their own cost and in ignorance of the new plan of making fortunes on the profits of what they owed. A new theory, not found in the works on political economy, was broached. It was found out that the prejudice in favor of the metals (brass excluded) was an absurd superstition; and that, in reality, any thing else, which the parties interested in giving it currency chose, might serve as a representative of value and medium for exchange of property; and as gold and silver had served for a great number of years as representatives, the republican doctrine of rotation in office required they should give way. Accordingly it was decided that Rags, a very familiar character, and very popular and easy of access, should take their place. Rags belonged to the school of progress. He was representative of the then Young America. His administration was not tame. It was *very* spirited. It was based on the Bonapartist idea of keeping the imagination of the people excited. The leading fiscal idea of his system was to *democratize* capital, and to make, for all purposes of trade, credit and enjoyment of wealth, the man that had *no* money a little richer, if any thing, than the man that had a million. The principle of success and basis of operation, though inexplicable in the hurry of the time, is plain enough

387

now: it was faith. Let the public believe that a smutted rag is money, it is money: in other words, it was a sort of financial biology, which made, at night, the thing conjured for, the thing that was seen, so far as the patient was concerned, while the fit was on him—except that now a man does not do his trading when under the mesmeric influence: in the flush times he did.

This country was just settling up. Marvellous accounts had gone forth of the fertility of its virgin lands; and the productions of the soil were commanding a price remunerating to slave labor as it had never been remunerated before. Emigrants came flocking in from all quarters of the Union, especially from the slaveholding States. The new country seemed to be a reservoir, and every road leading to it a vagrant stream of enterprise and adventure. Money, or what passed for money, was the only cheap thing to be had. Every cross-road and every avocation presented an opening,—through which a fortune was seen by the adventurer in near perspective. Credit was a thing of course. To refuse it—if the thing was ever done—were an insult for which a bowie-knife were not a too summary or exemplary a means of redress. The State banks were issuing their bills by the sheet, like a patent steam printing-press *its* issues; and no other showing was asked of the applicant for the loan than an authentication of his great distress for money. Finance, even in its most exclusive quarter, had thus already got, in this wonderful revolution, to work upon the principles of the charity hospital. If an overseer grew tired of supervising a plantation and felt a call to the mercantile life, even if he omitted the compendious method of buying out a merchant wholesale, stock, house and good will, and laying down, at once, his bull-whip for the yard-stick— all he had to do was to go on to New-York, and present himself in Pearl street with a letter avouching his citizenship, and a clean shirt, and he was regularly given a through ticket to speedy bankruptcy.

Under this stimulating process prices rose like smoke. Lots in obscure villages were held at city prices; lands, bought at the minimum cost of government, were sold at from thirty to forty dollars per acre, and considered dirt cheap at that. In short, the country had got to be a full ante-type of California, in all except the gold. Society was wholly unorganized: there was no restraining public opinion, the law was well-nigh powerless—and religion scarcely was heard of except as furnishing the oaths and *technics* of profanity. The world saw a fair experiment of what it would have been, if the fiat had never been pronounced which decreed subsistence as the price of labor.

Money, got without work, by those unaccustomed to it, turned the heads of its possessors, and they spent it with a recklessness like that with which they gained it. The pursuits of industry neglected, riot and coarse debauchery filled up the vacant hours. "Where the carcass is, there will the eagles be gathered together"; and the eagles that flocked to the South-west, were of the same sort as the *black eagles* the Duke of Saxe-Weimar saw on his celebrated journey to the Natural Bridge. "The cankers of a long peace and a calm world"—there were no Mexican wars and filibuster expeditions in those days—gathered in the villages and cities by scores.

388

Even the little boys caught the taint of the general infection of morals; and I knew one of them—Jim Ellett by name—to give a man ten dollars to hold him up to bet at the table of a faro-bank. James was a fast youth; and I sincerely hope he may not fulfil his early promise, and some day be *assisted up still higher*.

The groceries—*vulgice*—doggeries, were in full blast in those days, no village having less than a half-dozen all busy all the time: gaming and horse-racing were polite and well patronized amusements. I knew a Judge to adjourn two courts (or court twice) to attend a horse-race, at which he officiated judicially and ministerially, and with more appropriateness than in the judicial chair. Occasionally the scene was diversified by a murder or two, which though perpetrated from behind a corner, or behind the back of the deceased, whenever the accused *chose* to stand his trial, was always found to have been committed in self-defence, securing the homicide an honorable acquittal *at the hands of his peers.*

The old rules of business and the calculations of prudence were alike disregarded, and profligacy, in all the departments of the *crimen falsi,*[3] held riotous carnival. Larceny grew not only respectable, but genteel, and ruffled it in all the pomp of purple and fine linen. Swindling was raised to the dignity of the fine arts. Felony came forth from its covert, put on more seemly habiliments, and took its seat with unabashed front in the upper places of the synagogue. Before the first circles of the patrons of this brilliant and dashing villainy, Blunt Honesty felt as abashed as poor Halbert Glendinning by the courtly refinement and supercilious airs of Sir Piercie Shafton.

Public office represented, by its incumbents, the state of public morals with some approach to accuracy. Out of sixty-six receivers of public money in the new States, sixty-two were discovered to be defaulters; and the agent, sent to look into the affairs of a peccant office-holder in the South-West, reported him *minus* some tens of thousands, but advised the government to retain him, for a reason one of Aesop's fables illustrates: the agent ingeniously surmising that the appointee succeeding would do his stealing without any regard to the proficiency already made by his predecessor; while the present incumbent would probably consider, in mercy to the treasury, that he *had* done *something* of the pious duty of providing for his household.

There was no petit larceny: there was all the difference between stealing by the small and the "operations" manipulated, that there is between a single assassination and an hundred thousand men killed in an opium war. The placeman robbed with the gorgeous magnificence of a Governor-General of Bengal.

The man of straw, not worth the buttons on his shirt, with a sublime audacity, bought lands and negroes, and provided times and terms of payment which a Wall-street capitalist would have to re-cast his arrangements to meet.

Oh, Paul Clifford and Augustus Tomlinson, philosophers of the road, practical and theoretical! if ye had lived to see those times, how great an improvement on your ruder scheme of distribution would these gentle arts have seemed; arts whereby, without risk, or loss of character, or the vulgar barbarism of personal violence, the same beneficial results flowed with no greater injury to the superstitions of moral education!

With the change of times and the imagination of wealth easily acquired came a change in the thoughts and habits of the people. "Old times were changed—old manners gone." Visions of affluence, such as crowded Dr. Samuel Johnson's mind, when advertising a sale of Thrale's Brewery, and casting a soft sheep's eye towards Thrale's widow, thronged upon the popular fancy. Avarice and hope joined partnership. It was strange how the reptile arts of humanity, as at a faro

389

[3] *Scandals.*

table, warmed into life beneath their heat. The *cacoethes accrescendi* [4] became epidemic. It seized upon the universal community. The pulpits even were not safe from its insidious invasion. What men anxiously desire they willingly believe; and all believed a good time was coming—nay, had come.

"Commerce was king"—and Rags, Tag and Bobtail his cabinet council. Rags was treasurer. Banks, chartered on a specie basis, did a very flourishing business on the promissory notes of the individual stockholders ingeniously substituted in lieu of cash. They issued ten for one, the *one* being fictitious. They generously loaned all the directors could not use themselves, and were not choice whether Bardolph was the endorser for Falstaff, or Falstaff borrowed on his own proper credit, or the funds advanced him by Shallow. The stampede towards the golden temple became general: the delusion prevailed far and wide that this thing was not a burlesque on commerce and finance. Even the directors of the banks began to have their doubts whether the intended swindle was not a failure. Like Lord Clive, when reproached for extortion to the extent of some millions in Bengal, they exclaimed, after the bubble burst, "When they thought of what they had got, and what they might have got, they were astounded at their own moderation."

The old capitalists for a while stood out. With the Tory conservativism of cash in hand, worked for, they couldn't reconcile their old notions to the new regime. They looked for the thing's ending, and *then* their time. But the stampede still kept on. Paper fortunes still multiplied—houses and lands changed hands—real estate see-sawed up as morals went down on the other end of the plank—men of straw, corpulent with bank bills, strutted past them on 'Change. They began, too, to think there might be something in this new thing. Peeping cautiously, like hedge-hogs out of their holes, they saw the stream of wealth and adventurers passing by—then, looking carefully around, they inched themselves half way out—then, sallying forth and snatching up a morsel, ran back, until, at last, grown more bold, *they* ran out too with their hoarded store, in full chase with the other unclean beasts of adventure. They never got back again. Jonah's gourd withered one night, and next morning the vermin that had nestled under its broad shade were left unprotected, a prey to the swift retribution that came upon them. They were left naked, or only clothed themselves with cursing (the Specie Circular on the United States Bank) as with a garment. To drop the figure: Shylock himself couldn't live in those times, so reversed was every thing. Shaving paper and loaning money at a usury of fifty per cent, was for the first time since the Jews left Jerusalem, a breaking business to the operator.

The condition of society may be imagined:—vulgarity—ignorance—fussy and arrogant pretension—unmitigated rowdyism—bullying insolence, if they did not rule the hour *seemed* to wield unchecked dominion. The workings of these choice spirits were patent upon the face of society; and the modest, unobtrusive, retiring men of worth and character (for there were many, perhaps a large majority of such) were almost lost sight of in the hurly-burly of those strange and shifting scenes.

390 Even in the professions were the same characteristics visible. Men dropped down into their places as from the clouds. Nobody knew who or what they were, except as they claimed, or as a surface view of their characters indicated. Instead of taking to the highway and magnanimously calling upon the wayfarer to stand

[4] *Bad habits increasing progressively.*

and deliver, or to the fashionable larceny of credit without prospect or design of paying, some unscrupulous horse-doctor would set up his sign as "Physician and Surgeon," and draw his lancet on you, or fire at random a box of his pills into your bowels, with a vague chance of hitting some disease unknown to him, but with a better prospect of killing the patient, whom or whose administrator he charged some ten dollars a trial for his markmanship.

A superannuated justice or constable in one of the old States was metamorphosed into a lawyer; and though he knew not the distinction between a *feetail* and a *female*, would undertake to construe, off-hand, a will involving all the subtleties of *uses and trusts*.

But this state of things could not last for ever: society cannot always stand on its head with its heels in the air.

The Jupiter Tonans of the White House saw the monster of a free credit prowling about like a beast of apocalyptic vision, and marked him for his prey. Gathering all his bolts in his sinewy grasp, and standing back on his heels, and waving his wiry arm, he let them all fly, hard and swift upon all the hydra's heads. Then came a crash, as "if the ribs of nature broke," and a scattering, like the bursting of a thousand magazines, and a smell of brimstone, as if Pandemonium had opened a window next to earth for ventilation,—and all was silent. The beast never stirred in his tracks. To get down from the clouds to level ground, the Specie Circular was issued without warning, and the splendid lie of a false credit burst into fragments. It came in the midst of the dance and the frolic—as Tam O'Shanter came to disturb the infernal glee of the warlocks, and to disperse the rioters. Its effect was like that of a general creditor's bill in the chancery court, and a marshalling of all the assets of the trades-people. Gen. Jackson was no fairy; but he did some very pretty fairy work, in converting the bank bills back again into rags and oak-leaves. Men worth a million were insolvent for two millions: promising young cities marched back again into the wilderness. The ambitious town plat was re-annexed to the plantation, like a country girl taken home from the city. The frolic was ended, and what headaches, and feverish limbs the next morning! The retreat from Moscow was performed over again, and "Devil take the hindmost" was the tune to which the soldiers of fortune marched. The only question was as to the means of escape, and the nearest and best route to Texas. The sheriff was as busy as a militia adjutant on review day; and the lawyers were mere wreckers, earning salvage. Where are ye now my ruffling gallants? Where now the braw cloths and watch chains and rings and fine horses? Alas! for ye—they are glimmering among the things that were—the wonder of an hour! They live only in memory, as unsubstantial as the promissory notes ye gave for them. When it came to be tested, the whole matter was found to be hollow and fallacious. Like a sum ciphered out through a long column, the first figure an error, the whole, and all the parts were wrong, throughout the entire calculation.

Such is a charcoal sketch of the interesting region—now inferior to none in resources, and the character of its population—during the FLUSH TIMES; a period constituting an episode in the commercial history of the world—the reign of humbug, and wholesale insanity, just overthrown in time to save the whole country from ruin. But while it lasted, many of our countrymen came into the South-West in time to get "a benefit." The *auri sacra fames* [5] is a catching disease. Many Vir-

[5] *Sacred hunger for gold.*

391

ginians had lived too fast for their fortunes, and naturally desired to recuperate: many others, with a competency, longed for wealth; and others again, with wealth, yearned—the common frailty—for still more. Perhaps some friend or relative, who had come out, wrote back flattering accounts of the El Dorado, and fired with dissatisfaction those who were doing well enough at home, by the report of his real or imagined success; for who that ever moved off, was not "doing well" in the new country, himself or friends being chroniclers?

Superior to many of the settlers in elegance of manners and general intelligence, it was the weakness of the Virginian to imagine he was superior too in the essential art of being able to hold his hand and make his way in a new country, and especially *such* a country, and at *such* a time. What a mistake that was! The times were out of joint. It was hard to say whether it were more dangerous to stand still or to move. If the emigrant stood still, he was consumed, by no slow degrees, by expenses: if he moved, ten to one he went off in a galloping consumption, by a ruinous investment. Expenses then—necessary articles about three times as high, and extra articles still more extra-priced—were a different thing in the new country from what they were in the old. In the old country, a jolly Virginian, starting the business of free living on a capital of a plantation, and fifty or sixty negroes, might reasonably calculate, if no ill luck befell him, by the aid of a usurer, and the occasional sale of a negro or two, to hold out without declared insolvency, until a green old age. His estate melted like an estate in chancery, under the gradual thaw of expenses; but in this fast country, it went by the sheer cost of living—some *poker* losses included—like the fortune of the confectioner in California, who failed for one hundred thousand dollars in the six months keeping of a candy-shop. But all the habits of his life, his taste, his associations, his education—every thing—the trustingness of his disposition—his want of business qualifications—his sanguine temper—all that was Virginian in him, made him the prey, if not of imposture, at least of unfortunate speculations. Where the keenest jockey often was bit, what chance had *he?* About the same that the verdant Moses had with the venerable old gentle man, his father's friend, at the fair, when he traded the Vicar's pony for the green spectacles. But how could he believe it? how *could* he believe that that stuttering, grammarless Georgian, who had never heard of the resolutions of '98, could beat him in a land trade? "Have no money dealings with my father," said the friendly Martha to Lord Nigel, "for, idiot though he seems, he will make an ass of thee." What a pity some monitor, equally wise and equally successful with old Trapbois' daughter, had not been at the elbow of every Virginian! "Twad frae monie a blunder free'd him—an' foolish notion."

If he made a bad bargain, how could he expect to get rid of it? *He* knew nothing of the elaborate machinery of ingenious chicane,—such as feigning bankruptcy—fraudulent conveyances—making over to his wife—running property—and had never heard of such tricks of trade as sending out coffins to the graveyard, with negroes inside, carried off by sudden spells of imaginary disease, to be "resurrected," in due time, grinning, on the banks of the Brazos.

The new philosophy, too, had commended itself to his speculative temper. He readily caught at the idea of a new spirit of the age having set in, which rejected the saws of Poor Richard as being as much out of date as his almanacs. He was already, by the great rise of property, compared to his condition under the old-

392

time prices, rich; and what were a few thousands of debt, which two or three crops would pay off, compared to the value of his estate? (He never thought that the value of property might come down, while the debt was a fixed fact.) He lived freely, for it was a liberal time, and liberal fashions were in vogue, and it was not for a Virginian to be behind others in hospitality and liberality. He required credit and security, and, of course, had to stand security in return. When the crash came, and no "accommodations" could be had, except in a few instances, and in those on the most ruinous terms, he fell an easy victim. They broke by neighborhoods. They usually endorsed for each other, and when one fell—like the child's play of putting bricks on end at equal distances, and dropping the first in the line against the second, which fell against the third, and so on to the last—all fell; each got broke as security, and yet few or none were able to pay their own debts! So powerless of protection were they in those times, that the witty H. G. used to say they reminded him of an oyster, both shells torn off, lying on the beach, with the sea-gulls screaming over them; the only question being, *which* should "gobble them up."

There was one consolation—if the Virginian involved himself like a fool, he suffered himself to be sold out like a gentleman. When his card house of visionary projects came tumbling about his ears, the next question was, the one Webster plagiarised—"Where am I to go?" Those who had fathers, uncles, aunts, or other like dernier resorts, in Virginia, limped back with feathers moulted and crest-fallen, to the old stamping ground, carrying the returned Californian's fortune of ten thousand dollars—six bits in money, and the balance in experience. Those who were in the condition of the prodigal, (barring the father, the calf—the fatted one I mean—and the fiddle,) had to turn their accomplishments to account; and many of them, having lost all by eating and drinking, sought the retributive justice from meat and drink, which might, at least, support them in poverty. Accordingly, they kept tavern, and made a barter of hospitality, a business, the only disagreeable part of which was receiving the money, and the only one I know of for which a man can eat and drink himself into qualification. And while I confess I never knew a Virginian, out of the State, to keep a bad tavern, I never knew one to draw a solvent breath from the time he opened house, until death or the sheriff closed it.

Others again got to be, not exactly overseers, but some nameless thing, the duties of which were nearly analogous, for some more fortunate Virginian, who had escaped the wreck, and who had got his former boon companion to live with him on board, or other wages, in some such relation that the friend was not often found at table at the dinings given to the neighbors, and had got to be called Mr. Flournoy instead of Bob, and slept in an out-house in the yard, and only read the *Enquirer* of nights and Sundays.

Some of the younger scions that had been transplanted early, and stripped of their foliage at a tender age, had been turned into birches for the corrective discipline of youth. Yes; many, who had received academical or collegiate educations, disregarding the allurements of the highway—turning from the gala-day exercise of ditching—scorning the effeminate relaxation of splitting rails—heroically led the Forlorn Hope of the battle of life, the corps of pedagogues of country schools—*academies*, I beg pardon for *not* saying; for, under the Virginia economy, every cross-road log-cabin, where boys were flogged from B-a-k-e-r to Constantinople, grew into the dignity of a sort of runt college; and the teacher

393

vainly endeavored to hide the meanness of the calling beneath the sonorous *sobriquet* of Professor. "Were there no wars?" Had *all* the oysters been opened? Where was the regular army? Could not interest procure service as a deck-hand on a steamboat? Did no stage-driver, with a contract for running at night, through the prairies in mid-winter, want help, at board wages, and sweet lying in the loft, when off duty, thrown in? What right had the Dutch Jews to monopolize *all* the peddling? "To such vile uses may we come at last, Horatio." The subject grows melancholy. I had a friend on whom this catastrophe descended. Tom Edmundson was a buck of the first head—gay, witty, dashing, vain, proud, handsome and volatile, and, withal, a dandy and lady's man to the last intent in particular. He had graduated at the University, and had just settled with his guardian, and received his patrimony of ten thousand dollars in money. Being a young gentleman of enterprise, he sought the alluring fields of South-Western adventure, and found them in this State. Before he well knew the condition of his exchequer, he had made a permanent investment of one-half of his fortune in cigars, Champagne, trinkets, buggies, horses, and current expenses, including some small losses at poker, which game he patronized merely for amusement; and found that it diverted him a good deal, but diverted his cash much more. He invested the balance, on private information kindly given him, in *"Choctaw Floats;"* a most lucrative investment it would have turned out, but for the facts: 1. That the Indians never had any title; 2. The white men who kindly interposed to act as guardians for the Indians did not have the Indian title; and 3dly, the land, left subject to entry, if the "Floats" had been good, was not worth entering. "These imperfections off its head," I know of no fancy stock I would prefer to a "Choctaw Float." "Brief, brave and glorious" was "Tom's young career." When Thomas found, as he did shortly, that he had bought five thousand dollars' worth of moonshine, and had no title to it, he honestly informed his landlord of the state of his "fiscality," and that worthy kindly consented to take a new buggy, at half price, in payment of the old balance. The horse, a nick-tailed trotter, Tom had raffled off; but omitting to require cash, the process of collection resulted in his getting the price of one chance—the winner of the horse magnanimously paying his subscription. The rest either had gambling offsets, or else were not prepared just at any one particular, given moment, to pay up, though always ready, generally and in a general way.

Unlike his namesake, Tom and his landlady were not—for a sufficient reason—very gracious; and so, the only common bond, Tom's money, being gone, Tom received "notice to quit" in regular form.

In the hurly-burly of the times, I had lost sight of Tom for a considerable period. One day, as I was travelling over the hills in Greene, by a cross-road, leading me near a country mill, I stopped to get water at a spring at the bottom of a hill. Clambering up the hill, after remounting, the summit of it brought me to a view, on the other side, through the bushes, of a log country school-house, the door being wide open, and who did I see but Tom Edmundson, dressed as fine as ever, sitting back in an arm-chair, one thumb in his waistcoat armhole, the other hand brandishing a long switch, or rather pole. As I approached a little nearer, I heard him speak out: "Sir—Thomas Jefferson, of Virginia, was the author of the Declaration of Independence—mind that. I thought everybody knew that—

even the Georgians." Just then he saw me coming through the bushes and entering the path that led by the door. Suddenly he broke from the chair of state, and the door was slammed to, and I heard some one of the boys, as I passed the door, say —"Tell him he can't come in—the master's sick." This is the last I ever saw of Tom. I understand he afterwards moved to Louisiana, where he married a rich French widow, having first, however, to fight a duel with one of her sons, whose opposition couldn't be appeased, until some such expiatory sacrifice to the manes of his worthy father was attempted; which failing, he made rather a *lame* apology for his zealous indiscretion—the poor fellow could make no other—for Tom had unfortunately fixed him for visiting his mother on crutches the balance of his life.

One thing I will say for the Virginians—I never knew one of them, under any pressure, extemporize a profession. The sentiment of reverence for the mysteries of medicine and law was too large for a deliberate quackery; as to the pulpit, a man might as well do his starving without the hypocrisy.

But others were not so nice. I have known them to rush, when the wolf was after them, from the counting-house or the plantation, into a doctor's shop or a law office, as if those places were the sanctuaries from the avenger; some pretending to be doctors that did not know a liver from a gizzard, administering medicine by the guess, without knowing enough of pharmacy to tell whether the stuff exhibited in the big-bellied blue, red and green bottles at the show-windows of the apothecaries' shops, was given by the drop or the half-pint.

Divers others left, but what became of them, I never knew any more than they know what becomes of the sora after frost.

Many were the instances of suffering; of pitiable misfortune, involving and crushing whole families; of pride abased; of honorable sensibilities wounded; of the provision for old age destroyed; of the hopes of manhood overcast, of independence dissipated, and the poor victim without help, or hope, or sympathy, forced to petty shifts for a bare subsistence, and a ground-scuffle, for what in happier days, he threw away. But there were too many examples of this sort for the expenditure of a useless compassion; just as the surgeon after a battle, grows case-hardened, from an excess of objects of pity.

My memory, however, fixes itself on one honored exception, the noblest of the noble, the best of the good. Old Major Willis Wormley had come in long before the *new era*. He belonged to the old school of Virginians. Nothing could have torn him from the Virginia he loved, as Jacopi Foscari, Venice, but the marrying of his eldest daughter, Mary, to a gentleman of Alabama. The Major was something between, or made of about equal parts, of Uncle Toby and Mr. Pickwick, with a slight flavor of Mr. Micawber. He was the soul of kindness, disinterestedness and hospitality. Love to every thing that had life in it, burned like a flame in his large and benignant soul; it flowed over in his countenance, and glowed through every feature, and moved every muscle in the frame it animated. The Major lived freely, was rather corpulent, and had not a lean thing on his plantations; the negroes; the dogs; the horses; the cattle; the very chickens, wore an air of corpulent complacency, and bustled about with a good-humored rotundity. There was more laughing, singing and whistling at "Hollywood," than would have set up a dozen Irish fairs. The Major's wife had, from a long life of affection, and the practice of the same pursuits, and the indulgence of the same feelings and tastes, got so much

395

like him, that she seemed a feminine and modest edition of himself. Four daughters were all that remained in the family—two had been married off—and they had no son. The girls ranged from sixteen to twenty-two, fine, hearty, whole-souled, wholesome, cheerful lasses, with constitutions to last, and a flow of spirits like mountain springs—not beauties, but good housewife girls, whose open countenances, and neat figures, and rosy cheeks, and laughing eyes, and frank and cordial manners, made them, at home, abroad, on horseback or on foot, at the piano or discoursing on the old English books, or Washington Irving's Sketch Book, a favorite in the family ever since it was written, as entertaining and as well calculated to fix solid impressions on the heart, as any four girls in the country. The only difficulty was, they were so much alike, that you were put to fault which to fall in love with. They were all good housewives, or women, rather. But Mrs. Wormley, or Aunt Wormley, as we called her, was as far ahead of any other woman in that way, as could be found this side of the Virginia border. If there was any thing good in the culinary line that she couldn't make, I should like to know it. The Major lived on the main stage road, and if any decently dressed man ever passed the house after sundown, he escaped by sheer accident. The house was greatly visited. The Major knew every body, and every body near him knew the Major. The stage coach couldn't stop long, but in the hot summer days, about noon, as the driver tooted his horn at the top of the red hill, two negro boys stood opposite the door, with trays of the finest fruit, and a pitcher of cider for the refreshment of the wayfarers. The Major himself being on the look-out, with his hands over his eyes bowing—as he only could bow—vaguely into the coach, and looking wistfully, to find among the passengers an acquaintance whom he could prevail upon to get out and stay a week with him. There wasn't a poor neighbor to whom the Major had not been as good as an insurer, without premium, for his stock, or for his crop; and from the way he rendered the service, you would think he was the party obliged—as he was.

This is not, in any country I have ever been in, a money-making business; and the Major, though he always made good crops, must have broke at it long ago, but for the fortunate death of a few Aunts, after whom the girls were named, who, paying their several debts of nature, left the Major the means to pay his less serious, but still weighty obligations.

The Major—for a wonder, being a Virginian—had no partisan politics. He could not have. His heart could not hold any thing that implied a warfare upon the thoughts or feelings of others. He voted all the time for his friend, that is, the candidate living nearest to him, regretting, generally, that he did not have another vote for the other man.

It would have done a Camanche Indian's heart good to see all the family together—grand-children and all—of a winter evening, with a guest or two, to excite sociability a little—not company enough to embarrass the manifestations of affection. Such a concordance—as if all hearts were attuned to the same feeling—the old lady knitting in the corner—the old man smoking his pipe opposite—both of their fine faces radiating in the pauses of the laugh, the jest, or the caress, the infinite satisfaction within.

It was enough to convert an abolitionist, to see the old Major when he came home from a long journey of two days to the county town; the negroes running in a string to the buggy; this one to hold the horse, that one to help the old man

396

out, and the others to inquire how he was; and to observe the benignity with which—the kissing of the girls and the old lady hardly over—he distributed a piece of calico here, a plug of tobacco there, or a card of *town* ginger-bread to the little snow-balls that grinned around him; what was given being but a small part of the gift, divested of the kind, cheerful, rollicking way the old fellow had of giving it.

The Major had given out his autograph (as had almost every body else) as endorser on three several bills of exchange, of even tenor and date, and all maturing at or about the same time. His friend's friend failed to pay as he or his firm agreed, the friend himself did no better, and the Major, before he knew any thing at all of his danger, found a writ served upon him, and was told by his friend that he was dead broke, and all he could give him was his sympathy; the which, the Major as gratefully received as if it was a legal tender and would pay the debt. The Major's friends advised him he could get clear of it; that notice of protest not having been sent to the Major's post-office, released him; but the Major wouldn't hear of such a defence, he said *his* understanding was, that he was to pay the debt if his friend didn't; and to slip out of it by a quibble, was little better than pleading the gambling act. Besides, what would the lawyers say? And what would be said by his old friends in Virginia, when it reached their ears, that he had plead want of notice, to get clear of a debt, when every body knew it was the same thing as if he had got notice. And if this defence were good at law, it would not be in equity; and if they took it into chancery, it mattered not what became of the case, the property would all go, and he never could expect to see the last of it. No, no; he would pay it, and had as well set about it at once.

The rumor of the Major's condition spread far and wide. It reached old N. D., "an angel," whom the Major had "entertained," and one of the few that ever travelled that road. He came, post haste, to see into the affair; saw the creditor; made him, upon threat of defence, agree to take half the amount, and discharge the Major; advanced the money, and took the Major's negroes—except the house-servants—and put them on his Mississippi plantation to work out the debt.

The Major's heart pained him at the thought of the negroes going off; he couldn't witness it; though he consoled himself with the idea of the discipline and exercise being good for the health of sundry of them who had contracted sedentary diseases.

The Major turned his house into a tavern—that is changed its name—put up a sign, and three weeks afterwards, you couldn't have told that any thing had happened. The family were as happy as ever—the Major never having put on airs of arrogance in prosperity, felt no humiliation in adversity; the girls were as cheerful, as bustling, and as light-hearted as ever, and seemed to think of the duties of hostesses as mere bagatelles, to enliven the time. The old Major was as profluent of anecdotes as ever, and never grew tired of telling the same ones to every new guest; and yet, the Major's anecdotes were all of Virginia growth, and not one of them under the legal age of twenty-one. If the Major had worked his negroes as he had those anecdotes, he would have been able to pay off the bills of exchange without any difficulty.

The old lady and the girls laughed at the anecdotes, though they must have heard them at least a thousand times, and knew them by heart; for the Major

397

told them without the variations; and the other friends of the Major laughed too; indeed, with such an air of thorough benevolence, and in such a truly social spirit did the old fellow proceed "the tale to unfold," that a Cassius like rascal that wouldn't laugh, whether he saw any thing to laugh at or not, ought to have been sent to the Penitentiary for life—half of the time to be spent in solitary confinement. (*1853*)

GEORGE WASHINGTON HARRIS

1814–1869

George Washington Harris was born in Pennsylvania, but at the age of five he moved to Knoxville, Tennessee, where he spent most of his life. After a short formal schooling he was apprenticed to a half-brother, a jeweler. But the Tennessee River had a fascination for him, and upon reaching his legal maturity, he managed to become captain of the first steamboat to make regular runs out of Knoxville. He assisted in transporting the Cherokee Indians from Tennessee, meanwhile advertising his ability as a craftsman "in the metals generally." After the Civil War, Harris became a railroad engineer. His death occurred suddenly and unexplainably on December 11, 1869, while he was a passenger on a train.

Harris is best known for his *Sut Lovingood Yarns* (1867), supposedly told by a rough but good-natured Tennessee mountaineer. The dialect of the tales is difficult to follow unless they are read aloud, yet the rough frontier humor they reflect is unmistakable. Comic—and often bawdy—situations are invariably underlined by a homely but sound philosophy. Harris' *Sut Lovingood's Travels with Old Abe Linkhorn*—first published in the *Nashville American*—shows the author a shrewdly entertaining critic of Lincoln.

Mrs. Yardley's Quilting

398

"Thar's one durn'd nasty muddy job, an' I is jis' glad enuf tu take a ho'n ur two, on the straingth ove hit."

"What have you been doing, Sut?"

"Helpin tu salt ole Missis Yardley down."

"What do you mean by that?"

"Fixin her fur rotten cumfurtably, kiverin her up wif sile, tu keep the buzzards frum cheatin the wurms."

"Oh, you have been helping to bury a woman."

"That's hit, by golly! Now why the devil can't I 'splain mysef like yu? I ladles out my words at randum, like a calf kickin at yaller-jackids; yu jis' rolls em out tu the pint, like a feller a-layin bricks—every one fits. How is it that bricks fits so clost enyhow? Rocks won't ni du hit."

"Becaze they'se all ove a size," ventured a man with a wen over his eye.

"The devil yu say, hon'ey-head! haint reapin-mersheens ove a size? I'd like tu see two ove em fit clost. Yu wait ontil yu sprouts tuther ho'n, afore yu venters tu 'splain mix'd questions. George, did yu know ole Missis Yardley?"

"No."

"Well, she wer a curious 'oman in her way, an' she wore shiney specks. Now jis' listen: Whenever yu see a ole 'oman ahine a par ove *shiney* specks, yu keep yer eye skinn'd; they am dang'rus in the extreme. Thar is jis' no knowin what they ken du. I hed one a-stradil ove me onst, fur kissin her gal. She went fur my har, an' she went fur my skin, ontil I tho't she ment tu kill me, an' wud a-dun hit, ef my hollerin hadent fotch ole Dave Jordan, a *bacheler*, tu my aid. He, like a durn'd fool, cotch her by the laig, an' drug her back'ards ofen me. She jis' kivered him, an' I run, by golly! The nex time I seed him he wer bald headed, an' his face looked like he'd been a-fitin wildcats.

"Ole Missis Yardley wer a great noticer ove littil things, that nobody else ever seed. She'd say right in the middil ove sumbody's serious talk: 'Law sakes! thar goes that yaller slut ove a hen, a-flingin straws over her shoulder; she's arter settin now, an' haint laid but seven aigs. I'll disapint *her*, see ef I don't; I'll put a punkin in her nes', an' a feather in her nose. An' bless my soul! jis' look at that cow wif the wilted ho'n, a-flingin up dirt an' a-smellin the place whar hit cum frum, wif the rale ginuine still-wurim twis' in her tail, too; what upon the face ove the yeath kin she be arter now, the ole fool? watch her, Sally. An' sakes alive; jis' look at that ole sow; she's a-gwine in a fas' trot, wif her empty bag a-floppin agin her sides. Thar, she hes stop't, an's a-listenin! massy on us! what a long yearnis grunt she gin; hit cum frum way back ove her kidneys. Thar she goes agin; she's arter no good, sich kerryin on means no good.'

"An' so she wud gabble, no odds who wer a-listenin. She looked like she mout been made at fust 'bout four foot long, an' the common thickness ove wimen when they's at tharsefs, an' then had her har tied tu a stump, a par ove steers hitched to her heels, an' then straiched out a-mos' two foot more—mos' ove the straichin cumin outen her laigs an' naik. Her stockins, a-hangin on the clothes-line tu dry, looked like a par ove sabre scabbards, an' her naik looked like a dry beef shank smoked, an' mout been ni ontu es tough. I never felt hit mysef, I didn't, I jis' jedges by looks. Her darter Sal wer bilt at fust 'bout the laingth ove her mam, but wer never straiched eny by a par ove steers an' she wer fat enuf tu kill; she wer taller lyin down than she wer a-standin up. Hit wer her who gin me the 'hump shoulder.' Jis' look at me; haint I'se got a tech ove the dromedary back thar bad? haint I humpy? Well, a-stoppin tu kiss that squatty lard-stan ove a gal is what dun hit tu me. She wer the fairest-lookin gal I ever seed. She allers

399

wore thick woolin stockins 'bout six inches too long fur her laig; they rolled down over her garters, lookin like a par ove life-presarvers up thar. I tell yu she wer a tarin gal enyhow. Luved kissin, wrastlin, an' biled cabbige, an' hated tite clothes, hot weather, an' suckit-riders. B'leved strong in married folk's ways, cradles, an' the remishun ove sins, an' didn't b'leve in corsets, fleas, peaners, nur the fashun plates."

"What caused the death of Mrs. Yardley, Sut?"

"Nuffin, only her heart stop't beatin 'bout losin a nine dimunt quilt. True, she got a skeer'd hoss tu run over her, but she'd a-got over that ef a quilt hadn't been mix'd up in the catastrophy. Yu see quilts wer wun ove her speshul gifts; she run strong on the bed-kiver question. Irish chain, star ove Texas, sun-flower, nine dimunt, saw teeth, checker board, an' shell quilts; blue, an' white, an' yaller an' black coverlids, an' callic-kercumfurts reigned triumphan' 'bout her hous'. They wer packed in drawers, layin in shelfs full, wer hung four dubbil on lines in the lof, packed in chists, piled on cheers, an' wer everywhar, even ontu the beds, an' wer changed every bed-makin. She told everybody she cud git tu listen tu hit that she ment tu give every durn'd one ove them tu Sal when she got married. Oh, lordy! what es fat a gal es Sal Yardley cud ever du wif half ove em, an' sleepin wif a husbun at that, is more nor I ever cud see through. Jis' think ove her onder twenty layer ove quilts in July, an' yu in thar too. Gewhillikins! George, look how I is sweatin' now, an' this is December. I'd 'bout es leif be shet up in a steam biler wif a three hundred pound bag ove lard, es tu make a bisiness ove sleepin wif that gal—'twould kill a glass-blower.

"Well, tu cum tu the serious part ove this conversashun, that is how the old quilt-mersheen an' coverlidloom cum tu stop operashuns on this yeath. She hed narrated hit thru the neighborhood that nex Saterday she'd gin a quiltin—three quilts an' one cumfurt tu tie. 'Goblers, fiddils, gals, an' whiskey,' wer the words she sent tu the men-folk, an' more tetchin ur wakenin words never drap't ofen an 'oman's tongue. She sed tu the gals, 'Sweet toddy, huggin, dancin, an' huggers in 'bundunce.' Them words struck the gals rite in the pit ove the stumick, an' spread a ticklin sensashun bof ways, ontil they scratched thar heads wif one han, an' thar heels wif tuther.

"Everybody, he an' she, what wer baptized b'levers in the righteousnes ove quiltins wer thar, an' hit jis' so happen'd that everybody in them parts, frum fifteen summers tu fifty winters, wer unannaums b'levers. Strange, warn't hit? Hit wer the bigges' quiltin ever Missis Yardley hilt, an' she hed hilt hundreds; everybody wer thar, 'scept the constibil an' suckit-rider, two dam easily-spared pussons; the numbers ni ontu even too; jis' a few more boys nur gals; that made hit more exhitin, fur hit gin the gals a chance tu kick an' squeal a littil, wifout runnin eny risk ove not gittin kissed at all, an' hit gin reasonabil grouns fur a few scrimmages amung the he's. Now es kissin an' fitin am the pepper an' salt ove all soshul getherins, so hit wer more espishully wif this ove ours. Es I swung my eyes over the crowd, George, I thought quiltins, managed in a morril an' sensibil way, truly am good things—good fur free drinkin, good fur free eatin, good fur free huggin, good fur free dancin, good fur free fitin, an' goodest ove all fur poperlation a country fas'.

"Thar am a fur-seein wisdum in quiltins, ef they hes proper trimmins: 'vittils, fiddils, an' sperrits in 'bundunce.' One holesum quiltin am wuf three old pray'r-

400

meetins on the poperlashun pint, purtickerly ef hits hilt in the dark ove the moon, an' runs intu the night a few hours, an' April ur May am the time chosen. The moon don't suit quiltins whar everybody is well acquainted an' already fur along in courtin. She dus help pow'ful tu begin a courtin match onder, but when hit draws ni ontu a head, nobody wants a moon but the ole mammys.

"The mornin cum, still, saft, sunshiney; cocks crowin, hens singin, birds chirpin, tuckeys gobblin—jis' the day tu sun quilts, kick, kiss, squeal, an' make love.

"All the plow-lines an' clothes-lines wer straiched tu every post an' tree. Quilts purvailed. Durn my gizzard ef two acres roun that ar house warn't jis' one solid quilt, all out a-sunnin, an' tu be seed. They dazzled the eyes, skeered the hosses, gin wimen the heart-burn, an' perdominated.

"To'ards sundown the he's begun tu drap in. Yearnis' needil-drivin cummenced tu lose groun; threads broke ofen, thimbils got los', an' quilts needed anuther roll. Gigglin, winkin, whisperin, smoofin ove har, an' gals a-ticklin one anuther, wer a-gainin every inch ove groun what the needils los'. Did yu ever notis, George, at all soshul gatherins, when the he's begin tu gather, that the young she's begun tu tickil one anuther an' the ole maids swell thar tails, roach up thar backs, an' sharpen thar nails ontu the bed-posts an' door jams, an' spit an' groan sorter like cats a-courtin? Dus hit mean *rale* rath, ur is hit a dare tu the he's, sorter kivered up wif the outside signs ove danger? I honestly b'leve that the young shes' ticklin means, 'Cum an' take this job ofen our hans.' But that swellin I jis' don't onderstan; dus yu? Hit looks skeery, an' I never tetch one ove em when they am in the swellin way. I may be mistaken'd 'bout the ticklin bisiness too; hit may be dun like a feller chaws poplar bark when he haint got eny terbacker, a-sorter better nur nun make-shif. I dus know one thing tu a certainty: that is, when the he's take hold the ticklin quits, an' ef yu gits one ove the ole maids out tu herself, then she subsides an' is the smoofes, sleekes, saft thing yu ever seed, an' dam ef yu can't hear her purr, jis' es plain!

"But then, George, gals an' ole maids haint the things tu fool time away on. Hits widders, by golly, what am the rale sensibil, steady-goin, never-skeerin, never-kickin, willin, sperrited, smoof pacers. They cum clost up tu the hoss-block, standin still wif thar purty silky years playin, an' the naik-veins a-throbbin, an' waits fur the word, which ove course yu gives, arter yu finds yer feet well in the stirrup, an' away they moves like a cradil on cushioned rockers, ur a spring buggy runnin in damp san'. A tetch ove the bridil, an' they knows yu wants em tu turn, an' they dus hit es willin es ef the idear wer thar own. I be dod rabbited ef a man can't 'propriate happiness by the skinful ef he is in contack wif sumbody's widder, an' is smart. Gin me a willin widder, the yeath over: what they don't know, haint worth larnin. They hes all been tu Jamakey an' larnt how sugar's made, an' knows how tu sweeten wif hit; an' by golly, they is always ready tu use hit. All yu hes tu du is tu find the spoon, an' then drink cumfort till yer blind. Nex tu good sperrits an' my laigs, I likes a twenty-five year ole widder, wif roun ankils, an' bright eyes, honestly an' squarly lookin into yurn, an' sayin es plainly es a partrige sez 'Bob White,' 'Don't be afraid ove me; I hes been thar; yu know hit ef yu hes eny sense, an' thar's no use in eny humbug, ole feller—cum ahead!'

401

"Ef yu onderstans widder nater, they ken save yu a power ove troubil, onsartinty, an' time, an' ef yu is interprisin yu gits mons'rous well paid fur hit. The very soun ove thar littil shoe-heels speak full trainin, an' hes a knowin click as they tap the floor; an' the rustil ove thar dress sez, 'I dar yu tu ax me.'

"When yu hes made up yer mind tu court one, jis' go at hit like hit wer a job ove rail-maulin. Ware yer workin close, use yer common, every-day moshuns an' words, an' abuv all, fling away yer cinamint ile vial an' burn all yer love songs. No use in tryin tu fool em, fur they sees plum thru yu, a durn'd sight plainer than they dus thru thar veils. No use in a pasted shut; she's been thar. No use in borrowin a cavortin fat hoss; she's been thar. No use in har-dye; she's been thar. No use in cloves, tu kill whisky breff; she's been thar. No use in buyin clost curtains fur yer bed, fur she hes been thar. Widders am a speshul means, George, fur ripenin green men, killin off weak ones, an makin 'ternally happy the soun ones.

"Well, es I sed afore, I flew the track an' got ontu the widders. The fellers begun tu ride up an' walk up, sorter slow, like they warn't in a hurry, the durn'd 'saitful raskils, hitchin thar critters tu enything they cud find. One red-comb'd, long-spurr'd, dominecker feller, frum town, in a red an' white gridiron jackid an' patent leather gaiters, hitched his hoss, a wild, skeery, wall-eyed devil, inside the yard palins, tu a cherry tree lim'. Thinks I, that hoss hes a skeer intu him big enuf tu run intu town, an' perhaps beyant hit, ef I kin only tetch hit off; so I sot intu thinkin.

"One aind ove a long clothes-line, wif nine dimunt quilts ontu hit, wer tied tu the same cherry tree that the hoss wer. I tuck my knife and socked hit thru every quilt, 'bout the middil, an' jis' below the rope, an' tied them thar wif bark, so they cudent slip. Then I went tu the back aind, an' ontied hit frum the pos', knottin in a hoe-handil, by the middil, tu keep the quilts frum slippin off ef my bark strings failed, an' laid hit on the groun. Then I went tu the tuther aind: thar wer 'bout ten foot tu spar, a-lyin on the groun arter tyin tu the tree. I tuck hit atwix Wall-eye's hine laigs, an' tied hit fas' tu bof stirrups, an' then cut the cherry tree lim' betwix his bridil an' the tree, almos' off. Now, mine yu thar wer two ur three uther ropes full ove quilts atween me an' the hous', so I wer purty well hid frum thar. I jis' tore off a palin frum the fence, an' tuck hit in bof hans, an' arter raisin hit 'way up yander, I fotch hit down, es hard es I cud, flat-sided to'ards the groun, an' hit acksidentally happen'd tu hit Wall-eye, 'bout nine inches ahead ove the root ove his tail. Hit landed so hard that hit made my hans tingle, an' then busted intu splinters. The first thing I did, wer tu feel ove mysef, on the same spot whar hit hed hit the hoss. I cudent help duin hit tu save my life, an' I swar I felt sum ove Wall-eye's sensashun, jis' es plain. The fust thing he did, wer tu tare down the lim' wif a twenty-foot jump, his head to'ards the hous'. Thinks I, now yu hev dun hit, yu durn'd wall-eyed fool! tarin down that lim' wer the beginin ove all the troubil, an' the hoss did hit hissef; my conshuns felt clar es a mountin spring, an' I wer in a frame ove mine tu observe things es they happen'd, an' they soon begun tu happen purty clost arter one anuther rite then, an' thar, an' tharabouts, clean ontu town, thru hit, an' still wer a-happenin, in the woods beyant thar ni ontu eleven mile frum ole man Yardley's gate, an' four beyant town.

"The fust line ove quilts he tried tu jump, but broke hit down; the nex one he ran onder; the rope cotch ontu the ho'n ove the saddil, broke at bof ainds, an'

402

went along wif the hoss, the cherry tree lim' an' the fust line ove quilts, what I hed proverdensally tied fas' tu the rope. That's what I calls foresight, George. Right furnint the frunt door he cum in contack wif ole Missis Yardley hersef, an' anuther ole 'oman; they wer a-holdin a nine dimunt quilt spread out, a-'zaminin hit, an' a-praisin hits purfeckshuns. The durn'd onmanerly, wall-eyed fool run plum over Missis Yardley, frum ahine, stompt one hine foot through the quilt, takin hit along, a-kickin ontil he made hits corners snap like a whip. The gals screamed, the men hollered wo! an' the ole 'oman wer toted intu the hous' limber es a wet string, an' every word she sed wer, 'Oh, my preshus nine dimunt quilt!'

"Wall-eye busted thru the palins, an' Dominicker sed 'im, made a mortal rush fur his bitts, wer too late fur them, but in good time fur the strings ove flyin quilts, got tangled amung em, an' the gridiron jackid patren wer los' tu my sight amung star an' Irish chain quilts; he went frum that quiltin at the rate ove thuty miles tu the hour. Nuffin lef on the lot ove the hole consarn, but a nine biler hat, a par ove gloves, an' the jack ove hearts.

"What a onmanerly, suddin way ove leavin places sum folks hev got, enyhow.

"Thinks I, well, that fool hoss, tarin down that cherry tree lim', hes dun sum good, enyhow; hit hes put the ole 'oman outen the way fur the balance ove the quiltin, an' tuck Dominicker outen the way an' outen danger, fur that gridiron jackid wud a-bred a scab on his nose afore midnite; hit wer morrily boun tu du hit.

"Two months arterwards, I tracked the route that hoss tuck in his kalamatus skeer, by quilt rags, tufts ove cotton, bunches ove har, (human an' hoss,) an' scraps ove a gridiron jackid stickin ontu the bushes, an' plum at the aind ove hit, whar all signs gin out, I foun a piece ove watch chain an' a hosses head. The places what know'd Dominicker, know'd 'im no more.

"Well, arter they'd tuck the ole 'oman up stairs an' camfired her tu sleep, things begun tu work agin. The widders broke the ice, an' arter a littil gigilin, goblin, an' gabblin, the kissin begun. *Smack!*—'Thar, now,' a widder sed that. *Pop!*—'Oh, don't!' *Pfip!*—'Oh, yu quit!' *Plosh!*—'Go *way* yu awkerd critter, yu kissed me in the eye!' anuther widder sed that. *Bop!* 'Now yu ar satisfied, I recon, big mouf!' *Vip!*—'That haint fair!' *Spat!*—'Oh, lordy! May, cum pull Bill away; he's a-tanglin my har.' *Thut!*—'I jis' d-a-r-e yu tu du that agin!' a widder sed that, too. Hit sounded all 'roun that room like poppin co'n in a hot skillet, an' wer pow'ful sujestif.

"Hit kep on ontil I be durn'd ef *my* bristils didn't begin tu rise, an' sumthin like a cold buckshot wud run down the marrow in my back-bone 'bout every ten secons, an' then run up agin, tolerabil hot. I kep a swallerin wif nuthin tu swaller, an' my face felt swell'd; an' yet I wer fear'd tu make a bulge. Thinks I, I'll ketch one out tu hersef torreckly, an' then I guess we'll rastil. Purty soon Sal Yardley started fur the smoke-'ous, so I jis' gin my head a few short shakes, let down one ove my wings a-trailin, an' sirkiled roun her wif a side twis' in my naik, steppin sidewise, an' a-fetchin up my hinmos' foot wif a sorter jerkin slide at every step. Sez I, 'Too coo-took a-too.' She onderstood hit, an stopt, sorter spreadin her shoulders. An' jis' es I hed pouch'd out my mouf, an' wer a-reachin forrid wif hit, fur the article hitsef, sunthin interfared wif me, hit did. George, wer yu ever ontu yer hans an' knees, an' let a hell-tarin big, mad ram, wif a ten-yard run, but yu yearnis'ly, jis' onst, right squar ontu the pint ove yer back-bone?"

403

"No, you fool; why do you ask?"

"Kaze I wanted tu know ef yu cud hev a realizin' noshun ove my shock. Hits scarcely worth while tu try tu make yu onderstan the case by words only, onless yu hev been tetched in that way. Gr-eat golly! the fust thing I felt, I tuck hit tu be a back-ackshun yeathquake; an' the fust thing I seed wer my chaw'r terbacker a-flyin over Sal's head like a skeer'd bat. My mouf wer pouch'd out, ready fur the article hitsef, yu know, an' hit went outen the roun hole like the wad outen a pop-gun—thug! an' the fust thing I know'd, I wer a flyin over Sal's head too, an' a-gainin on the chaw'r terbacker fast. I wer straitened out strait, toes hinemos', middil finger-nails foremos', an' the fust thing I hearn wer, 'Yu dam Shanghi!' Great Jerus-a-lam! I lit ontu my all fours jis' in time tu but the yard gate ofen hits hinges, an' skeer loose sum more hosses—kep on in a four-footed gallop, clean acrost the lane afore I cud straiten up, an' yere I cotch up wif my chaw'r terbacker, stickin flat agin a fence-rail. I hed got so good a start that I thot hit a pity tu spile hit, so I jis' jump'd the fence an' tuck thru the orchurd. I tell yu I dusted these yere close, fur I tho't hit wer arter me.

"Arter runnin a spell, I ventered tu feel roun back thar, fur sum signs ove what hed happened tu me. George, arter two pow'ful hardtugs, I pull'd out the vamp an' sole ove one ove ole man Yardley's big brogans, what he hed los' amung my coat-tails. Dre'ful! dre'ful! Arter I got hit away frum thar, my flesh went fas' asleep, frum abuv my kidneys tu my knees; about now, fur the fust time, the idear struck me, what hit wer that hed interfar'd wif me, an' los' me the kiss. Hit wer ole Yardley hed kicked me. I walked fur a month like I wer strad-dlin a thorn hedge. Sich a shock, at sich a time, an' on sich a place—jis' think ove hit! hit am tremenjus, haint hit? The place feels num, right now."

"Well, Sut, how did the quilting come out?"

"How the hell du yu 'speck me tu know? I warn't thar eny more." (*1867*)

Rare Ripe Garden-Seed

"I tell yu now, I minds my fust big skeer jis' es well as rich boys minds thar fust boots, ur seein the fust spotted hoss sirkis. The red top ove them boots am still a rich red stripe in thar minds, an' the burnin red ove my fust skeer hes lef es deep a scar ontu my thinkin works. Mam hed me a standin atwixt her knees. I kin feel the knobs ove her jints a-rattlin a-pas' my ribs yet. She didn't hev much petticoats tu speak ove, an' I hed but one, an' hit wer calliker slit frum the nap ove my naik tu the tail, hilt tugether at the top wif a draw-string, an' at the bottom by the hem; hit wer the handiest close I ever seed, an' wud be pow'ful cumfurtin in summer if hit warn't fur the flies. Ef they was good tu run in, I'd war one yet. They beats pasted shuts, an' britches, es bad es a feather bed beats a bag ove warnut shells fur sleepin on.

404

"Say, George, wudn't yu like tu see me intu one 'bout haf fadid, slit, an' a-walkin jis' so, up the middil street ove yure city chuch, a-aimin fur yure pew pen, an' hit chock full ove yure fine city gal friends, jis' arter the people hed sot down frum the fust prayer, an' the orgin beginin tu groan; what wud yu du in sich a margincy? say hoss?"

"Why, I'd shoot you dead, Monday morning before eight o'clock," was my reply.

"Well, I speck yu wud; but yu'd take a rale ole maid faint fus, rite amung them ar gals. Lordy! wudn't yu be shamed ove me! Yit why not ten chuch in sich a suit, when yu hesn't got no store clothes?

"Well, es I wer sayin, mam wer feedin us brats ontu mush an' milk, wifout the milk, an' es I wer the baby then, she hilt me so es tu see that I got my sheer. Whar thar ain't enuf feed, big childer roots littil childer outen the troff, an' gobbils up thar part. Jis' so the yeath over: bishops eats elders, elders eats common peopil; they eats sich cattil es me, I eats possums, possums eats chickins, chickins swallers wums, an' wums am content tu eat dus, an' the dus am the aind ove hit all. Hit am all es regilur es the souns frum the tribil down tu the bull base ove a fiddil in good tchune, an' I speck hit am right, ur hit wudn't be 'lowed.

" 'The sheriff!' his'd 'mam in a keen trimblin whisper, hit sounded tu me like the skreech ove a hen when she sez 'hawk,' tu her little roun-sturn'd, fuzzy, bead-eyed, stripid-backs.

"I actid jis' adzacly as they dus; I darted on all fours onder mam's petti-coatails, an' thar I met, face tu face, the wooden bowl, an' the mush, an' the spoon what she slid onder frum tuther side. I'se mad at mysef yet, fur rite thar I show'd the fust flash ove the nat'ral born durn fool what I now is. I orter et hit all up, in jestis tu my stumick an growin, while the sheriff wer levyin ontu the bed an' the cheers. Tu this day, ef enybody sez 'sheriff,' I feels skeer, an' ef I hears constabil menshun'd, my laigs goes thru runnin moshuns, even ef I is asleep. Did yu ever watch a dorg dreamin ove rabbit huntin? Thems the moshuns, an' the feelin am the rabbit's.

"Sheriffs am orful 'spectabil peopil; everybody looks up tu em. I never adzacly seed the 'spectabil part mysef. I'se too fear'd ove em, I reckon, tu 'zamin fur hit much. One thing I knows, no country atwix yere an' Tophit kin ever 'lect me tu sell out widders' plunder, ur poor men's co'n, an' the tho'ts ove hit gins me a good feelin; hit sorter flashes thru my heart when I thinks ove hit. I axed a passun onst, whan hit cud be, an' he pernounced hit tu be *onregenerit pride*, what I orter squelch in prayer, an' in tendin chuch on colleckshun days. I wer in hopes hit mout be 'ligion, ur sence, a-soakin intu me; hit feels good, enyhow, an' I don't keer ef every suckit rider outen jail knows hit. Sheriffs' shuts allers hes nettil dus ur fleas inside ove em when they lies down tu sleep, an' I'se glad ove hit, fur they'se allers discumfortin me, durn em. I scarcely ever git tu drink a ho'n, ur eat a mess in peace. I'll hurt one sum day, see ef I don't. Show me a sheriff a-steppin softly roun, an' a-sorter sightin at me, an' I'll show yu a far sampil ove the speed ove a express ingine, fired up wif rich, dry, rosiny skeers. They don't ketch me *much,* usin only human laigs es wepuns.

"Ole John Doltin wer a 'spectabil sheriff, monsusly so, an' hed the bes' scent fur poor fugatif devils, an' wimen, I ever seed; he wer sure fire. Well, he toted a warrun fur this yere skinful ove durn'd fool, 'bout that ar misfortnit nigger meetin bisness, ontil he wore hit intu six seperit squar bits, an' hed wore out much shoe leather a-chasin ove me. I'd foun a doggery in full milk, an' hated pow'ful bad tu leave that settilment while hit suck'd free; so I sot intu sorter try an' wean him off frum botherin me so much. I suckseedid so well that he not only

405

quit racin ove me, an' wimen, but he wer tetotaly spiled es a sheriff, an' los' the 'spectabil seckshun ove his karacter. Tu make yu fool fellers onderstan how hit wer done, I mus' interjuice yure minds tu one Wat Mastin, a bullit-headed yung blacksmith.

"Well, las' year—no hit wer the year afore las'—in struttin an' gobblin time, Wat felt his keepin right warm, so he sot intu bellerin an' pawin up dus in the neighborhood roun the ole widder McKildrin's. The more dus he flung up, the wus he got, ontil at las' he jis cudn't stan the ticklin sensashuns anutner minnit; so he put fur the county court clark's offis, wif his hans sock'd down deep intu his britchis pockets, like he wer fear'd ove pick-pockets, his back roach'd roun, an' a-chompin his teef ontil he splotch'd his whiskers wif foam. Oh! he wer yearnis' hot, an' es restless es a cockroach in a hot skillit."

"What was the matter with this Mr. Mastin? I cannot understand you, Mr. Lovingood; had he hydrophobia?" remarked a man in a square-tail coat, and cloth gaiters, who was obtaining subscribers for some forthcoming Encyclopedia of Useful Knowledge, who had quartered at our camp, uninvited, and really unwanted.

"What du yu mean by high-dry-foby?" and Sut looked puzzled.

"A madness produced by being bit by some rabid animal," explained Squaretail, in a pompous manner.

"Yas, hoss, he hed high-dry-foby *orful*, an' Mary McKildrin, the widder McKildrin's only darter, hed gin him the complaint; I don't know whether she bit 'im ur not; he mout a-cotch hit frum her bref, an' he wer now in the roach back, chompin stage ove the sickness, so he wer arter the clark fur a tickit tu the hospital. Well, the clark sole 'im a piece ove paper, part printin an' part ritin, wif a picter ove two pigs' hearts, what sum boy hed shot a arrer thru, an' lef hit stickin, printed at the top. That paper wer a splicin pass—sum calls hit a par ove licins—an' that very nite he tuck Mary, fur better, fur wus, tu hev an' tu hole tu him his heirs, an' ——"

"Allow me to interrupt you," said our guest; "you do not quote the marriage ceremony correctly."

"Yu go tu *hell*, mistofer; yu bothers me."

This outrageous rebuff took the stranger all aback, and he sat down.

"Whar wer I? Oh yes, he married Mary tight an' fas', an' nex day he wer abil tu be about. His coat tho', an' his trousis look'd jis' a skrimshun too big, loose like, an' heavy tu tote. I axed him ef he felt soun. He sed yas, but he'd welded a steamboat shaftez the day afore, an' wer sorter tired like. Thar he tole a durn lie, fur he'd been a-ho'nin up dirt mos' ove the day, roun the widder's garden, an' bellerin in the orchard. Mary an' him sot squar intu hous'-keepin, an' 'mung uther things he bot a lot ove *rar ripe garden-seed*, frum a Yankee peddler. Rar ripe co'n, rar ripe peas, rar ripe taters, rar ripe everything, an' the two yung durn'd fools wer dreadfully exercis'd 'bout hit. Wat sed he ment tu git him a rar ripe hammer an' anvil, an' Mary vow'd tu grashus, that she'd hev a rar ripe wheel an' loom, ef money wud git em. Purty soon arter he hed made the garden, he tuck a noshun tu work a spell down tu Ataylanty, in the railroad shop, es he sed he hed a sorter ailin in his back, an' he tho't weldin rail car-tire an' ingine axiltrees, wer lighter work nur sharpinin plows, an' puttin lap-links in trace-chains. So down he went, an' foun hit agreed wif him, fur he didn't cum back ontil the middil ove August. The fust thing he seed when he landid intu his cabin-door, wer a shoebox wif rockers onder hit, an' the nex thing he seed, wer Mary hersef, propped up in bed, an' the nex thing he seed arter that, wer a par ove littil rat-eyes a-shinin abuv the aind ove the quilt, ontu Mary's arm, an' the nex an' las' thing he seed wer the two littil rat-eyes aforesed, a-turnin intu two hundred thousand big green stars, an' a-swingin roun an' roun the room, faster an' faster, ontil they mix'd intu one orful green flash. He drap't intu a limber pile on the floor. The durn'd fool what hed weldid the steamboat shaftez hed fainted safe an' soun es a gal skeered at a mad bull. Mary fotch a weak cat-scream, an' kivered her head, an' sot intu work ontu a whifflin dry cry, while littil Rat-eyes gin hitssef up tu suckin. Cryin an' suckin bof at onst ain't far; mus' cum pow'ful strainin on the wet seckshun ove an' 'oman's constitushun; yet hit am ofen dun, an' more too. Ole Missis McKildrin, what wer a-nussin Mary, jis' got up frum knittin, an' flung a big gourd ove warter squar intu Wat's face, then she fotch a glass bottil ove swell-skull whiskey outen the three-cornered cup-board, an' stood furnint Wat, a-holdin hit in wun han, an' the tin-cup in tuther, waitin fur Wat tu cum to. She wer the piusses lookin ole 'oman jis' then, yu ever seed outside ove a prayer-meetin. Arter a spell, Wat begun tu move, twitchin his fingers, an' battin his eyes, sorter 'stonished like. That pius lookin statue sed tu him:

" 'My son, jis' take a drap ove sperrits, honey. Yu'se very sick, dumplin, don't take on darlin, ef yu kin help hit, ducky, fur poor Margarit Jane am mons'ous ailin, an' the leas' nise ur takin on will kill the poor sufferin dear, an yu'll loose yure tuckil ducky duv ove a sweet wifey, arter all she's dun gone thru fur yu. My dear son Watty, yu mus' consider her feelins a littil.' Sez Wat, a-turnin up his eyes at that vartus ole relick, sorter sick like—

" 'I is a-considerin em a heap, rite now.'

" 'Oh that's right, my good kine child.'

"Oh dam ef ole muther-in-lors can't plaster humbug over a feller, jis' es saft an' easy es they spreads a camrick hanketcher over a three hour ole baby's face; yu don't feel hit at all, but hit am thar, a plum inch thick, an' stickin fas es court-plaster. She raised Wat's head, an' sot the aidge ove the tin cup agin his lower teef, an' turned up the bottim slow an' keerful, a-winkin at Mary, hu wer a-peepin over the aidge ove the coverlid, tu see ef Wat *tuck the perskripshun,* fur a heap ove famerly cumfort 'pended on that ar ho'n ove sperrits. *Wun* ho'n allers saftens a man, the yeath over. Wat keep a-battin his eyes, wus nur a owl in daylight; at las' he raised hissef ontu wun elbow, an' rested his head in that han, sorter weak like. Sez he, mons'ous trimblin an' slow: 'Aprile—May—June—July—an' mos'—haf—ove—August,' a-countin the munths ontu the fingers ove tuther han, wif the thumb, a-shakin ove his head, an' lookin at his spread fingers like they warn't his'n, ur they wer nastied wif sumfin. Then he counted em agin, slower, Aprile—May—June—July—an', mos' haf ove August, an' he run his thumb atwixt his fingers, es meanin mos' haf ove August, an' look'd at the pint ove hit, like hit mout be a snake's head. He raised his eyes tu the widder's face, who wer standin jis' es steady es a hitchin pos', an' still a-warin that pius spression ontu her pussonal feturs, an' a flood ove saft luv fur Wat, a-shinin strait frum her eyes intu his'n. Sez he, 'That jis' makes four munths, an' mos' a half, don't hit, Missis McKildrin?' She never sed one word. Wat reached fur the hath, an' got a dead fire-coal; then he made a mark clean acrost a floorplank. Sez he, 'Aprile,' a-holdin down the coal ontu the aind ove the mark, like he wer fear'd hit mout blow away afore he got hit christened Aprile. Sez he, 'May'—an' he marked across the board agin; then he counted the marks, one, two, a-dottin at em wif the coal. 'June,' an' he marked agin, one, two, three; counted wif the pint ove the coal. He scratched his head wif the littil finger ove the han holdin the charcoal, an' he drawed hit slowly acrost the board agin, peepin onder his wrist tu see when hit reached the crack, an' sez he 'July,' es he lifted the coal; 'one, two, three, four,' countin frum lef tu right, an' then frum right tu lef. 'That haint but four, no way I kin fix hit. Ole Pike hissef cudn't make hit five, ef he wer tu sifer ontu hit ontil his laigs turned intu figger eights.' Then he made a mark, haf acrost a plank, spit on his finger, an' rubbed off a haf inch ove the aind, an' sez he, 'Mos' haf ove August.' He looked up at the widder, an' thar she wer, same es ever, still a-holdin the flask agin her bussum, an' sez he 'Four months, an' mos' a haf. *Haint enuf, is hit mammy?* hits jis' 'bout (lackin a littil) *haf enuf*, haint hit, mammy?'

"Missis McKildrin shuck her head sorter onsartin like, an' sez she, 'Take a drap more sperrits, Watty, my dear pet; dus yu mine buyin that ar rar ripe seed, frum the peddler?' Wat nodded his head, an' looked 'what ove hit,' but didn't say hit.

" 'This is what cums ove hit, an' four months an' a haf am rar ripe time fur babys, adzackly. Tu be sure, hit lacks a day ur two, but Margarit Jane wer allers a pow'ful interprizin gal, an' a yearly rizer.' Sez Wat,

" 'How about the 'taters?'

" 'Oh, *we* et 'taters es big es goose aigs, afore ole Missis Collinze's blossomed.'

" 'How 'bout co'n?'

" 'Oh, we shaved down roasin years afore hern tassel'd—'

" 'An' peas?'

" 'Yes son, we hed gobs an' lots in three weeks. Everything cums in adzackly half the time that hit takes the ole sort, an' yu *knows*, my darlin son, yu planted hit waseful. I tho't then yu'd rar ripe everything on the place. Yu planted *often*, too, didn't yu luv? fur fear hit wudn't cum up.'

" 'Ye-ye-s-s he—he did,' sed Mary a-cryin. Wat studied pow'ful deep a spell, an' the widder jis' waited. Widders allers wait, an' allers win. At las, sez he, 'Mammy.' She looked at Mary, an' winked these yere words at her, es plain es she cud a-talked em. 'Yu hearn him call me *mammy twiste*. I'se *got him* now. His back-bone's a-limberin fas', he'll own the baby yet, see ef he don't. Jis' hole still my darter, an' let yer mammy knead this dough, then yu may bake hit es brown es yu please.'

"'Mammy, when I married on the fust day ove Aprile'——The widder look'd oneasy; she tho't he mout be a-cupplin that day, his weddin, an' the idear, dam fool, tugether. But he warn't, fur he sed 'That day I gin ole man Collins my note ove han fur a hundred dullars, jew in one year arter date, the balluns on this lan. Dus yu think that ar seed will change the *time* eny, ur will hit alter the *amount?*' An' Wat looked at her powerful ankshus. She raised the whisky bottil way abuv her head, wif her thumb on the mouf, an' fotch the bottim down ontu her han, spat. Sez she, 'Watty, my dear b'lovid son, pripar tu pay *two* hundred dullars 'bout the fust ove October, fur hit'll be jew jis' then, *es* sure es that littil black-eyed angel in the bed thar, am yer darter.'

"Wat drap't his head, an' sed, *'Then hits a dam sure thing.'* Rite yere, the baby fotch a rattlin loud squall, (I speck Mary wer sorter figetty jis' then, an' hurt hit.) 'Yas,' sez Wat, a-wallin a red eye to'ards the bed; 'my littil she—what wer hit yu called her name, mammy?' 'I called her a sweet littil angel, an' she is wun, es sure es yu're her daddy, my b'loved son.' 'Well,' sez Wat, 'my littil sweet, patent rar ripe she angel, ef yu lives tu marryin time, yu'll 'stonish sum man body outen his shut, ef yu don't rar ripe lose hits vartu arter the fust plantin, that's all.' He rared up on aind, wif his mouf pouch'd out. He had a pow'ful forrid, fur-reachin, bread funnel, enyhow—cud a-bit the aigs outen a catfish, in two-foot warter, wifout wettin his eyebrows. 'Dod durn rar ripe seed, an' rar ripe pedlers, an' rar ripe notes tu the hottes' corner ove——'

" 'Stop Watty, *darlin,* don't swar; 'member yu belongs tu meetin.'

" 'My blacksmith's fire,' ainded Wat, an' he studied a long spell; sez he,

" 'Did you save eny ove that infunnel doubil-trigger seed?' 'Yas,' sez the widder, 'thar in that bag by the cupboard.' Wat got up ofen the floor, tuck a countin sorter look at the charcoal marks, an' reached down the bag; he went tu the door an' called 'Suke, muley! Suke, Suke, cow, chick, chick, chicky chick.' 'What's yu gwine tu du now, my dear son?' sed Missis McKildrin. 'I'se jis' gwine tu feed this actif *smart* truck tu the cow, an' the hens, that's what I'se gwine tu du. Ole muley haint hed a calf in two years, an' I'll eat sum rar ripe aigs.' Mary now venter'd tu speak: 'Husban, I ain't sure hit'll work on hens; cum an' kiss me my luv.' 'I haint sure hit'll work on hens, either,' sed Wat. 'They's powerful onsartin in thar ways, well es wimen,' an' he flung out a hanful spiteful like. 'Takin the rar ripe invenshun all tugether, frum 'taters an' peas tu notes ove han, an' childer, I can't say I likes hit much,' an' he flung out anuther hanful. 'Yer mam hed thuteen the ole way, an' ef this truck stays 'bout the hous', yu'se good fur twenty-six, maybe thuty, fur yu'se a pow'ful interprizin gal, yer mam sez,' an' he flung out anuther hanful, overhandid, es hard es ef he wer flingin rocks at a stealin sow. 'Make yere mine easy,' sed the widder; 'hit never works on married folks only the fust time.' 'Say them words agin,' sed Wat, 'I'se glad tu hear em. Is hit the same way wif notes ove han?' 'I speck hit am,' answer'd the widder, wif jis' a taste ove strong vinegar in the words, es she sot the flask in the cupboard wif a push.

"Jis' then ole Doltin, the sheriff, rid up, an' started 'stonished when he seed Wat, but he, quick es an 'oman kin hide a strange hat, drawed the puckerin-string ove that legil face ove his'n, an' fotch hit up tu the 'know'd yu wer at home,' sorter look, an' wishin Wat much joy, sed he'd fotch the baby a present, a par ove red shoes, an' a calliker dress, fur the luv he bore hits granmam. Missis Mc-Kildrin tole him what the rar ripe hed dun, an' he swore hit allers worked jis' that way, an' wer 'stonished at Wat's not knowin hit; an' they talked so fas', an' so much, that the more Wat listened the less he know'd.

"Arter the sheriff lef, they onrolled the bundil, an' Wat straitched out the calliker in the yard. He step't hit off keerfully, ten yards, an a littil the rise. He

409

puss'd up his mouf, an' blow'd out a whistil seven foot long, lookin up an' down the middil stripe ove the drygoods, frum aind tu aind. Sez he, 'Missis McKildrin, that'll make Rar Ripe a good *full* frock, won't hit?' 'Y-a-s,' sed she, wif her hans laid up along her jaw, like she wer studyin the thing keerfully. 'My son, I thinks hit will, an' I wer jis' a-thinkin ef hit wer cut tu 'vantage, thar *mout* be nuff lef, squeezed out tu make yu a Sunday shutin shut, makin the ruffils an' ban outen sumthin else.' 'Put hit in the bag what the rar ripe wer in, an' by mornin thar'll be nuff fur the ruffils an' bans, an' yu mout make the tail tu drag the yeath, wif- out squeezin ur pecin,' sez Wat, an' he put a few small wrinkils in the pint ove his nose, what seemed tu bother the widder tu make out the meanin ove; they look'd mons'ous like the outward signs ove an onb'lever. Jis' then his eyes sot fas' ontu sumthin a-lyin on the groun whar he'd onrolled the bundil; he walk'd up tu hit slow, sorter like a feller goes up tu a log, arter he thinks he seed a snake run onder. He walk'd clean roun hit twiste, never takin his eyes ofen hit. At las' he lifted hit on his instep, an' hilt out his laig strait at that widdered muther-in- lor ove his'n. Sez he, 'What mout yu call that? Red baby's shoes don't giner'lly hev teeth, dus they?' 'Don't yu *know* hits a tuckin comb, Watty? The store- keeper's made a sorter blunder, I speck,' sed that vartus petticoatful ove widder- hood. 'Maybe he hes; I'se durn sure I *hes*,' sed Wat, an' he wrinkil'd his nose agin, mons'ous botheringly tu that watchful widder. He scratched his head a spell; sez he, 'Ten yards an' the rise fur a baby's frock, *an' hit rar ripe at that, gits me;* an' that ar tuckin comb gits me wus.' 'Oh, fiddlesticks an' flusterashun,' sez she. 'Save the comb; baby'll soon want hit.' 'That's so, mammy, I'm dam ef hit don't,' an' he slip't his foot frum onder hit, an' hit scarcely totch the yeath afore he stomp't hit, an' the teeth flew all over the widder. He look'd like he'd been stompin a blowin adder, an' went apas' the 'oman intu the cabin, in a rale Aprile tucky gobbler strut. When he tore the rapper off the sheriff's present, I seed a littil bit ove white paper fall out. Onbenowenst tu enybody, I sot my foot ontu hit, an' when they went in I socked hit deep intu my pocket, an' went over tu the still-'ous. I tuck Jim Dunkin out, an' arter swarin 'im wif a uplifted han', tu keep dark, got him tu read hit tu me, ontil hit wer printed on the mindin seck- shun ove my brain. Hit run jis' so:

MY SWEET MARY:
     I mayn't git the chance tu talk eny tu yu, so when Wat gits home, an' axes enything 'bout the *comb* an' *calliker,* yu tell him yer mam foun the bundil in the road. She'll back yu up in that ar state- mint, ontil thar's enuf white fros' in hell tu kill snapbeans.

 Notey Beney.—I hope Wat'll stay in Atlanty ontil the merlenium, don't yu, my dear duv?

            Yures til deth,
            DOLTIN.

410

An' tu that ar las' remark he'd sot a big D. I reckon he ment that fur dam Wat.
 "Now, I jis' know'd es long es I hed that paper, I hilt four aces ontu the sheriff, an' I ment tu bet on the han, an' *go halves wif Wat,* fur I wer sorry fur him, he

wer so infunely 'posed upon. I went tu school tu Sicily Burns, tu larn 'oman tricks, an' I tuck a dirplomer, I did, an' now I'd jes' like tu see the pussonal feeters ove the she 'oman what cud stock rar ripe kerds on me, durn'd fool es I is. I hed a talk wif Wat, an' soon foun out that his mine hed simmer'd down intu a strong belief that the sheriff an' Mary wer doin thar weavin in the same loom.

"Then I show'd him my four aces, an' that chip made the pot bile over, an' he jis' 'greed tu be led by me, spontanashusly.

"Jis' think on that fac' a minnit boys; a man what hed sense enuf tu turn a hoss shoe, an' then nail hit on toe aind foremos', bein led by me, looks sorter like a plum tree barin tumil bug-balls, but hit wer jis' so, an' durn my pictur, ef I didn't lead him tu victory, strait along.

"Wat narrated hit, that he b'leved strong in rar ripe, frum beans, thru notes ove han, plum tu babys, an' that his cabin shud never be wifout hit. The widder wer cheerful, Mary wer luvin, an' the sheriff wer told on the sly, by ole Mister McKildrin's remainin, an' mos' pius she half, that Wat wer es plum blind es ef his eyes wer two tuckil aigs. So the wool grow'd over *his* eyes, ontil hit wer fit tu shear, an' *dam ef I warn't at the shearin.*

"Things, tharfore, went smoof, an' es quiet es a greased waggin, runnin in san. Hits allers so, jis' afore a tarin big storm.

"By the time littil Rar Ripe wer ten weeks ole, Doltin begun tu be pow'ful plenty in the neighborhood. Even the brats know'd his hoss's tracks, an' go whar he wud, the road led ni ontu Wat's, ur the widder's, tu git thar. My time tu play my four aces hed 'bout cum."

"And so has orderly bed time. I wish to repose," remarked the man of Useful Knowledge, in the square-tail coat, and cloth gaiters.

Sut opened his eyes in wonder.

"Yu wish tu du what?"

"I wish to go to sleep."

"Then why the h——l didn't yu say so? Yu mus' talk Inglish tu me, ur not git yersef onderstood. I warn't edikated at no Injun ur nigger school. Say, bunty, warn't yu standid deep in sum creek, when the taylure man put the string to yu, fur that ar cross atwix a rounabout an' a flour barril, what yu'se got on in place of a coat?"

My self-made guest looked appealingly at me, as he untied his gaiters, evidently deeply insulted. I shook my head at Sut, who was lying on his breast, with his arms crossed for a pillow, but with head elevated like a lizard's, watching the traveler's motions with great interest.

"Say, George, what dus repose mean? That wurd wer used at me jis' now."

"Repose means rest."

"Oh, the devil hit dus! I'se glad tu hear hit, I tho't hit wer pussonal. I kin repose now, mysef. Say, ole Onsightly Peter, repose sum tu, ef yu kin in that flour barril. I ain't gwine tu hunt fur yure har ontil mor——" and Sut slept. When morning broke, the Encyclopedia, or Onsightly Peter as Sut pronounced it, had

411

"Folded his tent like the Arab,
And as silently stole away."

(1867)

SPIRITUALS

Steal Away

Steal away, steal away, steal away to Jesus!
Steal away, steal away home,
I ain't got long to stay here.

My Lord, He calls me,
He calls me by the thunder,
The trumpet sounds within-a my soul,
I ain't got long to stay here.

Steal away, steal away, steal away to Jesus!
Steal away, steal away home,
I ain't got long to stay here.

Green trees a-bending, po' sinner stand a-trembling,
The trumpet sounds within-a my soul,
Oh, Lord, I ain't got long to stay here.

Lay Dis Body Down

I know moon-rise, I know star-rise,
    Lay dis body down;
I walk in de moonlight, I walk in de starlight,
    To lay dis body down.

I walk in de graveyard, I walk troo de graveyard,
    To lay dis body down.
I'll lie in de grass and stretch out my arms—
    Lay dis body down.

412

The spirituals in this group follow the versions appearing in The Book of American Negro Spirituals, *edited by James W. Johnson, The Viking Press, 1925.*

I go to de judgment in de evenin' of de day,
    When I lay dis body down;
And my soul and your soul will meet in de day
    When I lay dis body down.

Go Down, Moses

When Israel was in Egypt's land,
    Let my people go!
Oppress'd so hard dey could not stand,
    Let my people go!

Chorus
    Go down, Moses,
        Way down in Egypt's land.
    Tell ole Pha-raoh,
        Let my people go!

Thus say de Lawd, bold Moses said,
    Let my people go!
If not I'll smite your first-born dead,
    Let my people go!

No more shall dey in bondage toil,
    Let my people go!
Let dem come out wid Egypt's spoil,
    Let my people go!

Poor Pilgrim

I am a poor weary pilgrim,
    I sometimes know not where to roam—
I heard of a city called heaben,
    I'm strivin' to make it my home.

Sometimes I'm both tossed and driven,
    I sometimes know not where to roam,
I heard of a city called heaben,
    I'm strivin' to make it my home.

My friends and relations forsake me,
    And troubles roll round me so high,
I thought ob de kind voice of Jesus
    Sayin' "Poor pilgrim, I'm always nigh."

413

Nobody Knows de Trouble I've Seen

Nobody knows de trouble I've seen;
Nobody knows but Jesus.
Nobody knows de trouble I've seen;
Oh yes, Lord.

Sometimes I'm up, sometimes I'm down;
Oh yes, Lord.
Sometimes I'm almost to de groun';
Oh yes, Lord.

Although you see me gettin' 'long so,
Oh yes, Lord.
I got my troubles here below—
Oh yes, Lord.

Nobody knows de trouble I've seen;
Nobody knows but Jesus.
Nobody knows de trouble I've seen;
Oh yes, Lord.

Joshua Fit de Battle ob Jerico

Joshua fit de battle ob Jerico—Jerico—Jerico—
Joshua fit de battle ob Jerico,
And de walls came a-tumblin' down.

"Good mornin', Brudder Pilgrim,
Pray tell me where you boun';
O tell me where you travelin' to
'Cause dis enchanted groun'."

"My name it is Poor Pilgrim,
To Canaan I am boun';
Travelin' through dis wilderness
'Cause dis enchanted groun'."

You may talk about yo' King ob Gideon,
You may talk about yo' man ob Saul,
Dere's none like good ole Joshua,
At de battle ob Jerico.

Up to de walls ob Jerico
He marched wid spear in han',

414

"Go blow dem ram horns," Joshua cried,
"Kase de battle am in my han'."

Den de lam' ram sheep-horns begin to blow,
Trumpets begin to soun',
Joshua commanded de chillun to shout,
An' de walls came a-tumblin' down.

Dat mornin'—
Joshua fit de battle ob Jerico—Jerico—Jerico,
Joshua fit de battle ob Jerico,
An' de walls came a-tumblin' down.

Didn't Old Pharaoh Get Los'?

Isaac a ransom
While he lay upon an altar bound;
Moses an infant cast away,
By Pharaoh's daughter found.

Response
> Didn't old Pharaoh get los',
> get los', get los',
> Didn't old Pharaoh get los',
> In the Red Sea, True Believer,
> O didn't old Pharaoh get los',
> get los', get los',
> Didn't old Pharaoh get los',
> In de Red Sea?

Joseph by his false brethren sold,
God raised above them all;
To Hannah's child the Lord foretold
How Eli's house should fall.

De Lord said unto Moses—
"Go unto Pharaoh now,
For I have hardened Pharaoh's heart,
To me he will not bow."

Den Moses and Aaron,
To Pharaoh did go,
"Thus says de God of Israel,
Let my people go."

Old Pharaoh said, "Who is de Lord
Dat I should him obey?"

"His name it is Jehovah,
For he hears his people pray."

Hark! hear de children murmur,
Dey cry aloud for dread,
Down came the hidden manna,
De hungry soldiers fed.

Den Moses numbered Israel,
Through all de land abroad,
Sayin' "Children, do not murmur,
But hear de words of God."

Den Moses said to Israel,
As dey stood along de shore,
"Yo' enemies you see today
You'll never see no more."

Den down came raging Pharaoh,
Dat you may plainly see,
Old Pharaoh an' his host
Got los' in de Red Sea.

Den men an' women an' children
To Moses dey did flock;
Dey cried aloud for water,
An' Moses smote de rock.

An' de Lord spoke to Moses,
From Sinai's smoking top,
Sayin', "Moses lead de people,
Till I shall bid you stop."

415

Swing Low, Sweet Chariot

Swing low, sweet chariot,
Comin' for to carry me home.

I looked over Jordan and what did I see,
Comin' for to carry me home?
A band of angels comin' aftah me,
Comin' for to carry me home.

If you git there before I do,
Comin' for to carry me home,
Tell all my frien's I'm a-comin', too,
Comin' for to carry me home.

The brightes' day that ever I saw,
Comin' for to carry me home,
When Jesus washed my sins away,
Comin' for to carry me home.

I'm sometimes up an' sometimes down,
Comin' for to carry me home,
But still my soul feel heavenly-boun',
Comin' for to carry me home.

Singin' Wid a Sword in Ma Han'

Purtiest singin' ever I heard,
Way ovah on de hill,
De angels sing an' I sing too,
Singin' wid a sword in ma han', Lord,
Singin' wid a sword in ma han', Lord,
Singin' wid a sword in ma han'.

Purtiest shoutin' ever I heard,
Way ovah on de hill,
De angels shout an' I shout too,
Shoutin' wid a sword in ma han', Lord,
Shoutin' wid a sword in ma han', Lord,
Shoutin' wid a sword in ma han'.

416

Purtiest preachin' ever I heard,
Way ovah on de hill,
De angels preach an' I preach'd too,

Preachin' wid a sword in ma han', Lord,
Preachin' wid a sword in ma han', Lord,
Preachin' wid a sword in ma han'.

Purtiest mournin' ever I heard,
Way ovah on de hill,
De angels mourn an I mourn'd too,
Mournin' wid a sword in ma han', Lord,
Mournin' wid a sword in ma han', Lord,
Mournin' wid a sword in ma han'.

Purtiest prayin' ever I heard,
Way ovah on de hill,
De angels pray an' I pray'd too,
Prayin' wid a sword in ma han', Lord,
Prayin' wid a sword in ma han', Lord,
Prayin' wid a sword in ma han'.

CIVIL WAR SONGS

Dixie

I wish I was in de land ob cotton,
Old times dar am not forgotten;
  Look away! Look away! Look away! Dixie Land!
In Dixie Land whar I was born in,
Early on one frosty mornin',
  Look away! Look away! Look away! Dixie Land!

Chorus
  Den I wish I was in Dixie! Hooray! Hooray!
  In Dixie's Land we'll take our stand, to lib
    an' die in Dixie.
  Away! away! away down South in Dixie.
  Away! away! away down South in Dixie.

417

Ole missus marry "Will-de-weaber";
Willum was a gay deceaber;
   Look away, look away, look away, Dixie Land!
But when he put his arm around her,
He smiled as fierce as a forty-pounder;
   Look away, look away, look away, Dixie Land!

His face was sharp as a butcher's cleaber;
But dat did not seem to greab her;
   Look away, look away, look away, Dixie Land!
Ole missus acted de foolish part,
And died for a man dat broke her heart;
   Look away, look away, look away, Dixie Land!

Now here's a health to de next ole missus,
An' all the gals dat want to kiss us;
   Look away, look away, look away, Dixie Land!
But if you want to drive way sorrow,
Come hear dis song tomorrow;
   Look away, look away, look away, Dixie Land!

Dar's buckwheat cakes and Injin batter,
Makes you fat or a little fatter;
   Look away, look away, look away, Dixie Land!
Den hoe it down an' scratch your grabble,
To Dixie's land I'm bound to trabble;
   Look away, look away, look away, Dixie Land!

(Daniel Decatur Emmett — 1859)

Dixie

I.

Southrons, hear your country call you!
Up! lest worse than death befall you!
   To arms! to arms! to arms! in Dixie!
Lo! all beacon fires are lighted,
Let our hearts be now united!
   To arms! to arms! to arms! in Dixie!

Chorus
   Advance the flag of Dixie!
     Hurrah! Hurrah!
   For Dixie's land we'll take our stand,
     To live or die for Dixie!
   To arms! To arms!
     And conquer peace for Dixie!

418

    To arms! To arms!
      And conquer peace for Dixie!

II.

Hear the Northern thunders mutter!
Northern flags in South winds flutter!
    To arms! to arms! to arms! in Dixie!
Send them back your fierce defiance!
Stamp upon the cursed alliance!
    To arms! to arms! to arms! in Dixie!

III.

Fear no danger! shun no labor!
Lift up rifle, pike and sabre!
    To arms! to arms! to arms! in Dixie!
Shoulder pressing close to shoulder,
Let the odds make each heart bolder!
    To arms! to arms! to arms! in Dixie!

IV.

How the South's great heart rejoices,
At your cannon's ringing voices;
    To arms! to arms! to arms! in Dixie!
For faith betrayed and pledges broken,
Wrongs inflicted, insults spoken!
    To arms! to arms! to arms! in Dixie!

V.

Strong as lions, swift as eagles,
Back to their kennels hunt these beagles!
    To arms! to arms! to arms! in Dixie!
Cut the unequal bonds asunder!
Let them hence each other plunder!
    To arms! to arms! to arms! in Dixie!

VI.

Swear upon your country's altar,
Never to give up or falter;
    To arms! to arms! to arms! in Dixie!
Till the spoilers are defeated,
Till the Lord's work is completed.
    To arms! to arms! to arms! in Dixie!

VII.

Halt not till our Federation,
Secures among earth's Powers its station!
    To arms! to arms! to arms! in Dixie!
Then at peace and crowned with glory,
Hear your children tell the story!
    To arms! to arms! to arms! in Dixie!

419

VIII.

If the loved ones weep in sadness,
Victory soon shall bring them gladness.
    To arms! to arms! to arms! in Dixie!
Exultant pride soon banish sorrow;
Smiles chase tears away tomorrow,
    To arms! to arms! to arms! in Dixie!

(Albert Pike — 1861)

Maryland, My Maryland

The despot's heel is on thy shore,
        Maryland!
His torch is at thy temple door,
        Maryland!
Avenge the patriotic gore
That flecked the streets of Baltimore
And be the battle queen of yore,
        Maryland, my Maryland!

Hark to an exiled son's appeal,
        Maryland!
My Mother State, to thee I kneel,
        Maryland!
For life and death, for woe and weal,
Thy peerless chivalry reveal,
And gird thy beauteous limbs with steel,
        Maryland, my Maryland!

Thou wilt not cower in the dust,
        Maryland!
Thy beaming sword shall never rust,
        Maryland!
Remember Carroll's sacred trust,
Remember Howard's warlike thrust,
And all thy slumberers with the just,
        Maryland, my Maryland!

Come! 'tis the red dawn of the day,
        Maryland!
Come with thy panoplied array,
        Maryland!
With Ringgold's spirit for the fray,
With Watson's blood at Monterey,
With fearless Lowe and dashing May,
        Maryland, my Maryland!

Dear Mother! burst the tyrant's chain,
Maryland!
Virginia should not call in vain,
Maryland!
She meets her sisters on the plain—
"*Sic semper!*" 'tis the proud refrain
That baffles minions back amain,
Maryland!
Arise in majesty again,
Maryland, my Maryland!

Come! for thy shield is bright and strong,
Maryland!
Come! for thy dalliance does thee wrong,
Maryland!
Come to thine own heroic throng
Walking with Liberty along,
And chant thy dauntless slogan-song,
Maryland, my Maryland!

I see the blush upon thy cheek,
Maryland!
For thou wast ever bravely meek,
Maryland!
But lo! there surges forth a shriek,
From hill to hill, from creek to creek,
Potomac calls to Chesapeake,
Maryland, my Maryland!

Thou wilt not yield the Vandal toll,
Maryland!
Thou wilt not crook to his control,
Maryland!
Better the fire upon thee roll,
Better the shot, the blade, the bowl,
Than crucifixion of the soul,
Maryland, my Maryland!

I hear the distant thunder-hum,
Maryland!
The Old Line bugle, fife, and drum,
Maryland!
She is not dead, nor deaf, nor dumb;
Huzza! she spurns the Northern scum!
She breathes—she burns! she'll come! she'll come!
Maryland, my Maryland!

(*James Ryder Randall* — 1861)

421

The Bonnie Blue Flag

We are a band of brothers, and native to the soil,
Fighting for our liberty, with treasure, blood and toil;
    And when our rights were threatened, the cry rose near and far:
    Hurrah for the Bonnie Blue Flag that bears a Single Star!

Chorus
    Hurrah! Hurrah! for Southern rights, Hurrah!
    Hurrah for the Bonnie Blue Flag that bears a Single Star!

As long as the Union was faithful to her trust,
Like friends and like brethren kind were we and just;
    But now when Northern treachery attempts our rights to mar,
    We hoist on high the Bonnie Blue Flag that bears a Single Star.

First gallant South Carolina nobly made the stand;
Then came Alabama, who took her by the hand;
    Next, quickly Mississippi, Georgia, and Florida,
    All raised on high the Bonnie Blue Flag that bears a Single Star.

Ye men of valor, gather round the banner of the right,
Texas and fair Louisiana, join us in the fight:
    Davis, our loved President, and Stephens, statesman rare,
    Now rally round the Bonnie Blue Flag that bears a Single Star.

And here's to brave Virginia! The Old Dominion State
With the young Confederacy at length has linked her fate;
    Impelled by her example, now other States prepare
    To hoist on high the Bonnie Blue Flag that bears a Single Star.

Then cheer, boys, cheer, raise the joyous shout,
For Arkansas and North Carolina now have both gone out;
    And let another rousing cheer for Tennessee be given—
    The Single Star of the Bonnie Blue Flag has grown to be eleven.

Then, here's to our Confederacy; strong we are and brave,
Like patriots of old we'll fight our heritage to save;
    And rather than submit to shame, to die we would prefer—
    So cheer again for the Bonnie Blue Flag that bears a Single Star!

422

Chorus
    Hurrah! Hurrah! for Southern rights, Hurrah!
    Hurrah! for the Bonnie Blue Flag has gained the Eleventh Star.
                                     (*Harry B. Macarthy* — *1861*)

The Southern Cross

In the name of God! Amen!
 Stand for our Southern rights!
Arm, ye Southern men,
 The God of Battle fights!
Fling the invaders far,
 Hurl back their work of woe,
The voice is the voice of a brother,
 But the hands are the hands of a foe.
They come with a trampling army,
 Invading our native sod—
Stand, Southrons! fight and conquer!
 In the name of the Mighty God!

They're singing *our* song of triumph
 Which was made to make us free,
While they're breaking away the
 heartstrings
Of our nation's harmony.
Sadly it floateth from us,
 Sighing o'er land and wave,
Till mute on the lips of the poet,
 It sleeps in his Southern grave.
Spirit and song departed!
 Minstrel and minstrelsy!
We mourn thee, heavy-hearted,
 But we will, we shall be free!

They are waving *our* flag above us,
 With a despot's tyrant will;
With our blood they have stained its
 colors,
 And call it holy still.
With tearful eyes, but steady hand,
 We'll tear its stripes apart,
And fling them like broken fetters
 That may not bind the heart;
But we'll save our stars of glory,
 In the might of the sacred sign
Of Him who has fixed forever
 Our Southern Cross to shine.

Stand, Southrons! stand and conquer!
 Solemn and strong and sure!
The strife shall not be longer
 Than God shall bid endure.
By the life which only yesterday
 Came with the infant's breath,
By the feet which ere the morn may
 Tread to the soldier's death!
By the blood which cries to Heaven!
 Crimson upon our sod!
Stand, Southrons! stand and conquer!
 In the name of the Mighty God!
 (*Mrs. Ellen Key Blunt — 1862*)

Flight of Doodles

I come from old Manassas, with a pocket full of fun—
I killed forty Yankees with a single-barrelled gun;
It don't make a niff-a-stifference to neither you nor I,
Big Yankee, little Yankee, all run or die.

I saw all the Yankees at Bull Run,
They fought like the devil when the battle first begun,
But it don't make a niff-a-stifference to neither you nor I,
They took to their heels, boys, and you ought to see 'em fly.

I saw old Fuss-and-Feathers Scott, twenty miles away,
His horses stuck up their ears, and you ought to hear 'em neigh;

423

But it don't make a niff-a-stifference to neither you nor I,
Old Scott fled like the devil, boys; root, hog, or die.

I then saw a "Tiger," from the old Crescent City,
He cut down the Yankees without any pity:
Oh! it don't make a diff-a-bitterence to neither you nor I,
We whipped the Yankee boys, and made the boobies cry.

I saw South Carolina, the first in the cause,
Shake the dirty Yankees till she broke all their jaws;
Oh! it don't make a niff-a-stifference to neither you nor I,
South Carolina give 'em—boys; root, hog, or die.

I saw old Virginia, standing firm and true,
She fought mighty hard to whip the dirty crew;
Oh! it don't make a niff-a-stifference to neither you nor I,
Old Virginia's blood and thunder, boys; root, hog, or die.

I saw old Georgia, the next in the van,
She cut down the Yankees almost to a man;
Oh! it don't make a niff-a-stifference to neither you nor I,
Georgia's some in a fight, boys; root, hog, or die.

I saw Alabama in the midst of the storm,
She stood like a giant in the contest so warm;
Oh! it don't make a niff-a-stifference to neither you nor I,
Alabama fought the Yankees, boys, till the last one did fly.

I saw Texas go in with a smile,
But I tell you what it is, she made the Yankees bile;
Oh! it don't make a niff-a-stifference to neither you nor I,
Texas is the devil, boys; root, hog, or die.

I saw North Carolina in the deepest of the battle,
She knocked down the Yankees and made their bones rattle;
Oh! it don't make a niff-a-stifference to neither you nor I,
North Carolina's got the grit, boys; root, hog, or die.

Old Florida came in with a terrible shout,
She frightened all the Yankees till their eyes stuck out;
Oh! it don't make a niff-a-stifference to neither you nor I,
Florida's death on Yankees; root, hog, or die.

(Anonymous — Date unknown)

424   *Lee to the Rear*

Dawn of a pleasant morning in May,
Broke through the wilderness cool and grey,

While perched in the tallest tree-tops, the birds
Were carolling Mendelssohn's "Songs without words."

Far from the haunts of men remote,
The brook brawled on with a liquid note,
And Nature, all tranquil and lovely, wore
The smile of the spring, as in Eden of yore.

Little by little as daylight increased,
And deepened the roseate flush in the East—
Little by little did morning reveal
Two long glittering lines of steel;

Where two hundred thousand bayonets gleam,
Tipped with the light of the earliest beam,
And the faces are sullen and grim to see,
In the hostile armies of Grant and Lee.

All of a sudden, ere rose the sun,
Pealed on the silence the opening gun—
A little white puff of smoke there came,
And anon the valley was wreathed in flame.

Down on the left of the rebel lines,
Where a breastwork stands in a copse of pines,
Before the rebels their ranks can form,
The Yankees have carried the place by storm.

Stars and Stripes on the salient wave,
Where many a hero has found a grave,
And the gallant Confederates strive in vain
The ground they have drenched with their blood to regain!

Yet louder the thunder of battle roared—
Yet a deadlier fire on the columns poured—
Slaughter infernal rode with despair,
Furies twain, through the murky air.

Not far off in the saddle there sat,
A grey-bearded man in a black slouched hat;
Not much moved by the fire was he,
Calm and resolute Robert Lee.

Quick and watchful he kept his eye
On the bold rebel brigades close by,—
Reserves, that were standing (and dying) at ease,
While the tempest of wrath toppled over the trees.

For still with their loud, deep, bull-dog bay,
The Yankee batteries blazed away,

425

And with every murderous second that sped
A dozen brave fellows, alas! fell dead.

The grand old grey-beard rode to the space
Where death and his victims stood face to face,
And silently waved his old slouched hat—
A world of meaning there was in that!

"Follow me! Steady! We'll save the day!"
This, was what he seemed to say;
And to the light of his glorious eye
The bold brigades thus made reply—

"We'll go forward, but you must go back"—
And they moved not an inch in the perilous track:
"Go to the rear, and we'll send them to h——!"
And the sound of the battle was lost in their yell.

Turning his bridle, Robert Lee
Rode to the rear. Like the waves of the sea,
Bursting the dikes in their overflow,
Madly his veterans dashed on the foe.

And backward in terror that foe was driven,
Their banners rent and their columns riven,
Wherever the tide of battle rolled
Over the Wilderness, wood and wold.

Sunset out of a crimson sky,
Streamed o'er a field of ruddier dye,
And the brook ran on with a purple stain,
From the blood of ten thousand foemen slain.

Seasons have passed since that day and year—
Again o'er its pebbles the brook runs clear,
And the field in a richer green is drest
Where the dead of a terrible conflict rest.

Hushed is the roll of the rebel drum,
The sabres are sheathed, and the cannon are dumb,
And Fate, with his pitiless hand has furled
The flag that once challenged the gaze of the world;

426

But the fame of the Wilderness fight abides;
And down into history grandly rides,
Calm and unmoved as in battle he sat,
The grey-bearded man in the black slouched hat.

(*John Reuben Thompson* — *Date unknown*)

Goober Peas

WORDS BY A. PENDER   MUSIC BY P. NUTT

Sitting by the roadside on a summer day,
Chatting with my messmates, passing time away,
Lying in the shadow underneath the trees,
Goodness, how delicious, eating goober peas!

Chorus
>   Peas! Peas! Peas! Peas! eating goober peas!
>   Goodness, how delicious, eating goober peas!

When a horseman passes, the soldiers have a rule,
To cry out at their loudest, "Mister, here's your mule,"
But another pleasure enchantinger than these,
Is wearing out your grinders, eating goober peas!

Just before the battle the General hears a row,
He says, "The Yanks are coming, I hear their rifles now,"
He turns around in wonder, and what do you think he sees?
The Georgia militia eating goober peas!

I think my song has lasted almost long enough,
The subject's interesting, but the rhymes are mighty rough,
I wish this war was over, when free from rags and fleas,
We'd kiss our wives and sweethearts and gobble goober peas!

(Anonymous — Date unknown)

Do They Miss Me in the Trenches?

A VICKSBURG SONG

Do they miss me in the trenches, do they miss me,
>   When the shells fly so thickly around?
Do they know that I've run down the hillside
>   To hunt for my hole in the ground?
The shell exploded so near me,
>   It seemed best for me to run;
And altho' some laugh'd as I crawfished,
>   I could not discover the fun.

427

I often get up in the trenches,
>   When some Yank is near out of sight,
And fire a round or two at him,

To make the boys think I will fight;
But when the Feds commence shelling,
    I run to my hole down the hill—
I'll swear my legs never would stay there,
    Altho' all may stay there that will.

I'll save myself thro' the dread struggle,
    And when the great battle is o'er,
I'll claim my full rations of laurels,
    As always I've done heretofore.
I'll swear that I fought them as bravely
    As the best of my comrades who fell—
And swear to all others around me,
    That I never had fears of a shell.

(Anonymous — Date unknown)

The Virginians of the Valley

The knightliest of the knightly race,
    Who, since the days of old,
Have kept the lamp of chivalry
    Alight in hearts of gold;
The kindliest of the kindly band,
    Who, rarely hating ease,
Yet rode with Spotswood round the land,
    And Raleigh round the seas.

Who climbed the blue Virginian hills,
    Against embattled foes,
And planted there, in valleys fair,
    The lily and the rose;
Whose fragrance lives in many lands,
    Whose beauty stars the earth,
And lights the hearts of many homes
    With loveliness and worth.

We thought they slept! the sons who kept
    The names of noble sires,
And slumbered while the darkness crept
    Around the vigil fires.
But still the Golden Horse-shoe Knights
    Their Old Dominion keep,
Whose foes have found enchanted ground,
    But not a knight asleep.

(Francis Orray Ticknor — 1862?)

428

Little Giffen [1]

Out of the focal and foremost fire,
Out of the hospital walls as dire,
Smitten of grapeshot and gangrene,
Eighteenth battle and he sixteen—
Specter such as you seldom see,
Little Giffen of Tennessee.

"Take him and welcome," the surgeon said;
"Not the doctor can help the dead!"
So we took him and brought him where
The balm was sweet in our summer air;
And we laid him down on a wholesome bed;
Utter Lazarus, heel to head!

And we watched the war with abated breath,
Skeleton boy against skeleton death!
Months of torture, how many such!
Weary weeks of the stick and crutch,—
And still a glint in the steel-blue eye
Told of a spirit that wouldn't die,

And didn't! Nay! more! in death's despite
The crippled skeleton learned to write—
"Dear mother!" at first, of course, and then
"Dear Captain!" inquiring about the men.
Captain's answer: "Of eighty and five,
Giffen and I are left alive."

"Johnston pressed at the front," they say;—
Little Giffen was up and away!
A tear, his first, as he bade good-by,
Dimmed the glint of his steel-blue eye.
"I'll write, if spared!" There was news of fight,
But none of Giffen—he did not write!

I sometimes fancy that were I King
Of the courtly Knights of Arthur's ring,
With the voice of the minstrel in mine ear
And the tender legend that trembles here,
I'd give the best on his bended knee—
The whitest soul of my chivalry—
For Little Giffen of Tennessee.

(*Francis Orray Ticknor — 1867, 1879*)

429

[1] *This poem first appeared in 1867. The last stanza was rewritten and other minor alterations made before it was printed in Ticknor's* Poems *(1879).*

Stonewall Jackson's Way

Come, men, stack arms! Pile on the rails,
  Stir up the camp-fire bright;
No matter if the canteen fails,
  We'll make a roaring night.
Here Shenandoah brawls along,
Here burly Blue Ridge echoes strong,
To swell the brigade's rousing song,
  Of "Stonewall Jackson's way."

We see him now—the old slouched hat
  Cocked o'er his eye askew;
The shrewd, dry smile—the speech so pat,
  So calm, so blunt, so true.
The "Blue-Light Elder" knows 'em well.
Says he, "That's Banks, he's fond of shell;
Lord save his soul! We'll give him—" well,
  That's "Stonewall Jackson's way."

Silence! ground arms! kneel all! caps off!
  Old Blue Light's going to pray;
Strangle the fool that dares to scoff.
  Attention! it's his way!
Appealing from his native sod,
"Hear us, in power, Almighty God!
Lay bare thine arm, stretch forth thy rod,
  Amen." That's Stonewall's way.

He's in the saddle now! Fall in!
  Steady, the whole brigade!
Hill's at the ford, cut off; we'll win
  His way with ball and blade.
What matter if our shoes are worn?
What matter if our feet are torn?
Quick step! we're with him ere the dawn!
  That's Stonewall Jackson's way.

The sun's bright glances rout the mists
  Of morning—and, by George!
Here's Longstreet struggling in the lists,
  Hemmed in an ugly gorge,
Pope and his Yankees, whipped before,
"Bayonets and grape!" hear Stonewall roar.
"Charge, Stuart! pay off Ashby's score,
  In Stonewall Jackson's way."

Ah! maiden, wait, and watch, and yearn,
  For news of Stonewall's band!
Ah! widow, read with eyes that burn
  That ring upon thy hand!
Ah! wife, sew on, pray on, hope on!
Thy life shall not be all forlorn;
The foe had better ne'er been born
  That gets in Stonewall's way.

(John Williamson Palmer — 1866)

I'm a Good Old Rebel

O I'm a good old rebel,
  Now that's just what I am;
For the "fair land of freedom,"
  I do not care a damn;
I'm glad I fit against it,
  I only wish we'd won,
And I don't want no pardon,
  For anything I done.

I hate the Constitution,
  This great republic too;
I hate the freedman's buro,
  In uniforms of blue.
I hate the nasty eagle,
  With all his brags and fuss;
The lyin' thievin' Yankees,
  I hate 'em wuss and wuss.

I hate the Yankee nation
  And everything they do;
I hate the Declaration
  Of Independence, too.
I hate the glorious Union,
  'Tis dripping with our blood;
I hate the striped banner,
  I fit it all I could.

I followed old Marse Robert
  For four years near about,
Got wounded in three places,
  And starved on Point Lookout.
I cotch the roomatism
  A-campin' in the snow,
But if I killed a chance of Yankees,
  I'd like to kill some mo'.

Three hundred thousand Yankees
  Is stiff in Southern dust;
We got three hundred thousand
  Before they conquered us;
They died of Southern fever,
  And Southern steel and shot,
I wish it was three million
  Instead of what we got.

I can't take up my musket
  And fight 'em now no more;
But I ain't a-goin' to love 'em,
  Now that is certain sure.
And I don't want no pardon
  For what I was and am;
I won't be reconstructed,
  And I don't give a damn.

(Innes Randolph — Date unknown)

The Conquered Banner

431

Furl that Banner, for 'tis weary;
Round its staff 'tis drooping dreary;

Furl it, fold it, it is best:
For there's not a man to wave it,
And there's not a sword to save it,
And there's not one left to lave it
In the blood which heroes gave it;
And its foes now scorn and brave it;
    Furl it, hide it—let it rest.

Take that Banner down, 'tis tattered;
Broken is its staff and shattered;
And the valiant hosts are scattered,
        Over whom it floated high.
Oh! 'tis hard for us to fold it;
Hard to think there's none to hold it;
Hard that those, who once unrolled it,
        Now must furl it with a sigh.

Furl that Banner—furl it sadly;
Once ten thousands hailed it gladly,
And ten thousands wildly, madly,
        Swore it should forever wave;
Swore that foeman's sword should never
Hearts like theirs entwined dissever,
Till that flag should float forever
        O'er their freedom, or their grave!

Furl it! for the hands that grasped it,
And the hearts that fondly clasped it,
        Cold and dead are lying low;
And that Banner—it is trailing!
While around it sounds the wailing
        Of its people in their woe.

For, though conquered, they adore it!
Love the cold, dead hands that bore it!
        Weep for those who fell before it!
Pardon those who trailed and tore it!
But, oh! wildly they deplore it,
        Now who furl and fold it so.

Furl that Banner! True, 'tis gory,
Yet 'tis wreathed around with glory,
And 'twill live in song and story,
        Though its folds are in the dust:
For its fame on brightest pages,
Penned by poets and by sages,
Shall go sounding down the ages—
        Furl its folds though now we must.

432

Furl that Banner, softly, slowly,
Treat it gently—it is holy—
    For it droops above the dead.
Touch it not—unfold it never,
Let it droop there, furled forever,
    For its people's hopes are dead!

(Abram Joseph Ryan — 1865)

The Sword of Robert Lee

Forth from its scabbard pure and bright,
    Flashed the sword of Lee!
Far in the front of the deadly fight
High o'er the brave in the cause of Right
Its stainless sheen like a beacon light
    Led us to Victory.

Out of its scabbard where full long
    It slumbered peacefully,—
Roused from its rest by the battle's song,
Shielding the feeble, smiting the strong,
Guarding the right, avenging the wrong,
    Gleamed the sword of Lee.

Forth from its scabbard high in air
    Beneath Virginia's sky—
And they who saw it gleaming there
And knew who bore it knelt to swear,
That where that sword led, they would dare
    To follow and to die.

Out of its scabbard!—never hand
    Waved sword from stain as free,
Nor purer sword led braver band,
Nor braver bled for a brighter land,
Nor brighter land had a Cause so grand,
    Nor cause a chief like Lee.

Forth from its scabbard! how we prayed,
    That sword might victor be;—
And when our triumph was delayed,
And many a heart grew sore afraid,
We still hoped on while gleamed the blade
    Of noble Robert Lee.

Forth from its scabbard! all in vain
    Bright flashed the sword of Lee;—

433

'Tis shrouded now in its sheath again,
It sleeps the sleep of our noble slain;
Defeated yet without a stain,
    Proudly and peacefully.

(Abram Joseph Ryan — 1879)

A Land Without Ruins

"A land without ruins is a land without memories—a land without memories is a land without history. A land that wears a laurel crown may be fair to see; but twine a few sad cypress leaves around the brow of any land, and be that land barren, beautiless and bleak, it becomes lovely in its consecrated coronet of sorrow, and it wins the sympathy of the heart and of history. Crowns of roses fade—crowns of thorns endure. Calvaries and crucifixions take deepest hold of humanity —the triumphs of might are transient—they pass and are forgotten—the sufferings of right are graven deepest on the chronicle of nations."

Yes, give me the land where the ruins are spread,
And the living tread light on the hearts of the dead;
Yes, give me a land that is blest by the dust
And bright with the deeds of the down-trodden just.
Yes, give me the land where the battle's red blast
Has flashed to the future the fame of the past;
Yes, give me the land that hath legends and lays
That tell of the memories of long vanished days;
Yes, give me a land that hath story and song,
Enshrine the strife of the right with the wrong;
Yes, give me a land with a grave in each spot
And names in the graves that shall not be forgot;
Yes, give me the land of the wreck and the tomb—
There is grandeur in graves—there is glory in gloom;
For out of the gloom future brightness is born
As after the night comes the sunrise of morn;
And the graves of the dead with the grass overgrown
May yet form the footstool of liberty's throne,
And each single wreck in the war-path of might,
Shall yet be a rock in the temple of right.

(Abram Joseph Ryan — 1879)

part **3**

THE NEW SOUTH

1865-1918

part 3

THE NEW SOUTH

1865-1918

The New South

Reconstruction

The destitution of the South at the close of the Civil War is beyond the comprehension of most Americans today. Millions of people in the states which had comprised the Confederacy were without the necessities of life. Returning soldiers found their homes destroyed and their lands devastated. There was no money, little credit, and a serious shortage of manpower. A large percentage of white Southerners of fighting age had been killed or badly maimed, and many Negroes—free, but suddenly "displaced"—used their newly won freedom unwisely, going on prolonged vacations and sometimes stealing supplies from the meager stock of the whites.

The situation was aggravated by the actions of such radical Northern leaders as Thaddeus Stevens of Pennsylvania and Charles Sumner of Massachusetts, who, primarily for political ends, insisted that laws should be passed at once to make the Negroes socially, politically, and legally equal to their former masters. Had Lincoln lived, modern historians speculate, Reconstruction in the South might have been vastly different. During the war he had urged decisive and complete defeat, but afterwards he intended to restore the rights of citizenship to the people of the vanquished areas as soon as circumstances permitted. After the death of Lincoln, however, President Johnson was so bitterly opposed by members of the radical group that his humane proposals, from their inception, were doomed to defeat. He was impeached.

With national politics in the hands of vindictive and too-often unscrupulous men, Reconstruction measures were such as to rub salt into the still sensitive wounds made by the Civil War. On March 2, 1867, many of the Southern states were placed under military rule; on April 23 of the same year a law was passed requiring all voters to swear that they had not voluntarily participated in the "rebellion against the United States." Because of this act, the affairs of local government in the South were for the most part under the control of scalawags, carpetbaggers, and freed slaves.

The Freedman's Bureau, established by act of Congress in 1865, was authorized to distribute provisions, clothing, and fuel to relieve the suffering of the former slaves and their families. The Bureau's activities, however, went far beyond this original intention. Particularly objectionable, from the point of view of many white Southerners, was the attempt to provide homes for the Negroes by seizing the land that had been confiscated from Southern landowners and giving it, in plots of forty acres or less, to the freedmen. By persuading the Negroes to vote for the radical Republican candidates, members of this organization were able to control elections in many of the Southern states. Corruption in the South was so bad that the Ku Klux Klan was organized, under such leaders as General Nathan Bedford Forrest, to fight radical Reconstruction policies and to reëstablish white supremacy. These confused and troubled years in the South inspired the development of that unusual political unit, the "Solid South."

By a series of laws and by the use of military power, the radicals continued to dictate Southern policy throughout Grant's administrations. Beginning in 1874,

437

however, a number of occurrences brought about a healthier national attitude toward the South. In that year, first of all, the radicals were defeated at the polls; then the Supreme Court, following the election returns, reversed opinions issued a few years earlier and abolished the legal basis for the Reconstruction policies. One of the first acts of the newly elected Congress was to relinquish control of the Southern racial problems. Many Northern philanthropists, too, decided that the panacea for the South's ills was propaganda. They consequently spent millions of dollars sending "missionaries" to the South, buying books, and establishing schools and colleges in the "most backward section of our great country." Though sometimes misguided, their efforts raised considerably the educational level of the South.

The ante-bellum society versus the "New South"

Between 1870 and 1900 there arose in the South two conflicting ideological groups, and their opposing viewpoints received definite expression in the oratory, journalism, and literature of the last quarter of the nineteenth century. (This conflict characterizes much Southern thinking today. Although agrarianism would seem to be losing out, it is constantly reasserting itself.) The exponents of conservatism and agrarianism were opposed by a number of men who favored progress and industrialization for the South. This latter group, who represented what they called the "New South," included such prominent figures as Walter Hines Page, Henry W. Grady, Sidney Lanier, Booker T. Washington, George Washington Cable, and Joel Chandler Harris. The principal ideas on which these men were in general agreement may be summarized as follows: (1) since the war is over, past grievances should be forgotten and the former foes should work together for national solidarity; (2) although the South glories in its tragic past, it no longer mourns lost battles; (3) because the plantation system is no longer adequate to insure prosperity, it should be abandoned in favor of smaller farms and diversified agriculture; (4) if the South would industrialize, it would enjoy the material prosperity of the North.

According to this group, as Walter Hines Page expressed it, three ghosts haunted the Southern imagination and retarded the development of the region: the Confederacy, the fear of Negro domination, and religious intolerance. The cures they proposed were education, industrialization, and science. If the people would only realize that the issues of slavery and secession were dead, their argument ran, and if the section could be aroused from its lethargy and become ambitious and progressive, then all would be well. Too many Southerners, they insisted, were not aware that the South of mellow moonshine and magnolias—if it ever really existed—was forever exterminated by the Civil War.

Many of these men were confirmed optimists. That faint glimmer of material prosperity which could barely be perceived in the early 1880's would, they believed, completely obliterate the misery and hardships of a disastrous war and unwise Reconstruction policies. Henry W. Grady, the most typical representative of this progressive element, proposed that the solution to the entire problem lay in mutual understanding between the sections. After attracting the attention of Northerners and Southerners alike with his graphic accounts of the 1876 South

438

Carolina riots and the Florida election frauds of the same year, this animated Georgia journalist and orator gained national acclaim for his speech "The New South," delivered on December 22, 1886, before the New England society of New York. He was immediately accepted as the spokesman of a new era in the South, and the title of his address became the label of a vast movement in Southern thought. This and Grady's other addresses—"The South and Her Problem" (1887), "The Farmer and the Cities" (1889), and "The Negro" (1889)—are eloquent pleas for industrialization, improved methods of agriculture, and nationalism.

Another severe critic of traditional Southern policies was Walter Hines Page, editor of the Raleigh *State Chronicle* and the *Atlantic Monthly* and one of the founders of the publishing firm of Doubleday, Page and Company. Like Grady and Booker T. Washington, he advocated replacing the predominantly agrarian economy of the South with one that laid primary stress upon industrialization. His principal thesis, however, was the importance of education for the common man in any reform program. In the Old South, he said, education has been regarded as a luxury for the rich only, but "this civilization has been a failure. It is time now for a wiser statesmanship and a more certain means of grace." The South is replete with "Forgotten Men," men who cannot read or write. Democracy has never really existed in the South, but if the region ever expects to raise its economic level to that which prevails in other sections of the country it must provide education for the masses. The South is too much ruled by dead men's hands; what the section needs is a "few first-class funerals." Forget tradition, he reiterated, and share the material well-being of our Northern brethren.

In an article entitled "The New South," published in *Scribner's Monthly* (October 1880), Sidney Lanier allied himself, to some extent, with this progressive group. Lanier argued in this essay that the traditional cotton plantations, many of which had contained thousands of acres before the Civil War, should be replaced by a multitude of small farms stressing diversified agriculture. Independence and prosperity, he wrote, are within the grasp of the farmers of the region if they will concentrate on "small farming," which he defines as "meat and bread . . . pigs fed with home-made corn . . . eggs, chickens, peaches, water-mellons, the four extra sheep . . . two calves and a beef, a colt, who is now suddenly become, all by himself, a good serviceable horse; the four oxen . . . and a hundred other items, all representing income from a hundred sources to the small farmer." The farmer, in short, must become as nearly self-sustaining as he possibly can.

Many Southern writers in the immediate post-bellum period were also concerned with the problems of the Negro. George Washington Cable in *The Silent South* (1885) declared that the slaves had been freed in name only. In his native state of Louisiana and in the other Southern states where he lectured and traveled, he found the same intolerant and inhumane practices of the era before the Civil War still in existence. Joel Chandler Harris, in such stories as "Free Joe and the Rest of the World," indicated that he, too, was aware of the many problems presented by emancipation. The name that has become synonymous with Negro progress, however, is that of Booker T. Washington. As president of Tuskegee Institute in Alabama, he advocated a system of education which would fit the Negro for a useful and happy life. Although Washington agreed with Grady and

439

Walter Hines Page that prosperity in the South depended upon a high degree of industrialization, his primary contribution to the thinking of the New South movement was his suggestion for improving the deplorable circumstances of the Southern Negro by affording him facilities for thorough technical training. If every able Negro in the South were taught some useful skill and if the people of his race were relieved of the constant threat of poverty and fear, Washington believed, the Southern whites need not be afraid of a recurrence of "Black Republicanism." Washington also stressed the idea that segregation was essential for Negro progress. At the same time, however, there must be mutual understanding between the races and the Negroes must have more economic freedom and better educational opportunities.

This generally progressive attitude was opposed by a group of men who contended that more than a war had been lost in 1865. They believed, as John Donald Wade has expressed it, "that a philosophy of life had been destroyed." They accepted the South's defeat as final, but they did not repudiate the Southern cause. The literature of this group endeavored to express the spirit of the new age, but it sought to do so without sacrificing revered traditions. In the period immediately following the war, as one would expect, many Southern writers attempted to produce work distinctly Southern in content and almost exclusively Southern in appeal. Simms, Hayne, Timrod, Ticknor, and, for a time, Lanier tended to see the war as a disastrous holocaust in which principles had been defeated by brute force. With the exception of Lanier and Hayne, these men were dead by 1870, and Lanier by this time had compelling tendencies toward nationalism. There were two men, however—John Esten Cooke and Thomas Nelson Page—who continued to regard Southern problems as primarily sectional. Cooke, who had been producing novels with amazing regularity since long before the Civil War, wrote two of his best-known works in the "black raven days" of Reconstruction, *Surry of Eagle's Nest* (1866) and *Mohun* (1869). In both of these he idealized antebellum society. Cooke found nobility in the Cavalier life of Tidewater Virginia, and, with the exception of Thomas Nelson Page, became the most noted apologist for the aristocratic tradition.

Disgusted with the materialism he saw around him, Thomas Nelson Page followed Cooke's example and retreated to the "sweetest, purest, and most beautiful civilization" that America had ever known, that of the pre-Civil War South. Undoubtedly influenced by his aristocratic background, he was aware of the heritage the South stood to lose if it adopted the suggestions of his more progressive contemporaries. The advocates of the New South, he feared, would convert his beloved country into a "money worshipping domain" and discard the view that a civilized society must regard ethical principles and personal relationships as valuable.

The success of Page's *In Ole Virginia* (1877), comprising five tales in which he sympathetically treated Southern plantation life, encouraged him to turn his attention from law to literature. In dozens of subsequent fictional pieces, he depicted aspects of that idyllic life that was the South before the war. The focal character in many of his novels and stories is the Negro. Page glorified the "Uncles" and "Mammies," who, despite their newly acquired freedom, remained loyal to their old "Marsters." His romantic stories of dashing young sol-

440

diers stealing a farewell kiss from blushing young goddesses in the shadow of
the magnolia, or of the impressive Christmas festivities in the huge-columned
mansions, contained essentially the same social philosophy that he advanced in
his social essays. Here was a great civilization that would be completely forgotten
by the apostles of change unless it was carefully recorded. The needs of the freedmen, furthermore, could best be served by retaining the bonds of loyalty which
had existed between the slave and his master in the Old South.

Sidney Lanier

After the Civil War came the dreary pageant of a dispossessed and lost generation. Who was left, or who, still young among the survivors, felt it worth while to
come forward? By a sickening irony the South once more found itself where it
had stood in frontier days. It was a frontier again, though in a different way.
Carpetbaggers and scalawags instead of Indians were in the saddle, and even
after these were driven out, what remained but the grim job of building anew?
The South had to become Northernized, industrialized, or risk the decay Faulkner has described in certain of his novels. It had to do that or sink into the
degeneracy one associates with Erskine Caldwell's *Tobacco Road*.

What artist in the South could raise his voice in the face of antagonism from
the North and indifference and lethargy in his own section? The ideals of the
poets living at the end of the war—Francis Ticknor, Paul Hamilton Hayne, Henry
Timrod, William Gilmore Simms—were shattered by the disastrous days of Reconstruction, and all of them, except Hayne, soon died. The only poet of any
magnitude that the South produced in the post-war years was Sidney Lanier,
and even he was forced to sacrifice certain of his artistic principles and conform
to the rising tide of science and commercialism.

Lanier's literary efforts were not confined to one genre. In addition to his one
novel, *Tiger Lilies* (1867), he wrote a respectable body of literary criticism, and
his poetry is generally considered the best produced in America between Walt
Whitman and Edwin Arlington Robinson, excepting the work of Emily Dickinson.

Lanier's achievements in criticism were considerable. In his *English Novel*,
first published in 1883, he attempted to determine the merits of every English
novelist and his work. The important yardstick of measurement, however, was
the degree to which the narrative under consideration conformed to Victorian
morals and decorum. Basing his judgments upon strictly moral grounds, he discarded the works of Richardson and Fielding and came to the conclusion that
George Eliot was the "greatest of English novelists." Lanier also wrote a number
of essays in the complex field of English literature from the Anglo-Saxon *Beowulf* through the period of the Renaissance. What he found to say on this
broad subject still rewards study. Yet Lanier was poorly equipped both by
training and temperament to be a critic. His reading had been sporadic and
sketchy; his judgments were impressionistic and at times, it seems, intuitive.
Why, for example, would he proclaim William Drummond of Hawthornden "one
of the chief glories of the English tongue"? His efforts to relate earlier writings

441

to the age of Shakespeare, however ("Beowulf and Midsummer Night's Dream," "St. Juliana and Love's Labour's Lost," "The Music of Shakespeare's Time," and other studies), were well ahead of their day in scholarly and discriminating appreciation.

Lanier's most interesting contribution to criticism, perhaps, is his comment in *The Science of English Verse* (1880) on the relation of sound to sense in poetry. No one, he says,

> will find difficulty in accepting the assertion that when formal poetry . . . is repeated aloud it impresses itself upon the ear as verse only by means of certain relations existing among its component words considered purely as sounds. . . . If the least doubt upon this point should be entertained, it should be dispelled by observing that all ideas may be abolished out of a poem without disturbing its effect upon the ear as verse. This may be practically demonstrated by the simple experiment of substituting for the words of a formal poem any other words which preserve the accentuation, alliteration, and rhyme, but which convey no ideas to the mind—words of some foreign language not understood by the experimenter being the most useful for this purpose.

All this is interesting speculation; it antedates such performances as Edith Sitwell's *Façade* by more than half a century. But where does it leave poetry as a form of intelligent discourse? Lanier would eliminate even Poe's "pleasurable idea" from the poem; he would seemingly rank "Jabberwocky" with Marvell's "Coy Mistress." Poetry to him was pure, yet, paradoxically, at the same time a kind of verbal drug.

Lanier's greatest contribution to Southern letters is his poetry. For most of his productive life he insisted upon the identity of poetry and music, and many of his poems are merely experiments in which he was trying to put his theories into actual practice. Though he essentially agreed with Whitman's idea of democracy, he was convinced that Whitman was no poet. Whitman, he said, merely sketched suggestive outlines from which he could have written excellent poems if he had made them conform to a more orthodox pattern. Despite his own theories, then, Lanier was primarily a traditionalist from the standpoint of poetic forms.

On the basis of his dialect poem "Thar's More in the Man than Thar Is in the Land," as well as certain sections of his novel *Tiger Lilies*, Lanier has been associated with the local colorists. Although such poems as "The Marshes of Glynn" and "Song of the Chattahoochee" also encompass many of the characteristics usually associated with this type, Lanier's primary emphasis here was on pointing up the similarity between poetry and music. If we judge his work by how well he accomplished his intentions, "Symphony" and "Psalm of the West" are undoubtedly his most significant compositions. Because of the social philosophy expressed in such poems as "Corn" and "Symphony," Lanier has been acclaimed a forerunner of modern agrarianism. Certain agrarians, however, have denied the soundness of Lanier's pronouncements, insisting that his reactions to the social conflicts of the day were emotional rather than intellectual.

Attempting to evaluate Lanier's poetry, modern critics cite as inartistic his

442

grotesque comparisons, multiplicity of hyphenated words, repetition of favorite adjectives, vagueness of diction, labored lyrics, commonplace thought, and didacticism. On the other hand, they praise the fidelity of his landscape passages, the simplicity of his dialect poems, and his natural sense of melody. Professor Stanley Williams says of Lanier's poetry: "It carries us along in the rush of an emotion which cannot be translated into exact meanings, fulfilling the dictum of Coleridge that poetry gives the greatest pleasure when only generally and not perfectly understood. Such power Lanier's poetry sometimes displays in spite of its opaqueness of thought or eccentricity of technique. All nature is tense at the moment of sunrise; or we are lost in the music of the soaring violins; the reality of our emotion mocks the inadequacy of intellectual meaning; momentarily at least we are rapt in his 'strenuous sweet whirlwind.' "

Local color

The Southern writer of belles-lettres between 1870 and the turn of the century was compelled to produce stories and novels that appealed to Northern readers, for stories conceived and composed in the South still had to be published and circulated in the North. This situation naturally affected the trend of Southern letters during the last decades of the nineteenth century. Although Northern readers were intensely interested in eccentricities of Southern speech, manners, and codes of conduct, they insisted that the literature be non-partisan in letter and in spirit.

Faced by such a problem, these Southern writers might have followed the example of Poe and remained outside their tradition. Lacking his ability, however, and perhaps his inclination, many of them turned instead to exploiting the peculiarities of their region, with the expressed purpose of entertaining readers from all sections of the country.

Bret Harte is usually acclaimed the first of the local colorists, although local color was earlier evident in Sarah Kemble Knight's *Diary* or Byrd's remarks on the oddities of the backwoods people of North Carolina. But Harte turned his impressions into short-story form, a fact which seemed to excite authors all over the nation into something like wild emulation.

The cycle this wave of emulation took is well known. Southern writers began to exploit the rich traditions of their regions. George Washington Cable, Kate Chopin, and Grace Elizabeth King began to write about the Louisiana Creoles; Joel Chandler Harris produced his Uncle Remus books in Georgia; and Mary Noailles Murfree (writing under the pseudonym of Charles Egbert Craddock) and Sherwood Bonner celebrated, respectively, the mountaineers of Tennessee and the hillbillies of Mississippi. The trend as it developed in Virginia is best reflected in the plantation novels of Thomas Nelson Page and John Esten Cooke.

The unarticulated motive behind the movement seems to have run somewhat as follows. Here is a strange, new, and exciting section of the United States, although the characteristics which make it unique are fast disappearing. Thanks to the surrender at Appomattox, we shall soon be one nation again, a people

443

unified in behavior as well as in politics. Yet, not everything in the rapidly vanishing older society—the defeated society—is wholly bad. Much that prevailed in the period before the war, and that has not yet expired, is quaint and vastly charming. Let us set it down in print, capture it, before standardization comes to dominate everything.

Though many of these writers considered themselves mere depicters of life, flagrant violations of realism are readily apparent in their work. Thomas Nelson Page's portraits were idealized, and George Washington Cable concentrated on the bizarre and exotic. Yet it seems unfair to accuse them of insincerity or untruthfulness. They were, after all, neither historians nor reporters, but artists fashioning their fiction from selected aspects of a society that was rapidly vanishing. Though concerned, perhaps, with surface characteristics, their work is noteworthy for its accurate use of dialect, authentic presentation of character types, and careful descriptions of a particular way of life.

Three of these writers—Irwin Russell, Joel Chandler Harris, and Thomas Nelson Page—excelled in portraying the character of the Southern Negro. Of the three, Russell was the first to realize the literary possibilities of the Negro, and in his writing he endeavored to present the picturesque life of the Negro in southern Mississippi. His best poem, "Christmas Night in the Quarters," captures with amazing success the genuine exuberance and unrestrained joy of the Negro's festive spirit. The late Professor C. Alphonso Smith has noted that Russell's poem differs from others of its type in that "the Negro is the central character, the poem being written not to exploit him but to portray him; the dialect, both in its grammar and in its rhetoric, is an improvement on anything that had preceded it; and the mingling of humor and religion, though admirably true to life, had been hitherto unachieved."

Though Russell was the first to realize the literary value of the Negro, his untimely death prevented his giving a satisfactorily complete portrait of him. Russell's work is admirably complemented by that of Joel Chandler Harris, whose stories of the Negro were enthusiastically received in both North and South. Like Thomas Nelson Page, Harris depicted life on the pre-Civil War plantation, yet his point of emphasis was often quite different, for whereas Page attempted to present the social aspects of plantation life, Harris usually concentrated his attention upon the Negro. In some of his short stories he treated the problems of the dislocated post-bellum Negro, but his more characteristic Uncle Remus tales usually portray the slave. Harris' best work in Negro folklore and dialect is contained in *Uncle Remus: His Songs and His Sayings* (1880) and *Nights with Uncle Remus* (1883). Critics agree that a more authentic and artistic reproduction of the Negro dialect of middle Georgia has never been achieved.

Another local colorist, George Washington Cable, is usually credited with being the first to attract attention to the peculiarities of the Louisiana Creoles—although it is now a critical commonplace to accuse him of inaccuracies and exaggerations in his sketches. Grace Elizabeth King and Charles Gayarré, for example, have asserted that Cable chose the situations for his sketches not from Creole society, as he pretended, but from that of the Cajuns, reputed descendants of the Acadians. However this may be, it is readily apparent that his characters possess certain traits which set them apart from those created by his fellow local colorists.

444

Miss Murfree and Thomas Nelson Page, for instance, were careful to place their characters as typical members of certain traditional Southern classes—the mountaineer and the plantation aristocrat. Cable's creations, on the other hand—Jean Marie Poquelin, Posson Jone, 'Sieur George—represent a tradition that is less typically American. And whereas Russell, Murfree, and Bonner had chosen their subject matter from everyday situations, Cable tended to stress the unusual and exotic. Though often marked by slovenly and careless craftsmanship, his romantic narratives are always interesting, and, despite exaggerations, his characters vital and alive.

Another of the Southern local colorists to attract an avid following among readers of both North and South was Thomas Nelson Page, whose plantation stories have already been discussed. Although Page was often blind to the unpleasant aspects of plantation life, his fame has proved more lasting than Cable's for the reason that his material was not so limited in scope. Page set his novels and stories in the idyllic days of the Old Dominion and always handled his characters with the utmost sympathy. In fact, Page loved the plantation so much that he tended to idealize "Meh Lady," "Marse Chan," and "Uncle Edinburg." His Negro portraits are not realistic, but it should be remembered that they were not intended to be. Rather, they seek to represent a type—the loyal old slave whose utopian existence on the plantation was forever destroyed by the Civil War.

While Page was concerned with the values of the Old Tidewater aristocracy, Mary Noailles Murfree was depicting the mountaineers of her native Tennessee. Upon the publication of her first collection of stories, *In the Tennessee Mountains* (1884), and her first novel, *The Prophet of the Great Smoky Mountains* (1885), readers immediately became attached to these simple, down-to-earth folk, whose inherent goodness was apparently derived from their intimate contacts with nature. Miss Murfree attempted to reproduce exactly the customs and dialects of her region, and a modern reader seldom finishes one of her books without feeling that he has been associating with real mountaineers, though he may be distracted by the fact that her characteristically weak plots are too often impeded by lengthy descriptions of mountain scenery and that the dialect is often tedious.

Around the turn of the century another Southerner was establishing a reputation for local-color fiction that portrayed the interesting oddities of manners and customs peculiar to the section of America that he knew and loved. Although William Sydney Porter (O. Henry) is known chiefly for stories laid in New York City (see his *Four Million*), he wrote with equal brilliance about other parts of the country, notably the South. An eminent example is his story about Nashville, Tennessee, "A Municipal Report," for the writing of which his early Southern experience well fitted him.

Almost without exception, the literature produced in the South between 1865 and 1918 was given scope and direction by the strong sectional feelings that followed the Civil War. Much of the writing was journalistic propaganda inspired by the predominating social and political issue of the day—sectionalism versus nationalism. Although the period has left us few literary productions of major significance, the creative activities of such writers as Sidney Lanier, Thomas Nelson Page, George Washington Cable, and Joel Chandler Harris formed an important tributary to the present mighty stream of Southern literature.

445

JOHN ESTEN COOKE

1830–1886

John Esten Cooke, the younger brother of the poet and story writer Philip Pendleton Cooke, was born in Winchester, Virginia. He attended several local academies and distinguished himself as a member of their literary societies, but he did not go to college. Rather, he studied law in the office of his father, a noted lawyer of the Shenandoah Valley. Cooke was admitted to the bar in 1851 and practiced until the outbreak of the Civil War. He was among the first to volunteer for the Confederate forces and served with distinction throughout the conflict, surrendering with Lee at Appomattox. After the war he married Mary Francis Page and settled on her estate, "The Briars," where he divided his time between farming and writing.

John Esten Cooke's early stories and poems, like those of his elder brother Philip, appeared in the *Southern Literary Messenger*. The conflict in his mind as to whether he would devote his energies to law or to writing was not resolved until after the Civil War, although he had become convinced that he could earn his living with his pen as early as 1852, when he received ten dollars from Harper and Brothers for one of his stories. His conviction proved well founded, for he reputedly was the best paid Southern man of letters before 1870.

Although Cooke produced more than thirty volumes of novels, biographies, and histories, most of this work has been forgotten today. The most notable of his writings are *The Virginia Comedians* (1854), set in Williamsburg in 1765, and *Surry of Eagle's Nest* (1866), the most interesting of the seven books based on his Civil War experiences. His two biographies—*Stonewall Jackson: A Military Biography* (1866) and *A Life of Robert E. Lee* (1871)—are military rather than personal studies. Cooke's most important novel after 1866 was *The Heir of Gaymount* (1870), in which he recorded his efforts to adjust himself to a changing environment. The plantation system of the Old South, he said, must be replaced, or at least supplemented, by intensive farming, which he termed "the salvation of the post-war South."

In estimating Cooke's importance, his only biographer, John O. Beaty, writes: "He was a chivalric Cavalier who idealized the South and was unreservedly devoted to Virginia. His books are what he wished them to be—entertaining and

446

pure. His popularity has suffered somewhat from the unwinnowed abundance of his writings, but his best romances of colonial Virginia will unquestionably survive. . . . He will continue to be known as a social historian of late colonial Virginia and as a romantic Confederate captain, who used his military experience as a basis of fiction."

from *Surry of Eagle's Nest*

It is neither as social history nor as romanticism that Surry of Eagle's Nest *appeals to the modern reader, but simply as a narrative of Cooke's personal experiences in the Civil War. The many romantic elements in the plot (the most outstanding of which is the Gothic subplot of Fenwick and Mordaunt—the archvillain and the strong, silent, mysterious world-traveler) never become an integral part of the main sequence of military events.*

The material other than the romantic is not entirely autobiographical. Lieutenant Surry of the novel, Colonel Jackson's aide-de-camp, gives his age as twenty-five in 1861, whereas Cooke himself was thirty years old at the time the war broke out and, furthermore, never actually served on Jackson's staff. Cooke's own staff duties, however, gave him numerous opportunities to meet the principal commanders of the Confederate Army of Northern Virginia and his observations are undoubtedly based upon his personal experiences.

Chapter 131. The Last Greeting Between Stuart and Jackson

. . . At daylight, on the morning succeeding the events just narrated, Jackson put his column in motion, and directed his march over the same route which I had pursued on my way to find Stuart. At the Catherine Furnace he was observed and attacked by the advance force of the enemy, but, pushing on without stopping—his flank covered by the cavalry—he reached the Brock road, and, finally, the Orange plank-road.

Here I joined him at the moment when General Fitz Lee, who commanded the cavalry under Stuart, informed him that, by ascending a neighboring eminence, he could obtain a good view of the enemy's works. Jackson immediately rode to the point thus indicated, in company with General Fitz Lee and Stuart; and the works of Hooker were plainly descried over the tops of the trees.

The whole was seen at a glance, and, to attack to advantage, it was obviously necessary to move further still around the enemy's flank.

"Tell my column to cross that road," Jackson said to one of his aides; and the troops moved on steadily until they reached the Old Turnpike, at a point between the Wilderness Tavern and Chancellorsville.

Here instant preparations were made for attack. The force which Jackson had consisted of Rodes's, Colston's, and A. P. Hill's divisions—in all, somewhat less

447

than twenty-two thousand men—and line of battle was immediately formed for an advance upon the enemy. Rodes moved in front, Colston followed within two hundred yards, and Hill marched in column, with the artillery as a reserve.

Jackson gave the order to advance at about six in the evening, and, as the sinking sun began to throw its long shadows over the Wilderness, the long line of bayonets was seen in motion. Struggling on through the dense thickets on either side of the turnpike, the troops reached the open ground near Melzi Chancellor's —and there, before them, was the long line of the enemy's works.

Jackson rode in front, and, as soon as his lines were formed for the attack, ordered the works to be stormed with the bayonet.

At the word, Rodes rushed forward—the men cheering wildly—and, in a few moments, they had swept over the Federal earthworks, driving the Eleventh Corps in wild confusion before them. The woods swarmed with panic-stricken infantry, in utter confusion; artillery galloped off, and was overturned in ditches, or by striking against the trees. At one blow the entire army of Hooker, as events subsequently proved, was entirely demoralized.

Jackson pressed straight on upon the track of the flying enemy; and I soon discovered that he was straining every nerve to extend his left, and so cut off their retreat to the Rappahannock. Unavoidable delays, however, ensued. The lines of Rodes and Colston had been mingled in inextricable confusion in the charge; officers could not find their commands: before advancing further, it was absolutely necessary to halt and re-form the line of battle.

Rodes and Colston were, accordingly, ordered to stop their advance, re-form their divisions, and give way to Hill, who was directed to take the front with his fresh division, not yet engaged.

Before these orders could be carried out, it was nearly nine o'clock at night, and the weird scene was only lit up by the struggling beams of a pallid moon. On all sides the scattered troops were seen gathering around their colors again, and forming a new line of battle—and soon A. P. Hill was heard steadily advancing to take his place in front, for the decisive attack on Chancellorsville, about a mile distant.

Such was the condition of things, when General Jackson, accompanied by his staff and escort, rode in advance of his line down the road toward Chancellorsville, listening, at every step, for some indications of a movement in the Federal camps.

When nearly opposite an old wooden house, in the thicket by the roadside, he checked his horse to listen; and the whole cortege, General, staff, and couriers, remained for some moments silent and motionless, gazing toward the enemy.

From the narrative of what followed I shrink with a sort of dread, and a throbbing heart. Again that sombre and lugubrious Wilderness rises up before me, lit by the pallid moon; again the sad whippoorwill's cry; again I see the great soldier, motionless upon his horse—and then I hear the fatal roar of the guns which laid him low!

448 Jackson had halted thus, and remained motionless in the middle of the road, listening intently, when, suddenly, for what reason has never yet been discovered, one of his brigades in the rear, and on the right of the turnpike, opened a heavy fire upon the party.

Did they take us for Federal cavalry, or were they firing at random, under the excitement of the moment? I know not, and it is probable that the truth will never be known. But the fire had terrible results. Some of the staff were wounded; others threw themselves from their horses, who were running from the fire toward the Federal lines, not two hundred yards distant; and Captain Boswell, engineer upon the General's staff, was killed, and his body dragged by his maddened horse to Chancellorsville.

As the bullets whistled around him, Jackson wheeled his horse to the left, and galloped into the thicket. Then came the fatal moment. The troops behind him, on the left of the road, imagined that the Federal cavalry were charging; and, kneeling on the right knee, with bayonets fixed, poured a volley upon the General, at the distance of thirty yards.

Two balls passed through his left arm, shattering the bone, and a third through his right hand, breaking the fingers.

Mad with terror, his horse wheeled round and ran off; and, passing under a low bough, extending horizontally from a tree, Jackson was struck in the forehead, his cap torn from his head, and his form hurled back almost out of the saddle. He rose erect again, however; grasped the bridle with his bleeding fingers; and, regaining control of his horse, turned again into the high road, near the spot which he had left.

The fire had ceased as suddenly as it began, and not a human being was seen. Of the entire staff and escort, no one remained but myself and a single courier. The rest had disappeared before the terrible fire, as leaves disappear before the blasts of winter.

Jackson reeled in the saddle, but no sound had issued from his lips during the whole scene. He now declared, in faint tones, that his arm was broken; and, leaping forward, he fell into my arms.

More bitter distress than I experienced at that moment I would not wish to have inflicted upon my deadliest enemy. Nor was my anxiety less terrible. The lines of the enemy were in sight of the spot where the General lay. At any moment they might advance, when he would fall into their hands.

No time was to be lost. I sent the courier for an ambulance; and, taking off the General's military satchel and his arms, endeavored to stanch his wound. While I was thus engaged, I experienced a singular consciousness that other eyes than the General's were intently watching me. I can only thus describe the instinctive feeling which induced me to look up—and there, in the edge of the thicket, within ten paces of me, was a dark figure, motionless, on horseback, gazing at me.

"Who is that?" I called out.

But no reply greeted my address.

"Is that one of the couriers? If so, ride up there, and see what troops those are that fired upon us."

At the order, the dark figure moved; went slowly in the direction which I indicated; and never again appeared. Who was that silent horseman? I know not, nor ever expect to know.

I had turned again to the General, and was trying to remove his bloody gauntlets, when the sound of hoofs was heard in the direction of our own lines, and soon General A. P. Hill appeared, with his staff. Hastily dismounting, he ex-

449

pressed the deepest regret at the fatal occurrence, and urged the General to permit himself to be borne to the rear, as the enemy might, at any moment, advance.

As he was speaking, an instant proof was afforded of the justice of his fears.

"Halt! surrender! Fire on them, if they do not surrender!" came from one of the staff in advance of the spot, toward the enemy; and, in a moment, the speaker appeared, with two Federal skirmishers, who expressed great astonishment at finding themselves so near the Southern lines.

It was now obvious that no time was to be lost in bearing off the General, and Lieutenant Morrison, one of the staff, exclaimed: "Let us take the General up in our arms and carry him off!"

"No; if you can help me up, I can walk!" replied Jackson, faintly.

And, as General Hill, who had drawn his pistol and mounted his horse, hastened back to throw forward his line, Jackson rose to his feet.

He had no sooner done so, than a roar like thunder came from the direction of Chancellorsville, and a hurricane of shell swept the road in which we stood. A fragment struck the horse of Captain Leigh, of Hill's staff, who had just ridden up with a litter, and his rider had only time to leap to the ground when the animal fell. This brave officer did not think of himself, however; he hastened to Jackson, who leaned his arm upon his shoulder; and, slowly dragging himself along, his arm bleeding profusely, the General approached his own lines again.

Hill was now in motion, steadily advancing to the attack, and the troops evidently suspected, from the number and rank of the wounded man's escort, that he was a superior officer.

"Who is that?" was the incessant question of the men; but the reply came as regularly, "Oh, only a friend of ours."

"When asked, just say it is a Confederate officer!" murmured Jackson.

And he continued to walk on, leaning heavily upon the shoulders of the two officers at his side. The horses were led along between him and the passing troops; but many of the soldiers peered curiously around them, to discover who the wounded officer was.

At last one of them recognized him as he walked, bareheaded, in the moonlight, and exclaimed, in the most piteous tone I ever heard:

"Great God! that is General Jackson!"

"You are mistaken, my friend," was the reply of one of the staff; and, as he heard this denial of Jackson's identity, the man looked utterly bewildered. He said nothing more, however, and moved on, shaking his head. Jackson then continued to drag his feet along—slowly and with obvious pain.

At last his strength was exhausted, and it was plain that he could go no further. The litter, brought by Captain Leigh, was put in requisition, the General laid upon it, and four of the party grasped the handles and bore it on toward the rear.

Such, up to this moment, had been the harrowing scenes of the great soldier's suffering; but the gloomiest and most tragic portion was yet to come.

450

No sooner had the litter begun to move, than the enemy, who had, doubtless, divined the advance of Hill, opened a frightful fire of artillery from the epaulments near Chancellorsville. The turnpike was swept by a veritable hurricane of shell and canister—men and horses fell before it, mowed down like grass—and, where a moment before had been the serried ranks of Hill, the eye could now discern only riderless horses, men writhing in the death agony, and others seeking the shelter of the woods.

That sudden and furious fire did not spare the small party who were bearing off the great soldier. Two of the litter-bearers were shot, and dropped the handles to the ground. Of all present, none remained but myself and another; and we were forced to lower the litter to the earth, and lie beside it, to escape the terrific storm of canister tearing over us. It struck millions of sparks from the flint of the turnpike, and every instant I expected would be our last.

The General attempted, during the hottest portion of the fire, to rise from the litter; but this he was prevented from doing; and the hurricane soon ceased. He then rose erect, and, leaning upon our shoulders, while another officer brought on the litter, made his way into the woods, where the troops were lying down in line of battle.

As we passed on in the moonlight, I recognized General Pender, in front of his brigade, and he also recognized me.

"Who is wounded, Colonel?" he said.

"Only a Confederate officer, General."

But, all at once, he caught a sight of General Jackson's face.

"Oh! General!" he exclaimed, "I am truly sorry to see you are wounded. The lines here are so much broken that I fear we will be obliged to fall back!"

The words brought a fiery flush to the pale face of Jackson. Raising his drooping head, his eyes flashed, and he replied:

"You must hold your ground, General Pender! You must hold your ground, sir!"

Pender bowed, and Jackson continued his slow progress to the rear.

He had given his last order on the field.

Fifty steps further, his head sank upon his bosom, his shoulders bent forward, and he seemed about to fall from exhaustion. In a tone so faint that it sounded like a murmur, he asked to be permitted to lie down and die.

Instead of yielding to this prayer, we placed him again upon the litter—some bearers were procured—and, amid bursting shell, which filled the moonlit sky above with their dazzling coruscations, we slowly bore the wounded General on, through the tangled thicket, toward the rear.

So dense was the undergrowth that we penetrated it with difficulty, and the vines which obstructed the way more than once made the litter-bearers stumble. From this proceeded a most distressing accident. One of the men, at last, caught his foot in a grape-vine, and fell—and, in his fall, he dropped the handle of the litter. It descended heavily, and then, as the General's shattered arm struck the ground, and the blood gushed forth, he uttered, for the first time, a low, piteous groan.

We raised him quickly, and at that moment, a ray of moonlight, glimmering through the deep foliage overhead, fell upon his pale face and his bleeding form. His eyes were closed, his bosom heaved—I thought that he was about to die.

What a death for the man of Manassas and Port Republic. What an end to a career so wonderful! Here, lost in the tangled and lugubrious depths of this weird Wilderness, with the wan moon gliding like a ghost through the clouds—

451

the sad notes of the whippoorwill echoing from the thickets—the shell bursting in the air, like showers of falling stars—here, alone, without other witnesses than a few weeping officers, who held him in their arms, the hero of a hundred battles, the idol of the Southern people, seemed about to utter his last sigh! Never will the recollection of that scene be obliterated. Again my pulses throb, and my heart is oppressed with its bitter load of anguish, as I go back in memory to that night in the Wilderness.

I could only mutter a few words, asking the General if his fall had hurt him—and, at these words, his eyes slowly opened. A faint smile came to the pale face, and in a low murmur he said:

"No, my friend; do not trouble yourself about me!"

And again the eyes closed, his head fell back. With his grand courage and patience, he had suppressed all evidences of suffering; and, once more taking up the litter, we continued to bear him toward the rear.

As we approached Melzi Chancellor's, a staff-officer of General Hill recognized Jackson, and announced that Hill had been wounded by the artillery fire which had swept down the turnpike.

Jackson rose on his bleeding right arm, and exclaimed:

"Where is Stuart!"

As though in answer to that question, we heard the quick clatter of hoofs, and all at once the martial figure of the great cavalier was seen rapidly approaching.

"Where is General Jackson?" exclaimed Stuart in a voice which I scarcely recognized.

And suddenly he checked his horse right in front of the group. His drawn sabre was in his hand—his horse foaming. In the moonlight I could see that his face was pale, and his eyes full of gloomy emotion.

For an instant no one moved or spoke—and again I return in memory to that scene. Stuart, clad in his "fighting jacket," with the dark plume floating from his looped-up hat, reining in his foaming horse, while the moonlight poured on his martial features; and before him, on the litter, the bleeding form of Jackson, the face pale, the eyes half-closed, the bosom rising and falling as the life of the great soldier ebbed away.

In an instant Stuart had recognized his friend, and had thrown himself from his horse.

"You are dangerously wounded!"

"Yes," came in a murmur from the pale lips of Jackson, as he faintly tried to hold out his hand. Then his cheeks suddenly filled with blood, his eyes flashed, and, half rising from the litter, he exclaimed:

"Oh! for two hours of daylight! I would then cut off the enemy from United States Ford, and they would be entirely surrounded!"

Stuart bent over him, and their eyes met.

"Take command of my corps!" murmured Jackson, falling back; "follow your own judgment—I have implicit confidence in you!"

Stuart's face flushed hot at this supreme recognition of his courage and capacity—and I saw a flash dart from the fiery blue eyes.

"But you will be near, General! You will still send me orders!" he exclaimed.

"You will not need them," murmured Jackson; "to-night or early to-morrow

452

you will be in possession of Chancellorsville! Tell my men that I am watching them—that I am with them in spirit!"

"The watchword in the charge shall be, 'Remember Jackson!'"

And, with these fiery words, Stuart grasped the bleeding hand; uttered a few words of farewell, and leaped upon his horse. For a moment his sword gleamed, and his black plume floated in the moonlight; then he disappeared, at full speed, toward Chancellorsville.

At ten o'clock next morning he had stormed the intrenchments around Chancellorsville; swept the enemy, with the bayonet, back toward the Rappahannock; and as the troops, mad with victory, rushed through the blazing forest, a thousand voices were heard shouting:

"Remember Jackson!" (*1866*)

from *The Virginia Comedians*

The Virginia Comedians, *in the words of its author, "aims at presenting in a brief and rapid manner, some view, however slight, of the various classes of individuals who formed that Virginia of 1765."*

The plot is concerned with the efforts of Squire Effingham, the Virginia aristocrat, to arrange a marriage between Champ, his dissolute son, and Clare Lee, a neighbor's daughter. Just as progress is made in this affair, Champ loses interest in Clare and turns his attentions to Beatrice Hallam, the star of a theater troupe that is visiting Williamsburg. When Beatrice refuses Champ's proposal of marriage, he kidnaps her and takes her aboard a boat on the James River. After a wild fight, Beatrice is rescued by her cousin, Charles Waters, whom she later marries. Champ is forced to flee the country but later returns to marry Clare. The Virginia Comedians *is of interest primarily as an authentic portrayal of life and manners in pre-Revolutionary Virginia.*

Author's Preface to the 1883 Edition

In the autumn of 1752 the "Virginia Company of Comedians" played, at the Theatre near the Capitol in Williamsburg, Virginia, "The Merchant of Venice," the first dramatic representation in America.

It was the period of the culmination of the old social *régime*. A splendid society had burst into flower, and was enjoying itself in the sunshine and under the blue skies of the most beautiful of lands. The chill winds of the Revolution were about to blow, but no one suspected it. Life was easy, and full of laughter—of cordial greetings, grand assemblies, and the zest of existence which springs from the absence of care. Social intercourse was the joy of the epoch, and crowds flocked to the race-course, where the good horses were running for the cup, or to the cock-fight, where the favorite spangles fought to the death. The violins seemed to be ever playing—at the Raleigh Tavern, in Williamsburg, where young Jeffer-

453

son "danced with Belinda in the Apollo," and was happy; or in the great manor-houses of the planters clustering along the Lowland rivers. In town and country life was a pageant. His Excellency the royal Governor went in his coach-and-six to open the Burgesses. The youths in embroidered waistcoats made love to the little beauties in curls and roses. The "Apollo" rang with music, the theatre on Gloucester Street with thunders of applause; and the houses of the planters were as full of rejoicing. At Christmas—at every season, indeed—the hospitable old "nabob" entertained throngs of guests; and, if we choose to go back in fancy, we may see those Virginians of the old age amid their most characteristic surroundings. The broad board is spread with plenty; the wood-fires roar in the wide fire-places; the canary sparkles; the wax-lights flame, lighting up the Louis Quatorze chairs, the old portraits, the curious *bric-à-brac*, and the rich dresses of fair dames and gallant men. Care stands out of the sunshine of this brilliant throng, who roll in their chariots, dance the minuet, exchange compliments, and snatch the charm of the flying hours with no thought, one would say, but enjoyment, and to make the best of the little life we live below.

This is what may be seen on the surface of society under the old Virginia *régime;* but that social organization had reached a stage when the elements of disintegration had already begun their work. A vague unrest pervaded the atmosphere, and gave warning of the approaching cataclysm. Class distinctions had been immemorially looked upon as a part of the order of nature; but certain curious and restive minds began to ask if that was just, and to glance sidewise at the wealthy nabob in his fine coach. The English Church was the church of the gentry; it was not the church of the people. The "New Light" ministers began to talk about "sinegogues of Satan," and to tell the multitudes, who thronged to hear them preach in the fields, that the reverend parsons were no better than they should be. New ideas were on the march. The spirit of change was under the calm surface. The political agitation soon to burst forth was preceded by the social. The hour was near when the merry violins were to stop playing; when the "Apollo room" at the Raleigh would become the meeting-place of political conspirators; and the Virginians, waking from their dreams of enjoyment, were to be confronted by the hard realities of the new time.

Such was the period selected by the youthful writer of this volume for the picture he wished to attempt of that former society. When the story opens, the worthy "Virginia Comedians" have prospered. They have gone away, but have returned year after year, and are still playing at what is now the "Old Theatre near the Capitol." The winter still attracts the pleasure-loving Virginians to the vice-regal city, and throughout the theatrical season, beginning in the autumn, the playhouse is thronged with powdered planters, beautiful dames, honest yeomen, and indented servants. More than ever the spirit of unrest—social, political, and religious—pervades all these classes. Revolution is already in the air, and the radical sentiments of young Waters and the Man in the Red Cloak, in this volume, meet with thousands of sympathizers. On the surface the era is tranquil, but beneath is the volcano. Passion smoulders under the laughter; the home-spun coat jostles the embroidered costume; men are demanding social equality, as they will soon demand a republic; and the splendid old *régime* is about to vanish in the storms of the Revolution. . . .

454

Chapter 1. An Interior with Portraits

On a splendid October afternoon, in the year of our Lord 1763, two persons who will appear frequently in this history were seated in the great dining-room of Effingham Hall.

But let us first say a few words of this old mansion. Effingham Hall was a stately edifice not far from Williamsburg, which, as every body knows, was at that period the capital city of the colony of Virginia. The hall was constructed of elegant brick brought over from England: and from the great portico in front of the building a beautiful rolling country of hills and valleys, field and forest, spread itself pleasantly before the eye, bounded far off along the circling belt of woods by the bright waters of the noble river.

Entering the large hall of the old house, you had before you, walls covered with deers' antlers, fishing-rods, and guns: portraits of cavaliers, and dames and children: even carefully painted pictures of celebrated race-horses, on whose speed and bottom many thousands of pounds had been staked and lost and won in their day and generation.

On one side of the hall a broad staircase with oaken balustrade led to the numerous apartments above: and on the opposite side, a door gave entrance into the great dining-room.

The dining-room was decorated with great elegance:—the carved oak wainscot extending above the mantelpiece in an unbroken expanse of fruits and flowers, hideous laughing faces, and long foamy surges to the cornice. The furniture was in the Louis Quatorze style, which the reader is familiar with, from its reproduction in our own day; and the chairs were the same low-seated affairs, with high carved backs, which are now seen. There were Chelsea figures, and a sideboard full of plate, and a Japan cabinet, and a Kidderminster carpet, and huge andirons. On the andirons crackled a few twigs lost in the great country fireplace.

On the wall hung a dozen pictures of gay gallants, brave warriors, and dames, whose eyes outshone their diamonds:—and more than one ancestor looked grimly down, clad in cuirass and armlets, and holding in his mailed hand the sword which had done bloody service in its time. The lady portraits, as an invariable rule, were decorated with sunset clouds of yellow lace—the bright locks were powdered, and many little black patches set off the dazzling fairness of the rounded chins. Lapdogs nestled on the satin laps: and not one of the gay dames but seemed to be smiling, with her head bent sidewise fascinatingly on the courtly or warlike figures ranged with them in a long glittering line.

These portraits are worth looking up to, but those which we promised the reader are real.

In one of the carved chairs, if any thing more uncomfortable than all the rest, sits, or rather lounges, a young man of about twenty-five. He is very richly clad, and in a costume which would be apt to attract a large share of attention in our own day, when dress seems to have become a mere covering, and the prosaic tendencies of the age are to despise every thing but what ministers to actual material pleasure.

The gentleman before us lives fortunately one hundred years before our day:

455

and suffers from an opposite tendency in costume. His head is covered with a long flowing peruke, heavy with powder, and the drop curls hang down on his cheeks ambrosially: his cheeks are delicately rouged, and two patches, arranged with matchless art, complete the distinguished tout ensemble of the handsome face. At breast, a cloud of lace reposes on the rich embroidery of his figured satin waistcoat, reaching to his knees:—this lace is *point de Venise* and white, that fashion having come in just one month since. The sleeves of his rich doublet are turned back to his elbows, and are as large as a bushel—the opening being filled up, however, with long ruffles, which reach down over the delicate jewelled hand. He wears silk stockings of spotless white, and his feet are cased in slippers of Spanish leather, adorned with diamond buckles. Add velvet garters below the knee:—a little muff of leopard-skin reposing near at hand upon a chair—not omitting a snuffbox peeping from the pocket, and Mr. Champ Effingham, just from Oxford and his grand tour, is before you with his various surroundings.

He is reading the work which some time since attained to such extreme popularity, Mr. Joseph Addison's serial, "The Spectator,"—collected now for its great merits, into bound volumes. Mr. Effingham reads with a languid air, just as he sits, and turns over the leaves with an ivory paper cutter, which he brought from Venice with the plate glass yonder on the sideboard near the silver baskets and pitchers. This languor is too perfect to be wholly affected, and when he yawns, as he does frequently, Mr. Effingham applies himself to that task very earnestly.

In one of these paroxysms of weariness the volume slips from his hand to the floor.

"My book," he says to a negro boy, who has just brought in some dishes. The boy hastens respectfully to obey—crossing the whole width of the room for that purpose. Mr. Effingham then continues reading.

Now for the other occupant of the apartment. She sits near the open window, looking out upon the lawn and breathing the pure delicious air of October as she works. She is clad in the usual child's costume of the period (she is only eleven or twelve), namely, a sort of half coat, half frock, reaching scarcely below the knees; an embroidered undervest; scarlet silk stockings with golden clocks, and little rosetted shoes with high red heels. Her hair is unpowdered, and hangs in curls upon her neck and bare shoulders. Her little fingers are busily at work upon a piece of embroidery which represents or is to represent a white water dog upon an intensely emerald back-ground, and she addresses herself to this occupation with a business air which is irresistibly amusing, and no less pleasant to behold. There is about the child, in her movements, attitude, expression, every thing, a freshness and innocence which is only possessed by children. This is Miss Kate Effingham, whose parents died in her infancy, for which reason the little sunbeam was taken by the squire, her father's brother. . . .

Chapter 2. Squire Effingham

456

. . . The squire is a gentleman of fifty-five or sixty, with an open frank face, clear, honest eyes, and his carriage is bold, free, and somewhat pompous. He is clad much more simply than his eldest son, his coat having upon it not a particle of embroidery, and his long plain waistcoat buttoning up to the chin: below which a white cravat and an indication only of frill are visible. His limbs are cased in thick, strong and comfortable cloth, and woollen, and he wears boots, very large and serviceable, to which strong spurs are attached. His broad, fine brow, full of intelligence and grace, is covered by an old cocked hat, which, having lost the loops which held it in the three-cornered shape, is now rolled up upon each side; and his manner in walking, speaking, arguing, reading, is much after the description of his costume—plain, straightforward, and though somewhat pompous, destitute of finery and ornament. He is the head of a princely establishment, he has thousands of acres, and hundreds of negroes, he is a justice, and has sat often in the House of Burgesses: he is rich, a dignitary, every body knows it,—why should he strive to ape elegancies, and trouble himself about the impression he produces? He is simple and plain, as he conceives, because he is a great proprietor and can afford to wear rough clothes, and talk plainly.

His pomposity is not obtrusive, and it is tempered with so much good breeding and benevolence that it does not detract from the pleasant impression produced by his honest face. As he enters now that face is brown and red with exercise upon his plantation—and he comes in with cheerful smiles; his rotund person, and long queue gathered by a ribbon smiling no less than his eyes. . . .

Chapter 7. The Old Theatre near the Capitol

The "old Theatre near the Capitol," discoursed of in the manifesto issued by Mr. Manager Hallam, was so far *old*, that the walls were well-browned by time, and the shutters to the windows of a pleasant neutral tint between rust and dust color. The building had no doubt been used for the present purpose in bygone times, before the days of the "Virginia Gazette," which is our authority for many of the facts here stated, and in relation to the "Virginia Company of Comedians" —but of the former companies of "players," as my lord Hamlet calls them, and their successes or misfortunes, printed words tell us nothing, as far as the researches of the present Chronicle extend. That there had been such companies before, however, we repeat, there is some reason to believe; else why that addition "old" applied to the "Theatre near the Capitol." The question is submitted to the future social historians of the Old Dominion.

Within, the play-house presented a somewhat more attractive appearance. There was "box," "pit," and "gallery," as in our own day; and the relative prices were arranged in much the same manner. The common mortals—gentlemen and ladies—were forced to occupy the boxes raised slightly above the level of the stage, and hemmed in by velvet-cushioned railings—in front, a flower-decorated panel, extending all around the house,—and for this position were moreover compelled to pay an admission fee of seven shillings and sixpence. The demigods —so to speak—occupied a more eligible position in the "pit," from which they could procure a highly excellent view of the actors' feet and ankles, just on a level with their noses: to conciliate the demigods, this superior advantage had been offered, and the price for them was, further still, reduced to five shillings.

457

But "the gods" in truth were the real favorites of the manager. To attract them, he arranged the high upper "gallery"—and left it untouched, unincumbered by railing or velvet cushions, or any other device: all was free space, and liberal as the air: there were no troublesome seats for "the gods," and three shillings and nine pence was all that the managers would demand. The honor of their presence was enough.

From the boxes a stairway led down to the stage, and some rude scenes, visible at the edges of the green curtain, completed the outline.

When Mr. Lee and his daughters entered the box which had been reserved for them, next to the stage, the house was nearly full, and the neatness of the edifice was lost sight of in the sea of brilliant ladies' faces, and strong forms of cavaliers, which extended—like a line of glistening foam—around the semicircle of the boxes. The pit was occupied by well-dressed men of the lower class, as the times had it, and from the gallery proceeded hoarse murmurs and the unforgotten slang of London.

Many smiles and bows were interchanged between the parties in the different boxes; and the young gallants, following the fashion of the day, gathered at each end of the stage, and often walked across, to exchange some polite speech with the smiling dames in the boxes nearest.

Mr. Champ Effingham was, upon the whole, much the most notable fop present; and his elegant, languid, *petit maître* air, as he strolled across the stage, attracted many remarks, not invariably favorable. It was observed, however, that when the Virginia-bred youths, with honest plainness, called him "ridiculous," the young ladies, their companions, took Mr. Effingham's part, and defended him with great enthusiasm. Only when they returned home, Mr. Effingham was more unmercifully criticised than he would otherwise have been.

A little bell rang, and the orchestra, represented by three or four foreign-looking gentlemen, bearded and moustached, entered with trumpet and violin. The trumpets made the roof shake, indifferently, in honor of the *Prince of Morocco*, or *King Richard*, or any other worthy whose entrance was marked in the play-book "with a flourish." But before the orchestra ravished the ears of every one, the manager came forward, in the costume of *Bassanio*, and made a low bow. Mr. Hallam was a fat little man, of fifty or fifty-five, with a rubicund and somewhat sensual face, and he expressed extraordinary delight at meeting so many of the "noble aristocracy of the great and noble colony of Virginia," assembled to witness his very humble representation. It would be the chief end and sole ambition of his life, he said, to please the gentry, who so kindly patronized their servants—himself and his associates—and then the smiling worthy concluded by bowing lower than before. Much applause from the pit and gallery, and murmurs of approbation from the well-bred boxes, greeted this address, and, the orchestra having struck up, the curtain slowly rolled aloft. The young gallants scattered to the corners of the stage—seating themselves on stools or chairs, or standing, and the "Merchant of Venice" commenced. *Bassanio* having assumed a dignified and lofty port, criticised *Gratiano* with courteous and lordly wit: his friend *Antonio* offered him his fortune with grand magnanimity, in a loud singing voice, worthy the utmost commendation, and the first act proceeded on its way in triumph. (*1854, 1883*)

458

THOMAS NELSON PAGE

1853–1922

"That the social life of the Old South had its faults I am far from denying," said Thomas Nelson Page on one occasion, "but its virtues far outweighed them; its graces were never equalled. . . . It was, I believe, the purest, sweetest life ever lived." The task Page set for himself in his novels, stories, sketches, and poems was to preserve this past in print before it vanished forever from the recollections of men.

Descended from two of Virginia's most distinguished families and educated in the classical tradition requisite for a Southern gentleman, Page was unusually well equipped to perpetuate the Cavalier tradition. He attended Washington College during the presidency of Robert E. Lee, and that the tradition-conscious youth was impressed by his associations with this great Southern leader is indicated by Page's eulogistic biography, *Robert E. Lee: Man and Soldier* (1911). He left college, however, without taking a degree and enrolled at the University of Virginia, from which he received the LL.B. degree in 1874.

From the time he finished school until 1893, Page practiced law in Richmond and was active in the social and political activities of that city. On a trip abroad with his brother Rosewall in 1889, he was surprised to find that he had gained considerable fame in England as a writer. His reputation in America began to grow rapidly, partially as the result of an extended lecture and reading tour which he made with Francis Hopkinson Smith (1889–1893). In 1893 Page married Mrs. Florence Lathrop Smith (his first wife, Anna Selden Bruce, had died in 1886) and moved to Washington, where he remained until appointed Ambassador to Italy in 1913.

Page first achieved prominence in 1884, with the publication of "Marse Chan," although he had published previously a number of dialect poems. Three years later six of his stories appeared as *In Ole Virginia* and his reputation was firmly established. This work and the novel *Red Rock* (1898) are still held in high critical esteem. His best known books of social criticism are *The Old South* (1892) and *The Negro: The Southerner's Problem* (1904).

459

Despite his overemphasis on the attractive side of plantation life and his inability—or unwillingness—to see its faults, Page has been assured a secure place among Southern writers on the basis of his well-constructed plots and his skillful use of Negro dialect. With the exception of Joel Chandler Harris, the South has had no other writer who reproduced the speech of the Southern Negro with such ease and authenticity.

Marse Chan

One afternoon, in the autumn of 1872, I was riding leisurely down the sandy road that winds along the top of the water-shed between two of the smaller rivers of eastern Virginia. The road I was travelling, following "the ridge" for miles, had just struck me as most significant of the character of the race whose only avenue of communication with the outside world it had formerly been. Their once splendid mansions, now fast falling to decay, appeared to view from time to time, set back far from the road, in proud seclusion, among groves of oak and hickory, now scarlet and gold with the early frost. Distance was nothing to this people; time was of no consequence to them. They desired but a level path in life, and that they had, though the way was longer, and the outer world strode by them as they dreamed.

I was aroused from my reflections by hearing some one ahead of me calling, "Heah!—heah—whoo-oop, heah!"

Turning the curve in the road, I saw just before me a negro standing, with a hoe and a watering-pot in his hand. He had evidently just gotten over the "worm-fence" into the road, out of the path which led zigzag across the "old field" and was lost to sight in the dense growth of sassafras. When I rode up, he was looking anxiously back down this path for his dog. So engrossed was he that he did not even hear my horse, and I reined in to wait until he should turn around and satisfy my curiosity as to the handsome old place half a mile off from the road.

The numerous out-buildings and the large barns and stables told that it had once been the seat of wealth, and the wild waste of sassafras that covered the broad fields gave it an air of desolation that greatly excited my interest.

Entirely oblivious of my proximity, the negro went on calling "Whoo-oop, heah!" until along the path, walking very slowly and with great dignity, appeared a noble-looking old orange and white setter, gray with age, and corpulent with excessive feeding. As soon as he came in sight, his master began:

"Yes, dat you! You gittin' deaf as well as bline, I s'pose! Kyarnt heah me callin', I reckon? Whyn't yo' come on, dawg?"

The setter sauntered slowly up to the fence and stopped, without even deigning a look at the speaker, who immediately proceeded to take the rails down, talking meanwhile:

"Now, I got to pull down de gap, I s'pose! Yo' so sp'ilt yo' kyahn hardly walk. Jes' ez able to git over it as I is! Jes' like white folks—think 'cuz you's white and I's black, I got to wait on yo' all de time. Ne'm mine, I ain' gwi' do it!"

460

The fence having been pulled down sufficiently low to suit his dogship, he marched sedately through, and, with a hardly perceptible lateral movement of his tail, walked on down the road. Putting up the rails carefully, the negro turned and saw me.

"Sarvent, marster," he said, taking his hat off. Then, as if apologetically for having permitted a stranger to witness what was merely a family affair, he added: "He know I don' mean nothin' by what I sez. He's Marse Chan's dawg, an' he's so ole he kyahn git long no pearter. He know I'se jes' prodjickin' wid 'im."

"Who is Marse Chan?" I asked; "and whose place is that over there, and the one a mile or two back—the place with the big gate and the carved stone pillars?"

"Marse Chan," said the darky, "he's Marse Channin'—my young marster; an' dem places—dis one's Weall's, an' de one back dyar wid de rock gate-pos's is ole Cun'l Chahmb'lin's. Dey don' nobody live dyar now, 'cep' niggers. Arfter de war some one or nurr bought our place, but his name done kind o' slipped me. I nuver hearn on 'im befo'; I think dey's half-strainers. I don' ax none on 'em no odds. I lives down de road heah, a little piece, an' I jes' steps down of a evenin' and looks arfter de graves."

"Well, where is Marse Chan?" I asked.

"Hi! don' you know? Marse Chan, he went in de army. I was wid 'im. Yo' know he warn' gwine an' lef' Sam."

"Will you tell me all about it?" I said, dismounting.

Instantly, and as if by instinct, the darky stepped forward and took my bridle. I demurred a little; but with a bow that would have honored old Sir Roger, he shortened the reins, and taking my horse from me, led him along.

"Now tell me about Marse Chan," I said.

"Lawd, marster, hit's so long ago, I'd a'most forgit all about it, ef I hedn' been wid him ever sence he wuz born. Ez 'tis, I remembers it jes' like 'twuz yistiddy. Yo' know Marse Chan an' me—we wuz boys togerr. I wuz older'n he wuz, jes' de same ez he wuz whiter'n me. I wuz born plantin' corn time, de spring arfter big Jim an' de six steers got washed away at de upper ford right down dyar b'low de quarters ez he wuz a bringin' de Chris'mas things home; an' Marse Chan, he warn' born tell mos' to de harves' arfter my sister Nancy married Cun'l Chahmb'lin's Torn, 'bout eight years arfterwoods.

"Well, when Marse Chan wuz born, dey wuz de grettes' doin's at home you ever did see. De folks all hed holiday, jes' like in de Chris'mas. Ole marster (we didn' call 'im *ole* marster tell arfter Marse Chan wuz born—befo' dat he wuz jes' de marster, so)—well, de marster, his face fyar shine wid pleasure, an' all de folks wuz mighty glad, too, 'cause dey all loved ole marster, and aldo' dey did step aroun' right peart when ole marster was lookin' at 'em, dyar warn' nyar han' on de place but what, ef he wanted anythin', would walk up to de back poach, an' say he warn' to see de marster. An' ev'ybody wuz talkin' 'bout de young marster, an' de maids an' de wimmens 'bout de kitchen wuz sayin' how 'twuz de purties' chile dey ever see; an' at dinner-time de mens (all on 'em hed holiday) come roun' de poach an' ax how de missis an' de young marster wuz, an' ole marster come out on de poach an' smile wus'n a 'possum, an' sez, 'Thankee! Bofe doin' fust rate, boys;' an' den he stepped back in de house, sort o' laughin' to hisse'f, an' in a minute he come out ag'in wid de baby in he arms, all wrapped up in flannens an' things, an' sez, 'Heah he is, boys.' All de folks den, dey went up on de poach to look at 'im, drappin' dey hats on de steps an' scrapin' dey feets ez dey went up. An' pres'n'y ole marster, lookin' down at we

461

all chil'en all packed togerr down dyah like a parecel o' sheepburrs, cotch sight o' *me* (he knowed my name, 'cause I use' to hole he hoss fur 'im sometimes; but he didn' know all de chil'en by name, dey wuz so many on 'em), an' he sez, 'Come up heah.' So up I goes tippin', skeered like, an' de marster sez, 'Ain' you Mymie's son?' 'Yass, seh,' sez I. 'Well,' sez he, 'I'm gwine to give you to yo' young Marse Channin' to be his body-servant,' an' he put de baby right in my arms (it's de truth I'm tellin' yo'!), an' yo' jes' ought to a-heard de folks sayin', 'Lawd! marster, dat boy'll drap dat chile!' 'Naw, he won't,' sez marster; 'I kin trust 'im.' And den he sez: 'Now, Sam, from dis time you belong to yo' young Marse Channin'; I wan' you to tek keer on 'im ez long ez he lives. You are to be his boy from dis time. An' now,' he sez, 'carry 'im in de house.' An' he walks arfter me an' opens de do's fur me, an' I kyars 'im in in my arms, an' lays 'im down on de bed. An' from dat time I was tooken in de house to be Marse Channin's body-servant.

"Well, you nuver see a chile grow so!

"Pres'n'y he growed up right big, an' ole marster sez he must have some edication. So he sont 'im to school to ole Miss Lawry down dyar, dis side o' Cun'l Chahmb'lin's, an' I use' to go 'long wid 'im an' tote he books an' we all's snacks; an' when he larnt to read an' spell right good, an' got 'bout so-o big (measuring with his hand a height of some three feet), ole Miss Lawry she died, an' ole marster said he mus' have a man to teach 'im an' trounce 'im. So we all went to Mr. Hall, whar kep' de school-house beyant de creek, an' dyar we went ev'y day,—'cep Sat'd'ys of co'se, an' sich days ez Marse Chan din' warn' go, an' ole missis begged 'im off.

"Hit wuz down dyar Marse Chan fust took noticement o' Miss Anne.

"Mr. Hall, he teach gals ez well ez boys, an' Cun'l Chahmb'lin he sont his daughter (dat's Miss Anne I'm talkin' about). She wuz a leetle bit o' gal when she fust come. Yo' see, her ma wuz dead, an' ole Miss Lucy Chahmb'lin, she lived wid her brurr an' kep' house for 'im; an' he wuz so busy wid politics, he didn' have much time to spyar, so he sont Miss Anne to Mr. Hall's by a 'ooman wid a note.

"When she come dat day in de school-house, an' all de chil'en looked at her so hard, she tu'n right red, an' tried to pull her long curls over her eyes, an' den put bofe de backs of her little han's in her two eyes, an' begin to cry to herse'f. Marse Chan he was settin' on de een' o' de bench nigh de do', an' he jes' retched out an' put he arm roun' her an' drawed her up to 'im. An' he kep' whisperin' to her, an' callin' her name, an' coddlin' her; an' pres'n'y she took her han's down an' begin to laugh.

"Well, dey 'peared to tek' a gre't fancy to each urr from dat time. Miss Anne she warn' nuttin' but a baby hardly, an' Marse Chan he wuz a good big boy 'bout mos' thirteen year ole, I reckon. Hows'ever, dey sut'n'y wuz sot on each urr an' (yo' heah me!) ole marster an' Cun'l Chahmb'lin dey 'peared to like it 'bout well ez de chil'en. Yo' see, Cun'l Chahmb'lin's place j'ined ourn, an' it looked jes' ez nat'chal fur dem two chil'en to marry an mek it one plantation, ez it did fur de creek to run down de bottom from our place into Cun'l Chahmb'lin's. I don' rightly think de chil'en thought 'bout gittin' *mar'ied*, not den, no mo'n I thought 'bout mar'yin' Judy when she wuz a little gal at Cun'l Chahmb'lin's, runnin' 'bout de house, huntin' fur Miss Lucy's spectacles; but dey wuz good frien's from de start. Marse Chan he use' to kyar Miss Anne's books fur her ev'y day, an' ef de road wuz muddy or she was tired, he use' to tote her; an' 'twarn' hardly a day passed dat he didn' kyar her some'n' to school—apples or hick'y nuts, or some'n'. He wouldn' let none o' de chil'en tease her, nurr. Heh! One day, one o' de boys poke' he finger at Miss Anne, and arfter school Marse Chan he axed 'im 'roun' hine de school-house out o' sight, an' ef he didn' whup 'im!

"(Marse Chan, he wuz de peartes' scholar ole Mr. Hall hed, an' Mr. Hall he wuz mighty proud on 'im. I don' think he use' to beat 'im ez much ez he did de urrs, aldo' he wuz de head in all debilment dat went on, jes' ez he wuz in sayin' he lessons.)

"Heh! one day in summer, jes' fo' de school broke up, dyah come up a storm right sudden, an' riz de creek (dat one yo' cross' back yonder), an' Marse Chan he toted Miss Anne home on he back. He ve'y off'n did dat when de parf wuz muddy. But dis day when dey come to de creek, it had done washed all de lawgs 'way. 'Twuz still mighty high, so Marse Chan he put Miss Anne down, an' he took a pole an' waded right in. Hit took 'im long up to de shoulders. Den he waded back, an' took Miss Anne up on his head an' kyared her right over. At fust she was skeered; but he tol' her he could swim an' wouldn't let her git hu't, an' den she let 'im kyar her 'cross, she hol'in' his han's. I warn' 'long dat day, but he sut'n'y did dat thing!

"Ole marster he wuz so pleased 'bout it, he giv' Marse Chan a pony; an' Marse Chan rode 'im to school de day arfter he come, so proud, an' sayin' how he wuz gwine to let Anne ride behine 'im. When he come home dat evenin' he wuz walkin'. 'Hi! where's yo' pony?' said ole marster. 'I give 'im to Anne,' says Marse Chan. 'She liked 'im, an'—I kin walk.' 'Yes,' sez ole marster, laughin', 'I s'pose you's already done giv' her yo'se'f, an' nex' thing I know you'll be givin' her this plantation and all my niggers.'

"Well, about a fortnight or sich a matter arfter dat, Cun'l Chahmb'lin sont over an' invited all o' we all over to dinner, an' Marse Chan wuz 'spressaly named in de note whar Ned brought; an' arfter dinner he made ole Phil, whar wuz his ker'ige-driver, bring roun' Marse Chan's pony wid a little side-saddle on 'im, an' a beautiful little hoss wid a bran'-new saddle an' bridle on him; an' he gits up an' meks Marse Chan a gre't speech, an' presents 'im de little hoss; an' den he calls Miss Anne, an' she comes out on de poach in a little ridin' frock, an' dey puts her on her pony, an' Marse Chan mounts his hoss, an' dey goes to ride, while de grown folks is a-settin' on de poach an' a-laughin' an' chattin' an' smokin' dey cigars.

"Dem wuz good ole times, marster—de bes' Sam uver see! Dey wuz, in fac'! Niggers didn' hed nothin' 't all to do—jes' hed to 'ten' to de feedin' an' cleanin' de hosses, an' doin' what de marster tell 'em to do; an' when dey wuz sick, dey had things sont 'em out de house, an' de same doctor come to see 'em whar 'ten' to de white folks when dey wuz po'ly, an' all. Dyar warn' no trouble nor nuttin'.

"Well, things tuk a change arfter dat. Marse Chan he went to de bo'din' school, whar he use' to write to me constant. Ole missis use' to read me de letters, an' den I'd git Miss Anne to read 'em ag'in to me when I'd see her. He use' to write to her too, an' she use' to write to him too! Den Miss Anne she wuz sont off to school too. An' in de summer time dey'd bofe come home, an' yo' hardly know wherr Marse Chan lived at home or over at Cun'l Chahmb'lin's. He wuz over dyah constant! 'Twuz al'ays ridin' or fishin' down dyah in de river; or sometimes he'd go over dyah, an' 'im an' she'd go out an' set in de yard onder de trees; she settin' up mekin' out she wuz knittin' some sort o' bright-cullored some'n', wid de grarss growin' all up 'g'inst her, an' her hat th'owed back on her neck, an' he readin' to her out books; an' sometimes dey'd bofe read out de same book, fust one an' den turr. I use' to see 'em! Dat wuz when dey wuz growin' up like.

"Den ole marster he run for Congress, an' ole Cun'l Chahmb'lin he wuz put up to run 'g'inst ole marster by de Dimicrats; but ole marster he beat 'im. Yo' know he wuz gwine do dat! Co'se he wuz! Dat made ole Cun'l Chahmb'lin mighty mad, and dey stopt visitin' each urr reg'lar, like dey had been doin' all 'long. Den Cun'l Chahmb'lin he sort o' got in debt, an' sell some o' he niggers, an' dat's de way de fuss begun. Dat's whar de lawsuit come from. Ole marster he didn' like nobody to sell niggers, an' knowin' dat Cun'l Chahmb'lin wuz sellin' o' his, he writ an' offered to buy his M'ria an' all her chil'en, 'cause she hed mar'ied our Zeek'yel. An' don' yo' think, Cun'l Chahmb'lin axed ole marster mo' 'n th'ee niggers wuz wuth fur M'ria! Befo' old marster buy her, dough, de sheriff come an' levelled on M'ria an' a whole parecel o' urr niggers. Ole marster he went to de sale, an' bid for 'em; but Cun'l Chahmb'lin he got some one to bid 'g'inst ole marster. Dey wuz knocked out to ole marster dough, an' den dey hed a big lawsuit, an' ole marster was agwine to co't, off an' on, fur some years, till at lars' de co't decided dat M'ria belongst to ole marster. Ole Cun'l Chahmb'lin den wuz so mad he sued ole marster for a little strip o' lan' down dyah on de line fence, whar he said belongst to him. Evy'body knowed hit belongst to ole marster. Ef yo' go down dyah now, I kin show it to yo', inside de line fence, whar it hed done been uver sence long befo' Cun'l Chahmb'lin wuz born. But Cun'l Chahmb'lin was a mons'us perseverin' man, an' ole marster he wouldn' let nobody run over 'im. No, dat he wouldn'! So dey wuz agwine down to co't about dat, fur I don' know how long, till ole marster beat 'im agin.

"All dis time, yo' know, Marse Chan wuz agoin' back'ads and for'ads to college, an' wuz growed up a ve'y fine young man. He wuz a ve'y likely gent'man! Miss Anne she hed done mos' growed up too—wuz puttin' her hyar up like ole missis use' to put hers up, an' 'twuz jes' ez bright ez de sorrel's mane when de sun cotch on it, an' her eyes wuz gre't big dark eyes, like her pa's, on'y bigger an' not so fierce, an' 'twarn' none o' de young ladies ez purty ez she wuz. She an' Marse Chan still set a heap o' sto' by one 'nurr, but I don't think dey wuz easy wid each urr ez when he used to tote her home from school on he back. Marse Chan he use' to love de ve'y groun' she walked on, dough, is my 'pinion. Heh! His face 'twould light up whenever she come into chu'ch, or anywhere, jes' like de sun hed come th'oo a chink on it sudden'y.

"Den ole marster los' he eyes. D' yo' ever heah 'bout dat? Heish! Didn' yo'?

"Well, one night de big barn cotch fire. De stables, yo' know, wuz onder de big barn, an' all de hosses wuz in dyah. Hit 'peared to me like 'twarn' no time befo' all de folks an' de neighbors dey come, an' dey wuz a-totin' water, an' a-tryin' to save de po' critters, and dey got a heap on 'em out; but de ker'ige hosses dey would n' come out, an' dey wuz a-runnin' back'ads an' for'ads inside de stalls, a-nikerin' an' a-screamin', like dey knowed dey time hed come. Yo' could heah 'em in dyah so pitiful, an' pres'n'y ole marster said to Ham Fisher (he wuz de ker'ige-driver), 'Go in dyah, Ham, an' try to save 'em; don' let 'em bu'n to death.'

"An' Ham he went right in.

"An' jest arfter he got in, de shed whar it hed fus' cotch fell in, an' de sparks shot 'way up in de air; an' Ham didn' come back; an' de fire begin to lick out onder de eaves over whar de ker'ige hosses' stalls wuz. An' all of a sudden ole marster tu'ned an' kissed ole missis, who was standin' dyah nigh him, wid her face jes' ez white ez a sperit's, an', befo' anybody knowed what he wuz gwine do, jumped right in de do', an' de smoke come po'in' out behine 'im. Well, seh! I nuver 'spects to heah tell Jedgment sich a soun' ez de folks set up! Ole missis— she jes' drapt down on her knees in de mud an' prayed out loud.

"Hit 'peared like her pra'r wuz heard; for in a minit, right out de same do', kyain' Ham Fisher in his arms, come ole marster, wid his clo's all blazin'. Dey fling water on 'im, an' put 'im out; an', ef you b'lieve me, yo' wouldn' a-knowed 'twuz ole marster.

"Yo' see, he hed done find Ham Fisher done fall down in de smoke right by the ker'ige-hoss' stalls, whar he sont him, an' he hed to tote 'im back in his arms th'oo de fire what hed done cotch de front part o' de stable, and to keep de flame from gittin' down Ham Fisher' th'ote he had teck off his own hat and mashed it all over Ham Fisher' face, an' he hed kep' Ham Fisher from bein' so much bu'nt; but *he* wuz bu'nt dreadful! He beard an' hyar wuz all nyawed off, an' he face an' han's an' neck wuz scorified turrible. Well, he jes' laid Ham Fisher down, an' then he kind o' staggered for'ad, an' ole missis ketch' 'im in her arms.

"Ham Fisher, he warn' bu'nt so bad, an' he got out in a month or two; an' arfter a long time, ole marster he got well, too; but he wuz always stone blind arfter that. He nuver could see none from dat night.

"Marse Chan he comed home from college toreckly, an' he sut'n'y did nuss ole marster faithful—jes' like a 'ooman.

"Den he teck charge of de plantation arfter dat; an' I use' to wait on 'im jes' like when we wuz boys togerr; an' sometimes we'd slip off an' have a fox-hunt, an' he'd be jes' like he wuz in ole times, befo' ole marster got bline, an' Miss Anne Chahmb'lin stopt comin' over to our house, an' settin' onder de trees, readin' out de same book.

"He sut'n'y wuz good to me. Nuttin nuver made no diffunce 'bout dat! He nuver hit me a lick in his life—an' nuver let nobody else do it, nurr.

"I 'members one day, when he wuz a leetle bit o' boy, ole marster hed done tole we all chil'en not to slide on de straw-stacks; an' one day me an' Marse Chan thought ole marster hed done gone 'way from home. We watched him git on he hoss an' ride up de road out o' sight, an' we wuz out in de field a-slidin' an' a-slidin', when up comes ole marster. We start to run; but he hed done see us, an' he called us to come back; an' sich a whuppin' ez he did gi' us!

"Fust he took Marse Chan, an' den he teched me up. He nuver hu't me, but in co'se I wuz a-hollerin' ez hard ez I could stave it, 'cause I knowed dat wuz gwine mek him stop. Marse Chan he hed'n open he mouf long ez ole marster was tunin' 'im; but soon ez he commence warmin' me an' I begin to holler,

465

Marse Chan he bu'st out cryin', an' stept right in befo' ole marster, an' ketchin' de whup, said:

" 'Stop, seh! Yo' sha'n't whup 'im; he b'longs to me, an' ef you hit 'im another lick I'll set 'im free!'

"I wish yo' hed see ole marster! Marse Chan he warn' mo'n eight years ole, an' dyah dey wuz—old marster stan'in' wid he whup raised up, an' Marse Chan red an' cryin', hol'in' on to it, an' sayin' I b'longst to 'im.

"Ole marster, he raise' de whup, an' den he drapt it, an' broke out in a smile over he face, an' he chuck' Marse Chan onder de chin, an' tu'n right roun' an' went away, laughin' to hisse'f, an' I heah' 'im tellin' ole missis 'bout it dat evenin', an' laughin' 'bout it.

" 'Twan' so mighty long arfter dat when dey fust got to talkin' 'bout de war. Dey wuz a-dictatin' back'ads an' for'ds 'bout it fur two or th'ee years 'fo' it come sho' nuff, you know. Ole marster, he was a Whig, an' of co'se Marse Chan he teck after he pa. Cun'l Chahmb'lin, he wuz a Dimicrat. He wuz in favor of de war, an' ole marster and Marse Chan dey wuz agin' it. Dey wuz a-talkin' 'bout it all de time, an' purty soon Cun'l Chahmb'lin he went about ev'vywhar speakin' an' noratin' 'bout Ferginia ought to secede; an' Marse Chan he wuz picked up to talk agin' 'im. Dat wuz de way dey come to fight de duil. I sut'n'y wuz skeered fur Marse Chan dat mawnin', an' he was jes' ez cool!

"Yo' see, it happen so: Marse Chan he wuz a-speakin' down at de Deep Creek Tavern, an' he kind o' got de bes' of ole Cun'l Chahmb'lin. All de white folks laughed an' hoorawed, an' ole Cun'l Chahmb'lin—my Lawd! I t'ought he'd 'a' bu'st, he was so mad. Well, when it come to his tu'n to speak, he jes' light into Marse Chan. He call 'im a traitor, an' a ab'litionis', an' I don' know what all. Marse Chan, he jes' kep' cool till de ole Cun'l light into he pa. Ez soon ez he name ole marster, I seen Marse Chan sort o' lif' up he head. D' yo' ever see a hoss rar he head up right sudden at night when he see somethin' comin' to'ds 'im from de side an' he don' know what 'tis? Ole Cun'l Chahmb'lin he went right on. He say ole marster hed teach Marse Chan; dat ole marster wuz a wuss ab'litionis' dan he son. I looked at Marse Chan, an' sez to myse'f: 'Fo' Gord! old Cun'l Chahmb'lin better min'! an' I hedn' got de wuds out, when ole Cun'l Chahmb'lin scuse' ole marster o' cheatin' 'im out o' he niggers, an' stealin' piece o' he lan'—dat's de lan' I tole you 'bout. Well, seh, nex' thing I knowed, I heahed Marse Chan—hit all happen right 'long togerr, like lightnin' and thunder when they hit right at you!—I heah 'im say:

" 'Cun'l Chahmb'lin, what you say is false, an' yo' know it to be so. You have wilfully slandered one of de pures' an' nobles' men Gord ever made, an' nothin' but yo' gray hyars protects you.'

"Well, ole Cun'l Chahmb'lin, he ra'ed an' he pitch'd! He said he wan' too ole, an' he'd show 'im so.

" 'Ve'y well,' says Marse Chan.

"De meetin breke up den. I wuz hol'in' de hosses out dyar in de road by de een' o' de poach, an' I see Marse Chan talkin' an' talkin' to Mr. Gordon an' anurr gent'man, and den he come out an' got on de sorrel an' galloped off. Soon ez he got out o' sight he pulled up, an' we walked along tell we come to de road whar leads off to'ds Mr. Barbour's. He wuz de big lawyer o' de country. Dar he tu'ned

466

off. All dis time he hedn' sed a wud, 'cep' to kind o' mumble to hisse'f now and den. When we got to Mr. Barbour's, he got down an' went in. (Dat wuz in de late winter; de folks wuz jes' beginnin' to plough fur corn.) He stayed dyar 'bout two hours, an' when he come out Mr. Barbour come out to de gate wid 'im an' shake han's arfter he got up in de saddle. Den we all rode off.

" 'Twuz late den—good dark; an' we rid ez hard ez we could, tell we come to de ole school-house at ole Cun'l Chahmb'lin's gate. When we got deah, Marse Chan got down an' walked right slow 'roun' de house. Arfter lookin' roun' a little while an' tryin' de do' to see ef 't wuz shet, he walked down de road tell he got to de creek. He stop' dyar a little while an' picked up two or three little rocks an' frowed 'em in, an' pres'n'y he got up an' we come on home. Ez he got down, he tu'ned to me, an', rubbin' de sorrel's nose, said: 'Have 'em well fed, Sam; I'll want 'em early in de mawnin'.'

"Dat night at supper he laugh an' talk, an' he set at de table a long time. Arfter ole marster went to bed, he went in de charmber an' set on de bed by 'im talkin' to 'im an' tellin' 'im 'bout de meetin' an' e'vything; but he nuver mention ole Cun'l Chahmb'lin's name. When he got up to come out to de office in de yard, whar he slept, he stooped down an' kissed 'im jes' like he wuz a baby layin' dyar in de bed, an' he'd hardly let ole missis go at all.

"I knowed some'n wuz up, an' nex mawnin' I called 'im early befo' light, like he tole me, an' he dressed an' come out pres'n'y jes' like he wuz gwine to church. I had de hosses ready, an' we went out de back way to'ds de river.

"Ez we rid along, he said:

" 'Sam, you an' I wuz boys togerr, wa'n't we?'

" 'Yes,' sez I, 'Marse Chan, dat we wuz.'

" 'You have been ve'y faithful to me,' sez he, 'an' I have seen to it that you are well provided fur. You want to marry Judy, I know, an' you'll be able to buy her ef you want to.'

"Den he tole me he wuz gwoine to fight a duil, an' in case he should git shot, he had set me free an' giv' me nuff to tek keer o' me an' my wife ez long ez we lived. He said he'd like me to stay an' tek keer o' ole marster an' ole missis ez long ez dey lived, an' he said it wouldn' be ve'y long, he reckoned. Dat wuz de on'y time he voice broke—when he said dat; an' I couldn' speak a wud, my th'oat choked me so.

"When we come to de river, we tu'ned right up de bank, an' arfter ridin' 'bout a mile or sich a motter, we stopped whar dey wuz a little clearin' wid elder bushes on one side an' two big gumtrees on de urr, an' de sky wuz all red, an' de water down tow'ds whar the sun wuz comin' wuz jes' like de sky.

"Pres'n'y Mr. Gordon he come, wid a 'hogany box 'bout so big 'fore 'im, an' he got down, an' Marse Chan tole me to tek all de hosses an' go 'roun' behine de bushes whar I tell you 'bout—off to one side; an' 'fore I got 'roun' deah, ole Cun'l Chahmb'lin an' Mr. Hennin an' Dr. Call come ridin' from t'urr way, to'ds ole Cun'l Chahmb'lin's. When dey hed tied dey hosses, de urr gent'mens went up to whar Mr. Gordon wuz, an' arfter some chattin' Mr. Hennin step' off 'bout fur ez' cross dis road, or mebbe it mout be a little fur'er; an' den I see 'em th'oo de bushes loadin' de pistils, an' talk a little while; an' den Marse Chan an' ole Cun'l Chahmb'lin walked up an' dey gin' 'em de pistils in dey han's, an' Marse

Chan he stand wid his face right tow'ds de sun. I seen it shine on him jes' ez it come up over de low groun's, an' he look like he did sometimes when he come out of church.

"I wuz so skeered I couldn' say nuttin'. Ole Cun'l Chahmb'lin could shoot fust rate, an' Marse Chan he nuver missed.

"Den I heahed Mr. Gordon say, 'Gent'mens, is yo' ready?' and bofe of 'em sez, 'Ready,' jes' so.

"An' he sez, '*Fire*, one, two'—an' ez he said 'one,' ole Cun'l Chahmb'lin raised he pistil an' shot *right at* Marse Chan. De ball went th'oo his hat: I seen he hat sort o' settle on he head ez de bullit hit it! an' *he* jes' tilted his pistil up in de a'r an' shot—*bang*; an' ez de pistil went '*bang*,' he sez to Cun'l Chahmb'lin, 'I mek you a present to yo' fam'ly, seh!'

"Well, dey had some talkin' arfter dat. I didn't git rightly what 't wuz; but it 'peared like Cun'l Chahmb'lin he warn't satisfied, an' wanted to have anurr shot. De seconds dey wuz talkin', an' pres'n'y dey put de pistils up, an' Marse Chan an' Mr. Gordon shook han's wid Mr. Hennin an' Dr. Call, an' come an' got on dey hosses. An' Cun'l Chahmb'lin he got on his horse an' rode away wid de urr gent'mens, lookin' like he did de day befo' when all de people laughed at 'im.

"I b'lieve ole Cun'l Chahmb'lin wan' to shoot Marse Chan, anyways!

"We come on home to breakfast, I totin' de box wid de pistils befo' me on de roan. Would you b'lieve me, seh, Marse Chan he nuver said a wud 'bout it to ole marster or nobody! Ole missis didn' fin' out 'bout it for mo'n a month, an' den, Lawd! how she did cry and kiss Marse Chan; an' ole marster, aldo' he nuver say much, he wuz jes' ez please' ez ole missis: he call' me in de room an' made me tole 'im all 'bout it, an' when I got th'oo he gi' me five dollars an' a pyar of breeches.

"But ole Cun'l Chahmb'lin he nuver did furgive Marse Chan, an' Miss Anne she got mad too. Wimmens is mons'us onreasonable nohow. Dey's jes' like a catfish: you can n' tek hole on 'em like urr folks, an' when you gits 'm yo' can n' always hole 'em!

"What meks me think so? Heaps o' things—dis: Marse Chan he done gi' Miss Anne her pa jes' ez good ez I gi' Marse Chan's dawg sweet 'taters, an' she git mad wid 'im ez if he hed kill 'im stid o' sen'in 'im back to her dat mawnin' whole an' soun'. B'lieve me! she wouldn' even speak to him arfter dat!

"Don' I 'member dat mawnin'!

"We wuz gwine fox-huntin', 'bout six weeks or sich a matter arfter de duil, an' we meet Miss Anne ridin' 'long wid anurr lady an' two gent'mens whar wuz stayin' at her house. Dyah wuz always some one or nurr dyah co'tin' her. Well, dat mawnin' we meet 'em right in de road. 'Twuz de fust time Marse Chan had see her sence de duil, an' he raises he hat ez he pahss, an' she looks right at 'im wid her head up in de yair like she nuver see 'im befo' in her born days; an' when she comes by me, she sez, 'Good-mawnin', Sam!' Gord! I nuver see nuttin' like de look dat come on Marse Chan's face when she pahss 'im like dat. He gi' de sorrel a pull dat fotch 'im back settin down in de san' on he hanches. He ve'y lips wuz white. I tried to keep up wid 'im, but 'twarn no use. He sont me back home pres'n'y, an' he rid on. I sez to myself, 'Cun'l Chahmb'lin, don' yo' meet Marse Chan dis mawnin'. He ain' bin lookin' 'roun' de ole school-house, whar he an' Miss Anne use' to go to school to ole Mr. Hall togerr, to-day. He won' stan' no prodjickin' to-day.'

"He nuver come home dat night tell 'way late, an' ef he'd been fox-huntin' it mus' ha' been de ole red whar lives down in de greenscum mashes he'd been chasin'. De way de sorrel wuz gormed up wid sweat an' mire sut'n'y did hu't me. He walked up to de stable wid he head down all de way, an' I'se seen 'im go eighty miles of a winter day, an' prance into de stable at night ez fresh ez ef he hed jes' cantered over to ole Cun'l Chahmb'lin's to supper. I nuver see a hoss beat so sence I knowed de fetlock from de fo'lock, an' bad ez he wuz he want ez bad ez Marse Chan.

"Whew! he didn't git over dat thing, seh—he nuver did git over it!

"De war come on jes' den, an' Marse Chan wuz elected cap'n; but he wouldn' tek it. He said Firginia hadn' seceded, an' he wuz gwine stan' by her. Den dey 'lected Mr. Gordon cap'n.

"I sut'n'y did wan' Marse Chan to tek de place, cuz I knowed he wuz gwine tek me wid 'im. He wan' gwine widout Sam. An' beside, he look so po' an' thin, I thought he wuz gwine die.

"Of co'se, ole missis she heared 'bout it, an' she met Miss Anne in de road, an' cut her jes' like Miss Anne cut Marse Chan. Ole missis, she wuz proud ez any-body!

"So we wuz mo' strangers dan ef we hadn' live' in a hunderd miles of each urr. An' Marse Chan he wuz gittin' thinner an' thinner, an' Firginia she come out, an' den Marse Chan he went to Richmond an' listed, an' come back an' sey he wuz a private, an' he didn' know whe'r he could tek me or not. He writ to Mr. Gordon, hows'ever, an' 'twuz 'cided dat when he went I wuz to go 'long an' wait on him an' de cap'n too. I didn' min' dat, yo' know, long ez I could go wid Marse Chan, an' I like' Mr. Gordon, anyways.

"Well, one night Marse Chan come back from de offis wid a telegram dat say, 'Come at once,' so he wuz to start next mawnin'. He uniform wuz all ready, gray wid yaller trimmin's, an' mine wuz ready too, an' he had ole marster's sword, whar de State gi' 'im in de Mexikin war; an' he trunks wuz all packed wid ev'rything in 'em, an' my chist was packed too, an' Jim Rasher he druv 'em over to de depo' in de waggin, an' we wuz to start nex' mawnin' 'bout light. Dis wuz 'bout de las' o' spring, you know.

"Dat night ole missis made Marse Chan dress up in he uniform, an' he sut'n'y did look splendid, wid he long mustache an' he wavin' hyah an' he tall figger.

"Arfter supper he come down an' sez: 'Sam, I wan' you to tek dis note an' kyar it over to Cun'l Chahmb'lin's, an' gi' it to Miss Anne wid yo' own han's, an' bring me wud what she sez. Don' let any one know 'bout it, or know why you've gone.' 'Yes, seh,' sez I.

"Yo' see, I knowed Miss Anne's maid over at ole Cun'l Chahmb'lin's—dat wuz Judy,—an' I knowed I could wuk it. So I tuk de roan an' rid over, an' tied 'im down de hill in de cedars, an' I wen' 'roun' to de back yard. 'Twuz a right blowy sort o' night; de moon wuz jes' risin', but de clouds wuz so big it didn' shine 'cep th'oo a crack now an' den. I soon foun' my gal, an' arfter tellin' her two or three lies 'bout herse'f, I got her to go in an' ax Miss Anne to come to de do'. When she come, I gi' her de note, an' arfter a little while she bro't me anurr, an'

469

I tole her good-by, an' she gi' me a dollar, an' I come home an' gi' de letter to Marse Chan. He read it, an' tole me to have de hosses ready at twenty minits to twelve at de corner of de garden. An' jes' befo' dat he come out ez he wuz gwine to bed, but instid he come, an' we all struck out to'ds Cun'l Chahmb'lin's. When we got mos' to de gate, de hosses got sort o' skeered, an' I see dey wuz some'n or somebody standin' jes' inside; an' Marse Chan he jumpt off de sorrel an' flung me de bridle and he walked up.

"She spoke fust. 'Twuz Miss Anne had done come out dyar to meet Marse Chan, an' she sez, jes ez cold ez a chill, 'Well, seh, I granted your favor. I wished to reliebe myse'f of de obligations you placed me under a few months ago, when you made me a present of my father, whom you fust insulted an' then prevented from gittin' satisfaction.'

"Marse Chan he didn' speak fur a minit, an' den he said: 'Who is with you?' (Dat wuz ev'y wud.)

" 'No one,' sez she; 'I came alone.'

" 'My God!' sez he, 'you didn' come all through those woods by yourse'f at this time o' night?'

" 'Yes, I'm not afraid,' sez she. (An' heah dis nigger! I don' b'lieve she wuz.)

"De moon come out, an' I cotch sight o' her stan'in in dyah in her white dress, wid de cloak she had wrapped herse'f up in drapped off on de groun', an' she didn' look like she wuz 'feared o' nuthin'. She wuz mons'us purty ez she stood dyah wid de green bushes behine her, an' she hed jes' a few flowers in her breas'—right heah—and some leaves in her sorrel hyah; an' de moon come out an' shined down on her hyah an' her frock, an' peared like de light wuz jes' stan'in off it ez she stood dyah lookin' at Marse Chan wid her hed tho'd back, jes' like dat mawnin' when she pahss Marse Chan in de road widout speakin' to 'im, an' sez to me, 'Good-mawnin', Sam.'

"Marse Chan, he den tole her he hed come to say good-by to her, ez he wuz gwine 'way to de war nex' mawnin'. I wuz watchin' on her, an' I tho't, when Marse Chan tole her dat, she sort o' started an' looked up at 'im like she wuz mighty sorry, an' 'peared like she didn' stan' quite so straight arfter dat. Den Marse Chan he went on talkin' right fars' to her; an' he tole her how he had loved her ever sence she wuz a little bit o' baby mos', an' how he nuver 'membered de time when he hedn' hope' to marry her. He tole her it wuz his love for her dat hed made 'im stan' fust at school an' collige, an' hed kep' 'im good an' pure; an' now he wuz gwine 'way, wouldn' she let it be like 'twuz in ole times, an' ef he come back from de war wouldn' she try to think on him ez she use' to when she wuz a little guirl?

"Marse Chan he had done been talkin' so serious, he hed done tek Miss Anne' han', an' wuz lookin' down in her face like he wuz list'nin' wid his eyes.

"Arfter a minit Miss Anne she said somethin', an' Marse Chan he cotch her urr han' an' sez:

" 'But if you love me, Anne?'

"When he said dat, she tu'ned her head' way from 'im, an' wait' a minit, an' den she said—right clear:

" 'But I don't love yo'.' (Jes' dem th'ee wuds!) De wuds fall right slow—like dirt falls out a spade on a coffin when yo's buryin' anybody, an' seys, 'Uth to

470

uth.' Marse Chan he jes' let her hand drap, an' he stiddy hisse'f 'g'inst de gate-pos' an' he didn't speak torekly. When he did speak, all he sez wuz:

"'I mus' see you home safe.'

"I 'clar, marster, I didn' know 'twuz Marse Chan's voice tell I look at 'im right good. Well, she wouldn' let 'im go wid her. She jes' wrap' her cloak roun' her shoulders, an' wen' 'long back by herse'f, widout doin' more'n jes' look up once at Marse Chan leanin' dyah 'g'inst de gate-pos' in he sodger clo's, wid he eyes on de groun'. She said 'Good-by' sort o' sorf, an' Marse Chan, wid-out lookin' up, shake han's wid her, an' she wuz done gone down de road. Soon ez she got 'mos' 'roun de curve, Marse Chan he followed her, keepin' under de trees so ez not to be seen, an' I led de hosses on down de road behine 'im. He kep' 'long behine her tell she wuz safe in de house, an' den he come an' got on he hoss, an' we all come home.

"Nex' mawnin' we all come off to j'ine de army. An' dey wuz a-drillin' an' a-drillin' all 'bout for a while an' we went 'long wid all de res' o' de army, an' I went wid Marse Chan an' clean he boots an' look arfter de tent, an' tek keer o' him an' de hosses. An' Marse Chan, he wan' a bit like he use' to be. He wuz so solum an' moanful all de time, at leas' 'cep' when dyah wuz gwine to be a fight. Den he'd peartin' up, an' he alwuz ride at de head o' de company, 'cause he wuz tall; an' hit wan' on'y in battles whar all his company wuz dat *he* went, but he use' to volunteer whenever de cun'l wanted anybody to fine out anythin', an' 'twuz so dangersome he didn' like to mek one man go no sooner'n anurr, yo' know, an' ax'd who'd volunteer. *He* 'peared to like to go prowlin' aroun' 'mong dem Yankees, an' he use' to tek me wid 'im whenever he could. Yes, seh, he sut'n'y wuz a good sowger! He didn' mine bullets no more'n he did so many draps o'rain. But I use' to be pow'ful skeered sometimes. It jes' use' to 'pear like fun to him. In camp he use' to be so sorrerful he'd hardly open he mouf. You'd a' tho't he wuz seekin', he used to look so moanful; but jes' le' 'im git into dan-ger, an' he use' to be like old times—jolly an' laughin' like when he wuz a boy.

"When Cap'n Gordon got he leg shoot off, dey mek Marse Chan cap'n on de spot, 'cause one o' de lieutenants got kilt de same day, an' turr one (named Mr. Ronny) wan' no 'count, an' all de company said Marse Chan wuz de man.

"An' Marse Chan he wuz jes' de same. He didn' nuver mention Miss Anne's name, but I knowed he wuz thinkin' on her constant. One night he wuz settin' by de fire in camp, an' Mr. Ronny—he was de secon' lieutenant—got to talkin' 'bout ladies, an' he say all sorts o' things 'bout 'em, an' I see Marse Chan kinder lookin' mad; an' de lieutenant mention Miss Anne's name. He hed been courtin' Miss Anne 'bout de time Marse Chan fit de duil wid her pa, an' Miss Anne hed kicked 'im, dough he wuz mighty rich, 'cause he warn' nuthin' but a half-strainer, an' 'cause she like Marse Chan, I believe, dough she didn' speak to 'im; an' Mr. Ronny he got drunk, an' 'cause Cun'l Chahmb'lin tole 'im not to come dyah no more, he got mighty mad. An' dat evenin' I'se tellin' yo' 'bout, he wuz talkin', an' he mention Miss Anne's name. I see Marse Chan tu'n he eye 'roun' on 'im an' keep it on he face, and pres'n'y Mr. Ronny said he wuz gwine hev some fun dyah yit. He didn' mention her name dat time; but he said dey wuz all on 'em a parecel of stuck-up 'risticrats, an' her pa wan' no gent'man anyway, an'—I don' know what he wuz gwine say (he nuver said it), fur ez he got dat far Marse

471

Chan riz up an' hit 'im a crack, an' he fall like he hed been hit wid a fence-rail. He challenged Marse Chan to fight a duil, an' Marse Chan he excepted de challenge, an' dey wuz gwine fight; but some on 'em tole 'im Marse Chan wan' gwine mek a present o' him to his fam'ly, an' he got somebody to bre'k up de duil; twan' nuthin' dough, but he wuz 'fred to fight Marse Chan. An' purty soon he lef' de comp'ny.

"Well, I got one o' de gent'mens to write Judy a letter for me, an' I tole her all 'bout de fight, an' how Marse Chan knock Mr. Ronny over fur speakin' discontemptuous o' Cun'l Chahmb'lin, an' I tole her how Marse Chan wuz a-dyin' fur love o' Miss Anne. An' Judy she gits Miss Anne to read de letter fur her. Den Miss Anne she tells her pa, an'—you mind, Judy tells me all dis arfterwards, an' she say when Cun'l Chahmb'lin hear 'bout it, he wuz settin' on de poach, an' he set still a good while, an' den he sey to hisse'f:

" 'Well, he carn' he'p bein' a Whig.'

"An' den he gits up an' walks up to Miss Anne an' looks at her right hard; an' Miss Anne she hed done tu'n away her haid an' wuz makin' out she wuz fixin' a rose-bush 'g'inst de poach; an' when her pa kep' lookin' at her, her face got jes' de color o' de roses on de bush, and pres'n'y her pa sez:

" 'Anne!'

"An' she tu'ned roun', an' he sez:

"Do yo' want 'im?'

"An' she sez, 'Yes,' an' put her head on he shoulder an' begin to cry; an' he sez:

" 'Well, I won't stan' between yo' no longer. Write to 'im an' say so.'

"We didn' know nuthin' 'bout dis den. We wuz a-fightin' an a-fightin' all dat time; an' come one day a letter to Marse Chan, an' I see 'im start to read it in his tent, an' he face hit look so cu'ious, an' he han's trembled so I couldn' mek out what wuz de matter wid 'im. An' he fol' de letter up an' wen' out an' wen' way down 'hine de camp, an' stayed dyah 'bout nigh a hour. Well, seh, I wuz on de lookout for 'im when he come back, an', fo' Gord! ef he face didn' shine like a angel's! I say to myse'f, 'Um'm! ef de glory o' Gord ain' done shine on 'im!' An' what yo' 'spose 'twuz?

"He tuk me wid 'im dat evenin', an' he tell me he hed done git a letter from Miss Anne, an' Marse Chan he eyes look like gre't big stars, an' he face wuz jes' like 'twuz dat mawnin' when de sun riz up over de low groun', an' I see 'im stan'in' dyah wid de pistil in he han', lookin' at it, an' not knowin' but what it mout be de lars' time, an' he done mek up he mine not to shoot ole Cun'l Chahmb'lin fur Miss Anne's sake, what writ 'im de letter.

"He fol' de letter wha' was in his han' up, an' put it in he inside pocket—right dyah on de lef' side; an' den he tole me he tho't mebbe we wuz gwine hev some warm wuk in de nex' two or th'ee days, an' arfter dat ef Gord speared 'im he'd git a leave o' absence fur a few days, an' we'd go home.

"Well, dat night de orders come, an' we all hed to git over to'ds Romney; an' we rid all night till 'bout light; an' we halted right on a little creek, an' we stayed dyah till mos' breakfas' time, an' I see Marse Chan set down on de groun' 'hine a bush an' read dat letter over an' over. I watch 'im, an' de battle wuz a-goin' on, but we had orders to stay 'hine de hill, an' ev'y now an' den de bullets would cut de limbs o' de trees right over us, an' one o' dem big shells what goes '*Awhar—awhar—awhar!*' would fall right 'mong us; but Marse Chan he didn' mine it no mo'n nuttin'! Den it 'peared to git closer an' thicker, and Marse Chan he calls me, an' I crep' up, an' he sez:

" 'Sam, we'se goin' to win in dis battle, an' den we'll go home an' git married; an' I'se goin' home wid a star on my collar.' An' den he sez, 'Ef I'm wounded, kyah me home, yo' hear?' An' I sez, 'Yes, Marse Chan.'

"Well, jes' den dey blowed 'boots an' saddles,' an' we mounted; an' de orders come to ride 'roun' de slope, an' Marse Chan's comp'ny wuz de secon', an' when we got 'roun' dyah, we wuz right in it. Hit wuz de wust place uver dis nigger got in! An' dey said, 'Charge 'em!' an' my king! ef uver you see bullets fly, dey did dat day. Hit wuz jes' like hail; an' we wen' down de slope (I long wid de res') an' up de hill right to'ds de cannons, an' de fire wuz so strong dyah (dey hed a whole rigiment o' infintrys layin' down dyah onder de cannons) our lines sort o' broke an' stop; de Cun'l was kilt, an' I b'lieve dey wuz jes' 'bout to bre'k all to pieces, when Marse Chan rid up an' cotch hol' de fleg and hollers, 'Foller me!' an' rid strainin' up de hill 'mong de cannons. I seen 'im when he went, de sorrel four good lengths ahead o' ev'y urr hoss, jes' like he use' to be in a fox-hunt, an' de whole rigiment right arfter 'im. Yo' ain' nuver hear thunder! Fust thing I knowed, de roan roll' head over heels an' flung me up 'g'inst de bank like yo' chuck a nubbin over 'g'inst de foot o' de corn pile. An dat's what kep' me from bein' kilt, I 'spects. Judy she say she think 'twuz Providence, but I think 'twuz de bank. O' co'se, Providence put de bank dyah, but how come Providence nuver saved Marse Chan? When I look 'roun', de roan wuz layin' dyah by me, stone dead, wid a cannon-ball gone 'mos' th'oo him, an our men hed done swep' dem on t'urr side from de top o' de hill. 'Twan mo'n a minit, de sorrel come gallupin' back wid his mane flyin', an' de rein hangin' down on one side to his knee. 'Dyah!' says I, 'fo' Gord! I 'specks dey done kill Marse Chan, an' I promised to tek care on him.'

"I jumped up an' run over de bank, an' dyah, wid a whole lot o' dead mens, an' some not dead yit, onder one o' de guns wid de fleg still in he han', an' a bullet right th'oo he body, lay Marse Chan. I tu'n 'im over an' call 'im, 'Marse Chan!' but 'twan' no use, he was done gone home, sho' 'nuff.

"I pick' 'im up in my arms wid de fleg still in he han's, an' toted 'im back jes' like I did dat day when he wuz a baby, an' ole marster gin' 'im to me in my arms, an' sey he could trus' me, an' tell me to tek keer on 'im long ez he lived. I kyah'd 'im 'way off de battlefiel' out de way o' de balls, an' I laid 'im down onder a big tree till I could git somebody to ketch de sorrel for me. He was cotched arfter a while, an' I hed some money, so I got some pine plank an' made a coffin dat evenin', an' wrapt Marse Chan's body up in de fleg, an' put 'im in de coffin; but I didn' nail de top on strong, 'cause I knowed ole missis' wan' see 'im; an' I got a' ambulance an' set out for home dat night. We reached dyah de nex' evenin', arfter travellin' all dat night an' all nex' day.

"Hit 'peared like somethin' hed tole ole missis we wuz comin' so; for when we got home she wuz waitin' for us—done drest up in her best Sunday-clo'es, an' stan'n' at de head o' de big steps, an' ole marster settin' dyah bline in his big cheer—ez we druv up de hill to'ds de house, I drivin' de ambulance an' de sorrel leadin' long behine wid de stirrups crost over de saddle.

"She come down to de gate to meet us. We took de coffin out de ambulance an'

473

kyah'd it right into de big parlor wid de pictures in it, whar dey use' to dance in ole times when Marse Chan wuz a schoolboy, an' Miss Anne Chahmb'lin use' to come over, an' go wid ole missis into her chamber an' tek her things off. In dyah we laid de coffin on two o' de cheers, an' ole missis nuver said a wud; she jes' looked so ole an' white.

"When I had tell 'em all 'bout it, I tu'ned right 'roun' an' rid over to Cun'l Chahmb'lin's, 'cause I knowed dat wuz what Marse Chan he'd 'a' wanted me to do. I didn' tell nobody whar I was gwine, 'cause yo' know, none on 'em hadn' nuver speak to Miss Anne, not sence de duil, an' dey didn' know 'bout de letter.

"When I rid up in de yard, dyah wuz Miss Anne a-stan'in' on de poach watchin' me ez I rid up. I tied my hoss to de fence, an' walked up de parf. She knowed by de way I walked dyah wuz som'thin' de motter, an' she wuz mighty pale. I drapt my cap down on de een' o' de steps an' went up. She nuver opened her mouf; jes' stan' right still an' keep her eyes on my face. Fust, I couldn' speak; den I cotch my voice, an' I say, 'Marse Chan, he done got he furlough.'

"Her face was mighty ashy, an' she sort o' shook, but she didn' fall. She tu'ned roun' an' said, 'Git me de ker'ige!' Dat wuz all.

"When de ker'ige come roun' she hed put on her bonnet, an' wuz ready. Ez she got in, she sey to me, 'Hev yo' brought him home?' an' we drove 'long, I ridin' behine.

"When we got home, she got out, an' walked up de big walk—up to de poach by herse'f.

"Ole missis hed done fin' de letter in Marse Chan's pocket, wid de love in it, while I wuz 'way, an' she wuz a-waitin' on de poach. Dey sey dat wuz de fust time ole missis cry when she find de letter, an' dat she sut'n'y did cry over hit, pintedly.

"Well, seh, Miss Anne she walks right up de steps, mos' up to ole missis stan'in' dyah on de poach, an' jes' falls right down mos' to her, on her knees fust, an' den flat on her face right on de flo', ketchin' at ole missis' dress wid her two han's—so.

"Ole missis stood for 'bout a minit lookin' down at her, an' den she drapt down on de flo' by her, an' took her in bofe her arms.

"I couldn' see, I wuz cryin' so myse'f, an' ev'ybody wuz cryin'. But dey went in arfter a while in de parlor, an' shet de do'; an' I heahd 'em say, Miss Anne she tuk de coffin in her arms an' kissed it, an' kissed Marse Chan, an' call' 'im by his name, an' her darlin', an' ole missis lef' her cryin' in dyah tell some on 'em went in, an' found her done faint on de flo'.

"Judy she tell me she heah Miss Anne when she axed ole missis mout she wear mo'nin' fur 'im. I don' know how dat is; but when we buried 'im nex' day, she wuz de one whar walked arfter de coffin, holdin' ole marster, an' ole missis she walked next to 'em.

"Well, we buried Marse Chan dyah in de ole grabeyard, wid de fleg wrapped roun' 'im, an' he face lookin' like it did dat mawnin' down in de low groun's, wid de new sun shinin' on it so peaceful.

474

"Miss Anne she nuver went home to stay arfter dat; she stay wid ole marster an' ole missis ez long ez dey lived. Dat warn' so mighty long, 'cause ole marster he died dat Fall, when dey wuz fallerin' fur wheat—I had jes' married Judy den —an' ole missis she warn' long behine him. We buried her by him next summer. Miss Anne she went in de hospitals toreckly after ole missis died; an' jes b'fo' Richmond fell she come home sick wid de fever. Yo' nuver wud 'a' knowed her fur de same ole Miss Anne. She wuz light ez a piece o' peth, an' so white, 'cep' her eyes an' her sorrel hyah, an' she kep' on gittin' whiter an' weaker. Judy she sut'n'y did nuss her faithful. But she nuver got no betterment! De fever an' Marse Chan's bein' kilt hed done strain her, an' she died jes' fo' de folks wuz sot free.

"So we buried Miss Anne right by Marse Chan, in a place whar ole missis hed tole us to leave, an' dey's bofe on 'em sleep side by side over in de ole grabeyard at home.

"An' will yo' please tell me, marster? Dey tells me dat de Bible sey dyah won' be marryin' nor givin' in marriage in heaven, but I don' b'lieve it signifies dat —does you?"

I gave him the comfort of my earnest belief in some other interpretation, together with several spare "eighteen-pences," as he called them, for which he seemed humbly grateful. And as I rode away I heard him calling across the fence to his wife, who was standing in the door of a small whitewashed cabin, near which we had been standing for some time:

"Judy, have Marse Chan's dawg got home?" (*1884*)

from *The Old South* [1]

. . . Something more than twenty years ago there fell upon the South a blow for which there is no parallel among the casualties which may happen to an individual, and which has rarely in history befallen nations. Upon the euphemism of reconstruction an attempt was made after the war to destroy the South. She was dismembered, disfranchised, denationalized. The States which composed her were turned by her conquerors into military districts, and their governments were subverted to military tribunals. Virginia, that had given Washington, Jefferson, Henry, Nelson, the Lees, Madison, Marshall, and a host of others who had made the nation, became "District No. 1."

The South was believed to be no more. It was intended that she should be no more. But God in his providence had his great purpose for her and he called her forth. With the old spirit strong within her she renewed her youth like the eagles, fixed her gaze upon the sun, and once more spreading her strong pinions, lifted herself for another flight.

The outside world gazed astonished at her course, and said, this is not the Old South, but a new civilization, a New South.

The phrase by imperative inference institutes invidious comparison with and implies censure of something else—of some other order—of a different civilization.

That order, that civilization, I propose to discuss briefly this evening; to, so far as may be in the narrow limits of an address, repel this censure; show that

475

[1] The Old South *is a collection of social and political essays, many of which are slightly revised versions of speeches which Page had given earlier. The material reproduced here is an address which Page delivered at Washington and Lee University.*

comparison is absurd, and that the New South is, in fact, simply the Old South with its energies directed into new lines.

The civilization which is known by this name was as unique as it was distinct. It combined elements of the three great civilizations which since the dawn of history have enlightened the world. It partook of the philosophic tone of the Grecian, of the dominant spirit of the Roman, and of the guardfulness of individual rights of the Saxon civilization. And over all brooded a softness and beauty, the joint product of Chivalry and Christianity.

This individuality began almost with the first permanent Anglo-Saxon settlement of this continent; for the existence of its distinguishing characteristics may be traced from the very beginning of the colonial period. The civilization flourished for two hundred and fifty years, and until its vitality, after four years of invasion and war, expired in the convulsive throes of reconstruction.

Its distinctiveness, like others of its characteristics, was referable to its origin, and to its subsequent environing conditions.

Its tendency was towards exclusiveness and conservatism. It tolerated no invasion of its rights. It admitted the jurisdiction of no other tribunal than itself. The result was not unnatural. The world, barred out, took its revenge, and the Old South stands today charged with sterility, with attempting to perpetuate human slavery, and with rebellion.

That there was shortcoming in certain directions may not be denied; but it was not what is charged.

If, when judged by the narrow standard of mere, common materialism, the Southern civilization fell short, yet there is another standard by which it measured the fullest stature; the sudden supremacy of the American people today is largely due to the Old South, and to its contemned civilization.

The difference between the Southern civilization and the Northern was the result of the difference between their origins and subsequent surroundings.

The Northern colonies of Great Britain in America were the asylums of religious zealots and revolutionists who at their first coming were bent less on the enlargement of their fortunes than on the freedom to exercise their religious convictions, however much the sudden transition from dependence and restriction to freedom and license may in a brief time have tempered their views of liberty and changed them into proscriptors of the most tyrannical type.

The Southern colonies, on the other hand, were from the first the product simply of a desire for adventure, for conquest, and for wealth.

The Northern settlements were, it is true, founded under the law; but it was well understood that they contained an element which was not friendly to the government and that the latter was well satisfied to have the seas stretch between them. The Southern, on the other hand, came with the consent of the crown, the blessing of the Church, and under the auspices and favor of men of high standing in the kingdom. They came with all the ceremonial of an elaborate civil government—with an executive, a council deputed by authorities at home, and formal and minute instructions and regulations.

476

The crown hoped to annex the unknown land lying between the El Dorado, which Spain had obtained amid the summer seas, and the unbounded claims of its hereditary enemy, France, to the North and West.

The Church, which viewed the independence of the Northern refugees as schism, if not heresy, gave to this enterprise its benison in the belief that "the adventurers for the plantations of Virginia were the most noble and worthy advancers of the standard of Christ among the Gentiles." The company organized and equipped successive expeditions in the hope of gain; and soldiers of fortune, and gentlemen in misfortune, threw in their lot in the certainty of adventure and the probability that they might better their condition. Under such auspices the Southern colonies necessarily were rooted in the faith of the England from which they came—political, religious, and civil. Thus from the very beginning the spirit of the two sections was absolutely different, and their surrounding conditions were for a long time such as to keep them diverse. . . .

The South emerged from the Revolution mangled and torn, but free, and with the Anglo-Saxon spirit whetted by success and intensified. She emerged also with her character already established, and with those qualities permanently fixed which subsequently came to be known through their results as the Southern civilization.

Succeeding the Revolution came a period not very distinctly marked in the common idea of important steps, but full of hazard and equally replete with pregnant results—a period in which the loose and impotent Confederation became through the patriotism of the South this Union.

At last, the Constitution was somewhat of a compromise, and the powers not expressly delegated to Congress were reserved to each State in her sovereign capacity, and it was upon this basis simply that the Union was established.

It may throw light on the part that the South took in this to recall the fact that when the point was made that Virginia should relinquish her Northwestern territory, Virginia ceded to the country, without reservation, the territory stretching north to the Great Lakes and west to the Father of Waters. She granted it without consideration, and without grudging, as she had always given generously whenever she was called upon, and when she had stripped herself of her fairest domain, in retribution a third of the small part which she had retained was torn from her, without giving her even a voice to protest against it. There is no act of the Civil War, or of its offspring, the days of reconstruction, so arbitrary, so tyrannical, and so unjustifiable.

When the South emerged from the Revolutionary War, her character was definitely recognized as manifesting the qualities which combined to give her civilization the peculiar and strongly marked traits that have made it since distinctive among the English-speaking races. And in the succeeding years these traits became more and more prominent.

The guiding principle of the South had steadily been what may be termed public spirit; devotion to the rights and liberties of the citizen, the embodiment of which in a form of government was aptly termed the Commonwealth.

To this yielded even the aristocratic sentiment. The Southerner was attached to the British mode of inheritance, yet he did away with the law of primogeniture; he was devoted to the traditions of his Church, yet he declared for religious freedom, and not only disestablished the Church, but confiscated and made common the Church lands, and it is due to the South, today, that man is free to worship God according to his conscience wherever the true God is known and feared.

The South changed far less after its separation from Great Britain than did

477

the North. Indeed, the change was during the entire ante-bellum period comparatively small when viewed beside the change in the other portion of the country.

It has been said that it was provincial. It certainly did not so consider itself, for it held a self-esteem and self-content as unquestioning and sublime as that which pervaded Rome; and wherever the provinces were, they were to the Southerner assuredly beyond the confines of the Southern States. Yet the naked fact is, that, assuming provincialism to be what it has been aptly defined to be, "localism, or being on one side and apart from the general movement of contemporary life," the South was provincial.

African slavery, which had proven ill-adapted to the needs and conditions of the North, and consequently had disappeared more because of this fact than because of the efforts of the Abolitionists, had proved perfectly suited to the needs of the South.

The Negro flourished under the warm skies of the South, and the granaries and tobacco fields of Maryland and Virginia, the cotton fields of the Carolinas, Georgia, and Alabama, and the sugar plantations of the Mississippi States, bore ample testimony to his utility as a laborer. But the world was moving with quicker strides than the Southern planter knew, and slavery was banishing from his land all the elements of that life which was keeping stride with progress without. Thus, before the Southerner knew it, the temper of the time had changed, slavery was become a horror, and he himself was left behind and was in the opposition.

Changes came, but they did not affect the South—it remained as before or changed in less ratio; progress was made; the rest of the world fell into the universal movement; but the South advanced more slowly. It held by its old tenets when they were no longer tenable, by its ancient customs when, perhaps, they were no longer defensible. All interference from the outside was repelled as officious and inimical, and all intervention was instantly met with hostility and indignation. It believed itself the home of liberality when it was, in fact, necessarily intolerant—of enlightenment, of progress, when it had been so far distanced that it knew not that the world had passed by.

The cause of this was African slavery, with which the South is taunted as if she alone had instituted it. For this she suffered; for this, at last, she was forced to fight and pour out her blood like water.

Slavery had forced the South into a position where she must fight or surrender her rights.

The fight on the part of the North was for the power to adapt the Constitution to its new doctrine, and yet to maintain the Union; on the part of the South, it was for the preservation of guaranteed constitutional rights. Through the force of circumstances and under "an inexorable political necessity," the South found itself compelled to assume finally the defence of the system; but it was not responsible either for its origin or its continuance, and the very men who fought to prevent external interference with it had spent their lives endeavoring to solve the problem of its proper abolition.

The African slave trade, dating from about the year 1442 (although it did not flourish for a century or more), when it was begun by Anthony Gonzales, a Portuguese, was continued until the present century was well installed.

478

It was chartered and encouraged by Queen Elizabeth, and by her royal successors, against the protest of the Southern colonies, down to the time of the American Revolution. The first nation on the civilized globe to protest against it as monstrous was the Southern colony, Virginia. Twenty-three times her people protested to the crown in public acts of her Assembly.

One of the most scathing charges, brought by the writer of the Declaration of Independence against the crown, was that in which he arraigns the king of England for having "waged cruel war against human nature itself, violating its most sacred rights of life and liberty in the persons of a distant people who never offended him, captivating and carrying them into slavery in another hemisphere, or incurring a miserable death in their transportation thither.

"This piratical warfare, the opprobrium of infidel powers, is the warfare of the Christian king of Great Britain.

"Determined to keep open a market where men should be bought and sold, he has prostituted his negative for suppressing any legislative attempt to prohibit and restrain the execrable commerce," etc.

This clause was the product of Thomas Jefferson, a Southerner, and although it was stricken out in compliance with the wishes of two of the Southern colonies, yet substantially the same charge was made in the Constitution of Virginia, where in its preamble is set forth "the detestable and insupportable tyranny of the king of Great Britain, that he had prompted to rise in rebellion those very negroes whom by an inhuman use of his royal negative he had refused us permission to exclude by law."

If the South had at any previous time inclined to profit by the slave trade, it was only in common with the rest of Christendom—particularly with New England—when the most zealous and religious were participants in it; when the Duke of York, the future sovereign himself, was the head of the company chartered under the Great Seal of England, and when the queen-mother, the queen-consort, Prince Rupert, the Earl of Shaftesbury, and the leading men of the times were incorporators.

Even the godly John Newton was interested in the traffic.

In the South, however, long before Jefferson framed his famous arraignment of the king of Great Britain, protest on protest had been made against the iniquity, and all the ingenuity of those men who produced the Declaration of Independence and the Constitution of the United States had been exercised to bring it to an end.

The House of Burgesses often attempted to lay a duty of from £10 to £20 a head on the Negro slaves, and against the veto of the crown they continued to levy duties, until the oppression by the crown culminated, and "The gentlemen of the House of Burgesses and the body of merchants assembled in the old capital of Virginia on the 2d June, 1770, resolved, among other things, that we will not import or bring into the colony, or cause to be imported or brought into the colony, either by sea or land, any slaves, or make sale of any upon commission, or purchase any slave or slaves that may be imported by others, after the 1st day of November next, unless the same have been twelve months on the continent."

On the 1st of April, 1772, the House of Burgesses addressed a hot petition to the crown, "imploring his Majesty's paternal assistance in averting a calamity of a most alarming nature." It proceeds: "The importation of slaves into the col-

479

onies from the coast of Africa hath long been considered as a trade of great inhumanity, and under its present encouragement we have too much reason to fear will endanger the very existence of your Majesty's American dominions. We are sensible that some of your Majesty's subjects of Great Britain may reap emoluments from this sort of traffic, but when we consider that it greatly retards the settlement of the colonies with more useful inhabitants, and may in time have the most destructive influence, we presume to hope that the interest of a few will be disregarded when placed in competition with the security and happiness of such numbers of your Majesty's dutiful and loyal servants. Deeply impressed with these sentiments, we most humbly beseech your Majesty to remove all those restraints on your Majesty's governors of the colony which inhibit their assenting to such laws as might check so very pernicious a commerce."

It was not until the following year that the Philadelphia petition to the Pennsylvania Assembly was gotten up, and it accords the credit to the Southern colony by asking similar action with that of "the province of Virginia, whose House of Burgesses have lately petitioned the king."

On the 5th of October, 1778, Virginia passed an act forbidding the further importation of slaves, *by land or water,* under a penalty of £1000 from the seller and £500 from the buyer, and freedom to the slave: thus giving to the world the first example of an attempt by legislative enactment to destroy the slave trade.

When the vote was taken in the Federal Congress on the resolution to postpone the prohibition of the trade to the year 1808, Virginia used all her influence to defeat the postponement, and it was carried by New Hampshire, Massachusetts, and Connecticut voting with Maryland, the Carolinas, and Georgia. John Adams, writing of a speech of James Otis in 1761, says: "Nor were the poor negroes forgotten. Not a Quaker in Philadelphia, nor *Mr. Jefferson of Virginia,* ever asserted the rights of negroes in stronger terms. Young as I was and ignorant as I was, I shuddered at the doctrine he taught."

The final prohibition of the slave trade by act of Congress was brought about through the influence of President Jefferson and by the active efforts of Virginians. And greatly to the labors of the representatives from Virginia was due the final extinction of the vile traffic through the act of Congress declaring it to be piracy, five years before Great Britain took similar action with regard to her subjects.

Such is the actual record of the much-vilified South relating to the African slave trade, taken from official records.

Now as to slavery itself. We have seen how it was brought upon the South without its fault, and continued to be forced upon her against her protests. Let us for a moment investigate the facts connected with its continuance.

The gradual system of emancipation adopted at the North had undoubtedly led to many of the slaves being shipped off to the South and sold. When, therefore, after this "abolition," the movement, from being confined to the comparatively small band of liberators who were actuated by pure principle, extended to those who had been their persecutors, it aroused a suspicion at the South which blinded it to a just judgment of the case.

If the South maintained slavery unjustifiably, during its continuance, instead of its unnecessary horrors being, as is popularly believed, augmented by the natural brutality of the Southerner, the real facts are that the system was at the South perhaps fraught with less atrocity than it was whilst it continued at the North.

In the earliest period of the institution it was justified on the ground of the slaves being heathen, and a doubt was raised whether baptism would not operate to emancipate. At the South it was adjudicated that it did not so operate; but long prior to this act Negroes were admitted to the Church. In the leading colony at the North baptism was at the time expressly prohibited. The necessary concomitants of slavery were wretched enough, and the continuance of the system probed the curse of the fair land where it flourished, but to the African himself it was a blessing; it gave his race the only civilization it has had since the dawn of history.

The statutory laws relating to slavery at the South are held up as proof of the brutality with which they were treated even under the law. But these laws were not more cruel than were the laws of England at the period when they were enacted; they were rarely put into practical execution; and, at least, Southerners never tolerated wholesale burning at the stake as a legal punishment, as was done in New York as late as 1741, when fourteen Negroes were burnt at the stake on the flimsy testimony of a half-crazy servant girl; and as was done in Massachusetts as late as 1755, when a Negro was burnt for murder.

In the cotton and sugar States, where the Negroes were congregated in large numbers, and where a certain degree of absenteeism prevailed, there was naturally and necessarily more hardship.

African slavery was tolerated in Virginia and the Carolinas, but it received its first express legislative sanction from the Commonwealth of Massachusetts.

This Commonwealth, which has done so much to advance civilization, must bear the distinction of being the first American colony to proclaim slavery; to endorse the slave trade by legal sanction, and to build and equip the first slaveship which sailed from an American port. Even the *Mayflower*, whose timbers one might have supposed would be regarded as sanctified by the holy fathers whose feet first touched Plymouth Rock, was, according to tradition, turned to a more secular use, and is reported by general tradition to have been subsequently employed as an African slaver. Whether this be true or not, the first American slaver was the Salem ship *The Desire*, which was built and equipped at Marblehead in 1636, and was the prototype of a long line of slavers, in which, through many decades, continuing long after slavery was abolished in New England, and after the Southern States were piling protest on protest and act on act to inhibit the slave trade, New England shippers, in violation of law, plied their hellish traffic between the African coast and the slave-holding countries.

Whatever may have been the horrors of African slavery in the South, it was in its worst form and under its most inhuman surroundings a mild and beneficent system, benevolent in its features and philanthropic in its characteristics, when compared with the slave trade itself. The horrors of "the middle passage," when human beings, often to the number of eight or nine hundred, were "piled almost in bulk on water-casks," or were packed between the hatches in a space where there was "not room for a man to sit unless inclining his head forward, their

481

food half a pint of rice per day, with one pint of water," with "a blazing sun above, the boiling sea beneath, a withering air around," had never been equalled before, and in the providence of God will never be again.

It is not necessary to defend slavery, to defend the race which found it thrust upon it, contrary to what it deemed its rights, and which, after long and futile effort to rid itself of it, in accordance with what it held to be consistent at once with its rights and its security, refused to permit any outside interference. This was not primarily because it was wedded to slavery, but because it tolerated no invasion of its rights under any form or upon any pretext.

Vermont was the first State to lead off with emancipation in 1777. By the census of 1790 but seventeen slaves remained in the State. New Hampshire and Massachusetts failed to fix a statutory period; but the census of 1790 gives the former State 158 slaves, "and one of these was still reported in 1840."

Rhode Island and Connecticut [at] about the same time adopted a gradual plan of emancipation. The latter State held 2759 slaves in 1790—too many to admit of immediate emancipation.

Pennsylvania had by the same census 3737 slaves, and, recognizing the peril of injecting such a number of freedmen into the body politic, provided in 1780, by an act said to have been drafted by Benjamin Franklin, that all slaves born after that time should be free when they attained the age of twenty-eight years. The census of 1840 showed sixty-four still held in slavery.

In New York, by an act passed in 1799, the future issue of slaves were set free —males at the age of twenty-eight and females at the age of twenty-five years. In 1790 there were 21,324 slaves in the State. In 1800, before the act of emancipation could take effect, this number had fallen off [by] 981.

New Jersey in 1790 held 11,433 slaves. In 1804 her act of gradual emancipation was adopted. She had 674 slaves in 1840 and 236 in 1850.

This movement was largely owing in its inception to the efforts of the Quakers, who have devoted to peace those energies which others have given to war, and who have ever been moved by the spirit to take the initiative in all action which tends to the amelioration of the condition of the human race.

While this spirit of emancipation was passing over the North, the South, to whose action in asserting general freedom and universal civil equality was due the impulse, was stirring in the same direction. With her, however, the problem was far more difficult of solution, and although she addressed herself to it with energy and sincerity, she proved finally unequal to the task, and it was reserved, in the providence of an all-wise God, for the bitter scalpel of war to remove that which had served its purpose and was slowly sapping the lifeblood of the South.

In the New England and Northern States, there were, by the census of 1790, less than 42,000 slaves: in Virginia alone, by the same census, there were 293,427 slaves—about seven times the number contained in all the others put together.

How were they to be freed with advantage to the slaves and security to the State?

482   John Randolph of Roanoke described the situation aptly when he said we were holding a wolf by the ears, and it was equally dangerous to let go and to hold on.

The problem was stupendous. But it was not despaired of. Many masters manumitted their slaves, the example being set by numbers of the same benevolent sect to which reference has been made. By the census of 1781 there were in

Virginia 12,866 free negroes. Schemes of general emancipation of the slaves in Virginia had been proposed to the legislature by Jefferson in 1776; by William Craighead, and by Dr. William Thornton in 1785, whilst other schemes were proposed by St. George Tucker in 1796, by Thomas Jefferson Randolph in 1832, and by others from time to time. The vast body of slaves in the country, however, rendered it a matter so perilous as to prevent the schemes from ever being effectuated.

The most feasible plan appeared to be one that should lead to the colonization of the race in Africa; and the American Colonization Society was organized in Washington on the 1st of January, 1817, with Bushrod Washington president, and William H. Crawford, Henry Clay, John Taylor, and General John Mason [of Virginia], John Eager Howard, Samuel F. Smith, and John C. Herbert of Maryland, and Andrew Jackson of Tennessee among its vice-presidents.

Auxiliary societies were organized all over Virginia, John Marshall being the president of that established in Richmond, and ex-governors Pleasants and Tyler being vice-presidents. James Madison, James Monroe, and John Tyler all threw the weight of their great influence to carry out the purposes of the society and make it successful. Strange to say, every act on the part of the South leading towards liberation was viewed with suspicion by the Abolitionists of the North, and every step in that direction was opposed by them. Later a new and independent State organization was formed, called the Colonization Society of Virginia. Its president was John Marshall; its vice-presidents, James Madison, James Monroe, James Pleasants, John Tyler, Hugh Nelson, and others; and its roll of membership embraced the most influential men in the State.

Everything was looking towards the gradual but final extinction of African slavery. It was prevented by the attitude of the Northern Abolitionists. Their furious onslaughts, accompanied by the illegal circulation of literature calculated to excite the Negroes to revolt, and by the incursions of emissaries whose avowed object was the liberation of the slaves, but the effect of whose action was the instigation of the race to rise and fling off the yoke by rebellion and murder, chilled this feeling, the balance of political power came into question, and the temper of the South changed.

From this movement dates the unremittingly hostile attitude of the two sections towards each other. Before there had been antagonism; now there was open hostility. Before there had been conflicting rights, but they had been compromised and adjusted; from this time there was no compromise. The Northerner was a "miserable Yankee" and the Southerner was a "brutal slave-holder."

The two sections grew to be as absolutely separated as though a sea rolled between them. The antagonism increased steadily and became intensified. It extended far beyond the original cause, and finally became a factor in every problem, social and political, which existed in the whole land, affecting its results and often controlling its solution; forcing the two sections wider and wider apart, and eventually dividing them by an impassable gulf. Slavery, the prime cause, sank into insignificance in the multitudinous and potent differences which reared themselves between the two sections. It was employed simply as the battle-cry of the two opponents who stood arrayed against each other on a much broader question. The real fight was whether the conservative South should, with its doctrine of States rights, of original State sovereignty, rule the country according to a literal reading of the Constitution, or whether the North should govern according to a more liberal construction, adapted, as it claimed, by necessity to the new and more advanced conditions of the nation. Finally it culminated. After convulsions which would have long before destroyed a less stable nation, the explosion came.

The South, outraged at continual violation of the Constitution, declared that it would no longer act in unison with the North, and, after grave deliberation and hesitation, rendered proper by the magnitude of the step contemplated, the far Southern States exercised their sovereign right and dissolved their connection with the Union. Then came the President's call for troops, and finding themselves forced to secede or to make war upon their sister States, the border States withdrew.

The North made war upon the South, and, backed by the resources and the sentiment of the world, after four years compelled her to recede from her action.

Such in outline is the history of the South as it relates to slavery.

What has taken place since belongs partly to the New South and partly to the Old South.

The Old South made this people. One hundred years ago this nation, like Athene, sprang full panoplied from her brain.

It was the South that planned first the cooperation of the colonies, then their consolidation, and finally their establishment as free and independent States.

It was a Southerner, Henry, who first struck the note of independence. It was a Southerner, Nelson, who first moved, and the Convention of Virginia, a Southern colony, which first adopted the resolution "that the delegates appointed to represent this colony in General Congress be instructed to propose to that respectable body to declare the United Colonies free and independent States, absolved from all allegiance to or dependence on the crown or Parliament of Great Britain."

It was a Southerner, Henry, who first struck the note of independence. It was of her principle, *Virginia for Constitutional Liberty*.

It was a Southerner who wrote the *Declaration of Independence*.

These acts created revolution, and a Southerner led the armies of the revolutionists to victory; and when victory had been won it was to Southern intellect and Southern patriotism which created the Federal Constitution, that was due the final consolidation of the separated and disjointed elements extended along the Atlantic coast into one grand union of republics known as the United States.

From this time the South was as prominent in the affairs of the nation as she had been when she stood, a rock of defence, between the encroachments of the crown and the liberties of the colonies.

Of the Presidents who had governed the United States up to the time of the Civil War, the Old South had contributed Washington, Jefferson, Madison, Monroe, Jackson, Harrison, Tyler, Polk, and Taylor, and the cabinets had been filled with the representatives of the same civilization. In the only two wars which had ruffled the peaceful surface of the nation's course during this period the leading generals had been Southerners, and of the Chief Justices, John Marshall and Roger B. Taney had presided successively over the supreme bench of the United States from 1801, bringing to bear upon the decisions of that tribunal the force of their great minds, and the philosophic thought which is characteristic of the civilization of which they were such distinguished exponents.

Next to George Washington, John Marshall probably did more than any other one man to establish the principles on which this government is founded; for by his decisions he settled the mutual rights of the States on a firm and equitable basis, and determined forever those questions which might have strained the bonds of the young government.

To the South is due the fact that Louisiana is not now a French republic, and that the Mississippi rolls its whole length through the free land of the United States; to the South that the vast empire of Texas is not a hostile government; to the South is due the establishment of this Union in its integrity, and of the doctrines upon which it is maintained.

Thus in the council chamber and the camp, in the forum or on the field of battle, opposing invading armies or fighting for those principles which are ingrained in the very web and woof of our national life, the representatives of that contemned civilization always took the lead. In the great Civil War the two greatest men who stood for the Union, and to whom its preservation was due, were in large part the product of this civilization. Both Grant and Lincoln—the great general and the still greater President—sprang from Southern loins.

Can the New South make a better showing than this, or trace its lineage to a stronger source?

. . . Only study the course of the contest against the South and you cannot fail to see how she was conquered by the pen rather than by the sword; and how unavailing against the resources of the world, which the North commanded through the sympathy it had enlisted, was the valiance of that heroic army, which, if courage could have availed, had withstood the universe.

That Southern army was worn away as a blade is worn by use and yet retains its temper while but a fragment exists.

When the supreme moment came, the South had the world against her; the North had brought to its aid the sympathy of Christendom, and its force was as the gravitation of the earth—imperceptible, yet irresistible.

From their standpoint they were right, as we were right from ours. Slavery was a great barrier which kept out the light, and the North wrote of us in the main only what it believed.

If it was ignorant, it is our fault that it was not enlightened. We denied and fought, but we did not argue. Be this, however, our justification, that slavery did not admit of argument. Argument meant destruction.

The future historian of the Old South and of its civilization is yet to arise.

If in this audience tonight there be any young son of the South in whose veins there beats the blood of a soldier who perilled his life for that civilization which has been so inadequately outlined, and who, as he has heard from his mother's lips the story of his father's glorious sacrifice, has felt his pulses throb and his heart burn with noble aspiration, let him know that though he may never, like his father, be called upon to defend his principles with his life, yet he has before him a work not less noble, a career not less glorious: the true recording of that story, of that civilization whose history has never yet been written—the history of the Old South.

485

What nobler task can he set himself than this—to preserve from oblivion, or worse, from misrepresentation, a civilization which produced as its natural fruit Washington and Lee!

It is said that in all history there is no finer flight of human eloquence than that in which the Athenian orator aroused his countrymen by his appeal to the spirits of their sires who fell at Marathon. Shall not someone preserve the history of our fathers who fell in what they deemed a cause as sacred? Can any good come forth of a generation that believe that their fathers were traitors? I thank God that the sword of the South will nevermore be drawn except in defence of this Union; but I thank God equally that it is now without a stain. The time will come when the North as well as the South shall know that this Union is more secure because of the one heritage that our fathers have left us—the heritage of an untarnished sword.

If he shall feel the impulse stirring in his bosom to consecrate to this work the powers which have been nurtured at the nourishing breasts of this bountiful mother, there can be no fitter place for his sacrament than these hallowed walls— no better time than the present.

Within these sacred precincts three monuments meet his gaze. Each of them, by coincidence, is dedicated to the memory of one who had learnt by heart the lesson which that history teaches when rightly read,—the devotion of life to duty.

One of these was the leader of armies, the noblest character the South has produced, the great Lee; who, putting aside proffers of wealth and place and honor, gave himself to teaching the South the sublime beauty of devotion to duty—that lesson whose most admirable example was his own life. One was the surgeon, James M. Ambler, who refused to accept his life, and died amid the snows of the Lena Delta, pistol in hand, guarding the bodies of his dead comrades. Who does not remember the story of the young surgeon, kneeling amid the perpetual snows, pointing his dying comrades to Christ the crucified! The third, William E. Lynch, was a student, who while yet a lad put into action the same divine lesson, and to save a fellow-student plunged dauntless into the icy river and died, while yet a boy, a hero's death. All three speak to us this evening with sublime eloquence the heroic story of the Old South!

Here within these sacred walls, where the foremost soldier, the knightliest gentleman, the noblest man of his race, taught his sublime lesson, and his pupils learned to put it into such divine practice, the heart cannot but feel that the true story of their life must be told, the song must be sung, through the ages.

Not far off repose the ashes of another great soldier, Stonewall Jackson, the representative of the element that settled this valley, as Lee was representative of that which settled the tide-water. He flashed across the sky, a sudden meteor, and expired with a fame for brilliancy second only to Napoleon.

Near by him, and side by side with his own only son, Stonewall Jackson's aide-de-camp, Colonel Alexander S. Pendleton, slain in battle at the age of twenty-three, lies one to whom I owe a personal debt which I desire to acknowledge publicly tonight: General William Nelson Pendleton, a soldier who doffed the cassock for the uniform, and who lived a warrior-priest, leading his men in peace as he had done in war, and like his old commander, the highest type of the Christian soldier.

486

Standing here beside the sacred ashes of the noblest exponent of that civilization, which I have attempted to outline, delivering my message from this University, his grandest monument, I hail the future historian of the Old South. (*1892*)

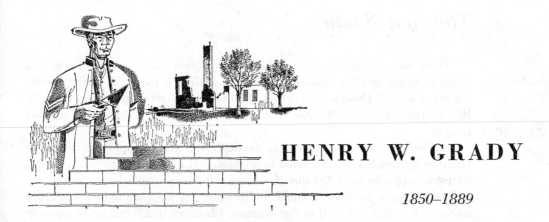

HENRY W. GRADY

1850–1889

Henry Woodfin Grady was born in Athens, Georgia, in May 1850. His father, a prosperous storekeeper, died in 1864 from wounds he received while serving as a major in the Confederate army. After the Civil War, Grady attended the University of Georgia. He took his degree in 1868 and during the following year studied law at the University of Virginia.

After writing a few informal letters to the *Atlanta Constitution*, Grady was invited to be a reporter on an excursion of newspapermen, and, having demonstrated his capabilities, became associate editor of the *Rome Courier*. In 1870 he became owner and editor of the *Commercial* in Rome and less than a year later bought out the *Rome Daily* and a weekly edition of the same paper.

Selling these journals in 1872, Grady became part owner of the *Atlanta Daily Herald*. The political opinions expressed in the *Herald* and the sensational—and sometimes unwise—publishing adventures of its owners led to its forced sale in 1876 and the loss of Grady's entire capital. Grady soon accepted a job with the *Atlanta Constitution* and there became associated with Evan P. Howell and Joel Chandler Harris. In 1880 he bought one-fourth of the *Constitution* with money lent him by Cyrus Field—a deal which resulted in the accusation by many that Grady had sold out to the moneyed interests. Accusations and denials are still occasionally heard.

In the course of his distinguished career, Grady became famous as the "Spokesman for the New South." In his editorials and speeches he argued that the problems of the South were to be solved only by the aid of outside capital, the encouragement of industry, the diversification of agriculture, and the development of the region's natural resources. He admonished Southerners to forget the "Lost Cause" and to look toward the future. Grady also worked to effect a reconciliation between the sections, at least partly because he realized that Northern capital was necessary to inaugurate the program of Southern develop-

487

ment he prescribed. His most famous bid for Northern cooperation was his speech, "The New South," delivered before the New England Society in New York on December 21, 1886. Its title quickly became the label for a vast movement in Southern thought.

The New South

"There was a South of slavery and secession—that South is dead. There is a South of union and freedom—that South, thank God, is living, breathing, growing every hour." These words, delivered from the immortal lips of Benjamin H. Hill, at Tammany Hall, in 1866, true then and truer now, I shall make my text tonight.

Mr. President and Gentlemen: Let me express to you my appreciation of the kindness by which I am permitted to address you. I make this abrupt acknowledgment advisedly, for I feel that if, when I raise my provincial voice in this ancient and august presence, I could find courage for no more than the opening sentence, it would be well if in that sentence I had met in a rough sense my obligation as a guest, and had perished, so to speak, with courtesy on my lips and grace in my heart. Permitted, through your kindness, to catch my second wind, let me say that I appreciate the significance of being the first Southerner to speak at this board, which bears the substance, if it surpasses the semblance, of original New England hospitality—and honors the sentiment that in turn honors you, but in which my personality is lost, and the compliment to my people made plain.

I bespeak the utmost stretch of your courtesy tonight. I am not troubled about those from whom I come. You remember the man whose wife sent him to a neighbor with a pitcher of milk, and who, tripping on the top step, fell with such casual interruptions as the landings afforded into the basement, and, while picking himself up, had the pleasure of hearing his wife call out: "John, did you break the pitcher?"

"No, I didn't," said John, "but I'll be dinged if I don't."

So, while those who call me from behind may inspire me with energy, if not with courage, I ask an indulgent hearing from you. I beg that you will bring your full faith in American fairness and frankness to judgment upon what I shall say. There was an old preacher once who told some boys of the Bible lesson he was going to read in the morning. The boys, finding the place, glued together the connecting pages. The next morning he read on the bottom of one page, "When Noah was one hundred and twenty years old he took unto himself a wife, who was"—then turning the page—"140 cubits long—40 cubits wide, built of gopher wood—and covered with pitch inside and out." He was naturally puzzled at this. He read it again, verified it, and then said: "My friends, this is the first time I ever met this in the Bible, but I accept this as an evidence of the assertion that we are fearfully and wonderfully made." If I could get you to hold such faith tonight I could proceed cheerfully to the task I otherwise approach with a sense of consecration.

Pardon me one word, Mr. President, spoken for the sole purpose of getting

488

into the volumes that go out annually freighted with the rich eloquence of your speakers—the fact that the Cavalier as well as the Puritan was on the continent in its early days, and that he was "up and able to be about." I have read your books carefully and I find no mention of that fact, which seems to me an important one for preserving a sort of historical equilibrium if for nothing else.

Let me remind you that the Virginia Cavalier first challenged France on the continent—that Cavalier, John Smith, gave New England its very name, and was so pleased with the job that he has been handing his own name around ever since —and that while Myles Standish was cutting off men's ears for courting a girl without her parents' consent, and forbade men to kiss their wives on Sunday, the Cavalier was courting everything in sight, and that the Almighty had vouchsafed great increase to the Cavalier colonies, the huts in the wilderness being as full as the nests in the woods.

But having incorporated the Cavalier as a fact in your charming little books, I shall let him work out his own salvation, as he has always done, with engaging gallantry, and we will hold no controversy as to his merits. Why should we? Neither Puritan nor Cavalier long survived as such. The virtues and good traditions of both happily still live for the inspiration of their sons and the saving of the old fashion. But both Puritan and Cavalier were lost in the storm of the first Revolution, and the American citizen, supplanting both and stronger than either, took possession of the republic bought by their common blood and fashioned to wisdom, and charged himself with teaching men government and establishing the voice of the people as the voice of God.

My friends, Dr. Talmage has told you that the typical American has yet to come. Let me tell you that he has already come. Great types, like valuable plants, are slow to flower and fruit. But from the union of these colonists, Puritans and Cavaliers, from the straightening of their purposes and the crossing of their blood, slow perfecting through a century, came he who stands as the first typical American, the first who comprehended within himself all the strength and gentleness, all the majesty and grace of this republic—Abraham Lincoln. He was the sum of Puritan and Cavalier, for in his ardent nature were fused the virtues of both, and in the depths of his great soul the faults of both were lost. He was greater than Puritan, greater than Cavalier, in that he was American, and that in his honest form were first gathered the vast and thrilling forces of his ideal government—charging it with such tremendous meaning and elevating it above human suffering that martyrdom, though infamously aimed, came as a fitting crown to a life consecrated from the cradle to human liberty. Let us, each cherishing the traditions and honoring his fathers, build with reverent hands to the type of this simple but sublime life, in which all types are honored, and in our common glory as Americans there will be plenty and to spare for your forefathers and for mine.

Dr. Talmage has drawn for you, with a master's hand, the picture of your returning armies. He has told you how, in the pomp and circumstance of war, they came back to you, marching with proud and victorious tread, reading their glory in a nation's eyes! Will you bear with me while I tell you of another army that sought its home at the close of the late war—an army that marched home in defeat and not in victory—in pathos and not in splendor, but in glory that equaled

489

yours, and to hearts as loving as ever welcomed heroes home! Let me picture to you the footsore Confederate soldier, as buttoning up in his faded gray jacket the parole which was to bear testimony to his children of his fidelity and faith, he turned his face southward from Appomattox in April 1865. Think of him as ragged, half-starved, heavy-hearted, enfeebled by want and wounds, having fought to exhaustion, he surrenders his gun, wrings the hands of his comrades in silence, and lifting his tear-stained and pallid face for the last time to the graves that dot old Virginia hills, pulls his gray cap over his brow and begins the slow and painful journey. What does he find—let me ask you who went to your homes eager to find, in the welcome you had justly earned, full payment for four years' sacrifice—what does he find when, having followed the battle-stained cross against overwhelming odds, dreading death not half so much as surrender, he reaches the home he left so prosperous and beautiful? He finds his house in ruins, his farm devastated, his slaves free, his stock killed, his barns empty, his trade destroyed, his money worthless, his social system, feudal in its magnificence, swept away; his people without law or legal status; his comrades slain, and the burdens of others heavy on his shoulders. Crushed by defeat, his very traditions are gone. Without money, credit, employment, material, or training; and beside all this, confronted with the gravest problem that ever met human intelligence—the establishing of a status for the vast body of his liberated slaves.

What does he do—this hero in gray with a heart of gold? Does he sit down in sullenness and despair? Not for a day. Surely God, who had stripped him of his prosperity, inspired him in his adversity. As ruin was never before so overwhelming, never was restoration swifter. The soldier stepped from the trenches into the furrow; horses that had charged Federal guns marched before the plow, and fields that ran red with human blood in April were green with the harvest in June; women reared in luxury cut up their dresses and made breeches for their husbands, and, with a patience and heroism that fit women always as a garment, gave their hands to work. There was little bitterness in all this. Cheerfulness and frankness prevailed. "Bill Arp" struck the key-note when he said: "Well, I killed as many of them as they did of me, and now I'm going to work." Of the soldier returning home after defeat and roasting some corn on the roadside, who made the remark to his comrades: "You may leave the South if you want to, but I am going to Sandersville, kiss my wife and raise a crop, and if the Yankees fool with me any more, I'll whip 'em again." I want to say to General Sherman, who is considered an able man in our parts, though some people think he is a kind of careless man about fire, that from the ashes he left us in 1864 we have raised a brave and beautiful city; that somehow or other we have caught the sunshine in the bricks and mortar of our homes, and have builded therein not one ignoble prejudice or memory.

But what is the sum of our work? We have found out that in the summing up the free Negro counts more than he did as a slave. We have planted the schoolhouse on the hilltop and made it free to white and black. We have sowed towns and cities in the place of theories, and put business above politics. We have challenged your spinners in Massachusetts and your iron-makers in Pennsylvania. We have learned that the $400,000,000 annually received from our cotton crop will make us rich when the supplies that make it are home-raised. We have reduced the commercial rate of interest from 24 to 6 per cent., and are floating 4 per cent. bonds. We have learned that one northern immigrant is worth fifty foreigners; and have smoothed the path to southward, wiped out the place where Mason and Dixon's line used to be, and hung out latchstring to you and yours. We have reached the point that marks perfect harmony in every household, when the husband confesses that the pies which his wife cooks are as good as those his mother used to bake; and we admit that the sun shines as brightly and the moon as softly as it did before the war. We have established thrift in city and country. We have fallen in love with work. We have restored comfort to homes from which culture and elegance never departed. We have let economy take root and spread among us as rank as the crabgrass which sprung from Sherman's cavalry camps, until we are ready to lay odds on the Georgia Yankee as he manufactures relics of the battlefield in a one-story shanty and squeezes pure olive oil out of his cotton seed, against any down-easter that ever swapped wooden nutmegs for flannel sausage in the valleys of Vermont. Above all, we know that we have achieved in these "piping times of peace" a fuller independence for the South than that which our fathers sought to win in the forum by their eloquence or compel in the field by their swords.

It is a rare privilege, sir, to have had part, however humble, in this work. Never was nobler duty confided to human hands than the uplifting and upbuilding of the prostrate and bleeding South—misguided, perhaps, but beautiful in her suffering, and honest, brave and generous always. In the record of her social, industrial and political illustration we await with confidence the verdict of the world.

But what of the Negro? Have we solved the problem he presents or progressed in honor and equity toward solution? Let the record speak to the point. No section shows a more prosperous laboring population than the Negroes of the South, none in fuller sympathy with the employing and land-owning class. He shares our school fund, has the fullest protection of our laws and the friendship of our people. Self-interest, as well as honor, demand that he should have this. Our future, our very existence depend upon our working out this problem in full and exact justice. We understand that when Lincoln signed the emancipation proclamation, your victory was assured, for he then committed you to the cause of human liberty, against which the arms of man cannot prevail—while those of our statesmen who trusted to make slavery the corner-stone of the Confederacy doomed us to defeat as far as they could, committing us to a cause that reason could not defend or the sword maintain in sight of advancing civilization.

Had Mr. Toombs said, which he did not say, "that he would call the roll of his slaves at the foot of Bunker Hill," he would have been foolish, for he might have known that whenever slavery became entangled in war it must perish, and that the chattel in human flesh ended forever in New England when your fathers— not to be blamed for parting with what didn't pay—sold their slaves to our fathers—not to be praised for knowing a paying thing when they saw it. The relations of the Southern people with the Negro are close and cordial. We remember with what fidelity for four years he guarded our defenseless women and children, whose husbands and fathers were fighting against his freedom. To his eternal credit be it said that whenever he struck a blow for his own liberty he fought in

491

open battle, and when at last he raised his black and humble hands that the shackles might be struck off, those hands were innocent of wrong against his helpless charges, and worthy to be taken in loving grasp by every man who honors loyalty and devotion. Ruffians have maltreated him, rascals have misled him, philanthropists established a bank for him, but the South, with the North, protests against injustice to this simple and sincere people. To liberty and enfranchisement is as far as law can carry the Negro. The rest must be left to conscience and common sense. It must be left to those among whom his lot is cast, with whom he is indissolubly connected, and whose prosperity depends upon their possessing his intelligent sympathy and confidence. Faith has been kept with him, in spite of calumnious assertions to the contrary by those who assume to speak for us or by frank opponents. Faith will be kept with him in the future, if the South holds her reason and integrity.

But have we kept faith with you? In the fullest sense, yes. When Lee surrendered—I don't say when Johnson surrendered, because I understand he still alludes to the time when he met General Sherman last as the time when he determined to abandon any further prosecution of the struggle—when Lee surrendered, I say, and Johnson quit, the South became, and has since been, loyal to this Union. We fought hard enough to know that we were whipped, and in perfect frankness accept as final the arbitrament of the sword to which we had appealed. The South found her jewel in the toad's head of defeat. The shackles that had held her in narrow limitations fell forever when the shackles of the Negro slave were broken. Under the old regime the Negroes were slaves to the South; the South was a slave to the system. The old plantation, with its simple police regulations and feudal habit, was the only type possible under slavery. Thus was gathered in the hands of a splendid and chivalric oligarchy the substance that should have been diffused among the people, as the rich blood, under certain artificial conditions, is gathered at the heart, filling that with affluent rapture but leaving the body chill and colorless.

The old South rested everything on slavery and agriculture, unconscious that these could neither give nor maintain healthy growth. The new South presents a perfect democracy, the oligarchs leading in the popular movement—a social system compact and closely knitted, less splendid on the surface, but stronger at the core—a hundred farms for every plantation, fifty homes for every palace—and a diversified industry that meets the complex need of this complex age.

The new South is enamored of her new work. Her soul is stirred with the breath of a new life. The light of a grander day is falling fair on her face. She is thrilling with the consciousness of growing power and prosperity. As she stands upright, full-statured and equal among the people of the earth, breathing the keen air and looking out upon the expanded horizon, she understands that her emancipation came because through the inscrutable wisdom of God her honest purpose was crossed, and her brave armies were beaten.

This is said in no spirit of time-serving or apology. The South has nothing for which to apologize. She believes that the late struggle between the States was war and not rebellion; revolution and not conspiracy, and that her convictions were as honest as yours. I should be unjust to the dauntless spirit of the South and to my own convictions if I did not make this plain in this presence. The South has nothing to take back. In my native town of Athens is a monument that

crowns its central hill—a plain, white shaft. Deep cut into its shining side is a
name dear to me above the names of men—that of a brave and simple man who
died in brave and simple faith. Not for all the glories of New England, from
Plymouth Rock all the way, would I exchange the heritage he left me in his soldier's death. To the foot of that I shall send my children's children to reverence
him who ennobled their name with his heroic blood. But, sir, speaking from the
shadow of that memory which I honor as I do nothing else on earth, I say that
the cause in which he suffered and for which he gave his life was adjudged by
higher and fuller wisdom than his or mine, and I am glad that the omniscient
God held the balance of battle in His Almighty hand and that human slavery was
swept forever from American soil, the American Union was saved from the
wreck of war.

This message, Mr. President, comes to you from consecrated ground. Every
foot of soil about the city in which I live is as sacred as a battle-ground of the
republic. Every hill that invests it is hallowed to you by the blood of your
brothers who died for your victory, and doubly hallowed to us by the blow of
those who died hopeless, but undaunted, in defeat—sacred soil to all of us—rich
with memories that make us purer and stronger and better—silent but staunch
witnesses in its red desolation of the matchless valor of American hearts and the
deathless glory of American arms—speaking an eloquent witness in its white
peace and prosperity to the indissoluble union of American States and the imperishable brotherhood of the American people.

Now, what answer has New England to this message? Will she permit the
prejudice of war to remain in the hearts of the conquerors, when it has died in
the hearts of the conquered? Will she transmit this prejudice to the next generation, that in their hearts which never felt the generous ardor of conflict it may
perpetuate itself? Will she withhold, save in strained courtesy, the hand which
straight from his soldier's heart Grant offered to Lee at Appomattox? Will she
make the vision of a restored and happy people, which gathered above the couch
of your dying captain, filling his heart with grace; touching his lips with praise,
and glorifying his path to the grave—will she make this vision on which the last
sigh of his expiring soul breathed a benediction, a cheat and delusion? If she
does, the South, never abject in asking for comradeship, must accept with dignity its refusal; but if she does not refuse to accept in frankness and sincerity
this message of good will and friendship, then will the prophecy of Webster, delivered in this very society forty years ago amid tremendous applause, become
true, be verified in its fullest sense, when he said: "Standing hand to hand and
clasping hands, we should remain united as we have been for sixty years, citizens
of the same country, members of the same government, united, all united now
and united forever." There have been difficulties, contentions, and controversies,
but I tell you that in my judgment,

"Those opened eyes,
Which like the meteors of a troubled heaven,
All of one nature, of one substance bred,
Did lately meet in th' intestine shock,
Shall now, in mutual well beseeming ranks,
March all one way."

(1886)

493

WALTER HINES PAGE

1855–1918

Walter Hines Page makes a striking contrast to his equally famous contemporary (and distant cousin), Thomas Nelson Page. Just as the Virginia novelist and romancer represented the ideal of the Old South, so Walter Hines Page—journalist, editor, orator, novelist, and diplomat—embraced the creed of the New South and attempted to destroy what seemed to him the false illusions about his native region. He agreed with Thomas Nelson Page that the South had a noble past and had produced many distinguished leaders before the Civil War; but that age, he believed, had passed and the South must now look toward the future.

Born near Raleigh, North Carolina, Page received a traditional liberal education, attending Bingham Academy at Mebane, North Carolina, Trinity College (now Duke University), Randolph Macon, and Johns Hopkins University, where he studied under Professor Basil L. Gildersleeve, who in his youth had been an active member of the literary group at Charleston. Page withdrew from the university in 1878 and began working on a newspaper. In 1882 he became editor and owner of the Raleigh *Chronicle,* but his editorials against the "Ghosts" which were strangling North Carolina and the rest of the South ("the Ghost of the Confederate dead, the Ghost of religious orthodoxy, and the Ghost of Negro domination") aroused much enmity against him. Discouraged by the apparent failure of his efforts, he moved to New York in 1885.

Here began one of the most distinguished journalistic careers in American history. After rescuing the tottering *Forum,* Page became associated with the *Atlantic Monthly* and, as Bliss Perry expresses it, "breathed the breath of life" into this staid aristocratic journal which was rapidly losing the splendid reputation it had enjoyed for almost a half century. Tiring of the magazine field, he helped to found the publishing firm of Doubleday, Page and Company. In 1902 he established *The World's Work,* which during the period of his editorship (lasting until 1913, when he was appointed Ambassador to England) became an important organ for his views about the South.

494

In his editorials, public addresses, and in his one novel, Page argued for the rebuilding of the South through education and industry. The education that Page advocated was not the classical instruction which he himself had received, but practical, vocational training. He warned Southerners that, in a period of grave crisis, the section was faced with a lack of leadership because of insufficient educational facilities and a too severe restriction upon thought and expression. His most important essays, "The Forgotten Man," "The School That Built a Town," and "The Rebuilding of Old Commonwealths" (published together in 1905 under the title of the last essay) contain the primary ideas that Page reiterated in his other writings. His only novel, *The Southerner, a Novel; Being the Autobiography of Nicholas Worth* (1909), is in large part autobiographical and presents an interesting account of life in the South after the Civil War. It is significant, too, because its point of view is one of nationalism, as opposed to the sectionalism of Thomas Nelson Page's novels.

Critics of Walter Hines Page have argued that he regarded Southern problems from the standpoint of an outsider; that he was interested in improving conditions in the South not from any deep-seated love for the region or loyalty to it, but because he believed that an illiterate, unhealthy, poverty-stricken South would weaken the entire nation. Such criticism is probably unjust. In spite of the fact that Page was nationalist in outlook and critical of many traditional Southern attitudes, his first loyalty was always to the South and his criticism was prompted by a genuine desire to strengthen and improve that region. He was, in the phrase of Edwin Mims, the "friendly critic of the South."

The Forgotten Man

The cordiality of your greeting touches me deeply.[1] I have not, as some old-time wanderers are said to have done, carried with me wherever I have gone a pot of my native earth; but I have carried with me always what the pot of earth would stand for. Your welcome is the more gratifying because you are kind enough to link me with the great cause for which your institution stands.

We have often reminded ourselves and informed other people that we have incalculable undeveloped resources in North Carolina, in our streams, our forests, our mines, our quarries, our soil—that Nature has been most bountiful; so that our undeveloped resources invite men under the pleasantest conditions to productive industry. And so they do. But there is one undeveloped resource more valuable than all these, and that is the people themselves. It is about the development of men that I shall speak, more particularly about the development of forgotten and neglected men.

In making an estimate of a civilization it is the neglected and forgotten man more than any other that must be taken into account. When you build a house, you make the foundation the strongest part of it, and the house, however ornate its architecture, can be no stronger than the foundation. In considering the level of the life of any community, you must not give undue value to any class of men. A community is not rich because it contains a few rich men, it is not healthful

495

From The Rebuilding of Old Commonwealths *by Walter Hines Page, Houghton Mifflin Company.*
[1] *This address was delivered in June 1897, at the State Normal and Industrial School for Women at Greensboro, North Carolina.*

because it contains a few strong men, it is not intelligent because it contains a few men of learning, nor is it of good morals because it contains good women—if the rest of the population also be not well-to-do, or healthful, or intelligent, or of good morals. The common people is the class most to be considered in the structure of civilization. Moreover, in proportion as any community in the organization of its society or in the development of its institutions lays emphasis on its few rich men, or its few cultivated men, it is likely to forget and to neglect its very foundations. It is not these small classes that really make the community what it is, that determine the condition of its health, the soundness of its social structure, its economic value and its level of life. The security and the soundness of the whole body are measured at last by the condition of its weakest part.

So much, if you please, to get the proper point of view. If you have been in the habit in your social studies of dividing men into classes and of considering some more important in possibilities to the common weal than others, your studies are not in keeping with the dominant democracy of our country and of our race. In any scheme of man-culture one man must be regarded of as great importance as another. The doctrine of equality of opportunity is at the bottom of social progress, for you can never judge a man's capacity except as he has opportunity to develop it. When we make a social study, we must come face to face with all the men who make up the social body, seeing them as they are, and not through the medium of our traditions nor by their estimates of themselves.

From this point of view let me make a very rapid and general survey of the culture of men in North Carolina—of the social structure and the social forces that have shaped our civilization.

In the days of our fathers the social structure was to a slight extent aristocratic, but it was much less aristocratic than the social structure was, for example, in Virginia or in South Carolina. The mass of the people were common people; they lived directly out of the soil and they had the manners and the virtues and the limitations of a simple agricultural population, which was much the same in the early part of the century in all countries where a livelihood was easily obtained. They were nearly all of English and Scotch, and Scotch-Irish stock. Most of them were sprung from peasants of sturdy qualities; a very few from gentlemen; and some were descended from forced and hired immigrants. Taken all together they were a common people, capable of as sound development as the population of any other State. But they were ignorant, as the common people in all lands were a hundred years ago.

The dominant idea of education was that it was a luxury for the rich, or a privilege of the well-born—if a necessity at all, a necessity only for the ruling class. This class-feeling in education was perceptible even within my recollection. When I was a pupil at the most famous school for boys in the State, a lad whose father had not had a military or political career was at a certain disadvantage. I recall a scene more ludicrous than any in Dickens when a thirteen-year-old companion of mine came to my room one day, shut the door and fell on the bed and wept—because his father was not a Colonel. I tried to comfort him by telling him that my father was not a Colonel either. So far from consoling him this information only gave him the less respect for me. I had not seen this weeping lad for more than twenty-five years, till I recently met him on the train. He was telling me of his children and I asked if he had ever reflected that his own children's father was not a Colonel. He recalled the incident as clearly as I recalled it. Learning might be acquired but there could be no true education in an atmosphere where such an incident could happen.

These things I mention not in blame of our ancestors. It is out of just such stock that the men came who today rule the world. But I mention these things because we ourselves have written and spoken much nonsense about ourselves and about our ancestors and have made ourselves believe that we were in some way different from other sturdy folk and that we were in some way better than other common people. Thus we have come to put a false value on our social structure, and we have never looked ourselves in the face and seen ourselves as others see us. This false view has done incalculable hurt. All social progress must begin with a clear understanding of men as they are. We are all common folk, then, who were once dominated by a little aristocracy, which, in its social and economic character, made a failure and left a stubborn crop of wrong social notions behind it—especially about education.

There lingers one very striking relic of the aristocratic structure of opinion in North Carolina—a certain timidity on the part of our leaders in dealing with the public, a timidity on the part of the leaders, which we have falsely called conservatism on the part of the people, a hesitation to trust the people's judgment. It cropped out humorously on this platform yesterday. Mr. Scarborough declared that our people were conservative—very conservative! You must consider what they are ready for and what they are not ready for, for they are very conservative. A half hour later, while narrating the career of Dorothea Dix, Mr. Carr showed how one woman of enthusiasm came here from Massachusetts and induced the State to spend for a single institution at one time (and that an asylum for the insane) a larger sum than the whole annual resources of the State government; and no man has from that day to this made objection to the expenditure. Our whole history is full of such incidents. Almost every noteworthy thing that we have done has been done in obedience to an impulse. Conservative? We are the most impulsive people imaginable. But if "conservatism" so overcomes any one who hears me in the very conservative things that I have to say, it must be understood that I speak only for myself. I speak out of my own ignorance only, and I speak, I regret to say, only as a spectator of your noble work.

In the old days when education was dominated by the aristocratic idea, the chief influences that shaped opinion were the stump and pulpit. From the stump two cardinal articles of faith were proclaimed. One was that a man must have liberty. Much was made of what was called personal liberty, and I think rightly. If any man sought an unfair advantage of another, the injured man was quick to assert his rights before the law, if, indeed, he did not assert it with his fists. This sturdy notion of liberty has been a great quality from the time of the Mecklenburg Declaration till today. If our fathers emphasized it too much let us forgive them, for we shall see presently that we also have need of some fighting qualities. Another article of faith proclaimed from the stump was that taxes were too high. From the days of King George to this day, the politicians of North Carolina have declaimed against taxes, thus laying the foundation of our

497

poverty. It was a misfortune for us that the quarrel with King George happened to turn on a question of taxation—so great was the dread of taxation that was instilled into us.

The other great educational force was the pulpit. Parts of the people were strongly inclined to an emotional kind of religion, and our historians tell us of great camp meetings and "revivals" that swept over whole counties, continued for weeks, and threw many persons into trances. More men lost their reason from religious troubles than from any other cause, except the lonely overwork of women. The latest book written and published in the State that I have happened to see is the autobiography of a notable religious maniac whom I knew in my boyhood. The more primitive and violent forms of religion took a deep hold on the people and (as is usually the case) without affecting their conduct at all.

Not only was the preacher a mighty man in our life, but there was in the old days a type of preacher who was an heroic man, a man who had all the qualities of the pioneer. He was ready any day to face the hardships of the wilderness or to stand in the presence of the Almighty. I doubt if we have ever produced other men as great as our pioneer preachers. They were cast in so large a mould, they dealt so directly with the fundamental emotions of men and with some of the great facts of the spiritual life, that they almost ranged themselves with the giants. I had rather have known one of these men than all the political and military heroes that we have since bred. The politician has been the greater popular hero, but the preacher has had much the greater influence. For a century he was by far our greatest man—the man of the largest original power and of the strongest character. He inherited the heroic qualities of the pioneers, and he led a life at once serene and active. He was a primitive sort of character, genuine and fearless. If our traditions overrate the political leaders that we have produced, they as greatly underrate the early preachers.

Now let us see what these two powers that ruled our fathers did for the education of the masses. The first conception of education was the aristocratic conception, and the first system of teaching was controlled by those who held political power; it was the old system of class education. It did not touch the masses. They had no part in it. They grew up with the idea that education was a special privilege: they did not aspire to it, did not believe that it was attainable, and at last they came to believe that it was not desirable, certainly that it was not necessary. They remained illiterate, neglected, forgotten. There was no substantial progress in broadening educational opportunities in North Carolina from the time of the colony till the beginning of the Civil War, except the noteworthy and noble work that was done just before the war to develop a public school system. This notable and noteworthy effort gives us good reason to hold those who made it, chief among whom was Calvin H. Wiley, in grateful remembrance.

I commend to you most earnestly as of the first importance a thorough study of our social beginnings and development—not always as it has been described by our historians, but from original sources. You will clear your mind of the hazy exaggerations that we get from tradition. Many traditional heroes will disappear, and many whose names have been forgotten or are seldom heard will re-appear as real heroes. Among these will be the group of men who strove forty years ago or more to establish a public school system. But their scheme, like Jefferson's own great scheme, was doomed to await a later time for its development.

Later than the aristocratic system of education and overlapping it, came the ecclesiastical system. In establishing and developing this, the preachers did valiant service. They were colporteurs and they carried religious books to the people. The churches established, besides preparatory schools for boys and girls, three schools for men which grew into colleges. At first they were established for the education of preachers, but they broadened their field of labour and became schools of general culture, and most admirable service they have done. The denominational educational movement was broader in its benefits than the old aristocratic educational movement had been, for these colleges were open to the common people and they proclaimed the desirability of general education. Still they were class institutions; each was a school of a sect. Universal education, universal free education, was not on their programme. Some men whom the State had neglected were now remembered by the churches, especially if they were of an emotional temperament and felt "called" to preach. The way towards general education was broadening, but the very conception of education was yet class conception. It was provided less for the sake of the people than for the sake of the church.

The forgotten man remained forgotten. The aristocratic scheme of education had passed him by. To a less extent, but still to the extent of hundreds of thousands, the ecclesiastical scheme also passed him by. The general level of education was almost as low as it had ever been. Both the aristocratic and the ecclesiastical plans held undisputed sway till a time within the memory of us all. But in the meantime education had been making more rapid conquests—developing in method and extending its benefits in other States and in other lands —than in any preceding time in the history of the world.

Tried by the tests of this progress, what have the aristocratic system and ecclesiastical system of education to show for themselves?

First, what did they do for their own favoured classes? North Carolina is one of the old thirteen States. The aristocratic system had free play here for nearly a hundred years, and the ecclesiastical system has had free play for at least half as long. They established our university and our denominational colleges. Excellent as these are, they do not rank with the best institutions of most of the other original thirteen States—of Virginia, nor of New Jersey, nor of New York, nor of Connecticut, nor of Massachusetts. Nor have they trained even a select body of scholars that have been or are in any way famous. Make another test: there are no great libraries in the State, nor do the people yet read, nor have the publishing houses yet reckoned them as their patrons, except the publishers of school books. By any test that may be made, both these systems of education failed even with the classes that they appealed to. One such test is the test of emigration from the State. In 1890 there were living in other States 293,000 persons who were born in North Carolina. One in eight of every native of the State then living had gone away. When we remember that almost every one of those emigrants went to States where taxes are higher and schools are more numerous and better and where competition is more fierce, and when we remember that they went away from a State that is yet sparsely settled and richer in natural opportunities than most of the States to which they went, the failure of these systems becomes painfully obvious.

If a slave brought $1,000 in old times, it ought to be safe to assume that every emigrant from the State has an economic value of $1,000. This emigration therefore had up to 1890 cost us $293,000,000—a fact that goes far to explain why we are poor. To take the places of these 293,000 emigrants, after twenty years of organized effort to induce immigration 52,000 immigrants born in other States had come here, a large proportion of whom had come for their health. But counting the sick and the dying at $1,000 each, we had still lost $241,000,000 by the transaction. This calculation gives a slight hint of the cost of ignorance and of the extravagance of keeping taxes too low.

Next, what did these systems of education do for the masses? In 1890, twenty-six percent of the white persons of the State were unable even to read and write. One in every four was wholly forgotten. But illiteracy was not the worst of it; the worst of it was the stationary social condition indicated by generations of illiteracy had long been the general condition. The forgotten man was content to be forgotten. He became not only a dead weight, but a definite opponent of social progress. He faithfully heard the politicians on the stump praise him for virtues that he did not have. The politician told him that he lived in the best State in the Union, told him that the other politician had some hare-brained plan to increase his taxes, told him as a consolation for his ignorance how many of his kinsmen had been killed in the war, told him to distrust anybody who wished to change anything. What was good enough for his fathers was good enough for him. Thus the forgotten man became a dupe, became thankful for being neglected. And the preacher told him that the ills and misfortunes of this life were blessings in disguise, that God meant his poverty as a means of grace, and that if he accepted the right creed all would be well with him. These influences encouraged inertia. There could not have been a better means to prevent the development of the people.

I have thus far spoken only of the forgotten man. I have done so to show the social and educational structure in proper perspective. But what I have come to speak about is the forgotten woman. Both the aristocratic and the ecclesiastical systems made provision for the women of special classes—the fortunately born and the religious well-to-do. But all the other women were forgotten. Let any man whose mind is not hardened by some worn-out theory of politics or of ecclesiasticism go to the country in almost any part of the State and make a study of life there, especially of the life of the women. He will see them thin and wrinkled in youth from ill prepared food, clad without warmth or grace, living in untidy houses, working from daylight till bed-time at the dull round of weary duties, the slaves of men of equal slovenliness, the mothers of joyless children— all uneducated if not illiterate. Yet even their condition were endurable if there were any hope, but this type of woman is encrusted in a shell of dull content with her lot; she knows no better and can never learn better, nor point her children to a higher life. If she be intensely religious, her religion is only an additional misfortune, for it teaches her, as she understands it, to be content with her lot and all its burdens, since they prepare her for the life to come.

500

Some *men* who are born under these conditions escape from them; a *man* may go away, go where life offers opportunities, but the women are forever help-less.

And this sight every one of you has seen, not in the countries whither we send missionaries, but in the borders of the State of North Carolina, in this year of grace. Nor is it an infrequent sight. There are thousands and thousands of such women in our population.

Now one of the two things is true—either these forgotten men and women are incapable of development, and belong to a lower order of intelligence than any other people of Anglo-Saxon stock; or our civilization, so far as they are con-cerned, has been a failure. Of course there is no doubt which of these supposi-tions is true; for these people are capable of development, capable of unlimited growth and elevation. But, if they be capable of development, then both the aristocratic and the ecclesiastical systems of society have failed to develop them.

Since both the politician and the preacher have failed to lift this life after a century of unobstructed opportunities, it is time for a wiser statesmanship and a more certain means of grace. And surely of all people the preacher and the politician ought, in common modesty, to be the last to oppose a new system of education for the development of the undeveloped masses.

But now the story brightens. These old educational systems having failed here, as they have failed in other States, the public-spirited, far-sighted and energetic young men, chief among them your own President and the President of the University, who came into activity ten years or more ago, began seriously to develop a public school system, first of course in the towns. They developed by their own earnestness the work that had been in part planned by men like Major Finger. One town followed another, levying a local tax to supplement the State tax. I doubt if such an educational revival was ever known in any other State, certainly nothing like it was ever known before in North Carolina. I am sure that you who have lived here continuously for the last ten years do not know how great the quickening of civilization has been. The level of life has been moved further upward in these ten years than it was moved in any preced-ing fifty years. I never come here but I am astonished at the changes I hear of. The civilization that you have today is different from the civilization of my own boyhood by a greater remove than that civilization was different from the civili-zation of fifty years before.

In my judgment there has been no other event in North Carolina since the formation of the American Union that is comparable in importance to this new educational progress. The movement now has such momentum that nothing can hinder the complete development of the public school system till every child is reached. When every inhabited township votes a local tax to supplement the State tax, the taxes you now levy will seem small and will be increased. Ac-cording to the last published reports of the Commissioner of Education, the total sum spent per year per pupil in the public schools was still lower in North Caro-lina than in any State except South Carolina. It was only $3.40. In Georgia it was nearly $6.50, in Virginia it was nearly $9, in Indiana it was $20, in Michigan nearly $20, in Wisconsin $21, in Minnesota nearly $30, in the new State of North Dakota it was nearly $33.50—nearly ten times the expenditure per pupil

501

that was made in North Carolina. None of these States is richer than your own in possibilities. The ability to maintain schools is in proportion rather to the appreciation of education than to the amount of wealth. We pay for schools not so much out of our purses as out of our state of mind. For example, there is a man in Moore County who had two children at school at the expense of somebody else. Although he did not pay their bills, he took them from school the other day because, he said, the charge for tuition was too high. He is the frankest and most faithful believer of our old-time economic creed that I have ever known.

As the movement to establish public schools everywhere gathers force, men of wealth will find that they can do no public service with their money so sure to bring lasting results as to build schoolhouses. The history of philanthropy shows that no public benefaction brings the same sure and permanent results as provision for the free education of the masses. The battle will be practically won when the whole State shall stand on this platform:

A public school system generously supported by public sentiment, and generously maintained by both State and local taxation, is the only effective means to develop the forgotten man, and even more surely the only means to develop the forgotten woman.

Even ten years ago, many men in North Carolina did not stand on this platform. Now I hear that few oppose such a programme, those few you will soon educate for sheer pity.

Standing in this institution today, it seems incredible that I myself can recall the opposition both of political leaders and of ecclesiastical leaders to free public schools. Nothing else ever made me so nearly hopeless. Thank Heaven, that opposition is passed. Or, if it be not wholly passed, and if any dupe of an old political fallacy say that we are too poor to increase our taxes for education, remember that the average amount paid now by every taxpayer is only $2.13; the average amount paid by each taxpayer in the poor State of Maine is $9.23; in Virginia $4.72, in Florida $5.93; in Iowa it is $15. Too poor to maintain schools? The man who says it is the perpetuator of poverty. It is the doctrine that has kept us poor. It smells of the alms-house and the hovel. It has driven more men and more wealth from the State and kept more away than any other political doctrine ever cost us—more even than the doctrine of Secession. Such a man is the victim of an ancient and harmful falsehood.

If any beggar for a church school oppose a local tax for schools or a higher school tax, take him to the huts of the forgotten women and children, and in their hopeless presence remind him that the church system of education has not touched tens of thousands of these lives, and ask him whether he think it wrong that the Commonwealth should educate them. If he think it wrong, ask him and ask the people plainly, whether he be a worthy preacher of the gospel that declares one man equal to another in the sight of God? Is not one man equal to another also in the sight of the Commonwealth? In all reasonableness, it is impossible to understand how any man can regard it as a Christian act to stand in the way of the State's elevating the neglected masses. Can any church afford to put itself in such a position? or, if it do, has it any right to complain if good men declare it an unchristian attitude? Even if you could respect the religion

502

of the man who objects to the elevation of the forgotten masses by public education, it is hard to respect his common sense; for does his church not profit by the greater enlightenment and prosperity that every educated community enjoys? This doctrine smells of poverty—poverty in living, poverty in thinking, poverty in the spiritual life.

The most sacred thing in the Commonwealth and to the Commonwealth is the child, whether it be your child or the child of the dull-faced mother of the hovel. The child of the dull-faced mother may, for all you know, be the most capable child in the State. At its worst, it is capable of good citizenship and a useful life, if its intelligence be quickened and trained. Several of the strongest personalities that were ever born in North Carolina were men whose very fathers were unknown. We have all known two such, who held high places in church and state. President Eliot said a little while ago that the ablest man that he had known in his many years' connection with Harvard University was the son of a brick mason. The child, whether it have poor parents or rich parents, is the most valuable undeveloped resource of the State.

But the day is past when worn-out theories hold us in captivity, and we owe its passing chiefly to the idea that this institution stands for. Our whole life will soon be delivered from the bondage of ignorance by our hitherto forgotten women. I am reminded of the story of the saving of a captured city by its gentlewomen. In an old translation of Montaigne it runs thus:

"The Emperor, Conradus, third of that name, having besieged Guelphe, Duke of Bavaria, what vile or base satisfaction soever was offered him, would yield to no other milder conditions, but only to suffer such gentle women as were with the Duke in the city (their honours safe) to issue out the town afoote, with such things as they could carry about them. They, with unrelenting courage, advised and resolved themselves (neglecting all their riches or jewels to carry their husbands, their children and the Duke himselfe, on their backs). The Emperor, perceiving the quaintnesse of their device, tooke so great pleasure in it that he wept for joy, and forthwith converted the former inexorable rage and mortall hatred he bare the Duke into so milde a relenting and gentle kindnesse, that thence he entreated both him and his, with all favour and courtesy."

You that know me will bear witness that I have not spoken of our fathers, nor of our political leaders, least of all of our religious leaders, in a spirit of ungrateful criticism. I have meant with all proper respect for them and for their good qualities and good works only to show that their systems have proved failures for our needs. Doubtless under the conditions of their lives they did the best they could do. But the conditions of our lives are different; and our duty is to accept our own conditions without illusions, to face our own problems like men, and when necessary with all respect for the past to lift dead men's hands from our life.

503

May I go forward a step further in the development of public education that must in due time follow this delivery from the bondage of the old systems? The extension of free preparatory schools in every part of the State is leading to the establishment of free high schools, such as already exist in some towns, as in Greensboro and in Durham, and in other larger towns. These will draw to themselves the intellectual interests of the whole community and make the public school system the pride of our people. I know towns where every enlightening interest centers in the high school. Lectures are given there on literature and on music and on practical subjects as well, by the most learned men and women. Parents pursue courses of study with their children. The whole life of such towns is lifted to a high intellectual level. In some such towns private schools exist only to train those boys and girls who are too dull or backward to keep pace with the rest—a sort of asylum for the stupid. My own sons are today preparing to enter Harvard University at the Cambridge Latin school, where the sons and daughters of the professors at Harvard are in the same classes, or may be, with the sons and daughters of draymen and hack-drivers. All have the same privileges and the same opportunities; and no pupil can buy even a book or a pencil; the city supplies them all. Every man pays for it in his taxes; and every man profits by it in the increased value of his property, in the higher wages he receives, as a higher and higher degree of skill in all work is developed, and a higher and higher level of trained life is reached. On their way home from school these pupils may stop at a magnificent public library and take from it any book they please free of charge, or spend the day in the large reading rooms, investigating any subject they may be interested in. So may any man or woman or child in the whole city, free of charge. The library building was the gift of a wealthy citizen. The books are paid for by my taxes and the taxes of other men there. Every town in Massachusetts, but about a dozen small and remote towns, has such a free library—the direct growth of a public school system. The States of New York and Michigan send travelling libraries of new books—collections of good literature—to any town that asks for them and has a public library of its own. After these hundred or two volumes have remained in one town the allotted time, they are sent on to another, and so on indefinitely—all at the State's expense.

When I have seen these things and profited by them, and when I know that men are every day going away from this old land that they love to get such advantages for themselves and for their children, can I listen to the mendicant whine of any ignorant political or ecclesiastical leader who says that my children had better not be educated at all if they cannot be bred with his narrow outlook on life?

Now look a little further yet along the line of development of the public school system. Following the high school may come (and I think ought to come), a still higher extension of State education—the wholly free University and Industrial Schools. When your University was established, the old political idea of education prevailed, and a restricted number of boys from each county was admitted free—and these only. This system discriminates in favour of a restricted number of youths and against all the rest. It is still only a partially free system. There is always a danger that the boys who pay, if it be known who they are, will regard those who do not pay as charity students. If all alike were free—as all in my judgment ought to be—no such danger could arise.

504

The old aristocratic system had a leaning towards charity as the ecclesiastical system has; and the view of education as a charity has always been one of the greatest weaknesses of both systems. Education pays the State. The more persons educated the better education pays the State. But to dole it out to a restricted number is to regard it as charity and to turn the State into an almsgiver. Most of the Eastern States, where the aristocratic idea was strongest, have stopped short of free universities; but many of the Western States have been wiser.

In the State of Michigan, for instance, a child of either sex may begin its education at a public school and pursue it through the State University without charge; and this University has become one of the strongholds of learning in the Union and one of our great schools. A similar system has been adopted in Kansas, in Texas, and in other States. Any child in any one of those great Commonwealths may have free training from infancy to maturity—free training in one of the most efficient systems of education ever devised by man. And this system has been constructed and developed almost within the lifetime of the youngest of us.

The opportunity exists in North Carolina to establish a similar system by a single effort and without any considerable increase of expenditure. We have our State University, most useful and vigorous under its recent President, and its present one, and we have our three larger and older denominational colleges—Davidson College with its solidity and old-time dignity, Wake Forest College, a striking demonstration of what people of moderate means may at any time do when they work with united purpose, and Trinity College with its new life made possible by its generous benefactors. We have all these and the other State schools and denominational schools for boys and for girls. If they could all be united into one great school, it would at once become by far the most efficient and noteworthy institution in the South. And there is no reason why it should not become one of the great seats of learning in the Union. If the doors of such an institution were thrown open free to every boy and girl in the State, and there were free schools to train them for it, we should no longer talk of forgotten men and women; and people from other States would seek homes here. These counties would be peopled at last by as useful and as cultivated a population as any in the United States.

Nor need the religious influence of any of the denominational colleges suffer by such a move when the time for it comes. Every one might have its own dormitory and religious supervision over pupils of its own sect. A definite movement of this sort has already been made where the denominational schools have shown a wish to become a part of the system of public education.

But I have wandered too far from the problems of the immediate present. Such things as I have spoken of, we may look for in the future. What may we not look for in the future? Whatever I might say in prophecy would be as inadequate as all that I might say in congratulation. Great changes come as silently as the seasons. I am no more sure of this spring time than I am of the rejuvenation of our society and the lifting up of our life. A revolution is in progress, and this institution is one of the first and best fruits of it. I declare in truth and soberness, that this is the most inspiring sight that I have ever seen in North

505

Carolina, for before the moral earnestness of well-trained women social illusions vanish and worn-out traditions fall away.

O earnest young Womanhood of the Commonwealth, we that had forgotten you now thankfully do you honour. Many a man with the patriotic spirit that is our inheritance has striven to lift dead men's hands from our stagnant life and has been baffled by a century's inertia. I speak the gladdest speech of my life when I say that *you* have lifted them. This institution and your presence is proof that the State has remembered the forgotten woman. You in turn will remember the forgotten child; and in this remembrance is laid the foundation of a new social order. The neglected people will rise and with them will rise all the people. (*1897*)

BOOKER T. WASHINGTON

c.1856–1915

Booker Taliaferro Washington, the son of a Negro cook on the plantation of James Burroughs, was born in Franklin County, Virginia. As a youth he worked in salt furnaces and coal mines until he was able to afford his schooling. He enrolled at Hampton Institute in 1872 and was graduated three years later. He taught for a time in Malden, West Virginia, and then went to Wayland Seminary in Washington, D. C., to continue his studies. In 1879 he returned to Hampton Institute as an instructor.

In May 1881 Washington was selected to head the newly founded Tuskegee Institute, an industrial training school for Negroes in Tuskegee, Alabama. Washington writes in his autobiography, *Up from Slavery*, that the school "opened with forty students in a dilapidated shanty near the coloured Methodist Church, with the church itself a sort of assembly room." Washington's entire life was devoted to an attempt to better the plight of the Negro in the South by giving him proficient industrial training and by promoting better understanding between the races. He traveled widely in connection with this work, lecturing both in America and Europe. So successful was his leadership at Tuskegee that at his death the institution had more than a hundred substantial buildings and over 2000 acres of local land, plus 25,000 acres in northern Alabama which it had received from Congress. Of Washington's many published works, his most important after *Up from Slavery* (1901) was *My Larger Education* (1911).

506

from *Up from Slavery*

Chapter 14. The Atlanta Exposition Address

The Atlanta Exposition, at which I had been asked to make an address as a representative of the Negro race, as stated in the last chapter, was opened with a short address from Governor Bullock. After other interesting exercises, including an invocation from Bishop Nelson, of Georgia, a dedicatory ode by Albert Howell, Jr., and addresses by the President of the Exposition and Mrs. Joseph Thompson, the President of the Woman's Board, Governor Bullock introduced me with the words, "We have with us to-day a representative of Negro enterprise and Negro civilization."

When I arose to speak, there was considerable cheering, especially from the coloured people. As I remember it now, the thing that was uppermost in my mind was the desire to say something that would cement the friendship of the races and bring about hearty cooperation between them. So far as my outward surroundings were concerned, the only thing that I recall distinctly now is that when I got up, I saw thousands of eyes looking intently into my face. The following is the address which I delivered:—

Mr. President and Gentlemen of the Board of Directors and Citizens.

One-third of the population of the South is of the Negro race. No enterprise seeking the material, civil, or moral welfare of this section can disregard this element of our population and reach the highest success. I but convey to you, Mr. President and Directors, the sentiment of the masses of my race when I say that in no way have the value and manhood of the American Negro been more fittingly and generously recognized than by the managers of this magnificent Exposition at every stage of its progress. It is a recognition that will do more to cement the friendship of the two races than any occurrence since the dawn of our freedom.

Not only this, but the opportunity here afforded will awaken among us a new era of industrial progress. Ignorant and inexperienced, it is not strange that in the first years of our new life we began at the top instead of at the bottom; that a seat in Congress or the state legislature was more sought than real estate or industrial skill; that the political convention or stump speaking had more attractions than starting a dairy farm or truck garden.

A ship lost at sea for many days suddenly sighted a friendly vessel. From the mast of the unfortunate vessel was seen a signal, "Water, water; we die of thirst!" The answer from the friendly vessel at once came back, "Cast down your bucket where you are." And a third and fourth signal for water was answered, "Cast down your bucket where you are." The captain of the distressed vessel, at last heeding the injunction, cast down his bucket, and it came up full of fresh, sparkling water from the mouth of the Amazon River. To those of my race who depend on bettering their condition in a foreign land or who underestimate the importance of cultivating friendly relations with the Southern white

507

From Up from Slavery, *by Booker T. Washington, Doubleday & Company, Inc.*

man, who is their next-door neighbour, I would say: "Cast down your bucket where you are"—cast it down in making friends in every manly way of the people of all races by whom we are surrounded.

Cast it down in agriculture, mechanics, in commerce, in domestic service, and in the professions. And in this connection it is well to bear in mind that whatever other sins the South may be called to bear, when it comes to business, pure and simple, it is in the South that the Negro is given a man's chance in the commercial world, and in nothing is this Exposition more eloquent than in emphasizing this chance. Our greatest danger is that in the great leap from slavery to freedom we may overlook the fact that the masses of us are to live by the productions of our hands, and fail to keep in mind that we shall prosper in proportion as we learn to dignify and glorify common labour and put brains and skill into the common occupations of life; shall prosper in proportion as we learn to draw the line between the superficial and the substantial, the ornamental gewgaws of life and the useful. No race can prosper till it learns that there is as much dignity in tilling a field as in writing a poem. It is at the bottom of life we must begin, and not at the top. Nor should we permit our grievances to overshadow our opportunities.

To those of the white race who look to the incoming of those of foreign birth and strange tongue and habits for the prosperity of the South, were I permitted I would repeat what I say to my own race, "Cast down your bucket where you are." Cast it down among the eight millions of Negroes whose habits you know, whose fidelity and love you have tested in days when to have proved treacherous meant the ruin of your firesides. Cast down your bucket among these people who have, without strikes and labour wars, tilled your fields, cleared your forests, builded your railroads and cities, and brought forth treasures from the bowels of the earth, and helped make possible this magnificent representation of the progress of the South. Casting down your bucket among my people, helping and encouraging them as you are doing on these grounds, and to education of head, hand, and heart, you will find that they will buy your surplus land, make blossom the waste places in your fields, and run your factories. While doing this, you can be sure in the future, as in the past, that you and your families will be surrounded by the most patient, faithful, law-abiding, and unresentful people that the world has seen. As we have proved our loyalty to you in the past, in nursing your children, watching by the sick-bed of your mothers and fathers, and often following them with tear-dimmed eyes to their graves, so in the future, in our humble way, we shall stand by you with a devotion that no foreigner can approach, ready to lay down our lives, if need be, in defence of yours, interlacing our industrial, commercial, civil, and religious life with yours in a way that shall make the interests of both races one. In all things that are purely social we can be as separate as the fingers, yet one as the hand in all things essential to mutual progress.

There is no defence or security for any of us except in the highest intelligence and development of all. If anywhere there are efforts tending to curtail the fullest growth of the Negro, let these efforts be turned into stimulating, encouraging, and making him the most useful and intelligent citizen. Effort or means so invested will pay a thousand per cent interest. These efforts will be twice blessed—"blessing him that gives and him that takes."

508

There is no escape through law of man or God from the inevitable:—

> The laws of changeless justice bind
> Oppressor with oppressed;
> And close as sin and suffering joined
> We march to fate abreast.

Nearly sixteen millions of hands will aid you in pulling the load upward, or they will pull against you the load downward. We shall constitute one-third and more of the ignorance and crime of the South, or one-third its intelligence and progress; we shall contribute one-third to the business and industrial prosperity of the South, or we shall prove a veritable body of death, stagnating, depressing, retarding every effort to advance the body politic.

Gentlemen of the Exposition, as we present to you our humble effort at an exhibition of our progress, you must not expect overmuch. Starting thirty years ago with ownership here and there in a few quilts and pumpkins and chickens (gathered from miscellaneous sources), remember the path that has led from these to the inventions and production of agricultural implements, buggies, steam-engines, newspapers, books, statuary, carving, paintings, the management of drug-stores and banks, has not been trodden without contact with thorns and thistles. While we take pride in what we exhibit as a result of our independent efforts, we do not for a moment forget that our part in this exhibition would fall far short of your expectations but for the constant help that has come to our educational life, not only from the Southern states, but especially from Northern philanthropists, who have made their gifts a constant stream of blessing and encouragement.

The wisest among my race understand that the agitation of questions of social equality is the extremest folly, and that progress in the enjoyment of all the privileges that will come to us must be the result of severe and constant struggle rather than of artificial forcing. No race that has anything to contribute to the markets of the world is long in any degree ostracized. It is important and right that all privileges of the law be ours, but it is vastly more important that we be prepared for the exercises of these privileges. The opportunity to earn a dollar in a factory just now is worth infinitely more than the opportunity to spend a dollar in an opera-house.

In conclusion, may I repeat that nothing in thirty years has given us more hope and encouragement, and drawn us so near to you of the white race, as this opportunity offered by the Exposition; and here bending, as it were, over the altar that represents the results of the struggles of your race and mine, both starting practically empty-handed three decades ago, I pledge that in your effort to work out the great and intricate problem which God has laid at the doors of the South, you shall have at all times the patient, sympathetic help of my race; only let this be constantly in mind, that, while from representations in these buildings of the product of field, of forest, of mine, of factory, letters, and art, much good will come, yet far above and beyond material benefits will be that higher good, that, let us pray God, will come, in a blotting out of sectional differences and racial animosities and suspicions, in a determination to administer absolute justice, in a willing obedience among all classes to the mandates of law.

509

This, this, coupled with our material prosperity, will bring into our beloved South a new heaven and a new earth.

The first thing that I remember, after I had finished speaking, was that Governor Bullock rushed across the platform and took me by the hand, and that others did the same. I received so many and such hearty congratulations that I found it difficult to get out of the building. I did not appreciate to any degree, however, the impression which my address seemed to have made, until the next morning, when I went into the business part of the city. As soon as I was recognized, I was surprised to find myself pointed out and surrounded by a crowd of men who wished to shake hands with me. This was kept up on every street on to which I went, to an extent which embarrassed me so much that I went back to my boarding place. The next morning I returned to Tuskegee. At the station in Atlanta, and at almost all of the stations at which the train stopped between that city and Tuskegee, I found a crowd of people anxious to shake hands with me.

The papers in all parts of the United States published the address in full, and for months afterward there were complimentary editorial references to it. Mr. Clark Howell, the editor of the Atlanta *Constitution*, telegraphed to a New York paper, among other words, the following, "I do not exaggerate when I say that Professor Booker T. Washington's address yesterday was one of the most notable speeches, both as to character and as to the warmth of its reception, ever delivered to a Southern audience. The address was a revelation. The whole speech is a platform upon which blacks and whites can stand with full justice to each other."

The Boston *Transcript* said editorially: "The speech of Booker T. Washington at the Atlanta Exposition, this week, seems to have dwarfed all the other proceedings and the Exposition itself. The sensation that it has caused in the press has never been equalled."

I very soon began receiving all kinds of propositions from lecture bureaus, and editors of magazines and papers, to take the lecture platform, and to write articles. One lecture bureau offered me fifty thousand dollars, or two hundred dollars a night and expenses, if I would place my services at its disposal for a given period. To all these communications I replied that my life-work was at Tuskegee; and that whenever I spoke it must be in the interests of the Tuskegee school and my race, and that I would enter into no arrangements that seemed to place a mere commercial value upon my services.

Some days after its delivery I sent a copy of my address to the President of the United States, the Hon. Grover Cleveland. I received from him the following autograph reply:—

Gray Gables, Buzzard's Bay, Mass.,
October 6, 1895.

510   Booker T. Washington, Esq.:

MY DEAR SIR: I thank you for sending me a copy of your address delivered at the Atlanta Exposition.

I thank you with much enthusiasm for making the address. I have read it with intense interest, and I think the Exposition would be fully justified if it did not do more than furnish the opportunity for its delivery. Your words cannot fail to delight and encourage all who wish well for your race; and if our coloured fellow-citizens do not from your utterances gather new hope and form new determinations to gain every valuable advantage offered them by their citizenship, it will be strange indeed.

Yours very truly,
GROVER CLEVELAND.

Later I met Mr. Cleveland, for the first time, when, as President, he visited the Atlanta Exposition. At the request of myself and others he consented to spend an hour in the Negro Building, for the purpose of inspecting the Negro exhibit and of giving the coloured people in attendance an opportunity to shake hands with him. As soon as I met Mr. Cleveland I became impressed with his simplicity, greatness, and rugged honesty. I have met him many times since then, both at public functions and at his private residence in Princeton, and the more I see of him the more I admire him. When he visited the Negro Building in Atlanta he seemed to give himself up wholly, for that hour, to the coloured people. He seemed to be as careful to shake hands with some old coloured "auntie" clad partially in rags, and to take as much pleasure in doing so, as if he were greeting some millionnaire. Many of the coloured people took advantage of the occasion to get him to write his name in a book or on a slip of paper. He was as careful and patient in doing this as if he were putting his signature to some great state document.

Mr. Cleveland has not only shown his friendship for me in many personal ways, but has always consented to do anything I have asked of him for our school. This he has done, whether it was to make a personal donation or to use his influence in securing the donations of others. Judging from my personal acquaintance with Mr. Cleveland, I do not believe that he is conscious of possessing any colour prejudice. He is too great for that. In my contact with people I find that, as a rule, it is only the little, narrow people who live for themselves, who never read good books, who do not travel, who never open up their souls in a way to permit them to come into contact with other souls—with the great outside world. No man whose vision is bounded by colour can come into contact with what is highest and best in the world. In meeting men, in many places, I have found that the happiest people are those who do the most for others; the most miserable are those who do the least. I have also found that few things, if any, are capable of making one so blind and narrow as race prejudice. I often say to our students, in the course of my talks to them on Sunday evenings in the chapel, that the longer I live and the more experience I have of the world, the more I am convinced that, after all, the one thing that is most worth living for— and dying for, if need be—is the opportunity of making some one else more happy and more useful.

The coloured people and the coloured newspapers at first seemed to be greatly pleased with the character of my Atlanta address, as well as with its reception.

511

But after the first burst of enthusiasm began to die away, and the coloured people began reading the speech in cold type, some of them seemed to feel that they had been hypnotized. They seemed to feel that I had been too liberal in my remarks toward the Southern whites, and that I had not spoken out strongly enough for what they termed the "rights" of the race. For a while there was a reaction, so far as a certain element of my own race was concerned, but later these reactionary ones seemed to have been won over to my way of believing and acting.

While speaking of changes in public sentiment, I recall that about ten years after the school at Tuskegee was established, I had an experience that I shall never forget. Dr. Lyman Abbott, then the pastor of Plymouth Church, and also editor of the *Outlook* (then the Christian Union), asked me to write a letter for his paper giving my opinion of the exact condition, mental and moral, of the coloured ministers in the South, as based upon my observations. I wrote the letter, giving the exact facts as I conceived them to be. The picture painted was a rather black one—or, since I am black, shall I say "white"? It could not be otherwise with a race but a few years out of slavery, a race which had not had time or opportunity to produce a competent ministry.

What I said soon reached every Negro minister in the country, I think, and the letters of condemnation which I received from them were not few. I think that for a year after the publication of this article every association and every conference or religious body of any kind, of my race, that met, did not fail before adjourning to pass a resolution condemning me, or calling upon me to retract or modify what I had said. Many of these organizations went so far in their resolutions as to advise parents to cease sending their children to Tuskegee. One association even appointed a "missionary" whose duty it was to warn the people against sending their children to Tuskegee. This missionary had a son in the school, and I noticed that, whatever the "missionary" might have said or done with regard to others, he was careful not to take his son away from the institution. Many of the coloured papers, especially those that were the organs of religious bodies, joined in the general chorus of condemnation or demands for retraction.

During the whole time of the excitement, and through all the criticism, I did not utter a word of explanation or retraction. I knew that I was right, and that time and the sober second thought of the people would vindicate me. It was not long before the bishops and other church leaders began to make a careful investigation of the conditions of the ministry, and they found out that I was right. In fact, the oldest and most influential bishop in one branch of the Methodist Church said that my words were far too mild. Very soon public sentiment began making itself felt, in demanding a purifying of the ministry. While this is not yet complete by any means, I think I may say, without egotism, and I have been told by many of our most influential ministers, that my words had much to do with starting a demand for the placing of a higher type of men in the pulpit. I have had the satisfaction of having many who once condemned me thank me heartily for my frank words.

The change of the attitude of the Negro ministry, so far as regards myself, is so complete that at the present time I have no warmer friends among any class

512

than I have among the clergymen. The improvement in the character and life of
the Negro ministers is one of the most gratifying evidences of the progress of the
race. My experience with them, as well as other events in my life, convinces me
that the thing to do, when one feels sure that he has said or done the right thing,
and is condemned, is to stand still and keep quiet. If he is right, time will show it.

In the midst of the discussion which was going on concerning my Atlanta
speech, I received the letter which I give below, from Dr. Gilman, the President
of Johns Hopkins University, who had been made chairman of the judges of
award in connection with the Atlanta Exposition:—

Johns Hopkins University, Baltimore,
President's Office, September 30, 1895.

DEAR MR. WASHINGTON: Would it be agreeable to you to be one of
the Judges of Award in the Department of Education at Atlanta? If so,
I shall be glad to place your name upon the list. A line by telegraph
will be welcomed.

Yours very truly,
D. C. GILMAN.

I think I was even more surprised to receive this invitation than I had been to
receive the invitation to speak at the opening of the Exposition. It was to be a
part of my duty, as one of the jurors, to pass not only upon the exhibits of the
coloured schools, but also upon those of the white schools. I accepted the position, and spent a month in Atlanta in performance of the duties which it en-
tailed. The board of jurors was a large one, consisting in all of sixty members.
It was about equally divided between Southern white people and Northern white
people. Among them were college presidents, leading scientists and men of letters, and specialists in many subjects. When the group of jurors to which I was
assigned met for organization, Mr. Thomas Nelson Page, who was one of the
number, moved that I be made secretary of that division, and the motion was
unanimously adopted. Nearly half of our division were Southern people. In
performing my duties in the inspection of the exhibits of white schools I was in
every case treated with respect, and at the close of our labours I parted from my
associates with regret.

I am often asked to express myself more freely than I do upon the political
condition and the political future of my race. These recollections of my experience in Atlanta give me the opportunity to do so briefly. My own belief is,
although I have never before said so in so many words, that the time will come
when the Negro in the South will be accorded all the political rights which his
ability, character, and material possessions entitle him to. I think, though, that
the opportunity to freely exercise such political rights will not come in any large
degree through outside or artificial forcing, but will be accorded to the Negro
by the Southern white people themselves, and that they will protect him in the
exercise of those rights. Just as soon as the South gets over the old feeling that
it is being forced by "foreigners," or "aliens," to do something which it does not
want to do, I believe that the change in the direction that I have indicated is

513

going to begin. In fact, there are indications that it is already beginning in a slight degree.

Let me illustrate my meaning. Suppose that some months before the opening of the Atlanta Exposition there had been a general demand from the press and public platform outside the South that a Negro be given a place on the opening programme, and that a Negro be placed upon the board of jurors of award. Would any such recognition of the race have taken place? I do not think so. The Atlanta officials went as far as they did because they felt it to be a pleasure, as well as a duty, to reward what they considered merit in the Negro race. Say what we will, there is something in human nature which we cannot blot out, which makes one man, in the end, recognize and reward merit in another, regardless of colour or race.

I believe it is the duty of the Negro—as the greater part of the race is already doing—to deport himself modestly in regard to political claims, depending upon the slow but sure influences that proceed from the possession of property, intelligence, and high character for the full recognition of his political rights. I think that the according of the full exercise of political rights is going to be a matter of natural, slow growth, not an over-night, gourd-vine affair. I do not believe that the Negro should cease voting, for a man cannot learn the exercise of self-government by ceasing to vote any more than a boy can learn to swim by keeping out of the water, but I do believe that in his voting he should more and more be influenced by those of intelligence and character who are his next-door neighbours.

I know coloured men who, through the encouragement, help, and advice of Southern white people, have accumulated thousands of dollars' worth of property, but who, at the same time, would never think of going to those same persons for advice concerning the casting of their ballots. This, it seems to me, is unwise and unreasonable, and should cease. In saying this I do not mean that the Negro should truckle, or not vote from principle, for the instant he ceases to vote from principle he loses the confidence and respect of the Southern white man even.

I do not believe that any state should make a law that permits an ignorant and poverty-striken white man to vote, and prevents a black man in the same condition from voting. Such a law is not only unjust, but it will react, as all unjust laws do, in time; for the effect of such a law is to encourage the Negro to secure education and property, and at the same time it encourages the white man to remain in ignorance and poverty. I believe that in time, through the operation of intelligence and friendly race relations, all cheating at the ballot box in the South will cease. It will become apparent that the white man who begins by cheating a Negro out of his ballot soon learns to cheat a white man out of his, and that the man who does this ends his career of dishonesty by the theft of property or by some equally serious crime. In my opinion, the time will come when the South will encourage all of its citizens to vote. It will see that it pays better, from every standpoint, to have healthy, vigorous life than to have that political stagnation which always results when one-half of the population has no share and no interest in the government.

As a rule, I believe in universal, free suffrage, but I believe that in the South we are confronted with peculiar conditions that justify the protection of the

514

ballot in many of the states, for a while at least, either by an educational test, a property test, or by both combined; but whatever tests are required, they should be made to apply with equal and exact justice to both races. (*1900*)

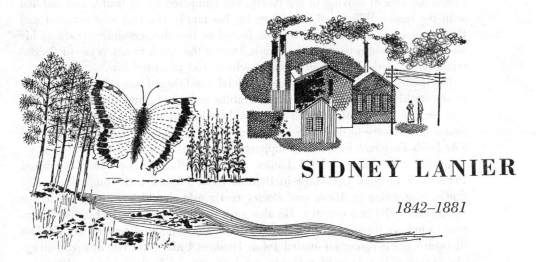

SIDNEY LANIER

1842–1881

Sidney Lanier was born in Macon, Georgia, on February 3, 1842. His mother was an accomplished musician, and from his earliest childhood Sidney displayed a great love for music. Having received his early education at a private academy, Lanier entered Oglethorpe University in January 1857. A small Presbyterian college near Milledgeville, it was an unpretentious place, as he was later to admit, but while there Lanier gained a lasting interest in scholarship through his contacts with one of his professors, James Woodrow, an uncle of Woodrow Wilson. Woodrow impressed upon his young student's mind the importance of science in modern thought and its relation to poetry and religion.

In 1860 Lanier was graduated from Oglethorpe at the head of his class and was appointed a tutor. His hopes to study in Germany, as Professor Woodrow had done, were frustrated by the advent of the Civil War, when he left the university and joined the Macon Volunteers. In 1863 he and his brother were transferred to the signal service, serving as mounted scouts along the James River. In August 1864 Sidney was given the dangerous assignment of signal officer on a blockade runner and on November 2 was captured and sent to prison at Fort Lookout, Maryland. The miserable conditions under which he lived there are described in *Tiger Lilies* (1867), a novel based upon his war experiences. During his imprisonment Lanier amused himself—and delighted his fellow prisoners— by playing upon his flute, which he had carried inside his coat sleeve while on active duty. During this period he also translated several poems from the German and formed a lasting friendship with the poet John Banister Tabb, who was in the same federal prison.

After four months, Lanier was exchanged and sent home to Macon seriously ill, never fully to regain his health. "Pretty much the whole of life," he wrote to Bayard Taylor in 1873, "has been not dying." Despite his war experiences, Lanier had no bitter sectional feelings. The times, however, were out of joint; there was no place in the post-war South for a man of Lanier's genius and tem-

515

permanent. He was convinced that the conception of the South he had held before the war—as a region destined to be the cultural center of the nation—had been a delusion. Struck by the intellectual sterility of the section, he seriously entertained the idea of moving to the North, but hampered by ill health and saddled with the responsibilities of providing for his family (he was now married and the father of four children), he was forced to live the remaining years of his short life in various parts of the South. During the "dark raven days" of Reconstruction he clerked in a hotel, taught school, and practiced law.

By 1873, despite his precarious financial condition, Lanier had determined to devote his declining energies to literature and music, and the few years left him were a period of feverish activity. In addition to his serious efforts, he found it necessary to do much hack work, such as *The Boy's King Arthur* and *The Boy's Froissart*, in order to support his family.

During the winter of 1874 Lanier played the flute in the newly organized Peabody Symphony Orchestra in Baltimore. He became a thorough student of music, contending in *Music and Poetry* that music should have its place in the life of every civilized country. He also gave readings from early English literature in private homes and in February 1879 was appointed lecturer on English literature at the recently founded Johns Hopkins University. His financial struggle seemed at last, in good measure, resolved, but not so the basic consideration of his health. The last book to appear before his premature death in 1881 was *The Science of English Verse* (1880).

Night and Day

The innocent, sweet Day is dead.
Dark Night hath slain her in her bed.
O, Moors are as fierce to kill as to wed!
—Put out the light, said he.

A sweeter light than ever rayed
From star of heaven or eye of maid
Has vanished in the unknown Shade.
—She's dead, she's dead, said he.

Now, in a wild, sad after-mood
The tawny Night sits still to brood
Upon the dawn-time when he wooed.
—I would she lived, said he.

Star-memories of happier times,
Of loving deeds and lovers' rhymes,
Throng forth in silvery pantomimes.
—Come back, O Day! said he.

(1866)

516

Thar's More in the Man Than Thar Is in the Land

I knowed a man, which he lived in Jones,
Which Jones is a county of red hills and stones,
And he lived pretty much by gittin' of loans,
And his mules was nuthin' but skin and bones,
And his hogs was flat as his corn-bread pones,
And he had 'bout a thousand acres o' land.

This man—which his name it was also Jones—
He swore that he'd leave them old red hills and stones,
Fur he couldn't make nuthin' but yallerish cotton,
And little o' *that*, and his fences was rotten,
And what little corn he had, *hit* was boughten
And dinged ef a livin' was in the land.

And the longer he swore the madder he got,
And he riz and he walked to the stable lot,
And he hollered to Tom to come thar and hitch
Fur to emigrate somewhar whar land was rich,
And to quit raisin' cock-burrs, thistles and sich,
And a wastin' ther time on the cussed land.

So him and Tom they hitched up the mules,
Pertestin' that folks was mighty big fools
That 'ud stay in Georgy ther lifetime out,
Jest scratchin' a livin' when all of 'em mought
Git places in Texas whar cotton would sprout
By the time you could plant it in the land.

And he driv by a house whar a man named Brown
Was a livin', not fur from the edge o' town,
And he bantered Brown fur to buy his place,
And said that bein' as money was skace,
And bein' as sheriffs was hard to face,
Two dollars an acre would git the land.

They closed at a dollar and fifty cents,
And Jones he bought him a waggin and tents,
And loaded his corn, and his wimmin, and truck,
And moved to Texas, which it tuck
His entire pile, with the best of luck,
To git thar and git him a little land.

But Brown moved out on the old Jones' farm,
And he rolled up his breeches and bared his arm,

517

And he picked all the rocks from off'n the groun',
And he rooted it up and he plowed it down,
Then he sowed his corn and his wheat in the land.

Five years glid by, and Brown, one day
(Which he'd got so fat that he wouldn't weigh),
Was a settin' down, sorter lazily,
To the bulliest dinner you ever see,
When one o' the children jumped on his knee
And says, "Yon's Jones, which you bought his land."

And thar was Jones, standin' out at the fence,
And he hadn't no waggin, nor mules, nor tents,
Fur he had left Texas afoot and cum
To Georgy to see if he couldn't git sum
Employment, and he was lookin' as hum-
Ble as ef he had never owned any land.

But Brown he axed him in, and he sot
Him down to his vittles smokin' hot,
And when he had filled hisself and the floor
Brown looked at him sharp and riz and swore
That, "whether men's land was rich or poor
Thar was more in the man than thar was in the land."

(*1866*)

Corn

Today the woods are trembling through and through
With shimmering forms, that flash before my view,
Then melt in green as dawn-stars melt in blue.
   The leaves that wave against my cheek caress
   Like women's hands; the embracing boughs express
   A subtlety of mighty tenderness;
   The copse-depths into little noises start,
   That sound anon like beatings of a heart,
   Anon like talk 'twixt lips not far apart.
   The beech dreams balm, as a dreamer hums a song;
   Through that vague wafture, expirations strong
   Throb from young hickories breathing deep and long
With stress and urgence bold of prisoned spring
     And ecstasy of burgeoning.
   Now, since the dew-plashed road of morn is dry,
   Forth venture odors of more quality
   And heavenlier giving. Like Jove's locks awry,
     Long muscadines

518

Rich-wreathe the spacious foreheads of great pines,
And breathe ambrosial passion from their vines.
   I pray with mosses, ferns and flowers shy
   That hide like gentle nuns from human eye
   To lift adoring perfumes to the sky.
I hear faint bridal-sighs of brown and green
Dying to silent hints of kisses keen
As far lights fringe into a pleasant sheen.
   I start at fragmentary whispers, blown
   From undertalks of leafy souls unknown,
   Vague purports sweet, of inarticulate tone.

Dreaming of gods, men, nuns and brides, between
Old companies of oaks that inward lean
To join their radiant amplitudes of green
   I slowly move, with ranging looks that pass
   Up from the matted miracles of grass
Into yon veined complex of space,
Where sky and leafage interlace
   So close, the heaven of blue is seen
   Inwoven with a heaven of green.

I wander to the zigzag-cornered fence
Where sassafras, intrenched in brambles dense,
Contests with stolid vehemence
   The march of culture, setting limb and thorn
   As pikes against the army of the corn.

There, while I pause, my fieldward-faring eyes
Take harvests, where the stately corn-ranks rise,
    Of inward dignities
And large benignities and insights wise,
    Graces and modest majesties.
Thus, without theft, I reap another's field;
Thus, without tilth, I house a wondrous yield,
And heap my heart with quintuple crops concealed.

Look, out of line one tall corn-captain stands
Advanced beyond the foremost of his bands,
   And waves his blades upon the very edge
   And hottest thicket of the battling hedge.
Thou lustrous stalk, that ne'er mayst walk nor talk,
   Still shalt thou type the poet-soul sublime
   That leads the vanward of his timid time
   And sings up cowards with commanding rhyme—
Soul calm, like thee, yet fain, like thee, to grow
By double increment, above, below;

519

Soul homely, as thou art, yet rich in grace like thee,
Teaching the yeomen selfless chivalry
That moves in gentle curves of courtesy;
Soul filled like thy long veins with sweetness tense,
By every godlike sense
Transmuted from the four wild elements.
Drawn to high plans,
Thou lift'st more stature than a mortal man's,
Yet ever piercest downward in the mold
And keepest hold
Upon the reverend and steadfast earth
That gave thee birth;
Yea, standest smiling in thy future grave,
Serene and brave,
With unremitting breath
Inhaling life from death,
Thine epitaph writ fair in fruitage eloquent,
Thyself thy monument.

As poets should
Thou hast built up thy hardihood
With universal food,
Drawn in select proportion fair
From honest mold and vagabond air;
From darkness of the dreadful night,
And joyful light;
From antique ashes, whose departed flame
In thee has finer life and longer fame;
From wounds and balms,
From storms and calms,
From potsherds and dry bones
And ruin-stones.
Into thy vigorous substance thou hast wrought
Whate'er the hand of Circumstance hath brought;
Yea, into cool solacing green hast spun
White radiance hot from out the sun.
So thou dost mutually leaven
Strength of earth with grace of heaven;
So thou dost marry new and old
Into a one of higher mold;
So thou dost reconcile the hot and cold,
The dark and bright,
And many a heart-perplexing opposite:
And so,
Akin by blood to high and low,
Fitly thou playest out thy poet's part,
Richly expending thy much-bruisèd heart
In equal care to nourish lord in hall,

520

Or beast in stall:
Thou took'st from all that thou might'st give to all.

O steadfast dweller on the selfsame spot
Where thou wast born, that still repinest not—
Type of the home-fond heart, the happy lot!—
  Deeply thy mild content rebukes the land
  Whose flimsy homes, built on the shifting sand
Of trade, forever rise and fall
With alternation whimsical,
  Enduring scarce a day,
  Then swept away
By swift engulfments of incalculable tides
Whereon capricious Commerce rides.
Look, thou substantial spirit of content!
Across this little vale, thy continent,
  To where, beyond the moldering mill,
  Yon old deserted Georgian hill
Bares to the sun his piteous aged crest
    And seamy breast,
  By restless-hearted children left to lie
  Untended there beneath the heedless sky,
  As barbarous folk expose their old to die.
Upon that generous-rounding side,
    With gullies scarified
  Where keen Neglect his lash hath plied,
Dwelt one I knew of old, who played at toil,
And gave to coquette Cotton soul and soil.
  Scorning the slow reward of patient grain,
  He sowed his heart with hopes of swifter gain,
  Then sat him down and waited for the rain.
He sailed in borrowed ships of usury—
A foolish Jason on a treacherous sea,
Seeking the Fleece and finding misery.
  Lulled by smooth-rippling loans, in idle trance
  He lay, content that unthrift Circumstance
  Should plow for him the stony field of Chance.
Yea, gathering crops whose worth no man might tell,
He staked his life on games of Buy-and-Sell,
And turned each field into a gambler's hell.
  Aye, as each year began,
  My farmer to the neighboring city ran;
Passed with a mournful anxious face
Into the banker's inner place;
Parleyed, excused, pleaded for longer grace;
  Railed at the drought, the worm, the rust, the grass;
  Protested ne'er again 'twould come to pass;
  With many an *oh* and *if* and *but alas*

521

Parried or swallowed searching questions rude,
And kissed the dust to soften Dives's mood.
At last, small loans by pledges great renewed,
   He issues smiling from the fatal door,
   And buys with lavish hand his yearly store
   Till his small borrowings will yield no more.
Aye, as each year declined,
With bitter heart and ever-brooding mind
He mourned his fate unkind.
   In dust, in rain, with might and main,
   He nursed his cotton, cursed his grain,
   Fretted for news that made him fret again,
Snatched at each telegram of Future Sale,
And thrilled with Bulls' or Bears' alternate wail—
In hope or fear alike forever pale.
   And thus from year to year, through hope and fear,
   With many a curse and many a secret tear,
   Striving in vain his cloud of debt to clear,
      At last
He woke to find his foolish dreaming past,
   And all his best-of-life the easy prey
   Of squandering scamps and quacks that lined his way
      With vile array,
From rascal statesman down to petty knave;
Himself, at best, for all his bragging brave,
A gamester's catspaw and a banker's slave.
   Then, worn and gray, and sick with deep unrest,
   He fled away into the oblivious West,
   Unmourned, unblest.

Old hill! old hill! thou gashed and hairy Lear
Whom the divine Cordelia of the year,
E'en pitying Spring, will vainly strive to cheer—
   King, that no subject man nor beast may own,
   Discrowned, undaughtered and alone—
Yet shall the great God turn thy fate,
And bring thee back into thy monarch state
   And majesty immaculate.
   Lo, through hot waverings of the August morn,
   Thou givest from thy vasty sides forlorn
   Visions of golden treasuries of corn—
Ripe largesse lingering for some bolder heart
That manfully shall take thy part,
   And tend thee,
   And defend thee,
With antique sinew and with modern art.

                     (1874)

522

The Symphony

"O Trade! O Trade! would thou wert dead!
The Time needs heart—'tis tired of head:
We're all for love," the violins said.
"Of what avail the rigorous tale
Of bill for coin and box for bale?
Grant thee, O Trade! thine uttermost hope:
Level red gold with blue sky-slope,
And base it deep as devils grope:
When all's done, what hast thou won
Of the only sweet that's under the sun?
Ay, canst thou buy a single sigh
Of true love's least, least ecstasy?"
Then, with a bridegroom's heart-beats trembling,
All the mightier strings assembling
Ranged them on the violins' side
As when the bridegroom leads the bride,
And, heart in voice, together cried:
"Yea, what avail the endless tale
Of gain by cunning and plus by sale?
Look up the land, look down the land
The poor, the poor, the poor, they stand,
Wedged by the pressing of Trade's hand
Against an inward-opening door
That pressure tightens evermore:
They sigh a monstrous foul-air sigh
For the outside leagues of liberty,
Where Art, sweet lark, translates the sky
Into a heavenly melody.
'Each day, all day' (these poor folks say),
'In the same old year-long, drear-long way,
We weave in the mills and heave in the kilns,
We sieve mine-meshes under the hills,
And thieve much gold from the Devil's bank tills,
To relieve, O God, what manner of ills?—
The beasts, they hunger, and eat, and die;
And so do we, and the world's a sty;
Hush, fellow-swine: why nuzzle and cry?
Swinehood hath no remedy
Say many men, and hasten by,
Clamping the nose and blinking the eye.
But who said once, in the lordly tone,
Man shall not live by bread alone
But all that cometh from the Throne?

523

Hath God said so?
But Trade saith *No:*
And the kilns and the curt-tongued mills say *Go!*
There's plenty that can, if you can't: we know.
Move out, if you think you're underpaid.
The poor are prolific; we're not afraid;
Trade is trade.'"
Thereat this passionate protesting
Meekly changed, and softened till
It sank to sad requesting
And suggesting sadder still:
"And oh, if men might some time see
How piteous-false the poor decree
That trade no more than trade must be!
Does business mean, *Die, you—live, I?*
Then 'Trade is trade' but sings a lie:
'Tis only war grown miserly.
If business is battle, name it so;
War-crimes less will shame it so,
And widows less will blame it so.
Alas, for the poor to have some part
In yon sweet living lands of Art,
Makes problem not for head, but heart.
Vainly might Plato's brain revolve it:
Plainly the heart of a child could solve it."

And then, as when from words that seem but rude
We pass to silent pain that sits abrood
Back in our heart's great dark and solitude,
So sank the strings to gentle throbbing
Of long chords change-marked with sobbing—
Motherly sobbing, not distinctlier heard
Than half wing-openings of the sleeping bird,
Some dream of danger to her young hath stirred.
Then stirring and demurring ceased, and lo!
Every least ripple of the strings' song-flow
Died to a level with each level bow
And made a great chord tranquil-surfaced so,
As a brook beneath his curving bank doth go
To linger in the sacred dark and green
Where many boughs the still pool overlean
And many leaves make shadow with their sheen.
But presently
A velvet flute-note fell down pleasantly
Upon the bosom of that harmony,
And sailed and sailed incessantly,
As if a petal from a wild-rose blown

Had fluttered down upon that pool of tone
And boatwise dropped o' the convex side
And floated down the glassy tide
And clarified and glorified
The solemn spaces where the shadows bide.
From the warm concave of that fluted note
Somewhat, half song, half odor, forth did float,
As if a rose might somehow be a throat:
"When Nature from her far-off glen
Flutes her soft messages to men,
   The flute can say them o'er again;
   Yea, Nature, singing sweet and lone,
Breathes through life's strident polyphone
The flute-voice in the world of tone.
   Sweet friends,
   Man's love ascends
To finer and diviner ends
Than man's mere thought e'er comprehends,
For I, e'en I,
As here I lie,
A petal on a harmony,
Demand of Science whence and why
Man's tender pain, man's inward cry,
When he doth gaze on earth and sky?
I am not overbold:
   I hold
Full powers from Nature manifold.
I speak for each no-tonguéd tree
That, spring by spring, doth nobler be,
And dumbly and most wistfully
His mighty prayerful arms outspreads
Above men's oft-unheeding heads,
And his big blessing downward sheds.
I speak for all-shaped blooms and leaves,
Lichens on stones and moss on eaves,
Grasses and grains in ranks and sheaves;
Broad-fronded ferns and keen-leaved canes,
And briery mazes bounding lanes,
And marsh-plants, thirsty-cupped for rains,
And milky stems and sugary veins;
For every long-armed woman-vine
That round a piteous tree doth twine;
For passionate odors, and divine
Pistils, and petals crystalline;
All purities of shady springs,
All shynesses of film-winged things
That fly from tree-trunks and bark-rings;

525

All modesties of mountain-fawns
That leap to covert from wild lawns,
And tremble if the day but dawns;
All sparklings of small beady eyes
Of birds, and sidelong glances wise
Wherewith the jay hints tragedies;
All piquancies of prickly burs,
And smoothnesses of downs and furs
Of eiders and of minevers;
All limpid honeys that do lie
At stamen-bases, nor deny
The humming-birds' fine roguery,
Bee-thighs, nor any butterfly;
All gracious curves of slender wings,
Bark-mottlings, fibre-spiralings,
Fern-wavings and leaf-flickerings;
Each dial-marked leaf and flower-bell
Wherewith in every lonesome dell
Time to himself his hours doth tell;
All tree-sounds, rustlings of pine-cones,
Wind-sighings, doves' melodious moans,
And night's unearthly under-tones;
All placid lakes and waveless deeps,
All cool reposing mountain-steeps,
Vale-calms and tranquil lotos-sleeps;—
Yea, all fair forms, and sounds, and lights,
And warmths, and mysteries, and mights,
Of Nature's utmost depths and heights,
—These doth my timid tongue present,
Their mouthpiece and leal instrument
And servant, all love-eloquent.
I heard, when 'All for love' the violins cried:
So, Nature calls through all her system wide,
Give me thy love, O man, so long denied.
Much time is run, and man hath changed his ways,
Since Nature, in the antique fable-days,
Was hid from man's true love by proxy fays,
False fauns and rascal gods that stole her praise.
The nymphs, cold creatures of man's colder brain,
Chilled Nature's streams till man's warm heart was fain
Never to lave its love in them again.
Later, a sweet Voice Love thy neighbor said;
Then first the bounds of neighborhood outspread
Beyond all confines of old ethnic dread.
Vainly the Jew might wag his covenant head:
'All men are neighbors,' so the sweet Voice said.
So, when man's arms had circled all man's race,

The liberal compass of his warm embrace
Stretched bigger yet in the dark bounds of space;
With hands a-grope he felt smooth Nature's grace,
Drew her to breast and kissed her sweetheart face:
Yea man found neighbors in great hills and trees
And streams and clouds and suns and birds and bees
And throbbed with neighbor-loves in loving these.
But oh, the poor! the poor! the poor!
That stand by the inward-opening door
Trade's hand doth tighten ever more,
And sigh their monstrous foul-air sigh
For the outside hills of liberty,
Where Nature spreads her wild blue sky
For Art to make into melody!
Thou Trade! thou king of the modern days!
    Change thy ways,
    Change thy ways;
Let the sweaty laborers file
    A little while,
    A little while,
Where Art and Nature sing and smile.
Trade! is thy heart all dead, all dead?
And hast thou nothing but a head?
I'm all for heart," the flute-voice said,
And into sudden silence fled,
Like as a blush that while 'tis red
Dies to a still, still white instead.

Thereto a thrilling calm succeeds,
Till presently the silence breeds
A little breeze among the reeds
That seems to blow by sea-marsh weeds:
Then from the gentle stir and fret
Sings out the melting clarionet,
Like as a lady sings while yet
Her eyes with salty tears are wet.
"O Trade! O Trade!" the Lady said,
"I too will wish thee utterly dead
If all thy heart is in thy head.
For O my God! and O my God!
What shameful ways have women trod
At beckoning of Trade's golden rod!
Alas when sighs are traders' lies,
And heart's-ease eyes and violet eyes
    Are merchandise!
O purchased lips that kiss with pain!
O cheeks coin-spotted with smirch and stain!

527

O trafficked hearts that break in twain!
—And yet what wonder at my sisters' crime?
So hath Trade withered up Love's sinewy prime,
Men love not women as in olden time.
Ah, not in these cold merchantable days
Deem men their life an opal gray, where plays
The one red Sweet of gracious ladies'-praise.
Now, comes a suitor with sharp prying eye—
Says, *Here, you Lady, if you'll sell, I'll buy:*
Come, heart for heart—a trade? What! weeping? why?
Shame on such wooers' dapper mercery!
I would my lover kneeling at my feet
In humble manliness should cry, *O sweet!*
I know not if thy heart my heart will greet:
I ask not if thy love my love can meet:
Whate'er thy worshipful soft tongue shall say,
I'll kiss thine answer, be it yea or nay:
I do but know I love thee, and I pray
To be thy knight until my dying day.
Woe him that cunning trades in hearts contrives!
Base love good women to base loving drives.
If men loved larger, larger were our lives;
And wooed they nobler, won they nobler wives."
There thrust the bold straightforward horn
To battle for that lady lorn.
With heartsome voice of mellow scorn,
Like any knight in knighthood's morn.
   "Now comfort thee," said he,
     "Fair Lady.
For God shall right thy grievous wrong,
And man shall sing thee a true-love song,
Voiced in act his whole life long,
   Yea, all thy sweet life long,
     Fair Lady.
Where's he that craftily hath said,
The day of chivalry is dead?
I'll prove that lie upon his head,
   Or I will die instead,
     Fair Lady.
Is Honor gone into his grave?
Hath Faith become a caitiff knave,
And Selfhood turned into a slave
   To work in Mammon's cave,
     Fair Lady?
Will Truth's long blade ne'er gleam again?
Hath Giant Trade in dungeons slain
All great contempts of mean-got gain

And hates of inward stain,
    Fair Lady?
For aye shall name and fame be sold,
And place be hugged for the sake of gold,
And smirch-robed Justice feebly scold
    At Crime all money-bold,
        Fair Lady?
Shall self-wrapt husbands aye forget
Kiss-pardons for the daily fret
Wherewith sweet wifely eyes are wet—
    Blind to lips kiss-wise set—
        Fair Lady?
Shall lovers higgle, heart for heart,
Till wooing grows a trading mart
Where much for little, and all for part,
    Make love a cheapening art,
        Fair Lady?
Shall woman scorch for a single sin
That her betrayer may revel in,
And she be burnt, and he but grin
    When that the flames begin,
        Fair Lady?
Shall ne'er prevail the woman's plea,
We maids would far, far whiter be
If that our eyes might sometimes see
    Men maids in purity,
        Fair Lady?
Shall Trade aye salve his conscience-aches
With jibes at Chivalry's old mistakes—
The wars that o'erhot knighthood makes
    For Christ's and ladies' sakes,
        Fair Lady?
Now by each knight that e'er hath prayed
To fight like a man and love like a maid,
Since Pembroke's life, as Pembroke's blade,
    I' the scabbard, death was laid,
        Fair Lady,
I dare avouch my faith is bright
That God doth right and God hath might.
Nor time hath changed His hair to white,
    Nor His dear love to spite,
        Fair Lady.
I doubt no doubts: I strive, and shrive my clay,
And fight my fight in the patient modern way
For true love and for thee—ah me! and pray
    To be thy knight until my dying day,
        Fair Lady."

529

Made end that knightly horn, and spurred away
Into the thick of the melodious fray.

And then the hautboy played and smiled,
And sang like any large-eyed child,
Cool-hearted and all undefiled.
    "Huge Trade!" he said,
"Would thou wouldst lift me on thy head
And run where'er my finger led!
Once said a Man—and wise was He—
Never shalt thou the heavens see,
Save as a little child thou be."
Then o'er sea-lashings of commingling tunes
The ancient wise bassoons,
    Like weird
    Gray-beard
Old harpers sitting on the high sea-dunes,
    Chanted runes:
"Bright-waved gain, gray-waved loss,
The sea of all doth lash and toss,
One wave forward and one across:
But now 'twas trough, now 'tis crest,
And worst doth foam and flash to best,
    And curst to blest.

"Life! Life! thou sea-fugue, writ from east to west,
    Love, Love alone can pore
    On thy dissolving score
    Of harsh half-phrasings,
    Blotted ere writ,
    And double erasings
    Of chords most fit.

"Yea, Love, sole music-master blest,
May read thy weltering palimpsest.
To follow Time's dying melodies through,
And never to lose the old in the new,
And ever to solve the discords true—
    Love alone can do.
And ever Love hears the poor-folks' crying,
And ever Love hears the women's sighing,
And ever sweet knighthood's death-defying,
And ever wise childhood's deep implying,
But never a trader's glozing and lying.

"And yet shall Love himself be heard,
Though long deferred, though long deferred:

O'er the modern waste a dove hath whirred:
Music is Love in search of a word."

(1877)

Song of the Chattahoochee

Out of the hills of Habersham,
Down the valleys of Hall,
I hurry amain to reach the plain,
Run the rapid and leap the fall,
Split at the rock and together again,
Accept my bed, or narrow or wide,
And flee from folly on every side
With a lover's pain to attain the plain
Far from the hills of Habersham,
Far from the valleys of Hall.

All down the hills of Habersham,
All through the valleys of Hall,
The rushes cried *Abide, abide,*
The willful waterweeds held me thrall,
The laving laurel turned my tide,
The ferns and the fondling grass said *Stay,*
The dewberry dipped for to work delay,
And the little reeds sighed *Abide, abide,*
Here in the hills of Habersham,
Here in the valleys of Hall.

High o'er the hills of Habersham,
Veiling the valleys of Hall,
The hickory told me manifold
Fair tales of shade, the poplar tall
Wrought me her shadowy self to hold,
The chestnut, the oak, the walnut, the pine,
Overleaning, with flickering meaning and sign,
Said, *Pass not, so cold, these manifold*
Deep shades of the hills of Habersham,
These glades in the valleys of Hall.

And oft in the hills of Habersham,
And oft in the valleys of Hall,
The white quartz shone, and the smooth brook-stone
Did bar me of passage with friendly brawl,
And many a luminous jewel lone
—Crystals clear or a-cloud with mist,

531

Ruby, garnet and amethyst—
Made lures with the lights of streaming stone
   In the clefts of the hills of Habersham,
   In the beds of the valleys of Hall.

   But oh, not the hills of Habersham,
   And oh, not the valleys of Hall
Avail: I am fain for to water the plain.
Downward the voices of Duty call—
Downward, to toil and be mixed with the main,
The dry fields burn, and the mills are to turn,
And a myriad flowers mortally yearn,
And the lordly main from beyond the plain
   Calls o'er the hills of Habersham,
   Calls through the valleys of Hall.

(1883)

The Marshes of Glynn

Glooms of the live-oaks, beautiful-braided and woven
With intricate shades of the vines that myriad-cloven
   Clamber the forks of the multiform boughs,—
      Emerald twilights,—
      Virginal shy lights,
Wrought of the leaves to allure to the whisper of vows,
When lovers pace timidly down through the green colonnades
Of the dim sweet woods, of the dear dark woods,
   Of the heavenly woods and glades,
That run to the radiant marginal sand-beach within
     The wide sea-marshes of Glynn;—

Beautiful glooms, soft dusks in the noon-day fire,—
Wildwood privacies, closets of lone desire,
Chamber from chamber parted with wavering arras of leaves,—
Cells for the passionate pleasure of prayer to the soul that grieves,
Pure with a sense of the passing of saints through the wood,
Cool for the dutiful weighing of ill with good;—

O braided dusks of the oak and woven shades of the vine,
While the riotous noon-day sun of the June-day long did shine
Ye held me fast in your heart and I held you fast in mine;
But now when the noon is no more, and riot is rest,
And the sun is a-wait at the ponderous gate of the West,
And the slant yellow beam down the wood-aisle doth seem
Like a lane into heaven that leads from a dream,—
Ay, now, when my soul all day hath drunken the soul of the oak,
And my heart is at ease from men, and the wearisome sound of the stroke

532

Of the scythe of time and the trowel of trade is low,
And belief overmasters doubt, and I know that I know,
And my spirit is grown to a lordly great compass within,
That the length and the breadth and the sweep of the marshes of Glynn
Will work me no fear like the fear they have wrought me of yore
When length was fatigue, and when breadth was but bitterness sore,
And when terror and shrinking and dreary unnamable pain
Drew over me out of the merciless miles of the plain,—

Oh, now, unafraid, I am fain to face
    The vast sweet visage of space.
To the edge of the wood I am drawn, I am drawn,
Where the gray beach glimmering runs, as a belt of the dawn,
    For a mete and a mark
      To the forest-dark:—
        So:
Affable live-oak, leaning low,—
Thus—with your favor—soft, with a reverent hand,
(Not lightly touching your person, Lord of the land!)
Bending your beauty aside, with a step I stand
On the firm-packed sand,
          Free
By a world of marsh that borders a world of sea.
    Sinuous southward and sinuous northward the shimmering band
    Of the sand-beach fastens the fringe of the marsh to the folds of the land.
Inward and outward to northward and southward the beach-lines linger and curl
As a silver-wrought garment that clings to and follows the firm sweet limbs of a
    girl.
Vanishing, swerving, evermore curving again into sight,
Softly the sand-beach wavers away to a dim gray looping of light.
And what if behind me to westward the wall of the woods stands high?
The world lies east: how ample, the marsh and the sea and the sky!
A league and a league of marsh-grass, waist-high, broad in the blade,
Green, and all of a height, and unflecked with a light or a shade,
Stretch leisurely off, in a pleasant plain,
To the terminal blue of the main.

Oh, what is abroad in the marsh and the terminal sea?
    Somehow my soul seems suddenly free
From the weighing of fate and the sad discussion of sin,
By the length and the breadth and the sweep of the marshes of Glynn.

Ye marshes, how candid and simple and nothing-withholding and free
Ye publish yourselves to the sky and offer yourselves to the sea!
Tolerant plains, that suffer the sea and the rains and the sun,
Ye spread and span like the catholic man who hath mightily won
God out of knowledge and good out of infinite pain
And sight out of blindness and purity out of a stain.

As the marsh-hen secretly builds on the watery sod,
Behold I will build me a nest on the greatness of God:
I will fly in the greatness of God as the marsh-hen flies
In the freedom that fills all the space 'twixt the marsh and the skies:
By so many roots as the marsh-grass sends in the sod
I will heartily lay me a-hold on the greatness of God:
Oh, like to the greatness of God is the greatness within
The range of the marshes, the liberal marshes of Glynn.

And the sea lends large, as the marsh: lo, out of his plenty the sea
Pours fast: full soon the time of the flood-tide must be:
Look how the grace of the sea doth go
About and about through the intricate channels that flow
      Here and there,
          Everywhere,
Till his waters have flooded the uttermost creeks and the low-lying lanes,
And the marsh is meshed with a million veins,
That like as with rosy and silvery essences flow
  In the rose-and-silver evening glow.
          Farewell, my lord Sun!
The creeks overflow: a thousand rivulets run
'Twixt the roots of the sod; the blades of the marsh-grass stir;
Passeth a hurrying sound of wings that westward whirr;
Passeth, and all is still; and the currents cease to run;
And the sea and the marsh are one.

How still the plains of the waters be!
The tide is in his ecstasy.
The tide is at his highest height:
      And it is night.
And now from the Vast of the Lord will the waters of sleep
Roll in on the souls of men,
But who will reveal to our waking ken
The forms that swim and the shapes that creep
      Under the waters of sleep?
And I would I could know what swimmeth below when the tide comes in
On the length and the breadth of the marvellous marshes of Glynn.

                                          (1878)

A Ballad of Trees and the Master

534

Into the woods my Master went,
Clean forspent, forspent.
Into the woods my Master came,
Forspent with love and shame.
But the olives they were not blind to Him,

The little gray leaves were kind to Him:
The thorn-tree had a mind to Him
When into the woods He came.

Out of the woods my Master went,
And He was well content.
Out of the woods my Master came,
Content with death and shame.
When Death and Shame would woo Him last,
From under the trees they drew Him last:
'Twas on a tree they slew Him—last
When out of the woods He came.

(*1880*)

Letters

To Robert S. Lanier

Oglethorpe University
April 26th 1857

Dear Father:

Mother's letter was received yesterday and was warmly welcomed as I had begun to think that you had all forgotten me. I intended answering it last night, but delayed writing, thinking that I might receive one from you to-day; not having received it I have concluded to waive formality and write again, as there is something, which if I do not tell you *quickly*, God knows, I fear it will break my heart. My Father, I have sinned! against your law of conduct which you laid down for my observance have I sinned! Yet without bad motive, without evil intent, without wrong feeling. But I shall not attempt to palliate my fault— although I might very plausibly. O, with what intensity of thoughts, with what deep and earnest reflection have I contemplated this, lately. But Father, bear with me, if possible while I tell you *all:* Often, last Term, when I would happen to be in need of some little affair, not having any money with me at the time, Willie, (who was my constant companion) would press it upon me, telling me that he did not need it, and that I could pay him back at any-time. Thus, (cheating myself with the delusive hope that I would be able to pay him out of my own pocket-money, without having to call on you for it) I often accepted it, until now I owe him about $15.00! It is with heart throbbing with the intensity of its anguish that I write you this, but Father, Mother said that you thought *I did not love you enough to place confidence in you,* and I MUST clear myself of *that*—therefore do I tell you all this, for I think that I *love you* and *Mother* with *all the filial affection that mortal ever possessed.* But I have not done yet. However, I believe this is not in violation of any of your rules. There is a *secret Literary* Society [1] here, an *old* and *time-honoured* one, existing with the high approval of the Faculty, composed only of the smartest members of the Senior and Junior Classes, (I am

535

[1] *The Thalian Literary Society.*

the only Soph. in it) which, in the middle of last Term elected me a member. This being told me by one of my most intimate friends, and he promising me upon his word of honor that there were no boys there, except those with whom I had been in the habit of associating, I joined;—and father, I assure you that *I have derived more benefit from that,* than any one of my Collegiate studies. We meet together in a nice room, read Compositions, declaim, and debate upon interesting subjects, being controlled by a strict Constitution and by-laws, which we have promised faithfully to observe upon our honor as gentlemen. This Society has concluded no longer to remain secret, and has sent on to have beautiful badges made for its members (we have twelve—it is limited to fifteen) and when these arrive we will all come out in them and thus it will be known. It was for *this (partly)* that I wrote to you for ten dollars: there are some other things which I need, such as Ink, writing-paper, a coat-brush, and a hair comb. I thought you understood why I did not mention these things as the bell for recitation was ringing and the Cars were whistling at the Depot, just as I finished the letter that far, and so I had to stop to get the letter on board in time to leave that day. The badge does not, by any means, cost near that amount, but as I wanted these other things I just wrote you for ten Dollars.

And now I have told you all. My Father, can you forgive me? If by hard study and good conduct I can in some measure atone for this, *God in Heaven knows* that I shall not be found wanting. This is what troubles me, Father. I know how hard you have to work to sustain the many burdens that are imposed upon you, and for me to be thus continually calling on you for money. O, Father you know not how *very much* it distresses me. I know you will be grieved at this: but if *you* are grieved at it, then what must be *my grief,* who am the cause of it all?

But I must close this letter. Father, please be certain and not breathe a word to any one about our Society as we are all pledged upon our honor not to divulge the existence of it, but I got permission to *tell you.* Give my love to all the folks at home, and rest assured that not a night passes but what the supplication, "God bless my Parents," ascends to the great mercy-seat, from the lips of their absent but loving son,

Sidney

Write soon.

To Walt Whitman

33 Denmead St., Baltimore, Md.
May 5th 1878

My dear Sir:

A short time ago while on a visit to New York I happened one evening to find your LEAVES OF GRASS in Mr. Bayard Taylor's library: and taking it with me to my room at the hotel I spent a night of glory and delight upon it. How it happened that I had never read this book before—is a story not worth the telling; but, in sending the enclosed bill to purchase a copy (which please mail to the above address) I cannot resist the temptation to tender you also my grateful thanks for such large and substantial thoughts uttered in a time when there are, as you say in another connection, so many "little plentiful mannikins skipping about in collars and tailed coats." [1] Although I entirely disagree with you in all points of your doctrine as is involved in those poetic exposures of the person which your pages so unreservedly make, yet I feel sure that I understand you therein, and my dissent in these particulars becomes a very insignificant consideration in the presence of that unbounded delight which I take in the bigness and bravery of all your ways and thoughts. It is not known to me where I can find another modern song at once so large and so naive: and the time needs to be told few things so much as the absolute personality of the person, the sufficiency of the man's manhood *to* the man, which you have propounded in such strong and beautiful rhythms. I beg you to count me among your most earnest lovers, and to believe that it would make me very happy to be of the least humble service to you at any time.

Sidney Lanier

To Robert S. Lanier

33 Denmead St. [Baltimore]
May 13th 1878

My dearest Father:

I am not quite so pushed for time this week, my lectures being now over for the season; and I am trying to rest my pen-arm a little, which has had a severe race of it for the last two months.

The Lecture-Committee of The Peabody Institute met last Friday and resolved to tender me their lecture-hall for the season of 1878–9. I am to deliver a series of lectures, extending from the 1st November to 1st April, two each week, under the auspices of the Peabody. Prest. Gilman (of Johns Hopkins University) has in the very kindest manner—and at a good deal of personal trouble—arranged to cooperate with me in such a manner as to make my course a very attractive one. During the second half-year of the series, when the progress of my lectures will have brought me to Shakespere, we are to have a sort of Shakesperean Revival: parallel with my own treatment of Shakespere. Prof. Childs of Harvard (who had been engaged by the Johns Hopkins University for a special course) will deliver a series of ten readings from Macbeth; Prof. Gildersleeve, (Greek prof. in Johns Hopkins) will give two lectures on the relation between the Greek drama and Shakespere's: Mr. Royce (Fellow of Johns Hopkins) will give two lectures on Shakespere in Germany: and two other gentlemen from Johns Hopkins will contribute lectures on their own specialties converging upon the same theme. We hope to wind up the whole with a beautiful spectacular exhibition representing an audience of Shakespere's times assembled on the stage while a play goes on.

It is proposed to sell a hundred subscription tickets to the whole course at twenty dollars each, and this is to be my remuneration.

It would thus seem that my next year's work is thus most delightfully mapped out. My lectures are to consist of ten introductory discourses on Literary Technic,

537

---

[1] *From Whitman's "Song of Myself."*

thirty on the less-known poetry of the Elizabeth Period, and ten on subjects connected with Shakespere—fifty in all. These are studies which I take such delight in pursuing that I can not well imagine a pleasanter prospect for my next season in Baltimore.

Meantime: it is necessary for me to devote the entire summer to the preparation of these lectures, and I am going to New York day after tomorrow for the purpose of making such fiscal arrangements as will enable me to do so. The carrying through of the whole project has been a matter of much work and thought, and the action of the Trustees is regarded as a great compliment to me.

This, together with my current lectures and the school, has kept me from realizing any avails with the magazines for three weeks past, and I am therefore at a small interregnum, just at present, in finances. I will need more than I have about me, when I start to New York, to leave some with Mary and for various household bills. If it should not arrive before day after tomorrow, I wish to draw on you for fifty dollars. Should you be without funds at the time the draft comes, please borrow from Mr. Plant for ten days,—in which time I will arrange to send it back to you if you *should* have to borrow.

I suppose you have seen my "Dove" in the May SCRIBNER's. I have not been able to get a copy of "Clover" for you.

We all send love to you and Mama. May is still a slave to the chills. The boys are well, and I continue in admirable condition. I hope the Court treats you well: but you have been so long and so uniformly successful that I am always expecting *some* temporary reverses.

Charley asks me to enclose these cards, which he has set up and printed with his own hands on his own printing-press. He wishes you to use them for visiting-cards. He has begun the business, and desires orders from any of your friends who wish cards printed in this style. His charge is eight cents a dozen. He will send you his business-card to put up in your office.

Your loving
S. L.

IRWIN RUSSELL

1853–1879

538

Irwin Russell was born on June 3, 1853, in Port Gibson, Mississippi. Shortly after his birth his parents moved to St. Louis, Missouri. Their sympathy for the Confederate cause brought them back to Port Gibson during the Civil War, but with the cessation of hostilities they returned to St. Louis, where they remained until young Russell graduated from St. Louis University in 1869. Russell seems to have been a brilliant, erratic youth. He could read at four and apparently enjoyed Milton at six. Seeking a life of adventure, he ran away a number of times, once to a sailor's boarding house in New Orleans and once to Texas. After graduating from college he studied law in Port Gibson and was admitted to the bar by special act of the Mississippi legislature, but his career as a lawyer was short and unsuccessful. Russell also tried his hand at writing poetry during this period, and the acceptance of a few of his poems by *Scribner's* encouraged him to seek a literary career in New York. He seemed to lack the inspiration for his Negro poetry in the North, however, and soon found himself without money or a job. In August 1879 he signed as a fireman on a steamship in order to work his way to New Orleans. Here he found a job as reporter for the *New Orleans Times*, but he died the following December, primarily of alcoholism.

Russell is generally regarded as the first Southern author to create a literary work in which the characters were all Negroes. Joel Chandler Harris says, in his introduction to the first edition of Russell's collected poems (1888), "Irwin Russell was among the first—if not the very first—of Southern writers to appreciate the literary possibilities of the negro character, and of the unique relations existing between the two races before the war, and was among the first to develop them. . . . The most wonderful thing about the dialect poetry of Irwin Russell is his accurate conception of the negro character. The dialect is not always the best,—it is often carelessly written,—but the negro is there, the old-fashioned, unadulterated negro, who is still dear to the Southern heart."

Christmas-Night in the Quarters

When merry Christmas-day is done,
And Christmas-night is just begun;
While clouds in slow procession drift,
To wish the moon-man "Christmas gift,"
Yet linger overhead, to know
What causes all the stir below;
At Uncle Johnny Booker's ball
The darkies hold high carnival.
From all the country-side they throng,
With laughter, shouts, and scraps of song,—
Their whole deportment plainly showing
That to the Frolic they are going.
Some take the path with shoes in hand,
To traverse muddy bottom-land;
Aristocrats their steeds bestride—
Four on a mule, behold them ride!
And ten great oxen draw apace
The wagon from "de oder place,"
With forty guests, whose conversation
Betokens glad anticipation.

539

Not so with him who drives: old Jim
Is sagely solemn, hard, and grim,
And frolics have no joys for him.
He seldom speaks but to condemn—
Or utter some wise apothegm—
Or else, some crabbed thought pursuing,
Talk to his team, as now he's doing:

Come up heah, Star! Yee-bawee!
　You alluz is a-laggin'—
Mus' be you think I's dead,
　An' dis de huss you's draggin'—
You's 'mos' too lazy to draw yo' bref,
　Let 'lone drawin' de waggin.

Dis team—quit bel'rin', sah!
　De ladies don't submit 'at—
Dis team—you ol' fool ox,
　You heah me tell you quit 'at?
Dis team's des like de 'Nited States;
　Dat's what I's tryin' to git at!

De people rides behin',
　De pollytishners haulin'—
Sh'u'd be a well-bruk ox,
　To foller dat ar callin'—
An' sometimes nuffin won't do dem steers,
　But what dey mus' be stallin'!

Woo bahgh! Buck-kannon! Yes, sah,
　Sometimes dey will be stickin';
An' den, fus thing dey knows,
　Dey takes a rale good lickin'.
De folks gits down: an' den watch out
　For hommerin' an' kickin'.

Dey blows upon dey hands,
　Den flings 'em wid de nails up,
Jumps up an' cracks dey heels,
　An' pruzently dey sails up,
An' makes dem oxen hump deysef,
　By twistin' all dey tails up!

_____

540

In this our age of printer's ink
'Tis books that show us how to think—
The rule reversed, and set at naught,
That held that books were born of thought.

We form our minds by pedants' rules,
And all we know is from the schools;
And when we work, or when we play,
We do it in an ordered way—
And Nature's self pronounce a ban on,
Whene'er she dares transgress a canon.
Untrammeled thus the simple race is
That "wuks the craps" on cotton places.
Original in act and thought,
Because unlearned and untaught.
Observe them at their Christmas party:
How unrestrained their mirth—how hearty!
How many things they say and do
That never would occur to you!
See Brudder Brown—whose saving grace
Would sanctify a quarter-race—
Out on the crowded floor advance,
To "beg a blessin' on dis dance."

————

O Mahsr! let dis gath'rin' fin' a blessin' in yo' sight!
Don't jedge us hard fur what we does—you knows it's Chrismus-night;
An' all de balunce ob de yeah we does as right's we kin.
Ef dancin's wrong, O Mahsr! let de time excuse de sin!

We labors in de vineya'd, wukin' hard an' wukin' true;
Now, shorely you won't notus, ef we eats a grape or two,
An' takes a leetle holiday,—a leetle restin'-spell,—
Bekase, nex' week, we'll start in fresh, an' labor twicet as well.

Remember, Mahsr,—min' dis, now,—de sinfulness ob sin
Is 'pendin' 'pon de sperret what we goes an' does it in:
An' in a righchis frame ob min' we's gwine to dance an' sing,
A-feelin' like King David, when he cut de pigeon-wing.

It seems to me—indeed it do—I mebbe mout be wrong—
That people raly *ought* to dance, when Chrismus comes along;
Des dance bekase dey's happy—like de birds hops in de trees,
De pine-top fiddle soundin' to de blowin' ob de breeze.

We has no ark to dance afore, like Isrul's prophet king;
We has no harp to soun' de cords, to holp us out to sing;
But 'cordin' to de gif's we has we does de bes' we knows,
An' folks don't 'spise de vi'let-flower bekase it ain't de rose.

You bless us, please, sah, eben ef we's doin' wrong to-night;
Kase den we'll need de blessin' more'n ef we's doin' right;

541

An' let de blessin' stay wid us, untel we comes to die,
An' goes to keep our Chrismus wid dem sheriffs in de sky!

Yes, tell dem preshis anguls we's a-gwine to jine 'em soon:
Our voices we's a-trainin' fur to sing de glory tune;
We's ready when you wants us, an' it ain't no matter when—
O Mahsr! call yo' chillen soon, an' take 'em home! Amen.

The rev'rend man is scarcely through,
When all the noise begins anew,
And with such force assaults the ears,
That through the din one hardly hears
Old fiddling Josey "sound his A,"
Correct the pitch, begin to play,
Stop, satisfied, then, with the bow,
Rap out the signal dancers know:

Git yo' pardners, fust kwattillion!
Stomp yo' feet, an' raise 'em high;
Tune is: "Oh! dat water-million!
Gwine to git to home bime-bye."
S'lute yo' pardners!—scrape perlitely—
Don't be bumpin' gin de res'—
Balance all!—now, step out rightly;
Alluz dance yo' lebbel bes'.
Fo'wa'd foah!—whoop up, niggers!
Back ag'in!—don't be so slow!—
Swing cornahs!—min' de figgers!
When I hollers, den yo' go.
Top ladies cross ober!
Hol' on, till I takes a dram—
Gemmen solo!—yes, *I's* sober—
Cain't say how de fiddle am.
Hands around!—hol' up yo' faces,
Don't be lookin' at yo' feet!
Swing yo' pardners to yo' places!
Dat's de way—dat's hard to beat.
Sides fo'w'd!—when you's ready—
Make a bow as low's you kin!
Swing acrost wid opp'site lady!
Now we'll let you swap ag'in:
Ladies change!—shet up dat talkin';
Do yo' talkin' arter while!
Right an' lef'!—don't want no walkin'—
Make yo' steps, an' show yo' style!

And so the "set" proceeds—its length
Determined by the dancers' strength;
And all agreed to yield the palm
For grace and skill to "Georgy Sam,"
Who stamps so hard, and leaps so high,
"Des watch him!" is the wond'ring cry—
"De nigger mus' be, for a fac',
Own cousin to a jumpin'-jack!"
On, on the restless fiddle sounds,
Still chorused by the curs and hounds;
Dance after dance succeeding fast,
Till supper is announced at last.
That scene—but why attempt to show it?
The most inventive modern poet,
In fine new words whose hope and trust is,
Could form no phrase to do it justice!
When supper ends—that is not soon—
The fiddle strikes the same old tune;
The dancers pound the floor again,
With all they have of might and main;
Old gossips, *almost* turning pale,
Attend Aunt Cassy's gruesome tale
Of conjurors, and ghosts, and devils,
That in the smoke-house hold their revels;
Each drowsy baby droops its head,
Yet scorns the very thought of bed:—
So wears the night, and wears so fast,
All wonder when they find it passed,
And hear the signal sound to go
From what few cocks are left to crow.
Then, one and all, you hear them shout:
"Hi! Booker! fotch de banjo out,
An' gib us *one* song 'fore we goes—
One ob de berry bes' you knows!"
Responding to the welcome call,
He takes the banjo from the wall,
And tunes the strings with skill and care,
Then strikes them with a master's air,
And tells, in melody and rhyme,
This legend of the olden time:

————————

Go 'way, fiddle! folks is tired o' hearin' you a-squawkin'.
Keep silence fur yo' betters!—don't you heah de banjo talkin'?
About de 'possum's tail she's gwine to lecter—ladies, listen!—
About de ha'r whut isn't dar, an' why de ha'r is missin':

543

"Dar's gwine to be a' oberflow," said Noah, lookin' solemn—
Fur Noah tuk the "Herald," an' he read de ribber column—
An' so he sot his hands to wuk a-cl'arin' timber-patches,
An' 'lowed he's gwine to build a boat to beat de steamah *Natchez*.

Ol' Noah kep' a-nailin' an' a-chippin' an' a-sawin';
An' all de wicked neighbors kep' a-laughin' an' a-pshawin';
But Noah didn't min' 'em, knowin' whut wuz gwine to happen:
An' forty days an' forty nights de rain it kep' a-drappin'.

Now, Noah had done cotched a lot ob ebry sort o' beas'es—
Ob all de shows a-trabbelin', it beat 'em all to pieces!
He had a Morgan colt an' sebral head o' Jarsey cattle—
An' druv 'em 'board de Ark as soon's he heered de thunder rattle.

Den sech anoder fall ob rain!—it come so awful hebby,
De ribber riz immejitly, an' busted troo de lebbee;
De people all wuz drownded out—'cep' Noah an' de critters,
An' men he'd hired to work de boat—an' one to mix de bitters.

De Ark she kep' a-sailin' an' a-sailin' *an'* a-sailin';
De lion got his dander up, an' like to bruk de palin';
De sarpints hissed; de painters yelled; tell, whut wid all de fussin',
You c'u'dn't hardly heah de mate a-bossin' 'roun' an' cussin'.

Now, Ham, de only nigger whut wuz runnin' on de packet,
Got lonesome in de barber-shop, an' c'u'dn't stan' de racket;
An' so, fur to amuse he-se'f, he steamed some wood an' bent it,
An' soon he had a banjo made—de fust dat wuz invented.

He wet de ledder, stretched it on; made bridge an' screws an' apron;
An' fitted in a proper neck—'twuz berry long an' tap'rin';
He tuk some tin, an' twisted him a thimble fur to ring it;
An' den de mighty question riz: how wuz he gwine to string it?

De 'possum had as fine a tail as dis dat I's a-singin';
De ha'r's so long an' thick an' strong,—des fit fur banjo-stringin';
Dat nigger shaved 'em off as short as wash-day-dinner graces;
An' sorted ob 'em by de size, f'om little E's to basses.

He strung her, tuned her, struck a jig,—'twuz "Nebber min' de wedder"—
She soun' like forty-lebben bands a-playin' all togedder;
Some went to pattin'; some to dancin': Noah called de figgers;
An' Ham he sot an' knocked de tune, de happiest ob niggers!

Now, sence dat time—it's mighty strange—dere's not de slightes' showin'
Ob any ha'r at all upon the 'possum's tail a-growin';

An' curi's, too, dat nigger's ways: his people nebber los' 'em—
For whar you finds de nigger—dar's de banjo an' de 'possum!

The night is spent; and as the day
Throws up the first faint flash of gray,
The guests pursue their homeward way;
And through the field beyond the gin,
Just as the stars are going in,
See Santa Claus departing—grieving—
His own dear Land of Cotton leaving.
His work is done; he fain would rest
Where people know and love him best.
He pauses, listens, looks about;
But go he must: his pass is out.
So, coughing down the rising tears,
He climbs the fence and disappears.
And thus observes a colored youth
(The common sentiment, in sooth):
"Oh! what a blessin' 'tw'u'd ha' been,
Ef Santa had been born a twin!
We'd hab two Chrismuses a yeah—
Or p'r'aps *one* brudder'd *settle* heah!"

(1888)

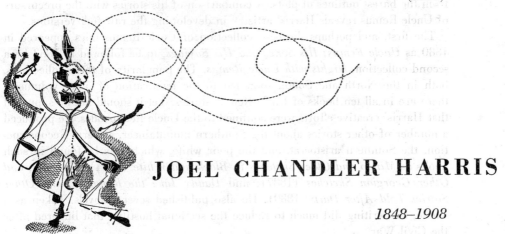

JOEL CHANDLER HARRIS

1848–1908

Joel Chandler Harris was born near Eatonton, Georgia, in December 1848. His mother, deserted by Joel's father (an Irish day-laborer with whom she had eloped), took in sewing to earn a living for herself and her son.

At thirteen, Harris went to "Turnwold" plantation to work as a printer for Joseph Addison Turner, editor of a weekly paper called *The Countryman*, which was possibly the only newspaper ever issued from a Southern plantation. Joel learned much at "Turnwold," both by working on the press and studying in Turner's large library. From Turner's slaves, particularly Old Harbert and Uncle

545

George Terrell, he continued to hear the Negro folk tales which had fascinated him in his early youth. As an author, Harris became even more dependent than his friend Mark Twain upon sources encountered in his childhood.

Following the Civil War, *The Countryman* was no longer published, for Turner was impoverished by the war and, furthermore, was unwilling to print a full paper unless he could freely express his rebel views. Harris, out of a job at "Turnwold," became a printer with the *Macon Telegraph*. In the course of the next few years he worked as private secretary to the editor of the *Crescent Monthly* in New Orleans, as editor of the *Monroe Advertiser* of Forsythe, Georgia, and as paragrapher for William Tappan Thompson's *Savannah Morning News*. He left Savannah in 1876, a refugee from the yellow fever epidemic, and took a position as an editorial paragrapher for the *Atlanta Constitution*. During the time that he was a member of the *Constitution's* staff, from 1876 until 1900, Harris helped Henry Grady to make that paper the most important outlet for the doctrines of the "New South." It was the *Constitution,* too, that first published his Uncle Remus stories. From 1907 until his death, in the following year, Harris was editor of *Uncle Remus's Magazine*.

In spite of his considerable accomplishments and the fame which he received, Harris was always extremely shy—so shy that in times of embarrassment he always stuttered. Once invited to lecture at Vanderbilt University, he replied, "I would not deliver a lecture in public for one million dollars." Harris always maintained that he was merely a transcriber of the Uncle Remus stories, but his critics and biographers have demonstrated that some of the tales were developed from the barest outlines of plots. A comparison of his stories with the precursors of Uncle Remus reveals Harris' artistry in developing the raw folk versions.

The first, and perhaps the best, collection of Uncle Remus tales appeared in 1880 as *Uncle Remus: His Songs and His Sayings,* to be followed in 1883 by a second collection, *Nights with Uncle Remus*. The popularity of these collections, both in the North and South, soon led to the publication of other volumes— there are in all ten books of Uncle Remus stories. Yet it should not be supposed that Harris' creative efforts were confined to the Uncle Remus tales. He produced a number of other stories about the Southern mountaineer, slavery, Reconstruction, the Southern aristocrat, and the poor white, which may be found in such books as *Mingo and Other Sketches in Black and White* (1884), *Free Joe, and Other Georgian Sketches* (1887), and *Daddy Jake the Runaway, and Other Stories Told After Dark* (1889). He also published several novels. Taken as a whole, his writing did much to reduce the sectional hostility that lingered after the Civil War.

Uncle Remus Initiates the Little Boy [1]

One evening recently, the lady whom Uncle Remus calls "Miss Sally" missed her little seven-year-old boy. Making search for him through the house and

---

[1] *"Uncle Remus Initiates the Little Boy," "The Wonderful Tar-Baby Story," "How Mr. Rabbit Saved His Meat,"* and *"Mr. Terrapin Shows His Strength"* appeared in the first collection of Uncle Remus tales, Uncle Remus: His Songs and His Sayings (*1880*).

through the yard, she heard the sound of voices in the old man's cabin, and, looking through the window, saw the child sitting by Uncle Remus. His head rested against the old man's arm, and he was gazing with an expression of the most intense interest into the rough, weather-beaten face, that beamed so kindly upon him. This is what "Miss Sally" heard:

"Bimeby, one day, arter Brer Fox bin doin' all dat he could fer ter ketch Brer Rabbit, en Brer Rabbit bin doin' all he could fer to keep 'im fum it, Brer Fox say to hisse'f dat he'd put up a game on Brer Rabbit, en he ain't mo'n got de wuds out'n his mouf twel Brer Rabbit come a lopin' up de big road, lookin' des ez plump, en ez fat, en ez sassy ez a Moggin hoss in a barley-patch.

" 'Hol' on dar, Brer Rabbit,' sez Brer Fox, sezee.

" 'I ain't got time, Brer Fox,' sez Brer Rabbit, sezee, sorter mendin' his licks.

" 'I wanter have some confab wid you, Brer Rabbit,' sez Brer Fox, sezee.

" 'All right, Brer Fox, but you better holler fum whar you stan'. I'm monstus full er fleas dis mawnin',' sez Brer Rabbit, sezee.

" 'I seed Brer B'ar yistiddy,' sez Brer Fox, 'en he sorter rake me over de coals kaze you en me ain't make frens en live naberly, en I told 'im dat I'd see you.'

"Den Brer Rabbit scratch one year wid his off hinefoot sorter jub'usly, en den he ups en sez, sezee:

" 'All a settin', Brer Fox. Spose'n you drap roun' ter-morrer en take dinner wid me. We ain't got no great doin's at our house, but I speck de old 'oman en de chilluns kin sorter scramble roun' en git up sump'n fer ter stay yo' stummuck.'

" 'I'm 'gree'ble, Brer Rabbit,' sez Brer Fox, sezee.

" 'Den I'll 'pen' on you,' sez Brer Rabbit, sezee.

"Nex' day, Mr. Rabbit an' Miss Rabbit got up soon, 'fo' day, en raided on a gyarden like Miss Sally's out dar, en got some cabbiges, en some roas'n years, en some sparrer-grass, en dey fix up a smashin' dinner. Bimeby one er de little Rabbits, playin' out in de backyard, come runnin' in hollerin', 'Oh, ma! oh, ma! I seed Mr. Fox a comin'!' En den Brer Rabbit he tuck de chilluns by der years en make um set down, en den him and Miss Rabbit sorter dally roun' waitin' for Brer Fox. En dey keep on waitin', but no Brer Fox ain't come. Atter 'while Brer Rabbit goes to de do', easy like, en peep out, en dar, stickin' fum behime de corn-der, wuz de tip-een' er Brer Fox tail. Den Brer Rabbit shot de do' en sot down, en put his paws behime his years en begin fer ter sing:

" 'De place wharbouts you spill de grease,
    Right dar youer boun' ter slide,
  An' whar you fine a bunch er ha'r,
    You'll sholy fine de hide.'

"Nex' day, Brer Fox sont word by Mr. Mink, en skuze hisse'f kaze he wuz too sick fer ter come, en he ax Brer Rabbit fer to come en take dinner wid him, en Brer Rabbit say he wuz 'gree'ble.

"Bimeby, w'en de shadders wuz at der shortes', Brer Rabbit he sorter brush up en santer down ter Brer Fox's house, en w'en he got dar, he hear somebody groanin', en he look in de do' en dar he see Brer Fox settin' up in a rockin' cheer all wrop up wid flannil, en he look mighty weak. Brer Rabbit look all 'roun', he

547

did, but he ain't see no dinner. De dish-pan wuz settin' on de table, en close by wuz a kyarvin' knife.

" 'Look like you gwineter have chicken fer dinner, Brer Fox,' sez Brer Rabbit, sezee.

" 'Yes, Brer Rabbit, deyer nice, en fresh, en tender,' sez Brer Fox, sezee.

"Den Brer Rabbit sorter pull his mustarsh, en say: 'You ain't got no calamus root, is you, Brer Fox? I done got so now dat I can't eat no chicken 'ceppin she's seasoned up wid calamus root.' En wid dat Brer Rabbit lipt out er de do' and dodge 'mong de bushes, en sot dar watchin' fer Brer Fox; en he ain't watch long, nudder, kaze Brer Fox flung off de flannil en crope out er de house en got whar he could cloze in on Brer Rabbit, en bimeby Brer Rabbit holler out: 'Oh, Brer Fox! I'll des put yo' calamus root out yer on dish yer stump. Better come git it while hit's fresh,' and wid dat Brer Rabbit gallop off home. En Brer Fox ain't never kotch 'im yit, en w'at's mo', honey, he ain't gwineter." (*1880*)

The Wonderful Tar-Baby Story

"Didn't the fox *never* catch the rabbit, Uncle Remus?" asked the little boy the next evening.

"He come mighty nigh it, honey, sho's you born—Brer Fox did. One day atter Brer Rabbit fool 'im wid dat calamus root, Brer Fox went ter wuk en got 'im some tar, en mix it wid some turkentime, en fix up a contrapshun wat he call a Tar-Baby, en he tuck dish yer Tar-Baby en he sot 'er in de big road, en den he lay off in de bushes fer to see what de news wuz gwineter be. En he didn't hatter wait long, nudder, kaze bimeby here comes Brer Rabbit pacin' down de road—lippity-clippity, clippity-lippity—dez ez sassy ez a jay-bird. Brer Fox, he lay low. Brer Rabbit come prancin' 'long twel he spy de Tar-Baby, en den he fotch up on his behime legs like he wuz 'stonished. De Tar-Baby, she sot dar, she did, en Brer Fox, he lay low.

" 'Mawnin'!' sez Brer Rabbit, sezee—'nice wedder dis mawnin',' sezee.

"Tar-Baby ain't sayin' nothin', en Brer Fox, he lay low.

" 'How duz yo' sym'tums seem ter segashuate?' sez Brer Rabbit, sezee.

"Brer Fox, he wink his eye slow, en lay low, en de Tar-Baby, she ain't sayin' nothin'.

" 'How you come on, den? Is you deaf?' sez Brer Rabbit, sezee. 'Kaze if you is, I kin holler louder,' sezee.

"Tar-Baby stay still, en Brer Fox, he lay low.

" 'Youer stuck up, dat's w'at you is,' says Brer Rabbit, sezee, 'en I'm gwineter kyore you, dat's w'at I'm a gwinter do,' sezee.

"Brer Fox, he sorter chuckle in his stummuck, he did, but Tar-Baby ain't sayin' nothin'.

" 'I'm gwineter larn you howter talk ter 'specttubble fokes ef hit's de las' ack,' sez Brer Rabbit, sezee. 'Ef you don't take off dat hat en tell me howdy, I'm gwineter bus' you wide open,' sezee.

"Tar-Baby stay still, en Brer Fox, he lay low.

"Brer Rabbit keep on axin' 'im, en de Tar-Baby, she keep on sayin' nothin', twel present'y Brer Rabbit draw back wid his fis', he did, en blip he tuck 'er side er de head. Right dar's whar he broke his merlasses jug. His fis' stuck, en he can't pull loose. De tar hilt 'im. But Tar-Baby, she stay still, en Brer Fox, he lay low.

" 'Ef you don't lemme loose, I'll knock you agin,' sez Brer Rabbit, sezee, en wid dat he fotch 'er a wipe wid de udder han', en dat stuck. Tar-Baby, she ain't sayin' nothin', en Brer Fox, he lay low.

" 'Tu'n me loose, fo' I kick de natal stuffin' outen you,' sez Brer Rabbit, sezee, but de Tar-Baby, she ain't sayin' nothin'. She des hilt on, en den Brer Rabbit lose de use er his feet in de same way. Brer Fox, he lay low. Den Brer Rabbit squall out dat ef de Tar-Baby don't tu'n 'im loose he butt 'er cranksided. En den he butted, en his head got stuck. Den Brer Fox, he sa'ntered fort', lookin' des ez innercent ez one er yo' mammy's mockin'-birds.

" 'Howdy, Brer Rabbit,' sez Brer Fox, sezee. 'You look sorter stuck up dis mawnin',' sezee, en den he rolled on de groun', en laughed en laughed twel he couldn't laugh no mo'. 'I speck you'll take dinner wid me dis time, Brer Rabbit. I done laid in some calamus root, en I ain't gwineter take no skuse,' sez Brer Fox, sezee."

Here Uncle Remus paused, and drew a two-pound yam out of the ashes.

"Did the fox eat the rabbit?" asked the little boy to whom the story had been told.

"Dat's all de fur de tale goes," replied the old man. "He mout, en den agin he moutent. Some say Jedge B'ar come 'long en loosed 'im—some say he didn't. I hear Miss Sally callin'. You better run 'long." (1880)

How Mr. Rabbit Saved His Meat

"One time," said Uncle Remus, whetting his knife slowly and thoughtfully on the palm of his hand, and gazing reflectively in the fire—"one time Brer Wolf—"

"Why, Uncle Remus!" the little boy broke in, "I thought you said the Rabbit scalded the Wolf to death a long time ago."

The old man was fairly caught and he knew it; but this made little difference to him. A frown gathered on his usually serene brow as he turned his gaze upon the child—a frown in which both scorn and indignation were visible. Then all at once he seemed to regain control of himself. The frown was chased away by a look of Christian resignation.

"Dar now! W'at I tell you?" he exclaimed as if addressing a witness concealed under the bed. "Ain't I done tole you so? Bless grashus! ef chilluns ain't gittin' so dey knows mo'n ole fokes, en dey'll spute longer you en spute longer you, ceppin der ma call um, w'ich I speck twon't be long 'fo' she will, en den I'll set yere by de chimbly-cornder en git some peace er mine. W'en ole Miss wuz livin'," continued the old man, still addressing some imaginary person, "hit 'uz mo'n enny her chilluns 'ud dast ter do ter come 'sputin' longer me, en Mars John'll tell you de same enny day you ax 'im."

"Well, Uncle Remus, you know you said the Rabbit poured hot water on the Wolf and killed him," said the little boy.

The old man pretended not to hear. He was engaged in searching among some scraps of leather under his chair, and kept on talking to the imaginary person. Finally, he found and drew forth a nicely plaited whip-thong with a red snapper all waxed and knotted.

"I wuz fixin' up a w'ip fer a little chap," he continued, with a sigh, "but, bless grashus! 'fo' I kin git 'er done, de little chap done grow'd up twel he know mo'n I duz."

The child's eyes filled with tears and his lips began to quiver, but he said nothing; whereupon Uncle Remus immediately melted.

"I 'clar' to goodness," he said, reaching out and taking the little boy tenderly by the hand, "ef you ain't de ve'y spit en image er ole Miss w'en I brung 'er de las' news er de war. Hit's des like skeerin' up a ghos' w'at you ain't fear'd un."

Then there was a pause, the old man patting the little child's hand caressingly.

"You ain't mad, is you, honey?" Uncle Remus asked finally, "kaze ef you is, I'm gwine out yere en butt my head 'gin de do' jam'."

But the little boy wasn't mad. Uncle Remus had conquered him and he had conquered Uncle Remus in pretty much the same way before. But it was some time before Uncle Remus would go on with the story. He had to be coaxed. At last, however, he settled himself back in the chair and began:

"Co'se, honey, hit mout er bin ole Brer Wolf, er hit mout er bin er n'er Brer Wolf; it mout er bin 'fo' he got kotch up wid, er it mout er bin atterwards. Ez de tale wer gun to me des dat away I gin it unter you. One time Brer Wolf wuz comin' 'long home fum a fishin' frolic. He s'anter 'long de road, he did, wid his string er fish 'cross his shoulder, wen fus news you know ole Miss Pa'tridge, she hop outer de bushes en flutter 'long right at Brer Wolf nose. Brer Wolf he say ter hisse'f dat ole Miss Pa'tridge tryin' fer ter toll 'im fum her nes', en wid dat he lay his fish down en put out inter de bushes whar ole Miss Pa'tridge come fum, en 'bout dat time Brer Rabbit, he happen 'long. Dar wuz de fishes, en dar wuz Brer Rabbit, en w'en dat de case w'at you speck a sorter innerpen'ent man like Brer Rabbit gwine do? I kin tell you dis, dat dem fishes ain't stay whar Brer Wolf put um at, en w'en Brer Wolf come back dey wuz gone.

"Brer Wolf, he sot down en scratch his head, he did, en study en study, en den hit sorter rush inter his mine dat Brer Rabbit bin 'long dar, en den Brer Wolf, he put out fer Brer Rabbit house, en w'en he git dar he hail 'im. Brer Rabbit, he dunno nuthin' 'tall 'bout no fishes. Brer Wolf he up'n say he bleedzd ter b'leeve Brer Rabbit got dem fishes. Brer Rabbit 'ny it up en down, but Brer Wolf stan' to it dat Brer Rabbit got dem fishes. Brer Rabbit, he say dat if Brer Wolf b'leeve he got de fishes, den he give Brer Wolf lief fer ter kill de bes' cow he got. Brer Wolf, he tuck Brer Rabbit at his word, en go off ter de pastur' en drive up de cattle en kill Brer Rabbit bes' cow.

"Brer Rabbit, he hate mighty bad fer ter lose his cow, but he lay his plans, en he tell his chilluns dat he gwineter have dat beef yit. Brer Wolf, he bin tuck up by de patter-rollers 'fo' now, en he mighty skeerd un um, en fus news you know, yer come Brer Rabbit hollerin' en tellin' Brer Wolf dat de patter-rollers comin'.

550

"'You run en hide, Brer Wolf,' sez Brer Rabbit, sezee, 'en I'll stay yer en take keer er de cow twel you gits back,' sezee.

"Soon's Brer Wolf hear talk er de patter-rollers, he scramble off inter de underbresh like he bin shot out'n a gun. En he want mo'n gone 'fo' Brer Rabbit, he whirl in en skunt de cow en salt de hide down, en den he tuck'n cut up de kyarkiss en stow it 'way in de smoke-'ouse, en den he tuck'n stick de een' er de cow-tail in de groun'. Atter he gone en done all dis, den Brer Rabbit he squall out fer Brer Wolf:

" 'Run yer, Brer Wolf! Run yer! Yo' cow gwine in de groun'! Run yer!'

"W'en ole Brer Wolf got dar, w'ich he come er scootin', dar wuz Brer Rabbit hol'in' on ter de cow-tail, fer ter keep it fum gwine in de groun'. Brer Wolf, he kotch holt, en dey 'gin a pull er two en up come de tail. Den Brer Rabbit, he wink his off eye en say, sezee:

" 'Dar! de tail done pull out en de cow gone,' sezee.

"But Brer Wolf he wer'n't de man fer ter give it up dat away, en he got 'im a spade, en a pick-axe, en a shovel, en he dig en dig fer dat cow twel diggin' wuz pas' all endu'unce, en ole Brer Rabbit he sot up dar in his front po'ch en smoke his seegyar. Eve'y time old Brer Wolf stuck de pick-axe in de clay, Brer Rabbit, he giggle ter his chilluns:

" 'He diggy, diggy, diggy, but no meat dar! He diggy, diggy, diggy, but no meat dar!'

"Kase all de time de cow wuz layin' pile up in his smoke-'ouse, en him en his chilluns wuz eatin' fried beef en inguns eve'y time dey mouf water.

"Now den, honey, you take dis yer w'ip," continued the old man, twining the leather thong around the little boy's neck, "en scamper up ter de big 'ouse en tell Miss Sally fer ter gin you some un it de nex' time she fine yo' tracks in de sugar-bairl." (*1880*)

Mr. Terrapin Shows His Strength

"Brer Tarrypin wuz de out'nes' man," said Uncle Remus, rubbing his hands together contemplatively, and chuckling to himself in a very significant manner; "he wuz de out'nes' man er de whole gang. He wuz dat."

The little boy sat perfectly quiet, betraying no impatience when Uncle Remus paused to hunt, first in one pocket and then in another, for enough crumbs of tobacco to replenish his pipe. Presently the old man proceeded:

"One night Miss Meadows en de gals dey gun a candy-pullin', en so many er de nabers come in 'sponse ter de invite dat dey hatter put de 'lasses in de wash pot in b'il'de fier in de yard. Brer B'ar, he hope [1] Miss Meadows bring de wood, Brer Fox, he men' de fier, Brer Wolf, he kep' de dogs off, Brer Rabbit, he grease de bottom er de plates fer ter keep de candy fum stickin', en Brer Tarrypin, he klum up in a cheer, en say he'd watch en see dat de 'lasses didn't bile over. Dey wuz all dere, en dey wern't cuttin' up no didos, nudder, kaze Miss Meadows, she done put her foot down, she did, en say dat w'en dey come ter her place dey hatter hang up a flag er truce at de front gate en 'bide by it.

"Well, den, w'iles dey wuz all a settin' dar en de 'lasses wuz a bilin' en a blubberin', dey got ter runnin' on talkin' mighty biggity. Brer Rabbit, he say he de swiffes'; but Brer Tarrypin, he rock 'long in de cheer en watch de 'lasses. Brer

551

---

[1] *Holp*; helped. (*Harris' note.*)

Fox, he say he de sharpes', but Brer Tarrypin he rock 'long. Brer Wolf, he say he de mos' suvvigus, but Brer Tarrypin, he rock en he rock 'long. Brer B'ar, he say he de mos' stronges', but Brer Tarrypin he rock, en he keep on rockin'. Bimeby he sorter shet one eye, en say, sezee:

" 'Hit look like 'periently dat de ole hardshell ain't nowhars 'longside er dis crowd, yit yer I is, en I'm de same man w'at show Brer Rabbit dat he ain't de swiffes'; en I'm de same man w'at kin show Brer B'ar dat he ain't de stronges',' sezee.

"Den dey all laff en holler, kaze it look like Brer B'ar mo' stronger dan a steer. Bimeby, Miss Meadows, she up'n ax, she did, how he gwine do it.

" 'Gimme a good strong rope,' sez Brer Tarrypin, sezee, 'en lemme git in er puddle er water, en den let Brer B'ar see ef he kin pull me out,' sezee.

"Den dey all laff g'in, en Brer B'ar, he ups en sez, sezee: 'We ain't got no rope,' sezee.

" 'No,' sez Brer Tarrypin, sezee, 'en needer is you got de strenk,' sezee, en den Brer Tarrypin, he rock en rock 'long, en watch de 'lasses a bilin' en a blubberin'.

"Atter w'ile Miss Meadows, she up en say, she did, dat she'd take'n loan de young men her bed-cord, en w'iles de candy wuz a coolin' in de plates, dey could all go ter de branch en see Brer Tarrypin kyar out his projick. Brer Tarrypin," continued Uncle Remus, in a tone at once confidential and argumentative, "wern't much bigger'n de pa'm er my han', en it look mighty funny fer ter year 'im braggin' 'bout how he kin out-pull Brer B'ar. But dey got de bed-cord atter w'ile, en den dey all put out ter de branch. W'en Brer Tarrypin fine de place he wanter, he tuck one een' er de bed-cord, en gun de yuther een' to Brer B'ar.

" 'Now den, ladies en gents,' sez Brer Tarrypin, sezee, 'you all go wid Brer B'ar up dar in de woods en I'll stay yer, en w'en you year me holler, den's de time fer Brer B'ar fer ter see ef he kin haul in de slack er de rope. You all take keer er dat ar een',' sezee, 'en I'll take keer er dish yer een',' sezee.

"Den dey all put out en lef' Brer Tarrypin at de branch, en w'en dey got good en gone, he dove down inter de water, he did, en tie de bed-cord hard en fas' ter wunner deze yer big clay-roots, en den he riz up en gin a whoop.

"Brer B'ar he wrop de bed-cord roun' his han', en wink at de gals, en wid dat he gin a big juk, but Brer Tarrypin ain't budge. Den he take bofe han's en gin a big pull, but, all de same, Brer Tarrypin ain't budge. Den he tu'n 'roun', he did, en put de rope cross his shoulders en try ter walk off wid Brer Tarrypin, but Brer Tarrypin look like he don't feel like walkin'. Den Brer Wolf he put in en hope Brer B'ar pull, but des like he didn't, en den dey all hope 'im, en, bless grashus! w'iles dey wuz all a pullin', Brer Tarrypin, he holler, en ax um w'y dey don't take up de slack. Den w'en Brer Tarrypin feel um quit pullin', he dove down, he did, en ontie de rope, en by de time dey got ter de branch, Brer Tarrypin, he wuz settin' in de aidge er de water des ez natchul ez de nex' un, en he up'n say, sezee:

" 'Dat las' pull er yone wuz a mighty stiff un, en a leetle mo'n you'd er had me,' sezee. 'Youer monstus stout, Brer B'ar,' sezee, 'en you pulls like a yoke er steers, but I sorter had de purchis on you,' sezee.

"Den Brer B'ar, bein's his mouf 'gun ter water atter de sweetnin', he up'n say he speck de candy's ripe, en off dey put atter it!' "

552

"It's a wonder," said the little boy, after a while, "that the rope didn't break."

"Break who?" exclaimed Uncle Remus, with a touch of indignation in his tone—"break who? In dem days, Miss Meadow's bed-cord would a hilt a mule."

This put an end to whatever doubts the child might have entertained. (*1880*)

Brother Rabbit and the Mosquitoes [1]

The next night Daddy Jack was still away when the little boy went to see Uncle Remus, and the child asked about him.

"Bless yo' soul, honey! don't ax me 'bout Brer Jack. He look lak he mighty ole en trimbly, but he mighty peart nigger, mon. He look lak he shufflin' 'long, but dat ole nigger gits over groun', sho'. Forty year ergo, maybe I mought er kep' up wid 'im, but I let you know Brer Jack is away 'head er me. He mos' sho'ly is."

"Why, he's older than you are, Uncle Remus!" the child exclaimed.

"Dat w'at I year tell. Seem lak hit mighty kuse, but sho' ez youer bawn Brer Jack is a heap mo' pearter nigger dan w'at ole Remus is. He little, yit he mighty hard. Dat's Brer Jack, up en down."

Uncle Remus paused and reflected a moment. Then he went on:

"Talkin' 'bout Brer Jack put me in min' 'bout a tale w'ich she sho'ly mus' er happen down dar in dat ar country war Brer Jack come fum, en it sorter ketch me in de neighborhoods er de 'stonishment 'kaze he aint done up'n tell it. I 'speck it done wuk loose fum Brer Jack 'membunce."

"What tale was that, Uncle Remus?"

"Seem lak dat one time w'en eve'ything en eve'ybody wuz runnin' 'long des lak dey bin had waggin grease 'pun um, ole Brer Wolf"—

The little boy laughed incredulously and Uncle Remus paused and frowned heavily.

"Why, Uncle Remus! how did Brother Wolf get away from Mammy-Bammy Big-Money?"

The old man's frown deepened and his voice was full of anger as he replied:

"Now, den, is I'm de tale, er is de tale me? Tell me dat! Is I'm de tale, er is de tale me? Well, den, ef I aint de tale en de tale aint me, den how come you wanter take'n rake me over de coals fer?"

"Well, Uncle Remus, you know what you said. You said that was the end of Brother Wolf."

"I bleedz ter 'spute dat," exclaimed Uncle Remus, with the air of one performing a painful duty; "I bleedz ter 'spute it. Dat w'at de tale say. Ole Remus is one nigger en de tale, hit's a n'er nigger. Yit I aint got no time fer ter set back yer en fetch out de oggyments."

Here the old man paused, closed his eyes, leaned back in his chair, and sighed. After a while he said, in a gentle tone:

"So den, Brer Wolf done dead, en yer I wuz runnin' on des same lak he wuz done 'live. Well! well! well!"

553

[1] *This story appeared in* Nights with Uncle Remus (*1883*).

Uncle Remus stole a glance at the little boy, and immediately relented.

"Yit," he went on, "ef I'm aint de tale en de tale aint me, hit aint skacely make no diffunce whe'er Brer Wolf dead er whe'er he's a high-primin' 'roun' bodder'n 'longer de yuther creeturs. Dead er no dead, dey wuz one time w'en Brer Wolf live in de swamp down dar in dat ar country whar Brer Jack come fum, en, mo'n dat, he had a mighty likely gal. Look lak all de yuther creeturs wuz atter 'er. Dey 'ud go down dar ter Brer Wolf house, dey would, en dey 'ud set up en court de gal, en 'joy deyse'f.

"Hit went on dis a-way twel atter w'ile de skeeters 'gun ter git monst'us bad. Brer Fox, he went flyin' 'roun' Miss Wolf, en he sot dar, he did, en run on wid 'er en fight skeeters des ez big ez life en twice-t ez natchul. Las' Brer Wolf, he tuck'n kotch Brer Fox slappin' en fightin' at de skeeters. Wid dat he tuck'n tuck Brer Fox by de off year en led 'im out ter de front gate, en w'en he git dar, he 'low, he did, dat no man w'at can't put up wid skeeters aint gwine ter come a-courtin' his gal.

"Den Brer Coon, he come flyin' 'roun' de gal, but he aint bin dar no time skacely 'fo' he 'gun ter knock at de skeeters; en no sooner is he done dis dan Brer Wolf show 'im de do'. Brer Mink, he come en try he han', yit he bleedz ter fight de skeeters, en Brer Wolf ax 'im out.

"Hit went on dis a-way twel bimeby all de creeturs bin flyin' 'roun' Brer Wolf's gal 'ceppin' it's ole Brer Rabbit, en w'en he year w'at kinder treatments de yuther creeturs bin ketchin' he 'low ter hisse'f dat he b'leeve in he soul he mus' go down ter Brer Wolf house en set de gal out one whet ef it's de las' ack.

"No sooner say, no sooner do. Off he put, en 'twa'n't long 'fo' he fine hisse'f knockin' at Brer Wolf front do'. Ole Sis Wolf, she tuck'n put down 'er knittin' en she up'n 'low, she did:

"'Who dat?'

"De gal, she 'uz stannin' up 'fo' de lookin'-glass sorter primpin', en she choke back a giggle, she did, en 'low:

"'Sh-h-h! My goodness, mammy! dat's Mr. Rabbit. I year de gals say he's a mighty prop-en-tickler [2] gentermun, en I des hope you aint gwine ter set dar en run on lak you mos' allers does w'en I got comp'ny 'bout how much soap-grease you done save up en how many kittens de ole cat got. I gits right 'shame' sometimes, dat I does!'"

The little boy looked astonished.

"Did she talk that way to her mamma?" he asked.

"*Shoo*, chile! 'Mungs' all de creeturs dey aint no mo' kuse creeturs dan de gals. Ole ez I is, ef I wuz ter start in dis minnit fer ter tell you how kuse de gals is, en de Lord wuz ter spar' me plum twel I git done, yo' head 'ud be gray, en Remus 'ud be des twice-t ez ole ez w'at he is right now."

"Well, what did her mamma say, Uncle Remus?"

"Ole Sis Wolf, she sot dar, she did, en settle 'er cap on 'er head, en snicker, en look at de gal lak she monst'us proud. De gal, she tuck'n shuck 'erse'f 'fo' de lookin'-glass a time er two, en den she tipt ter de do' en open' it little ways en peep out des lak she skeer'd some un gwine ter hit 'er a clip side de head. Dar stood ole Brer Rabbit lookin' des ez slick ez a race-hoss. De gal, she tuck'n laff, she did, en holler:

[2] *Proper and particular. (Harris' note.)*

" 'W'y law, maw! hit's Mr. Rabbit, en yer we bin 'fraid it 'uz some 'un w'at aint got no business 'roun' yer!'

"Ole Sis Wolf she look over 'er specks, en snicker, en den she up'n 'low:

" 'Well, don't keep 'im stannin' out dar all night. Ax 'im in, fer goodness sake.'

"Den de gal, she tuck'n drap 'er hankcher, en Brer Rabbit, he dipt down en grab it en pass it ter 'er wid a bow, en de gal say she much 'blige, 'kaze dat 'uz mo' den Mr. Fox 'ud er done, en den she ax Brer Rabbit how he come on, en Brer Rabbit 'low he right peart, en den he ax 'er wharbouts 'er daddy, en ole Sis Wolf 'low she go fine 'im.

" 'Twa'n't long 'fo' Brer Rabbit year Brer Wolf stompin' de mud off'n he foots in de back po'ch, en den bimeby in he come. Dey shuck han's, dey did, en Brer Rabbit say dat w'en he go callin' on he 'quaintunce, hit aint feel natchul 'ceppin' de man er de house settin' 'roun' some'rs.

" 'Ef he don't talk none,' sez Brer Rabbit, sezee, 'he kin des set up ag'in' de chimbly-jam en keep time by noddin'.'

"But ole Brer Wolf, he one er deze yer kinder mens w'at got de whimzies,[3] en he up'n 'low dat he don't let hisse'f git ter noddin' front er comp'ny. Dey run on dis a-way twel bimeby Brer Rabbit year de skeeters come zoonin' 'roun', en claimin' kin wid 'im."

The little boy laughed; but Uncle Remus was very serious.

"Co'se dey claim kin wid 'im. Dey claims kin wid folks yit, let 'lone Brer Rabbit. Manys en manys de time w'en I year um sailin' 'roun' en singin' out 'Cousin! Cousin!' en I let you know, honey, de skeeters is mighty close kin w'en dey gits ter be yo' cousin.

"Brer Rabbit, he year um zoonin'," the old man continued, "en he know he got ter do some mighty nice talkin', so he up'n ax fer drink er water. De gal, she tuck'n fotch it.

" 'Mighty nice water, Brer Wolf.' (*De skeeters dey zoon.*) [4]

" 'Some say it too full er wiggletails,[5] Brer Rabbit.' (*De skeeters, dey zoon en dey zoon.*)

" 'Mighty nice place you got, Brer Wolf.' (*Skeeters dey zoon.*)

" 'Some say it too low in de swamp, Brer Rabbit.' (*Skeeters dey zoon en dey zoon.*)

"Dey zoon so bad," said Uncle Remus, drawing a long breath, "dat Brer Rabbit 'gun ter git skeer'd, en w'en dat creetur git skeer'd, he min' wuk lak one er deze yer flutter-mills. Bimeby, he 'low:

" 'Went ter town t'er day, en dar I seed a sight w'at I never 'speckted ter see.'

" 'W'at dat, Brer Rabbit?'

" 'Spotted hoss, Brer Wolf.'

" '*No*, Brer Rabbit!'

" 'I mos' sho'ly seed 'im, Brer Wolf.'

"Brer Wolf, he scratch he head, en de gal she hilt up 'er han's en make great

555

---

[3] *In these latter days a man with the whimzies, or whimsies, is known simply as a crank.* (Harris' note.)

[4] *The information in parentheses is imparted in a low, impressive, confidential tone.* (Harris' note.)

[5] *Is it necessary to say that the wiggletail is the embryo mosquito?* (Harris' note.)

'miration 'bout de spotted hoss. (*De skeeters dey zoon, en dey keep on zoonin'.*) Brer Rabbit, he talk on, he did:

" ' 'Twa'n't des one spotted hoss, Brer Wolf, 't wuz a whole team er spotted hosses, en dey went gallin'-up [6] des lak yuther hosses,' sezee. 'Let 'lone dat, Brer Wolf, my grandaddy wuz spotted,' sez Brer Rabbit, sezee.

"Gal, she squeal en holler out:

" 'W'y, Brer Rabbit! aint you 'shame' yo'se'f fer ter be talkin' dat a-way, en 'bout yo' own-'lone blood kin too?'

" 'Hit's de naked trufe I'm a-ginin' [7] un you,' sez Brer Rabbit, sezee. (*Skeeter zoon en come closeter.*)

"Brer Wolf 'low 'Well—well—well!' Ole Sis Wolf, she 'low 'Tooby sho'ly, tooby sho'ly!' (*Skeeter zoon en come nigher en nigher.*) Brer Rabbit 'low:

" 'Yasser! Des ez sho' ez youer settin' dar, my grandaddy wuz spotted. Spotted all over. (*Skeeter come zoonin' up en light on Brer Rabbit jaw.*) He wuz dat. He had er great big spot right yer!' "

Here Uncle Remus raised his hand and struck himself a resounding slap on the side of the face where the mosquito was supposed to be, and continued:

"No sooner is he do dis dan ne'r skeeter come zoonin' 'roun' en light on Brer Rabbit leg. Brer Rabbit, he talk, en he talk:

" 'Po' ole grandaddy! I boun' he make you laff, he look so funny wid all dem spots en speckles. He had spot on de side er de head, whar I done show you, en den he had n'er big spot right yer on de leg,' sezee."

Uncle Remus slapped himself on the leg below the knee, and was apparently so serious about it that the little boy laughed loudly. The old man went on:

"Skeeter zoon en light 'twix' Brer Rabbit shoulder-blades. Den he talk:

" 'B'leeve me er not b'leeve me ef you min' to, but my grandaddy had a big black spot up yer on he back w'ich look lak saddle-mark.'

"Blip Brer Rabbit tuck hisse'f on de back!

"Skeeter sail 'roun' en zoon en light down yer beyan de hip-bone. He say he grandaddy got spot down dar.

"Blip he tuck hisse'f beyan de hip-bone.

"Hit keep on dis a-way," continued Uncle Remus, who had given vigorous illustrations of Brer Rabbit's method of killing mosquitoes while pretending to tell a story, "twel bimeby ole Brer Wolf en ole Sis Wolf dey lissen at Brer Rabbit twel dey 'gun ter nod, en den ole Brer Rabbit en de gal dey sot up dar en kill skeeters right erlong."

"Did he marry Brother Wolf's daughter?" asked the little boy.

"I year talk," replied Uncle Remus, "dat Brer Wolf sont Brer Rabbit wud nex' day dat he kin git de gal by gwine atter 'er, but I aint never year talk 'bout Brer Rabbit gwine. De day atterwuds wuz mighty long time, en by den Brer Rabbit moughter had some yuther projick on han'." [8] (*1883*)

556

[6] *Galloping. (Harris' note.)*
[7] *G hard as in give. (Harris' note.)*
[8] *This story, the funniest and most characteristic of all the negro legends, cannot be satisfactorily told on paper. It is full of action, and all the interest centres in the gestures and grimaces that must accompany an explanation of Brother Rabbit's method of disposing of the mosquitos. The story was first called to my attention by Mr. Marion Erwin, of Savannah, and it is properly a coast legend, but I have heard it told by three Middle Georgia negroes. (Harris' note.)*

Free Joe and the Rest of the World

The name of Free Joe strikes humorously upon the ear of memory. It is impossible to say why, for he was the humblest, the simplest, and the most serious of all God's living creatures, sadly lacking in all those elements that suggest the humorous. It is certain, moreover, that in 1850 the sober-minded citizens of the little Georgian village of Hillsborough were not inclined to take a humorous view of Free Joe, and neither his name nor his presence provoked a smile. He was a black atom, drifting hither and thither without an owner, blown about by all the winds of circumstances and given over to shiftlessness.

The problems of one generation are the paradoxes of a succeeding one, particularly if war, or some such incident, intervenes to clarify the atmosphere and strengthen the understanding. Thus, in 1850, Free Joe represented not only a problem of large concern, but, in the watchful eyes of Hillsborough, he was the embodiment of that vague and mysterious danger that seemed to be forever lurking on the outskirts of slavery, ready to sound a shrill and ghostly signal in the impenetrable swamps, and steal forth under the midnight stars to murder, rapine, and pillage,—a danger always threatening, and yet never assuming shape; intangible, and yet real; impossible, and yet not improbable. Across the serene and smiling front of safety, the pale outlines of the awful shadow of insurrection sometimes fell. With this invisible panorama as background, it was natural that the figure of Free Joe, simple and humble as it was, should assume undue proportions. Go where he would, do what he might, he could not escape the finger of observation and the kindling eye of suspicion. His lightest words were noted, his slightest actions marked.

Under all the circumstances it was natural that his peculiar condition should reflect itself in his habits and manners. The slaves laughed loudly day by day, but Free Joe rarely laughed. The slaves sang at their work and danced at their frolics, but no one ever heard Free Joe sing or saw him dance. There was something painfully plaintive and appealing in his attitude, something touching in his anxiety to please. He was of the friendliest nature, and seemed to be delighted when he could amuse the little children who had made a play-ground of the public square. At times he would please them by making his little dog Dan perform all sorts of curious tricks, or he would tell them quaint stories of the beasts of the field and birds of the air; and frequently he was coaxed into relating the story of his own freedom. The story was brief, but tragical.

In the year of our Lord 1840, when a negro-speculator of a sportive turn of mind reached the little village of Hillsborough on his way to the Mississippi region, with a caravan of likely negroes of both sexes, he found much to interest him. In that day and at that time there were a number of young men in the village who had not bound themselves over to repentance for the various misdeeds of the flesh. To these young men the negro-speculator (Major Frampton was his name) proceeded to address himself. He was a Virginian, he declared; and, to prove the statement, he referred all the festively inclined young men of Hillsborough to a barrel of peach-brandy in one of his covered wagons. In the minds of these young men there was less doubt in regard to the age and quality of the brandy than there was in regard to the negro-trader's birthplace. Major Framp-

557

ton might or might not have been born in the Old Dominion—that was a matter for consideration and inquiry—but there could be no question as to the mellow pungency of the peach-brandy.

In his own estimation, Major Frampton was one of the most accomplished of men. He had summered at the Virginia Springs; he had been to Philadelphia, to Washington, to Richmond, to Lynchburg, and to Charleston, and had accumulated a great deal of experience which he found useful. Hillsborough was hid in the woods of middle Georgia, and its general aspect of innocence impressed him. He looked on the young men who had shown their readiness to test his peach-brandy, as overgrown country boys who needed to be introduced to some of the arts and sciences he had at his command. Thereupon the Major pitched his tents, figuratively speaking, and became, for the time being, a part and parcel of the innocence that characterized Hillsborough. A wiser man would doubtless have made the same mistake.

The little village possessed advantages and seemed to be providentially arranged to fit the various enterprises that Major Frampton had in view. There was the auction-block in front of the stuccoed court-house, if he desired to dispose of a few of his negroes; there was a quarter-track, laid out to his hand and in excellent order, if he chose to enjoy the pleasures of horse-racing; there were secluded pine thickets within easy reach, if he desired to indulge in the exciting pastime of cock-fighting; and various lonely and unoccupied rooms in the second story of the tavern, if he cared to challenge the chances of dice or cards.

Major Frampton tried them all with varying luck, until he began his famous game of poker with Judge Alfred Wellington, a stately gentleman with a flowing white beard and mild blue eyes that gave him the appearance of a benevolent patriarch. The history of the game in which Major Frampton and Judge Alfred Wellington took part is something more than a tradition in Hillsborough, for there are still living three or four who sat around the table and watched its progress. It is said that at various stages of the game Major Frampton would destroy the cards with which they were playing, and send for a new pack, but the result was always the same. The mild blue eyes of Judge Wellington, with few exceptions, continued to overlook "hands" that were invincible—a habit they had acquired during a long and arduous course of training from Saratoga to New Orleans. Major Frampton lost his money, his horses, his wagons, and all his negroes but one, his body-servant. When his misfortune had reached this limit, the major adjourned the game. The sun was shining brightly, and all nature was cheerful. It is said that the major also seemed to be cheerful. However this may be, he visited the court-house and executed the papers that gave his body-servant his freedom. This being done, Major Frampton sauntered into a convenient pine thicket, and blew out his brains.

The negro thus freed came to be known as Free Joe. Compelled, under the law, to choose a guardian, he chose Judge Wellington, chiefly because his wife Lucinda was among the negroes won from Major Frampton. For several years Free Joe had what may be called a jovial time. His wife Lucinda was well provided for, and he found it a comparatively easy matter to provide for himself; so that, taking all the circumstances into consideration, it is not matter for astonishment that he became somewhat shiftless.

When Judge Wellington died, Free Joe's troubles began. The judge's negroes, including Lucinda, went to his half-brother, a man named Calderwood, who was a hard master and a rough customer generally—a man of many eccentricities of mind and character. His neighbors had a habit of alluding to him as "Old Spite"; and the name seemed to fit him so completely that he was known far and near as "Spite" Calderwood. He probably enjoyed the distinction the name gave him, at any rate he never resented it, and it was not often that he missed an opportunity to show that he deserved it. Calderwood's place was two or three miles from the village of Hillsborough, and Free Joe visited his wife twice a week, Wednesday and Saturday nights.

One Sunday morning he was sitting in front of Lucinda's cabin, when Calderwood happened to pass that way.

"Howdy, marster?" said Free Joe, taking off his hat.

"Who are you?" exclaimed Calderwood abruptly, halting and staring at the negro.

"I'm name' Joe, marster, I'm Lucindy's ole man."

"Who do you belong to?"

"Marse John Evans is my gyardeen, marster."

"Big name—gyardeen. Show your pass."

Free Joe produced the document, and Calderwood read it aloud slowly, as if he found it difficult to get at the meaning:

"To whom it may concern: This is to certify that the boy Joe Frampton has my permission to visit his wife Lucinda."

This was dated at Hillsborough, and signed *"John W. Evans."*

Calderwood read it twice, and then looked at Free Joe, elevating his eyebrows, and showing his discolored teeth.

"Some mighty big words in that there. Evans owns this place, I reckon. When's he comin' down to take hold?"

Free Joe fumbled with his hat. He was badly frightened.

"Lucindy say she speck you wouldn't min' my comin', long ez I behave, marster."

Calderwood tore the pass in pieces and flung it away.

"Don't want no free niggers 'round here," he exclaimed. "There's the big road. It'll carry you to town. Don't let me catch you here no more. Now, mind what I tell you."

Free Joe presented a shabby spectacle as he moved off with his little dog Dan slinking at his heels. It should be said in behalf of Dan, however, that his bristles were up, and that he looked back and growled. It may be that the dog had the advantage of insignificance, but it is difficult to conceive how a dog bold enough to raise his bristles under Calderwood's very eyes could be as insignificant as Free Joe. But both the negro and his little dog seemed to give a new and more dismal aspect to forlornness as they turned into the road and went towards Hillsborough.

After this incident Free Joe seemed to have clear ideas concerning his peculiar condition. He realized the fact that though he was free he was more helpless than any slave. Having no owner, every man was his master. He knew that he was the object of suspicion, and therefore all his slender resources (ah! how pitifully slender they were!) were devoted to winning, not kindness and appreciation, but toleration; all his efforts were in the direction of mitigating the

559

circumstances that tended to make his condition so much worse than that of the negroes around him—negroes who had friends because they had masters.

So far as his own race was concerned, Free Joe was an exile. If the slaves secretly envied him his freedom (which is to be doubted, considering his miserable condition), they openly despised him, and lost no opportunity to treat him with contumely. Perhaps this was in some measure the result of the attitude which Free Joe chose to maintain toward them. No doubt his instinct taught him that to hold himself aloof from the slaves would be to invite from the whites the toleration which he coveted, and without which even his miserable condition would be rendered more miserable still.

His greatest trouble was the fact that he was not allowed to visit his wife; but he soon found a way out of this difficulty. After he had been ordered away from the Calderwood place, he was in the habit of wandering as far in that direction as prudence would permit. Near the Calderwood place, but not on Calderwood's land, lived an old man named Micajah Staley and his sister Becky Staley. These people were old and very poor. Old Micajah had a palsied arm and hand; but, in spite of this, he managed to earn a precarious living with his turning-lathe.

When he was a slave Free Joe would have scorned these representatives of a class known as poor white trash, but now he found them sympathetic and helpful in various ways. From the back door of the cabin he could hear the Calderwood negroes singing at night, and he fancied he could distinguish Lucinda's shrill treble rising above the other voices. A large poplar grew in the woods some distance from the Staley cabin, and at the foot of this tree Free Joe would sit for hours with his face turned toward Calderwood's. His little dog Dan would curl up in the leaves near by, and the two seemed to be as comfortable as possible.

One Saturday afternoon Free Joe, sitting at the foot of this friendly poplar, fell asleep. How long he slept he could not tell; but when he awoke little Dan was licking his face, the moon was shining brightly, and Lucinda his wife stood before him laughing. The dog, seeing that Free Joe was asleep, had grown somewhat impatient, and he concluded to make an excursion to the Calderwood place on his own account. Lucinda was inclined to give the incident a twist in the direction of superstition.

"I'z settin' down front er de fireplace," she said, "cookin' me some meat, w'en all of a sudden I year sumpin at de do'—scratch, scratch. I tuck'n tu'n de meat over, en make out I aint year it. Bimeby it come dar 'gin—scratch, scratch. I up en open de do', I did, en, bless de Lord! dar wuz little Dan, en it look like ter me dat his ribs done grow tergeer. I gin 'im some bread, en den, w'en he start out, I tuck'n foller 'im, kaze I say ter myse'f, maybe my nigger man mought be some'rs 'roun'. Dat ar little dog got sense, mon."

Free Joe laughed and dropped his hand lightly on Dan's head. For a long time after that, he had no difficulty in seeing his wife. He had only to sit by the poplar tree until little Dan could run and fetch her. But after a while the other negroes discovered that Lucinda was meeting Free Joe in the woods, and information of the fact soon reached Calderwood's ears. He said nothing; but one day he put Lucinda in his buggy, and carried her to Macon, sixty miles away. He carried her to Macon, and came back without her; and nobody in or around Hillsborough, or in that section, ever saw her again.

560

For many a night after that Free Joe sat in the woods and waited. Little Dan would run merrily off and be gone a long time, but he always came back without Lucinda. This happened over and over again. The "willis-whistlers" would call and call, like phantom huntsmen wandering on a far-off shore; the screech-owl would shake and shiver in the depths of the woods; the night-hawks, sweeping by on noiseless wings, would snap their beaks as though they enjoyed the huge joke of which Free Joe and little Dan were the victims; and the whip-poor-wills would cry to each other through the gloom. Each night seemed to be lonelier than the preceding, but Free Joe's patience was proof against loneliness. There came a time, however, when little Dan refused to go after Lucinda. When Free Joe motioned him in the direction of the Calderwood place, he would simply move about uneasily and whine; then he would curl up in the leaves and make himself comfortable.

One night, instead of going to the poplar-tree to wait for Lucinda, Free Joe went to the Staley cabin, and, in order to make his welcome good, as he expressed it, he carried with him an armful of fat-pine splinters. Miss Becky Staley had a great reputation in those parts as a fortune-teller, and the school-girls, as well as older people, often tested her powers in that direction, some in jest and some in earnest. Free Joe placed his humble offering of light-wood in the chimney-corner, and then seated himself on the steps, dropping his hat on the ground outside.

"Miss Becky," he said presently, "whar in de name er gracious you reckon Lucindy is?"

"Well, the Lord he'p the nigger!" exclaimed Miss Becky, in a tone that seemed to reproduce, by some curious agreement of sight with sound, her general aspect of peakedness. "Well, the Lord he'p the nigger! haint you been a-seein' her all this blessed time? She's over at old Spite Calderwood's, if she's anywhere, I reckon."

"No'm, dat I aint, Miss Becky. I aint seen Lucindy in now gwine on mighty nigh a mont'."

"Well, it haint a-gwine to hurt you," said Miss Becky, somewhat sharply. "In my day an' time it wuz allers took to be a bad sign when niggers got to honeyin' 'roun' an' gwine on."

"Yessum," said Free Joe, cheerfully assenting to the proposition—"yessum, dat's so, but me an' my ole 'oman, we 'uz raise tergeer, en dey aint bin many days w'en we 'uz 'way fum one 'n'er like we is now."

"Maybe she's up an' took up wi' some un else," said Micajah Staley from the corner. "You know what the sayin' is, 'New master, new nigger.'"

"Dat's so, dat's de sayin', but taint wid my ole 'oman like 'tis wid yuther niggers. Me en her wuz des natally raise up tergeer. Dey's lots likelier niggers dan w'at I is," said Free Joe, viewing his shabbiness with a critical eye, "but I know Lucindy mos' good ez I does little Dan dar—dat I does."

There was no reply to this, and Free Joe continued—

"Miss Becky, I wish you please, ma'am, take en run yo' kyards en see sump'n n'er 'bout Lucindy; kaze ef she sick, I'm gwine dar. Dey ken take en take me up en gimme a stroppin', but I'm gwine dar."

Miss Becky got her cards, but first she picked up a cup, in the bottom of which were some coffee grounds. These she whirled slowly round and round, ending

561

finally by turning the cup upside down on the hearth and allowing it to remain in that position.

"I'll turn the cup first," said Miss Becky, "and then I'll run the cards and see what they say."

As she shuffled the cards the fire on the hearth burned slow, and in its fitful light the gray-haired, thin-featured woman seemed to deserve the weird reputation which rumor and gossip had given her. She shuffled the cards for some moments, gazing intently in the dying fire; then, throwing a piece of pine on the coals, she made three divisions of the pack, disposing them about in her lap. Then she took the first pile, ran the cards slowly through her fingers, and studied them carefully. To the first she added the second pile. The study of these was evidently not satisfactory. She said nothing, but frowned heavily; and the frown deepened as she added the rest of the cards until the entire fifty-two had passed in review before her. Though she frowned, she seemed to be deeply interested.

Without changing the relative position of the cards, she ran them over again. Then she threw a larger piece of pine on the fire, shuffled the cards afresh, divided them into three piles, and subjected them to the same careful and critical examination.

"I can't tell the day when I've seed the cards run this a-way," she said after a while. "What is an' what aint, I'll never tell you; but I know what the cards sez."

"W'at does dey say, Miss Becky?" the negro inquired, in a tone the solemnity of which was heightened by its eagerness.

"They er runnin' quare. These here that I'm a lookin' at," said Miss Becky, "they stan' for the past. Them there, they er the present; and the t'others, they er the future. Here's a bundle"—tapping the ace of clubs with her thumb—"an' here's a journey as plain as the nose on a man's face. Here's Lucinda"—

"Whar she, Miss Becky?"

"Here she is—the queen of spades."

Free Joe grinned. The idea seemed to please him immensely.

"Well, well, well!" he exclaimed. "Ef dat don't beat my time! De queen er spades! W'en Lucindy year dat hit'll tickle 'er, sho'!"

Miss Becky continued to run the cards back and forth through her fingers.

"Here's a bundle an' a journey, and here's Lucinda. An' here's ole Spite Calderwood."

She held the cards toward the negro and touched the king of clubs.

"De Lord he'p my soul!" exclaimed Free Joe with a chuckle. "De faver's dar. Yesser, dat's him! W'at de matter 'long wid all un um, Miss Becky?"

The old woman added the second pile of cards to the first, and then the third, still running them through her fingers slowly and critically. By this time the piece of pine in the fireplace had wrapped itself in a mantle of flame, illuminating the cabin and throwing into strange relief the figure of Miss Becky as she sat studying the cards. She frowned ominously at the cards and mumbled a few words to herself. Then she dropped her hands in her lap and gazed once more into the fire. Her shadow danced and capered on the wall and floor behind her, as if, looking over her shoulder into the future, it could behold a rare spectacle. After a while she picked up the cup that had been turned on the hearth. The coffee grounds, shaken around, presented what seemed to be a most intricate map.

"Here's the journey," said Miss Becky, presently; "here's the big road, here's rivers to cross, here's the bundle to tote." She paused and sighed. "They haint no names writ here, an' what it all means I'll never tell you. Cajy, I wish you'd be so good as to han' me my pipe."

"I haint no hand wi' the kyards," said Cajy, and he handed the pipe, "but I reckon I can patch out your misinformation, Becky, bekaze the other day, whiles I was a-fishin' up Mizzer Perdue's rolling-pin, I hearn a rattlin' in the road. I looked out, an' Spite Calderwood was a-drivin' by in his buggy, an' thar sot Lucinda by him. It'd in-about drapt out er my min'."

Free Joe sat on the door-sill and fumbled at his hat, flinging it from one hand to the other.

"You haint see um gwine back, is you, Marse Cajy?" he asked after a while.

"Ef they went back by this road," said Mr. Staley, with the air of one who is accustomed to weigh well his words, "it must 'a' bin endurin' of the time whiles I was asleep, bekaze I haint bin no furder from my shop than to yon bed."

"Well, sir!" exclaimed Free Joe in an awed tone, which Mr. Staley seemed to regard as a tribute to his extraordinary power of statement.

"Ef it's my beliefs you want," continued the old man, "I'll pitch 'em at you fair and free. My beliefs is that Spite Calderwood is gone an' took Lucindy outen the county. Bless your heart and soul! when Spite Calderwood meets the Old Boy in the road they'll be a turrible scuffle. You mark what I tell you."

Free Joe, still fumbling with his hat, rose and leaned against the door-facing. He seemed to be embarrassed. Presently he said:

"I speck I better be gittin' 'long. Nex' time I see Lucindy, I'm gwine tell 'er w'at Miss Becky say 'bout de queen er spades—dat I is. If dat don't tickle 'er, dey aint no nigger 'oman never bin tickle'."

He paused a moment, as though waiting for some remark or comment, some confirmation of misfortune, or, at the very least, some endorsement of his suggestion that Lucinda would be greatly pleased to know that she had figured as the queen of spades; but neither Miss Becky nor her brother said anything.

"One minnit ridin' in de buggy, 'longside er Mars Spite, en de nex' high-falutin' 'roun' playin' de queen er spades. Mon, deze yer nigger gals gittin' up in de pictur's; dey sholy is."

With a brief "Good-night, Miss Becky, Mars Cajy," Free Joe went out into the darkness, followed by little Dan. He made his way to the poplar, where Lucinda had been in the habit of meeting him, and sat down. He sat there a long time; he sat there until little Dan, growing restless, trotted off in the direction of the Calderwood place. Dozing against the poplar in the gray dawn of the morning, Free Joe heard Spite Calderwood's fox-hounds in full cry a mile away.

"Shoo!" he exclaimed, scratching his head, and laughing to himself, "dem ar dogs is des a-warmin' dat old fox up."

But it was Dan the hounds were after, and the little dog came back no more. Free Joe waited and waited, until he grew tired of waiting. He went back the next night and waited, and for many nights thereafter. His waiting was in vain, and yet he never regarded it as in vain. Careless and shabby as he was, Free Joe

563

was thoughtful enough to have his theory. He was convinced that little Dan had found Lucinda, and that some night when the moon was shining brightly through the trees, the dog would rouse him from his dreams as he sat sleeping at the foot of the poplar-tree, and he would open his eyes and behold Lucinda standing over him, laughing merrily as of old; and then he thought what fun they would have about the queen of spades.

How many long nights Free Joe waited at the foot of the poplar-tree for Lucinda and little Dan no one can ever know. He kept no account of them and they were not recorded by Micajah Staley or by Miss Becky. The season ran into summer and then into fall. One night he went to the Staley cabin, cut the two old people an armful of wood, and seated himself on the door-steps, where he rested. He was always thankful—and proud, as it seemed—when Miss Becky gave him a cup of coffee, which she was sometimes thoughtful enough to do. He was especially thankful on this particular night.

"You er still layin' off for to strike up wi' Lucindy out thar in the woods, I reckon," said Micajah Staley, smiling grimly. The situation was not without its humorous aspects.

"Oh, dey er comin', Mars Cajy, dey er comin', sho," Free Joe replied, "I boun' you dey'll come; en w'en dey does come, I'll des take en fetch um yer, whar you kin see um wid you own eyes, you en Miss Becky."

"No," said Mr. Staley, with a quick and emphatic gesture of disapproval. "Don't! don't fetch 'em anywheres. Stay right wi' 'em as long as may be."

Free Joe chuckled, and slipped away into the night, while the two old people sat gazing in the fire. Finally Micajah spoke:

"Look at that nigger; look at 'im. He's pine-blank as happy now as a kildee by a mill-race. You can't 'feze 'em. I'd in-about give up my t'other hand ef I could stan' flat-footed, an' grin at trouble like that there nigger."

"Niggers is niggers," said Miss Becky, smiling grimly, "an' you can't rub it out; yet I lay I've seed a heap of white people lots meaner'n Free Joe. He grins, —an' that's nigger,—but I've ketched his under jaw a-tremblin' when Lucindy's name uz brung up. An' I tell you," she went on bridling up a little, and speaking with almost fierce emphasis, "the Old Boy's done sharpened his claws for Spite Calderwood. You'll see it."

"Me, Rebecca?" said Mr. Staley, hugging his palsied arm; "me? I hope not."

"Well, you'll know it then," said Miss Becky, laughing heartily at her brother's look of alarm.

The next morning Micajah Staley had occasion to go into the woods after a piece of timber. He saw Free Joe sitting at the foot of the poplar, and the sight vexed him somewhat.

"Git up from there," he cried, "an 'go an' arn your livin'. A mighty purty pass it's come to, when great big buck niggers can lie a-snorin' in the woods all day, when t'other folks is got to be up an' a-gwine. Git up from there!"

Receiving no response, Mr. Staley went to Free Joe, and shook him by the shoulder; but the negro made no response. He was dead. His hat was off, his head was bent, and a smile was on his face. It was as if he had bowed and smiled when death stood before him, humble to the last. His clothes were ragged; his hands were rough and callous; his shoes were literally tied together with strings; he was shabby in the extreme. A passer-by, glancing at him, could have no idea that such a humble creature had been summoned as a witness before the Lord God of Hosts. (*1889*)

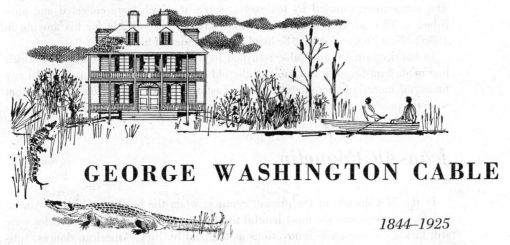

GEORGE WASHINGTON CABLE

1844–1925

George Washington Cable was born in New Orleans, Louisiana, the scene of his most popular stories and sketches. His father was never successful financially, and when he died in 1859, the family was left destitute, so that George, the oldest of several children, was forced to leave school and go to work. When war was declared two years later, he volunteered for service and distinguished himself in the Mississippi cavalry. After his return from the army, he held jobs as clerk, surveyor, and bookkeeper. In 1869, in order to earn some extra money, he began writing articles for the New Orleans *Picayune*. Cable's column of miscellany soon became so popular that it was made a daily feature, and its author was given full-time employment. His life as a reporter was very brief, however, for a few months later he was discharged, supposedly for refusing to report a theatrical performance which he considered indecent. His own version of the episode was, "I wanted to be always writing, and they wanted me to be always reporting. This didn't work well . . . and I went back to bookkeeping."

Cable was largely self-educated. There is a story that he studied his Latin, mathematics, and the Bible even while he was in the army. He taught himself French and began reading among the old city records, apparently with no intention of ever fashioning his investigation into fiction. Eventually, in reading the works of Dickens, Thackeray, Poe, Irving, Hugo, and Mérimée, he found a method for converting the materials of his research into imaginative stories. Thus, in much the same manner that Irving had used in exploiting New York history, Cable began to utilize the traditional legends of New Orleans.

Upon the suggestion of Edward King, *Scribner's Monthly* published one of Cable's Creole sketches, " 'Sieur George," in October 1873. Other stories appeared rather frequently in Eastern magazines for the next few years, and in 1879 seven of them were collected and issued as *Old Creole Days*. With the publication of *The Grandissimes* (1880) and *Madame Delphine* (1881) Cable's important creative writing was finished. For the next thirty years his work was

565

primarily that of the propagandist and social critic. He argued for the abolition of the convict-lease, for changes in the election laws, and for general prison reforms. He was most vehement in his protests against the injustices to the Negro. The antagonism aroused by his essays, some of which were collected and published as *The Silent South* (1885), was partially responsible for his moving in 1886 to New England, where he lived the remainder of his life.

In his declining years Cable returned to writing the romantic sketches which had made him famous, but most of the old charm and flavor had passed. In any final consideration, his literary fame must rest upon the Creole sketches that were the product of his early career.

Jean-Ah Poquelin

In the first decade of the present century, when the newly established American Government was the most hateful thing in Louisiana—when the Creoles were still kicking at such vile innovations as the trial by jury, American dances, anti-smuggling laws, and the printing of the Governor's proclamation in English—when the Anglo-American flood that was presently to burst in a crevasse of immigration upon the delta had thus far been felt only as slippery seepage which made the Creole tremble for his footing—there stood, a short distance above what is now Canal Street, and considerably back from the line of villas which fringed the river bank on Tchoupitoulas Road, an old colonial plantation-house half in ruin.

It stood aloof from civilization, the tracts that had once been its indigo fields given over to their first noxious wilderness, and grown up into one of the horridest marshes within a circuit of fifty miles.

The house was of heavy cypress, lifted up on pillars, grim, solid, and spiritless, its massive build a strong reminder of days still earlier, when every man had been his own peace officer and the insurrection of the blacks a daily contingency. Its dark, weather-beaten roof and sides were hoisted up above the jungly plain in a distracted way, like a gigantic ammunition-wagon stuck in the mud and abandoned by some retreating army. Around it was a dense growth of low water willows, with half a hundred sorts of thorny or fetid bushes, savage strangers alike to the "language of flowers" and to the botanist's Greek. They were hung with countless strands of discolored and prickly smilax, and the impassable mud below bristled with *chevaux de frise* of the dwarf palmetto. Two lone forest-trees, dead cypresses, stood in the centre of the marsh, dotted with roosting vultures. The shallow strips of water were hid by myriads of aquatic plants, under whose coarse and spiritless flowers, could one have seen it, was a harbor of reptiles, great and small, to make one shudder to the end of his days.

The house was on a slightly raised spot, the levee of a draining canal. The waters of this canal did not run; they crawled, and were full of big, ravening fish and alligators, that held it against all comers.

Such was the home of old Jean Marie Poquelin, once an opulent indigo planter, standing high in the esteem of his small, proud circle of exclusively male acquaintances in the old city; now a hermit, alike shunned by and shunning all

566

who had ever known him. "The last of his line," said the gossips. "His father lies under the floor of the St. Louis Cathedral, with the wife of his youth on one side, and the wife of his old age on the other. Old Jean visits the spot daily. His half-brother"—alas! there was a mystery; no one knew what had become of the gentle, young half-brother, more than thirty years his junior, whom once he seemed so fondly to love, but who, seven years ago, had disappeared suddenly, once for all, and left no clew of his fate.

They had seemed to live so happily in each other's love. No father, mother, wife to either, no kindred upon earth. The elder a bold, frank, impetuous, chivalric adventurer; the younger a gentle, studious, book-loving recluse; they lived upon the ancestral estate like mated birds, one always on the wing, the other always in the nest.

There was no trait in Jean Marie Poquelin, said the old gossips, for which he was so well known among his few friends as his apparent fondness for his "little brother." "Jacques said this," and "Jacques said that"; he "would leave this or that, or anything to Jacques," for "Jacques was a scholar," and "Jacques was good," or "wise," or "just," or "far-sighted," as the nature of the case required; and "he should ask Jacques as soon as he got home," since Jacques was never elsewhere to be seen.

It was between the roving character of the one brother, and the bookishness of the other, that the estate fell into decay. Jean Marie, generous gentleman, gambled the slaves away one by one, until none was left, man or woman, but one old African mute.

The indigo-fields and vats of Louisiana had been generally abandoned as unremunerative. Certain enterprising men had substituted the culture of sugar; but while the recluse was too apathetic to take so active a course, the other saw larger, and, at that time, equally respectable profits, first in smuggling, and later in the African slave-trade. What harm could he see in it? The whole people said it was vitally necessary, and to minister to a vital public necessity,—good enough certainly, and so he laid up many a doubloon, that made him none the worse in the public regard.

One day old Jean Marie was about to start upon a voyage that was to be longer, much longer, than any that he had yet made. Jacques had begged him hard for many days not to go, but he laughed him off, and finally said, kissing him:

"*Adieu, 'tit frère.*"

"No," said Jacques, "I shall go with you."

They left the old hulk of a house in the sole care of the African mute, and went away to the Guinea Coast together.

Two years after, old Poquelin came home without his vessel. He must have arrived at his house by night. No one saw him come. No one saw "his little brother"; rumor whispered that he, too, had returned, but he had never been seen again.

A dark suspicion fell upon the old slave-trader. No matter that the few kept the many reminded of the tenderness that had ever marked his bearing to the missing man. The many shook their heads. "You know he has a quick and fearful temper"; and "why does he cover his loss with mystery?" "Grief would out with the truth."

567

"But," said the charitable few, "look in his face; see that expression of true humanity." The many did look in his face, and, as he looked in theirs, he read the silent question: "Where is thy brother Abel?" The few were silenced, his former friends died off, and the name of Jean Marie Poquelin became a symbol of witchery, devilish crime, and hideous nursery fictions.

The man and his house were alike shunned. The snipe and duck hunters forsook the marsh, and the wood-cutters abandoned the canal. Sometimes the hardier boys who ventured out there snake-shooting heard a slow thumping of oar-locks on the canal. They would look at each other for a moment half in consternation, half in glee, then rush from their sport in wanton haste to assail with their gibes the unoffending, withered old man who, in rusty attire, sat in the stern of a skiff, rowed homeward by his white-headed African mute.

"O, Jean-ah Poquelin! O Jean-ah! Jean-ah Poquelin!"

It was not necessary to utter more than that. No hint of wickedness, deformity, or any physical or moral demerit; merely the name and the tone of mockery: "Oh Jean-ah Poquelin!" and while they tumbled one over another in their needless haste to fly, he would rise carefully from his seat, while the aged mute, with downcast face, went on rowing, and rolling up his brown fist and extending it toward the urchins, would pour forth such an unholy broadside of French imprecation and invective as would all but craze them with delight.

Among both blacks and whites the house was the object of a thousand superstitions. Every midnight, they affirmed, the *feu follet* [1] came out of the marsh and ran in and out of the rooms, flashing from window to window. The story of some lads, whose words in ordinary statements were worthless, was generally credited, that the night they camped in the woods, rather than pass the place after dark, they saw, about sunset, every window blood-red, and on each of the four chimneys an owl sitting, which turned his head three times round, and moaned and laughed with a human voice. There was a bottomless well, everybody professed to know, beneath the sill of the big front door under the rotten veranda; whoever set his foot upon that threshold disappeared forever in the depth below.

What wonder the marsh grew as wild as Africa! Take all the Faubourg Ste. Marie, and half the ancient city, you would not find one graceless dare-devil reckless enough to pass within a hundred yards of the house after nightfall.

The alien races pouring into old New Orleans began to find the few streets named for the Bourbon princes too strait for them. The wheel of fortune, beginning to whirl, threw them off beyond the ancient corporation lines, and sowed civilization and even trade upon the lands of the Graviers and Girods. Fields became roads, roads streets. Everywhere the leveller was peering through his glass, rodsmen were whacking their way through willow-brakes and rose-hedges, and the sweating Irishmen tossed the blue clay up with their long-handled shovels.

"Ha! that is all very well," quoth the Jean-Baptistes, feeling the reproach of an enterprise that asked neither co-operation nor advice of them, "but wait till they come yonder to Jean Poquelin's marsh; ha! ha! ha!" The supposed predicament so delighted them, that they put on a mock terror and whirled about in an assumed stampede, then caught their clasped hands between their knees in excess of mirth, and laughed till the tears ran; for whether the street-makers

568

[1] *will-of-the-wisp.*

mired in the marsh, or contrived to cut through old "Jean-ah's" property, either event would be joyful. Meantime a line of tiny rods, with bits of white paper in their split tops, gradually extended its way straight through the haunted ground, and across the canal diagonally.

"We shall fill that ditch," said the men in mud boots, and brushed close along the chained and padlocked gate of the haunted mansion. Ah, Jean-ah Poquelin, those were not Creole boys, to be stampeded with a little hard swearing.

He went to the Governor. That official scanned the odd figure with no slight interest. Jean Poquelin was of short, broad frame, with a bronzed leonine face. His brow was ample and deeply furrowed. His eye, large and black, was bold and open like that of a war-horse, and his jaws shut together with the firmness of iron. He was dressed in a suit of Attakapas cottonade, and his shirt, unbuttoned and thrown back from the throat and bosom, sailor-wise, showed a herculean breast, hard and grizzled. There was no fierceness or defiance in his look, no harsh ungentleness, no symptom of his unlawful life or violent temper; but rather a peaceful and peaceable fearlessness. Across the whole face, not marked in one or another feature, but as it were laid softly upon the countenance like an almost imperceptible veil, was the imprint of some great grief. A careless eye might easily overlook it, but, once seen, there it hung—faint, but unmistakable.

The Governor bowed.

"*Parlez-vous français?*" asked the figure.

"I would rather talk English, if you can do so," said the Governor.

"My name, Jean Poquelin."

"How can I serve you, Mr. Poquelin?"

"My 'ouse is yond'; *dans le marais là-bas.*" [2]

The Governor bowed.

"Dat *marais* billong to me."

"Yes, sir."

"To me; Jean Poquelin; I hown 'im meself."

"Well, sir?"

"He don't billong to you; I get him from me father."

"That is perfectly true, Mr. Poquelin, as far as I am aware."

"You want to make strit pass yond'?"

"I do not know, sir; it is quite probable; but the city will indemnify you for any loss you may suffer—you will get paid, you understand."

"Strit can't pass dare."

"You will have to see the municipal authorities about that, Mr. Poquelin."

A bitter smile came upon the old man's face:

"*Pardon, Monsieur,* you is not *le Gouverneur?*"

"Yes."

"*Mais,* yes. You har *le Gouverneur*—yes. Veh-well. I come to you. I tell you, strit can't pass at me 'ouse."

"But you will have to see"—

"I come to you. You is *le Gouverneur.* I know not the new laws. I ham a Fr-r-rench-a-man! Fr-rench-a-man have something *aller au contraire* [3]—he come

569

---

[2] *In the swamp over there.*
[3] *To complain about.*

at his *Gouverneur*. I come at you. If me not had been bought from me king like *bossals* [4] in the hold time, ze king gof—France would-a-show *Monsieur le Gouverneur* to take care his men to make strit in right places. *Mais*, I know; we billong to *Monsieur le Président*. I want you to do somesin for me, eh?"

"What is it?" asked the patient Governor.

"I want you to tell *Monsieur le Président*, strit—can't—pass—at—me—'ouse."

"Have a chair, Mr. Poquelin"; but the old man did not stir. The Governor took a quill and wrote a line to a city official, introducing Mr. Poquelin, and asking for him every possible courtesy. He handed it to him, instructing him where to present it.

"Mr. Poquelin," he said with a conciliatory smile, "tell me, is it your house that our Creole citizens tell such odd stories about?"

The old man glared sternly upon the speaker, and with immovable features said:

"You don't see me trade some Guinea nigga'?"

"Oh, no."

"You don't see me make some smugglin'?"

"No, sir; not at all."

"But, I am Jean Marie Poquelin. I mine me hown bizniss. Dat all right? Adieu."

He put his hat on and withdrew. By and by he stood, letter in hand, before the person to whom it was addressed. This person employed an interpreter.

"He says," said the interpreter to the officer, "he come to make you the fair warning how you muz not make the street pas' at his 'ouse."

The officer remarked that "such impudence was refreshing"; but the experienced interpreter translated freely.

"He says: 'Why you don't want?'" said the interpreter.

The old slave-trader answered at some length.

"He says," said the interpreter, again turning to the officer, "the marass is a too unhealth' for peopl' to live."

"But we expect to drain his old marsh; it's not going to be a marsh."

"*Il dit*"—The interpreter explained in French.

The old man answered tersely.

"He says the canal is a private," said the interpreter.

"Oh! *that* old ditch; that's to be filled up. Tell the old man we're going to fix him up nicely."

Translation being duly made, the man in power was amused to see a thundercloud gathering on the old man's face.

"Tell him," he added, "by the time we finish, there'll not be a ghost left in his shanty."

The interpreter began to translate, but—

"*J' comprends, J' comprends*," [5] said the old man, with an impatient gesture, and burst forth, pouring curses upon the United States, the President, the Territory of Orleans, Congress, the Governor and all his subordinates, striding out of the apartment as he cursed, while the object of his maledictions roared with merriment and rammed the floor with his foot.

570

[4] *Slaves or vassals.*
[5] *I understand.*

"Why, it will make his old place worth ten dollars to one," said the official to the interpreter.

" 'Tis not for de worse of de property," said the interpreter.

"I should guess not," said the other, whittling his chair,—"seems to me as if some of these old Creoles would liever live in a crawfish hole than to have a neighbor."

"You know what make old Jean Poquelin make like that? I will tell you. You know"—

The interpreter was rolling a cigarette, and paused to light his tinder; then, as the smoke poured in a thick double stream from his nostrils, he said, in a solemn whisper:

"He is a witch."

"Ho, ho, ho!" laughed the other.

"You don't believe it? What you want to bet?" cried the interpreter, jerking himself half up and thrusting out one arm while he bared it of its coat-sleeve with the hand of the other. "What you want to bet?"

"How do you know?" asked the official.

"Dass what I goin' to tell you. You know, one evening I was shooting some *grosbec*. I killed three; but I had trouble to fine them, it was becoming so dark. When I have them I star' to come home; then I got to pas' at Jean Poquelin's house."

"Ho, ho, ho!" laughed the other, throwing his leg over the arm of his chair.

"Wait," said the interpreter. "I come along slow, not making some noises; still, still"—

"And scared," said the smiling one.

"*Mais*, wait. I get all pas' the 'ouse. 'Ah!' I say; 'all right!' Then I see two thing' before! Hah! I get as cold and humide, and shake like a leaf. You think it was nothing? There I see, so plain as can be (though it was making nearly dark), I see Jean—Marie—Po-que-lin walkin' right in front, and right there beside of him was something like a man—but not a man—white like paint!—I dropp' on the grass from scared—they pass'; so sure as I live 'twas the ghos' of Jacques Poquelin, his brother!"

"Pooh!" said the listener.

"I'll put my han' in the fire," said the interpreter.

"But did you never think," asked the other, "that that might be Jack Poquelin, as you call him, alive and well, and for some cause hid away by his brother?"

"But there har' no cause!" said the other, and the entrance of third parties changed the subject.

Some months passed and the street was opened. A canal was first dug through the marsh, the small one which passed so close to Jean Poquelin's house was filled, and the street, or rather a sunny road, just touched a corner of the old mansion's dooryard. The morass ran dry. Its venomous denizens slipped away through the bulrushes; the cattle roaming freely upon its hardened surface trampled the superabundant undergrowth. The bellowing frogs croaked to westward. Lilies and the flower-de-luce sprang up in the place of reeds; smilax and poison-oak gave way to the purple-plumed iron-weed and pink spiderwort; the bindweeds ran everywhere blooming as they ran, and on one of the dead cypresses a giant creeper hung its green burden of foliage and lifted its scarlet

571

trumpets. Sparrows and red-birds flitted through the bushes, and dewberries grew ripe beneath. Over all these came a sweet, dry smell of salubrity which the place had not known since the sediments of the Mississippi first lifted it from the sea.

But its owner did not build. Over the willow-brakes, and down the vista of the open street, bright new houses, some singly, some by ranks, were prying in upon the old man's privacy. They even settled down toward his southern side. First a wood-cutter's hut or two, then a market gardener's shanty, then a painted cottage, and all at once the faubourg had flanked and half surrounded him and his dried-up marsh.

Ah! then the common people began to hate him. "The old tyrant!" "You don't mean an old *tyrant?*" "Well, then, why don't he build when the public need demands it? What does he live in that unneighborly way for?" "The old pirate!" "The old kidnapper!" How easily even the most ultra Louisianians put on the imported virtues of the North when they could be brought to bear against the hermit. "There he goes, with the boys after him! Ah! ha! ha! Jean-ah Poquelin! Ah! Jean-ah! Aha! aha! Jean-ah Marie! Jean-ah Poquelin! The old villain!" How merrily the swarming Américains echo the spirit of persecution! "The old fraud," they say—"pretends to live in a haunted house, does he? We'll tar and feather him some day. Guess we can fix him."

He cannot be rowed home along the old canal now; he walks. He has broken sadly of late, and the street urchins are ever at his heels. It is like the days when they cried: "Go up, thou bald-head," and the old man now and then turns and delivers ineffectual curses.

To the Creoles—to the incoming lower class of superstitious Germans, Irish, Sicilians, and others—he became an omen and embodiment of public and private ill-fortune. Upon him all the vagaries of their superstitions gathered and grew. If a house caught fire, it was imputed to his machinations. Did a woman go off in a fit, he had bewitched her. Did a child stray off for an hour, the mother shivered with the apprehension that Jean Poquelin had offered him to strange gods. The house was the subject of every bad boy's invention who loved to contrive ghostly lies. "As long as that house stands we shall have bad luck. Do you not see our peas and beans dying, our cabbages and lettuce going to seed and our gardens turning to dust, while every day you can see it raining in the woods? The rain will never pass old Poquelin's house. He keeps a fetich. He has conjured the whole Faubourg St. Marie. And why, the old wretch? Simply because our playful and innocent children call after him as he passes."

A "Building and Improvement Company," which had not yet got its charter, "but was going to," and which had not, indeed, any tangible capital yet, but "was going to have some," joined the "Jean-ah Poquelin" war. The haunted property would be such a capital site for a market-house! They sent a deputation to the old mansion to ask its occupant to sell. The deputation never got beyond the chained gate and a very barren interview with the African mute. The President of the Board was then empowered (for he had studied French in Pennsylvania and was considered qualified) to call and persuade M. Poquelin to subscribe to the company's stock; but—

"Fact is, gentlemen," he said at the next meeting, "it would take us at least twelve months to make Mr. Pokaleen understand the rather original features of our system, and he wouldn't subscribe when we'd done; besides, the only way to see him is to stop him on the street."

There was a great laugh from the Board; they couldn't help it. "Better meet a bear robbed of her whelps," said one.

"You're mistaken as to that," said the President. "I did meet him, and stopped him, and found him quite polite. But I could get no satisfaction from him; the fellow wouldn't talk in French, and when I spoke in English he hoisted his old shoulders up, and gave the same answer to everything I said."

"And that was—?" asked one or two, impatient of the cause.

"That it 'don't worse w'ile.' "

One of the Board said: "Mr. President, this market-house project, as I take it, is not altogether a selfish one; the community is to be benefited by it. We may feel that we are working in the public interest [the Board smiled knowingly], if we employ all possible means to oust this old nuisance from among us. You may know that at the time the street was cut through, this old Poquelann did all he could to prevent it. It was owing to a certain connection which I had with that affair that I heard a ghost story [smiles, followed by a sudden dignified check]—ghost story, which, of course, I am not going to relate; but I *may* say that my profound conviction, arising from a prolonged study of that story, is, that this old villain, John Poquelann, has his brother locked up in that old house. Now, if this is so, and we can fix it on him, I merely *suggest* that we can make the matter highly useful. I din't know," he added, beginning to sit down, "but that it is an action we owe to the community—hem!"

"How do you propose to handle the subject?" asked the President.

"I was thinking," said the speaker, "that, as a Board of Directors, it would be unadvisable for us to authorize any action involving trespass; but if you, for instance, Mr. President, should, as it were, for mere curiosity, *request* some one, as, for instance, our excellent Secretary, simply as a personal favor, to look into the matter—this is merely a suggestion."

The Secretary smiled sufficiently to be understood that, while he certainly did not consider such preposterous service a part of his duties as secretary, he might, notwithstanding, accede to the President's request; and the Board adjourned.

Little White, as the Secretary was called, was a mild, kindhearted little man, who, nevertheless, had no fear of anything, unless it was the fear of being unkind.

"I tell you frankly," he privately said to the President, "I go into this purely for reasons of my own."

The next day, a little after nightfall, one might have descried this little man slipping along the rear fence of the Poquelin place, preparatory to vaulting over into the rank, grass-grown yard, and bearing himself altogether more after the manner of a collector of rare chickens than according to the usage of secretaries.

The picture presented to his eye was not calculated to enliven his mind. The old mansion stood out against the western sky, black and silent. One long, lurid pencil-stroke along a sky of slate was all that was left of daylight. No sign of life was apparent; no light at any window, unless it might have been on the side of the house hidden from view. No owls were on the chimneys, no dogs were in the yard.

573

He entered the place, and ventured up behind a small cabin which stood apart from the house. Through one of its many crannies he easily detected the African mute crouched before a flickering pine-knot, his head on his knees, fast asleep.

He concluded to enter the mansion, and, with that view, stood and scanned it. The broad rear steps of the veranda would not serve him; he might meet some one midway. He was measuring, with his eye, the proportions of one of the pillars which supported it, and estimating the practicability of climbing it, when he heard a footstep. Some one dragged a chair out toward the railing, then seemed to change his mind and began to pace the veranda, his footfalls resounding on the dry boards with singular loudness. Little White drew a step backward, got the figure between himself and the sky, and at once recognized the short, broad-shouldered form of old Jean Poquelin.

He sat down upon a billet of wood, and, to escape the stings of a whining cloud of mosquitoes, shrouded his face and neck in his handkerchief, leaving his eyes uncovered.

He sat there but a moment when he noticed a strange, sickening odor, faint, as if coming from a distance, but loathsome and horrid.

Whence could it come? Not from the cabin; not from the marsh, for it was as dry as powder. It was not in the air; it seemed to come from the ground.

Rising up, he noticed, for the first time, a few steps before him a narrow foot-path leading toward the house. He glanced down it—ha! right there was some one coming—ghostly white!

Quick as thought, and as noiselessly, he lay down at full length against the cabin. It was bold strategy, and yet, there was no denying it, little White felt that he was frightened. "It is not a ghost," he said to himself. "I *know* it cannot be a ghost"; but the perspiration burst out at every pore, and the air seemed to thicken with heat. "It is a living man," he said in his thoughts. "I hear his footstep, and I hear old Poquelin's footsteps, too, separately, over on the veranda. I am not discovered; the thing has passed; there is that odor again; what a smell of death! Is it coming back? Yes. It stops at the door of the cabin. Is it peering in at the sleeping mute? It moves away. It is in the path again. Now it is gone." He shuddered. "Now, if I dare venture, the mystery is solved." He rose cautiously, close against the cabin, and peered along the path.

The figure of a man, a presence if not a body—but whether clad in some white stuff or naked the darkness would not allow him to determine—had turned, and now, with a seeming painful gait, moved slowly from him. "Great Heaven! can it be that the dead do walk?" He withdrew again the hands which had gone to his eyes. The dreadful object passed between two pillars and under the house. He listened. There was a faint sound of feet upon a staircase; then all was still except the measured tread of Jean Poquelin walking on the veranda, and the heavy respirations of the mute slumbering in the cabin.

The little Secretary was about to retreat, but as he looked once more toward the haunted house a dim light appeared in the crack of a closed window, and presently old Jean Poquelin came, dragging his chair, and sat down close against the shining cranny. He spoke in a low, tender tone in the French tongue, making some inquiry. An answer came from within. Was it the voice of a human? So unnatural was it—so hollow, so discordant, so unearthly—that the stealthy listener shuddered again from head to foot, and when something stirred in some bushes near by—though it may have been nothing more than a rat—and came scuttling through the grass, the little Secretary actually turned and fled. As he left the enclosure he moved with bolder leisure through the bushes; yet now and then he spoke aloud: "Oh, oh! I see, I understand!" and shut his eyes in his hands.

How strange that henceforth little White was the champion of Jean Poquelin! In season and out of season—wherever a word was uttered against him—the Secretary, with a quiet, aggressive force that instantly arrested gossip, demanded upon what authority the statement or conjecture was made; but as he did not condescend to explain his own remarkable attitude, it was not long before the disrelish and suspicion which had followed Jean Poquelin so many years fell also upon him.

It was only the next evening but one after his adventure that he made himself a source of sullen amazement to one hundred and fifty boys, by ordering them to desist from their wanton hallooing. Old Jean Poquelin, standing and shaking his cane, rolling out his long-drawn maledictions, paused and stared, then gave the Secretary a courteous bow and started on. The boys, save one, from pure astonishment, ceased; but a ruffianly little Irish lad, more daring than any had yet been, threw a big hurtling clod, that struck old Poquelin between the shoulders and burst like a shell. The enraged old man wheeled with uplifted staff to give chase to the scampering vagabond; and—he may have tripped, or he may not, but he fell full length. Little White hastened to help him up, but he waved him off with a fierce imprecation and staggering to his feet resumed his way homeward. His lips were reddened with blood.

Little White was on his way to the meeting of the Board. He would have given all he dared spend to have stayed away, for he felt too fierce and too tremulous to brook the criticisms that were likely to be made.

"I can't help it, gentlemen; I can't help you to make a case against the old man, and I'm not going to."

"We did not expect this disappointment, Mr. White."

"I can't help that, sir. No, sir; you had better not appoint any more investigations. Somebody'll investigate himself into trouble. No, sir; it isn't a threat, it is only my advice, but I warn you that whoever takes the task in hand will rue it to his dying day—which may be hastened, too."

The President expressed himself "surprised."

"I don't care a rush," answered little White, wildly and foolishly. "I don't care a rush if you are, sir. No, my nerves are not disordered; my head's as clear as a bell. No, I'm *not* excited."

A Director remarked that the Secretary looked as though he had waked from a nightmare.

"Well, sir, if you want to know the fact, I have; and if you choose to cultivate old Poquelin's society you can have one, too."

"White," called a facetious member, but White did not notice. "White," he called again.

"What?" demanded White, with a scowl.

"Did you see the ghost?"

"Yes, sir; I did," cried White, hitting the table, and handing the President a paper which brought the Board to other business.

The story got among the gossips that somebody (they were afraid to say little White) had been to the Poquelin mansion by night and beheld something appalling. The rumor was but a shadow of the truth, magnified and distorted as is the manner of shadows. He had seen skeletons walking, and barely had escaped the clutches of one by making the sign of the cross.

Some madcap boys with an appetite for the horrible plucked up courage to venture through the dried marsh by the cattle-path, and come before the house at a spectral hour when the air was full of bats. Something which they but half saw—half a sight was enough—sent them tearing back through the willow-brakes and acacia bushes to their homes, where they fairly dropped down, and cried:

"Was it white?" "No—yes—nearly so—we can't tell—but we saw it." And one could hardly doubt, to look at their ashen faces, that they had, whatever it was.

"If that old rascal lived in the country we come from," said certain Américains, "he'd have been tarred and feathered before now, wouldn't he, Sanders?"

"Well, now he just would."

"And we'd have rid him on a rail, wouldn't we?"

"That's what I allow."

"Tell you what you *could* do." They were talking to some rollicking Creoles who had assumed an absolute necessity for doing *something*. "What is it you call this thing where an old man marries a young girl, and you come out with horns and"—

"*Charivari?*" asked the Creoles.

"Yes, that's it. Why don't you shivaree him?" Felicitous suggestion.

Little White, with his wife beside him, was sitting on their doorsteps on the sidewalk, as Creole custom had taught them, looking toward the sunset. They had moved into the lately-opened street. The view was not attractive on the score of beauty. The houses were small and scattered, and across the flat commons, spite of the lofty tangle of weeds and bushes, and spite of the thickets of acacia, they needs must see the dismal old Poquelin mansion, tilted awry and shutting out the declining sun. The moon, white and slender, was hanging the tip of its horn over one of the chimneys.

"And you say," said the Secretary, "the old black man has been going by here alone? Patty, suppose old Poquelin should be concocting some mischief; he don't lack provocation; the way that clod hit him the other day was enough to have killed him. Why, Patty, he dropped as quick as *that!* No wonder you haven't seen him. I wonder if they haven't heard something about him up at the drug-store. Suppose I go and see."

"Do," said his wife.

She sat alone for half an hour, watching that sudden going out of the day peculiar to the latitude.

576

"That moon is ghost enough for one house," she said, as her husband returned. "It has gone right down the chimney."

"Patty," said little White, "the drug-clerk says the boys are going to shivaree old Poquelin to-night. I'm going to try to stop it."

"Why, White," said his wife, "you'd better not. You'll get hurt."

"No, I'll not."

"Yes, you will."

"I'm going to sit out here until they come along. They're compelled to pass right by here."

"Why, White, it may be midnight before they start; you're not going to sit out here till then."

"Yes, I am."

"Well, you're very foolish," said Mrs. White in an undertone, looking anxious, and tapping one of the steps with her foot.

They sat a very long time talking over little family matters.

"What's that?" at last said Mrs. White.

"That's the nine-o'clock gun," said White, and they relapsed into a long-sustained, drowsy silence.

"Patty, you'd better go in and go to bed," said he at last.

"I'm not sleepy."

"Well, you're very foolish," quietly remarked little White, and again silence fell upon them.

"Patty, suppose I walk out to the old house and see if I can find out anything."

"Suppose," said she, "you don't do any such—listen!"

Down the street arose a great hubbub. Dogs and boys were howling and barking; men were laughing, shouting, groaning, and blowing horns, whooping, and clanking cow-bells, whinnying, and howling, and rattling pots and pans.

"They are coming this way," said little White. "You had better go into the house, Patty."

"So had you."

"No. I'm going to see if I can't stop them."

"Why, White!"

"I'll be back in a minute," said White, and went toward the noise.

In a few moments the little Secretary met the mob. The pen hesitates on the word, for there is a respectable difference, measurable only on the scale of the half century, between a mob and a *charivari*. Little White lifted his ineffectual voice. He faced the head of the disorderly column, and cast himself about as if he were made of wood and moved by the jerk of a string. He rushed to one who seemed, from the size and clatter of his tin pan, to be a leader. "*Stop these fellows, Bienvenu, stop them just a minute, till I tell them something.*" Bienvenu turned and brandished his instruments of discord in an imploring way to the crowd. They slackened their pace, two or three hushed their horns and joined the prayer of little White and Bienvenu for silence. The throng halted. The hush was delicious.

"Bienvenu," said little White, "don't shivaree old Poquelin to-night; he's"—

"My fwang," said the swaying Bienvenu, "who tail you I goin' to chahivahi somebody, eh? You sink bickause I make a little playfool wiz zis tin pan zat I am *dhonk?*"

"Oh, no, Bienvenu, old fellow, you're all right. I was afraid you might not know that old Poquelin was sick, you know, but you're not going there, are you?"

"My fwang, I vay soy to tail you zat you ah dhonk as de dev'. I am *shem* of you. I ham ze servan' of ze *publique*. Zese *citoyens* goin' to wickwest Jean Poquelin to give to the Ursuline' two hondred fifty dolla' "—

577

"*Hé quoi!*" cried a listener, "*Cinq cent piastres, oui!*" [6]

"*Oui!*" said Bienvenu, "and if he wiffuse we make him some lit' *musique* ta-ra-ta!" He hoisted a merry hand and foot, then frowning, added: "Old Poquelin got no bizniz dhink s'much w'isky."

"But, gentlemen," said little White, around whom a circle had gathered, "the old man is very sick."

"My faith!" cried a tiny Creole, "we did not make him to be sick. W'en we say we going make *le charivari*, do you want that we hall tell a lie? My faith! 'sfools!"

"But you can shivaree somebody else," said desperate little White.

"*Oui!*" cried Bienvenu, "*et chahivahi* Jean-ah Poquelin tomo'w!"

"Let us go to Madame Schneider!" cried two or three, and amid huzzas and confused cries, among which was heard a stentorian Celtic call for drinks, the crowd again began to move.

"*Cent piastres pour l'hôpital de charité!*"

"Hurrah!"

"One hongred dolla' for Charity Hospital!"

"Hurrah!"

"Whang!" went a tin pan, the crowd yelled, and Pandemonium gaped again. They were off at a right angle.

Nodding, Mrs. White looked at the mantel-clock.

"Well, if it isn't away after midnight."

The hideous noise down street was passing beyond earshot. She raised a sash and listened. For a moment there was silence. Some one came to the door.

"Is that you, White?"

"Yes." He entered. "I succeeded, Patty."

"Did you?" said Patty, joyfully.

"Yes. They've gone down to shivaree the old Dutchwoman who married her step-daughter's sweetheart. They say she has got to pay a hundred dollars to the hospital before they stop."

The couple retired, and Mrs. White slumbered. She was awakened by her husband snapping the lid of his watch.

"What time?" she asked.

"Half-past three, Patty, I haven't slept a wink. Those fellows are out yet. Don't you hear them?"

"Why, White, they're coming this way!"

"I know they are," said White, sliding out of bed and drawing on his clothes, "and they are coming fast. You'd better go away from that window, Patty. My! what a clatter!"

"Here they are," said Mrs. White, but her husband was gone. Two or three hundred men and boys pass the place at a rapid walk straight down the broad, new street, toward the hated house of ghosts. The din was terrific. She saw little White at the head of the rabble brandishing his arms and trying in vain to make himself heard; but they only shook their heads, laughing and hooting the louder, and so passed, bearing him on before them.

Swiftly they pass out from among the houses, away from the dim oil lamps of the street, out into the broad starlit commons, and enter the willowy jungles of

[6] *What! . . . Five hundred piastres!*

578

the haunted ground. Some hearts fail and their owners lag behind and turn back, suddenly remembering how near morning it is. But the most part push on, tearing the air with their clamor.

Down ahead of them in the long, thicket-darkened way there is—singularly enough—a faint, dancing light. It must be very near the old house; it is. It has stopped now. It is a lantern, and is under a well-known sapling which has grown up on the wayside since the canal was filled. Now it swings mysteriously to and fro. A goodly number of the more ghost-fearing give up the sport; but a full hundred move forward at a run, doubling their devilish howling and banging.

Yes; it is a lantern, and there are two persons under the tree. The crowd draws near—drops into a walk; one of the two is the old African mute; he lifts the lantern up so that it shines on the other; the crowd recoils; there is a hush of all clangor, and all at once, with a cry of mingled fright and horror from every throat, the whole throng rushes back, dropping everything, sweeping past little White and hurrying on, never stopping until the jungle is left behind, and then to find that not one in ten has seen the cause of the stampede, and not one of the tenth is certain what it was.

There is one huge fellow among them who looks capable of any villany. He finds something to mount on, and, in the Creole *patois*, calls a general halt. Bienvenu sinks down, and, vainly trying to recline gracefully, resigns the leadership. The herd gather round the speaker; he assures them that they have been outraged. Their right peaceably to traverse the public streets has been trampled upon. Shall such encroachments be endured? It is now daybreak. Let them go now by the open light of day and force a free passage of the public highway!

A scattering consent was the response, and the crowd, thinned now and drowsy, straggled quietly down toward the old house. Some drifted ahead, others sauntered behind, but every one, as he again neared the tree, came to a stand-still. Little White sat upon a bank of turf on the opposite side of the way looking very stern and sad. To each newcomer he put the same question:

"Did you come here to go to old Poquelin's?"

"Yes."

"He's dead." And if the shocked hearer started away he would say: "Don't go away."

"Why not?"

"I want you to go to the funeral presently."

If some Louisianian, too loyal to dear France or Spain to understand English, looked bewildered, some one would interpret for him; and presently they went. Little White led the van, the crowd trooping after him down the middle of the way. The gate, that had never been seen before unchained, was open. Stern little White stopped a short distance from it; the rabble stopped behind him. Something was moving out from under the veranda. The many whisperers stretched upward to see. The African mute came very slowly toward the gate, leading by a cord in the nose a small brown bull, which was harnessed to a rude cart. On the flat body of the cart, under a black cloth, were seen the outlines of a long box.

"Hats off, gentlemen," said little White, as the box came in view, and the crowd silently uncovered.

"Gentlemen," said little White, "here comes the last remains of Jean Marie

579

Poquelin, a better man, I'm afraid, with all his sins,—yes, a better—a kinder man to his blood—a man of more self-forgetful goodness—than all of you put together will ever dare to be."

There was a profound hush as the vehicle came creaking through the gate; but when it turned away from them toward the forest, those in front started suddenly. There was a backward rush, then all stood still again staring one way; for there, behind the bier, with eyes cast down and labored step, walked the living remains —all that was left—of little Jacques Poquelin, the long-hidden brother—a leper, as white as snow.

Dumb with horror, the cringing crowd gazed upon the walking death. They watched in silent awe, the slow *cortège* creep down the long, straight road and lessen on the view, until by and by it stopped where a wild, unfrequented path branched off into the undergrowth toward the rear of the ancient city.

"They are going to the *Terre aux Lépreux*," said one in the crowd. The rest watched them in silence.

The little bull was set free; the mute, with the strength of an ape, lifted the long box to his shoulder. For a moment more the mute and the leper stood in sight, while the former adjusted his heavy burden; then, without one backward glance upon the unkind human world, turning their faces toward the ridge in the depths of the swamp known as the Leper's Land, they stepped into the jungle, disappeared, and were never seen again. (*1879*)

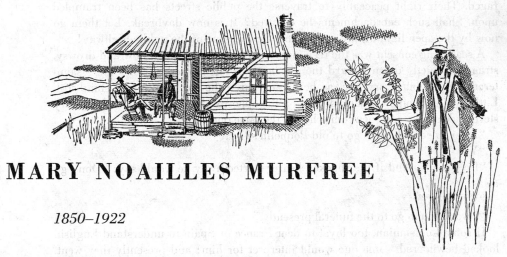

MARY NOAILLES MURFREE

1850–1922

The Murfree plantation of twelve hundred acres in Middle Tennessee and the colonial house in which Mary Noailles Murfree was born typify the aristocratic life she always lived. As a child she tended to be something of a recluse, and this inclination was strengthened when a childhood illness left her slightly lame. During her girlhood she spent a few months of each year visiting Beersheba summer resort in the Cumberland Mountains and—as proved important later—was greatly impressed by the mountaineers whom she saw there.

Miss Murfree received her first schooling in Nashville (where her father had moved the family in 1856), at the Nashville Female Academy and the school of Philip Fall. She later attended the Chegary Institute in Philadelphia. During the

Civil War and Reconstruction, the family plantations were almost completely ruined, but in 1872 the Murfrees moved back to the Grantland estate in Murfreesboro. Here Mary Noailles, in collaboration with her father, wrote her first stories. Her first publication, "Flirts and Their Ways," appeared in *Lippincott's* in May 1874, under the pseudonym of "R. Emmet Dembry."

Within four years Miss Murfree—now using the name "Charles Egbert Craddock"—was writing some of her best mountaineer stories for the *Atlantic Monthly*. The family moved to St. Louis in 1881, but her work was uninterrupted. A collection of her short stories from the *Atlantic* was published in 1884 as *In the Tennessee Mountains*. By the following year "Charles Egbert Craddock" had become a well-known name, and the disclosure of the true identity of that "gentleman" proved startling even to Thomas Bailey Aldrich, then editor of the *Atlantic*, who had been publishing her work for several years.

In 1885 Miss Murfree made a trip to Montvale Springs, Tennessee, to gather more material on the mountaineers, and in 1889 her family settled once again in its home state. By this time Mary Noailles Murfree, confronted by a public that had outgrown its taste for local color, was somewhat unsuccessfully trying her hand at the historical novel. Of the five books that she produced in this genre, *The Story of Old Fort Loudon* (1899) is perhaps the most noteworthy. Miss Murfree returned to her themes of local color in *The Windfall* (1907). In 1922, the year of her death, she was awarded an honorary degree as Doctor of Letters from the University of the South.

The best work of Mary Noailles Murfree clearly belongs to the category of local color, and the charms—together with the limitations—of that phase of American literature are evident in her writing. Her work was often didactic and her plots inferior, but despite her weaknesses, she achieved real triumphs of delineation in at least three of her volumes: *In the Tennessee Mountains* (1884), *The Prophet of the Great Smoky Mountains* (1885), a powerful study of a religious mountaineer, and *In the "Stranger People's" Country* (1891), perhaps the most finished of her works. In portraying the character of the isolated and eccentric Tennessee mountaineers, these stories represent an important facet of the local color movement.

The "Harnt" That Walks Chilhowee

June had crossed the borders of Tennessee. Even on the summit of Chilhowee Mountain the apples in Peter Giles's orchard were beginning to redden, and his Indian corn, planted on so steep a declivity that the stalks seemed to have much ado to keep their footing, was crested with tassels and plumed with silk. Among the dense forests, seen by no man's eye, the elder was flying its creamy banners in honor of June's coming, and, heard by no man's ear, the pink and white bells of the azalea rang out melodies of welcome.

"An' it air a toler'ble for'ard season. Yer wheat looks likely; an' yer gyarden truck air thrivin' powerful. Even that cold spell we-uns hed about the full o' the moon in May ain't done sot it back none, it 'pears like ter me. But, 'cording ter my way o' thinkin', ye hev got chickens enough hyar ter eat off every peabloom ez soon ez it opens." And Simon Burney glanced with a gardener's disapproval at the numerous fowls, lifting their red combs and tufted top-knots here and there among the thick clover under the apple-trees.

"Them's Clarsie's chickens,—my darter, ye know," drawled Peter Giles, a pale, listless, and lank mountaineer. "An' she hev been gin ter onderstand ez they hev got ter be kep' out 'n the gyarden; 'thout," he added indulgently,—" 'thout I'm a-plowin', when I lets 'em foller in the furrow ter pick up worms. But law! Clarsie is so spry that she don't ax no better 'n ter be let ter run them chickens off'n the peas."

Then the two men tilted their chairs against the posts of the little porch in front of Peter Giles's log cabin, and puffed their pipes in silence. The panorama spread out before them showed misty and dreamy among the delicate spiral wreaths of smoke. But was that gossamer-like illusion, lying upon the far horizon, the magic of nicotian, or the vague presence of distant heights? As ridge after ridge came down from the sky in ever-graduating shades of intenser blue, Peter Giles might have told you that this parallel system of enchantment was only "the mountings:" that here was Foxy, and there was Big Injun, and still beyond was another, which he had "hearn tell ran spang up into Virginny." The sky that bent to clasp this kindred blue was of varying moods. Floods of sunshine submerged Chilhowee in liquid gold, and revealed that dainty outline limned upon the northern horizon; but over the Great Smoky mountains clouds had gathered, and a gigantic rainbow bridged the valley.

Peter Giles's listless eyes were fixed upon a bit of red clay road, which was visible through a gap in the foliage far below. Even a tiny object, that ant-like crawled upon it, could be seen from the summit of Chilhowee. "I reckon that's my brother's wagon an' team," he said, as he watched the moving atom pass under the gorgeous triumphal arch. "He 'lowed he war goin' ter the Cross-Roads ter-day."

Simon Burney did not speak for a moment. When he did, his words seemed widely irrelevant. "That's a likely gal o' yourn," he drawled, with an odd constraint in his voice,—"a likely gal, that Clarsie."

There was a quick flash of surprise in Peter Giles's dull eyes. He covertly surveyed his guest, with an astounded curiosity rampant in his slow brains. Simon Burney had changed color; an expression of embarrassment lurked in every line of his honest, florid, hard-featured face. An alert imagination might have detected a deprecatory self-consciousness in every gray hair that striped the black beard raggedly fringing his chin.

"Yes," Peter Giles at length replied, "Clarsie air a likely enough gal. But she air mightily sot ter hevin' her own way. An' ef 't ain't give ter her peaceable-like, she jes' takes it, whether or no."

This statement, made by one presumably fully informed on the subject, might have damped the ardor of many a suitor,—for the monstrous truth was dawning on Peter Giles's mind that suitor was the position to which this slow, elderly widower aspired. But Simon Burney, with that odd, all-pervading constraint still prominently apparent, mildly observed, "Waal, ez much ez I hev seen of her goin's-on, it 'pears ter me ez her way air a mighty good way. An' it ain't comical that she likes it."

582

Urgent justice compelled Peter Giles to make some amends to the absent Clarissa. "That 's a fac'," he admitted. "An' Clarsie ain't no hand ter jaw. She don't hev no words. But then," he qualified, truth and consistency alike constraining him, "she air a toler'ble hard-headed gal. That air a true word. Ye mought ez well try ter hender the sun from shining ez ter make that thar Clarsie Giles do what she don't want ter do."

To be sure, Peter Giles had a right to his opinion as to the hardness of his own daughter's head. The expression of his views, however, provoked Simon Burney to wrath; there was something astir within him that in a worthier subject might have been called a chivalric thrill, and it forbade him to hold his peace. He retorted: "Of course ye kin say that, ef so minded; but ennybody ez hev got eyes kin see the change ez hev been made in this hyar place sence that thar gal hev been growed. I ain't a-purtendin' ter know that thar Clarsie ez well ez you-uns knows her hyar at home, but I hev seen enough, an' a deal more 'n enough, of her goin's-on, ter know that what she does ain't done fur *herself*. An' ef she will hev her way, it air fur the good of the whole tribe of ye. It 'pears ter me ez thar ain't many gals like that thar Clarsie. An' she air a merciful critter. She air mighty savin' of the feelin's of everything, from the cow an' the mare down ter the dogs, an' pigs, an' chickens; always a-feedin' of 'em jes' ter the time, an' never draggin', an' clawin', an' beatin' of 'em. Why, that thar Clarsie can't put her foot out'n the door, that every dumb beastis on this hyar place ain't a-runnin' ter git nigh her. I hev seen them pigs mos' climb the fence when she shows her face at the door. 'Pears ter me ez that thar Clarsie could tame a b'ar, ef she looked at him a time or two, she's so savin' o' the critter's feelin's! An' thar's that old yaller dog o' yourn," pointing to an ancient cur that was blinking in the sun, "he's older'n Clarsie, an' no 'count in the worl'. I hev hearn ye say forty times that ye would kill him, 'ceptin' that Clarsie purtected him, an' hed sot her heart on his a-livin' along. An' all the home-folks, an' everybody that kems hyar to sot an' talk awhile, never misses a chance ter kick that thar old dog, or poke him with a stick, or cuss him. But Clarsie!—I hev seen that gal take the bread an' meat off'n her plate, an' give it ter that old dog, ez 'pears ter me ter be the worst dispositionest dog I ever see, an' no thanks lef' in him. He hain't hed the grace ter wag his tail fur twenty year. That thar Clarsie air surely a merciful critter, an' a mighty spry, likely young gal, besides."

Peter Giles sat in stunned astonishment during this speech, which was delivered in a slow, drawling monotone, with frequent meditative pauses, but nevertheless emphatically. He made no reply, and as they were once more silent there rose suddenly the sound of melody upon the air. It came from beyond that tumultuous stream that raced with the wind down the mountain's side; a great log thrown from bank to bank served as bridge. The song grew momentarily more distinct; among the leaves there were fugitive glimpses of blue and white, and at last Clarsie appeared, walking lightly along the log, clad in her checked homespun dress, and with a pail upon her head.

She was a tall, lithe girl, with that delicately transparent complexion often seen among the women of these mountains. Her lustreless black hair lay along her forehead without a ripple or wave; there was something in the expression of her large eyes that suggested those of a deer,—something free, untamable, and yet gentle. " 'T ain't no wonder ter me ez Clarsie is all tuk up with the wild things,

583

an' critters ginerally," her mother was wont to say. "She sorter looks like 'em, I'm a-thinkin'."

As she came in sight there was a renewal of that odd constraint in Simon Burney's face and manner, and he rose abruptly. "Waal," he said, hastily, going to his horse, a raw-boned sorrel, hitched to the fence, "it's about time I war a-startin' home, I reckons."

He nodded to his host, who silently nodded in return, and the old horse jogged off with him down the road, as Clarsie entered the house and placed the pail upon a shelf.

"Who d' ye think hev been hyar a-speakin' of complimints on ye, Clarsie?" exclaimed Mrs. Giles, who had overheard through the open door every word of the loud, drawling voice on the porch.

Clarsie's liquid eyes widened with surprise, and a faint tinge of rose sprang into her pale face, as she looked an expectant inquiry at her mother.

Mrs. Giles was a slovenly, indolent woman, anxious, at the age of forty-five, to assume the prerogatives of advanced years. She had placed all her domestic cares upon the shapely shoulders of her willing daughter, and had betaken herself to the chimney-corner and a pipe.

"Yes, thar hev been somebody hyar a-speakin' of complimints on ye, Clarsie," she reiterated, with chuckling amusement. "He war a mighty peart, likely boy,— that he war!"

Clarsie's color deepened.

"Old Simon Burney!" exclaimed her mother, in great glee at the incongruity of the idea. "*Old Simon Burney!*—jes' a-sittin' out thar, a-wastin' the time, an' a-burnin' of daylight—jes' ez perlite an' smilin' ez a basket of chips—a-speakin' of complimints on ye!"

There was a flash of laughter among the sylvan suggestions of Clarsie's eyes,— a flash as of sudden sunlight upon water. But despite her mirth she seemed to be unaccountably disappointed. The change in her manner was not noticed by her mother, who continued banteringly,—

"Simon Burney air a mighty pore old man. Ye oughter be sorry fur him, Clarsie. Ye must n't think less of folks than ye does of the dumb beastis,—that ain't religion. Ye knows ye air sorry fur mos' everything; why not fur this comical old consarn? Ye oughter marry him ter take keer of him. He said ye war a merciful critter; now is yer chance ter show it! Why, air ye a-goin' ter weavin', Clarsie, jes' when I wants ter talk ter ye 'bout 'n old Simon Burney? But law! I knows ye kerry him with ye in yer heart."

The girl summarily closed the conversation by seating herself before a great hand-loom; presently the persistent thump, thump, of the batten and the noisy creak of the treadle filled the room, and through all the long, hot afternoon her deft, practiced hands lightly tossed the shuttle to and fro.

The breeze freshened, after the sun went down, and the hop and gourd vines were all astir as they clung about the little porch where Clarsie was sitting now, idle at last. The rain clouds had disappeared, and there bent over the dark, heavily wooded ridges a pale blue sky, with here and there the crystalline sparkle of a star. A halo was shimmering in the east, where the mists had gathered about the great white moon, hanging high above the mountains. Noiseless wings flitted

584

through the dusk; now and then the bats swept by so close as to wave Clarsie's hair with the wind of their flight. What an airy, glittering, magical thing was that gigantic spider-web suspended between the silver moon and her shining eyes! Ever and anon there came from the woods a strange, weird, long-drawn sigh, unlike the stir of the wind in the trees, unlike the fret of the water on the rocks. Was it the voiceless sorrow of the sad earth? There were stars in the night besides those known to astronomers: the stellular fireflies gemmed the black shadows with a fluctuating brilliancy; they circled in and out of the porch, and touched the leaves above Clarsie's head with quivering points of light. A steadier and an intenser gleam was advancing along the road, and the sound of languid footsteps came with it; the aroma of tobacco graced the atmosphere, and a tall figure walked up to the gate.

"Come in, come in," said Peter Giles, rising, and tendering the guest a chair. "Ye air Tom Pratt, ez well ez I kin make out by this light. Waal, Tom, we hain't furgot ye sence ye done been hyar."

As Tom had been there on the previous evening, this might be considered a joke, or an equivocal compliment. The young fellow was restless and awkward under it, but Mrs. Giles chuckled with great merriment.

"An' how air ye a-comin' on, Mrs. Giles?" he asked propitiatorily.

"Jes' toler'ble, Tom. Air they all well ter yer house?"

"Yes, they're toler'ble well, too." He glanced at Clarsie, intending to address to her some polite greeting, but the expression of her shy, half-startled eyes, turned upon the far-away moon, warned him. "Thar never war a gal so skittish," he thought. "She'd run a mile, skeered ter death, ef I said a word ter her."

And he was prudently silent.

"Waal," said Peter Giles, "what's the news out yer way, Tom? Ennything a-goin' on?"

"Thar war a shower yander on the Backbone; it rained toler'ble hard fur a while, an' sot up the corn wonderful. Did ye git enny hyar?"

"Not a drap."

" 'Pears ter me ez I kin see the clouds a-circlin' round Chilhowee, an' a-rainin' on everybody's corn-field 'ceptin' ourn," said Mrs. Giles. "Some folks is the favored of the Lord, an' t' others hev ter work fur everything an' git nuthin'. Waal, waal; we-uns will see our reward in the nex' worl'. Thar's a better worl' than this, Tom."

"That's a fac'," said Tom, in orthodox assent.

"An' when we leaves hyar once, we leaves all trouble an' care behind us, Tom; fur we don't come back no more." Mrs. Giles was drifting into one of her pious moods.

"I dunno," said Tom. "Thar hev been them ez hev."

"Hev what?" demanded Peter Giles, startled.

"Hev come back ter this hyar yearth. Thar's a harnt that walks Chilhowee every night o' the worl'. I know them ez hev seen him."

Clarsie's great dilated eyes were fastened on the speaker's face. There was a dead silence for a moment, more eloquent with these looks of amazement than any words could have been.

"I reckons ye remember a puny, shriveled little man, named Reuben Crabb,

585

ez used ter live yander, eight mile along the ridge ter that thar big sulphur spring," Tom resumed, appealing to Peter Giles. "He war born with only one arm."

"I 'members him," interpolated Mrs. Giles, vivaciously. "He war a mighty porely, sickly little critter, all the days of his life. 'T war a wonder he war ever raised ter be a man,—an' a pity, too. An' 't war powerful comical, the way of his takin' off; a stunted, one-armed little critter a-ondertakin' ter fight folks an' shoot pistols. He hed the use o' his one arm, sure."

"Waal," said Tom, "his house ain't thar now, 'kase Sam Grim's brothers burned it ter the ground fur his a-killin' of Sam. That warn't all that war done ter Reuben fur killin' of Sam. The sheriff run Reuben Crabb down this hyar road 'bout a mile from hyar,—mebbe less,—an' shot him dead in the road, jes' whar it forks. Waal, Reuben war in company with another evil-doer,—*he* war from the Cross-Roads, an' I furgits what he hed done, but he war a-tryin' ter hide in the mountings, too; an' the sheriff lef' Reuben a-lying thar in the road, while he tries ter ketch up with the t'other; but his horse got a stone in his hoof, an' he los' time, an' hed ter gin it up. An' when he got back ter the forks o' the road whar he hed lef' Reuben a-lyin' dead, thar war nuthin' thar 'ceptin' a pool o' blood. Waal, he went right on ter Reuben's house, an' them Grim boys hed burnt it ter the ground; but he seen Reuben's brother Joel. An' Joel, he tole the sheriff that late that evenin' he hed tuk Reuben's body out'n the road an' buried it, 'kase it had been lyin' thar in the road ever sence early in the mornin', an' he couldn't leave it thar all night, an' he hedn't no shelter fur it, sence the Grim boys hed burnt down the house. So he war obleeged ter bury it. An' Joel showed the sheriff a new-made grave, an' Reuben's coat whar the sheriff's bullet hed gone in at the back an' kem out'n the breast. The sheriff 'lowed ez they'd fine Joel fifty dollars fur a-buryin' of Reuben afore the cor'ner kem; but they never done it, ez I knows on. The sheriff said that when the cor'ner kem the body would be tuk up fur a 'quest. But thar hed been a powerful big frishet, an' the river 'twixt the cor'ner's house an' Chilhowee couldn't be forded fur three weeks. The cor'ner never kem, an' so thar it all stayed. That war four year ago."

"Waal," said Peter Giles, dryly, "I ain't seen no harnt yit. I knowed all that afore."

Clarsie's wondering eyes upon the young man's moonlit face had elicited these facts, familiar to the elders, but strange, he knew, to her.

"I war jes' a-goin' on ter tell," said Tom, abashed. "Waal, ever sence his brother Joel died, this spring, Reuben's harnt walks Chilhowee. He war seen week afore las', 'bout daybreak, by Ephraim Blenkins, who hed been a-fishin', an' war a-goin' home. Eph happened ter stop in the laurel ter wind up his line, when all in a minit he seen the harnt go by, his face white, an' his eye-balls like fire, an' puny an' one-armed, jes' like he lived. Eph, he owed me a haffen day's work; I helped him ter plow las' month, an' so he kem ter-day an' hoed along cornsider'ble ter pay fur it. He say he believes the harnt never seen him, 'kase it went right by. He 'lowed ef the harnt hed so much ez cut one o' them blazin' eyes round at him he couldn't but hev drapped dead. Waal, this mornin', 'bout sunrise, my brother Bob's little gal, three year old, strayed off from home while her mother war out milkin' the cow. An' we went a-huntin' of her, mightily worked

up, 'kase thar hev been a b'ar prowlin' round our cornfield twict this summer. An'
I went to the right, an' Bob went to the lef'. An' he say ez he war a-pushin' 'long
through the laurel, he seen the bushes ahead of him a-rustlin'. An' he jes' stood
still an' watched 'em. An' fur a while the bushes war still too; an' then they
moved jes' a little, fust this way an' then that, till all of a suddint the leaves
opened, like the mouth of hell mought hev done, an' thar he seen Reuben
Crabb's face. He say he never seen sech a face! Its mouth war open, an'
its eyes war a-startin' out'n its head, an' its skin war white till it war blue;
an' ef the devil hed hed it a-hangin' over the coals that minit it couldn't hev
looked no more skeered. But that war all that Bob seen, 'kase he jes' shet his eyes
an' screeched an' screeched like he war *de*stracted. An' when he stopped a second
ter ketch his breath he hearn su'thin' a-answerin' him back, sorter weak-like, an'
thar war little Peggy a-pullin' through the laurel. Ye know she's too little ter talk
good, but the folks down ter our house believes she seen the harnt, too."

"My lord!" exclaimed Peter Giles. "I 'low I couldn't live a minit ef I war ter
see that thar harnt that walks Chilhowee!"

"I know I couldn't," said his wife.

"Nor me, nuther," murmured Clarsie.

"Waal," said Tom, resuming the thread of his narrative, "we hev all been
a-talkin' down yander ter our house ter make out the reason why Reuben Crabb's
harnt hev sot out ter walk *jes' sence his brother Joel died,*—'kase it war never
seen afore then. An' ez nigh ez we kin make it out, the reason is 'kase thar's nobody lef' in this hyar worl' what believes he warn't ter blame in that thar killin' o'
Sam Grim. Joel always swore ez Reuben never killed him no more'n nuthin';
that Sam's own pistol went off in his own hand, an' shot him through the heart
jes' ez he war a-drawin' of it ter shoot Reuben Crabb. An' I hev hearn other men
ez war a-standin' by say the same thing, though them Grims tells another tale; but
ez Reuben never owned no pistol in his life, nor kerried one, it don't 'pear ter
me ez what them Grims say air reasonable. Joel always swore ez Sam Grim war a
mighty mean man,—a great big feller like him a-rockin' of a deformed little critter, an' a-mockin' of him, an' a-hittin' of him. An' the day of the fight Sam jes'
knocked him down fur nuthin' at all; an' afore ye could wink Reuben jumped up
suddint, an' flew at him like an eagle, an' struck him in the face. An' then Sam
drawed his pistol, an' it went off in his own hand, an' shot him through the heart,
an' killed him dead. Joel said that ef he could hev kep' that pore little critter
Reuben still, an' let the sheriff arrest him peaceable-like, he war sure the jury
would hev let him off; 'kase how war Reuben a-goin' ter shoot ennybody when
Sam Grim never left a-holt of the only pistol between 'em, in life, or in death?
They tells me they hed ter bury Sam Grim with that thar pistol in his hand; his
grip war too tight fur death to unloose it. But Joel said that Reuben war sartain
they'd hang him. He hedn't never seen no jestice from enny one man, an' he
couldn't look fur it from twelve men. So he jes' sot out ter run through the woods,
like a painter or a wolf, ter be hunted by the sheriff, an' he war run down an' kilt
in the road. Joel said *he* kep' up arter the sheriff ez well ez he could on foot,—fur
the Crabbs never hed no horse,—ter try ter beg fur Reuben, ef he war cotched,
an' tell how little an' how weakly he war. I never seen a young man's head turn
white like Joel's done; he said he reckoned it war his troubles. But ter the las'

587

he stuck ter his rifle faithful. He war a powerful hunter; he war out rain or shine, hot or cold, in sech weather ez other folks would think thar war n't no use in tryin' ter do nuthin' in. I'm mightily afeard o' seein' Reuben, now, that's a fac'," concluded Tom, frankly; " 'kase I hev hearn tell, an' I believes it, that ef a harnt speaks ter ye, it air sartain ye're bound ter die right then."

" 'Pears ter me," said Mrs. Giles, "ez many mountings ez thar air round hyar, he mought hev tuk ter walkin' some o' them, stiddier Chilhowee."

There was a sudden noise close at hand: a great inverted splint-basket, from which came a sound of flapping wings, began to move slightly back and forth. Mrs. Giles gasped out an ejaculation of terror, the two men sprang to their feet, and the coy Clarsie laughed aloud in an exuberance of delighted mirth, forgetful of her shyness. "I declar' ter goodness, you-uns air all skeered fur true! Did ye think it war the harnt that walks Chilhowee?"

"What's under that thar basket?" demanded Peter Giles, rather sheepishly, as he sat down again.

"Nuthin' but the duck-legged Dominicky," said Clarsie, "what air bein' broke up from settin'." The moonlight was full upon the dimpling merriment in her face, upon her shining eyes and parted red lips, and her gurgling laughter was pleasant to hear. Tom Pratt edged his chair a trifle nearer, as he, too, sat down.

"Ye ought n't never ter break up a duck-legged hen, nor a Dominicky, nuther," he volunteered, " 'kase they air sech a good kind o' hen ter kerry chickens; but a hen that is duck-legged an' Dominicky too oughter be let ter set, whether or no."

Had he been warned in a dream, he could have found no more secure road to Clarsie's favor and interest than a discussion of the poultry. "I'm a-thinkin'," she said, "that it air too hot fur hens ter set now, an' 't will be till the las' of August."

"It don't 'pear ter me ez it air hot much in June up hyar on Chilhowee,— thar's a differ, I know, down in the valley; but till July, on Chilhowee, it don't 'pear ter me ez it air too hot ter set a hen. An' a duck-legged Dominicky air mighty hard ter break up."

"That's a fac'," Clarsie admitted; "but I'll hev ter do it, somehow, 'kase I ain't got no eggs fur her. All my hens air kerryin' of chickens."

"Waal!" exclaimed Tom, seizing his opportunity, "I'll bring ye some ter-morrer night, when I come agin. We-uns hev got eggs ter our house."

"Thanky," said Clarsie, shyly smiling.

This unique method of courtship would have progressed very prosperously but for the interference of the elders, who are an element always more or less adverse to love-making. "Ye oughter turn out yer hen now, Clarsie," said Mrs. Giles, "ez Tom air a-goin' 'ter bring ye some eggs ter-morrer. I wonder ye don't think it's mean ter keep her up longer 'n ye air obleeged ter. Ye oughter remember ye war called a merciful critter jes' ter-day."

Clarsie rose precipitately, raised the basket, and out flew the "duck-legged Dominicky," with a frantic flutter and hysterical cackling. But Mrs. Giles was not to be diverted from her purpose; her thoughts had recurred to the absurd episode of the afternoon, and with her relish of the incongruity of the joke she opened upon the subject at once.

"Waal, Tom," she said, "we'll be hevin' Clarsie married, afore long, I'm a-thinkin'." The young man sat bewildered. He, too, had entertained views concerning Clarsie's speedy marriage, but with a distinctly personal application; and this frank mention of the matter by Mrs. Giles had a sinister suggestion that perhaps her ideas might be antagonistic. "An' who d'ye think hev been hyar ter-day, a-speakin' of compli*mints* on Clarsie?" He could not answer, but he turned his head with a look of inquiry, and Mrs. Giles continued, "He is a mighty peart, likely boy,—*he* is."

There was a growing anger in the dismay on Tom Pratt's face; he leaned forward to hear the name with a fiery eagerness, altogether incongruous with his usual lack-lustre manner.

"Old Simon Burney!" cried Mrs. Giles, with a burst of laughter. "*Old Simon Burney!* Jes' a-speakin' of compli*mints* on Clarsie!"

The young fellow drew back with a look of disgust. "Why, he's a old man; he ain't no fit husband fur Clarsie."

"Don't ye be too sure ter count on that. I war jes' a-layin' off ter tell Clarsie that a gal oughter keep mighty clar o' widowers, 'thout she wants ter marry one. Fur I believes," said Mrs. Giles, with a wild flight of imagination, "ez them men hev got some sort'n trade with the Evil One, an' he gives 'em the power ter witch the gals, somehow, so's ter git 'em ter marry; 'kase I don't think that any gal that's got good sense air a-goin' ter be a man's second ch'ice, an' the mother of a whole pack of step-chil'ren, 'thout she air under some sort'n spell. But them men carries the day with the gals, ginerally, an' I'm a-thinkin' they're banded with the devil. Ef I war a gal, an' a smart, peart boy like Simon Burney kem around a-speakin' of compli*mints*, an' sayin' I war a merciful critter, I'd jes' give it up, an' marry him fur second ch'ice. Thar's one blessin'," she continued, contemplating the possibility in a cold-blooded fashion positively revolting to Tom Pratt: "he ain't got no tribe of chil'ren fur Clarsie ter look arter; nary chick nor child hev old Simon Burney got. He hed two, but they died."

The young man took leave presently, in great depression of spirit,—the idea that the widower was banded with the powers of evil was rather overwhelming to a man whose dependence was in merely mortal attractions; and after he had been gone a little while Clarsie ascended the ladder to a nook in the roof, which she called her room.

For the first time in her life her slumber was fitful and restless, long intervals of wakefulness alternating with snatches of fantastic dreams. At last she rose and sat by the rude window, looking out through the chestnut leaves at the great moon, which had begun to dip toward the dark uncertainty of the western ridges, and at the shimmering, translucent, pearly mists that filled the intermediate valleys. All the air was dew and incense; so subtle and penetrating an odor came from that fir-tree beyond the fence that it seemed as if some invigorating infusion were thrilling along her veins; there floated upward, too, the warm fragrance of the clover, and every breath of the gentle wind brought from over the stream a thousand blended, undistinguishable perfumes of the deep forests beyond. The moon's idealizing glamour had left no trace of the uncouthness of the place which the daylight revealed; the little log house, the great overhanging chestnut-oaks, the jagged precipice before the door, the vague outlines of the distant ranges, all suffused with a magic sheen, might have seemed a stupendous altorilievo in silver repoussé. Still, there came here and there the sweep of the

589

bat's dusky wings; even they were a part of the night's witchery. A tiny owl perched for a moment or two amid the dew-tipped chestnut-leaves, and gazed with great round eyes at Clarsie as solemnly as she gazed at him.

"I'm thankful enough that ye hed the grace not ter screech while ye war hyar," she said, after the bird had taken his flight. "I ain't ready ter die yit, an' a screech-ow*el* air the sure sign."

She felt now and then a great impatience with her wakeful mood. Once she took herself to task: "Jes' a-sittin' up hyar all night, the same ez ef I war a fox, or that thar harnt that walks Chilhowee!"

And then her mind reverted to Tom Pratt, to old Simon Burney, and to her mother's emphatic and oracular declaration that widowers are in league with Satan, and that the girls upon whom they cast the eye of supernatural fascination have no choice in the matter. "I wish I knowed ef that thar sayin' war true," she murmured, her face still turned to the western spurs, and the moon sinking so slowly toward them.

With a sudden resolution she rose to her feet. She knew a way of telling fortunes which was, according to tradition, infallible, and she determined to try it, and ease her mind as to her future. Now was the propitious moment. "I hev always hearn that it won't come true 'thout ye try it jes' before daybreak, an' a-kneelin' down at the forks of the road." She hesitated a moment and listened intently. "They'd never git done a-laffin' at me, ef they fund it out," she thought.

There was no sound in the house, and from the dark woods arose only those monotonous voices of the night, so familiar to her ears that she accounted their murmurous iteration as silence too. She leaned far out of the low window, caught the wide-spreading branches of the tree beside it, and swung herself noiselessly to the ground. The road before her was dark with the shadowy foliage and dank with the dew; but now and then, at long intervals, there lay athwart it a bright bar of light, where the moonshine fell through a gap in the trees. Once, as she went rapidly along her way, she saw speeding across the white radiance, lying just before her feet, the ill-omened shadow of a rabbit. She paused, with a superstitious sinking of the heart, and she heard the animal's quick, leaping rush through the bushes near at hand; but she mustered her courage, and kept steadily on. "'T ain't no use a-goin' back ter git shet o' bad luck," she argued. "Ef old Simon Burney air my fortune, he'll come whether or no,—ef all they say air true."

The serpentine road curved to the mountain's brink before it forked, and there was again that familiar picture of precipice, and far-away ridges, and shining mist, and sinking moon, which was visibly turning from silver to gold. The changing lustre gilded the feathery ferns that grew in the marshy dip. Just at the angle of the divergent paths there rose into the air a great mass of indistinct white blossoms, which she knew were the exquisite mountain azaleas, and all the dark forest was starred with the blooms of the laurel.

She fixed her eyes upon the mystic sphere dropping down the sky, knelt among the azaleas at the forks of the road, and repeated the time-honored invocation:—

590 "Ef I'm a-goin' ter marry a young man, whistle, Bird, whistle. Ef I'm a-goin' ter marry an old man, low, Cow, low. Ef I ain't a-goin' ter marry nobody, knock, Death, knock."

There was a prolonged silence in the matutinal freshness and perfume of the woods. She raised her head, and listened attentively. No chirp of half-awakened bird, no tapping of woodpecker, or the mysterious death-watch; but from far along the dewy aisles of the forest, the ungrateful Spot, that Clarsie had fed more faithfully than herself, lifted up her voice, and set the echoes vibrating. Clarsie, however, had hardly time for a pang of disappointment. While she still knelt among the azaleas her large, deer-like eyes were suddenly dilated with terror. From around the curve of the road came the quick beat of hastening footsteps, the sobbing sound of panting breath, and between her and the sinking moon there passed an attenuated, one-armed figure, with a pallid, sharpened face, outlined for a moment on its brilliant disk, and dreadful starting eyes, and quivering open mouth. It disappeared in an instant among the shadows of the laurel, and Clarsie, with a horrible fear clutching at her heart, sprang to her feet.

Her flight was arrested by other sounds. Before her reeling senses could distinguish them, a party of horsemen plunged down the road. They reined in suddenly as their eyes fell upon her, and their leader, an eager, authoritative man, was asking her a question. Why could she not understand him? With her nerveless hands feebly catching at the shrubs for support, she listened vaguely to his impatient, meaningless words, and saw with helpless deprecation the rising anger in his face. But there was no time to be lost. With a curse upon the stupidity of the mountaineer, who couldn't speak when she was spoken to, the party sped on in a sweeping gallop, and the rocks and the steeps were hilarious with the sound.

When the last faint echo was hushed, Clarsie tremblingly made her way out into the road; not reassured, however, for she had a frightful conviction that there was now and then a strange stir in the laurel, and that she was stealthily watched. Her eyes were fixed upon the dense growth with a morbid fascination, as she moved away; but she was once more rooted to the spot when the leaves parted and in the golden moonlight the ghost stood before her. She could not nerve herself to run past him, and he was directly in her way homeward. His face was white, and lined, and thin; that pitiful quiver was never still in the parted lips; he looked at her with faltering, beseeching eyes. Clarsie's merciful heart was stirred. "What ails ye, ter come back hyar, an' foller me?" she cried out, abruptly. And then a great horror fell upon her. Was not one to whom a ghost should speak doomed to death, sudden and immediate?

The ghost replied in a broken, shivering voice, like a wail of pain, "I war a-starvin',—I war a-starvin'," with despairing iteration.

It was all over, Clarsie thought. The ghost had spoken, and she was a doomed creature. She wondered that she did not fall dead in the road. But while those beseeching eyes were fastened in piteous appeal on hers, she could not leave him. "I never hearn that 'bout ye," she said, reflectively. "I knows ye hed awful troubles while ye war alive, but I never knowed ez ye war starved."

Surely that was a gleam of sharp surprise in the ghost's prominent eyes, succeeded by a sly intelligence.

"Day is nigh ter breakin'," Clarsie admonished him, as the lower rim of the moon touched the silver mists of the west. "What air ye a-wantin' of me?"

There was a short silence. Mind travels far in such intervals. Clarsie's thoughts had overtaken the scenes when she should have died that sudden terrible death: when there would be no one left to feed the chickens; when no one would care if the pigs cried with the pangs of hunger, unless, indeed, it were time for them to be fattened before killing. The mare,—how often would she be taken from the plow, and shut up for the night in her shanty without a drop of water, after her hard day's work! Who would churn, or spin, or weave? Clarsie could not understand how the machinery of the universe could go on without her. And Towse, poor Towse! He was a useless cumberer of the ground, and it was hardly to be supposed that after his protector was gone he would be spared a blow or a bullet, to hasten his lagging death. But Clarsie still stood in the road, and watched the face of the ghost, as he, with his eager, starting eyes, scanned her open, ingenuous countenance.

"Ye do ez ye air bid, or it'll be the worse for ye," said the "harnt," in the same quivering, shrill tone. "Thar's hunger in the nex' worl' ez well ez in this, an' ye bring me some vittles hyar this time ter-morrer, an' don't ye tell nobody ye hev seen me, nuther, or it'll be the worse for ye."

There was a threat in his eyes as he disappeared in the laurel, and left the girl standing in the last rays of moonlight.

A curious doubt was stirring in Clarsie's mind when she reached home, in the early dawn, and heard her father talking about the sheriff and his posse, who had stopped at the house in the night, and roused its inmates, to know if they had seen a man pass that way.

"Clarsie never hearn none o' the noise, I'll be bound, 'kase she always sleeps like a log," said Mrs. Giles, as her daughter came in with the pail, after milking the cow. "Tell her 'bout'n it."

"They kem a-bustin' along hyar a while afore day-break, a-runnin' arter the man," drawled Mr. Giles, dramatically. "An' they knocked me up, ter know ef ennybody hed passed. An' one o' them men—I never seen none of 'em afore; they's all valley folks, I'm a-thinkin'—an' one of 'em bruk his saddle-girt' a good piece down the road, an' he kem back ter borrer mine; an' ez we war a-fixin' of it, he tole me what they war all arter. He said that word war tuk ter the sheriff down yander in the valley—'pears ter me them town-folks don't think nobody in the mountings hev got good sense—word war tuk ter the sheriff 'bout this one-armed harnt that walks Chilhowee; an' he sot it down that Reuben Crabb warn't dead at all, an' Joel jes' purtended ter hev buried him, an' it air Reuben hisself that walks Chilhowee. An' thar air two hunderd dollars blood-money reward fur ennybody ez kin ketch him. These hyar valley folks air powerful cur'ous critters,—two hunderd dollars blood-money reward fur that thar harnt that walks Chilhowee! I jes' sot myself ter laffin' when that thar cuss tole it so solemn. I jes' 'lowed ter him ez he couldn't shoot a harnt nor hang a harnt, an' Reuben Crabb hed about got done with his persecutions in this worl'. An' he said that by the time they hed scoured this mounting, like they hed laid off ter do, they would find that that thar puny little harnt war nuthin' but a mortal man, an' could be kep' in a jail ez handy ez enny other flesh an' blood. He said the sheriff 'lowed ez the reason Reuben hed jes' taken ter walk Chilhowee sence Joel died is 'kase thar air nobody ter feed him, like Joel done, mebbe, in the nights; an' Reuben always war a pore, one-armed, weakly critter, what can't even kerry a gun, an' he air driv by hunger out'n the hole whar he stays, ter prowl round the cornfields an' hencoops ter steal suthin',—an' that's how he kem ter be seen frequent. The sheriff 'lowed that Reuben can't find enough roots an' yerbs ter keep

592

him up; but law!—a harnt eatin'! It jes' sot me off ter laffin'. Reuben Crabb hev been too busy in torment fur the las' four year ter be a-studyin' 'bout eatin'; an' it air his harnt that walks Chilhowee."

The next morning, before the moon sank, Clarsie, with a tin pail in her hand, went to meet the ghost at the appointed place. She understood now why the terrible doom that falls upon those to whom a spirit may chance to speak had not descended upon her, and that fear was gone; but the secrecy of her errand weighed heavily. She had been scrupulously careful to put into the pail only such things as had fallen to her share at the table, and which she had saved from the meals of yesterday. "A gal that goes a-robbin' fur a hongry harnt," was her moral reflection, "oughter be throwed bodaciously off'n the bluff."

She found no one at the forks of the road. In the marshy dip were only the myriads of mountain azaleas, only the masses of feathery ferns, only the constellated glories of the laurel blooms. A sea of shining white mist was in the valley, with glinting golden rays striking athwart it from the great cresset of the sinking moon; here and there the long, dark, horizontal line of a distant mountain's summit rose above the vaporous shimmer, like a dreary, sombre island in the midst of enchanted waters. Her large, dreamy eyes, so wild and yet so gentle, gazed out through the laurel leaves upon the floating gilded flakes of light, as in the deep coverts of the mountain, where the fulvous-tinted deer were lying, other eyes, as wild and as gentle, dreamily watching the vanishing moon. Overhead, the filmy, lace-like clouds, fretting the blue heavens, were tinged with a faint rose. Through the trees she caught a glimpse of the red sky of dawn, and the glister of a great lucent, tremulous star. From the ground, misty blue exhalations were rising, alternating with the long lines of golden light yet drifting through the woods. It was all very still, very peaceful, almost holy. One could hardly believe that these consecrated solitudes had once reverberated with the echoes of man's death-dealing ingenuity, and that Reuben Crabb had fallen, shot through and through, amid that wealth of flowers at the forks of the road. She heard suddenly the far-away baying of a hound. Her great eyes dilated, and she lifted her head to listen. Only the solemn silence of the woods, the slow sinking of the noiseless moon, the voiceless splendor of that eloquent day-star.

Morning was close at hand, and she was beginning to wonder that the ghost did not appear, when the leaves fell into abrupt commotion, and he was standing in the road, beside her. He did not speak, but watched her with an eager, questioning intentness, as she placed the contents of the pail upon the moss at the roadside. "I'm a-comin' agin ter-morrer," she said, gently. He made no reply, quickly gathered the food from the ground, and disappeared in the deep shades of the woods.

She had not expected thanks, for she was accustomed only to the gratitude of dumb beasts; but she was vaguely conscious of something wanting, as she stood motionless for a moment, and watched the burnished rim of the moon slip down behind the western mountains. Then she slowly walked along her misty way in the dim light of the coming dawn. There was a footstep in the road behind her; she thought it was the ghost once more. She turned, and met Simon Burney, face to face. His rod was on his shoulder, and a string of fish was in his hand.

"Ye air a-doin' wrongful, Clarsie," he said sternly. "It air agin the law fur folks ter feed an' shelter them ez a-runnin' from jestice. An' ye'll git yerself inter

593

trouble. Other folks will find ye out, besides me, an' then the sheriff'll be up hyar arter ye."

The tears rose to Clarsie's eyes. This prospect was infinitely more terrifying than the awful doom which follows the horror of a ghost's speech.

"I can't help it," she said, however, doggedly swinging the pail back and forth. "I can't gin my consent ter starvin' of folks, even ef they air a-hidin' an' a-runnin' from jestice."

"They mought put ye in jail, too,—I dunno," suggested Simon Burney.

"I can't holp that, nuther," said Clarsie, the sobs rising, and the tears falling fast. "Ef they comes an' gits me, and puts me in the pen'tiary away down yander, somewhars in the valley, like they done Jane Simpkins, fur a-cuttin' of her step-mother's throat with a butcherknife, while she war asleep,—though some said Jane war crazy,—I can't gin my consent ter starvin' of folks."

A recollection came over Simon Burney of the simile of "hendering the sun from shining."

"She hev done sot it down in her mind," he thought, as he walked on beside her and looked at her resolute face. Still he did not relinquish his effort.

"Doin' wrong, Clarsie, ter aid folks what air a-doin' wrong, an' mebbe *hev* done wrong, air powerful hurtful ter everybody, an' henders the law an' jestice."

"I can't holp it," said Clarsie.

"It 'pears toler'ble comical ter me," said Simon Burney, with a sudden perception of a curious fact which has proved a marvel to wiser men, "that no matter how good a woman is, she ain't got no respect fur the laws of the country, an' don't sot no store by jestice." After a momentary silence he appealed to her on another basis. "Somebody will ketch him arter a while, ez sure ez ye air born. The sheriff's a-sarchin' now, an' by the time that word gits around, all the mounting boys'll turn out, 'kase thar air two hunderd dollars blood-money fur him. An' then he'll think, when they ketches him,—an' everybody'll say so, too,—ez ye war constant in feedin' him jes' ter 'tice him ter comin' ter one place, so ez ye could tell somebody whar ter go ter ketch him, an' make them gin ye haffen the blood-money, mebbe. That's what the mounting will say, mos' likely."

"I can't holp it," said Clarsie, once more.

He left her walking on toward the rising sun, and retraced his way to the forks of the road. The jubilant morning was filled with the song of birds; the sunlight flashed on the dew; all the delicate enameled bells of the pink and white azaleas were swinging tremulously in the wind; the aroma of ferns and mint rose on the delicious fresh air. Presently he checked his pace, creeping stealthily on the moss and grass beside the road rather than in the beaten path. He pulled aside the leaves of the laurel with no more stir than the wind might have made, and stole cautiously through its dense growth, till he came suddenly upon the puny little ghost, lying in the sun at the foot of a tree. The frightened creature sprang to his feet with a wild cry of terror, but before he could move a step he was caught and held fast in the strong grip of the stalwart mountaineer beside him. "I hev kem hyar ter tell ye a word, Reuben Crabb," said Simon Burney. "I hev kem hyar ter tell ye that the whole mounting air a-goin' ter turn out ter sarch fur ye; the sheriff air a-ridin' now, an' ef ye don't come along with me they'll hev ye afore night, 'kase thar air two hunderd dollars reward fur ye."

594

What a piteous wail went up to the smiling blue sky, seen through the dappling leaves about them! What a horror, and despair, and prescient agony were in the hunted creature's face! The ghost struggled no longer; he slipped from his feet down upon the roots of the tree, and turned that woful face, with its starting eyes and drawn muscles and quivering parted lips, up toward the unseeing sky.

"God A'mighty, man!" exclaimed Simon Burney, moved to pity. "Why n't ye quit this hyar way of livin' in the woods like ye war a wolf? Why n't ye come back an' stand yer trial? From all I've hearn tell, it 'pears ter me ez the jury air obleeged ter let ye off, an' I'll take keer of ye agin them Grims."

"I hain't got no place ter live in," cried out the ghost, with a keen despair.

Simon Burney hesitated. Reuben Crabb was possibly a murderer,—at the best could but be a burden. The burden, however, had fallen in his way, and he lifted it.

"I tell ye now, Reuben Crabb," he said, "I ain't a-goin' ter holp no man ter break the law an' hender jestice; but ef ye will go an' stand yer trial, I'll take keer of ye agin them Grims ez long ez I kin fire a rifle. An' arter the jury hev done let ye off, ye air welcome ter live along o' me at my house till ye die. Ye air no-'count ter work, I know, but I ain't a-goin' ter grudge ye fur a livin' at my house."

And so it came to pass that the reward set upon the head of the harnt that walked Chilhowee was never claimed.

With his powerful ally, the forlorn little spectre went to stand his trial, and the jury acquitted him without leaving the box. Then he came back to the mountains to live with Simon Burney. The cruel gibes of his burly mockers that had beset his feeble life from his childhood up, the deprivation and loneliness and despair and fear that had filled those days when he walked Chilhowee, had not improved the harnt's temper. He was a helpless creature, not able to carry a gun or hold a plow, and the years that he spent smoking his cob-pipe in Simon Burney's door were idle years and unhappy. But Mrs. Giles said she thought he was "a mighty lucky little critter: fust, he hed Joel ter take keer of him an' feed him, when he tuk ter the woods ter pertend he war a harnt; an' they do say now that Clarsie Pratt, afore she war married, used ter kerry him vittles, too; an' then old Simon Burney tuk him up an' fed him ez plenty ez ef he war a good workin' hand, an' gin him clothes an' houseroom, an' put up with his jawin' jes' like he never hearn a word of it. But law! some folks dunno when they air well off."

There was only a sluggish current of peasant blood in Simon Burney's veins, but a prince could not have dispensed hospitality with a more royal hand. Ungrudgingly he gave of his best; valiantly he defended his thankless guest at the risk of his life; with a moral gallantry he struggled with his sloth, and worked early and late, that there might be enough to divide. There was no possibility of a recompense for him, not even in the encomiums of discriminating friends, nor the satisfaction of tutored feelings and a practiced spiritual discernment; for he was an uncouth creature, and densely ignorant.

595

The grace of culture is, in its way, a fine thing, but the best that art can do— the polish of a gentleman—is hardly equal to the best that Nature can do in her higher moods. (*1884*)

WILLIAM SYDNEY PORTER

1862–1910

William Sydney Porter (O. Henry) was born of a well-established family in Greensboro, North Carolina. He left school at the age of fifteen and worked for five years as a clerk in his uncle's drugstore in Greensboro. In 1882, because of ill health, he moved to a ranch in Texas, where he is said to have developed into a "regular bronco buster." An interest in journalism later led him to Austin, where he married and acquired a magazine, *The Iconoclast* (changed by Porter to *The Rolling Stone*), from the sensational W. C. Brand. He divided his time between his journalistic activities and a job as a bank clerk in Austin.

The Rolling Stone failed after only a year, and in February 1896 Porter was charged with having embezzled $4,702.94 from his bank—he had apparently used the money to keep his magazine alive. Bond was posted, but before the trial came up Porter fled to Honduras. He returned to this country after hearing that his wife was incurably ill, and was tried and sentenced to three years in the penitentiary at Columbus, Ohio.

Prison conditions proved wretched. "Suicides are as common as picnics here," he said. "The men are regarded as animals without soul or feeling." Yet the experience did not embitter Porter in any permanent way; indeed, it may be said to have established him as an author. While in prison he began to write short stories under the pen name of "O. Henry"—a name the author had first applied to a favorite cat. Twelve of his stories are known to have been written before his release in 1900.

From 1902 until his death in 1910, Porter spent most of his time in New York. He contributed to *McClure's* and was under contract to the *New York World* to supply "one story a week for one hundred dollars a story." Porter gathered materials for these highly popular narratives by making frequent visits to bars, brothels, river-front cafés, race tracks, and illegally staged prize fights. His New York stories were collected as *The Four Million* (1906) and *The Voice of the City* (1908). A tribute was paid to Porter's contribution to the field of American letters in 1918, when the Society of Arts and Letters founded the O. Henry Memorial Award for the best American short story published each year.

A Municipal Report

The cities are full of pride,
Challenging each to each—
This from her mountainside,
That from her burthened beach.—R. Kipling.

Fancy a novel about Chicago or Buffalo, let us say, or Nashville, Tennessee! There are just three big cities in the United States that are "story cities"—New York, of course, New Orleans, and, best of the lot, San Francisco.—*Frank Norris.*

East is East, and West is San Francisco, according to Californians. Californians are a race of people; they are not merely inhabitants of a State. They are the Southerners of the West. Now, Chicagoans are no less loyal to their city; but when you ask them why, they stammer and speak of lake fish and the new Odd Fellows Building. But Californians go into detail.

Of course they have, in the climate, an argument that is good for half an hour while you are thinking of your coal bills and heavy underwear. But as soon as they come to mistake your silence for conviction, madness comes upon them, and they picture the city of the Golden Gate as the Bagdad of the New World. So far, as a matter of opinion, no refutation is necessary. But dear cousins all (from Adam and Eve descended), it is a rash one who will lay his finger on the map and say "In this town there can be no romance—what could happen here?" Yes, it is a bold and a rash deed to challenge in one sentence history, romance, and Rand and McNally.

NASHVILLE.—A city, port of delivery, and the capital of the State of Tennessee, is on the Cumberland River and on the N. C. & St. L. and the L. & N. railroads. This city is regarded as the most important educational centre in the South.

I stepped off the train at 8 P.M. Having searched thesaurus in vain for adjectives, I must, as a substitution, hie me to comparison in the form of a recipe.

Take of London fog 30 parts; malaria 10 parts; gas leaks 20 parts; dewdrops gathered in a brick yard at sunrise, 25 parts; odor of honeysuckle 15 parts. Mix.

The mixture will give you an approximate conception of a Nashville drizzle. It is not so fragrant as a moth-ball nor as thick as peasoup; but 'tis enough—'twill serve.

I went to a hotel in a tumbril. It required strong self-suppression for me to keep from climbing to the top of it and giving an imitation of Sidney Carton. The vehicle was drawn by beasts of a bygone era and driven by something dark and emancipated.

I was sleepy and tired, so when I got to the hotel I hurriedly paid it the fifty

597

cents it demanded (with approximate lagniappe, I assure you). I knew its habits; and I did not want to hear it prate about its old "marster" or anything that happened "befo' de wah."

The hotel was one of the kind described as "renovated." That means $20,000 worth of new marble pillars, tiling, electric lights and brass cuspidors in the lobby, and a new L. & N. time table and a lithograph of Lookout Mountain in each one of the great rooms above. The management was without reproach, the attention full of exquisite Southern courtesy, the service as slow as the progress of a snail and as good-humored as Rip Van Winkle. The food was worth traveling a thousand miles for. There is no other hotel in the world where you can get such chicken livers *en brochette*.

At dinner I asked a Negro waiter if there was anything doing in town. He pondered gravely for a minute, and then replied: "Well, boss, I don't really reckon there's anything at all doin' after sundown."

Sundown had been accomplished: it had been drowned in the drizzle long before. So that spectacle was denied me. But I went forth upon the streets in the drizzle to see what might be there.

> It is built on undulating grounds; and the streets are lighted by electricity at a cost of $32,470 per annum.

As I left the hotel there was a race riot. Down upon me charged a company of freedmen, or Arabs, or Zulus, armed with—no, I saw with relief that they were not rifles, but whips. And I saw dimly a caravan of black, clumsy vehicles; and at the reassuring shouts, "Kyar you anywhere in the town, boss, fuh fifty cents," I reasoned that I was merely a "fare" instead of a victim.

I walked through long streets, all leading uphill. I wondered how those streets ever came down again. Perhaps they didn't until they were "graded." On a few of the "main streets" I saw lights in stores here and there; saw street cars go by conveying worthy burghers hither and yon; saw people pass engaged in the art of conversation, and heard a burst of semi-lively laughter issuing from a soda-water and ice-cream parlor. The streets other than "main" seemed to have enticed upon their borders houses consecrated to peace and domesticity. In many of them lights shone behind discreetly drawn window shades, in a few pianos tinkled orderly and irreproachable music. There was, indeed, little "doing." I wished I had come before sundown. So I returned to my hotel.

> In November, 1864, the Confederate General Hood advanced against Nashville, where he shut up a National force under General Thomas. The latter then sallied forth and defeated the Confederates in a terrible conflict.

598 All my life I have heard of, admired, and witnessed the fine marksmanship of the South in its peaceful conflicts in the tobacco-chewing regions. But in my hotel a surprise awaited me. There were twelve bright, new, imposing, capacious brass cuspidors in the great lobby, tall enough to be called urns and so wide-mouthed that the crack pitcher of a lady baseball team should have been able to throw a ball into one of them at five paces distant. But, although a terrible battle

had raged and was still raging, the enemy had not suffered. Bright, new, imposing, capacious, untouched, they stood. But, shades of Jefferson Brick! the tile
floor—the beautiful tile floor! I could not avoid thinking of the battle of Nashville, and trying to draw, as is my foolish habit, some deductions about hereditary marksmanship.

Here I first saw Major (by misplaced courtesy) Wentworth Caswell. I knew
him for a type the moment my eyes suffered from the sight of him. A rat has no
geographical habitat. My old friend, A. Tennyson, said, as he so well said almost
everything:

> *Prophet, curse me the blabbing lip,*
> *And curse me the British vermin, the rat.*

Let us regard the word "British" as interchangeable *ad lib*. A rat is a rat.

This man was hunting about the hotel lobby like a starved dog that had forgotten where he had buried a bone. He had a face of great acreage, red, pulpy,
and with a kind of sleepy massiveness like that of Buddha. He possessed one
single virtue—he was very smoothly shaven. The mark of the beast is not in-
delible upon a man until he goes about with a stubble. I think that if he had not
used his razor that day I would have repulsed his advances, and the criminal
calendar of the world would have been spared the addition of one murder.

I happened to be standing within five feet of a cuspidor when Major Caswell
opened fire upon it. I had been observant enough to perceive that the attacking
force was using Gatlings instead of squirrel rifles, so I sidestepped so promptly
that the major seized the opportunity to apologize to a noncombatant. He had
the blabbing lip. In four minutes he had become my friend and had dragged me
to the bar.

I desire to interpolate here that I am a Southerner. But I am not one by profession or trade. I eschew the string tie, the slouch hat, the Prince Albert, the
number of bales of cotton destroyed by Sherman, and plug chewing. When the
orchestra plays "Dixie" I do not cheer. I slide a little lower on the leather-
cornered seat and, well, order another Würzburger and wish that Longstreet
had—but what's the use?

Major Caswell banged the bar with his fist, and the first gun at Fort Sumter
re-echoed. When he fired the last one at Appomattox I began to hope. But then
he began on family trees, and demonstrated that Adam was only a third cousin
of a collateral branch of the Caswell family. Genealogy disposed of, he took up,
to my distaste, his private family matters. He spoke of his wife, traced her descent back to Eve, and profanely denied any possible rumor that she may have
had relations in the land of Nod.

By this time I began to suspect that he was trying to obscure by noise the
fact that he had ordered the drinks, on the chance that I would be bewildered
into paying for them. But when they were down he crashed a silver dollar loudly
upon the bar. Then, of course, another serving was obligatory. And when I had
paid for that I took leave of him brusquely; for I wanted no more of him. But
before I had obtained my release he had prated loudly of an income that his wife
received, and showed a handful of silver money.

When I got my key at the desk the clerk said to me courteously: "If that man

599

Caswell has annoyed you, and if you would like to make a complaint, we will have him ejected. He is a nuisance, a loafer, and without any known means of support, although he seems to have some money most of the time. But we don't seem to be able to hit upon any means of throwing him out legally."

"Why, no," said I, after some reflection; "I don't see my way clear to making a complaint. But I would like to place myself on record as asserting that I do not care for his company. Your town," I continued, "seems to be a quiet one. What manner of entertainment, adventure, or excitement, have you to offer to the stranger within your gates?"

"Well, sir," said the clerk, "there will be a show here next Thursday. It is—I'll look it up and have the announcement sent up to your room with the ice water. Good-night."

After I went up to my room I looked out the window. It was only about ten o'clock, but I looked upon a silent town. The drizzle continued, spangled with dim lights, as far apart as currants in a cake sold at the Ladies' Exchange.

"A quiet place," I said to myself, as my first shoe struck the ceiling of the occupant of the room beneath mine. "Nothing of the life here that gives color and good variety to the cities in the East and West. Just a good, ordinary, hum-drum, business town."

> Nashville occupies a foremost place among the manufacturing centres of the country. It is the fifth boot and shoe market in the United States, the largest candy and cracker manufacturing city in the South, and does an enormous wholesale drygoods, grocery, and drug business.

I must tell you how I came to be in Nashville, and I assure you the digression brings as much tedium to me as it does to you. I was traveling elsewhere on my own business, but I had a commission from a Northern literary magazine to stop over there and establish a personal connection between the publication and one of its contributors, Azalea Adair.

Adair (there was no clue to the personality except the handwriting) had sent in some essays (lost art!) and poems that had made the editors swear approvingly over their one o'clock luncheon. So they had commissioned me to round up said Adair and corner by contract his or her output at two cents a word before some other publisher offered her ten or twenty.

At nine o'clock the next morning, after my chicken livers *en brochette* (try them if you can find that hotel), I strayed out into the drizzle, which was still on for an unlimited run. At the first corner I came upon Uncle Cæsar. He was a stalwart Negro, older than the pyramids, with gray wool and a face that reminded me of Brutus, and a second afterwards of the late King Cettiwayo. He wore the most remarkable coat that I ever had seen or expect to see. It reached to his ankles and had once been a Confederate gray in colors. But rain and sun and age had so variegated it that Joseph's coat, beside it, would have faded to a pale monochrome. I must linger with that coat, for it has to do with the story— the story that is so long in coming, because you can hardly expect anything to happen in Nashville.

Once it must have been the military coat of an officer. The cape of it had vanished, but all adown its front it had been frogged and tasseled magnificently. But now the frogs and tassels were gone. In their stead had been patiently stitched (I surmised by some surviving "black mammy") new frogs made of cunningly twisted common hempen twine. This twine was frayed and disheveled. It must have been added to the coat as a substitute for vanished splendors, with tasteless but painstaking devotion, for it followed faithfully the curves of the long-missing frogs. And, to complete the comedy and pathos of the garment, all its buttons were gone save one. The second button from the top alone remained. The coat was fastened by other twine strings tied through the buttonholes and other holes rudely pierced in the opposite side. There was never such a weird garment so fantastically bedecked and of so many mottled hues. The lone button was the size of a half-dollar, made of yellow horn and sewed on with coarse twine.

This Negro stood by a carriage so old that Ham himself might have started a hack line with it after he left the ark with the two animals hitched to it. As I approached he threw open the door, drew out a feather duster, waved it without using it, and said in deep, rumbling tones:

"Step right in, suh; ain't a speck of dust in it—jus' got back from a funeral, suh."

I inferred that on such gala occasions carriages were given an extra cleaning. I looked up and down the street and perceived that there was little choice among the vehicles for hire that lined the curb. I looked in my memorandum book for the address of Azalea Adair.

"I want to go to 861 Jessamine Street," I said, and was about to step into the hack. But for an instant the thick, long, gorilla-like arm of the Negro barred me. On his massive and saturnine face a look of sudden suspicion and enmity flashed for a moment. Then, with quickly returning conviction, he asked, blandishingly: "What are you gwine there for, boss?"

"What is that to you?" I asked, a little sharply.

"Nothin', suh, jus' nothin'. Only it's a lonesome kind of part of town and few folks ever has business out there. Step right in. The seats is clean—jes' got back from a funeral, suh."

A mile and a half it must have been to our journey's end. I could hear nothing but the fearful rattle of the ancient hack over the uneven brick paving; I could smell nothing but the drizzle, now further flavored with coal smoke and something like a mixture of tar and oleander blossoms. All I could see through the streaming windows were two rows of dim houses.

> The city has an area of 10 square miles; 181 miles of streets, of which 137 miles are paved; a system of waterworks that cost $2,000,-000, with 77 miles of mains.

Eight-sixty-one Jessamine Street was a decayed mansion. Thirty yards back from the street it stood, outmerged in a splendid grove of trees and untrimmed shrubbery. A row of box bushes overflowed and almost hid the paling fence from sight; the gate was kept closed by a rope noose that encircled the gate post and the first paling of the gate. But when you got inside you saw that 861 was a shell, a shadow, a ghost of former grandeur and excellence. But in the story, I have not yet got inside.

601

When the hack had ceased from rattling and the weary quadrupeds came to a rest I handed my jehu his fifty cents with an additional quarter, feeling a glow of conscious generosity as I did so. He refused it.

"It's two dollars, suh," he said.

"How's that?" I asked. "I plainly heard you call out at the hotel, 'Fifty cents to any part of the town.'"

"It's two dollars, suh," he repeated obstinately. "It's a long ways from the hotel."

"It is within the city limits and well within them," I argued. "Don't think that you have picked up a greenhorn Yankee. Do you see those hills over there?" I went on, pointing toward the east (I could not see them, myself, for the drizzle); "well, I was born and raised on their other side. You old fool nigger, can't you tell people from other people when you see 'em?"

The grim face of King Cettiwayo softened. "Is you from the South, suh? I reckon it was them shoes of yourn' fooled me. They is somethin' sharp in the toes for a Southern gen'l'man to wear."

"Then the charge is fifty cents, I suppose?" said I, inexorably.

His former expression, a mingling of cupidity and hostility, returned, remained ten seconds, and vanished.

"Boss," he said, "fifty cents is right; but I *needs* two dollars, suh; I'm *obleeged* to have two dollars. I ain't *demandin'* it now, suh, after I knows whar you's from; I'm jus' sayin' that I *has* to have two dollars to-night and business is mighty po'."

Peace and confidence settled upon his heavy features. He had been luckier than he had hoped. Instead of having picked up a greenhorn, ignorant of rates, he had come upon an inheritance.

"You confounded old rascal," I said, reaching down to my pocket, "you ought to be turned over to the police."

For the first time I saw him smile. He knew; *he knew;* HE KNEW.

I gave him two one-dollar bills. As I handed them over I noticed that one of them had seen parlous times. Its upper right-hand corner was missing, and it had been torn through in the middle, but joined again. A strip of blue tissue paper, pasted over the split, preserved its negotiability.

Enough of the African bandit for the present: I left him happy, lifted the rope, and opened the creaky gate.

The house, as I said, was a shell. A paint brush had not touched it in twenty years. I could not see why a strong wind should not have bowled it over like a house of cards until I looked again at the trees that hugged it close—the trees that saw the battle of Nashville and still drew their protecting branches around it against storm and enemy and cold.

Azalea Adair, fifty years old, white-haired, a descendant of the cavaliers, as thin and frail as the house she lived in, robed in the cheapest and cleanest dress I ever saw, with an air as simple as a queen's, received me.

602

The reception room seemed a mile square, because there was nothing in it except some rows of books, on unpainted white-pine bookshelves, a cracked marble-topped table, a rag rug, a hairless horsehair sofa, and two or three chairs. Yes, there was a picture on the wall, a colored crayon drawing of a cluster of pansies. I looked around for the portrait of Andrew Jackson and the pine-cone hanging basket but they were not there.

Azalea Adair and I had conversation, a little of which will be repeated to you. She was a product of the old South, gently nurtured in the sheltered life. Her learning was not broad, but was deep and of splendid originality in its somewhat narrow scope. She had been educated at home, and her knowledge of the world was derived from inference and by inspiration. Of such is the precious, small group of essayists made. While she talked to me I kept brushing my fingers, trying, unconsciously, to rid them guiltily of the absent dust from the half-calf backs of Lamb, Chaucer, Hazlitt, Marcus Aurelius, Montaigne, and Hood. She was exquisite, she was a valuable discovery. Nearly everybody nowadays knows too much—oh, so much too much—of real life.

I could perceive clearly that Azalea Adair was very poor. A house and a dress she had, not much else, I fancied. So, divided between my duty to the magazine and my loyalty to the poets and essayists who fought Thomas in the valley of the Cumberland, I listened to her voice which was like a harpsichord's, and found that I could not speak of contracts. In the presence of the nine Muses and the three Graces one hesitated to lower the topic to two cents. There would have to be another colloquy after I had regained my commercialism. But I spoke of my mission, and three o'clock of the next afternoon was set for the discussion of the business proposition.

"Your town," I said, as I began to make ready to depart (which is the time for smooth generalities) "seems to be a quiet, sedate place. A home town, I should say, where few things out of the ordinary ever happen."

> It carries on an extensive trade in stoves and hollow ware with the West and South, and its flouring mills have a daily capacity of more than 2,000 barrels.

Azalea Adair seemed to reflect.

"I have never thought of it that way," she said, with a kind of sincere intensity that seemed to belong to her. "Isn't it in the still, quiet places that things do happen? I fancy that when God began to create the earth on the first Monday morning one could have leaned out one's window and heard the drops of mud splashing from His trowel as He built up the everlasting hills. What did the noisiest project in the world—I mean the building of the tower of Babel—result in finally? A page and a half of Esperanto in the *North American Review*."

"Of course," said I, platitudinously, "human nature is the same everywhere; but there is more color—er—more drama and movement and—er—romance in some cities than in others."

"On the surface," said Azalea Adair. "I have traveled many times around the world in a golden airship wafted on two wings—print and dreams. I have seen (on one of my imaginary tours) the Sultan of Turkey bowstring with his own hands one of his wives who had uncovered her face in public. I have seen a man in Nashville tear up his theatre tickets because his wife was going out with her face covered—with rice powder. In San Francisco's Chinatown I saw the slave girl Sing Yee dipped slowly, inch by inch, in boiling almond oil to make her swear she would never see her American lover again. She gave in when the boiling oil had reached three inches above her knee. At a euchre party in East Nashville the other night I saw Kitty Morgan cut dead by seven of her schoolmates and lifelong friends because she had married a house painter. The boiling oil was sizzling as high as her heart; but I wish you could have seen the fine little smile that she carried from table to table. Oh, yes, it is a hum-drum town. Just a few miles of red brick houses and mud and stores and lumber yards."

Some one had knocked hollowly at the back of the house. Azalea Adair breathed a soft apology and went to investigate the sound. She came back in three minutes with brightened eyes, a faint flush on her cheeks, and ten years lifted from her shoulders.

"You must have a cup of tea before you go," she said, "and a sugar cake."

She reached and shook a little iron bell. In shuffled a small Negro girl about twelve, barefoot, not very tidy, glowering at me with thumb in mouth and bulging eyes.

Azalea Adair opened a tiny, worn purse and drew out a dollar bill, a dollar bill with the upper right-hand corner missing, torn in two pieces and pasted together again with a strip of blue tissue paper. It was one of those bills I had given the piratical Negro—there was no doubt of it.

"Go up to Mr. Baker's store on the corner, Impy," she said, handing the girl the dollar bill, "and get a quarter of a pound of tea—the kind he always sends me—and ten cents' worth of sugar cakes. Now, hurry. The supply of tea in the house happens to be exhausted," she explained to me.

Impy left by the back way. Before the scrape of her hard, bare feet had died away on the back porch, a wild shriek—I was sure it was hers—filled the hollow house. Then the deep, gruff tones of an angry man's voice mingled with the girl's further squeals and unintelligible words.

Azalea Adair rose without surprise or emotion and disappeared. For two minutes I heard the hoarse rumble of the man's voice; then something like an oath and a slight scuffle, and she returned calmly to her chair.

"This a roomy house," she said, "and I have a tenant for part of it. I am sorry to have to rescind my invitation to tea. It is impossible to get the kind I always use at the store. Perhaps to-morrow Mr. Baker will be able to supply me."

I was sure that Impy had not had time to leave the house. I inquired concerning street-car lines and took my leave. After I was well on my way I remembered that I had not learned Azalea Adair's name. But to-morrow would do.

The same day I started in on the course of iniquity that this uneventful city forced upon me. I was in the town only two days, but in that time I managed to lie shamelessly by telegraph, and to be an accomplice—after the fact, if that is the correct legal term—to a murder.

As I rounded the corner nearest my hotel the Afrite coachman of the polychromatic, nonpareil coat seized me, swung open the dungeony door of his peripatetic sarcophagus, flirted his feather duster and began his ritual: "Step right in, boss. Carriage is clean—jus' got back from a funeral. Fifty cents to any——"

And then he knew me and grinned broadly. " 'Scuse me, boss; you is de gen'l'man what rid out with me dis mawnin'. Thank you kindly, suh."

"I am going out to 861 again to-morrow afternoon at three," said I, "and if you will be here, I'll let you drive me. So you know Miss Adair?" I concluded, thinking of my dollar bill.

"I belonged to her father, Judge Adair, suh," he replied.

"I judge that she is pretty poor," I said. "She hasn't much money to speak of, has she?"

For an instant I looked again at the fierce countenance of King Cettiwayo, and then he changed back to an extortionate old Negro hack driver.

"She ain't gwine to starve, suh," he said, slowly. "She has reso'ces, suh; she has reso'ces."

"I shall pay you fifty cents for the trip," said I.

"Dat is puffeckly correct, suh," he answered, humbly. "I jus' *had* to have dat two dollars dis mawnin', boss."

I went to the hotel and lied by electricity. I wired the magazine: "A. Adair holds out for eight cents a word."

The answer that came back was: "Give it to her quick, you duffer."

Just before dinner "Major" Wentworth Caswell bore down upon me with the greetings of a long-lost friend. I have seen few men whom I have so instantaneously hated, and of whom it was so difficult to be rid. I was standing at the bar when he invaded me; therefore I could not wave the white ribbon in his face. I would have paid gladly for the drinks, hoping thereby, to escape another; but he was one of those despicable, roaring, advertising bibbers who must have brass bands and fireworks attend upon every cent that they waste in their follies.

With an air of producing millions he drew two one-dollar bills from a pocket and dashed one of them upon the bar. I looked once more at the dollar bill with the upper right-hand corner missing, torn through the middle, and patched with a strip of blue tissue paper. It was my dollar again. It could have been no other.

I went up to my room. The drizzle and the monotony of a dreary, eventless Southern town had made me tired and listless. I remember that just before I went to bed I mentally disposed of the mysterious dollar bill (which might have formed the clue to a tremendously fine detective story of San Francisco) by saying to myself sleepily: "Seems as if a lot of people here own stock in the Hack-Drivers' Trust. Pays dividends promptly, too. Wonder if——" Then I fell asleep.

King Cettiwayo was at his post the next day, and rattled my bones over the stones out to 861. He was to wait and rattle me back again when I was ready.

. Azalea Adair looked paler and cleaner and frailer than she had looked on the day before. After she had signed the contract at eight cents per word she grew still paler and began to slip out of her chair. Without much trouble I managed to get her up on the antediluvian horsehair sofa and then I ran out to the sidewalk and yelled to the coffee-colored Pirate to bring a doctor. With a wisdom that I had not suspected in him, he abandoned his team and struck off up the street afoot, realizing the value of speed. In ten minutes he returned with a grave, gray-haired, and capable man of medicine. In a few words (worth much less than eight cents each) I explained to him my presence in the hollow house of mystery. He bowed with stately understanding, and turned to the old Negro.

"Uncle Cæsar," he said, calmly, "run up to my house and ask Miss Lucy to

605

give you a cream pitcher full of fresh milk and half a tumbler of port wine. And hurry back. Don't drive—run. I want you to get back sometime this week."

It occurred to me that Dr. Merriman also felt a distrust as to the speeding powers of the land-pirate's steeds. After Uncle Cæsar was gone, lumberingly, but swiftly, up the street, the doctor looked me over with great politeness and as much careful calculation until he had decided that I might do.

"It is only a case of insufficient nutrition," he said. "In other words, the result of poverty, pride, and starvation. Mrs. Caswell has many devoted friends who would be glad to aid her, but she will accept nothing except from that old Negro, Uncle Cæsar, who was once owned by her family."

"Mrs. Caswell!" said I, in surprise. And then I looked at the contract and saw that she had signed it "Azalea Adair Caswell."

"I thought she was Miss Adair," I said.

"Married to a drunken, worthless loafer, sir," said the doctor. "It is said that he robs her even of the small sums that her old servant contributes toward her support."

When the milk and wine had been brought the doctor soon revived Azalea Adair. She sat up and talked of the beauty of the autumn leaves that were then in season and their height of color. She referred lightly to her fainting seizure as the outcome of an old palpitation of the heart. Impy fanned her as she lay on the sofa. The doctor was due elsewhere, and I followed him to the door. I told him that it was within my power and intentions to make a reasonable advance of money to Azalea Adair on future contributions to the magazine, and he seemed pleased.

"By the way," he said, "perhaps you would like to know that you have had royalty for a coachman. Old Cæsar's grandfather was a king in Congo. Cæsar himself has royal ways, as you may have observed."

As the doctor was moving off I heard Uncle Cæsar's voice inside: "Did he git bofe of dem two dollars from you, Mis' Zalea?"

"Yes, Cæsar," I heard Azalea Adair answer, weakly. And then I went in and concluded business negotiations with our contributor. I assumed the responsibility of advancing fifty dollars, putting it as a necessary formality in binding our bargain. And then Uncle Cæsar drove me back to the hotel.

Here ends all of the story as far as I can testify as a witness. The rest must be only bare statements of facts.

At about six o'clock I went out for a stroll. Uncle Cæsar was at his corner. He threw open the door of his carriage, flourished his duster, and began his depressing formula: "Step right in, suh. Fifty cents to anywhere in the city—hack's puffickly clean, suh—jus' got back from a funeral——"

And then he recognized me. I think his eyesight was getting bad. His coat had taken on a few more faded shades of color, the twine strings were more frayed and ragged, the last remaining button—the button of yellow horn—was gone. A motley descendant of kings was Uncle Cæsar!

About two hours later I saw an excited crowd besieging the front of the drug store. In a desert where nothing happens this was manna; so I wedged my way inside. On an extemporized couch of empty boxes and chairs was stretched the mortal corporeality of Major Wentworth Caswell. A doctor was testing him for the mortal ingredient. His decision was that it was conspicuous by its absence.

606

The erstwhile Major had been found dead on a dark street and brought by curious and ennuied citizens to the drug store. The late human being had been engaged in terrific battle—the details showed that. Loafer and reprobate though he had been, he had been also a warrior. But he had lost. His hands were yet clinched so tightly that his fingers could not be opened. The gentle citizens who had known him stood about and searched their vocabularies to find some good words, if it were possible, to speak of him. One kind-looking man said, after much thought: "When 'Cas' was about fo'teen he was one of the best spellers in the school."

While I stood there the fingers of the right hand of "the man that was," which hung down the side of a white pine box, relaxed, and dropped something at my feet. I covered it with one foot quietly, and a little later on I picked it up and pocketed it. I reasoned that in his last struggle his hand must have seized that object unwittingly and held it in a death grip.

At the hotel that night the main topic of conversation, with the possible exceptions of politics and prohibition, was the demise of Major Caswell. I heard one man say to a group of listeners:

"In my opinion, gentlemen, Caswell was murdered by some of these no-account niggers for his money. He had fifty dollars this afternoon which he showed to several gentlemen in the hotel. When he was found the money was not on his person."

I left the city the next morning at nine, and as the train was crossing the bridge over the Cumberland River I took out of my pocket a yellow horn overcoat button the size of a fifty-cent piece, with frayed ends of coarse twine hanging from it, and cast it out of the window into the slow, muddy waters below.

I wonder what's doing in Buffalo! (1910)

607

part **4**

THE MODERN RENAISSANCE

1918 to the present

The Modern Renaissance

The Southern renaissance in letters

To many Southern people of 1865, the loss of the Civil War was the major material calamity in American history. Their slaves had been emancipated (slaves were property) and much of their land had been pillaged. The picture of what conditions actually were becomes concrete when one considers it in terms of a single subject, that of higher education. Dr. L. C. Garland, later first Chancellor of Vanderbilt, wrote his father from the University of Alabama in the fall of 1865: "The University buildings are all burned." He had returned to teach with a single colleague; one student appeared for registration. At the University of Georgia conditions were no better. Windows and buildings were battered in and Greek columns riddled with gunfire. The University of South Carolina was closed for four years. In 1870, thirty-six students were enrolled at the University of North Carolina, which did not open its doors again until 1875. William and Mary, the oldest Southern college, did not operate between 1881–1887.

The astonishing economic recovery the region has made since those days, along with the circumstances which have attended it, has provoked some of our finest modern writing. Certain authors have rejoiced in the modern industrialization, arguing in effect that the South has decided to join the twentieth century and mount the bandwagon of Progress. Others have deprecated the large-scale transformation of Southern life on the score that not everything our ancestors believed in was wholly bad. Still others have invited us, in their fictions, to face contemporary issues and forget our traditions entirely. These several attitudes, with all kinds of individual variations among authors themselves, have a way of stimulating people interested in writing.

The change in Southern life from a predominantly agricultural economy has certainly followed the pattern of the general industrialization of Western society —indeed, of World society. If a given people today is not preëminent in Science, for example, it must forfeit its position of leadership. For America, and more particularly for the South, this lesson has been learned the hard way. Offering relatively large areas of inexpensive land suitable for aviation fields and factories and (with air conditioning widely prevalent) conditions as comfortable for skilled labor as those elsewhere in the nation, the South was *bound*—or as some critics of the turn of events might say, *fated*—to be in considerable measure industrialized. The railroad terminals of Atlanta and the night flares of the furnaces of Birmingham are symbols of a South that is radically altered. The writers have made their own evaluations, which, collectively considered, represent their diverse judgments about the modern South and modern civilization generally.

It is an obsession with reality which has preoccupied many Southern authors. "Isn't this the way it is, or the way it was?" they seem to ask themselves. "And if this is so, must we not try to give it—in so far as words can render anything— an honest representation in language?" Here, in a broad sense, is the theme of recent Southern literature. While individual authors may write with a charming indifference to the existence of one another, in the sum of their efforts can be found an attempt to present the total scene—the inherent tragedies and comedies

611

—and to tell us what we are and have been as a people. This quest for identity has brought about something that might be termed a Southern renaissance. *None Shall Look Back* is the title of one of Caroline Gordon's novels. It must be considered ironically in this sense: we are all looking back constantly, to discover what we are, and why.

The Southern writer has continued to find his principal theme in the Civil War and its aftermath, when conceived in terms of its total implications. From the history of his region and from his personal experience, he has developed an acute awareness that civilizations are mortal, just as men are. The basis of the modern Southern renaissance, perhaps, rests in this sense of the everlasting imminence of death—to a society and to the individual. Mortality might to an important degree be called an underlying theme of *all* great literature, for the simple reason that it is a universal experience. If authors do not possess this sense in terms of their own history, they must arrive at it—as with Housman or Hardy—by instinct. Southern authors have held a unique place among American writers in that they have been able to learn it both ways—through their personal history and through contemplating the history of their people.

The question of belief is another important element in the renaissance. The Southern writer, for the most part, has been loath to discard the ideals of past generations. If he is no longer able to accept completely his grandfather's beliefs, he is nevertheless ready to defend them as worthy ones, at least in the light of their times. Andrew Lytle has phrased the issue in a somewhat different way. He is writing about John Crowe Ransom, but his remarks apply as well to talents as diverse as those of William Faulkner and Stark Young. Tennessee, after the Civil War, Lytle says, was a chastened society:

> The people had believed so absolutely in the support of a just God for a just cause that when this cause went down to defeat, it became plain to all that they had sinned. Out of this grew a great questioning of the heart and a genuine humility before the fact of defeat. Religious debates were held all over the countryside, and they were heartily attended. Certainly [Ransom's] training derived from a coherent view of life. It was the last possible moment to get so completely this kind of education, for this was a historic moment everywhere in the Western world, the latter part of the Nineteenth and the first part of the Twentieth Centuries. It was the last moment of equilibrium, of peace and the enjoyment of the peaceful arts. It was the last time a man could know who he was. Or where he was from. It was the last time a man, without having to think, could say what was right and what was wrong. For almost overnight, with the automobile as a symbol of the change, the community disappeared.[1]

612 It is impossible to say with any certainty what brought the Southern renaissance about, why writers throughout the region became suddenly articulate. John Crowe Ransom advanced some interesting conjectures on this score in an article in *The Virginia Quarterly Review*:

[1] *Reprinted from* The Sewannee Review (*Summer 1948*).

The Southern artists in going modern offer us their impression of a general decay, and that is not a pleasant thing to think about. But another impression which they offer is that, if the old illusions are spent, they do not rush to commit themselves to new ones, and prefer, on the whole, to go down under standards which, if tattered and disreputable, may still be technically said to fly. It is a stubborn attitude, and trying to readers of a certain cast.

It is in this sense, I think, that the Southern writers have gone modern. They reflect decay; their convictions have gone, while their tastes and habits still linger. And here is a strange thing, that the South in its strength never bloomed into art so luxuriantly as now, when the tree is old and dry. A biological notion about that sort of thing became fixed in my mind when I was a little boy, though I think it has no scientific recommendation. There was an apple tree which dropped its limbs one by one as the seasons went by, and finally crashed to earth in a storm. But its apples seemed to grow finer every year to the end, and to be much superior to the apples of the other and healthier trees. I had the feeling that the flavor was better even though the apples tended to be faulty, and could not always be eaten. Are the works of art like those apples, reaching their best when the society behind them is under sentence of death? I offer that as a rhetorical question, not proposing to answer it. But there must be many Southerners waiting like myself to hear the right explanation of the skimpiness of Southern art in those very days when the Southern tradition was unquestioned; and we must feel chastened when we remark that an admired brilliancy in the contemporary display tends nearly always to coincide with a deep-seated decadence.[2]

This diagnosis is familiar; it has been advanced to explain, among others, the Greek renaissance and that of Elizabethan England. It would seem that the aftermath of all major wars becomes a period of fundamental self-appraisal: "Why did it happen, and what has happened to me and to the friends I have cherished?" Anybody interested in an answer to such a question and interested in writing as well has found his basic subject.

One more general consideration about the Southern renaissance seems worth mentioning:[3] it is likely that it would never have occurred without the vigorous movement in criticism which preceded it and which has continued to parallel it. This does not mean Southern criticism exclusively. Academicians like Stuart P. Sherman, Paul Elmer More, Irving Babbitt, and W. C. Brownell are involved— along with such creative talents as Henry James, T. S. Eliot, Ford Madox Ford, and certain French figures of the late nineteenth century. Early Southern literature lacked a vigorous critical tradition, though we should except the penetrating but meager essays of Timrod and the arbitrary, if more extensive, pronouncements of Poe. Collectively considered, modern critics have made our most recent authors more conscious of what they were doing; the process of creation and a critical evaluation of the work being created have tended constantly to accompany and modify each other, with rewarding results.

613

[2] *Reprinted from* The Virginia Quarterly Review (*Spring 1935*).
[3] *Other observations about the modern renaissance have been made in the Foreword.*

The Fugitive and Agrarian movements

The literary magazines of the South have played an important role in shaping Southern literary history and Southern thought during the period following the First World War. While many of these magazines have been short-lived and, in a financial sense, unrewarding, they have provided an important stimulus to Southern literature and may in part account for the development of the modern literary renaissance. The majority of modern Southern writers, particularly the poets, first won recognition through their contributions to one or another of these periodicals.

Perhaps one of the most important and widely remembered of the "little" Southern magazines was *The Fugitive,* a magazine of verse and brief critical commentaries on the state of letters in general. In its pages were published some of the first works of John Crowe Ransom, Allen Tate, Robert Penn Warren, and Merrill Moore. The intention of this magazine was set out explicitly in its first number: "The *Fugitive* flees from nothing faster than the high-caste Brahmins of the Old South." Donald Davidson expanded this comment in a letter to Corra Harris:

> If there is a significance in the title . . . it lies perhaps in the senti-
> ment of the editors . . . to flee from the extreme of conventionalism
> whether old or new. They hope to keep in touch with and to utilize in
> their work the best qualities of modern poetry, without at the same time
> casting aside as unworthy all that is established as good in the past.

Publication of *The Fugitive* began in April 1922 and ended in December 1925, after a total of nineteen numbers had appeared. Its short life may be explained by the fact that many of its editors were becoming increasingly prominent authors in their own right and could no longer devote the necessary time to continue the project.

By the time *Fugitives: An Anthology* was published in 1928, certain members of the original group had achieved national recognition. Not only had dozens of their poems been reprinted in the most widely read collections; several of the number had put out their own books. Ransom had published *Chills and Fever, Grace Before Meat,* and *Two Gentlemen in Bonds.* Donald Davidson was known as the author of *An Outland Piper* and *The Tall Men;* Laura Riding had brought out *The Close Chaplet* and *Voltaire;* Stanley Johnson, *Professor;* Ridley Wills, *Hoax* and *Harvey Landrum.* Five of the original group—Ransom, Davidson, Tate, Warren, and Moore—were also represented in the standard index of contemporary verse, Louis Untermeyer's *Modern American Poetry.* It was only natural, therefore, that *The Fugitive* should attract serious critical attention.

At this same time plans of a much more ambitious nature were being matured by a few members of the Fugitive group, with the assistance of certain friends who were historians, political scientists, and students of philosophy. These men were profoundly concerned with the dominant cultural presuppositions of American life and, particularly, with the relation of the South to those presuppositions. It is important to realize that this interest, which received national attention later as the Agrarian Movement, was in no sense directly related to the Fugitive enter-

614

prise. Of the sixteen Fugitives, only four—Ransom, Davidson, Tate, and Warren
—were represented in *I'll Take My Stand*, the symposium published by the Agrarian group in 1930. The remaining twelve were either hostile or indifferent to the
entire program, or too preoccupied to do more than follow its development privately. In addition to the four Fugitives, the contributors to *I'll Take My Stand*
included the following eight Southerners: Lyle Lanier, Frank Lawrence Owsley,
John Donald Wade, Henry B. Kline, Andrew Lytle, H. C. Nixon, John Gould
Fletcher, and Stark Young.

The statement of principles which introduced *I'll Take My Stand* is generally
known. Its main thesis may be summarized briefly as follows: All of the contributors "tend to support a Southern way of life against what may be called the
American or prevailing way; and all as much as agree that the best terms in which
to represent the distinction are contained in the phrase, Agrarian *versus* Industrial." While acknowledging the principle of political unity as final and desirable,
these twelve Southerners refused to accept the surrender of the South's "moral,
social and economic autonomy" to the more widely prevalent industrial ideal.
This statement of principles, together with the accompanying essays, precipitated
a more widespread controversy, perhaps, than has attended any Southern book
ever printed. Copies of editorials, newspaper articles, and letters-of-protest from
every part of the country virtually deluged the authors. The symposium was not
the kind of document which a person seriously interested in the nature of a capitalistic economy could examine without profound misgivings. The statement of
William S. Knickerbocker, editor of the *Sewanee Review*, was typical of the reaction the book received. He termed it "the most audacious book ever written by
Southerners . . . the most challenging book published since Henry George's
Progress and Poverty." H. L. Mencken assailed it in his *American Mercury*, and
a second time in the *Virginia Quarterly Review*. "So Did Canute" was the caption given to Henry Hazlitt's lengthy attack in the *Nation*, meaning that the
Agrarians would be no more successful than that fabulous king in stemming
the tide of "Progress." Gerald W. Johnson attacked their program in an article in
Harper's, and Howard Mumford Jones disparaged it before a large audience in
Dallas, Texas. The Agrarians were Neo-Confederates, ran the charges; they were
Poets, Fugitives, Escapists, "sufferers from nostalgic vapors," romanticists unwilling to face the realities of modern life. *I'll Take My Stand*, according to one
of its contributors, came to be more thoroughly denounced and misapprehended
by more people who had never read it than any other volume in American literature.

Another magazine, the *American Review*, published in New York, was responsible for giving further expression to the ideas of the original Agrarian group
and certain younger followers who had been attracted to their point of view. This
magazine, a successor to the *Bookman*, was founded in 1933 by Seward Collins,
who announced in his first issue that the Agrarians, along with such English Distributionists as G. K. Chesterton and Hilaire Belloc, were thinkers to whose ideas
he wished principally to devote space. The *American Review* proved important
in another sense, for it led indirectly to the publication of a second symposium,
Who Owns America? (1936). The contributors included a number of Distributionists and American Catholics interested in land reform, virtually all of whom
had previously appeared more than once in the pages of the *American Review*.

615

Literary criticism

The "New Criticism" has been gaining momentum in recent years throughout the United States and in England. It probably received part of its impetus from the *explication de text* in France, which preceded its general vogue with us. Broadly speaking, it might be termed a revolt against hurried and careless reading. "What does a given passage of literature actually *say* or *mean?*" is the question which proponents of this approach are constantly raising. These critics have, by implication and practice, invited us to look more closely at the printed page and to examine and evaluate it. *Scrutiny,* an English publication, and *The Explicator* in this country might be termed interesting manifestations of this revolt. T. S. Eliot, Yvor Winters, I. A. Richards, R. P. Blackmur, Kenneth Burke, and John Crowe Ransom are important pioneers in the movement. Cleanth Brooks and Robert Penn Warren have succeeded in popularizing it on a college level, through the publication of their texts, *Understanding Poetry* and *Understanding Fiction,* and through elaborations in later individual essays and volumes.

Brooks' emphasis is almost always upon specific texts. "If literary history has not been emphasized," he remarks in *The Well Wrought Urn* (1947), "it is not because I discount its importance . . . It is rather that I have been anxious to see what residuum, if any, is left after we have referred the poem to its cultural matrix." He is out of sympathy with the view that "every poem is an expression of its age," that we "must judge it by the canons of its age." Such an attitude, he suggests, tends to make the poetry of the past "significant merely as cultural anthropology." The debate between Brooks and the traditional scholars is thus fairly joined, although he states both positions in extreme terms.

The first chapter of *The Well Wrought Urn* develops an interesting thesis—that the language of poetry is the language of paradox:

> We may approach the problem in this way: the poet has to work by analogies. All of the subtler states of emotion, as I. A. Richards has pointed out, necessarily demand metaphor for their expression. The poet must work by analogies, but the metaphors do not lie in the same plane or fit neatly edge to edge. There is a continual tilting of the planes; necessary overlappings, discrepancies, contradictions. Even the most direct and simple poet is forced into paradoxes far more often than we think, if we are sufficiently alive to what he is doing.
>
> But in dilating on the difficulties of the poet's task, I do not want to leave the impression that it is a task which necessarily defeats him, or even that with his method he may not win a fine precision. To use Shakespeare's figure, he can
>
> > *with assays of bias*
> > *By indirections find directions out.*

Shakespeare had in mind the game of lawnbowls in which the bowl is distorted, a distortion which allows the skillful player to bowl a curve. To elaborate the figure, science makes use of the perfect sphere and its attack can be direct. The method of art can, I believe, never be direct—is always indirect.[4]

One is rather pointedly reminded of John Crowe Ransom's statement in *The World's Body* (1938): "The aesthetic forms are a technic of restraint, not of efficiency. . . . I suggest, therefore, that an art is usually, and probably of necessity, a kind of obliquity; that its fixed form proposes to guarantee the roundabout of the artistic process, and the 'aesthetic distance.' "

Brooks' insistent demand is that we read poetry with care.

> Much modern poetry is difficult. Some of it may be difficult because the poet is snobbish and definitely wants to restrict his audience, though this is a strange vanity and much rarer than Max Eastman would have us think. Some modern poetry is difficult because it is bad—the total experience remains chaotic and incoherent because the poet could not master his material and give it a form. Some modern poetry is difficult because of the special problems of our civilization. But a great deal of modern poetry is difficult for the reader simply because so few people, relatively speaking, are accustomed to reading *poetry as poetry*. The theory of communication throws the burden of proof upon the poet, overwhelmingly and at once. The reader says to the poet: Here I am; it's your job to 'get it across' to me—when he ought to be assuming the burden of proof himself.

It might be remarked that the reader-inertia this critic so accurately sets forth represents no special conspiracy against the art form he is discussing. The same indifference is evident in the case of style—the sentence by sentence structure—in the work of prose writers. The whole problem may be rooted in the simple truth that no two individuals can perfectly communicate with each other. Brooks and William Empson, for example, interpret certain key passages of Gray's "Elegy" in fundamentally different ways. It is this kind of expert disagreement which explains, though it does not justify, the disposition of the average reader to insist upon a thread of meaning in a poem and which leaves him dissatisfied when he fails to discover it. This skeletal meaning he can share with others; it contributes to the satisfaction he feels upon discovering himself anew as a social being. Yet it is valuable to remember Brooks' warning: "We can very properly use paraphrase [that is, a prose summary of content] provided that we know what we are doing. But it is highly important that we know what we are doing and that we see plainly that the paraphrase is not the real core of meaning which contributes the essence of the poem."

The overall limitations of this approach to literature have been frequently noticed. Perhaps, in substance, they may be summarized in these questions: Why demand of a reader that he suppress his sense of history? How will it hurt him to know that Milton's "Lycidas" was written in the tradition of the pastoral elegy, and that the poet felt honor-bound to respect its conventions? Many scholars

617

[4] *Excerpts from* The Well Wrought Urn *by Cleanth Brooks reprinted by permission of Harcourt, Brace and Company, Inc., copyright, 1947.*

have argued that the more we know about an author and his age, the more clearly we can comprehend him and his work.

The controversy centering about the issue of how poetry should be read will undoubtedly continue for a long time—as long as poetry or any other kind of literature is appreciated in a serious way. Parallels in the other art forms—whether in sculpture, painting, music, or the drama—become evident on a moment's reflection. These divergent points of view are what mainly keep the creative arts alive.

Folk trends

The recent widespread interest in folk customs and traditions has been nowhere more evident than in the efforts of scholars to study and collect the great wealth of Southern folk literature. The discoveries resulting from these investigations have to a striking degree pointed up the richness of the Southern tradition. This "movement"—it may almost be termed such—began approximately thirty years ago and has grown in interest and excitement ever since. A pioneer in the field, although he himself wrote little, was C. Alphonso Smith of Virginia. Other more recent and important pioneers have been Reed Smith of South Carolina; George Pullen Jackson of Tennessee; and John Avery Lomax of Texas. Paralleling the work of these scholars has been the founding of folklore societies in every Southern state. These societies issue regular quarterlies or bulletins, and the material that they continue to uncover seems inexhaustible.

Our present-day creative authors have used these findings on what might be termed a modern level, in so far as narrative and dramatic techniques are concerned. What is worth remembering, however, is the fact that earlier Southern men of letters also took advantage of the possibilities of their folk tradition, both for tragic and comic representations of human experience. William Gilmore Simms, Thomas Nelson Page, and Joel Chandler Harris acquired the folk tradition almost as effortlessly and as unconsciously as they acquired their physical growth—and this is to name only a few nineteenth-century authors who recognized its importance some years before Paul Green, DuBose Heyward, Julia Peterkin, Thomas Wolfe, Elizabeth Madox Roberts, William Faulkner, Donald Davidson, Caroline Gordon, and Eudora Welty, among others, began to explore and to use this material in their several ways.

Perhaps the most important characteristic of all folk literature is that it is essentially an oral literature. The countless folk tales which recently have been collected—ghost and animal stories and tall tales—have existed for generations, but rarely in printed form. Excellent as many written versions of folk tales are, the oral versions were necessarily somewhat changed in being transcribed. The audience, setting, and spontaneity of the narrator have been lost, and with them much of the original charm and flavor of the tales. Folk tales, like folksongs, are the product not of a single literary artist, but of a great number of re-creating transmitters, which means that the collector has no standard version of a tale from which to work. Most collectors have chosen a typical oral version of a tale and tried to render it into words as faithfully as possible, although a few have deliberately altered the stories to make them conform to the sophisticated tastes of modern readers.

Currently, the most popular type of folk literature is the folksong. In terms of source, Southern folksongs are chiefly of two kinds—those of native American origin and those that are variants of much older British pieces. There are several varieties of folksongs, though none is sharply defined: ballads (impersonal narrative songs), ballad songs (more subjective), love songs, spirituals, laments, comic songs, lullabies, dance songs, work songs, and occupational songs (of the farmer, the sailor, the cowboy, the lumberman). The term *ballad* might be most undebatably applied to the older British pieces, texts of most of which were published by Professor Child in *The English and Scottish Popular Ballads* (1882–1898), together with perhaps no more than two or three American items. Love songs are often courting songs or perhaps songs about unrequited love, in which case they merge into the lament (dirges, jail-house songs, blues). Spirituals include folk hymns, revival songs, and "shouts." Work songs differ from occupational songs in being sung or grunted by manual laborers while they are actually performing some sort of repetitive work. Poetically, the finest folksongs current in the South today are survivals of the old-world ballads. Of Child's 305 separate ballads, upwards of eighty have been found in oral tradition in the South. Two of the folksongs reprinted in this text, "Barbara Allen" and "Lord Thomas and Fair Eleandor," are American versions of Child ballads.

The airs to which folk poems are sung are traditionally nonharmonic and constitute a flexible melodic accompaniment, remarkably well-suited to the poetry. Folk tunes recognize no allegiance to the modern tempered or chromatic scale of tones, nor do they necessarily maintain their original meter throughout. Many of the melodies which are still sung in the South are neither major nor harmonic minor in tonality, but modal like medieval ecclesiastical music. An extraordinary illustration of this vestigial tendency is found in the folk-hymn tunes of the *Sacred Harp*, of which some, although appearing on the page in minor, are performed by the singers unconsciously in the Dorian mode.

It is the wonderful relationship between folk poetry and music that lifts the ballad to its unique position as an art form. Tune and text are welded inseparably together into a single end-product. The musical meter intensifies and enriches the prosodic reading of the poem; there is even a correlation between vowel and tone pitch level. The fundamental rhythm movement of a tune may change during its course in order best to fit stanzaic architecture, and the tune itself may vary from stanza to stanza to suit the demands of the text. Ornaments —grace notes and vocal twists—are attached to the tune at points directed partly by the poetry. In short, fluid flexibility between text and tune is foremost in the performance of the traditional folk singer.

The specific sources of folksongs of American origin can be isolated with some accuracy because of relatively recent research, although the problem is often difficult. One of the earliest songs, "Springfield Mountain," apparently originated because of the death of "Lieutenant Myrick's only son," who was bitten by a rattlesnake in Massachusetts, in 1761. It is sung today, with many variants in the South, almost as often as favorite English ballads. Although "Casey Jones" is believed to have been adapted from an older ballad, the wreck described took place in 1900. Many of the more pretentious American folksongs were written by newspaper men and poetasters in the wake of the events they commemorate. Without doubt, many of them—including spirituals, revival hymns, blues, and

619

work songs—were orally composed out of what is not inaccurately called "inspiration."

The sources of the traditional ballads and other old-world folksongs are lost in uncertainty, but various theories have been formulated to explain the nature of their origin. The "communal" theory argues that the beginning of the ballad was in the choral dance, with one or more leaders composing and singing stanzas in the heat of group inspiration and the dancers joining in on the chorus; the "minstrel" theory supposes that some ballads were orally devised by illiterate geniuses among the people; and the "literary" theory suggests that some were written by recognized or hack poets of the day, among whose gifts were a strong sense of rhythm and the common touch.

Whatever their precise origin, the ballads passed into the memories of singers and, sometimes, reciters. Unwritten transmission thereupon began, to terminate generations later in a collector's notebook. But collection is not the end of a ballad. Since no two versions of a folksong are ever identical, there is even now no such thing as an established text. Thus in a very real sense, the folksong—like all folk literature—exists in its variants. In spite of their necessary limitations, however, the collectors of folk literature have performed a valuable service in preserving and making available to a wide audience an important literary and cultural heritage which might otherwise have been lost.

Stark Young

Unlike many modern Southern authors who have taken as their theme a South marked by decadence and violence, Stark Young writes of the genteel South of charming tradition—the South of good taste and good breeding, of gay parties, belles, courtly planters, and an endless array of relatives. Some of Young's most succinct statements about his region can be found in his critical essays, among the most important of which is "Not in Memoriam, But in Defense." Here he vigorously defends certain traditional attitudes and customs, which have long been "the flower of Southern civilization," against the encroachments of a modern, industrial society. In defending the old Southern life, he is asking Southerners to temper their acceptance of the new epoch with the values they have learned from their own tradition, to preserve what was good in the past and combine it with what is good in the present.

Young's defense of the aristocratic South takes into account its shortcomings:

> The aristocratic implied with us a certain long responsibility for others; a habit of domination; a certain arbitrariness; certain ideas of personal honor, with varying degrees of ethics, *amour propre*, and the fantastic. And it implied the possession of no little leisure. Whether that was a good system or not is debatable. I myself think it, if we had to make a choice strictly between either one or the other, better than a society of bankers and bankers' clerks, department-store communities, manufacturers and their henchmen and their semi-slaves, and miserable little middle-class cities . . . This way of life meant mutuality of interests among more people, an innate code of obligations, and a cer-

620

tain openness of life. It meant self-control that implied not the expression of you and your precious personality, not the pleasures of suffering or of denying your own will; you controlled yourself in order to make the society you lived in more decent, affable, and civilized and yourself more amenable and attractive.[5]

Young illustrates the values and attitudes he would defend more specifically in "Encaustics for Southerners" (*Virginia Quarterly Review*, April 1935), in a series of ten sketches, each on the order of a "case history."

The attitudes expressed in Young's essays and critical statements are characteristic of the point of view found throughout his fiction. The pattern of his novels observes roughly the following chronological arrangement: *Heaven Trees*, 1830; *So Red the Rose*, 1860 through the aftermath of war; *The Torches Flare*, the early nineteen-twenties; and *River House*, a period two years later. The same family names recur in all four books. Young's novels may be said to deal with three questions: What was the nature of the Southern tradition before it was violated? In what ways was it affected by the Civil War and Reconstruction? What is its place in society today?

Heaven Trees is concerned with the first question, the elements of tradition. To define any tradition is an abstract problem, but the characteristic qualities of the Southern tradition are present in all of Young's books: family pride, a moral code, close family ties, an enjoyment and use of leisure, fine homes and gardens, the *noblesse oblige* attitude of master toward slave. These are its basis. Young summarily terms it "the art of living." It was an art practiced during the past century and in many places to the present day, at a sacrifice of certain of the more formally recognized arts.

In *Heaven Trees*, the author defines the traditional Southern attitude toward family:

If confusion reigns in these pages of so many aunts and uncles, fathers, mothers and cousins, it is little wonder; we hardly had it straight ourselves. When visitors from far away asked for the right plan of the family we always said it was all the family and might go at that if the visitor liked; the very essence of family life, uncle George said, was confusion. Though sometimes, too, when these visitors inquired, I laid our states of kinship more plainly out for them. . . . The truth, however, was that in my heart they were all the same kin to me, and I remember them as I do the garden at Heaven Trees, as flowers one after another, rather than a system of branches and family trees.[6]

The opinions of many of Young's characters seem frequently an expression of his own, as they may be traced in his essays. Hugh McGehee in *So Red the Rose* is talking to Duncan Bedford, after the latter's return from the war:

Democracy, a good theory, a great human right, which works out none too well; slavery, a great human wrong, which works out none too

621

[5] From "Not in Memoriam, But in Defense" by Stark Young, in I'll Take My Stand, *Harper & Brothers*, 1930.
[6] From Heaven Trees by Stark Young, *Charles Scribner's Sons*, 1936.

badly. I endorsed democracy, I condemned slavery; and here I am with my house burned down and my coloured people free, deceived with false promises, mixed up and robbed. Mr. Mack [a Northern speculator who had come South] and his crew won't consume me . . . these men just haven't enough life behind them to match me. I mean by "life" tradition, forefathers, and a system of living. . . . It's as if I stood on the ground and they didn't. . . . I've noticed that our people her'n this country—by way of defending themselves, I reckon—have already begun boasting of what they had, their former splendor and so on. But what they would do better to speak would be not what they had but what they have loved.[7]

This is an argument that Young makes recurrently, both in his fiction and in his prose criticism.

The Torches Flare is the story of Eleanor Dandridge, a Mississippi girl who becomes successful on the Broadway stage. While in New York she has an affair with Arthur Lane, a native Kentuckian. Bohemianism proved acceptable in New York, but when Lane follows Eleanor home, the illicit affair becomes sordid to her; she cannot in conscience practice deception upon her provincial father and aunt. The traditional South has asserted itself in the bones, as it were, of a person who would outwardly try to escape it. For Arthur the tradition was a disgusting, senseless impediment; for Eleanor it involved the intangible issue of conscience.

Similarly in *River House*, Major Dandridge, "a man now close to sixty, tall and slender, with a proud head," wonders what has happened to the world. "I might ask—are there any more codes at all these days? There are no codes to follow anymore. There's only the individual case, you decide it for yourself. That's all right if you are an exceptional being. But for most people a society depends on a code and without a code they are lost." [8]

These are the things that Stark Young has been saying and representing in his fiction and even, if intuitively, in his painting and dramatic criticism. As a literary artist, he has created a prose style rich and varied in its cadence. It seldom falters into mere graceful lyricism or showmanship; it seldom becomes too artificial or obvious. The reason for this may be that Young has a great deal to say about a period immediate in time. Perhaps his engrossing predilection for detail tends to bewilder a reader looking for a story with a clean and lively plot. One should go to his writing, primarily, to find a set of mind, a way of apprehending one's personal past, with all its follies, affectionate absurdities, and unspectacular grandeurs. Young never deserts or repudiates his people, out of the conviction, once expressed, that "people who give up their own land too readily need careful weighing, exactly as do those who are so with their convictions."

Thomas Wolfe

622

Perhaps the most striking impression conveyed by the writings of Thomas Wolfe is that here was an immense, if undisciplined, talent—exuberant, inexhaust-

[7] *From* So Red the Rose *by Stark Young, Charles Scribner's Sons, 1934.*
[8] *From* River House *by Stark Young, Charles Scribner's Sons, 1929.*

ible, romantic, narcissistic, essentially melancholy. His is the story of a man at odds with an environment which at once bewildered and fascinated him. As some critics have reminded us, Wolfe wrote too much and too loosely, leaving to his editors, Maxwell Perkins and, later, Edward C. Aswell, the strenuous task of imposing a semblance of order upon his sprawling manuscripts. It may sometimes seem that his editors were charitable in their inclusions, yet to have cut Wolfe's material more drastically would have involved a fundamental misrepresentation of his mind. For Wolfe speaks for his age in a way which only the vital but half-articulate genius can portray it: he is the dissociated individual, "lost, lost, lost." T. S. Eliot gave us such a representation in "The Love Song of J. Alfred Prufrock"; he is likewise evident in Allen Tate's "Ode to the Confederate Dead" and in Eudora Welty's little girl, Ellen, in *Delta Wedding*. Yet Eliot, Tate, Welty, and others projected their characters into the formal pattern of art: Eliot, as a person, is no more a Prufrock than Shakespeare was a King Lear or an Othello. Wolfe, on the other hand, *is* the Eugene Gant of *Look Homeward, Angel* and the George Webber of *You Can't Go Home Again*.

Another outstanding characteristic of Wolfe is that he wanted to represent everything in his writing—the poetry, the geography, the social strata which his broad, rich, passionate land afforded. He had a consuming lust for every kind of experience and he had to get it all down in his writing. On deciding to become an author, Wolfe wrote to his mother: "I will go everywhere and see everything. I will meet all the people I can. I will think all the thoughts, feel all the emotions I am able, and I will write, write, write." This effort at all-inclusiveness is a solidly established tradition in American literature—witness the writing of Walt Whitman. The price it exacts has always been that of structural confusion, a certain formlessness which most modern authors have tried to avoid. They have studied Flaubert, Henry James, Conrad, Ford Madox Ford, and others, together with the exegetes of these authors in criticism. But Wolfe, though he tried to learn from the example of other writers, found nothing outside of himself to use as a guide. He had to put down his material as he felt it and to progress, in the matter of form, by trial and error. While his work lacks the conventional novel form, when viewed as a whole it does, nonetheless, have a form of its own. As Edward C. Aswell has pointed out, Wolfe's writings present a larger form, that of life itself. His work, if taken in its entirety without regard to how the various pieces are put together, tells the single story of Eugene Gant and George Webber—or of Thomas Wolfe.

Most of Wolfe's writing exhibits an intensely perceptive sense, which one may or may not equate with poetry. John Hall Wheelock, in his introduction to *The Face of a Nation,* calls Wolfe "a born poet, the author of some of the most magnificent dithyrambic passages in literature," quoting as an example:

> Each of us is all the sums he has not counted; subtract us into nakedness and night again and you shall see begin in Crete four thousand years ago the love that ended yesterday in Texas.

Wolfe immediately repeats the idea:

> The seed of our destruction will blossom in the desert, the elixir of our cure grows by a mountain rock, and our lives are haunted by a Georgia

623

slattern because a London cutpurse went unhung. Each moment is the print of forty thousand years.

It is difficult to say in what precise sense these statements can be termed poetry. Similar paragraphs may be found in authors like DeQuincey, passages lyrical in the same way. They arouse in the reader a vague recollection of his racial history, a recollection which is superimposed upon the context of the sentences themselves. They do not, however, necessarily warrant the claim of being poetry.

Wolfe's ever-recurring theme is that of man's loneliness. Nowhere, perhaps, is this theme more succinctly articulated than in his essay "God's Lonely Man":

> He knows that dark time is flowing by him like a river. The huge, dark wall of loneliness is around him now. It encloses and presses in upon him, and he cannot escape. And the cancerous plant of memory is feeding at his entrails, recalling hundreds of forgotten faces and ten thousand vanished days, until all life seems as strange and insubstantial as a dream. Time flows by him like a river, and he waits in his little room like a creature held captive by an evil spell. And he will hear, far off, the murmurous drone of the great earth, and feel that he has been forgotten, that his powers are wasting from him while the river flows, and that all his life has come to nothing. He feels that his strength is gone, his power withered, while he sits there drugged and fettered in the prison of his loneliness.[9]

Wolfe once wrote to Maxwell Perkins: "Man was born to live, to suffer, and to die, and what befalls him is a tragic lot. There is no denying this is the final end. *But we must, dear Fox, deny it all along the way.*" Is the right word *deny* or *comprehend*? And in the act of comprehension should we not rather seek to understand ourselves in relation to the ultimate fact about human experience— the fact of its transience? Wolfe appears to have been a man who would have said to almost every moment's experience: "Stay, thou art so fair."

Wolfe is usually discussed as a "world figure"; as a Southern figure he has been too often ignored or misinterpreted. In a letter to his mother, he wrote of one of his early works: "I spared Boston . . . no more than the South, which I love, but which I nevertheless pounded." In some of his statements about "those people who shout 'Progress, Progress, Progress'—when what they mean is more Ford automobiles, more Rotary clubs, more Baptist Ladies Social Unions," Wolfe seemed to ally himself not only with the point of view of Sinclair Lewis, but also with that of the Agrarians. In *The Hills Beyond* he indicates, simultaneously, a love for the South and a critical attitude toward it. The selections reprinted in this text show Wolfe frequently working in the vein of the Old Southwest humorists. "The Great Schism" is a study of the mountain rural and the urban South, or, as Wolfe says, "the history of those who stayed at home, and of those who went to town."

624

The Hills Beyond is of interest, too, in that it shows a considerable change in Wolfe's artistic method since the writing of his first-published novel, *Look Home-*

[9] *From "God's Lonely Man," in* The Hills Beyond *by Thomas Wolfe, Harper & Brothers, 1941.*

ward, Angel (1929). Edward C. Aswell, in his notes on Wolfe, has effectively described the change found in the later work:

> In some parts of it the style is lean and bare beyond anything one would have expected to find in Wolfe. There is both a gain and a loss in this—a gain in compactness along with objectivity; a loss of the lyrical and poetic intensity of his earlier writing. (Tom said it was good for a young man to sing, and also good for an older man to want something else so much that he would stop singing.)

Wolfe's most avid readers will probably continue to remember his flow of language. Unfortunately, it is impossible to determine what direction he would have taken had he reached his full maturity as an artist. But whatever is the final estimate of Wolfe's artistic method, readers will return to his books for as long a time as loneliness continues to eat at man's heart.

William Faulkner

The primary considerations about William Faulkner are that readers return to him again and again in an effort to assess his meaning and that his meaning is constantly in a condition of change, like the world itself. He presents the story of a conquered people, of a society which—if in part conceived in violence—evolved a code of honor based upon a sense of property, of human dignity and worth. Faulkner writes about the South because it is a region he knows at first hand, both traditionally and through personal experience. But beyond this, his work is a judgment upon the human race. He gives us his own tragic vision of man's fate as man.

Faulkner's total situation is conceived in terms of four families: the Sartorises, the Compsons, the Sutpens, and the Snopeses. The Sartoris and Compson families—and even the Sutpens, by extension—are aristocratic and traditional. All three clans were destroyed, both economically and spiritually, by the Civil War and its aftermath. Their inheritors, the Snopeses, take over because theirs are the ruthless and unscrupulous methods of our own age. No code of honor is comprehensible to them, nor can the descendants of the aristocracy compete with them, for they are impotent in the use of the weapons of aggrandizement which must accompany success in the modern South and, by implication, in the modern world.

George Marion O'Donnell, in an essay in the *Kenyon Review* (Summer 1939), defined the major issue in Faulkner's work for the first time. It was O'Donnell who stated the conflict sharply in terms of two types of characters: "They are Sartorises and Snopeses, whatever the family names may be. And in the spiritual geography of Mr. Faulkner's work there are two worlds: the Sartoris world and the Snopes world. In all of his successful books, he is exploring these two worlds in detail, dramatizing the inevitable conflict between them." The one family acts traditionally, morally, responsibly; the other only out of self-interest—animalistically, amorally. A character in *The Unvanquished* remarks, "General Johnson

625

or General Forrest wouldn't have took a Snopes into his army at all"; this epitomizes what O'Donnell calls the Faulkner Myth. By *myth* this critic means any set of assumptions, or constructs, which enables an author to conceive of his subject matter coherently in imaginative terms. To strict historians, these assumptions may be distortions of fact; yet they need not be distortions of that fundamental reality which it is the business of the creative artist to communicate.

Malcolm Cowley's more extended study of Faulkner in the *Sewanee Review* (Summer 1945) and the *Portable Faulkner* (1946) leans heavily upon O'Donnell's analysis, though it is rewarding in its own right. Cowley divides Faulkner's novels into five cycles: "One about the planters and their descendants, one about the townspeople of Jefferson, one about the poor whites, one about the Indians . . . and one about the Negroes." Cowley notices also the curious combination in Faulkner's work of two major traditions in American letters: the "tradition of psychological horror, often close to symbolism, that begins with Charles Brockden Brown, our first professional novelist, and extends through Poe, Melville, Henry James (in his later stories), Stephen Crane, and Hemingway; and the other tradition of frontier humor and realism, beginning [in its written, not its oral form] with Augustus Longstreet's *Georgia Scenes* and having Mark Twain as its best example."

O'Donnell and Cowley have defined the central problem in Faulkner's work. It is interesting to see how it appears when set out concretely in *The Sound and the Fury* (1929), which Faulkner is said to regard as his best work. The novel is in four parts and is the story of four members of the doomed Compson family. The first action deals with Benjy, a thirty-three-year-old idiot, whose mind is that of a child of five. He was christened Maury, a name his father continues to use, but was rechristened Benjamin by his brother Quentin ("Benjamin, our lastborn, sold into Egypt"). Benjy, Faulkner remarks in his notes on the family, loves three things: "the pasture which was sold to pay for Candace's wedding and to send Quentin to Harvard, his sister Candace, [and] firelight." He

> lost none of them because he could not remember his sister but only the loss of her, and firelight was the same bright shape as going to sleep, and the pasture [which had been made into a golf course] was even better sold than before because now he and T. P. [a Negro boy] could not only follow timeless along the fence the motions which it did not even matter to him were humanbeings swinging golfsticks, T. P. could lead them to clumps of grass or weeds where there would appear suddenly in T. P.'s hand small white spherules which competed with and even conquered what he did not even know was gravity and all the immutable laws . . .[10]

All time and space are confused in Benjy's mind; he knows only the craving for pure sensation—a craving which Faulkner might term the disease of the modern world. Benjy, confusing the golfer's shout of "caddie" with the name of his lost sister Candace ("Caddy"), who has taken care of him, becomes, by extension, the author's characterization of his generation.

626

[10] *Excerpts from William Faulkner's notes to* The Sound and the Fury *reprinted by permission of Random House, Inc. Copyright, 1946, by William Faulkner.*

The astonishing verisimilitude of detail in Benjy's part of the story tends to deceive the reader, for this is "a tale told by an idiot," and an audience brought up on the well-made novel wants to know how Benjy could be capable of the telling. The answer is that the section is pure myth. This remarkable fusion of myth with realism has been achieved by other modern writers—witness Eudora Welty —but never more successfully than by Faulkner.

The second part of *The Sound and the Fury* is Quentin's story, the last complex day in the life of this guilt-obsessed youth at Harvard. He awakens and hears the ticking of his grandfather's watch:

> It was propped against the collar box and I lay listening to it. Hearing it, that is. I don't suppose anybody ever deliberately listens to a watch or a clock. You don't have to. You can be oblivious to the sound for a long while, then in a second of ticking it can create in the mind unbroken the long diminishing parade of time you didn't hear. Like Father said down the long and lonely lightrays you might see Jesus walking, like. And the good Saint Francis that said Little Sister Death, that never had a sister.[11]

Determined to take his own life, Quentin first mutilates the watch:

> I went to the dresser and took up the watch, with the face still down. I tapped the crystal on the corner of the dresser and caught the fragments of glass in my hand and put them into the ashtray and twisted the hands off and put them in the tray. The watch ticked on . . . not knowing any better.

Quentin's obsession is his sister Caddy—promiscuous, turned virtually whore— who is pregnant by one of the town men, Dalton Ames. Hoping to give some dignity to her disgrace—to make of it a sin, not a trifling accident—Quentin had declared to his father that the unborn child was his own, that he was guilty of incest. At a picnic he attends, Quentin—drunk—is beaten up by Gerald, an amateur boxer who had been boasting of his prowess with women. Quentin's roommate explains the occasion: "The first I knew was when you jumped up all of a sudden and said, 'Did you ever have a sister? Did you?' and when he said No, you hit him."

Part III is the story of Jason Compson, who is a bastard and knows it; "You are a Bascomb despite your name," his mother once tells him. Jason is the breadwinner of the family. He supports his distracted mother, Benjy, and Caddy's illegitimate and whorish daughter Quentin, in addition to "a whole damn kitchen full of niggers." Jason was not able to go to Harvard, as Quentin had done. With his own money, which he had saved from his meager wages as a store clerk, he had sent himself "to a Memphis school where he had learned to class and grade cotton and so establish his own business . . . with which he assumed the entire burden of the rotting family and the rotting house."

Jason Compson is one of the most complex characters in Faulkner's work. He

627

[11] *Excerpts from* The Sound and the Fury *reprinted by permission of Random House, Inc. Copyright, 1929, 1930, by William Faulkner.*

represents that last desperate gesture of pride in a family name—not truly his own —that has become to the outside world synonymous with degeneracy. He is mean, grasping, hard, calculating, and for most purposes illiterate; yet he will not surrender, despite his most fierce and bitter personal denials of interest in whatever is considered conventionally respectable. In his own notes, Faulkner traces Jason's history to its culmination. He is described, after his mother's death, as

> moving into a pair of offices up a flight of stairs above the supplystore containing his cotton ledgers and samples, which he had converted into a bedroom-kitchen-bath, in and out of which on weekends there could be seen a big plain friendly brazenhaired pleasantfaced woman no longer very young, in round picture hats and (in its season) an imitation fur coat, the two of them, the middleaged cottonbuyer and the woman whom the town called, simply, his friend from Memphis, seen at the local picture show on Saturday night and on Sunday morning mounting the apartment stairs with paper bags from the grocer's containing loaves and eggs and oranges and cans of soup, domestic, uxorious, connubial, until the late afternoon bus carried her back to Memphis. He was emancipated now. He was free. "In 1865," he would say, "Abe Lincoln freed the niggers from the Compsons. In 1933, Jason Compson freed the Compsons from the niggers."

So for him ran the world of Jefferson, "where life lived too with all its incomprehensible passion and turmoil and grief and fury and despair."

Dilsey, the Negro cook, is the strongest character in the last section of *The Sound and the Fury*. Faulkner's note about her—which may be said to apply to all the Negroes in the book—seems cryptic, yet the meaning is unmistakable: "They endured." This was his summation of human experience. We endure it or we are destroyed by it. Dilsey runs the Compson house and is the single principle of order within it.

In this final section the action is once more concerned with Jason, this time with his futile effort to find his niece Quentin, who stole all his savings and ran off with a circus employee. Why had he not kept his money in a bank? "Because to him a banker too was just one more Compson." Faulkner seems here to be rendering the retributive irony which almost invariably accompanies perverse human experience. Jason deserved whatever calamities befell him. Similarly, Popeye, in *Sanctuary*, is hanged on the charge of having committed an act of which he is innocent, though he deserved such a death for numerous other reasons. It is this irony—the unpredictable fall of the dice, which somehow seems at last to follow a principle of averages—that defines the moral sense of William Faulkner and that invests his major theme with a sense of dignity and unarguable conviction.

In his brief Nobel speech a more mature Faulkner is talking. One should think of him as a man of questing and always restless imagination, with which all creative writers of the first rank have been blessed, or cursed. What he has written about the Negro, for example, reflects the complexity of the problem which has occupied the attention of people of both races. Far more of his evil characters have been "white" people than have been "black" people, although nobody is ever totally depraved in his books. Even in the case of Popeye, a sense of elemental compassion is evoked in the mind of an attentive reader: "The poor bastard," the reader is made to feel, "the poor impotent, pitiful bastard." The theme of man's sufferings and triumphs in the face of his inevitable physical tragedy is implicit in all of Faulkner's important work.

Robert Penn Warren

Of the many men of letters identified with the Southern literary renaissance in recent decades, Robert Penn Warren is probably the most versatile; he is a poet, critic, novelist, short-story writer, and dramatist. As a creative writer, Warren comes close to being all-inclusive in the sense that he refuses to limit his sensibility. Yet to compare him with Whitman on this score would be meaningless, for Warren has absorbed the formal disciplines of the schools. Probably no writer doing significant work in this generation is more learned.

One should begin any comment upon Warren's work with a consideration of his poetry, which is intrinsically as rewarding as his prose, although it has been overshadowed by popular success in the latter form. Reiterated in Warren's verse —as in his fiction—are the themes of Man's Personal History (or Conscience), of Time's Violence, and of the Lost Innocence which the frail reproachful *alter ego* of childhood never permits the restless and acquisitive adult to forget. In a sense his poems are all subjective pieces, despite whatever brilliant objectivity may be found in particular details.

In one of Warren's early poems, "The Return: An Elegy," the poet is coming back from a distant place to the home in which his mother lies dead, and the recalcitrant images which flood his mind insistently violate the sanctity of the occasion:

> Calcium phosphate lust speculation faith treachery
> it walked upright with habitation and a name
> *Tell me its name* . . .
>
> I have a name: I am not blind.
> Eyes, not blind, press to the Pullman pane
> Survey the driving dark and silver taunt of rain
> *What will I find*
>
> What will I find beyond the snoring pine?
> O eyes locked blind in death's immaculate design
> Shall fix their last distrust in mine.

The irony, the dogged unwillingness to avoid the full context of the experience evokes the following brutal passage:

629

> Give me the nickels off your eyes
> from your hands the violets

> let me bless your obsequies
> if you possessed conveniently enough three eyes
> then I could buy a pack of cigarettes.

Again,

> the old bitch is dead
> What have I said! [12]

reinforces the complex tone of the situation the poet is trying faithfully to render, as on the train he pursues "past culvert cut fill embankment semaphore" the ghostly parallels. Warren's is the method of irony. It is a deliberate attempt to include the discordant and contradictory without evasions. Such poetry, when successful, may be said to achieve an added dimension.

The richly figurative context of Warren's prose is of a piece with his poetry. Few modern writers can command with so little apparent effort the limitless possibilities of the English language. He has inherited, of course, the rewards of the revolution in diction—the repudiation of the "poetic" or otherwise "special" language—which Eliot and his contemporaries undertook some thirty years ago. But Warren has profited by their experiments in much the same way that Shakespeare learned from Kyd and Marlowe; he has taken from them what he could use within the framework of his own imagination.

As a novelist, Warren has dealt primarily with the problems of twentieth-century civilization: *Night Rider* is set in 1905, *At Heaven's Gate* in 1929, and *All the King's Men* in 1935. Only in *World Enough and Time* does he explore an earlier period.

What does Warren say in his fiction; what is his vision of reality? Basically, his theme is the Problem of Evil. The artist holds an advantage over the philosopher with respect to this question, in that he is not obligated to attempt a solution; his responsibility is to present the problem in human and concrete terms. Warren's characters are constantly violating the original innocence of their natures; their experiences are, in sum, the record of these violations, whether they are committed in the interest of outwardly plausible and even noble causes or through a blind lust for temporal power.

"There must be a new innocence for us to be stayed by," exclaims the protagonist in "Original Sin," one of Warren's finest poems. But it is actually his own past self which this individual remembers and from the violation of which his conscience can never escape. This condition is inevitable; it is a part of man's estate. Whether the particular individual involved is a scholar, like Dr. Adam Stanton, or a man of action, like Willie Stark, does not matter. Sue Murdock, in *At Heaven's Gate*, cries as she looks in the mirror, "Oh I wasn't like this. I wasn't like this always!" And Jack Burden, thinking about the deaths of Willie Stark and Adam Stanton, recalls Willie's last words: "It might have been different, Jack. You got to believe that." These are all words which imply a violation of that same innocence which preoccupies the narrator of "Original Sin."

630   Actually all of Warren's moderns seem to be doomed—Percy Munn, Sue Murdock, Willie Stark, and others—primarily because they are "dissociated." Those

[12] *From* Selected Poems 1923–1943 *by Robert Penn Warren, copyright, 1944, by Harcourt, Brace and Company, Inc.*

characters who are able to preserve a measure of integrity have mores rooted in an earlier and alien tradition, a simpler tradition in the sense that its way of life possessed form and meaning—Willie Proudfit in *Night Rider*, Ashby Windham in *At Heaven's Gate*, Cass Mastern in *All the King's Men*. In the broad sense of the term, the tradition which all these characters represent is agrarian.

To dismiss Warren's juxtaposition of values as myth, as opposed to the factual realities of history, represents a major failure on the part of the reader's imagination. Many of our most significant writers have thought in terms of myths—Milton had his Christian myth, Yeats his myth about the cycles of history, and Eliot his about the inferiority of the present to the past. The important question to consider is what insights into human nature does any given author afford us, once we have suspended our disbelief and accepted his vision in its own terms.

Even if damned, the moderns in Warren's fiction are never stereotyped villains. It is this author's fundamental and instinctive awareness of the human frailties in *all* people that makes his characters rewarding subjects for contemplation, at whatever level one elects to consider them.

WILLIAM ALEXANDER PERCY

1885–1942

Born in Greenville, Mississippi, William Alexander Percy lived most of his life in the heart of the Delta country. He spent his boyhood on his father's cotton plantation, acquiring, as he says in *Lanterns on the Levee* (1941), a love of nature and an appreciation of literature, the latter from the various private tutors whom his father—mistrusting the public school system—had employed to instruct him. In 1900 he matriculated at the University of the South, chosen, he said, because "it was fairly near and healthy and genteel and inexpensive." After graduating in 1904, he spent a year abroad before enrolling in the Harvard Law School. In 1908 he returned to Greenville to practice law with his father.

Upon the death of his father, Percy inherited 3343 acres of fertile Delta land. Cotton was the principal crop grown upon this land and tenant farmers were the chief source of labor. Percy's defense of this system of farming is well known. In answer to his critics' charge that he was an "unreconstructed Southerner," he insisted that share-cropping was the fairest and most humane way by which the plantation could be operated. The first selection from *Lanterns on the Levee* printed in this book is the author's answer to those persons who consider the South the major economic problem of the nation and regard the system of share-cropping as infamous.

In addition to the autobiographical *Lanterns on the Levee*, Percy is the author of four volumes of poetry: *Sappho in Levkas* (1915), *In April Once* (1920), *Enzio's Kingdom* (1924), and *Selected Poems* (1930).

from *Lanterns on the Levee*

Chapter 21. Planters, Share-Croppers, and Such

632
Father was the only great person I ever knew and he would not have been great without Mother. They died two years after the flood, mercifully within a few weeks of each other. Without them my life seemed superfluous.

Holt, a hunting partner of Father's and an ex-slave, came up to the office to express his grief. I met him in the hall, but he motioned me to Father's desk, saying: "Set there where he sot. That's where you b'long." He took the chair across the desk from me, filling it and resting his strong hands on the heavy cane he always carried and needed. He was a magnificent old man with massive shoulders and a noble head. For some minutes he struggled silently, sitting there in what had been Father's office, then he let the tears gush unhindered from his eyes and the words from his heart: "The roof is gone from over my head and the floor from under my feet. I am out in the dark and the cold alone. I want to go where he is." He rose and hobbled out. Many of us felt that way.

From Father I inherited Trail Lake, a three-thousand-acre cotton plantation, one of the best in the county and unencumbered. I was considered well-to-do for our part of the state. Father loved the land and had put into it the savings of a lifetime. Perhaps he loved it because he and his brothers and sisters had been born on it and had passed their childhood among country things. His grandfather had obtained title to the Percy Place about 1850. It was a patch of woods then and many slaves had to labor many months before it could properly be termed a cotton plantation. This grandfather, whom the family affectionately, but rather disrespectfully, referred to as Thomas G., had been the favorite son of old Don Carlos and had married a famous beauty from Huntsville named Maria Pope. If you had lived as long as I have with that oil painting of him in the library over the fireplace, you could easily deduce why Maria and Don Carlos loved him. It reticently and through a fume of chiaroscuro reveals a personable young chap in a black stock and a black waistcoat adorned with four stylish brass buttons. At first perhaps you won't notice his smile, but it's there, all right, at the corner of his mouth, very shadowy and knowing, a little hurt but not at all bitter. It's by that smile I really know him, and not by his descendants, who mostly are the kind you like to descend with, or by the tender trusting references to him in Don Carlos's will. Though I've always lived with the remnant of his brown English library (each leather volume numbered and marked with the book-plate bearing his name sans crest or escutcheon) and always loved his enormous mahogany dining-room table with its carved legs and brass claws, around which all of us have eaten meals together going on six generations now, it's not they but his smile that makes him a familiar and a confidant of mine— that and the fact he cut no very great figure in the world. He isn't a demanding ancestor.

He seems to have felt that if he raised his sons to be gentlemen he would have done his full Christian duty by them and indeed by life. Training in a profession, though ornamental, was unnecessary for a gentleman, but of course you couldn't be one at all unless you owned land. Therefore, Thomas G. casually made doctors of his two older boys, Walker and LeRoy, and a lawyer of Fafar, after whom I was named, but having done that, without, of course, expecting them to practice medicine or law, he settled down gravely to the really serious business of getting them a plantation. He decided on a place in the Delta, paid for it, manned it with enough slaves to clear and cultivate it, and shipped his sons, all three of them, down to live on it.

When I was a youngster, I quite often spent the week-end on this plantation of theirs, which is still called the Percy Place. Already the slave quarters looked

633

ramshackly, the woods had disappeared, the loamy creek land seemed thin, and the residence, from which the ells had fallen away, was ugly and plain, more full of room than anything else and split amidships by an enormous drafty hall, a very cave for coolness and emptiness.

I am sure in these days and times no wise father would dare bundle off three sons, two of them married, and expect them to live forever after under the same roof without kicking it off. Uncle Walker was married to Aunt Fannie, Fafar to Mur, and Uncle LeRoy (whom everybody loved and the youngsters called Uncle Lee) was the bachelor—scholar and gallivanter of the trio and so destined to endure gracefully occasional admonitions and rakings over the coals from his young sisters-in-law. Yet all reports agree that the Percy household was not only amiable but full of fun. Apparently they were a cheery lot who liked life.

Then the war came, and everything changed. By the time of the surrender Uncle Walker had died, Uncle Lee had been stricken with paralysis, and when Fafar, the youngest and the soldier of the three, returned, it was to a diminished and penniless household of which he found himself the head and the bread-winner. The women and children and sick were still clinging to the place, but there wasn't a servant or a field-hand on it. All the slaves had left. I suppose he and Mur must have done some pretty tragic planning together the night he got home. Mur brought out from hiding the last of the plantation's horses, Fafar mounted this priceless, unlovely steed—his name was Bill Jack—and jogged off to Greenville, which then was a mere river-landing at the end of ten miles of impassable road. Fafar was over thirty years old and a Colonel of a defeated army. He hung out a shingle announcing to the bankrupt countryside that W. A. Percy had opened offices for the practice of law. In time he became one of Mississippi's famous lawyers, but Father said that right from the start he always managed to collect more clients than fees.

Fafar was fifty-five years old when he died. Long before his death people had been calling him "Old Colonel Percy" and "The Gray Eagle." His life had been crowded with usefulness and honor, but it ended when he was fifty-five. That is my age now. When I consider all he did and all I haven't done, I feel the need of taking a good long look at Thomas G., debonair and wistful, expecting nothing.

Of course the stage that Fafar trod after the war was no ordinary stage, and the play no ordinary play. Those days you had to be a hero or a villain or a weakling—you couldn't be just middling ordinary. The white people in the whole Delta comprised a mere handful, but there were hordes of Negroes. Poor wretches! For a thousand years and more they had been trained in tribal barbarism, for a hundred and more in slavery. So equipped, they were presented overnight with freedom and the ballot and told to run the river country. They did. They elected Negroes to every office. We had a Negro sheriff, Negro justices of the peace, Negro clerks of court. There were no white officials, not even carpetbaggers. It was one glorious orgy of graft, lawlessness, and terrorism. The desperate whites though negligible in number banded together to overthrow this regime and chose Fafar as their leader. His life work became the re-establishment of white supremacy. That work required courage, tact, intelligence, patience; it also required vote-buying, the stuffing of ballot-boxes, chicanery,

634

intimidation. Heart-breaking business and degrading, but in the end successful. At terrific cost white supremacy was re-established." Some of us still remember what we were told of those times, and what we were told inclines us to guard the ballot as something precious, something to be withheld unless the fitness of the recipient be patent. We are the ones I suppose who doubt despairingly the fitness of Negroes and (under our breath be it said) of women.

Father considered Fafar superior to any human being he had ever known: he insisted he had a finer mind, a greater gusto, a warmer love of people, and a more rigid standard of justice than any of his sons. But for Fafar's efforts at running the plantation Father had only amused and tolerant scorn.

It appears that Fafar practiced law in order to be able to practice husbandry. He retained title to the Percy Place by paying its taxes with fees. But never, never, during all the years he managed it, did it yield one penny of profit. Father contended the reason for this deplorable result was Fafar's inability to say no to any Negro in wheedling mood. I suspect, however, the main reason was the low price of cotton and the South's economic collapse following Gettysburg.

After the first fine frenzy of emancipation, although Negro politicians and carpetbaggers were riding high and making prosperity look like sin, the rank and file of ex-slaves, the simple country Negroes, found themselves faring exceedingly ill. They had freedom, but nothing else. It's a precious possession, but worthless commercially. The former slave-holders had land, but nothing else. It's as precious, nearly, as freedom, but without plow and plowmen equally worthless. On ex-slave and ex-master it dawned gradually that they were in great need of one another—and not only economically, but, curiously enough, emotionally. Holt killed a Yankee officer for insulting Colonel Howell Hines, his old master. Fafar had Negro friends without whose information and advice he and the other political rebels of the time would have suffered under this reign of scalawaggery even more grievously than they did. To each plantation drifted back puzzled, unhappy freedmen who had once worked it as slaves and who were discovering that though slaves couldn't go hungry, freedmen could and did. Ex-slaves returned to the Percy Place and asked for a chance to make a crop on it. Fafar had little to offer them except good land and leadership. He puzzled over what was just to do and what he could do. He concluded by offering his ex-slaves a partnership with him. The terms of it were simple.

In simple words, about like these, he explained it to them:

I have land which you need, and you have muscle which I need; let's put what we've got in the same pot and call it ours. I'll give you all the land you can work, a house to live in, a garden plot and room to raise chickens, hogs, and cows if you can come by them, and all the wood you want to cut for fuel. I'll direct and oversee you. I'll get you a doctor when you are sick. Until the crop comes in I'll try to keep you from going hungry or naked in so far as I am able. I'll pay the taxes and I'll furnish the mules and plows and gear and whatever else is necessary to make a crop. This is what I promise to do. You will plant and cultivate and gather this crop as I direct. This is what you will promise to do. When the crop is picked, half of it will be mine and half of it yours. If I have supplied you with money or food or clothing or anything else during this year, I will charge it against your half of the crop. I shall handle the

635

selling of the cotton and the cottonseed because I know more than you do about their value. But the corn you may sell or eat or use for feed as you like. If the price of cotton is good, we shall both make something. If it is bad, neither of us will make anything, but I shall probably lose the place and you will lose nothing because you have nothing to lose. It's a hard contract these hard times for both of us, but it's just and self-respecting and if we both do our part and have a little luck we can both prosper under it.

This was the contract under which Fafar operated the Percy Place during his lifetime, under which Mur operated it after his death, under which Father operated it from the time of her death to the time it was sold. It changed in no essential during all those years except that with better times the promise to keep the Negroes from going hungry and cold became a fixed obligation to lend them a stated amount of money each month from the first of March, when planting started, to the first of September, when cottonseed money began coming in. After the place had been worked for years under this arrangement—years during which nobody grew rich and nobody suffered for necessities—Father decided that it was getting run down, it was too old, it was worn out. Miserable, but feeling foresighted and awfully business-like, he sold the Percy Place.

I rode through it last week and the crop was twice as big as either Fafar or Father had ever raised on it. Modern methods of farming, government-inspired diversification of crops, and the use of fertilizer have made it more productive than when Thomas G.'s sons planted their first cotton crop in its virgin soil with slave labor.

Let no one imagine that because Father sold the Percy Place he was landless. Far from it. Instead, he'd been watching longingly the new part of the county, the Bogue district, and little by little, bit by bit, over a period of ten years, he'd been buying a plantation there. It was his very own, his creation, and he loved it. He started with a batch of virgin timber and cleared that. Next he won in the cotton market and put the winnings into that section of Doctor Atterbury's, good land and mostly in cultivation. Then he added the desolate-looking deadening along Deep Slough. At last he bought the Cheek Place and the Ross Place. In all he finally acquired title to a single block of land of over three thousand acres—some cleared, some half-cleared, some in cultivation, part of it paid for, part mortgaged, most of it magnificent ridge-land, a few hundred acres swampy and sour. He named it Trail Lake after a singularly dilapidated-looking slough which meandered half-heartedly into the center of the place before petering out from sheer inertia. When I was going to Sewanee the whole property looked ragged and unkempt, full of fallen logs and charred stumps, standing and prone. It was at the end of the world, in a turkey and panther country. You could reach it only by a rocking impromptu trainlet called the Black Dog. The trip from Greenville and back required twenty-four hours.

Trail Lake was so far from anywhere, so inaccessible to "the law" and to the infrequent neighbors, that the Negroes ran off one manager after another and terrified the whole countryside. Father almost lost the place because the Negroes wouldn't let any white man stay on it. At last, in desperation, he sent down a young manager from Arkansas, Billy Hardie, who shot a tenant the day of his arrival and single-handed dispersed a crap game his first Saturday night. Quiet ensued. It's a pleasant country, but even now not safe. If you haven't got a few pioneer virtues thrown in with the run-of-the-mill sort you'd better move on to a more cultured environment.

I have no love of the land and few, if any, pioneer virtues, but when Trail Lake became mine after Father's death, I must confess I was proud of it. I could reach it in three quarters of an hour. It was a model place: well drained, crossed by concrete roads, with good screened houses, a modern gin, artesian-well water, a high state of cultivation, a Negro school, a foolish number of churches, abundant crops, gardens and peach trees, quantities of hogs, chickens, and cows, and all the mules and tractors and equipment any place that size needed.

Father had operated it under the same contract that Fafar used on the Percy Place. The Negroes seemed to like it and I certainly did. I happen to believe that profit-sharing is the most moral system under which human beings can work together and I am convinced that if it were accepted in principle by capital and labor, our industrial troubles would largely cease. So on Trail Lake I continue to be partners with the sons of ex-slaves and to share fifty-fifty with them as my grandfather and Father had done.

In 1936 a young man with a passion for facts roved in from the University of North Carolina and asked to be allowed to inspect Trail Lake for the summer. He was Mr. Raymond McClinton, one of Doctor Odum's boys, and the result of his sojourn was a thesis entitled "A Social-Economic Analysis of a Mississippi Delta Plantation." That's coming pretty stout if you spend much of your time trying to forget facts and are stone-deaf to statistics. But some of his findings were of interest even to me, largely I suspect because they illustrated how Fafar's partnership-contract works in the modern world. In 1936, the year Mr. McClinton chose for his study, the crop was fair, the price average (about twelve cents), and the taxes higher than usual. Now for some of his facts:

Trail Lake has a net acreage of 3,343.12 acres of which 1,833.66 are planted in cotton, 50.59 are given to pasture, 52.44 to gardens, and the rest to corn and hay. The place is worked by 149 families of Negroes (589 individuals) and in 1936 yielded 1,542 bales of cotton. One hundred and twenty-four of the families work under Fafar's old contract, and twenty-five, who own their stock and equipment, under a similar contract which differs from the other only in giving three-fourths instead of one-half of the yield to the tenant. The plantation paid in taxes of all kinds $20,459.99, a bit better than $6.00 per acre; in payrolls for plantation work $12,584.66—nearly $4.00 an acre. These payrolls went to the Negroes on the place. The 124 families without stock of their own made a gross average income of $491.90 and a net average income of $437.64. I have lost Mr. McClinton's calculation of how many days of work a plantation worker puts in per year, but my own calculation is a maximum of 150 days. There is nothing to do from ginning time, about October the first, to planting time, about March the fifteenth, and nothing to do on rainy days, of which we have many.

These figures, as I read them, show that during an average year the 124 families working on Trail Lake for 150 days make each $437.64 clear, besides having free water and fuel, free garden plot and pasturage, a monthly credit for six months to cover food and clothing, a credit for doctor's bills and medicine, and a house to live in. The Negroes who receive this cash and these benefits are simple unskilled laborers. I wonder what other unskilled labor for so little re-

637

ceives so much. Plantations do not close down during the year and there's no firing, because partners can't fire one another. Our plantation system seems to me to offer as humane, just, self-respecting, and cheerful a method of earning a living as human beings are likely to devise. I watch the limber-jointed, oily-black, well-fed, decently clothed peasants on Trail Lake and feel sorry for the telephone girls, the clerks in chain stores, the office help, the unskilled laborers everywhere—not only for their poor and fixed wage but for their slave routine, their joyless habits of work, and their insecurity.

Even with a place like Trail Lake, it's hard to make money farming. Although I kept myself helpfully obscure during the first years of my plantation-ownership, retaining the same excellent employees and following Father's practices, I began losing money almost at once, and in two years (they were depression years for everybody, I must confess) I had lost over a hundred thousand dollars and Trail Lake was mortgaged to the hilt. For the next four or five years I was in such a stew and lather getting that mortgage reduced and taxes paid, I lost track of goings-on in the outside world and missed the first tide of talk about share-croppers. Those hundred and twenty-four families of mine with $437.64 in their jeans worked "on the shares" and called themselves "croppers," but I wasn't familiar with the term "share-croppers." As used by the press, it suggested to me no Delta group and I assumed vaguely that share-croppers must be of some perverse bucolic genus that probably originated in Georgia and throve in Oklahoma. But one day I read that the President of the United States had excoriated bitterly and sorrowfully "the infamous share-cropper system." I asked a Washington friend of mine in what locality that system of farming prevailed. He knocked the breath out of me by answering: "On Trail Lake." I woke to the discovery that in pseudo-intellectual circles from Moscow to Santa Monica the Improvers-of-the-world had found something new in the South to shudder over. Twenty years ago it had been peonage. In the dark days when the collapse of the slave-trade almost bankrupted good old New England, it had been slavery. Now it was the poor share-croppers—share-croppers over the whole South, but especially in the Delta. That very partnership of Fafar's which had seemed to me so just and practical now was being denounced as avaricious and slick—it was Mr. Roosevelt's "infamous system." We who had operated our plantations under it since carpetbag days were taunted now with being little better than slave-drivers by the carpetbaggers' progeny and kin. Obviously we are given to depravity down here: the South just won't do. In spite of prayers and advice from the "holier-than-thou's" it's always hell-bent for some deviltry or other. At this moment there's another of those great moral daybreaks on, and its east is Washington. In the glow I realize that Fafar and Mur, Father and I suffered from moral astigmatism—for all I know, from complete moral blindness: we were infamous and didn't even suspect it. Well, well, well. That makes a Southerner feel pretty bad, I reckon.

Notwithstanding an adage to the contrary, truth, as I've observed it, is one of the least resilient of herbs. Crushed to earth, it stays crushed; once down, it keeps down, flatter than anything except an oat field after a wind-storm. The truth about share-croppers has been told and retold, but, being neither melodramatic nor evidential of Southern turpitude, it isn't believed. I am not a well-informed person, but I know the truth about share-cropping and in this chapter

638

I have told enough for earnest seekers to infer what it is; I have not done this, however, in the naïve hope that my words will do the slightest good or change the views of a single reader; my reason is other and quite unworthy: there's a low malicious pleasure in telling the truth where you know it won't be believed. Though rightly considered a bore and a pest in the best Trojan circles, Cassandra, no doubt, had her fun, but, at that, not nearly so much as the Knights of the Bleeding Heart who in politics and literature years from now will still be finding it fetching and inexpensive to do some of their most poignant public heart-bleeding over the poor downtrodden share-croppers of the deep South.

Share-cropping is one of the best systems ever devised to give security and a chance for profit to the simple and the unskilled. It has but one drawback—it must be administered by human beings to whom it offers an unusual opportunity to rob without detection or punishment. The failure is not in the system itself, but in not living up to the contractual obligations of the system—the failure is in human nature. The Negro is no more on an equality with the white man in plantation matters than in any other dealings between the two. The white planter may charge an exorbitant rate of interest, he may allow the share-cropper less than the market price received for his cotton, he may cheat him in a thousand different ways, and the Negro's redress is merely theoretical. If the white planter happens to be a crook, the share-cropper system on that plantation is bad for Negroes, as any other system would be. They are prey for the dishonest and temptation for the honest. If the Delta planters were mostly cheats, the results of the share-cropper system would be as grievous as reported. But, strange as it may seem to the sainted East, we have quite a sprinkling of decent folk down our way.

Property is a form of power. Some people regard it as an opportunity for profit, some as a trust; in the former it breeds hubris, in the latter, noblesse oblige. The landed gentry of Fafar's time were of an ancient lineage and in a sober God-fearing tradition. Today many have thought to acquire membership in that older caste by acquiring land, naked land, without those ancestral hereditaments of virtue which change dirt into a way of life. On the plantation where there is stealing from the Negro you will generally find the owner to be a little fellow operating, as the saying goes, "on a shoe-string," or a nouveau riche, or a landlord on the make, tempted to take more than his share because of the mortgage that makes his title and his morals insecure. These, in their pathetic ambition to imitate what they do not understand, acquire power and use it for profit; for them the share-cropper system affords a golden opportunity rarely passed up.

Two courses of action would be effective against unworthy landlords: the Negroes could and should boycott such landlords, quietly and absolutely; the government could and should deny government benefits to the landlord who will not put the terms of his contract in writing, who will not carry out those terms and who will not permit the government to prove by its own inspection that they have been carried out. In place of these suggested remedies, I can only recommend changing human nature. All we need anywhere in any age is character: from that everything follows. Leveling down's the fashion now, but I remember the bright spires—they caught the light first and held it longest.

So much that was fine and strong went into the making of this Delta of ours!

639

So much was conquered for us by men and women whose names we have forgotten! So much had to be overcome before ever this poor beautiful unfinished present was turned over to us by the anonymous dead—malaria and yellow fever, swamp-water and rain-water and river-water, war and defeat, tropic heat and intemperate cold, poverty and ignorance, economic cruelty and sectional hatred, the pathos of a stronger race carrying on its shoulders a weaker race and from the burden losing its own strength! They must have been always in the front line fighting for us, those builders of the Delta; they could never have stopped long enough to learn of leisure and safety the graces of peace. But there are those who live in fear as in a native element, and they are beautiful with a fresh miraculous beauty. It is watching for unseen death that gives a bird's eyes their glancing brilliance. It is dodging eternal danger that makes his motions deft and exquisite. His half-wit testament to the delight of living, terror has taught him that, shaking the melody from his dubious innocent throat. Perhaps security is a good thing to seek and a bad thing to find. Perhaps it is never found, and all our best is in the search.

Chapter 22. Fode

People are divided into Leaners and Leanees: into oaks more or less sturdy and vines quite, quite clinging. I was never a Leaner, yet, although seldom mistaken for one, I find people are constantly feeling impelled to protect me. Invariably they are right and I accept their proffered ministrations gratefully. I cannot drive a car or fix a puncture or sharpen a pencil or swim or skate or give a punch in the jaw to the numerous parties who need punching. My incompetency is almost all-inclusive, but it must have a glow, for it attracts Samaritans from miles around. I have been offered a very fine, quick-working poison for use on my enemies or myself; I have had my rifle carried by a soldier who disliked me, just because I was all in; a bootlegger once asked me to go partners with him because I looked seedy; a top sergeant, icy with contempt, put together my machine-gun when its disjecta membra unassembled would have returned me in disgrace to America; a red-headed friend of mine had to be restrained from flinging a red-headed enemy of mine into the river for some passing insolence; an appreciable percentage of the hard-boiled bastards of the world have patched tires, blown life into sparkplugs, pushed, hauled, lifted, hammered, towed, and sweated for me because they knew that without their aid I should have moldered indefinitely on some wretched, can-strewn landscape. If you mix incompetency with a pinch of the wistful and a heap of good manners, it works pretty well. Men of goodwill are all over the place, millions of them. It is a very nice world—that is, if you remember that while good morals are all-important between the Lord and His creatures, what counts between one creature and another is good manners. A good manner may spring from vanity or a sense of style; it is a sort of pleasant fiction. But good manners spring from well-wishing; they are fundamental as truth and much more useful. No nation or stratum of society has a monopoly on them and, contrary to the accepted estimate, Americans have more than their share.

The righteous are usually in a dither over the deplorable state of race relations

640

in the South. I, on the other hand, am usually in a condition of amazed exultation over the excellent state of race relations in the South. It is incredible that two races, centuries apart in emotional and mental discipline, alien in physical characteristics, doomed by war and the Constitution to a single, not a dual, way of life, and to an impractical and unpracticed theory of equality which deludes and embitters, heckled and misguided by pious fools from the North and impious fools from the South—it is incredible, I insist, that two such dissimilar races should live side by side with so little friction, in such comparative peace and amity. This result is due solely to good manners. The Southern Negro has the most beautiful manners in the world, and the Southern white, learning from him, I suspect, is a close second.

Which reminds me of Ford. (He pronounces his name "Fode" with enormous tenderness, for he is very fond of himself.)

In the South every white man worth calling white or a man is owned by some Negro, whom he thinks he owns, his weakness and solace and incubus. Ford is mine. There is no excuse for talking about him except that I like to. He started off as my caddy, young, stocky, strong, with a surly expression, and a smile like the best brand of sunshine. For no good reason he rose to be my chauffeur; then house-boy; then general factotum; and now, without any contractual relation whatever, my retainer, which means to say I am retained for life by him against all disasters, great or small, for which he pays by being Ford. It was not because of breaking up the first automobile, coming from a dance drunk, or because of breaking up the second automobile, coming from a dance drunk, that our contractual relation was annulled, but for a subtler infamy. I was in the shower, not a position of dignity at best, and Ford strolled in, leaned against the door of the bathroom, in the relaxed pose of the Marble Faun, and observed dreamily: "You ain't nothing but a little old fat man."

A bit of soap was in my eye and under the circumstances it was no use attempting to be haughty anyway, so I only blurted: "You damn fool."

Ford beamed: "Jest look at your stummick."

When one had fancied the slenderness of one's youth had been fairly well retained! Well, taking advantage of the next dereliction, and one occurred every week, we parted; that is to say, I told Ford I was spoiling him and it would be far better for him to battle for himself in this hostile world, and Ford agreed, but asked what he was going to do "seeing as how nobody could find a job nohow." As neither of us could think of the answer, I sent him off to a mechanics' school in Chicago. He returned with a diploma and a thrilling tale of how nearly he had been married against his vehement protest to a young lady for reasons insufficient surely in any enlightened community with an appreciation of romance. With Ford's return the demand for mechanics fell to zero—he always had an uncanny effect on the labor market—so he took to house-painting. His first week he fell off the roof of the tallest barn in the county and instead of breaking his neck, as Giorgione or Raphael would have done, he broke only his ankle and had to be supplied with crutches, medical care, and a living for six weeks. It was then that I left for Samoa.

641

But I should not complain. Ford has never learned anything from me, but I am indebted to him for an education in more subjects and stranger ones than I took at college, subjects, however, slightly like those the mock-turtle took from the Conger eel. The first lesson might be called "How Not to Faint in Coils." Ford observed:

"You don't understand folks good as I does." I was appalled. "You sees what's good in folks, but you don't see what's bad. Most of the time I'se a good boy, then I goes nigger, just plain nigger. Everybody do that, and when they does, it hurts you." I was pulverized. It may not have taken a wicked person to think that, but it certainly took a wicked one to say it.

That I have any dignity and self-respect is not because of but in spite of Ford. We were returning from a directors' meeting in a neighboring town and he was deeply overcast. At last he became communicative:

"Mr. Oscar Johnston's boy says Mr. Oscar won't ride in no car more'n six months old and he sho ain't goin' to ride in nothin' lessen a Packard."

I received this calmly, it was only one more intimation that my Ford was older than need be and congenitally unworthy. Ford continued:

"He says Mr. Oscar says you ain't got near as much sense as your pa." I agreed, heartily. "He says you ain't never goin' to make no money." I agreed, less heartily. "En if you don't be keerful you goin' to lose your plantation." I agreed silently, but I was nettled, and observed:

"And you sat there like a bump on a log, saying nothing, while I was being run down?"

"Well, I told him you had traveled a lot, a lot more'n Mr. Oscar; you done gone near 'bout everywhere, en he kinder giggled and says: 'Yes, they tells me he's been to Africa,' en I says: 'He is,' en he says: 'You know why he went to Africa?' en I says: ' 'Cause he wanted to go there,' en he says: 'That's what he tells you, but he went to Africa to 'range to have the niggers sent back into slavery.' "

I exploded: "And you were idiot enough to believe that?"

"I'se heard it lots of times," Ford observed mildly, "but it didn't make no difference to me, you been good to me en I didn't care."

Having fancied I had spent a good portion of my life defending and attempting to help the Negro, this information stunned me and, as Ford prophesied, it hurt. But hiding my wounded vanity as usual in anger, I turned on Ford with:

"You never in your life heard any Negro except that fool boy of Oscar Johnston's say I was trying to put the Negroes back in slavery."

"Lot of 'em," reiterated Ford.

"I don't believe you," I said. "You can't name a single one."

We finished the drive in silence; spiritually we were not en rapport.

The next morning when Ford woke me he was wreathed in smiles, suspiciously pleased with himself. He waited until one eye was open and then announced triumphantly:

"Louisa!" (pronounced with a long *i*).

"What about Louisa?" I queried sleepily.

"She says you'se goin' to send the niggers back into slavery!"

642 Louisa was our cook, the mainstay and intimate of the household for fifteen years.

"God damn!" I exploded, and Ford fairly tripped out, charmed with himself.

I dressed thoughtfully and repaired to the kitchen. My intention was to be gentle but desolating. Louisa weighs over three hundred, and despite a physical allure I can only surmise from the stream of nocturnal callers in our back yard, she distinctly suggests in her general contour a hippopotamus. When I entered the kitchen I found her pacing ponderously back and forth through the door that opens on the back gallery. It seemed a strange procedure—Louisa was not given to exercise, at least not of that kind. The following colloquy ensued:

"Louisa, what are you doing?"

"I stuck a nail in my foot."

"Why don't you go to the doctor?"

"I'se gettin' the soreness out."

"You can't walk it out."

"Naw, suh, the nail is *drawing* it out."

"What nail?"

"The nail I stepped on."

"Where is it?"

Louisa pointed to the lintel of the door. A nail hung from it by a piece of string; under it Louisa was pacing. I left her pacing. I didn't mention slavery then or later.

My bitter tutelage didn't conclude here. In late autumn we drove to the plantation on settlement day. Cotton had been picked and ginned, what cash had been earned from the crop was to be distributed. The managers and bookkeeper had been hard at work preparing a statement of each tenant's account for the whole year. As the tenant's name was called he entered the office and was paid off. The Negroes filled the store and overflowed onto the porch, milling and confabulating. As we drove up, one of them asked: "Whose car is dat?" Another answered: "Dat's *us* car." I thought it curious they didn't recognize my car, but dismissed the suspicion and dwelt on the thought of how sweet it was to have the relation between landlord and tenant so close and affectionate that to them my car was their car. Warm inside I passed through the crowd, glowing and bowing, the lord of the manor among his faithful retainers. My mission concluded, I returned to the car, still glowing. As we drove off I said:

"Did you hear what that man said?"

Ford assented, but grumpily.

"It was funny," I continued.

"Funnier than you think," observed Ford sardonically.

I didn't understand and said so.

Ford elucidated: "He meant that's the car *you* has bought with *us* money. They all knew what he meant, but you didn't and they knew you didn't. They wuz laughing to theyselves."

A few days later the managers confirmed this version of the meaning of the phrase and laughed. I laughed too, but not inside.

Yet laughter singularly soft and unmalicious made me Ford's debtor more even than his admonitions and revelations. I still think with gratitude of an afternoon which his peculiarly Negro tact and good manners and laughter made charming. I was in what Ford would call "low cotton." After a hellish day of details and beggars, my nerves raw, I phoned for Ford and the car. On climbing in I asked dejectedly:

"Where shall we drive?"

643

Ford replied: "Your ruthers is my ruthers" (what you would rather is what I would rather). Certainly the most amiable and appeasing phrase in any language, the language used being not English but deep Southern.

"Let's try the levee," I suggested.

Although nothing further was said and Ford asked no questions, he understood my depression and felt the duty on him to cheer me up. He drove to my favorite spot on the levee and parked where I could watch across the width of waters a great sunset crumbling over Arkansas. As I sat moody and worried, Ford, for the first and only time in his life, began to tell me Negro stories. I wish I could imitate his exact phrases and intonations and pauses, without which they are poor enough stories; but, in spite of the defects of my relaying, anyone can detect their Negro quality, care-free and foolish and innocent—anyone, that is, who has lived among Negroes in the South.

Here are the three I remember in something approximating Ford's diction:

"There wuz a cullud man en he died en went to hevven en the Lawd gevvum all wings, en he flew en he flew" (here Ford hunched his shoulders and gave a superb imitation of a buzzard's flight). "After he flew round there fur 'bout a week he looked down en saw a reel *good*-lookin' lady, a-settin' on a cloud. She wuz *reel* good-lookin'. En he dun the loop-the-loop.

"The Lawd cum en sez: 'Don't you know how to act? There ain't nuthin' but nice people here, en you beehavin' like that. Git out.' But he told the Lawd he jest didn't know en he wuzzent never gonner do nuthin' like that no mo', en please let him stay. So the Lawd got kinder pacified en let him stay. En he flew en he flew. En after he had been flying round fur 'bout a week, he ups en sees that same good-lookin' lady a-settin' on a cloud en he jest couldn't hep it—he dun the loop-the-loop.

"So the Lawd stepped up en he sez: 'You jest don't know how to act, you ain't fitten fur to be with decent folks, you'se a scanlus misbeehavor. Git out.' En he got.

"He felt mighty bad en hung round the gate three or four days tryin' to ease up on St. Peter, but St. Peter 'lowed there wuzn't no way, he jest couldn't let him in en the onliest way he might git in wuz to have a *conference* with the Lawd. Then the man asked if he couldn't 'range fur a conference en they had a lot of back-and-forth. En finally St. Peter eased him in fur a conference." (Ford loved that word, it made him giggle.) "But the Lawd wuz mad, He wuz mad sho-nuff, he wuz hoppin' mad en told him flat-footed to git out en stay out. Then the cullud man sez:

" 'Well, jest remember this, Lawd: while I wuz up here in yo' place I wuz the flyin'est fool you had.' "

Since the thirteenth century no one except Ford and his kind has been at ease in heaven, much less confident enough of it to imagine an aeroplane stunt there. And I do hope that good-looking lady saw the loop-the-loop.

644

The second story is just as inconsequential:

"A fellow cum to a cullud man en promised him a whole wagen-load of watermelons if he would go en set by hisself in a hanted house all night long.

Well, the man he liked watermelons en he promised, though he sho didn't like no hanted house, en he sho didn't wanter see no hants. He went in en drug up a cheer en set down en nuthin' happened. After so long a time, in walked a black cat en set down in front of him en jest looked at him. He warn't so skeered because it warn't much more'n a kitten, en they both uvvem jest set there en looked at each uther. Then ernurther cat cum in, a big black 'un, en he set by the little 'un en they jest set there lookin' at him, en ain't sed nuthin'. Then ernurther one cum en he wuz big as a dawg en all three uvvem jest set there en looked at him en sed nuthin'. Ernurther one cum, still bigger, en ernurther, en ernurther, en the last one wuz big as a hoss. They all jest set there in a row en sed nuthin' en looked at him. That cullud man he wuz plum skeered en he had ter say sumpin so he 'lowed all nice en p'lite:

" 'Whut us gwiner do?'

"En the big 'un sed: 'Us ain't gwiner do nuthin', till Martin comes.'

"The cullud man says reel nice en p'lite: 'Jest tell Martin I couldn't wait,' en he busted out the winder en tore down the big road fast as he could en faster, en he ain't never taken no more interest in watermelons since."

"But, Ford," I asked, "who was Martin?"

"I dunno," said Ford and chuckled, "but I reckon he wuz big as er elly-fant."

I reckon so too, and twice as real, so far as I am concerned.

And now the last:

"A cullud man cum to the white folks' house in the country en sed to the man:

" 'Boss, I'se hongry; gimme sumpin t'eat.'

"The man sed: 'All right, go round to the back do' en tell the cook to feed you.'

"The cullud man sed: 'Boss, I'se neer 'bout starved, I ain't et fur a whole week.'

"The man sed: 'All right, all right, go round to the kitchen.'

"The cullud man sed: 'Boss, if you gimme sumpin t'eat I'll split up all that stove wood you got in yo' back yard.'

"The man sed: 'All right, all right, go en git that grub like I tole yer.'

"So he went. After 'bout three hours the man went to his back yard en saw the cullud man, who wuz jest settin'. So he sed:

" 'Has you et?'

"En he sed: 'Yassir.'

"En he sed: 'Has you chopped up that wood-pile?'

"En he sed: 'Boss man, if you jest let me res' round till dinner time, after dinner I'll go en chop out that patch of cotton fur you.'

"So the man sed: 'All right, but don't you fool me no more.'

"After the cullud man had et him a big dinner he started out to the cotton patch en he met him a cooter [a mud-turtle] en the cooter sed to him:

" 'Nigger, you talks too much.'

"The nigger goes tearin' back to the big house en when he gits there the man cums out en sez:

" 'Nigger, has you chopped out that cotton?'

"En the nigger sez:

645

" 'Lawd, boss, I wuz on my way, fo' God I wuz, en I met a cooter en he started talkin' to me en I lit out from there en here I is.'

"The boss man was plenty riled and he sez:

" 'Nigger, take me to that cooter en if he don't start talkin', I'se goin' to cut your throat frum year to year.' "

"So they bof uvvem started fur the cotton patch en there in the middle of the big road set that cooter. En he never opened his mouth, he ain't sed nuthin'. So the man hopped on the nigger en whupped him sumpin scand'lous en left fur the big house mighty sore at niggers en cooters. Well, the cullud man wuz neer 'bout through breshing hisself off en jest fo' moseying on off when the cooter poked his head out en looks at him en sez:

" 'Nigger, I tole you you talks too much.' "

Can it be wondered at, now that Ford is sojourning in the North beyond the infamous housing conditions of the South, comfortable and healthy in his own little room with four young Negro roommates, a single window to keep out the cold and a gas burner for cooking and heat—can it be wondered, if now when the phone rings and the operator's voice says: "Detroit, calling collect," that I accept the charge, although I know who it is and why he is calling? It is Ford and he is drunk and he is incoherently solicitous for me and mine and for his mother and wants to come home and needs five dollars. I reply I am glad to hear his voice, which is true, and hope he is well, and advise him to be a good boy and stick to his job, and a letter will follow or shall I wire? Of course, he has no job, except with the W.P.A., to which he has attached himself by fictions and frauds with which all good Southern darkies with itching feet are familiar. I hope the government supports him as long and as loyally as I did, because if it doesn't, I must. I must because Ford is my fate, my Old Man of the Sea, who tells me of Martin and admonishing cooters and angels that do the loop-the-loop, my only tie with Pan and the Satyrs and all earth creatures who smile sunshine and ask no questions and understand.

I wish my parting with him could have been happier or that I could forget it. He had abandoned his truck in a traffic jam and forfeited his job, one that I had procured for him with much difficulty and some misrepresentation. Then he had got looping drunk and last, against all precedent and propriety, he had come to see me; it was late at night when he arrived, stumbling and weeping. He threw himself across the couch and sobbed without speaking. I could not get him up or out, and he wouldn't explain his grief. At last he quieted down and, his face smeared with tears, managed to gasp:

"You cain't do no good, Mr. Will. It don't make no difference how hard I tries or how good I bees, I ain't never gonner be nuthin' but jest Fode."

I wish I had never heard him say that. There are some truths that facing does not help. Something had brought home to Ford the tragedy of himself and of his race in an alien world. Had he been in South Africa or Morocco or Harlem or Detroit, his pitiful cry would have been equally true, equally hopeless and unanswerable. What can we do, any of us, how can we help? Let the man who has the answer cry it from the house-tops in a hundred languages. But there will be no crier in the night, and it is night for all the Fords of the world and for us who love them. (*1941*)

646

RICHARD WRIGHT

1908–

The unhappy childhood of Richard Wright began on a plantation near Natchez, Mississippi. His earliest remembrance, he writes in his autobiography, *Black Boy* (1945), was the desire for more food. When the boy was only five, his father deserted the family, forcing the mother to place her son in an orphanage temporarily. Five years later his mother became totally paralyzed, and Richard spent the remainder of his childhood with relatives. At the age of fifteen he went to Memphis, Tennessee, where he earned a meager living doing odd jobs until he finally secured a position as postal clerk.

Convinced that he must leave the South if he was ever to realize his ambition to become a writer, Wright moved to Chicago in 1934 and, a few years later, to New York. After several unrewarding efforts, he was able to devote his full time to writing as a member of one of the Federal Writers' Projects. He first received recognition in 1938, when he won a $500 award from *Story* magazine for *Uncle Tom's Children*, a group of four stories. The next year, as a Guggenheim Fellow, he wrote *Native Son*, an immediate best seller and a Book-of-the-Month-Club selection. Wright's thesis as developed in this novel is that the cause of most racial crimes can be traced to the environment in which the Negro is forced to live. Wright uses a similar argument in *Black Boy*, the story of the writer's difficult but successful struggle to break into the charmed circle of authorship, in the face of mistreatment by the whites and the often hostile attitude of his own race.

from *Black Boy*

Chapter 6

The next day at school I inquired among the students about jobs and was given the name of a white family who wanted a boy to do chores. That afternoon, as soon as school had let out, I went to the address. A tall, dour white woman

647

talked to me. Yes, she needed a boy, an honest boy. Two dollars a week. Mornings, evenings, and all day Saturdays. Washing dishes. Chopping wood. Scrubbing floors. Cleaning the yard. I would get my breakfast and dinner. As I asked timid questions, my eyes darted about. What kind of food would I get? Was the place as shabby as the kitchen indicated?

"Do you want this job?" the woman asked.

"Yes, ma'am," I said, afraid to trust my own judgment.

"Now, boy, I want to ask you one question and I want you to tell me the truth," she said.

"Yes, ma'am," I said, all attention.

"Do you steal?" she asked me seriously.

I burst into a laugh, then checked myself.

"What's so damn funny about that?" she asked.

"Lady, if I was a thief, I'd never tell anybody."

"What do you mean?" she blazed with a red face.

I had made a mistake during my first five minutes in the white world. I hung my head.

"No, ma'am," I mumbled. "I don't steal."

She stared at me, trying to make up her mind.

"Now, look, we don't want a sassy nigger around here," she said.

"No, ma'am," I assured her. "I'm not sassy."

Promising to report the next morning at six o'clock, I walked home and pondered on what could possibly have been in the woman's mind to have made her ask me point-blank if I stole. Then I recalled hearing that white people looked upon Negroes as a variety of children, and it was only in the light of that that her question made any sense. If I had been planning to murder her, I certainly would not have told her and, rationally, she no doubt realized it. Yet habit had overcome her rationality and had made her ask me: "Boy, do you steal?" Only an idiot would have answered: "Yes, ma'am. I steal."

What would happen now that I would be among white people for hours at a stretch? Would they hit me? Curse me? If they did, I would leave at once. In all my wishing for a job I had not thought of how I would be treated, and now it loomed important, decisive, sweeping down beneath every other consideration. I would be polite, humble, saying yes sir and no sir, yes ma'am and no ma'am, but I would draw a line over which they must not step. Oh, maybe I'm just thinking up trouble, I told myself. They might like me . . .

The next morning I chopped wood for the cook stove, lugged in scuttles of coal for the grates, washed the front porch and swept the back porch, swept the kitchen, helped wait on the table, and washed the dishes. I was sweating. I swept the front walk and ran to the store to shop. When I returned the woman said:

"Your breakfast is in the kitchen."

"Thank you, ma'am."

I saw a plate of thick, black molasses and a hunk of white bread on the table. Would I get no more than this? They had had eggs, bacon, coffee . . . I picked up the bread and tried to break it; it was stale and hard. Well, I would drink the molasses. I lifted the plate and brought it to my lips and saw floating on the surface of the black liquid green and white bits of mold. Goddamn . . . I can't eat this, I told myself. The food was not even clean. The woman came into the kitchen as I was putting on my coat.

"You didn't eat," she said.

"No, ma'am," I said. "I'm not hungry."

"You'll eat at home?" she asked hopefully.

"Well, I just wasn't hungry this morning, ma'am," I lied.

"You don't like molasses and bread," she said dramatically.

"Oh, yes, ma'am, I do," I defended myself quickly, not wanting her to think that I dared criticize what she had given me.

"I don't know what's happening to you niggers nowadays," she sighed, wagging her head. She looked closely at the molasses. "It's a sin to throw out molasses like that. I'll put it up for you this evening."

"Yes, ma'am," I said heartily.

Neatly she covered the plate of molasses with another plate, then felt the bread and dumped it into the garbage. She turned to me, her face lit with an idea.

"What grade are you in school?"

"Seventh, ma'am."

"Then why are you going to school?" she asked in surprise.

"Well, I want to be a writer," I mumbled, unsure of myself; I had not planned to tell her that, but she had made me feel so utterly wrong and of no account that I needed to bolster myself.

"A what?" she demanded.

"A writer," I mumbled.

"For what?"

"To write stories," I mumbled defensively.

"You'll never be a writer," she said. "Who on earth put such ideas into your nigger head?"

"Nobody," I said.

"I didn't think anybody ever would," she declared indignantly.

As I walked around her house to the street, I knew that I would not go back. The woman had assaulted my ego; she had assumed that she knew my place in life, what I felt, what I ought to be, and I resented it with all my heart. Perhaps she was right; perhaps I would never be a writer; but I did not want her to say so.

Had I kept the job I would have learned quickly just how white people acted toward Negroes, but I was too naïve to think that there were many white people like that. I told myself that there were good white people, people with money and sensitive feelings. As a whole, I felt that they were bad, but I would be lucky enough to find the exceptions.

Fearing that my family might think I was finicky, I lied to them, telling them that the white woman had already hired a boy. At school I continued to ask about jobs and was directed to another address. As soon as school was out I made for the house. Yes, the woman said that she wanted a boy who could milk a cow, feed chickens, gather vegetables, help serve breakfast and dinner.

"But I can't milk a cow, ma'am," I said.

"Where are you from?" she asked incredulously.

"Here in Jackson," I said.

649

"You mean to stand there, nigger, and tell me that you live in Jackson and don't know how to milk a cow?" she demanded in surprise.

I said nothing, but I was quickly learning the reality—a Negro's reality—of the white world. One woman had assumed that I would tell her if I stole, and now this woman was amazed that I could not milk a cow, I, a nigger who dared live in Jackson . . . They were all turning out to be alike, differing only in detail. I faced a wall in the woman's mind, a wall that she did not know was there.

"I just never learned," I said finally.

"I'll show you how to milk," she said, as though glad to be charitable enough to repair a nigger's knowledge on that score. "It's easy."

The place was large; they had a cow, chickens, a garden, all of which spelled food and that decided me. I told her that I would take the job and I reported for work the next morning. My tasks were simple but many; I milked the cow under her supervision, gathered eggs, swept, and was through in time to serve breakfast. The dining-room table was set for five; there were eggs, bacon, toast, jam, butter, milk, apples . . . That seemed promising. The woman told me to bring the food in as they called for it, and I familiarized myself with the kitchen so that I could act quickly when called upon. Finally the woman came into the dining room followed by a pale young man who sat down and stared at the food.

"What the hell!" he snarled. "Every morning it's these damn eggs for breakfast."

"Listen, you sonofabitch," the woman said, sitting too, "you don't have to eat 'em."

"You might try serving some dirt," he said, and forked up the bacon.

I felt that I was dreaming. Were they like that all the time? If so, I would not stay here. A young girl came and flopped into her chair.

"That's right, you bitch," the young man said. "Knock the food right out of my goddamn mouth."

"You know what you can do," the girl said.

I stared at them so intently that I was not aware that the young man was watching me.

"Say, what in hell are you glaring at me for, you nigger bastard?" he demanded. "Get those goddam biscuits off that stove and put 'em on the table."

"Yes, sir."

Two middle-aged men came in and sat down. I never learned who was in the family, who was related to whom, or if it was a family. They cursed each other in an amazingly offhand manner and nobody seemed to mind. As they hurled invectives, they barely looked at each other. I was tense each moment, trying to anticipate their wishes and avoid a curse, and I did not suspect that the tension I had begun to feel that morning would lift itself into the passion of my life. Perhaps I had waited too long to start working for white people; perhaps I should have begun earlier, when I was younger—as most of the other black boys had done—and perhaps by now the tension would have become an habitual condition, contained and controlled by reflex. But that was not to be my lot; I was always to be conscious of it, brood over it, carry it in my heart, live with it, sleep with it, fight with it.

The morning was physically tiring, but the nervous strain, the fear that my actions would call down upon my head a storm of curses, was even more damaging. When the time came for me to go to school, I was emotionally spent. But I clung to the job because I got enough to eat and no one watched me closely and measured out my food. I had rarely tasted eggs and I would put hunks of yellow butter into a hot skillet and hurriedly scramble three or four eggs at a time and gobble them down in huge mouthfuls so that the woman would not see me. And I would take tumblers of milk behind a convenient door and drain them in a swallow, as though they contained water.

Though the food I ate strengthened my body, I acquired another problem: I had fallen down in my studies at school. Had I been physically stronger, had not my new tensions sapped my already limited energy, I might have been able to work mornings and evenings and still carry my studies successfully. But in the middle of the day I would grow groggy; in the classroom I would feel that the teacher and the pupils were receding from me and I would know that I was drifting off to sleep. I would go to the water fountain in the corridor and let cold water run over my wrists, chilling my blood, hoping in that way to keep awake.

But the job had its boon. At the midday recess I would crowd gladly into the corner store and eat sandwiches with the boys, slamming down my own money on the counter for what I wanted, swapping descriptions of the homes of white folks in which we worked. I used to divert them with vivid word pictures of the cursing family, their brooding silences, their indifference toward one another. I told them of the food I managed to eat when the woman's back was turned, and they were filled with friendly envy.

The boys would now examine some new article of clothing I had bought; none of us allowed a week to pass without buying something new, paying fifty cents down and fifty cents per week. We knew that we were being cheated, but we never had enough cash to buy in any other way.

My mother began a rapid recovery. I was happy when she expressed the hope that someday soon we might have a home of our own. Though Granny was angry and disgusted, my mother began to attend a Methodist church in the neighborhood, and I went to Sunday school, not because my mother begged me to—which she did—but to meet and talk with my classmates.

In the black Protestant church I entered a new world: prim, brown, puritanical girls who taught in the public schools; black college students who tried to conceal their plantation origin; black boys and girls emerging self-consciously from adolescence; wobbly-bosomed black and yellow church matrons; black janitors and porters who sang proudly in the choir; subdued redcaps and carpenters who served as deacons; meek, blank-eyed black and yellow washerwomen who shouted and moaned and danced when hymns were sung; jovial, potbellied black bishops; skinny old maids who were constantly giving rallies to raise money; snobbery, clannishness, gossip, intrigue, petty class rivalry, and conspicious displays of cheap clothing . . . I liked it and I did not like it; I longed to be among them, yet when with them I looked at them as if I were a million miles away. I had been kept out of their world too long ever to be able to become a real part of it.

Nevertheless, I was so starved for association with people that I allowed my-

651

self to be seduced by it all, and for a few months I lived the life of an optimist. A revival began at the church and my classmates at school urged me to attend. More because I liked them than from any interest in religion, I consented. As the services progressed night after night, my mother tried to persuade me to join, to save my soul at last, to become a member of a responsible community church. Despite the fact that I told them I could never feel any religion, the boys of my gang begged me to "come to God."

"You believe in God, don't you?" they asked.

I evaded the question.

"But this is a new day," they said, pulling down the corners of their lips. "We don't holler and moan in church no more. Come to church and be a member of the community."

"Oh, I don't know," I said.

"We don't want to push you," they said delicately, implying that if I wanted to associate with them I would have to join.

On the last night of the revival, the preacher asked all of those who were members of the church to stand. A good majority of those present rose. Next the preacher called upon the Christians who were not members of any church to stand. More responded. There remained now but a few young men who, belonging to no church and professing no religion, were scattered sheepishly about the pews. Having thus isolated the sinners, the preacher told the deacons to prevail upon those who lived "in darkness to discuss the state of their souls with him." The deacons sped to their tasks and asked us to go into a room and talk with a man "chosen and anointed of God." They held our arms and smiled as they bent and talked to us. Surrounded by people I knew and liked, with my mother's eyes looking pleadingly into mine, it was hard to refuse. I followed the others into a room where the preacher stood; he smiled and shook our hands.

"Now, you young men," he began in a brisk, clipped tone, "I want all of you to know God. I'm not asking you to join the church, but it's my duty as a man of God to tell you that you are in danger. Your peril is great; you stand in the need of prayer. Now, I'm going to ask each of you a personal favor. I want you to let the members of this church send up a prayer to God for you. Now, is there any soul here so cold, so hard, so lost, that he would say no to that? Can you refuse to let the good people of this community pray for you?"

He paused dramatically and no one answered. All the techniques of his appeal were familiar to me and I sat there feeling foolish, wanting to leap through the window and go home and forget about it. But I sat still, filled more with disgust than sin.

"Would any man in this room dare fling no into God's face?" the preacher asked.

There was silence.

"Now, I'm going to ask all of you to rise and go into the church and take a seat on the front bench," he said, edging on to more definite commitments. "Just stand up," he said, lifting his hands, palms up, as though he had the power to make us rise by magic.

"That's it, young man," he encouraged the first boy who rose.

652

I followed them and we sat like wet ducks on a bench facing the congregation. Some part of me was cursing. A low, soft hymn began.

This may be the last time, I don't know . . .

They sang it, hummed it, crooned it, moaned it, implying in sweet, frightening tones that if we did not join the church then and there we might die in our sleep that very night and go straight to hell. The church members felt the challenge and the volume of song swelled. Could they sing so terrifyingly sweet as to make us join, burst into tears and drop to our knees? A few boys rose and gave their hands to the preacher. A few women shouted and danced with joy. Another hymn began.

It ain't my brother, but it's me, oh, Lord,
Standing in the need of prayer . . .

During the singing the preacher tried yet another ruse; he intoned mournfully, letting his voice melt into the singing, yet casting his words above it:

"How many mothers of these young men are here tonight?"

Among others, my mother rose and stood proudly.

"Now, good sweet mothers, come right down in front here," said the preacher.

Hoping that this was the night of my long-deferred salvation, my mother came forward, limping, weeping, smiling. The mothers ringed their sons around, whispering, pleading.

"Now, you good sweet mothers, symbols of Mother Mary at the tomb, kneel and pray for your sons, your only sons," the preacher chanted.

The mothers knelt. My mother grabbed my hands and I felt hot tears scalding my fingers. I tried to stifle my disgust. We young men had been trapped by the community, the tribe in which we lived and of which we were a part. The tribe, for its own safety, was asking us to be at one with it. Our mothers were kneeling in public and praying for us to give the sign of allegiance. The hymn ended and the preacher launched into a highly emotional and symbolic sermon, recounting how our mothers had given birth to us, how they had nursed us from infancy, how they had tended us when we were sick, how they had seen us grow up, how they had watched over us, how they had always known what was best for us. He then called for yet another hymn, which was hummed. He chanted above it in a melancholy tone:

"Now, I'm asking the first mother who really loves her son to bring him to me for baptism!"

Goddam, I thought. It had happened quicker than I had expected. My mother was looking steadily at me.

"Come, son, let your old mother take you to God," she begged. "I brought you into the world, now let me help to save you."

She caught my hand and I held back.

"I've been as good a mother as I could," she whispered through her tears.

"God is hearing every word," the preacher underscored her plea.

653

This business of saving souls had no ethics; every human relationship was shamelessly exploited. In essence, the tribe was asking us whether we shared its feelings; if we refused to join the church, it was equivalent to saying no, to placing ourselves in the position of moral monsters. One mother led her beaten and frightened son to the preacher amid shouts of amen and hallelujah.

"Don't you love your old crippled mother, Richard?" my mother asked. "Don't leave me standing here with my empty hands," she said, afraid that I would humiliate her in public.

It was no longer a question of my believing in God; it was no longer a matter of whether I would steal or lie or murder; it was a simple, urgent matter of public pride, a matter of how much I had in common with other people. If I refused, it meant that I did not love my mother, and no man in that tight little black community had ever been crazy enough to let himself be placed in such a position. My mother pulled my arm and I walked with her to the preacher and shook his hand, a gesture that made me a candidate for baptism. There were more songs and prayers; it lasted until well after midnight. I walked home limp as a rag; I had not felt anything except sullen anger and a crushing sense of shame. Yet I was somehow glad that I had got it over with; no barriers now stood between me and the community.

"Mama, I don't feel a thing," I told her truthfully.

"Don't you worry; you'll grow into feeling it," she assured me.

And when I confessed to the other boys that I felt nothing, they too admitted that they felt nothing.

"But the main thing is to be a member of the church," they said.

The Sunday of the baptism arrived. I dressed in my best and showed up sweating. The candidates were huddled together to listen to a sermon in which the road of salvation was mapped out from the cradle to the grave. We were then called to the front of the church and lined up. The preacher, draped in white robes, dipped a small branch of a tree in a huge bowl of water and hovered above the head of the first candidate.

"I baptize thee in the name of the Father, the Son, and the Holy Ghost," he pronounced sonorously as he shook the wet branch. Drops trickled down the boy's face.

From one boy to another he went, dipping the branch each time. Finally my turn came and I felt foolish, tense; I wanted to yell for him to stop; I wanted to tell him that all this was so much nonsense. But I said nothing. The dripping branch was shaken above my head and drops of water wet my face and scalp, some of it rolling down my neck and wetting my back, like insects crawling. I wanted to squirm, but I held still. Then it was over. I relaxed. The preacher was now shaking the branch over another boy's head. I sighed. I had been baptized.

Even after receiving the "right hand of fellowship," Sunday school bored me. The Bible stories seemed slow and meaningless when compared to the bloody thunder of pulp narrative. And I was not alone in feeling this; other boys went to sleep in Sunday school. Finally the boldest of us confessed that the entire thing was a fraud and we played hooky from church.

654

As summer neared, my mother suffered yet another stroke of paralysis and again I had to watch her suffer, listen to her groans, powerless to help. I used to lie awake nights and think back to the early days in Arkansas, tracing my mother's life, reliving events, wondering why she had apparently been singled out for so much suffering, meaningless suffering, and I would feel more awe than I had ever felt in church. My mind could find no answer and I would feel rebellious against all life. But I never felt humble.

Another change took place at home. We needed money badly and Granny and Aunt Addie decided that we could no longer share the entire house, and Uncle Tom and his family were invited to live upstairs at a nominal rental. The dining room and the living room were converted into bedrooms and for the first time we were squeezed for living space. We began to get on each other's nerves. Uncle Tom had taught school in country towns for thirty years and as soon as he was under the roof he proceeded to tell me what was wrong with my life. I ignored him and he resented it.

Rattling pots and pans in the kitchen would now awaken me in the mornings and I would know that Uncle Tom and his family were getting breakfast. One morning I was roused by my uncle's voice calling gently but persistently. I opened my eyes and saw the dim blob of his face peering from behind the jamb of the kitchen door.

"What time have you?" I thought he asked me, but I was not sure.

"Hunh?" I mumbled sleepily.

"What time have you got?" he repeated.

I lifted myself on my elbow and looked at my dollar watch, which lay on the chair at the bedside.

"Eighteen past five," I mumbled.

"Eighteen past five?" he asked.

"Yes, sir."

"Now, is that the right time?" he asked again.

I was tired, sleepy; I did not want to look at the watch again, but I was satisfied that, on the whole, I had given him the correct time.

"It's right," I said, snuggling back down into my pillow. "If it's a little slow or fast, it's not far wrong."

There was a short silence; I thought he had gone.

"What on earth do you mean, boy?" he asked in loud anger.

I sat up, blinking, staring into the shadows of the room, trying to see the expression on his face.

"What do I mean?" I asked, bewildered. "I mean what I said." Had I given him the wrong time? I looked again at my watch. "It's twenty past now."

"Why, you impudent black rascal!" he thundered.

I pushed back the covers of the bed, sensing trouble.

"What are you angry about?" I asked.

"I never heard a sassier black imp than you in all my life," he spluttered.

I swung my feet to the floor so that I could watch him.

"What are you talking about?" I asked. "You asked me the time and I told you."

" 'If it's a little fast or slow, it's not far wrong,' " he said, imitating me in an angry voice, sarcastic voice. "I've taught school for thirty years, and by God I've never had a boy say anything like that to me."

655

"But what's wrong with what I said?" I asked, amazed.

"Shut up!" he shouted. "Or I'll take my fist and ram it down your sassy throat! One more word out of you, and I'll get a limb and teach you a lesson."

"What's the matter with you, Uncle Tom?" I asked. "What's wrong with what I said?"

I could hear his breath whistling in his throat; I knew that he was furious.

"This day I'm going to give you the whipping some man ought to have given you long ago," he vowed.

I got to my feet and grabbed my clothes; the whole thing seemed unreal. I had been confronted so suddenly with the struggle that I could not pull all the strings of the situation together at once. I did not feel that I had given him cause to say I was sassy. I had spoken to him just as I spoke to everybody. Others did not resent my words, so why should he? I heard him go out of the kitchen door and I knew that he had gone into the back yard. I pulled on my clothes and ran to the window; I saw him tearing a long, young, green switch from the elm tree. My body tightened. I was damned if he was going to beat me with it. Until a few days ago he had never lived near me, had never had any say in my rearing or lack of rearing. I was working, eating my meals out, buying my own clothes, giving what few pennies I could to Granny to help out in the house. And now a strange uncle who felt that I was impolite was going to teach me to act as I had seen the backward black boys act on the plantations, was going to teach me to grin, hang my head, and mumble apologetically when I was spoken to.

My senses reeled in protest. No, that could not be. He would not beat me. He was only bluffing. His anger would pass. He would think it over and realize that it was not worth all the bother. Dressed, I sat on the edge of the bed and waited. I heard his footsteps come onto the back porch. I felt weak all over. How long was this going to last? How long was I going to be beaten for trifles and less than trifles? I was already so conditioned toward my relatives that when I passed them I actually had a nervous tic in my muscles, and now I was going to be beaten by someone who did not like the tone of voice in which I spoke. I ran across the room and pulled out the dresser drawer and got my pack of razor blades; I opened it and took a thin blade of blue steel in each hand. I stood ready for him. The door opened. I was hoping desperately that this was not true, that this dream would end.

"Richard!" he called me in a cold, even tone.

"Yes, sir!" I answered, striving to keep my tension out of my voice.

"Come here."

I walked into the kitchen, my eyes upon him, my hands holding the razors behind my back.

"Now, Uncle Tom, what do you want with me?" I asked him.

"You need a lesson in how to live with people," he said.

"If I do need one, you're not going to give it to me," I said.

"You'll swallow those words before I'm through with you," he vowed.

"Now, listen, Uncle Tom," I said, "you're not going to whip me. You're a stranger to me. You don't support me. I don't live with you."

"You shut that foul mouth of yours and get into the back yard," he snapped.

He had not seen the razors in my hand. I ducked out the kitchen door and jumped lightly off the porch to the ground. He ran down the steps and advanced with the lifted switch.

656

"I've got a razor in each hand!" I warned in a low, charged voice. "If you touch me, I'll cut you! Maybe I'll get cut too, but I'll cut you, so help me God!"

He paused, staring at my lifted hands in the dawning light of morning. I held a sharp blue edge of steel tightly between thumb and forefinger of each fist.

"My God," he gasped.

"I didn't mean to hurt your feelings this morning," I told him. "You insist I did. Now, I'll be damned if I'm going to be beaten because of your hurt feelings."

"You're the worst criminal I ever saw," he exclaimed softly.

"If you want to fight, I'll fight. That's the way it'll be between us," I told him.

"You'll never amount to anything," he said, shaking his head and blinking his eyes in astonishment.

"I'm not worried about that," I said. "All I want you to do is keep away from me, now and always . . ."

"You'll end on the gallows," he predicted.

"If I do, you'll have nothing to do with it," I said.

He stared at me in silence; evidently he did not believe me, for he took a step forward to test me.

"Put those razors down," he commanded.

"I'll cut you! I'll cut you!" I said, hysteria leaping into my voice, my hands slicing out with points of steel as I backed away.

He stopped; he had never in his life faced a person more grimly determined. Now and then he blinked his eyes and shook his head.

"You fool!" he bellowed suddenly.

"I'll make you bloody if you hit me!" I warned him.

His chest heaved and his body seemed to droop.

"Somebody will yet break your spirit," he said.

"It won't be you!"

"You'll get yours someday!"

"You won't be the one to give it to me!"

"And you've just been baptized," he said heavily.

"The hell with that," I said.

We stood in the early morning light and a touch of sun broke on the horizon. Roosters were crowing. A bird chirped near-by somewhere. Perhaps the neighbors were listening. Finally Uncle Tom's face began to twitch. Tears rolled down his cheeks. His lips trembled.

"Boy, I'm sorry for you," he said at last.

"You'd better be sorry for yourself," I said.

"You think you're a man," he said, dropping his arm and letting the switch drag in the dust of the yard. His lips moved as he groped for words. "But you'll learn, and you'll learn the hard way. I wish I could be an example to you . . ."

I knew that I had conquered him, had rid myself of him mentally and emotionally; but I wanted to be sure.

"You are not an example to me; you could never be," I spat at him. "You're a warning. Your life isn't so hot that you can tell me what to do." He repaired chairs for a living now, since he had retired from teaching. "Do you think I want to grow up and weave the bottoms of chairs for people to sit in?"

657

He twitched violently, trying to control himself.

"You'll be sorry you said that," he mumbled.

He turned his tall, lean, bent body and walked slowly up the steps. I sat on the porch a long time, waiting for my emotions to ebb. Then I crept cautiously into the house, got my hat, coat, books, and went to work, went to face the whims of the white folks. (*1945*)

FRANK LAWRENCE OWSLEY

1890–

A native of Montgomery County, Alabama, Frank Lawrence Owsley received his B.S. and M.S. degrees from Alabama Polytechnic Institute in 1911 and 1912 and his A.M. and Ph.D. degrees from the University of Chicago in 1917 and 1924. After completing his studies at Auburn, he taught history and Latin at his alma mater and at the Agricultural School in Wetumpka, Alabama. He also served one year as director of an agricultural experiment station in Wetumpka. In 1919 Owsley accepted a position in the history department at Birmingham-Southern College, and the following year moved to Vanderbilt University, where he served as a member of the Department of History until 1949. He is now Friedman Professor of History at the University of Alabama.

Throughout his career, Professor Owsley has strongly supported the philosophical tenets of the Nashville Agrarians. As the foremost scholar-historian of the group, he has done sound and interesting research on the structure of the government of the Confederacy and on the economic basis of the agricultural South. He has also made an intensive study of land ownership and management in the South before the Civil War. The results of his research are found in such publications as *States Rights in the Confederacy* (1925), *King Cotton Diplomacy —The Foreign Relations of the Confederate States of America* (1931), and *The Plain Folk of the Old South* (1949).

Professor Owsley, however, is more than an historical scholar. He uses his knowledge of history as a basis for his thesis that regionalism is still a vital factor in American life, particularly in Southern life. He has demonstrated that the outstanding conflicts of the Civil War and Reconstruction periods have a relevance to present-day issues. Excellent as his longer works are, Owsley is perhaps at his best in such essays as the following: "The Irrepressible Conflict" (*I'll Take My Stand*, 1930), "The Seven Pillars of Agrarianism" (*The American*

658

Review, 1935), "The Foundations of Democracy" (*The Southern Review*, 1936), and the selection chosen for this text, "The Fundamental Cause of the Civil War."

The Fundamental Cause of the Civil War: Egocentric Sectionalism

Before attempting to say what were the causes of the American Civil War, first let me say what were not the causes of this war. Perhaps the most beautiful, the most poetic, the most eloquent statement of what the Civil War was not fought for is Lincoln's Gettysburg Address. That address will live as long as Americans retain their love of free government and personal liberty; and yet in reassessing the causes of the Civil War, the address whose essence was that the war was being fought so "that government of the people, by the people and for the people shall not perish from the earth" is irrelevant. Indeed, this master-piece of eloquence has little if any value as a statement of the basic principles underlying the war.

The Civil War was not a struggle on the part of the South to destroy free government and personal liberty nor on the part of the North to preserve them. Looked at from the present perspective of the world-wide attempt of the totalitarians to erase free governments and nations living under such governments from the face of the earth, the timeworn stereotype that the South was attempting the destruction of free government and the North was fighting to preserve it seems very unrealistic and downright silly. In the light of the present-day death struggle against the most brutal form of despotism ever known, the Civil War, as far as the issue of free government was involved, was a sham battle. Indeed, both northern and southern people in 1861 were alike profoundly attached to the principles of free government. A systematic study of both northern and southern opinion as expressed in their newspapers, speeches, diaries, and private letters, gives irrefutable evidence in support of this assertion. Their ideology was demo-cratic and identical. However, theoretical adherence to the democratic principles is not sufficient evidence that democratic government exists. I believe that I shall not be challenged in the assertion that the economic structure of a section or a nation is the foundation upon which its political structure must rest. For this reason, therefore, it will be necessary to know what the economic foundations of these sections were. Was the economic structure of the North such as to support a political democracy in fact as well as in form? And was the economic structure of the South such as to permit the existence of free government? By utilizing the county tax books and the unpublished census reports a reasonably accurate and specific picture of wealth structure of the ante-bellum South, and to some extent that of the other sections has been obtained. As has been generally known, the Northwest was agricultural and its population was predominantly composed of small farmers, though a considerable minority were large farmers comparable with the larger southern planters. It seems that in 1860 about 80 per cent of the farmers in the Old Northwest were landowners. A fairly large fraction of

659

From The Journal of Southern History, *1941. Used by permission of the publishers.*

the remaining farm population in that area were either squatters upon public lands or were the members of landowning families. Only a small per cent were renters. In those regions farther west the ownership of land was not as widespread because farmers had not yet completed their titles to the lands that they had engrossed. Taken as a whole the people of the Northwest were economically self-sufficient. They could not be subjected to economic coercion and, hence, they were politically free. Their support of free government—as they understood it—was effective.

The northeastern section of the United States had already assumed its modern outlines of a capitalistic-industrial society where the means of production were either owned or controlled by a relatively few. That is to say, New England and the middle states were fast becoming in essence a plutocracy whose political ideology was still strongly democratic; but the application of this democratic ideology was being seriously hampered by the economic dependence of the middle and lower classes upon those who owned the tools of production. The employee unprotected by government or by strong labor organizations was subject in exercising his political rights to the undue influence of the employer.

To sum up: the economic structure of the Northwest was an adequate foundation for free government; but that of the East, though still supporting democratic ideals, was often too weak to sustain these ideals in actual government.

Turning to the South, which was primarily agricultural, one finds the situation completely contradictory to what has usually been assumed. While the plutocracy of the East owned or controlled the means of production in industry and commerce, the so-called slave oligarchy of the South owned scarcely any of the land outside the Black Belt and only about 25 per cent of the land in the Black Belt. Actually, the basic means of production in the Black Belt and in the South as a whole was well distributed among all classes of the population. The overwhelming majority of southern families in 1860 owned their farms and livestock. About 90 per cent of the slaveholders and 70 per cent of the nonslaveholders owned the land which they farmed. The bulk of slaveholders were small farmers, not oligarchs. While taken together they owned more slaves and more land than the large planters, taken individually the majority of slaveholders owned from one to four slaves and less than three hundred acres of land. The nonslaveholders —70 per cent of whom, as just noted, were landowners—were not far removed economically from the small slaveholders. While the majority of slaveholders possessed from one to three hundred acres of land, 80 per cent of the landed nonslaveholders owned from one to two hundred acres of land and 20 per cent owned from two hundred to a thousand. To repeat: the basic fact disclosed in an analysis of the economic structure of the South, based upon the unpublished census reports and tax books, is that the overwhelming majority of white families in the South, slaveholders and nonslaveholders (unlike the industrial population of the East) owned the means of production. In other words, the average Southerner like the average Westerner possessed economic independence; and the only kind of influence that could be exercised over his political franchise by the slave oligarchy was a strictly persuasive kind. The South, then, like the Northwest, not only held strongly to the democratic ideology; it had a sound economic foundation for a free government.

If the destruction of democratic government by the South and its preservation

660

by the North were not the causes of the Civil War, what then were the causes? The immediate answer to this question is that in 1861 the southern people desired and attempted to establish their independence and that the North took up arms to prevent the South from establishing this independence. This is only another way of saying that by 1861 the South had developed a Southern nationalism. The war for Southern independence was and remains unique: it is the only war ever fought upon the principle of the right of a people to choose their own government, for the purpose of separating from a government founded upon this principle. Looking immediately behind this desire of the South to establish a separate government, and of the North to prevent it, we discover a state of mind in both sections which explains their conduct. This state of mind may be summed up thus: by the spring of 1861 the southern people felt it undesirable and danger- ous to continue to live under the same government with the people of the North. So profound was this feeling among the bulk of the southern population that they were prepared to fight a long and devastating war to accomplish a separa- tion. On the other hand, the North was willing to fight a war to retain their reluctant fellow citizens under the same government with themselves.

That state of mind, which manifested itself in a desire of the South to separate from the North, and a desire on the part of the North to conquer and break the South, we may well call a war psychology. Its origin was in the sectional character of the United States. In other words, Southern nationalism and the resultant Civil War had one basic cause: sectionalism. But to conclude that sectionalism was the cause of the Civil War, and at the same time insist—as has usually been done—that the Civil War was the climax of an irrepressible con- flict is to seem to accept a pessimistic view of the future of the United States. For if the ante-bellum conflict was irrepressible and the Civil War unavoidable, we are faced with future irrepressible conflicts, future civil wars, and ultimate disintegration of the nation into its component sections. I say this because I do not see any way by which sectionalism can be erased from the political, economic, racial, and cultural maps of the United States. Our national state was built, not upon the foundations of a homogeneous land and people, but upon geographical sections inhabited severally by provincial, self-conscious, self-righteous, aggressive, and ambitious populations of varying origins and diverse social and economic systems; and the passage of time and the cumulative effects of history have accentuated these sectional patterns. That is to say, the United States has always been and probably will always be more of an empire than a national state.

Before accepting the possibility of future wars and national disintegration as inevitable because of the irrepressible conflict between permanent sections, let me hasten to say that there are two types of sectionalism: there is that egocentric, destructive sectionalism where conflict is always irrepressible; and there is that constructive sectionalism where good will prevails—two types as opposite from one another as good is opposite from evil, as the benign is from the malignant. It was the egocentric, the destructive, malignant type of sectionalism that de- stroyed the Union in 1861, and that would do so again if it existed over a long period of time.

Before discussing that destructive sectionalism which caused the Civil War, some observations should be made of the constructive type, since, as I have

661

suggested, the very nature of the American state makes one or the other type of sectionalism inevitable. The idea of either good or bad sectionalism as an enduring factor in American national life has received scant consideration by historians as a rule, either because they have desired to justify the conduct of their section on occasion as being the manifestation of nationalism when in truth it was sectionalism writ large; or because they have apparently been unable to reconcile sectionalism with nationalism.

Since sectionalism from the very nature of our country must remain a permanent and basic factor in our national life, we should look it in the face and discriminate between the good and the bad features. Above all else, we should recognize the fact that sectionalism when properly dealt with, far from being irreconcilable with nationalism, is its strongest support. It is only the malignant, destructive type that conflicts with nationalism or loyalty to the national state or empire. Great Britain once failed to make this distinction and to grasp the fact that the American colonials could be good Americans and good Britishers at the same time, and the result was the loss of the American colonies. After the lesson learned from the American Revolution, the British mind has grasped the fact that good Canadians or good Australians are all the better Britishers because of their provincial or—may I say?—sectional loyalty. Provincialism, dominionism, and, in the case of the United States, sectionalism, far from excluding nationalism, when properly recognized and not constantly frowned upon, and the interests of sections ignored and their ambitions frustrated, are powerful supports of nationalism. Such provincialism or sectionalism becomes a national asset. It is a brake upon political centralization and possible despotism. It has proven and will prove to be, if properly directed, a powerful force in preserving free institutions. It gives color, variety, and vitality to all segments of the national state. Because of this vitality in all its parts, the United States, unlike France, whose lifeblood seems to flow entirely through Paris, would prove a difficult country to subjugate by a foreign enemy, and its government and society more difficult, if not impossible, to overthrow by violent revolution. It is because Great Britain has, as the result of her lesson learned from the American Revolution, fostered a good sectionalism within her empire, that she stood alone in 1940–41 and baffled the orderly mind of the Germans and defied conquest. By loosening the ties that bind the component parts of this straggling union of colonies and dominions, Great Britain has made these bonds all the stronger. She and her commonwealth of nations—her sections—thus live in all their parts. Tragically, the American people failed to learn adequately the very lesson that they so thoroughly taught Great Britain: that local differences and attachments were natural, desirable, and formed the very rootbed of patriotism; indeed, that such differences, when given decent recognition, greatly strengthened nationalism and the national state. It was this failure to recognize or respect local differences and interests—in other words, the failure to recognize sectionalism as a fundamental fact of American life—that contributed most to the development of that kind of sectionalism which destroyed national unity and divided the nation.

662

There were three basic manifestations of that egocentric sectionalism which disrupted the Union in 1861. First was the habit of the dominant section—that is, the section which had the larger share in the control of the Federal government—of considering itself the nation, its people the American people, its interests the national interests (in other words, the habit of considering itself the sole possessor of nationalism, when, indeed, it was thinking strictly in terms of one section) and conversely the habit of the dominant section of regarding the minority group as factional, its interests and institutions and way of life as un-American, unworthy of friendly consideration, and even the object of attack.

The second manifestation of this egocentric sectionalism that led to the Civil War was the perennial attempt of a section to gain or maintain its political ascendency over the Federal government by destroying the sectional balance of power which, both New England and the South maintained, had been established by the three-fifths ratio clause in the Federal constitution.

The third and most dangerous phase of this sectionalism, perhaps the *sine qua non* of the Civil War, was the failure to observe what in international law is termed the comity of nations, and what we may by analogy designate as the comity of sections. That is, the people in one section failed in their language and conduct to respect the dignity and self-respect of the people in the other section. These three manifestations of sectionalism were so closely related that at times they can be segregated only in theory and for the sake of logical discussion. Indeed, as I have suggested, all were manifestations of that egocentric sectionalism that caused a section to regard itself as the nation.

Let me review some familiar facts of American history that illustrate each of these phases of sectionalism. During the first twelve years of the government under the Federal Constitution, the old commercial-financial aristocracy of New England, with the aid of the same classes of people scattered throughout the urban centers of the seaboard, controlled the national government through the instrumentality of the Federalist party. An analysis of the chief measures of the Federalist regime and of the mental processes behind their enactments—as disclosed in speeches and letters and newspaper editorials—reveals the dominant section, New England, with its compact, homogeneous population, its provincial outlook, thinking, talking, and acting as if it were the United States; its way of life, its economic system, and its people the only real Americans; while the remainder of the country, the people, and their interests and ways of life were alien and un-American. Most of the laws enacted during the control of the New England Federalists were considered by the South and much of the middle states as being for the sole benefit of the commercial and banking interests of the East, and as injurious, even ruinous, to the agricultural sections. In order to give constitutional sanction to these centralizing sectional laws, the Federalist party under the brilliant leadership of Alexander Hamilton evolved the doctrine of implied powers, which seemed to the agricultural sections, by this time under the leadership of Thomas Jefferson, to be pulling the foundations from under constitutional government. This sectional and centralizing policy of the New England-dominated Federalist party culminated in the Alien and Sedition Laws, which were met by the Virginia and Kentucky Resolutions. These resolutions may be regarded as a campaign document to be used in ousting the Federalists and New England from power. They were also a threat of the minority section to withdraw from the Union should Federalist New England continue in power, and continue its policy of ignoring the agricultural sections of the country or of running roughshod over their interests.

663

The overthrow of New England's control of the national government by the Jeffersonian party in 1800 resulted in a twenty-four-year regime of the Virginia dynasty, during fifteen years of which—that is, until after the War of 1812—the government was distinctly dominated by the South and Southwest. If Hamilton had been positive that the welfare of the nation depended upon reinforcing and maintaining by special government favor the capitalistic system of the East, Jefferson was more positive that democratic and constitutional government and the welfare of the American people depended upon maintaining the supremacy in government and society of a landowning farmer-people whose center of gravity was in the South and middle states. To Jefferson, commerce, finance, and industry were only necessary evils to be maintained purely as conveniences and handmaidens of agriculture. Such a doctrinaire conception of government and society boded ill for New England; and the period from 1801 until the end of the War of 1812 was filled with laws, decrees, and executive acts that seemed to threaten the economic and social existence of that section. One measure in particular seemed to be destined to end forever in favor of the South the sectional balance of power, namely, the purchase of Louisiana. During all this time New England's standing committee on secession, the Essex Junto, was maneuvering to bring about the withdrawal of New England from the Federal Union; nor is there any sufficient reason to suppose that it would not have eventually succeeded in the disruption of the Union had not the ending of the war with Great Britain brought a termination of the policies that seemed so detrimental to the social and economic interests of the East; and had not the outburst of genuine nationalism at the victorious ending of the war actually resulted in the adoption of measures distinctly favorable to New England. The point I wish to emphasize is that the rise to power of the South and middle states was marked by the same egocentric sectionalism which characterized the dominance of Federalist New England: the agricultural sections thought of themselves as the United States, thought of the American farmers as the only simon-pure Americans, and looked upon the interests of the agricultural population as the national interests.

It is not the ambition of this essay to attempt a summary of the ante-bellum history of the United States; but simply to use the twelve-year sectional regime of the Federalists and about the same length of rule by the Jeffersonian party to illustrate that tendency of the dominant section to consider itself the United States and its people the American people, and by the same token to ignore or treat with contempt the peculiar needs of the minority sections.

The second manifestation of that egocentric sectionalism which led to the American Civil War was the attempt of one section to gain a permanent ascendency by destroying the sectional balance of power or by permanently undermining the prestige of the other section. Let me pause for a moment, in discussing the overthrow of the balance of power, and review very briefly just how and why there had been an approximate balance of power established between the slaveholding and nonslaveholding states during the constitutional convention. The delegates to the convention, from both the northern and southern sections of the country, were unanimously in favor of a constitution that would establish a much stronger and more effective government than that which had so signally broken down under the Articles of Confederation. There was a

664

fundamental difference, however, as to what specific powers should be granted to this new government. New England and the capitalistic segments of the middle states were above all else determined that the new government should be able to control foreign and interstate commerce and to make commercial treaties that could be enforced. The agricultural sections of the country looked with considerable disfavor upon such a grant of powers. The South was so much opposed that it quietly passed out the word that it would never enter a Union where commerce was so thoroughly controlled by the national government unless it were assured a position of approximate political equality in that government. Otherwise, the power over commerce would be used by the North, dominated by the East, for its sole benefit and to the detriment of agriculture and the South.

Finally, the balance of power was worked out by the technique of counting three fifths of the slaves in apportioning representation in Congress and in the electoral college. This was called the three-fifth compromise between the North, which wanted to count all the slaves in apportioning direct taxes and none in apportioning representatives, and the South, which wanted to count all the slaves in making up representation and none in making up taxation. But an examination of the speeches and correspondence of the delegates indicates that it was also, and more important, a means of giving the South approximate equality in the Federal government in return for granting New England's profound desire to have the Federal government control interstate and international commerce.

That the sectional balance of power should be obtained by the process of counting three fifths of the slaves in determining representation was a natural but unfortunate arrangement. It was natural inasmuch as the Southerner regarded his slave as a human being and as part of the population; it was unfortunate in that it quickly identified the political influence of the South with the institution of slavery, and in doing so it went far toward engendering or increasing hostility in New England and finally in the whole North toward both slavery and the South.

As long as New England was able to dominate the Federal government there was no important opposition to the theoretical balance of power obtained by the three-fifths ratio; but when New England lost her status with the collapse of the Federalist party, her leaders immediately seized upon the three-fifth ratio as the explanation. During the period that ended with the Hartford Convention and the treaty of peace the New England leaders were unceasing in their attack upon "slave representation," as they called it. At the Hartford Convention it formed the leading grievance. The convention demanded an unconditional repeal.

During this same time Jefferson purchased the Louisiana territory, not for the purpose of destroying the sectional balance of power, but complacent in the belief that it would do so. We thus behold, during the earlier Jeffersonian period, the spectacle of the agricultural South and the commercial East tampering with the sectional balance of power. Of course, permanent balance of power was impossible in a rapidly expanding country, and both sections must have realized that eventually the forces of nature would tip the balance in favor of one section or the other or in favor of a section not yet born. Such eventualities were regarded as remote and were not permitted to disturb the peace of mind. It was the overthrow of the sectional balance by artificial, political methods which

665

caused uneasiness and wrath, for it indicated intersectional ill will or gross selfishness.

The Missouri controversy, 1819–1820, marked the decline of the agitation by the Northeast to repeal the three-fifths ratio clause as a means of weakening the political power of the South and inaugurated the second and final phase of the struggle of the North to destroy by artificial methods the sectional balance of power. This second phase was to prevent the formation and admission into the Union of any more slave states, which meant, from the political and social point of view, the exclusion of southern states. While the demand for exclusion was based partly upon what we may call moral reasons, Rufus King and the other northern leaders in this debate were quite frank in asserting that the Missouri debate was a struggle between the slave and free states for political power.

The first two phases of that sectionalism which led to the Civil War, while causing a slow accumulation of sectional grievances, were not marked during the thirty years prior to the Missouri debates by excessive ill will or serious disregard for the comity of sections. Indeed, up until the time of the Missouri debates, despite the rivalry of sections which almost disrupted the Union, there was maintained a certain urbanity and self-restraint on the part of the leaders of the rival sections; for as long as the founding fathers lived and exercised in-fluence over public affairs, there seems to have been a common realization—indeed, a common recollection—that the nation had been founded upon the principle of mutual tolerance of sectional differences and mutual concessions; that the nation had been constructed upon the respect of each section for the institutions, opinions, and ways of life of the other sections. But the years laid the founding fathers low, and their places were taken by a new and impatient generation who had no such understanding of the essence of national unity. The result was that urbanity, self-restraint, and courtesy—the ordinary amenities of civilized intercourse—were cast aside; and in their gracious place were sub-stituted the crude, discourteous, and insulting language and conduct in inter-sectional relations so familiar in the recent relations between the totalitarian nations and the so-called democracies. It was the Missouri debates in which intersectional comity was first violated; and it was the political leaders of the East, particularly the New Englanders and those of New England origin, who did it when they denounced in unmeasured terms slavery, the slaveholder, and southern society in general. It is noteworthy that the Southern leaders, with the exception of one or two, including John Randolph, ignored this first violent, denunciatory, insulting language of the Northerners during and immediately after the Missouri controversy; ignored them at least in that no reply in kind was made with the possible exception of two or three, including John Randolph, who demanded that the South withdraw from the Union before it was too late. The private correspondence of the Southerners, however, reveals them as resent-ful and apprehensive of future bad relations with the North.

666 Ten years after the Missouri Compromise debates the moral and intellectual leaders of the North, and notably those of New England origin, took up the language of abuse and vilification which the political leaders of that section had first employed in the Missouri debates. Quickly the political leaders re-sumed the tone of the Missouri controversy: and thus was launched the so-called anti-slavery crusade, but what in fact was a crusade against the southern people. For over three decades this attack upon slavery and the entire structure of southern society grew in volume and in violence. (A discussion of the motives behind this crusade would lead us far afield and into bitterly controversial questions. It does seem clear, however, that political and economic considerations were thoroughly mingled with the moral and religious objection to slavery.) One has to seek in the unrestrained and furious invective of the totalitarians to find a near parallel to the language that the Abolitionists and their political fellow travelers used in denouncing the South and its way of life. Indeed, as far as I have been able to ascertain, neither Dr. Goebbels nor Virginio Gayda nor other Axis propaganda agents ever plumbed the depths of vulgarity and obscenity reached and maintained by George Bourne, Stephen Foster, Wendell Phillips, Charles Sumner, and other Abolitionists of note. Let me cite a few of these—most of them are too indecent to quote. Phillips characterized the South as "one great brothel, where half a million women are flogged to prostitution." Bourne raised Phillips' estimate and insisted that there were a million slave women in the South who constituted "one vast harem where men-stealers may prowl, corrupt and destroy." However, Bourne was not satisfied with implicating the entire white male population of the South in the charge of miscegenation; he gave what he claimed were authentic examples of the same practice among the young white women of the South and insinuated that such practices were common. Foster and Bourne both attacked the morality of the southern ministry. Bourne said that the pulpits of the South were often filled with "man stealing, girl selling, pimping and slave manufacturing preachers," and that the churches were "synagogues of Satan." It would be far better, he insisted, "to transfer the inmate from the state prison, and the pander from the brothel to the pulpit" than permit a southern minister "to teach us righteousness and purity" in a northern church. Foster, in a book significantly entitled the *Brotherhood of Thieves*, charged that the Methodist Church was "more corrupt than any house of ill fame in New York," arguing that the fifty thousand adult female slaves who were members of that church "were inevitably doomed to lives of prostitution" under the penalty of being scourged to death. Foster, Bourne, Phillips, William Lloyd Garrison, Theodore Parker—indeed, most of the Abolitionists—put forward such attacks upon southern morality. No one was spared in this charge. All crimes were laid at the door of these people: they were kidnapers, man-stealers, pimps, robbers, assassins, freebooters, much more "despicable than the common horse thief." Good taste permits no real analysis of this torrent of coarse abuse; but let it be said again that nothing equal to it has been encountered in the language of insult used between the nations today— even those at war with one another.

This crusade against the South has often been brushed aside as the work of a few unbalanced fanatics. Such is not the case at all. The genuine Abolitionists were few in number in the beginning; but just as radicalism today has touched so many of the intellectuals of the East, so did abolitionism touch the intellectuals of the East and of the North generally. So did it touch the moral and political leaders. The effects upon the minds of those millions who did not consider themselves Abolitionists were profound. In time the average Northerner accepted in whole or in part the abolitionist picture of southern people: they became mon-

667

sters, and their children became not children but young monsters. Such a state of mind is fertile soil for war. The effect upon the minds of the southern people was far more profound, since they were recipients of this Niagara of insults and threats. To them the northern people were a combination of mad fanatics and cold-blooded political adventurers. As years passed, slow and consuming fury took hold of the southern people; and this fury was combined with a deadly fear which John Brown's raid confirmed: a fear that most of the northern people not only hated the southern people but would willingly see them exterminated. This fear was further confirmed when such a kindly philosopher as Ralph Waldo Emerson approved of the incendiary John Brown, by likening him to Jesus.

The political, intellectual, and moral leaders of the South did not remain silent under the abuse of the crusaders and the fellow travelers and well-wishers, but replied in a manner that added fuel to the roaring flames which were fast consuming the last vestiges of national unity. The language of insult which the so-called fire-eaters employed, however, was not usually coarse or obscene in comparison with that of the Abolitionists; it was urbane and restrained to a degree—but insulting. Thus in language of abuse and insult was jettisoned the comity of sections: And let me repeat that peace between sections as between nations is placed in jeopardy when one section fails to respect the self-respect of the people of another section. (*1941*)

PAUL GREEN

1894–

Paul Green was born March 17, 1894, near Lillington, N. C. As a youth he worked in the fields on his father's farm, in close contact with the Negro and white laborers—people of the type whom he later portrayed so realistically and sympathetically in his regional folk dramas. Green attended Buies Creek Academy and the University of North Carolina, from which he graduated in 1921. He completed two years of graduate study, first at Chapel Hill and then at Cornell. While at Cornell he published his first volume of one-act plays.

668

In 1923 Green returned in a teaching capacity to the University of North Carolina, where he is now Professor of Dramatic Art. As a writer, he has experimented with the short story and the novel as well as the drama, but his reputation rests primarily upon his plays. He is perhaps the most widely known student of the late Frederick H. Koch, whose classes in folk drama at Chapel Hill and whose student company of Carolina Playmakers did highly important work in presenting to Southern audiences relatively neglected characters in Southern life, such as the tenant farmers, mill hands, moonshiners, and mountaineers.

Green has done a great deal of work in experimenting with new forms in the drama and is particularly noteworthy for his use of music in the folk drama. His most esteemed plays include *In Abraham's Bosom*, for which he was awarded a Pulitzer prize in 1927; *The House of Connelly* (1931); *Roll Sweet Chariot* (1934); and *Hymn to the Rising Sun* (1935).

In Abraham's Bosom [1]

Scene I

In the turpentine woods of eastern North Carolina, forty years ago, near a spring at the foot of a hill. The immediate foreground is open and clear save for a spongy growth of grass and sickly ground creepers. In the rear a wide-spreading tangle of reeds, briars, and alder bushes shuts around the spring in a semi-circle. At the right front the great body of a pine, gashed and barked by the turpentine farmer's axe, lifts straight from the earth. To the left a log lies rotting in the embrace of wild ivy. Maples, bays, dogwoods and other small trees overrun by tenacious vines raise their leafy tops to shade the spot. Through interstices in the undergrowth one can see the pine forest stretching away until the eye is lost in a colonnade of trees. The newly scraped blazes on the pines show through the brush like the downward spreading beards of old men, suggestive of the ancient gnomes of the woods, mysterious and forever watchful.

At the left front four tin dinner pails hang on a limby bush. The sound of axes against the trees, accompanied by the rhythmically guttural "han—n—h! han—n—h!" of the cutters comes from the distance. One of the laborers breaks into a high mournful song—

> *Oh, my feets wuh wet—wid de sunrise dew,*
> *De morning star—wuh a witness too.*
> *'Way, 'way up in de Rock of Ages,*
> *In God's bosom gwine be my pillah.*

Presently there is a loud halloo near at hand, and another voice yodels and cries, Dinner time—m-m—e! Git yo' peas, ev'ybody! *Voices are heard nearer, a loud burst of laughter, and then three full-blooded Negroes shuffle in carrying long thin-bladed axes, which they lean against the pine at the right. They are dressed in nondescript clothes, ragged and covered with the glaze of raw turpentine. As they move up to the spring they take off their battered hats, fan themselves, and*

669

Reprinted with the kind permission of Paul Green, copyright 1926.
[1] *A revised version of* In Abraham's Bosom *appears in* Out of the South, *a volume of plays by Paul Green, published by Harper & Brothers, 1939.*

wipe the streaming sweat from their brows. Two of them are well-built and burly, one stout and past middle age with some pretension to a thin scraggly mustache, the second tall and muscled, and the third wiry, nervous and bandy-legged. They punctuate their conversation with great breaths of cool air.

YOUNG NEGRO. Monkey walking in dis woods.

OLDER NEGRO. Yah, Jaboh progueing round and 'bout um.

LITTLE NEGRO. While us res' he roos' high in pine tree.

YOUNG NEGRO. Fall on Puny's back 'bout th'ee o'clock, git um down. Hee—hee.

PUNY. Ain't no monkey kin ride me, tell you.

[*They stand fanning themselves.*]

OLDER NEGRO. Dat nigger tough, ain't you, Puny?

PUNY. Tough as whitleather, tough 'y God! [*He gets down on his belly at the spring.*] Mouf 'bout to crack, kin drink dis heah spring dry.

OLDER NEGRO [*slouching his heavy body towards the pool*]. Hunh, me too. Dat axe take water same lak a sawmill.

[*He lies down flat and drinks with the other. The water can be heard gluking over the cataract of their Adam's apples. The* YOUNGER NEGRO *opens his torn and sleeveless undershirt and stands raking the sweat from his powerful chest with curved hand.*]

YOUNG NEGRO [*after a moment*]. Heigh, Puny, you'n Lije pull yo' guts out'n dat mud-hole and let de engineer take a drink.

[*With a sudden thought of devilment he steps quickly forward and cracks their heads together.* PUNY *starts and falls face foremost in the spring.* LIJE, *slow and stolid, saves himself, crawls slowly upon his haunches and sits smiling good-naturedly, smacking his lips and sucking the water from the slender tails of his mustache.*]

LIJE [*cleaning his muddy hands with a bunch of leaves*]. Nunh—unh, not dis time, my boy.

YOUNG NEGRO [*scrambling to his feet, strangling and sputtering*]. Damn yo' soul, why you push me, Bud Gaskins?

BUD [*a threatening note slipping into his laugh*]. Hyuh, hyuh, don't you cuss at me, bo.

PUNY. Why'n't you 'pose on somebody yo' size? Bedder try Lije dere.

[BUD *gets down and begins drinking.*]

LIJE [*drawling*]. Don't keer 'f 'e do. Ducking good foh you dis hot weather.

PUNY [*helplessly*]. Allus picking at me. Wisht, wisht——

BUD. Heah I is lying down. Come on do whut you wisht. [PUNY *makes no reply but turns off, wiping his face on his shirt sleeve, and staring morosely at the ground.* BUD *gets to his feet.*] Yah, reckon you sail on me and I jam yo' haid in dat spring lak a fence post and drownd you.

PUNY [*his anger smouldering*]. Talk is cheap, black man, cheap!

[*Suddenly afraid of his boldness in replying, he turns and looks at* BUD *in a weak pleading defiance.*]

670

BUD [*making a frightening movement towards him*]. Mess wid me a-jowing and I knock yo' teef th'ough yo' skull.

LIJE. Hyuh, Bud, you let Puny 'lone.

[*He moves over to his bucket, gets it and sits down on the log at the left.*]

BUD [*turning for his bucket with a movement of disgust*]. Sho' I ain't gwine hurt him—po' pitiful bow-legs.

[PUNY *clenches his hands as if stung to the quick, and then beaten and forlorn reaches for his bucket, the weak member of the herd. He throws off his overall jacket, revealing himself stripped to the waist, and sits down at the pine tree.*]

LIJE [*laying out his food and singing*].

> 'Way, 'way up in de Rock of Ages,
> In God's bosom gwine be my pillah.

BUD [*looking at* PUNY's *bony bust*]. Uhp, showing off dat 'oman's breas' o' yo'n, is you? Haw-haw.

PUNY [*in sheer ineffectuality now answering him blandly*]. Gwine cool myse'f.

LIJE. Me too, peoples. [*He loosens his belt, pulls out his shirt-tails, undoes his shirt, and pats his belly.*] Lawd, Bud, you sho' led us a race dis mawning on dem dere boxes. Musta sweat a peck er mo'.

BUD [*taking his bucket and sitting on the ground near the center*]. Race? Hunh, wait till fo' o'clock dis evening, you gwine call foh de ca'f rope, sho' 'nough. [*Tickled at the tribute to his powers.*] And po' Puny, de monkey have rid him to deaf.

PUNY. Ain't no monkey rid me, I tells you. Little but loud. Be raght dere when de hawn blows.

BUD. Mought, and you slubbering yo' work. I cawners my boxes lak de Colonel calls foh. You des' gi' 'em a lick and a promise. Ain't it so, Lije?

LIJE [*swallowing a hunk of bread*]. Dunno, dunno. He do all right, reckon.

PUNY. Putt us in de cotton patch, and I kin kill you off de way a king snake do a lizard.

BUD. Picking cotton! Dat 'oman and chillun's job. No reg'lar man mess wid dat. [*Waving his hand at the woods behind him.*] Turpentiming's de stuff.

[*They fall to eating heartily, peas, side-meat, molasses poured in the top of the bucket-lid from a bottle, bread and collards. The axe of a fourth hand is heard still thudding in the forest.*]

LIJE [*jerking his bread-filled hand behind him*]. Whyn't Abe come on? Time he eating.

BUD. Let him rair. 'On't hurt hisse'f a-cutting. Gitting to be de no 'countest hand I ever see.

LIJE. Useter could cut boxes lak a house afiah.

PUNY. And hack! Lawd, dat nigger could hack.

LIJE. De champeen o' de woods and de swamps.

PUNY. Bedder'n Bud, bedder'n all. Knowed him to dip eight barrels many day.

BUD. Cain't he'p whut has been. Ain't wuth my ol' hat now. Colonel Mack say so too. And I heahd Mr. Lonnie talking rough to him over at de weaving house day 'fo' yistiddy 'bout his gitting trifling heah lately.

PUNY. Been gitting no' count since two yeah' 'go. De time when de white folks hang dat Charlie Sampson on a telegram pole—him whut 'tacked a white 'oman, and dey shoot him full o' holes, ayh Lawd!

671

BUD. Dey did. And dat Abe gut his neck stretched hadn't been foh de Colonel. Fool went down dere in de night and cut dat nigger down and bury 'im hese'f.

LIJE [*looking around him*]. 'Twon't do to mess wid white folks and dey r'iled up.

BUD. You said it, bruvver.

PUNY [*looking around him*]. Won't do. Keep to yo' work, da's all.

BUD. Yeh, work, work foh 'em. Git yo' money and yo' meat, push on th'ough, axe no questions, no sass, keep to yo' work.

LIJE. Nigger keep mouf shet, let white man do talking. He safe den.

BUD. Safe! You done said. No telegram poles, no shooting, no fiah burn um.

PUNY. Safe is best.

[*They lapse into silence under the touch of worry, something undefinable, something not to be thought upon. They swallow their food heavily. Presently* LIJE *stops and looks at the ground.*]

LIJE. Abe ain't safe.

BUD. Eyh?

LIJE [*gesturing vaguely behind him*]. Abe talk too much.

BUD [*nodding*]. He do, talk too much to white folks.

PUNY. Cain't he'p it, I bet.

BUD. Kin too. Didn't talk much 'fore dat boy wuh hung. Worked hard den and say nothing.

LIJE. Sump'n on he mind. Sump'n deep, worry 'im, trouble——

BUD. Trouble 'bout de nigger, wanter rise him up wid eddication—fact!

PUNY. Hunh, rise him up to git a rope roun' his neck. Git buried in he own graveyard, don't mind out. Nigger's place down de bottom.

BUD. Raght on de bottom wid deir hand and legs, muscle power, backbone, down wid de rocks and de shovels and de digging, dat's de nigger. White man on top.

LIJE. You's talking gospel.

PUNY. Abe say he gwine climb. I heah him tell de Colonel dat.

BUD. Fo' God! Whut Colonel say?

PUNY. He ain't say nothing, des' look at 'im.

LIJE. Abe is bad mixed up all down inside.

BUD. White and black make bad mixtry.

LIJE. Do dat. [*Thumping on his chest.*] Nigger down heah. [*Thumping his head.*] White mens up heah. Heart say do one thing, head say 'nudder. Bad, bad.

PUNY. De white blood in him coming to de top. Dat make him want-a climb up and be sump'n. Nigger gwine hol' him down dough. Part of him take adder de Colonel, part adder his muh, 'vision and misery inside.

LIJE. Ssh!

PUNY [*starting and looking around*]. Colonel Mack he daddy, everybody knows. Lak as two peas, see de favor.

BUD [*bitingly*]. Talk too much! Little bird carry news to de Colonel and he fall on you and scrush you. Ain't nigger, ain't white whut ail him. Dem damn books he gut to studying last yeah or two. Cain't go to de woods widdout 'em. Look up dere on his bucket, foh Christ sake. [*He points to the remaining tin bucket in the bush. A small book is lying on the top under the handle. Snorting.*] 'Rifmatic I bet. Give a nigger a book and des' well shoot him. All de white folks tell you dat.

672

PUNY [*pouring molasses on his bread*]. He sma't dough, in his haid. Dat nigger gut sense.

LIJE. Has dat. Gitting so he kin cipher raght up wid de Colonel.

PUNY [*looking at* BUD]. Bet some day Colonel Mack put him woods boss over us.

BUD. Ain't no nigger gwine boss me, hoss-cake. Split his haid open wid my axe.

LIJE [*leaning back and emitting a halloo*]. Heighp, you Abe! Dinner! Gwine cut all day?

BUD. Gi' him de full title and he'll heah you.

LIJE [*grinning*]. Aberham, Aberham McCranie!

PUNY. Yeh, you, Aberham Lincoln, whut drapped de nigger he freedom from de balloon, you better git yo' grub!

[*An answering shout comes out of the forest.*]

BUD. Trying to cut past time, mebbe us'll think he sma't.

PUNY. Don't keer whut you think, Bud, gitting so he look down on you and de rest of us.

BUD. Damn yo' runty soul, whut you know 'bout it? Ain't no nigger living kin look down on me and git by wid it. Do, and I make 'em smell o' dat.

[*He clenches his heavy fist and raises it to heaven.*]

PUNY. Jesus! Dat Abe take you up in one hand and frail yo' behime to a blister.

LIJE. Whut make you two black-gyard so much?

BUD [*to* PUNY]. Keep on, keep on, little man. Some dese days you gwine come missing.

[*He crams a handful of cornbread into his mouth.*]

LIJE [*drawling*]. Try a little fist and skull and work de bile out'n yo' systems. [*Looking off and singing.*]

Dark was de night and cold de ground. . . .

BUD [*spitting in scorn*]. Ain't gwine bruise my fistes on his old skull. Don't 'spec' to notice him no mo'. [*He falls to eating in huge mouthfuls.*] But he bedder quit th'owing dat Abe in my face, I tells him dat.

PUNY. Don't see why dat make you mad.

BUD. It do dough. I don't lak him and his uppity ways, I don't.

PUNY. Hunh, and you was one o' de fust to brag on him foh goin' on sho't rations so de Colonel buy him books and learn 'im to teach school.

BUD. Sho't rations. Ain't no sho't rations, and dat Goldie gal bringing him pies and stuff eve'y day. Be here wid a bucket in a few minutes, I betcha. Fool love de ve'y ground he squat on! And he look down on her caze her ign'ant. And teach school! Been heahing dat school teaching business de whole yeah. He ain't gwine teach no school. Niggers 'on't send to him, dey 'on't. Niggers don't want no schooling.

PUNY. Mought. Abe tol' me dis mornin' dat de Colonel gwine fix it wid de 'missioners or something in town to-day. I know whut de matter wid you, Bud. Hee-hee.

BUD. Whut?

673

PUNY [*hesitating*]. Abe come riding by in de two-hoss coach. Us'll be bowing and a-scraping. Us'll pull off'n our hats and be "Howdy, Mister Aberham." [BUD *turns and looks at him with infinite scorn, saying nothing.*] And Bud? [BUD *makes no answer.*] Bud?

BUD. Whut?

PUNY. Dat Goldie business whut worrying you, hee-hee. She love Abe and—

BUD [*bounding up and kicking* PUNY'S *bucket and food into the bushes*]. Damn yo' lousy soul, minner mind stomp you in de dirt!

[*He towers over the terrified* PUNY, *who lies flat on his back whimpering.*]

PUNY. Don't hit me, Bud. Foh Gohd's sake! I des' joking.

LIJE. Go at it, fight it out. [*Singing as he watches them.*]

> De bones in de grave cried Ca'vary
> De night King Jesus died.

BUD [*kicking dirt at* PUNY *and going back to his bucket*]. Done told him now. Ain't gwine say no mo'! Next time be my fist rammed down his th'oat, and turn him wrong side out'ards.

[ABE *comes in at the right, carrying his axe. He is a young Negro, with a touch of the mulatto in him, of twenty-five or six, tall and powerfully built, dressed much like the others in cap and turpentine-glazed clothes. He puts his axe by the pine at the right, pulls off his cap and fans himself, while he pinches his sweaty shirt loose from his skin. His shaggy head, forehead and jaw are marked with will and intelligence. But his wide nostril and a slumbrous flash in his eye that now and then shows itself suggest a passionate and dangerous person when aroused. From the change in the actions of the others when he enters it is evident that they respect and even fear him.*]

ABE. What's de trouble 'tween you and Puny, Bud?

BUD [*sullenly*]. Ain't no trouble.

PUNY [*crawling around on the ground and collecting his spilled food*]. Ain't nothing, Abe, I des' spilled my rations.

[ABE *gets his book down and seats himself in the shade at the left. He begins working problems, using a stub of a pencil and a sheet of crumpled paper.*]

LIJE. Puny, I got some bread left you kin have.

[*He pulls a harp from his pocket and begins to blow softly.*]

PUNY [*straightening out his mashed bucket and closing it*]. I don't want nothing else, Lije. Et all I kin hold. [*After a moment.*] Putt yo' bucket up foh you.

[*He gets* LIJE'S *bucket and hangs it along with his own in the limby bush.* BUD *eats in silence, puts up his bucket, gets a drink from the spring, and resumes his seat, hanging his head between his knees.* PUNY *goes to the spring and drinks.*]

BUD [*pouring snuff into his lip*]. Don't fall in an' git drownded, Puny.

PUNY. Want some water, Lije?

[*He goes to the log, curls himself up in the shade beside it and prepares to sleep.*]

LIJE [*stirring lazily*]. Believe I does.

[*He goes to the spring and drinks, returns to the pine tree and sits down.*]

PUNY. Ain't you g'in' eat no dinner, Abe?

674

[ABE *makes no reply.*]

LIJE. Call him again. [*Touching his head with his finger.*] Deep, deep up dere.

PUNY. Heigh, Abe, bedder eat yo' grub.

ABE [*starting*]. You call me?

PUNY. You so deep stud'in' didn't heah me. Bedder eat yo' dinner. Git full o' ants settin' up dere.

ABE. I goin' to eat later.

BUD. Yeh, when Goldie come.

ABE. Hunh!

BUD. You heahd me.

ABE [*irritably*]. Don't let me heah no mo'.

BUD. Hunh?

ABE. You heahd me. [PUNY *snickers from his log with audible delight.* LIJE *waits a moment and then lies down.* BUD *reaches out and tears a bush from the ground and casts it angrily from him.*] I'll eat my dinner when it please me, you gentlemens allowing. [*There is a touch of anger in his voice which he apparently regrets on second thought, for he goes on more kindly.*] Goldie said she goin' to fetch me sump'n t' eat today. I got to work dis problem. Been on it two days now. Cain't git it out'n my head. Ain't been able to sleep two nights. [BUD *sits staring and spitting straight before him. Presently* LIJE *begins to snore, then* PUNY *follows.* ABE *goes on with his figuring.* BUD *turns over on the ground and goes to sleep.* ABE *becomes more and more absorbed in the problem he is working. He mutters to himself.*] How many sheep? How many sheep? [*He clutches at his hair, gnaws his pencil, and turns to the back of his book.*] Answer say fifteen. Cain't make it come out fifteen, cain't, seem lak, to save me. Man must have answer wrong. Six go into fo'teen, three, no, two times and—two over. [*His voice dies away as he becomes lost in his work. Presently his face begins to light up. He figures faster. Suddenly he slaps his knee.*] Dere whah I been missing it all de time. I carried two 'stid o' one. Blame fool I is. [*He hits the side of his head with his knuckle. In his excitement he calls out.*] Puny, I gitting dat answer. [*But* PUNY *is snoring away. In a moment he throws down his book with beaming face.*] I got it, folkses, I got it. Fifteen! Dat white man know whut he doing, he all time git dem answer right. [*He turns expectantly towards* LIJE.] I got it, Lije. [LIJE *makes no answer. He turns towards* PUNY *again, starts to speak but sees he is asleep.*] Bud! [*But* BUD *makes no answer. The heavy breathing of the sleepers falls regularly upon his ears. His face sinks into a sort of hopeless brooding.*] Yeh, sleep, sleep, sleep yo' life away. I figger foh you, foh me, foh all de black in de world to lead 'em up out'n ignorance. Dey don't listen, dey don't heah me, dey in de wilderness, don't wanta be led. Dey sleep, sleep in bondage. [*He bows his head between his knees.*] Sleep in sin. [*Presently.*] Time me to eat.

[*He reaches for his bucket and is about to open it when* PUNY *springs high into the air with a squeak of terror, and begins rolling over and over in the leaves and briars.*]

675

PUNY. Come heah, folkses, come heah git dis thing off'n me.

[*He clutches at his breeches.* LIJE *and* BUD *start up out of their sleep.*]

LIJE. Who dat run-mad man?

BUD. Dat damn Puny, sump'n in he britches!

ABE. Be still, Puny, I git it out. [*He goes up to the frightened* PUNY, *reaches down his trousers and pulls out a mouse.*] Nothing but a little bitty old field mice.

[*He throws the mouse into the thicket.* LIJE *and* BUD *break into roaring laughter.* PUNY *sits down exhausted, fanning himself angrily.*]

PUNY. Laugh, laugh, all o' you. Dat thing bite same as mud turkle. Yeh, funny, funny, lak hell to you.

[*He snaps his mouth closed and fans himself the more furiously. A loud shout comes from off the left.*]

ABE. Stop yo' laughing, I heah somebody hollering.

[*A second halloo comes down the hill.*]

PUNY. Dat de Colonel and Mr. Lonnie!

BUD. Sound lak 'em. Da's who 'tis.

ABE [*going off at the left*]. Heah we is, Colonel Mack, at de spring eating dinner! [*He comes back.*] Colonel Mack and Mr. Lonnie coming on down heah.

PUNY. Co'se. Gut to see how many boxes us cleaned up dis mawning.

ABE. He tell me 'bout de school now. [*He stirs around him in his excitement.*] Mebbe dat his main business heah in de middle o' de day.

BUD. Hunh, mebbe. Gut some special work want done. Wanter hurry us to it, dat's whut.

[*The sound of voices is heard approaching from the left, and almost immediately the* COLONEL *and his son* LONNIE *come in. The* COLONEL *carries a riding whip. He is a stout, run-down old Southerner with all the signs of moral and intellectual decadence upon him. Lechery, whiskey, and levity of living have taken their toll of him, and yet he has retained a kind of native good-naturedness. His shirt front and once pointed beard are stained with the drippings of tobacco juice. There is something in his bearing and in the contour of his face that resembles* ABE. *His son, a heavyish florid young man of twenty-three or four, walks behind him.*]

COLONEL [*in a high jerky voice*]. Snoozing, hanh?

ABE. Just finishing our dinner, suh.

PUNY. Us 'bout to wuk over-time to-day, Colonel.

COLONEL. Not likely, I reckon. Say, I want you fellows, all four of you, to get over to the swamp piece on Dry Creek. Boxes there are running over, two quarts in 'em apiece, prime virgin. [*They begin to move to their feet.*] No, I don't mean to go right now. Gabe's coming by on the big road here [*jerking his whip towards the rear*] with a load of barrels and the dippers in about a half-hour. Meet him out there.

LONNIE. Yeh, we want to git the wagons off to Fayetteville to-night.

COLONEL. How you get on cornering this morning, Bud?

BUD. Purty good, suh. Us fo' done 'bout all dat pastuh piece, suh.

COLONEL. Fine, fine. That's the way. Puny and Lije stay with you?

BUD. Raght dere eve'y jump.

LIJE. Yessuh, yessuh!

PUNY. When he gi' de call we gi' 'im de 'sponse eve'y time, suh. Yes, suh, us kept 'im crowded.

COLONEL. We got to git on, Lonnie. Want to see how the scrape's coming over on Uncle Joe's Branch. Be up on the road there in half a' hour.

676

LONNIE [*stopping as they go out*]. Got so you doing any better work lately, Abe?

ABE [*starting*]. Suh!

LONNIE. You heard me.

ABE. I didn't understand you, Mr. Lonnie.

LONNIE. You understood me all right. [*Pointing to the book on the ground.*] Let them damned books worry you still?

COLONEL. Come on, Lonnie.

ABE [*stammering*]. I dunno—I——

COLONEL. Still holding out on short rations, ain't you, Abe?

[*There is the least hint of pride in the* COLONEL'S *voice.*]

ABE [*somewhat confused*]. I studying whut I kin, slow go, slow go.

COLONEL. Stick to it. You the first nigger I ever see so determined. But then you're uncommon! [*The* COLONEL *moves on.*] Come on, Lonnie.

ABE [*following somewhat timidly after him*]. Colonel Mack, did di—you— what'd dey say over dere 'bout that little school business?

COLONEL. Bless my soul, 'bout to forgit it. I talked it over with the board and most of 'em think maybe we'd better not try it yet.

ABE [*his face falling*]. When dey say it might be a good time? I gitting right 'long wid dat 'rithmetic and spelling and reading. I kin teach de colored boys and gals a whole heap right now, and I'll keep studying.

COLONEL [*impatiently*]. Oh, I dunno. Time'll come mebbe. Mebbe time won't come. Folks is quare things y' know.

[*He moves on.*]

ABE. Cain't you git 'em to let me try it awhile? Reckon——

COLONEL. I don't know, I tell you. Got my business on my mind now.

LONNIE. He's done told you two or three times; can't you hear?

ABE [*his eyes flashing and his voice shaking with sudden uncontrollable anger*]. Yeh, yeh, I hear 'im. Dem white folks don't keer—dey——

LONNIE [*stepping before him*]. Look out! none of your sass. Pa's already done more for you than you deserve. He even stood up for you and they laughing at him there in town.

ABE [*trembling*]. Yeh, yeh, I knows. But dem white folks don't think—I going to show 'em, I——

LONNIE [*pushing himself before him*]. Dry up. Not another word.

ABE [*his voice breaking almost into a sob*]. Don't talk to me lak dat, Mr. Lonnie. Stop him, Colonel Mack, 'fore I hurt him.

[*The other Negroes draw off into a knot by the pine tree, mumbling in excitement and fear.*]

COLONEL. Stop, Lonnie! Abe, don't you talk to my son like that.

LONNIE. By God, I'm going to take some of the airs off'n him right now. You've gone around here, sorry, worthless—worse every day for the last year. What you need is a good beating, and I'm gonna give it to you.

[*He steps backwards and snatches the whip from his father's hand.*]

677

COLONEL. Stop that, Lonnie!

LONNIE. Keep out of this yourself. [*He comes towards* ABE.] I'll beat his black hide off'n him.

ABE. Keep 'im back dere, Colonel Mack. I mought kill him! Keep 'im off.

LONNIE. Kill him! All right, do it, damn you!

[*He strikes* ABE *across the face with his whip. With a snarl* ABE *springs upon him, tears the whip from his hands and hurls him headlong into the thicket of briars and bushes. Then he stands with his hands and head hanging down, his body shaking like one with the palsy.*]

PUNY [*screaming*]. You done kilt Mr. Lonnie! Oh, Lawdy, Lawdy!

COLONEL [*running to* LONNIE *who is crawling up out of the mud with his clothes and skin torn. He is sobbing and cursing*]. Are you hurt? How bad are you hurt?

LONNIE. Let me git at that son of a bitch and I'll kill him dead. [*Moaning.*] Oh, I'll beat his brains out with one o' them axes.

COLONEL. If you ain't dead, you'd better keep your hands off'n him. I'll fix him. [*He reaches down and picks up the whip—thundering.*] Git down on your knees, Abe! Git down, you slave! I'm gonna beat you.

[ABE *jerks his head up in defiance, but before the stern face of the* COLONEL *his strength goes out of him. He puts his hands up in supplication.*]

ABE. Don't beat me, Colonel Mack, don't beat me wid dat whip!

COLONEL. Git down on your knees! I've beat many a slave, and I'll show you how it feels.

[*He strikes him several blows.*]

ABE [*falling on his knees*]. Oh, Lawd, have muhcy upon me!

[*The* COLONEL *begins to beat him blow upon blow.* PUNY, BUD *and* LIJE *stand near the pine in breathless anxiety.*]

PUNY. De Colonel'll kill 'im!

BUD [*seizing his arm*]. Shet dat mouf, nigger!

COLONEL [*as he brings the whip down*]. Let this be a lesson to you to the end of your life!

ABE [*his back twitching under the whip, his voice broken*]. Muhcy, Colonel Mack, muhcy!

COLONEL. You struck a white man, you struck my son.

ABE [*raising his tear-stained face*]. I yo' son too, you my daddy.

[*He throws himself down before him, embracing his feet. The* COLONEL *lowers the whip, then drops it behind him.*]

LONNIE [*his voice husky with rage*]. You hear what he say? Hear what he called you?

[*He seizes the whip and in a blind rage strikes the prostrate* ABE *again and again.*]

COLONEL [*stepping between them*]. Stop it! Give me that whip. [LONNIE *nervelessly hesitates and then reluctantly hands him the whip.*] Go on back out to the road and wait for me. Trot! [LONNIE *in disgust and rage finally goes off at the left nursing his face in his arms.*] Get up, Abe. Get up, I say.

[ABE *sits up, hugging his face between his knees. The* COLONEL *wets his handkerchief in the spring, and with his hands on* ABE'S *head bathes the bruises on his neck and shoulders.*]

ABE [*in a voice grown strangely dignified and quiet*]. Thank 'ee, thank 'ee, Colonel Mack.

COLONEL [*breathing heavily*]. Thanky nothing. I had to beat you, Abe, had to. Think no more about it. Dangerous thing, hitting a white man. But this is the end

678

of it. Won't be no law, nothing but this. Put some tar and honey on yourself to-night and you'll be all right to-morrow. [*The bushes are suddenly parted at the rear and a tall sinuous young mulatto woman bounds through. She carries a bucket in her hand. At the sight of the* COLONEL *bathing* ABE'S *head and neck she rushes forward with a low cry. The* COLONEL *turns towards her.*] Now, Goldie, ain't no use cutting up. Abe been in a little trouble. Nothing much.

GOLDIE [*moaning*]. I heahd de racket and I 'fraid somebody being kilt. Is you hurt bad, Abe, honey babe? [*She bends tenderly over him, her hand running over his hair.*] Who hurt you, honey, who hurt you?

COLONEL [*handing* GOLDIE *his handkerchief*]. Look after him, Goldie. [*He goes out at the left calling.*] Wait a minute, Lonnie!

GOLDIE. Whut dey do to you, Abe? Who hurt you? [*All the time she is rubbing his neck, dabbing his shoulders with the handkerchief, and cooing over him.*] Why'n you kill dem white mens if dey hurt you? You kin do it, break 'em lak broomstraws.

ABE [*standing up*]. Ain't nobody hurt me. I crazy dat's whut, crazy in de haid. Ain't nobody hurt me.

GOLDIE [*clinging to him*]. You is hurt, hurt bad. Look at yo' po' neck and shoulders. Look at 'em beat wid great whales on 'em!

ABE [*growling*]. Ain't nobody hurt me, I tell you.

GOLDIE. Lay yo'se'f down heah and let me smoove off yo' forehead and put some cold water on dat mark crost yo' face. Please'm, Abe.

ABE [*suddenly crying out in a loud voice*]. I ain't nothing, nothing. Dat white man beat me, beat me like a dawg. [*His voice rising into a wail.*] He flail me lak a suck-egg dawg! [*He rocks his head from side to side in a frenzy of wrath.*] Lemme git to him! [*He falls on his knees searching in the leaves and finds a stone.* GOLDIE *stands wringing her hands and moaning. He jumps to his feet, raising the stone high above his head.*] Lemme git to him, I scrush his God-damn head lak a eggshell!

[*He moves to the left to follow the* COLONEL. GOLDIE *throws her arms around his neck.*]

GOLDIE. No, no, you ain't gwine out dere, Abe, Abe!

PUNY [*crying out*]. Stop him, Bud! Lije, keep him back!

LIJE [*coming from the pine tree*]. Hyuh, now you, Abe, stop dat.

BUD [*moving quickly before him and blocking his path*]. Stop dat, fool. You gwine fix it to git yo'se'f hung up on a telegram pole. Body be so full o' holes, sift sand.

GOLDIE [*sobbing*]. Don't do it, Abe, sugar babe. [*Throws herself upon his breast.*]

BUD [*reaching toward her*]. Seem lak you take yo'se'f off'n dat man!

ABE [*pulling her arms from around him*]. Lemme loose, lemme loose. [*After a moment he throws the stone down.*] I ain't going do nothing.

[*He sits down on the log at the left, holding his head in his hands.*]

GOLDIE [*bringing her bucket*]. Hyuh, eat sump'n, Abe, you feel better. I gut some pie and some cake in heah foh you.

PUNY [*stepping back and forth in senseless excitement*]. Somebody gwine git kilt at dis mess, somebody——

ABE [*pushing* GOLDIE *away*]. I ain't want nothing t' eat, ain't hongry.

679

LIJE. Bedder eat, Abe. Git yo' stren'th back.

ABE [*savagely*]. Ain't hongry, I keep telling you.

[GOLDIE *drops on her knees beside him and laying her head in his lap clasps her arms around him.*]

GOLDIE [*sobbing softly*]. Oh, boy, boy, why dey beat you up so? Whut you do to 'em?

ABE. Fool, fool I is. Crazy, dat's it.

BUD [*sharply*]. He g'in Mr. Lonnie and de Colonel back talk. Cain't sass white mens and git 'way wid it. Abe orter know better.

[LIJE *wanders over to the right blowing his harp softly and forlornly.*]

PUNY [*sitting down on the ground*]. Cain't be done, Abe. Cain't.

BUD [*stripping leaves from a bush and watching* GOLDIE *as she carries on over* ABE]. Hyuh, 'oman, stop dat rairing. [*Muttering to himself.*] Nevah see two bigger fools.

[ABE *puts his hands mechanically on* GOLDIE'S *shoulders and begins stroking her.*]

ABE. Stop it, baby. Ain't no use to cry.

[PUNY *sits with his mouth open in astonishment watching them.* LIJE *lays himself back on the ground and blows his harp, apparently no longer interested.*]

BUD [*jealousy rising within him*]. Heigh, Goldie, git up from dat man's lap. He ain't keer nothing foh you. [GOLDIE'S *sobs die away and she is quiet.*] He say you foolish many time. He look down on you.

GOLDIE [*raising her tear-stained face*]. How you know? You jealous, Bud Gaskins. He better man dan you. Wuth whole town of you. [*Catching* ABE *by the hand and picking up her bucket.*] Come on, come on, honey, le's go off dere in de woods and eat our dinner by ourse'ves!

BUD [*coming up to her*]. Hyuh, you stay out'n dat woods wid him, nigger.

ABE [*standing up*]. Yeh, yeh, I come wid you.

[*He moves as one in a dream, and reaches out and pushes* BUD *behind him.*]

GOLDIE [*her face alight, a sort of reckless and unreal abandonment upon her*]. I knows where dere's a cool place under a big tree. And dey's cool green moss dere and soft leaves. Le's go dere, boy. I gwine tend to you and feed you. [*She moves across towards the right, leading* ABE *like a child.*] We make us a bed dere, honey. [LIJE *sits up watching them.*] Us fohgit de 'membrance o' all dis trouble. [*A kind of ecstasy breaking in her voice.*] Dere de birds sing and we hear de little branch running over de rocks. Cool dere, sweet dere, you kin sleep, honey, rest dere, baby. Yo' mammy, yo' chile gwine love you, make you fohgit.

ABE [*moved out of himself*]. Yeh, yeh, I come wid you. I don't keer foh nothing, not nothing no mo'. You, des' you'n me.

GOLDIE. Ain't no worl', ain't no Lije and Bud, nobody. Us gwine make us a 'biding place and a pillah under dat green tree. [*In sweet oblivion.*] Feel yo' arms around me, my lips on yo'n. We go singing up to heaben, honey, togedder—togedder.

680

[*They go off, her voice gradually dying away like a nun's chant.*]

BUD [*breaking a sapling in his grasp*]. Gwine off, gwine off in de woods togedder dere lak hawgs.

PUNY [*bounding up, his body shaking in lascivious delight*]. I gwine watch 'em—hee-hee—I gwine watch 'em.

LIJE [*knocking him back*]. Bedder stay out'n dat woods. Abe kill you.

PUNY [*standing up by the pine tree*]. Kin see 'em, her still a-leading 'im.

LIJE [*standing up and peering off to the right*]. Dere on de cool moss and de sof' green leaves.

BUD [*stripping the limbs from the top of the broken sapling*]. Ain't gwine look. Dey fools, bofe fools. [*Raging out.*] Dere she go playing de hawg. Didn't know she lak dat. [*He sucks in his breath with the sound of eating something.*] Wisht to Gohd I knowed she lak dat. I de man foh her. Bud Gaskins. I tame her, Gohd damn her, I tame her down and take dat speerit out'n her.

[*He crowds out his chest and walks up and down.*]

PUNY [*grasping LIJE's arm*]. Cain't hardly see 'em no mo', kin you?

LIJE. Kin hardly.

BUD [*his anger and jealousy disappearing in physical emotion and vulgar curiosity*]. Whah dey now?

LIJE [*pointing*]. Dere, dere, dey crossing de branch now.

PUNY [*breathlessly*]. I see 'em. I see 'em. He arm 'round her now, her head on he shoulder. [*He capers in his excitement.*] Lawd! Lawd!

BUD [*with a loud brutal laugh as he slaps LIJE on the back*]. On de sof' green moss.

LIJE [*laughing back and dragging his harp across his mouth*]. Whah de leaves is cool.

PUNY. Cain't see 'em no mo'. [*He whirls about and turns a handspring.*] Whoopee, folkses! Gwine run away wid myse'f!

BUD [*his eyes shining*]. Down whah de branch water run.

[*He shuffles a jig among the leaves.*]

LIJE [*blowing upon his harp*]. Singing raght up to heaben!

[*He plays more wildly as they all drop into a barbaric dance that gradually mounts into a dionysiac frenzy.*]

PUNY. Heaben!

BUD. Jesus, Lawd, Fadder and Son!

LIJE [*singing loudly as they dance, the music running into a quick thumping rhythm*].

> My feets wuh wet wid de sunrise dew,
> De mawning stah wuh a witness too.
> 'Way, 'way up in de Rock of Ages,
> In God's bosom gwine be my pillow.

[*They gambol, turn and twist, run on all fours, rear themselves up on their haunches, cavort like goats.*]

PUNY. In God's bosom—hanh!

BUD. In who bosom?

LIJE. In who bosom, bubber!

[*A loud halloo comes down from the hill in the rear, unnoticed by them.*]

PUNY. In Goldie's bosom. Hee-hee-hee.

BUD and LIJE. Haw-haw-haw! Hee-hee-hee! In God's bosom gwine be my pillah.

681

[*The halloo is repeated.*]

LIJE. Hyuh, dere dat Gabe calling us. Better git, or de Colonel have dat stick on our back.

[*They gather up their buckets and axes.* PUNY *clambers up the pine a few feet and drops to the ground.*]

BUD. Kin see?

PUNY. See nothing. Hee-hee!

LIJE. Gut to leave 'em now. Abe ketch it 'gin don't mind out. He not coming wid us.

BUD. He done foh now. Dat gal gut him hard and fast. [*Snorting scornfully.*] Books, books! Rise 'em up, lak hell!

LIJE. I done told you. Heart say dis, head say dat. Bad mixtry. Bad. Crazy!

PUNY [*shouting*]. Heigh, you Gabe! Coming!

[*They move out at the rear up the hill, singing, laughing and jostling each other.*]

> 'Way, 'way down by de sweet branch water
> In her bosom gwine be he pillah!

Hee-hee—haw—haw—! [*Their loud brutally mocking laughter floats back behind them.*]

Scene II

A spring day about three years later, in ABRAHAM MCCRANIE'S *two-room cabin. The room is roughly built of framed material and unceiled. To the right front is a fireplace with a green oakwood fire going. A wood box is to the right of the chimney. To the left rear of the room is a bed, and at the left center rear a door leads out to the porch. To the right of the door a window gives a view of wide-stretched cotton fields. Below the window close to the wall is a rough homemade chest with several books on it, and hanging between it and the door is a sort of calendar, with the illustration of a slave leaving his chains behind and walking up a hill towards the sunrise. There is a caption at the top of the print in large letters—*"WE ARE RISING." *Several old dresses, bonnets, and coats hang on the nails in the joists in the right rear. A door in the right center leads into the kitchen. At the left front is a dilapidated old bureau, small pieces of wood taking the place of lost casters. The top drawer is open, sagging down like a wide lip, with stray bits of clothing hanging over the edge. A bucket of water and a pan are on the bureau. There are several splint-bottomed chairs and a rocker in the room.*

When the curtain rises MUH MACK *is sitting by the fire rocking a bundle in her arms. She is a chocolate-colored Negress of near sixty, dressed in a long dirty wrapper, and barefooted. Her graying hair is wrapped in pigtails and stands around her head Medusa-like. A long snuff-stick protrudes from her mouth, and now and then the fire sputters with a frying noise as she spits into it.* GOLDIE'S *long gaunt form lies stretched on the bed at the left partly covered by a sheet, her head hanging off on her arm. She is constantly raising in her languid hand a stick with a paper tied to it to shoo away the flies.* MUH MACK *rocks and sings.*

682

MUH MACK.

> Oohm—oohm—hoonh—oohm—oohm—
> Dis heah baby de pu'tiest baby,
> Pu'tiest baby in de lan'.
> He gwine grow up champeen sojer,
> Mammy's honey, onlies' man.
> Oohm—oohm—hoonh—oohm—oohm—

GOLDIE [*in a tired voice*]. How he coming now?

MUH MACK [*shaking her finger and wagging her head at the bundle*]. Done seen um grow. Look at me lak he know me.

GOLDIE [*with a long sigh*]. I so tiahed, tiahed. Seem lak I kin sleep forever.

MUH MACK. Lie and sleep, sleep. Git yo' stren'th.

GOLDIE. I tiahed but cain't sleep. [*She lapses into silence. The old woman rocks and sings. Presently GOLDIE raises her head.*] Whut day to-day?

MUH MACK. Sa'd'y.

GOLDIE. Seem lak I cain't 'member nothing. Whut day he come?

MUH MACK. He come a-Chuesday.

GOLDIE. Dat make him—le's see, how old?

MUH MACK. Fo' day now.

GOLDIE [*suddenly sitting up with a gasp*]. Dem udder two die, one th'ee days, udder'n fo'.

MUH MACK. Nanh—nanh, lie back down. Dis heah baby live be a hundred. He strong, he muscled. Dem udder po' little 'uns puny, bawn to die. De mark was on 'em f'om de fust.

GOLDIE [*bending her head between her knees and weeping softly*]. Dey was so pitiful and liddle. I cain't fohgit how dey feel and fumble foh me wid deir liddle hands and dey hongry.

MUH MACK [*irritably*]. Bless Gohd, crying adder dem, and gut dis fine 'un heah. Lay yo'se'f down on dat bed and res'.

GOLDIE. Cain't fohgit 'em, cain't.

MUH MACK. Hunh, mought as well and dey done plowed in de ground.

GOLDIE [*her tears beginning to flow again*]. Yeh, yeh, dey is! Abe didn't try to keep Mr. Lonnie f'om cutting down dem plum bushes and plowing up dat hedgerow. I hold it 'gin him long as I live.

MUH MACK. Why foh? De dead's de dead. Let de earf hab 'em. Let cotton grow over 'um. No use mo'ning. Think on de living.

GOLDIE. Po' Abe, 'on't his fault dough. He proud, stand by see white mens plow over 'em, say nothin', 'on't beg foh his babies.

MUH MACK. Cain't blame 'im! He stiff neck. God break his spirit. Gi' 'im two dead 'uns to fetch 'im down. He bedder humble now. [*Talking half to herself.*] He talk proud lak, gwine raise up big sons, leader 'mong men. Fust 'un come thin, liddle lak a rat. He hate 'im. He die. God call 'im. Second come, Ol' Moster keep him liddle, thin. He die too. Abe gitting down to sackcloff and ashes in he mind, mebbe. God see him down crying foh muhcy, He send dis 'un, strong. Israel man. He gwine flourish, he gwine wax.

GOLDIE [*stretching herself out on the bed*]. Abe say dis 'un gwine die too, same lak de udders. He don't look at 'im, pay no 'tention.

683

Muh Mack. Hunh, he will dough when he see 'im fleshen up wid he sucking.

Goldie. Whah he?

Muh Mack. Went down in de new ground planting cawn. Won't make nothing dough and it de light o' de moon. He be heah directly foh he dinner.

Goldie. Po' Abe wuk too hard.

Muh Mack [snorting]. Wuk too hahd de mischief! Ain't wuk whut ail him. He studyin' ol' books and mess too much. Crap shows it.

Goldie. He don't look well, neiver.

Muh Mack. Cain't look well and worry all time. [A step is heard on the porch.] Dere he now. Take dis baby. Gut to put dinner on de table.

[She takes the baby over to Goldie, lays it by her side, goes out at the right, and is heard rattling dishes and pans in the kitchen.]

Goldie [crooning over her baby]. Now you go sleep, res' yo'se'f, git strong and grow gre't big.

[Abe comes in at the rear carrying a hoe and a file. He is barefooted and dressed in overalls, ragged shirt and weather-stained straw hat. Sitting down near the center of the room, he begins filing his hoe.]

Abe [without looking around]. How you come on?

Goldie. Better, I reckon. [With a sharp gasp.] Hyuh, why you fetch dat hoe in de house?

Abe [paying no attention to her query]. Baby still living, hunh?

Goldie. Abe, take dat hoe out'n dis house. Mought bring bad luck on you. [Raising herself up in bed.] Mought bring sump'n on de baby.

Abe. Cain't swub dem new-ground bushes wid no dull hoe.

Goldie [pleading]. Take it out'n de house, I say.

Abe. When I damn ready.

Goldie [calling]. Muh Mack! Muh Mack!

Muh Mack [coming to the door at the right]. What ails you? [She sees Abe filing his hoe.] Lawd he'p us! Throw dat thing out, throw it out! Ain't gut no sense. Goldie too weak to be worried up.

Abe. Aw right den. I finish wid it now. Set o' fools. Eve'ything got a sign 'tached to it. Ign'ant, bline!

[He throws the hoe out through the rear door and gets a book from the chest and begins reading.]

Muh Mack. Back at dem books, Lawd, never see sich.

[She goes scornfully back to the kitchen.]

Abe [half growling]. Says heah niggers gut to git out'n dem 'spicions and being 'fraid. Ain't no signs wid evil and good in 'em. I read dat last night. [Reading and halting over the words.] "The Negro is a superstitious person. There are signs and wonders in the weather, some fraught with evil, some with good. He plants his crops according to the moon, works and labors under the eye of some evil spirit of his own imagining." [Closing the book with a bang.] Heah dat?

684 Goldie. I heah but don't mind it. Mean nothing. White man wrote it, and he don't know.

Abe. Dat's jest it; he do know. Nigger one don't know. Dat book wrote foh you, Muh, and all de rest of de bline.

GOLDIE. Put up dem ol' books. Seem lak you keer mo' foh 'em dan you do dis heah baby, and he a fine boy chile.

ABE [*throwing the book back on the chest*]. What he nohow? Ain't 'rested in 'im. Ain't no use being. He be dead in week. God done cuss me and my household. No luck at nothing. Cain't raise chillun, cain't raise crap, nothing. Ain't dry weather, wet. Ain't wet, dry. Heah May month and cold 'nough foh freeze. [*He stretches his feet to the fire.*] De damn crows down dere on de creek pulling up my cawn faster'n I kin plant it. [*He rocks his head.*] Jesus!

GOLDIE [*pleading*]. Abe, honey, don't git down. Things coming better now. Dis boy gwine make you feel better. Heah he lie now des' smiling lak he onderstand me. [*Bending over the baby.*] Yeh you is gwine grow up and take trouble off'n yo' po' daddy. Yeh, you is.

ABE [*holding his head in his arms*]. Listen to dat talk, listen dere. [*Bitterly.*] 'Oman know. She know. Heah I am wid no money to buy me shoes. [*Holding up his dust-stained foot.*] Dere you is, foot, cut wid glass, full o' b'rars, wo' out stumping de roots and snags, and I cain't buy nothing to kiver you wid.

GOLDIE. De Colonel give you shoes, you ax him.

ABE. Ain't gwine ax him nothing, not nothing. [*Suddenly clenching his fist and hitting his thigh.*] Dat man beat me, beat me at de spring th'ee yeah ago, I ain't fohgit. [*He gets up and strides over to the bed and looks down at the suckling infant.*] Dere you lie drinking yo' grub in. What you keer? Nothing.

[*He lays his hand roughly on the baby and pinches him. The child lets out a high thin wail.*]

GOLDIE [*beating his hand off*]. Quit dat pinching dat baby. Quit it!

ABE [*laughing brutally as he walks up and down the floor*]. Yeh, you fight over 'im now and he be plowed in de ground lak de udders in a month. Hee-hee! Ain't dis a hell of a mess! It sho' God is. And us ain't got 'nough to feed a cat. You'n Muh cook and slay and waste fast I make it. Note at de sto' done tuck up, crap done all mortgaged up 'head o' time. Cain't make ends meet, cain't. [*Throwing his hands out hopelessly.*] Ayh God! [*Stopping.*] He cain't heah me.

GOLDIE [*wretchedly*]. Oh, Abe, we git on somehow, us will. And Muh'n me don't waste. I be up wid you in de fields by de middle o' de week. Po' chile, you need sleep, need rest.

ABE. Make no difference. Wuk our guts out do no good. I tell you, gal, de nigger is down, down. De white man up dere high, setting up wid God, up dere in his favor. He git eve'ything, nigger git de scraps, leavings. [*Flaring out.*] Ain't no God foh de nigger, dat's white man's God. Dat come to me down in de new ground.

[*He sits down again, tapping his feet on the floor.*]

GOLDIE [*wiping her eyes*]. Honey, you gut to stop talking lak dat. Cain't be bad luck allus. I'se 'feared when you talk dat wild talk. God heah it he do. [MUH MACK *comes and stands in the door.*] He mought be doing all dis to make us good, make us humble down befo' him.

ABE. Humble down, hell! Look at de udder niggers den. Dey shout and carry on in de church, pray and pay de preachers in deir blindness. Dey humble. What do God do? Starve 'em to deaf. Kill 'em off lak flies wid consumption. Dey dying 'long de river same as de chillun in de wilderness.

685

MUH MACK. You blaspheaming, da's whut you doing. No wonder Gohd take yo' babies 'way, no wonder he make yo' mule die, blast down yo' plans and send de crows and cold weather and root lice to destroy yo' craps. [*Her eyes flashing.*] You gut to change yo' ways. Some day he gwine re'ch down from de clouds and grab you by de scruff o' de neck and break you cross he knee. He gi'n you fine baby chile, you don't thank him. You gut to fall down, pray, git low, git humble. [*Her voice rises into a semi-chant.*] You dere, Jesus, heah my prayer. Dis heah sinner, he weeked, he blaspheam. Save him and save dis po' liddle baby.

GOLDIE [*weeping over the child*]. Do, Lawd, heah our prayer.

[ABE *sits down in his chair and stares moodily into the fire.*]

MUH MACK [*crying out*]. Dem dere ol' books cause it, da's whut. Burn um up, burn um wid fiah. Yo' wild talk gwine make de Upper Powers drap lightning on dis house, gwine destroy all of us. [*She wraps her arms before her, mumbling and swaying from side to side. Suddenly she raises her head and striding over to the chest shakes her fist at the books and kicks them.*] You de trouble. I hates de sight o' you, and I wish dere wa'n't nary one o' you in de worl'.

ABE [*throwing her back*]. Look out, 'oman! Don't you tech my books!

MUH MACK. You mash my arm!

[*With a wail she goes out at the right and is heard sobbing in the kitchen.*]

GOLDIE. Oh, you struck huh! Abe—Abe——

[*She sits up in the bed rocking the baby and quieting him. A heavy step sounds on the porch.* ABE *sits before the fire smoothing out the leaves of a book, as a voice calls from the outside.*]

VOICE. Heigh, you, Abe!

GOLDIE [*quickly*]. Dat de Colonel out dere, Abe.

ABE [*going to the door*]. Yes, suh, dat you, Colonel Mack?

COLONEL [*coming in*]. Yes. How you come on, all of you? [*He looks around the room and at the bed. Three years have worked a great change in him. He is stouter, his face mottled, and he walks with difficulty, propped on a stick.*] Been wanting to see that fine baby, Abe.

ABE [*quietly*]. Yes, suh, yes, suh.

MUH MACK [*coming in*]. And he sho' is a fine 'un. [*Standing near the* COLONEL.] Fine and strong same lak Abe when he wuh bawn.

COLONEL. What's the matter, Goldie? Ain't been fighting, have you all? Who was that making a racket in here?

GOLDIE [*keeping her head lowered*]. I all right, Colonel Mack.

MUH MACK [*wiping her eyes*]. Ain't no row, Colonel. Want you to 'suade dat Abe git rid o' dem ol' books. 'Nough trouble come on us 'count of um.

COLONEL [*laughing*]. The devil, let him keep his books. He's the only nigger in the whole country worth a durn. Let me see the baby. [GOLDIE *shows the baby.*] That's a fine un, Abe. He'll live. Let me feel him. [*Holding him up.*] Heavy, gracious!

[MUH MACK *looks at him intently and there is the vaguest touch of malice in her voice as she speaks.*]

MUH MACK. Lawd, it all comes to me ag'in. Jest sech a day as dis thirty yeah ago you come down heah and hold Abe up dat-a-way.

COLONEL [*looking through the window a long while*]. Time hurries on, it goes by in a hurry. [ABE *looks before him with an indefinable expression on his face.*

686

A constrained silence comes over them and the COLONEL *takes a sort of refuge in gazing intently at the child. Once or twice he clears his throat.*] Yes, Callie, we're getting old.

[*For an instant all differences are passed away and they are four human beings aware of the strangeness of their lives, conscious of what queer relationships have fastened them together.*]

MUH MACK [*starting*]. Yes, suh, we ain't gut much longer.

[*The baby begins to cry and the* COLONEL *smiles.*]

COLONEL. Here, take him, Goldie. Favors Muh Mack, don't favor you, Abe.

ABE. Yes, suh.

COLONEL [*drawing a heavy, folded paper from his pocket slowly and with weighty dignity.*] I got a little surprise for you'n Goldie, Abe. [*He puts on his spectacles, opens the paper and starts to read.*] "Whereas"—[*He stops as if convulsed with pain, and presently goes on.*] "I devise to Abraham McCranie a house and tract of land containing twenty-five acres and formerly known as the 'Howington place,' to him and his heirs forever." [*Hesitating a moment and folding the paper together.*] Then follows a description of the place in course and distance, Abe, which I won't read. It's all signed up and recorded in the court-house.

[*He feels around him heavily for his stick.*]

ABE [*incredulously*]. Whut dat? Dat foh me?

COLONEL. Yes, for you. A deed to this house and twenty-five acres of land, yours.

[*He holds out the paper to* ABE.]

ABE [*taking it with trembling hands*]. Lawd, Colonel Mack, whut I gwine say?

COLONEL. Say nothing. Say thanky if you want to.

ABE [*overcome*]. Thanky, suh, thanky, suh.

COLONEL. Shake hands on it, Abe.

ABE [*wiping his hand on his shirt*]. Thanky, suh.

[*The* COLONEL *looks at his bent head with strange intentness, and then drops* ABE's *hand.*]

GOLDIE. Oh, Colonel Mack!

[*Her eyes are shining with thankfulness.*]

MUH MACK. Abe, you's gut land, boy, you owns you a piece o' land, Glory!

[*She runs up to the* COLONEL *and covers his hands with kisses.*]

COLONEL [*waving her off*]. Nothing, nothing to do for him. He deserves it. [*Looking straight at* ABE.] You do, boy. I want to see you go forward now. You had a hard time the last three years.

GOLDIE. He has, po' boy. He had it hard since de day he married me.

COLONEL. Hunh. He couldn't a done better nowhere. I know. [*The* COLONEL *picks up his stick which he has laid across the bed.*] Well, I got to move on. [*He stops near the door.*] And, Abe, how's your book business coming on?

ABE. I—I studying and reading now and den. Most too tiahed every night dough to do much.

COLONEL. Don't give up like Lonnie. Sent him to school, and sent him to school, even tried him at the university, won't stay. He ain't worth a damn, that's what. [*Turning toward the door and stopping again.*] Well, I've got another little surprise for you in celebration of that fine boy.

687

[*He looks down and taps on the floor.*]

ABE [*excitedly*]. Whut is it, Colonel Mack, suh?

COLONEL. How'd you like to try your hand at teaching a little school next fall?

[MUH MACK *throws up her hands.*]

GOLDIE [*breathlessly*]. Oh, me!

ABE [*in confusion*]. Teach school? Yessuh, I——

COLONEL. I'm going to have that old Quillie house fixed up and put some benches in it and a blackboard. I'll get two Negroes to serve with me on the school board and we'll try you out. [*Smiling queerly.*] I been reading your books, too, Abe.

ABE [*with a great breath*]. I gwine teach school—at last!

COLONEL [*going shakily out at the door*]. Yes, at last. Now don't forget your crop, Abe, and study yourself to death.

ABE [*following him*]. Colonel Mack, you, you—I—I——

COLONEL. Take care of that baby. Raise him up right. And, Abe, don't forget you ain't gonna have no easy time. I'll get a lot of cussing for this, well as you. Go on eat your dinner. [*He stops on the porch and calls.*] Here, Goldie, take this fifty cents and buy the boy a stick of candy. [*He steps to the door and throws the coin on the bed.*] Take care of him and don't kill him on collards and beans.

[*He goes off.*]

ABE [*calling after him*]. I ain't, Colonel, I gwine raise him. I gwine make a man——[*He stops and stands watching the old man going in the lane. Then he turns and stumbles into the room with shining face.*] I—I fohgives him all. I don't 'member dat beating by de spring no mo'.

GOLDIE [*reaching out from the bed and grasping his hand*]. Oh, honey babe, our troubles's ended. We gwine—we gwine have 'nough t'eat and you gwine be happy.

[*She turns over in the bed and begins to cry softly.*]

ABE [*patting her shoulders*]. Dere, dere, don't you cry, chile. [*He wipes his eyes with his sleeve.*] I been mean man. [*In a husky voice.*] I treat my gal mean, blaspheam 'gin de Lawd. I gwine do better, I——[*A sob chokes in his throat.*]

MUH MACK [*coming up to him and clasping her arms around him*]. Bless de Lawd, you gwine do bedder now.

[*She sits down in a chair and bows her head in her lap.*]

GOLDIE. He good man, de Colonel. He too good to us. Raise us up, help us.

ABE [*vaguely*]. Up! Lift me up! Up! Up tow'd de sun! [*He glances at the calendar.*] Dat whup don't hurt no mo'. De 'membrance is passed away. [*Thumping on his breast.*] Ain't no mo' bitter gall in heah. Peace. It come all suddent over me. [*He suddenly falls on his knees by the bed in a sobbing burst of prayer.*] O God, God of de po' and of de sinful!

MUH MACK [*whispering*]. Yea, our God.

ABE. De black man's God, de white man's God, de one and only God, heah me, heah my prayer.

688 MUH MACK [*swaying and moaning*]. Heah 'im, Jesus!

GOLDIE [*softly*]. We dy chillun, Lawd.

ABE. Dy little chillun, and you pow'ful. You de Almighty, us de dust in dy hand. Us po' and weak, us nothing. Lak de grasshopper, lak de po' fee-lark, swept away in de storm. Man gut no stren'th in um, no muscle kin raise him, 'cepting yo' power. He walk in de wind, de wind take 'im away. Let dere be fiah, and de fiah burn um. It devour 'im. Same lak de broomstraw he fall befo' it. Man cain't stand. He lost, lost. Shet in de grave, shet till de judgment.

MUH MACK. Jesus! Jesus!

GOLDIE [*piteously*]. Jesus!

ABE. He fall in de winter. He lie down in de summer. De spring come and find him gone.

MUH MACK. Ha' muhcy, our Fadder.

GOLDIE [*whispering*]. Jesus, fohgive 'im.

ABE [*his voice rising into a chant*]. De dirt stop up his po' mouf. Peace come to him in de ground. And de friends do cry, dey wail and beat deir breas'. Dey call foh deir love' ones, and dey don't answer. Deir tongue make no mo' speech, from de graveyard, from de deep grave.

MUH MACK. Yea, Lawd!

ABE. Dey gone at de planting, gone at de harvest. De hoe dull wid rust, de harness wait on de peg, de bridle break, de collar hang dere useless. Dey ain't no mo' hoeing, ain't no mo' plowing, no shoe track in de furrow. Man gone, same lak a whisper, hushed in de graveyard, in de deep grave.

MUH MACK. Oh, ha' muhcy 'pon us.

GOLDIE. Muhcy!

ABE [*raising his head up, his eyes closed*]. Heah us, heah us, heah me dis day, heah my po' prayer. Fohgive me my sins, my blaspheamy. Wipe out de evil o' my weeked days. Purify, make clean, fohgit de 'membrance o' my transgression. Now heah I do humble down, I do cohnfess. Lift me, raise me, up, up!

MUH MACK. Hallelujah!

GOLDIE. Amen.

ABE [*bowing his head in a storm of grief*]. Re'ch down yo' hand and gimme stren'th. Now I draw nigh, I feel yo' sperit. Save me, save me now! [MUH MACK *and* GOLDIE *pray and moan aloud. Presently* ABE *stands up and cries out exultantly.*] He save me, he done save me! He done fohgive me!

MUH MACK [*clapping her hands wildly*]. Bless de Lawd, bless um!

GOLDIE [*faintly*]. Thank Jesus, save my baby and my husban'.

[ABE *is silent a moment, his face working with emotion. He turns and bends down over the bed.*]

ABE. Po' little fellow, he sleep and rest. [*He puts his arms around* GOLDIE *and she clings to him.*] Honey chile, I changed. I gwine take new holt. From dis day I begins. I sorry foh all de past. [*He loosens her arms from around his neck and stands up, a strange set look on his face.*] I gwine keep heart now, look up, rise. I gwine lead. [*Looking down at the baby.*] I gwine raise him up a light unto peoples. He be a new Moses, he bring de chillun out of bondage, out'n sin and ign'ance.

[*He turns suddenly and goes to the bucket at the left, pours some water out in a pan and sets it on the bed. Then he bends down and lifts the baby in his hand.* MUH MACK *looks up, drying her eyes.*]

GOLDIE. Whut dat, Abe? Whut dat you doing?

ABE [*dipping his hand in the water and holding the child aloft, his face lighted up in a beatific smile*]. On dis day I names you Douglass. You gwine be same lak him. Yeh, better. You gwine be a light in darkness, a mighty man. [*He dips his*

689

hand into the water and sprinkles the child.] I baptize you and consecrate you to de salvation ob my people dis day! Amen!

[*The women stare at him transfixed, caught out of themselves. He bends his head and stands with the child stretched before him as if making an offering to some god.*]

Scene III

Winter of the same year. The old Quillie house, a Negro cabin of one bare room, now fitted up as a school-house. At the left center is a squat rusty cast-iron stove, the pipe of which reels up a few feet and then topples over into an elbow to run through the wall. A box of pine knots rests on the floor by it. Four or five rough pine benches, worn slick by restless students, stretch nearly the length of the room, ending towards a small blackboard nailed to the wall in the rear center. Between the benches and the blackboard is the teacher's rickety table with a splint-bottomed chair behind it. To the right rear is a small window, giving a glimpse of brown broomsedge stretching up a gentle hill, and beyond, a ragged field of stripped cornstalks, gray now and falling down in the rot of winter rains. To the left rear is a door opening to the outside.

The curtain rises on the empty room. Presently ABRAHAM McCRANIE *comes in, carrying a tin lunch bucket and two or three books. He is wearing an old overcoat and a derby hat, both making some claims to a threadbare decency. He sets the bucket and books on the table and hangs his coat and hat on a nail in the wall at the right; then comes back to the stove, revealing himself dressed in baggy trousers, worn slick with too much ironing, heavy short coat, cheap shirt, and a celluloid collar with no tie. With his pocket-knife he whittles some shavings from a pine knot and starts a fire in the stove. He looks at his watch, beats his hands together from cold, and stirs about the room, his brow wrinkled in thought and apparent worry. Again and again he goes to the door and stares out expectantly. Looking at his watch the second or third time, he goes and rings a farm bell, the cord of which hangs down by the door outside.*

ABE [*shouting toward the empty fields as the bell booms*]. Books! Books! Come in to books! [*He returns and sits down by the stove.*] No scholars in sight. [*With a sigh he goes to the board and writes laboriously across the top:* "January 21. An idle brain is the devil's workshop." *While he is writing, three Negro students come in carrying a bucket and a book or two each—a lazy slumbrous girl of eighteen or twenty, a stout thick-lipped youth about the same age, and a little serious-faced ragged boy of ten.* ABE'S *face brightens at the sight of them.*] Good morning, chillun. Late. Everybody a little late.

STUDENTS [*standing uncertainly around the stove*]. Good morning, Mr. Mack.

ABE [*finishing his writing*]. This will be our motto foh to-day. [ABE'S *speech has improved somewhat. When he speaks with conscious deliberation he substitutes "this" for "dis," "that" for "dat," and so on. But when in a hurry or excited he drops back into his old methods. He addresses the little boy.*] Read it, Eddie, out loud.

690

EDDIE [*eagerly*]. I kin read it, Mr. Mack. [*In a slow and halting voice he reads.*] "A' idle brain is the devul's wukshop."

ABE. Good, fine. Kin you read it, Neilly?

NEILLY [*boldly*]. Yeh, suh, read it raght off.

ABE. And how 'bout you, Lanie?

LANIE [*dropping her heavy-lidded eyes*]. I kin too.

[*She and* NEILLY *look at each other with a fleeting smile over some secret between them.* EDDIE *gazes up at them, his lips moving silently as if over something to be told which he dare not utter.*]

ABE [*pulling out his watch*]. Twenty minutes to nine. Whah the other scholars? [*No one answers.* NEILLY *gives the girl a quick look and turns deftly on his heel and kicks the stove, sticking up his lips in a low whistle.*] You see the Ragland chillun on the road, Lanie?

LANIE [*enigmatically*]. Yessuh, I see 'em.

[ABE *goes to the door and rings the bell again.*]

ABE. Books! Books! Come in to books. [*He turns back into the room and stands pondering.*] How 'bout the Maffis chillun?

NEILLY. Ain't coming!

ABE. Dey say so?

NEILLY. Yessuh.

ABE [*shortly*]. Take yo' seats. We'll go on wid our lessons if nobody else don't come. [*He goes to his table.*]

EDDIE [*pulling excitedly at* LANIE'S *dress*]. G'won, ax him whut he gwine do.

LANIE [*snatching herself loose from him*]. Shet up. Ain't my business.

ABE. Put yo' buckets up and take yo' seats and listen to the roll-call. All the late ones ketch it on the woodpile and sweeping up the school-yard. [*Eyeing them.*] I said take yo' seat.

[EDDIE *hurries to his seat.*]

NEILLY. Ain't gwine have no school, is we?

ABE. Hunh?

NEILLY. Ain't gwine be no mo' school.

[LANIE *giggles.*]

ABE [*with a worried note in his voice*]. Going have school same as usual. Seem lak all of 'em late dough. Take yo' seats, time foh the spelling lesson. Won't have de scripture reading dis mawning.

NEILLY. De rest of 'em done quit school.

[LANIE *giggles again.*]

ABE. Stop dat giggling and go to yo' seat. [*She moves to her seat sulkily.*]

EDDIE [*in a high frightened quaver*]. Mr. Mack, dey all say de school ain't gwine run no mo' and dey ain't coming.

ABE. How dey hear it? I ain't heard it. [*No one answers.*] Whah'd you folks get all dis news, Neilly?

NEILLY. Dey was all talking it down de road. We wouldn't a-come eiver, but Eddie dah beg me and Lanie so hard to come wid 'im. Ain't no mo' folks coming dough.

ABE [*hitting the table with his fist*]. Sump'n' up. Dey got to show me fo' I quits, dey got to show me. Putt up yo' buckets and things, we going have school.

691

[*They reluctantly set down their buckets near the wall and stand waiting.*] Take yo' seats, I say, and listen to yo' name. [*He pulls out a cheap arm-and-hammer memorandum book and begins calling the roll.*] Lanie Horton.

LANIE. Presunt.

[*She looks around at the bare seats and gives her senseless giggle.*]

ABE. Vanderbilt Jones, absent; 'Ona May Jordon, absent; Jane Matthews, absent; Sister Matthews, absent; Jennie McAhlister, absent; Neilly McNeill.

NEILLY. Present. [*He smiles at* LANIE.]

ABE. Arthur Ragland, absent. Didn't 'spect him back nohow. Dora Ragland, absent; Nora Ragland, absent; Eddie Williams.

EDDIE. Prizzunt.

[ABE *sits drumming on the table and staring before him. The students twist about on their seats in embarrassment.*]

ABE [*roughly*]. Spelling lesson! [*The three move out and stand in a line before him.*] How many of you been over it as least fo' times? [EDDIE *raises his hand.*]

EDDIE. I been over it nine times fo'w'd and six back'ards.

ABE. You, Neilly?

NEILLY. I been over it onct and part twict, Mr. Mack.

ABE. Lanie?

LANIE. I dunno hardly.

ABE. Have you studied it any?

LANIE [*pouting*]. I done lost my book somewhah.

ABE. And you wuh supposed to be head to-day. You'n Neilly kin clean up the paper and sweep 'round the well at recess. Le's see yo' book, Eddie. [EDDIE *hands him his book.*] Eddie you got a head-mark yistiddy; so you foot to-day. [*Opening the book.*] The first word is "chew," chew, lak vittles, Lanie, "chew."

LANIE. C-c. C-u, "chew."

ABE. One mo' trial.

LANIE [*pondering a long while*]. I cain't spell dat.

ABE. Yes, you kin. Try it.

LANIE. C-h-u, "chew."

ABE. Next.

NEILLY [*smiling ruefully*]. Too hahd foh me. Des' well pass on.

ABE [*working his jaws up and down*]. Watch me wuk my jaws. That's chew, chewing. Spell at it, Neilly, "chew."

NEILLY [*scratching his head and nervously boring the floor with the toe of his shoe*]. Cain't do it, cain't fohm no letters in my head.

ABE. I'll have to pass it den.

NEILLY [*taking a hopeless shot at it*]. S-s. S-u, "chew." No, dat wrong. I seed dat word on de page, but cain't remember it now. I cain't spell it. Gi' it to Eddie, he kin.

ABE. All right, Eddie.

692   EDDIE. C-h-e-w—"chew."

[*He darts around* NEILLY *and* LANIE *and stands triumphantly at the head of the class.*]

ABE. I goin' send you back to yo' seats to study twenty minutes. Then come back heah and don't you make no such mess of it. I'll put the writing lesson up while you study. [*They go to their seats.*] Lanie, you look wid Eddie in his book. [*He turns to the board and begins to write down the copy models. As he writes, the students mumble over their words in a drone.* NEILLY *and* LANIE *begin talking to each other in low whispers.* EDDIE *is lost in his book.* LANIE *suddenly giggles out loud, and* ABE *turns quickly from his board.*] Heigh you, Lanie, stand up in dat corner over thah. School isn't out yit.

LANIE. I ain't done nothing. [*Half audibly.*] "Isn't!"

ABE. Don't talk back. Stand in de corner wid yo' face to de wall. Hyuh, Eddie, you read in dis reader and let her have yo' book.

[LANIE *creeps over to the corner and mouths over her lesson.* ABE *finishes his apothegm,* "A Wise man will rise with the sun, or before it." *He is finishing another,* "Wise children will imitate the manners of polite people," *when there is a stir at the door and* PUNY AVERY *comes in, swallowed up in a teamster's coat and carrying a long blacksnake whip in his hand.*]

PUNY. Good mawning.

ABE. Good morning, Mr. Avery.

[*At the appellation of* "Mister," PUNY *stuffs his cap against his mouth to hide a grin.*]

PUNY. How you come on, Mr. McCranie? Kin I warm my hands a minute? Freezing col' setting on dat waggin seat.

[*He moves up to the stove and stretches his hands above it.*]

ABE. Help yo'se'f. Be a snow fo' night, I believe.

PUNY. Yeh, or—look lak it.

[*He warms himself, and* ABE *sits at the table watching him questioningly. Now and then his gaze drops upon the whip.*]

ABE. Hauling lumber over the river?

PUNY. Is dat. [*Looking at* LANIE *in the corner.*] Whut she do?

ABE. Misbehaved.

PUNY. Seem lak yo' school kinda thin. [ABE *says nothing.*] Been gettin' thinner ev'y since de colonel died last fall, ain't it?

ABE. Been dropping off some since then.

PUNY. Whah all de rest o' de scholars?

ABE. Haven't showed up yet.

PUNY. Uhm.

ABE. Why you want to know, might I ask.

PUNY [*authoritatively*]. Already know. And foh yo' own good I come by to tell you and to bring you a message.

ABE [*looking at him intently and then waving his hand at the three students*]. You chillun kin go out and have recess now. Mr. Avery wants to see me on a little business. [LANIE *and* NEILLY *get their coats and walk out.* EDDIE *remains crouched in his seat, unconscious of his surroundings.*] What message you got foh me?

PUNY. You des' well quit de school business raght heah and now. Dey ain't gwine send to you no mo'.

ABE. What's the trouble?

PUNY. Trouble! You gone and done it, you has, when you beat Will Ragland's boy yistiddy. Will so mad he kin kill you.

ABE [*anger rising in his voice*]. Needn't think I'm skeahed of him.

693

PUNY. I knows you ain't. But you wants to keep on teaching, don't you?

ABE. Yeh, and I'm going to.

PUNY. Nunh-unh, you ain't neiver. Will went 'round last night and gut everybody to say dey won't gwine send to you no mo'. Dey ain't gwine stand foh no nigger beating deir young 'uns.

ABE [angrily]. I had a right to beat him. I couldn't make him work no other way, and 'sides he told a lie to me. Said he didn't eat up po' little Sis Maffis' dinner. Several of 'em seen him do it.

PUNY. Cain't he'p it. You beat 'im so dey had to have a doctor foh him, and Will done gone to de sher'ff to git out papers foh you.

ABE [starting out of his chair]. Gwine have me 'rested?

PUNY. He is dat. And mo', I reckon. And my advice to you is to git f'om heah. As a member of de school boa'd I say, bedder leave.

ABE. He think he kin run me 'way?

PUNY. Don't know what he think. Know I wouldn't lak to lie in no white man's jail-house, dat's me.

ABE. De otheh members of de boa'd know 'bout it?

PUNY. Us had a meeting last night.

ABE. What dey say?

PUNY [fumbling in his pockets]. Dey all side wid Will, 'count o' de beating and 'count o' dat speech you made in chu'ch last Sunday.

ABE. Wuh Mr. Lonnie dere?

PUNY. He dere and he send dis heah writing to you.

[He pulls a note from his pocket and hands it to ABE, who opens it excitedly.]

ABE [clenching his fist]. Dat man say heah—God——He say de boa'd done all 'cided de school got to stop. [He tears the note to pieces and throws it on the floor.] He say dere he know a good job in Raleigh at public wuk he kin git me. [Bitterly.] Say I do better at dat dan farming or school. [Pacing the floor, he throws his hand above his head.] Nanh, anh—suh, I sets a oaf on high, I ain't going let 'em run me off. Dey cain't skeah me. Dey cain't run me off lak I stole sump'n'. [He turns on PUNY with blazing eyes and EDDIE now watches him terrified.] Why you all vote dat way? Whyn't you stand up and vote foh me? You know I trying do right. You weak, coward, no backbone.

PUNY [backing toward the door]. I ain't gut nothing 'gin you, Abe. Why you 'buse me?

ABE. Git out o' heah. All o' you down on me. Dat speech was so. It was right. Dat beating was right. [Crying out.] I ain't gwine give in. Dey cain't run me. You cain't run me. I fight 'em. I stay heah. Let 'em putt me in de jail, I last till de jail rot down. [He moves menacingly toward PUNY, who flees through the door and slams it after him.] I come through deir bars, deir iron won't hold me. I'll git dere, I'll come. My flesh will be as tough as deir iron! [He goes to the table and picks up his books. He opens the Bible and stands thinking. Dropping into his chair, he sits with his elbow on the table and his chin in his hand, gazing into the distance. The anger and bitterness gradually pass from his face.] Dat man's talk, proud. Cain't push through 'thout help—[putting his hand on the Bible]—'thout help from up there. [He bows his head on the table. EDDIE begins to sob and, leaving his seat timidly, approaches ABE's bent form, gulping and

694

wiping his nose and eyes with his sleeve. ABE *looks up and puts his arm around him.*] Son, this heah's the last of this school. But we cain't stop, we got to keep on. [EDDIE *leans his head against him, his sobs increasing.*] Got to keep studying, got to keep climbing. [*After a moment he stands up and writes across the board,* "This school is stopped for a while." LANIE *and* NEILLY *come inquiringly in.*] Chillun, ain't goin' to be no mo' school till mebbe next yeah. You kin go home. [LANIE *giggles and* NEILLY *looks at him with familiar condescension.*] But I wants to dismiss with a word of prayer. [*At a sign from him,* EDDIE *falls on his knees by the table. He gets down at his chair.*] Our Father, where two or three is gathered——[NEILLY *and* LANIE *look at him, pick up their buckets and scurry out giggling and laughing.* ABE *springs to his feet, his face blank with astonishment. He calls after them furiously.*] Heigh, heigh, you!

[*They are heard going off, their sharp laughter softening in the distance.*]

NEILLY. 'Fo' Gohd, he down on his knees!

LANIE [*her voice growing faint*]. Yeh, and he 'bout kilt Arth yistiddy.

NEILLY. Haw—haw—haw.

LANIE. Hee—hee—hee.

[*Their voices die away.*]

Scene IV

Fifteen years later. A room in the poverty-stricken Negro section of Durham, North Carolina, as it was then. When the curtain rises, GOLDIE *is washing at a tub placed on a goods-box at the left of the room.* MUH MACK *is seated at the fireplace at the right, bent under a slat bonnet and dozing. Pots and pans are piled around the hearth and a kettle is singing on the fire. Several garments are hanging on chairs before the fire drying.*

To the left rear is a bed with a pile of rough-dried clothes on it. A door at the center rear leads into another room. To the right of the door is a low chest with books and dishes set upon it. At the right front by the chimney is a small window letting in the sickly light of a dying winter day. In the center of the room is a small eating-table covered with a greasy, spotted oil-cloth.

For several minutes neither of the women says anything. GOLDIE *washes heavily at the tub, her body bent and disfigured with the years of toil and poverty and the violence of childbirth. She wrings out a garment and takes it to the fireplace.*

GOLDIE [*lifelessly*]. Move yo'se'f, Muh. Lemme hang up dis shirt.

MUH MACK [*testily as she moves her chair with her body*]. Lemme 'lone. Cain't sleep, rest—nothing.

[GOLDIE *drags up a chair, hangs the shirt on it and returns to her washing. Her movements are slow, ox-like, and in her eyes now and then comes a sort of vacant look as if some deadening disease has had its way within her brain, or as if trouble and worry have hardened her beyond the possibility of enthusiasm or grief any more. Between her eyes a deep line has furrowed itself, a line often found on the foreheads of those who think a great deal or those who are forgetting how to think at all. And her mouth has long ago fastened itself into a*

695

drawn anguished questioning that has no easeful answer in the world. She washes away at the tub, the garment making a kind of flopping sound against the board. After a moment she calls to MUH MACK.]

GOLDIE. Gitting neah 'bout day-down, Muh. Time to start supper.

MUH MACK [*whom age and poverty have made meaner than before*]. Yeh, yeh, it is, and I gut to git it, I reckon.

GOLDIE [*making an effort to hurry*]. Yeh, Mis' Duke got to have her clothes to-morrow, I done said.

MUH MACK [*getting slowly to her feet*]. Oh, me my! My leg done gone to sleep! [*She fumbles among the pans on the hearth.*] Yo' water hyuh all gwine bile 'way.

GOLDIE. Gimme hyuh!

[*She takes the kettle and pours the water into the tub and then goes on scrubbing the clothes.*]

MUH MACK. Whut I gwine cook?

GOLDIE. Make some cawn bread, and dey's a little piece o' Baltimo' meat in de chist.

[MUH MACK *arranges her pan on the fire with much grumbling and growling and goes over to the chest.*]

MUH MACK [*knocking the pile of books off with a bang*]. Heah dem ol' books of Abe's piled right hyuh in de way. Minner mind to burn 'em up. Allus whah dey ain't got no business.

GOLDIE [*abstractedly*]. Yeh, yeh. Always minner mind to burn 'em.

[MUH MACK *opens the chest and pulls out a small piece of white meat.*]

MUH MACK. Hunh, look at dis, will you? Ain't mo'n 'nough to fill my old hollow toof. I et dat old meat and cawn bread till it makes me heave to look at it.

GOLDIE. Dat all dey is.

MUH MACK. Dat won't make a mou'ful foh Abe. Whut we gwine eat?

GOLDIE. Abe won't eat it nohow, and I don't want nothing. You'n Douglass kin eat it.

MUH MACK. Bofe of you gwine die if you don't eat. Dat Abe been living off'n cawfee and bread two weeks now. No wonder he look lak a shadow and cain't ha'f do his work.

GOLDIE. Cain't eat when you ain't gut it.

MUH MACK. Well, starving ain't gwine give you stren'th to git no mo'. How you gwine keep washing foh folks and you don't eat?

GOLDIE [*bowing her head in weariness over the tub, her voice rising with sudden shrillness*]. Oh, Lawd Gohd in heaven, I don't know.

MUH MACK. Calling on Gohd ain't gwine he'p you git no supper eiver. [*Throwing the meat back into the chest and slamming the lid.*] Well, I ain't gwine cook dat old mess. I'll set right heah by dis fiah and starve wid you and Abe.

GOLDIE [*drying her hands on her apron*]. I gut des' one mo' fifty-cent piece in dat pocketbook. I'll git it and run out and buy some liver den. Po' Abe gut to live somehow. [*She goes out at the rear and returns immediately holding an empty ragged purse in her hand.*] Whah my ha'f dollar! Whah is it?

MUH MACK [*dropping into a chair by the fire*]. Hunh, needn't ax me. Ain't seed it.

696

GOLDIE [*sitting down and rocking back and forth*]. Somebody stole it. [*Turning upon* MUH MACK.] You done gin it to dat Douglass.

MUH MACK. Ain't.

GOLDIE. Yeh, you has, you has.

MUH MACK [*beating the floor with her foot*]. Ain't, I tell you.

GOLDIE [*staggering to her feet*]. And he off somewhah's spending it foh icecream and mess.

MUH MACK. Don't keer 'f I did. Po' boy do widdout all de time.

GOLDIE [*falling on the tub with renewed vigor*]. Cain't cry now!

MUH MACK. G'won down dere and git dat man to let you have sump'n' on a credit. You can pay 'im to-morrow when Mis' Duke pay you.

GOLDIE. He done said he ain't gwine let us have no mo' widdout de money.

MUH MACK. Mebbe Abe fetch sump'n' when he come.

GOLDIE. How kin he and dey don't pay 'im off till to-morrow evening?

MUH MACK [*suddenly crying out with a whimper*]. Look lak us gwine starve spite of all. I wants to go back home. I wants to go back to home. Mr. Lonnie won't let us do widdout.

GOLDIE. I been wanting to go back foh fifteen yeah, but Abe's gwine die fo' he go back.

MUH MACK [*beating her hands together in her lap*]. Crazy, crazy! He de biggest fool in de whole world.

GOLDIE. Needn't keep talking 'bout Abe. [*Bravely and hopelessly.*] He doing de best he kin.

MUH MACK [*her anger rising*]. Dere you set, Goldie McCranie, and say dat, after he done drug you f'om pillar to post foh fifteen yeah. Doing de best he kin! He ain't nothing, des' wuss'n nothing! He des' a plumb fool. But he mammy wuh a fool befo' 'im. Da's how come he in dis worl'.

GOLDIE. Stop dat. He sick, been sick a long time, po' fellow, and he keep trying.

MUH MACK. Sick! He wa'n't sick back dere when he got into co't and lost all his land trying to git dem lawyers to keep 'im out'n jail, and he beat dat Will Ragland's boy ha'f to death. [GOLDIE *bows her head in her hands, swaying from side to side.*] De devil in him! Dat's what.

GOLDIE [*wretchedly*]. You done sot dere by dat fiah and told me dat same tale time and ag'in, day in, day out. I don't want to heah it no mo'.

MUH MACK. Unh-unh. And I reckon you will dough. Wuh he sick, and he cutting up a rust in Raleigh and de niggers and white folks runnin' him out'n dere? It was old Scratch in him dere too. I tells you.

GOLDIE. Dey didn't treat 'im right over dere.

MUH MACK. Hunh. No, dey didn't. And dey didn't treat him raght in Greensboro, did dey? Same old tale dere, gitting in a row wid somebody and ha' to leave. He's mean, mean lak sump'n' mad at de world.

GOLDIE [*tossing her head about her*]. I dunno. I dunno. He orter nevah married me and gut tied down. Seem lak things all go wrong, crosswise foh him.

MUH MACK [*staring at her*]. Hunh. Things'll be crosswise wid 'im till dey straighten 'im out in de grave. Dem's my words. [*Blowing her nose in her skirt and half weeping.*] If all dat shooting and killing in Wilmington wouldn't make 'im do better, nothing in de Gohd's world kin.

697

GOLDIE [*moaning*]. Stop dat talking. I cain't beah it.

MUH MACK. Dat's des' whut you orter stop doing, stop beahing it. Gather up yo' duds and take me'n Douglass and whop off'n leave 'im, dat's what you orter do.

GOLDIE [*beating herself with her fists*]. I ain't. I ain't. I gwine stay by 'im.

MUH MACK. Co'se you gwine stay by 'im—and starve too. Foh dat's whut you'll do. Whut he don't spend on medicine he do on dem old lodges and sich and books and newspapers. And gits turned out'n eve'y one of 'em foh his speeches and wild talk, he do. [*With grim satisfaction.*] Shoveling dat coal down at de power house reckon'll hold him down foh a while. [*With an after-thought.*] Hold 'im down till somebody crack his haid wid a shovel and tu'n 'im off. [*Stirring the fire and then folding her hands.*] I done said my say-so now. Do no good, 'caze you so wropped up in de fool.

GOLDIE [*flaring out*]. No, it won't do no good. I gwine stick by him. [*Rising and turning to her work again.*] Dey ain't never done 'im right. Dey all been down on him f'om de fust.

MUH MACK [*shrilly*]. And'll be till de last. Otheh niggers makes a living foh deir fambly. Why don't he? Allus gut his eyes on sump'n' else.

GOLDIE. He gwine be a big man yit. Dem udder niggehs do de dirty work and take whut dey kin git. Dey de low-down trash. [*Her voice trembling.*] He gwine git him a big school some dese days.

MUH MACK [*laughing scornfully*]. Hee-hee—hee. Listen at him. He cain't teach nothing. De niggeh school teachers round hyuh know mo'n a minute dan Abe do in a week. Dey been to college at Raleigh and Greensboro and no telling whah. And dey gut some sense 'sides deir learning. Dat li'l Eddie Williams has. He done gone th'ough dat Shaw school in Raleigh and is off doing big wuk. Why couldn't Abe do sump'n' lak dat!

GOLDIE [*her voice breaking*]. Shet up, I tell you.

MUH MACK [*sulkily*]. Aw right den, but dat talk don't fill yo' stomach. [*Pulling a walking stick from the chimney corner.*] I gwine go down to Liza's and ax her to gi' me some supper.

[*She groans and creaks to her feet.*]

GOLDIE. You been down to Liza's till she's tiahed o' feeding you.

MUH MACK [*waving her stick in the air*]. Well, you feed me den.

GOLDIE. Wait'll Douglass come f'om school and I'll git him to go down to de cawner and try to git some meat f'om dat man.

MUH MACK. Done past time foh Douglass to be heah. Mought not come till late.

GOLDIE [*drying her hands again and patting her hair*]. I'll go den. You putt de kittle on foh some cawfee and set de table and I'll be right back. [*Far off a muffled whistle blows.*] Dere's de power house whistle. Abe be heah soon. Light de lamp and putt on de table. [*She goes out.*]

MUH MACK [*somewhat mollified, calling after her*]. Aw raght.

698

[*She puts her stick back in the corner, fills the kettle and stirs stiffly about her, bringing plates to the table and laying out the knives and forks. She hobbles into the room at the rear and returns with a lamp without any chimney, which she lights at the fireplace and places on the table. While she is engaged in making coffee over the fire,* DOUGLASS *strolls in. He is a young Negro in short trousers, fifteen or sixteen years old, black as* MUH MACK *and with something of a wild and worthless spirit already beginning to show in his face. He carries two ragged books under his arm.*]

DOUGLASS [*dropping the books by the door and kicking them toward the chest*]. Heigh!

MUH MACK [*jumping*]. Who?—hee—hee, you skeahed me, honey. [*She stands up and looks at him indulgently*]. Whah you been so late?

DOUGLASS. Oh, round and about. Stopped by de hot dawg stand awhile chewing de rag wid some fellows.

MUH MACK. How many dem sa'sage things you eat?

DOUGLASS. Dunno. Sev'al.

MUH MACK [*leaning forward, her eyes shining with anticipation*]. Whut you fotch me to eat?

DOUGLASS. I wanted to bring you sump'n', but——

MUH MACK. You mean you ain't bought me nothing wid dat fifty cents?

DOUGLASS. I fool-lak matched wid some ub'm down dere and had to set 'em up.

MUH MACK. And I so hongry I cain't see straight!

DOUGLASS [*nonchalantly*]. I cain't he'p it.

MUH MACK [*threateningly*]. I gwine tell yo' daddy on you.

DOUGLASS [*looking at her*]. Hunh, you better not. Do and I won't play nary piece foh you in—in two weeks mebbe.

MUH MACK [*turning to her cooking*]. Yo' muh know 'bout it.

DOUGLASS. Why you tell her?

MUH MACK. She guessed at it. She knowed you tuck dat money soon's she found it gone.

DOUGLASS [*alarmed*]. Pap don't know, do he?

MUH MACK. Not yit. He ain't come f'om wuk. [*He turns back into the room at the rear and reappears with a guitar. Sitting down wonderfully at ease, he begins strumming.*] Lawd, Lawd, honey, gi' us a piece 'fo' yo' daddy comes. [*He falls to playing and* MUH MACK *begins to pat the floor and skip happily now and then as she moves about the fireplace.*] Hee-hee—dat bedder'n eating.

DOUGLASS [*hugging up the "box" and throwing back his head in abandon*]. Hee-hee—ain't it dough! [*He turns and scowls at the books lying on the floor, and begins singing to them.*] Dem old books—[*Strum, strum*] lying in de corner, [*Strum, strum.*] Dem old books—[*Strum, strum*] lying in de corner—[*Strum, strum.*] Lie dere, babies, lie dere! Hee-hee—Muh Mack, I kin make music raght out'n my haid. [*He goes on throwing his fingers across the strings.*]

MUH MACK. You kin, honey, you sho'ly kin.

[*She sits listening happily. He wraps himself over the guitar, his fingers popping up and down the neck of the instrument with marvelous dexterity. His bowed head begins to weave about him rhythmically as he bursts into snatches of song.*]

DOUGLASS [*singing*].

699

> *Look down, look down dat lonesome road,*
> *De hacks all dead in line.*
> *Some give a nickel, some give a dime*
> *To bury dis po' body o' mine.*

MUH MACK [*staring at him*]. I declah! I declah! Listen at dat chile.

DOUGLASS. Ne'h mind, ne'h min' me. [*Modulating with amazing swiftness from key to key.*] And dere was po' Brady. Po' old Brady.

MUH MACK. Yeh, Brady, dey laid him down to die.

DOUGLASS [*singing*].

> *Oh, Brady, Brady, you know you done me wrong,*
> *You come in when de game was a-goin' on!*
> *And dey laid po' Brady down.*
>
> *Wimmens in Gawgy dey heard de news*
> *Walking 'bout in deir little red shoes,*
> *Dey glad, dey glad po' Brady dead.*
>
> *When I close my eyes to ketch a liddle sleep,*
> *Po' old Brady about my bed do creep,*
> *One mo', des' one mo' rounder gone.*

[*While he is singing and playing,* ABE *comes suddenly in at the rear dragging a heavy wooden box in one hand and carrying a dinner-pail in the other. He is dirty and begrimed with coal dust.*]

ABE [*shouting*]. Put up dat box! [DOUGLASS *bounds out of his chair as if shot and backs away from him.*] Put down dat damn guitah, you good-foh-nothing!

[ABE *hangs his cap and dinner-pail on a nail by the door and comes heavily across to the fire. His face is haggard and old and his shoulders have grown humped with the going of time.* DOUGLASS *slips out with his guitar and presently creeps in and sits stealthily on the chest.* ABE *lays the goods box on the floor and breaks it up and places pieces of it on the fire. Then he sits down and stretches out his feet and stares moodily before him.* MUH MACK *hurries around making bread, frying the hated side meat, and arranging the table.*]

MUH MACK [*tremulously*]. How you feeling? You come quick adder de whistle——

ABE. Ah, feel lak I'll stifle in heah. [*He strikes his breast once and then follows it with a fury of savage blows.*] Cain't git no wind down in dat b'iler house. [*He drags his hand wearily across his brow and shakes his head as if clearing his eyes of a fog.*] Whah Goldie?

MUH MACK. Gone out to de cawner to git some meat. Time she back.

ABE. How long fo' supper?

MUH MACK. Soon's she gits back and we kin cook de meat.

ABE [*pulling off his shoes and setting them in the corner*]. I' going to lie down a minute till my head clears up. Feel lak it'll blow off at de top. [*Grasping his chair, he staggers to his feet and goes across the room. At the door he stops and looks down at* DOUGLASS.] I' going to tend to you in a little bit.

[DOUGLASS *quails before him.* ABE *goes out and slams the door.*]

MUH MACK. Whut de name o' Gohd ail him now? Wus'n ever.

DOUGLASS [*whimpering*]. He gwine beat me! He'll kill me.

[*The bed is heard creaking in the rear room as* ABE *lies down.*]

MUH MACK. Whut'n de world foh?

[*She stands tapping her hands together helplessly.*]

DOUGLASS. He done heahed sump'n' on me. Oh, he gwine beat me to deaf.

700

[ABE *is heard turning in his bed again, and he immediately appears in the door.*]

ABE. Shet up dat whimpering. Git over dere and start washing on dem clothes foh yo' po' mammy. [DOUGLASS *darts over and begins rubbing at the board and sniffling.*] Dry up, I tell you.

[ABE *turns back to his bed.*]

MUH MACK [*sitting to the fire and rocking back and forth in her anxiety*]. Oh, Lawd—Lawd!

[*She hides her head in her skirt grumbling and moaning. Presently* GOLDIE *comes in.*]

GOLDIE [*coming over to the tub*]. Look out, son, lemme git at 'em.

[*She falls to washing feverishly.*]

MUH MACK [*looking up*]. Whah dat meat, Goldie?

GOLDIE. Dat man look at me and laugh, dat's whut. [*Turning angrily toward* DOUGLASS.] You went and——

MUH MACK [*throwing out her hand in alarm*]. Nanh, nanh, Goldie. [*Lowering her voice and nodding to the rear.*] Abe in dere. He find out 'bout dat, he kill de boy. Done say he gwine beat 'im foh sump'n' 'nother.

GOLDIE. When he come?

MUH MACK. He des' dis minute gut heah.

GOLDIE [*in alarm*]. He wuss off, I bet. [*She hurries into the room and is heard talking softly and kindly to* ABE. *He answers her with indistinct growls. In a moment* GOLDIE *returns.*] Putt whut you gut on de table and le's eat. [*She goes on with her washing.*] Abe ain't feeling well. Hadder eat whut he kin, I reckon.

[MUH MACK *puts the bread, coffee and meat on the table.*]

MUH MACK. Come on, you all.

GOLDIE. Come on in, Abe. [ABE *enters in his undershirt and trousers.*] G'won and eat, I don't want nothing.

ABE [*almost falling in his chair*]. Come on and set whedder you can or not. [GOLDIE *takes her place at the table.*] Come on, Douglass.

DOUGLASS. I don't want nothing eiver.

[MUH MACK *draws up her chair.*]

ABE. Don't make no difference. I said come on. [DOUGLASS *gets a chair and takes his place.* ABE *surveys the fare before him.*] Dis all you got foh a working man and he sick?

GOLDIE. I didn' have no money and——

[*She turns away her head to hide her tears.*]

ABE [*kindly as he reaches out and touches her shoulders*]. Neveh mind, honey chile. [*He closes his eyes with weariness and sits brooding. Presently he raises his head.*] Well, neveh you mind, I ain't hungry. [*Looking at her sadly.*] But you must be plumb wore out wid all dat washing and all. [*Dropping his head.*] Le's have de blessing. Oh, Lawd, we thank Thee foh what we have befo' us. Make us truly thankful foh all Thy gifts and save us at last, we humbly beg, foh Christ's sake, Amen! [*After the blessing is over* GOLDIE *still keeps her head bowed, her shoulders heaving with sobs.* MUH MACK *pours out the coffee and hands it round.* ABE *calls to* GOLDIE.] Come on eat sump'n', Goldie, you feel better, you git yo' stren'th back. Drink some this coffee. [GOLDIE, *bursting into wild sobs, goes and sits by the fire.*] What's de matter, chile?

701

MUH MACK. She done wukked to deaf and nothing to wuk on, dat's whut.

ABE [drinking down a cup of steaming coffee at a gulp]. Po' me some mo' of dat! [GOLDIE's sobs gradually die away.] Come on, honey, don't cry no mo'.

[GOLDIE stands up and looks toward the table with anguished face.]

GOLDIE. Abe, Abe honey babe, whut us gwine do?

[She buries her face in her hands.]

ABE. You done heahed sump'n', ain't you?

GOLDIE. Yeh, yeh, Liza told me. Jim done come f'om de power house and told her.

ABE [dully]. Neveh mind. Come on drink some coffee. We talk 'bout dat directly. I got sump'n' else to tell you, too.

MUH MACK [staring at him in fear]. Whut dat happen at de power house?

ABE. I tell you when I git good and ready. Come on, Goldie, chile. [GOLDIE wipes her eyes and returns to the table to drink her coffee.] Befo' we gits on what happened wid me, I got a question to ax dis young gentleman. [Looking across at DOUGLASS.] Why don't you eat?

DOUGLASS [falteringly]. I ain't hongry.

ABE. Try and see do you want anything.

DOUGLASS. I cain't eat nothing.

ABE. How come?

DOUGLASS. I des' don't want nothing.

ABE [bitterly]. I reckon I know how come. Dis evening I pass on the other side of de street and see you down dere at dat drink stand settin' up dem wuthless niggers wid yo' mammy's good money. [Savagely.] Oh, yeh, I know dat's whah you got it. I see you last night watching her putt it away.

GOLDIE. Please don't have no mo' row, Abe.

ABE. I ain't gwine beat 'im foh dat, nunh-unh. Sump'n' else he's goin' to ketch it foh. [Raging out.] De teacher stop me on de street and tell me you doing wuss'n ever in yo' books and she done had to putt you back in third reader. [Swallowing his third cup of coffee down with a hunk of bread, he stands up and stares into the distance.] Heah we done labor and sweat foh you, fix foh you to rise up and be sump'n'. Eight yeah you been going to school and you won't work, you won't learn. [He strikes the table with his fist, and the lamp flickers and almost goes out.] You ain't no good. Onct I thought you gwine go on, climb, rise high and lead.

[He seizes him by the collar and, lifting him from the floor, shakes him like a rag.]

DOUGLASS [sputtering and choking]. Pap, papa!

MUH MACK [whining in terror]. Stop dat! You kill him!

ABE. I teach you to fool wid dem low niggers! I git you out'n dem trifling ways or I'll break yo' back in two. [He sits down and jerks the boy across his knee and begins beating him blindly.] I name you foh a great man, a man what stand high lak de sun, and you turn out to be de lowest of de low! Change yo' name, dat's what you better do. [With a cuff he hurls him across the room, where he falls sobbing and wailing on the floor.] Shet dat fuss up! [DOUGLASS' sobs gradually cease. GOLDIE starts toward him, but ABE jerks her back.] Let 'im lie dere, de skunk and coward.

[GOLDIE turns despairingly to her washing again. ABE moves to the fire and

702

sits down, pulling a wrinkled newspaper out of his pockets, while MUH MACK *rocks and slobbers and moans.*]

MUH MACK. You need de law on you, Abe McCranie. You beat dat po' baby——

ABE. Shet up! You what gwine ruin him. He takes adder you and yo' trifling.

MUH MACK. Oh, I gwine leave heah, find me 'nudder place to stay.

ABE. We all got to git another place to stay.

GOLDIE. Le's go back home, Abe! Le's go back.

MUH MACK. Ha' we gut to leave 'caze whut you done down at de power house? [*Wringing her hands.*] Whut you do down dere? Oh, Lawd!

ABE. Ain't no use waking up de neighborhood wid yo' yelling. I didn't do nothing but stand up foh my rights. A white man sass me and I sass back at him. And a crowd of 'em run me off. Won't be able to git no other job in dis town, God damn it! [*Standing up and shaking his fist.*] God damn de people in dis town! Dem wid deir 'bacco warehouses, and cotton mills, and money in de bank, you couldn't handle wid a shovel! Yeh, dey mortgage up God's great world and shet out de po'!

MUH MACK. Le's go back home. De Colonel fix it in his will so us could have a place to come back to. Mr. Lonnie'll rent us some land.

GOLDIE [*coming over to* ABE'S *chair and dropping on her knees beside him*]. Abe, Abe, le's go back. Please do. Le's go back whah we growed up. Ain't no home foh us in no town. We gut to git back to de country. Dat's whah we belong.

[*She lays her head in his lap.*]

ABE [*looking down at her in sudden tenderness*]. Yeh, yeh, honey. We is gwine back. Adder all dese yeahs I knows now de town ain't no place foh us. Fifteen yeah we been trying to make it and couldn't. Dat's what I was going to tell you. All de signs been ag'in us. I orter knowed it after three or fo' yeahs. Back home de place foh us. Back in our own country. [*Staring before him and a smile suddenly sweetening the hardness of his face.*] We go back dere and take a new start. We going to build up on a new foundation. Took all dese yeahs to show me. [*His voice rising in a sort of nervous exultation.*] Dere's whah my work is cut out to be. It come to me dis evening while I walked on de lonesome street. [*Standing up.*] Seem lak sump'n' spoke to me and said go back down on de Cape Fair River. I heard it plain lak a voice talking. "Dese streets and dese peoples ain't yo' peoples. Yo'n is de kind what works and labors wid de earf and de sun. Dem who knows de earth and the fullness thereof. Dere's whah yo' harvest is to be." And den when I come face to face wid de ruining of my boy, in my anger I see de way clear. We going back, we going back. And dere at last I knows I'm going to build up and lead! And my boy going to be a man. [*Looking at* DOUGLASS *with a hint of pleadingness.*] Ain't it so?

[*But* DOUGLASS *only stares at him coldly and afraid.*]

GOLDIE [*smiling up at him*]. I knows you will. I feel it des' de way you do. I keep telling Muh Mack some day you gwine git dere.

ABE [*gazing down at her*]. Dese yeahs all been sent foh our trial, ain't dey, honey?

GOLDIE. Yeh, yeh, we been tried all foh a purpose.

ABE. And now we ready, ain't we, honey?

GOLDIE. We ready to go back and start all over.

703

MUH MACK [*repeating uncertainly*]. To start all over.

ABE. To build us a monument from generation unto generation.

GOLDIE [*softly, the tears pouring from her eyes*]. Yeh, yeh.

ABE. And all dis sin and tribulation and sorrow will be forgot, passed away, wiped out till de judgment, won't it, chile?

GOLDIE. It will, oh, I knows it will. We done suffered our share and Old Moster gwine be good to us now.

ABE. Good! Yeh, good!

[*He sits with bowed head.*]

Scene V

Three years later. The same as Scene Two, in ABE's *cabin on the McCranie farm. The room shows some sign of improvement over its former state. There is a lambrequin of crêpe paper on the mantel, a wooden clock, and at the right a home-fashioned bookcase with books and magazines. On the rear wall is the same colored print with the caption of the rising slave.*

ABE *is seated at a table near the front writing by a lighted lamp. He is better dressed and more alert than formerly. Further back and to the left of the fireplace sits* MUH MACK *dozing and quarreling in her rocking chair. Her head and face are hid under the same slat-bonnet, and a dirty pink "fascinator" is draped over her bony shoulders. Her huge snuff brush protrudes from her lips and now and then describes a sort of waving motion when she moves her jaws in sleep. Between her knees she clasps her walking-stick.*

Through the window at the rear come bright streaks from the orange afterglow of the west. The November sun has set and the sky near the horizon is fading into a deep gloom under an approaching cloudiness. In the oaks outside the sparrows going to roost pour out a flooding medley of sharp calls resembling the heavy dripping of rain from eaves. For a moment ABE *continues his writing and then lays down his pencil and replenishes the fire. He returns to his chair and sits drumming absently on the table.*

ABE. When Goldie coming back, Muh?

[*His speech is gentle and more cultivated.*]

MUH MACK [*starting out of her sleep*]. Whut you say?

ABE. When Goldie coming back from Mr. Lonnie's?

MUH MACK. When she git done o' dat washing and arning, po' thing.

ABE. Seem like it's time she was back.

MUH MACK. Whut you keer 'bout her and you setting dere all day wuking at dat old speech mess.

ABE. You going to cook any supper?

MUH MACK. Supper! You ax dat and know I cain't git out'n my chaih wid de stiffness and misery. You'll hadder eat cold.

ABE. I've done looked. Ain't nothing cold.

MUH MACK. Den you'll hadder wait till she come. Po', po' thing, wid all her trouble wonder she able to cook or work or do anything.

[*She returns to her snoozing and* ABE *picks up his pencil again and gnaws at it as he works on his speech. Soon he stops and begins tapping on the table.*]

ABE. What trouble she got now?

MUH MACK [*astounded*]. You ax dat and you fixing to bring mo' trouble on us wid yo' schooling and mess. And wid Mr. Lonnie down on you 'bout de crap ag'in. Lawd, Lawd! And who dat won't let his po' boy putt foot in de home? Keep 'im driv' off lak a homeless dawg.

[*She wipes her eyes with a dirty rag.*]

ABE. You talk, but this time they won't be no failing. The school is going through. Then I can talk to Mr. Lonnie. Six men done already promised a thousand dollars. Cain't fail this time, nosuh.

MUH MACK. You don't 'serve nothing, and won't let po' Douglass come back to see his mammy. [*Brightly.*] Dem men mebbe ain't promised. Dey talking.

ABE [*sharply*]. I know. . . . You needn't say another word about it. [*Concerned with the speech.*] I won't let Douglass darken my door.

[MUH MACK *stirs from her doze and sniffles into her rag, wiping the rheumy tears from her eyes.* ABE *turns to his writing. He writes more and more rapidly as he nears the end. Presently he throws down his pencil and stretches his arms back of his head with a weary, happy yawn. He looks towards* MUH MACK *and speaks exultantly.*]

ABE. That's the best I've ever done. They can't go against that, they can't this time.

MUH MACK [*sleepily, rubbing her eyes and speaking coldly*]. Thank God you's finished yo' speech and'll soon be outen my sight and I kin git a liddle nap.

ABE [*not noticing her*]. That crowd's going to listen to me to-night.

MUH MACK. Mebbe dey will, but you's talked yo' life away, and it hain't come to nothing.

ABE [*looking at the speech*]. I've done my best this time. All I got from books and experience is there, and the truth's in it. [*He gathers the closely written sheets together.*] I tell 'em——[*He turns to his speech and begins to read as he rises from his chair.*] I say, ladies and gentlemen [*he takes no notice of* MUH MACK'S *disgust, as she turns away from him*], this night is going to mean much in the lives of each and every one of us, big and little.

MUH MACK. Hit won't ef dey treats dey chil'en lak you treats yo' one.

ABE [*hurrying on*]. It marks the founding of the Cape Fair Training School, an institution that will one day be a light to other institutions around about. It is to be our aim here, with the few teachers and facilities we can provide, to offer education to the colored children amongst us and offer it cheap. [*He turns toward* MUH MACK *and speaks with more spirit, as if his audience were directly before him. But she turns her back to him and blinks in the fire.*] Looking over the country, ladies and gentlemen, we see eight million souls striving in slavery, yea, slavery, brethren, the slavery of ignorance. And ignorance means being oppressed, both by yourselves and by others—hewers of wood and drawers of water.

[*He picks up his pencil and crosses out a word.*]

MUH MACK [*sarcastically*]. Dey hain't nobody been in slavery since de surrenduh. If dey is, how come? And I reckon de hewers o' woods and de drawers o' water is 'bout free as anybody.

705

ABE [*continuing his speech without noticing her*]. Ignorance means sin, and sin means destruction, destruction before the law and destruction in a man's own heart. The Negro will rise when his chareckter is of the nature to cause him to rise—for on that the future of the race depends, and that chareckter is mostly to be built by education, for it cannot exist in ignorance. Let me repeat again, ladies and gentlemen. We want our children and our grandchildren to march on towards full lives and noble chareckters, and that has got to come, I say, by education. We have no other way. We got to live and learn—and think, that's it. [*He strides in front of the old woman, who has dozed off again under his eloquence. She raises her head with a jerk when he thunders at her.*] A little over forty years ago the white man's power covered us like the night. Through war and destruction we was freed. But it was freedom of the body and not freedom of the mind. And what is freedom of the body without freedom of the mind? It means nothing. It don't exist. [*Throwing his arm out in a long gesture.*] What we need is thinking people, people who will not let the body rule the head. And again I cry out, education. I been accused of wanting to make the Negro the equal of the white man. Been run from pillar to post, living in poverty because of that belief. But it is false. I never preached that doctrine. I don't say that the colored ought to be made equal to the white in society, now. We are not ready for it yet. But I do say that we have equal rights to educating and free thought and living our lives. With that all the rest will come. [*Pointing to the bookcase.*] Them books there show it. [*Caught up in the dreams of his life, he pours out a roll of words and beats the air with his fists.*] Ladies and gentlemen, what's to hinder us from starting a great center of learning here, putting our time and our hope and money and labor into it and not into the much foolishness of this life. What little education I got was by light 'ood knots, and after reading and studying all these years, I am just a little ways along. We must give the children of the future a better chance than we have had. With this one school-building we can make a good start. Then we can get more teachers later on, more equipment, and some day a library where the boys and girls can read about men that have done something for the world. And before many years pass we will be giving instruction in how to farm, how to be carpenters, how to preach, how to teach, how to do anything. [*Forgetful of his written page, he shouts.*] And what will stop us in the end from growing into a great Negro college, a university, a light on a hill, a place the pride of both black and white. [*He stands a moment, lost in thought. Turning through the leaves of his speech, he looks towards* MUH MACK, *who sits hid under her bonnet.*] Ain't that the truth, Muh Mack? Ain't it? [*Anxiously.*] They can't stand out against that, can they? Ain't that a speech equal to the best of the white, ain't it? [*He coughs.*]

MUH MACK. Lawd Jesus! You's enough to wake de daid. And you brung on yo' cough ag'in.

ABE [*fiercely*]. I tell you it's going through. I believe the people here are with me this time.

706   MUH MACK. Sounds like de same old tale. [*Bitterly.*] You's made dem dere speeches from Wilmington and Greensboro to I don' know where. It's foolishnesses, and you knows it. [ABE *arranges the leaves of his speech without listening to her.*] Time you's learning dat white is white and black is black, and

Gohd made de white to allus be bedder'n de black. It was so intended from de beginning.

ABE [*staring at her and speaking half aloud*]. We been taught and kept believing that for two hundred years. [*Blazing out.*] But it's a lie, a lie, and the truth ain't in it.

MUH MACK [*going on in her whining, irritating voice*]. Yeh, all yo' life you's hollered Lawd and followed Devil, and look whut it's brung you to. Ef you'd a putt as much time on picking cotton lately as you has on dat speech, you wouldn't have Mr. Lonnie down on you de way he is. De truf's in dat all right.

ABE [*trying to control his nervousness and anger*]. I ain't a farmer. My business is with schools. [*Hotly.*] Can't you learn nothing? You dribbling old——, here for twenty years you've heard me talk the gospel and it ain't made no impression on you. [*He turns away, realizing the vanity of his words to her. He speaks to himself and the shadows of the room.*] That speech is so! It's so, and I got to speak it that-a-way. [*He looks about him with burning eyes and pleads as if with an unseen power.*] The truth's there. Can't you see it? [*His nostrils quiver and he goes on in a kind of sob, calling to the unbeliever hiding within the dark.*] God A'mighty knows they ain't no difference at the bottom. Color hadn't ought to count. It's the man, it's the man that lasts. [*Brokenly.*] Give us the truth! Give us the truth!

[*He coughs slightly, and a queer baffled look creeps over his face. For the moment he seems to sense ultimate defeat before a hidden, unreachable enemy.*]

MUH MACK [*looking at the clock and snapping*]. Thought you's bound to be at de Quillie house by six o'clock. It's done near 'bout time. Git on. I wants my nap.

[*She pours snuff into her lip and turns to her snoozing again. With a hurried look at the clock,* ABE *crams his speech into his pocket, gets a plug hat from the desk, and blows out the lamp. The room is filled with great leaping shadows from the darting flames of the fireplace.*]

ABE [*at the door*]. You remember what I said about Douglass.

MUH MACK. Git on, git on. [*Whining sarcastically.*] Sho' you'll be a light on de hill and de pride o' de land—and you won't even let a po' old woman see her boy.

ABE [*turning back*]. Damn him! If he puts his foot in this house he'd better not let me get hold of him. They ain't no man, flesh of my flesh or not, going to lie rotten with liquor and crooks around me. That's what I been talking against for twenty years. I drove him off for it and I'd do it again. Just because a little time's passed ain't no reason I've changed.

MUH MACK. He mought a changed and want to do bedder.

ABE [*coming back into the room*]. Changed enough so he like to got arrested in town yesterday and it his first day back.

MUH MACK [*pleading in a high quavering voice*]. But I gut to see him. He's been gone two yeah.

ABE. Let him come if he dares. You ruint him with your tales and wuthless guitar playing and I don't want nothing more to do with him.

MUH MACK [*mumbling to herself*]. I's gwine see him 'fo' he goes 'way back yander ef I has to crawl slam over de river.

707

ABE [*with brightening eye*]. You heard me. He ain't no longer mine, and that's the end of it.

MUH MACK [*bursting into a rage*]. And yo' ain't none o' mine. You's gut all de high notions of old Colonel Mack and de white folks and don't keer nothing foh yo' own. Git on. [*He stands looking at the floor, hesitating over something.*] Whut you skeered of, de dark?

ABE [*shuddering and going across the room and getting an old overcoat from a nail*]. Yes, I'm afraid of it. You're right, I'm none of yours, nor my own mother either. You know what I am—no, I dunno whut I am. Sometime I think that's de trouble. [*Sharply.*] No, no, de trouble out there, around me, everywhere around me. [*The despondent look comes back to his face and he speaks more calmly.*] I'll cut across the fields the near way. And tell Goldie not to worry. I'll be back by ten with the school good as started. [*At the door he turns back again and calls to the old woman earnestly.*] Muh Mack, don't let her worry, don't. [*But the old woman is asleep.*] Let her sleep, let us all sleep.

[*He goes out softly, closing the door behind him.*]

Scene VI

An hour later the same evening. A sandy country road twists out of the gloom of scrubby oaks and bushes at the rear and divides into a fork, one branch turning sharply to the left and the other to the right. The moon has risen low in the east, casting a sickly drunken light over the landscape through the flying clouds. To the left in a field of small loblolly pines the dim outline of a barn can be seen. The tops and the branches of the larger trees move like a vast tangle of restless arms, and the small bushes and grasses hug the earth under the wind's blustering. Down the road in the distance come the sounds of running footsteps. And farther off, almost out of hearing, the halloo as of some one pursuing. The footsteps thump nearer, and presently ABE *staggers up out of the darkness and falls panting in the edge of the bushes at the right. His hat is gone and his clothes torn. The shouts sound fainter in the night and gradually die away.*

ABE *crawls to his knees and stares back at the road, his breath coming in great gasps. His learning and pitiful efforts at cultural speech have dropped away like a worn-out garment and left him a criminal.*

ABE. Reckon, reckon dey leave me 'lone now, de damn cutth'oats! [*Holding his sides with his hands and rocking his head in pain.*] Oh, my breast feel lak it'll bust. Yeh, I outrun you, you po' white trash. [*Clambering wildly to his feet and staring up the road.*] But you done fix me now. You done got all de underholt and lay me on de bottom. [*Looking up at the sky and raising his fist above his head.*] Dere dat moon looking on it all so peaceful lak. It don't know, it can't feel what dey done to me. [*Bursting out with a loud oath.*] God damn 'em to hell! Dem white sons of bitches! Dey don't gi' me no chance. Dey stop every crack, nail up every do' and shet me in. Dey stomp on me, squash me, mash me in de ground lak a worm. [*His voice breaking into a sob.*] Dey ain't no place foh me. I lost, ain't no home, no 'biding place. [*He throws himself down on the ground and lays his cheek to the earth. Unseen by him, a light begins to*

708

twinkle at the barn. He sits up and looks intently at the ground.] Seem lak dis earf feel sweet to me. It warm me lak it feel sorry. [*Laying his hand on it as if it were a being.*] Ground, you is my last and only friend. You take me in, you keep me safe from trouble. Wisht I could dig me a hole now and cover me up and sleep till de great judgment day, and nobody never know whah I gone.

[LONNIE MCCRANIE, *stout and middle-aged, comes in at left with a lantern.*]

LONNIE. Heigh there!

ABE [*bounding up*]. Keep back, whoever you is. Stay back dere, white man.

LONNIE [*peering forward*]. Who's that cutting up crazy here in the night?

ABE. Ain't nobody, nobody.

LONNIE. Well, by God, Abe, what's the matter?

ABE. That you, Mr. Lonnie?

LONNIE. Yeh. What'n the world's the matter? I was out there at the barn and heard the awfulest racket. Somebody talking like they was crazy.

ABE. Trouble, Mr. Lonnie, trouble.

LONNIE. Trouble, what sort of trouble? [*Coming closer and holding up his light before* ABE.] Great goodness, you're wet as water.

ABE [*straightening up*]. I all right now. Got to go on.

[*He makes a drunken step on the road toward the right.* LONNIE *gets quickly before him.*]

LONNIE. Where you going?

ABE. I going to leave heah, going clean away.

LONNIE. No, you're not. Tell me what's the matter.

ABE. Dem white men run me away from the Quillie house.

LONNIE. That's what the shouting was about, was it?

ABE. Mebbe so, suh.

LONNIE. Uh-huh. You were down there 'bout your school business, anh?

ABE. I wa'n't doing no harm. I was going to talk to 'em 'bout our school foh next year, and when I got there dey was a crowd of low-down white men dere——

LONNIE. Look out, mind how you talk.

ABE. I minding all right. When I got there, they done run them lazy niggers off and told me I had to go. [*Grimly.*] Dey couldn't skeer me, though. I went on in de house and started my speech. And den——[*Throwing out his arms wildly.*] Mr. Lonnie, help me git back at 'em. Help me git de law on 'em.

LONNIE. What'd they do?

ABE. Dey fell on me and beat me and told me I got to git out of de country. And dey run me off. But I reckon some of 'em got dey heads cracked. [*His body swaying with weakness.*] What I going to do? I don't know what.

LONNIE. Go on home and behave yourself.

ABE [*his voice almost cracking*]. I ain't done nothing. I tell you.

LONNIE [*roughly*]. Serves you right. I've told you time and again to quit that messing about and look after your crop and keep in your place. But you won't, you won't. I reckon you'll stay quiet now awhile.

ABE [*pleading with him*]. But I done right. I ain't done nothing to be beat foh.

LONNIE. The devil you ain't! I've been off to-day all around the country trying to get hands to pick out your cotton. It's falling out and rotting in the fields.

709

ABE. But I ain't lost no time from the cotton patch, 'cepting two or three days and I was sick den. I been sick all to-day.

LONNIE. You needn't talk back to me. If you're sick, what are you doing out tonight and getting yourself beat half to death? Yeh, I reckon I know such tales as that. And you needn't fool with the crop no more. I done levied on it and am going to have it housed myself.

ABE [*moving toward him*]. You mean you tuck my crop away from me?

LONNIE. Don't talk to me like that, I tell you. [*A fit of coughing seizes* ABE.] Call it taking away from you if you want to. I'm done of you. Next year you can hunt another place.

ABE [*his face working in uncontrollable rage*]. Den you's a damn thief, white man.

LONNIE [*yelling*]. Stop that!

ABE [*moving toward him*]. Now I'm going to pay somebody back. I going to git even.

LONNIE. Stop! I'll bust yo' head open with this lantern.

ABE [*with a loud laugh*]. Yeh, yeh, hit me. Yo' time done come.

[*He makes a movement toward* LONNIE, *who swings his lantern aloft and brings it crashing down on his head. The light goes out and the two rocking forms are seen gripping each other's throats under the moon.*]

LONNIE. Let go—let go——

[ABE *gradually crushes him down to the ground, choking him.*]

ABE [*gnashing his teeth and snarling like a wild animal*]. I choke you, I choke yo' guts out'n yo' mouf. [*He finally throws* LONNIE'S *limp body from him, and then falls upon it, beating and trampling the upturned face.*] Dere you lie now. Dead! [*His voice trails high into a croon.*] I wipe out some de suffering of dis world now! [*Standing up and drawing away from the body.*] I—I—git even, I pay 'em back. [*He begins wiping his hands feverishly upon his trousers.*] Blood! Blood, de white man's blood all over me. [*Screaming out in sudden fear.*] I done kilt somebody! Oh, Lawd, Mr. Lonnie! Mr. Lonnie! [*He falls on his knees by the body.*] What's de matter? Wake up, wake up! . . . Pshaw, he's asleep, fooling. [*Springing to his feet.*] He's dead, dead. [*The wind groans through the trees like the deep note of some enormous fiddle and then dies away with a muffled boom across the open fields.* ABE *stands frozen with horror.*] Listen at dat wind, will you! Mercy, dat his spirit riding it and crying! [*He falls prone upon the earth moaning and rocking. In a moment he sits up and holds his head tightly in his hands.*] O—oh, seem lak my head done turnt to a piece o' wood, seem lak cold as ice. [*He slaps his forehead queerly with his open palms.*] De whole world done seem turnt upside down, everything going round me lak a wheel. [*As he stares wonderingly around and gropes before him like one dreaming, the branches of the trees seem to change their characteristics and become a wild seething of mocking, menacing hands stretched forth from all sides at him. He snatches up a piece of broken fence rail and snarls at them.*] Don't tech me, I kill you! [*He stands in an attitude of defense and the branches seem to regain their normal appearance. Stupefied, he lets the rail fall to the ground and then wraps his arms spasmodically across his face.*] O Lawd, I going crazy, dat's what! [*He bends over jerking and shivering. Presently from the left he sees*

710

appear a shadowy cortège of raggle-taggle country gentry, men and boys carry-
ing muskets, sticks and stones. Their faces, illumined by the moon, are set and
frozen in the distortion of hate and revenge. In the midst of them is a young
Negro being dragged along with a rope around his neck. Abe *starts back with a*
gasp.] What's dis? Whah am I? [*Suddenly terrified.*] Lawd, dat's a lynching!
. . . It's de night o' dat lynching. And dat dere's Charlie—Charlie Sampson.
[*Seizing the rail.*] What you white mens doing? [*Crying out.*] Dat you, Charlie!
I come save you! [*The group appear to pass silently down the road at the rear,*
the prisoner throwing out his arms and clawing the air as he is dragged onward.
Abe *springs forward at them and swings his rail through the air. It lands on*
the ground with a thud. He shrieks.] Ghosts! Dey's ha'nts! Dey ain't no peoples!
[*He stands rooted in his tracks as they disappear down the road. After a moment*
out of the underbrush at the left steal two shadowy figures dressed in the fashion
of the late fifties. One is a young good-looking Negress of twenty, the other a
dandified young white man about thirty. As they move across the scene at the
rear, the man looks guiltily around him as if in fear of being surprised. The
woman stops and points to the thicket at the right. He nods and motions her to
move on. Abe *looks up and sees them stealing away. He leaps to his feet and*
stares at them in stupefaction.] Who dat 'oman and white man? [*With a joyous*
cry he rushes forward.] Mammy! Mammy! Dat you! Dis heah's Abe, yo' boy!
Mammy! [*The figures begin entering the thicket.*] Mammy! Dat you, Colonel
Mack? Whah you going? Stay heah, help me, I——[*The man and the woman*
disappear in the bushes. Abe *stands with his mouth open, staring after them.*]
Whut's all dis? Must be anudder dream—a dream. Sump'n' quare. [*He moves*
cautiously forward and parts the bushes and starts back with a loud oath.] God
damn 'em! Dey dere lak hawgs! [*The fearful truth breaks upon him and he*
shrieks.] Stop it! Stop dat, Mammy, Colonel Mack! [*Rushing toward the bushes*
again and stopping as if spellbound.] Stop dat, I tell you, dat's me! Dat's me!

[*He stumbles backward over the body of* Lonnie McCranie *and, shrieking,*
rushes down the road at the left.]

Scene VII

Thirty minutes later. Douglass *has arrived and with* Muh Mack *before the*
fire is giving an account of his travels. He is now about nineteen years old, and
has developed into a reckless dissipated youth, dressed in the cheap flashy clothes
of a sport.

Douglass [*turning toward* Muh Mack *with a bitter smile*]. Yeh, I says it and
I says it ag'in. Let dem dere Norveners putt Pap in print foh what he's trying to
do foh de niggers. Ef dey could see him now down a po' dirt fahmer dey'd not
think he's such a sma't man. Let him read his books and git new ide's. Dey
won't change de nigger in him, not by a damn sight. He's raght down working
a tenant and dat's where he belongs. Git me? Ah, him off to-night making his
speeches. I bet to Christ dis heah's his last 'un.

Muh Mack. Foh God's sake don' carry on so. Come on and tell me some mo'

711

'bout de places you been since you left heah. [*He sits looking in the fire.*] Whut —whut's de matter? You hain't been usual so ficey-lak wid yo' pap. You been drinking?

DOUGLASS [*laughing sweetly*]. Yeh, I been drinking. And I gut cause to cuss de whole works out. [*Looking at her fiercely.*] Listen heah. Let dis slip in yo' yur, foh you'd heah it soon enough. You never has swung a' eight-pound hammer, steel driving day adder day in the br'iling sun, has you? And you hain't never done it wid a ball and chain on you ca'se you is marked dang'us, has you? and dat foh a whole yeah long? Well, I has.

MUH MACK [*in astonishment*]. You been on de roads since you left?

DOUGLASS [*recklessly*]. I has dat and wo' de convict clo'es des' ca'se in my drunkenness I 'gun to preach some o' his doctrines 'bout dere being no difference 'twixt de cullud and de white. I knowed bedder. But I was drunk and had hearn so many o' his speeches. De judge said he'd des' stop my mouf foh a month. And I gut a knife one day and stobbed a gyard to de hollow. And dey gin me twelve months foh dat.

MUH MACK [*admiring his prowess*]. You allus was one whut fou't at de drap o' de hat.

DOUGLASS [*disgustedly*]. Yeh, a damn fool, and I ain't fohgit how he run me off'n heah and beat me! [*Bursting out with shining eyes.*] Hain't I gut cause to hate him and want to git him down?

MUH MACK. Gittin' on de roads ain't much, Douglass.

DOUGLASS. No, it ain't much to lie in de jug, is it? You do it and you ain't never gwine have no more peace. De cops is allus watching you. You gits de look and dey knows you. Dey tried to 'rest me yistiddy over dere, and I hadn't done nothing. And de old man was knowing to it too. But I's learnt what he'll never learn and it's dis—dat we belongs down wid de pick and de sludge hammer and de tee-arn and de steam shovel, and de heavy things—at de bottom doing de dirty work foh de white man, dat's it. And he ain't gwine stand foh us to be educated out'n it nuther. He's gwine keep us dere. It pays him to. I sees it. And adder all dese yeahs Pap keeps on trying to teach dat men is men. Some white man's gwine shoot his lights out one dese days, see ef dee don't. [*With a reckless forgetful-ness.*] And so I says gimme a fast time, a liddle gin to drown down all my troubles in, and den——[*He goes over to the door and gets his guitar.*] A liddle music to top it off wid. How about it, Muh Mack?

MUH MACK [*straining her eyes through the shadows*]. Whut you gut dere? [*Jubilantly.*] Lawd, Lawd! Ef you ain't brung yo' box wid you! And I ain't heerd nothing but dem sporrers by de do' and dat old rain crow in de hollow since you left two yeah back. Play her, boy, play her.

[*By this time he has sat down by the fire strumming.*]

DOUGLASS [*tuning up while* MUH MACK *sits in a quiver of excitement*]. Lemme play yo' old piece. My 'oman in Rocky Mount said 'twas de onliest chune.

MUH MACK. Dat's it! Dat's it! Lawd, gimme de "Band." I useter be put in de middle every time foh dat step. Dance all day, dance all night, des' so I's home by de broad daylight. Chile, I c'd natch'ly knock de wool off'n 'em.

[*As* DOUGLASS *plays she chuckles and whines with delight and almost rises from her seat. He starts in a quiet manner gradually working up to a paroxysm*

712

of pantomime and song. MUH MACK *begins doing the Jonah's Band Party step with her heels and toes while sitting.* DOUGLASS *spreads his wriggling feet apart, leans forward with closed eyes, and commences the "call," with the old woman's quavery slobbering voice giving the "sponse."*]

CALL. Sech a kicking up san'!

SPONSE. Jonah's ban'!

[*This is repeated; then comes the command to change steps.*]

> Hands up, sixteen, and circle to de right,
> We's gwine git big eatings heah to-night.
>
> Sech a kicking up san'! Jonah's Ban'!
> Sech a kicking up san'! Jonah's Ban'!
>
> Raise yo' right foot, kick it up high,
> Knock dat Mobile buck in de eye.
>
> Sech a kicking up san'! Jonah's Ban'!
> Sech a kicking up san'! Jonah's Ban'!
>
> Stan' up, flat-foot. Jump dem bars.
> Karo backwards lak a train o' cyars.
>
> Sech a kicking up san'! Jonah's Ban'!
> Sech a kicking up san'! Jonah's Ban'!
>
> Dance roun', 'oman, show 'em de p'int,
> Dem yudder coons don'ter how to coonj'int.

[*By this time* DOUGLASS *is playing a tattoo on the wood of his box and carrying on the tune at the same time.* MUH MACK *has risen from her chair. With her dress to her knees, defying her years, she cuts several of the well-remembered steps. At sight of her bare and thin dry shanks the delirious* DOUGLASS *bursts into loud mocking guffaws and only plays faster.*

The door opens at the right and GOLDIE *comes timidly in. Her face is worn and haggard, and the strained vacant look in her eyes has deepened.* MUH MACK *stops and creeps guiltily to her chair.* DOUGLASS *tapers off his music and stops. For a moment* GOLDIE *stands astonished in the door, holding a bulky tow-sack in her hand. She drops the sack and hurries over to* DOUGLASS.]

GOLDIE. Muhcy me! I knowed 'twas you soon's I heard de guitar. And sech carrying-ons!

DOUGLASS [*rising confusedly as she comes up to him*]. How you, Mam?

[*She puts her hand shyly on his arm and then clings convulsively to him, her shoulders heaving with restrained sobs. He lays one arm around her and stands looking tenderly and somewhat foolishly down at her. It is evident that in his way he cares for her. She suddenly raises her head, dries her eyes with her apron, and fetches wood from the box.*]

GOLDIE [*punching the fire*]. Why'n't you let me know Douglass'd come, Muh Mack?

MUH MACK. He des' come.

713

DOUGLASS [*laying his box on the bed*]. Mam, you set in dis char. You must be cold.

[*She sits down wearily, and he stands with his back to the fire. MUH MACK picks up her snuff-brush and slyly begins to dip from her tin box.*]

GOLDIE [*with a sudden start of terror*]. You hain't seed yo' pap, has you?

DOUGLASS. No'm, I ain't seed 'im. I found out he done gone to de Quillie house 'fo' I come. I slipped in heah and found Muh Mack asleep. Lawd, I skeahed her wid a fiah coal.

GOLDIE [*suddenly reaching out and clutching his hand to her face*]. Don't you and yo' pap have no trouble. Don't agg him on. He—he—ain't well and might rile easy. We—we kin see one 'nother off.

DOUGLASS. Oh, I'se gwine be partickler. Now don't worry no mo'. It's awright.

GOLDIE [*slowly getting up*]. You all set while I fix you some supper. I got something good foh Abe and de rest of us. Lemme show you. [*She brings the bag, sits down in the chair and takes out a big meaty ham-bone. MUH MACK eyes it hungrily. Naïvely.*] Ain't dat de finest dough? And I gut a hawg haid, too, and collards and cracklings.

DOUGLASS [*angrily*]. Dat's de way wid dem damn—wid dem white folks. Dey works you to death and den shoves dey old skippery meat off on you foh pay.

GOLDIE [*a worried look coming over her face*]. You hadn't ort to say dat, Douglass. Mr. Lonnie gi'n me it—all of it. And he paid me cash foh my work. Abe'll have a new bottle o' medicine Monday. [*She fingers the food childishly, and DOUGLASS turns away with a smothered oath. Putting the food back into the bag, she stands up.*] Now I'll git you some supper.

DOUGLASS. I cain't stay foh no supper. I promised to eat down de road wid Joe Day. Le's set and talk, ca'se we don't have much time and you can cook adder I'm gone.

GOLDIE [*hesitating*]. Well—lemme put dese heah in de kitchen den.

[*She goes out at the right.*]

DOUGLASS [*turning sharply to MUH MACK*]. What's de matter wid Mam?

MUH MACK. Won't we des' a-having of a time when she broke in?

DOUGLASS. Cut out de damn jowing. What makes Mam act so quare?

MUH MACK [*surprised*]. Do how? She acts awright.

DOUGLASS. She don't. She acts sort o' lost lak—wropped up in something.

[*He scratches his head perplexed.*]

MUH MACK. Ef dey's anything wrong wid her, it's 'count o' trouble, I reckin.

DOUGLASS. De hell-fi'ed fool! He's drug her to death wid his wildishness.

MUH MACK. And ef it's trouble dat ails her, I reckin as how you's done yo' shur in bringing it on.

[*He swallows his reply as GOLDIE comes in. She lights the lamp, then sits down and begins staring in the fire.*]

DOUGLASS [*after turning from one side to the other*]. Mammy, whut's de matter wid you?

714 GOLDIE [*brushing her hand across her face and looking up as she wipes the tears from her eyes*]. Lawd bless you, chile, dey ain't nothing. I's des' happy to be wid you.

[*She catches his hand and holds it a moment, then drops it and begins to look in the fire again. DOUGLASS watches her intently a moment and then turns away as if somewhat awed by her manner. There is a noise of some one's coming up on the porch.*]

MUH MACK [*crying out in fear*]. Dat's him, Douglass! I knows his step. Dat's yo' pap.

[GOLDIE *stands up, wringing her hands and crying silently as* DOUGLASS *gets his guitar and hurries into the kitchen. The door at the left opens and* ABE *enters.*]

GOLDIE [*leaning forward and rousing the fire*]. Did everything turn out—— [MUH MACK *suddenly screams.* GOLDIE *looks up and cries out.*] Oh!

[ABE *comes toward the fire. His face is bruised, his clothes torn to shreds, and he sways as he walks.*]

MUH MACK [*rising from her chair*]. Dey's been adder him! Dey's been adder him!

ABE [*snarling at her*]. Shet up yo' damn yowling, will you? and don't be rousing de neighborhood. I'm not dying yit.

[GOLDIE *stands a moment terror-stricken and then runs up to him.*]

GOLDIE. You's hurt, hurt bad, Abe, po' baby!

ABE [*pushing her back*]. Ain't hurt much. No time to doctor me now. [*He stands before the fire.* MUH MACK *collapses in her chair. He is no longer the reformer and educator, but a criminal, beaten and hunted.*] I come to tell you to git away—[*Panting.*] to—to leave, leave!

GOLDIE [*sobbing and burying her face in her hands*]. Whut's happened! Whut's happened!

MUH MACK [*swaying in her chair and crying to herself*]. Lawdy-a-muhcy on us! Lawd-a-muhcy!

[*For a moment he stands before the women silent, with closed eyes.*]

ABE [*looking at the motto on the wall and repeating the words dully*]. We are rising! [*Echoing.*] We are rising!—He didn't know what he said, he didn't. [*He staggers and grips the mantel and stands listening as if to far-away sounds. He turns desperately to the cowering women.*] Git your clothes and leave. You got to go, I tell you everything's finished at de end.

GOLDIE [*wailing*]. What happened at de schoolhouse?

ABE [*pushing his bruised hand across his forehead*]. I cain't, cain't quite think—yeh, they was a crowd of white men at de door with dough-faces on. Said wa'n't going to be no meeting. Dey beat me, run me off. And dey give me till to-morrow to git outen de country. You got to git away, foh it's worse'n dat—oh, it is! [*Calmly and without bitterness.*] Who you reckon set 'em on me? Who you think it was told 'em about de trouble I been in before? Yeh, and he made it out terribler'n it was. Douglass told 'em . . . He done it. My own flesh and blood. No! No! he was but ain't no more! [*Gloomily.*] But I don't blame him—dey ain't no blaming nobody no longer.

GOLDIE [*fiercely*]. He didn't—he wouldn't turn ag'in' his own pa.

ABE [*sternly*]. Hush! He did though. But it don't matter to-night. And you got to leave. [*Half screaming and tearing at the mantel.*] Now! Now, I tell you.

GOLDIE [*between her sobs*]. Did you—who hurt you?

ABE. I tell you I've done murder, and dey coming for me.

[MUH MACK *sits doubled up with fear, her head between her arms. With a sharp gasp* GOLDIE *ceases weeping and sits strangely silent.*]

MUH MACK. Murder! Oh, Lawd-a-muhcy! [*She mumbles and sobs in her rag.*]

715

ABE. Dey drove me away from de meeting. I come back by the road mad. [*He gasps.*] Every white man's hand ag'in' me to de last. And Mr. Lonnie come out to de road when I passed his house and begun to abuse me about de crop. He struck at me, and I went blind all of a sudden and hit him wid my fist. Den we fou't. [*His voice growing shrill.*] And I hit him and hit him. I beat his head in. I killed him dead, dead! I beat on and on until all de madness went out of me and de dark was everywhere. Den I seed a sight——[*He stops, aghast at the remembrance.*] I left him dere in the night dead on de ground. Dey done found 'im— I heah 'em crying up dere in de night. Dey's coming to git me. [*He holds out his bruised hands.*] His blood's still shining on dem hands. [*He turns his head away in fear.*]

MUH MACK [*in a high whine of terror*]. My God a-mighty! You kilt yo' own flesh!

ABE [*turning wrathfully upon her*]. Yeh, yeh, some bitch went a-coupling wid a white man! And I seed it—seed it! [*He drops his hands helplessly. A sort of terror comes upon him.*] Oh, Lawd God! I'm anudder Cain. I tell you I—I scrushed his head in and beat it till I put out de stars wid blood. Mercy! Mercy! [*With his hands still held before him, he stands with bowed head. After a moment he looks up and speaks calmly, almost resignedly, his dignity coming back to him.*] This is the way it was meant to be, and I'm glad it's ended. [*He stands with his fists to his temples, and then flings out his arms in a wide gesture.*] Oh, but damn 'em! Don't dey know I want to do all for de best. [*Shaking his fist at the shadows.*] I tell you, I tell you I wanted—I've tried to make it come right. [*Lowering his head.*] And now it's come to dis.

[DOUGLASS *comes in from the kitchen and stands away before him, his face filled with shame and fear.* ABE *looks at him without interest.*]

DOUGLASS. Befo' God, Pap, I—I didn't mean no sech happenings. I never thought——

ABE [*eyeing him coldly*]. Who you? [*More loudly.*] A leader, a king among men! [*To the women.*] Here's Douglass and you can go wid him.

[DOUGLASS *turns back into the kitchen and instantly runs out. His eyes are staring with fear.*]

DOUGLASS [*in a throaty whisper*]. Come on, Mam! [*Twisting his cap in terror.*] Dey's coming. I heerd 'em from de kitchen do'. Dey's coming. Run, Pap! God have muhcy!

[MUH MACK *hobbles to him and tries to pull him through the door at the right. He looks back towards his mother.*]

MUH MACK. Come on! Come on!

DOUGLASS. Mam, Mam, don't stay heah!

ABE [*raising* GOLDIE *from her chair*]. Go on wid him. You ain't to blame foh nothing.

[*He pushes her toward* DOUGLASS. *But she turns and throws her arms around him, clinging silently to his breast.*]

MUH MACK [*pulling* DOUGLASS]. I heahs 'em. Dat's dem coming.

[*With an anxious look at* GOLDIE, DOUGLASS *hurries with* MUH MACK *through the door and into the fields.* ABE *places* GOLDIE *back into her chair and stands looking at her. He catches her by the shoulders and shakes her.*]

ABE. Tell me, what is it, Goldie! What ails you, gal? [*She sits looking dumbly*

716

at him and he draws away from her. Presently there is a sound of stamping feet outside, and voices slip in like the whispering of leaves. A stone is thrown against the house, then another and another. One crashes through the window and strikes the lamp. The room is left in semi-darkness. ABE *with a sob of overwhelming terror falls upon his knees. Twisting his great hands together, he casts up his eyes and cries in a loud voice.*] God, God, where is you now! Where is you, God! [*He begins half sobbing and chanting.*] You has helped befo', help me now. Is you up dere? Heah my voice! [*Fear takes possession of him.*] Blast me, Lawd, in yo' thunder and lightning, if it is yo' will! Ketch me away in de whirlwind, foh I'm a sinner. Yo' will, yo' will, not mine. Let fiah and brimstone burn me to ashes and scatter me on de earf. [*Gasping.*] I've tried, I've tried to walk de path, but I'm po' and sinful. . . . Give me peace, rest—rest in yo' bosom—if it is dy will. Save me, Jesus, save me!

[*He falls sobbing to the floor.*]

Voice [*outside*]. Come out of there, you dirty nigger! [*A shudder runs through him, and his sobs grow less violent.*] Come out! Come out!

[*Another stone crashes through the room. As if ashamed of his weakness,* ABE *rises from the floor. He speaks firmly to the shadows.*]

ABE. In the end it was so intended. [*Looking around him.*] And I end here where I begun. [*He bursts out in a loud voice.*] Yet they're asleep, asleep, and I can't wake 'em!

VOICES.
He's in there.
I hear him talking.
He's done talking now, goddam him!
We'll show him the law all right.
He's got a gun!
Shoot him like a dog.

ABE [*wiping his brow and again speaking in the rôle of the educator trying to convince his everlastingly silent hearers*]. But they'll wake, they'll wake—a crack of thunder and deep divided from deep—a light! A light, and it will be! [GOLDIE *still sits hunched over in her chair. As he speaks he goes to the door at the left.*] We got to be free, freedom of the soul and of the mind. Ignorance means sin and sin means destruction. [*Shouting.*] Freedom! Freedom! [*Lifting up his voice.*] Yea, yea, it was writ, "Man that is born of woman is of few days and full of trouble. . . ." Lak de wind wid no home. Ayh, ayh, nigger man, nigger man——[*He opens the door.*] I go talk to 'em, I go meet 'em——

VOICE. Hell! Look out! There he is!

ABE. Yea, guns and killings is in vain. [*He steps out on the porch.*] What we need is to—to—[*His words are cut short by a roar from several guns. He staggers and falls with his head in the doorway*]—and we must have—have——

[*At the sound of the guns,* GOLDIE *springs to her feet. For an instant everything is still. Then several shots are fired into* ABE's *body.*]

VOICE. Quit the shooting. He's dead as a damned door! Now everybody get away from here—no talking, no talking. Keep quiet—quiet.

[*There is the sound of shuffling footsteps and men leaping the fence. Voices come back into the room.*]

VOICES.

717

Yeh, mum's it.

He won't raise no more disturbances!

[*The voices grow more faint.*]

What a bloody murder he done!

He's still now, by God!

It's the only way to have peace, peace.

Peace, by God!

[GOLDIE *moves toward the door where* ABE *lies. Halfway across the room she stops and screams and then drops down beside his body.*

The wind blows through the house setting the sparks flying.]

(1926)

FOLK TALES

The Bell Witch of Tennessee and Mississippi

A written version of the legend of the Bell Witch appeared as early as 1894, when M. V. Ingram published in Clarksville, Tennessee, An Authenticated History of the Famous Bell Witch: The wonder of the 19th Century, and Unexplained Phenomenon of the Christian Era: The Mysterious Talking Goblin that Terrorized the West End of Robertson County, Tennessee, Tormenting John Bell to His Death: The Story of Betsy Bell, Her Lover and the Haunting Sphinx. When Donald Davidson began teaching near the home of the Bell family in Springfield, Tennessee, in 1910, he frequently heard versions of the legend about the Witch, and in 1930, Harriet Parks Miller published The Bell Witch of Middle Tennessee, *again in Clarksville. The text selected for this volume was collected and written by Arthur Palmer Hudson and Peter Kyle McCarter in 1934.*

Back in the days before the War there lived somewhere in old North Carolina a man by the name of John Bell. Bell was a planter and was well-fixed. He had a good-sized plantation and a dozen niggers of field-hand age, and mules and cows and hogs a-plenty. His family was made up of his wife, a daughter thirteen or

718

From The Journal of American Folklore, *Vol. XLVII, 1934, collected by Arthur Palmer Hudson and Peter Kyle McCarter. Reprinted by permission of the American Folklore Society. The collectors' footnotes have been omitted.*

fourteen years old they say was mighty pretty, and two or three young-uns that don't figure much in this story. Until he hired him an overseer, Bell got along fine.

The overseer was a Simon Legree sort of fellow, always at sixes and sevens with other folks, and especially with the niggers. He didn't even mind jawing with his boss. They say Mr. Bell was half a mind to fire the scoundrel and hire another one. But he tended to his business. He had a way with the women-folks. Some say he had an eye open for Mary, the daughter. And Mrs. Bell stood up for him. So he stayed on for a good while, and the longer he stayed the uppiter he got. Whenever he and Bell had a row—and their rows got bigger and bitterer—the overseer went out and blacksnaked three or four niggers, for they were the only critters in the shape of man that he could abuse without a come-back. He was the worst kind of a bully, and a man of high temper, in fact, a regular overseer of the kind you hear about in Yankee stories.

Mr. Bell had a tall temper too, and the men did not spend a lot of time patting each other on the back and bragging about each other's good points. A stand-up fight was bound to come off.

It did. Some say it was about the way the overseer had beat up one of the niggers. Some say it was about something Mr. Bell heard and saw from behind a cotton-house one day when Mary rode through the field where the overseer was working a gang of niggers. Bell went away blowing smoke from his pistol barrel, and mumbling something about white trash. The overseer didn't go away at all.

Of course Bell was brought into court, but he plead self-defense, and the jury let him off. He went home, hired him another overseer, and allowed that everything was settled. But the truth was that everything was now plumb unsettled.

That year and the next and the next the crops on the Bell place were an out-an-out failure: bumblebee cotton and scraggly tobacco and nubbin corn. His mules died of colic or some strange disease like it. His cows and hogs got sick of something the horse-doctors couldn't cure. He had to sell his niggers one by one, all except an old woman. Finally he went broke. He got what he could for his land—lock, stock, and barrel—and moved with his family to Tennessee. They say that where he settled down the town of Bell, Tennessee, was named for him. Anyway, he bought him a house and a patch of land near the home of old Andy Jackson, who had knocked off from being President and was living in a big house called The Hermitage.

Not long after the move to Tennessee, strange things began to happen in the Bell home. The children got into the habit of tumbling, or being tumbled, out of bed at least once a week, and of waking up every morning with every stitch of the bed-clothes snatched off and their hair all tangled and mussed up. Now for young-uns to tumble out of bed and to wake up in the mornings with their heads uncombed is a mighty strange thing, and the Bells realized it. The children couldn't explain this carrying-on, for they were always asleep till they hit the floor; and it was a peculiar fact that they were never tumbled out while awake.

The old nigger woman told them it was the ha'nt of the overseer Mr. Bell had killed that was pestering the children. She was as superstitious as any other nigger, and she said she had always felt jubous about what the ha'nt of a man like the overseer would do. But she had spunk, and one day she allowed she would find out whether she was right by spending the night under the young-uns' bed.

719

In the middle of the night Mr. and Mrs. Bell were fetched out of their bed by a squall like a pant'er's. When they lit a lamp and ran into the room, they found the old nigger woman sprawled in the middle of the floor, dripping cold sweat like an ash-hopper, her face gray-blue as sugar-cane peeling, and her eyes like saucers in a dish-pan. She was stiff-jointed and tongue-tied. When they got her sitting up and her tongue loosened, she screeched: "Hit's him! Hit's him! Fo' Gawd, hit's him! Hit peenched me all over, stuck pins in me, snatched de keenks outen ma haiuh, an' whup me, Lawd Gawd, how hit whup me, whup me limber an' whup me stiff, whup me jes' lack *him*. Ain' gwine back dauh no mo', ain' gwine back dauh no mo'.' "

The Bells were so scared they told some of the neighbors. Old Andy Jackson heard about it and decided to ride over. He didn't take any stock in ha'nts, and as he rode through the gate he spoke his mind out loud about tarnation fools that believed nigger tales about them. He hadn't got the words out of his mouth before something whaled him over the head and skipped his hat twenty or thirty yards back down the road. Old Andy didn't say any more. He motioned his nigger boy to hand him his hat, and he went away from there.

It seems like the Witch could get hungry like folks, and was satisfied with folks' grub. But it had to be the best. One day the old nigger woman came tearing into the front room where Mrs. Bell was quilting and said the Witch was back in the kitchen drinking up all the sweet milk.

Mrs. Bell was scared and said the old woman was lying.

"Come see fo' yo'se'f, missus. Come see fo' yo'se'f. Ah was back dauh a-mixin' up de biscuit, an' Ah retched ovah to git a cup o' miu'k, an' fo' Gawd, de cup was in de middle o' de auh, an' de miu'k was a-runnin' rat outen hit—an' hit wa'n't gwine nowheah, missus—hit wa'n't gwine nowheah. Jes' run outen de cup, an' den Ah couldn' see hit no mo'.' "

"You're just seeing things," said Mrs. Bell.

"Jes' whu Ah ain' doin'—ain' seein' de miu'k. Go on back in de kitchen efen you don' believe hit. Go on back dauh an' look fo' yo'se'f. . . . No, ma'am, Ah hain' gwine back in dat place. No, ma'am, dat ha'nt kin guzzle an' bile up all de miu'k de cows evah give 'fo' Ah raise mah finger to stop hit."

Mrs Bell went back into the kitchen and looked. There was a cup there that had had milk in it, and the milk was gone, sure as shootin'. She was now as scared as the old nigger woman, and sent right away for her husband to come out of the field.

They couldn't figure out how a ghost could drink milk, or what becomes of the milk if he does. Does the milk dry up into the ghost of itself? If not, where does it go when the ghost swallows it? Ghosts can't be seen. At least, this one couldn't. They could see through where it was. If they could see through it, why couldn't they see the milk as plain when it was inside the ghost as when it was outside? The old nigger woman said the milk was running out of the cup, but it "wa'n't gwine nowheah." An old Holy Roller preacher from down in Talla-hatchie bottom who rode over to talk about it argued that if the old woman's tale was so milk must be of a higher class than folks. When it turns into the soul of itself, it leaves nothing behind; but folks leave behind a corpse that must be covered up with dirt right away. Folks argued about it on front galleries in the summer time and around the fire in winter—but they didn't argue about it on the Bells' front gallery or by the Bells' fire. And the preachers preached about it at camp meetings.

But the Witch didn't let up on the Bells' grub. No one ever saw it; but lots of times some member of the family would see something to eat dive out of the cupboard or pop out of the safe. The Witch's favorite was cream, and he got to skimming it from every pan in the spring-house. The Bells were never able to get any butter from the churning.

Mr. Bell might have stood for having his young-uns' rest disturbed and his old nigger woman all tore up this way, but he couldn't stand for letting the ghost eat him out of house and home. So he called the family together and allowed he would move again—this time to Mississippi, where land was rich and cheap. Mrs. Bell raised up.

"Pa," said she, "it seems like to me we have been gettin' along tolerable well here. I don't see any use moving away. What would be to keep the Witch from following us down there?"

"Nothing in the world," spoke up a hide-bottomed chair from a corner of the room. "I'll follow you wherever you go," the Chair went on. "And I'll tell you what: if you stay on here, I won't bother you much; but if you go traipsing off to Mississippi—well, you'll wish you hadn't."

Mr. Bell was scared and bothered, but he studied a while and screwed up his courage enough to ask the Witch why he couldn't live where he pleased. But there was no answer. He asked some more questions. But the Chair had lapsed into the habit of silence that chairs have.

Mary, Mr. Bell's daughter, was now old enough to argue with the old folks about things. She was pretty as a spotted puppy, they say, and had lots of spunk and took after her pa. She sided with him. Girls always like to be moving. So when the family got over its scare about the Chair they argued back and forth. But finally Mrs. Bell and what they remembered about the Witch got the upper hand. Mr. Bell and Mary gave up the idea of moving to Mississippi—for a while anyway.

And for a while the Witch eased up on them. It even did some good turns. One day Mr. Bell was talking of visiting a family across the creek where he had heard everybody was sick. "I have just come from there," said a Voice from the eight-day clock, and went on to tell how well everybody was and what everybody was doing. Later Mr. Bell met up with a member of the family and learned that everything the Witch said was so.

Maybe because she had taken sides with him in the argument about going to Mississippi, the Witch was partial to Mrs. Bell. The old nigger woman said the ha'nt sided with her because she had stood up for the overseer when Mr. Bell wanted to fire him in North Carolina.

One Christmas time the family was invited to a taffy-pulling. Mrs. Bell was sick and couldn't go. They talked about whether they ought to go off and leave their mammy feeling poorly. Mr. Bell was invited too, and they needed him to do the driving; so Mary and the children begged him to take them. Mrs. Bell told them to go ahead, she didn't need them and could make out all right. So they all piled into the wagon and started.

But before they got far one of the wagon wheels flew off and let the axle down into the road with a bump. It looked like a common accident, and the old man

721

climbed down and put the wheel back on the axle and stuck the linchpin in. He looked at all the other linchpins and saw they were on all right. Before long another wheel flew off. They looked on the ground for the linchpin but couldn't find it there. Mr. Bell whittled a new one, and when he went to put the wheel back on he found the old one in place. He fixed the wheel and drove off again, telling all of the children to watch all of the wheels. Soon they saw something like a streak of moonshine dart around the wagon, and all four wheels flew off, and the wagon dropped kersplash into a mud-hole. They put them back on, turned round, and drove back home, going quiet and easy, like sitting on eggs.

When they got there, they found their mammy sitting up by the Christmas tree eating a plate of fresh strawberries, and feeling lots better.

Other pranks were laid to the Witch. Often when the old man and the boys would go to the stable to catch the horses and mules for the day's plowing or a trip to town, the critters would back their ears and rare and kick and stomp like hornets or yellow-jackets were after them. Some morning they would be puny as chickens with the pip, and caked with sweat and mud, and their manes and tales tangled in witch-locks. The neighbors said that off and on they met an unbridled and barebacked horse, and the horse would stop, and something on his back that they couldn't see would talk to them—but not long—they had business the other way.

Maybe because Mary had sided with her pa against her mammy and the Witch, the Witch was harder on her after the argument than on anybody else. She would wake up in the middle of the night, screaming and crying that something cold and heavy had been sitting on her breast, sucking her breath and pressing the life out of her.

One time she was getting ready to go to a play-party. Some of the young sprouts were waiting for her in the front room. While she was combing her long, black hair, it suddenly was full of cuckleburs. She tugged and pulled and broke the comb to untangle it, and when she couldn't, she leaned on the bureau and cried.

"I put them in your hair," said the Witch from the looking-glass. "You've got no business going to the party. Stay here with me. I can say sweet things to you."

She screamed, and the young fellows rushed in the room, and when she told them about the Voice they shot at the glass with their pistols. But the glass didn't break. And the Witch caught every bullet and pitched it into their vest pockets and laughed. So they called it a draw and went out of there. And Mary stayed at home.

Mary was now mighty near grown. She had turned out to be a beautiful woman. She had lots of beaux. But whenever one of them screwed himself up to the point of popping the question he always found that the words stuck in his throat and his face and ears burned. For young fellows these were strange signs. But it was always that way. And none of them seemed to be able to ask Mary the question. They laid it on the Witch, and finally quit hitching their horses to the Bell fence.

All but one. His name was Gardner. He was a catch for any girl, smart as a briar, good-looking, easy-going and open-hearted, and the owner of rich bottom land, a passel of niggers, and a home as big as the courthouse, with columns as

722

tall and white. He got all wrapped up in Mary, and they say Mary was leaning to him.

The way of the Witch with him was different, more businesslike. Maybe it was because the Witch realized this was the man Mary was setting her heart on. One night when Gardner was walking up the row of cedars in the Bell yard to see Mary, something he couldn't see reached out from a big cedar and touched him on the shoulder, and a voice said, "Wait a minute." Gardner was afraid to wait, but he was more afraid to run. So he waited.

"You might as well understand, here and now, that you are not going to have Mary Bell."

"Why not?" Gardner asked.

"You might have guessed from all that's happened round here. I'm in love with her myself. It's going to be hard to get her consent, and it may be harder to get the old man's. But she's not going to marry you. I'll see to that. If you open your mouth about it to-night, you'll be dead as a door-nail before morning."

Gardner studied a while and said, "If you'd only come out like a man."

The cedar tree stepped out and snatched his hat off and stomped it.

"Well, I reckon I'll have to lay off for a while," says Gardner. "But I do love her, and I'd go to the end of the world for . . . ."

"Well, you don't have to go that far, and it wouldn't do you any good if you did, and if you love her the only way you can keep her out of hell is to get out yourself. If you keep on hanging round here, I'll make it hell for you. Now this is how far you go. Pack up your traps and get out of the country, hide and hair. Go any place you think the Bells won't hear tell of you—and go before breakfast. If you slip out quiet without raising any rookus I'll never pester you again. What's more, on the day you get married I'll give you a pair of new boots you'll be proud of all your life."

Gardner couldn't see why the Witch's promise of a pair of wedding boots was in the same class as the threat of death before breakfast, but he didn't split hairs, and he didn't argue any more. He picked up his hat, sneaked back to his horse, and rode off.

He never said or wrote a thing to the Bells about what had happened, part because he was scared, but more because he was ashamed of being scared. He left the neighborhood before sunup and moved to the western part of the state. He got somebody else to sell out for him. They say the town of Gardner, where he settled, was named after him when he got old and respected.

After he had been there a while he fell in love with a girl and got engaged to her. And they say that when he was dressing for the wedding he couldn't find his boots. He looked high and low, every place a pair of boots was liable to be and lots of places where they couldn't possibly be, but no boots could he find. He was about to give up and go to his wedding in his sock feet, when a Voice told him to crawl out from under the bed and look in the bed. And there between the sheets he found a pair of shiny new boots. He put them on and went his way rejoicing and thinking of how well a ghost kept his word, and wondering if the boots would ever wear out and if they were like the Seven-League boots he had read about in old McGuffey.

But they looked like natural boots. He told some of his friends how he had got them. They thought he was a liar. But they had to own up they were wrong. One day Gardner's house-boy made a mistake and carried them instead of another pair to a cobbler. The cobbler said they were in perfect shape, that they were not made by mortal hands, and that the soles were sewed on in a way that no man or man-made machine could have stitched them. And there is a lady in this neighborhood who has seen the boots.

While Gardner's mind was getting mossed over about Mary, Mr. Bell decided again to move to Mississippi. It looked like his move from North Carolina was jumping from the frying pan into the fire, but he figured maybe the skillet wouldn't be any hotter. Gardner's break-up with Mary and Mary not marrying hung heavy on his mind. Mrs. Bell raised up again, telling him about rolling stones. And the Witch horned in. By this time the family got used to the Witch and would talk free with him, but respectful. Every time the question came up there was a row between Mr. Bell and Mary on one side and Mrs. Bell and the Witch on the other. The old nigger woman told Mr. Bell the ha'nt didn't want him to move because he was afraid of witch hunters in Mississippi. She said there were powerful ones down there.

And so one winter after the crops had petered out on him again, he sold his place dirt cheap. But the old nigger woman told him to wait till spring to start. She said Easter was early that year and there would be plenty of time to pitch a crop. Good Friday would be a good day to leave, she said, for the ha'nt would have to go back to his grave and stay three days under the ground and would be puny-like several days more. While he was in good working order he could be in two or three places at once and be in any of them in the bat of an eye, but then he would have to lie low, and that would give them plenty of start. So Mr. Bell early on Good Friday stacked his furniture and duds in a couple of wagons, climbed into the front one with Mary, put the old nigger woman and his biggest boy into the hind one, and told Mrs. Bell, "Git in with old Patsy if you're a-comin', and don't forgit the young-uns."

And that was the way the Bell family came to Mississippi. Mr. Bell bought him a little place in Panola County, ten miles east of Batesville on the Oxford road. He was all ready to begin life over again without supernatural interference.

But the Witch made a quick come-back, not before the family got there, but before they moved into their new home.

When Mr. Bell first got to Batesville, or Panola as they called it then, he left the family there and went out to look at the land he aimed to buy. When he got a place that suited him, he went back to town for his family and stuff. There was some sort of hitch, and the wagons did not get started till late in the evening. As the wagons moved slowly out of town, dark clouds began to roll up in the south and west, and before they had gone three miles the storm broke. Dark came on earlier than usual, for the clouds hid the sun. The rain beat down on the wagon covers. Every now and then the lightning flashes lit up the swaying trees on each side of the road, the draggle-tailed horses, and the road itself,—a long, muddy creek,—and then it was dark as a stack of black cats. The folks all stopped talking. There was nothing to listen to but the beating rain and the thunder and the suck of the horses' feet and the wheels in the mud.

All at once the hind wagon, with the family in it, slid to the side of the road and sunk into the mud up to the bed. Mr. Bell saw it in a lightning flash and came back. It couldn't be moved; the horses had no foothold, and the wheels were in too deep. The fix they were in wasn't dangerous, but it was mighty uncomfortable.

And then the Witch took a hand.

"If you'll go back to your wagon and stop your cussin'," said the empty dark beside the wagon, "I'll get you out. Hump it back to your wagon now—light a shuck!"

Mr. Bell waded back and crawled in.

And then the horses and the wagon and the furniture and the family and the dog under the wagon and the calf tied behind and everything else but the mud on the wheels riz up about eight feet high and floated down the road till they were just behind the front wagon, and then they settled down easy and went on home without any trouble.

The family got settled down in their two-story double-loghouse amongst the cedars on the Oxford road.

A few nights later, the Witch spoke up from one of the andirons and told Mr. and Mrs. Bell he was in love with Mary. He said he wanted to marry her. Mr. Bell was shocked and surprised. He explained, respectful but emphatic like, that he could never dream of letting a daughter of his marry a ghost, not even so noble a ghost like the one he was talking with.

"I got a claim on you, John Bell," said the Witch. "I got a claim on you and on yours. I got a claim." And his voice was deep and hollowlike.

This was a point Mr. Bell maybe didn't want to hear any more about. So he said, "Have you spoken to Mary?"

"No, not spoken."

"Well, how do you know she would have you?"

"I don't. But I haven't got any reason to believe she wouldn't love me. She's never seen me. She doesn't know whether she would or not. Maybe she would consider it an honor to be married to a ghost. Not many girls are, you know. Why, it would make her famous."

"I don't want any daughter of mine getting famous that way. And besides, what if you were to have children? What in the world do you reckon they'd be like? Like you or her? Maybe half good human meat and bone, and the other half sight unseen. Or maybe they'd be the vanishin' kind and goin' round here and raisin' hell invisible. Do you think I want a passel of soap-suds young-uns floatin' round here and poppin' up into puffs of wind every time I p'inted to the stovewood pile or sprouts on a ditch bank? Not on your life. I reckon plain flesh and blood's good enough for Mary."

"But, John Bell, I love Mary. And remember. Remember."

"So do I, and that's why I'm not a-goin' to let you marry her. Why, when she got old and hard-favored I reckon you'd quit her for some young hussy. You could do it easy enough. Mary'd have a hard time keepin' up with a stack of wind and a voice, and I'd have a hard time trackin' down and shootin' a low-down, no-count dust devil. When Mary marries, she marries a man that's solid and alive in body."

"I gather, John Bell, that you're opposed to me courting your daughter. But she's the one to say, and I'm going to talk to her about it. You'll be my father-in-law yet, or you'll be a-mourning, a-mourning."

725

"But what kind of wedding would it be like?" Mrs. Bell put in. "Think of it. Mary standing in front of the preacher and the preacher saying, 'Do you take this woman?' to a vase of flowers. And the ring floating down to Mary from the hanging-lamp maybe, or rising up from under a bench. I won't stand for it. I've stood for a lot of things, and you can't say I haven't been a friend to you. But I won't stand for Mary being a laughing-stock and disgrace to the family."

"If we're a-goin' to add to this family," Mr. Bell took up, "we're a-goin' to be able to see what we're addin'. I don't even know what shape you've got, if any."

"Oh, I can give you some idea what shape I have. I'll let you shake hands with me. But you must promise not to squeeze. We're very delicate, especially when we touch folks. Here, hold out your hand, and I'll put mine in it."

Mr. Bell held out his hand, felt something, and grabbed it. It was, he said later, the hand of a new-born baby—soft and crinkly and warm and just about the size of a new-born baby's hand.

"How big are you all over?" he asked.

"I can't tell you that."

"Well, there's one other thing I want to know. How do you get into this house any time you want to when every window and door is locked and barred? Do you ooze through the walls?"

"No. It's a lot easier than that. If you'll watch the corner of the ceiling up there, you'll see."

And all the rest of his life Mr. Bell swore to trustworthy witnesses that he saw the corner of the ceiling raised a good three feet and then let down again —all without the slightest racket.

"Do you mean to tell me that anything with a hand like that can h'st the top off of the house that a-way?"

"Sure," came the answer. "But—about Mary. I'm going to talk to her right off."

"Don't," said Mr. Bell. "Do you want to drive her crazy?"

But the meeting was over, for there was no answer. And the fire had died down, and the andiron looked glum.

The story is kind of skimpy here. Nobody seems to know what the Witch said to Mary or what Mary said to the Witch.

But the family noticed next day that she was drooping and wasn't minding what was going on around her. For days she wandered about the house and up and down the yard under the gloomy old cedars, like somebody sleep-walking. And the color left her face, and deep in her wide-open black eyes was a far-away look, like she was trying to see something that ought to be but wasn't there. Every day she got up later and went to bed earlier.

And finally there came a day when she didn't get up at all. In the evening a screech-owl hollered in a cedar right by the gallery.

That night her fever was high, and by midnight she was raving. "We've put off seein' a doctor too long," said Mrs. Bell.

"The roads like they are, it'll take me two hours goin' and him and me two

726

hours comin'," said Mr. Bell. "It'll be might' nigh daylight before we get back. But I reckon you're right, and I'll go as quick as I can saddle a horse."

"No use," said a Voice. "All the doctors and medicines in the world won't cure her. But if you want one, I'll get him, and get him a lot quicker than you can."

The doctor got there just as the old eight-day clock struck one. "I heard somebody hollering at my window about midnight, telling me to come out here right away. When I got to the door, nobody was there; but I thought I'd better come anyway." He was a young doctor just starting out. "Say, what kind of road overseer and gang do you fellows have out this way? Last time I came over this road, about Christmas, it was the worst I ever saw. Why, I picked up a Stetson hat in the middle of a mud-hole near the four-mile board, and by George there was a man under it. 'You're in the middle of a bad fix, old man,' I said. 'Hell,' he said, 'that ain't nothin' to the fix this mule's in under me.' I had to lift up my feet half the way to keep them from dragging in the mud by the horse's belly. But to-night my horse skimmed over it in an hour. Well, who's sick out here?"

"It's her mind and nerves," he told them after he had questioned them and examined Mary. "I won't conceal from you, she's in pretty bad shape. And medicine won't do her any good. You've just got to be gentle and careful with her. Humor her and be patient with her. I'll give her something to put her to sleep when she gets like this. Watch her close and don't let her get lonesome. She's young and strong and ought to come round in time."

But she never did. For a month she lay there on the bed, looking at nothing and yet straining to see something. Something too far off. At night her pa and ma took turns sitting up. They didn't want the neighbors in. They called the doctor back a few times, but he shook his head and said he couldn't do any more. So they would watch and wait, wanting to do something, but helpless.

One night her ma was sitting there, holding Mary's hand and stroking the dark hair back from her forehead. Suddenly Mary pushed her mother away and sat up and looked across the foot of the bed, as if somebody was standing there.

"Mamma," she whispered, "Mamma. . . . I see him . . . at last . . . And I think . . . I think . . . I'm going . . . to love him."

And she died with the only expression of happiness they had seen on her face in months.

Some folks have tried to explain Mary's strange death. A few say the Witch tortured her continually and kept her in such constant terror that her mind was affected. Others have heard that a school teacher ventriloquist that was jealous of Gardner played tricks on her and the family, and then when she wouldn't have him tormented and frightened her to death. Some believe she was in love with the overseer from the first, and then when he was killed she was in love with the Witch and didn't want to live because she knew she would never be happy with him until she too became a ghost.

But she died, just the same. And they say that on the day of the funeral, when the coffin was carried from the house to a wagon a great black bird flew down from the sky and hung in the air just above the wagon. And around its

727

neck was a bell that tolled in the mournfullest tone ever heard by the ear of man. And when the funeral procession began to move, the great bird floated just in front of it all the way to the graveyard and circled round and round the grave during the burial, the bell tolling all the while. And when the mound was rounded up, the bird swung high up in the air and flew away to the west and finally became just a little speck above the treetops and disappeared. But long after it was gone the mourning notes of the bell floated back to those who stood and watched. (*1934*)

Fiddler's Dram

Talk about your fiddlers—why, in yonder's times we *had* fiddlers around here! None of your modern-age make-shifters that whip all the tunes till a body can't tell "Rabbit in the Pea Patch" from "Bull Amongst the Yearlings." Nor in them days they didn't make the fiddle sound like a jug full of hungry mosquitoes, neither! No siree! They just made the sweetest music this direction from heaven.

And in all yonder time I verily know there never was a finer hand to fiddle than Ples Haslock. He fiddled for all the square dances and play-parties anywheres around. No gathering of whatever kind amounted to much unless Ples was there, with his long solemn face and them light blue far-shot eyes, patting his foot and ripping away on his fiddle and calling the figgers.

> "*Gents, hands in your pockets, back to the wall,*
> *Take a chaw tobaccer and balance all!*
> *Ladies, do-se-do with the gents you know,*
> *Swing your corner and-a here we go!*"

He wasn't no old billygoat fiddler with crazy ways and a cracked voice. He was right young and by nature handsome. All the girls sighed, but Ples just didn't deal in women. He said, "Give me my fiddle and a place to pat my foot and they's nothing else in creation I crave." His daddy had got an old fiddlebox in a bunch of junk he'd traded from an Irish Gypsy for a nag is how Ples got started fiddling. He made his own strings out of catamount guts and the bow from the tail hairs of mare colts. Then he teached his self to fiddle till he laid it plumb over any of the old heads.

Since his daddy died, Ples lived at home by his self over near Post Oak, but he was a man that just didn't stay home much. He liked to ramble and visit around. Wheresoever he went, he was twice as welcome as anybody. He had word of all the latest things and happenings and he could keep a family spell-charmed to the midwarp of the night telling tales he made out of his head. He'd make the young'uns eldershoot flutes and cornstalk fiddles, and, when asked to, he'd get out his own old fiddle and make it talk—I *mean* talk! You'd sweared to hear it that there was a live mockingbird singing in that fiddlebox or a buzzing cowfly or maybe a little peeping chicken. He could take and mock

From God Bless the Devil: Liars' Bench Tales, *collected by James R. Aswell, University of North Carolina Press, 1940.*

cats fighting or old gossip women gabbing till folks fell in the floor laughing. And he could fiddle the old tunes to where the meanest man in the county would break under and cry all down his face.

Nothing was too good for Ples Haslock when he visited around. He was welcomed by high and low as long as he wanted to stay and they begged him to stop longer when he fancied to go.

They had fiddling contests then, but it got so there wasn't a heap of contest to them. Everybody come to know that Ples Haslock was going to win hands down. He always walked off with the gallon jimmyjohn of fine oak-chartered drinking whiskey they give for the prize. Why, it come to the point where they had to give another jug for second prize or they'd never had nobody in the contest but Ples. The other fiddlers only tried to outbeat each other. None of them had any show at all against Ples and they purely all knowed it.

So what happened one time but the wall of the jail at Dukedom fell out and the county court didn't have no money in the poke to fix it. When the squires figgered to get up a fiddling contest to raise the money, everybody says, "We'll have to send over to Post Oak and tell Ples Haslock and notify him."

Coot Kersey was the best fiddler near and around Dukedom and Coot says, "He may can't come this time. I hear he's a sick man. Down with heart dropsy is what I hear."

"Don't you *hope* so, Coot?" they says, and laughed him to a fair deadstand.

The County Court Clerk says, "I've got to drive my rig over to Post Oak on business tomorrow. I'll tell Ples and notify him."

So the County Court Clerk dropped his hitching block in front of Ples Haslock's the next day and called, "Heyo! You to home, Ples?"

Nobody answered him, so he walked through the weeds to the house, a one-room shack that looked like a good strong puff of air would blow it over. The clapboards was dropping off and the shingles curled up every which way like the feathers of an old Dominecker hen.

When the County Court Clerk climbed the shaky steps to the porch, Ples woke up inside and said, "Who's there?"

"Just me," says the County Court Clerk and give out his name.

"Well come right in!" says Ples. "Ain't seen you since I don't rightly know when. How're you folks living at Dukedom?"

"Pretty fair, Ples. Can't complain."

The room was one big clutteration of old clothes, pots and pans, and junk, and Ples was setting up in a mess of dirty comforts on his bed at the far end.

Everything else might be knocking around just anywheres it lit, but Ples didn't care a whet so long as his fiddle was safe. He never let go of that fiddle— had it now beside him in bed, running his fingers over it like you'd pet a child. It give the County Court Clerk a shock to see how like death Ples looked, green-faced and shrunk, with big brown liver splotches on his face and hands. He had gone down mightily, but his eyes was just as blue-bright as ever. His nose looked natural. It always had been big and bony.

County Court Clerk said, "How're you feeling, Ples?"

"Well," says he, "I could say I was down in the back. I could say I don't know what I'd do if it wasn't for them kind people that neighbor me round. I could say it and I *do* say it. Three times a day some good neighbor woman

729

brings me some nice something to eat and sets a spell talking. The menfolks come over at night and see that I ain't fell out of bed to my harm. Between whiles, I just lay around and play my fiddle."

"I'd heared you was ailing," says the County Court Clerk.

"It's for a fact," says Ples. "Heart dropsy runs in the Haslock line. Here of late I've been having night flotations too. But seems like I'm coming around some. Aim to be up and on my feet soon."

The County Court Clerk was of two minds whether to tell him about the contest but now he figgered it wouldn't do no harm. So he come out about the jail wall and the contest and notified Ples that it would be held at the Dukedom school two weeks come a Monday.

Minute he heard that, Ples peartened up mightily. "I'll be there!" he says. "When the roll is called at Dukedom, Ples Haslock will be there certain sure!"

So the County Court Clerk visited awhile and then had to be on his way. "We'll be looking for you, Ples," he says.

"Get your fiddler's dram ready," says Ples, "for I virtuously aim to win it."

Well, the night of the contest most everybody in the county come to Dukedom in their Sunday best and tramped into the schoolhouse and settled in their seats. Everybody was in a looking-forward mood. You know how them gatherings are. A heap of shouting and high joking back and forth. Old gossip-trots running from one group to another with the latest. Young bloods standing around talking loud and the girls giggling and sneaking looks at them. Little mustards running up and down the aisles, snatching things from each other, having rooster-fights at the back of the hall, and raising a general rumpus. Little girls setting with their folks and sticking out their tongues at the boys when nobody was looking. Babies crying, people coughing, and the lye soap smell pretty strong.

The crowd was getting restless. Little boys, and some not so little, begun whistling and banging desks for things to get started.

Old Judge Huley Dunlap was the chairman of the committee and he come out on the stage and give out that the contest was fixing to start. Then he put on his glasses and read off the names of the fiddlers, seven in all.

When he got through, everybody commenced yelling, "How about Ples Haslock?"

"Well," says Judge Dunlap, "we'd hoped he could make it, but till yet he ain't showed up. He's been laid up in bed lately and I reckon he couldn't stand the trip over here from Post Oak. Anybody that wants to can get their admission back at the door."

Some folks grumbled but everybody stayed set and things quieted down.

So the seven fiddlers come out on the stage and taken seats and the contest was ready to break out.

Everybody knowed that five of the seven fiddlers might as well not have got in the contest. They was plain everyday set-in-a-rocker-and-scratch-aways. The contest was between Coot Kersey and Old Rob Reddin, number six and seven. With Ples Haslock down and out, Coot and Old Rob was the best fiddlers you could find anywhere around and about in the county. Everybody figgered Old Rob was the likely one, not because his fiddling was fancier than Coot's but because of the crazy way he carried on.

The five sorry fiddlers sawed away and got through without nobody paying attention in special. Coot and Old Rob would do the real fiddling and they come last.

There was a big laugh when Coot's turn come. Everybody always felt like laughing when they saw Coot. The way his head bobbed up and down on his long red wrinkled neck with every step he took, the way his chin ran back and his nose beaked out, and the way a long tag of his hair kept wattling down to the bridge of his nose put everybody in mind of an old turkey gobbler. Coot gobbled when he talked, too.

But one thing sure—Coot could make a fiddle sing. He was the dead serious kind of fiddler. Had to have his fiddle set just right across his knees before he'd commence, but let him get started and he sure fiddled. His piece was "Leather Britches." He went at it like a boy killing snakes, whipping and scraping away and stamping his foot till he'd worked up a pouring sweat. When he'd finished, he was as limp as an old rag. He drawed down a powerful claphand from the listeners.

The gathering set up smart when it come Old Rob Reddin's turn and he hobbled to the front of the stage. Folks started grinning before he'd done a thing. Old Rob was as funny to look at as Coot Kersey, but not because he put you in mind of no bird or animal. He was a lard-fat little man and when he walked his stomach wobbled in front of him. He'd never been heard to open his mouth without some real funny humor-saying rolling out. If ever by accident he was to have a mournful spell and say anything serious, people would've laughed at him just the same. Seeing Old Rob meant laughing like falling in the creek meant getting wet.

So Old Rob he plumped his self down in the fiddler's chair. He laid his fiddle on his lap and winked at his wife that was setting down front. All on a sudden he yelled, "Hold to your seats, folks! I'm driving wild!"

He give the gathering time to stop howling. Then he lit in fiddling "Hell Turned Loose in Georgia." The way he carried on, a body'd thought he was having some sort of fit if they hadn't knowed better. When he drawed a high note he'd open his mouth wide, run his eyebrows to his hairline, and shoot his neck up. On low ones he'd bend almost to the floor. Every once in so often he'd throw his bow into the air. While it was coming down he'd bawl out things like "*Eating* hogeye!" and "I *love* chittlins!" and "Ladies, where *was* your man last Saturday night!"

Everybody was still shouting and stamping and whistling when Old Rob come down off the platform. No need to hold the jimmyjohn over the different fiddlers' heads to see who'd get the most applauding. A deaf and dumb blind man could easy see Old Rob had that contest.

Like everybody, the judges was so taken up with watching Old Rob cut capers because he'd won that they didn't see Ples Haslock till he'd already started playing. The first anybody knowed he was anywheres about was when a fiddle begun on the stage.

The crowd looked to see who it was, and there sat Ples in the chair with his fiddle across his knees, his bow weaving over the strings, and his foot patting steady. Yes, there he set with his eyes shut and his head nodding in time with his foot.

731

It was a dumbfounder, all right. For just a minute the gathering thought maybe they was seeing things. But there he was, Ples Haslock, all drawed and pale from sickness, fiddling in the contest just a snatch before it was too late.

The minute folks seen it *was* Ples, the hall got still as time in a grave.

It was about nine o'clock when Ples started in and he fiddled over an hour. It was straight honest fiddling—none of your stunts on the strings like Coot Kersey, none of that loud fool-blabber that was Old Rob Reddin's stock in trade.

Folks there had heard fiddlers that could make them laugh and fiddlers that could make them cry, but Ples this night didn't do neither one. When you listened to him you nearly forgot who you was. You just set limp in your seat while your mind tried to remember something cloudy and away far off, something you'd never really seen or done.

Ples played "Poor Wayfaring Stranger" and "The Two Sisters" and "The Elfin Knight" and a dozen or more.

When Ples Haslock did stop, it verily did look like the crowd was going to tear the whole place down and scatter the pieces. They heaved to their feet and whooped, whistled, screamed, and bellered and hammered on the desks. Kept it up while Judge Huley Dunlap handed Ples the jimmyjohn of fine red drinking whiskey and said, "I hereby present and award to Ples Haslock this prize which may he enjoy it as much as the good people of Dukedom done his fiddling." Leastways they seen Judge Dunlap's mouth flapping and knowed he was saying something like that.

Well, Ples stood up, holding his fiddle and his bow under his left arm and heisting the jimmyjohn with a crooked finger of his right hand. He flipped that jimmyjohn over his shoulder, jerked the corncob out of the mouth of it with his teeth, and taken a long pull, his fiddler's dram.

Right then come a crash. For the chair, the jimmyjohn and Ples and his fiddle all landed in a heap on the floor.

Man, woman, and child run up onto the stage. But Judge Huley Dunlap made them stand back. "Get a doctor!" he says. "This man is done for, or near it. I can't feel no heart-beat at all."

So they hushed down and stood looking at Ples where he laid there on the stage.

"Think of it!" they says. "Poor Ples coming thirty miles to Dukedom with the last life in him just to win this contest!"

"He sure was a man that liked to fiddle!"

"Would you look at his clothes," says somebody. "All covered with clay, they are. From the looks of it, he must have walked all the way and through the swamp at that."

They kept saying, "It's the beat of all ever happened in Dukedom!"

Before long the doctor come hustling in and knelt down and examined over Ples. He said, "How'd he get in here?"

So they told him. Judge Dunlap says, "He just keeled over dead before our eyes, poor man."

"Keeled over my granny!" says the doctor. "This here man has been dead for forty-eight hours at the very least. And from the clay he's got on his clothes, I'd say buried, too." (*1940*)

732

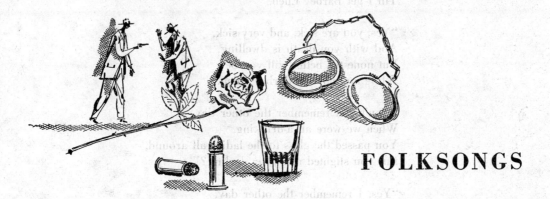

FOLKSONGS

Barbara Allen

Way down South where I came from
Is where I got my learning.
I fell in love with a pretty little girl,
And her name is Barbey Ellen.

I courted her for seven years,
And I asked her if she would marry.
With a bowed down head and a sweet little smile,
She never made no answer.

Early along in the spring,
When the red roses were blooming,
A young man on his death bed lay
For the love of Barbey Ellen.

He sent his servant to the town
To a place where she was dwelling:
"My master is love-sick and sent for you,
If your name is Barbey Ellen."

She slightly talked and slowly walked
And slowly went unto him.
"Young man, young man, I heard you were sick,
For the love of me, your darling."

"Yes, I am sick, and very sick
And with me death is dwelling

733

"Barbara Allen" from Folk-Songs from the Southern Highlands, *compiled by Mellinger Edward Henry. J. J. Augustin, publisher, 1938.*

And none the better will I be,
Till I get Barbey Ellen."

"Yes, you are sick, and very sick,
And with you death is dwelling,
But none the better will you be
While my name is Barbey Ellen.

"Don't you remember the other day
When we were all a-drinking,
You passed the glass to the ladies all around,
But you slighted me, your darling?"

"Yes, I remember the other day,
When we were all a-drinking:
I passed the glass to the ladies all around,
But all for you, my darling."

He turned his pale face to the wall,
His back he turned towards them:
"Adieu, adieu, to all this world,
But be kind to Barbey Ellen."

She had not rode five miles from town,
Till she heard the death bells ringing,
And every lick, it seemed to strike:
"Hard hearted Barbey Ellen."

She looked east, she looked west,
Till she saw the pale corpse coming:
"Lay him down, lay him down,
And let me look upon him."

The more she looked, the worse she got
Till she bursted out in crying:
"Young man, young man, you died for me,
I will die for you tomorrow."

They buried Sweet Willie in one church yard,
And Barbey in the other,
And out of Barbey's breast sprang a red, red rose,
And out of his a brier.

They grew and grew to such a length of height,
Till they could not grow no higher;
And there they tied in a true-lover's knot
And the rose run around the brier.

Lord Thomas and Fair Eleandor

"Come rede us fathers, come rede us mothers,
Come riddle us two in one,
Say shall I bring the brown girl home
And leave fair Eleandor alone?"

"The brown girl, she has house and land,
Fair Eleandor, she has none.
Therefore, I charge you with my blessings
To bring the brown girl home."

He called out his waiting maids,
By one, by two, by three,
"Go bridle and saddle my milk-white steed,
Fair Eleandor I must see."

He rode till he came to fair Eleandor's house,
He tingled at the ring.
There was none more ready than fair Eleandor herself,
To rise and let him in.

"Bad news, bad news, bad news," said he,
"Bad news I have brought to thee,
I have come to invite you to my wedding,
And that is bad news to thee."

"Lord Thomas, Lord Thomas, Lord Thomas," said she,
"Bad news you have brought me,
For I thought I was to be the bride,
And you the bridegroom were to be.

"Come rede us fathers, come rede us mothers,
Come riddle us both in one,
Say shall I go to Lord Thomas's wedding,
Or shall I stay at home?"

She called out her waiting maids,
By one, by two, by three,
"Go bridle and saddle my milk-white steed,
Lord Thomas's wedding I'll see."

735

"Lord Thomas and Fair Eleandor" from Master's thesis by Mildred Haun (Vanderbilt University, 1937).

She dressed her maidens all in red,
She dressed herself in green,
And every town that she passed through,
They took her to be some queen.

She rode till she came to Lord Thomas's hall,
She tingled at the ring.
There was none more ready than Lord Thomas himself,
To rise and let her in.

He took her by the lily-white hand,
And led her across the hall,
Set her down at the head of the table,
Among the gentry all.

"Lord Thomas, Lord Thomas, Lord Thomas," said she,
"Your bride is a wonderful coun,
When you could have married as fair a young lady
As e'er the sun shone on."

The brown girl, she had a pen knife,
It was both keen and sharp.
Between the long ribs and the short,
She pierced fair Eleandor's heart.

Lord Thomas was walking across the hall,
He spied fair Eleandor's face.
'What is the matter, fair Eleandor?" said he,
"You look so wonderfully pale."

"But look, but look, but look," said she,
"But look and you shall see,
That I am standing in a puddle,
My blood running down by me."

He took the brown girl by the hand,
And led her across the hall,
With his bright sword, cut off her head,
And stove it against the wall.

He gave one look to the two ladies,
And marked a place on his breast,
"Here goes three loving ones," he cried,
"God send them all to rest."

He put the crystal to the floor,
The point into his heart.

There never was three lovers did meet,
That ever so soon did part.

"My friends, my friends, go dig my grave,
Go dig it both wide and deep,
And bury fair Eleandor in my arms,
The brown girl at my feet."

Casey Jones

Come all you rounders if you want to hear
The story of a brave engineer.
Casey Jones was the rounder's name,
On the six-eight wheeler he won his fame.

The caller called Casey at half-past four;
He kissed his wife at the station door;
He mounted to the cabin with his orders in his hand,
He took a farewell trip to that promised land.

Chorus
Casey Jones! Mounted to the cabin,
Casey Jones! With his orders in his hand,
Casey Jones! Mounted to the cabin
And took that farewell trip to the promised land.

"Put in your water and shovel in your coal;
Put your head out the window, watch them drivers roll.
I'll run her till she leaves the rail,
'Cause I'm eight hours late with that western mail."

He looked at his watch and his watch was slow;
He looked at the water and the water was low;
He turned to the fireman and then he said,
"We're going to reach Frisco, if we'll all be dead."

Chorus
Casey Jones! Going to reach Frisco,
Casey Jones! If we'll all be dead.
Casey Jones! Going to reach Frisco,
We're going to reach Frisco, but we'll all be dead.

Casey pulled up that Reno hill,
He tooted for the crossing; it was awful shrill.
The switchman knew by the engine's moans
That the man at the throttle was Casey Jones.

737

He pulled up within two miles of the place;
Number Four stared him right in the face;
Turned to the fireman, said, "Boy, you'd better jump,
'Cause there's two locomotives that's going to bump."

Chorus

Casey Jones! Two locomotives!
Casey Jones! That's a-going to bump!
Casey Jones! Two locomotives!
There's two locomotives that's a-going to bump.

Casey mumbled just before he died,
"There's two more railroads that I'd like to ride."
Fireman said, "What can they be?"
"The Southern Pacific and the Santa Fe."

Mrs. Jones sat on her bed a-sighing,
Just received a message that poor Casey was dying,
Said, "Go to bed, children, and hush your crying,
'Cause you got another papa on the Salt Lake Line."

Chorus

Mrs. Casey Jones! Got another papa!
Mrs. Casey Jones! On the Salt Lake Line!
Mrs. Casey Jones! Got another papa!
You've got another papa on the Salt Lake Line.

Why Can't I Take Love Easy?[1]

Why can't I take love easy
As the leaves upon the tree?
They only fade and wither.
So is his love for me.

He is just as nice as a flower.
But he does not care for me.
But still I'll always love him
Wherever he may be.

Chorus

I don't know why I love him.
For he does not care for me.
But still my mind will wonder
Wherever he may be.

He may go across the ocean.
He may go across the sea.
He may travel this wide world over.
He'll never find another like me.

738   "*Why Can't I Take Love Easy*" *from Master's thesis by Mildred Haun (Vanderbilt University, 1937).*
[1] *Miss Haun says of this ballad, "I have included the little lyric, 'Why Can't I Take Love Easy?' because of its similarity with W. B. Yeats' poem 'An Old Song Resung' which, he said in a note in one of the earlier editions, 'is an extension of three lines sung to me by an old woman of Bollisodare.'..."*

Kennie Wagner

There was a man in Tennessee,
Kennie Wagner was his name.
He got into bad company,
A murderer he became.

'Twas down in Mississippi,
The trouble it began,
For Kennie got a pistol
And shot him down a man.

They took poor Kennie to the jail;
It was on Christmas day.
There was no man to go his bail,
But he made his get-a-way.

He went to see his sister
Away up in Tennessee.
And there they caught poor Kennie
And took his liberty.

They backed him to the river front
On one mild April day
And there poor Kennie drew his gun;
Two sheriffs he did slay.

They took him back to trial.
At last the judge did say,
"Your sentence shall be death, my son."
But Kennie got away.

Kennie Wagner's Surrender

I'm sure you've heard my story
From the Kennie Wagner song,
How down in Mississippi
I took the road that was wrong.

It was down in Mississippi
Where I murdered my first man,
The sheriff there at Lincolnsville
Took his rightful stand.

I went from Mississippi
To the state of Tennessee;
Two men went down before me,
Here they took my liberty.

I wandered through the country,
But I never could find rest,
Till I went to Texana
Away out in the West.

Again I started drinking
And again I pulled my gun,
And in a single moment
The deadly work was done.

The sheriff there was a woman,
But she got the drop on me.
I quit the game and surrendered,
And gave up my liberty.

I'm now in Mississippi
And soon shall know my stay,
I'm waiting for my trial,
But I do not dread my fate.

For still the sun is shining,
And the sky is blue and clear,
But my heart is not returning
For I do not dread the chair.

I've had my worldly pleasure,
I've faced a many a man,
But it was down in Mississippi
Where a woman called my hand.

Young men, young men, take warning,
O, take my last advice,
If you start the game in life's run,
You must surely pay the price.

739

"Kennie Wagner" and "Kennie Wagner's Surrender" from Master's thesis by Mildred Haun (Vanderbilt University, 1937).

Leo Frank and Mary Phagan

Little Mary Fagen,
She went to town one day:
She went to the pencil factory
To get her weekly pay.

She left her home at eleven;
She kissed her mother goodbye;
Not once did the poor girl think
She was going off to die.

Leo Frank met her
With a brutish heart and grin;
He says to little Mary:
"You'll never see home again."

Down on her knees fell
To Leo Frank and pled.
He picked a stick from the trash pile
And beat her o'er the head.

The tears rolled down her cheeks,
The blood rolled down her back;
For she remembered telling her mother
What time she would be back.

Nemphon was the watchman;
He went to wind his key;
Away down in the basement
Was nothing he could see.

They phoned for the officers;
Their names I do not know;

They came to the pencil factory,
Says to Nemphon, "You must go."

They took him to the jail house;
They bound him in his cell;
The poor old innocent negro
Had nothing he could tell.

Mother sits a-weeping;
She weeps and mourns all day
And hopes to meet her darling
In a better land some day.

Come, all ye good people,
Wherever you may be,
Suppose that "little Mary"
Belonged to you or me.

I have an idea in my mind
When Frankie comes to die
And stands examination
In the courthouse in the sky,

He'll be so astonished
To what the angels say
And how he killed little Mary
Upon that holiday.

Judge Roan passed a sentence;
He passes it very well;
The Christian doers of heaven
Sent Leo Frank to hell.

Rowan County Troubles

Come on young men and ladies, mothers and fathers too.
I'll relate to you the hist'ry of the Rowan County Crew,
Concerning bloody Rowan and her many heinous deeds.
Now friends please give attention, remember how it reads.

740

"Leo Frank and Mary Phagan" from Folk-Songs from the Southern Highlands, compiled by Mellinger Edward Henry. J. J. Augustin, publisher, 1938.
"Rowan County Troubles" from Ballad Makin' in the Mountains of Kentucky by Jean Thomas, The Traipsin' Woman. Published by Henry Holt and Company, 1939.

It was in the month of August upon election day,
John Martin he was wounded, they say by Johnny Day,
Martin could not believe it, he could not think it so;
He thought it was Floyd Tolliver that struck the fatal blow.

They shot and killed Sol Bradley, a sober innocent man,
He left his wife and loving children to do the best they can,
They wounded young Ad Sizemore; although his life was saved
He seemed to shun the grog shops since he stood so near the grave.

Martin did recover, some months had come and past,
In the town of Morehead those men both met at last;
Tolliver and a friend or two about the streets did walk,
He seemed to be uneasy and with no one wished to talk.

He walked in Judge Carey's grocery and stepped up to the bar,
But little did he think, dear friends, that he met the fatal hour;
The sting of death was near him, Martin rushed in at the door,
A few words passed between them concerning a row before.

The people soon were frightened began to rush out of the room,
A ball from Martin's pistol laid Tolliver in the tomb.
His friends soon gathered round him, his wife to weep and wail;
Martin was arrested and soon confined in jail.

He was put in the jail of Rowan there to remain a while,
In the hands of law and justice to bravely stand his trial.
The people all talked of lynching him, at present though they failed,
The prisoner's friends soon moved him into the Winchester jail.

Some persons forged an order, their names I do not know,
The plan was soon agreed upon, for Martin they did go;
Martin seemed discouraged, he seemed to be in dread,
"They have sought a plan to kill me," to the jailer Martin said.

They put the handcuffs on him, his heart was in distress,
They hurried to the station, stepped on the night express.
Along the line she lumbered at her usual speed;
They were only two in numbers to commit the dreadful deed.

Martin was in the smoking car accompanied by his wife,
They did not want her present when they took her husband's life;
When they arrived at Farmers they had no time to lose,
A band approached the engineer and bid him not to move.

741

They stepped up to the prisoner with pistols in their hands,
In death he soon was sinking, he died in iron bands.

His wife soon heard the horrid sound; she was in another car,
She cried, "Oh Lord! they've killed him!" when she heard the pistol fire.

The death of these two men has caused great trouble in our land,
Caused men to leave their families and take the parting hand.
Retaliating, still at war they may never, never cease,
I would that I could only see my land once more in peace.

They killed the deputy sheriff, Baumgartner was his name,
They shot him from the bushes after taking deliberate aim;
The death of him was dreadful, it may never be forgot,
His body pierced and torn with thirty-three buckshot.

I compose this as a warning. Oh! beware, young men!
Your pistols may cause trouble, on this you may depend;
In the bottom of a whisky glass the lurking devils dwell,
It burns the breast of those who drink, it sends their souls to hell.

Old Joe Clark

I went on the mountain top,
I give my horn a blow.
I thought I heard Suzanna say
Yonder comes my beau.

Fare you well, old Joe Clark,
Get along old Joe.
Fare you well, old Joe Clark,
Good-bye, Betty Brown.

Chorus
Fare you well, old Joe Clark,
Fare you well, I say,
Fare you well, old Joe Clark,
And good-bye, Betty Brown.

I wish I was in Tennessee
Sitting in a big arm chair,
One arm around a whisky jug
The other one round my dear.

The prettiest girl I ever saw
Went running around the house

With a dog skin all round her neck
The tail was in her mouth.

I went down to Joe Clark's,
Joe Clark was not at home;
I eat all old Joe's meat
And left old Joe the bone.

I wish I was an apple
A-hanging on the tree,
And every time my true love past
She'd take a bite of me.

I climbed up the old oak tree
And she climbed up the gum;
I never saw a pretty girl
But what I loved her some.

I would not marry an old maid,
I will tell you the reason why:
Her neck is so long and skinny
I am afraid she would never die.

742

"Old Joe Clark" from Devil's Ditties by Jean Thomas, The Traipsin' Woman. Published by W. Wilbur Hatfield.

Old Smoky

On top of Old Smoky, all covered with snow
I lost my true lover by courting too slow.

While courting is pleasure and parting is grief,
A false hearted lover is worse than a thief.

A thief they will rob you and take what you have,
But a false hearted lover will take you to the grave.

The grave will decay you, will turn you to dust,
Only one boy out of a hundred a poor girl can trust.

They'll tell you they love you to give your heart ease;
As soon as your back's turned, they'll court who they please.

'Tis raining, 'tis hailing, this dark stormy night;
Your horses can't travel for the moon gives no light.

Go, put up your horses and give them some hay;
Come, sit down beside me as long as you can stay.

My horses aren't hungry; they won't eat your nay;
My wagon is loaded; I'll feed on my way.

As sure as the dewdrops fall on the green corn,
Last night he was with me; tonight he is gone.

I'll go back to Old Smoky, to the mountain so high,
Where the wild birds and turtle doves can hear my sad cry.

Way down on Old Smoky all covered in snow,
I lost my blue eyed boy by courting too slow.

I wrote him a letter of roses and lines;
He sent it back to me all twisted in twine.

He says, "You keep your love letters, and I'll keep mine;
You write to your true love and I'll write to mine.

"I'll go to old Georgia; I'll write you my mind;
My mind is to marry you and leave you behind."

Turnip Greens

Had a dream the other night—
Dreamed that I could fly,

743

"Old Smoky" from Folk-Songs from the Southern Highlands, compiled by Mellinger Edward Henry. J. J. Augustin, publisher, 1938.
"Turnip Greens" from Folksongs of Mississippi and Their Background, compiled by Arthur Palmer Hudson. The University of North Carolina Press, 1936.

Flapped my wings like a buzzard
And flew up to the sky.

St. Peter stood at the Golden Gate.
"From what place did you fly?"
I told him from Mississippi
I flew up to the sky.

He showed me through a telescope—
I don't know what that means—
I saw ten thousand people
Living on turnip greens.

They all looked so sassy,
Been living above their means,
And he kicked them down to the hot place
For stealing turnip greens.

Turnip greens, turnip greens,
Good old turnip greens,
Cornbread and buttermilk,
And good old turnip greens.

CLEANTH BROOKS

1906–

Cleanth Brooks, Jr. was born on October 16, 1906. A Kentuckian by birth, he spent most of his youth in Tennessee, where his father was a minister. Brooks studied at Vanderbilt University, from which he received his A.B. degree in 1928, and at Tulane, where he was awarded an M.A. degree the following year. He did further graduate study at Oxford as a Rhodes Scholar. From 1932 until 1947 Brooks taught at Louisiana State University as a member of the Department of English. During this period he also helped to found and edit *The Southern Review* (1935–1942). At the present time he is Professor of English at Yale University.

744

In cooperation with Robert Penn Warren, Brooks has published several college textbooks, which have pointed toward a new approach in the teaching of literature, based primarily upon a close study of the text itself. The first of these volumes, *Understanding Poetry*, appeared in 1938. It was followed by *Understanding Fiction* (1943) and *Understanding Drama* (1945), the latter with Robert Heilman as co-editor. Brooks' own best-known critical volumes are *Modern Poetry and the Tradition* (1939) and *The Well Wrought Urn* (1947). In the last-named volume, he employs a distinctive critical method to illuminate the poetry of Shakespeare, Wordsworth, Yeats, and others.

Another field which has attracted Brooks' interest and scholarship is that of Southern speech, with particular emphasis upon the origins of Southern speech patterns. The results of his research are to be found in such work as *The Relation of the Alabama-Georgia Dialect to the Provincial Dialects of Great Britain* (1935) and the essay which appears in this volume, *The English Language in the South*.

The English Language in the South

One of the prices of democracy and democratic education is that you want to speak like everybody else. And one of the ills of isolation—one, if you like, of the limitations of the provincial—is that you are nervous, or may become so, as to what is done in the great world outside. It follows, therefore, with regard to the South and Southern people, that sometimes they are not sure of themselves, that they abandon too readily their own guns, and are apt to be defenseless before accusations that are mainly limited, if not even ignorant. It is not necessary to speak a language that is archaic and out of tone with our present world. But, on the other hand, we are not obliged to be exactly like the general mass spread over the entire United States; nor must we, on a lower plane, seek that generalization of speech that represents everybody who is not anybody. Within limits, it is a good thing to speak your own way, the way of your own part of the world. It follows, therefore, that it is not a bad idea to look into the background of your inherited speech, with the mingled purposes of justification, defense, and, if need be, compromise. Tone of voice is one thing and so is rhythm. The present article is about the language spoken.

A Southern pronunciation—lumping it all together, despite the fact that in the South there are many different ways of speaking—is usually thought to have emanated from the Negro; on the lips of a Virginia girl, pleasantly quaint, like other relics of the influence of the Negro mammy, but corrupt English after all. This popular belief has from time to time acquired the dignity of publication. Dr. Embree, for example, in his *Brown America* unhesitatingly attributes the Virginia lady's accent to the influence of the Negro. The origins of Southern speech, however, cannot be accounted for under a theory of Negro influence. Moreover, Southern English is not a corrupt form of "standard English." To

745

make this point is to raise a number of questions with regard to the criterion of correct English—questions which divers people with their dogmatic assumptions on the subject never take into account.

In the first place, the speech of the Southern states represents an older form of English than that which is found in standard British English today. Indeed, it conforms rather closely to the description which A. J. Ellis gave in the last century of the behavior of the speech of a colony. The speech of a colony is conservative. It is in the language of the mother country that innovations are made. For example, few people other than professional students of the language know that the so-called broad *a*, heard in the British pronunciation of words like *path*, *staff*, *last*, and *dance*, is a later form than the vowel that is usually met with in these words in America. The broad *a*, most scholars agree, did not become fashionable in England until late in the eighteenth century. The settlement of America by Englishmen began early in the seventeenth. Obviously, the form used by Englishmen today could not have been the pronunciation carried over by the seventeenth century colonists.

It can be said that a large part of the United States is capable of making criticisms of Southern speech that are merely refined criticism; for the speech of other sections of this country is in its origins also seventeenth century English. Such criticisms are usually based on a hazy assumption that present "standard British" (the speech of the educated classes in London) is "correct," and that the nearer American speech approximates this, the more nearly correct it is. The assumption is not necessarily true, and only ignorance and fear can make us think so. What we can say, however, is that if American English is based originally on seventeenth century English, the South has clung more tenaciously to these original forms than have other parts of the country. Indeed, many of the pronunciations which are usually regarded as specifically "Negro" represent nothing more than older native English forms. The pronunciation, for example, of *get* as "git," so widespread in America and certainly not confined to the Negro, was the standard English form in the eighteenth century; and the pronunciation of *yellow* as "yal-uh" was also the polite eighteenth century pronunciation. Examples could be multiplied. To give only a few: *boil* pronounced as "bile"; *oblige* as "obleege"; *china* as "chainy." One remembers that Boswell remarks on Dr. Johnson's pronunciation of *heard* with the vowel of *hear*, and that Noah Webster prefers the pronunciation *hierd*, taking *heard* as merely an affectation that he has heard since the Revolution. In Anglo-Saxon it was *hierde* and often enough in Middle English. The so-called dropping of the *g* in final *-ing* as in "darlin'" for *darling* was perfectly correct in England itself in the eighteenth century, not to mention its practice nowadays by the British upper classes. Many a lord says "it don't." Matthew Arnold said "fascinatin'," not *fascinating*.

You will hear pronunciations in the South, however, which do not go back to any pronunciation in earlier *standard* English. This does not mean that they originated on our side of the Atlantic. They represent forms from the provincial dialects—pronunciations which occurred in the dialects of certain parts of England but which did not, as such dialectal forms occasionally did, obtain a footing in the standard language. These dialect forms are of great importance because they offer a possible means for determining the regions in England from which

746

came the colonists who set the speech pattern of the South. Joel Chandler Harris has Uncle Remus pronounce *until, unsettle,* etc., as "awn-til," "awn-settle," etc. *Un-* is still pronounced "awn" by dialect speakers in Devon. Uncle Remus pronounces *corner* as "cawnduh," inserting a *d* in it. The living dialects of Somerset and Devon give the same form. When Uncle Remus pronounces *whether,* he leaves out the *th,* but so do the dialects of Wiltshire, Dorset, Somerset, and Devon. Again, the word *seven* is frequently heard in the South as "sebn," but the same form occurs in a number of dialects of England, including those of the southwest. In the southwest of England, "gwine" occurs for *going.* Even the dropping of a final *d* as in *told,* "tole," or in *hand,* "han'," or of a final *t* as in *last,* "las'," is not a corruption. If it is a corruption at all, it is one which probably came into this country by passage across the Atlantic. Such forms are the regular developments in many of the living dialects of Great Britain.

As a matter of fact, a number of words in the South which appear to be new words entirely, represent in their origin merely dialectal forms of standard English: *roil* is a purely literary word, but "rile," which is related to it in the same way as "bile" to *boil,* is common. "Ingun" is a variant of *onion,* still to be found in many of the counties of England and Scotland. The word "frail," used in the South in the sense of a severe beating ("I'm going to *frail* the life out of him") has no relation to *frail* in the sense of "fragile." It is a development of *flail* which has occurred in many of the provincial dialects of Great Britain. The word "rare" as used in the phrase "rarin' to go" is related to the word *rear* in the same way that "quare" is related to *queer.* Both "rare" and "quare" are widely distributed through the dialects of Great Britain. "Peart" is a development of *pert* and must have been brought across the Atlantic by the early settlers, for it still exists in a number of English counties.

In this connection one may point out that the Southern *r* is connected with the south of England as well as with the Southern states of America. In this part of England the consonant *r* was lost very early, before consonants and at the end of words. From the seventeenth century onward this development had penetrated the standard language, and this treatment of *r,* far from being a slurring or a corruption, is the treatment standard in British English today. It is the normal treatment also in some other parts of America—eastern New England, for example. On the western edges of the Southern states, Midwestern influence has come in bringing the *r* with it; in the mountain regions of the South also (under Scotch-Irish influence?) the *r* is preserved.

As one instance after another of Southern speech traces itself back to England, either to earlier standard English or to provincialisms of the south and southwest counties, it rapidly becomes apparent that any theory of Negro influence must be abandoned. The Negro learned his speech from the colonists, who must have come predominantly from the English southwest. The Negro has then preserved many of these original forms, even after most of the whites have discarded them. This is not to state, of course, that Uncle Remus speaks the dialect of Hardy's peasants. But the fact that his dialect, wherever it deviates from modern British English, differs together along *with* the dialects of the southwest counties indicates that Southern speech has been colored by the English southwest.

The only alternative to this theory is to accept what amounts to a staggering

747

coincidence. The magnitude of the coincidence will be made more vivid by consideration of a few more specific cases. Take the Southern variants of *muskmelon*, for instance. *Melon* is often heard as "million" in the South, especially among Negroes; and *muskmelon* is frequently, even among whites, pronounced "mushmelon." The form "mushmillion," which Harris has Uncle Remus use, and which may still be heard among old people in the South in country districts, would accordingly be considered by most people as about as thoroughly "Negro" as a word could be. The form seems obviously to be a corruption. But one holding such a view will be disconcerted to find in the Oxford Dictionary precisely this form occurring in a passage written by one Jerome Horsey in 1591. . . .

The interpretation of the origin of Southern speech given above raises questions with regard to the origin of the speech used in other parts of the country. If the speech of the Southern states shows forms from seventeenth and eighteenth century standards and from the provincial dialects of England, why do not such forms appear in the states of the North? The answer, of course, is that they do. In James Russell Lowell's *Biglow Papers*, written in the New England rustic dialect, occur many spellings which indicate such pronunciations. We find even more parallelisms with Southern forms when we consult early New England records with their occasional spellings which indicate dialectal pronunciations, or else the remarks on pronunciation made by the early grammarians of this section. To take only a few examples collected by the late George Phillip Krapp in his *English Language in America*, "skase" for *scarce* must have occurred frequently in the earlier speech of this country, in the North as well as in the South. It probably derives from the southern part of England, where the *r* was lost early before consonants and at the end of words. *Itch* is pronounced "each" by Uncle Remus, but formerly it was so pronounced in parts of the North. "Drap" for *drop* and "crap" for *crop* are still frequently heard in the South, but such forms were once found in New England also; and in the case of both sections, their ultimate origin was probably in the dialects of the southwest of England.

Most scholars who have worked on the subject believe that the New England coast was predominantly influenced by the south and east counties of England. Pronunciations from the eastern counties, Norfolk, Suffolk, and Essex, are to be found there: for example, the pronunciation of *whole* as something resembling "hull," *stone* resembling "stun," etc. The evidence would seem to indicate, however, in my opinion, considerable influence from the counties of the southwest as well. The influence of the southwest, as has been pointed out, seems dominant in the South, though some forms occurring in Virginia seem to point back to the eastern counties, and other influences may be present in other parts of the South. At any rate, the language of both New England and the South— whatever differences existed between them—in the eighteenth century must have differed very considerably from the British English of today. The marked difference between eastern New England and the South did not exist at this period. These differences came later, and came, not with laziness and corruption in the South, but with innovation in New England through the influence of spelling, the elocution book, and the diligence of the New England schoolma'am. Probably no other part of the English-speaking world in any one period has produced so many spelling books and dictionaries as New England produced in the early nineteenth century.

There is also evidence to indicate that New England has consciously imitated British pronunciation by taking over from it later developments of the qualities of certain vowel sounds, and imposing them in whole classes of words like *corn, morning, short, thorn,* etc., which were distinguished in pronunciation from words like *divorce, store, pork, fort,* etc. The first group had an *aw* vowel, the second a long *o.* Today in British pronunciation, both groups have *aw,* but this development did not take place in England until the nineteenth century. Consequently, the appearance of examples of the present-day British pronunciation in New England (or elsewhere in America) suggests a late imitation of British English.

This difference in attitude toward speech in New England on the one hand and the South on the other is an indication of more fundamental cultural differences. The desire to cultivate "correctness" of speech, the reliance on spelling, the diligence of the New England schoolma'am, may, if you choose to do so, be interpreted as marks of the cultural continuity existing between the New England and the Old. They are susceptible, however, of another account, not quite so favorable, perhaps; they may be interpreted as symptoms of a feeling of cultural inferiority—of anxiety, that is, as to status. But it might be more graceful to let a New Englander speak in this matter of New England's dependence on the mother land. Henry Adams, writing of the mid-nineteenth century, says: "The tone of Boston society was colonial. The true Bostonian always knelt in self-abasement before the majesty of English standards; far from concealing it as a weakness, he was proud of it as his strength."

The attitude of the South (again speaking in relative terms) was quite different. The South never had quite the reverence for the written word which prevailed in New England. Like England itself, especially among country families and the aristocracy in general, it was content to rest the criterion of speech on a living oral tradition. Unconsciously at least and by its very lack of extreme self-consciousness, the South ceased to be a colony. Whatever general conclusion one may wish to draw, it would be hard to deny that the attitude toward speech in the South exhibits a culture in a very healthy state. The continuity between class and class and even between race and race was not severed by that artificial and irritating barrier, a *class* dialect.

The influence of spelling has, of course, exerted itself on Southern speech, but less than it has on that of most other sections of the country. Otherwise, there has been little or no attempt to keep up with the later developments of British English. Many Southerners, educated persons as well as the uneducated, consistently pronounce *better* as "bedduh," *bottle* as "boddle," etc., thus carrying on regularly in their speech a development largely to be found in the dialects of the English southwest. "Taripin" is the almost universal pronunciation of *terrapin,* for few allow themselves to be browbeaten by the spelling. As a matter of fact, *terrapin* is in origin an Algonquin Indian word, and the earliest form seems to have had an *a* rather than an *e.*

749

The student of language is supposed to be completely objective—to describe conditions rather than to prescribe standards. But perhaps he may be allowed to affect standards, at least in one regard: by giving a true description when a false description is being made the basis for prescriptions. On one fact, scholars are agreed: that the standard of speech for a country is that of the "best" speakers, the educated speakers, of that country. British English is undoubtedly correct for the modern Englishman. It is not correct, by virtue of that reason at least, for the Virginian or Tennessean. Moreover, in trying to find a standard for modern America, the best authorities are agreed that there is no virtue in trying to impose an artificial and synthetic criterion. If the Virginian is not to be forced into imitation of the Oxford don, there is logically no reason for him to be forced into imitation of Boston—or, for that matter, of Chicago or Hollywood.

If the South—or, for that matter, any other sections of the country—under the influence of the radio, the talking pictures, or other "cultural" forces, cares to abandon its characteristic speech, the pronunciation then adopted by the educated speakers of the region will, of course, then be the standard. But that adoption need not be made under the delusion that something poor is being abandoned for something "better." Certainly the heritage the South possesses is not one to be ashamed of—neither the seventeenth century standard forms, nor the coloring of Devon, Somerset, and Dorset. The men of the west country were active in the conquest and settlement of America. One of the most prominent of them, Sir Walter Raleigh, was not ashamed of his provincial accent, even at Elizabeth's court. John Aubrey, the gossipy biographer of the seventeenth century, tells us that he heard one of Raleigh's contemporaries say that "notwithstanding his so great mastership in style and his conversation with the learnedest and politest persons, yet he spake broad Devonshire to dying day." It would be odd, indeed, if Raleigh's fellow countrymen, mariners, adventurers, and colonists, not courtiers at all, had not bequeathed forms of their sturdy speech to their descendants in the New World.

"*Gy* pronounced *gj* in such a word as *garden,* found in Virginia and sometimes in other eastern parts of the South, is traced back to Leicester, northwest Oxford, Hereford, north Derby; *ky* pronounced *kj* in *card*—found also in Maine as well as the South—goes back to west Somerset, Aberdeen, and north Derby.

"Through the South and New England, in the colloquial speech of educated and cultivated people the suffix -*ing* as in *going* commonly -*in'*. . . . This characteristic of eighteenth century speech is not quite so evident in the South generally as it is on the Eastern Shore of Virginia and on the New England coast, where the syllable containing -*in'* has a stronger stress. For example, *pudding*, which generally becomes 'pudn' colloquially, is on the Eastern Shore and in New England 'pudin.' In *going* ('goin') the second syllable is not obscured. In the South generally, this 'loss of g' may seem slovenly; on the Eastern Shore and in New England the *g* is lost precisely ('pudin,' for example, instead of the Southern 'pudn').

"No one should feel ashamed of this ancient and honorable pronunciation." [1]

(*1937*)

---

[1] *William Cabell Greet, "Southern Speech" in* Culture in the South, *p. 609. (Brooks' note.)*

JOHN CROWE RANSOM

1888–

John Crowe Ransom was born in Pulaski, Tennessee, on April 30, 1888. He received his A.B. degree from Vanderbilt University in 1909 and, after teaching for a short time in a secondary school in Mississippi, went to Oxford as a Rhodes Scholar. Beginning in 1914, Ransom taught for twenty-three years in the Department of English at Vanderbilt, where he was an important influence in the Fugitive and Agrarian movements. In 1937 he left Vanderbilt to become Carnegie Professor of Poetry at Kenyon College and to edit *The Kenyon Review*, which immediately became one of the most advanced critical quarterlies appearing in English.

Ransom's publications have been various. He has been active to an outstanding degree in the usually divergent fields of literary criticism, poetry, and social commentary. He has issued three important volumes of poetry in addition to his *Selected Poems* (1945). They are *Poems About God* (1919), *Chills and Fever* (1924), and *Two Gentlemen in Bonds* (1926). His *God Without Thunder* (1930) is a book-length essay which sets forth the unhappy consequences of Western Man's surrender to the modern deity, Science. Through this surrender, the author contends, God has been robbed of His thunder, which is His mystery.

During the last decade and a half, Ransom's primary interest has been literary criticism. The books which best define his critical position are *The World's Body* (1938) and *The New Criticism* (1941). A serious student should also study Ransom's essays and editorial comments in *The American Review* (1933–1938) and *The Kenyon Review*, as well as the symposia *I'll Take My Stand* (1930) and *Who Owns America?* (1936), to which he contributed.

Bells for John Whiteside's Daughter

751

There was such speed in her little body,
And such lightness in her footfall,

It is no wonder that her brown study
Astonishes us all.

Her wars were bruited in our high window.
We looked among orchard trees and beyond,
Where she took arms against her shadow,
Or harried unto the pond

The lazy geese, like a snow cloud
Dripping their snow on the green grass,
Tricking and stopping, sleepy and proud,
Who cried in goose, Alas,

For the tireless heart within the little
Lady with rod that made them rise
From their noon apple dreams, and scuttle
Goose-fashion under the skies!

But now go the bells, and we are ready;
In one house we are sternly stopped
To say we are vexed at her brown study,
Lying so primly propped.

(1924)

Janet Waking

Beautifully Janet slept
Till it was deeply morning. She woke then
And thought about her dainty-feathered hen,
To see how it had kept.

One kiss she gave her mother,
Only a small one gave she to her daddy
Who would have kissed each curl of his shining baby;
No kiss at all for her brother.

"Old Chucky, Old Chucky!" she cried,
Running on little pink feet upon the grass
To Chucky's house, and listening. But alas,
Her Chucky had died.

It was a transmogrifying bee
Came droning down on Chucky's old bald head

752

And sat and put the poison. It scarcely bled,
But how exceedingly

And purply did the knot
Swell with the venom and communicate
Its rigour! Now the poor comb stood up straight
But Chucky did not.

So there was Janet
Kneeling on the wet grass, crying her brown hen
(Translated far beyond the daughters of men)
To rise and walk upon it.

And weeping fast as she had breath
Janet implored us, "Wake her from her sleep!"
And would not be instructed in how deep
Was the forgetful kingdom of death.

(1927)

Dead Boy

The little cousin is dead, by foul subtraction,
A green bough from Virginia's aged tree,
And neither the country kin love the transaction
Nor some of the world of outer dark, like me.

He was not a beautiful boy, nor good, nor clever,
A black cloud full of storms too hot for keeping,
A sword beneath his mother's heart,—yet never
Woman bewept her babe as this is weeping.

A pig with a pasty face, I had always said.
Squealing for cookies, kinned by pure pretense
With a noble house. But the little man quite dead,
I can see the forebears' antique lineaments.

The elder men have strode by the box of death
To the wide flag porch, and muttering low send round
The bruit of the day. O friendly waste of breath!
Their hearts are hurt with a deep dynastic wound.

He was pale and little, the foolish neighbors say;
The first-fruits, saith the preacher, the Lord hath taken;

753

But this was the old tree's late branch wrenched away,
Aggrieving the sapless limbs, the shorn and shaken.

(1927)

Spectral Lovers

By night they haunted a thicket of April mist,
As out of the rich ground strangely come to birth,
Else two immaculate angels fallen on earth.
Lovers they knew they were, but why unclasped, unkissed?
Why should two lovers go frozen asunder in fear?
And yet they were, they were.

Over the shredding of an April blossom
Her thrilling fingers touched him quick with care;
Of many delicate postures she cast a snare;
But for all the red heart beating in the pale bosom,
Her face as of cunningly tinctured ivory
Was hard with an agony.

Stormed by the little batteries of an April night,
Passionate being the essence of the field,
Should the penetrable walls of the crumbling prison yield
And open her treasure to the first clamorous knight?
"This is the mad moon, and must I surrender all?
If he but ask it, I shall."

And gesturing largely to the very moon of Easter,
Mincing his steps, and swishing the jubilant grass,
And beheading some field-flowers that had come to pass,
He had reduced his tributaries faster,
Had not considerations pinched his heart
Unfitly for his art.

"Am I reeling with the sap of April like a drunkard?
Blessed is he that taketh this richest of cities;
But it is so stainless, the sack were a thousand pities;
This is that marble fortress not to be conquered,
Lest its white peace in the black flame turn to tinder
And an unutterable cinder."

754

They passed me once in April, in the mist.
No other season is it, when one walks and discovers
Two clad in the shapes of angels, being spectral lovers,

Trailing a glory of moon-gold and amethyst,
Who touch their quick fingers fluttering like a bird
Whose songs shall never be heard.

(1924)

Necrological

The friar had said his paternosters duly
And scourged his limbs, and afterwards would have slept;
But with much riddling his head became unruly,
He arose, from the quiet monastery he crept.

Dawn lightened the place where the battle had been won,
The people were dead—it is easy, he thought, to die—
These dead remained, but the living all were gone,
Gone with the wailing trumps of victory.

The dead men wore no raiment against the air,
Bartholomew's men had spoiled them where they fell;
In defeat the heroes' bosoms were whitely bare,
The field was white like meads of asphodel.

Not all were white; some gory and fabulous
Whom the sword had pierced and then the grey wolf eaten;
But the brother reasoned that heroes' flesh was thus,
Flesh fails, and the postured bones lie weather-beaten.

The lords of chivalry were prone and shattered,
The gentle and the bodyguard of yeomen;
Bartholomew's stroke went home—but little it mattered,
Bartholomew went to be stricken of other foemen.

Beneath the blue ogive of the firmament
Was a dead warrior, clutching whose mighty knees
Was a leman, who with her flame had warmed his tent,
For him enduring all men's pleasantries.

Close by the sable stream that purged the plain
Lay the white stallion and his rider thrown.
The great beast had spilled there his little brain,
And the little groin of the knight was spilled by a stone.

The youth possessed him then of a crooked blade
Deep in the belly of a lugubrious knight;

755

He fingered it well, and it was cunningly made;
But strange apparatus was it for a Carmalite.

Then he sat upon a hill and hung his head,
Riddling, riddling, and lost in a vast surmise,
And so still that he likened himself unto those dead
Whom the kites of Heaven solicited with sweet cries.

(1924)

Prelude to an Evening

Do not enforce the tired wolf
Dragging his infected wound homeward
To sit tonight with the warm children
Naming the pretty kings of France.

The images of the invaded mind
Being as monsters in the dreams
Of your most brief enchanted headful,
Suppose a miracle of confusion:

That dreamed and undreamt become each other
And mix the night and day of your mind;
And it does not matter your twice crying
From mouth unbeautied against the pillow.

To avert the gun of the swarthy soldier,
For cry, cock-crow, or the iron bell
Can crack the sleep-sense of outrage,
Annihilate phantoms who were nothing.

But now, by our perverse supposal,
There is a drift of fog on your mornings;
You in your peignoir, dainty at your orange-cup,
Feel poising round the sunny room

Invisible evil, deprived and bold.
All day the clock will metronome
Your gallant fear; the needles clicking,
The heels detonating the stair's cavern.

Freshening the water in the blue bowls
For the buckberries with not all your love,

You shall be listening for the low wind,
The warning sibilance of pines.

You like a waning moon, and I accusing
Our too banded Eumenides,
You shall make Noes but wanderingly,
Smoothing the heads of the hungry children.

(1945)

Poets Without Laurels

The poets I refer to in the title are the "moderns": those whom a small company of adept readers enjoys, perhaps enormously, but the general public detests; those in whose hands poetry as a living art has lost its public support.

Consequently I do not refer to such poets as Edna St. Vincent Millay and Robert Frost, who are evidently influenced by modernism without caring to "go modern" in the sense of joining the revolution; which is very much as if they had stopped at a mild or parlor variety of socialism, when all about them the brave, or at least the doctrinaire, were marching under the red banner. Probably they are wise in their time; they have laurels deservedly and wear them gracefully. But they do not define the issue which I wish to discuss. And still less do I refer to poets like E. A. Robinson, Sturge Moore, and John Masefield, who are even less modern; though I have no intention of questioning their laurels either. I refer to poets with no laurels.

I do not wish to seem to hold the public responsible for their condition, as if it had suddenly become phlegmatic, cruel, and philistine. The poets have certainly for their part conducted themselves peculiarly. They could not have estranged the public more completely if they had tried; and smart fellows as they are, they know very well what they have been doing, and what they are still stubborn in doing, and what the consequences are.

For they have failed more and more flagrantly, more and more deliberately, to identify themselves with the public interests, as if expressly to renounce the kind affections which poets had courted for centuries. Accordingly, they do not only encounter public indifference, they sometimes encounter active hostility. A Pulitzer committeeman, I hear, says about some modernist poet whose book is up for judgment: "He will never get the award except over my dead body." The violence of the remark seems to exceed the occasion, but it is not exceptional.

Poets used to be bards and patriots, priests and prophets, keepers of the public conscience, and naturally men of public importance. Society crowned them with wreaths of laurel, according to the tradition which comes to us from the Greeks and is perpetuated by official custom in England—and in Oklahoma. Generally the favor must have been gratefully received. But modern poets are of another breed. It is as if all at once they had lost their prudence as well as their

757

piety, and formed a compact to unclasp the chaplet from their brows, inflicting upon themselves the humility of delaureation, and retiring from public responsibility and honors. It is this phenomenon which has thrown critical theory into confusion.

Sir Philip Sidney made the orthodox defense of poetry on the ground of the poet's service to patriotism and virtue:

> He doth not only show the way, but giveth so
> sweet a prospect into the way, as will
> entice any man to enter into it.

And what was the technique of enticement?

> With a tale forsooth he cometh unto you, with a
> tale which holdeth children from play,
> and old men from the chimney corner.

The poets, therefore, told entrancing tales, which had morals. But the fact was, also, that the poets were not always content to win to virtue by indirection, or enticement, but were prepared to preach with almost no disguise, and to become sententious and repetitious, and the literature which they created is crowded with precise maxims for the moralists. There it stands on the shelves now. Sometimes the so-called poet has been only a moralist with a poetic manner. And all the poets famous in our tradition, or very nearly all, have been poets of a powerful moral cast.

So I shall try a preliminary definition of the poet's traditional function on behalf of society: he proposed to make virtue delicious. He compounded a moral effect with an aesthetic effect. The total effect was not a pure one, but it was rich, and relished highly. The name of the moral effect was goodness; the name of the aesthetic effect was beauty. Perhaps these did not have to co-exist, but the planners of society saw to it that they should; they called upon the artists to reinforce morality with charm. The artists obliged.

When they had done so, the public did not think of attempting to distinguish in its experience as reader the glow which was aesthetic from the glow which was moral. Most persons probably could not have done this; many persons cannot do it today. There is yet no general recognition of the possibility that an aesthetic effect may exist by itself, independent of morality or any other useful set of ideas. But the modern poet is intensely concerned with this possibility, and he has disclaimed social responsibility in order to secure this pure aesthetic effect. He cares nothing, professionally, about morals, or God, or native land. He has performed a work of dissociation and purified his art.

There are distinct styles of "modernity," but I think their net results, psychologically, are about the same. I have in mind what might be called the "pure" style and what might be called the "obscure" style.

758 A good "pure" poem is Wallace Stevens' "Sea Surface Full of Clouds"—famous perhaps, but certainly not well known. I shall have to deal with it summarily. Time and place: "In that November off Tehuantepec." The poem has five uniform stanzas, presenting as many surface effects beheld at breakfast time "after the slopping of the sea by night grew still." The first surface made one think of rosy chocolate and gilt umbrellas; the second, of chophouse chocolate and sham umbrellas; the third, of porcelain chocolate and pied umbrellas; the fourth, of musky chocolate and frail umbrellas; the fifth, of Chinese chocolate and large umbrellas. Nothing could be more discriminating than these details, which induct us respectively into the five fields of observation. The poem has a calculated complexity, and its technical competence is so high that to study it, if you do that sort of thing, is to be happy. That it has not been studied by a multitude of persons is due to a simple consideration which strikes us at once: the poem has no moral, political, religious, or sociological values. It is not about "res publica," the public thing. The subject matter is trifling.

Poetry of this sort, as it was practiced by some French poets of the nineteenth century, and as it is practiced by many British and American poets now, has been called pure poetry, and the name is accurate. It is nothing but poetry; it is poetry for poetry's sake, and you cannot get a moral out of it. But it was to be expected that it would never win the public at large. The impulse which led readers to the old poetry was at least as much moral as it was aesthetic, while the new poetry cannot count on any customers except those specializing in strict aesthetic effects. But the modern poets intend to rate only as poets, and would probably think it meretricious to solicit patronage by making moral overtures.

As an example of "obscure" poetry, though not the most extreme one, I cite Allen Tate's "Death of Little Boys." Here are some of its verses:

> Then you will touch at the bedside, torn in two,
> Gold curls deftly intricate with gray
> As the windowpane extends a fear to you
> From one peeled aster drenched with the wind all day. . . .

> Till all the guests, come in to look, turn down
> Their palms; and delirium assails the cliff
> Of Norway where you ponder, and your little town
> Reels like a sailor drunk in his rotten skiff.

There is evidently a wide difference between Stevens and Tate, as poets. Tate has an important subject, and his poem is a human document, with a contagious fury about it: Stevens, pursuing purity, does not care to risk such a subject. But Tate, as if conscious that he is close to moralizing sententiousness, builds up deliberately, I imagine, an effect of obscurity; for example, he does not care to explain the private meaning of his windowpane and his Norwegian cliff; or else, by some feat, he permits these bright features to belong to his total image without permitting them to reveal any precise meaning, either for himself or for his reader. Stevens, however, is objective from beginning to end; he completes all his meanings, knowing these will have little or no moral importance.

Pure or obscure, the modern poet manages not to slip into the old-fashioned moral-beautiful compound. If pure, he will not consider a subject which lends itself to moralization; that is, a subject of practical interest. It is his chief problem to find then a subject which has any interest at all. If, however, he prefers the other road, he may take the subject nearest his own humanity, a subject

759

perhaps of terrifying import; but in treating it will stop short of all moral or theoretical conclusions, and confuse his detail to the point where it leaves no positive implications.

To be more technical: it is as if the pure poet presented a subject and declined to make any prediction about it or even to start predication; and as if the obscure poet presented a subject in order to play with a great deal of important predication without ever completing any.

Personally, I prefer the rich obscure poetry to the thin pure poetry. The deaths of little boys are more exciting than the sea surfaces. It may be that the public preference, however, is otherwise. The public is inclined simply to ignore the pure poetry, because it lacks practical usefulness; but to hate the obscure poetry, because it looks important enough to attend to, and yet never yields up any specific fruit. Society, through its spokesmen the dozens of social-minded critics, who talk about the necessity of "communication," is now raging with indignation, or it may be with scorn, against the obscure poetry which this particular generation of poets has deposited. Nevertheless, both types of poetry, obscure as well as pure, aim at poetic autonomy; that is, speaking roughly, at purity.

Modern poetry in this respect is like modern painting. European painting used to be nearly as social a thing as poetry. It illustrated the themes prescribed by the priests, whether popularly (Raphael) or esoterically and symbolically (Michelangelo); did the portraits of kings and cardinals, and the scenes of battles and great occasions; worked up allegorical and sentimental subjects. But more or less suddenly it asserted its independence. So we find Impressionists, doing the most innocent tricks with landscapes and mere objects; and we find Cézanne, painting so many times and so lovingly his foolish little bowl of fruits. The procedure was a strange one for the moral laity, who could detect nothing of importance there; and indeed nothing of public importance was there, only matters of technical interest to painters, and to persons who found painting sufficient. Later, and today, we find painters taking up the most heroic human material again in the most promising manner, yet arriving at no explicit meaning and, on the whole, simply playing with its powerful symbols. (Not all painters, of course.)

Apostate, illaureate, and doomed to outlawry the modern poets may be. I have the feeling that modernism is an unfortunate road for them to have taken. But it was an inevitable one. It is not hard to defend them from imputations against their honor and their logic. It is probably a question of whether we really know them, and understand their unusual purpose, and the powerful inhibitions they impose upon themselves.

But let us approach the matter from a slightly different angle. Poets have had to become modern because the age is modern. Its modernism envelops them like a sea, or an air. Nothing in their thought can escape it.

Modern poetry is pure poetry. The motive behind it cannot be substantially different from the motive behind the other modern activities, which is certainly the driving force of all our modernism. What is its name? "Purism" would be exact, except that it does not have the zealous and contriving sound we want. "Platonism" would do, provided there were time to come to an agreement about the essential meaning of Plato's act. I think the name "Puritanism" will describe

760

this motive, if I may extend a little a term whose application in history has been mostly religious and moral.

Our period differs outwardly from other periods because it first differs inwardly. Its spiritual temper is puritanical; that is, it craves to perfect the parts of experience separately or in their purity, and is a series of isolated perfections. These have often been brilliant. But perhaps the modern program, on the whole, is not the one under which men maintain their best health and spirits. A little fear to that effect is beginning to cloud the consciousness of the brilliant moderns.

And here I conclude my defense of the modern poet. He is a good workman, and his purpose is really quite orthodox in its modernism. But it is no better.

The development of modern civilization has been a grand progression in which Puritanism has invaded first one field and then another.

The first field perhaps was religion. The religious impulse used to join to itself and dominate and hold together nearly all the fields of human experience; politics, science, art, and even industry, and by all means moral conduct. But Puritanism came in the form of the Protestant Reformation and separated religion from all its partners. Perhaps the most important of these separations was that which lopped off from religion the aesthetic properties which simple-hearted devotees and loving artists had given it. The aesthetic properties constituted the myth, which to the temperamental Protestants became superstition, and the ceremonial, which became idolatry. Under the progressive zeal of the Reformation the being of God has become rarefied in the degree that it has been purified, until we find difficulty in grasping it, and there are people who tell me, just as there are people who tell the reader, that religion as a living force here in the Western world is spent. Theology is purer or more abstract than ever before, but it would seem to belong exclusively to theologians, and it cannot by itself assemble together all those who once delighted in the moral precepts, the music and the pomp, the social communion, and the concrete Godhead, of the synthetic institution which was called religion.

Next, or perhaps at the same time, Puritanism applied itself to morality. Broad as the reach of morality may be, it is distinct enough as an experience to be capable of purification. We may say that its destiny was to become what we know as sociology, a body of positivistic science. It had to be emancipated from its religious overlords, whose authority, after all, was not a moral one. Then it had to be emancipated from the dictates of taste, or aesthetic, and this latter emancipation was the harder, and perhaps the more needless. The Greeks, though they were incipient Puritans, scarcely attempted it. They had a compound phrase meaning "beautiful-good," which even their philosophers used habitually as the name of something elemental and indissoluble. Suspicion was aroused in Greeks by a goodness which could not produce beauty, just as to a man like Spenser the idea of virtue was incomplete until it flowered into poetic form, and just as to the sympathetic French artist our new American liberty was not quite won until identifiable with an able-bodied demi-goddess lifting a torch. The splitting up of the moral-beautiful compound for the sake of the pure moral article is visibly at work in the New Testament, and in the bourgeois cult of plainness in seventeenth-century England, and in the finicky private life of a Puritan moralist like Kant, and today in moral or sociological

761

treatises (and authors) which neither exhibit nor discuss charm. Now, it is true that we moralize with "maximum efficiency" when we do it technically, or abstractly, but when that comes to be the rule we no longer approach a moral discussion with anything but a moral interest. To be moral is no longer to be "decent," and it looks as if moral appeal had become something less wide and less instant than it was.

Then Puritanism worked upon politics. I am not prepared to go deeply into this, but it is evident that purification consisted in taking the state away from the church, from the monarch, from the feudal aristocracy, from any other concrete attachments, in order that it might propel itself by the force of pure statecraft. Progress in this direction meant constitutionalism, parlimentarianism, republicanism. A modern state like ours is transparent in the perfection of its logic. But that does not make it the more realistic. It is obliged to count upon a universal and continuous will on the part of the citizens to accept an abstract formula of political action. But such a will may not be there. The population, not being composed exclusively of politicians, is inclined to delegate statecraft to those who profess it. The old mixed states had a greater variety of loyalties to appeal to.

Puritanism is an ideal which not all persons are strong enough to realize, but only those with great power of concentration. Its best chance of success lies in individual projects. Accordingly, Puritanism fairly came into its own in the vast multitude of private enterprises which go together to make modern science. Galileo and Kepler found science captive to religious dogma. America, the paradise of puritanism, was not yet in being, but England was; and there presently, while other Puritanisms were going on, Lord Bacon was able to anticipate the complete emancipation of science by virtue of its adoption of the pure experimental method. Now, there have been other incubi besides religion resting upon science at one time or another; and chiefly the tendency of poetry to haunt its deliberations. Poetry is a figurative way of expression, science is a technical or abstract way; but since science employs language, the figurative associations are hard to keep out. In earlier days poetry kept close to science, and it did not seem so strange if Lucretius wanted to set forth the body of accepted science in verse. But poetry now cannot attend science into its technical labyrinth. The result is greater success for scientists, but not necessarily their greater happiness as men; and the general understanding on our part that we will follow science if we are scientists, but otherwise will leave it to the scientists.

It was but one step that Puritanism had to go from there into the world of business, where the material sciences are systematically applied. The rise of the modern business world is a development attendant upon the freedom which it has enjoyed; upon business for business's sake, or pure business, or "laissez faire," with such unconditioned principles as efficiency, technological improvement, and maximum productivity. If I wished to attack the record of business, I should by now have been long anticipated. It is common opinion that business as a self-contained profession has created business men who are defective in their humanity; that the conduct of business has made us callous to personal relations and to social justice; and that many of the occupations which business has devised are, in the absence of aesthetic standards, servile.

All these exclusions and specializations, and many more, have been making

762

modern life what it is. It is significant that every specialization on the list has had to resist the insidious charms of aesthetic experience before its own perfection could arise. (Evidently the aesthetic interest is remarkably catholic among our faculties in its affinities; ready to attach itself easily to almost any sort of moment; a ubiquitous element in experience, it might be thought, which it would be unhealthy to cast out.) But the energy of so deep an impulse as Puritanism had to flow through all the channels, and to come to its last outlet in a pure art, a pure poetry. Those who have not observed the necessity may choose to hold its predestined agents the poets in contempt, or in amazement. The poets are in the spirit of their time. On the one hand, they have been pushed out of their old attachments, whereby they used to make themselves useful to public causes, by the specialists who did not want the respective causes to be branded amateurism. On the other hand, they are moved by a universal tendency into their own appropriate kind of specialization, which can be, as they have been at pains to show, as formidable as any other.

Considerations of this kind, I feel sure, have been more or less precisely within the intuition of all modern poets, and have motivated their performance. Technically, they are quite capable of writing the old compound poetry, but they cannot bring themselves to do it; or rather, when they have composed it in unguarded moments, as modern poets still sometimes do, they are under the necessity of destroying it immediately. There is no baffling degree of virtuosity in the old lines,

> Roll on, thou deep and dark blue Ocean, roll!
> Ten thousand fleets sweep over thee in vain:
> Man marks the earth with ruin, his control
> Stops with the shore.

The modern poet can accomplish just as elegant a rumination as this; but thinks it would commit him to an anachronism, for this is the style of an older period. In that period, though it was a comparatively late one, and though this poet thought he was in advance of it, the prophets of society were still numbering and tuning their valuable reflections before they saw fit to release them; and morality, philosophy, religion, science, and art could still meet comfortably in one joint expression, though perhaps not with the same distinction they might have gained if they had had their pure and several expressions. A passage of Byron's if sprung upon an unsuspecting modern would be felt immediately as "dating"; it would be felt as something that did very well for those dark ages before the modern mind achieved its own disintegration and perfected its faculties serially.

Even as readers, we must testify readily to the force of this time-principle. We sometimes pore over an old piece of poetry for so long that we fall under its spell and forget that its spirit is not our spirit. But we began to read it in a peculiar manner; by saying to ourselves, This is early Greek epic, This is seventeenth-century English drama. By means of one of the ripest and subtlest powers in us, that is, the historical sense, we made an adaptation of our minds to its mind, and were able to suspend those centuries which had intervened. Those centuries had made our minds much more knowing and at the same time, it is to

763

be feared, much less suggestible. Yet it is not exactly with our own minds that we are reading the old poetry; otherwise we could not read it. For when we come back to our own world there begins to function in us a different style of consciousness altogether. And if we had begun to read a poetry of this old sort by saying, This was written last night by the poet around the corner, we could not have put up with it. If we throw away impatiently a contemporaneous poetry which displays archaisms of diction, what will we do with that which displays archaisms of temper? It looks spurious; for we require our art, and the living artists require it too, to be as contemporaneous as our banking or our locomotion.

What, then, is the matter with a pure poetry? The question is really more theoretical than practical. A school, an age, is involved by such a question, not merely some small poem or poet. And there is nothing the matter with this particular branch of purity which is not the matter with our other modern activities. All are affected by Puritanism, just as the vegetation is affected, generally and indifferently, by the climate.

It is impossible to answer the question categorically because the items are intangible. But we find ourselves reasoning about it as well as we can, which is as follows:

You may dissociate the elements of experience and exploit them separately. But then at the best you go on a schedule of small experiences, taking them in turn, and trusting that when the rotation is complete you will have missed nothing. And at the worst you will become so absorbed in some one small experience that you will forget to go on and complete the schedule; in that case you will have missed something. The theory that excellence lies in the perfection of the single functions, and that society should demand that its members be hard specialists, assumes that there is no particular harm in missing something. But I do not see why. A maniac with a fixed idea is a variety of specialist, and an absorbing specialty is a small mania.

As for poetry, it seems to me a pity that its beauty should have to be cloistered and conventual, if it is "pure," or teasing and evasive, if it is "obscure." The union of beauty with goodness and truth has been common enough to be regarded as natural. It is the dissociation which is unnatural and painful.

But when we talk about simple and compound experiences, we are evidently employing a chemical mode of speech to represent something we cannot quite make out. Units of consciousness are hard to handle scientifically; it takes more science than we have. Max Eastman thinks the future of literary criticism is bound up with the future of psychology, and very likely it is; but it is difficult to share his sanguine expectations of that science. It cannot become as effective a science as chemistry.

Nevertheless, I shall make a tentative argument from the analogy of chemistry. Lemonade is only a mechanical mixture, not very interesting to chemists. Aside from the water, a drop of lemonade contains lemon and sugar in no standard proportions. If it tastes too sour, add sugar and if it tastes too sweet, add lemon. (And do not forget to stir the mixture.) No matter what the final proportions, you still detect in the lemonade the sweet taste and the sour; though this is too abstract a matter to bother about if the lemonade is satisfactory, for in that case you simply drink it.

764

Table salt, however, is a true chemical compound; a molecule of it is NaCl. Understanding this, you do not claim to know the taste either of sodium or of chlorine when you say you are acquainted with the taste of salt. Whatever the Na was and however it tasted by itself, it gave up that identity when it compounded with Cl; and *vice versa*.

NaCl is found in the state of nature, where it is much commoner than either of its constituents. But suppose the chemists decided to have nothing to do with NaCl because of its compoundness, and undertook to extract from it the pure Na and Cl to serve on the table. Suppose they made war on all the natural compounds, broke them down into the hundred or so atomic elements, and asked us to live on these alone. The beneficiaries would regard this service as well-meaning but mistaken.

But we provide the necessities for our minds and affections with more harshness than we dare use on our stomachs and bodies—so inferior in precision is our knowledge of minds to our knowledge of bodies. Poets are now under the influence of a perfectly arbitrary theory which I have called Puritanism. They pursue A, an aesthetic element thought always to have the same taste and to be the one thing desirable for poets. They will not permit the presence near it of M, the moral element, because that will produce the lemonade MA, and they do not approve of lemonade. In lemonade the A gets itself weakened and neutralized by the M.

But it is possible that MA is not a drop of lemonade after all, but a true molecule, into which the separate M and the separate A have disappeared and out of which an entirely new taste is born. The effects which we attribute to a poet like Virgil, or Milton, are on the following order: pious, philosophical, imaginative, sonorous, and the like. But perhaps the effect which we actually receive from the poetry is not that of an aggregate or series or mechanical mixture of distinct properties but only the single effect of a compound. In that event the properties will exist separate only in our minds, by a later act of qualitative analysis, and they will not really be in the poetry in their own identities.

Is the old-fashioned full poetry a mechanical mixture like lemonade or a chemical compound like table salt? That is probably the most important question which the modern critics have opened up to speculation. There are many corollary questions along with it, like these: When does the display of doctrine in poetry incur the charge of didacticism? And must the poet also bear arms— that is, like the economist and the social reformer, view his performance in the light of a utility rather than an end?

Now some poetry, so-called, is not even lemonade, for the ingredients have not been mixed, much less compounded. Lumps of morality and image lie side by side, and are tasted in succession. T. S. Eliot thinks that this has been the character of a great deal of English poetry since the age of Dryden. Such poetry occupies some of the best room in the library, and takes up some of the best time of the earnest student of literature. It is decidedly one of the causes of that revulsion of feeling on the part of the modern poet which drives him away from the poetic tradition.

When our critical theory is complete, perhaps we shall be able to distinguish various combinations of elements passing for poetry; thus, poetry by assemblage, poetry by mixture, and poetry by composition. The last of these sound the best.

765

I suggest that critics and philosophers fix their most loving attention upon certain natural compounds in human experience. But I say so diffidently, and not too hopefully. It will take a long time to change the philosophical set which has come over the practice of the poets. The intellectual climate in which they live will have to be altered first. (*1938*)

DONALD DAVIDSON

1893–

Donald Davidson was born in Campbellsville, Tennessee, on August 18, 1893. He received his A.B. and M.A. degrees from Vanderbilt University. After serving in World War I as an officer in the A.E.F., he became a member, in 1920, of the Department of English at Vanderbilt, where he is still teaching. For six years (1924–1930) he served as literary editor of the Nashville *Tennessean*. Since 1931, Davidson has taught at the summer sessions of the Bread Loaf School of English in Middlebury, Vermont.

Davidson is nationally recognized for his work as a creative writer, editor, historian, and critic, as well as an outstanding teacher. His two-volume work, *The Tennessee* (1946, 1948), in the Rivers of America Series is generally regarded as the best of those distinguished studies. As a poet, Davidson issued two volumes of verse—*An Outland Piper* (1924) and *The Tall Men* (1927)—before publishing his *Lee in the Mountains* (1938), which might be termed his "Selected Poems." This volume was reissued by Charles Scribner's Sons in 1950.

Davidson has been an outstanding spokesman for his region, and was one of the founders and leaders of the Fugitive and Agrarian movements at Vanderbilt. He was one of twelve prominent Southerners who published the symposium, *I'll Take My Stand* (1930). In *The Attack on Leviathan* (1938), Davidson voices his opposition to the increasing centralization of economic and political power. The intention of this book is perhaps best stated in its preface: "When these agencies [those of the national government] are discovered in the act of arranging such intimate matters as one's income tax, or the education of one's children, or the veritable root and stock of his life, it is time for the layman to put aside his awe and ask whether these people really know what they are talking about, or whether they are, after all, not divine, but perhaps as fallibly human as oneself."

Lee in the Mountains

Walking into the shadows, walking alone
Where the sun falls through the ruined boughs of locusts
Up to the president's office. . . .
                                    Hearing the voices
Whisper, *Hush, it is General Lee!* And strangely
Hearing my own voice say, *Good morning, boys.*
(*Don't get up. You are early. It is long*
Before the bell. You will have long to wait
On these cold steps. . . .)

                        The young have time to wait.
But soldiers' faces under their tossing flags
Lift no more by any road or field,
And I am spent with old wars and new sorrow.
Walking the rocky path, where steps decay
And the paint cracks and grass eats on the stone.
It is not General Lee, young men . . .
It is Robert Lee in a dark civilian suit who walks,
An outlaw fumbling for the latch, a voice
Commanding in a dream where no flag flies.

My father's house is taken and his hearth
Left to the candle-drippings where the ashes
Whirl at a chimney-breath on the cold stone.
I can hardly remember my father's look, I cannot
Answer his voice as he calls farewell in the misty
Mounting where riders gather at gates.
He was old then—I was a child—his hand
Held out for mine, some daybreak snatched away,
And he rode out, a broken man. Now let
His lone grave keep, surer than cypress roots,
The vow I made beside him. God too late
Unseals to certain eyes the drift
Of time and the hopes of men and a sacred cause.
The fortune of the Lees goes with the land
Whose sons will keep it still. My mother
Told me much. She sat among the candles,
Fingering the *Memoirs,* now so long unread.

767

And as my pen moves on across the page
Her voice comes back, a murmuring distillation
Of old Virginia times now faint and gone,
The hurt of all that was and cannot be.

Why did my father write? I know he saw
History clutched as a wraith out of blowing mist
Where the tongues are loud, and a glut of little souls
Laps at the too much blood and the burning house.
He would have his say, but I shall not have mine.
What I do is only a son's devoir
To a lost father. Let him only speak.
The rest must pass to men who never knew
(But on a written page) the strike of armies,
And never heard the long Confederate cry
Charge through the muzzling smoke or saw the bright
Eyes of the beardless boys go up to death.
It is Robert Lee who writes with his father's hand—
The rest must go unsaid and the lips be locked.

If all were told, as it cannot be told—
If all the dread opinion of the heart
Now could speak, now in the shame and torment
Lashing the bound and trampled States—

If a word were said, as it cannot be said—

I see clear waters run in Virginia's Valley
And in the house the weeping of young women
Rises no more. The waves of grain begin.
The Shenandoah is golden with new grain.
The Blue Ridge, crowned with a haze of light,
Thunders no more. The horse is at plough. The rifle
Returns to the chimney crotch and the hunter's hand.
And nothing else than this? Was it for this
That on an April day we stacked our arms
Obedient to a soldier's trust? To lie
Ground by heels of little men,
Forever maimed, defeated, lost, impugned?
And was I then betrayed? Did I betray?

If it were said, as still it might be said—
If it were said, and a word should run like fire,
Like living fire into the roots of grass,
The sunken flag would kindle on wild hills,
The brooding hearts would waken, and the dream
Stir like a crippled phantom under the pines,

And this torn earth would quicken into shouting
Beneath the feet of ragged bands—
                                    The pen
Turns to the waiting page, the sword
Bows to the rust that cankers and the silence.

Among these boys whose eyes lift up to mine
Within gray walls where droning wasps repeat
A hollow reveille, I still must face,
Day after day, the courier with his summons
Once more to surrender, now to surrender all.
Without arms or men I stand, but with knowledge only
I face what long I saw, before others knew,
When Pickett's men streamed back, and I heard the tangled
Cry of the Wilderness wounded, bloody with doom.

The mountains, once I said, in the little room
At Richmond, by the huddled fire, but still
The President shook his head. The mountains wait,
I said, in the long beat and rattle of siege
At cratered Petersburg. Too late
We sought the mountains and those people came.
And Lee is in mountains now, beyond Appomattox,
Listening long for voices that never will speak
Again; hearing the hoofbeats come and go and fade
Without a stop, without a brown hand lifting
The tent-flap, or a bugle call at dawn,
Or ever on the long white road the flag
Of Jackson's quick brigades. I am alone,
Trapped, consenting, taken at last in mountains.

It is not the bugle now, or the long roll beating.
The simple stroke of a chapel bell forbids
The hurtling dream, recalls the lonely mind.
Young men, the God of your fathers is a just
And merciful God Who in this blood once shed
On your green altars measures out all days,
And measures out the grace
Whereby alone we live;
And in His might He waits,
Brooding within the certitude of time,
To bring this lost forsaken valor
And the fierce faith undying
And the love quenchless
To flower among the hills to which we cleave,
To fruit upon the mountains wither we flee,
Never forsaking, never denying

769

His children and His children's children forever
Unto all generations of the faithful heart.

(*1938*)

Sanctuary

You must remember this when I am gone,
And tell your sons—for you will have tall sons,
And times will come when answers will not wait.
Remember this: if ever defeat is black
Upon your eyelids, go to the wilderness
In the dread last of trouble, for your foe
Tangles there, more than you, and paths are strange
To him, that are your paths, in the wilderness,
And were your fathers' paths, and once were mine.

You must remember this, and mark it well
As I have told it—what my eyes have seen
And where my feet have walked beyond forgetting.
But tell it not often, tell it only at last
When your sons know what blood runs in their veins.
And when the danger comes, as come it will,
Go as your fathers went with woodsman's eyes
Uncursed, unflinching, studying only the path.

First, what you cannot carry, burn or hide.
Leave nothing here for *him* to take or eat.
Bury, perhaps, what you can surely find
If good chance ever bring you back again.
Level the crops. Take only what you need:
A little corn for an ash-cake, a little
Side-meat for your three days' wilderness ride.
Horses for your women and your children,
And one to lead, if you should have that many.
Then go. At once. Do not wait until
You see *his* great dust rising in the valley.
Then it will be too late.
Go when you hear that he has crossed Will's Ford.
Others will know and pass the word to you—
A tap on the blinds, a hoot-owl's cry at dusk.

770

Do not look back. You can see your roof afire
When you reach high ground. Yet do not look.

Do not turn. Do not look back.
Go further on. Go high. Go deep.

The line of this rail-fence east across the old-fields
Leads to the cane-bottoms, Back of that,
A white-oak tree beside a spring, the one
Chopped with three blazes on the hillward side.
There pick up the trail. I think it was
A buffalo path once or an Indian road.
You follow it three days along the ridge
Until you reach the spruce woods. Then a cliff
Breaks, where the trees are thickest, and you look
Into a cove, and right across, Chilhowee
Is suddenly there, and you are home at last.
Sweet springs of mountain water in that cove
Run always. Deer and wild turkey range.
Your kin, knowing the way, long there before you
Will have good fires and kettles on to boil,
Bough-shelters reared and thick beds of balsam.
There in tall timber you will be as free
As were your fathers once when Tryon raged
In Carolina hunting Regulators,
Or Tarleton rode to hang the old-time Whigs.
Some tell how in that valley young Sam Houston
Lived long ago with his brother, Oo-loo-te-ka,
Reading Homer among the Cherokee;
And others say a Spaniard may have found it
Far from De Soto's wandering turned aside,
And left his legend on a boulder there.
And some that this was a sacred place to all
Old Indian tribes before the Cherokee
Came to our eastern mountains. Men have found
Images carved in bird-shapes there and faces
Moulded into the great kind look of gods.
These old tales are like prayers. I only know
This is the secret refuge of our race
Told only from a father to his son,
A trust laid on your lips, as though a vow
To generations past and yet to come.
There, from the bluffs above, you may at last
Look back to all you left, and trace
His dust and flame, and plan your harrying
If you would gnaw his ravaging flank, or smite
Him in his glut among the smouldering ricks.
Or else, forgetting ruin, you may lie
On sweet grass by a mountain stream, to watch
The last wild eagle soar or the last raven

771

Cherish his brood within their rocky nest,
Or see, when mountain shadows first grow long,
The last enchanted white deer come to drink.

(*1938*)

Still Rebels, Still Yankees

At a meeting of Southern writers in Charleston some years ago, Laurence Stallings looked belligerently around him and expressed an ardent preference for a "Balkanized America." "What I like about Charleston," he said, "is that it has resisted Abraham Lincoln's attempts to put the country into Arrow Collars. If the South had won the war, the country would have had lots more color."

The rebelliousness of Mr. Stallings need not compel us to suspect him of being an unreconstructed Southerner disguised as a man of letters, who is looking for artistic reasons to justify what arms and politics once failed to secure. Discontent with the uniformity of America is common enough; what is not common is the knowledge that this uniformity, a byword ever since James Bryce looked at the American commonwealth through the spectacles of the Gilded Age, is more a myth than a reality.

As a myth, it probably represents the wishful thinking of those who, for their own designs, want America to become uniform. Actually America is not yet uniform; very likely it is less uniform than it once was, and far more Balkanized than Mr. Stallings dreams. The unreconstructed Southerners have done their part in keeping it Balkan; but there are unreconstructed Yankees, too, and other unreconstructed Americans of all imaginable sorts, everywhere engaged in preserving their local originality and independence.

The only people who do not know this are certain experts who do most of the current talking about American society. They live in a sociological pickle of statistics and progress. They are eternally looking for what they call "social values," but they strangely confine their research to libraries and graduate "projects" at the larger universities. They avoid the places where social values may be encountered in the flesh. If they stumble upon a living social value, walking visibly about some spot of earth and drawing its nutriment from a tradition embodied in the houses, speech, crafts, music, folklore, and wisdom of an actual people, their rule is to denounce it as an anachronism and to call for its extermination. For them, nothing must grow according to its nature, but things "develop" by laboratory formulae, which are obtained by inspecting the reactions of the most abnormal and depressed specimens of humankind, too weak to protest against sociological vivisection.

Those of us who still believe in the map of the United States know that it marks the residence of some diverse Americans who had better not go unacknowledged. In Vermont, for instance, are people who are still Yankees; and in Georgia, and elsewhere, there are still Rebels. I remember talking with a

772

From The Attack on Leviathan *by Donald Davidson, University of North Carolina Press, 1938. Used by permission of the author.*

certain Virginian who watched a Vermont sunset with me, one summer evening. As the sun passed below the distant Adirondacks, we looked at the Green Mountains around us, and at the trim Vermont fields where all the weeds were flowers and all the grass was hay. In the clear detail of the afterglow we saw the forests of spruce and balsam and maple, and spoke of how the very wilderness, in this New England state, had uprightness and order. The woods were as snug and precise as a Yankee kitchen—no ragged edges, no sprawling, nothing out of place. In the clearings the farmhouses were all painted; and the barns were painted, too. The streams were orthodox streams, almost model streams, with water always translucent and stones rounded and picturesquely placed among moss and ferns. They were often called "brooks"—a word that for Southerners existed only on the printed page.

On this land, the Virginian said, the Yankees had looked so intimately and long that, like the man in Hawthorne's story of the Great Stone Face, they had become the image of what they contemplated. The Yankee genius of Vermont was upright, vertical, and no doubt Puritan. Where the landscape itself enforced consistency and order, how could the people concede much virtue to inconsistency and irregularity? The forebears of the Vermont Yankee had once failed to understand how Southerners could be devoted both to slavery and democracy. That old failure of understanding did not seem queer, or worth more than a passing sigh, to two Southerners who stood looking at sunset upon a land whose gentled wildness suggested the urgent possibility of a well-ordered universe, cut to a discreet Yankee pattern. But the human geography of America had now become a patricolored thing, sprawling across the continent in a crazy-quilt of provinces, or sections, each with its private notion of a universe. No longer, as in the sixties, could the Yankee make bold to set up a general pattern for the entire Union. He had enough to do if he would defend and preserve what was peculiarly his own—his very own, surely, in upper New England. In such a purpose of preservation the two Southerners at last could make bold to sympathize, even to help if possible. But preservation could not be achieved without recognizing a principle of diversity in American life. Only by such means could one make any sense out of Lamar's famous epigram in his eulogy on Sumner, "My countrymen, know one another and you will love one another"; it ceased to have meaning if America was to be subjugated to the ideal of uniformity, or to the ideal universe that some one section might generate.

But how could the principle of diversity be inculcated? On the negative side, certain false images, the product of legend or propaganda, must somehow be counterbalanced. Regrettably enough, some of the fairest legends caused the greatest embarrassment. To the Virginian I recalled the horror of a good lady from the Middle West, who was motoring from Washington to Richmond. Mount Vernon was all right, she thought; there the legend was safely frozen. But beyond, on the road to Richmond, what had become of all the great mansions she had read about, the cotton fields with Negroes caroling, the old gentlemen in goatees and white vests, sipping mint juleps in the shade? They were not visible. There were only a few scattered shacks and tumbledown barns in miles of impenetrable wilderness that looked for all the world as it must have looked when John Smith first invaded it. If she could have encountered the legend,

773

the lady would have been content. But not seeing it or knowing how to locate it, she was smitten with a housewifely desire to get at this ragged land with a good broom and whisk it into seemliness.

Other sojourners had been anxious to do a far more drastic tidying-up. The Harlan County visitors, the Scottsboro attorneys, the shock troops of Dayton and Gastonia asked no questions about the genius of place. Wherever they went on their missions of social justice, they carried with them a legend of the future, more dangerously abstract than the legend of the past, and sternly demanded that the local arrangements be made to correspond with it, at whatever cost. The local arrangements, indeed, might well bear some mending. And yet the only America that the visitors offered as a model was an overgrown urban America, forever in process of becoming one laboratory experiment after another.

What could be done about all this? Our answers were shrouded in darkness as we walked back to the log fires and good company of a New England inn. The Virginian, after the fashion of good Southerners who do not want to let anybody know the uncertainty of their minds under modern conditions, did not propose any answer. Instead, he told several good stories. They were his courteous and delightful way of saying that he was being pounded between his own unyielding loyalty and the howling respectability of the great world.

If any answer is to be found, if anything positive is to be done, it must surely be through a laborious process of discovering America all over again. When one looks at America, not to see how it does or does not fit the synthetic ideals proposed for its future, but only with the modest purpose of detecting the realities—let us say the social values—that persist in local habitations, he soon realizes that comparisons are more fruitful than condemnations. More specifically, when one has the good fortune to go directly from a summer in Vermont to an autumn and winter in Middle Georgia, he forms a clear picture of sectional differences. This picture is not in the least favorable to the notion that the diverse America of the Rebels and Yankees is in any immediate danger of being submerged.

If on coming to Vermont I had consulted the modern legend of New England that vaguely haunted my mind, I would have received the iconoclastic shock which our advanced thinkers argue is the first step toward salvation. Had not a New England migrant to the South assured me that his ancestral acres were now inhabited by Montenegrins, who had turned them into a goat farm? Had not the sepulchral Eugene O'Neill and others told tales of the poverty and decadence of New England life? The farms were deserted, it was said; the immigrants and mill towns had come; the Yankees had left for parts unknown, or, remaining, had become degenerate. Even the loyalty of Robert Frost gave no comfortable assurance, if one accepted the New York aleck's criticism of *North of Boston;* though there were many wistful asides in which Frost put forth the guarded wisdom of a not yet daunted soul. The New England of Whittier and Webster was supposed to be extinct; it had been replaced by Puritan-baiters and F. Scott Fitzgeraldites who drank cocktails and read Proust when not conducting the insurance business of the United States.

But if the Vermont that I saw was in the least representative of New England, this composite picture was a wild detraction. In Vermont, if nowhere else, a New England like that of Whittier and Webster miraculously persisted, a reality

774

capable of reducing a Southerner almost to despairing envy. I could understand what led Walter Hines Page, a quarter of a century ago, to disparage his native North Carolina and fall in love with New England. But the time was past when one needed to disparage or praise in the interest of the America Page dreamed about, for in the 1930's it seemed impossible of realization, or, where realized, already past saving. To one who did not accept Lincoln's quaint idea that the United States must become "all one thing or all the other," it seemed more than ever true that the unity of America must rest, first of all, on a decent respect for sectional differences.

If Vermont and Georgia could be taken in a broad way to stand for New England and the deep South, one could easily trace out the most general differences. The Vermont towns, like the Vermont landscape, were swept and garnished, as if the Day of Judgment might at any moment summon them into the presence of the celestial inspector. They looked as if Vermonters lived by the adage "Handsome is as handsome does," and one could reflect that this proverb might well have issued from some collaborative effort of Poor Richard and Jonathan Edwards. The most delightful of Southern towns was almost certain to mix a little squalor with its grandeurs. Here, what a Southerner most particularly noticed, was the neatly painted aspect of everything, the absence of ramshackle buildings and litter, the white steeples of churches, the shipshapeness of streets, yards, garages, barber shops, and public buildings. By some special benison of God and the New England conscience, not a billboard had been allowed to sprout between Bennington and the Canadian border. Perhaps by the same double grace, not a weed sprouted, either. All the weeds had turned into ferns and buttercups. Vermont farms were Currier and Ives prints of what good farms ought to look like, with orchards and brooks in exactly the right place and gates that did not need mending. In the background were lakes and mountains where one would put them if he were Aladdin or Wordsworth. It was not surprising to be told that hardly a poison snake, and no poison ivy, existed in the state of Vermont; or to find that there were excellent trails running the whole length of the Green Mountains, with fingerposts at every wilderness crossroads, and tin huts, with beds, firewood, and caretaker, atop of the highest peak. A few nagging irregularities of nature, like blackflies and mosquitoes, seemed really blasphemous in a land to which God had given a monopoly of all things good and precise. No wonder, with all this beneficence around them, that the Yankees remembered the *Mayflower* and forgot John Smith, honored Bunker Hill and neglected King's Mountain. If they could claim such priority in the benevolence of God, their proprietary feeling toward the Revolutionary War and their almost hereditary claim to the direction of the United States government were by comparison insignificant appurtenances, theirs as a matter of course and by general presumption.

Although I did not hold very devotedly to the economic determinism of modern historians, it was a temptation to say that the people were a great deal like the land. There was the climate, which put keenness into a Southerner's veins. Summer was short, and one had to make the most of it; winter was severe, and one had to keep shield and buckler perpetually ready against it—in that matter was God benevolent or ruthless? Short summers and cold winters made the Vermont Yankee frugal and careful. He must watch his corners. If he were caught napping, he would perish. So much and no more was the gift of his seasons; so much and no more was the rule of his nature. And one had to watch over his neighbor as well as work with him if the general security were not to be imperiled by some outrageous letting down of bars. Very likely, the New England civic conscience derived as much from the imperatives of climate as from the Puritan tradition; the one egged on the other.

No great check had ever been put upon the development of qualities that the Southerners recognized as ineradicably Yankee. History had been as kind to the Yankee as God had been kind. Since Revolutionary times no great sudden change had ever swept over these peaceful towns and this quiet landscape. Industrialism had come slowly and somewhat agreeably upon a people who had the ingenuity to use it and the moral force to make it behave. How could they who thought they knew how to tame the monster realize that he might walk unshackled and ravening elsewhere? The Yankees, indeed, had never tasted defeat. Since Burgoyne's expedition no invader had come upon them to ravage and destroy. They had freed the Negroes, replying "I can" to duty's "Thou must"; but they were fortunately exempt from the results of emancipation, for no Negroes lived among them to acquaint them with the disorder of unashamed and happy dirt. One knew that a slum in New England would be a well-managed slum, and that New Englanders would comprehend Secretary Perkins's horror at the lack of plumbing in unreformed America and her notion of saving the barefoot South by building shoe factories. For in New England humanitarianism was the natural flower of good sense. In a land where everything was so right, it was hard to imagine a perverse land where so much could be so wrong without disturbing either a people's composure or their happiness.

But in the plantation country of Middle Georgia the social values required a different yardstick. The genius of Georgia was stretched out, relaxed and easy, in keeping with the landscape, which required a large and horizontal view of mundane affairs. The Georgian assumed that God would have sense and heart enough to take into consideration, when Judgment Day came around, a good deal besides external and man-made appearances. God was a gentleman, indeed, who would certainly know, without being told, that one was a person, a somebody, doing his best among some rather amazing arrangements that had better not be talked about too much. The climate might or might not predispose the Georgia Rebel to laziness; the fact was, he worked and fretted more than the Yankee knew. But the Rebel idea was never to seem to work and fret. You must not let your work ride you, was the saying. In plain truth, you did not need to. The land was bountiful, and the Lord would provide, and in event of the Lord's failure or displeasure you could always fall back on your kinfolks.

Where the seasons were all mixed up, so that autumn merged into spring without any sharp demarcation, and you might have a dubious summer in the middle of winter, it became almost a point of honor not to worry too much about provision. There was no need to watch corners when something was growing all the time. Almost anything would grow in Middle Georgia, and almost everything did grow, including weeds whose invasions could not possibly be repelled from every roadside and ditch if they were to be kept out of cotton and corn.

The Georgia landscape had a serene repose that lulled a man out of all need

776

of conscience. It was anything but swept and garnished. It could be mild or majestic or genial and savage depending on what view you got of pines against red earth, or Negro cabins underneath their chinaberry trees, or sedge grass running into gullies and thence to impenetrable swamps, or deserted mansions lost in oak groves and magnolias. Rivers were muddy and at times unrestrained; they got out of bounds, as all things natural did here. In the pine barrens you might get an impression of desolation and melancholy; but things could grow lushly too, with the overpowering vegetable passion that harrowed the Puritan soul of Amy Lowell when she visited the Magnolia Gardens at Charleston. But finally, it was a well-tilled country, where you were forever seeing the Negro and his mule against the far horizon, or the peach orchards bursting into an intoxicating pink.

The seasons were full of charms and intimidations. Spring, with its dogwood blossoms and soft airs, might deliver a tornado or a flood; summer, full of grown corn and harvest ease, might turn into dusty drouth. The woods that lured you to enter and gave nuts and flowers for the taking were full of hidden terrors. Sit on a mossy bank without precaution, and in a few hours you might be on fire with chigoe bites. Stoop to pick a flower, and you might find a rattlesnake. Indoors the housewife had to fight cockroaches and flies; outdoors were hawks, polecats, weasels, possums, coons, and other varmints to harry the henhouse. Precision, for the Georgian, must rank among the Utopian virtues. If New England encouraged man to believe in an ordered universe, Georgia—and a good deal of the South besides—compelled him to remember that there were snakes in Eden. Nature, so ingratiating and beautiful, which bound the Georgian to his land with a love both possessive and fearful, was a fair but dreadful mistress, unpredictable and uncontrollable as God. The New Englander knew exactly where to find nature yielding, and he could make his arrangements accordingly. But the Georgian never knew. His safest policy was to relax, and he readily developed a great degree of tolerance for irregularity in nature and man. At his lowest level, this quality made him lackadaisical and trifling. In this he differed from the New England Yankee, who became a perfectionist, and then at his worst might turn into zealot, strangely intolerant even while, as idealist, he argued for tolerance.

History, like God and nature, had been both generous and unkind to Georgia and the South. The Georgia Rebel must approach his early history through a bloody link of war and reconstruction that was hazy and bygone to the Vermont Yankee. Defeat had possessed him and had rubbed deep into his wounds. Around him were the visible reminders of destruction and humiliation. His land had been ravaged and rebuilt, and he had been told to forget. But he would not and could not forget, and was therefore torn between his loyalty and his awareness that the great world was bored with his not forgetting. He had been rebuked for being inept at administering a newfangled government that he did not understand or like any too well, and in which he had been allowed to participate only by a kind of negligent afterthought. Turning desperately to the industrial civilization against which he had once taken arms, he had played it as a hedge against the problematic future. Though agrarian at heart, he had been forced to wonder whether the ingenious Yankee might not be right after all.

Thus he remembered the faith and hankered after the fleshpots at the same

777

time. But industrialism, declining to be treated as a mere hedge, began Sherman's march to the sea all over again. It piled ugliness upon wreckage and threw the old arrangements out of kilter. The United Daughters of the Confederacy and the Kiwanis Club flourished side by side. Mule wagon and automobile, fundamentalism and liberalism, education and illiteracy, aristocratic pride and backwoods independence disproved the axiom that two bodies cannot occupy the same space. Cities that preserved the finest flavor of the old régime had to be approached over brand-new roads where billboards, tourist camps, filling stations, and factories broke out in a modernistic rash among the water oaks and Spanish moss. And everywhere was the Negro, a cheerful grinning barnacle tucked away in all the tender spots of Southern life, not to be removed without pain, not to be cherished without tragedy. The Georgian, when reproached for his intolerance, told himself that actually nobody outdid him in fond tolerance of the Negro. Lynchings, the work of hotheads and roustabouts, were regrettable; but what did a few lynchings count in the balance against the continual forbearance and solicitude that the Georgian felt he exercised toward these amiable children of cannibals, whose skins by no conceivable act of Congress or educational program could be changed from black to white. The presence of the Negro, which had its advantages in agriculture and domestic service, made the Georgian's life both comfortable and ramshackle; it gave him devoted servants and social problems, cheap labor and hideous slums, an endless flow of folklore and anecdote, and eternal apprehension for the future. But in his own way the Georgian respected the Negro as another irregularity, taking a human and personal form, that had somehow to be lived with. He distrusted all ready-made prescriptions for bringing about regularity. In Georgia, life went along horizontally: you never crossed a bridge until you came to it—and maybe not then.

But sociologists not only cross bridges; they build all imaginable kinds of new ones. The picture of America, as sociologically reformed, does not contemplate any great concessions to Yankee uprightness or Rebel relaxation. Indeed, the sociologist, armed with science, is ready to follow reformation with transformation. In the vast inevitable working of the social forces, sectional differences become irrelevant. With a cold smile the sociologist pronounces a death sentence upon Rebel and Yankee alike. Not that they matter very much—but they will have to yield!

When he talks like this, I am perversely compelled to remember the individuals I have seen, Brother Jonathan of Vermont and Cousin Roderick of Georgia, whom I cannot imagine as yielding to the puny weapons flourished by our social philosophers. They are local incarnations of the Old Adam. They are the immovable bodies that can furnish the irresistible social forces with an incalculable meeting. They are human beings, undebatably alive; and they are different.

Brother Jonathan lives in Yankeetown—for a place name is often a "town" in New England, and less often a "ville" or a "burg" as in the South. He is a wizened little chip of a man, with blue eyes and a bald head, and he looks frail enough for any northwest wind to blow away. But there is not a wind on this planet strong enough to blow Brother Jonathan off his mountain farm. If any wind contrived to do so, he would climb right back again in the matter-of-fact way that Robert Frost describes in *Brown's Descent*—he would "bow with grace to natural law, and then go round it on his feet."

Brother Jonathan is past seventy years, and his wife Priscilla is well over sixty, but between them they still manage to do most of the daily work, in house and field, for a two-hundred-acre farm, most of which is in woodland and meadow. Nathaniel, their adopted son, helps some now and then; but Nathaniel, who is carpenter, mechanic, cabinetmaker, mountain guide, and tax collector combined, is busy putting up the new house into which he and Sophronia, his wife, will soon move—they are building it extra large, to take in summer boarders. Sophronia helps Priscilla as much as she can, but she has her own small children to look after. Later on, Brother Jonathan hopes to get a twelve-year-old boy from the orphanage, who will do the chores for his keep. But now, Brother Jonathan must be up at daylight to start the kitchen fire and milk the cows. If it is haying time, he is out in the meadow early with the mowing machine, which he has sharpened and greased with his own hands or repaired at his own smithy if it needs repairing. The mower bumps and clicks through the rough meadow, tossing the little man to and fro as he warily skirts the outcrops of stone that will have to be circled with a scythe to get the last wisp of hay.

Later, he changes the patient old horses from mower to wagon and starts in with a pitchfork. It is a sight to see him navigating the loaded wagon from the upper field to the barn, past jutting boulders and through deep ruts. But his pace is easy; he keeps it up all day without undue perspiration or agony, and after supper cuts his wood and milks his cows again in unruffled calm. He does not seem tired or bored. As he milks, he philosophizes to the listening stranger. Yes, times are not what they were, but a man can get along if he will be careful and honest. Foolish people, of course, never know how to manage. The harm all comes from people of no character that do things without regard to common decency. The stars are shining when he takes the pails of milk into the kitchen. Under the hanging oil lamp he reads the Burlington *Free Press* or *The Pathfinder* until he begins to nod.

All the arrangements on Brother Jonathan's farm are neat and ingenious—the arrangements of a man who has had to depend largely on his own wits and strength. The barn is cleverly arranged in two stories, with a ramp entering the upper story for the convenience of Brother Jonathan and his hay wagons, and running water on the lower story, for the convenience of the animals. One well, near the barn, is operated by a windmill; it supplies the stock. Another well, higher up, supplies the house, for Brother Jonathan has a bathroom in the upper hall and faucets in the kitchen. He has no telephone or electric lights. A man can dig and pipe his own well, and they are finished; but telephone and electric lights, not being home contrivances, require a never ending tribute to Mammon. He has his own sawmill and his own workshop, where he can mend things without losing time and money on a trip to the village. His garage, occupied at present by Nathaniel's four-year-old car (which is not being used!), contains a carpenter's bench and a small gas engine rigged to do sawing and turning. There are pelts drying on the walls.

779

The house is built to economize space and retain heat. For all its modest proportions, it is convenient and comfortable. The kitchen is spacious and well equipped. The pantry and cellar are stored with vegetables, fruits, and meats that Priscilla has put up with her own hands. The dining-room, with its long table covered with spotless oilcloth, is eating-room, living-room, and children's playground combined. Here all gather after supper: the women with their tatting and embroidery; the lively dark-eyed boy from the village, with his homemade fiddle; a summer boarder or two, or a visiting relative; and always Brother Jonathan with his newspaper. In one corner is a reed organ, on which Brother Jonathan occasionally plays hymns. In another corner is a desk, filled with miscellaneous papers, books, and old magazines. On the walls hang a glass frame containing butterflies, the gift of a wandering entomologist; an 1876 engraving of General Washington being welcomed at New York, with the pictures of all the Presidents, up to Hayes, around the border; and a faded photograph of a more youthful Brother Jonathan with his fellow baggage-clerks, taken in the days when he went west and got a job in Chicago. Brother Jonathan talks of Chicago sometimes, but he never reveals why he, unlike many other Yankees, came back to Vermont.

The temper of the household is a subdued and even pleasantness which the loud alarms and excursions of the world do not penetrate very far. The progress of Nathaniel's new house; the next morning's arrangements for gathering vegetables and canning; what Brother Jonathan shall say in the speech he is to make at the approaching celebration of the Timothys' golden wedding—such topics take precedence over the epic contentions of Mr. Roosevelt. Priscilla may go so far as to marvel that anybody can doubt the goodness of Mr. Hoover. (She does not add, as she well might, that Mr. Roosevelt, as a "Yorker," inherits the distrust of Vermont.) Or Brother Jonathan may warm up to politics enough to announce his everlasting distrust for liquorish Al Smith and to confess that, out of firm disapproval for vice, he has once or twice bolted the Republican ticket and voted for the Prohibition party's candidate. But in the South, he supposes, he would be as good a Democrat as the next one. They are all curious about the South—about Negroes—and whether the Southern people still have hard feelings against the North (on this point they seem a little anxious and plaintive). But the talk soon shifts to the Green Mountain Boys, from one of whom Brother Jonathan is descended, or to stories of his childhood, when bears were as thick as porcupines are now—he tells of how seven bears were once killed in the same tree. In these stories Brother Jonathan may put in a dry quip or two, by way of garnishment. He has a store of homely jokes and extended metaphors, to which he frequently adds a humorous gloss to be sure the stranger gets the point. Then maybe there is a game of anagrams—or on another evening, a corn roast, with a few cronies and kinfolks from the village, who talk the clipped Yankee-talk that seems, to Southern ears, as pure an English as can be, with only a little of the twang that dialect stories have taught one to expect.

Brother Jonathan is not dogmatic to the point of testiness, but he is firmly rationalistic on many points. He declares it incredible, for instance, that Catholics can believe in transubstantiation—how can bread and wine *actually* turn into the blood and body of Jesus Christ? Yet oddly enough, Brother Jonathan is neither Congregationalist nor Unitarian, but Methodist, and does not mind repeating the Apostles' Creed, with its formidable references to the Trinity and

780

the Resurrection. I am led to suspect that it is not the doctrine but the authority to which Brother Jonathan is temperamentally hostile. He is used to depending on himself; he does not like to be told things. And his independence is of a piece with the whole conduct of his life. Years ago, when a famous local character eccentrically bought up all the surrounding woodland and farm land and turned it into a forest reserve which he bequeathed to a neighboring college, Brother Jonathan did not sell out. He held on then, he holds on now, with a possessiveness that would be the despair of communists. He will continue to hold on, as long as trees yield maple syrup—which he will never, never basely dilute with cane syrup—and boarders return summer after summer.

For Brother Jonathan belongs in spirit to the old republic of independent farmers that Jefferson wanted to see flourish as the foundation of liberty in the United States. To conserve that liberty he has his own Yankee arrangements: the "town," which the Southerner had to learn consisted of a village and a great deal of contiguous territory up to the next "town line"; and the town meeting, at which Brother Jonathan could stand up and tell the government what he thought about it. Of the uses of town meetings Priscilla has something to say, which comes, I reflect, with a little feminine sauciness. A certain individual, she relates, was criticized for not painting the "community house," as he had been employed to do; and when he excused himself on the ground that paint was lacking, his own wife sprang up in the town meeting and cried: "Don't believe a word he says. That paint's setting in the cellar this minute!"

But the Southerner could reflect that such family intimacy might have civic advantages. Brother Jonathan's local government is composed of nobody more Olympic or corrupt than his own neighbors and relations. For him it is not something off yonder, and he visualizes the national government (though a little too innocently) as simply an enlarged town meeting, where good management ought to be a matter of course: it maintains a library, it looks after roads, it sees that taxes are paid and well spent. If the state government does not behave, Nathaniel himself will run for the legislature and see that it does behave.

In all this there was much for a Southerner to savor seriously and learn about —as he savored and learned about the strange food that appeared on Brother Jonathan's table: doughnuts for breakfast, maple syrup on pie and cereal, the New England boiled dinner, the roasting ears that were really roasted in the old Indian fashion. Just as Brother Jonathan's menu suited the soil and the people, so his tidiness and responsibility suited the unobtrusive integrity of his character. With emphasis, one could say: Vermont is upright, vertical, and, even yet, Puritan—why not?

And almost two thousand miles away, with an unconcern about the state of the world that parallels but differs from Brother Jonathan's, Cousin Roderick of Rebelville is achieving another salvation somehow not recorded in the auguries of socialistic planning. Autumn is beginning, the scuppernongs are ripe, and he invites everybody to come over and join him in the scuppernong arbor. In the late afternoon a merry crew gather around the great vine, laughing and banter- ing as they pick the luscious grapes and crush them against their palates. Sister Caroline is there, with a figure as trim and a wit as lively at eighty as it must have been at twenty. Young Cousin Hector and his wife are there—they are

781

"refugeeing" from the industrial calamity that overtook them in a Northern city. And there are numerous other vague cousins and sisters and children, all munching and passing family gossip back and forth between bites. Cousin Roderick's own Dionysian laughter goes up heartiest of all among the leaves, as he moves to and fro, rapidly gathering grapes and pressing them upon the visitors. "Oh, you are not going to quit on us," he says. "You must eat more than *that*. Scuppernongs never hurt a soul." The scuppernong vine, he declares, is a hundred years old and nearly always fruitful. But not so old, never so fruitful, puts in Sister Caroline, as the scuppernong vine at the old place, that as barefoot children they used to clamber over.

Then the meeting is adjourned to Cousin Roderick's great front porch, where one looks out between white columns at sunset clouds piling up into the deep blues and yellows of a Maxfield Parrish sky. Down the long street of Rebelville, between the mighty water oaks set out by Cousin Roderick's kin after the Confederate War, the cotton wagons are passing, heaped high with the white mass of cotton and a Negro or two atop, and the talk goes on, to the jingle of trace chains and the clop of mule hoofs on the almost brand-new state highway, which is so much better for rubber tires than mule hoofs. Over yonder lives Cousin Roderick's Aunt Cecily, a widow, the single indomitable inhabitant of a stately mansion where economics has not yet prevailed against sentiment. Next door is Uncle Burke Roderick, a Confederate veteran who at ninety still drives his horse and buggy to the plantation each morning; he is the last survivor of three brothers who were named Pitt, Fox, and Burke, after their father's eighteenth century heroes. All around, indeed, are the Roderick kin, for Cousin Roderick, whose mother married a Bertram, bears the family name of his mother's people, a numerous clan who, by dint of sundry alliances and ancient understandings, attend to whatever little matters need attention in the community affairs of Rebelville, where Jefferson's "least government" principle is a matter of course. Before supper, or after, some of the kinfolks may drop in, for there is always a vast deal of coming and going and dropping in at Cousin Roderick's.

As he takes his ease on the porch, Cousin Roderick looks to be neither the elegant dandy nor the out-at-elbows dribbler of tobacco juice that partisans have accredited to the Southern tradition. He is a fairly tall, vigorous man, plainly dressed, with the ruddiness of Georgia sun and good living on his face. His eyes are a-wrinkle at the corners, ready to catch the humor of whatever is abroad. His hand fumbles his pipe as he tells one anecdote after another in the country drawl that has about as much of Mark Twain and Sut Lovingood in it as it has of the elisions and flattenings supposed to belong to Southern patrician speech. In fact, though he is really patrician (as the female members of his family can assure you) he does not look anything like the Old Colonel of legend, and in spirit he, too, belongs to the Jeffersonian constituency. He has some of the bearing of an English squire, and a good deal of the frontier heartiness that Augustus Baldwin Longstreet depicted in *Georgia Scenes*. He assumes that the world is good-humored and friendly until it proves itself otherwise. If it does prove otherwise, there is a glint in his eye that tells you he will fight.

Cousin Roderick is the opposite of Chaucer's Man of Law, who ever seemed busier than he was. Cousin Roderick is busier than he seems. His air of negligence, like his good humor, is a philosophical defense against the dangerous surprises that life may turn up. Really, he is not negligent. He does not work with his own hands, like Brother Jonathan, or his Southern brothers of up-country and bluegrass; but in the past he has worked aplenty with his hands and knows how it should be done. On his several tracts of land, the gatherings of inheritance and purchase, are some one hundred and fifty Negroes whom he furnishes housing, food, and a little money; they do his labor—men, women, children together—they are his "hands." He is expected to call them by name, to get them out of jail, to doctor them, even sometimes to bury them when "lodge dues" may have lapsed. They are no longer his slaves; but though they do not now utter the word, they do not allow him to forget that he has the obligations of a master.

As Cousin Roderick makes the "rounds" of his fields—no more on horseback, as of old, but in a battered Chevrolet—he sets forth his notions of economy. As for the depression, that is no new thing in Rebelville. People here have got used to ruination. After the Confederate War came Reconstruction, Tom Watson, and the Populist turmoil of the nineties; a while later, the peach boom and its collapse; then the Florida boom with its devastations; and now, this new depression. Like most of his kin, Cousin Roderick has simply retreated into the plantation economy. He tells how, when he was a young fellow just beginning to take charge, his father came out to the plantation one day and asked for a ham. Cousin Roderick explained that hogs were up to a good price; he had sold the entire lot, on the hoof, and had good money in the bank. "Sir," said the old man, "let me never again catch you without hams in your smokehouse and corn in your crib. You've got to make this land take care of itself." "And that," says Cousin Roderick, "is what I aim to do." From the land he feeds his own family, the hundred and fifty Negroes, and the stock. Whatever is left, when taxes and upkeep are deducted, is the profit. Anything that grows, he will plant: asparagus, peaches, pecans, onions, peppers, tomatoes, and of course the great staple crops, grain, hay, and cotton. Especially cotton, for no matter how low the price, cotton is money. It is ridiculous, he thinks, to talk of getting people who are hard-up for money to reduce cotton acreage. For his part, Cousin Roderick intends to make every bale his land will produce. But if cotton fails, he still can sell cattle, or cabbage, or timber from his baronial holdings. Land is the only abiding thing, the only assurance of happiness and comfort. He wants more land, not less.

One suspects that Cousin Roderick, however hard-pressed he may be at the bank, is fundamentally right. If he is not right, how does he manage, in these times, to send a daughter to college, and entertain his friends, and keep a cheerful face before the world? The portraits of his ancestors, looking down from their frames above great-grandfather's sideboard or his wife's new grand piano, eternally assure Cousin Roderick that he is right. They won this Eden of sandy earth and red clay, where all things grow with a vigor that neither winter nor drouth can abate. Not soon, not soon will their son give it up.

To the designs of experts who want to plan people's lives for them, Cousin Roderick gives no more than the indulgent attention of a naturally kindhearted man. He reads the anxious thunderings of the young men who reproduce, in the

783

Macon *Telegraph*, the remote dynamitical poppings of the *New Republic*, and is unmoved; the young men are like the mockingbird who sat on the cupola of the courthouse while court was in session and so learned to sing: *Prisoner-look-upon-the-jury! Jury-look-upon-the-prisoner!* GUILTY! GUILTY! GUILTY! It is a little incredible that so much planning should need to be done. Don't people know how they want to live? As for politics, long since it became tawdry and uncertain. Politics is for lawyers. Cousin Roderick would no more think of running for the legislature than he would think of moving to China. In that, perhaps, he lamentably differs from his ancestors. But in Rebelville political action is generally no more than a confirmation of what has been talked around among the clans. If you really want things done, you speak quietly to Cousin So-and-So and others that pass the word to everybody that counts. And then something is done.

In Rebelville the politics and economics of the bustling world become a faint whisper. All that matters is to see one's friends and relatives and pass from house to house, from field to field, under Georgia skies; to gather at a simple family dinner where only three kinds of bread and four kinds of meat are flanked by collards, sweet potatoes, corn, pickles, fruits, salads, jams, and cakes; or at a barbecue for fifty or more, for which whole animals are slaughtered and, it would seem, entire pantries and gardens desolated; or to sit with the wise men in front of the store, swapping jokes and telling tales hour after hour; or to hunt for fox, possum, coon, and quail, in swamp and field; or (for the ladies) to attend meetings of U.D.C.'s, and missionary societies; or church service, or district conference or the tender ceremonies of Confederate Memorial Day, or the high school entertainment; or to hear the voices of Negroes, sifting through the dusk, or the mockingbird in moonlight; or to see the dark pines against sunset, and the old house lifting its columns far away, calling the wanderer home. The scuppernongs are gone, and cotton is picked. But already the pecans are falling. And planting begins again while late roses and chrysanthemums are showing and, even in the first frosts, the camellias are budding, against their December flowering. What though newspapers be loud and wars and rumors threaten—it is only an academic buzzing, that one must yet tolerate for manners' sake. Sowing and harvest go together, and summer runs into winter, and in Georgia one is persuaded to take the horizontal view.

By some it may be said that dark clouds hang over Yankeetown and Rebelville —and clouds of menace, maybe of destruction. I do not deny their presence, but my story is not of such clouds. In this strange modern world it may be observed that men talk continually of the good life without producing a specimen of it, to convince an inquirer. Brother Jonathan and Cousin Roderick do not talk about the good life. They lead it. If government is intended to serve human interests, what does it propose to do about them? I cannot believe that a government or a science which ignores or depreciates them is very trustworthy. I believe that government and science will fail unless they are taken into account. They, and others, are the incarnations of the principle of diversity through which the United States have become something better than Balkan, and without which the phrase "my country" is but a sorry and almost meaningless abstraction. (*1938*)

784

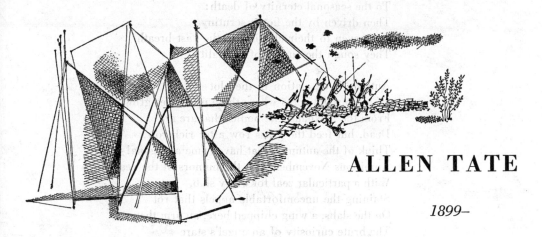

ALLEN TATE

1899–

Allen Tate was born in Clarke County, Kentucky, on November 16, 1899, and was graduated from Vanderbilt University in 1922. In 1924 he married Caroline Gordon, the novelist. Tate is one of the most influential among serious contemporary Southern authors. Internationally recognized as a poet and critic, Tate has also won acclaim as a biographer, novelist, and as editor of the *Sewanee Review* (1944–1946). His appearances on the "Invitation to Learning" radio programs during 1940 and 1941 established him as an important commentator on the classic books of Western Man. Tate has taught English at Southwestern University, North Carolina College for Women, Princeton, the University of Chicago, New York University, and the Kenyon School of English. He is at present a professor at the University of Minnesota.

Among Tate's most outstanding volumes are his two biographies, *Stonewall Jackson: The Good Soldier* (1928) and *Jefferson Davis: His Rise and Fall* (1929); his one novel, *The Fathers* (1938); *Poems—1922–1947*; and his volumes of criticism, *Reactionary Essays on Poetry and Ideas* (1936), *Reason in Madness* (1941), and *The Limits of Poetry* (1949).

Along with Donald Davidson, John Crowe Ransom, and others, Tate was an important influence in both the Fugitive and Agrarian movements. He was one of the founders of *The Fugitive* and served as its co-editor (1922–1925).

Ode to the Confederate Dead

> Row after row with strict impunity
> The headstones yield their names to the element,
> The wind whirrs without recollection;
> In the riven troughs the splayed leaves
> Pile up, of nature the casual sacrament

785

To the seasonal eternity of death;
Then driven by the fierce scrutiny
Of heaven to their election in the vast breath,
They sough the rumor of mortality.

Autumn is desolation in the plot
Of a thousand acres where these memories grow
From the inexhaustible bodies that are not
Dead, but feed the grass row after rich row.
Think of the autumns that have come and gone!—
Ambitious November with the humors of the year,
With a particular zeal for every slab,
Staining the uncomfortable angels that rot
On the slabs, a wing chipped here, an arm there:
The brute curiosity of an angel's stare
Turns you, like them, to stone,
Transforms the heaving air
Till plunged to a heavier world below
You shift your sea-space blindly
Heaving, turning like the blind crab.

　　Dazed by the wind, only the wind
　　The leaves flying, plunge

You know who have waited by the wall
The twilight certainty of an animal,
Those midnight restitutions of the blood
You know—the immitigable pines, the smoky frieze
Of the sky, the sudden call: you know the rage,
The cold pool left by the mounting flood,
Of muted Zeno and Parmenides.
You who have waited for the angry resolution
Of those desires that should be yours tomorrow,
You know the unimportant shrift of death
And praise the vision
And praise the arrogant circumstance
Of those who fall
Rank upon rank, hurried beyond decision—
Here by the sagging gate, stopped by the wall.

　　Seeing, seeing only the leaves
　　Flying, plunge and expire

Turn your eyes to the immoderate past,
Turn to the inscrutable infantry rising
Demons out of the earth—they will not last.
Stonewall, Stonewall, and the sunken fields of hemp,

Shiloh, Antietam, Malvern Hill, Bull Run.
Lost in that orient of the thick and fast
You will curse the setting sun.

     Cursing only the leaves crying
     Like an old man in a storm

You hear the shout, the crazy hemlocks point
With troubled fingers to the silence which
Smothers you, a mummy, in time.

            The hound bitch
Toothless and dying, in a musty cellar
Hears the wind only.

         Now that the salt of their blood
Stiffens the saltier oblivion of the sea,
Seals the malignant purity of the flood,
What shall we, who count our days and bow
Our heads with a commemorial woe
In the ribboned coats of grim felicity,
What shall we say of the bones, unclean,
Whose verdurous anonymity will grow?
The ragged arms, the ragged heads and eyes
Lost in these acres of the insane green?
The gray lean spiders come, they come and go;
In a tangle of willows without light
The singular screech-owl's tight
Invisible lyric seeds the mind
With the furious murmur of their chivalry.

     We shall say only the leaves
     Flying, plunge and expire

We shall say only, the leaves whispering
In the improbable mist of nightfall
That flies on multiple wing:
Night is the beginning and the end
And in between the ends of distraction
Waits mute speculation, the patient curse
That stones the eyes, or like the jaguar leaps
For his own image in a jungle pool, his victim.

What shall we say who have knowledge
Carried to the heart? Shall we take the act
To the grave? Shall we, more hopeful, set up the grave
In the house? The ravenous grave?

787

                                        Leave now
     The shut gate and the decomposing wall:
     The gentle serpent, green in the mulberry bush,
     Riots with his tongue through the hush—
     Sentinel of the grave who counts us all!
                                        (*1926–1936*) [1]

The Mediterranean

           Quem das finem, rex magne, dolorum? [2]

     Where we went in the boat was a long bay
     A slingshot wide, walled in by towering stone—
     Peaked margin of antiquity's delay,
     And we went there out of time's monotone:

     Where we went in the black hull no light moved
     But a gull white-winged along the feckless wave,
     The breeze, unseen but fierce as a body loved,
     That boat drove onward like a willing slave:

     Where we went in the small ship the seaweed
     Parted and gave to us the murmuring shore
     And we made feast and in our secret need
     Devoured the very plates Aeneas bore:

     Where derelict you see through the low twilight
     The green coast that you, thunder-tossed, would win
     Drop sail, and hastening to drink all night
     Eat dish and bowl—to take that sweet land in!

     Where we feasted and caroused on the sandless
     Pebbles, affecting our day of piracy,
     What prophecy of eaten plates could landless
     Wanderers fulfil by the ancient sea?

     We for that time might taste the famous age
     Eternal here yet hidden from our eyes
     When lust of power undid it stuffless rage;
     They, in a wineskin, bore earth's paradise.

     Let us lie down once more by the breathing side

788

Of Ocean, where our live forefathers sleep
As if the Known Sea still were a month wide—
Atlantis howls but is no longer steep!

What country shall we conquer, what fair land
Unman our conquest and locate our blood?
We've cracked the hemispheres with careless hand!
Now, from the Gates of Hercules we flood

Westward, westward till the barbous brine
Whelms us to the tired land where tasseling corn,
Fat beans, grapes sweeter than muscadine
Rot on the vine: in that land were we born.

(*1937*)

Shadow and Shade

The shadow streamed into the wall—
The wall, break-shadow in the blast;
We lingered wordless while a tall
Shade enclouded the shadow's cast.

The torrent of the reaching shade
Broke shadow into all its parts,
What then had been of shadow made
Found exigence in fits and starts

Where nothing properly had name
Save that still element the air,
Burnt sea of universal frame
In which impounded now we were:

I took her hand, I shut her eyes
And all her shadow clove with shade,
Shadow was crushed beyond disguise
But, being fear, was unafraid.

I asked fair shadow at my side:
What more shall fiery shade require?
We lay there in the immense tide
Of shade and shadowy desire

And saw the dusk assail the wall,
The black surge, mounting, crash the stone!

789

Companion of this lust, we fall,
I said, lest we should die alone.
(*1937*)

The Wolves

There are wolves in the next room waiting
With heads bent low, thrust out, breathing
As nothing in the dark: between them and me
A white door patched with light from the hall
Where it seems never (so still is the house)
A man has walked from the front door to the stair.
It has all been forever. A beast claws the floor.
I have brooded on angels and archfiends
But no man has ever sat where the next room's
Crowded with wolves, and for the honor of man
I affirm that never have I before. Now while
I have looked for the evening star at a cold window
And whistled when Arcturus spilt his light,
I've heard the wolves scuffle, and said: So this
Is man; so—what better conclusion is there—
The day will not follow night, and the heart
Of man has a little dignity, but less patience
Than a wolf's, and a duller sense that cannot
Smell its own mortality. (This and other
Meditations will be suited to other times
After dog silence howls my epitaph)
Now remember courage, go to the door,
Open it and see whether coiled on the bed
Or cringing by the wall a savage beast
Maybe with golden hair, with deep eyes
Like a bearded spider on a sunlit floor
Will snarl—and man can never be alone.
(*1937*)

Literature as Knowledge

Matthew Arnold's war on the Philistines was fought, as everybody knows; but nobody thinks that it was won. Arnold conducted it in what he considered to be the scientific spirit. The Philistines had a passion for "acting and instituting," but they did not know "what we ought to act and to institute." This sort of

790

knowledge must be founded upon "the scientific passion for knowing." But it must not stop there. Culture, which is the study of perfection and the constant effort to achieve it, is superior to the scientific spirit because it includes and passes beyond it. Arnold was, in short, looking for a principle of unity, but it must be a unity of experience. There was before him the accumulating body of the inert, descriptive facts of science, and something had to be done about it.

Yet if it is true, as T. S. Eliot said many years ago, that were Arnold to come back he would have his work to do over again, he would at any rate have to do it very differently. His program, culture added to science and perhaps correcting it, has been our program for nearly a century, and it has not worked. For the facts of science are not inert facts waiting for the poet, as emblematic guardian of culture, to bring to life in the nicely co-operative enterprise of scientist and poet which the nineteenth century puts its faith in. In this view the poet is merely the scientist who achieves completeness. "It is a result of no little culture," Arnold says, "to attain to a clear perception that science and religion are two wholly different things." Religion had yielded to the "fact" of science, but poetry on a positive scientific base could take over the work of religion, and its future was "immense." The "fact" had undermined religion, but it could support poetry.

Although Arnold betrayed not a little uneasiness about this easy solution, it was his way of putting literature upon an equal footing with science. If Arnold failed, can we hope to succeed? Whether literature and science considered philosophically, as Coleridge would phrase it, are the same thing, or different but equal, or the one subordinate to the other, has become a private question. It does not concern the public at large. While Arnold's poet was extending the hand of fellowship to the scientist, the scientist did not return the greeting; for never for an instant did he see himself as the inert and useful partner in an enterprise of which he would not be permitted to define the entire scope. He was not, alas, confined to the inertia of fact; his procedure was dynamic all along; and it was animated by the confident spirit of positivism which has since captured the modern world.

Had he been what Arnold thought he was, how conveniently the partnership would have worked! For what was Arnold's scientist doing? He was giving us exact observation and description of the external world. The poet could give us that, and he could add to it exact observation and description of man's inner life, a realm that the positivist would never be so bold as to invade. But the poet's advantage was actually twofold. Not only did he have this inner field of experience denied to the scientist, he had a resource which was his peculiar and hereditary right—figurative language and the power of rhetoric.

If the inert fact alone could not move us, poetic diction could make it moving by heightening it; for poetry is "thought and art in one." This is an injustice to Arnold; he was a great critic of ideas, of currents of ideas, of the situation of the writer in his time; and from this point of view his theory of poetry is of secondary importance. But since I am now interested in the failure, ours as well as his, to understand the relation of poetry and science, it has been necessary to put his poetic theory in terms that will bring out its defects. On one side it is an eighteenth-century view of poetic language as the rhetorical vehicle of ideas; and it is connected with Arnold's famous definition of religion as "morality

791

touched with emotion." Poetry is descriptive science or experience at that level, touched with emotion.

If Arnold had taste, he had very simple analytical powers, and we are never quite convinced by his fine quotations from the poets. Why is this so? Because he admires good things for bad reasons; or because at any rate his reasons invariably beg the question. In the famous passage on Dryden and Pope in "The Study of Poetry" these poets are not poetic because they are not *poetic*. (Arnold himself is responsible for the italics.) And he looks to us for immediate assent to a distinction between a "prose" classic and a "poetic" classic that has not been actually made. He cites his "touchstones" for the purpose of moving us, and the nice discrimination of feeling which awareness of the touchstones induces will permit us to judge other passages of verse in terms of feeling. The "high seriousness" is partly the elevated tone, a tone which is a quality of the poet's feeling about his subject: it is the poet's business to communicate it to the reader.

This attitude, this tone, centers in emotion. But its relation to what it is about, whether it is external to the subject or inherent in it, Arnold refuses to make clear. The high seriousness may be said to reflect the subject, which must have Aristotelian magnitude and completeness. Arnold had a shrewd sense of the disproportions of tone and subject which he developed into a principle in the Preface to the 1853 edition of his poems. He was suppressing the very fine "Empedocles on Aetna" because, he said, it has no action; it is all passive suffering; and passive suffering is not a proper subject for poetry. (A view that has been revived in our time by the late W. B. Yeats.) Action, then, is the subject of the greatest poetry. This conviction is so strong—who will question its rightness, *as far as it goes?*—that he actually puts into quotation marks words which are not quoted from anybody at all but which represent for him the consensus of the ancients on the importance of action: " 'All depends upon the subject; choose a fitting action, penetrate yourself with the feeling of its situations; this done, everything else will follow.' " But will everything else follow? Does a great style follow? To a gift for action Shakespeare "added a special one of his own; a gift, namely, of happy, abundant, and ingenious expression. . . ." I think we should attend closely here to the words "added" and "ingenious," for they reveal Arnold's view of the function of language. And suppose you have lyric poetry which may be, like Arnold's own fine lyrics, more meditative than dramatic, and more concerned with the futility of action than with action itself? It has never, I believe, been pointed out that the Preface of 1853 cuts all the props from under lyric poetry. The lyric at its best is "dramatic," but there is no evidence that Arnold thought it so; for the lyric, though it may be a moment of action, lacks magnitude and completeness; it may be the beginning, or the middle, or the end, but never all three. What, then, is the subject of the lyric? Is it all feeling, nothing but feeling? It is feeling about "ideas," not actions; and the feeling communicates "power and joy."

This gross summary of Arnold's poetics omits all the sensitive discriminations that he felt in reading the poets; it omits all but the framework of his thought. Yet the framework alone must concern us on this occasion. Arnold is still the great critical influence in the universities, and it is perhaps not an exaggeration of his influence to say that debased Arnold is the main stream of popular appreciation of poetry. It would be fairer to say that Arnold the critic was superior to his critical theory; yet at the distance of three generations we may look back upon his lack of a critical dialectic—he even had a certain contempt for it in other critics—as a calamity for that culture which it was his great desire to strengthen and pass on.

His critical theory was elementary, and if you compare him with Coleridge a generation earlier, he represents a loss. His position is nearer to the neo-classicism of Lessing, whom he praises in *Culture and Anarchy* for humanizing knowledge, a leveling-off of distinctions of which Lessing as a matter of fact was not guilty. He shares with Lessing the belief—but not its dialectical basis—that the language of poetry is of secondary importance to the subject, that it is less difficult than the medium of painting, and that, given the action, all else follows.

This remnant of neo-classicism in Arnold has been ably discerned by Mr. Cleanth Brooks in *Modern Poetry and the Tradition.* I go into it here not to deny that action is necessary to the long poem; for Arnold's view contains a fundamental truth. But it is not the whole truth; asserted in his terms, it may not be a truth at all. The important question goes further. It is: What is the relation of language to the "subject," to the dramatic and narrative subject as action, or to the lyrical subject as "idea"? The question may be pushed even further: Is it possible finally to distinguish the language from the subject? Are not subject and language one?

For Arnold the subject is what we commonly call the prose subject; that is to say, as much of the poetic subject as we can put into ordinary prose. The poet takes it up at the level at which the scientist—or Arnold's simulacrum of him—takes it: the level of observation and description. The poet now puts it into language that will bring the inert facts to life and move us. The language is strictly what Mr. Richards calls the "vehicle"—it does not embody the subject; it conveys it and remains external to it.

For what are action and subject? The positivists have their own notion of these terms; and their language of physical determinism suits that notion better than the poet's. The poet's language is useless.

II

Is it not easy to see how such a poetics gives the case for poetry away to the scientist? Not to Arnold's straw scientist, who politely kept to his descriptive place and left to literature man's evaluation of his experience; but to the scientist as he is: a remarkably ingenious and dynamic fellow whose simple fanaticism brooks no compromise with his special projects. Whatever these on occasion may be, he demands an exact one-to-one relevance of language to the objects and the events to which it refers. In this relevance lies the "meaning" of all terms and propositions in so far as they are used for the purpose of giving us valid knowledge. It is, of course, knowledge for action; and apart from this specific purpose, the problem of meaning is not even a real problem.

"Meaning" has been replaced by a concept of "operational validity"—that is to say, the "true" meaning of a term is not its definition; it is the number of statements containing it which can be referred to empirically observed events.

793

Along with meaning and definition, universals also disappear; and with universals, cognition. A proposition does not represent an act of knowing by a knower—that is, a mind; it is, in a chemical metaphor, the expression of an interaction among certain elements of a "situation."

This advanced position in the philosophy of science has been set forth in the new *International Encyclopedia of Unified Science*, which is being published serially at the University of Chicago. Of great interest from the point of view of literary criticism are the brilliant studies of "semiosis," or the functioning of language as "signs." Mr. Charles W. Morris's "Foundations for the Theory of Signs,"[1] is a model of exact exposition in a field of enormous complication. This field is popularly known as "semantics," but semantics in any exact sense is only one "dimension" of semiosis. In this brief glance at the aesthetic and critical implications of Mr. Morris's writings, his theory as a whole cannot be set forth.

Semiosis is the actual functioning of language in three dimensions which are located and described by means of the science of "semiotic." Semiotic, then, is the study of semiosis. The three dimensions in which all language, verbal, or mathematical, functions are: (1) the semantical, (2) the syntactical, and (3) the pragmatical; and the respective studies in these dimensions are semantics, syntactics, and pragmatics. It must be borne in mind that in semiosis the three dimensions are never separate; in semiotic they are distinguished abstractly for study. Semiotic looks towards the formation of rules which will govern the use of all language (signs), and it lays claim to an ultimate unification of all "knowledge."

That need not concern us here. Let us take a simple declarative sentence: "This county has an annual rainfall of fifty-one inches." From the semantical point of view the sentence designates certain conditions, or a situation: it is the "sign-vehicle" for that designation. If upon investigation we find that the situation actually exists, then it has not only been designated; it has also been *denoted*. From the syntactical point of view we are not concerned with what the sign-vehicle points to; for syntactics deals with the formal structure of the sentence, the relations of the words. From the pragmatical point of view the meaning of the sentence is the effect it has upon somebody who hears it or reads it. If I am about to buy a farm in this county, and learn that "this county has an annual rainfall of fifty-one inches," I may go elsewhere; at the moment I hear the sentence I may light a cigarette, or look the other way, or laugh or swear. All this behavior would be the functioning of the sign in the pragmatic dimension.

The complex possibilities of semiotic may not be evident in this crude summary. Mr. Morris says: "The sign vehicle itself is simply one object." It is an object that may function in other sign-vehicles; it may be designated, denoted, or reacted to; and the process is infinite. The identification of signs and their relations is equally complex. There are, for example, a characterizing sign, a symbolic sign, an indexical sign, and an iconic sign; and any of these, in certain contexts, may function as any other. I shall return to them presently.

794

The only philosophic criticism of this system that I have seen is Howard D. Roelofs's article in the symposium on the "New Encyclopedists," published in

[1] International Encyclopedia of Unified Science, *Vol. I. No. 2. (Tate's note.)*

the *Kenyon Review* (Spring 1939). Mr. Roelofs is concerned with Mr. Morris's rejection of the problem of universals and of cognition. It ought to be plain from my brief exposition of the pragmatic dimension of semiosis that the significant factor is what I *do*, not what I *think* leading to what I do; and that thus the bias of the science of semiotic is pragmatic in the ordinary sense, and even behavioristic. For Mr. Morris says: "A 'concept' [i.e., a universal] may be regarded as a semantical rule determining the use of characterizing signs." Mr. Roelofs's comment is interesting:

> Morris has no trouble with this problem [i.e., the problem of universals]. It is simply a rule of our language that such a term as "man" can be used as often as the conditions stated in its definition are fulfilled. That makes the term a universal. If we then ask how it happens those conditions are in fact frequently fulfilled, we are informed, "It can only be said the world is such." And those who are tempted by this fact to believe that universals are somehow objective, functioning in nature, are silenced with a threat: to talk as if universals were entities in the world is "to utter pseudo-thing sentences of the quasi-semantical type.". . . the heart of the problem is dismissed with a phrase and a language rule offered as a solution.

The bearing of Mr. Roelofs's criticism will be plainer in a moment. Now Mr. Morris, in discussing the syntactical dimension, says: "Syntactics, as the study of the syntactical relations of signs to one another *in abstraction* from the relations of signs to objects or to interpreters [persons], is the best developed of all the branches of semiotic." Exactly; because syntactics comes out of traditional formal logic and grammar, and because it "deliberately neglects what has here been called the semantical and the pragmatical dimensions of semiosis."

The rôle of syntactics in the semiotic science remains somewhat obscure; it seems to consist in a number of "transformation rules"—that is, in formulas by which given expressions in words, numbers, or symbols can be changed into equivalent but formally different expressions. What power of the mind there may be which enables us in the first place to form these expressions nowhere appears. (I daresay this statement is of the quasi-semantical type.) But Mr. Morris tells us how we are to think of the rules of the three dimensions of semiotic:

> Syntactical rules determine the sign relations between sign vehicles; semantical rules correlate sign vehicles with other objects; pragmatical rules state the conditions in the interpreters under which the sign vehicle is a sign. Any rule when actually in use operates as a type of behavior, and in this sense there is a pragmatical component in all rules.

If we imagine with Mr. Roelofs a situation in which semiosis is functioning, we shall see pretty clearly the behavioristic tendency of the science of semiotic; and we shall also see in what sense "there is a pragmatical component in all rules." A simplified process of semiosis, or the actual functioning of signs, is

795

very easy to state. There is first of all the sign, which we get in terms of a sign-vehicle. It looks two ways; first, it points to something, designates something; and, secondly, what is designated elicits a response from persons who are present. The thing pointed to is thus the *designatum;* the response is the *interpretant.* By implication there is an interpreter, a person, a mind; but Mr. Morris is consistently vague about him: he is not a technical factor, he is a superfluous entity, in semiosis. That is to say, not only is he not needed in order to explain the functioning of signs; he would embarrass the explanation. Mr. Roelofs makes this clear, as follows:

> The innocent reader will take the analysis of the use of signs to be the analysis of a cognitive process. The correctness of the analysis as far as it goes conceals the fact that cognition itself has been eliminated. Consider this illustration. A maid enters the room and says to the three persons present, "The doctor called." One person thereupon takes a pen and writes a line in a dairy; the second goes to a telephone and makes a call; the third says, "Did he?" According to the analysis offered by Morris, the words uttered by the maid are the sign-vehicle. The actual call of the doctor is the denotatum.[2] The three persons are the interpreters, and their three different actions are the interpretants, the responses of the interpreters to the denotatum via the sign-vehicle. No one is likely to deny these factors are present. It should be noted that the interpretants, to the extent that they are a sequence of physical actions, can be perceived. It should also be noted that such sequences of action are not cognitions . . . they are "interpretants," but their being such depends upon the cognitions of the interpreters. These responses are not themselves knowledge. They do depend upon knowledge, and that is precisely what Morris leaves out. . . . Morris objects to the term "meaning." This is not surprising. His analysis leaves out meaning in the primary sense of meaning. This is not to say that meanings are "like marbles" [Morris's phrase]. Meanings, indeed, like knowledge in general, are a unique kind of thing. There is literally nothing like knowledge except knowledge itself.

I have quoted Mr. Roelofs at length because what he has to say about the problem of cognition bears directly upon the semiotic version of the aesthetic problem. He sums up his argument:

> The procedure culminates in eliminating not only universals, but cognition itself. Just as the answer to the problem of universals is that they do not exist [that is, they are only a semantical rule], the answer to the problem of knowledge is that there is no such thing. There are responses, but no cognition; there is a language, but not knowledge. Knowledge cannot be reduced to exclusively perceptual terms. There-

796

---

[2] Denotata *are real things;* designata *may be pointed to, but they are not necessarily real. For example, the Phoenix' "spicy nest." The doctor's call is a* designatum *which is also a* denotatum—*it's "real." (Tate's note.)*

fore it does not exist. This is not empiricism. *It is positivism.* [Italics mine.]

In this positivist technique for the analysis of language, the interpreting mind, the cognizing intelligence, is lost in the perceptual account of its external behavior. Mr. Morris says: "In general, from the point of view of behavior, signs are 'true' in so far as they correctly determine the expectations of the users, and so release more fully the behavior which is implicitly aroused in the expectation or interpretation."

In Mr. Morris's aesthetics there is an aesthetic sign. Does it implicitly—or explicitly—arouse expectations in terms of behavior? Does it correctly determine our expectations? Is the aesthetic sign "true" in that it is a determinant of our behavior? Mr. Morris is not unequivocal in his answers to these questions.

III

No—and yes, replies Mr. Morris, in two essays [3] the cunning and scholastic ingenuity of which make even the beautiful essay on the general theory of signs look amateurish. No, he says, because the aesthetic sign is a special sort of sign: it is *iconic.* It does not correctly determine our behavior. Yes, because it bears the formidable responsibility of showing us what we ought to try to get out of our behavior. The function of the aesthetic sign is nothing less than the "vivid presentation" of *values,* a presentation that is not only vivid, but *immediate—* without mediation—for direct apprehension. The iconic sign, in other words, designates without denoting; or if it does denote anything its *denotatum* is already in its own "properties." "In certain kinds of insanity," writes Mr. Morris, "the distinction between the designatum and the denotatum vanishes; the troublesome world of existences is pushed aside, and the frustrated *interests* [italics mine] get what satisfaction they can in the domain of signs. . . ." Likewise *designata* and *denotata* become in aesthetics the same thing; but in this logical shuffle, worthy of a thirteenth-century *doctor subtilis,* the aesthetic sign is never confused "with the object it designates." It is that alone which saves it from the ignominy of insanity.

The difficulties of this theory must already be apparent. First, the difference between insanity and art is the hair's-breadth line, in the interpreter's response to the sign, between substituting the sign for reality and maintaining the distinction between sign and reality. The first question that one must ask, then, is this: With what does the interpreter make this distinction? If the distinction is not inherent in the nature of the sign, does the interpreter not perform an act of cognition? If the distinction is a mere interpretant, a behavioristic response, why do we not respond to a work of art uniformly; and why is that uniform response in every case not insane *unless we are capable of a primary act of knowledge,* of simply knowing the difference?

Secondly, if art is the realm of values—that is, if the peculiar nature of the aesthetic sign is that it shall convey values—the values must be inherent in the

797

[3] *"Esthetics and the Theory of Signs," in* The Journal of Unified Science, *VIII, 1–3, pp. 131–150; and "Science, Art, and Technology,"* The Kenyon Review, *I, 4, pp. 409–423. (Tate's note.)*

aesthetic sign, and must therefore compel in the interpreter the distinction between value and insanity; so that there is no possibility that the interpreter, who is incapable of cognition, will confuse the mere sign with reality. For the nature of the sign must determine the interpretant, or response.

There must therefore be a special "differentia" for the aesthetic sign that distinguishes it from all other signs whatever. "Lyric poetry," Mr. Morris says, "has a syntax and uses terms which designate things, but the syntax and the terms are so used that what stand out for the reader are values and evaluations." [4] Does not Mr. Morris confess his difficulty when he uses the vague metaphorical expression, "stand out," and the even more vague "so used"? Just what is this use? It is significant that in Mr. Morris's two articles on aesthetics, in which the word poetry frequently appears, there is no actual analysis of a passage or even of a line of verse; and not even a quotation from any poem in any language. He contents himself with assertions that the future of semiotic in the field of poetry is immense, and that only the work has to be done.

Now, if the contradiction that I have pointed out in general terms exists, we may see its origin if we examine further Mr. Morris's idea of the aesthetic sign. It is a special variety of the iconic sign. To illustrate this it will be sufficient to relate the iconic to the characterizing sign, and to distinguish the icon from the symbol.

> A characterizing sign [he says] characterizes that which it can denote. Such a sign may do this by exhibiting in itself the properties an object must have to be denoted by it, and in this case the characterizing sign is an *icon;* if this is not so, the characterizing sign may be called a *symbol.* A photograph, a star chart, a model, a chemical diagram, are icons, while the word "photograph," the names of the stars and of chemical elements are symbols.

The terminology is quite special. Icon is the Greek (εἰχών) for a sculptured figure. Ordinarily a symbol is what Mr. Morris claims for the icon: it exhibits in itself the qualities it stands for—like Christ on the Cross; or it represents by convention something other than itself, like πr^2 for the circumference of a circle. But here the terms are roughly equivalent, icon to image, symbol to concept; but only roughly, since in Mr. Morris's list of symbols "photograph" is not any particular photograph, while the name of a star must be the name of a particular star. There is a fundamental obscurity, that we shall have to pass over, in attributing to verbal language a thoroughly *iconic* property. In the list of icons, there are *a* photograph, *a* star chart, *a* model, *a* chemical diagram—all of them spatial and perceptual objects; but, while language is always used in a spatial setting, words appear in temporal sequence, and have only the spatial character of their occasion. We cannot *see* the properties of words in the words. We have simply got to know *what* the words convey. The phrase "a star chart" is not a star chart itself. Mr. Morris appears to have found in the term *icon,* at any rate so far as it pertains to aesthetics, merely a convenient evasion of the term *image;* for image would doubtless have held him to the old ontological aesthetics.

798

[4] *"Foundations for the Theory of Signs,"* p. 58. *(Tate's note.)*

The essay, "Esthetics and the Theory of Signs," deals with the specific problem "of stating the differentia of the esthetic sign." Mr. Morris is constantly reminding us that iconic signs appear in all discourse, and that all discourse is by no means aesthetic discourse. Yet the special function of the iconic sign makes it possible for us to use it as the aesthetic sign; and that function is stated in a "semantical rule":

> The semantical rule for the use of an iconic sign is that it denotes any object which has the properties (in practice, a selection from the properties) which it itself has. Hence when an interpreter apprehends an iconic sign-vehicle he apprehends directly what is designated; here mediated and unmediated taking account of certain properties both occur; [5] put in still other terms, every iconic sign has its own sign-vehicle among its denotata.

This is a difficult conception; perhaps it can be illustrated with a few lines of verse:

> That time of year thou mayst in me behold
> When yellow leaves, or none, or few do hang
> Upon those boughs which shake against the cold . . .

According to Mr. Morris, the sign-vehicle here would be the leaves hanging on the boughs. This verbal sign-vehicle has the "properties" of the natural objects which it designates; and that which it denotes in the designation itself. That is, leaves-bough does not point to a definite situation or condition beyond itself: we get "directly what is designated" because it is of the nature of the iconic sign to contain its own *denotatum*. (I have simplified this analysis by ignoring "That time of year," which I believe would make it impossible to apply Mr. Morris's terms coherently.)

The treatment of the iconic sign in semiotic is mysterious. If any generalization about it is legitimate, we may surmise that certain terms, which Mr. Morris calls "primary terms," are untranslatable; that is to say, they cannot be handled by any principle of reduction; they have a certain completeness and finality. They denote themselves; certain iconic signs seem to be such terms. They are sign-vehicles for images, and our apprehension of them is direct. For while the iconic sign may denote something beyond itself, its specific character as an iconic sign is that part of what it denotes as the sign itself. "These facts," says Mr. Morris, "taken alone, do not delimit the esthetic sign, for blueprints, photographs, and scientific models are all iconic signs—but seldom works of art." He continues in a passage of great interest:

> If, however, the designatum of an iconic sign be a *value* [italics mine] (and of course not all iconic signs designate values), the situation is changed: there is now not merely the designation of value properties

799

---

[5] *There seems to be evidence in this clause that Mr. Morris is not interested in syntactics. (Tate's note.)*

(for such designation takes place even in science), nor merely the functioning of iconic signs (for these as such need not be esthetic signs), but there is the direct apprehension of value properties through the very presence of that which itself has the value it designates.

There are thus three steps in the "delimitation" of the aesthetic sign: First, it is an iconic sign; secondly, it is an iconic sign which designates a value; thirdly, it is an iconic sign which designates a value in the sign itself, so that our "apprehension" of that value is unmediated, that is, *direct.*

The difficulties created by this aesthetic doctrine are slippery and ambiguous. We may, for convenience, see them in two ways. The first set of problems lies in the term "apprehension"; the second, in the term "value."

The primary meaning of apprehension is a grasping or a taking hold of. What does Mr. Morris mean? If it means taking hold of by means of perception, we are asked to see ourselves *perceiving a value;* but a value cannot be an object of perception. If, however, apprehension means a direct, unmediated knowledge of a value, then there is an act of evaluation involved which implies the presence of a knowing mind. For the implied "semantical rule" for the aesthetic sign obviously forbids us to check the value wholly in terms of a situation external to the properties of the sign itself. We have got to *know* the value in itself; and only in an act of cognition can we know it. But if Mr. Morris means by apprehension the response, or mere "interpretant," of semiosis, it is difficult to see how a mere response can be semantically correct unless the sign-vehicle points to a situation outside itself in terms of which the response is relevant. If there is no such situation, is not the interpretant a piece of insanity?

I cannot see how there can be any direct apprehension unless there is an agency to do the apprehending; and the interpretant is not an agent, it is a response. "One additional point may be noted to confirm the sign status of the work of art: The artist often draws attention to the sign-vehicle in such a way as to prevent the interpreter from merely reacting to it as an object and not as a sign. . . ." Mr. Morris's phrases, "in such a way," "so used that," remain painfully evasive. What is that way? Now, if the preventive factor is inherent in the work of art, why did not the birds refrain from trying to eat the grapes in Zeuxis's picture? The citizens of Athens did not mistake the sign-vehicle for an object. Why? Because they *knew* the difference.

Mr. Morris's theory of value will further illuminate his difficulty. It is an "interest" theory of value for which he acknowledges an indebtedness to the pragmatic tradition of Mead and Dewey. Objects, according to this ancient theory, have value in relation to interests. "Values," says Mr. Morris, "are consummatory properties of objects or situations which answer to the consummation of interested acts." If I satisfy my hunger by eating a banana, the banana has value in relation to the specific interest, hunger. Does it follow that we have similar aesthetic interests, which we similarly satisfy? No specific aesthetic interest appears in semiosis. The aesthetic satisfaction proceeds from the frustration of "real" interests, from the blockage of interests as they drive onward to real "consummations." The aesthetic sign is a value that has not been consummated. Art is the expression of what men desire but are not getting.

There are two passages in "Esthetics and the Theory of Signs" which reveal the fundamental ambiguity in Mr. Morris's conception of the aesthetic sign as a "value." We shall be struck, I believe, by the remarkable parallel between Mr. Morris's view of the aesthetic medium and the neo-classical view, which we saw in Matthew Arnold.

> Even though the complexity of the total icon is so very great that no denotatum (other than the esthetic sign vehicle itself) can in actuality be found, the work of art can still be considered a sign—for there can be designation without denotation.

But can the aesthetic sign—and this is the center of the problem—designate an interest "value" if it does not point to an interest? It seems to me that it cannot be a value in any "interest" theory of value whatever. And when the aesthetic sign is so complex that it does not lead to denotation, is not this complexity a semantical failure so great that Mr. Morris actually ought to take it to an institution for the insane?

The traditional prestige of the arts is formidable; so, rather than commit himself to his logic of the aesthetic sign as a designation of a value which cannot be located and which thus cannot be an interest-value, he offers us the ordinary procedure of positivism; that is to say, he shows us how we may reduce the aesthetic sign to a *denotatum* after all.

> Since a statement must say something about something, it must involve signs for locating what is referred to, and such signs are ultimately indexical signs [i.e., "pointing" signs]. An iconic sign in isolation cannot then be a statement, and a work of art, conceived as an iconic sign, cannot be true in the semantical sense of the term. Nevertheless, the statement that a work of art is "true" might under analysis turn out to be an elliptical form of syntactical, semantical, or pragmatical statements. Thus semantically it might be intended to affirm that the work in question actually is iconic of the value structure of a certain object or situation. . . .

The work of art is elliptical and iconic; that is, it is an image from which the semantical dimension is omitted, or in which it remains vague. By translating the icon, by expanding it and filling it in with a *denotatum*, we construct a situation external to the work of art: a situation which replaces it. In the usual terms of literary criticism, this situation is the "subject" which exists outside the language of the poem. For the language is merely "iconic of" this ordinary prose subject.

So a neo-classical theory of poetic language not only gave the case for poetry away to the scientist; it has become the foundation of the scientists' theory of poetry. When Mr. Richards remarked, in *Science and Poetry*, that we were now getting on a large scale "genuine knowledge" which would soon reduce poetry to the level of the "pseudo-statement," we could not see how right he was. Right —from the point of view of neo-classical theory. So long as the scientific pro-

801

cedure was observation, description, and classification, it was not very different from the procedure of common sense and its feeling for the reality of ordinary experience. As late as the first edition (1892) of *The Grammar of Science*, Karl Pearson said: "The aesthetic judgment pronounces for or against the interpretation of the creative imagination according as that interpretation embodies or contradicts the phenomena of life, which we ourselves have observed." But from the point of view of Unified Science, this principle of common-sense observation will no longer serve; it does not go far enough. And so we have a dilemma. Since the language of poetry can be shown to be not strictly relevant to objects and situations as these are presented by the positivist techniques, poetry becomes either nonsense or hortatory rhetoric.

The semiotic approach to aesthetics "has the merit of concreteness"; yet we have seen that Mr. Morris never quite gets around to a specific work of art. In "Science, Art, and Technology," he distinguishes three primary forms of discourse and relates them to the three dimensions of semiosis:

1. Scientific discourse: semantical dimension.
2. Aesthetic discourse: syntactical dimension.
3. Technological discourse: pragmatical dimension.

We have seen that the iconic sign is semantically weak; so the aesthetic sign, a variety of iconic sign, must function primarily at the syntactical level; that is, if we look at it "indexically" it "points" first of all to itself. Looking at the aesthetic sign from this point of view, we are forced to see that it wholly lacks cognitive content, and it is subject to the operation of "transformation rules." Does the "concreteness" of the semiotic approach to art consist in this? Again, is the syntactical dimension that in which direct apprehension of the aesthetic sign is possible? Once more it must be said that this direct apprehension seems impossible unless there is an agency of apprehension—a knowing mind; without this we get only an "interpretant," which is conceivable only at the pragmatic level; and if the interpretant is intelligible, it is so in terms of semantical relevance, or of the scientific form of discourse. For Mr. Morris himself confesses: ". . . in so far as the knowledge of value which art gives is the more than the having of value [i.e., is the *knowing* of value] there is no reason to suppose that this knowledge is *other than scientific in character*."

It is significant here that Mr. Morris conceives the character of poetry in the relation of pragmatics and semantics. What is our response to poetry and how do we behave when we read it: what, in a word, does it lead to? There is a certain uneasy piety in the extravagant claim that poetry is the realm of values; and there is no way, I think, to get around the conclusion that, since the values are not attached to reality, they are irresponsible feelings. They are, in fact, rhetoric. And it is also significant that for Mr. Morris the study of rhetoric is a branch of pragmatics; it is even a kind of technological instrument. For, in the essay, "Science, Art, and Technology," poetry seems to acquire its main responsibility in the technological function of telling us what we *ought* to want and do. Here again neo-classical didacticism appears in terms of a rigorous instrumentalism.

Does the language of poetry mean what it says, or does it mean the "situation" that we get from it in a process of reduction? Although we have seen Mr. Morris's bias, we have also seen that he has not made up his mind: he would like to have it both ways. The origin of this dilemma is remote. But there is always "the sad ghost of Coleridge beckoning from the shades."

IV

The famous Chapter XIV of *Biographia Literaria* has been the background of the criticism of poetry for more than a hundred years. Its direct influence has been very great; its indirect influence, through Poe upon Baudelaire, and through the French symbolists down to contemporary English and American poets, has perhaps been even greater. This chapter is the most influential statement on poetry ever formulated by an English critic: its insights, when we have them, are ours, and ours too its contradictions. Yet the remarkable "definition" of poetry, which I shall now quote, is not, as we shall presently see, the chief source of the aesthetic dilemma that we inherit today. (That source is another passage.) Here is the definition:

A poem is that species of composition, which is opposed to works of science, by proposing for its *immediate* object pleasure, not truth; and from all other species—(having this object in common with it)—it is distinguished by proposing to itself such delight from the *whole*, as is compatible with a distinct gratification from each component *part*.

Much of the annoyance and misunderstanding caused by this passage has not been Coleridge's fault; but is rather due to the failure of literary men to observe the accurate use of *species*. For Coleridge is giving us a strict Aristotelian definition of a *species* within a given *genus*. It is not a qualitative statement, and it does not answer the question: *What* is poetry? The *whatness* of poetry does not come within the definition; and I believe that nowhere else does Coleridge offer us an explicit qualitative distinction between poetry and other "species of composition" which may be "opposed" to it.

For what is Coleridge saying? (I have never seen a literal reading of the passage by any critic.) There is the generic division: composition. A poem is a species within the genus; but so is a work of science. How are the two species distinguished? By their immediate objects. It is curious that Coleridge phrases the passage as if a poem were a person "proposing" to himself a certain end, pleasure; so for *object* we have got to read *effect*. A poem, then, differs from a work of science in its immediate effect upon us; and that immediate effect is pleasure. But other species of composition may aim at the effect of pleasure. A poem differs from these in the relation of part to whole: the parts must give us a distinct pleasure, moment by moment, and they are not to be conceived as subordinate to the whole; they make up the whole.

If there is an objective relation of part to whole, Coleridge does not say what it is; nor does he distinguish that relation in terms of any specific poetic work. It is strictly a quantitative analogy taken, perhaps, from geometry. And the only purpose it serves is this: in the paragraph following the "definition" he goes on to say that "the philosophic critics of all ages coincide" in asserting that

803

beautiful, isolated lines or distichs are not a poem, and that neither is "an unsustained composition" of uninteresting parts a *"legitimate* poem." What we have here, then, is a sound but ordinary critical insight; but because it is merely an extension of the pleasure principle implicit in the "definition," we are not prepared by it to distinguish objectively a poem from any other form of expression. The distinction lies in the effect, and it is a psychological effect. In investigating the differentia of poetry—as Mr. Morris would put it—we are eventually led away from the poem into what has been known since Coleridge's time as the psychology of poetry.

The difficulties of this theory Coleridge seems not to have been aware of; yet he illustrates them perfectly. In the second paragraph after the famous definition he writes this remarkable passage:

> The first chapter of Isaiah—(indeed a very large portion of the whole
> book)—is poetry in the most emphatic sense; yet it would be no less
> irrational than strange to assert, that pleasure, not truth, was the im-
> mediate object of the prophet. In short, whatever specific import we
> attach to the word, Poetry, there will be found involved in it, as a
> necessary consequence, that a poem of any length neither can be, nor
> ought to be, all poetry. Yet if an harmonious whole is to be produced,
> the remaining parts must be preserved in keeping with the poetry;
> and this can no otherwise be effected than by such a studied selection
> and artificial arrangement, as will partake of one, though not a peculiar
> property of poetry. And this again can be no other than the property of
> exciting a more continuous and equal attention than the language of
> prose aims at, whether colloquial or written.

This is probably the most confused statement ever uttered by a great critic, and it has probably done more damage to critical thought than anything else said by any critic. Isaiah is poetry in "the most emphatic sense," although his immediate object (effect) is truth. It will be observed that, whereas in the definition our attention is drawn to a species of composition, a poem, we are here confronted with the personage, Isaiah, who does have the power of proposing an object; and Isaiah's immediate object is truth. But are we to suppose that the effect of the poem and the object of the prophet are to be apprehended in the same way? Is our experience of truth the same as our experience of pleasure? If there is a difference between truth and pleasure, and if an immediate effect of pleasure is the specific "property" of poetry (how a property can be an effect it is difficult to see), how can the first chapter of Isaiah be poetry at all? It cannot be, looked at in these terms; and as a matter of fact Coleridge rather slyly withdraws his compliment to Isaiah when he goes on to say that a "poem of any length neither can be, nor ought to be, all poetry." Isaiah is not all poetry; he is partly truth, or even mostly truth. And the element of truth, while it is strictly speaking insubordinate and unassimilable, can be used by means of an artificial arrangement—meter. There is no doubt that meter does on the whole what Coleridge attributes to it: it demands a "continuous and equal attention." Does he mean to say that the insubordinate element of truth—insubordinate to the immediate effect of pleasure—should be given such conspicuous emphasis? Or does he perhaps mean that the attention will be fixed upon the metrical pattern, so that the nonpoetic element will be less conspicuous?

Coleridge's theory of meter is not quite pertinent here: in the later and more elaborate discussion of meter in *Biographia Literaria* there is the general conclusion that meter is indispensable to poetry. In Chapter XIV, now being examined, he speaks of meter as "an artificial arrangement . . . not a peculiar property of poetry."

There is, then, in Coleridge's poetic theory a persistent dilemma. *He cannot make up his mind whether the specifically poetic element is an objective feature of the poem, or is distinguishable only as a subjective effect.* He cannot, in short, choose between metaphysics and psychology. His general emphasis is psychological, with metaphysical ambiguities.

The distinction between Fancy and Imagination is ultimately a psychological one: he discusses the problem in terms of separate faculties, and the objective poetical properties, presumably resulting from the use of these faculties, are never defined, but are given only occasional illustration. (I have in mind his magnificent analysis of "Venus and Adonis," the value of which lies less perhaps in the critical principles he supposes he is illustrating, than in the perfect taste with which he selects the good passages for admiration.) When Coleridge speaks of the "esemplastic power" of the Imagination, it is always a "faculty" of the mind, not an objective poetic order. When he says that a poem gives us "a more than usual state of emotion with more than usual order," we acknowledge the fact, without being able to discern in the merely comparative degree of the adjective the fundamental difference between the poetic and the philosophic powers which Coleridge frequently asserts, but which he nowhere objectively establishes. The psychological bias of his "system" is perfectly revealed in this summary passage of Chapter XIV:

> My own conclusions on the nature of poetry, in the strictest use of the word, have been in part anticipated in some of the remarks on the Fancy and Imagination in the early part of this work. What is poetry? —is so nearly the same question with, what is a poet?—that the answer to the one is involved in the solution to the other. For it is a distinction resulting from the poetic genius itself, which sustains and modifies the images, thoughts, and emotions of the poet's own mind.

There can be little doubt that Coleridge's failure to get out of the dilemma of Intellect-or-Feeling has been passed on to us as a fatal legacy. If the first object of poetry is an effect, and if that effect is pleasure, does it not necessarily follow that truth and knowledge may be better set forth in some other order altogether? It is true that Coleridge made extravagant claims for a poetic order of truth, and it is upon these claims that Mr. I. A. Richards has based his fine book, *Coleridge on Imagination:* Mr. Richards's own testimony is that the claims were not coherent. The coherent part of Coleridge's theory is the fatal dilemma that I have described. Truth is only the secondary consideration of the poet, and from the point of view of positivism the knowledge, or truth, that poetry gives us is immature and inadequate. What of the primary consideration of the poet— pleasure?

805

Pleasure is the single qualitative feature of Coleridge's famous definition; but it is not *in* the definition objectively. And with the development of modern psychology it has ceased to be qualitative, even subjectively. It is a *response*. The fate of Coleridge's system, then, has been its gradual extinction in the terminology of experimental psychology. The poetry has been extinguished in the poet. The poetic "effect" is a "response" to a "stimulus"; and in the early works of Mr. Richards we get for the first time the questions, rigorously applied: Is the poetic response relevant to the real world? Is it relevant to action? Poetry has come under the general idea of "operational validity." So we must turn briefly to Mr. Richards.

V

In *Science and Poetry* (1926) Mr. Richards condensed in untechnical language the position that he had set forth in detail earlier, in *The Principles of Literary Criticism*. The positivist side of Mr. Richards's thought at that time is plainly revealed in a passage like this:

> You contrive not to laugh [in church]; but there is no doubt about the activity of the impulses in their restricted form. The much more subtle and elaborate impulses which a poem excites are not different in principle. *They do not show themselves as a rule, they do not come out into the open, largely because they are so complex.* [Italics mine.] When they have adjusted themselves to one another and become organized into a coherent whole, the needs concerned may be satisfied. *In a fully developed man a state of readiness for action will take the place of action when the full appropriate situation for action is not present.*[6] [Mr. Richards's italics.]

The mere state of readiness for action is the poetic experience in terms of value and relevance. The readiness points to the "direct apprehension" of an interest-value in Mr. Morris's sense; but the failure of the action to come off, the lack of the "full appropriate situation for action," indicates the absence of a *denotatum*. We receive the designation of a value without being provided with a situation in which we can act upon it. The remarkable parallel between Mr. Richards's early theories of poetry and the recent theories of Mr. Morris need not detain us. It is enough to point out that Mr. Richards anticipated fifteen years ago everything that Mr. Morris's science of semiotic has to say about the language of poetry.

I have italicized a sentence, in the quotation from Mr. Richards, for two reasons: first, the vagueness of the language is significant; secondly, the idea of the coherent whole into which the "impulses" are organized has no experimental basis in terms of impulses. Mr. John Crowe Ransom remarks that Mr. Richards never shows us *how* this ordering act of poetry upon our minds takes place, and then proceeds to discern the reason for Mr. Richards's vague statements about the conduct of poetic stimulation and response:

806

> Most readers will retort, of course, that in the very large majority of cases the spiritual happenings are the only happenings we have ob-

[6] *Science and Poetry*, pp. 28–29. *(Tate's note.)*

served, and *the neural happenings are simply what the behaviorists would like to observe.* [Italics mine.] At present the mental datum is the fact and the neural datum is the inference.[7]

In throwing out the mental fact Mr. Richards in his early writings preceded Mr. Morris in his rejection of the cognitive powers of the mind. I do not suggest any direct influence from Mr. Richards upon Mr. Morris, although Mr. Morris has acknowledged the work of his predecessor: it is easier to relate these men to a much wider movement. That movement is positivism, and it is more than a strict scientific method.

It is a general attitude towards experience. If it is not, why should Mr. Richards have attempted in his early criticism to represent the total poetic experience and even the structure of poetry in one of the positivist languages—experimental psychology? It was representation by analogy. The experimental basis for such a representation was wholly lacking. Mr. Richards, had we listened hard enough, was saying in *The Principles of Literary Criticism* and *Science and Poetry* that here at last is what poetry would be if we could only reduce it to the same laboratory technique that we use in psychology; and without warning to the unwary reader, whose credulity was already prepared by his own positivist *zeitgeist,* Mr. Richards went on to state "results" that looked like the results of an experiment; but the experiment had never been made. It had been inferred. The "impulses" that we feel in response to a poem, says Mr. Richards, "do not show themselves as a rule." There is no scientific evidence that they have ever shown themselves to Mr. Richards or to anybody else. Mr. Richards like a good positivist was the victim of a deep-seated compulsive analogy, an elusive but all-engrossing assumption that all experience can be reduced to what is actually the very limited frame of reference supplied by a doctrine of correlation, or of the relevance of stimulus to response. This early procedure of Mr. Richards's was not even empiricism, for in empiricism the cognitive intelligence is not eliminated in the pursuit of verifiable facts. Mr. Richards, like Mr. Morris after him, eliminated cognition without demonstrating experimentally the *data* of his behavioristic poetics. So this doctrine was not empiricism: it came out of the demi-religion of positivism. The poetry had been absorbed into a pseudo-scientific jargon, no more "relevant" to poetry than the poetic pseudo-statement was relevant to the world: the net result was zero from both points of view.

I have put this brief commentary on Mr. Richards's early poetics in the past tense because it is no longer his poetics. From 1926, the year of *Science and Poetry,* he has come a long way. It is perhaps not an extravagant claim to make for Mr. Richards's intellectual history, that it will probably turn out to be the most instructive, among critics, of our age. His great intellectual powers, his learning, his devotion to poetry—a devotion somewhat frustrated but as marked fifteen years ago as now—are qualities of an intellectual honesty rare in any age. In exactly ten years, from 1926, he arrived, in *The Philosophy of Rhetoric* (1936), at such a statement as this:

807

[7] *"A Psychologist Looks at Poetry,"* The World's Body, p. 147. *This essay is the most searching examination of Mr. Richards's position—or positions—that I have seen; but it does somewhat less than full justice to Mr. Richards's insights. (Tate's note.)*

> So far from verbal language being a "compromise for a language of intuition"—a thin, but better-than-nothing, substitute for real experience—language, well used, is a *completion* and does what the intuitions of sensation by themselves cannot do. Words are the meeting points at which regions of experience which can never combine in sensation or intuition, come together. They are the occasion and means of that growth which is the mind's endless endeavor to order itself. That is why we have language. *It is no mere signalling system.* [Italics mine.] It is the instrument of all our distinctively human development, of everything in which we go beyond the animals. [Pp. 130–131.]

These words should be read and re-read with the greatest care by critics who still cite the early Richards as the continuing head of a positivist tradition in criticism. There is, in this passage, first of all, an implicit repudiation of the leading doctrine of *The Principles of Literary Criticism.* The early doctrine did look upon poetic language as a "substitute for real experience," if by experience is meant responses relevant to scientifically ascertained facts and situations: this early doctrine, as I have indicated, anticipated in psychological terms Mr. Morris's poetic doctrine of designation without *denotatum,* of value without consummation of value, of interpretant without an interpreter. Mr. Richards's more familiar equivalents of the semiotic terms were: pseudo-statement without referents; poetry as the orderer of our minds, as the valuer, although the ordering mysteriously operated in fictions irrelevant to the real world; a response, a behavioristic "readiness for action," without a knowing mind.

Language, says Mr. Richards, "is no mere signalling system." With that sentence the early psychological doctrine is discreetly put away. Is it too much to assume that the adjective "signalling" may indicate the relation of Mr. Richards's present views to the pragmatic bias of Mr. Morris's aesthetics? He speaks of the inadequacy of "sensation" and "intuition," and of the equal inadequacy of "intuitions of sensation." Is not the mere sensation Mr. Morris's interpretant, the intuition of sensation his iconic sign? What is the "completion" which language "well used" can achieve beyond sensation and intuition?

It is doubtless knowledge of a kind that we can discuss only if we assume the action of a knowing mind. Of what is it the completion? In the paragraph following the passage that I have just quoted, Mr. Richards cites Coleridge:

> Are not words parts and germinations of the plant? And what is the law of their growth? In something of this sort I would destroy the old antithesis of Words and Things: elevating, as it were, Words into Things and living things too.

This attribution to the language of poetry of a special kind of "life" goes back to Mr. Richards's *Coleridge on Imagination* (1935), the most ambitious attempt of a modern critic to force into unity the antithesis of language and subject, of pleasure and truth. It is an antithesis which, as we have seen, has harassed critical theory since the time of Coleridge. Mr. Richards's book may be looked upon as an effort to finish Coleridge's own uncompleted struggle with this neo-

808

classical dilemma. This is not the place to describe the entire nature and scope of his effort, or to estimate it. A single chapter of the book, "The Wind Harp," contains the clearest presentation of the antithesis that I have seen by a modern critic.

There are "two doctrines," he says, which have tended to flourish independently—"And yet, neither is intelligible, apart from Imagination." He continues:

The two doctrines can be stated as follows:
1. The mind of the poet at moments . . . gains an insight into reality, reads Nature as a symbol of something behind or within Nature not ordinarily perceived.
2. The mind of the poet creates a Nature into which his own feelings, his aspirations and apprehensions, are projected.

Now the positivist sciences have denied all validity to the first doctrine: as a proposition, in the many forms in which it may be stated, it is strictly meaningless. For the sole effective procedure towards nature is the positivist. The second doctrine is the standard poetics of our time: projection of feeling. The confusion and contradiction that we saw in Mr. Morris and in the early Richards came of trying to square a theory of interest-value with a theory of emotional projection which was not firmly based upon positivist knowledge. That contradiction is the clue to the "unintelligibility" of the doctrines if held separately. If you take the first alone, eliminating the second, you eliminate the "mind," and you get pure positivism: in thus eliminating cognition you lose "everything in which we go beyond the animals." If you take the second alone, and eliminate the external world in any of the four meanings [8] that Mr. Richards gives to the phrase, you have a knowing mind without anything that it can know.

Before the development of the positivist procedures towards nature, the pressure of this dilemma was not seriously felt. We have seen in Matthew Arnold (the determined anti-dialectician) the belief that the subject is external to the language—a merely common-sense view inherited from neo-classical theory. The poetic subject was the world of ordinary experience; but as soon as the subject —Nature—became the field of positivism, the language of poetry ceased to represent it; ceased, in fact, to have any validity, or to set forth anything real. (The world of positivism is a world without minds to know the world; and yet Mr. Morris does not hesitate to assert that his Unified Science will save the world. For whom will it be saved?)

What is this Imagination which Mr. Richards says will make the two doctrines intelligible? No doubt it becomes in his hands something different from Coleridge's conception of it: it closely resembles an Hegelian synthesis, which joins the opposites in a new proposition in which their truths, no longer contradictory, are preserved.

809

They are [says Mr. Richards of the two doctrines] neither consequences of *a priori* decisions, nor verifiable as the empirical statements of sci-

[8] Coleridge on Imagination, *pp. 157–8. (Tate's note.)*

ence are verifiable; and all verifiable statements are independent of them. But this does not diminish in the least their interest, or that of the other senses in which they may be true.

With that we are almost ready to leave Mr. Richards, who offers no final solution of the problem of the unified imagination. "It is the privilege of poetry," he says finely, "to preserve us from mistaking our notions either for things or for ourselves. *Poetry is the completest mode of utterance.*" [9] It is neither the world of verifiable science nor a projection of ourselves; yet it is *complete*. And because it is complete knowledge we may, I think, claim for it a unique kind of responsibility, and see in it at times an irresponsibility equally distinct. The order of completeness that it achieves in the great works of the imagination is not the order of experimental completeness aimed at by the positivist sciences, whose responsibility is directed towards the verification of limited techniques. The completeness of science is an abstraction covering an ideal of co-operation among specialized methods. No one can have an experience of science, or of a single science. For the completeness of *Hamlet* is not of the experimental order, but of the experienced order: it is, in short, of the mythical order. And here Mr. Richards can give us a final insight. Myths, he says,

> . . . are no amusement or diversion to be sought as a relaxation and an escape from the hard realities of life. They are these hard realities in projection, their symbolic recognition, co-ordination and acceptance. . . . The opposite and discordant qualities in things in them acquire a form. . . . Without his mythologies man is only a cruel animal without a soul . . . a congeries of possibilities without order and aim.[10]

Man, without his mythologies, is an interpretant. Mr. Richards's books may be seen together as a parable, as a mythical and dramatic projection, of the failure of the modern mind to understand poetry on the assumptions underlying the demi-religion of positivism. We do not need to reject the positive and rational mode of inquiry into poetry; yet even from Mr. Morris we get the warning lest we substitute the criticism for the poem, and thus commit ourselves to a "learned ignorance." We must return to, we must never leave, the poem itself. Its "interest" value is a cognitive one; it is sufficient that here, in the poem, we get knowledge of a whole object. If rational inquiry is the only mode of criticism, we must yet remember that the way we employ that mode must always powerfully affect our experience of the poem. I have been concerned in this commentary with the compulsive, almost obsessed, application of an all-engrossing principle of pragmatic reduction to a formed realm of our experience, the distinction of which is its complete knowledge, the full body of the experience that it offers us. However we may see the completeness of poetry, it is a problem less to be solved than, in its full import, to be preserved. (*1941*)

810

[9] Ibid., *p. 163. (Tate's note.)*
[10] Ibid., *pp. 171–172. (Tate's note.)*

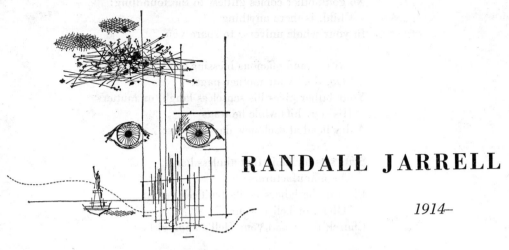

RANDALL JARRELL

1914–

Randall Jarrell was born May 16, 1914, in Nashville, Tennessee, but spent most of his childhood in California and the Middle West. A graduate of Vanderbilt University, he has taught English at Kenyon College, the University of Texas, and the Woman's College of the University of North Carolina. He has also served as literary editor of the *Nation*. His rather severe critical essays and reviews of the works of fellow poets have proved uniformly interesting.

Jarrell is one of the most gifted of the younger Southern poets. Certainly no one, in the South or elsewhere, has registered the shattering impact of World War II upon the sensibilities of men more poignantly than he. In an early volume of poetry, *Blood for a Stranger* (1942), Jarrell begins to define his preoccupation with the dogged-out individual whose way of life—whether child, soldier, or refugee—has been violated. He writes with a tragic penetration that is rare in our time. Jarrell's most recent collections of poetry are *Little Friend, Little Friend* (1945), *Losses* (1948), and *The Seven League Crutches* (1951).

The Head of Wisdom [1]

> The little Will comes naked to its world
>   Without a rag of wit;
> Church, State, the crazy categories
>   Crowd to the straw where it
> Weeps under the family's fondling;
>
> The shepherds baa, the Magi smell like camels,
>   Hark, how Herod's agents sing!

811

"The Head of Wisdom" and *"For an Emigrant"* from Blood for a Stranger *by Randall Jarrell,* copyright, 1942, by Harcourt, Brace and Company, Inc.
[1] *This poem is written for Katherine Louise Lyle Starr, who was born May 16, 1940. The head is Beethoven's. (Jarrell's note.)*

No godmother comes giftless to the foundling:
    Child, is there anything
In your whole universe to spare you

Its witless and officious blessing?
    "Do, do," your mother nags,
Your father gives his senseless laugh, or mutters
    His sour hits while he wags
A dry head at each new day's errors;

State sets a rifle in that aimless hand;
    The manufacturers
Bid for the labors of its fruitless years;
    "Obey, or hell is yours,"
Church tells; and your Hell's apologists—

King, priest, philosopher, the lean professors—
    Tell, tell, and tell. You see.
Learn it all—the lies, the hunger, and the blood:
    The peoples' history;
What we said; and all that we knew instead;

Learn it; but wisdom is more than knowing
    What we knew, what we said,
The famous errors of the famous dead.
    The maned and erring head
Holds, under the truth, under the lies,

Something stronger than either; the great stare
    Of the magnificent eyes
Dazzles, is dazzled with more than tears;
    No surprise
Warms the ruined face: the wilderness

Of confusion, of desolation, the helpless laughter
    Of the wise break free
From the mouth open in the dying face—
    Child, *here* is history,
Here is knowledge, is wisdom—see! see!

                              (*1942*)

For an Emigrant

812

In that bad year and city of your birth
They traded bread for bank notes weight for weight,
And nothing but the statues kept the smile

The waltzers wore once: excluding, innocent,
The face of old and comfortable injustice.
And if you wept,
Dropped red into a city where the husbandless
And fatherless were crying too, who cared
For one more cry or one more child? You grew;

Time put words into your mouth, and you put sugar
Upon your windowsill and waited for a brother—
The stork was greedy, ate, brought nothing in return.
And life was thinking of you, took you back to Prague;
At school there, timid, boisterous, you spoke
The unaccustomed Czech—
The children laughed at you. But you were learning
New worlds and a new life, the old
City and its new country too were learning
Man's strength: to be just; yes, to be free.

"I saw summer in my time." Summer is ending.
The storms plunge from the tree of winter, death
Moves like an impulse over Europe. Child,
What man is just or free?—but fortunate,
Warm in time's hand, turning and trusting to his face?
And that face changes.
Time is a man for men, and He is willing.
For many a new life, for others death. Already
He buys His trench-coat, falls, writes His big book;

Points here, points here: to Jews, the wicked friends—
His words are the moments of a man's life.
And now the men march. One morning you woke
And found Vienna gone, your father said:
"Us next!" And you were next.
Us next!
Cried map and mouth, oppressors and oppressed,
The appeasers as they gave your life—but you were gone.
"I have a tongue, a city." *What is your name?*
"My name is what my name was." *You have no name.*

So the dream spoke to you: in Zurich, Paris,
In London on a lawn; the unbefriending sea
Cried to you, "Stranger!"—superb, inhospitable,
The towers of the island turned their gaze
Past the girl who stared up to the great statue:
So green, so gay. . . .
That is how you came. Your face shows white
Against the dark time, your words are indistinct,
One cry among so many, lost in the great sound

813

Of degradation and agony, the peoples dying.
The net was laid for you; and you are free.
Free—to be homeless, to be friendless, to be nameless,
To stammer the hard words in the foreign night,
To remember; and free also, child,
To love and to be loved,
To see in one face the land, the tongue, the time—
Blind with your joy, to whisper: Happiness
Is possible and difficult: to learn at last
New words and a new country, a new love.

II

(In augmentation)

If I could only stop there—stop telling there,
Stop time there; fix those eyes upon their life,
The answerers and answered; fix in their light dream
The lips parting for their laugh, the grateful and faultless
And stupid laughter of the child, the joy of ignorance;
But you must wake, poor Beauty.
And here where Locke's page sparkled white as dew
The woman's face must come, to choose and suffer
And lose its beauty and at last find beautiful

Its death. . . . You escaped from nothing; the westering soul
Finds Europe waiting for it over every sea.
The statue in the harbor stretched its hand
Above you in His gesture, He is here
To turn on you in love or in denunciation
The eyes that are your own.
If they are evil, they are evil really,
As a child's are evil: blind in the unbearable
Magnificence of bronze; so absolute in their assurance
Of power and of innocence: the statue's eyes.

And what looks timidly from their clear depths
Is the child's loneliness, his passionate rejection
Of his own helplessness and pain, the man's
Denial of the knowledge he cannot endure.
The mouth says: "I made me, I shall last, be sure.
Time is my will.
Surely the tears are iron within my eyes.
Look, and find life here about my lips—
Who has not loved me? I shall never die."

814

And not those lips alone. O what mouth will not shape,
Blood wash and spittle moisten, tongue caress
That lie and all man's versions of that lie?
—The facets of the look the lives are mirroring,

The maze where all of us are wandering: that History
Where nothing is not repeated.
Where mistress and Mother fuse at last into a face,
And Time and my father and the terrible finger
Of all I cannot face and must adore—

The Accuser, the Appeaser, the inhuman Judge—
Are Hitler: a separate peace: the real history
Where there is nothing that can cause except my lies,
Where there is nothing that can list except my life,
Where there is nothing. . . . *That* is the world
You must escape from: The America where each
Can think still, "I am innocent."
But there is guilt enough for all: existence is guilt enough.
Because of us, because of what we did or did not do,
See, the men die. "And they are the innocent?"

Irremediably. They? Those innocents whom we forgive
Because their failure is intolerable, the final guilt
Only forgiving hides from us? Forgive today
And the next day fail, and die, and be forgiven?
Forgive, forgive? Forgive no one.
Understand and blame.
"But I am all of them. That face, that world is mine."
Change, then. Learn what you can, love what you can: when
　　　they kill you,
Let them look at your face and remember your life
And cry—"You stranger, you damned stranger!"

　　　　　　　　　　　　　　　　　　(*1942*)

ELLEN GLASGOW

1874–1945

Ellen Glasgow was born in Richmond, Virginia, on April 22, 1874. She was **815** privately educated, to a large extent by reading in her father's library. Her literary achievement comprises twenty novels seriously executed over a period approximating half a century. Her career is without parallel among women fictionists in the modern South.

Shortly before her death, in *A Certain Measure*, Miss Glasgow favored her readers with a considered statement about her ideas on the art of the novel and about life in her part of the country. The purpose of fiction, she declared, is "the communication of ideas, of feeling, of vital experience. Beyond this a novel is entitled to be anything, from a treatise on philosophy to an affair of the heart." It is "experience illuminated." When Ellen Glasgow began as an author, she felt herself undertaking "a solitary revolt against the formal, the false, the affected, the sentimental, and the pretentious in Southern writing. I had no guide." In her first book the central character was an illegitimate poor white. An elderly kinsman, having read the novel, declared it incredible "that a well-brought-up Southern girl should even know what a bastard is." Thus, Ellen Glasgow's role was from the beginning that of a rebel against certain presuppositions of her tradition. It seems to have been a role of immense personal satisfaction. ("It is true that the South disapproved of *Life and Gabriella* [1916]," she said, "but I had lived long enough in that section to know that the South would instinctively disapprove of the living.") When *The Voice of the People* was published in 1900, as Stuart P. Sherman remarked years later, "Realism crossed the Potomac."

The broad plan of Ellen Glasgow's work may be simply described, for it falls into three clearly conceived categories. She proposed first to write, in a series of novels, a social history of private and public life in Virginia from 1850 to 1912. *The Battle-Ground, Deliverance, The Romance of a Plain Man, Virginia,* and *Life and Gabriella* belong to this period which, in later years, she termed "another life." Three important "novels of the country" followed. They were *The Miller of Old Church, Barren Ground,* and *Vein of Iron.* Finally came her novels of the city: *The Sheltered Life, The Romantic Comedians, They Stooped to Folly,* and *In This Our Life,* for which she was awarded a Pulitzer Prize in 1942. *Barren Ground* (1925), *The Sheltered Life* (1932), and *The Shadowy Third* (short stories, 1925) represent her most successful performances.

Miss Glasgow's statement about *The Sheltered Life,* probably her best-known work, clarifies her conception of its primary value: "What I saw, as my novel unfolded, was a complete reversal of a classic situation. For once, in Southern fiction, the betrayed woman would become the victor instead of the victim. In the end she would triumph through that deep instinct for survival, which had ceased to be a negative quality and had strengthened into a dynamic force. She would be hardened by adversity, but hard things, as she said, are the last things to decay. . . . The only thing that mattered was her triumph over circumstances."

from The Sheltered Life

The Sheltered Life *is divided into three parts, from the second of which this selection is taken. The setting of the novel is in Queenborough, a typical Southern city, shortly before the outbreak of the first World War. The bare plot runs as follows:*

816

Jenny Blair Archbald was only a little girl when she began to fancy George Birdsong, an attractive but none too successful lawyer who had married Eva Howard, the most beautiful woman of her generation. Making over old evening dresses and thriftily managing her home, Eva declared herself well content with the great love which had been vouchsafed her with marriage—well content, even though the child Jenny Blair heard rumors that George Birdsong was keeping the mulattress, Memoria, whom he had rescued from a burning shanty.

Eva Birdsong's bright-faced acceptance of her lot was the admiration of everyone who knew her, especially of the aged General David Archbald, Jenny Blair's grandfather. It is General Archbald and Jenny Blair who, from widely divergent points of view, observe the events of the story.

Memoria was not the only mistress with whom George Birdsong shared his affections; but not until Eva surprised him in an embrace with Jenny Blair did the illusion of love with which she had sheltered her life fall completely away. Seeing her husband as he really was, she killed him. Jenny, for her part, weeping in the arms of her grandfather, cried that she had not meant anything, had not meant anything in the world.

The Deep Past

"Yes, it is true," said old General Archbald, for he had passed his eighty-third birthday, and had found that phrases, like events, often repeat themselves, "you can't mend things by thinking."

Though thought may have created life in the beginning, though the whole visible world may hang suspended in an invisible web of mind, one could not by taking heed mend the smallest break, not the tiniest loosened thread in the pattern. All the thinking in the world, he mused, with a sense of unreality as vague as smoke, could not help Eva Birdsong. For months he had suspected that something was wrong. Not more than ten days ago, he had seen her stop suddenly in the midst of a sentence, while a shiver ran through her body, the smile twisted and died on her lips, and she looked at him with the eyes of a woman in torture. Then she had seemed, by sheer strength of will, to drive the spasm away, to keep the returning pain at a distance. "What is it, Eva?" he had asked, and she had answered with a laugh of protest, "Oh, nothing." That was all, "Oh, nothing." Yet he had not been satisfied; he had felt uneasy and agitated; he had known in his heart that something was wrong with her. And now he had just heard that they had taken her to the hospital.

"They have given her morphine," Mrs. Archbald was saying, "and George telephoned me that she will be operated on in the morning. If you'll go up late this afternoon, she thinks she will be able to talk to you. There is something she has on her mind." Arrested by the pain in his eyes, she added, "I sometimes think, Father, that Eva is more to you than any one in the world."

With his hands clasped on the ebony crook of his walking-stick, he stood on the front porch and blinked up at his daughter-in-law, while William (an old dog now, but carrying his years well) waited for him to go out into the April sunshine in Jefferson Park.

"Is there danger?" he asked, without answering her question. For it was true

817

that Eva was more than a daughter, and nothing is so hard to speak aloud as the truth.

"There is, of course, always danger. For a year she has been really ill; but you know how long it took us to make her submit even to an examination."

"Yes, I know." The brooding eyes beneath the sardonic eyebrows did not waver.

"It does seem exaggerated to carry modesty to the point of endangering one's life. But with Eva, I think, it was less her own shrinking than the feeling that George might—well, might——Oh, I don't know, of course, but she told me once he had a horror of what he called maimed women."

"Any man worth his salt would think first of her health."

"That is exactly what George said to me an hour ago. But women, especially romantic women like Eva," she added sagaciously, "make the mistake of measuring a man's love by his theories. She told me about it the day she was seized with that dreadful pain and I telephoned for Doctor Bridges." She broke off abruptly, with the feeling probably, the General reminded himself, that she was giving away some solemn league and covenant of woman.

If only she would tell him more! While the thought crossed his mind, he flinched and raised his eyes to the clement sky. If only she would tell him nothing! After all, there was wisdom in an era that smothered truth in words. For truth, in spite of the stern probings of science, is an ugly and a terrible thing.

"If women could begin to realize," he said, "how little what a man thinks has to do with what he feels."

"Had I ever doubted that, the way George has risen to this crisis would have convinced me. He seems to feel the pain more than Eva does. For three nights he has sat up with her, and he refused to go to bed even after he fell asleep in his chair. The night nurse made him lie down on a couch last night; but he looks dreadfully haggard this morning, and his nerves are on edge. No man," she concluded emphatically, "could have shown a greater devotion."

"I can well believe that."

"Then why——? Why——?"

"Those other things, my dear, have nothing to do with his marriage."

Mrs. Archbald looked puzzled. "But that is just what I mean. There have been so many things in his life that have had nothing to do with his marriage."

The General sighed with the usual male helplessness before the embarrassing logic of the feminine mind. "Well, George has the kindest heart in the world. But even the kindest heart in the world sometimes fails to get the better of nature. All that side of his life has no more to do with his devotion to Eva than if—than if it were malaria from the bite of a mosquito. That's what women, especially women like Eva, are never able to understand."

"No wonder. It seems so illogical."

"Men aren't logical creatures, my dear. Nor, for that matter, is life logical." Then he asked, "Have you seen Isabella to-day?"

818 "Yes, she stopped as she was taking little Erminia to the dentist. There's something wrong with her teeth. It's such a pity, for she is a beautiful child."

"All three of them are beautiful children. Nature seems to be on the side of Isabella. Well, so am I, if only because she let our family skeleton out of the closet. The only way to be rid of a skeleton is to drag it into the light and clothe it in flesh and blood."

Mrs. Archbald looked puzzled. "I don't understand, Father."

"I didn't mean you to, my dear, but Isabella would. She is like every other Archbald, only more so, and though she is happily unaware of it, the more so has been her salvation."

Seven years before, three days after the renewal of her engagement to Thomas Lunsford, Isabella had taken the morning train to Washington, and had returned the next afternoon as the wife of Joseph Crocker. "Life is too short," she had explained, with the dash of coarseness that embarrassed her sister and her sister-in-law, "not to have the right man for your first husband at least. As for what people say—well, if talk could kill, I should have been dead long ago." Etta had been prostrated; but Mrs. Archbald had been too busy readjusting the Crockers' station in life to give way to prejudice. When so few standards remained unimpaired, the distinction between plain people and quiet people was almost obliterated by the first important step from the Baptist Communion to the Episcopal Church. And everything, of course, was made easier because Joseph had so little religion. . . .

"You look tired, Father," Mrs. Archbald remarked, when she had studied him for a moment. "Hadn't you better lie down?"

"No, I like to feel the sun on me, and so does William. We'll sit in the park awhile and then walk up to the hospital."

"Jenny Blair will go with you. She can wait downstairs while you are in Eva's room. The child is so distressed. She has always adored Eva."

"Every one adores her."

"Well, try not to worry. Something tells me that she will come through. Doctor Bridges feels very hopeful."

"He would naturally—but maimed for life——" his voice trembled.

"We must try not to think of that. If only she comes through it well." Then after a moment's thought, she added cheerfully, "It isn't as if she were a younger woman and still hoped to have children. She is forty-two, and has been married almost twenty years. One would never suspect that to look at her."

After she finished, he lingered a moment, hoping and fearing that she might, if only by accident, become more explicit. Was she shielding Eva's modesty from him, an old man, who would have loved her had she been stripped bare not only of modesty but of every cardinal virtue? Or was such evasion merely an incurable habit of mind? Would George tell him the truth? Or was it conceivable that George did not know?

"Will Jenny Blair come in time?" he asked, pricked by sudden fear. "I should not like to be late."

"Why, you've at least two hours, Father, and if Jenny Blair isn't back in time, I'll go with you myself."

"But I don't need anybody. I am able to go alone." No man needed protection less; but because he had lived a solitary male among women, he could never escape it, and because these women depended upon him, he had remained at their mercy. It was impossible to wound the feelings of women who owed him the bread they ate and the roof over their heads, and so long as he did not

819

hurt their feelings, they would be stronger than he was. Always, from earliest childhood, he mused, with a curious resentment against life, he had been the victim of pity. Of his own pity, not another's. Of that double-edged nerve of sympathy, like the aching nerve in a tooth, which throbbed alive at the sight of injustice or cruelty. One woman after another had enslaved his sympathy more than his passion, and never had she seemed to be the woman his passion demanded.

Well, it is over, he thought, and knew that it would never be over. Again this secret hostility swept through his nerves, surprising him by its vehemence. Was it possible that he was beginning to break in mind before the infirmities of the flesh had attacked a single physical organ? Only yesterday, Bridges had told him that a man of sixty might be proud of his arteries. Only yesterday! And to-day he was annoyed by this queer tingling in his limbs, by this hollow drumming which advanced along his nerves and then receded into the distance. "Let us sit down a bit, William," he murmured, walking very erect, with a proper pride in his straight back and thighs and his well-set-up figure for a man of his years. "I suppose this bad news about Eva has disturbed me. I'd rather lose my right arm than have anything happen to her."

Dropping down on a green bench in the park, beneath a disfigured tulip tree, which was putting out into bud, he tried to imagine her ill, suffering, and waiting calmly for that dreaded hour under the knife. But no, she chose, as always capriciously, her own hour and mood to return to him. Never had he seen her cast aside her armour of gaiety. Never, among all the women he had known, had she asked him for sympathy. Never once had she tried to take care of him. For all her loveliness, she was, he found himself thinking aloud to William, curled up on the grass by the bench, a strong soul in affliction. A strong soul, still undefeated by life, she came to him now. She came to him out of the pale green distance, out of the flying clouds, out of the April bloom of the sky. Even to-day, he mused proudly, there wasn't a girl in Queenborough who was worthy to step into her shoes. Not one of them. Not Jenny Blair, a vivid little thing, but lacking in queenliness.

Resting there, with his tired old hands clasped on the crook of his stick, he told himself that Eva Birdsong in her prime, before misfortune had sapped her ardent vitality, would have put to shame all the professional beauties of Paris or London. Why, he had seen Mrs. Langtry, and had considered her deficient in presence. "Eva would have had all London at her feet," he meditated, without jealousy, since his devotion, at eighty-three, was of the mind alone. Or was this deception? Did one go down into the grave with the senses still alive in the sterile flesh? Well, no matter. The thread had snapped, and the question had floated out of his thoughts. Airy and fragile as mist, he watched it blown away into the April world, into that windy vastness which contained the end of all loving and all living.

At least she had had, he pondered, sitting beside a triangular flower-bed, beneath the pale buds on the tulip tree, what she believed that she wanted. True, her life might have been easier if they hadn't been poor. Yet being poor, which kept her from parties where she once shone so brilliantly, had saved her also from brooding, from that fatal introspection which is the curse of women and poets. She had not had time to fall out of love. She had not had time to discover that George was unworthy.

Or was it conceivable, as Cora suspected, that Eva knew the truth, and was merely preserving appearances? No, he could not believe this, he mused, poking the end of his stick into a tuft of young dandelions. Yet, while he rejected Cora's suspicion, he admitted that life would be more agreeable if women could realize that man is not a monogamous animal, and that even a man in love does not necessarily wish to love all the time. Certainly, there would be less unhappiness abroad in the world if good women could either accept or reject the moral nature of man. Over and over, he had seen the faithful lover lose to the rake in an affair of the heart. Over and over, he had seen a miracle of love that failed to make a conversion. Yet he knew, having much experience to build on, that even loose-living men are not all of one quality. It was not a simple question of merit. The diversity went deeper, far down through the nature of man into nature itself. George had lived according to life; his very faults were the too lavish defects of generosity. He was generous with himself always, and with his money whenever he was affluent. Not without a pang, the General remembered that long ago, when he was caught on the verge of financial ruin, George alone among his sympathetic friends had offered him help. The year before George had inherited his father's modest estate, and he would have sacrificed this fortune to save a friend from disaster. Later on, to be sure, he had speculated unwisely and lost his inheritance—but it was not of this that the General was thinking while he poked at the dandelions.

He saw George, with his thick wind-blown hair, his smiling eyes, his look of virile hardness, of inexhaustible energy. Well favoured enough if you judged by appearances, and did women, or men either for that matter, ever judge by anything else? But it was more than George's fine features, ruddy skin, and friendly grey eyes that made one reluctant to blame him. Yes, there was something more, some full-bodied virtue, some compensating humanity. "But I am human too," thought old General Archbald, "and what good has it done me?". . .

As a child, at Stillwater, they had called him a milksop, because he saw visions in the night and wanted to be a poet. The sight of blood sickened him; yet his grandfather assured him, with truth, that hunting had given greater pleasure to a greater number of human beings than all the poetry since Homer. Pity, said the men who had none, is a woman's virtue; but he had known better than this. A poet's virtue, it may be. He was not sure. So much virtue passed into a poet when he was dead; when his immortal part was bound in English calf and put into a library. Little girls, however, were not pitiful. Little girls were as savage as boys, only weaker. They had never failed to torment him. They had laughed when he was made sick; they had mocked at his visions; they had stolen his poems and used them for curl-papers. Strange, the images that were dragged up like bits of shell, in a net of the memory! All his life curl-papers had remained, for him, the untidy symbol of an aversion. No, little girls were not gentle. And even his tender-hearted mother, who nursed her servants in illness, and had never used the word "slave" except in the historical sense—even his mother was incapable of the pity that becomes a torment to the

821

nerves. She accepted meekly, as an act of God's inscrutable wisdom, all the ancient wrongs and savage punishments of civilization. . . .

Again General Archbald sighed and prodded the dandelions. Again the thread snapped and a flock of unrelated images darted into his mind. . . .

"Where did the boy get his tomfool ideas?" his robust grandfather inquired sternly. "Was he born lacking?"

"Not lacking, Father," his mother protested, "but different. Some very nice people," she added, with an encouraging glance at her peculiar child, "are born different. He may even turn out to be a poet."

"Do you think," his father asked in a troubled tone, "that we had better try changing his tutor? Is it possible that Mr. Davis has infected him with new-fangled ideas?"

His mother shook her head in perplexity, for it distressed her that one of her sons should be deficient in manliness. "But the other boys are all manly. Even if Mr. Davis has talked of abolition, after giving us his word that he would treat the—the institution with respect, I have never heard that New Englanders disliked bloodshed. I thought, indeed, it was exactly the opposite. Don't you remember I opposed your engaging Mr. Davis because I had always heard the Puritans were a hard and cruel people? Perhaps," she confessed bravely, "he may inherit his eccentric notions from me. Though I try to be broad-minded, I can't help having a sentiment against cock-fights."

"Pooh! Pooh!" his grandfather blustered, for he belonged to the Georgian school of a gentleman. "Would you deprive the lower classes of their favourite sport? As for this young nincompoop, I'll take him deer-hunting to-morrow. If he is too much of a mollycoddle to kill his buck, we'll try to scare up a fawn for him."

A famous hunter in his prime, the old gentleman still pursued with hounds any animal that was able to flee. Fortunately, game was plentiful and game laws unknown in the fields and forests of Stillwater. For nothing escaped his knife or his gun, not the mole in the earth, not the lark in the air. He could no more look at a wild creature without lusting to kill than he could look at a pretty girl without lusting to kiss. Well, it was a pity he had not lived to enjoy the war; for the killing nerve, as his grandson had once said of him, was the only nerve in his body. Yet he had fallen in love with a woman because of her fragile appearance; and when she had gone into a decline after the birth of her fifth child, and had lost her reason for a number of years, he had remained still devoted to her. Against the advice of his family and his physician, he had refused to send her away, and had kept her, behind barred windows, in the west wing of the house. To be sure, when she died, he had married again within seven months; but only his first wife, though he had buried two others, had given him children, and through her the strain of melancholy had passed into the Archbald blood. . . .

From his father, with filial patience, "For my part, I try not to kill a doe or a fawn."

"Fiddlesticks, sir! You talk like an abolitionist. Didn't the Lord provide negroes for our servants and animals for our sport? Haven't you been told this from the pulpit? I hope, sir, I shan't live to see the day when every sort of sport is no longer welcome at Stillwater." Even the field hands in the quarters, General

Archbald remembered, had their "coon or possum dawgs," and went rabbit chasing on holidays when there were no cock-fights. High or low, good or bad, manners at Stillwater were a perpetual celebration of being alive. No other way of living had ever seemed to him so deeply rooted in the spirit of place, in an established feeling for life. Not for happiness alone, not for life at its best only, but for the whole fresh or salty range of experience. There was, too, a quality, apart from physical zest, that he had found nowhere else in the world, a mellow flavour he had never forgotten.

Naturally, as a child, he did not hunt or shoot with his grandfather; but several weeks later on, on a brilliant November morning, he watched a buck at bay pulled down by the hounds in a rocky stream. He could not remember how it had happened. By accident, probably, when he was out with his tutor. At first, watching the death, he had felt nothing. Then, in a spasm, the retch of physical nausea. For the eyes of the hunted had looked into his at the end; and that look was to return to him again and again, as a childish fear of the dark returns to the grown man when his nerves are unstrung. In how many faces of men, women, children, and animals, all over the world, had he seen that look of the hunted reflected? A look of bewilderment, of doubt, of agony, of wondering despair; but most of all a look that is seeking some God who might, but does not, show mercy. All over the world! North, South, East, West. On the heights, in the desert.

With blood on his hands and a savage joy inflaming his face, his grandfather strode over to smear stains on a milksop. "If you don't like the taste of blood better than milk, you'll have to be blooded. Hold still, sir, I say, and be blooded." Then, as the blood touched him, the boy retched with sickness, and vomited over the anointing hand and the outstretched arm. "Damn you, sir!" the old gentleman bellowed, while he wiped away the mess with his silk handkerchief. "Go back to the nursery where you belong!"

Still retching, furious and humiliated because he had been born a milksop, the boy rode home with his tutor. "I don't love people!" he sobbed passionately. "I don't love people!" Was it fair to blame him because he had been born different? Was anybody to blame for the way God had let him be born?

How close that day seemed to him now, that day and others at Stillwater. The more distant a scene, the clearer it appeared in his vision. Things near at hand he could barely remember. Even yesterday was smothered in fog. But when he looked far back in the past, at the end of seventy years or more, the fog lifted, and persons and objects started out in the sunken glow on the horizon. Instead of diminishing with time, events in the deep past grew larger, and the faces of persons long dead became more vivid and lifelike than life itself. "It is old age," he thought wearily. "It is a sign of old age to lack proper control." Or was the cause deeper still? he mused, while the shadow of a bird flitted over the grass and was gone. Was this second self of his mind, as variable as wind, as nebulous as mist, merely the forgotten consciousness of the poet who might have been? Sitting here in the spring sunshine, was he living again, was he thinking again, with that long buried part of his nature? For his very words, he realized, were the words of that second self, of the self he had always been in dreams and never been in reality. Again the bird flitted by. He did not know. He could not tell. No matter how hard he tried, it was impossible to keep his thoughts

823

from rambling back into the past. It was impossible to trace a connection between the past and present. Was he growing, in his old age, like poor Rodney, who had surrendered to shadows? Better let the past disappear, and hold firmly to the bare structure of living.

For an instant his look wandered from the trees in the park to the few carriages and many motor cars in Washington Street. Yes, the world was changing rapidly, and he wondered what was waiting ahead. He could remember when Queenborough had the charm of a village; but now, wherever he looked, he found ugliness. Beauty, like every other variation from type, was treated more or less as a pathological symptom. Did Americans, especially Southerners, prefer ugliness? Did ugliness conform, he pondered fancifully, to some automatic aesthetic spring in the dynamo? But even if the scientific method destroyed beauty, there would be no more great wars, only little wars that no one remembered, said John Welch. What, indeed, would be left to fight about when people thought alike everywhere, and exact knowledge had spread in a vast cemetery for ideals all over the world?

So John Welch, being very advanced in opinion, would argue for hours; but when argument was ended, old General Archbald could not see that human nature was different from what it had been in his youth. To be sure, idealism, like patriotism, appeared to diminish with every material peace between conflicts; but he was near enough to the Spanish War, and indeed to the Civil War, to realize that the last battle has never been fought and the last empty word has never been spoken. Not that it mattered. All he knew now was that he was too old to bother about life. He was too old to bother about cruelty, which he had seen all over the world, in every system invented by man; which he had seen in a velvet mask, in rags, and naked except for its own skin. Yes, he was too old to suffer over the evils that could not be cured. Only, whenever he listened to John Welch assailing the present order, he was reminded of his own revolt against slavery in the eighteen fifties. The reformers of that age had believed that all the world needed was to have negro slavery abolished. Yet negro slavery was gone, and where it had been, John said, another system had ushered in the old evils with a clean, or at least a freshly wiped face. What the world needed now, cried the modern reformers, like John Welch, was the new realism of science. For one confirmed habit had not changed with the ages. Mankind was still calling human nature a system and trying vainly to put something else in its place.

But a world made, or even made over, by science was only a stark and colourless spectacle to old David Archbald. A thin-lipped world of facts without faith, of bones without flesh. Better the red waistcoats and the soulful vapouring of early Romanticism. Better even the excessive sensibility of mid-Victorian aesthetics. Since he belonged to the past, if he belonged anywhere, his mental processes, it seemed, were obliged to be disorderly. When he said, "I am more than myself," when he said, "Life is more than living," when he blundered about "the nature of reality," he was still, or so John Welch declared, harping on a discredited idealism. "Transcendental!" John would snap when he meant "Nonsense!"

Glancing from the street to the sky, while the thread broke again, General Archbald reflected that it was easy to be an idealist in this pleasant spring of the year 1914, and to look with hope, if not with confidence, to the future. It was true that the familiar signs of uneasiness were abroad in the world. There was trouble not only in China and Mexico, where one naturally expected trouble to be, but among a part at least of the population of Europe. Power everywhere was growing more arrogant, and unrest more unrestful. Socialism was springing up and taking root in soil that appeared sterile. In Great Britain, Ulster and the suffragettes were disturbing a peace that turned in its broken sleep and dreamed of civil war. Nearer home, pirates had deserted the seas and embarked afresh as captains of industry.

But in the realm of ideas, where hope reigned, the prospect was brighter. There the crust of civilization, so thin and brittle over the world outside, was beginning to thicken. Religion and science, those hoary antagonists, were reconciled and clasped in a fraternal embrace. Together, in spite of nationalism, in spite even of nature, they would build, or invent, the New Jerusalem for mankind. In that favoured province, smooth, smiling, well-travelled, there would be neither sin nor disease, and without wars all the ancient wrongs would be righted. Nobody, not even the old sunning themselves on green benches, would be allowed to ramble in mind.

Well, perhaps. . . . No harm could come, he supposed, of a sanguine outlook. Only—only, did not that outlook approach a little too close to a formula? Were material ends all the world needed to build on? Was passion, even in the old, a simple problem of lowering your blood pressure and abandoning salt? Could a man discard his thinking self as lightly as he discarded the doctrine of an ultimate truth? When John said, "A green bench is only a green bench," was he wiser than old David Archbald, who replied, "A green bench is not the green bench I touch"? True, men no longer wrangled in public halls over the nature of reality. But he could not see that exact knowledge and precision of language had improved the quality of mankind. Well, the wonder in every age, he supposed, was not that most men were savage, but that a few men were civilized. Only a few in every age, and these few were the clowns in the parade. . . .

Suddenly, while he meditated, it seemed to him that the shape of the external world, this world of brick and asphalt, of men and women and machines moving, broke apart and dissolved from blown dust into thought. Until this moment he had remembered with the skin of his mind, not with the arteries; but now, when the concrete world disappeared, he plunged downward through a dim vista of time, where scattered scenes from the past flickered and died and flickered again. At eighty-three, the past was always like this. Never the whole of it. Fragments, and then more fragments. No single part, not even an episode, complete as it had happened.

In each hour, when he had lived it, life had seemed important to him; but now he saw that it was composed of things that were all little things in themselves, of mere fractions of time, of activities so insignificant that they had passed away with the moment in which they had quivered and vanished. How could any one, he asked, resting there alone at the end, find a meaning, a pattern? Yet, though his mind rambled now, he had walked in beaten tracks in his maturity. His soul, it is true, had been a rebel; but he had given lip-homage, like other men all over the world, to creeds that were husks. Like other men all

825

over the world, he had sacrificed to gods as fragile as the bloom of light on the tulip tree. And what was time itself but the bloom, the sheath enfolding experience? Within time, and within time alone, there was life—the gleam, the quiver, the heartbeat, the immeasurable joy and anguish of being. . . .

The trail plunged straight and deep into the November forest. There was the tang of woodsmoke far off in a clearing. Frost was spun over the ground. The trees were brilliant with the yellow of hickory, the scarlet of sweet gum, the wine-red of oaks.

Why was he here? How had he come? Was he awake or asleep? Ah, he knew the place now. A forest trail at Stillwater. But they had left Stillwater fifty years ago. Well, no matter. No matter that he was a boy and an old man together, or that the boy wanted to be a poet. It was all the same life. A solitary fragment, but the same fragment of time. Time was stranger than memory. Stranger than his roaming again through this old forest, with his snack and a thin volume of Byron tucked away in his pocket. Here was the place he had stopped to eat his snack, while his pointer puppies, Pat and Tom, started game in the underbrush.

Then, as he stood with his head up and his eyes on the westering sun through the trees, he knew that he was watched. He knew that there were eyes somewhere among the leaves, and that these eyes, the eyes of the hunted, were watching him. It was the look in the eyes of the dying buck, but now it was everywhere. In the trees, in the sky, in the leaf-strewn pool, in the underbrush, in the very rocks by the trail. All these things reflected and magnified to his quivering nerves the look of the hunted. Because of the fear in his nerves, he cried out, expecting no answer. But before his call ended, there was a stir in the woods; the leaves scattered; and through the thick branches, he met the eyes of a runaway slave. Ragged, starved, shuddering, a slave crouched on the forest mould, and stared at the bread and meat in the boy's hand. When the food was given to him, he gulped it down and sat watching. Haggard with terror and pain, a dirty rag wrapping his swollen jaw, his clothes as tattered as the shirt of a scarecrow, he had been driven by hunger and cold up from the swamps. His breath came with a wheezing sound, and his flesh shed the sour smell of a wild animal. (A sour smell and a filthy rag after nearly seventy years!)

For weeks—for months, even, he may have lain hidden; but the deep swamps were far away, and he was the first fugitive slave to come within the boundaries of Stillwater. Beyond speech, beyond prayer, nothing remained in his eyes but bewilderment. "Nobody will hurt you," the boy said, emptying his pockets of the cornbread he had brought for the puppies. "Nobody will hurt you," he repeated, as if the creature were deaf or inarticulate. While he gave the promise, a wave of courage, of daring, of high adventure, rushed over him. For the second time in his young life he was defying the established order, he was in conflict with the moral notions of men. Is it true, he asked himself now, that man's pity and man's morality are for ever in conflict? Is it true that pity is by nature an outlaw? Well, he liked to think that he had not hesitated; no, not for an instant.

Again that day he had returned to the hidden place in the forest. He had brought clothes taken from the old garments in his father's and his grandfather's closets, food that he had found put away in the pantry, and a little wine that had been left over in the glasses at lunch. From his own bed he had stolen a blanket, and from his grandfather's "body servant" he had borrowed, as if in jest, the "ticket" that permitted Abram Jonas to visit his wife in another county. "When it is over, they will have to know," the boy thought, as he trudged back into the forest with the help he had come to fetch. "When it is over."

And then what had happened? His memory faded, died down to ashes, and shot up more brightly. Two mornings later, he had set out in an old buggy, with a decently clothed servant on the seat at his side. Miles away, screened from the turnpike, he had put a knapsack of food and the money he was saving to buy a colt into the hands of the runaway. "Your name is Abram Jonas. This is a paper that says so. You belong to Gideon Archbald, and you are going to visit your wife in Spottsylvania. Do you remember that? What is your name? Say it once more." "Abram Jonas, marster." "You'd better repeat it as you go along. I am Abram Jonas. Here is the paper that says so." "I'se Abram Jonas, marster. Dis heah is de paper." The fugitive looked up at him, first with the fear of the hunted, then with a dawning intelligence. "Thanky, marster," and turning, he had limped away from the turnpike into a forest trail. What had become of him? Had he escaped? Was he caught? Did he drop down like an animal and die of the shuddering misery of life?

After all these years General Archbald was still curious. But no word had come. Only silence. Only silence, and the feeling that he had taken his stand against the forces men about him called civilization. He had defied not only the moral notions of his age and his place, but the law and the Constitution and the highest court in the land. The truth came out at last when the real Abram Jonas asked for the return of his "ticket"; and, as a measure of discipline, David's father sent his youngest son abroad to be educated. He was sixteen then; and years afterwards, when he left Oxford, he had lived in Paris and London. Ironically, he had begun to think of himself as a stranger in his world and his age. Yet when the war came, he was drawn back to his own. He was drawn back to fight for old loyalties. After the war he had endured poverty and self-denial and, worst of all, darned clothes for a number of years. Then, while he was still burdened by defeat, he had compromised Erminia and proposed to her the next morning. Well, the past was woven of contradictions. For eighty-three years he had lived two lives, and between these two different lives, which corresponded only in time, he could trace no connection. What he had wanted, he had never had; what he had wished to do, he had never done. . . .

A fog clouded his mind, and he heard a voice like his own remark testily, "Rambling is a sign of age, but I can't keep hold of the present." He couldn't keep hold of yesterday, of last month, of last year, of the faces he knew best, of the features even of his wife, which had grown vague since her death. Now, at the end, all faces of women, even the faces of women he had slept with, looked alike to him. All faces of women, except, perhaps—he wasn't sure—the face of Eva Birdsong. "No, I can't remember," he repeated, while this suppressed irritation clotted his thoughts. "I'm too old to remember that anything, especially any woman, made a difference in life."

Then, softly, while he was thinking this, the fog in his mind dispersed, and the crowd of women's faces melted to air, and reassembled in a solitary face he had not forgotten. Fifty years—nearer sixty years now—since he had lost her.

827

What was the use, he pondered resentfully, in dragging back that old memory, that old passion? Why couldn't the dead stay dead when one had put them away? Half a century of dust! Yet she came to him, unspoiled by time, out of the drifting haze of the present. Was it because he had loved her alone? Or did she shine there, lost, solitary, unforgotten, merely because she was farther away than the others? Not that it mattered. The cause was unimportant beside the vast significance of that remembrance.

But why, after all, had he loved her? Even when he had fallen in love with her that April in England, he could not point to a single perfection and say, "I love her because she is beautiful, or brilliant, or gifted." There was nothing unusual about her, his friends had remarked wonderingly. Dozens of women he knew in London were handsomer, or wittier, or more conspicuously good. Small, shy, pale, she was utterly lacking in the presence so much admired by English society in the eighteen fifties.

When he first met her, she was married to the wrong man, and was the mother of two delicate children. Had he fallen in love with a veiled emptiness, a shadow without substance? Yet her blue eyes, as soft as hyacinths, had promised joy that was infinite. Or had he loved her because he had seen in her face the old fear and bewilderment of the hunted? Had her memory endured because it was rooted not in desire but in pity? Happier loves, lighter women, he had forgotten. No matter what people say, he thought moodily, it takes more than going to bed with a woman to fix her face in one's mind. For this woman alone he had loved and lost without wholly possessing. Yet she was there when he turned back, clear, soft, vivid, with some secret in her look that thrilled, beckoned, and for ever eluded him. Her eyes were still eloquent with light; the promised joy was still infinite; the merest glimmer of a smile had outlasted the monuments of experience.

Yet like everything else in his life, important or unimportant, his passion seemed, when it occurred, to come at the wrong moment. He had intended to leave London; his ticket to Paris was in his pocket; his bags were packed. Then a tooth had begun to ache—a tooth he had lost only last year—and he had decided to stay over a day or two and consult an English dentist who had once treated him for an abscess. Not an act of God, he told himself (unless a twinge of pain were an act of God), but a toothache had decided his destiny. Had the pain come a day later, just one sunrise and one sunset afterwards, he might have escaped. But falling as it did in that infinitesimal pin point of time, his fate had been imprisoned in a single luminous drop of experience.

Looking back, he had often wondered why there had been no suspicion of danger, no visible or invisible warning that he was approaching the crossroads. Even the voice of his old friend was not ruffled when she met him on his way to the dentist and asked him to dinner. Some one had dropped out at the last moment. Tony Bracken (he had not forgotten that it was Tony Bracken) had been summoned to the deathbed of his great-uncle, and since Tony was the heir, he was obliged, naturally, to go when he was summoned. So, in spite of an occasional twinge, young David had braced himself with whiskey, applied laudanum to his tooth, and set out on an adventure beside which all the other occasions of his life were as flat as balloons that are pricked.

Even then, if she had not stood alone in that particular spot, between a lamp

828

and a window, he might never have noticed her. "I wonder who she is," he thought, observing her loneliness; and then, as she raised her lowered lashes and he met her gaze, "She looks frightened." Was he called or driven when he went straight to her through the crowded room? Was it pity or the compulsion of sex that awakened while he watched her hesitate, bite her lip with a nervous tremor, and try in vain to think of something to say? "What can have frightened her?" he thought, as his hand closed over hers. Her eyes held him, and he asked, "Are you alone?" She shook her head. "No, my husband is with me." Her husband! Well, most women had husbands, especially most women one met at dinner in London. It was too late after that first look to think of a husband. It was too late to think even of children. In the end her marriage had won, as dead sounds inevitably win over living voices; but while he stood there and looked into her upturned face, that sulky, well-set-up sportsman and his two vague children had no part in the moment. Nothing mattered to him but the swift, tumultuous, utterly blissful sense of recognition—of now, here, this is my hour. Not the indefinite perhaps, to-morrow, some day in the future. The world, so colourless an instant before, had become alive to the touch. People and objects, sights, sounds, scents even, were vibrating with light.

And now, after sixty years, he could see that moment as clearly and coldly as if it were embedded in crystal. What is memory, a voice asked on the surface of thought, that it should outlast emotion? For he remembered, but he could feel nothing. Nothing of the old rapture, the wildness, the illusion of love's immortality. He still mused with remorseful sympathy of Erminia, whom he had never loved, whose death had brought him release; but the burning ecstasy of desire had left only emptiness. Only emptiness, and the gradual chill of decay. Why had it happened? What was the meaning of it all? he demanded, caught within the twisting vision of age. Why had passion strong enough to ruin his life forsaken him while he lived? Why had it left only two diminished shapes, performing conventional gestures in a medium that was not time—that was not eternity? Did they still exist, those diminished shapes, in a timeless reality? Were they blown off from time into some transparent substance superior to duration? Did he survive there and here also? Which was the real David Archbald, the lover in memory, or the old man warming his inelastic arteries in the April sunshine? Or were they both merely spirals of cosmic dust, used and discarded in some experimental design? . . .

For an hour, a single hour, of her love he would have given his life when he was young. Her death had left a jagged rent in the universe. Yet if she returned to him now, he knew that it would mean only an effort—only the embarrassment that comes to persons who have loved and separated when they were young, and then meet again, unexpectedly, after they have grown old apart. Strangely enough, if any woman were to return from the dead, he preferred that she should be Erminia. Were the dead like that to the old? Were the intenser desires obliterated by the duller sensations? Joy, longing, disappointment, personalities that impinged upon one another, and then, separating, left only a faint outline of dust. Life was not worth the trouble, he thought. Life was not worth the pang of being, if only that faint outline remained. For the passion of his youth had ended as swiftly as it had begun, and at first he had not even suspected that the

829

vehement craving was love. Helpless, bewildered, he had struggled blindly in the grasp of a power he could not resist and could not understand. All he knew was that her presence brought the world into beauty, that his whole being was a palpitating ache for her when she was absent. Inarticulate, passive, without the compelling ardour of sex, she had exercised that ruthless tyranny over desire. Or was it true, as he had sometimes imagined, that he himself was a rare, or perhaps a solitary, variation from sex? Were his deeper instincts awakened only by pity? As the generations went on, would there be others and still others of his breed born into an aging world? Was he more civilized than the average race of males, or simply more white-livered, as his virile grandfather believed? Well, he was too old, he repeated stubbornly, and life was too long over, to bother about what couldn't be helped. All he asked now was to sit in the April sunshine and wait for death with William beside him.

But was it really long over? What if it were true that some fragment of his lost ecstasy still survived there, burning with its own radiance, beyond that dim vista of time? What if it were true that such bliss, such agony, such unavailing passion, could never end? All that spring and a part of the summer they had met secretly and joyously; and their secret joy had overflowed into the visible world. The landscape in which they moved borrowed the intense, quivering brightness of a place seen beneath the first or the last sunbeams. Spring was as fair as it looks to a man about to be hanged. Never again were the fields so starry with flowers, the green so luminous on the trees, the blue of the April sky so unearthly.

Years afterwards (sometimes as a young man in a strange bed, or again in the long fidelity to a wife he had never desired) a flitting dream of that English spring would flood his heart with an extraordinary delight. For a moment, no longer, since he invariably awoke while the joy flickered and died. Always, except in dreams, the past had escaped him. The anguish alone had stayed by him in the beginning, closer than the flesh to his bones or the nerves to his brain. And even in sleep, his bliss, when it returned, was only the tremor of light before a dawn that never approached.

Would it have been different if she had lived? For she had not lived, and he could never know what his life might have been without that ugly twist in the centre. They had planned to go away together, he devoured by love and longing, she fearful, passive, yielding mutely to that implacable power. In July, they would go to Venice and begin life over in Italy. The tickets were bought; her few boxes were at the station; the compartment was reserved; and then the merest accident had detained them. In the middle of that last night, while she was destroying her letters, one of the children had awakened with a sore throat. The nurse had come for her; she had sat till dawn beside the crib in the nursery; and when morning came she had lost the courage for flight. Fear, the old fear of life, of the unknown, had triumphed over them both.

For an eternity, it seemed to him, he walked the station platform. The guard shut the doors fast; the train drew out slowly. Still he watched with an intolerable ache of desolation while the engine was sliding over the straight track to the gradual curve in the distance. Then, turning away, he wandered, distraught with misery, out into the street. Why? why? why? he demanded of a heaven that seemed as unstable as water. Overhead, low, flying clouds scudded like foam

830

driven by wind. In the country, he walked for hours through rain vague as suspense, soft, fine, slow as mist falling. Afterwards, she wrote that the struggle was over; she could not give up her children—and in the early autumn he heard from a stranger that she had drowned herself in a lake. Lost, vanished, destroyed by the fear for which he had loved her in the beginning!

When he knew that she was dead, he went alone into the country, to the secret places where they had met and loved in the spring. In his memory, these places shone out suddenly, one after another, as scattered lights come out in a landscape at dusk. The woods, the fields, the stream where cowslips bloomed, the grey bench with its blurred marking, the flowers, the bright grass. Now it was spring, but in this flickering scene, he walked there in autumn. Everything returned to him; the falling leaves, the trail of autumn scents in the air, everything but the vital warmth in his agony. Yet he knew, while this light flashed out and moved on again, through the encompassing darkness, that the form, if not the essence, of his passion had lain hidden somewhere beneath the surface of life.

In his anguish, he had flung himself beyond time, beyond space, beyond the boundaries of ultimate pain. A panic stillness was in the air; the whole external world, the blue sky, the half-bared trees, the slow fall of the leaves, the grass sprinkled with bloom,—all this was as hollow as a bubble blown from a pipe. Nothing remained alive, nothing but his despair in a universe that was dead to the touch. Again and again, he had cried her name in this panic stillness. He had cried her name; but she was gone; she could never return. Not though he waited for ever in the place she had left, could she return to him. In the end, she had escaped the terror of life. She had escaped his love and his pity. She had escaped into hollowness. But while the light shone in that vacant place, every twig on the trees, every blade of grass stood out illuminated.

Then this also had passed. Anguish, he discovered, was scarcely less brief than joy. The light went out and moved on again. Days, weeks, months, years passed, and a thick deposit of time hardened into a crust of despair over his wound. "I do not wish to forget," he said, and in forming the thought had already begun to forget and to recover. Yet, though he enjoyed life again, he never lost entirely the feeling that he was crippled in spirit, that there was a twisted root, an ugly scar, at the source of his being. The poet had died in him, and with the poet had died the old living torment of pity. When he sailed home to fight with his people, he found that the hunted buck, the driven slave, the killing of men in battle, left him more annoyed than distressed. Nothing, not even death, not even dying, seemed important; yet it was amazing to discover how much pleasure could come after one had ceased to expect happiness. Little things began to matter supremely. A smile, a kiss, a drink, a chance encounter in love or war. Appetite, he told himself, with gay cynicism, had taken the place of desire; and it was well that it should be so. There was much to be said in favour of living if only one were careful not to probe deeply, not to touch life on the nerve. If only one were careful, too, not to shatter the hardened crust of despair.

Even so, there were moments, there were hours when he was visited by the old sensation of something missing, as if he were part of a circle that was bent and distorted and broken in pieces. Life, as well as himself, seemed to be crippled, to have lost irrevocably a part of the whole. Still, in the solitude of the

831

night, he would awake from his dream of a bliss that hovered near but never approached, and think, with a start of surprise, "If I awoke and found her beside me, would all the broken pieces come together again? Should I find that life was simple and right and natural and whole once more?" Then the dream, the surprise, the pang of expectancy, would fade and mingle and dissolve into emptiness. Like a man hopelessly ill who realizes that his malady is incurable, he would distract his mind with those blessed little things of life that bear thinking about. Well, he was used to it now, he would repeat again and again; he was used to the ache, the blankness, even to the stab of delight which pierced him in sleep. He had accepted the sense of something missing as a man accepts bodily disfigurement. After the first years of his loss, he was prepared, he felt, for all the malicious pranks grief can play on the memory. He was prepared even for those mocking resemblances that beckoned him in the street, for those arrowy glimpses of her in the faces of strange women, for that sudden wonder, poignant as a flame, "What if the past were a delusion! What if she were within reach of my arms!" No, it had been many years, thirty, almost forty years, since life had so mocked him.

He had fought through the war. Strange, how insignificant, how futile, any war appeared to him now! He could never, not even when he took an active part in one, understand the fascination war exercised over the human mind. Then, when it was over, he had let life have its way with him. Though the poet in him was lost, he became in later years a prosperous attorney, and a member in good standing, so long as one did not inquire too closely, of the Episcopal Church. . . .

Sitting there in the pale sunshine, so carefully brushed and dressed by his man Robert, he told himself that, in spite of the ugly twist in the centre, he had had a fair life. Nothing that he wanted, but everything that was good for him. Few men at eighty-three were able to look back upon so firm and rich a past, upon so smooth and variegated a surface. A surface! Yes, that, he realized now, was the flaw in the structure. Except for that one defeated passion in his youth, he had lived entirely upon the shifting surface of facts. He had been a good citizen, a successful lawyer, a faithful husband, an indulgent father; he had been, indeed, everything but himself. Always he had fallen into the right pattern; but the centre of the pattern was missing. Once again, the old heartbreaking question returned. Why and what is human personality? An immortal essence? A light that is never blown out? Or a breath, a murmur, the rhythm of molecular changes, scarcely more than the roving whisper of wind in the tree-tops?

A multitude of women people the earth: fair women, dark women; tall women, short women; kind women, cruel women; warm women, cold women; tender women, sullen women—a multitude of women, and only one among them all had been able to appease the deep unrest in his nature. Only one unit of being, one cluster of living cells, one vital ray from the sun's warmth, only one ripple in the endless cycle of time or eternity, could restore the splintered roots of his life, could bring back to him the sense of fulfilment, completeness, perfection. A single personality out of the immense profusion, the infinite numbers! A reality that eluded analysis! And yet he had been happy as men use the word happiness.

Rarely, since his youth, had he remembered that something was missing, that he had lost irrevocably a part from the whole, lost that sense of fulfilment not only in himself but in what men call Divine goodness. Irrevocably—but suppose, after all, the loss were not irrevocable!

Suddenly, without warning, a wave of joy rose from the unconscious depths. Suppose that somewhere beyond, in some central radiance of being, he should find again that ecstasy he had lost without ever possessing. For one heartbeat, while the wave broke and the dazzling spray flooded his thoughts, he told himself that he was immortal, that here on this green bench in the sun, he had found the confirmation of love, faith, truth, right, Divine goodness. Then, as swiftly as it had broken, the wave of joy spent itself. The glow, the surprise, the startled wonder, faded into the apathetic weariness of the end. He was only an old man warming his withered flesh in the April sunshine. "My life is nearly over," he thought, "but who knows what life is in the end?"

A cloud passed overhead; the changeable blue of the sky darkened and paled; a sudden wind rocked the buds on the tulip tree; and in the street, where life hurried by, a pillar of dust wavered into the air, held together an instant, and then sank down and whirled in broken eddies over the pavement. (*1932*)

JAMES BRANCH CABELL

1879–

James Branch Cabell was born in Richmond, Virginia, on April 14, 1879. He was graduated in 1898 from William and Mary College, where, during his last year as an undergraduate, he served as an instructor in French and Greek. Cabell worked a short time as a journalist, in Richmond and New York, and spent two years in the coal mines of West Virginia before turning seriously to the writing of fiction.

The wit and general tone of disillusionment which inform Cabell's novels proved a source of wide interest, especially during the decade of the 1920's. The vogue his writing enjoyed was also due, in part, to his frank but never vulgar treatment of sex and to a general skepticism regarding its moral sanctity. What Cabell had to say was set down with a kind of consummate artistry; a study of his style would be rewarding to any young student of English prose. His antecedents in style are such classic masters of English as Charles Lamb and Sir Thomas Browne.

833

Cabell's best-known novels are *The Rivet in Grandfather's Neck* (1915), *Jurgen* (1919), and *The Way of Ecben* (1929). He has also written poetry, plays, essays, and criticism; his best nonfictional works include *Beyond Life* (1919), *Straws and Prayer-Books* (1924), and *Let Me Lie* (1947).

from Let Me Lie

Almost Touching the Confederacy

I

Always afterward it was to seem odd, to look back upon the childhood of that myth which you, during your own childhood, were permitted to witness among those of your elders who defined themselves, without any thought of vainglory, or of being contradicted, as belonging to the best families of Virginia. Like Ulysses before King Alcinous in your *Old Greek Stories Simply Told,* or like Aeneas at Carthage in *Stories of Old Rome,* your elders, to every side of you, were engaged in retelling the tragedy in which their own part had not been minor. No more than for young George Washington, in your *Child's History of Virginia,* was it conceivable for anyone of them ever to consider perverting the truth consciously. That they were wholly in earnest as to everything which concerned the sacred Lost Cause for which their lives had been risked, and their fortunes demolished, went equally, as people phrase it, without saying.

So you meant only that, every now and then, you wondered about your elders and the two different ways in which they talked.

The atmosphere of the Richmond of your childhood, to a very marked degree, was elegiac. The Confederacy had fallen, which was bad enough in all conscience; and, which appeared to have been far more horrible, Reconstruction had followed. Herewith one employs the word "horrible" on account of the backwardness of the English language, which, as yet, has not produced any adjective better qualified to express the more lenient aspects of Reconstruction, as your elders viewed Reconstruction. Not until a long while afterward did you have any special notion as to what "Reconstruction" might signify, precisely, because when you first began to remember things you knew only that it had let loose strange monsters, which were called Carpet-baggers; and that these had acted real mean to everybody in Richmond, and over in Petersburg also.

II

When your elders talked about The War they reminded you of those prophets and the several other people in nightgowns who, according to the full-page picture in your *Book of Bible Stories,* had sat down by the rivers of Babylon; nor in later years did you change this opinion, materially. You did not mean that your elders behaved in this way upon the banks of the James River or near the Canal. That was where you went fishing.

834

Instead, it was before the tall writing desks of their grandfathers, or between a dignified pitcher of ice water and a flag of the Confederacy on a gold-painted pole, that your elders sat down very solemnly; and they lamented together, in memoirs and upon memorial days, when they remembered their Zion, that South which had been, and which now was at one with Babylon.

They spoke—not without any ardor, nor did they shun the more sturdy graces of elocution—as to a paradise in which they had lived once upon a time, and in which there had been no imperfection, but only beauty and chivalry and contentment. They spoke of womanhood, and of the brightness of hope's rainbow, and of the tomb, and of right upon the scaffold, and of the scroll of fame, and of stars, and of the verdict of posterity. But above all did they speak of a thin line of heroes who had warred for righteousness' sake in vain, and of four years' intrepid battling, even from the McLean farmlands at Bull Run to the McLeans' parlor at Appomattox.

When your elders spoke as to General Robert E. Lee, it was in the tones which other, less fortune-favored nations reserve for divinity, because a god, or at any rate a demigod, had come forth from the Northern Neck of Virginia to dwell in the Confederate States of America; and they who spoke had beheld with their own eyes his serene glory. There was no flaw in it when, upon tall iron-gray Traveller, he had ridden among them, like King Arthur returned from out of Avalon, attended by the resplendent Launcelots and Tristrams and Gareths and Galahads, who, once upon a time, had been the other Confederate generals.

And about yet another sublime and gracious being, who resembled wise Merlin, your elders spoke also, calling him Jefferson Davis, and telling about his downfall, and about his imprisonment in a place which was more discomfortable than Broceliande. All this had happened to Mr. Davis, so you learned gradually, after a great host of very bad people called Yankees, who reminded you of Mordred's "great host" in the last chapter of the book that Uncle Landon gave to you one Christmas, had seized on the fair kingdom which really and truly belonged to General Robert E. Lee.

And still later, those Carpet-baggers had come, right into Richmond. Only they were not at all like big caterpillars or large bugs, it was explained to you. They were much worse.

III

It was confusing, the way in which your elders talked about things which no great while before you were born had happened in Richmond.—Because you lived in Richmond: and Richmond was not like Camelot. Richmond was a modern city, with sidewalks and plumbing and gas light and horse cars.

You could see for yourself that damsels in green kirtles and fire-breathing dragons and champions in bright armor did not go up and down the streets of Richmond, but only some hacks and surreys, and oxcarts hauling tobacco, or it might be a doctor in his buggy, and sometimes a herd of sheep or of cows (which spilled all over the brick sidewalks and had to be shouted at by men with long sticks), or the boys that were bigger than you were, riding most enviably upon tall bicycles; or perhaps it was just the man with a hand bell and a little grindstone in a sort of thin wheelbarrow who sharpened your mother's carving knives and scissors, or the hokey-pokey man, or some colored people

835

that were selling fine fresh vegetables out of their cart, or the organ-grinder with his monkey dressed in unforgettably dusty red velvet.

Anyhow, there were not in Richmond any such old-time things as falchions and guerdons and varlets. Richmond was a progressive and up-to-date city which had re-arisen triumphantly, like a phoenix from out of its ashes, so everybody said. Richmond was not at all like Camelot or Caerleon upon Usk; and so you found it kind of curious that the way in which your elders talked, upon platforms, reminded you of your *Stories of the Days of King Arthur*, by Charles Henry Hanson, with Illustrations by Gustave Doré.

That was a real nice book, you thought at this season. It was a grayish-blue and rather small book. Upon the cover of it was a brickdust-colored picture of Sir Gawaine, with an edifice of curly plumage on top of his helmet, and ostentatiously undulant for a good distance behind it also, as he rode toward the Green Chapel, which "was the most perilous place in the world"; and "this compilation contains"—so did the chapter that was called "Preface" tell you— "an epitome of the Arthurian Legends," in which (as was declared farther on) "no occasional allusions and episodes which make them unfit to be placed in the hands of juvenile readers . . . have been retained."

You liked this book very much. But you could not understand why almost everything that in public your elders said about The War seemed, somehow, to have come out of this book.

IV

Moreover, you noticed that your elders did not speak in the same way when they were just talking to one another in your father's drugstore, or in your mother's dining-room at Sunday night supper (when everybody ate out of the best plates, which had a different sort of bright colored bird painted upon each one of them), or when your elders were playing whist in the big and high-ceilinged pale-brown back-parlor of your grandfather's house, down upon Governor Street. When, with all eight of the gas jets lighted overhead, in the gleaming copper and crystal-hung chandelier, your elders played whist, pensively and without any excitations, then they used to save time, and avoid argument, by turning up the very last card in the pack so as to find out at once what was going to be trumps. And upon such reflective occasions they would talk differently about The War and the people who had been in it.

They would speak, for instance, of Abraham Lincoln. You recollected afterward that never did you hear them speak, in private, as to Abraham Lincoln with enmity. If your elders had found in his life a great deal which demanded praise, then they must have withstood these demands with success; but his death was regretted—upon grounds that were wholly practical, so you observed later—as having been to the South a misfortune. Had Abraham Lincoln lived, the South would have been dealt with more mercifully and more decently, said your elders. That he was a poor-white and untidy person they said also; he, in short, was tacky: but the man was well-meaning.

Those stories which your elders had heard, and which they repeated urbanely, as to his private life, were rather curious sounding sometimes. You did not understand, for some while to come, what the joke was about in a number of them; and he seemed, too, to have had a lot of fathers.

836

Yet these anecdotes, if spiced with derision, remained unflavored by malice. Your elders did but laugh—"high and disposedly"—to remember that small-town lawyer whom those Yankees had thought fit to be their President. He, in the opinion of your elders, most certainly was.

That Mr. Lincoln had displayed any element of greatness, was a suspicion which did not occur to your elders. Mr. Lincoln was regretted unresonantly, without raising one's polite soft voice, as a shrewd but not unamiable politician, whose death, which was an ill-advised affair in the manner of its occurrence also, had happened to expose a conquered South to the oppression that he, living, would have opposed. Young Booth, in brief, through the most excellent of motives, had made a tragic blunder. That, so nearly as you could word this matter, during the long years which were to come later, seemed to be the opinion of your elders as to what, in their belief, had been Mr. Lincoln's unfortunate and involuntary importance. They almost always called him "Mr. Lincoln," with formal politeness.

And in the cause of vividness, you came by-and-by to regret this opinion. You would have preferred to record that your elders spoke with a more lively emotion about Abraham Lincoln, either as an heroic enemy or as an abhorred enemy. But in point of fact they did not, because at no time were they much interested in their fallen opponent, as a person, either one way or the other.

"Young Booth, through the most excellent of motives, had made a tragic blunder." Such, one can but repeat, was the verdict of well-bred Virginia as to Abraham Lincoln's murder, at a time when you were still in short trousers and long stockings stragglingly divorced by a neutral zone of chapped flesh.—For John Wilkes Booth had been admired as an actor and liked as a person, immediately before the War Between the States, when for some two years he had figured handsomely, in and about Virginia's capital city, as a member of Mr. Kunkel's Stock Company; Virginia did not know Lincoln except by reports, the most of which were ungrandiose; and moreover, not even the most highly gifted of your elders was able quite to anticipate a re-united republic's final verdict as to the unfortunate commemoration of your birthday a good fourteen years ahead of time. You, it is to be feared, thought, while your elders talked, that the most interesting thing about this sort of mixed-up sounding Mr. Lincoln was, after all, his having been shot on your birthday.

Such memories troubled you, by-and-by, after your knowledge as to Abraham Lincoln's now accepted importance had been enlarged; and you became perturbed when you tried to imagine anyone of your once familiar elders, who had known John Wilkes Booth, as being buttonholed by Mr. Carl Sandburg during Mr. Sandburg's gathering of the needed data for his definitive large Life of Lincoln.

"Sir," Mr. Sandburg would inquire of your boyhood's acquaintance, just as Mr. Sandburg has inquired of the present age, "who was this Booth? What was he like? In what kind of a green-poison pool of brain and personality had the amazing and hideous crime arisen?"

"Why, I can but tell you—" the well-bred Virginian would reply.

"—For out of a mediocre fame and a second-rate reputation as a mimic," Mr. Sandburg would continue, "this Booth has wrapped the letters of his name with a weird infamy synonymous with Enemy of Mankind. His name on a

837

thousand occasions is to go unspoken with loathing for the unspeakable and untouchable; a pitiless, dripping, carnivorous, slathered, subhuman and anti-human beast mingling snake and tiger; the unmentionable; the American Judas with a brain that was a haunted house of monsters of vanity, of vampires and bats of hallucination."

—To which the Virginian would answer in winged words such as, after reflection, you preferred not to imagine, because in permitting them to pass the barrier of his teeth, he might laugh (also Homerically) on account of some superficial differences between Middle Western rhetoric in anything which concerns Lincoln and the South's rhetoric as to the Confederacy. Yet it seemed to you that instead of laughing he would say, just as he did of old,—

"Young Booth, suh, through the most excellent of motives, made a tragic blunder."

And the Virginian, the unchangeable Virginian of the 1880's, would thus dismiss the entire matter serenely.

v

—For the main business in life of your elders was to create a myth which was not intimately concerned with the perhaps equally great myth of Lincoln, and which in consequence did not need to clash with it. They were creating (so did you decide later), in the same instant that they lamented the Old South's extinction, an Old South which had died proudly at Appomattox without ever having been smirched by the wear and tear of existence. They perverted no facts consciously; but they did omit, from their public utterances or from their printed idyllic narratives, with the tact of a correctly reared person, any such facts as appeared undesirable—without, of course, ever disclaiming these facts.

A gentleman, in brief, does not tell lies. There is no ruling which denies to him a judicious amount of reticence.

So you noticed, for example, when in private your elders talked about him who had reminded you of wise Merlin, that they did not really like this Mr. Jefferson Davis or admire very many of his doings. They stated their reasons, in terms which you found to be incomprehensible and of no large interest, because you were wondering why Mr. Davis appeared to be an entirely different person when people talked about him upon platforms. And some of the more prominent knights of the Confederate Round Table seemed to have been like that also, when, at supper or during those leisured whist games, your elders spoke about them.

Your elders told then of how one of these heroes had been a trifle too drunk to sit upon his horse at any time during the battle which made him famous, and so had not been able to take part in this special battle. And nobody blamed him, of course, for what was really a rather good joke on the strapping dare-devil: it was just a bit of bad luck which might have happened to almost anyone. Quite otherwise did your elders discourse as to another illustrious person, who, so they said, had hid in a barn when he ought to have been fighting; and who had been forced, quietly, to get out of Virginia, and to go north, where, in addition to being made a judge, he had become a professional Confederate veteran with a prestige so enormous that it still nurtures his descendants. None envied him these glories; nor did anyone wish to remove his bogus lustre from out of that which, upon platforms, your elders called the eternal roster of fame. It was simply that he could not ever come back to Virginia.

Your elders spoke also as to the final words of a more authentic hero, which, it appeared, were not the soldierly utterance that is set down in every Confederate Arthuriad, but a request for the bedpan; as to with how large thrift yet another pre-eminent idol of the Confederacy had behaved in renting out his renown, for advertising purposes, to a pack of gamblers, year after year; as to the manner in which an out-at-elbows paladin had apostatized in order to become an ambassador; and as to the quaint fury with which a half-dozen or more ex-chieftains of the Lost Cause were now publishing a surplus of inconvenient candors in their depreciations of one another.

Nor was this by any means all that which your elders talked about, in their quiet and matter-of-fact and half amused voices, when they spoke as to the divinities, and as to the wives of these divinities, whom in public they worshipped.

To a child, who could not understand that for the health of human ideals every national myth needs to be edited and fostered with an unfailing patience, the discrepancy was puzzling; but you did reason it out, by-and-by. Your elders were not telling any lies, either in private or upon memorial days, about their technically unstained and superhuman heroes, or at least not exactly. It was just that grown people told only a part of the truth when they climbed up on platforms, and did not talk about things which were not nice, such as getting drunk, or like bedpans.

VI

And it seemed to you remarkable, in later years, that you could not recall hearing your elders talk about any of the Union generals, except only a very little bit about a General Sherman, who burned up houses, and perhaps slightly more than that about an oddly named General Beast Butler, who appeared to have stolen some teaspoons. That which your elders said as to "Mr. Lincoln" has been recorded; but they did not talk much about Abraham Lincoln, either. They liked better to talk about their own people. And if constantly they derided Yankees, or if in particular they denounced the wicked doings of Carpet-baggers, yet, as you remembered it afterward, to neither one of these evil races was granted the distinction of surnames. So did they remain to you, at this time, an anonymous and unaccounted-for "great host" such as at Salisbury Plain had destroyed King Arthur.

Your elders, in brief, were not mad with the armies and the leaders of the armies that had invaded and seized upon the fair kingdom which really and truly belonged to General Robert E. Lee. They just kind of made fun of them. They were not even very much interested in those Yankee soldiers who had killed off a lot of your own uncles and cousins. It was only when they talked about Carpet-baggers. Carpet-baggers must have been rather like ogres, or perhaps they were churls and fell caitiffs, you decided.—Because you were getting sort of sleepy. It must be mighty near nine o'clock. Anyhow, whenever grown-up people talked about Carpet-baggers they would get mad as a wet hen.

But that did not last for more than a little while. Pretty soon they would go back to talking, almost as if they were sitting in church instead of right here in

839

your grandfather's back-parlor, about what a real fine place all the South used to be, and Virginia in particular.

VII

They were making history after a time-approved fashion. Even in the same instant that, westward and northward, about the benign figure of Abraham Lincoln, as the messiah of the United States of America, was being assembled an epitome of legends in which no "occasional allusions and episodes which made them unfit to be placed in the hands of juvenile readers . . . have been retained," just so in Virginia was being edited and amended and enhanced, after the same chaste manner of Charles Henry Hanson, our own epic of the Old South. In both instances, loyalty required of each myth's makers that more or less should be left out, and that an appreciable deal should be recolored, for the good of mankind at large. And in both instances, the reshapers and the editors of these national myths, with the naive duplicity of all other devout artists in fiction, even while they observed with some human pride how very far they had bettered veracity, yet, in part, believed their romanticizing to be wholly veracious.

You found it difficult to explain, this bifold mood in which human beings create, as though by instinct, the one sort of history which their descendants can find profitable; and which alone, because of this mood, their descendants do acquire and try to keep faith with. You at least could not ever explain this half-mythopoeic and half-critical frame of mind, not quite intelligibly, not even to yourself.

You knew only that, in Richmond, during your childhood, you had seen this dual mood about its beneficent labors. And you knew also, very much as you had observed in talking about the colonizing of Virginia, that for anyone of us to investigate, in the bleak light of common-sense, these two twin noble myths of the Old South's perfection and of Abraham Lincoln's perfection, or to contemn yet any other legend about our forefathers' perfection, to become not unworthy of which a delusion may spur us, would be to repeat the unthrift of prying Ham and of ill-judging Esau, those deficient inheritors.

—For each one of them, as you recalled from afar your long-perished *Book of Bible Stories*, had lost all which rightfully had belonged to him. That meant something rather important, you decided. It meant that for human beings it might be wiser, even at the price of some inconsistency, to maintain the beliefs that were agreeable and inspiring and magnanimous.

Is of Southern Ladies

I

840   That, without any fear of succeeding, the intrepid native Virginian will dauntlessly attempt to conceal his superiority to everybody else, remains a tribal virtue which has not escaped the comment of anthropologists. He treads among the commonalty of other commonwealths, it has been remarked, with the meticulous and maddening courtesy of M. le Duc upon a casual visit to the peasantry of this or the other of his minor estates. And yet not really for this Virginian version of politeness is any living Virginian who, let us say, can remember when Grover Cleveland occupied the White House at all blameworthy. Rather is this an enforced trait which has been developed in the man's nature by two circumstances such as through no precautions could he have avoided.

The one circumstance is that throughout the first years of his life (during which his character was taking form, irretrievably) he was reared as a godling who could not, not even in the false teeth of parental reproof, be wrong as to anything. The second circumstance is that he knows there has been reserved for him in heaven a very special place.

In short, he once had a mammy.

II

With a forlorn sense of impotence, one pauses here to reflect that, nowadays, in no household anywhere does one find an authentic mammy; so that whosoever speaks as to this vanished subdivision of fauna needs to depend upon a scant number of sexagenarians to divine exactly what he may be talking about.— For the mammy, the true mammy, the mammy *au vieille roche,* is now extinct, along with the passenger pigeon and the bison and the hack driver; but in the Richmond of the 1880's a mammy still ruled over every household in which there were children.

So in no part of Richmond were mammies infrequent; but it was in Monroe Park that you noted them, upon clear afternoons, in full panoply. To every bench there would be two or three mammies; alongside most of the benches sprawled a baby carriage formed of rotund and elaborately betwisted wickerwork, of which the occupant was screened by a vividly blue veil; and whatever it was that mammies talked about, for some two hours, with a serene and oriental indolence, between their slow outbursts of sedate Olympian chuckles, you did not ever hear, because you were playing, in common with a select number of yet other children, under the uncompromising surveillance of all these mammies. Any one of them, at any instant, might direct toward you the attention of Sister Nelson with an acerb shrillness.

And besides that, when you played in Monroe Park, you had to be careful not ever, upon any imaginable pretext, to get your nice clean linen suit messed up; because, otherwise, you became just the most aggravating child that ever was.

III

These ladies wore white caps and large white aprons, befrilled proudly. They ran, rather, to stoutness; and to steel-rimmed spectacles they accorded a perceptible vogue. Each one of them was—legally, at any rate—a Negress. Each one of them some twenty years earlier had been a slave; but now they were tyrants. Not for one quarter-instant would I suggest that their despotism was often, or indeed ever, unkindly. I mean merely that none dared to assail the authority of the mammies of Richmond within the borders of their several kingdoms; and that this was especially true of the parents who paid to each one of them ten dollars a month.

841

I grant that in every household—in order, it is my theory, to cajole into self-complacence the cook and the house girl—the children's mammy was ranked, through a jocose flight of fancy, as being one of the servants.—For that, most precisely, is what a mammy was at no time whatever, except only upon the courteous principle by which a monarch elects, in state papers or in formal proclamations, to describe himself as being the servant of his people.

In brief, the mammy was a Virginian institution which, under the encroachments of democracy, has vanished; she survives only in the heart's core of her fosterlings; and she is not comprehensible any longer except by those who have need to remember her forever. The children of Virginia, so nearly as I can understand their unhappy estate, are looked after nowadays, more or less, by a visitant duchess, more or less Negroid, who stays with them for as long as the job contents her; and who passes on by-and-by to another nursery somewhere else. Her place is then filled, for a month or it may be for two months, by some other nomad; and later, by yet another. Thus Amurath to Amurath succeeds, barbarically. It must be, for these luckless children, rather like living in a world which every once in a while shoots off into space and finds an alien sun about which to revolve. It is, at any rate, a state of affairs which does not bear thinking about, by us who once had a mammy.

IV

And so, while in theory I would like for a fair number of these children to be dealt with competently, by Mrs. Louisa Nelson, yet to the other side, Mrs. Nelson was my mammy; and she was by me regarded with an affection which, during some sixty years of research work, I have not found any other person to merit. Were she alive today, I with an incivic stoicism would observe every brat upon earth in transit toward a state reformatory rather than permit Mrs. Nelson to leave me.—For she was my mammy once, now, and forever afterward; so that I must decline, even in thought, to be severed from her by the dictates of altruism.

—Although, of course, she had not always been Mrs. Nelson. In fact, at the beginning, which was about 1820, she was just Louisa, when she belonged to Miss Patsy Brander. She was Miss Patsy's own colored girl; and every night she used to sleep in old Miss Patsy's room, in a trundle bed which enduring the day you stuck under Miss Patsy's big bed. That was so you could wait on Miss Patsy Brander, in case she wanted something, or if Miss Patsy got took sick in the night. She did, right often. And so Miss Patsy had a little stepladder to get in and out of bed with.

All this was sort of before Mammy had married up with Mr. Cornelius Winston, who belonged to Miss Patsy too; and he was mighty handsome. He was always pleasant spoken. He toted fair with the high and the low. He was a fine good man. Mr. Winston was just the finest man that anybody ever knew. So he and Mammy were real happy together, in those bad old slavery times; and their daughter was named Kizzy. But Miss Patsy Brander up and died; and when her ownings got settled, Mr. Cornelius Winston was sold off to be the head butler for a white gentleman, that fancied him a heap, out West.

That was why Mammy did not ever see Mr. Winston again until after The

842

War. He came back to her then, to find out how she and Kizzy were getting along; and he and Mr. Solomon liked each other very much.

Mr. Solomon Simms was the other gentleman that Mammy was married to by this time. And Mr. Winston had married up too, to a colored lady in Kentucky; so he brought her picture along with him, and a picture of both the children, to let Mammy see what his family looked like. Mr. Winston was always mighty thoughtful. They were nice enough children; they took after Mr. Winston, you could tell that right off. The boy was his very living spit and image. But if you wanted an honest and true to God opinion, that fat, greasy-mouthed colored woman was kind of onery-looking. Anyhow, Mr. Winston and Mr. Simms got along fine; and Mr. Winston stayed with them, out on the farm over in Powhatan County, for about two weeks.

After Mr. Winston went away, he sent back some presents for Kizzy, and along with them came a necklace of real coral beads for little Julia Simms, so as to keep her from having croup. Julia was Mammy's other daughter. You could always count on Mr. Winston to act handsome. And that was the last that Mammy ever heard about him. She most surely would have liked to find out what did become of Mr. Winston, when she had his street address out in Kentucky too, where he was setting up at catering and waiting on white people's parties; but then she and Mr. Winston never could get around to learning just how to read and write, what with all the other things they had to do.

And presently Mr. Simms, that nebulous and, as one somehow felt, that rather shiftless farmer—concerning whom, to the best of your recollection, you at no time heard anything quite definite, except only his delight in being honored with a visit by Mr. Winston, his all-gifted predecessor—Mr. Solomon Simms of Powhatan took sick and died. That was how Mammy came to marry Mr. Jeremiah Nelson, who was just as smart as you make them. He was right dark-complected, though.

Mr. Nelson was a city gentleman. He was born and brought up in Richmond. He had rooms upon St. James Street. He worked for the *Richmond Evening State*. He packed papers.

One imagines, nowadays, this must mean that Mr. Jeremiah Nelson used to tie up, with very shaggy brown twine, and to deposit within the *State's* delivery wagons, those oblong bundles of printed matter which, later, at about five o'clock in the afternoon, when people were watering their front yards, and Mammy was wheeling John's baby carriage back home from Monroe Park, and you and Robert were walking alongside her, were flung out upon the red brick sidewalk, with an unforgettable massive slumping noise, and came pretty close to you sometimes, so that you held on to Mammy's skirts, while the enormous Percheron horse which drew the white-and-blue covered wagon continued its unhurried trotting toward wherever it was going.

One is not certain. One does not even know upon what principle those big bundles of newspapers were flung out upon the pavement, or who took charge of them afterward. One knows only that Mr. Nelson packed papers for the *Richmond Evening State* until the final 1870's, which was when Mr. Jeremiah Nelson died.

And to the very last, let it be observed, Mr. Nelson acted with more force of

843

character than was displayed by Mr. Solomon Simms—who, so far as it can be remembered, did not even die of anything in particular. But Mr. Jeremiah Nelson died of pneumonia, just like that, and almost before you could snap your fingers, along about three days after he caught a bad cold in a snow storm; and it showed how careful you ought to be about not forgetting your rubbers.

That was why Mr. Nelson's widow kind of thought she might try working out, for a sort of change. She retained the rooms upon St. James Street. But she came to my parents when their first child was a month old, and when she was fifty-two, and she remained with us for the rest of her life.

V

It is a trait to be dwelt upon, the fact that after some threescore years of existence, Mrs. Nelson came to us when she was fifty-two, because never during the time that one knew her did her age vary. She was fifty-two. If pressed as to this point, through any ignoble considerations of arithmetic, or if reminded, with an unmannerly precision, as to the unusual number of years throughout which she had stayed fifty-two, she would so far yield as to concede that anyhow she was about fifty-two. Beyond that, there was no budging her, not even in her most lenient moments.

Now, technically, Mrs. Louisa Nelson was a Negress; but it is not conceivable that anybody ever said so in her presence, not even after she had become very deaf. She elected instead to rank as a colored person; and her color, to be precise, was the just not golden yellow of peanut butter. As to her parents it is not remembered that Mrs. Nelson ever spoke, but her features were unmistakably Indian; her eyes had the alert black gleam of undried ink; her nose hooked slightly; her lips were thin. She too was thin; and until she had passed eighty, a ramrod would have seemed, in comparison with Mrs. Nelson, to be liquescent. Upon her flat left breast, except only when she visited Monroe Park, or during yet more stately occasions which called for an appearance in her black silk dress, she wore two or three needles with thread in them; she had wholly beautiful white crinkly hair; and she smelled very pleasantly with an indefinable odor which I can but describe as that of musk flavored with cloth.

She must have had Negro blood, but in her exterior there was not any trace of it. She most certainly had a great deal of Caucasian blood; and one imagines that every drop of it was aristocratic. Mrs. Nelson, in any case, was.

She likewise was that patron saint who performed miracles for your comfort tirelessly; and who served as an efficient mediator between you and powers which (in academic theory) were stronger than Mrs. Nelson, such as unfamiliar policemen and God and large dogs and your parents. Parents were well enough in their place, and you loved both of them; but, relatively, their place was remote; and in it they now and then were engaged, with an irresponsible graveness, by grown-up affairs in which you were not interested.

Mrs. Nelson had no such frivolous avocations. To her children (a heading under which she did not include Julia and Kizzy, or any of Kizzy's descendants, but restricted to your two brothers and you) she devoted twenty-four hours of each day—excluding only her Sunday afternoons and her Thursday evenings out. She went then to her rooms upon St. James Street. She was Head of the Sub-obinate Department of the Tents of Ham and the Daughters of David; and upon

844

St. James Street the members of this organization were accustomed to confer with Sister Nelson as to matters which she could not talk to you about, because they were Lodge secrets.

You did not mind the Sunday afternoons, when company came in or else you went out with your parents somewhere, and were allowed to be company yourself, and to let people see your raising, just as Mrs. Nelson had told you to do. But Thursday evenings were lonesome, after you had gone to bed, and the gas jet out in the hall had been turned down, and when both your brothers were asleep. Robert talked in his sleep a great deal, but that was not any help. As you remembered it afterward, there was always a soft-coal fire in the room upon those long Thursday evenings; and this made the shadow of the mantelpiece, upon the wall above it, jump every which way, like a big black chained-up Something, such as might be a Carpet-bagger, that was trying to get loose with no friendly intentions.

So you did not ever quite fall asleep until after Mrs. Nelson came in at twenty minutes after eleven. She said that you ought to have been asleep long ago. She asked if you children had been good children, and not kept everything in a swivet the first minute her back was turned. She brought you a glass of water, because you said you were sort of thirsty. That was so you could touch her. Then she got into her bed, which was next to your bed; and you went to sleep in less than no time, because everything was all right now that Mammy was back.

VI

So long as Mrs. Nelson stayed near you, all matters tended to straighten themselves out satisfactorily. Even when you were sick-in-bed (for until you were at least ten years old you thought of this condition as being one word) she saw to it that you were not very sick, and had a plenty of boiled custard, and in fact, rather enjoyed yourself. But she remained rigid. She was not touched to the quick, nor did she condole, when you were sick-in-bed. It was her official attitude upon all such occasions that you were just upsetting the house from top to bottom by being sick-in-bed.—For there was not anywhere one minim of tenderness in Mrs. Nelson's nature, nor any reasonableness either, but only an unlimited devotion to her children.

So did it follow that at all times her ideas as to corporal punishment stayed sound and unshakable. To begin with, she did not ever concede that in any circumstances any one of her children had been bad; at utmost, the small accused might have been, it was allowed fair-mindedly, sort of mischeevous, but then, good Lord, what child would not be, when folks started in to upset him like that without attending to their own business? Through this dashing gambit, any parentally discussed punishment, instead of figuring as the result of a misdemeanor, was left unmasked as the true cause of it.

The child had been mischeevous because folks who were more than twice as big, and who did not know how to keep their temper, had started in to spank him, and what child, what child anywhere upon this earth, would not be? That, and that alone, was just simply what the indignant dark lawyer for the defence wanted to ask of Dr. Cabell and Miss Annie; and did ask, freezingly.

Moreover, should the incriminated parent remain deaf to remorse, then

845

promptly the exposed rear of the condemned was shielded by both of Mrs. Nelson's lean and wiry, peanut-butter-colored hands. Nor from this strategic position was she detachable. So the foiled parent, or it might be both parents, withdrew. And Mrs. Nelson, triumphant but still icily offended, began to speak as to the convenience and the accessibility of her rooms upon St. James Street.

VII

Throughout twenty-five years these rooms remained the weapon which made her always, at the last pinch, invincible.—For Mrs. Nelson did not have to stay where folks did not like her ways. She did not intend to go on slaving where people were not satisfied. And so, about once every month, we learned that she was going back home, the very first thing tomorrow morning, to live in her rooms over on St. James Street without being stormed at and fussed with enough to run anybody clean crazy.

I do not think that at any time she had the least intention of doing this. But the knowledge that she, after all, was free to desert us for those rooms upon St. James Street kept every one of her dependents in a proper state of subjection throughout the quarter of a century.—For Mrs. Nelson, of course, like all other authentic mammies, after her children had become too old to require a nurse, retained an anonymous ranking as a general assistant in our household affairs—and, at need, as their autocrat.

In title, to be sure, she remained Mammy. But so far as went her indoor pursuits, she merely swept, and dusted, and sewed, and excelled in darning, and delighted to wait at table in her black silk dress whensoever we had company. She tended the ill; she now and then cooked meals, but only when a creative urge to cook was upon her; and she "laundered"—if that verb be still in current usage—with a perfection which to the present age is unknown. In fine, Mrs. Nelson, after her actual retirement as a mammy, did everything; but always, it must be recorded, upon her own terms.

—Which reminds me to record likewise that Mrs. Nelson, what with all the other things she had to do, still did not ever quite get around to learning just how to read and write. So she remained unfamiliar with novels as to the South of yesterday, and she did not ever hear about any mammies who termed their children "my precious lamb," or "my own baby," or "honey chile," or yet something else of a nature no less affectionate and revolting. I am rather glad of this fact: for in Mrs. Nelson's eyes, these graceless if not actively immoral women would have ceased to figure as colored ladies; and in a brief philippic they would have been dismissed, I am wholly certain, as niggers who were just plumb idiots.

VIII

So then did the fourth part of a century pass by without forcing us to conceive of a life without Mrs. Nelson, or to face the notion of any existence thus maimed and bone-bare. Nor did we, until her death, when she was about eighty-five, had left us no choice; and for my part, it is a notion to which, after forty-and-some years of deliberation, I have not as yet become reconciled.

It should be recorded that upon the last day of her life, she told the attendant physician she was fifty-two; as well as that, upon this same heart-breaking

846

Sunday, when she was not permitted to leave her bed, she assured me that, the very first moment she got over this sort of sinking spell, she meant to go straight spang back to her rooms, over on St. James Street, and not be a bother to us, when once she was out of this bed, praise the Lord.

—Because it was getting right far past the time for her little biddy bed to be pushed back under Miss Patsy's big bed. That was why she was trying to get up, Mrs. Nelson explained. So please be good kind folks and let her get out of bed.

She, who had been indomitable, now spoke half timidly. She did not know any one of us. In her last thoughts we figured as unfamiliar, and it might be cruel, white persons who were interfering with the proper duties of Miss Patsy Brander's own colored girl, under the presidency of Andrew Jackson, now that Mrs. Nelson had put out of mind those twenty-five years of tyrannic devotion which she had given to us, "her children," and of which no mortal that ever lived could hope to be worthy. She had forgotten about Julia, and about Kizzy, and about her three husbands, even Mr. Cornelius Winston. With a child's fitful and half-hushed persistence, she repeated that Miss Patsy Brander wanted to have her room kept right enduring the day time; and it was in this way that Mrs. Nelson left us, in an attempt to wait upon her first mistress, who had been buried for somewhat more than sixty years.

IX

Almost at random I have set down these recollections, as to an illiterate and hard-headed and great-hearted Negress, just as I thought about them, and without any re-arrangement or recoloring, because to my judgment Mrs. Nelson explains several generations of not humble-minded Virginians. Every one of these Virginians once had his mammy; by her he was taught, from infancy onward, to regard himself as an all-superior person; by her he was spoiled, completely and forever; and by her, as he very well foreknows, he by-and-by is going to be put in his right heavenly place, not unseverely, with an injunction, for the good Lord's sake, to behave himself now, and to let people see his raising.

In view of these circumstances, I submit, the aforesaid Virginian should not, in common reason, be required to affect any mock modesty. He is of the elect; he willy-nilly has been made a sophomore seraph; and for him to deny the fact would be a sacrilege.

—For do you but consider the plight of my own generation. It is wholly certain that all those mammies who once foregathered in Monroe Park are now assembled on an eternally clear afternoon somewhere in heaven. It is just such a partly Hebraic and partly Baptist heaven as they expected, because God, if that were necessary, will have rebuilded it especially so as to prevent their being disappointed. But they will not be seated upon thrones unsociably. Instead, there will have been provided an infinity of broad benches, with room upon every one of them for three persons inclining toward stoutness; these benches will be molded of bright gold, I imagine; and they will be decorated suitably with all the gems which St. John mentions.

Nor will any one of these dark angels wear a long white robe such as, to a respectable colored person, could not but indecorously suggest nightgear. They instead will all wear black silk dresses of the very best quality, as well as be-frilled caps and large aprons, and extra-large, loose golden slippers. And every-

847

where about them, but always under their uncompromising surveillance, will be frolicking obediently a throng of deceased Virginian lawyers and bankers and physicians and tobacconists and clergymen and, I daresay, a few convicts.— For the fact has been explained to Jehovah, quite firmly, that while upon earth all these Virginians, at their very worst, were just sort of mischeevous.

So then do the mammies of the 1880's as yet talk lazily together forever and ever, between their slow benignant chuckles, while these blessed spirits await the complete return of their children. And eventually, some one or the other of them will be inquiring—without, I am afraid, any special enthusiasm,—

"Ain't that your Jeemes, Sis' Nelson?"

Everything will be all right then. (*1947*)

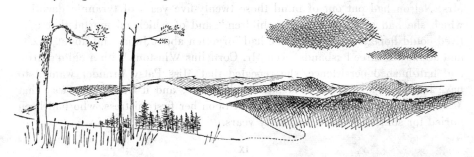

ELIZABETH MADOX ROBERTS

1886–1941

A descendant of Kentucky pioneers, Elizabeth Madox Roberts was born October 30, 1886, in Perrysville, Kentucky, near Springfield. Her childhood was spent in Kentucky and in the mountains of Colorado. Miss Roberts attended the University of Chicago, from which she received a Ph.B. degree in 1921, and then left for New York with the intention of becoming a writer. Her first publication was *Under the Tree* (1922), a group of lyrics about childhood. In 1926 she published her first novel, *The Time of Man,* a study of the poor whites of the Pigeon River country and of their desire for greener pastures. After completing this novel, Miss Roberts spent a number of years in California before returning to her native Kentucky. In 1928 she received the John Reed Memorial Prize from *Poetry Magazine* and two years later was awarded a short-short story prize in the O. Henry memorial volume.

In all essential respects the people whom Elizabeth Madox Roberts portrayed were of the mountaineer stock previously described by James Lane Allen and Mary Noailles Murfree. But her use of local color—and perhaps the term is misleading in her case—is more subtle. Miss Roberts' stories contain fewer archaic words, less action, more introspection, and more complete characterization. Her themes are more philosophic and less obvious than those of the older school, and she exhibits a lyricism and mysticism, especially evident in her novel, *He Sent Forth a Raven* (1935). In an article on Miss Roberts published in the *Sewanee Review* (October 1937), F. Lamar Janney asserts that she has tran-

848

scended the local colorists by adding a quality of universality. "The Pigeon River country," he writes, "with its poor, illiterate children of the earth who happen to live there, is the scene for a universal drama. The characters are not viewed primarily as members of a certain race or class or as natives of a specific locality, but as figures in a universal pageant where race, color, nationality and region are of secondary importance. Though they happen to be poor whites of central Kentucky 'with all the circumstances of their time and place about them,' they mirror human truth, human values, valid for all time."

Miss Roberts' publications include two volumes of short stories, *The Haunted Mirror* (1932) and *Not by Strange Gods* (1941); three volumes of poetry, the last of which was *Song in the Meadow* (1940); and seven novels: *The Time of Man* (1926), *My Heart and My Flesh* (1927), *Jingling in the Wind* (1928), *The Great Meadow* (1930), *A Buried Treasure* (1931), *He Sent Forth a Raven* (1935), and *Black Is My Truelove's Hair* (1938).

On the Mountainside

There was a play-party at the schoolhouse at the bottom of the cove. Newt Reddix waited outside the house, listening to the noises as Lester Hunter, the teacher, had listened to them—a new way for Newt. Sound at the bottom of a cove was different from sound at the top, he noticed, for at the top voices spread into a wide thinness. Before Lester came, Newt had let his ears have their own way of listening. Sounds had then been for but one purpose—to tell him what was happening or what was being said. Now the what of happenings and sayings was wrapped about with some unrelated feeling or prettiness, or it stood back beyond some heightened qualities.

"Listen!" Lester had said to him one evening, standing outside a house where a party was going forward. "Listen!" And there were footsteps and outcries of men and women, happy cries, shrill notes of surprise and pretended anger, footsteps on rough wood, unequal intervals, a flare of fiddle playing and a tramp of dancing feet. Down in the cove the sounds from a party were different from those that came from a house on the side of a hill, the cries of men bent and disturbed, distorted by the place, by the sink and rise of land. While he listened, the knowledge that Lester Hunter would soon go out of the country, the school term being over, brought a loneliness to his thought.

He went inside the schoolhouse and flung his hat on the floor beside the door; he would take his part now in the playing. His hat was pinned up in front with a thorn and was as pert a hat as any of those beside the door, and no one would give it dishonor. The schoolteacher was stepping about in the dance, turning Corie Yancey, and the fiddle was scraping the top of a tune. For him the entire party was filled with the teacher's impending departure.

"Ladies change and gents the same," the fiddler called, his voice unblended with the tune he played. Newt fell into place when an older man withdrew in his favor and gave him Ollie Mack for his partner. The teacher danced easily, bent

849

to the curve of the music, neglectful and willing, giving the music the flowing lightness of his limp body.

Newt wanted to dance as the teacher did, but he denied himself and kept the old harsh gesture, pounding the floor more roughly now and then with a deeply accented step. He wanted to tread the music lightly, meeting it halfway, but he would not openly imitate anybody. While he danced he was always, moment by moment, aware of the teacher, aware of him standing to wait his turn, pulling his collar straight, pushing his hands into the pockets of his coat, looking at Ollie Mack when she laughed, looking full into her face with pleasure, unafraid. The teacher had given an air to the dance, and had made it, for him, more bold in form, more like itself or more true to its kind, more gentle in courtesy. Lester had come from one of the low counties of the rolling plain where the curving creeks of the Pigeon River spread slowly, winding broadly to gather up many little rills. Newt had learned somewhere, in his own blood, to hate the lower country for its pleasantness. There the fields rolled out smoothly and the soil was deep. The grass of any roadside was bluegrass mingled, perhaps, with rich weeds. Fat cattle, fine beasts, ate in the mythical pastures. Smooth roads ran between the farms. Dancing, shaking his body stiffly with the beat of the fiddle, Newt saw that Lester took his partner's hand lightly, that he gave equal courtesy to all the women, calling them ladies. He wanted to be as the teacher was, but he could not. The dance drawing to an end, he realized again that in two days more the teacher would go, for he had set his head upon some place far away, down in the settlements, among the lower counties from which he had come six months earlier.

There was pie for a treat, baked by Marthy Anne Sands and brought to the schoolhouse in a great hickory basket. Standing about eating the pie, all were quiet, regretting the teacher's going. Newt wove a vagrant path in and out among them, hearing the talk of the older men and women.

"My little tad, the least one, Becky, is plumb bereft over 'im," one said, a woman speaking.

"Last year at the school there wasn't hardly anybody would go, and look at this. I had to whop Joel to make him stay on the place one day to feed and water the property whilst I had to go. Hit appears like Joel loves book-sense since Les Hunter come up the mountain."

"What makes you in such a swivet to go nohow?" one asked.

"Did you come up the gorge to borrow fire you're in such a swivet to get on?"

"There's a big meeten over to Kitty's branch next light moon. Why don't you stay? No harm in you to be broguen about a small spell."

"You could loafer around a spell and wait for the meeten."

"Big meeten. And nohow the meeten needs youens to help sing."

"What's he in such a swivet to go off for?"

"I got to go. I got to see the other end of the world yet."

"What's he a-sayen?"

"I got to go to the other end of the world."

"That's too far a piece."

"That surely undoubtedly is a right smart piece to go."

"He could stay a spell at my place and welcome. I'd be real proud to have him stay with my folks a spell. And Nate, he'd keep youens a week, that I right well know. Youens could loafer around awhile as well as not."

"He always earns his way and more, ever since he kem up the mountain, always earns his keep, anyhow."

"I've got to go. I'm bound for the other end of this old globe. I'm obliged all the same, but I got a heap to see yet. I'm bound to go."

Newt plowed the corn in the rocky field above the house where he lived, one horse to the plow, or he hoed where the field lay steepest. The teacher was gone now. On Sunday Newt would put on his clean shirt his mother had washed on Friday, and climb up the gorge to the head of the rise and meet there Tige English and Jonathan Evans. Then they would go to see Lum Baker's girls. He would contrive to kiss each girl before the night fell and Lum would cry out: "Come on, you gals now, and milk the cow brutes." Or sometimes they would go down the way to see Corie Yancey and Ollie Mack. To Newt all the place seemed still since the teacher had left, idle, as if it had lost its uses and its future. Going to the well for water he would stare at the winch, at the soft rot of the bucket, at the stones inside the well curb, or he would listen intently to the sounds as the vessel struck the water or beat against the stones.

The noises gave him more than the mere report of a bucket falling into a well to get water; they gave him some comprehension of all things that were yet unknown. The sounds, rich with tonality, as the bucket struck the water, rang with some strange sonority and throbbed with a beat that was like something he could not define, some other, unlike fiddle playing but related to it in its unlikeness. A report had come to him from an outside world and a suspicion of more than he could know in his present state haunted him. He cried out inwardly for the answer, or he looked about him and listened, remembering all that he could of what Lester Hunter had taught—capitals of countries, seaports, buying and selling, nouns, verbs, numbers multiplied together to make other numbers. Now he looked intently and listened. He detected a throb in sound, but again there was a beat in the hot sun over a moist field. One day he thought that he had divined a throb in numbers as he counted, a beat in the recurrences of kinds, but this evaded him. He listened and looked at the well happenings, at the house wall, at the rail fence, at the barn, at the hills going upward toward the top of the gorge.

On every side were evasions. These sights and sounds could not give him enough; they lay flat against the air; they were imbedded within his own flesh and were sunk into his own sense of them. He would stare at the green and brown moss on the broken frame of the well box and stare again at the floating images in the dark of the well water. The rope would twine over the axle as he turned the wooden handle, and the rounds of the rope would fall into orderly place, side by side, as he knew too casually and too well. Since the teacher had gone the place had flattened to an intolerable staleness that gave out meager tokens of withheld qualities and beings—his mother leaning from the door to call him to dinner, his sister dragging his chair to the table and setting his cup beside his place, the old dog running out to bark at some varmint above in the brush. He could hardly separate the fall of his own bare foot from the rock door-step over which he had walked since he could first walk at all. His thirst

851

and his water to drink were one now. His loneliness, as he sat to rest at noon beside the fence, merged and was identified with the still country from brush-grown slope to brush-grown slope.

His father began to clear a new patch below the house; they grubbed at the roots all day when the corn was laid by. One morning in September, when the sun, moving south, was just getting free of Rattlesnake Hill, it came to him that he would go down to the settlements, that he would go to Merryman. All summer he had known that there was a school at Merryman, but he had not thought to go there, for he had no money. It came to him as a settled fact that he would go there and look about at the place. Three high ridges with numberless breaks and gorges intervened; he had heard this said by men who knew or had heard of what lay beyond. The determination to set forth and the wish to go came to him at one instant. "My aim, hit's to go there," he said. "I lay off to do that-there, like I say."

He remembered the teacher more clearly at this moment, saw him in a more sharply detailed picture; his own breath jerked deeply inward as he was himself related, through his intended departure, to the picture. Hunter was remembered cutting wood for the schoolhouse fire, sweethearting the girls and turning them lightly in the dance, or sitting by the fire at night, reading his book, holding the page low to the blaze. He was remembered hallooing back up the mountain the day he left, his voice calling back as he went down the ridge and he himself answering until there was not even a faint hollow whoopee to come up the slope. By the fire Newt had often taken Hunter's book into his hands, but he could never read the strange words nor in any way know what they meant when they were read, for they had stood four-square and hostile against his understanding. His father's voice would fall dully over the slow clearing: "You could work on this-here enduren the while that I cut the corn patch."

He knew that he would go. His determination rejected the clearing, knowing that he would be gone before the corn was ready to cut. It rejected the monotonous passing of the days, the clutter of feet on the stones by the door, the dull, inconspicuous corn patch above. He would walk, taking the short cut over the mountains. Two ridges to go and then there would be a road for his feet, some one had said. He announced his plan to his father one day while they leaned over their grub hoes. There was no willingness offered, but his mind was set, and three days later he had established his plan. His mother had washed his shirts clean and had rolled them into a bundle with his spare socks, and she had baked him bread and a joint of ham. She and his sister stood by the doorway weeping after he had driven back the dog and had shouted his goodbye.

It was a mid-afternoon and the sun beat down into the cove where he traveled. He worked his way through the thick-set laurel, struggling to keep his bundle tied to his shoulders where the brush stood most dense.

The dry clatter of the higher boughs came to his ears, but it was so mingled with the pricking snarls of the twigs on his face that the one sense was not divided from the other. "This durned ivy," he said when the laurel held him back. He matched his strength against boughs or he flashed his wits against snarls and rebounds, hot and weary, tingling with sweat and with the pricking twigs. Pushed back at one place where he tried to find an opening, he assailed

852

another and then another, throwing all his strength angrily against the brush and tearing himself through the mesh with *god-damns* of relief. A large shaded stone that bulged angrily out of the mountainside gave him a space of rest. He stretched himself on the slanting rock, his face away from the sun, and lay for an hour, thinking nothing, feeling the weariness as it beat heavily upon his limbs.

"I'm bodaciously tired," he said, after a long period of torpor. "Could I come by a spring branch, I'd drink me a whole durned quart of it."

Another tree-grown mountain arose across the cove, misty now in the afternoon and in the first haze of autumn, and beyond lay other blue mountains, sinking farther and farther into the air. Back of him it was the same; he had been on the way two weeks now. Before him he knew each one would be dense with laurel until he came to the wagon road. He took to the pathless way after his hour of rest, going forward. When the sun was setting behind Bee Gum Mountain, he saw a house down in the cove, not far as the crow would fly but the distance of two hours' going for him. When he saw the cabin he began to sing, chanting:

> Right hands across and howdy-do,
> Left and back and how are you.
>
> Oh, call up yo' dog, oh, call up yo' dog,
> Ring twang a-whoddle lanky day.

The sight of the house quickened his desire for Merryman and the cities and counties in the settlements, and this desire had become more definite in his act of going. His wish was for sure, quick gestures and easy sayings that would come from the mouth as easily as breath. There were for him other things, as yet unrelated to any one place—men playing ball with a great crowd to watch, all the crowd breaking into a laugh at one time; men racing fine horses on a hard, smooth track; music playing; men having things done by machinery; lovely girls not yet imagined; and things to know beyond anything he could recall, and not one of them too fine or too good for him. He sang as he went down the slope, his song leaping out of him. He had heard it said that the lights of Merryman could be seen from Coster Ridge on a clear night, and Coster was now visible standing up in the pale air, for a man had pointed him the way that morning. Singing, he set himself toward the house at the bottom of the cove.

Night was falling when he called "Hello" at the foot of Bee Gum Mountain. The man of the house asked his name and told his own, making him welcome. Supper was over, but the host, whose name was Tom Bland, ordered Nance, his woman, to give the stranger a snack of biscuit bread and bacon, and this Newt ate sitting beside the fire. Another stranger was sitting in the cabin, an old man who kept very still while Nance worked with the utensils, his dim eyes looking into the fire or eyeing Newt, who stared back and searched the looks of the stranger. Then Tom told Nance how they would sleep that night, telling her to give the old man her place in the bed beside himself.

"You could get in bed along with the young ones," he said to her. "The boy here, he could sleep on a shakedown alongside the fireplace."

From gazing into the fire the old stranger would fall asleep, but after a moment he would awake, opening dim, ashamed eyes that glanced feebly at

853

Newt, faintly defying him. Then Nance put some children to bed, her own perhaps, and sat quietly in the corner of the hearth, her hands in her lap. Newt had looked at the host, acquainting himself with him. He was a strong man, far past youth, large-boned and broad-muscled. His heavy feet scraped on the floor when he moved from his chair to the water bucket on the window sill. Newt saw that he on his side had been silently searching out the old stranger. After a while the host and the old man began to talk, Tom speaking first.

"There's a sight of travel now."

"Hit's a moven age."

Between each speech there was a slow pause as each saying was carefully probed before the reply was offered.

Tom said: "Two in one night, and last week there was one come by." And then after a while he asked: "Where might youens be bound for, stranger?"

"I'm on my way back," the man said.

There was a long season of quiet. The ideas were richly interspersed with action, for Nance softly jolted back and forth in her chair, her bare feet tapping lightly on the boards of the floor.

"You been far?" Tom asked.

"I been a right far piece. I been to the settlements in Froman county, and then I been to the mines around Tateville and Beemen."

Newt bit nervously at his knuckles and looked at the man, taking from him these signs of the world. The fire burned low, and breaking the long silence Tom said once or twice: "There's a sight of travel now." Newt looked at the old man's feet in their patched shoes, feet that had walked the streets in towns. Indefinite wonders touched the man's feet, his crumpled knees, and his crooked hands that were spread on his lap.

Then Tom said: "Froman, I reckon that's a prime good place to be now."

"Hit may be so, but I wouldn't be-nasty my feet with the dust of hit no longer. Nor any other place down there. I'm on my way back."

The old man's voice quavered over his words toward the close of this speech, and after a little while he added, his voice lifted: "Hit's a far piece back, but a man has a rather about where he'd like to be." Finally he spoke in great anger, his arm raised and his hand threatening: "I've swat my last drop of sweat in that-there country and eat my last meal's victuals. A man has a rather as to the place he likes to be."

This thought lay heavily over the fireplace, shared by all but uncomprehended by Nance, whose skin was rich with blood and life. She sat complacently rocking back and forth in her small chair.

After the long quiet which surrounded this thought the old man began to speak softly, having spent his passion: "I'm on my way back. I been in a study a long time about goen back but seems like I couldn't make hit to go. Work was terrible pressen. But now I'm on my way back where I was borned and my mammy and pappy before me. I was a plumb traitor to my God when I left the mountains and come to the settlements. Many is the day I'd study about that-there and many is the night I lay awake to study about the way back over Coster Ridge, on past Bear Mountain, past Hog Run, past Little Pine Tree, up and on past Louse Run, up, then on over Long Ridge and up into Laurel, into Grady Creek and on up the branch, past the Flat Rock, past the saw-mill, past

854

the grove of he-balsams, and then the smoke a-comen outen the chimney and the door open and old Nomie's pup a-comen down the road to meet me. I'd climb the whole way whilst I was a-layen there, in my own mind I would, and I'd see the ivy as plain as you'd see your hand afore your face, and the coves and the he-balsams. In my own mind I'd go back, a step at a time, Coster, Bear Mountain and the Bee Gum, Little Pine Tree, Louse Run, Grady, and I'd see the rocks in the way to go, and a log stretched out in my way maybe. I wouldn't make hit too easy to go. Past Bear Mountain, past Hog Run and the cove, scratchen my way through ivy brush. Then I'd come to myself and there I'd be, a month's travel from as much as a sight of the Flat Rock, and I'd groan and shake and turn over again. I was a traitor to my God."

Nance laid a little stick on the fire, with a glance at Tom, he allowing it without protest. Then she sat back in her stiff chair with a quick movement, her bare feet light on the boards. The old man was talking again.

"Where my mammy was borned before me and her mammy and daddy before again. And no water in all Froman or Tateville but dead pump waters, no freestone like you'd want. How could a man expect to live? Many's the night I've said, could I be on the shady side of the Flat Rock, up past the saw-mill, up past the grove of he-balsams, where the spring branch runs out over the horse-shoe rock, and could I get me one drink of that-there cold crystal water I'd ask ne'er thing more of God Almighty in life."

"I know that-there very spring branch," Newt now said. He was eager to enter the drama of the world, and his time now had come. "I know that-there very place. You come to a rock set on end and a hemlock bush set off to the right, she-balsams all off to the left like."

"Mankind, that's just how hit's set. I believe you been right there!"

"A mountain goes straight up afore you as you stand, say this-here is the spring, and the water comes out and runs off over a horse-shoe rock."

"Mankind, that's just how hit's set. I do believe you know that-there very place. You say hit's there just the same?"

"I got me a drink at that-there very spring branch Tuesday 'twas a week ago."

"You drank them waters!" And then he said after a period of wonder: "To think you been to that very spring branch! You been there!"

"We can burn another stick," Tom said, as if in honor of the strange event, and Nance mended the fire again. Outside Newt heard dogs howling far up the slope and some small beast cried.

"To think you been there! You are a-setten right now in hearen of my voice and yet a Tuesday 'twas a week ago you was in the spot I call home. Hit's hard to study over. You come down the mountain fast. That country is powerful hard goen."

"Yes, I come right fast."

"I couldn't make hit back in twice the time and more. Hard goen it was. What made you travel so hard, young man?"

"I'm a-maken hit toward the settlements."

"And what you think to find in the settlements, God knows! What you think to see, young man?"

"Learnen. I look to find learnen in the settlements."

855

In the pause that followed the old man gazed at the hearth as if he were looking into time, into all qualities, and he fell momentarily asleep under the impact of his gaze. But presently he looked at Newt and said: "And to think you tasted them waters Tuesday 'twas a week ago!"

"You come to a rock set on end, and here's the hemlock off to the right like, and here to the left goes the gorge."

The old man was asleep, his eyes falling away before the fire. But he waked suddenly and said with kindling eyes, his hand uplifted: "You come from there at a master pace, young man, come from the place I hope to see if God Almighty sees fitten to bless me afore I lay me down and die. You walked, I reckon, right over the spot I pined to see a many is the year, God knows, and it was nothing to you, but take care. The places you knowed when you was a little shirt-tail boy won't go outen your head or outen your recollections."

Then he said, another outbreak after a long pause, his hand again uplifted: "I reckon you relish learnen, young man, and take a delight in hit, and set a heap of store by the settlements. But the places you knowed when you was a little tad, they won't go outen your remembrance. Your insides is made that way, and made outen what you did when you was a shirt-tail boy, and you'll find it's so. Your dreams of a night and all you pine to see will go back. You won't get shed so easy of hit. You won't get shed."

Newt looked into the fire and a terror grew into his thought. He saw minutely the moss on the well curb and the shapes in which it grew, and saw the three stones that lay beside the well, that lifted his feet out of the mud. The sound made by the bucket in the well as it rocked from wall to wall, as it finally struck the water, rolled acutely backward into his inner hearing. He saw the rope twine over the beam as he turned the wooden handle, drawing the full bucket to the top. Three long steps then to the door of the house, the feel of the filled bucket drawing at his arm. Up the loft ladder to his room, his hands drawing up his body, the simple act of climbing, of emerging from some lower place to a higher, and he was buried in the act, submerged in a deep sense of it.

"You may go far and see a heap in life," the old stranger said, slowly, defiantly prophetic, "you may go far, but mark me as I say it, the places you knowed when you was a little tad will be the strongest in your remembrance. It's true, whoever you are and whatever land you come from. Your whole insides is made outen what you done first."

Newt saw in terror what he saw as he gazed into the sinking embers. His mother calling him from the house door, calling him to come to his dinner, her hand uplifted to the door frame. His sister, a little girl, dragging his chair in place and pushing his cup up against the plate. His tears for them dimmed the fire to a vague, red, quivering glow. The floating images in the dark of the well water, the bright light of the sky in the middle as a picture in a frame, and his own head looking into the heart of the picture—these were between him and the fire, moving more inwardly and dragging himself with them as they went. He was bereft, divided, emptied of his every wish, and he gazed at the fire, scarcely seeing it.

There was moving in the room, figures making a dim passage of shadows behind him. Presently he knew that the old man had gone to his sleeping place and that Nance was spreading quilts on the floor to the side of the fireplace. Her

856

strong body was pleasant to sense as she flung out the covers and pulled them into line, and a delight in the strange room, the strange bed, welled over him. His breath was then set to a fluted rhythm as he drew suddenly inward a rich flood of air, a rhythm flowing deeply until it touched the core of his desire for the settlements, laid an amorous pulse on his determination to go there. Learning was the word he cherished and kept identified with his quickened breath. He remembered that the lights of Merryman and the settlements would be brightly dusted over the low valley when he reached Coster.

By the end of the week he would, his eager breath told him, be looking down on to the farther valleys. (*1932*)

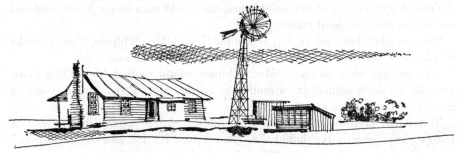

KATHERINE ANNE PORTER

1894–

Katherine Anne Porter is a native of Indian Creek, Texas, where she was born May 15, 1894. She was brought up in Texas and Louisiana, receiving her education in private schools. From 1920 until 1937 she spent much of her time traveling, living intermittently in Mexico, in various parts of the United States, and in Europe. In 1931 she received a Guggenheim Fellowship and in 1944 was made a consultant in Regional Literature at the Library of Congress.

Writing has been the one major interest in Miss Porter's life. She started writing as a young child, but made no effort to publish any of her work until she was thirty. A meticulous craftsman, she has taken great pains to perfect her style. She has established herself as a restrained and sensitive author, and certain of her short stories are generally recognized as being the most subtle that the present generation of writers has produced. The best-known collections of Miss Porter's fiction are *The Flowering Judas and Other Stories* (1930), *Pale Horse, Pale Rider* (1939), and *The Leaning Tower* (1944).

He

Life was very hard for the Whipples. It was hard to feed all the hungry mouths, it was hard to keep the children in flannels during the winter, short as it

857

was: "God knows what would become of us if we lived north," they would say: keeping them decently clean was hard. "It looks like our luck won't never let up on us," said Mr. Whipple, but Mrs. Whipple was all for taking what was sent and calling it good, anyhow when the neighbours were in earshot. "Don't ever let a soul hear us complain," she kept saying to her husband. She couldn't stand to be pitied. "No, not if it comes to it that we have to live in a wagon and pick cotton around the country," she said, "nobody's going to get a chance to look down on us."

Mrs. Whipple loved her second son, the simple-minded one, better than she loved the other two children put together. She was forever saying so, and when she talked with certain of her neighbours, she would even throw in her husband and her mother for good measure.

"You needn't keep on saying it around," said Mr. Whipple, "you'll make people think nobody else has any feelings about Him but you."

"It's natural for a mother," Mrs. Whipple would remind him. "You know yourself it's more natural for a mother to be that way. People don't expect so much of fathers, some way."

This didn't keep the neighbours from talking plainly among themselves. "A Lord's pure mercy if He should die," they said. "It's the sins of the fathers," they agreed among themselves. "There's bad blood and bad doings somewhere, you can bet on that." This behind the Whipples' backs. To their faces everybody said, "He's not so bad off, He'll be all right yet. Look how He grows!"

Mrs. Whipple hated to talk about it, she tried to keep her mind off it, but every time anybody set foot in the house, the subject always came up, and she had to talk about Him first, before she could get on to anything else. It seemed to ease her mind. "I wouldn't have anything happen to Him for all the world, but it just looks like I can't keep Him out of mischief. He's so strong and active, He's always into everything, He was like that since He could walk. It's actually funny sometimes, the way He can do anything, it's laughable to see Him up to His tricks. Emly has more accidents, I'm forever tying up her bruises, and Adna can't fall a foot without cracking a bone. But He can do anything and not get a scratch. The preacher said such a nice thing once when he was here. He said, and I'll remember it to my dying day, 'The innocent walk with God—that's why He don't get hurt.'" Whenever Mrs. Whipple repeated these words, she always felt a warm pool spread in her breast, and the tears would fill her eyes, and then she could talk about something else.

He did grow and He never got hurt. A plank blew off the chicken house and struck Him on the head and He never seemed to know it. He had learned a few words, and after this He forgot them. He didn't whine for food as the other children did, but waited until it was given Him; He ate squatting in the corner, smacking and mumbling. Rolls of fat covered Him like an overcoat, and He could carry twice as much wood and water as Adna. Emly had a cold in the head most of the time—"she takes that after me," said Mrs. Whipple—so in bad weather they gave her the extra blanket off His cot. He never seemed to mind the cold.

Just the same, Mrs. Whipple's life was a torment for fear something might happen to Him. He climbed the peach trees much better than Adna and went skittering along the branches like a monkey, just a regular monkey. "Oh, Mrs.

Whipple, you hadn't ought to let Him do that. He'll lose His balance sometime. He can't rightly know what He's doing."

Mrs. Whipple almost screamed out at the neighbour. "He *does* know what He's doing! He's as able as any other child! Come down out of there, you!" When He finally reached the ground she could hardly keep her hands off Him for acting like that before people, a grin all over His face and her worried sick about Him all the time.

"It's the neighbours," said Mrs. Whipple to her husband. "Oh, I do mortally wish they would keep out of our business. I can't afford to let Him do anything for fear they'll come nosing around about it. Look at the bees, now. Adna can't handle them, they sting him up so; I haven't got time to do everything, and now I don't dare let Him. But if He gets a sting He don't really mind."

"It's just because He ain't got sense enough to be scared of anything," said Mr. Whipple.

"You ought to be ashamed of yourself," said Mrs. Whipple, "talking that way about your own child. Who's to take up for Him if we don't, I'd like to know? He sees a lot that goes on, He listens to things all the time. And anything I tell Him to do He does it. Don't never let anybody hear you say such things. They'd think you favoured the other children over Him."

"Well, now I don't, and you know it, and what's the use of getting all worked up about it? You always think the worst of everything. Just let Him alone, He'll get along somehow. He gets plenty to eat and wear, don't He?" Mr. Whipple suddenly felt tired out. "Anyhow, it can't be helped now."

Mrs. Whipple felt tired too, she complained in a tired voice. "What's done can't never be undone, I know that good as anybody; but He's my child, and I'm not going to have people say anything. I get sick of people coming around saying things all the time."

In the early fall Mrs. Whipple got a letter from her brother saying he and his wife and two children were coming over for a little visit next Sunday week. "Put the big pot in the little one," he wrote at the end. Mrs. Whipple read this part out loud twice, she was so pleased. Her brother was a great one for saying funny things. "We'll just show him that's no joke," she said, "we'll just butcher one of the sucking pigs."

"It's a waste and I don't hold with waste the way we are now," said Mr. Whipple. "That pig'll be worth money by Christmas."

"It's a shame and a pity we can't have a decent meal's vittles once in a while when my own family comes to see us," said Mrs. Whipple. "I'd hate for his wife to go back and say there wasn't a thing in the house to eat. My God, it's better than buying up a great chance of meat in town. There's where you'd spend the money!"

"All right, do it yourself then," said Mr. Whipple. "Christamighty, no wonder we can't get ahead!"

The question was how to get the little pig away from his ma, a great fighter, worse than a Jersey cow. Adna wouldn't try it: "That sow'd rip my insides out all over the pen." "All right, old fraidy," said Mrs. Whipple, "*He's* not scared. Watch *Him* do it." And she laughed as though it was all a good joke and gave Him a little push towards the pen. He sneaked up and snatched the pig right

859

away from the teat and galloped back and was over the fence with the sow raging at His heels. The little black squirming thing was screeching like a baby in a tantrum, stiffening its back and stretching its mouth to the ears. Mrs. Whipple took the pig with her face stiff and sliced its throat with one stroke. When He saw the blood He gave a great jolting breath and ran away. "But He'll forget and eat plenty, just the same," thought Mrs. Whipple. Whenever she was thinking, her lips moved making words. "He'd eat it all if I didn't stop Him. He'd eat up every mouthful from the other two if I'd let Him."

She felt badly about it. He was ten years old now and a third again as large as Adna, who was going on fourteen. "It's a shame, a shame," she kept saying under her breath, "and Adna with so much brains!"

She kept on feeling badly about all sorts of things. In the first place it was the man's work to butcher; the sight of the pig scraped pink and naked made her sick. He was too fat and soft and pitiful-looking. It was simply a shame the way things had to happen. By the time she had finished it up, she almost wished her brother would stay at home.

Early Sunday morning Mrs. Whipple dropped everything to get Him all cleaned up. In an hour He was dirty again, with crawling under fences after a possum, and straddling along the rafters of the barn looking for eggs in the hay-loft. "My Lord, look at you now after all my trying! And here's Adna and Emly staying so quiet. I get tired trying to keep you decent. Get off that shirt and put on another, people will say I don't half dress you!" And she boxed Him on the ears, hard. He blinked and blinked and rubbed His head, and His face hurt Mrs. Whipple's feelings. Her knees began to tremble, she had to sit down while she buttoned His shirt. "I'm just all gone before the day starts."

The brother came with his plump healthy wife and two great roaring hungry boys. They had a grand dinner, with the pig roasted to a crackling in the middle of the table, full of dressing, a pickled peach in his mouth and plenty of gravy for the sweet potatoes.

"This looks like prosperity all right," said the brother, "you're going to have to roll me home like I was a barrel when I'm done."

Everybody laughed out loud, it was fine to hear them laughing all at once around her table. Mrs. Whipple felt warm and good about it. "Oh, we've got six more of these; I say it's as little as we can do when you come to see us so seldom."

He wouldn't come into the dining room, and Mrs. Whipple passed it off very well. "He's timider than my other two," she said, "He'll just have to get used to you. There isn't everybody He'll make up with, you know how it is with some children, even cousins." Nobody said anything out of the way. "Just like my Alfy here," said the brother's wife. "I sometimes got to lick him to make him shake hands with his own grand-mammy."

So that was over, and Mrs. Whipple loaded up a big plate for Him first, before everybody. "I always say He ain't to be slighted, no matter who else goes without," she said, and carried it to Him herself. "He can chin Himself on the top of the door," said Emly, helping along. "That's fine, He's getting along fine," said the brother.

They went away after supper. Mrs. Whipple rounded up the dishes, and sent the children to bed and sat down and unlaced her shoes. "You see?" she said to

Mr. Whipple. "That's the way my whole family is. Nice and considerate about everything. No out-of-the-way remarks—they *have* got refinement. I get awfully sick of people's remarks. Wasn't that pig good?"

Mr. Whipple said, "Yes, we're out three hundred pounds of pork, that's all. It's easy to be polite when you come to eat. Who knows what they had in their minds all along?"

"Yes, that's like you," said Mrs. Whipple. "I don't expect anything else from you. You'll be telling me next that my own brother will be saying around that we make Him eat in the kitchen! Oh, my God!" She rocked her head in her hands, a hard pain started in the very middle of her forhead. "Now it's all spoiled, and everything was so nice and easy. All right, you don't like them and you never did—all right, they'll not come here again soon, never you mind! But they *can't* say He wasn't dressed every lick as good as Adna—oh, honest, sometimes I wish I was dead!"

"I wish you'd let up," said Mr. Whipple. "It's bad enough as it is."

It was a hard winter. It seemed to Mrs. Whipple that they hadn't ever known anything but hard times, and now to cap it all a winter like this. The crops were about half of what they had a right to expect; after the cotton was in it didn't do much more than cover the grocery bill. They swapped off one of the plough horses, and got cheated, for the new one died of the heaves. Mrs. Whipple kept thinking all the time it was terrible to have a man you couldn't depend on not to get cheated. They cut down on everything, but Mrs. Whipple kept saying there are things you can't cut down on, and they cost money. It took a lot of warm clothes for Adna and Emly, who walked four miles to school during the three-months session. "He sets around the fire a lot, He won't need so much," said Mr. Whipple. "That's so," said Mrs. Whipple, "and when He does the outdoor chores He can wear your tarpaullion coat. I can't do no better, that's all."

In February He was taken sick, and lay curled up under His blanket looking very blue in the face and acting as if He would choke. Mr. and Mrs. Whipple did everything they could for Him for two days, and then they were scared and sent for the doctor. The doctor told them they must keep Him warm and give Him plenty of milk and eggs. "He isn't as stout as he looks, I'm afraid," said the doctor. "You've got to watch them when they're like that. You must put more cover onto Him, too."

"I just took off His big blanket to wash," said Mrs. Whipple, ashamed. "I can't stand dirt."

"Well, you'd better put it back on the minute it's dry," said the doctor, "or He'll have pneumonia."

Mr. and Mrs. Whipple took a blanket off their own bed and put His cot in by the fire. "They can't say we didn't do everything for Him," she said, "even to sleeping cold ourselves on His account."

When the winter broke He seemed to be well again, but He walked as if His feet hurt Him. He was able to run a cotton planter during the season.

"I got it all fixed up with Jim Ferguson about breeding the cow next time," said Mr. Whipple. "I'll pasture the bull this summer and give Jim some fodder in the fall. That's better than paying out money when you haven't got it."

861

"I hope you didn't say such a thing before Jim Ferguson," said Mrs. Whipple. "You oughtn't to let him know we're so down as all that."

"Godamighty, that ain't saying we're down. A man is got to look ahead sometimes. *He* can lead the bull over today. I need Adna on the place."

At first Mrs. Whipple felt easy in her mind about sending Him for the bull. Adna was too jumpy and couldn't be trusted. You've got to be steady around animals. After He was gone she started thinking, and after a while she could hardly bear it any longer. She stood in the lane and watched for Him. It was nearly three miles to go and a hot day, but He oughtn't to be so long about it. She shaded her eyes and stared until colored bubbles floated in her eyeballs. It was just like everything else in life, she must always worry and never know a moment's peace about anything. After a long time she saw Him turn into the side lane, limping. He came on very slowly, leading the big hulk of an animal by a ring in the nose, twirling a little stick in His hand, never looking back or sideways, but coming on like a sleep-walker with His eyes half-shut.

Mrs. Whipple was scared sick of bulls; she had heard awful stories about how they followed on quietly enough, and then suddenly pitched on with a bellow and pawed and gored a body to pieces. Any second now that black monster would come down on Him, my God, He'd never have sense enough to run.

She mustn't make a sound nor a move; she mustn't get the bull started. The bull heaved his head aside and horned the air at a fly. Her voice burst out of her in a shriek, and she screamed at Him to come on, for God's sake. He didn't seem to hear her clamour, but kept twirling His switch and limping on, and the bull lumbered along behind him as gently as a calf. Mrs. Whipple stopped calling and ran towards the house, praying under her breath: "Lord, don't let anything happen to Him. Lord, you *know* people will say we oughtn't to have sent Him. You *know* they'll say we didn't take care of Him. Oh, get Him home, safe home, safe home, and I'll look out for Him better! Amen."

She watched from the window while He led the beast in, and tied him up in the barn. It was no use trying to keep up, Mrs. Whipple couldn't bear another thing. She sat down and rocked and cried with her apron over her head.

From year to year the Whipples were growing poorer and poorer. The place just seemed to run down of itself, no matter how hard they worked. "We're losing our hold," said Mrs. Whipple. "Why can't we do like other people and watch out for our best chances? They'll be calling us poor white trash next."

"When I get to be sixteen I'm going to leave," said Adna. "I'm going to get a job in Powell's grocery store. There's money in that. No more farm for me." "I'm going to be a school teacher," said Emly. "But I've got to finish the eighth grade, anyhow. Then I can live in town. I don't see any chances here." "Emly takes after my family," said Mrs. Whipple. "Ambitious every last one of them, and they don't take second place for anybody."

When fall came Emly got a chance to wait on table in the railroad eating-house in the town near by, and it seemed such a shame not to take it when the wages were good and she could get her food too, that Mrs. Whipple decided to let her take it, and not bother with school until the next session. "You've got plenty of time," she said. "You're young and smart as a whip."

With Adna gone too, Mr. Whipple tried to run the farm with just Him to help. He seemed to get along fine, doing His work and part of Adna's without noticing it. They did well enough until Christmas time, when one morning He slipped on the ice coming up from the barn. Instead of getting up He thrashed round and round, and when Mr. Whipple got to Him, He was having some sort of fit.

They brought Him inside and tried to make Him sit up, but He blubbered and rolled, so they put Him to bed and Mr. Whipple rode to town for the doctor. All the way there and back he worried about where the money was to come from: it sure did look like he had about all the troubles he could carry.

From then on He stayed in bed, His legs swelled up double their size, and the fits kept coming back. After four months, the doctor said, "It's no use, I think you'd better put Him in the County Home for treatment right way. I'll see about it for you. He'll have good care there and be off your hands."

"We don't begrudge Him any care, and I won't let Him out of my sight," said Mrs. Whipple. "I won't have it said I sent my sick child off among strangers."

"I know how you feel," said the doctor. "You can't tell me anything about that, Mrs. Whipple. I've got a boy of my own. But you'd better listen to me. I can't do anything more for Him, that's the truth."

Mr. and Mrs. Whipple talked it over a long time that night after they went to bed. "It's just charity," said Mrs. Whipple, "that's what we've come to, charity! I certainly never looked for this."

"We pay taxes to help support the place just like everybody else," said Mr. Whipple, "and I don't call that taking charity. I think it would be fine to have Him where He'd get the best of everything . . . and besides, I can't keep up with these doctor bills any longer."

"Maybe that's why the doctor wants us to send Him—he's scared he won't get his money," said Mrs. Whipple.

"Don't talk like that," said Mr. Whipple, feeling pretty sick, "or we won't be able to send Him."

"Oh, but we won't keep Him there long," said Mrs. Whipple. "Soon's He's better, we'll bring Him right back home."

"The doctor has told you and told you time and time again He can't ever get better, and you might as well stop talking," said Mr. Whipple.

"Doctors don't know everything," said Mrs. Whipple, feeling almost happy. "But anyhow, in the summer Emly can come home for a vacation, and Adna can get down for Sundays: we'll all work together and get on our feet again, and the children will feel they've got a place to come to."

All at once she saw it full summer again, with the garden going fine, and new white roller shades up all over the house, and Adna and Emly home, so full of life, all of them happy together. Oh, it could happen, things would ease up on them.

They didn't talk before Him much, but they never knew just how much He understood. Finally the doctor set the day and a neighbour who owned a double-seated carry-all offered to drive them over. The hospital would have sent an ambulance, but Mrs. Whipple couldn't stand to see Him going away looking so sick as all that. They wrapped Him in blankets, and the neighbour and Mr. Whipple lifted Him into the back seat of the carry-all beside Mrs. Whipple, who had on her black shirt-waist. She couldn't stand to go looking like charity.

"You'll be all right, I guess I'll stay behind," said Mr. Whipple. "It don't look like everybody ought to leave the place at once."

863

"Besides, it ain't as if He was going to stay forever," said Mrs. Whipple to the neighbour. "This is only for a little while."

They started away, Mrs. Whipple holding to the edges of the blankets to keep Him from sagging sideways. He sat there blinking and blinking. He worked His hands out and began rubbing His nose with His knuckles, and then with the end of the blanket. Mrs. Whipple couldn't believe what she saw; He was scrubbing away big tears that rolled out of the corners of His eyes. He snivelled and made a gulping noise. Mrs. Whipple kept saying, "Oh, honey, you don't feel so bad, do you? You don't feel so bad, do you?" for He seemed to be accusing her of something. Maybe He remembered that time she boxed His ears, maybe He had been scared that day with the bull, maybe He had slept cold and couldn't tell her about it; maybe He knew they were sending Him away for good and all because they were too poor to keep Him. Whatever it was, Mrs. Whipple couldn't bear to think of it. She began to cry too, frightfully, and wrapped her arms tight around Him. His head rolled on her shoulder: she had loved Him as much as she possibly could, there were Adna and Emly who had to be thought of too, there was nothing she could do to make up to Him for His life. Oh, what a mortal pity He was ever born.

They came in sight of the hospital, with the neighbour driving very fast, not daring to look behind him. (*1930*)

CAROLINE GORDON

1895–

Caroline Gordon was born in Kentucky on October 6, 1895. She received her earliest education from her father, who conducted a school for boys in Clarksville, Tennessee. In 1916 she was graduated from Bethany College, where she was awarded the honorary degree of Litt.D. thirty years later. She has taught creative writing at the Woman's College of the University of North Carolina and at Columbia University. In 1924 Miss Gordon married the poet and critic, Allen Tate.

864 Caroline Gordon's solid reputation is based upon her achievement in prose fiction, a form in which she has few superiors. Her fine sensibility and craftsmanship should be readily apparent in the selection which appears in this book. Miss Gordon's novels include *Penhally* (1931), the story of several generations on a Kentucky plantation and one of her best-known books; *Aleck Maury, Sportsman*

(1934); *None Shall Look Back* (1937), a novel of the Civil War; *The Garden of Adonis* (1937); *Green Centuries* (1941); and *The Women on the Porch* (1944). A collection of her short stories, *The Forest of the South*, appeared in 1945. With her husband Miss Gordon has also published *The House of Fiction* (1949), a critical anthology of short stories.

The Captive

We were up long before daybreak and were loading the horses at first dawn streak. Even then Tom was a mind not to go.

"This ginseng it don't have to get to the station," he said, "and as for the money it'll bring, we can git along without that."

"We've been without salt for three weeks now," I told him.

"Thar's worse things than doing without salt," Tom said.

I knowed if he got to studying about it he wouldn't go and I was bound he should make the trip, Indians or no Indians. I slapped the lead horse on the rump. "G' long," I said, "I'd as soon be scalped now and have done with it as keep on thinking about it all the time."

Tom rode off without saying anything more, and I went on in the house and set about my morning work. The children was all stirring by that time. Joe, he felt mighty big to be the only man on the place and he was telling 'em what he'd do if any Indians was to come.

"You better hush that up," I says. "Can't you git your mind off them Indians a minute?"

All that morning, though, I was thinking about what Tom had said and wishing he hadn't had to go. Seems like I was riding with him most of the day.

"Now he's at West Fork," I'd say to myself, and then after I'd done some more chores, "He'll be about at the crossroads now or maybe Sayler's tavern." I knowed, though, it warn't much use to be following him that way in my mind. It'd be good dark before he could git home, and my thinking about it wouldn't hurry him none.

It was around ten o'clock that I heard the first owl hooting. Over on the mountain it seemed like. Joe was in the yard feeding the chickens and he stopped stock-still when he heard it and throwed back his head.

"You hear that, Mammy?" he said.

I knowed then thar must be something wrong with the call, or a boy like Joe wouldn't have noticed it.

I spoke up sharp, though. "I heard it," I says, "and I could hear a heap of other things ef'n I had time to stand around with my years open. How long you reckon it's going to take you to git them chickens fed?"

We both went on about our business without more talk, but all the time I was saying to myself that ef'n I could git through this day and see Tom Wiley riding in at the gate one more time I'd be content to bide without salt the rest of my natural life. I knowed it wouldn't do to let down before the children, though, and

865

I kept 'em all busy doing one thing and another till dinner time. It began to rain while we was eating our dinner and it rained a long time. After it stopped raining the fog settled down, so thick you could hardly see your hand before you. And all the time the owls was calling. Calling back and forth from one mountain to the other. My littlest girl, Martha, got scared; so I made all the children stay in the house and play by the fire whilst I started in on a piece of cloth I'd had in the loom a long time and never could seem to finish. Red it was with a stripe running through it. I aimed to make both the girls a dress out of that piece before the winter set in.

By that time the fog had risen as high as the top of the ridges and the whole house was swallowed up in it. The children kept teasing, saying it was good dark now and couldn't they have a candle.

"Yes," I said, "we here all by ourselves and you want to go lighting candles, so they can't help finding the house."

One of the gals got to crying. "Who's coming?" she said. "Mammy, who you think's coming?"

I seen then I'd got 'em stirred up and I'd have to settle 'em, for seems like I couldn't stand to be worrying like I was and the children crying too. I give them all a lump of sugar around and got 'em started on a play-party. I made out I had the headache and if they was going to sing they'd have to sing low. Hog-Drovers it was they was playing.

> "Hog-drovers, hog-drovers, hog-drovers we air,
> A-courtin' your darter so sweet and so fair.
> Kin we git lodgin' here, O here,
> Kin we git lodgin' here?"

I got 'em started to frolicking and playing and then I went back to my work. But I couldn't git my mind off something a man said to me once when we was out hunting on the Hurricane, and I made him go right in on a bear without waiting for the other men folks to come up.

"You're brash, Jinny," he said, "you're brash and you always been lucky, but one of these times you going to be too brash."

Sitting there listening to them owls calling, and wondering how much longer it'd be before Tom got home, I got to thinking that maybe this was the time I was too brash. For I knowed well thar warn't another woman in the settlements would have undertook to stay on that place all day with nothing but a passel of children. Still I said to myself it's done now and thar ain't no undoing it. And the first thing I know Tom will be back, and tomorrow morning it'll fair up, and I'll be thinking what a goose I was to get so scared over nothing.

The children was still singing.

> "Oh, this is my darter that sets by my lap.
> No pig-stealin' drover kin git her from pap.
> You can't git lodgin' here, O here,
> You can't git lodgin' here."

I got up and looked out the window. Seemed to me the fog was lifting a little. A man was coming up the path. I knew it was a white man by the walk, but I didn't know it was John Borders till he stepped upon the porch.

The first thing he asked was where was Tom.

"Gone to the station with a load of ginseng," I told him. "I'm looking for him back now any minute."

He stood there looking off towards the mountain. "How long them owls been calling?" he asked.

"Off and on all evening," I said, "but owls'll hoot, dark days like this."

"Yes," he said, "and some owls'll holler like wolves and gobble like turkeys and ever' other kind of varmint. Jinny, you better git them children and come over to our house. Ain't no telling when Tom'll be back."

Just then an owl hooted and another one answered him from somewhere on top of the ridge. We both listened hard. It sounded like a real owl calling to his mate, but I was good and scared by that time and I thought I'd best go over to the Borderses'. It was my judgment, though, that thar warn't any hurry. Indians hardly ever come round before nightfall.

I told John that if he'd wait till I'd fastened up the stock I'd go back with him. He said that while I was doing that he'd walk out in the woods a little way. He'd been looking all day for some strayed sheep and hadn't found no trace of them, but he thought they might be herded up in that gulley by the spring. He went off down the path and I fastened the front door and went out the back way. I didn't fasten the back door, but I kept my eye on it all the time I was worrying with the cattle. Joe, he was along helping me. The cow was standing there at the pen; so I stopped and milked her while Joe went up in the triangle to look for the heifer. He found her all right and brought her up to the cowpen just as I finished milking. We fastened both cows up in the stable and Joe went over and saw that all the chickens was up and fastened the door on them. Then we started back to the house with the milk.

We were halfway up the path when we heard the Indians holler. We started for the house on a dead run. I could see Indians in the yard, and one Indian was coming around to the house to the back door. I ran faster and slipped in the door ahead of him. Joe was right behind me. The room was so full of Indians that at first I couldn't see any of my children. The Indians was dancing around and hollering and hacking with their tomahawks. I heard one of the children screaming but I didn't know which one it was. An Indian caught me around the waist but I got away from him. I thought, I have got to do something. I fell down on my knees and crawled around between the Indians' legs, they striking at me all the time, till I found Martha, my littlest one, in the corner of the loom. She was dead and I crawled on a little way and found Sadie. She was dead, too, with her skull split open. The baby was just sitting there holding on to the bar of the loom. I caught him in my bosom and helt him up to me tight; then I got to my feet. Joe was right behind me all the time and he stood up when I did. But an Indian come up and brained him with a tomahawk. I seen him go down and I knowed I couldn't git any more help from him. I couldn't think of anything to do; so I worked my way over towards the door, but there was two or three Indians standing on the porch and I knowed there was no use running for it. I just stood there holding the baby while the Indians pulled burning logs out of the fire on to the floor. When the blaze had sprung up they all come out on to the porch.

I made a break and got some way down the path, but an Indian run after me

867

and caught me. He stood there, holding me tight till the other Indians come up; then he laid his hand on my head and he touched the baby too. It seemed he was claiming me for his prisoner. He had rings on his arms and ankles, and trinkets in his ears. I knew he was a chief and I thought he must be a Shawnee. I could understand some of what he said.

He was telling them they better hurry and git away before Tice Harman come home. Another Indian stepped up. I knew him—a Cherokee that comes sometimes to the station. Mad Dog they called him. Tice Harman had killed his son. It come to me that they had been thinking all along that they was at Tice Harman's. I jerked my arm away from the Shawnee chief.

"You think you're burning Tice Harman's house," I said. "This ain't Tice Harman's house. It's Tom Wiley's. Tom Wiley. Tom Wiley never killed any Indians."

They looked at each other and I think they was feared. Feared because they had burned the wrong house, but feared too of Tice Harman. Mad Dog said something and laid his hand on his tomahawk, but the old chief shook his head and took hold of my arm again. He spoke, too, but so fast I couldn't tell what he was saying. The Cherokee looked mad but he turned around after a minute and called to the other Indians and they all left the house and started off through the woods. Mad Dog went first and half a dozen young Indians after him. The old chief and I came last. He had hold of my arm and was hurrying me along, and all the time he kept talking, telling me that he had saved my life, that I was to go with him to his town to be a daughter to him to take the place of a daughter that had died.

I didn't take in much that he was saying. I kept looking back towards the burning house, thinking maybe they wasn't all dead before the Indians set fire to it. Finally I couldn't stand it no longer and I asked the old Shawnee. He pointed to one of the young Indians who was going up the ridge ahead of us. I seen something dangling from his belt and I looked away quick. I knowed it was the scalps of my children.

II

We went up over the ridge and then struck north through the woods. I didn't take much notice of where we was going. I had all I could do to keep Dinny quiet —he warn't but ten months old. I let him suck all the way but it didn't do much good. We went so fast it'd jolt out of his mouth and he'd cry louder than ever. The Shawnee would grab my arm and say the other Indians would kill him sure if he kept that up. Finally I got his head down inside the waist of my dress and I helt him up against me so tight he couldn't cry, and then I was scared he'd smother, but the Shawnee wouldn't let me stop to find out.

We went on, up one valley and down another, till finally we come out on level land at the foot of a mountain. The old chief made me go first, right up the mountainside. It was worse there than it was in the woods. The laurel and the ivy was so thick that sometimes he'd have to reach ahead of me and break a way through. My arms got numb and wouldn't hold the baby up. It was lucky for me I was crawling up a mountain. I would put him up ahead of me and then crawl to him, and in this way my arms would get a little ease of the burden. The old chief didn't like this, though, and ever' time it happened he'd slap me and tell me to go faster, go faster or they would surely kill the baby.

We got to the top of the mountain, somehow, and started down. My legs were hurting me now worse than my arms. It was going so straight down the mountainside. The back of my legs got stiff and would jerk me up every time I set my foot down, what they call stifled in a horse. I got on, somehow, though, all through that night and for most of the next day. It was near sundown when we stopped, in a rockhouse [1] at the head of a creek. The Indians must have thought they was too far for any white men to follow them. They made up a big fire and walked around it pretty careless. Two of the young Indians went off in the woods. I heard a shot and they come back dragging a little deer. They butchered it and sliced it down the middle, and slung the two haunches over the fire on forked sticks. The tenderer parts they broiled on rocks that they heated red-hot in the coals. A young buck squatted down by the fire and kept the venison turning. Soon the smell of rich meat cooking rose up in the air. The juices begun dripping down into the blaze and I thought it was a shame for all that gravy to go to waste. I asked the Shawnee to lend me a little kittle he had, and I hung it on a forked stick and caught the juices as they fell, and then poured them back over the meat. When they turned brown and rich I caught the gravy in the little kittle and sopped my fingers in it and let the baby suck them.

The old chief, Crowmocker, smiled like he thought a lot of me. "White woman know," he said. "White woman teach Indian women. You make rum?"

I said I didn't know how to make rum, but there was plenty in the settlements and if he would take me back, take me just within a mile or two of the clearing, I'd undertake to furnish him and his men with all the rum they could drink.

He laughed. "White people promise," he said. "You in your cabin you forget poor Indian."

The Cherokee, Mad Dog, had been sitting there broiling the deer nose on a rock that he had got red-hot in the flames. When it was brown he brought it over and gave it to me. Then he went back and sat down, sullen like, not saying anything. The fire shone on his black eyes and on his long beak of a nose. When he moved, you could see the muscles moving, too, in his big chest and up and down his nekkid legs. An Indian woman would have thought him a fine-looking man, tall and well formed in every way, but it frightened me to look at him. I was glad it was the old chief and not him that had taken me prisoner. I was glad, too, that the chief was old. I'd heard tell how particular the Indians was about things like that. I thought the old chief would likely do what he said and keep me for his daughter, but if it was Mad Dog he would have me for his wife.

I thought the meat never would get done, but it finally did. The Indians give me a good-size piece off the haunch and I ate it all, except a little piece I put in Dinny's mouth. He spit it out, but I kept putting it back till he got some good of it. Then I took him down to the creek and scooped up water in my hands for him. He'd been fretting because my milk was giving out, but the water and the juice from the meat quieted him a little. After we'd both had all the water we could drink I went back up the hill and sat down on a log with Dinny laying across my knees. It felt good to have his weight off my arms, but I was afraid to take my

869

[1] *A rockhouse is not a cave, but a place sheltered by an overhanging ledge of rock.* (Miss Gordon's note.)

hands off him. I was feared one of them might come up and snatch him away from me any minute.

He laid there a while a-fretting and then he put his little hand up and felt my face.

"Sadie . . . ," he said. "Sadie . . ."

Sadie was the oldest girl. She played with him a lot and fondled him. He'd go to her any time out of my arms.

I hugged him up close and sang him the song Sadie used to get him to sleep by. "Lord Lovell, he stood at the castle gate," I sang and the tears a-running down my face.

"Hush, my pretty," I said, "hush. Sadie's gone, but Mammy's here. Mammy's here with baby."

He cried, though, for Sadie and wouldn't nothing I could do comfort him. He cried himself hoarse and then he'd keep opening his little mouth but wouldn't no sound come. I felt him and he was hot to the touch. I was feared he'd fret himself into a fever, but there wasn't nothing I could do. I helt his arms and legs to the blaze and got him as warm as I could, and then I went off from the fire a little way and laid down with him in my arms.

The Indians kept putting fresh wood to the fire till it blazed up and lit the whole hollow. They squatted around it, talking. After a while half a dozen of them got up and went off in the woods. The light fell far out through the trees. I could see their nekkid legs moving between the black trunks. Some of them was dragging up down timber for the fire and some kept reaching up and tearing boughs off the trees. They come back trailing the green boughs behind them. Two or three other Indians come over and they all squatted down and begun stripping the leaves off the switches and binding them into hoops. An Indian took one of the scalps off his belt—Sadie's light hair, curling a little at the ends and specked now all over with blood. I watched it fall across the bough of maple. I watched till they began stretching the scalp on the hoop and then I shut my eyes.

After a while Crowmocker come over and tied me with some rawhide thongs that he took off his belt. He tied me up and tight and it felt good to have the keen thongs cutting into me. I strained against them for a while and then I must have dropped off to sleep. I woke myself up hollering. I thought at first it was the Indians hollering, and then I knew it was me. I tried to stop but I couldn't. It would start way down inside me and I would fight to hold it in, but before I knew it my mouth would be wide open and as soon as I'd loose one shriek another would start working its way up and there wasn't nothing I could do to hold it back. I was shaking, too, so hard that the baby rolled out of my arms and started crying.

The old chief got up from where he was sleeping and come over. He stood there looking down at me and then he lighted a torch and went off in the woods a little way. He brought some leaves back with him and he put them to boil in his little kittle. He made me drink some tea from the leaves and he gave the baby some too, and after a while we both went off to sleep.

III

I woke with the old chief shaking me by the arm and telling me it was time to get up. I was still sort of lightheaded and for a minute I didn't know where I was. It was raining hard and so dark you couldn't tell whether it was good day. The Indians had built a fire up under the ledge and was broiling the rest of the venison. I laid there and I saw the light shine on their nekkid legs and the tomahawks hanging from their belts, and I knew where I was and all that had happened.

The old chief untied the thongs and I stood up with Dinny in my arms. They gave me a little piece of venison and some parched corn. My lips was so swelled I couldn't chew, but I swallowed the corn and I put the meat in my mouth and sucked it till it went away. I felt milk in my breasts and I was glad for the baby. I gave him his dinny but he wouldn't suck. He wouldn't hardly open his eyes. I thought that was from the tea the old Indian had given us and I feared he'd got too much. He was still hot to the touch and I thought he might have got a fever from laying out all night in the rain. I tore off part of my top skirt and I made a sort of sling that I put around my shoulders to carry him in; and I made a cover, too, out of part of the cloth to keep the rain off his little face.

Soon as we had finished eating, the Indians stomped out the fire and scattered the ashes so you couldn't have told there had ever been a camp there, and we started off through the woods.

We hadn't gone far before two of the young Indians left us. I thought they was most likely going back over the trail to watch if anybody was following us. I heard them saying that the folks at the settlement would be sure to send out a party. Some of the Indians thought it wouldn't do no good because the heavy rains had washed out the trail so nobody could find it. But Mad Dog said Tice Harman could follow any trail. I never knew before the Indians was so feared of Harman. They said he was the best hunter among the Long Knives, that he could go as far and stand as much as any Indian, and that they would like for him to come and live with them and be one of their warriors. Mad Dog said now that the only thing was to go so fast and go so far that even Tice Harman couldn't come up with us. He said "O-hi-yo" several times and I judged they meant to make for one of the towns on the river.

It stopped raining after a while but it didn't do much good. It was level ground we was traveling over and the water was standing everywhere, so that half the time you was wading. I knew we was some place high up in the hills, but afterwards I couldn't have told what country I had passed over. I went with my head down most of the time, not seeing anything but the black trunks of the trees going by and the yellow leaves floating in the puddles. Beech woods we must have been in because the leaves was all yellow and little.

We went on like that all day, not stopping to eat anything except some parched corn that the old chief took out of his bag and handed around to us still traveling. Late that evening we come to a water hole. One of the Indians shot a bear and we stopped and built a fire under a cliff. The Indians hadn't no more'n butchered the meat when two scouts come running into camp. They said that white men were following us, on horseback. The Indians all looked scared at this. Crowmocker stood there talking to Mad Dog about what we had best do. I went over and stood by them. Mad Dog said that they ought to kill the child and change the course, that they would have to go faster than ever now and I couldn't keep up, carrying the baby. Crowmocker showed him the sling I had made and said the baby wasn't no burden to me now. He said he had brought me this far and

871

was going to carry me on to his town to teach his women how to weave cloth like the dress I had on.

He told Mad Dog that and then he motioned to me and said "Go!" I started off, top speed, through the trees. Behind me I could hear the Indians stomping around in the leaves to cover up the signs of the fire. I went on as fast as I could, but every now and then an Indian would shoot past me. Pretty soon they was all ahead except the old chief.

We went down hill towards a hollow that had a little branch running through it. Mad Dog was in the lead, the other Indians right on his heels, jumping over down logs and bushes quick as cats. The old chief stayed by me, and when I'd slow up getting over a log or fall down in the bushes he'd jerk me on to my feet again.

The branch was narrow but running deep with the rains. Mad Dog started wading downstream and the other Indians after him, single file. They hadn't slowed up much and water splashed high. I could see their legs moving through the splashing water. The old chief by my side was breathing hard. I knowed he was winded but I thought he would wind quicker than the others. I thought I would keep moving as long as I saw the Indians' legs going on.

The Indian that was in front of me stepped in a hole up to his waist. When he come out of it he took two three steps and stood still. I knowed then that Mad Dog had stopped and I knowed he would be coming back down the line. I looked up, but the sides of the gulley was too steep. I turned and ran back upstream fast as I could. I heard the breathing close behind me and I knowed it was the old chief, and then there was a big splashing and I knowed Mad Dog was after me.

I left the water and ran sideways up the gulley. The breathing was closer now. I tried to run faster and I caught my foot in a root. They was on me as soon as I went down. Mad Dog grabbed me by both arms. Crowmocker got there a second after, but Mad Dog already had hold of Dinny. I caught at his legs and tried to push them out from under him but he kicked me away. I got up and went at him again but he kicked me down. He kicked me again and then he went on up the side of the gulley till he come to a big tree and he held the baby by the feet and dashed his brains out.

I rolled over on my face and I laid there flat on the ground till the old chief come up. He pulled me to my feet and said we would have to run on fast, that the white men were following us on horses. I said no, I wouldn't go, I would stay there with my baby; but he and another Indian took me by the arms and drug me down the stream spite of all I could do.

We went on down the branch a good way. Towards dark we came out on the banks of a river. Water was standing halfway up the trunks of big trees. I saw the current, running fast and covered with black drift, and I didn't believe even an Indian could get across that raging river. But they didn't stop a minute. Crowmocker fell back and two young Indians took hold of my arms and carried me out into the water. The current caught us and swept us off our feet. I couldn't swim much on account of my clothes, but the two young Indians held onto my wrists and carried me on between them. The other Indians come right in after us. They held their guns up high over their heads and swum like boys treading water. I could see their heads bobbing all around me through the black drift and I

872

couldn't see nothing to keep all of us from drowning. They managed to keep out of the drift somehow, though, and all the time they was working towards the other bank till finally we come out in dead water at the mouth of a creek. The Indians that was holding me up stopped swimming all of a sudden, and I knowed then that we must have got across. It was so dark by that time that I couldn't see nothing hardly. I got out of the water as best I could and a little way up the creek bank. I fell down there 'mongst some willows. I saw the Indians come up out of the water shaking themselves like dogs, and I saw them falling down all around me, and then my eyes went shut.

IV

The old chief woke me up at the first dawn streak. I heard him and I felt him shaking me, but I didn't get up. As soon as I opened my eyes the pain in my feet started up. I touched one foot to the ground and it throbbed worse'n tooth-ache. I knew I couldn't travel any that day and I·didn't care. I turned over on my back and laid there looking up at the sky. It had cleared off during the night and the stars was shining. The sky was all a pale gray except for one long sulphur-colored streak where day was getting ready to break. Behind me the Indians was looking to their guns and settling their tomahawks in their belts. I watched their heads and shoulders moving against that yellow light, and I saw one of them take his tomahawk out and heft it and then try the blade with his finger. I thought that if I just kept on laying there that maybe he would be the one to finish me off, and then I thought Mad Dog was quicker and would beat him to it.

The old chief was still shaking me. "Get up, Jinny. Day come."

"No," I said, "I ain't going to get up."

He took me by the shoulders and tried to pull me to my feet but I slimped back on the ground. I spoke to him in Shawnee.

"My feet bleed and I cannot travel. Let me die."

He leaned over and looked at my feet and then he called to one of the young Indians to bring him some white oak bark. When the bark come he boiled it over the fire and then he took the liquor from the bark and cooled it with more water and poured it over my feet.

The other Indians had finished scattering the fire and was starting out through the willows, but Crowmocker just sat there pouring that stuff on my feet. I could feel the swelling going down and after a while I touched my feet to the ground. It didn't hurt nothing like it had, and I got up and we started off. He give me some parched corn and I ate it, walking. He said we would have to travel fast to catch up with the other Indians. I asked him if the white people was still follow-ing us and he laughed and said no white men could get across that river. I owned to myself that they couldn't, and I didn't think any more about them coming after me. I thought the Indians would probably take me so far away that I'd never again see a white face.

We caught up with the other Indians towards dark. That night we slept in a canebrake by a little river. A buffalo was wallowing in the river as we come up. One of the Indians shot him. They butchered him there in the water and drug big slabs of the meat up the bank with ropes cut from the hide. We must have been in Indian country by this time. They didn't seem to think it made no differ-

873

ence how much noise they made. They made up a big fire to one side of the brake and they was half the night cooking the meat and eating. I went to sleep under a tree with them singing and yelling all around me.

When I woke up the next morning they was having a council. They talked till the sun was high and then they split up into two parties. Mad Dog and three of the young bucks left us and swum across the river. The rest of us kept on up the bank. We traveled all that day through the cane and then we struck a divide and followed it into another valley. We had run out of everything to eat by this time except the strings of jerked meat that they all carried slung around their necks. We stayed two three days at a buffalo lick, hoping to kill some game, but none came and we went on.

Most of the leaves was off the trees by this time and the nights was real cold. I knew it was some time in October that the Indians come and burned our house, but I didn't know how long we'd been on the trail and I didn't have no idea what country we was in. •

One morning we come out in some deep narrows just above where two creeks flowed together. A wild-looking place with tumbling falls and big rocks laying around everywhere. I looked up at the cliffs over our heads and I couldn't believe my eyes. They was *painted*: deer and buffalo and turtles big as a man, painted in red and in black on the rock. Some of the young Indians acted like they had never been there before either. They would keep walking around looking at things and sometimes stand and stare at the pictures of wild beasts that was painted everywhere on the smooth rock.

The old chief took a way up the side of the cliffs, the rest of us following. The young Indians went up like deer, but I had to pull myself up by the laurel and ivy that grew down in between the rocks. We walked along a narrow ledge and come to a rockhouse. It was the biggest rockhouse ever I seen, run all along one side of the cliff. The old chief uncovered an iron pot from where it was hid in a lot of trash in one corner of the cave and showed me how to set it up on forked sticks. He said that I would have to do all the work around the camp from now on the way Indian women did, and when the spring rains come and melted the snows he would take me to his town on the Tenassee and I would learn more about Indian ways and be adopted into the tribe in place of his dead daughter.

I thought if he took me there I would never get away and I had it in mind to make a break for it first chance I got. I got hold of two strings of jerked meat and I kept them tied around my waist so I'd be ready when the time came. I thought I would wait, though, and maybe I would find out how far it was to the settlements. I would lie there in my corner of the cave at night, making out I was asleep and listen to them talking around the fire. I heard them call the names of the creeks that flowed through that valley—Big Paint and Little Mudlick; and further off was another creek, Big Mudlick, where they went sometimes to hunt. The names was strange to me and I never could tell from their talk how far it was to the settlements or even which way to go. I had an idea that the place I was in was secret to the Indians, for it was a wonder to see and yet I had never heard any white body tell of it. I asked Crowmocker what the pictures of deer and buffalo and bear was for and he said they was the Indians' fathers and that I would learn about them when I was adopted into the tribe.

Once he pointed some mounds out to me and said they was graves. He said that he and his people always stopped when they come this way to visit the graves of their fathers that was all over the valley.

A spell of fine weather come, late in the fall. Indian summer they call it. We looked out one day and bees was swarming on the cliffside. Crowmocker was mad when he saw them. He said it meant that the white people were coming; that when bees swarmed out of season they was running away from the white people who had scared all the game out of the country and made it so that even bees couldn't live in it. I asked would the white people find their way into this valley and he said they couldn't—that it was a way known only to Indians; that if a white man ever set foot in it the great bear would come down off the wall and crush him in his paws. He said, though, that there would be fighting soon over all the land and a lot of bloodshed.

I knowed that was all foolishness about the bear, but I thought likely as not there would be fighting and I wanted to get away worse than ever. One morning I was down in the hollow by myself, gathering wood, and I thought that was the time. Three of the Indians had gone off hunting and I knowed the others was laying up in the cave asleep. I didn't think anybody would be following me, for a while, anyhow. I started off, slipping from tree to tree, and I got quite a ways up the hollow. I knowed wasn't nobody following me, but I would keep looking back over my shoulder all the time. I got to thinking. I didn't have no way to kill no game, and nothing to eat but them two strings of jerked meat. I didn't even know how far I'd have to go before I came to any settlement. Worst of all, I didn't even know which way to take. Likely as not I'd starve to death in the woods, or freeze if the weather turned. I'd better stay with the Indians, where at least I could sleep warm and eat, if it wasn't nothing but parched corn. I picked up my load of wood and I got back to camp quick as I could, and didn't none of them ever know I'd been away.

I never tried it again, but sometimes I'd sit there on the edge of the cliff and pick out the way I'd take if I did go. There was a ridge covered with black pines rose up right in front of the rockhouse. I thought if I could once get up there I could get down into the valley easy. I hadn't never been over there, but I knew what the country would be like. I saw myself slipping along through that divide, around the foot of the mountain and over some more mountains till I'd come out on a clearing. I'd slip up to some cabin, towards dark. They'd think I was an Indian at first, maybe, and then they'd see my eyes was light and they'd take me in and keep me till I could get back to my own folks again.

We stayed in that rockhouse a long time. The leaves all fell off the trees, and one or two light snows fell, but the real cold weather was late coming. The Indians hunted just enough to keep us in meat. They said the pelts was thin that year and not worth taking. Sometimes they would take me along to bring in the game, but mostly they left me to work by myself. When cold weather set in we built big fires in the cave and it was warm inside like a house. When the Indians wasn't hunting they would lie around on buffalo skins and sleep. The smoke was terrible and the smell of Indians was all over everything. At first it bothered me, but after a while I got so I didn't notice it.

I wasn't in the cave much, even in bad weather. I had to gather all the firewood. The Indians didn't have no axe and I couldn't get nothing but dead

875

branches. There wasn't much down timber on the cliffside; so I'd mostly go up over the cliffs when I was hunting wood. There was a barren there, flat as the palm of your hand and covered with a thin kind of grass. It had plenty of trees on it but they was all twisty and stunted by the wind. The only sizable tree was a big elm. It was peeled for thirty or forty feet and had a rattlesnake painted on it—a monster snake coiling up around the trunk. You could see that snake from everywhere on the barren. I was feared to look at it. The Indians seemed to think a lot of it. Sometimes they would go up there at night and I would hear them singing and dancing and calling to the snake.

Somewhere on the barren there was lead mines. The Indians never let me go to them, but they would go off and stay two-three hours and come back with big balls of lead. They made me smelt it out for bullets. I had to have a mighty fire. It would take me days and days to get up enough wood. I would heap it up in a big pile and then I would kindle the fire and keep it going for hours. When the lead melted, it ran down through little ditches into holes that I had dug to form the bullets. It would take the lead a long time to melt. Sometimes I would be up on the barren from sunup to sundown.

I would sit there and think about my husband and my children. I would wonder whether Tom went out in the woods hunting ginseng the way he used to do, and was he still looking for me or had give me up for dead. When I thought of Tom the house would be there, too, not burning down the way it was last time I saw it, but standing with the rooms just the way they always was. I could see both rooms plain, even to the hole that was burnt in the floor when a big log fell out one night. The children would be playing in and out of the house like they did. It was like they was all living; it was only me that was gone away.

I would think back, too, over things that happened long before ever I was grown and married to Tom Wiley. There was a man named Rayburn stayed at the settlement one winter. Lance Rayburn. A big, strong man and a mighty hunter. We ate bear of his shooting all that fall. He was handy with snares too, and took over a hundred beaver down in the bottom. He courted me some that winter, sitting in front of the fire after the old folks was in bed. I laughed and went on with him, but Tom Wiley had just started a-courting me and all the time my mind was on him more'n it was on the stranger.

Come time for Rayburn to pack up his pelts to take to the station, he saved one out for me. Beaver, and extra fine and soft. He give it to my sister, Sarah, and told her to hand it to me when I come to the house. She made one of the children bring it down to the creek where I was boiling clothes. I laid it there on the grass and I would stop and look at it as I went back and forth with my clothes, and sometimes I would wipe my hands dry and lay them on the soft fur for pleasure in the feel. But all the time I knowed I wasn't going to keep it. When Rayburn come towards me through the willows I went to meet him with the pelt in my hands.

876

"Keep this," I said, "and give it to some girl where you're going."

"Don't you want it?" he asked.

"I ain't taking nothing from you."

He stood there looking at me and all of a sudden his eyes narrowed up like a cat's. "You're full young to be marrying," he said.

"I ain't too young to know my own mind," I told him and before I thought I laughed.

He come towards me, and before I knowed what he was up to he was on me and trying to bear me to the ground. He was a strong man but I was stout, too, and I stood up to him. We was rassling around in the bushes quite some while before he got me down, and then he had to keep both his hands on my chest. I laid there right still, looking up at him.

"What you reckon my pappy'll say when I tell him about this?" I asked.

He laughed. "I ain't a-feared of no Sellards that ever walked," he said, "but that Tom Wiley ain't no manner of man for you," he said.

"You can talk against Tom Wiley and you can hold me here till Doomsday," I told him, "but it ain't going to do you no good. I ain't going to have none of you no matter what happens."

His face kind of changed. Looked like it hurt him to hear me say it. He got up off me right away and he picked the beaver pelt up from where it lay in the grass and he throwed it hard as he could into the creek.

"It'll git to my girl that way fast as any other," he said.

I watched the pelt floating down the water and on to a rock and then off again. When I turned around he was out of sight and he was gone when I got back to the house. He stayed at the station a while and then he went off in the mountains hunting bear and wasn't never heard of again. Some said he was killed by wild beasts. A rifle and a cap that they said was his'n was found up in the hills. The man that found the rifle kept it, but they give the cap to the Borderses. Wouldn't nobody wear it, and Sally hung it up in the dog alley. I used to look at it ever' time I passed and wonder whether it had ever been on Lance Rayburn's head and was he dead or still living. And sometimes I'd wonder how it'd been if I'd married him instead of Tom, but I knowed all the time I wouldn't never have married nobody but Tom because he was the one I fancied from the time I was a chap, living neighbor to the Wileys, back in the Roanoke country.

I thought about Lance Rayburn and I thought about a lot of other folks that had come to the settlement and stayed and then gone on and wouldn't anybody know whether they was living still or dead. And I thought about people dead long ago, my old granny back in Carolina, ninety-eight years old and turned simple. She'd sit in the chimney corner all day long singing, the likeliest tunes!

"Pa'tridge in the pea patch," she'd sing and call me to her and fondle me, liking gals, she said, always better than boys.

> "Pa'tridge in the pea patch
> Pickin' up the peas.
> Long comes the bell cow
> Kickin' up her heels . . ."

"Oh . . . h, the bell cow," she'd sing and catch me by my little shimmy tail. "O . . . O . . . hh, the bell cow . . ." and hist me up over the arm of her chair. "O . . . O . . . hh, the bell cow, kickin' up her heels. Call the little gal to milk her in the pail."

I used to call those songs to mind when I had to go down to the lick for salt. It was a place I didn't like to go. A deep hollow with three sulphur springs and

877

a lick that covered nigh an acre of ground. The biggest lick ever I seen in my life. The way was white with the bones of beasts, and in between the piled up bones the long furrows that the buffalo made licking the ground for salt. I would walk down those furrows to the spring and fill my bucket with the salty water and go back up the hill to where my kettle was slung between two little birches. Sitting there waiting for the water to boil, I couldn't keep my eyes off the bones. I would take them up in my hand and turn them over and over, wondering what manner of beasts they had belonged to.

Once I made myself a little beast, laying all the bones out on some lacy moss, the front feet stiff like it was galloping off in the woods, the hind legs drawn up under him. A hare it might have been or a little fawn. Or maybe a beast that nobody ever heard of before.

They was beasts come to that lick one time or another not known to man. Bigger'n buffalo they must have been. One thighbone, I mind, longer'n I was and twice as big around as two good-sized men.

I thought of a man used to be around the station, Vard Wiley, second cousin to Tom. Folks said he was the biggest liar in the settlements. He would stay off in the woods hunting day after day and never bring in no game except maybe a brace of wild turkeys. And he told tall tales about a lick bigger'n any lick around those parts, where the beasts come up in tens of thousands. He would lay up in a tree all day and watch 'em he said, and not take a shot for wonder. There was beasts used there, he said, ten times the size of buffalo. He offered to take anybody there and show them the bones, and when they asked him why he didn't bring them back to the settlement he said couldn't no man carry them, nor no two horses.

Folks laughed at him, and the children round the settlement used to sing a song:

"Vard Wiley's gone west, Vard Wiley's gone east,
A-huntin' the woods for a monster beast.

He'll make him a tent out of the wild beast's hide
And all the king's horses can stable inside.

He'll make him a wagon out of solid bone
And it'll take ten oxen to draw it home."

I called that song to mind and I thought how if I ever saw Vard Wiley again I'd go up to him and say I knew him to be a truthteller, and all the people would laugh at me maybe, the way they did Vard Wiley, but all the time I would be knowing it was the truth.

I thought, too, of other tales he told and of jokes he played. Of the time he borrowed my dress and sunbonnet and shawl and went and sat on the creek bank when the schoolmaster was in swimming. He sat there all evening with the sunbonnet hiding his face and old Mister Daugherty shaking his fist at him. "You hussy! You brazen hussy! Don't you know I'm nekkid?" and finally when he come up out of the water nekkid as the day he was born Vard took out after him and run him clean to the house. Old Mister Daugherty went around saying they was a woman ought to be run out of the settlements, and Vard would talk to him and make out it was me. But Old Man Daugherty knowed wouldn't none

878

of Hezekiah Sellards' daughters be carrying on like that. He was bound it was a woman from Ab's Valley.

I would think about 'em sitting there and arguing about how the hussy ought to be run out of the settlements, and I would laugh all by myself there in the woods. Throw back my head and laugh and then feel silly when the woods give back the echo.

I done a lot of work while I was with the Indians. It was hard on me at first but I got used to it. It was better after Mad Dog left us. The old chief was like a father to me, and the young ones knowed I belonged to him and didn't bother me none. I slept off by myself in a fur corner of the cave and he would wake me up at daybreak and tell me what there was to do that day. He took pains to show me how to flesh pelts and cure them, and he showed me how to split a deer sinew for thread and how to make a whistle to call deer out of birch bark and sticks. And after I got so I could sew skins good he had me make him a pair of leggings and trim them with porcupine quills—porcupine quills colored with some roots he got out of the woods.

It bothered him the way I looked and he made me paint my face the way the Indians did. Fixed me up some of the red root mixed with bear's grease, and after I'd been putting it on my face for a while you couldn't told me from an Indian woman, except for my light eyes.

He'd stay in the cave with me sometimes all day, his buffalo hide wrapped around him so tight that his knees was up against him like a chair. He'd sit there and rock back and forth on his heels and talk while I worked. Down in the hollow the young braves would be practicing their war whoops. He would listen to them and laugh.

"Our young men give the war whoop loudly to cover up their fear of the enemy. It was not so when I was young. There was joy in the war whoop then."

He said he was a chief but he might have been something better. He might have been a medicine man. He had the gift of it from his grandmother. His own mother died when he was born, he said, and his old granny raised him. He told me about how she would take him into the woods with her looking for yarbs and roots, and how she knew where everything grew and which roots would be good to take and which had no strength in them. He said that after I was adopted into the tribe he would tell some of her secrets to me, but the Spirit would be angry if a white woman knew them.

I asked him wouldn't I still be a white woman after I was adopted into the tribe but he said no, the white blood would go out of me and the Spirit would send Indian blood to take its place, and then I would feel like an Indian and know all the Indian ways and maybe get to be a wise woman like his old granny.

He told me about his youngest daughter and how she come by her death, following what she thought was a fawn bleating. They found her days afterward, three enemy arrows in her. Her death had been paid for with three scalps of warriors, and he would say that he didn't grieve over her, but I knew he did. I got to feeling sorry for him sometimes to have lost his daughter that meant so much to him, and then I would think how I had lost all my children and my husband and I would cry, dropping tears on the skin I was sewing.

I got so after a while that the Indian way of doing things seemed natural to me. I thought nothing of seeing dark faces around me all the time, but in the

879

night sometimes I would dream of white faces. White faces coming towards me through the trees. Or sometimes I would be in a house again and look up all of a sudden and all the faces in the room would be white.

One white face was always coming to me in my dreams: Tice Harman, the man whose house the Indians thought they was burning the day they burned ours. I always thought that if anybody came to save me it would be Tice Harman. I could see him plain in my dreams. A little man, wouldn't weigh more'n a hundred and twenty pounds, but he had a big head. A big head and a big beak of a nose and long yellow hair down to his shoulders. His eyes was blue and in my dreams they glittered like ice. I would dream about Tice Harman and when I waked I would think what I'd heard said of him—how he could go further and stand more than any man in the settlements, and how he loved to fight Indians better'n eat when he was hungry. I would think, too, of how folks said he would bring trouble on the settlements shooting that Indian down when there warn't really no use in it; and I would think that since it was him that brought all my trouble on me, maybe it would be him that would get me away from the Indians. But time went on and nobody came, and after a while I got so I didn't think much about it.

One evening I was gathering wood on the cliffside and I heard a lot of whooping and hollering down near the mouth of the creek. The Indians come out from where they was sleeping back in the cave and stood looking over the falls. A long whoop came and the old chief put his hands to his mouth and answered it. There was more whooping back and forth, and then Mad Dog came up the trail by the falls with about twenty Indians following him. They was painted for war and marched single file, all except the last six or eight. They was in pairs and in the middle of them a white man, walking with his hands tied behind him. A white man? A boy. Couldn't have been more'n eighteen years old.

I had to step out of the path to let them by. The dead branches rustled in my hands. The prisoner turned his head. He looked straight into my eyes. It was like he didn't know I was there. I spoke to him.

"I can't do nothing," I said. "I'm a white woman, but I can't do nothing. Christ!" I said, "there ain't nothing I can do."

He kept on looking at me but he didn't say nothing. They was hurrying him past. I dropped the branches and run after them. Mad Dog called to one of the young bucks and he caught me and held me. I fought him, but he held me till they had all gone up the path.

I went on to the rockhouse and kindled up the fire. After a while Mad Dog come down and told me to cook up some meat quick as I could. There would be singing and dancing he said; they would want meat all night long.

I looked at him. "A present," I said. "A present for Kagahye-liske's daughter. Give me this boy. He is not good for anything but to gather wood."

His eyes was fierce. "Boy?" he said. "He has this day killed my brother." Then he laughed and smoothed my hair. "Jinny," he said, "pretty Jinny."

880

I made out I had to see to the fire and walked away. I put some bear meat on to boil and I told him I would call him when it was done, and he went on back up the path.

There was a moon coming. I sat there waiting for the meat to boil and watched it rise over the pines. Up on the barren the Indians was dragging up all the dead branches they could find into one pile. After a while I looked up over the rockhouse and saw the sky all light and I knew they had kindled the fire.

The stamping and yelling went on, and every now and then a gun would go off. Then there was running around the tree. You could hear the feet pounding and the long calls. "Ai . . . yi . . . Ai . . . yi . . . Ai . . . yi . . ." One for each man that had died that day. And the sharp cry for the scalp taking. They would act it all out and the boy standing there watching. He was dazed, though; he wouldn't see it for what it was. He wouldn't know what they was doing, might not know what they was going to do. There on the path he looked at me and didn't know me for a white woman. I ought to have found out his name and where he come from. I ought to have done that much. But he wouldn't have answered. And what good would it do his folks . . . if I ever saw white folks again. Mad Dog's hand on my hair. "Pretty Jinny . . . pretty Jinny . . ."

The flames shot up and lit the whole valley. The moon looked cold where it hung over the pines. I kept the fire up under the kittle but I couldn't sit still. I walked back and forth in the rockhouse, back and forth, back and forth, waiting for the shrieks to start.

They was a long time coming. I thought maybe it was already going on. Indians can stand there burning and not make a sound, and there have been white men that could. But this was just a boy . . .

The first shriek was long and then they come short and quick, one right after the other. I got over in a corner of the rockhouse and held on tight to a big rock. After a while I let go of the rock and put both fingers in my ears and then I was feared to take them out, thinking it might not be over yet. The Indians was still yelling and stamping. The young ones kept running down and grabbing up chunks of meat from the boiling pot and carrying them up to the barren. I could see the old chief's shadow where he stood on the edge of the cliff calling to the new moon.

When he came down to the rockhouse Mad Dog was with him. They stood there dipping meat up out of the kittle. Mad Dog talked.

"It is too much. For five hundred brooches I could buy a girl of the Wild-Cats, young and swift, a fine worker in beads. A girl like a moonbeam, daughter of a mighty warrior."

His eyes was black in the circles of paint. His tongue showed bright between his painted lips. The red lines ran from his forehead down the sides of his cheeks to make gouts of blood on his chin.

A devil. A devil come straight from hell to burn and murder. Three white men killed that day and the boy brought back to torture. It was him that killed them, him that yelled loudest when the boy was burning. Him that set fire to my house and burned my children . . .

I saw him running through the woods, white men after him. I saw him fall, a dozen bullets in him. But he wouldn't be dead. He would lay there bleeding and look at me out of his painted eyes, and I would go up and stomp on him, stomp him into the dirt . . .

My hands shook so I dropped the sticks I was carrying. I was up near enough now to hear all they was saying. Mad Dog was taking little silver brooches out of a buckskin bag. He poured them out in a pile on a rock and then counted

881

them. The old chief stood there till he got through counting; then he swept them all up into a bag he took from around his neck.

"Brother," he said, "the woman is yours."

Mad Dog had left the fire and was coming towards me. I ran over and caught hold of the old chief's arm. I called him by his Indian name.

"Kagahye-liske, do not give me to this man. He has killed my children and burned my house."

He looked down at me and it was like he'd never seen me before. His face, not painted, was as cruel as the Cherokee's, the eyes bloodshot and the whole face swollen from the meat he had eaten.

"The war whoop drowns sorrow," he said. "This chief is my brother and a mighty warrior. He has this day killed three white men."

I hung on to his arm. "Keep me for one of the young men of your village," I said. "The Cherokee are old women. You have said so and you have promised. You have promised to take me with you wherever you go."

He shook my hands off. "A promise," he said, "to a white coward! Go to your work."

He turned around like he was going to leave the cave. I run after him and caught hold of his knees, but he broke away. Mad Dog come and tied me up tight with thongs that he cut from buffalo hide, and then they both went on up to the barren where the other Indians was still screeching and stamping.

The screeching and stamping went on far into the night. The fire under the kittle went out and it was dark except for a little light from the moon. I laid there on the floor, listening to the Indians and thinking about how it would be when Mad Dog came down to take me for his wife. I laid there, expecting him to come any minute, but the singing and dancing went on and he didn't come, and after a while I went to sleep.

V

The white boy that they had burned came to me while I was asleep. He came carrying a lamp that was made from the bleached skull of a sheep. The brain hollow was filled with buffalo fat and there was a wick in it burning bright. He came walking between the trees like he didn't have need to look where he was going. His hair was light like I had seen it when he passed me there on the path, but it was long, too, like Tice Harman's. His eyes were the same eyes that had looked at me there on the path.

I said to him what I had said there. "I couldn't do nothing," I said. "There wasn't nothing I could do."

He didn't speak—only made signs for me to follow him. I got up and walked after him. The rawhide thongs was still on me but they didn't bind any more and I moved as easy and as light as he did. He went down by the falls and clomb up over the hill to where the elm tree stood that had the big rattlesnake painted on it. He walked past the elm tree and struck out through the black pines that was all over that ridge. Sometimes he would go so fast that I couldn't keep up with him, and then I would stand still and after a while I would see the light flickering through the trees and I would go on to where he was waiting for me. We went on through the pine woods and started down the side of the ridge. I heard water running somewhere far down below. I thought that would be Mudlick creek, but when I got to it it was a branch I'd never seen before. We crossed it and went on up a path through a clearing. There was little shrubs all around like the ones up on the barren, and in the middle of them was a house. It was my house and yet it wasn't. White all over and the walls so thin you could see the light from the lamp shining through the logs.

People was walking around in the yard and sitting on the doorstep. They moved to let me go through the door, but they didn't speak to me and I didn't speak to them.

The men that was sitting in front of the fire playing draughts didn't even look up when I came in. I went over to the hearth and tried to dry out my clothes. I stood there holding out my hands but didn't no heat come. I looked at the logs and they was white like the timbers of the house, and the same light came from them. I saw that the men playing didn't have no lamp and yet there was light all around them.

People kept walking in and out of the cabin, men and women and little children. I would go up to them and look in their faces, but there wasn't nobody there I knew. I walked round and round the room. Every now and then the people would move out of the way and I would catch a sight of the walls. White, with patches of green on them. I put my hand up and felt one of the logs. It was round and cold to the touch. No log at all, but bleached bone. I knew then that all the house was bone, the floor and the walls and the chimney, even the table that the men was playing on, all made from the big bones down at the lick.

One of the men at the table stretched his arm out and pulled me over to him. He had on a beaver cap and his face under it was pale like he'd been in the woods a long time. He looked at me and I saw it was Lance Rayburn. He sang, pulling me up over the arm of his chair:

> "Oh . . . the bell cow, kicking up her heels,
> Call the little gal to milk her in the pail . . ."

Fiddling started up somewhere and all fell to dancing. They danced to one of my old granny's tunes:

> "They was an old lord lived in a northern countree,
> Bowee down, bowee down . . ."

There was bowing back and forth and balancing, and there was figures called, but wasn't no women dancing anywhere. I would see something going by and think it was a woman's skirt, but when I got up to it it would be fur or feathers dangling from a belt and all the faces around was dark, not like they was at first.

The great flames went leaping up the chimney, and all of a sudden I knew that they had built that fire to burn somebody by. I looked around for the one they was going to burn but he wasn't there. I said they will burn me next, and I saw what they would tie me to—the rattlesnake tree, going straight up from the table through the roof.

I went to the door and I saw through the black trunks a light flickering. I run and Mad Dog and the old chief was after me the way they was that day in the hollow. I thought they will kill me now when I go down, and I run faster and

883

then they was both gone away and I was walking through pine woods, the light flickering on ahead of me.

I walked on and come to a creek that ran along between wide banks of cane. The light shone on the water and made it light as mist. I stepped in, not knowing whether it was water or mist, and I could feel it coming up around my knees, water and yet not water. I moved along through it light as the wind till I come to where the creek forked. I could see the two forks and the white trunks of the sycamores along the bank, but I didn't know which way to go.

The light was all around me. I could see it shining on the reeds and on the little leaves of the cane and on the water where it broke on the rocks. Behind me there was voices talking.

"Jinny Wiley . . . Jinny Wiley, that was stolen and lived with the Indians . . ."

And then it was the old chief talking to the new moon:

"The white people . . . The white people are all over the land. The beaver makes no more dams and the buffalo does not come to the lick. And bees swarm here in the ancient village. Bees swarm on the graves of our fathers . . ."

The light that had been around me was gone. It was shining now through the tree trunks down a fork of the creek. I waded towards it through the light water, the voices following, and then they was gone away and I was standing at the foot of a high mountain. I looked up and I saw the light flickering at the top and I clomb towards it, pulling myself up by the scrubs and holly bushes.

I got up on the mountain top but the young man wasn't there. I walked out on to the edge of a cliff and he was by my side. He said "Look, Jinny!" and the flame of his lamp leaped up and lighted the whole valley and I looked across a river and I saw a fort. I saw the roofs of the houses and the stockade and the timber burned back over the rifle range, and I saw men and women walking around inside the stockade.

I said: "I'm a-going over there," but the young man wasn't with me no more, and the dark that was all around was the inside of the rockhouse.

VI

When I woke up the next morning the Indians had a big fire going and was all sitting around eating. I laid there and made out I was still asleep. They had found trace of buffalo down at the lick and was making ready for a big hunt. I thought maybe they would take me along to bring in the game the way they did sometimes, and then I heard Mad Dog say they would leave me tied up in the cave till they got ready to start for their town.

I was laying with my face turned up and I was feared they could tell by my eyes that I wasn't asleep. I give a kind of groan and rolled over on my side. I laid there not moving while the talking went on all around me. Once footsteps come over to the corner where I was laying and I heard something slap down on the ground right by me but I didn't give any sign and the footsteps went away.

I laid there so still that I went to sleep again with the talking and the making ready for the hunt still going on. I was waked up by a kind of roaring sound. At first I thought it was the falls and then I knowed the falls wouldn't sound

884

that loud. I opened my eyes. The Indians was all gone and there was a big storm blowing up.

I laid there watching the pine tops lash back and forth in the wind, and the dream I'd had come back into my mind as plain as if it was something that had happened. I thought it was sent to me on purpose to tell me that now was the chance to get away. I knowed that if the Indians come back with any game that night they'd feast high again and was more than likely to take me up on the barren and burn me like they done that boy.

I sat up. A piece of meat was lying on the floor right by me. That meant that the Indians would be all gone all day and maybe another day. If I could only get free of the thongs I might get a long way off before they knew I was gone.

There was a knife stuck in a crack of the rock where they laid the meat. If I could only get hold of that! I rolled over and over till I got to the rock and I managed to get up on my knees, though the thongs cut into me bad. I could see the handle of the knife sticking up out of the crack and I laid my face down flat on the rock and tried to catch hold of it with my teeth. But it was too far down and all I did was get my mouth full of grit and sand. I gave up and laid down again. The wind wasn't as high as it had been, but the rain was coming down hard. It blew way back into the cave. I laid there with the big drops spattering in my face and a thought came to me. I rolled over to where the rain was pouring down off the roof and I laid there till I was soaked through. All the time I kept straining at the thongs and I could feel them giving a little, the way leather does when it's wet. I kept on, getting them looser and looser till finally I worked my way out of them and stood up free.

I listened and I couldn't hear anything but the roaring of the wind and the beating of the rain on the ledge. I tiptoed to the end of the cave and looked down the path. But I couldn't see any sign of living creature. I dug the knife out from between the rocks and I took the piece of cooked meat and a little kittle that the old chief had left laying around, and I went off out of the other end of the cave and along the cliffside.

I kept to the path a little way and then I struck off through the trees down the hillside. The ground was wet and slid from under my feet in big chunks. I caught on to the trees all the way to keep myself from falling. When I got to the bottom I could look back and see where I'd come, as plain as if I'd blazed a trail. I knowed I'd have to strike water. I run in among some pines and come to a wet weather branch. I waded right in. It was swift water and full of holes. I would step in one every now and then and go down, but I kept on as fast as I could. I felt all the time like the Indians was after me. I knowed they had gone south towards the salt lick and I knowed the whole cliffside and the barren was between me and them, but all the time I felt like they was right behind me. When I looked over my shoulder the top boughs of the rattlesnake tree showed from the barren. I was glad when I rounded a bend and it was out of sight.

When I come to where the branch flowed into the creek I didn't know which way to go, and then I thought that in my dream I was following water and I struck right down the stream. It was harder going here than it was in the branch. The snows melting had filled all the dry weather branches, and muddy water kept running in till you couldn't tell nothing about the depth. It was good

885

I was going downstream, but even then the current was a hindrance to me, reaching in and sweeping me off my feet sometimes into a hole that I would have a time getting out of. More'n once I was in danger of drowning.

I kept on like this all day. When it was drawing towards dark I crawled up on the bank under some cedars and I laid there and I ate a good-sized piece of the cooked meat I had brought with me. The rain had fallen off to a light drizzle and there was some color in the sky, sign of a clear day tomorrow. There was a flight of little birds over the water and then round and round the tops of the cedars. Some of them lit in the boughs of the tree I was laying under. I could hear them flying in and out and the quick cries and then the twittering as they settled down to roost. It was dark under the trees but the streak of light stayed on the water. I laid here and watched it fade and I wished I could stay there where the cedar boughs was like a little house. I wished I could stay there and not run no more. I thought I would maybe sleep a few minutes and then I could go on faster. But when I shut my eyes I would think I heard the Indians coming through the trees and after a little I got up and went on again.

I tried wading some more but I couldn't make it in the pitch dark. I got up on the bank of the creek and pushed my way through the bushes as best I could. Sometimes the undergrowth would be so thick I couldn't make it, and then I would have to get down in the water again. All the way I was worrying about losing time following the bending and twisting of the creek, and then I would think that was the only sure way to get out of the hill country and I had best stick to water, spite of all the bending.

Some time during the night I lost my way from the creek and wandered in the pitch dark into a marsh that was all along the creek bottom. More like a bog it was. I couldn't seem to get out of it no matter what I did. I stood there bogged to the knees and I couldn't even hear the creek running—nothing but the wind soughing in the trees. And I thought what a lone place it was and if I came on quicksand, as was more than likely, I could go down and even my bones never be found. And I thought of how Lance Rayburn's bones might have been laying all this time in some hollow of the mountain and nothing maybe but squirrels or deer ever going near the place, and it seemed to me I might better have stayed with the Indians. But I knew it wouldn't be no use going back now. They would put the fire to me sure.

I stood there and I heard some wild thing passing. Pit pat pit pat it went; feet falling on dry ground. I pulled out of the muck and made towards the sound, and a deer or something broke through the thicket and went off through the woods.

I followed and come out on high ground, a slope covered with pine needles. I throwed myself down flat on my face. I must have gone off to sleep. When I come to myself light was growing through the trees, and all around me I could hear twigs snapping and little rustlings. I got up quick, thinking it was the Indians coming, and then I felt foolish, knowing it was only game stirring at break of day. I saw two deer go by, moving slow over the brown pine needles. The air was so still they didn't get a whiff of me till they was out of the thicket. The buck wheeled so quick he almost knocked the doe over, and then they was both clattering off over the hill.

886

I went down to the creek bank and washed my face and let the water run over my wrists where they was scratched by the branches. I ate the last of my meat sitting there on a rock. When I got ready to go I found out that one of my strings of jerked meat had slipped off during the night. I couldn't hardly believe it at first. I stood up and felt all over my clothes time and again but it warn't there.

"Well," I said, "it's gone and they ain't no use crying over it, but I wish to God it'd a been the little piece."

I got in the water and started wading again. The creek was shallow for about half a mile and then it run into a bigger creek. The two of them run on before me and I didn't know which way to go. I stood there looking. The sun was up and it shone on the water. I watched the riffles break on the black rocks where the sun caught them, and the place was not the same place I had seen in the dream and yet it was the same because of the light that was over everything.

I remembered the way I took in the dream. "Left I'll go," I said, "like it was in the dream, and if it don't turn out right it's no fault of mine."

I went on, wading half the time. All that day I was thinking about something to eat. Seems like everything good I ever had to eat in my life come back to torment me that day. The smell of herring, cooking, bothered me most. I would see myself, a chap, back in the Roanoke country, broiling herrings over the coals the way children did when their mammy wouldn't give them anything else to eat between meals. I would go over it all, time and again, the herrings hanging in rows in the smokehouse, like tobacco in a barn, and us climbing up on a slab of wood to get at them.

"Three," Dinny, that's my oldest brother, 'd say every time. "Three. You might as well get one apiece while you're at it."

I thought, too, about people wasting things, of a woman I knew used to give all her buttermilk to her pig, and I thought how it was shameful to have no mind for them that might be starving. And I thought how if I could have that pig's dinner one time, or even a moldy piece of bread, the kind I'd thrown away many a time as not good enough for the dogs. And yet I'd been as wasteful as any of them in my day—worse, even, with game. I used to go hunting just for the fun of it. Seemed like there warn't nothing I liked better than sighting down a rifle. Warn't none of the Sellards or Damron boys a better shot than I was, and I could throw a knife with the best of them. That time John and Dick and me and the two Damrons went to Sinking Fork on a big hunt I shot eighteen wild gobblers, and when we loaded up and they was more'n we could carry it was me that said to leave them laying, that there warn't no use in breaking yourself down and the woods full of gobblers like they was. I thought about them gobblers more'n once that day and Lord, how I wished I could git my hands on a rifle butt just one more time.

I threwed my knife once or twice at some small game, mostly rabbits, but it was a rusty old thing and not fitted to the hand the way a knife has to be to turn proper. One rabbit that I hit square in the middle got up and skittered off like nothing had happened, and I seed then it was a waste of time to throw at them.

Late that evening I come on some forward wild greens in a sheltered place on

887

the creek bank. I went down on my knees and I gathered every shoot. I found some punk and I went up to a rockhouse on the side of the hill and I built a little fire way in under the ledge the way I'd seen the Indians do. I knowed it was craziness to build a fire, but it might be days before I'd come on any wild greens again. "I'll eat," I said, "varmints or no varmints."

I put my greens on to boil in the little kittle with a piece of the jerked meat and I sat there, thinking about how Indians would go up on a cliff to sight over the country and how the least little smoke curling up would be a sign to them. Once I was on the point of putting the fire out but I couldn't bring myself to do it. I feared to feed it much and yet I'd catch myself putting dead twigs to it. It was a long time before the bubbles started rising up in that little old kittle. I sat there rocking on my heels and talking to them.

"Bile," I said, "bile. God's sake, can't you bile no faster'n that? And me setting here starving."

I ate up ever' mite of the greens and I drank the pot liquor and licked the kittle and then I put out down the hill as fast as I could. I could feel my stomach tight under my waist band and strength coming up in me from the vittles and I run faster than I'd ever run before. It was dark under the trees but there was still light down the water courses. I thought how in some cleared place or in a town it wouldn't be dark for two or three hours yet and I saw myself in such a place, moving around and talking to people but staying always in the light. And I said to myself, if I ever got into such a cleared place again it'd be hard to get me to set foot in the woods.

The creek I was following was a master tumbler. Straight down it went over big rocks and the water white everywhere with its dashing. Once I thought I would leave it and strike out through the woods again, and then I thought falling water'd take me out of the hills quicker'n anything else and I'd best stick to it long as I could.

I went on and then all of a sudden I come upon something that froze my guts cold: the print of a foot by the water. I knowed it would be a moccasin but I stooped down and looked at it good. I told myself it might be a white man— might be a hunter wearing moccasins like most of 'em did; but I went on a little way and there was three-four footprints in some wet sand and all of 'em was moccasins. I thought then the game was up or would be directly, but I run on. I run on. I couldn't think of nothing else to do.

It was still light when I come out on a big rock by some little falls. I stood there looking and I couldn't believe my eyes. A broad river ran there before me and clearings here and there on the bank and right across from the rock I was standing on a fort: a blockhouse with a stockade fence around it and the timber burned back over the rifle range.

I got off the rock and I run down towards the water. A woman and some children was walking along outside the stockade. I called to the woman. She give one look at me and turned and run inside the fort, the children after her. I saw the gate swing to behind them and I knowed they had shot the bolt.

I tore off my petticoat and I waved it over my head and I yelled loud as I could.

"Let me in! Let me in, I tell you!"

I could see heads at the upper story and one somebody standing up on a stump to look over the stockade. But nobody answered and there wasn't no sign of the gate opening.

I looked over my shoulder. The woods was dark behind me and they wasn't no signs of Indians, but I knowed they'd be coming any minute. I felt like I knowed the place in the woods they was at now. I saw them trotting, trotting through the trees, one after another, the way they went.

I thought, I'll have to do something quick or they'll git me sure, after all my trouble. I started in to swim it but I couldn't make no headway against that current. I saw I would be drowning in a minute, and I swum hard and got back to shallow water. It come to me then that the folks in the fort didn't know who I was. I stood up in the water and I yelled, loud as I could.

"I'm Jinny Wiley . . . Jinny Wiley that the Indians stole."

The echo come back to me from the woods, but there warn't no sound from the fort. Then the gate opened a little way and an old man come out with a gun in his hand. He stood there looking at me and he turned around and said something to the folks in the fort and then he started down the path. I watched him coming down over the rifle range, an old man, gray-haired and feeble enough to a been my grandsire. I shouted at him.

"You can't do it. Send some young body over."

He stood on the bank and shouted back at me, his old voice quavering across the water:

"Where'd you come from?"

I jumped up and down and shrieked, top of my voice:

"God's sakes, man, you going to let me die right here before your eyes? I'm white! White, I tell you!"

"All of 'em's gone but me," he said, "and they ain't no canoe."

"Make a raft," I told him.

He nodded his head up and down. I could see his old gray beard a-shaking. "You better be ready to swim for it," he said. "I don't know as I can git across."

He called to the women in the fort and they come and brought an axe. They was a dead mulberry tree on the bank and they went to work felling it. The old man went off in the woods and come back with some grapevine. When the tree fell it split into three logs and he tied them together with grapevine and then he and the women rolled them down to the water. They handed him two rifles and he laid them on the raft and started poling. The current caught him and he was going downstream. Yelling had started behind me somewhere in the woods. The Indians was coming.

I run down the bank till I got even with the raft and I swum out and clomb abroad. The old man poled hard. We got halfway out in the river and then the vines begun to come loose and the raft was spreading apart. I knelt down and held the logs together with my hands as best as I could. The old man fell down on his knees and started praying.

" 'Tain't no use," he said, "we can't make it."

I looked over my shoulder. The Indians was swarming down towards the water. I knowed they'd be swimming directly. The old man was still praying. I took the pole away from him.

"Go on and pray, you old fool," I said. "I'm a-going to git across this river."

I put all the strength I had into it and we made some headway. The yelling

889

was closer now. The Indians was in the water. A shot rung out. I hoped to God one of 'em was hit. I poled harder and I seen some willow boughs ahead of me. I reached out and grabbed hold of 'em and we pulled ourselves to shore.

We went up over the rifle range fast as we could. I looked back once. The Indians had left the water and was standing on the bank. I heard Mad Dog calling:

"Whoopee! . . . whoopee! . . . pretty Jinny!"

We went through the gate. I heard the bolt shoot home and I knowed I was inside the fort. I fell down on the ground and the women and children come crowding. The Indians was still yelling. I sat up and the high stockade fence was all around me.

"Lord God," I said, "I was lucky to git away from them Indians!" (*1945*)

ERSKINE CALDWELL

1903–

Erskine Caldwell was born on December 17, 1903, at White Oak, Coweta County, Georgia. His mother was a school teacher and his father a Presbyterian minister who had migrated from Ireland. Caldwell's youth was spent traveling throughout the South (it was his father's duty as secretary of his denomination to go from parish to parish), so that most of his education was given him by his mother. He later attended Erskine College (1920–1921), the University of Virginia (1922, 1925–1926), and the University of Pennsylvania (1924). Both during his schooling and afterward, Caldwell experimented with a great variety of occupations—he has held as many as fifteen different types of jobs. In addition to his literary activities, he has worked as a stagehand, a cotton picker, a night cook and waiter, a soft-drink dispenser, and a professional football player.

Caldwell's controversial literary career began in 1929 with the publication of *The Bastard*. Much of his work has been criticized as being unnecessarily sordid, but his books have nevertheless enjoyed an amazing popularity. The stage version of his *Tobacco Road* ran for 3180 consecutive performances, to establish a new record as the longest run in the history of the American theater. Caldwell's admirers see in his work the virtues of simplicity, excellent narration, imagination, and humor. His severest critics construe his stories as an indictment of the South.

In 1933 Caldwell was awarded the *Yale Review* award for fiction for his short story, "Country Full of Swedes." He has published a total of twenty-four books, of which some of the most important are *Tobacco Road* (1932), *God's Little Acre* (1933), *Kneel to the Rising Sun and Other Stories* (1935), *Georgia Boy* (1943), and *Tragic Ground* (1944).

Candy-Man Beechum

It was ten miles out of the Ogeechee swamps, from the saw mill to the top of the ridge, but it was just one big step to Candy-Man. The way he stepped over those Middle Georgia gullies was a sight to see.

"Where you going, Candy-Man?"

"Make way for these flapping feet, boy, because I'm going to see my gal. She's standing on the tips of her toes waiting for me now."

The rabbits lit out for the hollow logs where those stomping big feet couldn't touch them.

"Don't tread on no white-folks' toes, Candy-Man," Little Bo said. "Because the white-folks is first-come."

Candy-Man Beechum flung a leg over the rail fence just as if it had been a hoe-handle to straddle. He stood for a minute astride the fence, looking at the black boy. It was getting dark in the swamps, and he had ten miles to go.

"Me and white-folks don't mix," Candy-Man told him, "just as long as they leave me be. I skin their mules for them, and I snake their cypress logs, but when the day is done, I'm long gone where the white-folks aint are."

Owls in the trees began to take on life. Those whooing birds were glad to see the setting sun.

The black boy in the mule yard scratched his head and watched the sun go down. If he didn't have all those mules to feed, and if he had had a two-bit piece in his pocket, he'd have liked to tag along with Candy-Man. It was Saturday night, and there'd be a barrelful of catfish frying in town that evening. He wished he had some of that good-smelling cat.

"Before the time aint long," Little Bo said, "I'm going to get me a gal."

"Just be sure she aint Candy-Man's, boy, and I'll give you a helping hand."

He flung the other leg over the split-rail fence and struck out for the high land. Ten miles from the swamps to the top of the ridge, and his trip would be done. The bushes whipped around his legs, where his legs had been. He couldn't be waiting for the back-strike of no swamp-country bushes. Up the log road, and across the bottom land, taking three corn rows at a stride, Candy-Man Beechum was on his way.

There were some colored boys taking their time in the big road. He was up on them before they had time to turn their heads around.

"Make way for these flapping feet, boys," he shouted. "Here I come!"

"Where you going, Candy-Man?"

891

They had to do a lot of running to keep up with him. They had to hustle to match those legs four feet long. He made their breath come short.

"Somebody asked me where I'm going," Candy-Man said. "I got a yellow gal, and I'm on my way to pay her some attention."

"You'd better toot your horn, Candy-Man, before you open her door. The yellow gals don't like to be taken by surprise."

"Boy, you're tooting the truth, except that you don't know the why-for of what you're saying. Candy-Man's gal always waits for him right at the door."

"Saturday-night bucks sure have to hustle along. They have to strike pay before the Monday-morning whistle starts whipping their ears."

The boys fell behind, stopping to blow and wheeze. There was no keeping up, on a Saturday night, with the seven-foot mule skinner on his way.

The big road was too crooked and curvy for Candy-Man. He struck out across the fields, headed like a plumb-line for a dishful of frying catfish. The lights of the town came up to meet him in the face like a swarm of lightning-bugs. Eight miles to town, and two more to go, and he'd be rapping on that yellow gal's door.

Back in the big road, when the big road straightened out, Candy-Man swung into town. The old folks riding, and the young ones walking, they all made way for those flapping feet. The mules to the buggies and the sports in the middle of the road all got aside to let him through.

"What's your big hurry, Candy-Man?"

"Take care my dust don't choke you blind, niggers. I'm on my way."

"Where to, Candy-Man?"

"I got a gal what's waiting on her toes. She don't like for to be kept waiting."

"Better slow down and cool those heels, Candy-Man, because you're coming to the white-folks' town. They don't like niggers stepping on their toes."

"When the sun goes down, I'm on my own. I can't be stopping to see what color people be."

The old folks clucked, and the mules began to trot. They didn't like the way that big coon talked.

"How about taking me along, Candy-Man?" the young bucks begged. "I'd like to grab me a chicken off a henhouse roost."

"Where I'm going I'm the cock of the walk. I gouge my spurs in all strange feathers. Stay away, black boy, stay away."

Down the street he went, sticking to the middle of the road. The sidewalks couldn't hold him when he was in a hurry like that. A plateful of frying catfish, and he would be on his way. That yellow gal was waiting, and there was no time to lose. Eight miles covered, and two short ones to go. That saw-mill fireman would have to pull on that Monday-morning whistle like it was the rope to the promised land.

The smell of the fish took him straight to the fish-house door. Maybe they were mullets, but they smelled just as good. There wasn't enough time to order up a special dish of fins.

892

He had his hand on the restaurant door. When he had his supper, he would be on his way. He could see that yellow gal waiting for him only a couple of miles away.

All those boys were sitting at their meal. The room was full of hungry people just like him. The stove was full of frying fish, and the barrel was only half-way used. There was enough good eating for a hundred hungry men.

He still had his hand on the fish-house door, and his nose was soaking it in. If he could have his way about it, some of these days he was going to buy a barrel of catfish and eat them every one.

"What's your hurry, Candy-Man?"

"No time to waste, white-boss. Just let me be."

The night policeman snapped open the handcuffs, and reached for his arms. Candy-Man stepped away.

"I reckon I'd better lock you up. It'll save a lot of trouble. I'm getting tired of chasing fighting niggers all over town."

"I never hurt a body in all my life, white-boss. And I sure don't pick fights. You must have the wrong nigger, white-boss. You sure has got me wrong. I'm just passing through for to see my gal."

"I reckon I'll play safe and lock you up till Monday morning just the same. Reach out your hands for these cuffs, nigger."

Candy-Man stepped away. His yellow gal was on his mind. He didn't feel like passing her up for no iron-bar jail. He stepped away.

"I'll shoot you down, nigger. One more step, and I'll blast away."

"White-boss, please just let me be. I won't even stop to get my supper, and I'll shake my legs right out of town. Because I just got to see my gal before the Monday-morning sun comes up."

Candy-Man stepped away. The night policeman threw down the handcuffs and jerked out his gun. He pulled the trigger at Candy-Man, and Candy-Man fell down.

"There wasn't no cause for that, white-boss. I'm just a big black nigger with itching feet. I'd a heap rather be traveling than standing still."

The people came running, but some of them turned around and went the other way. Some stood and looked at Candy-Man while he felt his legs to see if they could hold him up. He still had two miles to go before he could reach the top of the ridge.

The people crowded around, and the night policeman put away his gun. Candy-Man tried to get up so he could be getting on down the road. That yellow gal of his was waiting for him at her door, straining on the tips of her toes.

"White-boss, I sure am sorry you had to go and shoot me down. I never bothered white-folks, and they sure oughtn't bother me. But there ain't much use in living if that's the way it's going to be. I reckon I'll just have to blow out the light and fade away. Just reach me a blanket so I can cover my skin and bones."

"Shut up, nigger," the white-boss said. "If you keep on talking, I'll just have to pull out my gun again and hurry you on."

The people drew back, so they would not stand too close. The night policeman put his hand on the butt of his gun, where it would be handy in case.

"If that's the way it's to be, then make way for Candy-Man Beechum, because here I come." (*1935*)

893

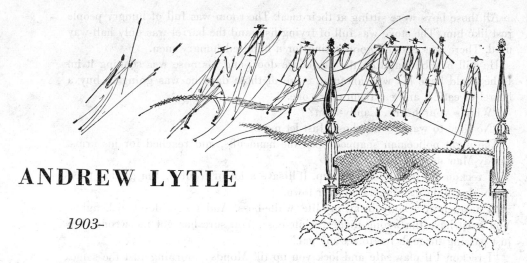

ANDREW LYTLE

1903-

Andrew Nelson Lytle was born in Murfreesboro, Tennessee, December 26, 1903. He received his A.B. degree from Vanderbilt University in 1925, studied for a time in France, and spent a year at Yale as a student in George Pierce Baker's famous school of drama. From 1940 until 1942 he held a Guggenheim Fellowship for creative writing in fiction. Lytle has taught at the University of the South (Sewanee) and at the Universities of Iowa and Florida. During the year 1942–1943 he was managing editor of the *Sewanee Review*.

Lytle's work, though not prolific, is uniformly finished and dramatic to an intense degree. In addition to several memorable short stories, his work includes *Bedford Forrest and His Critter Company* (1931) and three novels—*The Long Night* (1936), *At the Moon's Inn* (1941), and *A Name for Evil* (1946). An important influence in the Agrarian movement, he was also a contributor to *I'll Take My Stand* (1930) and *Who Owns America?* (1936).

Mister McGregor

"I want to speak to Mister McGregor."

Yes, sir, that's what he said. Not marster, but MISTER MCGREGOR. If I live to be a hundred, and I don't think I will, account of my kidneys, I'll never forget the feelen that come over the room when he said them two words: Mister Mc-Gregor. The air shivered into a cold jelly; and all of us, me, ma, and pa, sort of froze in it. I remember thinken how much we favored one of them waxwork figures Sis Lou had learnt to make at Doctor Price's Female Academy. There I was, a little shaver of eight, standen by the window a-blowen my breath on it so's I could draw my name, like chillun'll do when they're kept to the house with a cold. The knock come sudden and sharp, I remember, as I was crossen a T. My heart flopped down in my belly and commenced to flutter around in my breakfast; then popped up to my ears and drawed all the blood out'n my nose except a

894

From The Virginia Quarterly Review, *Summer, 1935. Used by permission of the author.*

little sack that got left in the point to swell and tingle. It's a singular thing, but the first time that nigger's fist hit the door I knowed it was the knock of death. I can smell death. It's a gift, I reckon, one of them no-count gifts like good conversation that don't do you no good no more. Once Cousin John Mebane come to see us, and as he leaned over to pat me on the head—he was polite and hog-friendly to everybody, chillun and poverty-wropped kin especial—I said, Cousin John, what makes you smell so funny? Ma all but took the hide off'n me; but four days later they was dressen him in his shroud. Then I didn't know what it was I'd smelled, but by this time I'd got better acquainted with the meanen.

Ma was rollen tapers for the mantel. She stiffened a spell like she was listenen for the North wind to rise; rolled out a taper and laid it down. She went to the door and put her hand square on the knob; hesitated like she knew what was comen; then opened it. There stood Rhears. He was the coachman. Him and his wife Della was ma's pets. The both of'm was give to ma by her pa at the marryen; and in a way that folks don't understand no more, they somehow become a part of her. Ma liked horses that wanted to run away all the time, and Rhears was the only nigger on the place that could manage'm. He was a powerful, dangerous feller. He'd killed the blacksmith and two free niggers in the other county before ma brought him to Long Gourd. His shoulders jest but stretched across the openen, as he stood there in a respectful-arrogant sort of way with a basket-knife in his hand.

"What do you want, Rhears?" his mistress asked.

"I want to speak to Mister McGregor," he said.

Pa had been scratchen away at his secretary. At "Mister" the scratchen stopped. That last scratch made more noise in my ears than the guns at Shiloh. Without a word, without even looken behind him, pa stood up and reached for his gun. The secretary was close to the fireplace and had a mirror over it. He didn't waste no time, but he didn't hurry none either. He just got up, took off his specs, and laid them as careful on the secretary, just like he meant to set'm in one special place and no other place would do. He reached for the gun and turned.

Rhears warn't no common field hand. He was proud, black like the satin in widow-women's shirt-waists, and spoiled. And his feelens was bad hurt. The day before, pa had whupped Della, and Rhears had had all night to fret and sull over it and think about what was be-en said in the quarters and how glad the field hands was she'd been whupped. He didn't mean to run away from his home like any blue-gum nigger. He jest come a-marchen straight to the house to settle with pa before them hot night thoughts had had time to git cooled down by the frost.

Pa turned and walked towards him. He still moved as steady and solemn. I watched the even distance each boot-heel made and calculated that two more steps would put him up to the threshold. Just to look at him you might have thought he was a-goen towards the courthouse to pay his taxes or walken down the aisle to his pew. All of a sudden he come to a stop. Ma's brown silk skirt had spread out before him. I looked up. There she was, one hand tight around the gun stock, the othern around the barrel. Her left little finger, plunged like a hornet's needle where the skin drew tight over pa's knuckles, made the blood drop on the bristly hairs along his hand; hang there; then spring to the floor. She held there the time it took three drops to bounce down and splatter. That blood put a spell on me.

A gold shiver along ma's dress made me look quick at their faces. Her hair was a shade darker than the dress she was wearen and slicked down around her ears. There wasn't no direct sun on it, but a light sorghum color slipped up and down as if it was playen on grease. The light might have come from her eyes, for they was afire. She was always fine to look at, although her face wasn't soft enough to rightly claim her beautiful. But she would have taken the breeches away from any ordinary man, I tell you. She'd rather manage folks than eat. Pa ought to have let her do a sight more of it than he did. She was happier than I ever seen her the time he went to the legislature. But he didn't take to politics somehow. He said the government rooms smelled too strong of tobacco. He was a mighty clean man, the cleanest I ever come across. Took a washen once a day reg'lar. When I come to think about ma, I see her a-studyen about somethen, with a wrinkle in her eyes. She didn't have to tell the servants not to bother her then. They stayed out of her way or went tippen around if their work took'm near her.

Well, pa saw he couldn't get his gun out of her grip without acting ungentlemanly. He gave her a curious look and a low bow; then turned it loose. Taken off his coat and folden it, he laid it across a chair. Ma was marbly-pale when she stepped out of the way, but she moved easy and steady.

For a long time I never could make out the meanen of them looks, nor why ma done what she done. And she never set us right about it. She wasn't the explainen kind, and you can bet nobody never asked. I'd just as soon've asked the devil to pop his tail. It's bothered me a heap in my time, more'n it's had any right to. I reckon it's because I always think about it when I'm taperen off. That's a time when a man gits melancholy and thinks about how he come not to be president and sich-like concerns. Well, sir, when I'd run through all my mistakes and seen where if I'd a-done this instead of that how much better off I'd be today, and cuss myself for drinken up my kidneys, I'd always end up by asken myself why that woman acted like that. I've knowed a sight of women in my day, knowed'm as the Bible saints knowed'm, as well as in a social and business way; and I'm here to say, sir, they are stuffed with dynamite, the puniest of'm.

It was a question of authority, and a time when whuppen was out of the argyment. All you had to do was look at Rhears and that basket-knife sharpened thin like a dagger, a-hangen as innocent agen his pant leg, to see he didn't mean to take no whuppen. He must have felt in his Afrykin way that pa had betrayed him. Folks jest didn't whup their house servants, and Rhears was a-meanen to teach pa his manners. Niggers can think straight up to a certain point, and beyond that the steadiest of'm let their senses fly like buckshot, high to scatter. It never struck him that Della needed her whuppen. No, sir, he was jest a-standen in the door tellen pa he warn't his marster.

896 Now ma might have thought that pa ought, with his proper strength, to show him who his marster was. There ain't no doubt but what he had to show it in some way, or he might as well have sold all his niggers for any work he could a got out'n them. Still it was a powerful big risk to run. And it was plain she was a-meanen for him to run it.

Anyway, that was the construction the kin put on it, and it was natural they would. But it never satisfied me. I got it in my head that Rhears warn't the only person on Long Gourd who didn't claim pa his marster. Before I tell you what I mean, give me a little taste of that shuck juice—half a glass'll do, jest enough to settle the dust in my belly. I'm about to choke to death with the drought.

Aah . . . that's sweet to the taste. Now, sir. You'll excuse me if I lean over and whisper this. *That other body was ma.* I know it ain't a-goen to sound right, for she and pa had the name of be-en a mighty loven couple. But a man and woman can fight and still love. Most of'm enjoy fighten. I ain't never seen one get wore out with it. They can go on with a fight for years. Can git fat on it. When they win out, they put the man down amongst the chillun and give him a whuppen when he forgits his manners or sasses back. But if he's stout enough to put her and keep her in her place, she don't hold it agin him. She's proud to think she picked such a game one. That's how come I never married. I'm peaceful by nature. Ain't but one thing ever gits me fighten mad: that's putten salt in my whisky. That riles me. I'll fight a elyplant then.

Well, sir, that morning Della was late. Ma had had to send for her twice, and she come in looken like the hornets stung her. She fluffed down to her sewen and went to work in a sullen way, her lip stuck out so far it looked swole. And they ain't nothen meaner-looken than a blue-black, shiney lip of a sullen nigger woman. It looks like a devil's pillow.

Directly ma said, "Della, take out that seam and do it over again."

"Take it out yourself, if it don't suit," she flounced back.

In a second pa was on his feet: "Woman, lay down that sewen and come with me."

Them was his words; and if a nigger can git pale, Della done it. She seen right away what a mistake she'd made. She fell on the floor and commenced to grab at ma's skirts. "Don't let him whup me, Mistiss. Don't let him." For a while ma didn't say a word.

"Get up off that floor and come with me," said pa again.

"Mister McGregor, what are you going to do with this girl?"

Pa never made her no answer. He walked over and lifted Della up by the arm.

"Don't you tech me: you don't dare tech me. I belongs to Mistiss."

Pa shuck her till her teeth rattled; then she stopped her jumpen and goen on and stood there a-tremblen like a scared horse.

"Mister McGregor," come ma's even tones, "you're not going to punish that girl. She's mine."

And with that pa turned and said in a hard, polite way he never used before to ma: "And so are you mine, my dear." Then he nodded to Della to go before him, and she went.

When he came back, ma was standen in the middle of the floor just where he had left her. She hadn't moved a peg. She just stood there, stiff as a poker, her head thrown up and her eyes as wide as a hawk's.

"I have whipped Della and sent her to the field for six months. If at the end of that time she has learned not to forget her manners, she may take up again her duties here. In the meantime, so you will not want, I've sent for P'niny. If you find her too old or in any way unsuitable, you may take your choice of the young girls."

897

He waited a breath for her answer and when it didn't come, got on his horse and went runnen over the back road down to the fields. No other words passed between them that day. At supper the meal went off in quick order. There wasn't no good old-fashioned table talk. Everybody was as polite to one another as if they was visiten. Ma sat at the foot, froze to her chair. Pa at the head like a judge expecten shooten in the court. We knew somethen was bound to blow up and bust; and I do believe if somebody had tromped on a hog bladder, we chillun'd a jumped under the table.

Next mornen it come. That bow of pa's, as he let go of the gun, was his answer to the challenge. For you might almost say pa had whupped ma by proxy. And here was Rhears, agen by proxy, to make him answer for it . . . a nigger and a slave, his mistress's gallant, a-callen her husband and his marster to account for her. I don't reckon they'd been any such mixed-up arrangement as that before that time; and I know they ain't since.

I scrouched back in the corner and watched, so scared my eyes turned loose in their sockets. If Jesus Christ had a touched me on the shoulder and said, "Come on, little boy, and git your harp," I'd a no more looked at him than if he'd a been my dog come to lick me. For pa and Rhears was a-eyen one another. This fight was to be accorden to no rules. I saw straight off it would start fist and skull and work into a stomp and gouge. If pa didn't manage to git that knife away from the nigger, it would be cut and grunt as well.

Pa was the slimberer of the two, but he wouldn't a looked it away from Rhears. From necked heel up he was six feet—no, six feet four—and his boots raised him an ench higher. Right away he took a quick easy step forward, and both of'm tied their muscles together. Rhears tightened his fingers around the knife. I looked at pa's breeches. They fit him tight; and the meat rolled up, snapped, then quivered under the cloth. His butt give in at the sides and squeezed away its sitten-down softness. His waist drawed in and pumped the wind into his chest, a-pushen out his shoulders just as easy and slow. I don't believe you could have found a man in the whole cotton country hung together any purtier.

Pa, quick-like, sunk his hand in and around the black flesh of Rhears' neck. The knife swung backwards, but pa grabbed it with his left hand before it could do its damage. A breath, and Rhears was a-spinnen round the room. The basket-knife lay in the door as still as any of the pine floor boards. This rattled the nigger some. He had figured on gitten Mister McGregor in the door, where he could a used the knife to advantage. Fighten in his mistress's room, a place he didn't feel at home in, rattled him some more. So before he could come to himself good, pa lambed a blow into his black jaw. It was a blow fit to down a mule, but Rhears shook his head and run in to close; changed quick; dropped low and butted. Four quick butts jambed pa agen the wall, where he saved his guts by grabben Rhears' shoulders—to hold. That kinky hunk of iron slowed down. Both men shook under the strain. The noise of destruction held up. All you could hear was a heavy-pumpen blowen, like to wind-broke horses drawen a killen load . . . then a rippen cry from Rhears' coat—and it was good broadcloth— as it split both ways from the small of his back. Both men drawed in their breaths for a long second.

Sudden-like pa's head and chest went down and forward. His feet pressed agen the wall. Slow as candy pullen he broke the nigger's holt on the front

898

muscles of his thighs. But that nigger's grip never give. No, sir. What give was two drippen hunks of leg meat. Just the second that holt was broke pa shifted neat and shoved hard. Rhears smashed a sewen table top into kindlen wood before he hit the wall. That table saved his neck, or I'm as good a man as I used to be. Before he could get his bearens, pa was a-pounden his head into the hard pine floor. I looked for the brains to go a-splatteren any time, and I begun to wonder how far they would slide on the floor's smooth polish. But God never made but one thing tougher'n a nigger's head—and that's ironwood. Slowly Rhears raised up and, with a beautiful strain of muscles, got to his feet. Then him and pa went round the room. It looked like that bangen had set the nigger crazy. A stranger comen into the room would a thought he was set on breaken up ever stick of furniture, a-usen pa for his mallet. Once the two of'm come close to ma, so close the wind they made blowed her skirts; but never a peg did she move. She held as rigid as a conjure woman.

Directly the nigger begun to wear some. All that crazy spurt of energy hadn't done him no good. Gradually pa's feet touched the floor more and more; then they didn't leave it. The panten got heavier, more like bellows. A chair got in their way. They went over it. They did a sight of rollen—up to the door crowded with house servants, all a-looken like they had fell in the ash-hopper. You could follow how far they'd rolled by the sweat on the floor. It looked like a wet mop had been run by a triflen hand. Then, sir, my hairs straightened up and drawed in to hide under the scalp. Rhears had ended up on top and was a-shiften to gouge. Pa looked all wore down. I tried to holler to ma to shoot, but my throat was as parched as it is right this minute. . . . Thank you, sir. You are very generous.

Have you ever seen a long dead limb stretched between sky and droppen sun? Well, that's how still ma held on to that gun of pa's. I couldn't stand to see them black thumbs go down. As I turned my head, I heard the nigger holler. Pa had jerked up his knee and hit him in a tender spot. He fell back and grabbed himself. It must have been an accident, for pa made no move to take advantage of the break. He just lay there and let Rhears take hold of himself and git at pa's throat. I never seen such guts in nobody, nigger or white man. Bump went pa's head on the floor. Bump and agen. Ever time he lifted pa, he squeezed tighter. Ever time he come down he pushed him forward.

It had been one of them frosty December mornens, and a fire had been burnen in the chimney since first light. The front stick had been burned in two and left between it and the back stick a heap of red and blue hickory coals. They don't make no hotter fire than that. I saw right away what Rhears had in mind. Every time he bumped my father's head against the floor, he was that much nearer the hearth. Pa wriggled and jerked, but his wind was cut and the black blood ran into his eyes. Those heavy black hands growed deep in the red, greasy flesh of pa's neck.

They moved slower towards the fire, for pa had at last clamped his legs in a way to slow'm down. Then I saw him reach for his pocket. Rhears didn't see this move. His eyes was bucked on what they had in mind to do, and the heat from the hickory logs made'm swell with a dark, dry look of battle luck. After some fumblen pa finally brought out his knife. He opened it in a feeble way over the nigger's back, and let it rip and tear through his ribs. The blood first oozed;

899

then spouted. It fell back from the knife like dirt from a turnen plow. Then pa made a jab back of the kidneys. That done for him. He grunted, turned loose and rolled over like a hunk of meat.

Staggering to his feet, pa went over and leaned agen the mantel. Directly Rhears spoke up, so low you could hardly hear him:

"Marster, if you hadn't got me, I'd a got you."

Then he shook with a chill, straightened out, and rolled back his eyes. Mister McGregor looked at him a minute before he turned to his wife. And then no words passed his mouth. He reached out his hand and she walked over and handed him the gun. He reached over the mantel and, his arms a tremblen, set the gun back in its rack.

"Bring me a pan of warm water, the turpentine, and the things out of my medicine chest." That was ma speaken, sharp and peremptory, to the servants in the doorway. "And take this body out of here," she added in a tone she used when the girl Sally failed to dust behind the furniture.

"Sit down in that chair, Mister McGregor, so I can dress your wounds."

Pa done what she told him. She worked away at him with deft, quick fingers. Directly I hears her in a off-hand way, her head benden over and her hands busy wrappen:

"Colonel Winston will be through here on the way South. I think it would be best to sell him Della."

"I think that, my dear," said pa, "would be the most sensible thing to do." (*1935*)

Jericho, Jericho, Jericho

She opened her eyes. She must have been asleep for hours or months. She could not reckon; she could only feel the steady silence of time. She had been Joshua and made it swing suspended in her room. Forever she had floated above the counterpane; between the tester and the counterpane she had floated until her hand, long and bony, its speckled-dried skin drawing away from the bulging blue veins, had reached and drawn her body under the covers. And now she was resting, clear-headed and quiet, her thoughts clicking like a new-greased mower. All creation could not make her lift her thumb or cross it over her finger. She looked at the bed, the bed her mother had died in, the bed her children had been born in, her marriage bed, the bed the General had drenched with his blood. Here it stood where it had stood for seventy years, square and firm on the floor, wide enough for three people to lie comfortable in, if they didn't sleep restless; but not wide enough for her nor long enough when her conscience scorched the cool wrinkles in the sheets. The two foot posts, octagonal-shaped and mounted by carved pieces that looked like absurd flowers, stood up to comfort her when the world began to crumble. Her eyes followed down the posts and along the basket-quilt. She had made it before her marriage to the General, only he wasn't a general then. He was a slight, tall young man with a rolling mustache and perfume in his hair. A many a time she had seen her young love's locks dripping

From The Southern Review, *Spring, 1936. Used by permission of the author.*

with scented oil, down upon his collar. . . . She had cut the squares for the baskets in January, and for stuffing had used the letters of old lovers, fragments of passion cut to warm her of a winter's night. The General would have his fun. *Miss Kate, I didn't sleep well last night. I heard Sam Buchanan make love to you out of that farthest basket. If I hear him again, I mean to toss this piece of quilt in the fire.* Then he would chuckle in his round, soft voice; reach under the covers and pull her over to his side of the bed. On a cold and frosting night he would sleep with his nose against her neck. His nose was so quick to turn cold, he said, and her neck was so warm. Sometimes her hair, the loose, unruly strands at the nape, would tickle his nostrils and he would wake up with a sneeze. This had been so long ago, and there had been so many years of trouble and worry. Her eyes, as apart from her as the mirror on the bureau, rested upon the half-tester, upon the enormous button that caught the rose-colored canopy and shot its folds out like the rays of the morning sun. She could not see but she could feel the heavy cluster of mahogany grapes that tumbled from the center of the headboard—out of its vines curling down the sides it tumbled. How much longer would these never-picked grapes hang above her head? How much longer would she, rather, hang to the vine of this world, she who lay beneath as dry as any raisin. Then she remembered. She looked at the blinds. They were closed.

"You, Ants, where's my stick? I'm a great mind to break it over your trifling back."

"Awake? What a nice long nap you've had," said Doctor Ed.

"The boy? Where's my grandson? Has he come?"

"I'll say he's come. What do you mean taking to your bed like this? Do you realize, beautiful lady, that this is the first time I ever saw you in bed in my whole life? I believe you've taken to bed on purpose. I don't believe you want to see me."

"Go long, boy, with your foolishness."

That's all she could say, and she blushed as she said it—she blushing at the words of a snip of a boy, whom she had diapered a hundred times and had washed as he stood before the fire in the round tin tub, his little back swayed and his little belly sticking out in front, rosy from the scrubbing he had gotten. *Mammy, what for I've got a hole in my stummick; what for, Mammy?* Now he was sitting on the edge of the bed calling her beautiful lady, an old hag like her, beautiful lady. A good-looker the girls would call him, with his bold, careless face and his hands with their fine, long fingers. Soft, how soft they were, running over her rough, skinny bones. He looked a little like his grandpa, but somehow there was something missing . . .

"Well, boy, it took you a time to come home to see me die."

"Nonsense. Cousin Edwin, I wouldn't wait on a woman who had so little faith in my healing powers."

"There an't nothing strange about dying. But I an't in such an all-fired hurry. I've got a heap to tell you about before I go."

The boy leaned over and touched her gently. "Not even death would dispute you here, on Long Gourd, Mammy."

He was trying to put her at her ease in his carefree way. It was so obvious a pretending, but she loved him for it. There was something nice in its awkwardness, the charm of the young's blundering and of their efforts to get along in the

901

world. Their pretty arrogance, their patronizing airs, their colossal unknowing of what was to come. It was a quenching drink to a sin-thirsty old woman. Somehow his vitality had got crossed in her blood and made a dry heart leap, her blood that was almost water. Soon now she would be all water, water and dust, lying in the burying ground between the cedar—and fire. She could smell her soul burning and see it. What a fire it would make below, dripping with sin, like a rag soaked in kerosene. But she had known what she was doing. And here was Long Gourd, all its fields intact, ready to be handed on, in better shape than when she took it over. Yes, she had known what she was doing. How long, she wondered, would his spirit hold up under the trials of planting, of cultivating, and of the gathering time, year in and year out—how would he hold up before so many springs and so many autumns. The thought of him giving orders, riding over the place, or rocking on the piazza, and a great pain would pin her heart to her backbone. She wanted him by her to train—there was so much for him to know: how the south field was cold and must be planted late, and where the orchards would best hold their fruit, and where the frosts crept soonest—that now could never be. She turned her head—who was that woman, that strange woman standing by the bed as if she owned it, as if . . .

"This is Eva, Mammy."

"Eva?"

"We are going to be married."

"I wanted to come and see—to meet Dick's grandmother . . ."

I wanted to come see her die. That's what she meant. Why didn't she finish and say it out. She had come to lick her chops and see what she would enjoy. That's what she had come for, the lying little slut. The richest acres in Long Gourd valley, so rich hit'd make yer feet greasy to walk over'm, Saul Oberly at the first tollgate had told the peddler once, and the peddler had told it to her, knowing it would please and make her trade. *Before you die.* Well, why didn't you finish it out? You might as well. You've given yourself away.

Her fierce thoughts dried up the water in her eyes, tired and resting far back in their sockets. They burned like a smothered fire stirred up by the wind as they traveled over the woman who would lie in her bed, eat with her silver, and caress her flesh and blood. The woman's body was soft enough to melt and pour about him. She could see that; and her firm, round breasts, too firm and round for any good to come from them. And her lips, full and red, her eyes bright and cunning. The heavy hair crawled about her head to tangle the poor, foolish boy in its ropes. She might have known he would do something foolish like this. He had a foolish mother. There warn't any way to avoid it. But look at her belly, small and no-count. There wasn't a muscle the size of a worm as she could see. And those hips—

And then she heard her voice: "What did you say her name was, Son? Eva? Eva Callahan, I'm glad to meet you, Eva. Where'd your folks come from, Eva? I knew some Callahans who lived in the Goosepad settlement. They couldn't be any of your kin, could they?"

"Oh, no, indeed. My people . . ."

"Right clever people they were. And good farmers, too. Worked hard. Honest —that is, most of 'em. As honest as that run of people go. We always gave them a good name."

902

"My father and mother live in Birmingham. Have always lived there."

"Birmingham," she heard herself say with contempt. They could have lived there all their lives and still come from somewhere. I've got a mule older'n Birmingham. "What's your pa's name?"

"Her father is Mister E. L. Callahan, Mammy."

"First name not Elijah by any chance? Lige they called him."

"No. Elmore, Mammy."

"Old Mason Callahan had a son they called Lige. Somebody told me he moved to Elyton. So you think you're going to live with the boy here."

"We're to be married . . . that is, if Eva doesn't change her mind."

And she saw his arm slip possessively about the woman's waist. "Well, take care of him, young woman, or I'll come back and han't you. I'll come back and claw your eyes out."

"I'll take very good care of him, Mrs. McCowan."

"I can see that." She could hear the threat in her voice, and Eva heard it.

"Young man," spoke up Doctor Edwin, "you should feel powerful set up, two such women pestering each other about you."

The boy kept an embarrassed silence.

"All of you get out now. I want to talk to him by himself. I've got a lot to say and precious little time to say it in. And he's mighty young and helpless and ignorant."

"Why, Mammy, you forget I'm a man now. Twenty-six. All teeth cut. Long trousers."

"It takes a heap more than pants to make a man. Throw open them blinds, Ants."

"Yes'm."

"You don't have to close the door so all-fired soft. Close it naturally. And you can tip about all you want to—later. I won't be hurried to the burying ground. And keep your head away from that door. What I've got to say to your new master is private."

"Listen at you, Mistiss."

"You listen to me. That's all. No, wait. I had something else on my mind— what is it? Yes. How many hens has Melissy set? You don't know. Find out. A few of the old hens ought to be setting. Tell her to be careful to turn the turkey eggs every day. No, you bring them and set them under my bed. I'll make sure. We got a mighty pore hatch last year. You may go now. I'm plumb worn out, boy, worn out thinking for these people. It's that that worries a body down. But you'll know all about it in good time. Stand out there and let me look at you good. You don't let me see enough of you, and I almost forget how you look. Not really, you understand. Just a little. It's your own fault. I've got so much to trouble me that you, when you're not here, naturally slip back in my mind. But that's all over now. You are here to stay, and I'm here to go. There will always be Long Gourd, and there must always be a McCowan on it. I had hoped to have you by me for several years, but you would have your fling in town. I thought it best to clear your blood of it, but as God is hard, I can't see what you find to do in town. And now you've gone and gotten you a woman. Well, they all have to do it. But do you reckon you've picked the right one—you must forgive the frankness of an old lady who can see the bottom of her grave—I

903

had in mind one of the Carlisle girls. The Carlisle place lies so handy to Long Gourd and would give me a landing on the river. Have you seen Anna Belle since she's grown to be a woman? I'm told there's not a better housekeeper in the valley."

"I'm sure Anna Belle is a fine girl. But Mammy, I love Eva."

"She'll wrinkle up on you, Son; and the only wrinkles land gets can be smoothed out by the harrow. And she looks sort of puny to me, Son. She's powerful small in the waist and walks about like she had worms."

"Gee, Mammy you're not jealous are you? That waist is in style."

"You want to look for the right kind of style in a woman. Old Mrs. Penter Matchem had two daughters with just such waists, but 'twarnt natural. She would tie their corset strings to the bed posts and whip'm out with a buggy whip. The poor girls never drew a hearty breath. Just to please that old woman's vanity. She got paid in kind. It did something to Eliza's bowels and she died before she was twenty. The other one never had any children. She used to whip'm out until they cried. I never liked that woman. She thought a whip could do anything."

"Well, anyway, Eva's small waist wasn't made by any corset strings. She doesn't wear any."

"How do you know, sir?"

"Well . . . I . . . What a question for a respectable woman to ask."

"I'm not a respectable woman. No woman can be respectable and run four thousand acres of land. Well, you'll have it your own way. I suppose the safest place for a man to take his folly is to bed."

"Mammy!"

"You must be lenient with your Cousin George. He wanders about night times talking about the War. I put him off in the west wing where he won't keep people awake, but sometimes he gets in the yard and gives orders to his troops. 'I will sweep that hill, General'—and many's the time he's done it when the battle was doubtful—'I'll sweep it with my iron brooms'; then he shouts out his orders, and pretty soon the dogs commence to barking. But he's been a heap of company for me. You must see that your wife humors him. It won't be for long. He's mighty feeble."

"Eva's not my wife yet, Mammy."

"You won't be free much longer—the way she looks at you, like a hungry hound."

"I was just wondering," he said hurriedly. "I hate to talk about anything like this . . ."

"Everybody has a time to die, and I'll have no maudlin nonsense about mine."

"I was wondering about Cousin George . . . if I could get somebody to keep him. You see, it will be difficult in the winters. Eva will want to spend the winters in town. . . ."

He paused, startled, before the great bulk of his grandmother rising from her pillows, and in the silence that frightened the air, his unfinished words hung suspended about them.

After a moment he asked if he should call the doctor.

It was some time before she could find words to speak.

"Get out of the room."

904

"Forgive me, Mammy. You must be tired."

"I'll send for you," sounded the dead voice in the still room, "when I want to see you again. I'll send for you and—the woman."

She watched the door close quietly on his neat square back. Her head whirled and turned like a flying jennet. She lowered and steadied it on the pillows. Four thousand acres of the richest land in the valley he would sell and squander on that slut, and he didn't even know it and there was no way to warn him. This terrifying thought rushed through her mind, and she felt the bed shake with her pain, while before the footboard the spectre of an old sin rose up to mock her. How she had struggled to get this land and keep it together—through the War, the Reconstruction, and the pleasanter after days. For eighty-seven years she had suffered and slept and planned and rested and had pleasure in this valley, seventy of it, almost a turning century, on this place; and now that she must leave it . . .

The things she had done to keep it together. No. The one thing. . . . From the dusty stacks the musty odor drifted through the room, met the tobacco smoke over the long table piled high with records, reports. Iva Louise stood at one end, her hat clinging perilously to the heavy auburn hair, the hard blue eyes and the voice:

"You promised Pa to look after me"—she had waited for the voice to break and scream—"and you have stolen my land!"

"Now, Miss Iva Louise," the lawyer dropped his empty eyes along the floor, "you don't mean . . ."

"Yes, I do mean it."

Her own voice had restored calm to the room: "I promised your pa his land would not be squandered."

"My husband won't squander my property. You just want it for yourself."

She cut through the scream with the sharp edge of her scorn: "What about that weakling's farm in Madison? Who pays the taxes now?"

The girl had no answer to that. Desperate, she faced the lawyer: "Is there no way, sir, I can get my land from the clutches of this unnatural woman?"

The man coughed; the red rim of his eyes watered with embarrassment: "I'm afraid," he cleared his throat, "you say you can't raise the money. . . . I'm afraid—"

That trapped look as the girl turned away. It had come back to her, now trapped in her bed. As a swoon spreads, she felt the desperate terror of weakness, more desperate where there has been strength. Did the girl see right? Had she stolen the land because she wanted it?

Suddenly, like the popping of a thread in a loom, the struggles of the flesh stopped, and the years backed up and covered her thoughts like the spring freshet she had seen so many times creep over the dark soil. Not in order, but as if they were stragglers trying to catch up, the events of her life passed before her sight that had never been so clear. Sweeping over the mounds of her body rising beneath the quilts came the old familiar odors—the damp, strong, penetrating smell of new-turned ground; the rank, clinging, resistless odor of green-picked feathers stuffed in a pillow by Guinea Nell, thirty-odd years ago; tobacco on the mantel, clean and sharp like smelling salts; her father's sweat, sweet like stale oil; the powerful ammonia of manure turned over in a stall; curing hay in the wind;

905

the polecat's stink on the night air, almost pleasant, a sort of commingled scent of all the animals, man and beast; the dry smell of dust under a rug; the over-strong scent of too-sweet fruit trees blooming; the inhospitable wet ashes of a dead fire in a poor white's cabin; black Rebeccah in the kitchen; a wet hound steaming before a fire. There were other odors she could not identify, over-whelming her, making her weak, taking her body and drawing out of it a choking longing to hover over all that she must leave, the animals, the fences, the crops growing in the fields, the houses, the people in them. . . .

It was early summer, and she was standing in the garden after dark—she had heard something after the small chickens. Mercy and Yellow Jane passed beyond the paling fence. Dark shadows—gay, full voices. *Where you gwine, gal? I dunno. Jest a-gwine. Where you? To the frolic, do I live. Well, stay off'n yoe back to-night.* Then out of the rich, gushing laughter: *All right, you stay off'n yourn. I done caught de stumbles.* More laughter.

The face of Uncle Ike, head man in slavery days, rose up. A tall Senagalese, he was standing in the crib of the barn unmoved before the bush-whackers. *Nigger, whar is that gold hid? You better tell us, nigger. Down in the well; in the far-place. By God, you black son of a bitch, we'll roast ye alive if you air too contrary to tell. Now, listen ole nigger, Miss McCowan ain't nothen to you no more. You been set free. We'll give ye some of it, a whole sack. Come on, now—* out of the dribbling, leering mouth—*whar air it?* Ike's tall form loomed towards the shadows. In the lamp flame his forehead shone like the point, the core of night. He stood there with no word for answer. As she saw the few white beads of sweat on his forehead, she spoke.

She heard her voice reach through the dark—*I know your kind. In better days you'd slip around and set people's barns afire. You shirked the War to live off the old and weak. You don't spare me because I'm a woman. You'd shoot a woman quicker because she has the name of being frail. Well, I'm not frail, and my Navy Six an't frail. Ike, take their guns.* Ike moved and one of them raised his pistol arm. He dropped it, and the acrid smoke stung her nostrils. *Now, Ike, get the rest of their weapons. Their knives, too. One of us might turn our backs.*

On top of the shot she heard the soft pat of her servants' feet. White eyeballs shining through the cracks in the barn. Then: *Caesar, Al, Zebedee, step in here and lend a hand to Ike.* By sun the people had gathered in the yard. Uneasy, silent, they watched her on the porch. She gave the word, and the whips cracked. The mules strained, trotted off, skittish and afraid, dragging the white naked bodies bouncing and cursing over the sod: *Turn us loose. We'll not bother ye no more, lady. You ain't no woman, you're a devil.* She turned and went into the house. It is strange how a woman gets hard when trouble comes a-gobbling after her people.

Worn from memory, she closed her eyes to stop the whirl, but closing her eyes did no good. She released the lids and did not resist. Brother Jack stood before her, handsome and shy, but ruined from his cradle by a cleft palate, until he came to live only in the fire of spirits. And she understood, so clear was life, down to the smallest things. She had often heard tell of this clarity that took a body whose time was spending on the earth. Poor Brother Jack, the gentlest of men, but because of his mark, made the butt and wit of the valley. She saw him leave for school, where he was sent to separate him from his drinking com-

906

panions, to a church school where the boys buried their liquor in the ground and sipped it up through straws. His letters: *Dear Ma, quit offering so much advice and send me more money. You send barely enough to keep me from stealing.* His buggy wheels scraping the gravel, driving up as the first roosters crowed. *Katharine, Malcolm, I thought you might want to have a little conversation.* Conversation two hours before sun! And down she would come and let him in, and the General would get up, stir up the fire, and they would sit down and smoke. Jack would drink and sing, *If the Little Brown Jug was mine, I'd be drunk all the time and I'd never be sob-er a-gin*—or, *Hog drovers, hog drovers, hog drovers we air, a-courting your darter so sweet and so fair.* They would sit and smoke and drink until she got up to ring the bell.

He stayed as long as the whiskey held out, growing more violent towards the end. She watered his bottles; begged whiskey to make camphor—*Gre't God, Sis Kate, do you sell camphor? I gave you a pint this morning.* Poor Brother Jack, killed in Breckinridge's charge at Murfreesboro, cut in two by a chain shot from an enemy gun. All night long she had sat up after the message came. His body scattered about a splintered black gum tree. She had seen that night, as if she had been on the field, the parties moving over the dark field hunting the wounded and dead. Clyde Bascom had fallen near Jack with a bad hurt. They were messmates. He had to tell somebody; and somehow she was the one he must talk to. The spectral lanterns, swinging towards the dirge of pain and the monotonous cries of *Water,* caught by the river dew on the before-morning air and held suspended over the field in its acrid quilt. There death dripped to mildew the noisy throats . . . and all the white relief parties, moving, blots of night, sullenly moving in the viscous blackness.

Her eyes widened, and she looked across the foot posts into the room. There was some mistake, some cruel blunder; for there now, tipping about the carpet, hunting in her wardrobe, under the bed, blowing down the fire to its ashes until they glowed in their dryness, stalked the burial parties. They stepped out of the ashes in twos and threes, hunting, hunting and shaking their heads. Whom were they searching for? Jack had long been buried. They moved more rapidly; looked angry. They crowded the room until she gasped for breath. One, gaunt and haggard, jumped on the foot of her bed; rose to the ceiling; gesticulated; argued in animated silence. He leaned forward; pressed his hand upon her leg. She tried to tell him to take it off. Cold and crushing heavy, it pressed her down to the bowels of the earth. Her lips trembled, but no sound came forth. Now the hand moved up to her stomach; and the haggard eyes looked gravely at her, alert, as if they were waiting for something. Her head turned giddy. She called to Dick, to Ants, to Doctor Ed; but the words struck her teeth and fell back in her throat. She concentrated on lifting the words, and the burial parties sadly shook their heads. Always the cries struck her teeth and fell back down. She strained to hear the silence they made. At last from a great distance she thought she heard . . . *too late . . . too late.* How exquisite the sound, like a bell swinging without ringing. Suddenly it came to her. She was dying.

907

How slyly death slipped up on a body, like sleep moving over the vague boundary. How many times she had laid awake to trick the unconscious there. At last she would know . . . But she wasn't ready. She must first do something about Long Gourd. That slut must not eat it up. She would give it to the hands first. He must be brought to understand this. But the spectres shook their heads. Well let them shake. She'd be damned if she would go until she was ready to go. She'd be damned all right, and she smiled at the meaning the word took on now. She gathered together all the particles of her will; the spectres faded; and there about her were the anxious faces of kin and servants. Edwin had his hands under the cover feeling her legs. She made to raise her own hand to the boy. It did not go up. Her eyes wanted to roll upward and look behind her forehead, but she pinched them down and looked at her grandson.

"You want to say something, Mammy?"—she saw his lips move.

She had a plenty to say, but her tongue had somehow got glued to her lips. Truly it was now too late. Her will left her. Life withdrawing gathered like a frosty dew on her skin. The last breath blew gently past her nose. The dusty nostrils tingled. She felt a great sneeze coming. There was a roaring; the wind blew through her head once, and a great cotton field bent before it, growing and spreading, the bolls swelling as big as cotton sacks and bursting white as thunderheads. From a distance, out of the far end of the field, under a sky so blue that it was painful-bright, voices came singing, *Joshua fit the battle of Jericho, Jericho, Jericho—Joshua fit the battle of Jericho, and the walls come a-tumbling down.* (1936)

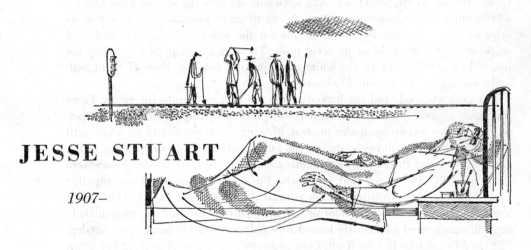

JESSE STUART

1907–

Jesse Hilton Stuart was born on W-Hollow, a farm near Riverton, Kentucky, August 8, 1907, and received his early education in a one-room country schoolhouse. Even as a young boy his main ambition was to become a writer. Stuart worked to put himself through Lincoln Memorial University, where he received a B.A. degree in 1929, and then taught school for a time. He studied one year as a graduate student at Vanderbilt University (1931–1932), but never completed his Master's degree. (The notes for his thesis were destroyed in a dormitory fire and he lacked the money necessary to continue with his work.) While in residence, however, he wrote an autobiography for his senior professor, Dr. Edwin Mims, which he later published as *Beyond Dark Hills* (1938).

Stuart's experience has been varied and strenuous: he has done farm labor, industrial labor, and janitorial work, and has served in the Navy. He is a prolific writer, working successfully in the forms of poetry, the short story, and the novel, and has received many literary awards. He has contributed to numerous magazines and lectured widely in this country.

Stuart's best compositions in both poetry and fiction have retained an autobiographical flavor, though he knows how to make his stories dramatic and exciting. The fundamental honesty of his autobiographical statements should be a first consideration of anyone interested in seriously appraising his vigorous and unmistakable talents. To call him "an American Burns" is to recognize only one aspect of his apparently inexhaustible energies as an author. In addition to his autobiography, Stuart's most rewarding volumes are the following: *Head o' W-Hollow* (short stories, 1936), *Man with a Bull-Tongued Plow* (poems, 1934), *Taps for Private Tussie* (1943), *Tales from the Plum Grove Hills* (short stories, 1946), and *The Thread That Runs So True* (1949).

Uncle Jeff

Pa and Finn and me are on our way to see Uncle Jeff. Uncle Jeff is in a railroad hospital at Ferton, West Virginia, and he is likely to kick the bucket. Don't know though, Pa said Uncle Jeff was tough as an old rooster. But there must be somethin wrong. He sent for Pa. And Pa takes us along, he says, to help him get about in the city and to find the hospital. Pa hates the town, for he can't read and he gets mixed up in signs. Pa never knows where he is goin unless he asks someone and he says he hates to be askin everybody he meets where this is and that is. So Pa up-and-takes us boys. And we are glad to go with him.

"I told Brother Jeff," says Pa, "to quit that damn railroad when they offered him the little pension that time. That would have been better'n stickin it out for a few dollars on the month and endin up in a hospital among strangers where a body don't know a soul."

"What is the matter with Uncle Jeff, Pa," I said, "that he is about to die?"

"He is a broke-down man," said Pa with tears in his eyes. "He is like I am. Look at me—I am a broke-down man. If you follow workin on a section long as your Uncle Jeff, then you would have one foot in the grave and the other ready to slide in too. He's been on that Chatworth section for thirty-three years. Could have been a boss if he had had the education. Can't read. Just like I am. Now you boys see that it pays to take education. I couldn't take it for there was none offered here in these Kentucky hills when I was a boy."

"Wasn't Uncle Jeff in a wreck one foggy mornin on a motor car?" asked Brother Finn.

"Yes," said Pa, "Brother Jeff and eighteen more men were hit by a Big Sandy train. The car was in the fog and the train was in it too and they didn't see each other. Your Uncle Jeff leaped like a frog or he would a been where some of the others are today. Part of the motor car and some of the men flew through the air and lit on them like a bird. Brother Jeff was knocked cold as a icicle. When he

909

woke up they had him in the railroad hospital in Ferton where we are goin now. Brother Jeff has not been well since. He is not able to work. He is like a horse too old to plow but has to pull the plow just the same. I am a horse too broke-down to pull the plow, but I have to pull it just the same."

"We are in Ferton now," says Brother Finn, "we are in West Virginia."

And Pa says: "Yes, West Virginia, look how these damn big-headed people hold their heads up above us. It is not like back over there in Kentucky. I went to work in the mines up in Cattle Branch, West Virginia, when I was sixteen years old and the place where I boarded had so many bedbugs I had to leave. I'd like to tell these people about the bedbugs they got in this State—more than any State in the Union."

Pa asks Finn to read the signs. Brother Finn is younger than I am, but he can read. He has been to school and he can cipher some and read pretty well. He is not like Pa.

But here we go. People do look at us and Pa gets hot behind his collar. Pa is not as big as we are. He walks between us with a big gray overcoat on that strikes him around the ankles. I found the overcoat in an old house and gave it to him. I believe he sorty thinks I stole it. Finn is almost a head above the crowd and my old blue overcoat just strikes him about five inches above the knees. But Finn looked right good in it. I have a new overcoat and I look better than Pa or Brother Finn. Pa's hair is out a little long and it rolls up a little at the edge of his thick felt black cap. I don't have on a hat. Finn has on a gray felt hat. And we walk up the street toward the hospital.

Pa says: "Ferton is a big town. Look at these big houses that cover a square."

Pa likes to see flashin signs. He asks Finn to read them for him. Finn reads the signs for Pa since Finn reads better than I do.

Then Pa says: "It took a lot of money to build that house. It took piles of money—a flour barrel of money. I'd like to see all the money it took in one pile. I'd like to be in it with a coal scoop for five minutes and I'd have all I could shovel. I'd never go back out on that section. Boys, look at these houses, won't you. Damned if they ain't a plum sight."

We do not ride a street car to the hospital. We walk to it to save the money. We will need the money gettin back home and Finn and me have planned somethin for Pa. We are goin to surprise Pa. He has never seen a picture show and we intend to take him to one after we leave the hospital. We are now in sight of the hospital.

Pa says: "Here is the place they had Brother Jeff before. Walk right in, boys— I've been here at this place before."

And we walk in behind Pa. He walks up to a desk where a woman in a white dress is writin somethin on a piece of paper.

Pa says, "Jeff Powderjay in this hospital?"

"Jeff Powderjay? Yes, he is here."

"I want to see him," says Pa.

"He is too bad to let anyone see him," says the woman and she looks mean out of a pair of nose-glasses.

"Beats all," says Pa. "A man comes forty miles and can't see his dyin brother."

"Well, you can't see him," says the woman, "and that's that."

"Well, by God I will see him," says Pa, "or they'll be more patients in this hospital than you already got."

I saw Pa was gettin hot behind the collar and so I whispered to Finn: "Get a hold of Pa before he gets us all into it. You can do more with him than I can."

Finn takes Pa by the arm and says, "Come on, Pa, and let's see the hospital doctor. He'll let us see Uncle Jeff."

Down the corridor we take Pa until we come to a sign that says DOCTOR.

"Here," says Finn. "Wait a minute." And Finn finds him.

"You want to see Jeff Powderjay?" says the doctor. "It is good that you have come to see him. None of his kin have come to see him and he will not get back to Kentucky alive, I am afraid."

"Can we see him?" asks Pa.

"Yes," says the doctor and he leads the way with a bunch of keys in his little soft hand.

"Look at that hand, won't you," says Pa. "What if he worked like I have to, tampin ties and layin tee rails. Makin sod lines and makin right-of-way. He wouldn't have hands like that. Look," and Pa shows us his hands—hands that we have seen and felt so many times before.

"Here we are," says the doctor. "You'll find Jeff Powderjay right in that room." He opens the door and walks away.

Pa goes in first. "Hello, Jeff," he says, "do you know me?"

"Know you?" says Uncle Jeff. "Know you? What do you think I am? I'd know you in hell, Mick. You are boy number eleven, and I am number ten. Ain't that right?"

"Yes," says Pa. "And we are supposed to have the same Mama and Pappie— and I believe we have. Pa was a scoundrel, but Mama was a decent woman."

"Yes," says Uncle Jeff. "And you come up to see me kick the bucket."

"I come to see you," says Pa.

"Well, I am goin to kick the damn bucket this time," says Uncle Jeff.

Finn doesn't say a word. Pa and Uncle Jeff are doin all the talkin. But Uncle Jeff spies Finn.

"Come over here, you little son-of-a-gun," he says. "You look for all the world like your Pap. Come over here and say good-by and old-Satan-bless-you-Uncle Jeff. And you," pointin to me, "come over here, you big son-of-a-gun and say good-by and Satan-bless-you to your Uncle Jeff."

I see it is gettin under Pa's skin. Pa is twistin and squirmin in his chair. Pa doesn't do that unless somethin is gougin at his heart.

Pa says, "Take it easy, Jeff."

And Uncle Jeff says: "Take it easy, hell. It is that big-tailed thing they got waitin on me. She is tryin to kill me too soon. She knows I ain't goin to get out of this hole this time. I got out once before—and I prayed to God to get out. Now I am cussin and prayin for the Devil to get me."

"The Devil?" says Pa.

"Yes, the Devil," says Uncle Jeff. "I want to go somewhere and the Lord won't have me. I've been prayin to die ever since I got broke down in that wreck and God won't take me. I guess the Devil will. I want to go some place."

I wish that Uncle Jeff would let loose of my hand. He is holdin to my hand and

911

talkin to Pa. His hand is soft and warm and wrinkled like a thawed-out black snake. His lips have fallen down at the corners, beard is over his face—a white and red-sandy beard. His eyes are the color of faded slate.

"Give me a chew of red-horse," says Uncle Jeff. "A damn liar, Mick. Doctor says no—but give me a chew of red-horse, and I'll give you a cup of water in hell."

Tears come to Pa's eyes and he says to Finn, "I'll give him a chew even if that doctor throws me out of this hospital."

"That is what I want—it tastes sweet," says Uncle Jeff. "You know I am glad that I have chewed tobacco. It has been enjoyment to me all my life. It is that damn big-tailed nurse. She is tryin to kill me. I want to go back over on the Big Sandy and die there. I want to go back home to die, back where Pap and Ma died. I am goin back too."

"Now lay in the bed, Jeff—you can't get up," Pa is coaxing Uncle Jeff. "Lay still and you'll be able to get home by next week."

"Goddamn you, Mick, don't sit up there and lie to me like that. You ain't foolin nobody, not even yourself. You know more than that, surely. The Devil, the Lord and the ground are goin to get me—maybe one, maybe all three. I hate to leave my little children by my second wife—but goddamn her she is a bitch and I know it, a bitch. That bachelor can run her all he damn pleases. He has run her and I know it—the-son-of-a-bitch."

And I say to my brother Finn while Pa and Uncle Jeff are talkin, "I remember Uncle Jeff before he married his second wife. He was a handsome man then. He was a young man in the bloom of life. He married Aunt Tinnie, as pretty a woman as ever the Kentucky sun shone on. They had three children by that marriage, Daisy, Silva, and Jewel. Then Aunt Tinnie died and lost her fourth baby with her dead body, you understand. Uncle Jeff worked on the section and raised three girls until they married and had homes of their own. He always said he would never bring a stepmother in over his 'three little dears.' He had a time hirin a girl to take care of them and buyin food for them on a section man's wages, but he did. He raised three fine girls too. Then they left him in the old house alone. So he goes and marries this last wife. An old man and a young woman. Results. You see, you know."

"I remember Uncle Jeff givin me candy and showin me how to fight bitin dogs," says Finn. "That was when he used to come and visit us livin on the Collins' place."

And now Pa and Uncle Jeff are talkin louder than ever.

"We had the measles together, Mick," says Uncle Jeff, "and they had us down in the left-hand corner of that big room instead of the back room, I remember. And you looked through a crack in the wall and saw the only turkey Ma had, and you said, 'How about eatin that turkey, Jeff?' And I said, 'W'y that is a go, all you'll have to do is say the word to Ma.' And you said the word to Ma. She killed that turkey for us. I'll never forget it. You got anything you wanted because you was her baby—you was child number eleven."

"That is right," says Pa. "After Ma died the girls found some cake she had put away for me. I was her baby."

"The nurse is comin," says Finn.

"Keep that goddamn big-tailed thing out of this room," says Uncle Jeff. "Keep her out, Mick."

"Time to take your medicine. Time the visitors should leave, too," says the nurse.

"Time for you to get out of here and stay out of here," says Uncle Jeff.

"He is out of his head," says Pa.

"You are a goddamn liar, Mick, and you know you are," says Uncle Jeff. "I am just not goin to get out of here alive and I want to get out of here alive and die back over on Big Sandy. And I don't like a goddamn gown to sleep in. Look at this—looks like a mother-hubbard on me. And I don't want that damn medicine.

"I've done that all my life," says Uncle Jeff. "I've took my medicine—thirty-three years of it on a section and the last part of it with a crooked woman. I've had all the damn medicine I want. I'd sooner be in hell. It doesn't matter a damn to me. I ain't been such a mean man. I'm not such a good one. I've always had trouble gettin right and wrong straightened out."

"You are goin to take your medicine?" asks the nurse.

"No, by God."

"Die then."

"That's what I am goin to do and you are goin to do."

But the doctor comes in. "My good man, take your medicine," he says.

And Uncle Jeff says, "Don't ever send that damn woman back in here. She don't know what it is all about."

The doctor laughs and says, "No, she doesn't know what it is all about."

"Now, Mick," says Uncle Jeff, "you didn't bring the scissors back you borrowed that time—you promised to bring them back Saturday."

"Out of his head," says Pa—"out of his head sure as God made little green apples."

"But, Mick, you can give me them scissors in hell. I'm not out of my head. You're goin home, I see. We will not meet here again—we'll meet in hell. Bring them scissors."

Pa holds his shriveled snake-like hand and wipes the tears with his other hand.

"Good-by, Uncle Jeff," I say.

"Good-by, Uncle Jeff," says Finn.

"You boys don't work on no goddamn railroad," says Uncle Jeff.

We walk out holdin Pa. He is a little chicken-hearted and he says: "Brother Jeff is a goner. That work has got him. The time he got hurt they offered him five hundred dollars for compromise and if they had paid him that he didn't get to keep his job. So he took the job. Look at him now. He is a dead man. He had thirty-three years of it. I have had nineteen. Look at me—a wreck. I never was stout as Jeff. Jeff was the best man among us boys."

We go down the Ferton street holding to Pa. Pa is nervous. I have never seen him this nervous before.

"It is three hours before we can get a bus out of here, Pa," I say, "what do you say we see a show?"

"I never saw one of them things and I don't want to see one," says Pa.

"We got to spend some time some place."

913

"Well, just as you say, then," says Pa. "Not as I care, but looks to me like we are goin to be late about gettin back home and doin up the work. Cows to milk, hogs to feed, mules to put in the barn, and your Ma can't do all that work. It is killin her.

"Fine building," says Pa, "wish I owned it, but it took money to build a show house like this. Even to velvet rugs for the feet."

Pa sets between us in the theater. He likes the news flashes. "Funny how they do that," he says. "I'll have one on the boys Monday mornin. They won't believe me when I tell them about this."

And the picture shows a man's wife in love with another man. They slip to a hotel. "Just like Jeff's wife exactly," says Pa to Finn. "That woman ought to have her kneck wrong off, doin like that."

"Be quiet, Pa," says Finn. "You are in the theater and people will hear what you say."

"I don't care if they do," says Pa. "A woman like that ought to be shot. She is just like Brother Jeff's wife, only she slips to a hotel and Jeff's wife slips to the brush back up there on Big Sandy."

When we start to leave the theater Pa says: "The power of man is mighty to do a thing like that. But the Bible says man will grow weaker and wiser, and damned if I don't believe it. The boys won't believe me when I tell them all of this."

And we go on out where the bright lights of Ferton are flickerin. We catch the bus back to Kentucky.

Pa says: "Work not done up or anythin. Here it is dark. We got about thirty more miles to go and walk four miles after we leave the main road."

Over the silent, cold earth and back home. The stars shine in the heavens. But we need a lantern to see how to throw the fodder over to the cows. We feed the cows and the mules, slop the hogs and get in the wood.

"Jeff and me used to do this at home," says Pa, "but we'll never do it any more together. I'll be the next one—I'll be the next to go. If you boys ever work on a section I'll hant you from the grave. Get the least wages in the world and do the hardest work. The men that set up in the engines and ride get five times much as I get. I've worked like a dog and will come down to the end unless you boys take me and your Ma in—come down to the poorhouse. Goddamn a poorhouse to hell! Our section is not far from the poorhouse and they got bastard babies over there, people crazy as hell and pregnant mothers. Got the damnest mixup over there you ever saw. What if I would have to go there in the end and take your Ma? Wouldn't that be awful? I couldn't stand to take her there the way she has worked and bore my children. This is a hard world after all. Think of it, so much to have and so hard to get. Yet, there is plenty—plenty, but not for me nor my kind. I can't read. I ain't been no place. I never had a chance to go to school. Now I have to take what I can get. Poorhouse may be all I'm able to get."

914 It is the next afternoon. The rain is fallin and low black clouds, it seems, just scud above the leafless timber. The wind whips through the saw briars. The cows, standin humped up in the barn lot, chew on the ends of old cornstalks. The mules run alongside the fence and bite each other's necks and snicker.

"Sign of fallen weather," says Pa, "when mules play—and sign of a death when two mules ride each other.

"Just as I expected," says Pa, when Finn reads the telegram sayin that Brother Jeff is dead.

"Gettin up in the paper to get a telegram," says Finn.

"Because of that telegram," says Pa, "somebody will have to go to the poor-house or the orphans' home. That fellow that runs Jeff's wife might take her now, but he won't take the children. They'll have to give them away or send them to the orphans' home. Jeff dies a pauper after thirty-three years of hard work. I can't keep his children. I can't take them. I'll do well to raise what I got."

We see Pa gettin ready. He puts on his old blue suit—his Sunday suit he bought from Lark Jenkins second-handed. He puts on one of Finn's shirts and black bow tie. He takes a black hat out of the trunk and brushes it up a little. He wears it. Ma says he looks real nice. Pa walks out into the rain with all his good clothes on. He is goin to catch Number 8.

Pa has a pass and he can ride right up on Big Sandy. That is one thing they do. They haul him free. But he has to ride in one of the poor coaches—one for the poor people. But Pa is poor and he doesn't mind. He wouldn't know how to act with them Big Bugs on that train in a coach where a man is hired to wipe your shoes off as you leave the coach.

We see Pa go. We see him cross the pasture, go between the wires of a barb-wire fence, then to the ridge road. We see him leavin in the rain.

We do not want to go. We understand that Pa is a little nervous. Uncle Jeff's house is a little two-room shack and part of us would have to sleep in a bed made down on the floor unless some of the neighbors would invite us to stay with them. Pa's other brother, Uncle Joe, used to invite us, but Uncle Joe and Uncle Jeff had trouble about their wives fightin and they have not spoken to each other since last June. Uncle Joe's wife called Uncle Jeff's wife a slut. Finn and I don't go. We leave it up to Pa.

Finn and I, we understand. We were up to Uncle Jeff's last Decoration Day. Pa, Uncle Joe, Uncle Jeff, Finn and me all went to hunt Grandma's grave. We went up the hollow back of Uncle Jeff's house and through heavy timber where the squirrels played right before our eyes. There was a white fuzz from the leaves of such dense foliage that it choked us to breathe it.

"Here," said Uncle Joe, "I used to carry Micky—you and Jeff back in 1882. We had this in corn that year and Pap built that rail fence you see there. He split them rails and built that fence back then."

Pa stopped and picked up a rail. "The hands that split them rails tanned my jacket with a hickory withe a many a time. He worked like a brute and died a pauper," he said.

We gathered the wild flowers—the wild bleeding heart, the wild snowballs, the mountain daisies as we went along. Pa, Uncle Jeff and Uncle Joe helped us. Uncle Joe had to walk with a cane. We walked slowly through the woods, partin our way through the dense undergrowth of greenbriers and ferns and wild snowball bushes that lapped across a once traveled path.

915

"This is the right road," said Uncle Joe, "though I ain't been to Ma's grave since she was buried. I never wanted to go back. We have to go out here and through where Pap took that last forty-acre lease from Steve Bocock back in '93. It's all growed up till you wouldn't know it."

There was a dim toe-path leadin down through woods that looked as if they were the trees that Adam roamed among.

"And Grandpa cleared this up once?" I asked.

"Yes," said Uncle Joe. "We farmed this, cleared it up and got it in the first year. Put a rail fence around it to boot."

We followed the dim path through the ferns and under the tall trees. Uncle Joe carried the basket and parted brush with his cane. Soon we came to a point out in a grass field that sloped gently down to a little valley stream of water.

"Over there is where Ma is laid," said Uncle Joe.

When we got there no one could definitely locate her grave. Pa said: "Call old Joe Blevins over here. He knows. He still owns this farm, don't he?"

"Yes," said Uncle Joe.

"Boys," said Joe Blevins, "there are eleven of youn'ns buried here and your Ma is in the middle. She is number six. There are five before her and five after. Right here is the place at this sunken sankfield mound."

Uncle Joe spilled his basket of flowers there.

Uncle Jeff said: "We three brothers are all that's left. I'll be the next to come here. I can't work any more and when a good horse gets so he can't stand work then he's through. You know that. Now right here is where I'll be put. You see to it, Mick."

It was by a little peach tree. Finn stood under it in the bright spring sun and I pulled off a few of its green leaves and one of its old but not shedded blossoms and crumbled them in my hand.

As the rain keeps fallin here and Pa has just gone out of sight now, I understand. They will haul Uncle Jeff on a wagon around the skirts of that hill we walked over. It will be a long haul, but they will haul him to that point and dig his grave by that peach tree. The rain will be fallin perhaps. It will be white rain and will soak down where I crumbled the peach tree leaves and the faded blossoms last year. Dirt will be piled high there. Pa will be there.

"Wonder if Uncle Jeff's wife will be there?" I think.

It is best to let Pa go, for this is bad weather to sleep on a floor. We don't want to do it. We know where Uncle Jeff will be planted for he told Pa and Pa will see to that. It will be where the green peach tree leaves and the pink peach tree blossoms were crumbled down last year. There will not be the sound of a train whistle back there. (1936)

Another April

"Now, Pap, you won't get cold," Mom said as she put a heavy wool cap over
his head.

"Huh, what did ye say?" Grandpa asked, holding his big hand cupped over his ear to catch the sound.

From Tales from the Plum Grove Hills *by Jesse Stuart, published by E. P. Dutton & Co., Inc., New York. Copyright, 1946, Jesse Stuart.*

"Wait until I get your gloves," Mom said, hollering real loud in Grandpa's ear. Mom had forgotten about his gloves until he raised his big bare hand above his ear to catch the sound of Mom's voice.

"Don't get 'em," Grandpa said, "I won't ketch cold."

Mom didn't pay any attention to what Grandpa said. She went on to get the gloves anyway. Grandpa turned toward me. He saw that I was looking at him.

"Yer Ma's a-puttin' enough clothes on me to kill a man," Grandpa said, then he laughed a coarse laugh like March wind among the pine tops at his own words. I started laughing at them not at Grandpa's words. He thought I was laughing at them and we both laughed together. It pleased Grandpa to think that I had laughed with him over something funny that he had said. But I was laughing at the way he was dressed. He looked like a picture of Santa Claus. But Grandpa's cheeks were not cherry-red like Santa Claus' cheeks. They were covered with white thin beard—and above his eyes were long white eyebrows almost as white as percoon petals and very much longer.

Grandpa was wearing a heavy wool suit that hung loosely about his big body but fitted him tightly round the waist where he was as big and as round as a flour barrel. His pant legs were as big 'round his pipestem legs as emptied meal sacks. And his big shoes, with his heavy wool socks dropping down over their tops, looked like sled runners. Grandpa wore a heavy wool shirt and over his wool shirt he wore a heavy wool sweater and then his coat over the top of all this. Over his coat he wore a heavy overcoat and about his neck he wore a wool scarf.

The way Mom had dressed Grandpa you'd think there was a heavy snow on the ground but there wasn't. April was here instead and the sun was shining on the green hills where the wild plums and the wild crab apples were in bloom enough to make you think there were big snowdrifts sprinkled over the green hills. When I looked at Grandpa and then looked out the window at the sunshine and the green grass I laughed more. Grandpa laughed with me.

"I'm a-goin' to see my old friend," Grandpa said just as Mom came down the stairs with his gloves.

"Who is he, Grandpa?" I asked, but Grandpa just looked at my mouth working. He didn't know what I was saying. And he hated to ask me the second time.

Mom put the big wool gloves on Grandpa's hands. He stood there just like I had to do years ago, and let Mom put his gloves on. If Mom didn't get his fingers back in the glove-fingers exactly right Grandpa quarreled at Mom. And when Mom fixes his fingers exactly right in his gloves the way he wanted them Grandpa was pleased.

"I'll be a-goin' to see 'im," Grandpa said to Mom. "I know he'll still be there."

Mom opened our front door for Grandpa and he stepped out slowly, supporting himself with his big cane in one hand. With the other hand he held to the door facing. Mom let him out of the house just like she used to let me out in the spring. And when Grandpa left the house I wanted to go with him, but Mom wouldn't let me go. I wondered if he would get away from the house—get out of Mom's sight—and pull off his shoes and go barefooted and wade the creeks like I used to do when Mom let me out. Since Mom wouldn't let me go with Grandpa, I watched him as he walked slowly down the path in front of our house. Mom stood there watching Grandpa too. I think she was afraid that he would fall. But

917

Mom was fooled; Grandpa toddled along the path better than my baby brother could.

"He used to be a powerful man," Mom said more to herself than she did to me. "He was a timber cutter. No man could cut more timber than my father; no man in the timber woods could sink an ax deeper into a log than my father. And no man could lift the end of a bigger saw log than Pap could."

"Who is Grandpa goin' to see, Mom?" I asked.

"He's not goin' to see anybody," Mom said.

"I heard 'im say that he was goin' to see an old friend," I told her.

"Oh, he was just a-talkin'," Mom said.

I watched Grandpa stop under the pine tree in our front yard. He set his cane against the pine tree trunk, pulled off his gloves and put them in his pocket. Then Grandpa stooped over slowly, as slowly as the wind bends down a sapling, and picked up a pine cone in his big soft fingers. Grandpa stood fondling the pine cone in his hand. Then, one by one, he pulled the little chips from the pine cone—tearing it to pieces like he was hunting for something in it—and after he had torn it to pieces he threw the pine-cone stem on the ground. Then he pulled pine needles from a low-hanging pine bough and he felt of each pine needle between his fingers. He played with them a long time before he started down the path.

"What's Grandpa doin'?" I asked Mom.

But Mom didn't answer me.

"How long has Grandpa been with us?" I asked Mom.

"Before you's born," she said. "Pap has been with us eleven years. He was eighty when he quit cuttin' timber and farmin'; now he's ninety-one."

I had heard her say that when she was a girl he'd walk out on the snow and ice barefooted and carry wood in the house and put it on the fire. He had shoes but he wouldn't bother to put them on. And I heard her say that he would cut timber on the coldest days without socks on his feet but with his feet stuck down in cold brogan shoes and he worked stripped above the waist so his arms would have freedom when he swung his double-bitted ax. I had heard her tell how he'd sweat and how the sweat in his beard would be icicles by the time he got home from work on the cold winter days. Now Mom wouldn't let him get out of the house for she wanted him to live a long time.

As I watched Grandpa go down the path toward the hog pen he stopped to examine every little thing along his path. Once he waved his cane at a butterfly as it zigzagged over his head, its polka-dot wings fanning the blue April air. Grandpa would stand when a puff of wind came along, and hold his face against the wind and let the wind play with his white whiskers. I thought maybe his face was hot under his beard and he was letting the wind cool his face. When he reached the hog pen he called the hogs down to the fence. They came running and grunting to Grandpa just like they were talking to him. I knew that Grandpa couldn't hear them trying to talk to him but he could see their mouths working and he knew they were trying to say something. He leaned his cane against the hog pen, reached over the fence, and patted the hogs' heads. Grandpa didn't miss patting one of our seven hogs.

As he toddled up the little path alongside the hog pen he stopped under a blooming dogwood. He pulled a white blossom from a bough that swayed over the path above his head, and he leaned his big bundled body against the dogwood while he tore each petal from the blossom and examined it carefully. There wasn't anything his dim blue eyes missed. He stopped under a redbud tree before he reached the garden to break a tiny spray of redbud blossoms. He took each blossom from the spray and examined it carefully.

"Gee, it's funny to watch Grandpa," I said to Mom, then I laughed.

"Poor Pap," Mom said, "he's seen a lot of Aprils come and go. He's seen more Aprils than he will ever see again."

I don't think Grandpa missed a thing on the little circle he took before he reached the house. He played with a bumblebee that was bending a windflower blossom that grew near our corncrib beside a big bluff. But Grandpa didn't try to catch the bumblebee in his big bare hand. I wondered if he would and if the bumblebee would sting him, and if he would holler. Grandpa even pulled a butterfly cocoon from a blackberry briar that grew beside his path. I saw him try to tear it into shreds but he couldn't. There wasn't any butterfly in it, for I'd seen it before. I wondered if the butterfly with the polka-dot wings, that Grandpa waved his cane at when he first left the house, had come from this cocoon. I laughed when Grandpa couldn't tear the cocoon apart.

"I'll bet I can tear that cocoon apart for Grandpa if you'd let me go help him," I said to Mom.

"You leave your Grandpa alone," Mom said. "Let 'im enjoy April."

Then I knew that this was the first time Mom had let Grandpa out of the house all winter. I knew that Grandpa loved the sunshine and the fresh April air that blew from the redbud and dogwood blossoms. He loved the bumblebees, the hogs, the pine cones, and pine needles. Grandpa didn't miss a thing along his walk. And every day from now on until just before frost Grandpa would take this little walk. He'd stop along and look at everything as he had done summers before. But each year he didn't take as long a walk as he had taken the year before. Now this spring he didn't go down to the lower end of the hog pen as he had done last year. And when I could first remember Grandpa going on his walks he used to go out of sight. He'd go all over the farm. And he'd come to the house and take me on his knee and tell me about all that he had seen. Now Grandpa wasn't getting out of sight. I could see him from the window along all of his walk.

Grandpa didn't come back into the house at the front door. He tottled around back of the house toward the smokehouse and I ran through the living room to the dining room so I could look out at the window and watch him.

"Where's Grandpa goin'?" I asked Mom.

"Now never mind," Mom said. "Leave your Grandpa alone. Don't go out there and disturb him."

"I won't bother 'im, Mom," I said. "I just want to watch 'im."

"All right," Mom said.

But Mom wanted to be sure that I didn't bother him so she followed me into the dining room. Maybe she wanted to see what Grandpa was going to do. She stood by the window and we watched Grandpa as he walked down beside our smokehouse where a tall sassafras tree's thin leaves fluttered in the blue April wind. Above the smokehouse and tall sassafras was a blue April sky—so high you couldn't see the sky-roof. It was just blue space and little white clouds floated upon this blue.

When Grandpa reached the smokehouse he leaned his cane against the sassa-

919

fras tree. He let himself down slowly to his kneees as he looked carefully at the ground. Grandpa was looking at something and I wondered what it was. I just didn't think or I would have known.

"There you are, my good old friend," Grandpa said.

"Who is his friend, Mom?" I asked.

Mom didn't say anything. Then I saw.

"He's playin' with that old terrapin, Mom," I said.

"I know he is," Mom said.

"The terrapin doesn't mind if Grandpa strokes his head with his hand," I said.

"I know it," Mom said.

"But the old terrapin won't let me do it," I said. "Why does he let Grandpa?"

"The terrapin knows your Grandpa."

"He ought to know me," I said. "But when I try to stroke his head with my hand, he closes up in his shell."

Mom didn't say anything. She stood by the window watching Grandpa and listening to Grandpa talk to the terrapin.

"My old friend, how do you like the sunshine?" Grandpa asked the terrapin.

The terrapin turned his fleshless face to one side like a hen does when she looks at you in the sunlight. He was trying to talk to Grandpa; maybe the terrapin could understand what Grandpa was saying.

"Old fellow, it's been a hard winter," Grandpa said. "How have you fared under the smokehouse floor?"

"Does the terrapin know what Grandpa is sayin'?" I asked Mom.

"I don't know," she said.

"I'm awfully glad to see you, old fellow," Grandpa said.

He didn't offer to bite Grandpa's big soft hand as he stroked his head.

"Looks like the terrapin would bite Grandpa," I said.

"That terrapin has spent the winters under that smokehouse for fifteen years," Mom said. "Pap has been acquainted with him for eleven years. He's been talkin' to that terrapin every spring."

"How does Grandpa know the terrapin is old?" I asked Mom.

"It's got 1847 cut on its shell," Mom said. "We know he's ninety-five years old. He's older than that. We don't know how old he was when that date was cut on his back."

"Who cut 1847 on his back, Mom?"

"I don't know, child," she said, "but I'd say whoever cut that date on his back has long been under the ground."

Then I wondered how a terrapin could get that old and what kind of a looking person he was who cut the date on the terrapin's back. I wondered where it happened—if it happened near where our house stood. I wondered who lived here on this land then, what kind of a house they lived in, and if they had a sassafras with tiny thin April leaves on its top growing in their yard, and if the person that cut the date on the terrapin's back was buried at Plum Grove, if he had farmed these hills where we lived today and cut timber like Grandpa had—and if he had seen the Aprils pass like Grandpa had seen them and if he enjoyed them like Grandpa was enjoying this April. I wondered if he had looked at the dogwood blossoms, the redbud blossoms, and talked to this same terrapin.

"Are you well, old fellow?" Grandpa asked the terrapin.

The terrapin just looked at Grandpa.

"I'm well as common for a man of my age," Grandpa said.

"Did the terrapin ask Grandpa if he was well?" I asked Mom.

"I don't know," Mom said. "I can't talk to a terrapin."

"But Grandpa can."

"Yes."

"Wait until tomatoes get ripe and we'll go to the garden together," Grandpa said.

"Does a terrapin eat tomatoes?" I asked Mom.

"Yes, that terrapin has been eatin' tomatoes from our garden for fifteen years," Mom said. "When Mick was tossin' the terrapins out of the tomato patch, he picked up this one and found the date cut on his back. He put him back in the patch and told him to help himself. He lives from our garden every year. We don't bother him and don't allow anybody else to bother him. He spends his winters under our smokehouse floor buried in the dry ground."

"Gee, Grandpa looks like the terrapin," I said.

Mom didn't say anything; tears came to her eyes. She wiped them from her eyes with the corner of her apron.

"I'll be back to see you," Grandpa said. "I'm a-gettin' a little chilly; I'll be gettin' back to the house."

The terrapin twisted his wrinkled neck without moving his big body, poking his head deeper into the April wind as Grandpa pulled his bundled body up by holding to the sassafras tree trunk.

"Good-by, old friend!"

The terrapin poked his head deeper into the wind, holding one eye on Grandpa, for I could see his eye shining in the sinking sunlight.

Grandpa got his cane that was leaned against the sassafras tree trunk and hobbled slowly toward the house. The terrapin looked at him with first one eye and then the other. (*1946*)

EUDORA WELTY

1909–

Eudora Welty was born in Jackson, Mississippi, on April 13, 1909. She attended the Mississippi State College for Women and received her B.A. degree from the University of Wisconsin in 1929. She also studied for one year (1930–1931) in the School of Advertising at Columbia University before returning to

Jackson, where she worked at several jobs in the field of journalism. Miss Welty first received notice when her short stories began to appear in such "little" Southern magazines as the *Southern Review*. She also became a contributor to *Harper's Bazaar* and *The Atlantic Monthly*. A number of her stories have been widely acclaimed by critics as evidencing a rare and sensitive talent.

In 1941 Miss Welty published her first collection of short stories, *A Curtain of Green,* with a critical preface written by Katherine Anne Porter. In the same year she received an O. Henry Memorial Award for her story, "A Worn Path." Since that time Miss Welty has published several books, including *The Robber Bridegroom* (1942), a fantasy; *The Wide Net* (1943), short stories; *Delta Wedding* (1946), a series of connected stories built around the fictional town of Morgana; and *The Golden Apples* (1949), a novel.

Old Mr. Marblehall

Old Mr. Marblehall never did anything, never got married until he was sixty. You can see him out taking a walk. Watch and you'll see how preciously old people come to think they are made—the way they walk, like conspirators, bent over a little, filled with protection. They stand long on the corners but more impatiently than anyone, as if they expected traffic to take notice of them, rear up the horses and throw on the brakes, so they can go where they want to go. That's Mr. Marblehall. He has short white bangs, and a bit of snapdragon in his lapel. He walks with a big polished stick, a present. That's what people think of him. Everybody says to his face, "So well preserved!" Behind his back they say cheerfully, "One foot in the grave." He has on his thick, beautiful, glowing coat—tweed, but he looks as gratified as an animal in its own tingling fur. You see, even in summer he wears it, because he is cold all the time. He looks quaintly secretive and prepared for anything, out walking very luxuriously on Catherine Street.

His wife, back at home in the parlor standing up to think, is a large, elongated old woman with electric-looking hair and curly lips. She has spent her life trying to escape from the parlorlike jaws of self-consciousness. Her late marriage has set in upon her nerves like a retriever nosing and puffing through old dead leaves out in the woods. When she walks around the room she looks remote and nebulous, out on the fringe of habitation, and rather as if she must have been cruelly trained—otherwise she couldn't do actual, immediate things, like answering the telephone or putting on a hat. But she has gone further than you'd think: into club work. Surrounded by other more suitably exclaiming women, she belongs to the Daughters of the American Revolution and the United Daughters of the Confederacy, attending teas. Her long, disquieted figure towering in the candlelight of other women's houses looks like something accidental. Any occasion, and she dresses her hair like a unicorn horn. She even

922

sings, and is requested to sing. She even writes some of the songs she sings ("O Trees in the Evening"). She has a voice that dizzies other ladies like an organ note, and amuses men like a halloo down the well. It's full of a hollow wind and echo, winding out through the wavery hope of her mouth. Do people know of her perpetual amazement? Back in safety she wonders, her untidy head trembles in the domestic dark. She remembers how everyone in Natchez will suddenly grow quiet around her. Old Mrs. Marblehall, Mr. Marblehall's wife: she even goes out in the rain, which Southern women despise above everything, in big meat biscuit-colored galoshes, for which she "ordered off." She is only looking around—servile, undelighted, sleepy, expensive, tortured Mrs. Marblehall, pinning her mind with a pin to her husband's diet. She wants to tempt him, she tells him. What would he like best, that he can have?

There is Mr. Marblehall's ancestral home. It's not so wonderfully large—it has only four columns—but you always look toward it, the way you always glance into tunnels and see nothing. The river is after it now, and the little back garden has assuredly crumbled away, but the box maze is there on the edge like a trap, to confound the Mississippi River. Deep in the red wall waits the front door—it weighs such a lot, it is perfectly solid, all one piece, black mahogany. . . . And you see—one of *them* is always going in it. There is a knocker shaped like a gasping fish on the door. You have every reason in the world to imagine the inside is dark, with old things about. There's many a big, deathly looking tapestry, wrinkling and thin, many a sofa shaped like an S. Brocades as tall as the wicked queens in Italian tales stand gathered before the windows. Everything is draped and hooded and shaded, of course, unaffectionate but close. Such rosy lamps! The only sound would be a breath against the prisms, a stirring of the chandelier. It's like old eyelids, the house with one of its shutters, in careful working order, slowly opening outward. Then the little son softly comes and stares out like a kitten, with button nose and pointed ears and little fuzz of silky hair running along the top of his head.

The son is the worst of all. Mr. and Mrs. Marblehall had a child! When both of them were terribly old, they had this little, amazing, fascinating son. You can see how people are taken aback, how they jerk and throw up their hands every time they so much as think about it. At least, Mr. Marblehall sees them. He thinks Natchez people do nothing themselves, and really, most of them have done or could do the same thing. This son is six years old now. Close up, he has a monkey look, a very penetrating look. He has very sparse Japanese hair, tiny little pearly teeth, long little wilted fingers. Every day he is slowly and expensively dressed and taken to the Catholic school. He looks quietly and maliciously absurd, out walking with old Mr. Marblehall or old Mrs. Marblehall, placing his small booted foot on a little green worm, while they stop and wait on him. Everybody passing by thinks that he looks quite as if he thinks his parents had him just to show they could. You see, it becomes complicated, full of vindictiveness.

But now, as Mr. Marblehall walks as briskly as possible toward the river where there is sun, you have to merge him back into his proper blur, into the little party-giving town he lives in. Why look twice at him? There has been an old Mr. Marblehall in Natchez ever since the first one arrived back in 1818—

923

with a theatrical presentation of Otway's *Venice*, ending with *A Laughable Combat between Two Blind Fiddlers*—an actor! Mr. Marblehall isn't so important. His name is on the list, he is forgiven, but nobody gives a hoot about any old Mr. Marblehall. He could die, for all they care; some people even say, "Oh, is he still alive?" Mr. Marblehall walks and walks, and now and then he is driven in his ancient fringed carriage with the candle burners like empty eyes in front. And yes, he is supposed to travel for his health. But why consider his absence? There isn't any other place besides Natchez, and even if there were, it would hardly be likely to change Mr. Marblehall if it were brought up against him. Big fingers could pick him up off the Esplanade and take him through the air, his old legs still measuredly walking in a dangle, and set him down where he could continue that same old Natchez stroll of his in the East or the West or Kingdom Come. What difference could anything make now about old Mr. Marblehall—so late? A week or two would go by in Natchez and then there would be Mr. Marblehall, walking down Catherine Street again, still exactly in the same degree alive and old.

People naturally get bored. They say, "Well, he waited till he was sixty years old to marry, and what did he want to marry for?" as though what he did were the excuse for their boredom and their lack of concern. Even the thought of his having a stroke right in front of one of the Pilgrimage houses during Pilgrimage Week makes them only sigh, as if to say it's nobody's fault but his own if he wants to be so insultingly and precariously well-preserved. He ought to have a little black boy to follow around after him. Oh, his precious old health, which never had reason to be so inspiring! Mr. Marblehall has a formal, reproachful look as he stands on the corners arranging himself to go out into the traffic to cross the streets. It's as if he's thinking of shaking his stick and saying, "Well, look! I've done it, don't you see?" But really, nobody pays much attention to his look. He is just like other people to them. He could have easily danced with a troupe of angels in Paradise every night, and they wouldn't have guessed. Nobody is likely to find out that he is leading a double life.

The funny thing is he just recently began to lead this double life. He waited until he was sixty years old. Isn't he crazy? Before that, he'd never done anything. He didn't know what to do. Everything was for all the world like his first party. He stood about, and looked in his father's books, and long ago he went to France, but he didn't like it.

Drive out any of these streets in and under the hills and you find yourself lost. You see those scores of little galleried houses nearly alike. See the yellowing China trees at the eaves, the round flower beds in the front yards, like bites in the grass, listen to the screen doors whining, the ice wagons dragging by, the twittering noises of children. Nobody ever looks to see who is living in a house like that. These people come out themselves and sprinkle the hose over the street at this time of day to settle the dust, and after they sit on the porch, they go back into the house, and you hear the radio for the next two hours. It seems to mourn and cry for them. They go to bed early.

924

Well, old Mr. Marblehall can easily be seen standing beside a row of zinnias growing down the walk in front of that little house, bending over, easy, easy, so as not to strain anything, to stare at the flowers. Of course he planted them!

They are covered with brown—each petal is a little heart-shaped pocket of dust. They don't have any smell, you know. It's twilight, all amplified with locusts screaming; nobody could see anything. Just what Mr. Marblehall is bending over the zinnias for is a mystery, any way you look at it. But there he is, quite visible, alive and old, leading his double life.

There's his other wife, standing on the night-stained porch by a potted fern, screaming things to a neighbor. This wife is really worse than the other one. She is more solid, fatter, shorter, and while not so ugly, funnier looking. She looks like funny furniture—an unornamented stairpost in one of these little houses, with her small monotonous round stupid head—or sometimes like a woodcut of a Bavarian witch, forefinger pointing, with scratches in the air all around her. But she's so static she scarcely moves, from her thick shoulders down past her cylindered brown dress to her short, stubby house slippers. She stands still and screams to the neighbors.

This wife thinks Mr. Marblehall's name is Mr. Bird. She says, "I declare I told Mr. Bird to go to bed, and look at him! I don't understand him!" All her devotion is combustible and goes up in despair. This wife tells everything she knows. Later, after she tells the neighbors, she will tell Mr. Marblehall. Cymbal-breasted, she fills the house with wifely complaints. She calls, "After I get Mr. Bird to bed, what does he do then? He lies there stretched out with his clothes on and don't have one word to say. Know what he does?"

And she goes on, while her husband bends over the zinnias, to tell what Mr. Marblehall (or Mr. Bird) does in bed. She does tell the truth. He reads *Terror Tales* and *Astonishing Stories*. She can't see anything to them: they scare her to death. These stories are about horrible and fantastic things happening to nude women and scientists. In one of them, when the characters open bureau drawers, they find a woman's leg with a stocking and garter on. Mrs. Bird had to shut the magazine. "The glutinous shadows," these stories say, "the red-eyed, muttering old crone," "the moonlight on her thigh," "an ancient cult of sun worshipers," "an altar suspiciously stained. . . ." Mr. Marblehall doesn't feel as terrified as all that, but he reads on and on. He is killing time. It is richness without taste, like some holiday food. The clock gets a fruity bursting tick, to get through midnight—then leisurely, leisurely on. When time is passing it's like a bug in his ear. And then Mr. Bird—he doesn't even want a shade on the light, this wife moans respectably. He reads under a bulb. She can tell you how he goes straight through a stack of magazines. "He might just as well not have a family," she always ends, unjustly, and rolls back into the house as if she had been on a little wheel all this time.

But the worst of them all is the other little boy. Another little boy just like the first one. He wanders around the bungalow full of tiny little schemes and jokes. He has lost his front tooth, and in this way he looks slightly different from Mr. Marblehall's other little boy—more shocking. Otherwise, you couldn't tell them apart if you wanted to. They both have that look of cunning little jugglers, violently small under some spotlight beam, preoccupied and silent, amusing themselves. Both of the children will go into sudden fits and tantrums that frighten their mothers and Mr. Marblehall to death. Then they can get anything they want. But this little boy, the one who's lost the tooth, is the

925

smarter. For a long time he supposed that his mother was totally solid, down to her thick separated ankles. But when she stands there on the porch screaming to the neighbors, she reminds him of those flares that charm him so, that they leave burning in the street at night—the dark solid ball, then, tonguelike, the wicked, yellow, continuous, enslaving blaze on the stem. He knows what his father thinks.

Perhaps one day, while Mr. Marblehall is standing there gently bent over the zinnias, this little boy is going to write on a fence, "Papa leads a double life." He finds out things you wouldn't find out. He is a monkey.

You see, one night he is going to follow Mr. Marblehall (or Mr. Bird) out of the house. Mr. Marblehall has said as usual that he is leaving for one of his health trips. He is one of those correct old gentlemen who are still going to the wells and drinking the waters—exactly like his father, the late old Mr. Marblehall. But why does he leave on foot? This will occur to the little boy.

So he will follow his father. He will follow him all the way across town. He will see the shining river come winding around. He will see the house where Mr. Marblehall turns in at the wrought-iron gate. He will see a big speechless woman come out and lead him in by the heavy door. He will not miss those rosy lamps beyond the many-folded draperies at the windows. He will run around the fountains and around the japonica trees, past the stone figure of the pigtailed courtier mounted on the goat, down to the back of the house. From there he can look far up at the strange upstairs rooms. In one window the other wife will be standing like a giant, in a long-sleeved gathered nightgown, combing her electric hair and breaking it off each time in the comb. From the next window the other little boy will look out secretly into the night, and see him—or not see him. That would be an interesting thing, a moment of strange telepathies. (Mr. Marblehall can imagine it.) Then in the corner room there will suddenly be turned on the bright, naked light. Aha! Father!

Mr. Marblehall's little boy will easily climb a tree there and peep through the window. There, under a stark shadeless bulb, on a great four-poster with carved griffins, will be Mr. Marblehall, reading *Terror Tales*, stretched out and motionless.

Then everything will come out.

At first, nobody will believe it.

Or maybe the policeman will say, "Stop! How dare you!"

Maybe, better than that, Mr. Marblehall himself will confess his duplicity— how he has led two totally different lives, with completely different families, two sons instead of one. What an astonishing, unbelievable, electrifying confession that would be, and how his two wives would topple over, how his sons would cringe! To say nothing of most men aged sixty-six. So thinks self-consoling Mr. Marblehall.

You will think, what if nothing ever happens? What if there is no climax, even to this amazing life? Suppose old Mr. Marblehall simply remains alive, getting older by the minute, shuttling, still secretly, back and forth?

926 Nobody cares. Not an inhabitant of Natchez, Mississippi, cares if he is deceived by old Mr. Marblehall. Neither does anyone care that Mr. Marblehall has finally caught on, he thinks, to what people are supposed to do. This is it: they endure something inwardly—for a time secretly; they establish a past, a memory; thus they store up life. He has done this; most remarkably, he has even multiplied his life by deception; and plunging deeper and deeper he speculates upon some glorious finish, a great explosion of revelations . . . the future.

But he still has to kill time, and get through the clocking nights. Otherwise he dreams that he is a great blazing butterfly stitching up a net; which doesn't make sense.

Old Mr. Marblehall! He may have years ahead yet in which to wake up bolt upright in the bed under the naked bulb, his heart thumping, his old eyes watering and wild, imagining that if people knew about his double life, they'd die. (*1941*)

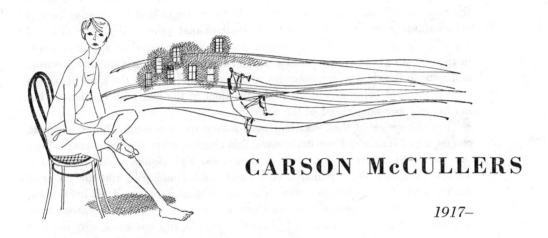

CARSON McCULLERS

1917–

Carson (Smith) McCullers was born in Columbus, Georgia, on February 17, 1917. She finished high school at an early age, and after two years of "loafing," set out for New York, where she planned to attend classes at Columbia University and the Juilliard Institute. She was seventeen at this time and seriously interested in music as well as in writing. During her second day in the city she lost all her tuition money on the subway and was forced to go to work. She held a number of part-time jobs, attended school at night, and wrote during her spare time. In 1935 *Story* magazine bought two of her short stories and she began to work at her writing more seriously. In the autumn of 1937 she married Reeves McCullers.

In 1940 Carson McCullers published her first novel, *The Heart Is a Lonely Hunter,* which proved an immediate success. This was followed by a short novel, *Reflections in a Golden Eye* (1941), and by *The Member of the Wedding* (1946). *The Ballad of the Sad Café* (1951) contains these three novels, the title-piece novella, and six short stories. Refashioned into a play in 1949, *The Member of the Wedding* had a highly successful New York run and in 1950 received the Critics Award as the best American play of the year. The detached melancholia of Carson McCullers' representations of character are a quiet commentary on her vision of human experience.

927

from *The Member of the Wedding*

Frankie Addams, "the member of the wedding," is twelve years old during the "crazy summer" when the narrative begins. A study of adolescence, the story centers around Frankie; Berenice, the Addams' Negro cook; and John Henry West, Frankie's young cousin.

. . . This was the summer when Frankie was sick and tired of being Frankie. She hated herself, and had become a loafer and a big no-good who hung around the summer kitchen: dirty and greedy and mean and sad. Besides being too mean to live, she was a criminal. If the Law knew about her, she could be tried in the courthouse and locked up in the jail. Yet Frankie had not always been a criminal and a big no-good. Until the April of that year, and all the years of her life before, she had been like other people. She belonged to a club and was in the seventh grade at school. She worked for her father on Saturday morning and went to the show every Saturday afternoon. She was not the kind of person ever to think of being afraid. At night she slept in the bed with her father, but not because she was scared of the dark.

Then the spring of that year had been a long queer season. Things began to change and Frankie did not understand this change. After the plain gray winter the March winds banged on the windowpanes, and clouds were shirred and white on the blue sky. April that year came sudden and still, and the green of the trees was a wild bright green. The pale wistarias bloomed all over town, and silently the blossoms shattered. There was something about the green trees and the flowers of April that made Frankie sad. She did not know why she was sad, but because of this peculiar sadness, she began to realize she ought to leave the town. She read the war news and thought about the world and packed her suitcase to go away; but she did not know where she should go.

It was the year when Frankie thought about the world. And she did not see it as a round school globe, with the countries neat and different-colored. She thought of the world as huge and cracked and loose and turning a thousand miles an hour. The geography book at school was out of date; the countries of the world had changed. Frankie read the war news in the paper, but there were so many foreign places, and the war was happening so fast, that sometimes she did not understand. It was the summer when Patton was chasing the Germans across France. And they were fighting, too, in Russia and Saipan. She saw the battles, and the soldiers. But there were too many different battles, and she could not see in her mind the millions and millions of soldiers all at once. She saw one Russian soldier, dark and frozen with a frozen gun, in Russian snow. The single Japs with slanted eyes on a jungle island gliding among green vines. Europe and the people hung in trees and the battleships on the blue oceans. Four-motor planes and burning cities and a soldier in a steel war helmet, laughing. Sometimes these pictures of the war, the world, whirled in her mind and she was dizzy. A long time ago she had predicted that it would take two months to

928

win the whole war, but now she did not know. She wanted to be a boy and go to the war as a Marine. She thought about flying aeroplanes and winning gold medals for bravery. But she could not join the war, and this made her sometimes feel restless and blue. She decided to donate blood to the Red Cross; she wanted to donate a quart a week and her blood would be in the veins of Australians and Fighting French and Chinese, all over the whole world, and it would be as though she were close kin to all of these people. She could hear the army doctors saying that the blood of Frankie Addams was the reddest and the strongest blood that they had ever known. And she could picture ahead, in the years after the war, meeting the soldiers who had her blood, and they would say that they owed their life to her; and they would not call her Frankie —they would call her Addams. But this plan for donating her blood to the war did not come true. The Red Cross would not take her blood. She was too young. Frankie felt mad with the Red Cross, and left out of everything. The war and the world were too fast and big and strange. To think about the world for very long made her afraid. She was not afraid of Germans or bombs or Japanese. She was afraid because in the war they would not include her, and because the world seemed somehow separate from herself.

So she knew she ought to leave the town and go to some place far away. For the late spring, that year, was lazy and too sweet. The long afternoons flowered and lasted and the green sweetness sickened her. The town began to hurt Frankie. Sad and terrible happenings had never made Frankie cry, but this season many things made Frankie suddenly wish to cry. Very early in the morning she would sometimes go out into the yard and stand for a long time looking at the sunrise sky. And it was as though a question came into her heart, and the sky did not answer. Things she had never noticed much before began to hurt her: home lights watched from the evening sidewalks, an unknown voice from an alley. She would stare at the lights and listen to the voice, and something inside her stiffened and waited. But the lights would darken, the voice fall silent, and though she waited, that was all. She was afraid of these things that made her suddenly wonder who she was, and what she was going to be in the world, and why she was standing at that minute, seeing a light, or listening, or staring up into the sky: alone. She was afraid, and there was a queer tightness in her chest.

One night in April, when she and her father were going to bed, he looked at her and said, all of a sudden: 'Who is this great big long-legged twelve-year-old blunderbuss who still wants to sleep with her old Papa.' And she was too big to sleep with father any more. She had to sleep in her upstairs room alone. She began to have a grudge against her father and they looked at each other in a slant-eyed way. She did not like to stay at home.

She went around town, and the things she saw and heard seemed to be left somehow unfinished, and there was the tightness in her that would not break. She would hurry to do something, but what she did was always wrong. She would call her best friend, Evelyn Owen, who owned a football suit and a Spanish shawl, and one would dress in the football suit and the other in the Spanish shawl and they would go down to the ten-cent store together. But that was a wrong thing and not what Frankie wanted. Or after the pale spring twilights, with the smell of dust and flowers sweet and bitter in the air, evenings of lighted windows and the long drawn calls at supper time, when the chimney swifts had

929

gathered and whirled above the town and flown off somewhere to their home together, leaving the sky empty and wide; after the long twilights of this season, when Frankie had walked around the sidewalks of the town, a jazz sadness quivered her nerves and her heart stiffened and almost stopped.

Because she could not break this tightness gathering within her, she would hurry to do something. She would go home and put the coal scuttle on her head, like a crazy person's hat, and walk around the kitchen table. She would do anything that suddenly occurred to her—but whatever she did was always wrong, and not at all what she had wanted. Then, having done these wrong and silly things, she would stand, sickened and empty, in the kitchen door and say:

'I just wish I could tear down this whole town.'

'Well, tear it down, then. But quit hanging around here with that gloomy face. Do something.'

And finally the troubles started.

She did things and she got herself in trouble. She broke the law. And having once become a criminal, she broke the law again, and then again. She took the pistol from her father's bureau drawer and carried it all over town and shot up the cartridges in a vacant lot. She changed into a robber and stole a three-way knife from the Sears and Roebuck Store. One Saturday afternoon in May she committed a secret and unknown sin. In the MacKeans' garage, with Barney MacKean, they committed a queer sin, and how bad it was she did not know. The sin made a shriveling sickness in her stomach, and she dreaded the eyes of everyone. She hated Barney and wanted to kill him. Sometimes alone in the bed at night she planned to shoot him with the pistol or throw a knife between his eyes.

Her best friend, Evelyn Owen, moved away to Florida, and Frankie did not play with anybody any more. The long and flowering spring was over and the summer in the town was ugly and lonesome and very hot. Every day she wanted more and more to leave the town: to light out for South America or Hollywood or New York City. But although she packed her suitcase many times, she could never decide to which of these places she ought to go, or how she would get there by herself.

So she stayed home and hung around the kitchen, and the summer did not end. By dog days she was five feet five and three-quarter inches tall, a great big greedy loafer who was too mean to live. She was afraid, but not as she had been before. There was only the fear of Barney, her father, and the Law. But even these fears were finally gone; after a long time the sin in the MacKeans' garage became far from her and was remembered only in her dreams. And she would not think of her father or the Law. She stuck close in the kitchen with John Henry and Berenice. She did not think about the war, the world. Nothing hurt her any longer; she did not care. She never stood alone in the back yard in order to stare up at the sky. She paid no attention to sounds and summer voices, and did not walk the streets of town at night. She would not let things make her sad and she would not care. She ate and wrote shows and practiced throwing knives against the side of the garage and played bridge at the kitchen table. Each day was like the day before, except that it was longer, and nothing hurt her any more.

So that Sunday when it happened, when her brother and the bride came to the house, Frankie knew that everything was changed; but why this was so, and what would happen to her next, she did not know. And though she tried to talk with Berenice, Berenice did not know either.

'It gives me this kind of a pain,' she said, 'to think about them.'

'Well, don't,' said Berenice. 'You done nothing but think and carry on about them all this afternoon.'

Frankie sat on the bottom step of the stairs to her room, staring into the kitchen. But although it gave her a kind of a pain, she had to think about the wedding. She remembered the way her brother and the bride had looked when she walked into the living room, that morning at eleven o'clock. There had been in the house a sudden silence, for Jarvis had turned off the radio when they came in; after the long summer, when the radio had gone on day and night, so that no one heard it any more, the curious silence had startled Frankie. She stood in the doorway, coming from the hall, and the first sight of her brother and the bride had shocked her heart. Together they made in her this feeling that she could not name. But it was like the feelings of the spring, only more sudden and more sharp. There was the same tightness and in the same queer way she was afraid. Frankie thought until her mind was dizzy and her foot had gone to sleep.

Then she asked Berenice: 'How old were you when you married your first husband?'

While Frankie was thinking, Berenice had changed into her Sunday clothes, and now she sat reading a magazine. She was waiting for the people who were due to meet her at six o'clock, Honey and T. T. Williams; the three of them were going to eat supper at the New Metropolitan Tea Room and sashay together around the town. As Berenice read, she moved her lips to shape each word. Her dark eye looked up as Frankie spoke, but, since Berenice did not raise her head, the blue glass eye seemed to go on reading the magazine. This two-sighted expression bothered Frankie.

'I were thirteen years old,' said Berenice.

'What made you get married so young for?'

'Because I wanted to,' said Berenice. 'I were thirteen years old and I haven't growed a inch since.'

Berenice was very short, and Frankie looked hard at her and asked: 'Does marrying really stop your growth?'

'It certainy do,' said Berenice.

'I didn't know that,' Frankie said.

Berenice had been married four different times. Her first husband was Ludie Freeman, a brickmason, and the favorite and best one of the four; he gave Berenice her fox fur, and once they had gone to Cincinnati and seen snow. Berenice and Ludie Freeman had seen a whole winter of Northern snow. They loved each other and were married for nine years, until the November he was sick and died. The other three husbands were all bad, each one worse than the one before, and it made Frankie blue just to hear about them. The first was a sorry old liquor-drinker. The next went crazy on Berenice: he did crazy things, had eating dreams in the night and swallowed a corner of the sheet; and what with one thing and another he distracted Berenice so much that finally

931

she had to quit him. The last husband was terrible. He gouged out Berenice's eye and stole her furniture away from her. She had to call the Law on him.

'Did you marry with a veil every time?' asked Frankie.

'Two times with a veil,' said Berenice.

Frankie could not keep still. She walked around the kitchen, although there was a splinter in her right foot and she was limping, her thumbs hooked in the belt of her shorts and her undershirt clinging and wet.

Finally she opened the drawer of the kitchen table and selected a long sharp butcher knife. Then she sat down and rested the ankle of her sore foot on her left knee. The sole of her foot was long and narrow, pitted with ragged whitish scars, as every summer Frankie stepped on many nails; Frankie had the toughest feet in town. She could slice off waxy yellow rinds from the bottoms of her feet, and it did not hurt her very much, although it would hurt other people. But she did not chisel for the splinter immediately—she just sat there, her ankle on her knee and the knife in her right hand, looking across the table at Berenice.

'Tell me,' she said. 'Tell me exactly how it was.'

'You know!' said Berenice. 'You seen them.'

'But tell me,' Frankie said.

'I will discuss it for the last time,' said Berenice. 'Your brother and the bride come late this morning and you and John Henry hurried in from the back yard to see them. Then next thing I realize you busted back through the kitchen and run up to your room. You came down with your organdie dress on and lipstick a inch thick from one ear to the next. Then you all just sat around up in the living room. It was hot. Jarvis had brought Mr. Addams a bottle of whiskey and they had liquor drinks and you and John Henry had lemonade. Then after dinner your brother and the bride took the three-o'clock train back to Winter Hill. The wedding will be this coming Sunday. And that is all. Now, is you satisfied?'

'I am so disappointed they couldn't stay longer—at least spend the night. After Jarvis being away so long. But I guess they want to be together as long as they can. Jarvis said he had some army papers to fill out at Winter Hill.' She took a deep breath. 'I wonder where they will go after the wedding.'

'On their honeymoon. Your brother will have a few days' leave.'

'I wonder where that honeymoon will be.'

'Well, I'm sure I don't know.'

'Tell me,' Frankie said again. 'Exactly what did they look like?'

'Look like?' said Berenice. 'Why, they looked natural. Your brother is a good-looking blond white boy. And the girl is kind of brunette and small and pretty. They make a nice white couple. You seen them, Foolish.'

Frankie closed her eyes, and, though she did not see them as a picture, she could feel them leaving her. She could feel the two of them together on the train, riding and riding away from her. They were them, and leaving her, and she was her, and sitting left all by herself there at the kitchen table. But a part of her was with them, and she could feel this part of her own self going away, and farther away; farther and farther, so that a drawn-out sickness came in her, going away and farther away, so that the kitchen Frankie was an old hull left there at the table.

932

'It is so queer,' she said.

She bent over the sole of her foot, and there was something wet, like tears or sweat drops on her face; she sniffled and began to cut for the splinter.

'Don't that hurt you none?' asked Berenice.

Frankie shook her head and did not answer. Then after a moment she said: 'Have you ever seen any people that afterward you remembered more like a feeling than a picture?'

'How you mean?'

'I mean this,' said Frankie slowly. 'I saw them O.K. Janice had on a green dress and green high-heel dainty shoes. Her hair was done up in a knot. Dark hair and a little piece of it was loose. Jarvis sat by her on the sofa. He had on his brown uniform and he was sunburned and very clean. They were the two prettiest people I ever saw. Yet it was like I couldn't see all of them I wanted to see. My brains couldn't gather together quick enough and take it all in. And then they were gone. You see what I mean?'

'You hurting yourself,' said Berenice. 'What you need is a needle.'

'I don't care anything about my old feet,' Frankie said.

It was only half-past six, and the minutes of the afternoon were like bright mirrors. From outside there was no longer the sound of whistling and in the kitchen nothing moved. Frankie sat facing the door that opened onto the back porch. There was a square cat-hole cut in a corner of the back door, and near-by a saucer of lavender sour milk. In the beginning of dog days Frankie's cat had gone away. And the season of dog days is like this: it is the time at the end of the summer when as a rule nothing can happen—but if a change does come about, that change remains until dog days are over. Things that are done are not undone and a mistake once made is not corrected.

That August Berenice scratched a mosquito bite under her right arm and it became a sore: that sore would never heal until dog days were over. Two little families of August gnats picked out the corners of John Henry's eyes to settle down in, and though he often shook himself and blinked, those gnats were there to stay. Then Charles disappeared. Frankie did not see him leave the house and walk away, but on the fourteenth of August, when she called him to his supper, he did not come, and he was gone. She looked for him everywhere and sent John Henry wailing out his name through all the streets of town. But it was the season of dog days and Charles did not come back again. Every afternoon Frankie said exactly the same words to Berenice, and the answers of Berenice were always the same. So that now the words were like an ugly little tune they sang by heart.

'If only I just knew where he has gone.'

'Quit worrying yourself about that old alley cat. I done told you he ain't coming back.'

'Charles is not alley. He is almost pure Persian.'

'Persian as I is,' Berenice would say. 'You seen the last of that old tom cat. He gone off to hunt a friend.'

'To hunt a friend?'

'Why, certainly. He roamed off to find himself a lady-friend.'

'You really think so?'

933

'Naturally.'

'Well, why don't he bring his friend home with him. He ought to know I would be only too glad to have a whole family of cats.'

'You seen the last of that old alley cat.'

'If only I just knew where he is gone.'

And so each gloomy afternoon their voices sawed against each other, saying the same words, which finally reminded Frankie of a raggedy rhyme said by two crazies. She would end by telling Berenice: 'It looks to me like everything has just walked off and left me.' And she would put her head down on the table and feel afraid.

But this afternoon Frankie suddenly changed all this. An idea came to her, and she put down the knife and got up from the table.

'I know what I ought to do,' she suddenly said. 'Listen.'

'I can hear.'

'I ought to notify the police force. They will find Charles.'

'I wouldn't do that,' said Berenice.

Frankie went to the hall telephone and explained to the Law about her cat. 'He is almost pure Persian,' she said. 'But with short hair. A very lovely color of gray and with a little white spot on his throat. He answers to the name of *Charles*, but if he don't answer to that, he might come if you call *Charlina*. My name is Miss F. Jasmine Addams and the address is 124 Grove Street.'

Berenice was giggling when she came back, a soft high giggle. 'Whew! They going to send around here and tie you up and drag you off to Milledgeville. Them fat blue police chasing tomcats around alleys and hollering: *Oh Charles, Oh come here, Charlina!* Sweet Jesus!'

'Aw, shut up,' Frankie said.

Berenice was sitting at the table; she had stopped giggling and her dark eye roved in a teasing way as she sloshed coffee into a white china saucer to cool.

'At the same time,' she said, 'I can't see how it is such a wise idea to trifle around with the Law. No matter for what reason.'

'I'm not trifling with the Law.'

'You just now set there and spelled them out your name and your house number. Where they can lay hold of you if ever they take the notion.'

'Well, let them!' said Frankie angrily. 'I don't care! I don't care!' and suddenly she did not care if anybody knew she was a criminal or not. 'Let them come get me for all I care.'

'I was just teasing you,' said Berenice. 'The trouble with you is that you don't have no sense of humor any more.'

'Maybe I'd be better off in jail.'

Frankie walked around the table and she could feel them going away. The train was traveling to the North. Mile after mile they went away, farther and farther away from the town, and as they traveled to the North, a coolness came into the air and dark was falling like the evening dark of wintertime. The train was winding up into the hills, the whistle wailing in a winter tone, and mile after mile they went away. They passed among themselves a box of bought store candy, with chocolates set in dainty, pleated shells, and watched the winter miles pass by the window. Now they had gone a long, long way from town and soon would be in Winter Hill.

934

'Sit down,' said Berenice. 'You make me nervous.'

Suddenly Frankie began to laugh. She wiped her face with the back of her hand and went back to the table. 'Did you hear what Jarvis said?'

'What?'

Frankie laughed and laughed.

'They were talking about whether to vote for C. P. MacDonald, and Jarvis said: *Why, I wouldn't vote for that scoundrel if he was running to be the dog-catcher*. I never heard anything so witty in my life.'

Berenice did not laugh. Her dark eye glanced down in a corner, quickly saw the joke, and then looked back at Frankie. Berenice wore her pink crepe dress and her hat with the pink plume was on the table. The blue glass eye made the sweat on her dark face look bluish also. Berenice was stroking the hat plume with her hand.

'And you know what Janice remarked?' asked Frankie. 'When Papa mentioned about how much I've grown, she said she didn't think I looked so terribly big. She said she got the major portion of her growth before she was thirteen. She did, Berenice!'

'O.K.! All right.'

'She said she thought I was a lovely size and would probably not grow any taller. She said all fashion models and movie stars—'

'She did not,' said Berenice. 'I heard her. She only remarked that you probably had already got your growth. But she didn't go on and on like that. To hear you tell it, anybody would think she took her text on the subject.'

'She said—'

'This is a serious fault with you, Frankie. Somebody just makes a loose remark and then you cozen it in your mind until nobody would recognize it. Your Aunt Pet happened to mention to Clorina that you had sweet manners and Clorina passed it on to you. For what it was worth. Then next thing I know you are going all around and bragging how Mrs. West thought you had the finest manners in town and ought to go to Hollywood, and I don't know what all you didn't say. You keep building on to any little compliment you hear about yourself. Or, if it is a bad thing, you do the same. You cozen and change things too much in your own mind. And that is a serious fault.'

'Quit preaching at me,' Frankie said.

'I ain't preaching. It is the solemn truth.'

'I admit it a little,' said Frankie finally. She closed her eyes and the kitchen was very quiet. She could feel the beating of her heart, and when she spoke her voice was a whisper. 'What I need to know is this. Do you think I made a good impression?'

'Impression? Impression?'

'Yes,' said Frankie, her eyes still closed.

'Well, how would I know?' said Berenice.

'I mean how did I act? What did I do?'

'Why, you didn't do anything.'

'Nothing?' asked Frankie.

'No. You just watched the pair of them like they was ghosts. Then, when they talked about the wedding, them ears of yours stiffened out the size of cabbage leaves——'

935

Frankie raised her hand to her left ear. 'They didn't,' she said bitterly. Then after a while she added. 'Someday you going to look down and find that big fat tongue of yours pulled out by the roots and laying there before you on the table. Then how do you think you will feel?'

'Quit talking so rude,' said Berenice.

Frankie scowled down at the splinter in her foot. She finished cutting it out with the knife and said, 'That would have hurt anybody else but me.' Then she was walking round and round the room again. 'I am so scared I didn't make a good impression.'

'What of it?' said Berenice. 'I wish Honey and T. T. would come on. You make me nervous.'

Frankie drew up her left shoulder and bit her lower lip. Then suddenly she sat down and banged her forehead on the table.

'Come on,' said Berenice. 'Don't act like that.'

But Frankie sat stiff, her face in the crook of her elbow and her fists clenched tight. Her voice had a ragged and strangled sound. 'They were so pretty,' she was saying. 'They must have such a good time. And they went away and left me.'

'Sit up,' said Berenice. 'Behave yourself.'

'They came and went away,' she said. 'They went away and left me with this feeling.'

'Hooee!' said Berenice finally. 'I bet I know something.'

The kitchen was silent and she tapped four times with her heel: one, two, three—*bang!* Her live eye was dark and teasing and she tapped with her heel, then took up the beating with a dark jazz voice that was like a song.

> Frankie got a crush!
> Frankie got a crush!
> Frankie got a crush!
> On the *Wedd*-ing!

'Quit,' said Frankie.

> Frankie got a crush!
> Frankie got a crush!

Berenice went on and on, and her voice was jazzed like the heart that beats in your head when you have fever. Frankie was dizzy, and she picked up the knife from the kitchen table.

'You better quit!'

Berenice stopped very suddenly. The kitchen was suddenly shrunken and quiet.

'You lay down that knife.'

'Make me.'

She steadied the end of the handle against her palm and bent the blade slowly. The knife was limber, sharp, and long.

936 'Lay it down, DEVIL!'

But Frankie stood up and took careful aim. Her eyes were narrowed and the feel of the knife made her hands stop trembling.

'Just throw it!' said Berenice. 'You just!'

All the house was very quiet. The empty house seemed to be waiting. And then there was the knife whistle in the air and the sound the blade made when it struck. The knife hit the middle of the stairway door and shivered there. She watched the knife until it did not shiver any longer.

'I am the best knife-thrower in this town,' she said.

Berenice, who stood behind her, did not speak.

'If they would have a contest I would win.'

Frankie pulled the knife from the door and laid it on the kitchen table. Then she spat on her palm and rubbed her hands together.

Berenice said finally: 'Frances Addams, you going to do that once too often.'

'I never miss outside of a few inches.'

'You know what your father said about knife-throwing in this house.'

'I warned you to quit picking with me.'

'You are not fit to live in a house,' said Berenice.

'I won't be living in this one much longer. I'm going to run away from home.'

'And a good riddance to a big old bad rubbage,' said Berenice.

'You wait and see. I'm leaving town.'

'And where you think you are going?'

Frankie looked at all the corners of the room, and then said, 'I don't know.'

'I do,' said Berenice. 'You going crazy. That's where you going.'

'No,' said Frankie. She stood very still, looking around the queerly pictured wall, and then she closed her eyes. 'I'm going to Winter Hill. I'm going to the wedding. And I swear to Jesus by my two eyes I'm never coming back here any more.'

She had not been sure that she would throw the knife until it struck and shivered on the stairway door. And she had not known that she would say these words until already they were spoken. The swear was like the sudden knife; she felt it strike in her and tremble. Then when the words were quiet, she said again:

'After the wedding I'm not coming back.'

Berenice pushed back the damp bangs of Frankie's hair and finally she asked: 'Sugar? You serious?'

'Of course!' said Frankie. 'Do you think I would stand here and swear that swear and tell a story? Sometimes, Berenice, I think it takes you longer to realize a fact than it does anybody who ever lived.'

'But,' said Berenice, 'you say you don't know where you're going. You going, but you don't know where. That don't make no sense to me.'

Frankie stood looking up and down the four walls of the room. She thought of the world, and it was fast and loose and turning, faster and looser and bigger than ever it had been before. The pictures of the War sprang out and clashed together in her mind. She saw bright flowered islands and a land by a northern sea with the gray waves on the shore. Bombed eyes and the shuffle of soldiers' feet. Tanks and a plane, wing broken, burning and downward-falling in a desert sky. The world was cracked by the loud battles and turning a thousand miles a minute. The names of places spun in Frankie's mind: China, Peachville, New Zealand, Paris, Cincinnati, Rome. She thought of the huge and turning world until her legs began to tremble and there was sweat on the palms of her hands. But still she did not know where she should go. Finally she stopped looking around the four kitchen walls and said to Berenice:

937

'I feel just exactly like somebody has peeled all the skin off me. I wish I had some cold good chocolate ice cream.'

Berenice had her hands on Frankie's shoulders and was shaking her head and staring with the live eye narrowed into Frankie's face.

'But every word I told you was the solemn truth,' she said. 'I'm not coming back here after the wedding.'

There was a sound, and when they turned they saw that Honey and T. T. Williams were standing in the doorway. Honey, though he was her foster brother, did not resemble Berenice—and it was almost as though he came from some foreign country, like Cuba or Mexico. He was light-skinned, almost lavender in color, with quiet narrow eyes like oil, and a limber body. Behind the two of them stood T. T. Williams, and he was very big and black; he was gray-haired, older even than Berenice, and he wore a church suit with a red badge in the buttonhole. T. T. Williams was a beau of Berenice, a well-off colored man who owned a colored restaurant. Honey was a sick, loose person. The army would not include him, and he had shoveled in a gravel pit until he broke one of his insides and could not do heavy work any more. They stood, the three of them, dark and grouped together in the door.

'What you all creep up like that for?' asked Berenice. 'I didn't even hear you.'

'You and Frankie too busy discussing something,' said T. T.

'I am ready to go,' said Berenice. 'I been ready. But do you wish a small little quickie before we start?'

T. T. Williams looked at Frankie and shuffled his feet. He was very proper, and he liked to please everybody, and he always wanted to do the right thing.

'Frankie ain't no tattle-tale,' said Berenice. 'Is you?'

Frankie would not even answer such a question. Honey wore a dark red rayon slack suit and she said: 'That sure is a cute suit you got on, Honey. Where did you get it?'

Honey could talk like a white school-teacher; his lavender lips could move as quick and light as butterflies. But he only answered with a colored word, a dark sound from the throat that can mean anything. 'Ahhnnh,' he said.

The glasses were before them on the table, and the hair-straightening bottle that held gin, but they did not drink. Berenice said something about Paris and Frankie had the extra feeling that they were waiting for her to leave. She stood in the door and looked at them. She did not want to go away.

'You wish water in yours, T. T.?' asked Berenice.

They were together around the table and Frankie stood extra in the door alone. 'So long, you all,' she said.

' 'Bye, Sugar,' said Berenice. 'You forget all that foolishness we was discussing. And if Mr. Addams don't come home by dark, you go on over to the Wests. Go play with John Henry.'

'Since when have I been scared of the dark?' said Frankie. 'So long.'

'So long,' they said.

938

She closed the door, but behind her she could hear their voices. With her head against the kitchen door she could hear the murmuring dark sounds that rose and fell in a gentle way. Ayee—ayee. And then Honey spoke above the idle wash of voices and he asked: 'What was it between you and Frankie when we come in the house?' She waited, her ear pressed close against the door, to hear what Berenice would say. And finally the words were: 'Just foolishness. Frankie was carrying on with foolishness.' She listened until at last she heard them go away.

The empty house was darkening. She and her father were alone at night, as Berenice went to her own home directly after supper. Once they had rented the front bedroom. It was the year after her grandmother died, when Frankie was nine. They rented the front bedroom to Mr. and Mrs. Marlowe. The only thing Frankie remembered about them was the remark said at the last, that they were common people. Yet for the season they were there, Frankie was fascinated by Mr. and Mrs. Marlowe and the front room. She loved to go in when they were away and carefully, lightly meddle with their things—with Mrs. Marlowe's atomizer which skeeted perfume, the gray-pink powder puff, the wooden shoe-trees of Mr. Marlowe. They left mysteriously after an afternoon that Frankie did not understand. It was a summer Sunday and the hall door of the Marlowes' room was open. She could see only a portion of the room, part of the dresser and only the footpiece of the bed with Mrs. Marlowe's corset on it. But there was a sound in the quiet room she could not place, and when she stepped over the threshold she was startled by a sight that, after a single glance, sent her running to the kitchen, crying: Mr. Marlowe is having a fit! Berenice had hurried through the hall, but when she looked into the front room, she merely bunched her lips and banged the door. And evidently told her father, for that evening he said the Marlowes would have to leave. Frankie had tried to question Berenice and find out what was the matter. But Berenice had only said that they were common people and added that with a certain party in the house they ought at least to know enough to shut a door. Though Frankie knew she was the certain party, still she did not understand. What kind of a fit was it? she asked. But Berenice would only answer: Baby, just a common fit. And Frankie knew from the voice's tones that there was more to it than she was told. Later she only remembered the Marlowes as common people, and being common they owned common things—so that long after she had ceased to think about the Marlowes or fits, remembering merely the name and the fact that once they had rented the front bedroom, she associated common people with gray-pink powder puffs and perfume atomizers. The front bedroom had not been rented since.

Frankie went to the hall hatrack and put on one of her father's hats. She looked at her dark ugly mug in the mirror. The conversation about the wedding had somehow been wrong. The questions she had asked that afternoon had all been the wrong questions, and Berenice had answered her with jokes. She could not name the feeling in her, and she stood there until dark shadows made her think of ghosts.

Frankie went out to the street before the house and looked up into the sky. She stood staring with her fist on her hip and her mouth open. The sky was lavender and slowly darkening. She heard in the neighborhood the sound of evening voices and noticed the light fresh smell of watered grass. This was the time of the early evening when, since the kitchen was too hot, she would go for a little while outdoors. She practiced knife-throwing, or sat before the cold-drink store in the front yard. Or she would go around to the back yard, and

939

there the arbor was cool and dark. She wrote shows, although she had outgrown all of her costumes, and was too big to act in them beneath the arbor; this summer she had written very cold shows—shows about Esquimaux and frozen explorers. Then when night had come she would go again back in the house.

But this evening Frankie did not have her mind on knives or cold-drink stores or shows. Nor did she want to stand there staring up into the sky; for her heart asked the old questions, and in the old way of the spring she was afraid.

She felt she needed to think about something ugly and plain, so she turned from the evening sky and stared at her own house. Frankie lived in the ugliest house in town, but now she knew that she would not be living there much longer. The house was empty, dark. Frankie turned and walked to the end of the block, and around the corner, and down the sidewalk to the Wests'. John Henry was leaning against the banisters of his front porch, with a lighted window behind him, so that he looked like a little black paper doll on a piece of yellow paper.

'Hey,' she said. 'I wonder when that Papa of mine is coming home from town.'

John Henry did not answer.

'I don't want to go back in that dark old ugly house all by myself.'

She stood on the sidewalk, looking at John Henry, and the smart political remark came back to her. She hooked her thumb in the pockets of her pants and asked: 'If you were going to vote in an election, who would you vote for?'

John Henry's voice was bright and high in the summer night. 'I don't know,' he said.

'For instance, would you cast your vote for C. P. MacDonald to be mayor of this town?'

John Henry did not answer.

'Would you?'

But she could not get him to talk. There were times when John Henry would not answer anything you said to him. So she had to remark without an argument behind her, and all by herself like that it did not sound so very smart: 'Why, I wouldn't vote for him if he was running to be dogcatcher.'

The darkening town was very quiet. For a long time now her brother and the bride had been at Winter Hill. They had left the town a hundred miles behind them, and now were in a city far away. They were them and in Winter Hill, together, while she was her and in the same old town all by herself. The long hundred miles did not make her sadder and make her feel more far away than the knowing that they were them and both together and she was only her and parted from them, by herself. And as she sickened with this feeling a thought and explanation suddenly came to her, so that she knew and almost said aloud: *They are the we of me.* Yesterday, and all the twelve years of her life, she had only been Frankie. She was an *I* person who had to walk around and do things by herself. All other people had a *we* to claim, all other except her. When Berenice said *we*, she meant Honey and Big Mama, her lodge, or her church. The *we* of her father was the store. All members of clubs have a *we* to belong to and talk about. The soldiers in the army can say *we*, and even the

940

criminals on chain-gangs. But the old Frankie had had no *we* to claim, unless it would be the terrible summer *we* of her and John Henry and Berenice—and that was the last *we* in the world she wanted. Now all this was suddenly over with and changed. There was her brother and the bride, and it was as though when first she saw them something she had known inside of her: *They are the we of me.* And that was why it made her feel so queer, for them to be away in Winter Hill while she was left all by herself; the hull of the old Frankie left there in the town alone.

'Why are you all bent over like that?' John Henry called.

'I think I have a kind of pain,' said Frankie. 'I must have ate something.'

John Henry was still standing on the banisters, holding to the post.

'Listen,' she said finally. 'Suppose you come on over and eat supper and spend the night with me.'

'I can't,' he answered.

'Why?'

John Henry walked across the banisters, holding out his arms for balance, so that he was like a little blackbird against the yellow window light. He did not answer until he safely reached the other post.

'Just because.'

'Because why?'

He did not say anything, and so she added: 'I thought maybe me and you could put up my Indian tepee and sleep out in the back yard. And have a good time.'

Still John Henry did not speak.

'We're blood first cousins. I entertain you all the time. I've given you so many presents.'

Quietly, lightly, John Henry walked back across the banisters and then stood looking out at her with his arm around the post again.

'Sure enough,' she called. 'Why can't you come?'

At last he said, 'Because, Frankie, I don't want to.'

'Fool Jackass!' she screamed. 'I only asked you because I thought you looked so ugly and so lonesome.'

Lightly John Henry jumped down from the banisters. And his voice as he called back to her was a clear child's voice.

'Why, I'm not a bit lonesome.'

Frankie rubbed the wet palms of her hands along the sides of her shorts and said in her mind: Now turn around and take yourself on home. But in spite of this order, she was somehow unable to turn around and go. It was not yet night. Houses along the street were dark, lights showed in windows. Darkness had gathered in the thick-leaved trees and shapes in the distance were ragged and gray. But the night was not yet in the sky.

'I think something is wrong,' she said. 'It is too quiet. I have a peculiar warning in my bones. I bet you a hundred dollars it's going to storm.'

John Henry watched her from behind the banister.

'A terrible terrible dog day storm. Or maybe even a cyclone.'

Frankie stood waiting for the night. And just at that moment a horn began to play. Somewhere in the town, not far away, a horn began a blues tune. The tune was grieving and low. It was the sad horn of some colored boy, but who

941

he was she did not know. Frankie stood stiff, her head bent and her eyes closed, listening. There was something about the tune that brought back to her all of the spring: flowers, the eyes of strangers, rain.

The tune was low and dark and sad. Then all at once, as Frankie listened, the horn danced into a wild jazz spangle that zigzagged upward with sassy nigger trickiness. At the end of the jazz spangle the music rattled thin and far away. Then the tune returned to the first blues song, and it was like the telling of that long season of trouble. She stood there on the dark sidewalk and the drawn tightness of her heart made her knees lock and her throat feel stiffened. Then, without warning, the thing happened that at first Frankie could not believe. Just at the time when the tune should be laid, the music finished, the horn broke off. All of a sudden the horn stopped playing. For a moment Frankie could not take it in, she felt so lost.

She whispered finally to John Henry West: 'He has stopped to bang the spit out of his horn. In a second he will finish.'

But the music did not come again. The tune was left broken, unfinished. And the drawn tightness she could no longer stand. She felt she must do something wild and sudden that never had been done before. She hit herself on the head with her fist, but that did not help any at all. And she began to talk aloud, although at first she paid no attention to her own words and did not know in advance what she would say.

'I told Berenice that I was leaving town for good and she did not believe me. Sometimes I honestly think she is the biggest fool that ever drew breath.' She complained aloud, and her voice was fringed and sharp like the edge of a saw. She talked and did not know from one word to the next what she would say. She listened to her own voice, but the words she heard did not make much sense. 'You try to impress something on a big fool like that and it's just like talking to a block of cement. I kept on telling and telling and telling her. I told her I had to leave this town for good because it is inevitable.'

She was not talking to John Henry. She did not see him any more. He had moved from the lighted window; but he was still listening from the porch, and after a little while he asked her:

'Where?'

Frankie did not answer. She was suddenly very still and quiet. For a new feeling had come to her. The sudden feeling was that she knew deep in her where she would go. She knew, and in another minute the name of the place would come to her. Frankie bit the knuckles of her fist and waited: but she did not hunt for the name of the place and did not think about the turning world. She saw in her mind her brother and the bride, and the heart in her was squeezed so hard that Frankie almost felt it break.

John Henry was asking in his high child voice: 'You want me to eat supper and sleep in the tepee with you?'

She answered: 'No.'

'You just a little while ago invited me!'

But she could not argue with John Henry West or answer anything he said. For it was just at that moment that Frankie understood. She knew who she was and how she was going into the world. Her squeezed heart suddenly opened and

942

divided. Her heart divided like two wings. And when she spoke her voice was sure.

'I know where I'm going,' she said.

He asked her: 'Where?'

'I'm going to Winter Hill,' she said. 'I'm going to the wedding.'

She waited, to give him a chance to say: 'I already knew that, anyhow.' Then finally she spoke the sudden truth aloud.

'I'm going with them. After the wedding at Winter Hill, I'm going off with the two of them to whatever place that they will ever go. I'm going with them.'

He did not answer.

'I love the two of them so much. We'll go to every place together. It's like I've known it all my life, that I belong to be with them. I love the two of them so much.'

And having said this, she did not need to wonder and puzzle any more. She opened her eyes, and it was night. The lavender sky had at last grown dark and there was slanted starlight and twisted shade. Her heart had divided like two wings and she had never seen a night so beautiful.

Frankie stood looking into the sky. For when the old question came to her—the who she was and what she would be in the world, and why she was standing there that minute—when the old question came to her, she did not feel hurt and unanswered. At last she knew just who she was and understood where she was going. She loved her brother and the bride and she was a member of the wedding. The three of them would go into the world and they would always be together. And finally, after the scared spring and the crazy summer, she was no more afraid. . . . (1946)

PETER TAYLOR

1917–

Peter Taylor was born in Trenton, Tennessee, on January 8, 1917. He studied at Vanderbilt University for one year, but transferred to Kenyon College in Gambier, Ohio, chiefly in order to study under John Crowe Ransom. He was graduated from Kenyon with an A.B. degree in 1940. During World War II he served as a sergeant in the United States Army.

A number of Taylor's short stories have appeared in *The New Yorker* and other magazines. A collection of them, *A Long Fourth and Other Stories* (1948) was enthusiastically received, as was his first novel, *A Woman of Means* (1950). At the present time Taylor is a Professor of English at the Woman's College of the University of North Carolina.

A Long Fourth

For over five years Harriet Wilson had been saying, "I'd be happier, Sweetheart, if BT were not even on the place." Harriet was a pretty woman just past fifty, and Sweetheart felt that she grew prettier as the years went by. He told her so, too, whenever she mentioned the business about BT or any other business. "I declare you get prettier by the year," he was accustomed to say. That was how the BT business had been allowed to run on so. Once she had pointed out to Sweetheart that he never said she grew wiser by the year, and he had replied, laughing, that it certainly did seem she would never be a judge of niggers. It was while they were dressing for breakfast one morning that he told her that, and she had quickly turned her back to him (which was the severest rebuke she was ever known to give her husband) and began to powder her neck and shoulders before the mirror. Then he had come over and put his hands on her pretty, plump shoulders and kissed her on the cheek saying, "But you're nobody's fool, darling."

Thinking of that had oftentimes been consolation to her when Sweetheart had prettied her out of some notion she had. But really she had always considered that she was nobody's fool and that she certainly was not merely a vain little woman ruled by a husband's flattery, the type her mother had so despised in her lifetime. She even found herself sometimes addressing her dead mother when she was alone. "It's not that I've become one of that sort of women in middle-age, Mama. It's that when he is so sweet to me I realize what a blessing that is and how unimportant other things are." For Harriet was yet guided in some matters by well remembered words of her mother who had been dead for thirty years. In other matters she was guided by the words of Sweetheart. In still others she was guided by what Son said. Her two daughters guided her in nothing. Rather, she was ever inclined to instruct them by quoting Mama, Sweetheart, or Son.

Their house was eight miles from downtown Nashville on the Franklin Pike, and for many years Sweetheart, who was a doctor, had had his own automobile for work and Harriet had kept a little coupe. But after the War began the doctor accepted gas-rationing rather conscientiously and went to and from his office in the interurban bus. "We eye-ear-nose-and-throat men don't have to make so many professional calls," he said. Harriet usually walked down to the Pike to meet him on the five-thirty bus in the evening.

It was a quarter of a mile from the Pike to the house, and they would walk up the driveway hand in hand. Harriet who said she lived in perpetual fear of turning her ankle on a piece of gravel kept her eyes on the ground when they

944

walked, and Sweetheart would usually be gazing upward into the foliage of the poplar trees and maples that crowded the lawn and overhung the drive or he would be peering straight ahead at the house which was an old fashioned single storey clapboard building with a narrow porch across the front where wisteria bloomed in June and July. Though they rarely had their eyes on each other during this walk they were always hand in hand and there was always talk. It was on one of these strolls, not a week before BT gave notice, that Harriet last uttered her old complaint: "I've always told you that I'd be happier, Sweetheart, if BT were not even on this place now that he's grown up."

"I know." He squeezed her hand and turned a smiling countenance to her.

"I don't think you do know," she said keeping her eyes on the white gravel. "He's grand on the outside, but all of them are grand on the outside. As long as we keep him I'm completely deprived of the services of a houseboy when I need one. When Son and his young lady come I don't know what I'll do. The girls are angels about things, but next week they should be entertaining Son and her, and not just picking-up after her. It seems so unreasonable, Sweetheart, to keep BT when we could have a nice, normal darkie that could do inside when I need him."

Sweetheart began swinging their joined hands merrily. "Ah, oh, now, BT's a pretty darned good darkie, just clumsy and runs around a bit."

Harriet looked up at her husband and stopped still as though she were afraid to walk with her eyes off her feet. "Sweetheart, you know very well it's not that." And making a face she held her nose and shuddered so acutely that he could feel it in the fingers of the hand he was holding.

"Well, there's nothing wrong that a little washing won't cure." He was facing her and trying now to take hold of her other hand.

"No, no, no, Sweetheart. It's constitutional with him. Last Monday I had him bathe before he came in to help old Mattie move the sideboard. Yet that room was unbearable for twenty minutes after he left. I *had* to get out, and I heard his Auntie Mattie say 'Whew!' Mattie knows it as well as I do and is just too contrary to admit it. I'm sure that's why she moved into the attic and left him the whole shack, but she's too contrary to admit it."

The doctor threw back his head and laughed aloud. Then for a time he seemed to be studying the foliage absently and he said that he reckoned poor old Mattie loved her little nephew a good deal. "I think it's touching," he said, "and I believe Mattie would leave us in a minute if we let BT go."

"Not a bit of it!" said Harriet.

"Nevertheless, he's a good nigger," her husband said, "and we can't judge Negroes the way we do white people, Harriet."

"Well, I should say *not!*" Harriet exclaimed.

Harriet was not a light sleeper but she complained that she often awoke in the night when there was something on her mind. On the last night of June that summer she awoke with a start and saw by the illuminated dial of her watch that it was three A.M. She rolled over on her stomach with great care not to disturb Sweetheart who was snoring gently beside her. This waking, she supposed, was a result of her worries about Son's coming visit and the guest he was bringing with him. And then Son was going to the Army on the day after the Fourth. She had been worrying for weeks about Son's going into the Army

945

and how he would fit in there. He was not like other men, more sensitive and had advanced ideas and was so intolerant of inefficiency and old fashioned things. This was what had broken her sleep, she thought; and then there was repeated the unheard of racket that had really awakened her.

Harriet grunted in her pillow, for she knew that it was her daughters quarreling again. A door slammed and she heard Kate's voice through the wall. "Oh, Goddy! Godamighty! Helena, won't you please shut up!" She knew at once the cause of the quarrel: Kate had been out this evening and had turned on the light when she came to undress. Poor thing certainly could not pin up her hair and hang up her dress in the dark. Yet it *was* an unreasonable hour. She wondered where the girls ever stayed till such a late hour. They were too old now to be quizzed about those things. But they were also too old to be quarreling so childishly. Why, when Harriet and her sister were their age they were married and had the responsibilities of their own families. What a shame it is, she thought, that my girls are not married, and it's all because of their height. Then Harriet rebuked herself for begrudging them one minute of their time with what few beaux they had.

For there really were so few tall men nowadays. In her own day there had been more tall men, and tall women were then considered graceful. Short dresses do make such a difference, she reflected, and my girls' legs are not pretty. Harriet was not tall herself, but Mama had been tall and Mama was known as one of the handsomest women that ever graced the drawing rooms of Nashville. But the girls were a little taller than even Mama had been. And they were smart like Mama. They read all the same books and magazines that Son did. Son said they were quite conversant. Nevertheless they must behave themselves while Son's friend was here. No such hours and no such quarrels! She did wish that Son had not planned to bring this girl down from New York, for he had said frankly that they were not in love, they were only friends and had the same interests. Harriet felt certain that Son would bring no one who was not a lady, but what real lady, she asked herself, would edit a birth-control magazine? Just then Sweetheart rolled over and in his sleep put his arm about her shoulders. So she began to think of all her blessings. Something reminded her that she had not said her prayers before going to bed, and so with his arm about her she said the Lord's Prayer and went off to sleep.

She forgot to speak to the girls the next day about their quarreling, but on the following day she was determined to mention it. Sweetheart had left for town in his car since he was to meet Son's and Miss Prewitt's train that afternoon. Harriet was in the front part of the house wearing a long gingham wrapper and her horn-rimmed spectacles. In one hand she clasped the morning paper and a few of the June bills which had come in that morning's mail. The house was in good order and in perfect cleanliness, for she and the girls and Mattie had spent the past three days in putting it so.

946   These days had been unusually cool with a little rain in the morning and again in the afternoon. Otherwise Harriet didn't know how they could have managed a general housecleaning in June. The girls had really worked like Trojans, making no complaint but indirectly. Once when it began to rain after a sultry noon hour Helena had said, "Well, thank God for small favors." Kate, when she broke her longest fingernail on the curtain rod, screamed a word that Harriet would not even repeat in her mind. But they had been perfect angels about helping. Their being so willing, so tall and so strong is really compensation, Harriet kept telling herself, for not having the services of a houseboy. They had tied their heads up in scarfs, pulled on their garden slacks and done all a-man's-work of reaching the highest ledges and light fixtures and even lifting the piano and the dining room table.

They had spent last evening on the big screened porch in back, had eaten supper and breakfast there too, so there was not a thing to be done to the front part of the house this morning. In the living room she looked about with a pleasant, company smile for the polished floor and gave an affected little nod to the clean curtains. All she did was to disarrange some of the big chairs which Mattie had fixed in too rigid a circle. Mama used to warn Harriet against being superficial in her housekeeping. "The main thing is comfort, dearest," and Harriet knew that she had a tendency to care for the cleanliness and order. So she even put the hearth rug at a slight angle. Then she went to the window and observed that a real July sun was rising today, so she pulled-to the draperies and went from window to window shutting out the light till the whole front part of the house was dark.

The girls slept late that morning. They had earned their rest, and Harriet went tiptoeing about the house listening for them to call for the breakfast that old Mattie had promised to serve them in bed. When ten o'clock came she had picked-up in her room, given a last dusting to Son's room and to the guest room, and Mattie had swept the screened porch and was through in the kitchen. It was time to go to market. Mattie had much to do that day and it was not planned for her to go marketing with Harriet. But the girls had been such angels that Harriet and Mattie agreed they should be allowed to sleep as late as their hearts desired.

Mattie put on her straw and in Harriet's presence she was on the back porch giving BT some last instructions. BT was cleaning six frying-size chickens from their own yard. Later he must peel potatoes and gather beans, lettuce, tomatoes and okra from what was known as the girls' victory garden. He was acknowledged a good hand at many services which could be rendered on the back porch, and his schedule there over the coming holiday week-end was a full one. "Have you cleaned up the freezer?" Harriet asked him. She too was standing with her hat on. She was looking critically at the naked chicken on which his black hands were operating with a small paring knife. Before he answered concerning the freezer she had turned to Mattie and said, "Don't serve the necks tonight, Mattie." Meanwhile BT had crossed the porch and brought back the big wooden bucket of the ice-cream freezer. The bucket itself had been scrubbed wonderfully clean, and with eyes directed toward her but focused for some object that would have been far behind her, BT exhibited the immaculate turner and metal container from within. "It does look grand, BT," Harriet admitted.

She was about to depart when she heard one of the girls' voices through their window across the way. (The rear of the house was of an U-shape with the big pantries and the kitchen in one wing and the bedrooms in the other.) Harriet went down through the yard and looked in the girls' window. She was astonished to find the room in complete order and the girls fully dressed and each seated

947

on her own bed reading. Harriet's eyes were immediately filled with tears. She thought of how hard they had worked this week and with what unaccustomed deference they had treated her, calling her "Mama" sometimes instead of Mother, sometimes even being so playful as to call her "Mammy." And this morning they had not wanted to be a bother to anyone. Further, they were reading something new so that they would be conversant with Son and Miss Prewitt. Kate jumped from the bed and said, "Why, Mammy, you're ready to go to market. I'll be right with you." Harriet turned from the window and called to Mattie to take off her straw, for Miss Kate was going to market with her.

But she didn't begin to walk toward the garage at once. The tears had left her eyes, and she stood thinking quite clearly of this change in her daughters' behavior. She was ashamed of having thought it would be necessary to mention their quarreling and their late hours to them. Perhaps they had worried as much as she about Son's going into the Army and probably they were as eager to make him proud of his family before Miss Prewitt.

As all of her concern for the success of the visit cleared away she began to think of what a pity it was that Son and Miss Prewitt were not in love. She would have suspected that it might really be a romance except that the girls assured her otherwise. They told her that Son did not believe in marriage and that he certainly would not subject his family and the people of Nashville to the sort of thing he did believe in. This girl was merely one of the people he knew in his publishing business. And thinking again of all Son's advanced ideas and his intolerance she could not but think of the unhappiness he was certain to know in the Army. And more than this there would be no weekly telephone calls for her and perhaps no letters and no periodic visits home. He would be going away from them all and he might just be missing and never be brought home for burial. Her imagination summoned for comfort the warmth of Sweetheart's smile and the feel of his arm about her, but there was little comfort even there.

When they returned from market they found Helena on the back porch peeling the potatoes. "What on earth is Helena doing?" Kate asked before they got out of the coupe. Harriet frowned and pressed the horn for BT to come and get the groceries. Then the tall daughter and the short little mother scrambled out of the car and hurried toward the porch. Almost as soon as the coupe appeared Helena had stood up. She took three long strides to the edge of the porch. When her mother and sister drew near, her eyes seemed ready to pop out of her head. Her mouth which was large and capable of great expansions was full open. Yet the girl was speechless.

Harriet was immediately all a tremble and she felt the blood leaving her lips. To herself she said, "Something terrible has—" Then simultaneously she saw that Helena's eyes were fixed on something behind Kate and herself and she heard old Mattie's broken voice calling to her, "Miss Harriet! Oh, Missie, Missie!" She turned about quickly, dropping her eyes to her feet to make sure of her footing, and now looking up she saw the old Negro woman running toward her with her big faded kitchen apron clasped up between her clean, buff colored hands.

The old fashioned appellative "Missie" told Harriet a great deal. She handed

Kate her purse and put out her arms to receive Mattie, for she knew that her old friend was in deep trouble. The Negress was several inches taller than Harriet but she threw herself into her little mistress's arms and by bending her knees slightly and stooping her shoulders she managed to rest her face on the bosom of the white eyelet dress while she wept. Harriet held her so for a time with her arms about her and patting her gently between the shoulder blades and just above the bow knot of her apron strings. "Now, now, Mattie," she whispered, "Maybe it's not as bad as it seems. It's something about BT, isn't it? What is it, Mattie, honey?"

"Oh, oh, oh, he gwine leave."

The voice seemed so expressive of the pain in that heart that Harriet could think only of the old woman's suffering and not at all of the cause. "My poor Mattie," she said.

But her sympathy only brought forth more tears and deeper sobs. "My little nephew is gwine leave his old auntie who raised him up when nobody els'd tech him." Harriet did not even hear what Mattie was saying now, but she perceived that her own sympathy was encouraging self-pity and thus giving the pain a double edge. And so she tried to think of some consolation.

"Maybe he won't go after all, Mattie."

Saying this she realized the bearing of BT's departure upon the holiday week-end of which this was the very eve. Then she told herself that indeed Mattie's little nephew would not go after all. "He won't go," she said, "I tell you, Mattie, he won't go if I have any power of constraining him." Her blue eyes shone thoughtfully as she watched the two girls who were now making the last of several trips to bring the groceries from the back of the coupe.

"Oh, oh, oh, yes'm he will, Missie. He's gwine Tuesday. It's the war, an' y' can't stop 'm. He gwine work at th'air fact'ry 'cause the draf membuhs don't want 'm much. But ifn he don't work at th'air fact'ry they'll have to take 'im, want 'im or not." And while his auntie was speaking BT appeared from the door of the unpainted cabin from which Mattie had come. He was still wearing the white coat which he always wore on the back porch, and plainly intended to continue his work through the week-end. He ran over to the car where Kate was unloading the last of the groceries and relieved her of her armful.

Harriet's relief was great. BT would be here through Monday! She began to caress Mattie again and to speak softly in her ear. Her eyes and her thoughts, however, were upon BT. He was a big—neither muscular nor fat, merely big— black, lazy-looking Negro. As he came along the brick walk toward her he kept his eyes lowered to the bundle of groceries. He was what Harriet's Mama would have called a field nigger and had never learned any house manners at all. His face, to her, had ever seemed devoid of expression. He had grown up here on their suburban acreage and had been hardly more than twenty miles distant in his lifetime, but Harriet felt that she had held less converse with him than with any of the men who used to come for short intervals and do the work when BT was still a child. He worked hard and long and efficiently here on their small acreage, she knew, and on Saturday nights he usually got drunk down at the Negro settlement and sometimes spent the later part of that night and all day Sunday in the county jail. There had been times when he had stolen pieces of Sweetheart's and Son's clothing off the wash line, and you dare not lose any

949

change in the porch chairs. Sometimes too they would find that he was keeping some black female thing out in the shack for a week at a time, toting food to her from the kitchen. The female things he kept were not Negro women who might have been useful about the place but were real prostitutes from Nashville (Who else would have endured the smell there must be in that shack?), and Dr. Wilson was ever and anon having to take him to Nashville for the shots. But all of that sort of thing was to be expected, admitted Harriet, and it was not that which caused her antipathy, over and above his constitutional affliction, toward him. BT was simply wanting in those qualities which she generally found appealing in Negroes. He had neither good manners nor the affectionate nature nor the appealing humor that so many niggers have.

As he passed her there at the foot of the porch steps the odor he diffused had never seemed more repugnant and never so strong when outside the house. Mattie raised her tear streaked brown face, knowing it was BT surely more from his odor than from his footstep, and as he followed the two girls to the kitchen door she called after him, "BT, don't leave old Auntie!" Then she looked at her mistress with what Harriet acknowledged to be the sweetest expression she had ever beheld in a Negro's countenance. "Miss Harriet," she said as though stunned at her own thoughts, "it's like you losin' Mr. Son. BT is gwine too."

The small white woman abruptly withdrew her arms from about her servant. The movement was made in one fearful gesture which included the sudden contraction of her lips and the widening of her bright eyes. "Mattie!" she declaimed, "how dare you? That will be just exactly enough from you!" And now her eyes moved swiftly downward and to the porch steps. Without another glance at the woman she had been holding to her bosom she went up on the porch and, avoiding the kitchen where the girls were, she went along the porch up into the U of the house and entered the dark dining room. While she walked her face grew hot and cold alternately as her indignation rose and rose again. When she reached her own room in the far wing of the house she closed the door and let the knob turn-to in her hand. She pulled off her hat and dropped it on her dressing table among her toilet articles and handkerchief box and stray ends of gray hair that were wrapped around a hairpin. And she went and sat down in a rocking chair near the foot of the bed and began to rock. "Like Son! Like Son!"

The very chair had violence in its rocking motion. Several times Harriet might have pushed herself over backward but for lacking the strength in her small legs. Not since she was a little child had such rage been known to her bosom, and throughout the half hour of her wildest passion she was rather aware of this. This evidence of a choleric temperament was so singular a thing for her that she could not but be half conscious of its very singularness and could not but be taking note of herself as her feelings rose and convulsed in their paroxysm. She wondered first that she had refrained from striking Mattie out in the yard and she remarked it humorlessly that only the approaching holiday had prevented her. The insinuation had been sufficiently plain without Mattie's putting it into words. It was her putting it into words that earned Harriet's wrath. The open comparison of Son's departure to that of the sullen, stinking, thieving, fornicating black BT was an injury for which Son could not avenge himself, and she felt it her bounden duty to in some way make that black woman feel the grossness of her wrong and ultimately to drive her off the premises. And it was in this vein, this very declamatory language, this elevated tone with which Harriet expressed herself in the solitude of her room. She was unconsciously trying to use the language and the rhetoric of her mother and of the only books with which she had ever had much acquaintance. Between the moments when she even pictured Mattie's being tied and flogged or thought of Mama's uncle who shot all of his niggers before he would free them and of the Negro governor of North Carolina and the Negro senate rolling whiskey barrels up the capitol steps, of the rape and uprisings in Memphis and the riots in Chicago, between these thoughts she would actually consider the virtue of her own wrath. And recalling her Greek classes at Miss Hood's school she thought without a flicker of humor of Achilles' indignation.

Not the least of the offence was the time that Mattie had chosen. Harriet was powerless to act until this long Fourth of July was over. She meant to endure the presence of that Ethiopian woman and that ape of a man through Sunday and Monday, till her own boy had had his holiday and gone to join the Army. His last visit must not be marred, and she resolved to tell no one—not even Sweetheart—of what had occurred. The holiday would be almost intolerable to her now, but she stopped her furious rocking and with her feet set side by side on the carpet she resolved to endure it in silence for his sake who was the best of all possible sons. Sweat was running down her forehead, and her little hands hung limp and cold.

People in Nashville had been saying for a week how Son would be missed. More than most boys, even those who had not left Nashville to work in New York or St. Louis, Son would be missed by his family when he went to the Army. People said that he had been a model son while he was growing up. And after his own talents and ability took him away to New York he had been so good about keeping in touch. He had written and telephoned and visited home regularly. That was what the older people remarked. And the young people no less admired the faithfulness and consideration he showed his parents. He had carried all the honors in his classes at school and at the University and had not grieved his parents with youthful dissipation as most Nashville boys do. What the young people thought especially fine was that, being the intellectual sort which he certainly was, he had been careful never to offend or embarrass his family with the peculiar, radical ideas which he would naturally have. After he left Nashville he had never sent home magazines in which his disturbing articles appeared, not even to his sisters who pretended to have the same kind of mind. And finally when the wild stories about his private and semi-public activities began to come back to Nashville and circulate among people, people were not so displeased with these stories as they were pleased to find on his next visit that he behaved as of old while in Nashville.

He was a tall, fair headed young man, softly spoken, and he dressed conventionally. When he came into his mother's front hall that Saturday afternoon on the second of July he was still wearing the seersucker suit in which he had traveled. Harriet was not at the door to greet him, but as she came from her room she could hear amid the flurry of greetings his polite voice asking in his formal way if she were well. She met him at the door of the parlor and as she threw her arms about him she found herself unable to restrain her tears.

951

She thought, of course, that her weeping would subside in a moment and she did not even hide her face in her handkerchief. She tried to speak to him and then pushing him a little aside she tried to say something to the young woman he had brought with him. But the sight of Miss Prewitt there beside Sweetheart seemed to open new valves and it seemed that she was beginning to choke. When she had first seen Son in the doorway his very appearance had confirmed the justice of her outraged feelings this afternoon. When she saw the ladylike young woman in a black traveling dress and white gloves (as an example of his taste) it occurred to her that she had even underestimated the grossness of Mattie's reflection upon him. Her weeping became so violent now and was so entirely a physical thing that it seemed not to correspond to her feelings at all. First she tried to stifle and choke down her tears physically. This failing, she tried to shame herself into composure, thinking of what a vulgar display Mama would have called this. Presently she recognized that her state was already hysteria. Sweetheart rushed forward and supported her, and Son tried to hold one hand which she was waving about.

They walked her slowly to her room speaking to her gently. All the while she was trying at moments to think of the reason for this collapse. It was not—as they would all believe—Son's going into the Army. It could not be simply the scene she had had with her cook that afternoon. Could it be that she had always hated this black, servant race and felt them a threat to her son and her family? Such ridiculous thoughts! Then she was alternately laughing and weeping, and they put her on her bed. Sweetheart attended her and then sat holding her hand til she was absolutely quiet. Later the girls took their turns at sitting with her. All she could remember about Son that afternoon was hearing him say, out in the hall it seemed, "How unlike Mother."

It was late in the evening before they would let her move from her bed or leave her room. But by ten o' clock Sweetheart was convinced that her fretting there in bed was more harmful than a little company up in the front room would be. She declared herself to be quite recovered and after a bit of washing and powdering she presented herself to the four young people who were playing bridge in the parlor.

"Well, well, have a seat," Son said extending his left hand to her.

His manner was casual, as was that of the others—studiedly so. For they wanted to make her comfortable. Even Miss Prewitt restrained her attentions, pretending to be absorbed in the cards although she was dummy. "The girls have given us a good trimming tonight," she said.

When Miss Prewitt spoke, Harriet observed that she had extremely crooked teeth which had been brought more or less into line probably by wearing bands as a child. Her face was rather plain but her cheeks had a natural rosiness to them and her eyes though too small were bright and responsive. She wore no make-up and was redolent of no detectable perfume or powder. And before she sat down in the chair which Sweetheart drew up for her Harriet had perceived that the girl took no pains with her hair which hung in a half-bob with some natural wave.

"We're teaching these Yankees a thing or two," Helena said winking playfully at Kate.

"Will you listen to that?" Miss Prewitt smiled and revealed to Harriet a pleasant manner and an amiable, ladylike nature. "Your daughters keep calling their own brother and myself Yankees. But of course it's partly his fault, for I learn that he didn't write you that I'm from Little Rock, myself, and that I'm on my way home for a visit."

"Isn't that man-like?" Harriet said.

Now Son dropped his last three trumps on the table and proclaimed that that was "game." He suggested that they quit playing, but Harriet insisted that they complete the rubber. Helena began to deal the cards. For a time no one spoke. Harriet pretended to gaze about the room but she could hardly keep her eyes off Miss Prewitt. For though she found her extremely agreeable she perceived that the possibility of any romantic attachment between her and Son was out of the question. The tie between them was doubtless what the girls called an intellectual friendship. In her own girlhood people would have called it Platonic, but then they would have laughed about it. Mama had always said there could be no such relationship between young men and young women. Sweetheart always showed the smutty and cynical side to his nature when such things were discussed. Yet in some matters Son surely knew more than either Mama or Sweetheart. She had of course never, herself, known such a friendship with a man and just now she was really trying to imagine the feelings that two such friends would have for one another.

Until Miss Prewitt had spoken and thus started that train of thought in her mind Harriet had been wondering how dinner came off and whether Mattie served the chicken necks. But now her thoughts had been diverted and her nerves were somewhat relieved. It was she who finally broke the silence. "For Heaven's sake," she said, "let's not be so reserved. You're all being so careful of my feelings that Miss Prewitt will think I have a nervous ailment. My dear, that's the first time in my life I've ever carried on so. You just mustn't judge me by that scene I made. I have no sympathy with women who carry on so."

Then Sweetheart and the children did begin to tease her and make light of her carrying-on. Presently the conversation became animated and she was soon calling Miss Prewitt "Ann" as the girls did. Helena and Kate, she had never seen more cordial to a stranger than to Ann. She had never, indeed, seen them sweeter with one another. It was not until they had played their last card and had shaken hands across the table in acknowledgment of their complete victory that the strangeness of their behavior occurred to Harriet. It had been many a day since they had sat down at the same bridge table, for if they were partners they usually ended by calling each other "stupid" and if they were not partners they not infrequently accused each other of cheating.

Now Harriet felt herself trembling again and she was unable to follow the conversation. After a few minutes she said, "I think what we all need is a good night's sleep." The girls agreed at once, and so did Sweetheart. But Son suggested that he and Ann would like to sit up and talk for a while. Nobody seemed to take exception to this but Sweetheart who gave a little frown and shrugged his shoulders. Then he led Harriet off to their room, and the girls followed inquiring if there was anything they could do for Mother. As Harriet left the parlor she glanced back and observed that Ann's legs were as large and graceless as two fire plugs.

Sweetheart was in bed before her and lay there watching her own preparations at the dressing table. She felt that she was barely able to conceal from him the difficulty she had in rolling her hair and pulling on the net. But when she turned to put off the light she found him fast asleep.

She was standing in the dark for a moment and she heard the voices of Son and Ann out on the porch. Without even considering her action she stepped to the window and listened to their lowered voices.

"She's a very pretty and attractive little woman," Ann was saying, "but from things you had said I was not quite prepared to find her such a nervous woman."

"That's true. But I don't think she really is a nervous woman," Son said slowly. "I believe nobody was more surprised than herself at what happened this afternoon."

"It's not just what happened this afternoon. She was trembling most of the time in the living room tonight."

"I can't imagine what it is. Something seems to have come over her. But there's no visible change. She hasn't aged any. I looked for it in her hair and in the skin about her neck and in her figure." It hardly seemed possible to Harriet that this was Son talking about herself.

"She's certainly past her menopause, isn't she?"

"Oh, certainly. Several years ago when I was still in school."

"That's rather early."

"Yes. . . . Yes."

"The girls are much more conventional than I imagined, much less independent, more feminine.—"

"Something," Son emphasized, "seems to have come over them, too."

"They're too young for any sort of frustration, I suppose."

This whispered but clearly audible conversation caused Harriet to feel herself alienated from all around her. It was Son's disinterested tone and objectiveness. Her mind returned to Mattie. She wondered how she and BT would behave through the week-end. And now looking out into the back yard where the moon was shining on the shingled roof of the cabin and through the trees to the porch steps she considered again the words she had used to Mattie out there this afternoon.

The girls had planned a small party for Monday night which was July Fourth. It was not to be at the Country Club, where they had always before preferred to entertain, but at the house. But on Sunday night one of Son's old friends named Harry Buchanan had invited the group to supper at the Club. Harry was married and had two small children.

At the breakfast table Sunday morning Helena said to Ann, "We didn't plan anything for last night because we knew you two would be tired from traveling. But we're having a few friends to the house tomorrow night, and tonight the Buchanans"—she hesitated and closed her eyes significantly—"have asked us to supper at the Club. I don't know why some people must entertain at clubs and hotels."

"It all sounds quite festive," Ann said.

"Yes, I'm afraid 'festive' is the word," said Kate. "When people ask you to a hotel or a club, instead of to their home, if the occasion's not 'festive' or 'gala' what can it be? I don't take such an invitation as a great compliment."

Ann said nothing. Son looked over his pink grapefruit, perplexed. Harriet was completely mystified now by the things her daughters were saying. It sounded like pure nonsense to her although she was pleased to see them in such accord. She could not say that she disagreed with them, but it did sound like nonsense because it was the very reverse of ideas they usually expressed. Perhaps it was because they were growing older and more like herself. "One never realizes when one's children are growing up," she thought. But whether or not she agreed with them in principle she did think it ungracious and unkind of them to speak that way about Son's friend who was entertaining them tonight.

"Kate," she said, "the Buchanans have two small children and their house is so small."

The two daughters laughed. "Dear, dear Mama," Helena said, "you're such a Christian. You wouldn't say anything against *any*body on Sunday, would you?"

"Let me ask you this, Mama," said Kate. "Would your Mother have liked entertaining visitors at a Golf Club?"

Harriet shook her head. "That was long ago when Mama entertained, and it was not the custom then."

"There you are. We're only thinking as you've taught us to think, Mama, when we think that many of the customs and ways that used to pertain in Nashville were better than what is replacing them."

Harriet asked herself if that was what she had taught them to think. She didn't know she had taught them to think anything. But her only real interest in the matter was the defense of Harry Buchanan whose wife's mother, she presently said, was a dear friend of hers and was from one of Nashville's loveliest families and certainly knew how to "do." Then Helena asked with apparent artlessness what her dear friend's maiden name had been. And the question led to a prolonged discussion between the girls and their mother and even their father of the kinship of various Nashville families. Nothing yet had amazed Harriet more than the knowledge of those kinships and connections which Helena and Kate proceeded to display.

"Why, you two girls," Sweetheart said in his innocence, "are getting to rival your Mother in matters of who's kin to who." But Harriet was observing Son and Ann who remained silent and kept their eyes on their food. She herewith resolved that she would make it her special task during the remainder of the visit to avoid such talk since it seemed to cause a mysterious antagonism between the young people.

After breakfast Son and Ann left for a walk about the premises in the company of Sweetheart who wanted to show them his orchards and his four acres of oats and the old cotton patch where he had had BT put in lespedeza this year. They were also to see his poultry and the Jersey cow whose milk at breakfast had tasted of wild onions. He urged Helena and Kate to come along and show off the vegetable garden where they had worked and directed BT's labor. But the girls declined, saying that they were through with outdoor life until the weather was cool again. Harriet said to herself, "They're perfect angels and don't want to leave the housework to me this morning."

Later Sweetheart came back to the house and settled himself on the porch with the Sunday morning paper while Son and Ann walked down the Pike toward the Confederate Monument. Harriet debated the question of going to church. Sweetheart advised against it in view of her nervous agitation. Then she dis-

955

missed the idea, for she dared not reject Sweetheart's advice in such matters, though for a while there did linger the thought of how restful church service would seem. When the straightening up was done the girls went to their reading again and Harriet made a visit to the kitchen that she had been postponing all morning.

"Mattie," she said, "do you have everything?" Mattie was seated at a kitchen table with her back to the swinging door through which Harriet had entered, and she did not turn around. The table was in the center of the huge, shadowy kitchen. Directly beyond the table was the doorway to the back porch, through which opening Harriet could see BT also working at a table.

"I reckon," Mattie answered after a moment. There was no movement of her head when she spoke. And her head was not bent over the table. She seemed to be staring through the doorway at BT. She was seated there on a high, unpainted wooden stool which she had long ago had BT make for her (though she had complained at the time of having to pay him for it out of her own stocking), and since BT had selfishly made the stool to accommodate his own long legs Mattie's stockinged feet drooped, rather than dangled, above her old slippers that had fallen one upon the other on the linoleum.

She was not wearing her white cap or white serving apron, so there was absolutely no relief to her black dress and her head of black hair. She was the darkest object in the whole of the dark old fashioned kitchen—blacker even than the giant range stove whereon the vegetables were boiling and in which a fire roared that kept the kitchen so hot that Harriet had hesitated to step beyond the door sill. Harriet looked about to see if the windows were open and found them all open but that window where the winter icebox was built on, and she knew Mattie would not open that window while there were so many tomatoes and heads of cabbage and lettuce to keep fresh.

In the kitchen there was only the sound of water boiling. Through the back door she could see BT in the bright sunlight on the porch and hear the regular thumping of his knife on the table as he chopped a cocoanut for the ambrosia. He seemed to be unaware of or totally indifferent to Mattie's gaze upon him. Harriet stepped back into the pantry and let the door swing shut drawing a hot breeze across her face. The two Negroes doubtless had been sitting like that for hours without a word between them. It was a picture she was not able to forget.

Among the family friends the Wilson girls were admired no less than Son though they were considered to have more temperament. (By this it was meant that they occasionally displayed bad temper in public.) They were spoken of as devoted daughters and thoroughly capable and energetic young women. Helena who was known generally as the blonde Wilson girl, though her brown hair was only a shade lighter than Kate's, sometimes taught classes at Miss Hood's school during the winter. She usually substituted, and could teach mathematics, art appreciation or modern literature to the seniors. During the winter when there were more colds and throat trouble, Kate helped with the receiving and secretarial work at Sweetheart's office.

They had large, round pleasant faces which often seemed identical to strangers. Their voices were considered identical by everyone outside the family, even by close family friends who often remarked that they didn't speak with the vulgar drawl that so many Nashville girls have adopted. Their vocabulary and their accents were more like those of their mother. They pronounced girl as "gull" as all Nashville ladies once used to do. And so it was often shocking to a stranger after hearing their slightly metallic but very feminine and old fashioned voices to turn and discover that both girls were over six feet tall. Their ages were "in the vicinity of thirty," as was Son's, and they too never seemed to have considered matrimony.

As Harriet was returning from the kitchen her ear recognized Kate's familiar touch at the piano. It was by the bass that she could always distinguish the girls' playing; Kate's was a little the heavier but with more variations. She was playing accompaniment to the ballad *Barbara Allen*, and presently Helena's straining falsetto could be heard. Then as Harriet passed through the hall she saw through the open front door Son and Ann walking up the straight driveway from the Pike. Son wore white linen trousers and a white shirt open at the collar. Ann looked very fresh and youthful in a peasant-like shirtwaist and skirt, though the flare of the skirt did accentuate the heaviness of her legs. They walked over the white gravel beneath the green canopy of the trees and the picture was framed in the semi-circle of lavender wisteria that blossomed round the entrance to the porch. The prettiness of it made Harriet sigh. It seemed that her sorrow over Son's going into the Army would not be so great if she could believe that he and Ann were in love. This old house and the surrounding woods and pastures had always seemed to her the very setting for romance. From the time when her girls had first begun to have a few beaux she had considered what a felicitous setting the swing on the front porch or the old iron bench down by the fence stile would be for the final proposal; and during her walks with Sweetheart in the evenings she would sometimes look about the lawn trying to fix upon the best spot for a garden wedding. Now the sight of Son and Ann in this pretty frame only reminded her of their unnatural and strange relationship. They were walking far apart and Ann was speaking with deliberation and gesturing as she spoke. But apparently at the first glimpse of Harriet, Ann broke off speaking. And Harriet perceived in an instant that there was at least a trouble of some kind in their relationship. She recollected now that though Son had not been talking he had been shaking his head from side to side as though in exasperation.

Kate was still playing and Helena singing (after her fashion) when they entered the parlor. Son was not long able to restrain his laughter although he had actually pressed his hand over his mouth. When his laughter finally did explode the two girls sprang up from the piano bench. Their mother stood paralyzed, expecting a greater explosion of temper from them. But they only smiled with a shamefaced expression that was utterly artificial. Ann had turned to Son and was remonstrating with him. "I really should think you'd be ashamed," she said.

"Why, he's completely shameless and unchivalrous," Helena said with the same false expression of tolerance and good nature on her face. It was this expression which the faces of both girls were affecting that stunned and mystified Harriet beyond all bounds. She knew now that they were in league to accomplish some purpose. She could see that they were fully prepared for Son's reaction and that it was even desired.

"Hush, Son, you idiot," Kate smiled. Then turning to Ann: "That old ballad

957

is one Mama taught us when we were children. Of course none of us have Mama's music, but we weren't expecting an audience." And finally she addressed her sister, "The only trouble is, Helena, you were not singing the right words—not the words Mama taught us."

"No," Son derided, "you were singing from the Oxford Book of Verse."

"I know," Helena admitted with her feigned modesty and frankness. "But, Mama," she said to Harriet, "sing us your version—the real Tennessee version."

And they all began to insist that Harriet play and sing. At first she would not, for she felt that she was being a dupe to her two daughters. It was for this that the whole scene had been arranged! If she could avoid it she would not assist them in any of their schemings. If there was to be antagonism between her children she was not going to take sides. At breakfast the girls had led her to support their criticism of country club life and modern ways by bringing in Mama's opinions. Now her singing of an old ballad would somehow support their cause.

But Son and Ann were insisting as well. She looked at Son and he said, "Please do sing." So if her singing was what they all wanted, how could she refuse? Perhaps it would make them forget whatever was the trouble. Besides, Harriet loved so to be at the piano singing the old songs that were fixed so well in her ear and in her heart.

As she sat down before the piano Helena ran to get Sweetheart, for he would never forgive them if Mother sang without his hearing it. She would also get Mattie who loved hearing her mistress sing above all else. Then Helena returned with her father saying that Mattie would listen from the pantry.

So as Sweetheart took his stand by the upright piano and watched her with that rare expression of alertness in his eyes and as the young people grouped themselves behind her Harriet began to play and sing. Her soprano voice came as clear and fresh as when she was nineteen. When she had finished *Barbara Allen* she followed with other ballads almost without being asked. Anyone listening could tell how well she enjoyed singing the old songs that her Grandpa had taught her long ago and how well she remembered the lyrics and the melody, never faltering in the words or hesitating on the keyboard. But her lovely, natural talent was not merely of the music. She seemed actually to experience the mood of each song. And her memory and ear for the soft vowels and sharp consonants of the mountain dialect were such that what was really a precise rendition seemed effortless. All her family and their guest stood round remarking on the sweet, true quality of her voice.

At the dinner table the girls began to talk again of who was kin to whom in Nashville. "Mamma," Kate said, "I didn't know till the other day that Miss Liza Parks is Mrs. Frazier Dalton's aunt. She's one of that Parks family who used to live at Cedar Hill."

Harriet could hardly resist saying that Miss Liza was also second cousin to Mr. Bob Ragsdale. But without even looking at Kate she said, "Now, what interest could that be to Ann? Tell us, Ann, how you liked Sweetheart's little farm."

"Oh, it's a beauty," Ann said. "And his methods are quite modern. He even rotates his crops and paints his barn. Dr. Wilson is certainly no backward Southern farmer. BT showed us the garden, and I think BT is a wonder."

958

"He's grand on outside work," Harriet said.

The two girls began to laugh, and Harriet frowned at them.

"Son has told me," Ann whispered to Harriet, for Mattie was passing in and out of the room, "about the poor fellow's peculiarity. He's going away for the duration, I understand, but when he comes back why doesn't he try to get a farm of his own and make a real business of it? You can tell he has a genuine love of farming, and he's quite intelligent, isn't he? He ought to——"

"Now, Ann," Son interrupted, "how on earth is a poor Negro just going to reach out and get himself a farm? How can you ask such a question with all your knowledge of conditions?"

"I was thinking that Dr. Wilson would help him. Wouldn't you, Doctor?"

"Yes, of course, if he wanted——"

The girls were laughing together again. "That's just it," Helena said, "*if* BT wanted to. But he's a gentleman's nigger, Ann. He worships Daddy, and Daddy couldn't live without him. It's a very old-fashioned relationship, you know what I mean? It's the same with Mother and Mattie." At this point Mattie came in. She was serving the last of the four vegetable dishes. Nobody spoke while she was in the room. The picture of Mattie and BT in the kitchen this morning returned to Harriet, and she found herself thinking again of what she had said to Mattie yesterday in the yard. The brooding expression in Mattie's eyes and her repeated glances at Son as she passed round the table suggested anew the hateful comparison she had drawn. But Harriet could not feel such strong resentment now. She told herself that it was because she saw now how great was the real difference between her Son and Mattie's little nephew. It was too absurd even to consider. She must have been out of her head yesterday! Her nerves had been on edge. That was the answer. And Mattie had spoken to her about that foul-scented BT just when she was grieving most about Son's going into the Army. Today the real pain of that grief had left her. It would doubtless return. But why, she considered, had it left her now? It seemed that his putting on a uniform was as unreal and indifferent a matter to her as the mysterious life he led in New York and his intellectual friendship with Ann Prewitt and this conversation they were having at her table. Last night she had overheard Son and Ann discussing herself as objectively as they were now discussing BT and Negro "conditions." Then she rebuked herself and allowed that Son simply lived on a higher plane. She felt that she should be ashamed to understand so little about her son and about her daughters and the antagonism there was between the young people.

When Mattie had left the room Kate said, "Yes, it's quite the same with Mattie and Mama. Yesterday Mattie was upset by some bad news and she came and threw herself into Mama's arms and wept like a child. It seems to me that's what they really are: a race of children, a medieval peasantry. They're completely irresponsible and totally dependent upon us. I really feel that Southern white people have a great responsibility——"

"We are responsible," Ann Prewitt said, "for their being irresponsible and dependent, if that's what you mean, Kate."

"Oh, that's *not* what she means," said Helena. "Their whole race is in its childhood, Ann, with all the wonders and charm of childhood. And it needs the protection, supervision, discipline and affection that can be given only by South-

959

ern white people who have a vital relationship and traditional ties with them. The poor nigs who I feel for are those in Chicago and New York who have no white families to turn to."

Ann was looking at Son to see if he were going to make an argument of this. But Son said only, "What do you think of that, Ann?"

With an aggrieved, shy glance at Son she said, "I think it's a lot of nonsense. But that's only my opinion."

"Well, it's my opinion too," said Son. "The people in the South cannot expect to progress with the rest of the nation until they've forgotten their color line. The whole system has got to be changed. In some strange way it hinders the whites more than the blacks. When BT was in the garden with us this morning I felt that this was his home more than mine and that it was because of him that I feel no real tie to this place. Even when we were children it was so. . . . The whole system has got to be changed . . . somehow . . . some way."

"Somehow!" Ann exclaimed. Then she lowered her eyes and seemed to regret having spoken.

"You have a definite idea of how, then?" Helena asked.

"Equality: economic and social."

"You can't be serious," the girls said in one voice.

"Of course, she's serious," Son rejoined. Ann was silent. She appeared to have resolved not to speak again.

"You two are speaking as New Yorkers now," Helena began, "not as Southerners. Didn't it ever occur to you that the South has its own destiny? It has an entirely different tradition from the rest of the country. It has its own social institutions and must be allowed to work out its own salvation without interference."

"Sister," Son laughed, "you're beginning to sound not merely old-fashioned but unreconstructed."

"Then unreconstructed it is," defied Kate with a gallant smile. "Who can say that the Southern States were wrong to fight for their way of life?"

"For slavery, Kate?"

"The Southern master was morally responsible which is more than can be said for the industrial sweat-shopper."

Now Son slapped his hand over his mouth and presently his vehement laughter burst forth. He pushed his chair a little way from the table and said, "Now the cat's out of the bag! I know what you girls have been reading and who you've probably been seeing—those fellows at the University in Nashville. You know who I mean, Ann! Why, Ann, I've brought you into a hotbed of Southern reactionaries. How rich! How really rich this is! Now I know what you girls have been trying to put across. You and all Southern gentlemen and gentlewomen are the heirs and protectors of the great European traditions—the agrarian tradition, I should say. That's what all of this family pride and *noblesse oblige* means. And Ann here, my comrade, believes that come the Revolution it will all be changed over night. How rich!"

960

His laughter was curiously contagious and there did seem to be a general relief among all. "And now, my wise brother," asked Kate, "what do you believe?"

Ann and the two sisters were managing to smile at one another, for Son's derision had united them temporarily. While Son was trying to get his breath

Ann leaned across the table and said, "He believes nothing that's any credit to him. He's been reading *The Decline of the West!* A man his age!"

Harriet was utterly dismayed, though she did sense that the incomprehensible antagonism had reached its crisis and that the worst was over. At least the young people understood each other now. But as they were leaving the table she wished, for the first time in many years, that she could be alone for a while this afternoon. She wanted to remember how Son and Helena and Kate had been when they were children—the girls quarreling over scraps from her sewing or playing dolls on the porch and Son begging to go off swimming with BT when the creek was still cold in May.

Everybody slept late on the morning of the Fourth of July. Sweetheart was still snoring gently at nine-thirty. He awoke when Harriet started the electric fan. "I'm so sorry, Sweetheart," she said, "but you looked so hot there I thought the fan might help." She was already half dressed, but before she had snapped the last snap in the placket of her dress Sweetheart had put on his clothes and shaved and gone out onto the porch. She smiled as she thought of it; and then she began to hurry, for Son's voice could now be heard on the porch. Besides there was a lot to be done in preparation for the supper party tonight. Probably the girls were already helping in the kitchen. They were being such angels this week-end!

She was smoothing the last corner of the counterpane when Kate came in.

"I feel like the devil," Kate said. She was wearing her silk negligee and her hair was uncombed and even matted in places. She was barefooted; and the girls always looked taller to Harriet when in their bare feet.

"And you look like the very devil," Harriet said.

"Thanks, dear." She sat down on the bed which Harriet had just now made. She struck a match on the bottom of the bedside table and lit the cigarette which she had brought with her. She patted the bed beside her indicating for Harriet to sit down. Harriet could always tell when the girls had been drinking a good deal the night before by the sour expression which the heavy sleep left on their features. She was long since accustomed to their drinking "socially," and to their smoking, but she still did not like to smell the whiskey on them next morning. She pulled up her rocking chair and sat down.

"Mother, I do wish that Helena wouldn't drink so much. She just doesn't know how."

Harriet only shook her head, saying nothing, for Helena would have a similar report about Kate later in the morning. The truce between them was evidently over. "How was the Buchanans' party?" she asked.

"It was pretty nice." Then she shrugged her shoulders. "I want to tell you about Ann."

"What is there to tell?"

"I thought you wanted to hear about the party!" Kate said sharply.

"I do."

"Well, listen, that's what I mean—how Ann behaved last night."

"She didn't misbehave?"

"I should say not. She's a perfect little lady, you know. A perfect parlor pink, as we suspected—Helena and I."

961

Parlor pink meant nothing to Harriet. She turned her face away toward the window to indicate that if Kate persisted in talking the kind of nonsense they talked at the table yesterday she didn't care to listen.

"She holds her liquor well, all right," Kate continued, "but after a few drinks she's not the quiet little mouse she is around here. She talks incessantly and rather brilliantly, I admit. And what I'm getting at is that when she talks Son seems to hang on her every word. He plainly thinks she's the cleverest woman alive."

"What does she talk about?"

"For one thing, she talked about birth control and its implications to Lucy Price who is a Catholic. She was really very funny about the Pope as the great papa who *doesn't* pay." Harriet had no full understanding of birth control itself, much less of its implications. And she knew that she was unreasonably prejudiced against Catholics. Why couldn't Kate talk about Ann without dragging in those things?

"She quotes Marx and Huxley and lots of young British poets. And all the while Son sits beaming with admiration as though she were Sappho or Margaret Sanger, herself."

"Is he in love with her then, Kate, if he does all that?"

"Not at all."

"And Ann, herself?"

"Hardly! She's not the type. She never looks at him."

Harriet sighed.

"But there's something between them," Kate said speculatively.

"I suppose intellectual friendships can have very deep feelings."

"Pooh," said Kate.

"Then the girl is in love with him, and he——"

"No, Mother. I don't believe it." But Harriet looked at her daughter with the matted hair and the sleep-creased face and the cigarette with its smoke drifting straight upward into the breathless air. *Her* girls had never been in love. And it isn't their height, she thought, and it isn't their legs. They're like Son, she thought, and it isn't in them. She got up from her chair and as she left Kate behind she met Helena at the door. Helena's face and hair and general attire were about the same as Kate's. "Kate's in there," Harriet said and brushed past the daughter who towered above her in the doorway. She went into the parlor to draw the draperies before the sun got too warm.

The day grew warm. You could almost hear the temperature rising if you stood still a minute. Harriet was so busy about the house that she thought it her activity that made her perspire. But now and then she would step out to the porch and slip on her spectacles to look at the thermometer. "What an awful day," she would say to Sweetheart who was sleeping in his chair.

The girls remained in their room until afternoon. Once or twice Harriet heard them speaking irritably to one another. When they finally appeared Helena turned on the radio in the parlor and Kate sat on the porch. They would show no interest in the coming party. They sulked about as though they had been disappointed or defeated in something.

"Quit buzzing around, Mother," Kate said. "There are only a dozen or so people coming and it's supposed to be informal."

"Oh, Goddy, I never saw so much commotion over a cold supper," Helena said.

Ann tried to help, but Harriet said, "There's nothing left to do. I just have to cut the melon balls and everything will be ready."

Later Sweetheart and Son went off to Nashville to pick up the whiskey at the hotel. Ann went along to make her Pullman reservations, for she was taking a train at one A.M. She said she had to be in Little Rock the next day.

Most of the guests parked their cars in the back yard alongside BT's shack or in front of the garage. As they arrived Son went out into the yard to greet them or welcomed them on the screened porch. Supper was served buffet style, and Sweetheart brought everybody two or three drinks before they began to eat. "We want you to have an appetite," he would say.

The guests were, for the most part, Son's old school friends and their wives. There were two young men of sufficient height to escort the girls from room to room. And there was a young professor from the University and his wife who had taught at Miss Hood's School with Helena. Son was most cordial to this couple, introducing himself to them in the yard since Helena was not present when they arrived. The young professor (he explained that he was really only a teaching-fellow), wore a small mustache and a dark bow tie with his linen suit. He was very timid and spoke only a few words in the course of the whole evening.

While dressing for the party Harriet observed in the mirror that her face showed the strain she had been under. She spread extra powder under her eyes and applied more rouge than was usual with her. When she had finished her toilet she removed all her personal things from the dressing table, opened a new box of powder, and brought from the closet shelf an ivory handmirror and comb and brush. The ladies were going to use this as a powder room. From the closet shelf she also brought four small pillows with lacy slipovers which she arranged on the bed.

She was arranging the pillows when Son knocked at her door. He entered with his own large glass in one hand and a small tumbler for her in the other. "It's mostly ginger-ale," he said, "and I thought it would cool you off. It's right hot tonight."

It is this moment, she thought, that I've been waiting for through the whole week-end. And in this moment she banished all the despair that had been growing in her feelings toward Son and the girls. The insufferable insolence with which Mattie had treated her today also seemed as nothing. He has come to tell me what is in his heart. Or at least he has come so that we may have a few minutes alone before he leaves for the Army tomorrow. She glanced up at the childhood pictures of him which with pictures of the girls and a few of Mama and Papa and of Sweetheart covered one wall of her room. She pointed to a picture taken when he was thirteen wearing a skull cap on the back of his head and a sleeveless sweater. "That's my favorite," she said. "I began to notice a new look in your eyes when you were that age."

963

Son looked at the picture. Then his eyes roved indifferently over the other pictures there. "Well," he said, "I'd better go out and see that the girls are not sticking hat pins in Ann just to see how she reacts. Or at least not miss seeing it, myself, if they do."

The guests were beginning to leave by eleven-thirty. Harriet was sitting in a straight chair on the front porch. She had been sitting there in the dark for an hour with her hands folded in her lap. Sweetheart was slumped down among the pillows on the swing near by, asleep. The party had all been vague, like a dream of some event she dreaded, to Harriet. After Son left her standing alone before the gallery of pictures in her room she was hardly able to go into the house and meet the guests. There were no tears and no signs of nervous agitation. Rather, she felt herself completely without human emotion of any sort as she lingered there in her room for a long while. When finally she did go forward and take her place by the buffet in the dining room she pretended to be preoccupied with the food so that the guests would not notice how little concern she had for them. There were things she had planned to watch for this evening; but those things had become trivial and remote.

Early in the evening most of the party was gathered in the parlor and much of the conversation referred to things that had been said and done last night. Harry Buchanan urged Ann to express her views on something, but Ann declined. Several times Son was asking Ann what she thought about this or that, and always it seemed that Ann spoke two or three monosyllables which were followed by silence. Conversation between Son and the young professor did not materialize, and the girls did not try to draw him out as Harriet had expected. Ann and the professor were once heard talking about the "fragrance" of the wisteria. Helena took her tall, stooped young man to sit on the screened porch. Kate took hers to the chairs on the lawn. Now and then the two beaux appeared in the house on their way to the pantry with tall, empty glasses. Nothing could stir Harriet from her torpor, not even the information that in the middle of the evening BT had put on his hat and gone off to the settlement or to Nashville.

When she realized that the guests were beginning to go she placed her hand on Sweetheart's knee and said, "People are leaving, Sweetheart." He followed her into the hall and the two of them stood smiling and nodding and shaking hands of guests amid a hubbub of giddy and even drunken talk about Son's going into the Army. As the last of the automobiles pulled away, backing and turning in the gravel before the garage with its headlamps flashing on BT's shack and on the house and then on the trees and the white gravel of the driveway, someone called back, "Goodbye, Private Wilson!"

Harriet stood on the screened porch after the headlamps had gone round the house leaving the yard in darkness. While she was there she saw the light go off in the kitchen. The back door closed, and presently Mattie's dark figure moved sluggishly across the yard to the shack. There was no window on the near side of the little cabin, but when Mattie had put on the light inside, Harriet could see a square of light which a small window threw on the thick, green mint bed over by the fence. "She's going to wait up for BT," Harriet said. And now she went through the house and into the warm kitchen to see in what state Mattie had left things.

The dishes were not washed but they were stacked neatly on the table and in the sink. The back door was locked, and Harriet unlocked it so that Mattie could come in that way to go to her bed in the attic room above the kitchen. "Poor thing is so distracted she locked herself out," she said. She stood with her hand on the knob for a minute, for she wanted to go out and see Mattie. She could not bring herself to go.

When she came into the parlor she found that Ann had changed to her traveling dress. Helena and Kate were sprawled in two of the large chairs. Sweetheart was standing by the fireplace talking about train schedules to Little Rock. Ann was seated on the piano bench with her feet close together and her small delicate hands folded in her lap. Harriet had crossed the room and was taking her seat beside Ann when Son entered with the luggage.

"It's not quite time to go," Son said. He set the two bags by the hall door and drew up an odd chair. Harriet had taken one of Ann's hands between her own and was about to make a little farewell speech when Ann spoke.

She was looking into Harriet's face but as she spoke she turned her eyes to Son. "He thinks I have not behaved well tonight."

"Oh, for Heaven's sake, Ann," Son said turning in his chair and crossing his legs. Kate and Helena visibly collected their sprawled persons and looked attentively from Ann to Son.

"He does, indeed," said Ann. She stood up and walked to the mantel and stood at the other end from Sweetheart. "Very badly. He always thinks a person behaves badly who doesn't amuse him. He cares nothing for anything I say except when I'm talking theory of some kind. He was very willing to bring me here before your friends to express all manner of opinion which they and you find disagreeable while he behaves with conventional good taste. He even discouraged my bringing the proper clothes to make any sort of agreeable appearance. Yet see how smartly he's turned-out."

Son had now ceased to show any discomfort. He was watching Ann with the same interest that the girls showed. He was smiling when he interrupted her, "You are really drunk, Ann. But go on. You're priceless. You're rich. What else about me?"

"Nothing else about you," she said, undismayed. "But about me now. . . . We have had a very beautiful and very Platonic friendship. He has shown a marvelous respect for my intelligence and my virtue. And I, alas, have been so vulgar as to fall in love with him." She turned to Sweetheart who stood with his hands hanging limp at his sides and his mouth literally wide open. "It's a sad story, is it not, Doctor?" The doctor tried to smile.

Son rose from his chair saying, "Now it *is* time we go." And he and Ann left the room in such a hurry that Harriet was still seated when she heard them step out onto the porch. Then she jumped from her place on the piano bench and began to follow them.

But she had only reached the doorway to the hall when one of the girls said, "Mother, can't you see how drunk that gal really is?" As she stopped there in the hall her eyes fell on the mahogany umbrella rack where Sweetheart kept

965

his seven walking sticks. She counted the sticks and it seemed that there were only six of them. Then she counted them again and found that all seven were in their places. She counted them several times over, and each time there were still seven sticks in the rack.

Harriet was on her knees at her bedside. She had already repeated the Lord's Prayer twice but still was unable to think of the meaning of the words as she began it the third time. Her elbows were pressing into the soft mattress, and though the room was in darkness her eyes were closed. She was repeating the prayer slowly, moving her lips as she pronounced each word, when the fierce shout of a Negro woman seemed to break not only the silence but even the darkness. Sweetheart had sprung from the bed and put on the light. Harriet remained on her knees and watched him go to the closet shelf to get his pistol. "It's Mattie," he said. "It's Mattie screaming!"

"No, it's not Mattie," she said. "I don't think it was a scream either." Sweetheart turned his eyes to her with a suddenness that struck her dumb for a moment. When she was able to speak she said, "It's one of those women BT has." But the doctor had understood her before she spoke again and in his white pyjamas had already disappeared into the darkness of the hallway.

His hearing had been keen enough to detect that it was a Negro's voice. But his ear was not so sensitive as Harriet's. She was the only one in the house who knew that Mattie was waiting in the shack, and the shout had come distinctly from that quarter; but her ear was not deceived for an instant. She raised herself from her knees and faced her two daughters who had come to her door. She knew as well now as they would know when they were told a few minutes later what scene was taking place in the low doorway of that cabin. In her mind she saw the very shadows that were then being thrown on the green mint bed.

The first shout was followed by other distinct oaths. Now Mattie's and BT's voices could be heard mixing with that of the third Negro. So Harriet knew too that there had not yet been a cutting. "Hurry, Sweetheart," she called in a voice that hardly seemed her own. The girls stood watching her, and she stood motionless listening for every sound. Presently there came amid the voices the crunching sound of gravel under the wheels of her own coupe. Son was returning from the depot. She pushed herself between the girls and went to the window in their room. From there she could see that the incident was over. Sweetheart and Son stood in the bright lights from the headlamps of the automobile. They stood talking there for several minutes, and then Son came toward the house and Sweetheart went into the shack.

Son came into her room where she and the girls were waiting. His face was pale, but he was smiling. "It's not really anything," he said. "BT had brought one of his lady friends home, and his auntie would not receive her. I think his auntie even struck her. The lights of the car scared her off into the woods, and BT followed. Dad's bringing Mattie into the house."

Harriet put on her robe and went through the house to the kitchen. She waited there a long while watching the lights in the shack. Finally Sweetheart appeared on the stoop. He stood there in his white pyjamas for an endless time speaking into the doorway in such a quiet voice that she could not hear him.

When he did turn and see her at the kitchen he left the shack and came to her at once.

"You'll have to talk to Mattie," he said. "She doesn't want to come in the house, but of course she'll have to. That pair just might come back tonight."

Harriet gazed at him blankly for a moment and then closed her eyes. "I can't go," she said.

"Harriet? You'll have to go, Love. I'll go with you and wait at the door. The poor creature needs you."

"Did she ask for me?"

"No. She didn't think to. She's in a terrible state. She doesn't talk."

"Did you tell her I was coming?"

"Yes," he said, "and that's the only thing that made her even look at me."

Harriet turned away and moved toward the dining room. When he called to her she was at the swinging door and she said, "I'm going to dress."

"You've no need to dress," he said. He came round the kitchen table and stopped a few feet from her. She had never known him to speak to her in private from such a distance. "Harriet, why should this be so hard for you?"

There was no sympathy in the question, and actually he did not seem to want an answer to this precise question. He seemed to be making a larger and more general inquiry into her character than he had ever done before. She dropped her eyes to the floor and walked hurriedly by him to the back door. She paused there and said, "Wait here."

Mattie was seated on a squat, ladder back chair whose short legs had the look of being worn away through long usage. Her brown hands were resting on the black dress over each knee. A dim bulb hung on a cord almost at waist level, and the gray moths that flitted around it were lighting on Mattie's head. Harriet came in and stood directly before her. When she first tried to speak she felt that she was going to be nauseated by the awful smell of BT, a stench that seemed to be compounded of the smell of soiled and moldy clothing and the smell of condensed and concentrated human sweat. She even glanced about the room half expecting to find BT standing in one of the dark corners. "Mattie," she said at last, "I was unkind to you Saturday. You must not hold it against me."

Mattie raised her eyes to her mistress, and there was neither forgiveness nor resentment in them. In her protruding lower lip and in her wide nostrils there was defiance, but it was a defiance of the general nature of this world where she must pass her days, not of Harriet in particular. In her eyes there was grief and there was something beyond grief. After a moment she did speak, and she told Harriet that she was going to sit here all night and that they had all better go on to bed in the house. Later when Harriet tried to recall the exact tone and words Mattie had used—as her acute ear would normally have allowed her to do—she could not reconstruct the speech at all. It seemed as though Mattie had used a special language common to both of them but one they had never before discovered and could now never recover. Afterward they faced each other in uncommunicative silence for an indefinite time. Finally Harriet moved to the door again, but she looked back once more and she saw that besides the grief and hostility in Mattie's eyes there was an unspeakable loneliness for which she could offer no consolation.

967

When she told Sweetheart that Mattie still refused to leave the shack he sat down on the porch steps and said that he was going to keep watch for a while. She didn't try to dissuade him, and he said nothing more to her as she put her robe about his shoulders and went inside.

In her room she tried to resume her broken prayers. Then she lay on the bed with the light still burning and she longed to weep as she had done when she first saw Son in the doorway. Not a tear would come to her eyes. She thought of all the talking that Son and the girls had done and she felt that she was even beginning to understand what it had meant. But she sadly reflected that her children believed neither what Ann Prewitt or the professors at the University were offering them. To Harriet it seemed that her children no longer existed; it was as though they had all died in childhood as people's children used to do. All the while she kept remembering that Mattie was sitting out in that shack for the sole purpose of inhaling the odor in the stifling air of BT's room.

When Sweetheart finally came she was on her knees again at her bedside. She heard him put out the light and let himself down easily on the other side of the bed. When she opened her eyes it was dark and there was the chill of autumn night about the room. (*1946*)

STARK YOUNG

1881–

Stark Young was born in Como, Mississippi, October 11, 1881. Entering the University of Mississippi at the age of fourteen, he completed his undergraduate work in 1901 and the following year received an M.A. degree in English at Columbia University. Young's career has been remarkably varied. From 1904 to 1921 he taught English at the University of Mississippi, the University of Texas, and Amherst College. He then turned to a career in journalism, serving as associate editor of *The Theatre Arts Monthly,* as dramatic critic for *The New York Times,* and for twenty-two years (1925–1947) as a member of the editorial staff of *The New Republic.* He has been affiliated with the Agrarian group and was one of the contributors to *I'll Take My Stand* (1930).

Young has experimented with practically every form of literary expression, with considerable success. He has published collections of essays and poems, along with several volumes of dramatic criticism. He has written a number of plays and has also had experience as a director. His short stories have been favorably received and his novels—particularly *River House* (1929) and *So Red the Rose* (1934)—are still regarded as invaluable renderings of Mississippi plantation society. His other noteworthy publications include two novels, *Heaven Trees* (1926) and *The Torches Flare* (1927); a collection of short stories, *Feliciana* (1935); and *The Pavilion* (1951).

Encaustics for Southerners

Sette Frati

The Countess N—— comes from one of the richest and—it is pleasant to report —best bred families in New York; she is also discreet, Junior League, and educated. All this, of course, makes her reactions important. She looks in a curious way futile and mashed (I do not mean spiritually mashed). She is mashed, too, in the Pullman sense; which is to say that the artificial flowers on her abandoned, *de rigueur*, proper-shop gown look as if she had slept upon them. I do not say that, quite; for she looks really as if she had never slept with anything but meditations, analytical preoccupations, and laxatives.

Curiously enough, nevertheless, this mashed look extends to the impression that one gets of her whole nature. Life has wronged her (not to speak of the heinous glands) so that her whole aspect, face, arms, hands, back, and bosom— which are the parts her fashionable dressmaker decided on for exhibition— seems to announce already an inner constriction, and to promise a sallow withering very soon. She speaks firmly, shyly, and with a certain egotism that is sometimes characteristic of a person who is essentially solitary, no matter what husband or friends may do. One who was brought up so rich is likely to be spoiled, naturally; and being spoiled may well lead to some inner solitude.

She is married to a count with a great name, whose family seat is in the central part of Italy, not far from the village of Sette Frati, "Seven Brothers"— I'll wager she has dwelt upon that name; we shall see why later, perhaps—and in sight of cerulean lakes and private domains highly vegetous, to use Ben Jonson's word for it. In the winter they live in Rome.

I met the countess for the third time not long ago at dinner on Park Avenue in the same creases but a different dress, as if she slept the same way regardless of modistes—in other words, though a countess with one of the highest names in Europe, she has a democratic equality among the perpetually disheveled of this world. After dinner (one of those careful affairs in which the young hostess gets her hints for new dishes out of the recipes by celebrated chefs printed in the Sunday magazine sections) the countess found herself near me, and we began to talk of her life in Italy, ten years of it. That joyless, sallow expression

969

From The Virginia Quarterly Review, *April 1935. Reprinted with the kind permission of Stark Young and* The Virginia Quarterly Review.

makes me by contrast think of oleanders, wine, and a bright moon. It seems that to the count's beautiful estate in the country his family, which means also his mother and various nieces, nephews, visiting cousins, and so on, are wont to come during the summer season and presently to settle down. The count's family, in sum, spend months at the country place near Sette Frati.

One of the things that Teutonic foreigners never quite know of Italians is that they love the life *in campagna—in villeggiatura*,[1] as they sometimes call it. It is true that Italian poetry—since the Renaissance of shepherdesses and rills—is sadly lacking in the appreciation of nature. Their poets seem to have neglected to observe the primrose in its full fertility of human illustration. They have not sufficiently noted the hare, as the fine mist rises in his tracks behind him traversing the heather; nor have they exactly noted the passions of ashbuds during their blackness in the front of some month or other (Tennyson says March). The Italians have, alas, a tendency to condense nature or some natural effect to a phrase; which only shows their lack of profundity. They fire some notation of the natural world with passionate humanity; which only shows their classicism, their lack of botany, profundity, pantheism, and rapture. The poor things have noted the snail on the thorn, but failed to deduce from it that all's right with the world.

We must return, however, to the main fact of these summer stretches among the cypresses, lakes, peasants, and consanguinity, as the countess describes them to me.

From her accounts I gather that it is indeed a gloomy time for her. You are apt to have an aunt visiting, an uncle, a grandmother, cousins, with respected little cousins, and in the front portico people sitting long evenings, some of the peasants coming up perhaps, music sometimes (not very chic but, of course, the countess doesn't mind that); and then there are country visits, with simple diversions. I put all these things in one sentence because they remained in the countess's mind as a stream. Plainly, her summers *in villeggiatura* are duller than, dreaming of princes and palaces, she grew up to expect. I suppose to her it all seems to be a great to-do about nothing.

I do not mean to give a false impression of this very pleasant, slightly neurotic, unconsciously spoiled daughter of a high millionaire New York family of at least three generations in tradition (though I should add that their wealth enabled them to generate early) who is married thus into an ancient Italian life. But I must set down, before I leave her situation, my reflections on it in one simple Southern respect. The count should have married one of my cousins from the South.

Such a marriage would have been impossible, of course, because she would not have anything like a million, or even a quarter of a million. The count's family would have been devoted to her; I can see her now throwing her arms around some of those old aunts or uncles and grandmothers, and recognizing in them not a few of the same traditions on which she herself had been brought up. And as for sitting in the portico—which she would have called the gallery— she could have done that with the best of them. She would not constantly have asked herself what was there to do; she could even have lived without tennis.

[1] *In the country—on a picnic.*

She would not have needed to dash in a motorcar across country for luncheon. She would have understood, lying in bed at night, with the scent of the petunias rising from the garden below, that life, if it is to last, has a social scheme, has certain hard restrictions and finalities and orders, within which flourish all those affections, family loyalties, and uneventful times together that Southern people know the value of.

Yes, it is a pity that circumstances in this world did not allow the count to marry an American from the South. The poor countess bought what she wanted, but what was in what she bought she did not want. I can see the old Italian ladies thinking of how active their American countess was; not active in order to do anything really, but stirred to her center by the absence of anything to do. She had brought, however, a good dowry—*pazienza* [2]—one cannot have everything!

What shall we do? is plainly the countess's motto—not that she knows it. In Italian it is *che farò*, but, of course, to an Italian that suggests *che farò senza Euridice?* [3] What shall I do without Eurydice—that celebrated aria from Gluck's opera; or at least *che farò senza* something? I trust the difference is clear—what shall I do without something beloved, signifying an objective that feeds life. Which is quite another matter from "What shall I do?"

I can see one of my cousins now, if the Southern fortunes had remained so that the count could have afforded to marry her, sitting on the gallery, or terrace, of that Sette Frati villa, any afternoon or evening, and fitting exactly into the life and scene.

Culture in the Dirt Road

I have just been talking with Mrs. M——, and she reports to me the conversation of X, an acquaintance we both have in literary criticism—a great master, in fact, of stirring conclusions. The gist of it is that he has lately been on a visit to Nashville, and on his return has announced that, from what he had seen, he is about to decide that there never has been any culture in the South. About to decide.

Instead of leaping, as I doubtless should, to some endeavor that might head off an unfavorable decision on his part (a decision that would be offensive to the Chamber of Commerce), I find myself thinking of X's presence. A face, as it were, cumulous, with something both sullen and haughty about it that reminds you of a boil that has come to a head but refuses to burst, and a sound in his speech as if his nose were full of cotton seed. These, doubtless, are unfriendly comparisons, perhaps not even cultured save in a homely sense. What puzzles me is that X has assumed that the whole town of Nashville culled whatever were its loveliest aspects and laid them at his feet. Or does he think culture is waiting in the middle of, as we call it, the dirt road?

On the other hand, there is Z, who writes for a paper in one of the border

971

[2] *Patience.*
[3] *What shall I do without Euridice?*

states, half Northern, half Southern. He, it seems, has read some of my remarks on the city of Natchez. Now this culture and these fine people that I pretend existed in Natchez he doubts very much. He was in Natchez once, he says, for his newspaper, sent there to report a lynching. He must say he didn't see any of these fine people.

This is a most unfortunate moment for me socially; I cannot say to Z, "You should have let them know you were coming."

Return of the Native

Claribel grew up in Tennessee, an orphan under the roof of an aunt and uncle who fought like cats and dogs. We need not dwell on these unhappy years except to say that Claribel at twenty came to New York, began—somehow—her bookshop, was admired all up and down Park Avenue, seemed wistful to authors, and strove earnestly to forget her entire beginnings, which I suppose was natural.

Of late years, however, she has had a great number of rich friends who are buying plantations in South Carolina and Virginia, or living like lords (on the Riviera) in Florida, and they have often invited her down to these splendid demonstrations of estates and one-generation patriarchy. Furthermore she has heard of much biography, of fiction and of other matters in travel magazines, all dealing with the Southern material (every early fan window in Massachusetts having already been photographed). Going South has become very smart. How et cetera, et cetera, it all is! And how cheap it is! Restore the plantation great houses! C——, of the well-known soups, has opened up Belle Chasse, in the tidewater country. Claribel hears this at dinner parties.

"I'm all for the South," she has begun to say.

Richmond Lady Reading of Sad New York Lady

I watch Mrs. T—— as she reads the notice that Mrs. K—— is going to be obliged to have an auction, and that two of her houses in the country have been closed. Mrs. T—— is sad not from the house-closings, but because a circle of New York friends sitting there with her have been saying how hard it was for Mrs. K——, poor dear, no stables this summer, and so many responsibilities! Such a hard situation!

As I watch this scene I can hardly believe my eyes. Is it possible that little Mrs. T——, who is none too rich now, has completely forgotten her mother, in the days when they all made their lawn dresses, baked the cakes, and thought themselves lucky that they were not obliged even to do the washing? Her grandmother, after the Civil War, had to plow the field sometimes or else see her children starve—after, that is, she had sold what silver had been left from a handsome interment that baffled the general's men.

Still it is sad that Mrs. K—— will not be able to take out her hunters this season, and comparisons would be ungracious. It is better, as she herself recently

972

explained to me, that she and her daughter go to Europe this summer. To have the horses, et cetera, would cost $20,000 at least, she says, whereas the two of them can spend July and August in Europe for $10,000. I quote this to Mrs. T—— (my own grandfather was glad for a long time to take in $700 a year from his plantation) and like two fool Southerners we sit looking sadly at each other over Mrs. K——.

Sweet Defense

Miss Flora comes from the Charleston country; and, though she circulates in New York at a considerable rate, I am often struck by her helplessness. Far back in her spirit, sweet and most arrogant. A face gentle and ingratiating; an education floral and uncertain. And, I believe, a rather bad ear for sound.

At any rate, the other day at a fashionable New York club made up half of ladies and half of good addresses, I sat at the tea table listening to a gracious but grilling banter addressed to Miss Flora. She hearkened, blushed, smiled, poured more tea, and finally made a little speech which sounded like a quotation from a worn oration, though it was something about Southern aristocracy— bless her heart!

Now I should have advised something very different for Miss Flora, a bit of policy and a hint at sweet defense. First I should have said that our entire South has been filled up with somewhat frightened schoolteachers who learned to pronounce things out of books. Then I should have said, arm yourself, dear Miss Flora, with some international or historical illustrations. For example, there are scores of members of the English aristocracy who say *it don't, it ain't,* and so on, not to speak of a pronunciation of *girl* which amounts practically to "gal." When Miss Flora, following her own uncle, the old judge, says "jine" for *join,* "hyst" for *hoist,* "pint" for *point,* and so forth and so on—she's almost eighty and will likely be the last of her race to do these things—I should like her to be able to add that these are merely good Queen Anne pronunciations of such words, just as the word *roil* is still given the Queen Anne pronunciation, though people who don't know the difference have begun to spell it *rile.*

And for another example, I should like to hint to her, when she says "cha'ac-ter" or "Pa'is," that Byron, Lord Byron, and various members of his family always pronounced the name "Bi'on."

Nothing checks the newly learned bourgeois like tradition handed on, not read. Nothing snubs like snobbery. Once we got that in Miss Flora's head, she could execute the scheme with the most amiable malice, along with that violet smile that she has not yet lost.

Incarnation

973

H—— is a fine chap, sweet-tempered, good-hearted, and anxious not to be laughed at. He was, it seems, bright as a little child, very bright, so that you might have thought he would represent his family education. But now, with lazy time and scattered habitats in commercial towns North, his family education has to represent him.

I have lately observed H—— with a common friend of his and mine, a man that reviews books for a leading daily. A novel, it appears, has come out in which the author portrays a Virginia town with an assortment of backward citizens, a colonel, provincialism, old ideals, and the bunk, so the book seems to say, the bunk. The writer, I gathered from my reviewer friend—who had of course said this in print, there is no time to waste your stuff—showed in a fine, satirical manner, not uncommon in various pleasing Southern authors, that these fools in this Virginia town lived on lies. The proof of that lay chiefly in the fact that the old colonel was admired by the citizens as the embodiment of all that is chivalrous, honorable, and Southerngentleman—I make it one word in this case; but was, as a matter of fact, merely a pious fraud, none too any-thing of these high and boasted qualities attributed to him. The colonel (plus all the ideals grouped with him) was, therefore, the bunk. Proved.

I watched H——'s face, and have often thought since then of what may happen when you have neglected to think out your inheritance. What we could say to the reviewer is easy. His novel and his review prove nothing at all. I feel in fact like saying to him that plenty of babies kick in the womb before they are born; there is nothing intellectual or debunking about that.

The rebuttal of the novel's argument should be simple to H—— or to any Southern person who will take the trouble to dwell on his own things:

It is of only *incidental* consequence that these admirers of the colonel in the Virginia town, these believers in his embodiment of their ideals, were deluded in him. On that basis the novel is only finding out about Santa Claus. The point is not that the colonel did not truly represent these ideals. The significant point is what the ideals were, for which these townspeople sought an embodiment.

Aged Aunt and the Devil

My dear aunt, Miss R——, is at present confronted with a niece, Lola, who is very pretty, who has just married unhappily—some months ago, it was—and who is busily explaining the unhappiness of her situation and the egotistic con-volutions of her selfhood by quoting and explaining considerable sections of modern thought with which she has become acquainted.

"Goodness knows, I didn't bring up Lola," my aunt says of her dear niece, in a tone which implies you didn't get the ringworm from me, my dear.

The fact is that Lola was brought up by her uncle, her father's brother, who regarded all women, except the ugly ones, as sugar-coated fools from which male gallantry is to remove the sugar. As I remember, Lola says her uncle used to make her cut his nails, but I know little about that. At any rate, she says that, considering her early years, she has done the best she could. She will then give you a vast sketch of all the complexes, the inferiority complex and otherwise, that she suffers from because of her earlier life.

There are moments in the discussion when Lola quite embarrasses her aunt and a good many other people. On the other hand, certain more modern and sophisticated neighbors listen to her with attention. The truth is, as I have observed, however, they are not so much surprised at her knowledge of the science of psychology as they are at her knowledge of her early years. In sum, one may doubtless know all science, but how does one remember all these minutiae of the far and scattered past? How few could do that! I have talked with our aunt about Lola's explanations and condonements of herself; and we have agreed on one thing, which is that, pragmatically, it would be a great deal better for such people as Lola if they thought in terms of the old morality. In a word, though it might be less subtle, it would be a good thing if Lola stopped explaining all her tedious qualities, touchiness and egotism, by her adolescent history and adolescent brunts, and began to explain merely that she was full of the devil. If she said to me, I have a certain aroma because I have a piece of Limburger cheese in my pocket, I really do not believe that I should find it poignant. I am afraid I should say, "Take it out." I can scarcely—as I might with Limburger—ask Cousin Lola to remove all the early section of her life in this world. I could say, perhaps, since she knows these things so thoroughly, why not neglect various sections? But if she said she was full of the devil, I should have some hell-fire phraseology to hand, by inherited quotation. Full of the devil—that is old theology. The only devil I and my friends know is on the bottle of pepper sauce, a forked tail and so on. But, of course, the point for Lola is that old kirk devil.

If Lola should put her shortcomings—for which, so long as we are being archaic, we may as well say she should be lynched—down to the devil, it would be, of course, better practically, but far less intellectual perhaps. Good and useful nevertheless. Full as Lola is of modern thought, it will do no harm to remember that when we convert Lola to modern thought we convert modern thought to Lola. Unlucky old aunt!

However, Lola goes on, letting herself out with isms and complexes (Germanic origins). And those who know (and, by perplexity, pseudo-popular analyses, and natural kindness, admire) her say, "Such psychology! Such psychology!"

It reminds me of that little book of Sicilian travels where we read of the shrine with the Virgin's history depicted in it. In one scene the neighbors are gathered; St. Anna, the author tells us, has been prophesying all the morning and everybody says they never heard such prophecy in all their lives!

Loving Owner

She is a gentle little lady, with a proud nose. Once long ago her family was more than common rich, there in their South Carolina home. The plantations paid, and the city house that her grandfather built showed many luxurious furnishings, silver, portraits, and other tokens of good living and refinement. Of late years since nice people, even, have taken to opening their houses to touring strangers, thanks to gasoline and journalism, this lady has conducted many a visitor through —— ; I must not mention the name, but the stairs are graceful, the sofas with their damask are the originals; the inlaid papier-mâché, the rosewood with its roses carved on it, the silver, are still there, in part at least. There are also some porcelain figurines, chandeliers with crystal, gilt silver cake-baskets, and so on.

At first, when my friend showed people through the house—not quite all of it, including her own bedroom, where she has a basket in which sick and crippled chicks and goslings may sleep, a vase of peacock feathers, a puffed crazy-quilt and other items that, as a matter of fact, give the room a human vagary and charm such as no other part of the house presents—at first, when she showed the house, she spoke of *its age*. It was ancient, full of antiques. From that antique exclusiveness and that anemic phrase "Old Southern Home," she passed to the idea of fine, and then even to palatial. And so on from bad to worse. It was a sort of map, or tracing, of that method by which certain authors through certain decades built up a set of assumptions and élite nonsensicalities that almost made us Southerners ridiculous. And such bombast helped to provide a better market for books by Southern authors depicting us as degenerate, faking, and chivalry-fools, living on what is popularly called old stuff and bluff. This has become matter that raised eyebrows are not enough to dispose of, nor aristocratic scorn enough to dismiss.

Now I should like to advise my friend, there in her old house. She shows it graciously but is on the way to a certain pride of flesh, so to speak, a certain turning of the house's claims into her own private heraldries. I should like to say to her things like the following:

Dear friend and dear lady, you are not a Braganza, a Montmorency, a Hapsburg, Colonna, and so forth and so on; not immediately so at least. You are the descendant of a good line of fine people, related to the land, with a sense of responsibility to the society of which they make a part and which they intend to take a hand in ruling. For this class in the South, the life of the affections was believed in and followed; the family idea had meaning. My dear lady, I daresay you are aware (I know you are not, but wish to be courteous) that certain city writers have said we were merely Chinese in this. I hope you know that such writers (if you had ever heard of them) know just about as much about us as about China, which means they know nothing, but merely make of this their magazine copy or gin talk. I hope you know that Southern culture meant, not speaking Greek for the gentlemen and ladies and committing to memory the history of literature, but a certain sense of refinement in feeling, a desire for civilization and continuation, a wish to please, to harmonize human relationships and living, and perhaps we must admit, a determination to believe that for certain gentle results a little time (and even place in certain cases) must be added to money and push.

Now, what I want to say to you, my dear lady, is that your house is not a palace, not even important architecture. It shines mostly by the ensemble, the house plus the trees, the grounds, the Southern sky, and, may I say? such graces of its intrinsic life as you yourself are.

976 May I say, too, that most of these things of yours, these articles, bits of china, silver, and so on, can be bought on Third Avenue in New York, in the Victorian antique shops; and are, besides, not confined by any means to the South? In Europe there are miles of this very furniture that you possess, even to the inlaid tables, crystal-lustres, and vases. The whole supplication that I lay at your feet is for the purification of the vain human heart, and for the avoidance of our seeming a trifle innocent, or ridiculous, to outsiders. It can be expressed in a simple rearrangement of statement:

When you lead your visitor toward an object, please say, at best, "This is a thing we've always loved," which reverts to your own persuasion, instead of, "This is a fine ———, etc.," which invites what is called expertizing. Or say, "This is a piece of Sèvres of the First Empire." Or, if you wish to soar: "These my great-grandfather used to amuse himself having over from London." (Or Paris or Rome, according to taste.)

By this means two things may be accomplished: (1) A visitor from a nearby little town will not go away more ignorant and mixed up than ever over what is antique, what is distinguished or rare, what is a thing loved rather than a priceless thing. (2) People from sophisticated centers cannot go away smiling indulgently at us Southerners and our claims. (I am acquainted with plenty of people here in New York whom I should much prefer to have think my great-grandfather used to beat up Dresden cups when he had drunk too much Bourbon, than to have them think his great-grandson believes the three or four Dresden cups still left us to be unique in the world.)

At bottom this is most serious advice to my friend in her old house. I am asking her only to feature—as the journals and the films put it—her love of these old things for love's sake. For this is the way she has thought of them during most of her life. In fact, this is the way she really thinks of them now. She thinks thus now, despite our national money clichés that batter her brain, despite our advertising, our touristic movements that send endless riffraff into places they neither understand nor belong to.

In this lady's case, the joke is—and the tears of things too—that what she really wants is that the moment should go off, should be entertaining. (And, perhaps, a little to be the heroine of it, which is natural.) To make the moment go off, her instinct tells her that for most visitors nowadays the terms "rare" and "priceless" are the only terms that speak, that give the thrill.

The point of all this is that I want my friend to believe in her own spirit (apart from words). It is this in her that will convince, or at least touch, many of the poor visiting creatures from American cities, touring, rich and lost, defeated by their own smart adequacy in a world they have made empty for themselves of almost everything but the priceless.

If none of the above soulful arguments should stir this lady, then I hope she will heed me when I say that, if we can prevent it, nobody who is an outsider must go away feeling indulgent to "the poor creature's pride in her old things." She owes it to her South to see to it that they go away at least baffled, so to speak; wondering, for instance, if the last car they have bought—newest model —is quite enough.

Backward South

977

Not far from Baton Rouge, I have been talking to a man at a gasoline station, one of those sons of a Southern judge who are reduced to picking up what living they can. He gives me a discussion of communism as it appears here and there in our capitalistic North.

Some of those people, they tell him, he says, want to divide everything. What is there to divide? Does anybody want to pay our taxes?

I go home to dinner with him, and he begins to tell me how in his house they live, and him gettin' only a tiny bank salary.

Well, he says, you see they have a little land which pays its taxes and, now that the government bribes them not to farm it, provides also a bit of income. His wife is dead, but her mother takes care of the children. Then, too, the garden they would all work it—but would they?" At this he cackles. I explain down the street anyhow. "Now," he says, "I reckon if everybody owned the garden they would all work it—but would they?" At this he cackles. I explain that it is very fine to travel in Russia now, that everybody has work there, and that tourists, carefully steered, on a two weeks' orbit, see, besides museums and other distinguished matters, apartment houses with water taps in the halls, and are shown poor people wearing shoes. You don't mean it! he says. Now Celie, their cook, has got some shoes, but she won't wear them when she's at home. What she wants is her three dollars a week, and then she just plays with the children after dinner; they all ride the calf.

I try to make it all seem quite wrong and it keeps turning out quite right. Even the calf's sufferings fail me; it seems the calf's mighty fat. It must be that I cannot put the argument as it should be put.

From what they tell her, the grandmother says, some of those people up there must be going crazy.

"I read how one man said he didn't like his mother and all that. I reckon some mothers are bad, some sons too—my mother used to tell of a woman in Carolina who had a child so bad she used to ring a bell when they went through the streets." The two children propped at either side of their grandma now roar with laughter.

"I remember," she says, "my own dear son was no angel. Once in particular, he certainly was not. So I said, 'You just come on in this house and sit here with me; we're going to talk this thing out.' Of course we had some peach ice cream in the icebox and we ate that, though I said, 'We're going to talk this thing out.'"

The beginning of a solution for this household, I decide, would be to stop the grandmother and the father loving these children. If no mere Five-Year Plan could do that, well, the father and grandmother will in time die off.

It may very well be, of course, that we must plan for more than five years in order to make these children quit loving these older people.

"My children don't tell me any lies," their father says, "and we have a guitar, a banjo, a mandolin, and an accordion, and sit here on the porch when it's warm weather, you know—it's a regular band almost—and play. I've got good children."

It is not easy, I suppose, to resist such blandishments and simple, open confidence, even from a parent. I can scarcely shine against it. And so it looks as if the children might grow up benighted. I might find it hard to convince them how much better it would be to climb up on the state's lap and play tunes with comrades, citizens and citizenesses, on community-tuned guitars.

This is at least one thing that is meant by the Backward South.

978

Summer Night

S—— is a plumpish young man of twenty-five, regarded here in New York as of an amiable disposition. He comes from Louisiana, and the gallery of his father's house is in the shade of water oaks, old, wide, black-green, hanging with moss. I have seen his mother's picture on his desk; such a lovely, delicate, and possessive face! Beyond her, as she stands there in the photograph, is a rose garden, flower after flower; it must have been full summer in that place.

Two or three times I have heard S—— trying manfully and loyally to explain to his friends here a strange, close longing that he has for this country of his. He talks about the climate, the peace, the fresh fruit, everything, including the easy living with so many servants about and so few engagements.

I have long wanted to ask him why he does not merely say flatly that, though the day may be beautiful and not too brief there at home, the wonder of that Southern country is the evening and the nights. Something about those breathless summer nights, the leaves moving softly, the voices on the porch of those who love you. Nights soft and passionately repeated like a beloved name. Walks along the dusk of the streets in the little town, garden fragrancies, near stars, shadows, dogs at a distance barking, voices, and the knowledge that you are loved.

Lately I heard S—— say some of this, at least, to his blond roommate, who takes so much exercise that he is always exhausted and sleepy: "By God, I've written them that in June I'm comin' home!"

Days not too brief. Breathless summer nights. (*1935*)

Shadows on Terrebonne

The road from the highway to the Raymond house winds for two miles through cotton fields, sometimes with hedges alongside of Cherokee roses and honeysuckle; then comes the peach orchard, then at last the carriage-gate, of brick and iron, standing amid tall grass and palmettos that block the way. You drive nowadays through a side entrance near the old stable lot. To the right lies a pond, with willows, where once the swans floated above their white shadows but now only the frogs would be, no more swans these days and no more peach brandy. And then suddenly, after an avenue of water oaks, you make a turn and come on the house.

It is a rambling old house, though the front is rather correct and unexpected, with a small portico and white columns. The long central hall begins with glass and ends with glass. If you look from the front through the back door, you see, shimmering and far away, the dark mass of azalea bushes. In the hall and scattered through the rooms is the furniture that Joseph Carrière Raymond brought over from France when he built the house. There are books, pictures,

979

damasks, and vases, and a bust of Napoleon, who was then the rage; you get the impression that this Joseph Raymond on his wedding trip was an extravagant young man. The ceilings are high, with stucco ornaments, the walls all white. But the interior of the house is soon forgotten, once you pass through the hall door at the back and on to the terrace outside. Everything suddenly becomes quieter, the eye and the ear wait and listen. The birds that flutter in the garden hedges are fewer here; for instead of bushes and boughs, there is a stone terrace spreading out sixty or seventy feet. Old ivy beds, loose and vague as shades themselves, border this terrace, and from it spreads a greensward that slopes towards the water. The level bayou flows past, and from it comes the name of the house, Shadows on Terrebonne.

They said that Joseph Raymond built his house here rather than at his other places, Mantua Plantation, Silence Plantation, and Picayune Plantation, which his father had left him, because of the soft water flowing in Terrebonne Bayou. Joseph liked to see water keep its place, his sister, Mrs. Percy, said; by which her sharp tongue meant that brandy was highly esteemed by her brother. Wild fowl came, and the long moss hung down from the trees along the stream's edge. It was a bayou large enough for the smaller steamboats to travel up and down, stopping at the various plantations, each with its landing. The truth was a single steamboat, the *Lorient*, coming and going once a week, served their needs well enough. Slowly the bosom of the stream spread its ripples here and there where a reed or a bed of water-hyacinths stood up through the surface. Or now and then a small snake or water-bug streaked the smooth stretch of it, or a bird's wing, tipped slantwise, grazed the clear water. It was all like time itself, the shadows, the wings, the passing ripples, against the steady, still stream.

At one end of the garden, against this stillness and the stream with its reflections under the open sky, two columns stand. They are white marble with leafy capitals, in the Corinthian manner, more or less, but more extravagant in their design. They rise from a kind of terrace, or rather flight of steps; for there are three marble steps descending toward the bayou.

One end breaks off abruptly as if there had been more columns to be added. In places time and the rain through the moss in the branches above have stained the marble to a pale rose color. The columns are ten feet high perhaps; the years have softened both their fluted lines and the rich leafage of the capitals.

Joseph Raymond married Julie Thérèse Deslonde, one of a New Orleans family known for the beauty of both its men and women. To them at Shadows on Terrebonne were born a son and a daughter, Alfred Deslonde and Hélène. Alfred was seven years older than his sister. He was a proud, noble little boy, with a smile so sweet and eyes so straight and clear that everyone loved him. His Aunt Percy, coming down from Parish Assumption to visit at The Shadows and seeing this engaging manner and how easily it won everybody's favor and indulgence, thought that discipline would be wise, lest the boy be spoiled. 'Don't let any child grow up thinkin' the world belongs to him,' she said.

'Eh?' said his mother, thinking of the time she bent over to kiss him good night, lying in his small bed, and he said, 'I thought I heard a roseleaf popping.' It was only a game you played in the garden—you doubled up a rose petal and popped it against your lips—but how sweetly and gracefully whispered!

'Eh?' his mother said, politely, of course, but as if Aunt Percy could just answer that or stew in her own juice.

'I said my say.'

'When I see signs that Alfred is spoiled, then will be time enough. But have you ever seen a more generous child? Now tell me. Or eyes more eager? Why should I try to break his little will?'

'I reckon there's something in that.'

'It's true he hates to be stopped, but he brings the drawing to you as soon as it's completed; he'd give you his head.'

'I'm thinking of what life may do to Alfred some day. And I'm no fool, either.'

'He's the soul of honor, an honorable boy if one ever was, a lie's not in him. My father used to say that that was about all you have, honor was about all you can confront life with. Father had an old sword of his father's with an inscription in Spanish that said, Do not draw me without reason, do not sheathe me without honor. So you see.'

'I remember how that plagued sword rattled in the scabbard,' said the old lady, screwing up her eyes.

When Alfred was eleven they engaged a gentleman from Boston for his tutor. Long as he was with the family, there remained some mystery about this man; they gradually learned that he had been at one time an actor but before that, when he had money, he had been a great traveller. He never gave any distinct account of himself. He was a good Latin scholar and knew Greek and French in which language he sang many songs as well as in English and recited poetry with exquisite power. When he declaimed such lines as 'The mountains look on Marathon, and Marathon looks on the sea,' he would be so filled with it that he rose from his seat and held out his arms as if rapt. He slept in the same room with his pupil, so that the process of education was continually going on.

Then Monsieur Dumaine came for a while to stay at The Shadows, giving lessons in drawing to the two children, and to the children on the neighboring plantations, because Monsieur Dumaine wanted to earn money to go and study with David in Paris. Already Alfred, in place of study, had drawn pictures up and down the margins of his books, so that he became at once the artist's star pupil. This was not, of course, with the idea of becoming a painter, just say that and Alfred's father would have stopped the lessons! It was merely a way of acquiring an agreeable accomplishment—that was how they put it. A few years later found the boy at The Shadows growing into a youth very handsome, very much admired by his friends. His impetuous, high nature was eased and made charming by his sweet temper and natural talents. He was generous, he was given to trusting everyone, partly because of his bringing up. 'My father used to say,' Joseph Raymond said to him, 'never suspect people. It's better to be deceived or mistaken, which is only human after all, than to be suspicious, which is common, like trash.'

So the years went on, and the garden at The Shadows, which Joseph had planted at the time of his marriage, filled up with green and flowering plants. The quiet there seemed quieter for those rich green walls. The tall bamboo and

981

the long moss threw farther shadows than even the name of the place implied, over the smooth bayou. The herons and other wild fowl came in their season; and when the day dawned for it, flew away, nobody knew where. Even the plantation bells that called the field hands to and from work seemed to have grown mellow. The boy heard them softly along toward sundown; he would stand sometimes and hear the bell fading away among the rustling leaves.

In the spring of 1816 his sister Hélène, at fifteen, became engaged to a young man in Parish Avoyelles. And in that same season, Alfred, who was twenty-two, taking along with him a great deal more money than he could spend, made the voyage to France. The Deslondes, his mother's people, had a cousin there, an old marquis, who had written Latin verses and knew all the scholars in Paris. There was also in Paris a lady. Aunt Percy's husband's sister, whom the royal family favored because once the exiled Bourbon princes, travelling in Louisiana, had been guests of her father's. One of them, the Duc d'Orléans, was to become a long time afterward the king of France. At any rate, Alfred would know these cousins and would also see the world. He had spoken French from his infancy.

From Paris Alfred wrote letters home, about the concerts, the French nation and Europe, how kind people were to him, how he went to balls, evening parties, *fêtes champêtres*. In May a letter came that said he was going off on some Mediterranean ship. He would visit Greece and perhaps go farther, at least the Aegean Islands. In June, from Greece, he wrote that he had taken up his drawing again, he had made a sketch of the Corinth temples. Then he wrote that he was going to travel across some territory east of the Mediterranean; he would write more of this shortly. But the letters broke off, it was three months at The Shadows, far into the summer, in fact, they had heard nothing.

That was one of the yellow fever years, and when Alfred's packet of letters was brought to him at Marseilles, on his return to France, there was added to the pile Father Barbier's letter telling him of the death of his father and mother. The letter said that such calamities were not unique among stricken families, that it was God's will, and that the sooner Alfred returned the better. Picayune Plantation, which was the farthest distant as well as the largest had gone to Hélène, whose husband would take charge of it; but there were The Shadows, Silence, and Mantua to be managed.

Alfred came home that autumn burnt from the sun, handsomer than ever, bringing with him his Paris clothes and gifts that he had bought before his news reached him. He also brought a portfolio of drawings. Three of four of his kin who lived nearest had come to The Shadows and waited, so that they might be with Alfred when he first arrived. Of that homecoming to the family that loved him, of the romance of his travels and the glamor of his adventure and the surprise of it, which he had meant to tell them all, his mother especially, what was there to say? where was it gone? All through the empty parlors and the long hall the candles were lighted, and through the open doors at the back the soft wind from across the bayou brought in the garden fragrance; but there seemed nothing. In the midst of supper Father Barbier arrived.

It was a strange scene in the parlor an hour later that night, with the young

982

master of the plantation come home from abroad, his guests out of the kindness of their hearts entreating him to tell of his journey, and the portfolio of his drawings lying open on the table. The light of the tall candelabra fell on the sheets of paper as Alfred turned over one drawing after another. In a wide, unbroken desert, columns rose, a whole line of them, their flutings intact, the great leaves and garlands of their capitals still preserved. Or on another sheet were drawn the arches of an aqueduct going off into the distance, high arches, solitary, strong. Or here there was a single column on a great base, the capital gone and the shaft broken at the top and, in the ground beneath, long blocks of the entablature with its riotous ornament, under the black shadows of an Asiatic sun. In one of the drawings there was a whole temple shown, or at least a side of it; beyond the columns the wall of the shrine was still standing. It was drawn as if it were in moonlight, the sky pale and vague with a few stars, the earth lying rapt, but the temple shining out from its shadows, all as if there had been no years, no ruin, no ancient oblivion.

And so one by one the drawings appeared and seemed to make an agreeable entertainment for everyone. There were gasps of admiration, faint cries, polite questions. Father Barbier took the ruins for Greek and spoke of the glory that was Greece.

Certainly if these ancient monuments were Greek, Alfred had drawn them very badly; but he did not correct the gentle old priest who meant so well. Instead he began to explain to Father Barbier and his other guests that the drawings were not imaginary views, as they seemed to take them. They must not mistake these drawings for sheer embroideries or classical models.

Doubtless all men want to travel, Alfred said, and to have various seas and far roads bring them home again—*diverse maria et viae reportant,* as his old tutor had taught him from Catullus. Perhaps, also, his old tutor had filled him with the idea of Greece. However that was, he had gone there as a mere traveller along with travellers. And then one night in Athens he walked out past the city and down to the Piraeus harbor.

There was a café—a sort of arbor—by the waterside, where he sat down. It happened that beside him sat an Arab gentleman and, as people do, they fell to talking. In the course of it the Arab told Alfred of cities and temples in his country, across desert stretches or on the plains. Though they cared little about them, all his people knew of these things. But, so far as he had heard, nobody in Europe had ever reported them.

The Arab gentleman had a ring with a cornelian in it, scratched with Roman letters which his brother had picked up in a temple porch; he kept turning the ring on his finger. Next day Alfred sailed on the Levantine ship, arrived at the eastern end of the Mediterranean and journeying inland with his new acquaintance to the latter's town, hired escorts, dragomen with nothing to do otherwise, and set out, now along with some caravan, now along with his own party.

Everybody in the parlor listened to what Alfred said about the desert sands, the nights, the caravans, the sudden view of some ruined ancient city or temple columns; but they did not reopen the portfolio. It was clear that the drawings meant no more to them than chromos; in an upstairs hall at The Shadows was

983

there not the Lions of Luxor? His cousins' faces were full of goodness and affection. It never occurred to Alfred, at the time, that there could be anything prophetic in the way his kin and friends took his drawings.

It was during that Winter that Alfred set up the two columns at the garden end, by the water. From the stone platform, graded into steps, a row of columns was to rise. Through them the green vistas would be seen, the sheen of gardenia and camellia and oleander leaves, and Bayou Terrebonne. There was a young Italian in Thibodaux who knew how to work in marble and stone.

Sometimes in the evening Alfred would take out the drawings and divert himself by adding a few touches or making corrections in line and shading. As he looked at the drawings, there would come suddenly back the memory of his enthusiasm. He would see again the stone, the marbles, their antique beauty, in a forgotten land, under the vast skies. A breathless night, a great boon, the sky fretted with stars, and the solitary marbles standing.

He would sail for France, when the plantation's affairs were settled, by the end of April!

In those days you had to depend for your knowledge of distant lands on the reports of travellers. All you could know was what some traveller said or had drawn or painted. The rest could be only rumor. And thus his drawings would show people in the great world of learning and art things they had never seen, never even heard of.

The upshot of Paris was that Alfred took the drawings to his cousin, the old marquis, with the nose that was yellow from snuff, who sent him to the famous De Vaux in the Palais Royal, who, scenting a rich colonial, charged double, but in the end turned out plates that hit the drawings to a T. He was four months at it. The plates were bound into portfolios and Alfred sent them to the scholars recommended by his cousin and to some of the great ladies who had salons. A copy went, on the recommendations of Miss Percy, to the Duchess d'Angoulême, sister of the lost Dauphin and daughter of Louis XVI and Marie Antoinette. Thus, before many weeks, the drawings were seen by the best people, both in the learned circles and in society. What happened was that everybody saw the drawings of the temples, strange walls and columns, but nobody believed these things existed.

Monsieur the marquis had executed another affair beside De Vaux's engraving the plates, he had planned a marriage for his young cousin. As representative, so to speak, of the Louisiana branch of the family, he proposed to his old friend, the Vicomte Fernay (Victor Ernest Antoine Fernay), a great classical scholar but far from wealthy, an alliance between his rich young cousin and the vicomte's daughter, Artémise, about whom many people took sides, as to whether she had more beauty than brains or more brains than beauty. To a young man brought up on classical poetry the name itself was enough to go to one's head.

With romance the marquis' counsels proved even more successful than with engraving. His young cousin fell deeply in love with the girl and she with him. The two young people, properly chaperoned, spent many hours together during those four months while De Vaux chose to work on the engravings.

The vicomte, despite the entreaties of the more practical man (a good marriage in cold fact not being an everyday matter), turned out to be one of the worst critics of the drawings.

'In the first place,' the vicomte said to Alfred, 'if you saw these things you must have drawn them badly. Roman architecture is not so coarse, not those crude, bold carvings, cut so deep, not that heavy style.'

'With all due respect,' said the young man, 'I drew them as they are.'

'An affront to classic tradition,' the vicomte said. It was clear to Alfred that he had talked the whole thing over with other scholars.

'But, sir, these things are what I saw.'

'If they look as you depict them, these remains are degenerate architecture, that's all,' said the vicomte, the veins swelling on his forehead.

'I've never said they were important. Though, if you saw them as I did—how beautiful! All I say is that nobody has described them to us before.'

'Not important, certainly. But remarkably complete as you draw them. To survive thus extensively, one naturally asks what proof is there?'

'Proof, sir?' said Alfred, red in the face.

'It is generally known that the Roman Empire flourished in these countries you appear to have seen. And the ancient world, it seems—I know it only by report—is likely to be dotted with fallen shafts and broken marbles. But if there existed ruins so extensive as these you show, we'd know of them.'

'Tut, tut,' cried the little marquis, who had just come in and whose hand Artémise had hastened to take. 'All this over a cracked architrave! Let me remind you what Epictetus said, the grammarians, he said, who would set the very letters of the alphabet quarrelling together. And why should not a young man dream? Lord Byron wandered over classic lands, giving us their romance, but, of course, Byron couldn't draw. Why should not a young man, rapturous in the deserted ancient landscape, dream of Paris fame?

'Nonsense!' Alfred shouted, losing control of himself. 'Doubtless they too say the same, the noble ladies, the princess——' But seeing the distress on his cousin's vague old face, he stopped abruptly. 'I bid you all good day.' As he walked to the door he caught sight of Artémise, saw her eyes. The vicomte did not even glance at him.

Next day he received a formal note from Artémise's father breaking off the engagement. He wrote her every day for five days, and then the five notes were returned by the vicomte's servant. They were unopened.

'You will not see Artémise again,' said the marquis; 'this is Europe.'

So Paris would not believe his drawings! Alfred said to himself. They were too stupid, or too narrow, or too doubting in men's honor to give him even the benefit of the doubt. He made farewell visits to his cousins, the marquis and Miss Percy, and without adieus to anyone else, he boarded the *Liberté* at Boulogne and sailed for home. He had been absent almost a year.

Bad news, they say, travels fast. Word had already gone round New Orleans, at the parties and balls and among the gentlemen who met at the gambling-houses in Royal Street, or at the fencing academies in Exchange Alley, that Joseph Raymond and Thérèse Deslonde's son, Alfred, had published his classical drawings only to be smiled at by the Parisian scholars, who refused to believe the tale he told. A few older men like the bishop, the Chevalier Le Moyne, the

985

tutor, Mr. Edmonds, from Yale, or Mr. Henry Perrault, the bookseller, who were academically minded and wanted the logic of fact upheld, talked gravely to people about the matter. They too said that if any such classic remains existed, the scholars in Paris would have known it.

Otherwise, but for the brief gossip—this classical matter, and the vicomte's breaking off his daughter's engagement—nobody cared two straws, only Alfred himself. He had too much character to take on a profession of melancholy, too much pride to pity himself, and too much taste to go on with the argument for which no proof was likely. But he was hurt at the centre somewhere. They had broken something that sprang from a generous and honorable nature. In the cabinet room at The Shadows hung portraits of his father and mother. He had some of his drawings framed and hung in this room.

Years passed, and middle age came on Alfred Raymond. He was in his late fifties when his sister died and left to him her daughter Ellen—Nellie. The child was Hélène's youngest, born to her after forty; her other children had died, killed, so their cousin Thankful Percy said, by the nurses while Hélène was waltzing at Mardi Gras.

Ellen's father had been a man of fashion in his time and had gambled away most of his possessions. And his widow had not done very much to better what estate was left her, a part of which, Picayune Plantation, had long since gone to pay the mortgages; she liked a fine carriage-horse and she collected laces. So that, in the end, Ellen turned out to be by no means an heiress. The horses were sold, of course; the laces were in a box along with the velvet case of a parure of diamonds that would serve very well some day at a wedding, an event inevitable.

The little girl of ten came to live at Shadows on Terrebonne, bringing there her black mammy, Cydalise, whom her mother had willed to her along with the laces. She was given the chamber with the dressing-room, over the parlor, and here she and her mammy lived, and Ellen slept in the Empire bed whose rosewood frame would have held a dozen of her, lengthwise and crosswise. In fact, old Cydalise used to put two or three of the little cousins in with Ellen sometimes, when they came visiting; to watch over them all in one bed was easier.

Alfred saw the bed one night with three in it. 'Might as well get in yourself, Mammy,' he said, smiling at the old woman.

'Nah, suh, I ain' go be sleppin' wid no wildcats.'

'Considering how many beds there are in this house, the blue room, and Father's room, the room Aunt Percy always has——'

'Marse Alfred, I ain' lak de Bible proverb says. I puts all my eggs in one basket.'

'Mammy puts all her eggs in one basket,' Ellen cried, laughing and whirling over between the sheets.

'*Oui, mam'selle,* and you ain' washed the face. When your cher papa was a lil' boy at Grosse Tête he washed the face every night. I don' mean no cat lickin' either. I mean scrub.'

'Cher papa!' Ellen cried. 'But, Tante Cydalise, in the morning. Please!'

'Very well, for this once.'

Sometimes after supper, when the weather was mild, Ellen walked up and down on the terrace with her uncle. When he talked to her of those youthful scenes that he had known, the ancient walls, the sculptured images, the marble columns, they were tinged, it seemed to him, with the light that rose in Terrebonne from the moon and the dreaming clouds and water. Sometimes he thought it was her listening that made this so.

'Are they as tall as the columns in the garden, uncle?' said the little voice. 'Yes, Nellie.'

Meantime, if her uncle had been troubled as to whether or not Ellen would inherit the Deslonde beauty, a few years more served only to show how uselessly he had worried. The brown eyes were open and soft, luminous like a deer's, shadowed with passionate emphasis, strong with some loyalty of feeling, but shy and waiting.

By the time Ellen was seventeen it was clear that plenty of young men from the plantations around would have come oftener to The Shadows if she had so much as dropped a handkerchief. So far that seemed unlikely enough. Then in June, when her cousins came out to their plantation in Iberia, not far away from Terrebonne Parish, Ellen met a young man visiting there and fell in love. His name was Stewart Robard, and he lived at Randolph Gate in Parish Vermilion. His mother had been to school with her mother, and so it was the kind of love affair that pleased everyone. This young man, whose eyes were so gay, who sat his horse so well, who could shoot glass balls thrown in the air when there was a riding tournament, who was so often hunting in the pine woods or fishing in the Blanche Côte bays, would have come every day to The Shadows if he had lived near enough and if Ellen had let him. As it was, he came often those summer months, driving his claybank Arabians, and Nellie saw him also in New Orleans, at the D'Estrées'. But somehow nothing came of it.

She watched her uncle and Stewart together. They conversed like gentlemen, about the racing season, the hunting, the new roads in Parish St. Mary. But it seemed to her that neither of them said much that he cared to say.

'Do you think there are many people, Uncle Al,' she asked him one day, 'who say things to one that one likes? I mean that one likes to hear.'

'Sometimes,' he said, 'I think the point is not so much that we should like what people say to us. The point is that we should like what we say to them.'

Her sweet, perplexed heart whispered to her that this saying was like Uncle Alfred. How intelligent it was, it was something to think over!

She saw her uncle sometimes walking late in the evening up and down the terrace, saw the columns shining against the dusk, and beyond them the pale sheen of the bayou water.

'Darling Uncle Al,' she said to herself as she gazed at him from the curtains of the window, 'why do we not die? Why don't we fly south as the birds do? Uncle, I will stay by you, I'll never leave you.'

She would see him stop in his pacing and stand there with his arms folded, looking back at the house that his father had built and then at the two columns with their classic line against the dim fields beyond.

'I'll never leave you,' she thought.

She considered this in herself to be loyal and deep. 'Dear Uncle Alfred, what have they done to you? I won't leave you.'

The thought came to her, seeing the birds fly up from the bayou, of birds

987

drifting in the sky above the ancient marbles. At the same moment, she thought of Stewart Robard; and at the thought the lines of a ballad they had taught her long ago came back—

> Oh, gentle wind that bloweth south,
> Where my true love repaireth,
> Convey a kiss to his dear mouth,
> And tell me how he fareth.

'Y'all could sing, Miss Nell, ef you jes try,' Mammy said.

By virtue of her youth and her lovely heart's imagination, the story at Shadows on Terrebonne now turns toward Ellen. It belongs to her rather than to an old man grown tired now even of ironic peace, weary of all things, even of hope.

By June their beloved cousin Thankful Percy was saying that Ellen would be an old maid before she knew it. She was going on eighteen now, and her mother when she married was little better than sixteen. Could anybody imagine a girl kicking every man that courted her? But some way or other it was all Ellen's uncle's fault, trust a man! And truly it was plain as your nose on your face that Stewart Robard had graduated at the new State University in Mississippi and gone straight on home without stopping by The Shadows. Not even a mere pop call, Cousin Tank said.

The full summer came on in the Louisiana country. In the garden at Shadows on Terrebonne, rather neglected of late years and touched with extravagant growth, the roses had passed their prime, their fragrance mingled with the small grand duke jasmine and honeysuckle, and, when the sun was hot, with the sweet betsies. The lemon lilies were very sweet and the heliotrope. The red amaryllises, spread long ago beyond their beds, swung in heavy clusters; the water-hyacinths, pale as lilacs, crowded the edge of the bayou. At night the constellations shone close in the open sky; the stars spread out; and from the grass, the trees, the water, you heard the sounds of the small life there.

Sometimes the girl would begin a mimicry of these sounds: the cicadas; the bird across the bayou that was like a short flute-note, half finished; and the shrill tree frogs. Then pausing, she would listen to them all again as if they were her echoes.

Sometimes her uncle, seeing her crossing the green lawn to the bayou, thought of the saying that 'all heavenly things run on light feet.' Once when he repeated this to himself, it was autumn. All heavenly things run on light feet, he thought; and then he could hear the hush of falling leaves in such a silence as had not been before.

So the year 1859 passed into August; and in the orchard near the house Alfred Raymond, as he lay awake at night, heard the heavy fruit dropping to the ground. There came to him from the old orchard by that wing of the house the sound of fruit falling. 'Ripeness is all.' Did not Shakespeare say that? The apricots and pears, now and then, in the light wind, dropping to the ground. Ripeness is all—falling in the ripeness of summer. Another season would soon end, then another year.

A man thinks these things. But on the second Tuesday in the month, the *Lorient*, as she passed up the bayou, brought a visitor. Cydalise, whom nothing short of calamity could have prevented from watching for the boat every week, brought him into the hall where Ellen sat. The young man, still under thirty, was tall, with a high forehead and good, frank eyes. He made his apologies for not having written, but his time had been short. He had come because he had been on a journey, well, a sort of expedition, as it were, through the same country that her uncle had visited, so long ago, but now there was the camera to take along. He knew well her uncle's drawings, people had been too ignorant to believe them. He wanted to pay his respects and to present her uncle with an album of photographs.

He ran through the pages for her to see, while Cydalise went upstairs to announce the visitor.

'If it just won't smother me to death!' Ellen thought, as she felt her heart beating. She was in her own room now, and standing at the open window; but her heart beat like that.

There would be the photographs lying open on the table, her uncle and the young man gazing down on them up at the drawings on the walls. Here the camera had shown a scene, and here it appeared in her uncle's drawing. The line of columns, fluted, their capitals all graceful garlands and leaves, appeared in both. On the wall and in the album it was the same aqueduct, with the high arches going off into the distance, ruined but splendid. There was the same temple with the black shadows.

And so science, which everybody talked so much about these days, had supplied the proof.

What happens to our souls when nothing mocks them any more? Are they not free? And are not those who love us free then also?

She saw from the window the two columns at that end of the garden near the bayou. How long it was since her uncle had put them there, but had never finished his plan!

On the wall downstairs and on a page of the young man's photograph album would be the picture of the single column on a great base, she said to herself. But the shaft was broken, the long stone blocks of the magnificent entablature had fallen.

Outside it was past noon, and under the noon sky the garden lawn and the fields of the air were shadowless. The bayou was still as a mirror.

And yet——

She got up for the black writing-desk with mother-of-pearl flowers; and sitting down again, opened it on her knees.

'I do hope and believe'—she began, not writing the loved name just yet—'that you will forgive whatever—whatever I have not seemed to return in your true love. For there are other things, too, that are so strong. But now that life here is changed——' Then she said to herself that you would get the letter more like what you wanted if you waited. You could first just write his address on the envelope.

She began again, bending over the desk on her knees, and not letting her hand tremble—'Randolph Gate Plantation, Parish Vermilion.' (*1935*)

989

Reviews

In Abraham's Bosom [1]

The play now presented at the Garrick Theatre by the Provincetown Playhouse has for its theme a blend of aspiration, suffering, poignant futility and confusion. Its problem concerns the groping and defeated effort toward race freedom, growth and opportunity; and its material is full of pain, deep humanity and inherent drama. The figure who is to carry the main thread of this theme is a man half-white, half-black, troubled by white nerves and impulses, darkened in his soul with superstition, weakness and disease. He is Abraham McCranie, the son of Colonel McCranie and a colored woman, and the plot is a record of his story.

We see three Negroes in a wood where they have been chopping. They talk of Abe, the book-lover. Abe enters; he is apart from them, absorbed in his dream of an education and the salvation of his race. Goldie McAllister, also partly white, loves him, brings him food; and now, when Abe has been impudent to the son of his white father and struck him, and the father has given Abe a whipping, Goldie comforts him. The scene ends with their going to sit beneath the trees and the three other Negroes breaking into an orgy of excitement over this picture of love.

We see Abe then, after he has been married for a few years, the father of two puny children who have died and now of a son that is to be strong and the savior of his race. Fortune has deserted Abe, his crops are ruined, his spirit bitter, his family starving; for he is no farmer, what he wants is to teach a school. The Colonel comes and gives him the title to some land. Abe's bitterness changes; he sees the heavens open, sees himself as blest and on the road to his mission. We find him then in his school, a wretched sight, and then closing the school because of the attack to be made on him for cruelly beating one of his pupils who would not try to learn. He moves from town to town, talking his salvation theme and losing his jobs, hounded, sick, bewildered, brutal, fanatical, his weak and trifling son turned from the house. Muh Mack, the aunt who lives with him, scolding and complaining, only his wife faithful and slaving and starving for him, never losing her belief. Colonel McCranie's will has ordered that a place be always given him on the farm if he should wish to return. He goes back, his crop is again neglected, the cotton falls out of the bolls while he writes a speech for the inauguration of a new academy that shall be a light to his people. His son sets a low class of whites on him, he is hounded from the hall where he meant to speak. In the fields he lies, his pursuers outrun. Mr. Lonnie, the Colonel's son, comes to find out what the noise is. He tries to steady Abe, but when he tells him that he has taken his cotton crop and found pickers for it, Abe leaps at him, there is a scuffle, the white man is killed. In

Reprinted from Immortal Shadows by Stark Young; copyright 1948 by Charles Scribner's Sons; used by permission of the publishers.
[1] Young's review refers to the presentation of Paul Green's In Abraham's Bosom at the Garrick Theatre in New York City on February 13, 1927.

the last scene, Abe bursts in on his family, his pursuers arrive, as he opens the door he is shot down, his last cry is freedom, freedom. The curtain falls on his wife sobbing over him.

As I ponder this play it seems moving and profound. Certainly the course of its struggle is full of tragic despair: this poor, confused, violent high-souled creature beating out his life in vain against circumstance. There is, too, a certain wise balance of parts in the dramatic elements; the white people mean to be kind, but they are as lost in the midst of a race situation as the Negro is; they are moved now by human or affectionate impulse and now by a blind racial instinct and an arbitrary, desperate sense of self-preservation. The climaxes in the play are strong and bold. I seem, as I think of it, to have been present at a full, passionate story, told by a poet. Certainly this material that Mr. Green attempts is ambitious of power and devastation and beauty; we are in very deep waters with such subject matter as he employs.

But what I remember last is that for three-fifths of the time I was dissatisfied and often more than bored. The first act, up to that really inventive moment at the very last when the three Negroes dance about at the sight of the love between Abe and Goldie, was very nearly unbearable. With better acting, perhaps, *In Abraham's Bosom* might have been better. Of what acting there was, we may say that for more or less untrained actors, with little sense of technical projection, the company was perhaps passable; Miss Rose McClendon, by virtue of a certain sincerity or something in herself, was nearly always effective and often tragic.

The dialogue of this play, apart from some of the curtain climaxes, is flat and seems hastily written. Considering the bold, O'Neill sort of line that the treatment essays, the speeches are sometimes surprisingly false, borrowed, conventional. One of the best signs of promise in such a play as *In Abraham's Bosom* would lie in the ear; for nowhere in America is there better material for dialogue than in this world of Mr. Green's; nowhere is there a more special rhythm and flavor of speech than in the South, or more warmth and naïveté of words than in Negro speech. That Mr. Green made so little passion for the quivering beat of life that the words might carry, is a discouraging sign in what is obviously a marked theatre talent working with material that is wholly vibrant and freshly taken out of our American life.

The best places in this play of Negro life are those like that orgiastic end of the first act; or the scenes where the loose and worthless grandson with his jazz talent sings for his old aunt and the two of them prove to have one blood in their veins; or Abe's prayer when the land becomes his and he dedicates his baby to God and his race. In these there is an essence that is racial, dramatic and moving. These moments take themselves out of the hands of the actors, the pulse quickens, the glow of strangeness and beauty comes over the scene; and for a little we have the sense of a soul working and of poetic truth.

But it is between these moments that the trouble lies with Mr. Green's play. Between these high moments we cannot ask an equal tension and imagination; but we can ask more pains, more reduction of the play's progress to firm outlines that would go better with its bold technical aim. The tenderness of feeling in this work, the love of the country and soil in which this history

991

occurs, the courage of the character delineation and the range of sentiment, all deserve more care and choice on the author's part. The glow that is in these special passages could appear, though in smaller terms of course, in the speeches that lie between them. This play is of the kind that makes you wish it well; and you resent all the more the fact that the gloom that some of it spreads over you is not the gloom of tragedy, for that might be rich and stirring, but of casual form and bad writing. (*1927*)

The Tempest [1]

Margaret Breuning in her introduction to the new Hyperion book of Mary Cassatt, quotes Degas as saying, "I don't admit that a woman can draw so well as that." I confess I am inclined to go old-fashioned and say something of the sort about Miss Webster's production of *The Tempest*. Whatever may be the shortcomings of the occasion, you must be filled with wonder that one little woman, as it were, could pull all this together and send it off with such professional thoroughness. If you read the play again and see the problems involved for its presentation nowadays, you will better understand what is implied by my observation and may even take off your hat to her. Her results with the play are not in the direction of poetry, but do make a good show; and that in itself is something not to be despised.

Whether such is possible today or not, whether any sort of plausibility or absence of artiness could be achieved, is of course highly doubtful; but it is obvious that for *The Tempest* to get much of what Shakespeare intended, the Elizabethan stage is required, or something like it. There are three points involved. First is the fact that Shakespeare exists and is alive through the words, which, whatever may be his invention in other theatre elements, remain the chief point of supremacy in his genius. Second is the necessity for fluid scenes, no breaks or delays, so that the special lyricism of his form and movement may be achieved. Third is the close contact with the audience, which, if such are to reach us, the speed, the intricacy of expression and the variety in character require.

The matter of the quick changes and flow of scenes Miss Webster has solved well enough. Motley has designed a kind of rock mass on a revolving base that allows easy and continuous shifting of the scene. This is not an impressively imaginative creation, but it serves to good purpose. The first scene, however, of *The Tempest*, that of the ship's deck in the storm, Shakespeare for some reason has written in lines oddly difficult to speak out or catch the meaning of; at best they might be clear for us by being spoken on an apron stage, smack out among the audience, as the Elizabethan theatre knew how to do. Motley has a painted drop of a fancy ship, in which presently a transparent section shows the commo-

992

Reprinted from Immortal Shadows *by Stark Young; copyright 1948 by Charles Scribner's Sons; used by permission of the publishers.*
[1] *Young's review refers to the presentation of Shakespeare's* The Tempest *at the Alvin Theatre in New York City on January 25, 1945.*

tion on the deck. The scene spoken in the midst of this turns out to be confused, wasted and dull.

If you study the stage history of the play you will see that in divers epochs it was produced with many additions, cuttings and general changes, though the nineteenth century brought it round again closer to the Shakespeare text. Miss Webster has not cut very heavily or ironed matters out of the way until toward the end of the fourth act. There the interlude of the classic goddesses is left out, and the famous speech of Prospero's about our globe and all which it inherits dissolving, and we are such stuff as dreams are made on and our little life rounded with a sleep, is lifted out and put a whole act forward. Thus the finale of the play is changed from the sunny ending, with everybody happy, to an ending in which the characters go out and Prospero is left alone on the stage with his beautiful philosophic speech from the earlier scene. Whatever Shakespearean students may think of such alterations, the result is most effective, and is more lyric and moody, and thus more modern, than the text is or was intended to be.

As for the words, the character, of course, who most of all has the wings of words on which the play must be borne is Ariel. Miss Vera Zorina understands the role and gives herself to its sweet flight and delicacy of presence as perhaps nobody else in our theatre could. She adds to this as a matter of course her expert ballet movement, her beauty and her grace of conception.

Mr. Canada Lee's Caliban spoke often with a good metrical ear though his diction was much too insecure. He was neither malign, evil nor frightening but fitted well enough in the general plane of the occasion, which did not seek perhaps—certainly it did not achieve—poetic intensity or elevation. The two young people, Miranda and Ferdinand, Miss Frances Heflin and Mr. Vito Christi, were young players of an agreeable quality. In the light of the theatre around them on Broadway, we could hardly expect Miss Webster to teach them beautiful speech and style in a few weeks. Mr. Arnold Moss was a dignified and noble Prospero, with a good voice for the lines. And Mr. Paul Leyssac played the difficult and elusive and traditional role of the old councillor with his usual distinction, admirable speech and fine tone. The two comics, Trinculo and Stephano, so abundantly supplied with gusty, Elizabethan material by Shakespeare himself, were capitally played by Mr. George Voskovec and Mr. Jan Werich, until lately, we are told, among the prime favorites of the Czech-Slovakian theatre.

Serious students of *The Tempest* can find many interpretations of its meaning, all kinds of things about power, about freedom, spirit and matter, good and evil, and so on. It is best to begin that discussion merely with noting that *The Tempest* is one of those creations in art that achieve a truly fable form, which means that within it there are infinite implications that may be applied to life one way or another. I may add that on the starry, poetic side, *The Tempest* given by the children of the King-Coit School far surpasses any I know of.

So far as the themes of demons, beneficent spirits, witches and magic are concerned, nobody can arrive at any intelligent approach to *The Tempest* who thinks that either Shakespeare or his audience interpreted these scenes as most people nowadays are apt to do. Such people are likely to read *The Tempest* in the light of their childhood impressions of fairy tales and ghost stories. All that fantasy and naïve magic possibility that charmed them had in it little conviction

993

of reality. But this was not the case when *The Tempest* was written. To men of that time, and long before then and after, the spirit world was as close as technology today may be to us. Some of the best minds were concerned with the subject. For a list of books that were written, and an excellent study of pneumatology in Elizabethan drama, we can read Mr. Robert Hunter West's *The Invisible World*, published by the University of Georgia Press.   (*1945*)

THOMAS WOLFE

1900–1938

Thomas Wolfe was born October 3, 1900, in Asheville, North Carolina. His father was a "naturalized" Southerner and his mother a member of a prominent mountaineer clan. At fifteen, Wolfe entered the University of North Carolina, where he edited the college magazine and newspaper. While at Chapel Hill he also wrote a one-act play, "The Return of Buck Gavin," later published in one of the University's anthologies of Southern folk plays. Graduating in 1920, Wolfe went to Harvard University, where he became a member of George Pierce Baker's "47 Workshop"—at this time his ambition was to become a playwright. He received his M.A. degree from Harvard in 1922 and for six years, beginning in 1924, taught English at New York University, working seriously at his writing during his free time and completing his first novel, *Look Homeward, Angel*. He gave up his teaching permanently when he was awarded a Guggenheim Fellowship in 1930 and went to Europe, where he traveled widely and continued to write.

Wolfe was a prolific writer but was able to publish only four books—from what might almost be termed a "mountain" of manuscripts—before his untimely death in 1938. These were *Look Homeward, Angel* (1929), a lyrical account of his youth in Asheville; *Of Time and the River* (1935), in which a maturing hero begins to meet a non-provincial world; *From Death to Morning* (1935), a group of short selections; and *The Story of a Novel* (1936), a study of his own writing, which had appeared serially in *The Saturday Review of Literature* the preceding year. Some of Wolfe's best work has been published posthumously as *The Web and the Rock* (1939), *You Can't Go Home Again* (1940), and *The Hills Beyond* (1941).

994

The House of the Far and Lost[1]

In the fall of that year I lived out about a mile from town in a house set back from the Ventnor Road. The house was called a "farm"—Hill-top Farm, or Far-end Farm, or some such name as that—but it was really no farm at all. It was a magnificent house of the weathered gray stone they have in that country, as if in the very quality of the wet heavy air there is the soft thick gray of time itself, sternly yet beautifully soaking down forever on you—and enriching everything it touches—grass, foliage, brick, ivy, the fresh moist color of the people's faces, and old gray stone with the incomparable weathering of time.

The house was set back off the road at a distance of several hundred yards, possibly a quarter of a mile, and one reached it by means of a road bordered by rows of tall trees which arched above the road, and which made me think of home at night when the stormy wind howled in their tossed branches. On each side of the road were the rugby fields of two of the colleges and in the afternoon I could look out and down and see the fresh moist green of the playing fields, and watch young college fellows, dressed in their shorts and jerseys, and with their bare knees scurfed with grass and turf as they twisted, struggled, swayed, and scrambled for a moment in the scrimmage-circle, and then broke free, running, dodging, passing the ball as they were tackled, filling the moist air with their sharp cries of sport. They did not have the desperate, the grimly determined, the almost professional earnestness that the college teams at home have; their scurfed and muddy knees, their swaying scrambling scrimmages, the swift breaking away and running, their panting breath and crisp clear voices gave them the appearance of grown-up boys.

Once when I had come up the road in afternoon while they were playing, the ball got away from them and came bounding out into the road before me, and I ran after it to retrieve it as we used to do when passing a field where boys were playing baseball. One of the players came over to the edge of the field and stood there waiting with his hands upon his hips while I got the ball: he was panting hard, his face was flushed, and his blond hair tousled, but when I threw the ball to him, he said "Thanks very much!" crisply and courteously—getting the same sound into the word "very" that they got in "American," a sound that always repelled me a little because it seemed to have some scornful aloofness and patronage in it.

For a moment I watched him as he trotted briskly away on to the field again: the players stood there waiting, panting, casual, their hands upon their hips; he passed the ball into the scrimmage, the pattern swayed, rocked, scrambled, and broke sharply out in open play again, and everything looked incredibly strange, near, and familiar.

I felt that I had always known it, that it had always been mine, and that it was as familiar to me as everything I had seen or known in my childhood. Even

995

[1] This selection is reprinted as it appeared in Scribner's Magazine in 1934. Wolfe later made it a part of his novel, Of Time and the River (1935).

the texture of the earth looked familiar, and felt moist and firm and springy when I stepped on it, and the stormy howling of the wind in that avenue of great trees at night, was wild and desolate and demented as it had been when I was eight years old and could lie in my bed at night and hear the great oaks howling on the hill above my father's house.

The name of the people in the house was Coulson: I made arrangements with the woman at once to come and live there: she was a tall, weathered-looking woman of middle age, we talked together in the hall. The hall was made of marble flags and went directly out onto a gravelled walk.

The woman was crisp, cheerful, and worldly looking. She was still quite hand-some. She wore a well-cut skirt of woollen plaid, and a silk blouse: when she talked she kept her arms folded because the air in the hall was chilly, and she held a cigarette in the fingers of one hand. A shaggy brown dog came out and nosed upward toward her hand as she was talking and she put her hand upon its head and scratched it gently. When I told her I wanted to move in the next day, she said briskly and cheerfully:

"Right you are! You'll find everything ready when you get here!" Then she asked if I was at the university. I said no, and added, with a feeling of difficulty and naked desolation, that I was a "writer," and was coming there to work. I was twenty-four years old.

"Then I am sure that what you do will be *very, very* good!" she said cheer-fully and decisively. "We have had several Americans in the house before and all of them were very clever! All the Americans we have had here were very clever people," said the woman. "I'm sure that you will like it." Then she walked to the door with me to say good-bye. As we stood there, there was the sound of a small motor-car coming to a halt and in a moment a girl came swiftly across the gravel space outside and entered the hall. She was tall, slender, very lovely, but she had the same bright hard look in her eye the woman had, the same faint, hard smile around the edges of her mouth.

"Edith," the woman said in her crisp, curiously incisive tone, "this young man is an American—he is coming here tomorrow." The girl looked at me for a moment with her hard bright glance, thrust out a small gloved hand, and shook hands briefly, a swift firm greeting.

"Oh! How d'ye do!" she said. "I hope you will like it here." Then she went on down the hall, entered a room on the left, and closed the door behind her.

Her voice had been crisp and certain like her mother's, but it was also cool, young, and sweet, with music in it, and later as I went down the road, I could still hear it.

That was a wonderful house, and the people there were wonderful people. Later, I could not forget them. I seemed to have known them all my life, and to know all about their lives. They seemed as familiar to me as my own blood and I knew them with a knowledge that went deep below the roots of thought or memory. We did not talk together often, or tell any of our lives to one another. It will be very hard to tell about it—the way we felt and lived together in that house—because it was one of those simple and profound experiences of life which people seem always to have known when it happens to them, but for which there is no language.

And yet, like a child's half-captured vision of some magic country he has known, and which·haunts his days with strangeness and the sense of immanent, glorious re-discovery, the word that would unlock it all seems constantly to be almost on our lips, waiting just outside the gateway of our memory, just a shape, a phrase, a sound away the moment that we choose to utter it—but when we try to say the thing, something fades within our mind like fading light, and something melts within our grasp like painted smoke, and something goes forever when we try to touch it.

The nearest I could come to it was this: In that house I sometimes felt the greatest peace and solitude that I had ever known. But I always knew the other people in the house were there. I could sit in my sitting-room at night and hear nothing but the stormy moaning of the wind outside in the great trees, the small gaseous flare and jet from time to time of the coal fire burning in the grate—and silence, strong living lonely silence that moved and waited in the house at night—and I would always know that they were there.

I did not have to hear them enter or go past my door, nor did I have to hear doors close or open in the house, or listen to their voices: if I had never seen them, heard them, spoken to them, it would have been the same—I should have known they were there.

It was something I had always known, and had known it would happen to me, and now it was there with all the strangeness and dark mystery of an awaited thing. I knew them, felt them, lived among them with a familiarity that had no need of sight or word or speech. And the memory of that house and of my silent fellowship with all the people there was somehow mixed with an image of dark time. It was one of those sorrowful and unchanging images which, among all the blazing stream of images that passed constantly their stream of fire across my mind, was somehow fixed, detached, and everlasting, full of a sorrow, certitude, and mystery that I could not fathom, but that wore forever on it the old sad light of waning day—a light from which all the heat, the violence, and the substance of furious dusty day had vanished, and was itself like time, unearthly-of-the-earth, remote, detached, and everlasting.

And that fixed and changeless image of dark time was this: In an old house of time I lived alone, and yet had other people all around me, and they never spoke to me, or I to them. They came and went like silence in the house, but I always knew that they were there. I would be sitting by a window in a room, and I would know then they were moving in the house, and darkness, sorrow, and strong silence dwelt within us, and our eyes were quiet, full of sorrow, peace, and knowledge, and our faces dark, our tongues silent, and we never spoke. I could not remember how their faces looked, but they were all familiar to me as my father's face, and we had known one another forever, and we lived together in the ancient house of time, dark time, and silence, sorrow, certitude, and peace were in us. Such was the image of dark time that was to haunt my life thereafter, and into which, somehow, my life among the people in that house had passed.

In the house that year there lived, besides myself and Morison, the Coulsons, the father and mother and their daughter, and three men who had taken rooms together, and who were employed in a factory where motor-cars were made, two miles from town.

I think the reason that I could never forget these people later and seemed to

997

know them all so well was that there was in all of them something ruined, lost, or broken—some precious and irretrievable quality which had gone out of them and which they could never get back again. Perhaps that was the reason that I liked them all so much, because with ruined people it is either love or hate: there is no middle way. The ruined people that we like are those who desperately have died, and lost their lives because they loved life dearly, and had that grandeur that makes such people spend prodigally the thing they love the best, and risk and lose their lives because it is so precious to them, and die at length because the seeds of life were in them. It is only the people who love life in this way who die—and these are the ruined people that we like.

The people in the house were people who had lost their lives because they loved the earth too well, and somehow had been slain by their hunger. And for this reason I liked them all, and could not forget them later: there seemed to have been some magic which had drawn them all together to the house, as if the house itself was a magnetic centre for lost people.

Certainly, the three men who worked at the motor-car factory had been drawn together for this reason. Two were still young men in their early twenties. The third man was much older. He was a man past forty, his name was Nicholl, he had served in the army during the war and had attained the rank of captain.

He had the spare, alert, and jaunty figure that one often finds in army men, an almost professional military quality that somehow seemed to set his figure upon a horse as if he had grown there, or had spent a lifetime in the cavalry. His face also had the same lean, bitten, professional military quality: his speech, although good-natured and very friendly, was clipped, incisive, jerky, and sporadic, his lean weather-beaten face was deeply, sharply scarred and sunken in the flanks, and he wore a small cropped mustache, and displayed long frontal teeth when he smiled—a spare, gaunt, toothy, yet attractive smile.

His left arm was withered, shrunken, almost useless, part of his hand and two of the fingers had been torn away by the blast or explosion which had destroyed his arm, but it was not this mutilation of the flesh that gave one the sense of a life that had been ruined, lost, and broken irretrievably. In fact, one quickly forgot his physical injury: his figure looked so spare, lean, jaunty, well-conditioned in its energetic fitness that one never thought of him as a cripple, nor pitied him for any disability. No: the ruin that one felt in him was never of the flesh, but of the spirit. Something seemed to have been exploded from his life—it was not the nerve-centres of his arm, but of his soul, that had been destroyed. There was in the man somewhere a terrible dead vacancy and emptiness, and that spare, lean figure that he carried so well seemed only to surround this vacancy like a kind of shell.

He was always smartly dressed in well-cut clothes that set well on his trim spruce figure. He was always in good spirits, immensely friendly in his clipped spare way, and he laughed frequently—a rather metallic cackle which came suddenly and ended as swiftly as it had begun. He seemed, somehow, to have locked the door upon dark care and worry, and to have flung the key away— to have lost, at the same time that he lost more precious things, all the fretful doubts and perturbations of the conscience most men know.

Now, in fact, he seemed to have only one serious project in his life. This was to keep himself amused, to keep himself constantly amused, to get from

998

his life somehow the last atom of entertainment it could possibly yield, and in this project the two young men who lived with him joined in with an energy and earnestness which suggested that their employment in the motor-car factory was just a necessary evil which must be borne patiently because it yielded them the means with which to carry on a more important business, the only one in which their lives were interested—the pursuit of pleasure.

And in the way in which they conducted this pursuit, there was an element of deliberate calculation, concentrated earnestness, and focal intensity of purpose that was astounding, grotesque, and unbelievable, and that left in the mind of one who saw it a formidable and disquieting memory because there was in it almost the madness of desperation, the deliberate intent of men to cover up or seek oblivion at any cost of effort from some hideous emptiness of the soul.

Captain Nicholl and his two young companions had a little motor-car so small that it scuttled up the road, shot around and stopped in the gravel by the door with the abruptness of a wound-up toy. It was astonishing that three men could wedge themselves into this midget of a car, but wedge themselves they did, and used it to the end of its capacity, scuttling away to work in it in the morning, and scuttling back again when work was done, and scuttling away to London every Saturday, as if they were determined to wrest from this small motor, too, the last ounce of pleasure to be got from it.

Finally, Captain Nicholl and his two companions had made up an orchestra among them, and this they played in every night when they got home. One of the young men, who was a tall fellow with blond hair which went back in even corrugated waves across his head as if it had been marcelled, played the piano, the other, who was slight and dark, and had black hair, performed upon a saxophone, and Captain Nicholl himself took turns at thrumming furiously on a banjo, or rattling a tattoo upon the complex arrangement of trap drums, bass drums, and clashing cymbals that surrounded him.

They played nothing but American jazz music or sobbing crooner's rhapsodies or nigger blues. Their performance was astonishing. Although it was contrived solely for their own amusement, they hurled themselves into it with all the industrious earnestness of professional musicians employed by a night-club or a dance hall to furnish dance music for the patrons. The little dark fellow who played the saxophone would bend and weave prayerfully with his grotesque instrument, as the fat gloating notes came from its unctuous throat, and from time to time he would sway in a half circle, or get up and prance forward and back in rhythm to the music as the saxophone players in dance orchestras sometimes do.

Meanwhile the tall blond fellow at the piano would sway and bend above the keys, glancing around from time to time with little nods and smiles as if he were encouraging an orchestra of forty pieces or beaming happily and in an encouraging fashion at a dance floor crowded with paying customers.

While this was going on, Captain Nicholl would be thrumming madly on the strings of a banjo. He kept the instrument gripped somehow below his withered arm, fingering the end strings with his two good fingers, knocking the tune out with his good right hand, and keeping time with a beating foot. Then with a sudden violent movement he would put the banjo down, snatch up the sticks

999

of the trap drum, and begin to rattle out a furious accompaniment, beating the bass drum with his foot meanwhile, and reaching over to smash cymbals, chimes, and metal rings from time to time. He played with a kind of desperate fury, his mouth fixed in a strange set grin, his bright eyes burning with a sharp wild glint of madness.

They sang as they played, bursting suddenly into the refrain of some popular song with the same calculated spontaneity and spurious enthusiasm of the professional orchestra, mouthing the words of Negro blues and jazz with an obvious satisfaction, with an accent which was remarkably good, and yet which had something foreign and inept in it, which made the familiar phrases of American music sound almost as strange in their mouths as if an orchestra of skilful patient Japanese were singing them.

They sang:

> "Yes, sir! That's my baby
> Yes, sir! Don't mean maybe
> Yes, sir! That's my baby now!"

or:

> "Oh, it aint gonna rain no more, no more
> It aint gonna rain no more"

or:

> "I got dose blu-u-ues"—

the young fellow at the piano rolling his eyes around in a ridiculous fashion, and mouthing out the word "blues" extravagantly as he sang it, the little dark fellow bending forward in an unctuous sweep as the note came gloating fatly from the horn, and Captain Nicholl swaying sideways in his chair as he strummed upon the banjo strings, and improvising a mournful accompaniment of his own, somewhat as follows: "I got dose blu-u-ues! Yes, suh! Oh! I got dose blues! Yes, suh! I sure have got 'em—dose blu-u-ues—blu-u-ues—blu-u-ues!" —his mouth never relaxing from its strange fixed grin, nor his eyes from their bright set stare of madness as he swayed and strummed and sang the words that came so strangely from his lips.

It was a weird scene, an incredible performance, and somehow it pierced the heart with a wild nameless pity, an infinite sorrow and regret.

Something precious, irrecoverable had gone out of them, and they knew it. They fought the emptiness in them with this deliberate, formidable, and mad intensity of a calculated gaiety, a terrifying mimicry of mirth, and the storm wind howled around us in dark trees, and I felt that I had known them forever, and had no words to say to them—and no door.

There were four in the Coulson family: the father, a man of fifty years, the mother, somewhere in the middle forties, a son, and a daughter, Edith, a girl of twenty-two who lived in the house with her parents. I never met the son: he had completed his course at Oxford a year or two before, and had gone down to London where he was now employed. During the time I lived there the son did not come home.

1000

They were a ruined family. How that ruin had fallen on them, what it was, I never knew, for no one ever spoke to me about them. But the sense of their disgrace, of a shameful inexpiable dishonor, for which there was no pardon, from which there could never be redemption, was overwhelming. In the most astonishing way I found out about it right away, and yet I did not know what they had done, and no one ever spoke a word against them.

Rather, the mention of their name brought silence, and in that silence there was something merciless and final, something that belonged to the temper of the country, and that was far more terrible than any open word of scorn, contempt, or bitter judgment could have been, more savage than a million strident, whispering, or abusive tongues could be, because the silence was unarguable, irrevocable, complete, as if a great door had been shut against their lives forever.

Everywhere I went in town, the people knew about them, and said nothing—saying everything—when I spoke their names. I found this final, closed, relentless silence everywhere—in tobacco, wine, and tailor shops, in book stores, food stores, haberdashery stores—wherever I bought anything and gave the clerk the address to which it was to be delivered, they responded instantly with this shut finality of silence, writing the name down gravely, sometimes saying briefly "Oh! Coulson's!" when I gave them the address, but more often saying nothing.

But whether they spoke or simply wrote the name down without a word, there was always this quality of instant recognition, this obdurate, contemptuous finality of silence, as if a door had been shut—a door that could never again be opened. Somehow I disliked them more for this silence than if they had spoken evilly: there was in it something ugly, sly, knowing, and triumphant that was far more evil than any slyly whispering confidence of slander, or any open vituperation of abuse, could be. It seemed somehow to come from all the evil and uncountable small maggotry of the earth, the cautious little hatreds of a million nameless ciphers, each puny, pallid, trivial in himself, but formidable because he added his tiny beetle's ball of dung to the mountainous accumulation of ten million others of his breed.

It was uncanny how these clerk-like faces grave and quiet, that never spoke a word, or gave a sign, or altered their expression by a jot, when I gave them the address, could suddenly be alive with something secret, foul, and sly, could be more closed and secret than a door, and yet instantly reveal the naked, shameful, and iniquitous filth that welled up from some depthless source. I could not phrase it, give a name to it, or even see a certain sign that it was there, no more than I could put my hand upon a wisp of fading smoke, but I always knew when it was there, and somehow when I saw it my heart went hard and cold against the people who revealed it, and turned with warmth and strong affection toward the Coulson family.

There was, finally, among these grave clerk-like faces one face that I could never forget thereafter, a face that seemed to resume into its sly suave surfaces all of the nameless abomination of evil in the world for which I had no name, for which there was no handle I could grasp, no familiar places or edges I could get my hands upon, which slid phantasmally, oilily, and smokily away whenever I tried to get my hands upon it. But it was to haunt my life for years in dreams of hatred, madness, and despair that found no frontal wall for their attack, no word for their vituperation, no door for the shoulder of my hate—an evil world of phantoms, shapes, and whispers that was yet as real as death, as ever-present as man's treachery, but that slid away from me like smoke whenever I tried to meet, or curse, or strangle it.

This face was the face of a man in a tailor shop, a fitter there, and I could have battered that foul face into a bloody pulp, distilled the filthy refuse of his ugly life out of his fat swelling neck and through the murderous grip of my fingers if I could only have found a cause, a logic, and an act for doing it. And yet I never saw the man but twice, and briefly, and there had been nothing in his suave, sly careful speech to give offense.

Edith Coulson had sent me to the tailor's shop: I needed a suit and when I asked her where to go to have it made, she had sent me to this place because her brother had his suits made there and liked it. The fitter was a heavy shambling man in his late thirties: he had receding hair, which he brushed back flat in a thick pompadour, yellowish, somewhat bulging eyes, a coarse heavy face, loose-featured, red, and sensual, a sloping meaty jaw, and large discolored buck-teeth which showed unpleasantly in a mouth that was always half open. It was, in fact, the mouth that gave his face its sensual, sly, and ugly look, for a loose and vulgar smile seemed constantly to hover about its thick coarse edges, to be deliberately, slyly restrained, but about to burst at any moment in an open, evil, foully sensual laugh. There was always this ugly suggestion of a loose, corrupt, and evilly jubilant mirth about his mouth, and yet he never laughed or smiled.

The man's speech had this same quality. It was suave and courteous, but even in its most urbane assurances, there was something non-committal, sly, and jeering, something that slid away from you, and was never to be grasped, a quality that was faithless, tricky, and unwholesome. When I came for the final fitting it was obvious that he had done as cheap and shoddy a job as he could do; the suit was vilely botched and skimped, sufficient cloth had not been put into it, and now it was too late to remedy the defect.

Yet, the fitter gravely pulled the vest down till it met the trousers, tugged at the coat, and pulled the thing together where it stayed until I took a breath or moved a muscle, when it would all come apart again, the collar bulging outward from the shoulder, the skimpy coat and vest crawling backward from the trousers, leaving a hiatus of shirt and belly that could not be remedied now by any means.

Then, gravely he would pull the thing together again, and in his suave, yet oily, sly, and non-committal phrases, say:

"Um! Seems to fit you very well."

I was choking with exasperation, and knew that I had been done, because I had foolishly paid them half the bill already, and now knew no way out of it except to lose what I had paid, and get nothing for it, or take the thing, and pay the balance. I was caught in a trap, but even as I jerked at the coat and vest speechlessly, seized my shirt, and thrust the gaping collar in his face, the man said smoothly,

"Um! Yes! The collar. Should think all that will be all right. Still needs a little alteration." He made some chalk marks on me. "Should think you'll find it fits you very well when the tailor makes the alterations."

"When will the suit be ready?"

"Um. Should think you ought to have it by next Tuesday. Yes. I think you'll find it ready by Tuesday."

The sly words slid away from me like oil: there was nothing to pin him to or grasp him by, the yellowed eyes looked casually away and would not look at me, the sensual face was suavely grave, the discolored buck-teeth shone obscenely through the coarse loose mouth, and the suggestion of the foul loose smile was so pronounced now that it seemed that at any moment he would have to turn away with heavy trembling shoulders, and stifle the evil jeering laugh that was welling up in him. But he remained suavely grave and non-committal to the end, and when I asked him if I should come again to try it on, he said, in the same oily tone, never looking at me:

"Um. Shouldn't think that would be necessary. Could have it delivered to you when it's ready. What is your address?"

"The Far-end Farm—it's on the Ventnor Road."

"Oh! Coulson's!" He never altered his expression, but the suggestion of the obscene smile was so pronounced that now it seemed he had to out with it. Instead, he only said:

"Um. Yes. Should think it could be delivered to you there on Tuesday. If you'll just wait a moment I'll ask the tailor."

Gravely, suavely, he took the coat from me and walked back toward the tailor's room with the coat across his arm. In a moment, I heard sly voices whispering, laughing slyly, then the tailor saying:

"Where does he live?"

"Coulson's!" said the fitter chokingly, and now the foul awaited laugh did come—high, wet, slimy, it came out of that loose mouth, and choked and whispered wordlessly, and choked again, and mingled then with the tailor's voice in sly, choking, whispering intimacy, and then gasped faintly, and was silent. When he came out again his coarse face was red and swollen with foul secret merriment, his heavy shoulders trembled slightly, he took out his hand-kerchief and wiped it once across his loose half-opened mouth, and with that gesture wiped the slime of laughter from his lips. Then he came toward me suave, grave, and courteous, evilly composed, as he said smoothly:

"Should think we'll have that for you by next Tuesday, sir."

"Can the tailor fix it so it's going to fit?"

· "Um. Should think you'll find that everything's all right. You ought to have it Tuesday afternoon."

He was not looking at me: the yellowish bulging eyes were staring casually, indefinitely, away, and his words again had slid away from me like oil. He could not be touched, approached, or handled: there was nothing to hold him by, he had the impregnability of smoke or a ball of mercury.

As I went out the door, he began to speak to another man in the shop, I heard low words and whispered voices, then, gasping the word "Coulson's!" and the slimy, choking, smothered laughter as the street door closed behind me. I never saw him again. I never forgot his face.

1003

That was a fine house: the people in it were exiled, lost, and ruined people, and I liked them all. Later, I never knew why I felt so close to them, or remembered them with such warmth and strong affection.

I did not see the Coulsons often and rarely talked to them. Yet I felt as familiar and friendly with them all as if I had known them all my life. The house was wonderful as no other house I had ever known because we all seemed to be living in it together with this strange speechless knowledge, warmth, and familiarity, and yet each was as private, secret, and secure in his own room as if he occupied the house alone.

Coulson himself I saw least of all: we sometimes passed each other going in or out the door, or in the hall: he would grunt "Morning," or "Good Day," in a curt blunt manner, and go on, and yet he always left me with a curious sense of warmth and friendliness. He was a stocky well-set man with iron-gray hair, bushy eyebrows, and a red weathered face which wore the open color of the country on it, but also had the hard dull flush of the steady heavy drinker.

I never saw him drunk, and yet I think that he was never sober: he was one of those men who have drunk themselves past any hope of drunkenness, who are soaked through to the bone with alcohol, saturated, tanned, weathered in it so completely that it could never be distilled out of their blood again. Yet, even in this terrible excess one felt a kind of grim control—the control of a man who is enslaved by the very thing that he controls, the control of the opium eater who cannot leave his drug but measures out his dose with a cold calculation, and finds the limit of his capacity, and stops there, day by day.

But somehow this very sense of control, this blunt ruddy style of the country gentleman which distinguished his speech, his manner, and his dress, made the ruin of his life, the desperate intemperance of drink that smouldered in him like a slow fire, steadily, nakedly apparent. It was as if, having lost everything, he still held grimly to the outer forms of a lost standard, a ruined state, when the inner substance was destroyed.

And it was this way with all of them—with Mrs. Coulson and the girl, as well: their crisp, clipped friendly speech never deviated into intimacy, and never hinted at any melting into confidence and admission. Upon the woman's weathered face there hovered, when she talked, the same faint set grin that Captain Nicholl had, and her eyes were bright and hard, a little mad, impenetrable, as were his. And the girl, although young and very lovely, sometimes had this same look when she greeted any one or paused to talk. In that look there was nothing truculent, bitter, or defiant: it was just the look of three people who had gone down together, and who felt for one another neither bitterness nor hate, but that strange companionship of a common disgrace, from which love has vanished, but which is more secret, silent, and impassively resigned to its fatal unity than love itself could be.

And that hard bright look also said this plainly to the world: "We ask for nothing from you now, we want nothing that you offer us. What is ours is ours, what we are we are, you'll not intrude nor come closer than we let you see!"

1004

Coulson might have been a man who had been dishonored and destroyed by his women, and who took it stolidly, saying nothing, and drank steadily from morning until night, and had nothing for it now but drink and silence and acceptance. Yet I never knew for certain that this was so, it just seemed inescapable, and seemed somehow legible not only in the slow smouldering fire that burned out through his rugged weathered face, but also in the hard bright armor of the women's eyes, the fixed set grin around their lips when they were talking—a grin that was like armor, too. And Morison, who had referred to Coulson, chuckling, as a real "bottle-a-day-man," had added quietly, casually, in his brief, indefinite, but blurted-out suggestiveness of speech:

"I think the old girl's been a bit of a bitch in her day. . . . Don't know, of course, but has the look, hasn't she?" In a moment he said quietly, "Have you talked to the daughter yet?"

"Once or twice. Not for long."

"Ran into a chap at Magdalen other day who knows her," he said casually. "He used to come out here to see her." He glanced swiftly, slyly at me, his face reddening a little with laughter. "Pretty hot, I gather," he said quietly, smiling, and looked away. It was night: the fire burned cheerfully in the grate, the hot coals spurting in small gaseous flares from time to time. The house was very quiet all around us. Outside we could hear the stormy wind in the trees along the road. Morison flicked his cigarette into the fire, poured out a drink of whiskey into a glass, saying as he did so: "I say, old chap, you don't mind if I take a spot of this before I go to bed, do you?" Then he shot some seltzer in the glass, and drank. And I sat there, without a word, staring sullenly into the fire, dumbly conscious of the flood of sick pain and horror which the casual foulness of the man's suggestion had aroused, stubbornly trying to deny now that I was thinking of the girl all the time.

One night, as I was coming home along the dark road that went up past the playing field to the house, and that was bordered on each side by grand trees whose branches seemed to hold at night all the mysterious and demented cadences of storm, I came upon her suddenly standing in the shadow of a tree. It was one of the grand wild nights that seemed to come so often in the autumn of that year: the air was full of a fine stinging moisture, not quite rain, and above the stormy branches of the trees I could see the sky, wild, broken, full of scudding clouds through which at times the moon drove in and out with a kind of haggard loneliness. By that faint, wild, and broken light, I could see the small white oval of the girl's face—somehow even more lovely now just because I could not see it plainly. And I could see as well the rough gleaming bark of the tree against which she leaned.

As I approached, I saw her thrust her hand into the pocket of her overcoat, a match flared, and for a moment I saw Edith plainly, the small flower of her face framed in the wavering light as she lowered her head to light her cigarette.

The light went out, I saw the small respiring glow of her cigarette before the white blur of her face, I passed her swiftly, head bent, without speaking, my heart filled with the sense of strangeness and wonder which the family had roused in me.

Then I walked on up the road, muttering to myself. The house was dark when I got there, but when I entered my sitting-room the place was still warmly and softly luminous with the glow of hot coals in the grate. I turned the lights on, shut the door behind me, and hurled several lumps of coal upon the bedded coals. In a moment the fire was blazing and crackling cheerfully, and getting a

1005

kind of comfort and satisfaction from this activity, I flung off my coat, went over to the sideboard, poured out a stiff drink of scotch from a bottle there, and coming back to the fire, flung myself into a chair, and began to stare sullenly into the dancing flames.

How long I sat there in this stupor of sullen and nameless fury, I did not know, but I was sharply roused at length by footsteps light and rapid on the gravel, shocked into a start of surprise by a figure that appeared suddenly at one of my French windows that opened directly from my sitting-room to the level sward of velvet lawn before the house.

I peered through the glass for a moment with an astonished stare before I recognized the face of Edith Coulson. I opened the doors at once, she came in quickly, smiling at my surprise, and at the glass which I was holding foolishly, half-raised in my hand.

I continued to look at her with an expression of gape-mouthed astonishment and in a moment became conscious of her smiling glance, the cool sweet assurance of her young voice.

"I say!" she was saying cheerfully. "What a lucky thing to find you up! I came away without any key—I should have had to wake the whole house up— so when I saw your light—" she concluded briskly, "—what luck! I hope you don't mind."

"Why no-o, no," I stammered foolishly, still staring dumbly at her. "No—no-o —not at all," I blundered on. Then suddenly coming to myself with a burst of galvanic energy, I shut the windows, pushed another chair before the fire, and said:

"Won't you sit down and have a drink before you go?"

"Thanks," she said crisply. "I will—yes. What a jolly fire you have." As she talked she took off her coat and hat swiftly and put them on a chair. Her face was flushed and rosy, beaded with small particles of rain, and for a moment she stood before the mirror arranging her hair, which had been tousled by the wind.

The girl was slender, tall, and very lovely with the kind of beauty they have when they are beautiful—a beauty so fresh, fair, and delicate that it seems to be given to just a few of them to compensate for all the grimly weathered ugliness of the rest. Her voice was also lovely, sweet, and musical, and when she talked all the notes of tenderness and love were in it. But she had the same hard bright look in her eye that her mother had, the faint set smile around her mouth: as we stood there talking she was standing very close to me, and I could smell the fragrance of her hair, and felt an intolerable desire to put my hand upon hers and was almost certain she would not draw away. But the hard bright look was in her eye, the faint set smile around her mouth, and I did nothing.

"What'll you have?" I said. "Whiskey?"

"Yes, thank you," she said, with the same sweet crisp assurance with which she always spoke, "and a splash of soda." I struck a match and held it for her while she lit the cigarette she was holding in her hand, and in a moment returned to her with the drink. Then she sat down, crossed her legs, and for a moment puffed thoughtfully at her cigarette, as she stared into the fire. The storm wind moaned in the great trees along the road, and near the house, and suddenly a swirl of rain and wind struck the windows with a rattling blast. The girl stirred a little in her chair, restlessly, shivered:

"Listen!" she said. "What a night! Horrible weather we have here, isn't it?"

"I don't know. I don't like the fog and rain so well. But this—the way it is tonight—" I nodded toward the window—"I like it."

She looked at me for a moment.

"Oh," she said non-committally. "You do." Then, as she sipped her drink, she looked curiously about the room, her reflective glance finally resting on my table where there was a great stack of the ledgers in which I wrote.

"I say," she cried again. "What are you doing with all those big books there?"

"I write in them."

"Really?" she said, in a surprised tone. "I should think it'd be an awful bother carrying them around when you travel?"

"It is. But it's the best way I've found of keeping what I do together."

"Oh," she said, as before, and continued to stare curiously at me with her fair, lovely young face, the curiously hard, bright, and unrevealing glance of her eye. "I see. . . . But why do you come to such a place as this to write?" she said presently. "Do you like it here?"

"I do. As well as any place I've ever known."

"Oh! . . . I should think a writer would want a different kind of place."

"What kind?"

"Oh—I don't know—Paris—London—some place like that where there is lots of life—people—fun—I should think you'd work better in a place like that."

"I work better here."

"But don't you get awfully fed up sitting in here all day long and writing in those enormous books?"

"I do, yes."

"I should think you would . . . I should think you'd want to get away from it sometime."

"Yes. I do want to—every day—almost all the time."

"Then why don't you?" she said crisply. "Why don't you go off some week-end for a little spree. I should think it'd buck you up no end."

"It would—yes. Where should I go?"

"Oh, Paris, I suppose. . . . Or London! London!" she cried. "London is quite jolly if you know it."

"I'm afraid I don't know it."

"But you've *been* to London," she said in a surprised tone.

"Oh, yes. I lived there for several months."

"Then you know London," she said impatiently. "Of course you do."

"I'm afraid I don't know it very well. I don't know many people there—and after all, that's the thing that counts, isn't it?"

She looked at me curiously for a moment with the faint hard smile around the edges of her lovely mouth.

"—should think that might be arranged," she said with a quiet, an enigmatic humor. Then, more directly, she added: "That shouldn't be difficult at all. Perhaps I could introduce you to some people."

"That would be fine. Do you know many people there?"

"Not many," she said. "I go there—whenever I can." She got up with a swift decisive movement, put her glass down on the mantel and cast her cigarette into the fire. Then she faced me, looking at me with a curiously bold, an almost defiant directness of her hard bright eyes, and she fixed me with this glance for a full moment before she spoke.

"Good-night," she said. "Thanks awfully for letting me in—and for the drink."

"Good-night," I said, and she was gone before I could say more, and I had closed the door behind her, and I could hear her light swift footsteps going down the hall and up the steps. And then there was nothing in the house but sleep and silence, and storm and darkness in the world around me.

Mrs. Coulson came into my room just once or twice while I was there. One morning she came in, spoke crisply and cheerfully, and walked over to the window looking out upon the velvet lawn and at the dreary, impenetrable gray of foggy air. Although the room was warm, and there was a good fire burning in the grate, she clasped her arms together as she looked and shivered a little:

"Wretched weather, isn't it?" she said in her crisp tones, her gaunt weathered face and toothy mouth touched by the faint fixed grin as she looked out with her bright hard stare. "Don't you find it frightfully depressing? Most Americans do," she said, getting the sharp disquieting sound into the word.

"Yes. I do, a little. We don't have this kind of weather very often. But this is the time of year you get it here, isn't it? I suppose you're used to it by now?"

"Used to it?" she said crisply turning her hard bright gaze upon me. "Not at all. I've known it all my life but I'll never get used to it. It is a wretched climate."

"Still, you wouldn't feel at home anywhere else, would you? You wouldn't want to live outside of England."

"No?" she said, staring at me with the faint set grin around her toothy mouth. "Why do you think so?"

"Because your home is here."

"My home? My home is where they have fine days, and where the sun is always shining."

"I wouldn't like that. I'd get tired of sunlight all the time. I'd want some gray days and some fog and snow."

"Yes, I suppose you would. But then, you've been used to having fine days all your life, haven't you? With us, it's different. I'm so fed up with fog and rain that I could do without it nicely, thank you, if I never saw it again. . . . I don't think you could ever understand how much the sunlight means to us," she said slowly. She turned, and for a moment looked out the window with her hard bright stare, the faint set grin about her mouth. "Sunlight—warmth—fine days forever! Warmth everywhere—in the earth, the sky, in the lives of the people all around you nothing but warmth and sunlight and fine days!"

"And where would you go to find all that? Does it exist?"

"Oh, of course!" she said crisply and good-naturedly turning to me again. "There's only one place to live—only one country where I want to live."

"Where is that?"

1008

"Italy," she said. "That's my real home. . . . I'd live the rest of my life there if I could." For a moment longer she looked out the window, then turned briskly, saying:

"Why don't you run over to Paris some week-end? After all, it's only seven hours from London: If you left here in the morning you'd be there in time for dinner. It would be a good change for you. I should think a little trip like that would buck you up tremendously."

Her words gave me a wonderful feeling of confidence and hope: I think she had travelled a great deal, and she had the casual, assured way of speaking of a voyage that made it seem very easy, and filled one with a sense of joy and adventure when she spoke about it. When I tried to think of Paris by myself it had seemed very far away and hard to reach: London stood between it and me, and when I thought of the huge smoky web of London, the soft gray skies above me, and the enormous weight of lives that were hidden somewhere in that impenetrable fog, gray desolation and weariness of the spirit filled me. It seemed to me that I must draw each breath of that soft gray air with heavy weary effort, and that every mile of my journey would be a ghastly struggle through some viscous and material substance of soft heavy gray, that weighted down my steps, and filled my heart with desolation.

But when Mrs. Coulson spoke to me about it, suddenly it all seemed wonderfully easy and good. England was magically small, the channel to be taken in a stride, and all the thrill, the joy, the mystery of Paris mine again—the moment that I chose to make it mine.

I looked at her gaunt weathered face, her toothy mouth with the faint fixed grin, the hard bright armor of her eyes, and wondered how anything so clear, so sharp, so crisp, and so incisive could have been shaped and grown underneath these soft and humid skies that numbed me, mind and heart and body, with their thick numb substance of gray weariness and desolation.

A day or two before I left, Edith came into my room one afternoon bearing a tray with tea and jam and buttered bread. I was sitting in my chair before the fire, and had my coat off: when she came in I scrambled to my feet, reached for the coat and started to put it on. In her young crisp voice she told me not to, and put the tray down on the table, saying that the maid was having her afternoon away.

Then for a moment she stood looking at me with her faint and enigmatic smile.

"So you're leaving us?" she said presently.

"Yes. Tomorrow."

"And where will you go from here?" she said.

"To Germany, I think. Just for a short time—two or three weeks."

"And after that?"

"I'm going home."

"Home?"

"Back to America."

"Oh," she said slowly. "I see." In a moment, she added, "We shall miss you."

I wanted to talk to her more than I had ever wanted to talk to any one in my life, but when I spoke all that I could say, lamely, muttering, was:

"I'll miss you, too."

"Will you?" She spoke so quietly that I could scarcely hear her. "I wonder for how long?" she said.

"Forever," I said, flushing miserably at the sound of the word, and yet not knowing any other word to say.

The faint hard smile about her mouth was a little deeper when she spoke again.

"Forever? That's a long time, when one is young as you," she said.

"I mean it. I'll never forget you as long as I live."

"We shall remember you," she said quietly. "And I hope you think of us sometime—back here buried, lost, in all the fog and rain and ruin of England. How good it must be to know that you are young in a young country—where nothing that you did yesterday matters very much. How wonderful it must be to know that none of the failure of the past can pull you down—that there will always be another day for you—a new beginning. I wonder if you Americans will ever know how fortunate you are," the girl said.

"And yet you could not leave all this?" I said with a kind of desperate hope. "This old country you've lived in, known all your life. A girl like you could never leave a place like this to live the kind of life we have in America."

"*Couldn't* I?" she said with a quiet, but unmistakable passion of conviction. "There's nothing I'd like better."

I stared at her blindly, dumbly for a moment; suddenly all that I wanted to say, and had not been able to say, found release in a movement of my hands. I gripped her by the shoulders and pulled her to me, and began to plead with her:

"Then why don't you? I'll take you there!—Look here—" my words were crazy and I knew it, but as I spoke them, I believed all I said—"Look here! I haven't got much money—but in America you can make it if you want to! I'm going back there. You come, too—I'll take you when I go!"

She had not tried to free herself; she just stood there passive, unresisting, as I poured that frenzied proposal in her ears. Now, with the same passive and unyielding movement, the bright armor of her young eyes, she stepped away, and stood looking at me silently for a moment, the faint, hard smile at the edges of her mouth. Then slowly, with an almost imperceptible movement, she shook her head. "Oh, you'll forget about us all," she said quietly. "You'll forget about our lives here—buried in fog—and rain—and failure—and defeat."

"Failure and defeat won't last forever."

"Sometimes they do," she said with a quiet finality that froze my heart.

"Not for you—they won't!" I said, and took her by the hand again with desperate entreaty. "Listen to me—" I blundered on incoherently, with the old feeling of nameless shame and horror. "You don't need to tell me what it is—I don't want to know—but whatever it is for you—it doesn't matter—you can get the best of it."

1010 She said nothing, but just looked at me through that hard bright armor of her eyes, the obdurate finality of her smile.

"Good-bye," she said, "I'll not forget you either." She looked at me for a moment curiously before she spoke again. "I wonder," she said slowly, "if you'll ever understand just what it was you did for me by coming here."

"What was it?"

"You opened a door that I thought had been closed forever," she said, "a door that let me look in on a world I thought I should never see again—a new bright world, a new life and a new beginning—for us all. And I thought that was something which would never happen to any one in this house again."

"It will to you," I said, and took her hand again with desperate eagerness. "It can happen to you whenever you want it to. It's yours, I'll swear it to you, if you'll only speak."

She looked at me with her direct hard glance, an almost imperceptible movement of her head.

"I tell you I know what I'm talking about."

Again she shook her head.

"You don't know," she said. "You're young. You're an American. There are some things you'll never be old enough to know.—For some of us there's no return.—Go back," she said, "go back to the life you know—the life you understand—where there can always be a new beginning—a new life."

"And you—" I said dumbly, miserably.

"Good-bye, my dear," she said so low and gently I could scarcely hear her. "Think of me sometime, won't you—I'll not forget you." And before I could speak she kissed me once and was gone, so light and swift that I did not know it, until the door had closed behind her. And for some time, like a man in a stupor, I stood there looking out the window at the gray wet light of England.

The next day I went away, and never saw any of them again, but I could not forget them. Although I had never passed beyond the armor of their hard bright eyes, or breached the wall of their crisp, friendly, and impersonal speech, or found out anything about them, I always thought of them with warmth, with a deep and tender affection, as if I had always known them—as if, somehow, I could have lived with them or made their lives my own if only I had said a word, or turned the handle of a door—a word I never knew, a door I never found. (*1934*)

from The Hills Beyond

The first chapter of this work is a brief history of North Carolina and of Zachariah Joyner's election as governor. In Chapter four and the following, Wolfe traces the history of the Joyner family.

Chapter 2. Old Man of the Tribe

Zachariah Joyner was never one to indulge in the reverent pruning of family trees. When he was Governor of Old Catawba he often said that if people in the eastern part of the state would spend less time in thinking about where they

1011

From The Hills Beyond *by Thomas Wolfe, Harper & Brothers, 1941. Copyright 1941, by Maxwell Perkins as Executor.*

came from, and more in thinking about where they were going, they would be a lot easier to get along with.

He was also impatient of all attempts to dignify himself and his own family genealogically. In the heyday of his later fame, the Aborigines made some conciliating overtures to bring Catawba's most distinguished citizen into the fold. They did not quite dare hint that Zack had as good a right as anybody else to claim an ancestor in the Lost Colony, for they knew too well what he would say to that; but they did draw up quite a formidable account of the doings of the Joyners in the annals of history. They traced the name back to the Middle Ages. They even had one of the Joyners doing valiant service in defense of King Richard of the Lion Heart, when that great sovereign was surrounded by a murderous host of Saracens before the walls of old Jerusalem. They dug out others with baronial titles, and found some of them contending back and forth in the Wars of the Roses. There were Joyners who had fought loyally under the banners of King Charles, and others just as doggedly with Cromwell's men. From that point the earliest migrations of the family were traced to Virginia, thence to the coastal regions of Catawba, and finally to their stronghold in the mountain districts of the West. By dint of much contriving, the whole thing had been linked together in a kind of chain.

But Zachariah was not impressed. His comment on the document, when it was presented for his inspection and approval, was characteristically blunt and to the point:

"I don't know where we came from, and, what's more, I don't give a damn. The point is, we're here now."

There was not only good democracy in this, but the ring of sound truth, too. For the essential trait of the Joyner tribe was in those words. They were "here now," and Catawba would have been inconceivable without them. They were, in fact, a kind of native dragon seed. They may have had some other and more ancient antecedents, but in their magnificent quality of Now-ness—the quality of being what they were because they were where they were—they were so naturally a part of western Catawba, its life, its speech, its history, even the clay of its soil, that any other previous existence for them seemed fantastically detached, ghostly, and unreal.

Since every mother's son of us has got to come from somewhere, their lineage, no doubt, went back like everyone's to Father Adam, or to the origins of primeval man. So perhaps their ancestor was some prehistoric anthropoid. But if anyone wants to know who the founder of the family was, the answer is that it was old William Joyner, the father of Zack, and the sire of the whole clan. Even today the memory of old William is still kept alive in the hills, for in his own way he attained a legendary repute which almost equals that of his more celebrated son.

There is some doubt about William Joyner's antecedents, and no certainty whatever about where he came from. It is known that he came to Zebulon County because of a Revolutionary land grant. And the date of his coming is established. It was in 1793 when he took up his grant upon the south fork of what is now known as the Thumb Toe River. If he was not actually the first settler in that region, he was among the first. From this time on, people began

1012

to come in rapidly, and when William Joyner married, in 1798, the wife he took was the daughter of another settler who had recently arrived in the mountains.

Her name was Martha Creasman, and by her he had a family of seven. She died at the birth of her last child. Later, William married a second time. By this wife he had fourteen or sixteen children—for there were so many of them, and their destinies were so diverse, that even their number has been disputed. But of these matters, with all the ramifications of kinship and heredity they imply, it is our purpose to speak later. Here we shall tell a little more of William Joyner.

There were, in the earlier years of the present century, old men alive who could remember him; for he lived to a great old age, and there were people who were children in the 1840's who had seen him and had heard the stories men told of him. Even at that time, a hundred years ago, he was an almost legendary figure. The stories of his great physical strength, for example, were prodigious, and yet apparently were founded in substantial fact.

He was said to have been, particularly in his earlier years, a man of a hot temper, who liked a fight. There is a story of his fight with a big blacksmith: a quarrel having broken out between them over the shoeing of a horse, the blacksmith brained him with an iron shoe and knocked him flat. As William started to get up again, bleeding and half conscious, the blacksmith came at him again, and Joyner hit him while still resting on one knee. The blow broke the blacksmith's ribs and caved in his side as one would crack a shell.

He was known in his own day to be a mighty hunter; and old men who remembered him used to tell of the time he "chased the dogs the whole way over into Tennessee, and was gone four days and nights, and never knowed how fer from home he was."

There is also the story of his fight with a grizzly bear: the bear charged him at close quarters and there was nothing left for him to do but fight. A searching party found him two days later, more dead than living—as they told it, "all chawed up," but with the carcass of the bear: "and in the fight he had bit the nose off that big b'ar and chawed off both his years, and that b'ar was so tored up hit was a caution."

Then there is the story of the time when he walked off with enough leather on his back to shoe a regiment. The brother of Joyner's first wife owned a kind of trading post or country store, and had besides a pound of savage and ferocious dogs. It was the storekeeper's boast that no one but himself could manage these fierce animals, and certainly no one else had ever attempted to. People generally were afraid of them, and gave them a wide berth. Their owner was so proud of their untamed ferocity that on one occasion, when he was talking of his dogs to a group of men who were in his store, he offered any man who could subdue them "as much leather as he can tote out of here upon his back."

William Joyner was present and instantly accepted the challenge. In spite of the efforts of his friends to dissuade him, he went out to the pound, and, while the others watched, opened the gate and went in. The great dogs sprang snarling at him with bared fangs. According to the story, "he jest snapped his fingers once or twice," and the dogs whimpered and came crawling to him like a pack of curs. To add insult to injury, he is said to have stooped down and picked up two of the largest and most savage of the dogs and held them under his

1013

arms, "a-hangin' thar real foolish-like, like a couple of pigs." After walking about the pen with them a time or two, he tossed them down, snapped his fingers again, opened the gate, and walked out unscathed.

The storekeeper, although beaten and dumbfounded, was as good as his word. He pointed to the pile of leather in his store and told William he could take as much as he could carry. Joyner stood there while his companions heaped the leather on, and finally staggered out the door with eight hundred pounds of it on his shoulders.

There are many other stories about him, but these suffice to indicate the unusual qualities of his person, his great strength, and his undaunted courage. He was said by everyone who ever saw him to have been a person of remarkable gifts. Indeed, one does not have to probe a mystery to find an explanation for the amazing family he produced: the seed of all their talents was aware in him. Although he came to Zebulon with nothing but his rifle and his grant of land, within twenty years, through his ability as a shrewd trader, he had accumulated what was, in his time and place, a substantial property. He was the owner of a mill, to which his neighbors brought their corn for grinding. He increased his holdings until he owned and had under cultivation hundreds of acres of the most fertile land in the beautiful valley that now bears the name of Joyner's Creek. And eventually he became the owner of the largest and most flourishing trading post in the whole district.

From these beginnings came the start of the whole clan. It is true that Zachariah, in the later years of his political career, made frequent and eloquent reference, in the phrases of the orotund rhetoric of which he was a master, to "the little log cabin where I was born." It is further true that the little log cabin where Zachariah so often and so advantageously asserted he was born, still exists, kept piously by the State Historical Commission, in a condition of trimmed, sodded, planted, and be-flowered snugness that it assuredly did not know at the time when William Joyner lived in it. The State Highway Commission has likewise memorialized the sanctuary in a system of neat signs, which notify the modern pilgrim that he is now approaching "the birthplace of Zachariah Joyner—four miles."

It is unfortunate, perhaps, both for the lovers of sentiment and the believers in historic fact, that Zachariah was not born here at all. William Joyner did live here for years, and built the cabin with his own hands, with the assistance of some friendly Cherokees; but by the time of Zachariah's birth, his father was already a person of considerable substance, and in accordance not only with his new position, but with the expansive needs of his growing family, he had built the larger and much more substantial dwelling that adjoins it, and which also still exists. "The little log cabin where I was born," existed in Zachariah's childhood as a kind of outside kitchen; it was certainly in such a capacity that Zachariah himself must have known it, no matter how he remembered it later in the more imaginative flights of political oratory by which he gave it fame.

1014

In his later years, William Joyner having now become a man of weight and standing in the community, his wife tried, as wives of successful citizens are apt to do, to ameliorate some of his social imperfections. The story goes that she tried to get him to wear shoes in summertime—for apparently he was a man who liked bare feet, and when he went out to the fields to work, the weather and the season permitting, he always worked so.

Failing to win this really formidable concession, the worthy woman then attempted to persuade him "at least to put your shoes on when you come into the house." Her efforts even in this direction were not successful, for although he made some effort to please her, he "kept forgittin'." Failing in all this, she finally tried to prevail on him "for pity's sake, at least to put your shoes on when company comes." But this also proved too much, for she used to say despairingly: "I don't know what to do with him. I've begged an' I've pled an' he promises to try, but the minute we have company—even when the preacher's there—here he comes without his shoes, trampin' along out of the fields in his big feet."

As for "Bear" Joyner—for, after his famous encounter with the grizzly, he was known by this name—he would often say: "I thought I was marryin' me a wife, but I reckon what I done was to go an' git myself hitched to a black-smith. My advice to you young'uns is, if you ever go and git yourself married, make sure first whether you're marryin' a woman who is goin' to cook fer you, or one who is goin' to try to throw you down an' shoe you every time you come into the house."

He was a man of keen wit, and everyone who ever knew him said that he would have "gone far" if he had had the advantages of formal education. He was unable to read or write his own name until he was more than forty years old; but he learned how to do both in his later years. Indeed, he developed quite a taste for reading, and, limited as his facilities were, he managed to ac-quire a surprising store of bookish information.

Bear Joyner, like his famous son, was increate with myth, because the very nature of the man persuaded it. Such myths, then—*facts* most probably, indeed —as his bear-fighting, hunting, blacksmith-crushing, dog-mastering, and his in-stinctive shoelessness we have adduced to give the flavor of the man.

These things get into the story, make the picture. Yet it is not the Myth that falsifies the true identity of man (our debunking truth-tellers of the present notwithstanding—would to God they were themselves debunked!) The Myth is true. Let those who doubt it deny that Lincoln liked a joke, and had a gift for making one; split rails; was very strong; said h——l and d——n; so far as we can guess, was not averse to—; was pungent in his speech, and said his legs were long enough to reach the ground (which certainly was high sense); picked up the dirty pig; was chased out of doors by his wife—yes, and even when embar-rassed by the presence of surrounding ladies on a railroad platform, told a little boy who pointed to a certain word scrawled upon the wall by other little boys, that the thing it stood for was "a station, son . . . the name, son, of a certain station . . . a most important station . . . the station where more men get on and off than any other station in the world."

A myth, then, to like food and women, and to take a drink? . . . A myth to know the use of corncobs in the country? . . . To be able to say ———, and make a joke about it? . . . To be a lawyer, and have "a high and squeaky voice," and yet be able to speak *Gettysburg?*

O, little men, come, come!

1015

Then why the Myth?

The Myth is founded on *extorted* fact: wrenched from the context of ten thousand days, and rutted roads, the desolations of lost voices long ago, the rheumy nostrils in the month of March, the winter howling in the oak, the superfetation of the dreary wait, the vacancy of unremembered hours.

For it is not a question of having faith, or lack of it. It is a simple fact of seeing. Seeing, we are saved. Half-seeing, we are worse than blind. And wrong.

It is important, then, to know that William Joyner "chawed the b'ar." But it is even more important to know that William Joyner was a man who learned to read a book.

It may be that some later period in the human history will dispense with the whole necessity of print, and that book-reading, book-writing, book-publishing, all the ramified accessories that have accumulated since old Gutenberg, will (through some system of psychophones, printoscopes, empathic waves, or type telepathies; or what more of the strange and unbelievable we can wot not of) be as prehistoric as the dinosaur. But in William Joyner's day the thing was known—not only known, but, aside from speech, the swiftest and most common way of all communication; and the point is that, illiterate as he was until his fortieth year, unread, unlettered, not even knowing the look of his own name in common script—he learned it!

Why?

We do not know; and cannot guess the reason except that men sought India once, and braved inhuman seas beyond the world's edge, in their scallop shells; and looked at one another with "a wild surmise." As for all other antecedents— possible Joyners in the Middle Ages, with the Roses, or King Charles—let others search them: all things must have their precincts, and our own are there, in Old Catawba, with Bear Joyner, in the hills of home.

Whatever seed produced him, or what kernel of his own unknown heritage, the man was "there"—and not only "chawed the b'ar," but learned to read a book. And of all the facts that can be evidenced, of all the traits that bind the clan of William Joyner's seed together, none is more strange than its respect for learning.

Where did it come from?

In the century since old Bear Joyner's time, there have been some thousands of his name who have been dwellers in these hills. Some have been mountain folk, bowed down by poverty, who never learned to write, or to construe in print, their names. Others have been half-literate. Others have had the rudiments of education. Still others have risen in the world to places of commercial eminence: some have been lawyers, doctors, business men; there has been a preacher here and there; there has been more, much more, than an average sprinkling of "radical thinkers"—"atheists and agnostics" (that is to say, people who would openly debate the divinity of Jesus Christ, or the existence of "the after-life"); others who had "radical notions" (people who would challenge the accepted standards of law and property: there was one such who ran for Congress on the ticket of Eugene Debs, and got eight votes—it was said, however, that his sons and brothers did not vote for him). In the mountain districts to this day the Joyners have the reputation of being "queer." The word is not used scornfully, for generally, no matter what their station, the Joyners are respected folk.

But any variation from the norm in them does not astonish anyone: people have come to accept it casually and as a matter of expected fact. If a Joyner is an "atheist," an "agnostic," a "socialist," a "radical," it has come to be accepted because the Joyners are "queer" folk.

But again—why?

Boiled down to their essential element, all of these "eccentric" qualities which have, for a hundred years or more, caused their neighbors to accept the Joyners as belonging to their special type, and "queer," are nothing but the marks of an intensely heightened curiosity, a questioning, probing, debating, and examining intelligence that their neighbors did not have. There's the mystery—if mystery it be; indeed, the only mystery there is.

The Joyners have always been "individualists." But so are all mountain folk. Yet other mountain folk are individualistic more convenably. Most mountain folk are individuals within the narrow frame of a convention. True, they will go their own way, make their own law, "take nothing off of any man"—but all of this follows a close code. They are clannish, suspicious of the strange, world-lost, mistrustful of the outer world—conformant, really, in their non-conforming. For even when they go their way and kill their man, they are unquestioning of the special law of their own world.

In this respect the Joyners were all different from their neighbors, and the pattern of divergence was set by the founder of the clan. At a time when it was the convention for all men in the wilderness to be illiterate, in a place where the knowledge contained in books was of no earthly use, nothing would suit old Bear Joyner but that he must learn to read.

At a later time, as has already been stated, the genealogists of the Aborigines tried to account for Zachariah Joyner's distinction by tracing his line back to the Middle Ages. It was no use. The answer lay closer home. For no one ever really knew where his father came from. And it did not matter. Old Bear Joyner came from the same place, and was of the same kind, as all the other people in the mountains. But he was a man who learned to read. And there is the core of the whole mystery.

Chapter 3. The Great Schism

If, as Carlyle says, the history of the world is recorded in the lives of its great men, so, too, the spirit of a people is recorded in the heroes it picks. No better illustration of this fact could be found than in the life of Zachariah Joyner. Historically, his position is secure enough. True, his greatest fame is where he would himself have wished it to be—at home. His name has not attained the national celebrity of a Webster or Calhoun; no doubt most people outside Catawba would have difficulty in placing him. But historians will remember him as a leader in the affairs of his own state for almost fifty years; as an able and resourceful Governor; later, as one of the more forceful and colorful leaders of debate in the affairs of the United States Senate; and all in all, when the whole record of his life is weighed and estimated, as a man of great natural ability and intelligence, considering his place and time and situation.

He directed the affairs of his state through the Civil War, and he directed

1017

THE MODERN RENAISSANCE

them courageously and ably. In periods of stress he was unmoved by threat and unswayed by the hysterias of popular feeling. In the closing days of the Confederacy, when the armies were in desperate need, he curtly refused a demand from Jefferson Davis for almost seventy thousand suits of uniforms, shoes, and coats which the state owned and had in its possession. He refused bluntly and without apology, saying that the equipment would be used first of all for the rehabilitation of his own people; and although this act of rebellion brought down upon him bitter denunciation from all quarters, he stuck to his decision and refused to budge.

Later, in the darker days of Reconstruction, military occupation, black legislatures, and night riders, he rendered even greater service to his state. And he concluded a long life, full of honors and accomplishment, as a member of the nation's Senate, in which capacity he died, during Cleveland's last administration, in 1893.

All these facts are sufficiently well known to make his position in the nation's chronicle secure. But to people in Catawba his name means a great deal more than this. They are well acquainted with the story of his life, and the record of his offices as it has been outlined here. But these honors and accomplishments, splendid as they are, do not in themselves explain the place he holds in Catawba's heart. For he is their hero: in the most local and particular sense, they feel that he belongs to them, is of them, could in no conceivable way belong to anything else, is theirs and theirs alone. Therefore, they love him.

He was not only their own native Lincoln—their backwoods son who marched to glory by the log-rail route—he was their Crockett and Paul Bunyan rolled in one. He was not alone their hero; he was their legend and their myth. He was, and has remained so to this day, a kind of living prophecy of all that they themselves might wish to be; a native divinity, shaped out of their own clay, and breathing their own air; a tongue that spoke the words, a voice that understood and spoke the language, they would have him speak.

They tell a thousand stories about him today. What does it matter if many of the things which they describe never happened? They are true because they are the kind of things he would have said, the kind of things that would have happened to him. Thus, to what degree, and in what complex ways, he was created so in their imaginations, no one can say. How much the man shaped the myth, how much the myth shaped the man, how much Zack Joyner created his own folk, or how much his people created him—no one can know, and it does not matter.

For he was of them, and the rib; and they of him the body and the flesh. He was indigenous to them as their own clay, as much a part of all their lives as the geography of their native earth, the climate of their special weather. No other place on earth but Old Catawba could have produced him. And the people know this: therefore, again, they love him.

1018   In examining the history of that great man, we have collected more than eight hundred stories, anecdotes, and jokes that are told of him, and of this number at least six hundred have the unmistakable ring—or *smack*—of truth. If they did not happen—they *should* have! They belong to him: they fit him like an old shoe.

"But," the pedants cunningly inquire, "*did* they happen? Now, really, *did* they? Ah, yes, they *sound* like him—he *might* have said them—but that's not the point! *Did* he?"

Well, we are not wholly unprepared for these objections. Of the six hundred stories which have the smack of truth, we have actually verified three hundred as authentic beyond the shadow of a doubt, and are ready to cite them by the book—place, time, occasion, evidence—to anyone who may inquire. In these stories there is a strength, a humor, a coarseness, and a native originality that belonged to the man and marked his every utterance. They come straight out of his own earth.

As a result of our researches, we can state unequivocally that there is no foundation in fact for the story that one time, in answer to a lady's wish, he called out to a Negro urchin at a station curb, who had a donkey wagon and a load of peanuts:

"Boy! Back your ——— over here and show this lady your ——!"

But he certainly did make the speech in the United States Senate (in rejoinder to the Honorable Barnaby Bulwinkle) that is generally accredited to him, even though there is no account of it in the *Congressional Record*:

"Mr. President, sir, we are asked by the honorable gentleman to appropriate two hundred thousand dollars of the taxpayer's money for the purpose of building a bridge across Coon Creek in the honorable gentleman's district—a stream, sir, which I have seen, and which, sir, I assure you, I could ——— halfway across."

The Vice-President (pounding with his gavel): "The Senator is out of order."

Senator Joyner: "Mr. President, sir, you are right. If I was *in* order, sir, I could ——— the whole way across it!"

The last story that is told of Zachariah Joyner is that in his final days of illness (and, like King Charles, in dying, he was "an unconscionable time") he was aroused from coma one afternoon by the sound of rapid hoofs and wheels, and, looking wearily out of the window of his room, he saw the spare figure of his brother Rufus hastening toward the house. Even in his last extremity his humor did not forsake him, for he is said to have smiled wanly and feebly croaked:

"My God! I reckon it's all up with me! For here comes Rufe!"

People told the story later and, despite the grimness of the joke, they laughed at it; for the family trait to which it pointed was well known.

Bear Joyner, in his later years, after he had moved to Libya Hill, when told of the death of one of his sons in Zebulon by his second marriage, is known to have said:

"Well, I reckon some of the childern will attend the funeral." Here he considered seriously a moment, then nodded his head with an air of confirmation. "Hit's—hit's no more than right!" And after another pause he added virtuously: "If I was thar, *I'd go myself!*" And with these words, he wagged his head quite solemnly, in such a way as to leave no doubt about the seriousness of his intent.

Zachariah is reported, when asked the number of his kin, to have replied: "Hell, I don't know! You can't throw a rock in Zebulon without hitting one of them!" He reflected on his metaphor a moment, and then said: "However, let

1019

him that is without sin among you throw the first stone. I can't!" And with these words he turned virtuously away, scratching himself vigorously in the behind.

Again, when he responded to the greeting of a member of the audience after a political rally at which he had made a speech, he is reported to have said:

"My friend, your face looks familiar to me. Haven't I seen you somewhere before?"

To which the person so addressed replied: "Yes, sir. I think you have. I was yore pappy's ninth child by his second marriage, and you was his fourth 'un by his first. So I reckon you might say that you and me was both half-brothers, distantly removed."

The grimmest story in the whole Joyner catalogue, perhaps, is that old Bear Joyner, when reproached one time for a seeming neglect of his own brood, is reputed to have said to his inquisitor:

"My God Almighty! A man can plant the seed, but he cain't make the weather! I sowed 'em—now, goddamm 'em, let 'em grow!"

There is no reason to believe that either William or his children were as neglectful of each other as these stories indicate, yet they really do denote a trait—or failing—of the clan. The fault—if fault it be—has long been known in Catawba, where it is said that "the only thing that will bring 'em all together is a wedding or a funeral; and it has to be a good one to do that." And yet, this trait has been too easily interpreted. Many people have taken such stories as evidence that the Joyners were lacking in a sense of family feeling; but nothing could be further from the truth.

The truth is that no family ever lived that had a stronger sense of their identity. It is hard to describe the thing in more familiar terms, for the whole tribe violates the standards by which such things are commonly appraised. Of "affection," "love," "devotion," even "clannishness"—as these terms are generally accepted—the family seems to have had little. It is perfectly true that years have gone by when brothers have not seen or spoken to each other, even when they lived in the same town. It is also true that some have grown rich, indifferent to others who have struggled on in obscure poverty; that children have been born, and grown up, and gone away, scarcely familiar with the look of a cousin's face, the identity of a cousin's name.

Many people have observed these things and wondered at them, and then accepted them as further proof that the tribe was "queer." And yet, paradoxically, out of this very indifference came the family unity. From this very separateness came the deep and lasting sense of their identity. In a way, they reversed completely the old adage that if men refuse to hang together, they will all hang separately: of the Joyners it could rather be said that they hang separately because they know they hang together.

To find what produced their sense of "separateness" one must look into the history of the family.

1020

The many children of Bear Joyner by his two marriages—there were more than twenty by the lowest count—grew up in a community where every man had to look out for himself. As for old Bill himself, nothing in his earlier life had prepared him for the exacting duties of parenthood. Whatever his career had been before he came into the hill-bound fastnesses of Zebulon, it had been very hard. He is known to have said: "If a young'un don't learn to root afore fourteen, he never will. A hen'll scrabble for young chicks, but before they're fryin' size they've got to scratch for themselves."

Although he was a man of substance for his time and place, his means were not enough to give two dozen children an easy start in life. Moreover, it must be owned that, like so many men who have been widowed in first marriage, he ventured into a second because it was the best expedient to meet his need. And the fourteen or sixteen children who came later—well, it is a brutal fact, but it was a sowing of blind seed. They came. They just came. And that was all.

Perhaps it is unjust to emphasize the schism of this second marriage. And yet, a separation did exist. It is inevitable that this should have been. For one thing, the older children of Bear Joyner's first marriage were fairly well grown when he married for the second time, and when the children of the second brood began to come along. Again, the surviving children of the first—Zack, Robert, Hattie, Theodore, and Rufe—were, if not a different breed, yet of a separate clan. And they knew it. From the first, instinctively, they seemed to know it. It was not that, consciously, they felt themselves to be "superior"—a bitter accusation that was later made—and yet they seemed to feel they were. And—since the blunt truth must be spoken—in the light of their accomplishment, and in the world's esteem, they were.

Another fact—the Joyners, first to last, were a vainglorious folk. Even old William had his share of this defect, perhaps even more than the rest of them, for old men thirty years ago who could remember him, and who would pay due tribute to his prowess and his extraordinary gifts, would often add: "Well, he *knowed* that he was good. . . . He was remarkable, but he *knowed* that he was good. And he was bigoted. He could be bigoted; and he was overbearing, too. . . . And as for Zack," old men would smile when they said his name, "Well, there was Zack, too. He knowed that *he* was good. Zack was a wonder . . . but no one ever said he was a blushing violet."

The Joyners of this early flowering not only "knowed that they was good," but they made little effort to conceal it. Apparently, none of them—unless it was Robert—hid his light under a bushel. And the truth is, each of them, in his own way—even Theodore!—had a light to show.

The reasons? Well, the reasons were complex, but perhaps the first one was the consciousness they had of special heritage. Bear Joyner's first wife was a "special woman": she was a Creasman, and the Creasmans were "good people." The Joyners of the first lot were all proud of their Creasman ancestry. Of Martha Creasman herself there is little to be told except that she was a good wife, a quiet and hard-working mother, and a Presbyterian. This last fact, trifling as it seems, was all important: for it bespeaks a kind of denominational snobbishness which is still more prevalent than the world may know, and which the Joyners of the first lot never lost.

As to Bear Joyner's second wife, she was a Baptist. The first Joyners—Zack, and all the rest of them—were always careful to speak of her respectfully, but with a touch of unconscious patronage that was infuriating to "the country cousins" of the lesser breed:

"Well now, she was a mighty good woman, and all of that. . . . Of course"—

1021

with a kind of hesitant and regretful concessiveness—"she was a Baptist. . . . I reckon you might call her a kind of religious fanatic. . . . She had queer religious notions. . . . But she was a good woman. . . . She had some queer ideas, but she was a good mother to those children. . . . Now everyone will have to give her *that!*"

Here then, obviously, were the roots of the great schism. Bear Joyner himself seems to have shared unconsciously in this prejudice of his elder children. He had apparently always been somewhat in awe of his first wife: her family was well known, and there is reason to believe he felt he was making a considerable step forward in the world when he married her. Toward his second wife he had no such feeling: she was one of a hard-shell Baptist tribe, and there is a story that he met her at camp meeting. However that may be, he was "looking for a woman to keep house"; and it was pretty much in this capacity that he married her.

That she worked long and faithfully there can be no doubt; or that she was a patient, strong, enduring woman—"a good mother," as the elder Joyners always willingly admitted, to the numerous family that she now began to bring into the world.

As for Bear Joyner's older children by his previous marriage—Zack, Hattie, Robert, Theodore, and Rufe (Martha and George, the two remaining of the seven, had died in childhood)—they seem from the beginning to have been outside the sphere of their stepmother's control. Their strongly marked individualities had already been defined and shaped by the time their father married again. They had inherited, in liberal measure, his own strong character, his arrogant confidence in his own powers, a good measure of his color, his independence, his intelligence, his coarse and swingeing humor, his quick wit.

There is no evidence that they were consciously contemptuous of their new mother, but there is no doubt they felt superior to her. Even in a backwoods community theirs was a larger, bolder, more tolerant and experienced view of life than she had ever known; and her narrow prejudice, her cramped vision, her rigid small moralities (all products of an inheritance she couldn't help) simply amused them, aroused their ridicule and mirth.

Zachariah, especially, although in later years he always spoke feelingly of her excellent qualities, was particularly active in his humorous analysis of her. Her superstitions and prejudices amused him; the operations of her mind, and the narrow cells of her morality seemed grotesque and ludicrous to him; and he questioned, teased, examined her rather cruelly in order, as he said, "to see what made her tick."

Hers, indeed, poor woman, was a strange and contradictory code, and yet, because it was the only one she knew, she thought it was the only one there was: it seemed natural to her, and it never occurred to her to question it.

That harsh code to which she adhered was indigenous to America. It has not only done much to shape our lives and histories, but it persists to this day, and is at the root of much of the sickness, the moral complex of America. For example, she believed it was wrong to take a life "in cold blood," but it was not nearly so wrong as to take a drink. She was always warning her children against evil ways and loose living, and speaking of people who committed "all kinds of immorality and licentiousness"; but it would have come strangely to her ears to hear murder referred to as an immoral act. True, it was "an awful crime"—she could understand it in these terms because the Bible told about Cain and Abel, and taught that it was wicked to take life. But, privately, she did not consider it half as bad for a man to take a life as to take a drink, or—what was the most immoral act of all—to sleep with a woman who was not his wife.

Life-taking, the shedding of man's blood, was so much a part of the life of a pioneer community that it occasioned no surprise. To be sure, she would not openly defend the practice of killing, although in a surprising number of individual cases she was willing to defend it, becoming quite aroused, in fact, when Zachariah, with deceptive gravity, would point out that her own brother—whose life in other ways she esteemed at a model of the Christian virtues—had been quite handy with his gun in his hot youth, and was known to have killed three men:

"Now, Zach," she would cry angrily, "don't you go a-diggin' into that. Reese had his faults, like everyone, and I reckon maybe in his young days he may have been hot-tempered. But he's always led a good Christian and God-fearin' sort of life. He never drank or smoked or used bad language or ran around with women —like *some* people I know about." Here she glared accusingly at her erring stepson, who returned her look with an expression of bland innocence. "So don't you start on him: he's always been an upright, moral sort of man."

All of this amused Zachariah no end: he did not mean to be cruel to her, but, as she said, he was "always tormenting" her, rummaging gravely about in the confusing rag-bag of her moral consciousness to see what further mysteries would be revealed.

He is known to have spoken of the physical sharpness of her sense of smell, which really was amazing, and which all of her children inherited (she is said one time to have "smelled burning leaves five miles away upon the mountain, long before anyone else knowed there was a fire"):

"Well, she can smell fire and brimstone farther off than that. And Hell! If I took a drink in Libya Hill, she'd smell it on my breath before I crossed the county line!"

On another occasion, she is said to have called out to him the moment that he came into the house: "Zack Joyner! You've been drinkin' that bad, old, rotten, vile corn licker again. I can smell it on your breath!"

"Now, Mother," he answered temperately, "there is no bad, old, rotten, vile corn licker. Some is good—" he went on in a tone of judicious appraisal that she must have found very hard to take—"and some is better. But there is no bad!"

Again, when Bear Joyner returned from Libya Hill one day with this announcement:

"Well, Thad Burton's gone and done it again!"

"Gone and done what?" said Zachariah, looking up.

"Gone and killed a man," Bear Joyner answered.

"Oh!" said Zachariah with a relieved air, casting a sly look toward his stepmother, "I was afraid you were goin' to tell me he'd done something really bad, like gettin' drunk."

1023

Bear Joyner was no less adept than his sons in this sport of teasing his bewildered wife. It is said that having driven in with her one day from Zebulon, to see the boys who at that time were "keeping store" for him in Libya Hill, he went into the store and, finding Zack on duty there, the following conversation then took place between them:

"You boys been leadin' the Christ-life like your mother told you to?"

"Yes, sir," Zachariah said.

"Have you done your chores this mornin'?"

"Yes, sir."

"Watered the milk?"

"Yes, sir."

"Sanded the sugar?"

"Yes, sir."

"*Fixed* the scales?"

"Yes, sir."

"Well," said Bear, "you'd better call in Ted and Bob. Your mother's here, an' we're goin' to have prayers."

Finally there was the case of Harriet—the "Miss Hattie" of later years, for she never married—to add to the confusion and distress of William Joyner's second wife. Of all Bear Joyner's children, Hattie was the favorite. In her, perhaps, more than in any of the others he saw the qualities—the quick wit, the humor, the independence and intelligence—that in himself he most esteemed. It has been said she was his "love child"—a euphemism maybe for the fact that she was illegitimate—and that this accounted for her father's deeper care. At any rate, although her birth was hidden in an obscurity that was never cleared—for old Bear Joyner never spoke of it, and no one dared to speak of it to him—she was brought up as a member of his elder brood. The story goes that he was gone one time for several weeks upon a journey to the south, and that when he returned he brought the child with him. She was almost eight years old then, and Martha, the first wife, was still alive. The story goes that Joyner brought the child into the house—the family was at dinner, and the faces of the other children wonderingly turned—and sat her down beside them at the table.

"This," he said, "is your new sister. From this time on, she'll be one of the family, and you'll treat her so."

And this is all that was ever spoken. It is said that Martha, Joyner's first wife, took the child as one of her own; and in justice to the second wife, no matter what additional distress and confusion this new proof of Joyner wickedness may have caused that bewildered woman's soul, it was always freely acknowledged, most loyally of all by Harriet herself, as a further tribute to the woman's qualities, that she was a good mother, and brought the girl up as if she were "one of her own."

Historically, time-periods are most curiously defined: the world does not grow up together. The footpads that made Johnson carry his stick at night when he went out alone in London in the Eighteenth Century have been quite actively abroad in recent years in our own land. And as for "human life," a commodity which our editorial writers tell us they most jealously esteem, the security of human life in our own broad land—whether from murder, violence, or sudden death of every kind soever—is perhaps *almost* as great in America at the present time as it was in England at the period of Elizabeth, although our figures are by far the more bloody of the two.

And as for our own Dick Whittingtons—our country boys who went to town —there, too, we ape the European pattern; but we have been late.

The history of human celebrity for the most part is an urban one. In our own land, although children are taught that most of their great men "came from the country," it is not sufficiently emphasized that most of them also "went to town." Certainly, this has been true in America: the national history could almost be written in the lives of men who went to town.

Zachariah Joyner, in his later years, was very fond of using the log-cabin theme for politics, but if he had been more true to fact, he would have admitted that the turning point in his own career had come when he abandoned finally the world-lost fastnesses of Zebulon for the more urban settlement of Libya Hill. There, truly, was *his* starting point, his threshold, the step from which he gained his vantage, took off for the larger community of public life and general notice in which for fifty years he was to play so large a role.

And, in various ways, the same transitional experience was true of his more immediate family—his three brothers, who came with him. In one sense the whole history of the many Joyners, their divided lot and the boundary that separated the lowly from the great, might be stated in one phrase. It was the history of those who stayed at home, and of those who went to town.

As the years passed, the division of each group became more widely marked, the sense of unity more faint and far. Hill-bound, world-lost, locked in the narrow valleys and the mountain walls of Zebulon, the Joyners who remained at home became almost as strange and far away to those who lived in Libya Hill as if their home had been the Mountains of the Moon. True, they lived only fifty miles away, but as Bear Joyner had himself said so many years before, it was "the wrong way." It really was this sense of two directions that divided them. The Libya Hill Joyners were facing ever toward the world, and those in Zebulon away from it; and as years went by, it seemed that this directiveness became more marked than ever—the town Joyners ever more the world's men; those in Zebulon more withdrawn from the world.

By 1900, a whole century since William Joyner crossed the Blue Ridge and came down into the wilderness with his rifle and his grant of land, if some curious historian, gifted with immortality, could have returned there, he would have observed a change as startling as it was profound. He would have found the lives of the town Joyners (for by this time Libya Hill had grown to twelve thousand people) so greatly altered as to be scarcely recognizable; but he would have found the lives of the country Joyners scarcely changed at all.

True, some changes had occurred in Zebulon in those hundred years, but for the most part these were tragic ones. The great mountain slopes and forests of the section had been ruinously detimbered; the farm-soil on hill sides had eroded and washed down; high up, upon the hills, one saw the raw scars of old mica pits, the dump heaps of deserted mines. Some vast destructive "Suck" had been at work here; and a visitor, had he returned after one hundred years, would have been compelled to note the ruin of the change. It was evident that a huge compulsive greed had been at work: the whole region had been sucked and gutted, milked dry, denuded of its rich primeval treasures: something blind and ruthless had been here, grasped, and gone. The blind scars on the hills, the denuded slopes, the empty mica pits were what was left.

1025

And true, the hills were left—with these deteriorations; and all around, far-flung in their great barricades, the immense wild grandeur of the mountain wall, the great Blue Ridge across which they had come long, long ago; and which had held them from the world.

And the old formations of the earth were left: the boiling clamor of the rocky streams, the cool slant darkness of the mountain hollows. Something wild, world-lost, and lyrical, and special to the place called Zebulon was somehow left: the sound of rock-bright waters, birds calls, and something swift and fleeting in a wood; the way light comes and goes; cloud shadows passing on a hill; the wind through the hill grasses, and the quality of light—something world-lost, far, and haunting (special to the place as is the very climate of the soil) in the quality of light; and little shacks and cabins stuck to hill or hollow, sunken, tiny, in the gap; the small, heart-piercing wisps of smoke that coiled into the clear immensity of weather from some mountain shack, with its poignant evidence that men fasten to a ledge, and draw their living from a patch of earth—because they have been here so long and love it and cannot be made to leave; together with lost voices of one's kinsmen long ago—all this was left, but their inheritance was bare. Something had come into the wilderness, and had left the barren land.

And the people—ah, the people!—yes, the people!——

They were left! They were left "singing the same songs" (as college Doctors of Philosophy so gloatingly assure us) "their Elizabethan forebears sang"— which is a falsehood; and no glory—they should have made new and better ones for themselves. "Speaking the same tongue" their Elizabethan forebears spoke—which also is a falsehood; and they should have made a new one for themselves. "Living the same lives" their forebears lived a hundred years ago— which further is a falsehood. The lives their forebears lived were harsh and new, still seeking and explorative; their own lives often were just squalid, which should have been better.

What remained? It has been said, "The earth remains." But this was wrong. The earth had changed, the earth had eroded, the earth had washed down the gulleys in a billion runnels of red clay; the earth was gone.

But the people—ah, the people!—yes, the people! The people were still there!

Turned backwards now, world-lost, in what was once new land! Unseeking now, in what their forebears with blue vistas in their eyes, alone, in Indian country, sought! Turned in upon themselves, congruent as a tribe, all intermarried (so each man now was cousin to the very blood he took: each Cain among them brother to his very deed!)——

The people!—aye, the people! The people of Zack Joyner, and old Bear, who sought a world, and *found* it, that such as these might lose it; had wandered so that such as these should *stay*; had sought great vistas to the West, so that such as these remain——

The people! To be gloated over by exultant Ph.D's (who find in mountain shacks the accents of Elizabeth); to be gawked at by tourists (now the roads are good) in search of the rare picturesque; to be yearned over by consecrated school-marms "from the North"; have their "standards" "improved" by social service workers, who dote upon the squalor, ignorance, and poverty; lasciviously regret the degradations of the people's lot, and who do valiantly their little bit (God bless their little, little souls!) to help the people, teach the people, prop the people, *heal* the people, with their little salves (not too completely, else what are little salves and social service work about?)—and who therefore (in spite of dirt, filth, rickets, murder, lean-tos, children, syphilis, hunger, incest, and pellagra) love the people, adore the people, see underneath their "drawbacks" and their "lack of opportunities" all "the good" in people—because the people, at the bottom, "are so fine."

It is a lie! . . . Dear God! . . . Dear Jesus God, protect us, all men living, and the people, from such stuff as this!

The people are not "fine"—the people are not picturesque—the people——

Well, after a hundred years of it—denudings, minings, lootings, intermarryings, killings, dyings, bornings, livings, all the rest of it—the people—in spite of Smike, the lumber thief, who stole their hills; and Snead, his son, who stole their balladry; in spite of Gripe, who took their mica and their ore, and gave them "the lung-sickness" in exchange for it; despite Grace, Gripe's daughter, who now brings rubber condoms and tuberculin; and his wife, Gertrude, who schools them in hand-weaving—despite Gripe, Smike, and Grace, and all lovers of the picturesque soever—despite rickets, incest, syphilis, and sham—the people! —ah, the people!—well, the *people*——

"Why, goddamn it!" Zachariah Joyner roared—"I'll tell you what the people are! . . . The people . . . the *people!* . . . Why, goddamn it, sir, the people are the *people!*"

And so they are!—Smike, Gripe, rickets, Grace, and Snead—all forces to the contrary notwithstanding.

The people are the people.

And the Joyners—second Joyners; the humble, world-lost Joyners out in Zebulon—they're the people! (*1941*)

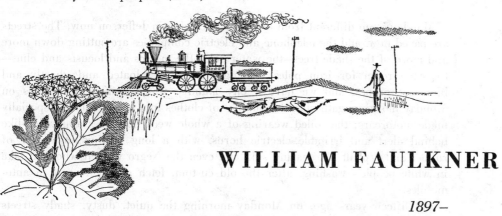

WILLIAM FAULKNER

1897–

William Faulkner (he spells his surname *Falkner* in *Who's Who*) was born in New Albany, Mississippi, September 25, 1897. Both of his parents came from Southern families which had suffered gravely during the Civil War. Faulkner attended school sporadically until World War I, when he enlisted in the Canadian Royal Air Force. When the war was over, he attended the University of Missis-

sippi at Oxford (1919–1921), but was never graduated. He drifted from one job
to another, working at intervals as a carpenter, house painter, book clerk, and
postmaster before settling down seriously to a career of writing. His first published pieces were poems and critical articles which appeared in *The New Republic* and *The Double Dealer*. Faulkner's reputation, however, rests upon his outstanding accomplishments in fiction.

Faulkner writes about the South, and his twin recurrent themes are those of
violence and of the disintegration of the ideals of valor and honor, a disintegration precipitated by the Civil War and its aftermath. His first major novel was
Sartoris, published in 1929 and the first of several novels set in the fictional town
of Jefferson—presumably, Oxford, Mississippi. The Sartorises themselves may be
taken loosely to represent the author's own family. A second novel in this group,
The Sound and the Fury, appeared in the same year. In 1931 Faulkner published *Sanctuary*, originally designed as a horror story but later revised and
made a part of the Jefferson cycle. This was the first of his books to attract
popular attention and probably remains his most widely read work. Faulkner's
other important novels include *As I Lay Dying* (1930), *Pylon* (1935), *Absalom, Absalom!* (1936), *Intruder in the Dust* (1948), and *Requiem for a Nun*
(1951). He has also issued several collections of short stories, many of them
closely related to the themes and characters of his novels: *These Thirteen*
(1931), *Doctor Martino and Other Stories* (1934), *The Unvanquished* (1938),
and *Go Down, Moses* (1942). Faulkner is regarded by many critics as the most
outstanding modern American fictionist. In 1950 he was awarded the Nobel Prize
for literature.

That Evening Sun Go Down

Monday is no different from any other weekday in Jefferson now. The streets
are paved now, and the telephone and electric companies are cutting down more
and more of the shade trees—the water oaks, the maples and locusts and elms—
to make room for iron poles bearing clusters of bloated and ghostly and
bloodless grapes, and we have a city laundry which makes the rounds on
Monday morning, gathering the bundles of clothes into bright-colored, specially
made motorcars: the soiled wearing of a whole week now flees apparition-like
behind alert and irritable electric horns, with a long diminishing noise of
rubber and asphalt like tearing silk, and even the Negro women who still take
in white people's washing, after the old custom, fetch and deliver it in automobiles.

But fifteen years ago, on Monday morning the quiet, dusty, shady streets
would be full of Negro women with, balanced on their steady, turbaned heads,
bundles of clothes tied up in sheets, almost as large as cotton bales, carried so
without touch of hand between the kitchen door of the white house and the
blackened washpot beside a cabin door in Negro Hollow.

1028

Nancy would set her bundle on the top of her head, then upon the bundle in turn she would set the black straw sailor hat which she wore winter and summer. She was tall, with a high sad face sunken a little where her teeth were missing. Sometimes we would go a part of the way down the lane and across the pasture with her, to watch the balanced bundle and the hat that never bobbed or wavered, even when she walked down into the ditch and up the other side and stooped through the fence. She would go down on her hands and knees and crawl through the gap, her head rigid, uptilted, the bundle steady as a rock or a balloon, and rise to her feet again and go on.

Sometimes the husbands of the washing women would fetch and deliver the clothes, but Jesus never did that for Nancy, even before Father told him to stay away from our house, even when Dilsey was sick and Nancy would come to cook for us.

And then about half the time we'd have to go down the lane to Nancy's cabin and tell her to come on and cook breakfast. We would stop at the ditch, because Father told us to not have anything to do with Jesus—he was a short black man, with a razor scar down his face—and we would throw rocks at Nancy's house until she came to the door, leaning her head around it without any clothes on.

"What yawl mean, chunking my house?" Nancy said. "What you little devils mean?"

"Father says for you to come on and get breakfast," Caddy said. "Father says it's over a half an hour now, and you've got to come this minute."

"I ain't studying no breakfast," Nancy said. "I going to get my sleep out."

"I bet you're drunk," Jason said. "Father says you're drunk. Are you drunk, Nancy?"

"Who says I is?" Nancy said. "I got to get my sleep out. I ain't studying no breakfast."

So after a while we quit chunking the cabin and went back home. When she finally came, it was too late for me to go to school. So we thought it was whiskey until that day they arrested her again and they were taking her to jail and they passed Mr. Stovall. He was the cashier in the bank and a deacon in the Baptist church, and Nancy began to say:

"When you going to pay me, white man? When you going to pay me, white man? It's been three times now since you paid me a cent—" Mr. Stovall knocked her down, but she kept on saying, "When you going to pay me, white man? It's been three times now since—" until Mr. Stovall kicked her in the mouth with his heel and the marshal caught Mr. Stovall back, and Nancy lying in the street, laughing. She turned her head and spat out some blood and teeth and said, "It's been three times now since he paid me a cent."

That was how she lost her teeth, and all that day they told about Nancy and Mr. Stovall, and all that night the ones that passed the jail could hear Nancy singing and yelling. They could see her hands holding the window bars, and a lot of them stopped along the fence, listening to her and to the jailer trying to make her stop. She didn't shut up until almost daylight, when the jailer began to hear a bumping and scraping upstairs and he went up there and found Nancy hanging from the window bar. He said that it was cocaine and not whiskey,

1029

because no nigger would try to commit suicide unless he was full of cocaine, because a nigger full of cocaine wasn't a nigger any longer.

The jailer cut her down and revived her; then he beat her, whipped her. She had hung herself with her dress. She had fixed it all right, but when they arrested her she didn't have on anything except a dress and so she couldn't make her hands let go of the window ledge. So the jailer heard the noise and ran up there and found Nancy hanging from the window, stark naked, her belly already swelling out a little, like a little balloon.

When Dilsey was sick in her cabin and Nancy was cooking for us, we could see her apron swelling out; that was before Father told Jesus to stay away from the house. Jesus was in the kitchen, sitting behind the stove, with his razor scar on his black face like a piece of dirty string. He said it was a watermelon that Nancy had under her dress.

"It never come off of your vine, though," Nancy said.

"Off of what vine?" Caddy said.

"I can cut down the vine it did come off of," Jesus said.

"What makes you want to talk like that before these chillen?" Nancy said. "Whyn't you go on to work? You done et. You want Mr. Jason to catch you hanging around his kitchen, talking that way before these chillen?"

"Talking what way?" Caddy said. "What vine?"

"I can't hang around white man's kitchen," Jesus said. "But white man can hang around mine. White man can come in my house, but I can't stop him. When white man want to come in my house, I ain't got no house. I can't stop him, but he can't kick me outen it. He can't do that."

Dilsey was still sick in her cabin. Father told Jesus to stay off our place. Dilsey was still sick. It was a long time. We were in the library after supper.

"Isn't Nancy through in the kitchen yet?" Mother said. "It seems to me that she has had plenty of time to finish the dishes."

"Let Quentin go and see," Father said. "Go and see if Nancy is through, Quentin. Tell her she can go on home."

I went to the kitchen. Nancy was through. The dishes were put away and the fire was out. Nancy was sitting in a chair, close to the cold stove. She looked at me.

"Mother wants to know if you are through," I said.

"Yes," Nancy said. She looked at me. "I done finished." She looked at me. "What is it?" I said. "What is it?"

"I ain't nothing but a nigger," Nancy said. "It ain't none of my fault."

She looked at me, sitting in the chair before the cold stove, the sailor hat on her head. I went back to the library. It was the cold stove and all, when you think of a kitchen being warm and busy and cheerful. And with a cold stove and the dishes all put away, and nobody wanting to eat at that hour.

"Is she through?" Mother said.

"Yessum," I said.

1030

"What is she doing?" Mother said.

"She's not doing anything. She's through."

"I'll go and see," Father said.

"Maybe she's waiting for Jesus to come and take her home," Caddy said.

"Jesus is gone," I said. "Nancy told us how one morning she woke up and Jesus had gone."

"He quit me," Nancy said. "Done gone to Memphis, I reckon. Dodging them city po-lice for a while, I reckon."

"And a good riddance," Father said. "I hope he stays there."

"Nancy's scaired of the dark," Jason said.

"So are you," Caddy said.

"I'm not," Jason said.

"You, Candace!" Mother said. Father came back.

"I am going to walk down the lane with Nancy," he said. "She says that Jesus is back."

"Has she seen him?" Mother said.

"No. Some Negro sent her word that he was back in town. I won't be long."

"You'll leave me alone, to take Nancy home?" Mother said. "Is her safety more precious to you than mine?"

"I won't be long," Father said.

"You'll leave these children unprotected, with that Negro about?"

"I'm going too," Caddy said. "Let me go, Father."

"What would he do with them, if he were unfortunate enough to have them?" Father said.

"I want to go, too," Jason said.

"Jason!" Mother said. She was speaking to Father. You could tell by the way she said the name. Like she believed that all day Father had been trying to think of doing the thing she wouldn't like the most, and that she knew all the time that after a while he would think of it. I stayed quiet, because Father and I both knew that Mother would want him to make me stay with her if she just thought of it in time. So Father didn't look at me. I was the oldest. I was nine and Caddy was seven and Jason was five.

"Nonsense," Father said. "We won't be long."

Nancy had her hat on. We came to the lane. "Jesus always been good to me," Nancy said. "Whenever he had two dollars, one of them was mine." We walked in the lane. "If I can just get through the lane," Nancy said, "I be all right then."

The lane was always dark. "This is where Jason got scaired on Hallowe'en," Caddy said.

"I didn't," Jason said.

"Can't Aunt Rachel do anything with him?" Father said. Aunt Rachel was old. She lived in a cabin beyond Nancy's, by herself. She had white hair and she smoked a pipe in the door, all day long; she didn't work any more. They said she was Jesus' mother. Sometimes she said she was and sometimes she said she wasn't any kin to Jesus.

"Yes, you did," Caddy said. "You were scairder than Frony. You were scairder than T. P. even. Scairder than niggers."

"Can't nobody do nothing with him," Nancy said. "He say I done woke up the devil in him and ain't but one thing going to lay it down again."

"Well, he's gone now," Father said. "There's nothing for you to be afraid of now. And if you'd just let white men alone."

"Let what white men alone?" Caddy said. "How let them alone?"

1031

"He ain't gone nowhere," Nancy said. "I can feel him. I can feel him now, in this lane. He hearing us talk, every word, hid somewhere, waiting. I ain't seen him, and I ain't going to see him again but once more, with that razor in his mouth. That razor on that string down his back, inside his shirt. And then I ain't going to be even surprised."

"I wasn't scaired," Jason said.

"If you'd behave yourself, you'd have kept out of this," Father said. "But it's all right now. He's probably in St. Louis now. Probably got another wife by now and forgot all about you."

"If he has, I better not find out about it," Nancy said. "I'd stand there right over them, and every time he wropped her, I'd cut that arm off. I'd cut his head off and I'd slit her belly and I'd shove—"

"Hush," Father said.

"Slit whose belly, Nancy?" Caddy said.

"I wasn't scaired," Jason said. "I'd walk right down this lane by myself."

"Yah," Caddy said. "You wouldn't dare to put your foot down in it if we were not here too."

II

Dilsey was still sick; so we took Nancy home every night until Mother said, "How much longer is this going on? I to be left alone in this big house while you take home a frightened Negro?"

We fixed a pallet in the kitchen for Nancy. One night we waked up, hearing the sound. It was not singing and it was not crying, coming up the back stairs. There was a light in Mother's room and we heard Father going down the hall, down the back stairs, and Caddy and I went into the hall. The floor was cold. Our toes curled away from it while we listened to the sound. It was like singing and it wasn't like singing, like the sounds that Negroes make.

Then it stopped and we heard Father going down the back stairs, and we went to the head of the stairs. Then the sound began again, in the stairway, not loud, and we could see Nancy's eyes halfway up the stairs, against the wall. They looked like cat's eyes do, like a big cat against the wall, watching us. When we came down the steps to where she was, she quit making the sound again, and we stood there until Father came back up from the kitchen, with his pistol in his hand. He went back down with Nancy and they came back with Nancy's pallet.

We spread the pallet in our room. After the light in Mother's room went off, we could see Nancy's eyes again. "Nancy," Caddy whispered. "Are you asleep, Nancy?"

Nancy whispered something. It was oh or no, I don't know which. Like nobody had made it, like it came from nowhere and went nowhere, until it was like Nancy was not there at all; that I had looked so hard at her eyes on the stairs that they had got printed on my eyeballs, like the sun does when you have closed your eyes and there is no sun. "Jesus," Nancy whispered. "Jesus."

"Was it Jesus?" Caddy said. "Did he try to come into the kitchen?"

"Jesus," Nancy said. Like this: Jeeeeeeeeeeeeeeesus, until the sound went out, like a match or a candle does.

"It's the other Jesus she means," I said.

"Can you see us, Nancy?" Caddy whispered. "Can you see our eyes too?"

"I ain't nothing but a nigger," Nancy said. "God knows. God knows."

"What did you see down there in the kitchen?" Caddy whispered. "What tried to get in?"

"God knows," Nancy said. We could see her eyes. "God knows."

Dilsey got well. She cooked dinner. "You'd better stay in bed a day or two longer," Father said.

"What for?" Dilsey said. "If I had been a day later, this place would be to rack and ruin. Get on out of here now, and let me get my kitchen straight again."

Dilsey cooked supper too. And that night, just before dark, Nancy came into the kitchen.

"How do you know he's back?" Dilsey said. "You ain't seen him."

"Jesus is a nigger," Jason said.

"I can feel him," Nancy said. "I can feel him laying yonder in the ditch."

"Tonight?" Dilsey said. "Is he there tonight?"

"Dilsey's a nigger too," Jason said.

"You try to eat something," Dilsey said.

"I don't want nothing," Nancy said.

"I ain't a nigger," Jason said.

"Drink some coffee," Dilsey said. She poured a cup of coffee for Nancy. "Do you know he's out there tonight? How come you know it's tonight?"

"I know," Nancy said. "He's there, waiting. I know. I done lived with him too long. I know what he is fixing to do 'fore he know it himself."

"Drink some coffee," Dilsey said. Nancy held the cup to her mouth and blew into the cup. Her mouth pursed out like a spreading adder's, like a rubber mouth, like she had blown all the color out of her lips with blowing the coffee.

"I ain't a nigger," Jason said. "Are you a nigger, Nancy?"

"I hellborn, child," Nancy said. "I won't be nothing soon. I going back where I come from soon."

III

She began to drink the coffee. While she was drinking, holding the cup in both hands, she began to make the sound again. She made the sound into the cup and the coffee splashed out onto her hands and her dress. Her eyes looked at us and she sat there, her elbows on her knees, holding the cup in both hands, looking at us across the wet cup, making the sound.

"Look at Nancy," Jason said. "Nancy can't cook for us now. Dilsey's got well now."

"You hush up," Dilsey said. Nancy held the cup in both hands, looking at us, making the sound, like there were two of them: one looking at us and the other making the sound. "Whyn't you let Mr. Jason telefoam the marshal?" Dilsey said. Nancy stopped then, holding the cup in her long brown hands. She tried to drink some coffee again, but it splashed out of the cup, onto her hands and her dress, and she put the cup down. Jason watched her.

"I can't swallow it," Nancy said. "I swallows but it won't go down me."

"You go down to the cabin," Dilsey said. "Frony will fix you a pallet and I'll be there soon."

"Won't no nigger stop him," Nancy said.

1033

"I ain't a nigger," Jason said. "Am I, Dilsey?"

"I reckon not," Dilsey said. She looked at Nancy. "I don't reckon so. What you going to do, then?"

Nancy looked at us. Her eyes went fast, like she was afraid there wasn't time to look, without hardly moving at all. She looked at us, at all three of us at one time. "You member that night I stayed in yawl's room?" she said. She told about how we waked up early the next morning, and played. We had to play quiet, on her pallet, until Father woke up and it was time to get breakfast. "Go and ask your maw to let me stay here tonight," Nancy said. "I won't need no pallet. We can play some more."

Caddy asked Mother. Jason went too. "I can't have Negroes sleeping in the bedrooms," Mother said. Jason cried. He cried until Mother said he couldn't have any dessert for three days if he didn't stop. Then Jason said he could stop if Dilsey would make a chocolate cake. Father was there.

"Why don't you do something about it?" Mother said. "What do we have officers for?"

"Why is Nancy afraid of Jesus?" Caddy said. "Are you afraid of Father, Mother?"

"What could the officers do?" Father said. "If Nancy hasn't seen him, how could the officers find him?"

"Then why is she afraid?" Mother said.

"She says he is there. She says she knows he is there tonight."

"Yet we pay taxes," Mother said. "I must wait here alone in this big house while you take a Negro woman home."

"You know that I am not lying outside with a razor," Father said.

"I'll stop if Dilsey will make a chocolate cake," Jason said. Mother told us to go out and Father said he didn't know if Jason would get a chocolate cake or not, but he knew what Jason was going to get in about a minute. We went back to the kitchen and told Nancy.

"Father said for you to go home and lock the door, and you'll be all right," Caddy said. "All right from what, Nancy? Is Jesus mad at you?" Nancy was holding the coffee cup in her hands again, her elbows on her knees and her hands holding the cup between her knees. She was looking into the cup. "What have you done that made Jesus mad?" Caddy said. Nancy let the cup go. It didn't break on the floor, but the coffee spilled out, and Nancy sat there with her hands still making the shape of the cup. She began to make the sound again, not loud. Not singing and not unsinging. We watched her.

"Here," Dilsey said. "You quit that, now. You get aholt of yourself. You wait here. I going to get Versh to walk home with you." Dilsey went out.

We looked at Nancy. Her shoulders kept shaking, but she quit making the sound. We watched her. "What's Jesus going to do to you?" Caddy said. "He went away."

Nancy looked at us. "We had fun that night I stayed in yawl's room, didn't we?"

"I didn't," Jason said. "I didn't have any fun."

"You were asleep in Mother's room," Caddy said. "You were not there."

"Let's go down to my house and have some more fun," Nancy said.

1034

"Mother won't let us," I said. "It's too late now."

"Don't bother her," Nancy said. "We can tell her in the morning. She won't mind."

"She wouldn't let us," I said.

"Don't ask her now," Nancy said. "Don't bother her now."

"She didn't say we couldn't go," Caddy said.

"We didn't ask," I said.

"If you go, I'll tell," Jason said.

"We'll have fun," Nancy said. "They won't mind, just to my house. I been working for yawl a long time. They won't mind."

"I'm not afraid to go," Caddy said. "Jason is the one that's afraid. He'll tell."

"I'm not," Jason said.

"Yes, you are," Caddy said. "You'll tell."

"I won't tell," Jason said. "I'm not afraid."

"Jason is going to tell," Caddy said. The lane was dark. We passed the pasture gate. "I bet if something was to jump out from behind the gate, Jason would holler."

"I wouldn't," Jason said. We walked down the lane. Nancy was talking loud.

"What are you talking so loud for, Nancy?" Caddy said.

"Who, me?" Nancy said. "Listen at Quentin and Caddy and Jason saying I'm talking loud."

"You talk like there was five of us here," Caddy said. "You talk like Father was here too."

"Who; me talking loud, Mr. Jason?" Nancy said.

"Nancy called Jason 'Mister,'" Caddy said.

"Listen how Caddy and Quentin and Jason talk," Nancy said.

"We're not talking loud," Caddy said. "You're the one that's talking like Father—"

"Hush," Nancy said; "hush, Mr. Jason."

"Nancy called Jason 'Mister' aguh—"

"Hush," Nancy said. She was talking loud when we crossed the ditch and stooped through the fence where she used to stoop through with the clothes on her head. Then we came to her house. We were going fast then. She opened the door. The smell of the house was like the lamp and the smell of Nancy was like the wick, like they were waiting for one another to begin to smell. She lit the lamp and closed the door and put the bar up. Then she quit talking loud, looking at us.

"What're we going to do?" Caddy said.

"What do yawl want to do?" Nancy said.

"You said we would have some fun," Caddy said.

There was something about Nancy's house; something you could smell besides Nancy and the house. Jason smelled it, even. "I don't want to stay here," he said. "I want to go home."

"Go home, then," Caddy said.

"I don't want to go by myself," Jason said.

"We're going to have some fun," Nancy said.

"How?" Caddy said.

1035

Nancy stood by the door. She was looking at us, only it was like she had emptied her eyes, like she had quit using them. "What do you want to do?" she said.

"Tell us a story," Caddy said. "Can you tell a story?"

"Yes," Nancy said.

"Tell it," Caddy said. We looked at Nancy. "You don't know any stories."

"Yes," Nancy said. "Yes, I do."

She came and sat in a chair before the hearth. There was a little fire there. Nancy built it up, when it was already hot inside. She built a good blaze. She told a story. She talked like her eyes looked, like her eyes watching us and her voice talking to us did not belong to her. Like she was living somewhere else, waiting somewhere else. She was outside the cabin. Her voice was inside and the shape of her, the Nancy that could stoop under a barbed wire fence with a bundle of clothes balanced on her head as though without weight, like a balloon, was there. But that was all. "And so this here queen come walking up to the ditch, where that bad man was hiding. She was walking up to the ditch, and she say, 'If I can just get past this here ditch,' was what she say . . ."

"What ditch?" Caddy said. "A ditch like that one out there? Why did a queen want to go into a ditch?"

"To get to her house," Nancy said. She looked at us. "She had to cross the ditch to get into her house quick and bar the door."

"Why did she want to go home and bar the door?" Caddy said.

IV

Nancy looked at us. She quit talking. She looked at us. Jason's legs stuck straight out of his pants where he sat on Nancy's lap. "I don't think that's a good story," he said. "I want to go home."

"Maybe we had better," Caddy said. She got up from the floor. "I bet they are looking for us right now." She went toward the door.

"No," Nancy said. "Don't open it." She got up quick and passed Caddy. She didn't touch the door, the wooden bar.

"Why not?" Caddy said.

"Come back to the lamp," Nancy said. "We'll have fun. You don't have to go."

"We ought to go," Caddy said. "Unless we have a lot of fun." She and Nancy came back to the fire, the lamp.

"I want to go home," Jason said. "I'm going to tell."

"I know another story," Nancy said. She stood close to the lamp. She looked at Caddy, like when your eyes look at a stick balanced on your nose. She had to look down to see Caddy, but her eyes looked like that, like when you are balancing a stick.

"I won't listen to it," Jason said. "I'll bang on the floor."

"It's a good one," Nancy said. "It's better than the other one."

"What's it about?" Caddy said. Nancy was standing by the lamp. Her hand was on the lamp, against the light, long and brown.

"Your hand is on that hot globe," Caddy said. "Don't it feel hot to your hand?"

Nancy looked at her hand on the lamp chimney. She took her hand away, slow. She stood there, looking at Caddy, wringing her long hand as though it were tied to her wrist with a string.

"Let's do something else," Caddy said.

"I want to go home," Jason said.

"I got some popcorn," Nancy said. She looked at Caddy and then at Jason and then at me and then at Caddy again. "I got some popcorn."

"I don't like popcorn," Jason said. "I'd rather have candy."

Nancy looked at Jason. "You can hold the popper." She was still wringing her hand; it was long and limp and brown.

"All right," Jason said. "I'll stay a while if I can do that. Caddy can't hold it. I'll want to go home again if Caddy holds the popper."

Nancy built up the fire. "Look at Nancy putting her hands in the fire," Caddy said. "What's the matter with you, Nancy?"

"I got popcorn," Nancy said. "I got some." She took the popper from under the bed. It was broken. Jason began to cry.

"Now we can't have any popcorn," he said.

"We ought to go home, anyway," Caddy said. "Come on, Quentin."

"Wait," Nancy said; "wait. I can fix it. Don't you want to help me fix it?"

"I don't think I want any," Caddy said. "It's too late now."

"You help me, Jason," Nancy said. "Don't you want to help me?"

"No," Jason said. "I want to go home."

"Hush," Nancy said; "hush. Watch. Watch me. I can fix it so Jason can hold it and pop the corn." She got a piece of wire and fixed the popper.

"It won't hold good," Caddy said.

"Yes it will," Nancy said. "Yawl watch. Yawl watch. Yawl help me shell some corn."

The popcorn was under the bed too. We shelled it into the popper and Nancy helped Jason hold the popper over the fire.

"It's not popping," Jason said. "I want to go home."

"You wait," Nancy said. "It'll begin to pop. We'll have fun then." She was sitting close to the fire. The lamp was turned up so high it was beginning to smoke.

"Why don't you turn it down some?" I said.

"It's all right," Nancy said. "I'll clean it. Yawl wait. The popcorn will start in a minute."

"I don't believe it's going to start," Caddy said. "We ought to start home, anyway. They'll be worried."

"No," Nancy said. "It's going to pop. Dilsey will tell um yawl with me. I been working for yawl long time. They won't mind if yawl at my house. You wait, now. It'll start popping any minute now."

Then Jason got some smoke in his eyes and he began to cry. He dropped the popper into the fire. Nancy got a wet rag and wiped Jason's face, but he didn't stop crying.

"Hush," she said. "Hush." But he didn't hush. Caddy took the popper out of the fire.

"It's burned up," she said. "You'll have to get some more popcorn, Nancy."

"Did you put all of it in?" Nancy said.

1037

"Yes," Caddy said. Nancy looked at Caddy. Then she took the popper and opened it and poured the cinders into her apron and began to sort the grains, her hands long and brown, and we watching her.

"Haven't you got any more?" Caddy said.

"Yes," Nancy said. "Yes. Look. This here ain't burnt. All we need to do is—"

"I want to go home," Jason said. "I'm going to tell."

"Hush," Caddy said. We all listened. Nancy's head was already turned toward the barred door, her eyes filled with red lamplight. "Somebody is coming," Caddy said.

Then Nancy began to make that sound again, not loud, sitting there above the fire, her long hands dangling between her knees; all of a sudden water began to come out on her face in big drops, running down her face, carrying in each one a little turning ball of firelight like a spark until it dropped off her chin. "She's not crying," I said.

"I ain't crying," Nancy said. Her eyes were closed. "I ain't crying. Who is it?"

"I don't know," Caddy said. She went to the door and looked out. "We've got to go now," she said. "Here comes Father."

"I'm going to tell," Jason said. "Yawl made me come."

The water still ran down Nancy's face. She turned in her chair. "Listen. Tell him. Tell him we going to have fun. Tell him I take good care of yawl until in the morning. Tell him to let me come home with yawl and sleep on the floor. Tell him I won't need no pallet. We'll have fun. You member last time how we had so much fun?"

"I didn't have fun," Jason said. "You hurt me. You put smoke in my eyes. I'm going to tell."

v

Father came in. He looked at me. Nancy did not get up.

"Tell him," she said.

"Caddy made us come down here," Jason said. "I didn't want to."

Father came to the fire. Nancy looked up at him. "Can't you go to Aunt Rachel's and stay?" he said. Nancy looked up at Father, her hands between her knees. "He's not here," Father said. "I would have seen him. There's not a soul in sight."

"He in the ditch," Nancy said. "He waiting in the ditch yonder."

"Nonsense," Father said. He looked at Nancy. "Do you know he's there?"

"I got the sign," Nancy said.

"What sign?"

"I got it. It was on the table when I come in. It was a hogbone with blood meat still on it, laying by the lamp. He's out there. When yawl walk out that door, I gone."

"Gone where, Nancy?" Caddy said.

"I'm not a tattletale," Jason said.

"Nonsense," Father said.

"He out there," Nancy said. "He looking through that window this minute, waiting for yawl to go. Then I gone."

"Nonsense," Father said. "Lock up your house and we'll take you on to Aunt Rachel's."

" 'Twon't do no good," Nancy said. She didn't look at Father now, but he looked down at her, at her long, limp, moving hands. "Putting it off won't do no good."

"Then what do you want to do?" Father said.

"I don't know," Nancy said. "I can't do nothing. Just put it off. And that don't do no good. I reckon it belong to me. I reckon what I going to get ain't no more than mine."

"Get what?" Caddy said. "What's yours?"

"Nothing," Father said. "You all must get to bed."

"Caddy made me come," Jason said.

"Go on to Aunt Rachel's," Father said.

"It won't do no good," Nancy said. She sat before the fire, her elbows on her knees, her long hands between her knees. "When even your own kitchen wouldn't do no good. When even if I was sleeping on the floor in the room with your chillen, and the next morning there I am, and blood—"

"Hush," Father said. "Lock the door and put out the lamp and go to bed."

"I scared of the dark," Nancy said. "I scared for it to happen in the dark."

"You mean you're going to sit right here with the lamp lighted?" Father said. Then Nancy began to make the sound again, sitting before the fire, her long hands between her knees. "Ah, damnation," Father said. "Come along, chillen. It's past bedtime."

"When yawl go home, I gone," Nancy said. She talked quieter now, and her face looked quiet, like her hands. "Anyway, I got my coffin money saved up with Mr. Lovelady." Mr. Lovelady was a short, dirty man who collected the Negro insurance, coming around to the cabins or the kitchens every Saturday morning, to collect fifteen cents. He and his wife lived at the hotel. One morning his wife committed suicide. They had a child, a little girl. He and the child went away. After a week or two he came back alone. We would see him going along the lanes and the back streets on Saturday mornings.

"Nonsense," Father said. "You'll be the first thing I'll see in the kitchen tomorrow morning."

"You'll see what you'll see, I reckon," Nancy said. "But it will take the Lord to say what that will be."

VI

We left her sitting before the fire.

"Come and put the bar up," Father said. But she didn't move. She didn't look at us again, sitting quietly there between the lamp and the fire. From some distance down the lane we could look back and see her through the open door.

"What, Father?" Caddy said. "What's going to happen?"

"Nothing," Father said. Jason was on Father's back, so Jason was the tallest of all of us. We went down into the ditch. I looked at it, quiet. I couldn't see much where the moonlight and the shadows tangled.

"If Jesus is hid here, he can see us, can't he?" Caddy said.

"He's not there," Father said. "He went away a long time ago."

"You made me come," Jason said, high; against the sky, it looked like Father had two heads, a little one and a big one. "I didn't want to."

1039

We went up out of the ditch. We could still see Nancy's house and the open door, but we couldn't see Nancy now, sitting before the fire with the door open, because she was tired. "I just done got tired," she said. "I just a nigger. It ain't no fault of mine."

But we could hear her, because she began just after we came up out of the ditch, the sound that was not singing and not unsinging, "Who will do our washing now, Father?" I said.

"I'm not a nigger," Jason said, high and close above Father's head.

"You're worse," Caddy said, "you are a tattletale. If something was to jump out, you'd be scairder than a nigger."

"I wouldn't," Jason said.

"You'd cry," Caddy said.

"Caddy," Father said.

"I wouldn't!" Jason said.

"Scairy cat," Caddy said.

"Candace!" Father said. (*1931*)

An Odor of Verbena

I

It was just after supper. I had just opened my *Coke* on the table beneath the lamp; I heard Professor Wilkins' feet in the hall and then the instant of silence as he put his hand to the door knob, and I should have known. People talk glibly of presentiment, but I had none. I heard his feet on the stairs and then in the hall approaching and there was nothing in the feet because although I had lived in his house for three college years now and although both he and Mrs. Wilkins called me Bayard in the house, he would no more have entered my room without knocking than I would have entered his—or hers. Then he flung the door violently inward against the doorstop with one of those gestures with or by which an almost painfully unflagging preceptory of youth ultimately aberrates, and stood there saying, "Bayard. Bayard, my son, my dear son."

I should have known; I should have been prepared. Or maybe I was prepared because I remember how I closed the book carefully, even marking the place, before I rose. He (Professor Wilkins) was doing something, bustling at something; it was my hat and cloak which he handed me and which I took although I would not need the cloak, unless even then I was thinking (although it was October, the equinox had not occurred) that the rains and the cool weather would arrive before I should see this room again and so I would need the cloak anyway to return to it if I returned, thinking 'God, if he had only done this last night, flung that door crashing and bouncing against the stop last night without knocking so I could have gotten there before it happened, been there when it did, beside him on whatever spot, wherever it was that he would have to fall and lie in the dust and dirt.'

1040

"Your boy is downstairs in the kitchen," he said. It was not until years later that he told me (someone did; it must have been Judge Wilkins) how Ringo had apparently flung the cook aside and come on into the house and into the library where he and Mrs. Wilkins were sitting and said without preamble and already turning to withdraw: "They shot Colonel Sartoris this morning. Tell him I be waiting in the kitchen" and was gone before either of them could move. "He has ridden forty miles yet he refuses to eat anything." We were moving toward the door now—the door on my side of which I had lived for three years now with what I knew, what I knew now I must have believed and expected, yet beyond which I had heard the approaching feet yet heard nothing in the feet. "If there was just anything I could do."

"Yes, sir," I said. "A fresh horse for my boy. He will want to go back with me."

"By all means take mine—Mrs. Wilkins'," he cried. His tone was no different yet he did cry it and I suppose that at the same moment we both realised that was funny—a short-legged deep-barrelled mare who looked exactly like a spinster music teacher, which Mrs. Wilkins drove to a basket phaeton—which was good for me, like being doused with a pail of cold water would have been good for me.

"Thank you, sir," I said. "We won't need it. I will get a fresh horse for him at the livery stable when I get my mare." Good for me, because even before I finished speaking I knew that would not be necessary either, that Ringo would have stopped at the livery stable before he came out to the college and attended to that and that the fresh horse for him and my mare both would be saddled and waiting now at the side fence and we would not have to go through Oxford at all. Loosh would not have thought of that if he had come for me, he would have come straight to the college, to Professor Wilkins', and told his news and then sat down and let me take charge from then on. But not Ringo.

He followed me from the room. From now until Ringo and I rode away into the hot thick dusty darkness quick and strained for the overdue equinox like a laboring delayed woman, he would be somewhere either just beside me or just behind me and I never to know exactly nor care which. He was trying to find the words with which to offer me his pistol too. I could almost hear him: "Ah, this unhappy land, not ten years recovered from the fever yet still men must kill one another, still we must pay Cain's price in his own coin." But he did not actually say it. He just followed me, somewhere beside or behind me as we descended the stairs toward where Mrs. Wilkins waited in the hall beneath the chandelier—a thin gray woman who reminded me of Granny, not that she looked like Granny probably but because she had known Granny—a lifted anxious still face which was thinking *Who lives by the sword shall die by it* just as Granny would have thought, toward which I walked, had to walk not because I was Granny's grandson and had lived in her house for three college years and was about the age of her son when he was killed in almost the last battle nine years ago, but because I was now The Sartoris. (The Sartoris: that had been one of the concomitant flashes, along with the *at last it has happened* when Professor Wilkins opened my door.) She didn't offer me a horse and pistol, not because she liked me any less than Professor Wilkins but because she was a woman and so wiser than any man, else the men would not have gone on with

1041

the War for two years after they knew they were whipped. She just put her hands (a small woman, no bigger than Granny had been) on my shoulders and said, "Give my love to Drusilla and your Aunt Jenny. And come back when you can."

"Only I don't know when that will be," I said. "I don't know how many things I will have to attend to." Yes, I lied even to her; it had not been but a minute yet since he had flung that door bouncing into the stop yet already I was beginning to realise, to become aware of that which I still had no yardstick to measure save that one consisting of what, despite myself, despite my raising and background (or maybe because of them) I had for some time known I was becoming and had feared the test of it; I remember how I thought while her hands still rested on my shoulders: *At least this will be my chance to find out if I am what I think I am or if I just hope; if I am going to do what I have taught myself is right or if I am just going to wish I were.*

We went on to the kitchen, Professor Wilkins still somewhere beside or behind me and still offering me the pistol and horse in a dozen different ways. Ringo was waiting; I remember how I thought then that no matter what might happen to either of us, I would never be The Sartoris to him. He was twenty-four too, but in a way he had changed even less than I had since that day when we had nailed Grumby's body to the door of the old compress. Maybe it was because he had outgrown me, had changed so much that summer while he and Granny traded mules with the Yankees that since then I had had to do most of the changing just to catch up with him. He was sitting quietly in a chair beside the cold stove, spent-looking too who had ridden forty miles (at one time, either in Jefferson or when he was alone at last on the road somewhere, he had cried; dust was now caked and dried in the tear-channels on his face) and would ride forty more yet would not eat, looking up at me a little red-eyed with weariness (or maybe it was more than just weariness and so I would never catch up with him) then rising without a word and going on toward the door and I following and Professor Wilkins still offering the horse and the pistol without speaking the words and still thinking (I could feel that too) *Dies by the sword. Dies by the sword.*

Ringo had the two horses saddled at the side gate, as I had known he would—the fresh one for himself and my mare father had given me three years ago, that could do a mile under two minutes any day and a mile every eight minutes all day long. He was already mounted when I realised that what Professor Wilkins wanted was to shake my hand. We shook hands; I knew he believed he was touching flesh which might not be alive tomorrow night and I thought for a second how if I told him what I was going to do, since we had talked about it, about how if there was anything at all in the Book, anything of hope and peace for His blind and bewildered spawn which He had chosen above all others to offer immortality, *Thou shalt not kill* must be it, since maybe he even believed that he had taught it to me except that he had not, nobody had, not even myself since it went further than just having been learned. But I did not tell him. He was too old to be forced so, to condone even in principle such a decision; he was too old to have to stick to principle in the face of blood and raising and background, to be faced without warning and made to deliver like by a highwayman out of the dark: only the young could do that—one still young enough to have his youth supplied him gratis as a reason (not an excuse) for cowardice.

So I said nothing. I just shook his hand and mounted too, and Ringo and I rode on. We would not have to pass through Oxford now and so soon (there was a thin sickle of moon like the heel print of a boot in wet sand) the road to Jefferson lay before us, the road which I had travelled for the first time three years ago with Father and travelled twice at Christmas time and then in June and September and twice at Christmas time again and then June and September again each college term since alone on the mare, not even knowing that this was peace; and now this time and maybe last time who would not die (I knew that) but who maybe forever after could never again hold up his head. The horses took the gait which they would hold for forty miles. My mare knew the long road ahead and Ringo had a good beast too, had talked Hilliard at the livery stable out of a good horse too. Maybe it was the tears, the channels of dried mud across which his strain-reddened eyes had looked at me, but I rather think it was that same quality which used to enable him to replenish his and Granny's supply of United States Army letterheads during that time—some outrageous assurance gained from too long and too close association with white people: the one whom he called Granny, the other with whom he had slept from the time we were born until Father rebuilt the house. We spoke one time, then no more:

"We could bushwhack him," he said. "Like we done Grumby that day. But I reckon that wouldn't suit that white skin you walks around in."

"No," I said. We rode on; it was October; there was plenty of time still for verbena although I would have to reach home before I would realise there was a need for it; plenty of time for verbena yet from the garden where Aunt Jenny puttered beside old Joby, in a pair of Father's old cavalry gauntlets, among the coaxed and ordered beds, the quaint and odorous old names, for though it was October no rain had come yet and hence no frost to bring (or leave behind) the first half-warm half-chill nights of Indian Summer—the drowsing air cool and empty for geese yet languid still with the old hot dusty smell of fox grape and sassafras—the nights when before I became a man and went to college to learn law Ringo and I, with lantern and axe and crokersack and six dogs (one to follow the trail and five more just for the tonguing, the music) would hunt possum in the pasture where, hidden, we had seen our first Yankee that after-noon on the bright horse, where for the last year now you could hear the whistling of the trains which had no longer belonged to Mr. Redmond for a long while now and which at some instant, some second during the morning Father too had relinquished along with the pipe which Ringo said he was smoking, which slipped from his hand as he fell. We rode on, toward the house where he would be lying in the parlor now, in his regimentals (sabre too) and where Drusilla would be waiting for me beneath all the festive glitter of the chandeliers, in the yellow ball gown and the sprig of verbena in her hair, hold-ing the two loaded pistols (I could see that too, who had had no presentiment; I could see her, in the formal brilliant room arranged formally for obsequy, not tall, not slender as a woman is but as a youth, a boy, is, motionless, in yellow, the face calm, almost bemused, the head simple and severe, the balancing sprig

1043

of verbena above each ear, the two arms bent at the elbows, the two hands shoulder high, the two identical duelling pistols lying upon, not clutched in, one to each: the Greek amphora priestess of a succinct and formal violence).

II

Drusilla said that he had a dream. I was twenty then and she and I would walk in the garden in the summer twilight while we waited for Father to ride in from the railroad. I was just twenty then: that summer before I entered the University to take the law degree which Father decided I should have and four years after the one, the day, the evening when Father and Drusilla had kept old Cash Benbow from becoming United States Marshal and returned home still unmarried and Mrs. Habersham herded them into her carriage and drove them back to town and dug her husband out of his little dim hole in the new bank and made him sign Father's peace bond for killing the two carpet baggers, and took Father and Drusilla to the minister herself and saw that they were married. And Father had rebuilt the house too, on the same blackened spot, over the same cellar, where the other had burned, only larger, much larger: Drusilla said that the house was the aura of Father's dream just as a bride's trousseau and veil is the aura of hers. And Aunt Jenny had come to live with us now so we had the garden (Drusilla would no more have bothered with flowers than Father himself would have, who even now, even four years after it was over, still seemed to exist, breathe, in that last year of it while she had ridden in man's clothes and with her hair cut short like any other member of Father's troop, across Georgia and both Carolinas in front of Sherman's army) for her to gather sprigs of verbena from to wear in her hair because she said verbena was the only scent you could smell above the smell of horses and courage and so it was the only one that was worth the wearing. The railroad was hardly begun then and Father and Mr. Redmond were not only still partners, they were still friends, which as George Wyatt said was easily a record for Father, and he would leave the house at daybreak on Jupiter, riding up and down the unfinished line with two saddlebags of gold coins borrowed on Friday to pay the men on Saturday, keeping just two cross-ties ahead of the sheriff as Aunt Jenny said. So we walked in the dusk, slowly between Aunt Jenny's flower beds while Drusilla (in a dress now, who still would have worn pants all the time if Father had let her) leaned lightly on my arm and I smelled the verbena in her hair as I had smelled the rain in it and in Father's beard that night four years ago when he and Drusilla and Uncle Buck McCaslin found Grumby and then came home and found Ringo and me more than just asleep: escaped into that oblivion which God or Nature or whoever it was had supplied us with for the time being, who had had to perform more than should be required of children because there should be some limit to the age, the youth at least below which one should not have to kill. This was just after the Saturday night when he returned and I watched him clean the derringer and reload it and we learned that the dead man was almost a neighbor, a hill man who had been in the first infantry regiment when it voted Father out of command: and we never to know if the man actually intended to rob Father or not because Father had shot too quick, but only that he had a wife and several children in a dirt-

1044

floored cabin in the hills, to whom Father the next day sent some money and she (the wife) walked into the house two days later while we were sitting at the dinner table and flung the money at Father's face.

"But nobody could have more of a dream than Colonel Sutpen," I said. He had been Father's second-in-command in the first regiment and had been elected colonel when the regiment deposed Father after Second Manassas, and it was Sutpen and not the regiment whom father never forgave. He was underbred, a cold ruthless man who had come into the country about thirty years before the War, nobody knew from where except Father said you could look at him and know he would not dare to tell. He had got some land and nobody knew how he did that either, and he got money from somewhere—Father said they all believed he robbed steamboats, either as a card sharper or as an out-and-out highwayman—and built a big house and married and set up as a gentleman. Then he lost everything in the War like everybody else, all hope of descendants too (his son killed his daughter's fiancé on the eve of the wedding and vanished) yet he came back home and set out singlehanded to rebuild his plantation. He had no friends to borrow from and he had nobody to leave it to and he was past sixty years old, yet he set out to rebuild his place like it used to be; they told how he was too busy to bother with politics or anything; how when Father and the other men organised the night riders to keep the carpet baggers from organising the Negroes into an insurrection, he refused to have anything to do with it. Father stopped hating him long enough to ride out to see Sutpen himself and he (Sutpen) came to the door with a lamp and did not even invite them to come in and discuss it; Father said, "Are you with us or against us?" and he said, "I'm for my land. If every man of you would rehabilitate his own land, the country will take care of itself" and Father challenged him to bring the lamp out and set it on a stump where they could both see to shoot and Sutpen would not. "Nobody could have more of a dream than that."

"Yes. But his dream is just Sutpen. John's is not. He is thinking of this whole country which he is trying to raise by its bootstraps, so that all the people in it, not just his kind nor his old regiment, but all the people, black and white, the women and children back in the hills who don't even own shoes— Don't you see?"

"But how can they get any good from what he wants to do for them if they are—after he has——"

"Killed some of them? I suppose you include those two carpet baggers he had to kill to hold that first election, don't you?"

"They were men. Human beings."

"They were Northerners, foreigners who had no business here. They were pirates." We walked on, her weight hardly discernible on my arm, her head just reaching my shoulder. I had always been a little taller than she, even on that night at Hawkhurst while we listened to the niggers passing in the road, and she had changed but little since—the same boy-hard body, the close implacable head with its savagely cropped hair which I had watched from the wagon above the tide of crazed singing niggers as we went down into the river —the body not slender as women are but as boys are slender. "A dream is not a very safe thing to be near, Bayard. I know; I had one once. It's like a loaded pistol with a hair trigger: if it stays alive long enough, somebody is going to be hurt. But if it's a good dream, it's worth it. There are not many dreams in the world, but there are a lot of human lives. And one human life or two dozen——"

"Are not worth anything?"

"No. Not anything.—Listen. I hear Jupiter. I'll beat you to the house." She was already running, the skirts she did not like to wear lifted almost to her knees, her legs beneath it running as boys run just as she rode like men ride.

I was twenty then. But the next time I was twenty-four; I had been three years at the University and in another two weeks I would ride back to Oxford for the final year and my degree. It was just last summer, last August, and Father had just beat Redmond for the State legislature. The railroad was finished now and the partnership between Father and Redmond had been dissolved so long ago that most people would have forgotten they were ever partners if it hadn't been for the enmity between them. There had been a third partner but nobody hardly remembered his name now; he and his name both had vanished in the fury of the conflict which set up between Father and Redmond almost before they began to lay the rails, between Father's violent and ruthless dictatorialness and will to dominate (the idea was his; he did think of the railroad first and then took Redmond in) and that quality in Redmond (as George Wyatt said, he was not a coward or Father would never have teamed with him) which permitted him to stand as much as he did from Father, to bear and bear and bear until something (not his will nor his courage) broke in him. During the War Redmond had not been a soldier, he had had something to do with cotton for the Government; he could have made money himself out of it but he had not and everybody knew he had not, Father knew it, yet Father would even taunt him with not having smelled powder. He was wrong; he knew he was when it was too late for him to stop just as a drunkard reaches a point where it is too late for him to stop, where he promises himself that he will and maybe believes he will or can but it is too late. Finally they reached the point (they had both put everything they could mortgage or borrow into it for Father to ride up and down the line, paying the workmen and the waybills on the rails at the last possible instant) where even Father realised that one of them would have to get out. So (they were not speaking then; it was arranged by Judge Benbow) they met and agreed to buy or sell, naming a price which, in reference to what they had put into it, was ridiculously low but which each believed the other could not raise—at least Father claimed that Redmond did not believe he could raise it. So Redmond accepted the price, and found out that Father had the money. And according to Father, that's what started it, although Uncle Buck McCaslin said Father could not have owned a half interest in even one hog, let alone a railroad, and not dissolve the business either sworn enemy or death-pledged friend to his recent partner. So they parted and Father finished the road. By that time, seeing that he was going to finish it, some Northern people sold him a locomotive on credit which he named for Aunt Jenny, with a silver oil can in the cab with her name engraved on it; and last summer the first train ran into Jefferson, the engine decorated with flowers and Father in the cab blowing blast after blast on the whistle when he passed Redmond's house; and there were speeches at the station, with more flowers and a Confederate flag and girls in white dresses and red sashes and a band, and Father stood on the pilot

of the engine and made a direct and absolutely needless allusion to Mr. Redmond. That was it. He wouldn't let him alone. George Wyatt came to me right
afterward and told me. "Right or wrong," he said, "us boys and most of the
other folks in this county know John's right. But he ought to let Redmond alone.
I know what's wrong: he's had to kill too many folks, and that's bad for a
man. We all know Colonel's brave as a lion, but Redmond ain't no coward
either and there ain't any use in making a brave man that made one mistake
eat crow all the time. Can't you talk to him?"

"I don't know," I said. "I'll try." But I had no chance. That is, I could have
talked to him and he would have listened, but he could not have heard me
because he had stepped straight from the pilot of that engine into the race for
the Legislature. Maybe he knew that Redmond would have to oppose him to
save his face even though he (Redmond) must have known that, after that train
ran into Jefferson, he had no chance against Father, or maybe Redmond had
already announced his candidacy and Father entered the race just because of
that, I don't remember. Anyway they ran, a bitter contest in which Father continued to badger Redmond without reason or need, since they both knew it
would be a landslide for Father. And it was, and we thought he was satisfied.
Maybe he thought so himself, as the drunkard believes that he is done with
drink; and it was that afternoon and Drusilla and I walked in the garden in
the twilight and I said something about what George Wyatt had told me and
she released my arm and turned me to face her and said, "This from you? You?
Have you forgotten Grumby?"

"No," I said. "I never will forget him."

"You never will. I wouldn't let you. There are worse things than killing men,
Bayard. There are worse things than being killed. Sometimes I think the finest
thing that can happen to a man is to love something, a woman preferably, well,
hard hard hard, then to die young because he believed what he could not help
but believe and was what he could not (could not? would not) help but be."
Now she was looking at me in a way she never had before. I did not know
what it meant then and was not to know until tonight since neither of us
knew then that two months later Father would be dead. I just knew that she
was looking at me as she never had before and that the scent of the verbena
in her hair seemed to have increased a hundred times, to have got a hundred
times stronger, to be everywhere in the dusk in which something was about to
happen which I had never dreamed of. Then she spoke. "Kiss me, Bayard."

"No. You are Father's wife."

"And eight years older than you are. And your fourth cousin too. And I
have black hair. Kiss me, Bayard."

"No."

"Kiss me, Bayard." So I leaned my face down to her. But she didn't move,
standing so, bent lightly back from me from the waist, looking at me; now it
was she who said, "No." So I put my arms around her. Then she came to me,
melted as women will and can, the arms with the wrist- and elbow-power to
control horses about my shoulders, using the wrists to hold my face to hers
until there was no longer need for the wrists; I thought then of the woman of
thirty, the symbol of the ancient and eternal Snake and of the men who have
written of her, and I realised then the immitigable chasm between all life and

1047

all print—that those who can, do, those who cannot and suffer enough because they can't, write about it. Then I was free, I could see her again, I saw her still watching me with that dark inscrutable look, looking up at me now across her down-slanted face; I watched her arms rise with almost the exact gesture with which she had put them around me as if she were repeating the empty and formal gesture of all promise so that I should never forget it, the elbows angling outward as she put her hands to the sprig of verbena in her hair, I standing straight and rigid facing the slightly bent head, the short jagged hair, the rigid curiously formal angle of the bare arms gleaming faintly in the last of light as she removed the verbena sprig and put it into my lapel, and I thought how the War had tried to stamp all the women of her generation and class in the South into a type and how it had failed—the suffering, the identical experience (hers and Aunt Jenny's had been almost the same except that Aunt Jenny had spent a few nights with her husband before they brought him back home in an ammunition wagon while Gavin Breckridge was just Drusilla's fiancé) was there in the eyes, yet beyond that was the incorrigibly individual woman: not like so many men who return from wars to live on Government reservations like so many steers, emasculate and empty of all save an identical experience which they cannot forget and dare not, else they would cease to live at that moment, almost interchangeable save for the old habit of answering to a given name.

"Now I must tell Father," I said.

"Yes," she said. "You must tell him. Kiss me." So again it was like it had been before. No. Twice, a thousand times and never like—the eternal and symbolical thirty to a young man, a youth, each time both cumulative and retroactive, immitigably unrepetitive, each wherein remembering excludes experience, each wherein experience antedates remembering; the skill without weariness, the knowledge virginal to surfeit, the cunning secret muscles to guide and control just as within the wrists and elbows lay slumbering the mastery of horses: she stood back, already turning, not looking at me when she spoke, never having looked at me, already moving swiftly on in the dusk: "Tell John. Tell him tonight."

I intended to. I went to the house and into the office at once; I went to the center of the rug before the cold hearth, I don't know why, and stood there rigid like soldiers stand, looking at eye level straight across the room and above his head and said "Father" and then stopped. Because he did not even hear me. He said, "Yes, Bayard?" but he did not hear me although he was sitting behind the desk doing nothing, immobile, as still as I was rigid, one hand on the desk with a dead cigar in it, a bottle of brandy and a filled and untasted glass beside his hand, clothed quiet and bemused in whatever triumph it was he felt since the last overwhelming return of votes had come in late in the afternoon. So I waited until after supper. We went to the diningroom and stood side by side until Aunt Jenny entered and then Drusilla, in the yellow ball gown, who walked straight to me and gave me one fierce inscrutable look then went to her place and waited for me to draw her chair while Father drew Aunt Jenny's. He had roused by then, not to talk himself but rather to sit at the head of the table and reply to Drusilla as she talked with a sort of feverish and glittering volubility—to reply now and then to her with that courteous intolerant pride

1048

which had lately become a little forensic, as if merely being in a political contest filled with fierce and empty oratory had retroactively made a lawyer of him who was anything and everything except a lawyer. Then Drusilla and Aunt Jenny rose and left us and he said, "Wait" to me who had made no move to follow and directed Joby to bring one of the bottles of wine which he had fetched back from New Orleans when he went there last to borrow money to liquidate his first private railroad bonds. Then I stood again like soldiers stand, gazing at eye level above his head while he sat half-turned from the table, a little paunchy now though not much, a little grizzled too in the hair though his beard was as strong as ever, with that spurious forensic air of lawyers and the intolerant eyes which in the last two years had acquired that transparent film which the eyes of carnivorous animals have and from behind which they look at a world which no ruminant ever sees, perhaps dares to see, which I have seen before on the eyes of men who have killed too much, who have killed so much that never again as long as they live will they ever be alone. I said again, "Father," then I told him.

"Hah?" he said. "Sit down." I sat down, I looked at him, watched him fill both glasses and this time I knew it was worse with him than not hearing: it didn't even matter. "You are doing well in the law, Judge Wilkins tells me. I am pleased to hear that. I have not needed you in my affairs so far, but from now on I shall. I have now accomplished the active portion of my aims in which you could not have helped me; I acted as the land and the time demanded and you were too young for that, I wished to shield you. But now the land and the time too are changing; what will follow will be a matter of consolidation, of pettifogging and doubtless chicanery in which I would be a babe in arms but in which you, trained in the law, can hold your own—our own. Yes. I have accomplished my aim, and now I shall do a little moral housecleaning. I am tired of killing men, no matter what the necessity nor the end. Tomorrow, when I go to town and meet Ben Redmond, I shall be unarmed."

III

We reached home just before midnight; we didn't have to pass through Jefferson either. Before we turned in the gates I could see the lights, the chandeliers—hall, parlor, and what Aunt Jenny (without any effort or perhaps even design on her part) had taught even Ringo to call the drawing room, the light falling outward across the portico, past the columns. Then I saw the horses, the faint shine of leather and buckle-glints on the black silhouettes and then the men too—Wyatt and other of Father's old troop—and I had forgot that they would be there. I had forgot that they would be there; I remember how I thought, since I was tired and spent with strain, *Now it will have to begin tonight. I won't even have until tomorrow in which to begin to resist.* They had a watchman, a picquet out, I suppose, because they seemed to know at once that we were in the drive. Wyatt met me, I halted the mare, I could look down at him and at the others gathered a few yards behind him with that curious vulture-like formality which Southern men assume in such situations.

"Well, boy," George said.

"Was it—" I said. "Was he——"

"It was all right. It was in front. Redmond ain't no coward. John had the

1049

derringer inside his cuff like always, but he never touched it, never made a move toward it." I have seen him do it, he showed me once: the pistol (it was not four inches long) held flat inside his left wrist by a clip he made himself of wire and an old clock spring; he would raise both hands at the same time, cross them, fire the pistol from beneath his left hand almost as if he were hiding from his own vision what he was doing; when he killed one of the men he shot a hole through his own coat sleeve. "But you want to get on to the house," Wyatt said. He began to stand aside, then he spoke again: "We'll take this off your hands, any of us. Me." I hadn't moved the mare yet and I had made no move to speak, yet he continued quickly, as if he had already rehearsed all this, his speech and mine, and knew what I would say and only spoke himself as he would have re- moved his hat on entering a house or used 'sir' in conversing with a stranger: "You're young, just a boy, you ain't had any experience in this kind of thing. Besides, you got them two ladies in the house to think about. He would under- stand, all right."

"I reckon I can attend to it," I said.

"Sure," he said; there was no surprise, nothing at all, in his voice because he had already rehearsed this: "I reckon we all knew that's what you would say." He stepped back then; almost it was as though he and not I bade the mare to move on. But they all followed, still with that unctuous and voracious formality. Then I saw Drusilla standing at the top of the front steps, in the light from the open door and the windows like a theatre scene, in the yellow ball gown and even from here I believe that I could smell the verbena in her hair, standing there motionless yet emanating something louder than the two shots must have been— something voracious too and passionate. Then, although I had dismounted and someone had taken the mare, I seemed to be still in the saddle and to watch my- self enter that scene which she had postulated like another actor while in the background for chorus Wyatt and the others stood with the unctuous formality which the Southern man shows in the presence of death—that Roman holiday engendered by mist-born Protestantism grafted onto this land of violent sun, of violent alteration from snow to heat-stroke which has produced a race impervious to both. I mounted the steps toward the figure straight and yellow and immobile as a candle which moved only to extend one hand; we stood together and looked down at them where they stood clumped, the horses too gathered in a tight group beyond them at the rim of light from the brilliant door and windows. One of them stamped and blew his breath and jangled his gear.

"Thank you, gentlemen," I said. "My aunt and my—Drusilla thank you. There's no need for you to stay. Goodnight." They murmured, turning. George Wyatt paused, looking back at me.

"Tomorrow?" he said.

"Tomorrow." Then they went on, carrying their hats and tiptoeing, even on the ground, the quiet and resilient earth, as though anyone in that house awake would try to sleep, anyone already asleep in it whom they could have wakened. Then they were gone and Drusilla and I turned and crossed the portico, her hand lying light on my wrist yet discharging into me with a shock like electricity that dark and passionate voracity, the face at my shoulder—the jagged hair with a verbena sprig above each ear, the eyes staring at me with that fierce exaltation. We entered the hall and crossed it, her hand guiding me without pressure, and

1050

entered the parlor. Then for the first time I realised it—the alteration which is death—not that he was now just clay but that he was lying down. But I didn't look at him yet because I knew that when I did I would begin to pant; I went to Aunt Jenny who had just risen from a chair behind which Louvinia stood. She was Father's sister, taller than Drusilla but no older, whose husband had been killed at the very beginning of the War, by a shell from a Federal frigate at Fort Moultrie, come to us from Carolina six years ago. Ringo and I went to Tennessee Junction in the wagon to meet her. It was January, cold and clear and with ice in the ruts; we returned just before dark with Aunt Jenny on the seat beside me holding a lace parasol and Ringo in the wagon bed nursing a hamper basket containing two bottles of old sherry and the two jasmine cuttings which were bushes in the garden now, and the panes of colored glass which she had salvaged from the Carolina house where she and Father and Uncle Bayard were born and which Father had set in a fanlight about one of the drawing room windows for her—who came up the drive and Father (home now from the railroad) went down the steps and lifted her from the wagon and said, "Well, Jenny," and she said, "Well, Johnny," and began to cry. She stood too, looking at me as I approached—the same hair, the same high nose, the same eyes as Father's except that they were intent and very wise instead of intolerant. She said nothing at all, she just kissed me, her hands light on my shoulders. Then Drusilla spoke, as if she had been waiting with a sort of dreadful patience for the empty ceremony to be done, in a voice like a bell: clear, unsentient, on a single pitch, silvery and triumphant: "Come, Bayard."

"Hadn't you better go to bed now?" Aunt Jenny said.

"Yes," Drusilla said in that silvery ecstatic voice, "Oh yes. There will be plenty of time for sleep." I followed her, her hand again guiding me without pressure; now I looked at him. It was just as I had imagined it—sabre, plumes, and all—but with that alteration, that irrevocable difference which I had known to expect yet had not realised, as you can put food into your stomach which for a while the stomach declines to assimilate—the illimitable grief and regret as I looked down at the face which I knew—the nose, the hair, the eyelids closed over the intolerance—the face which I realised I now saw in repose for the first time in my life; the empty hand still now beneath the invisible stain of what had been (once, surely) needless blood, the hands now appearing clumsy in their very inertness, too clumsy to have performed the fatal actions which forever afterward he must have waked and slept with and maybe was glad to lay down at last— those curious appendages clumsily conceived to begin with yet with which man has taught himself to do so much, so much more than they were intended to do or could be forgiven for doing, which had now surrendered that life to which his intolerant heart had fiercely held; and then I knew that in a minute I would begin to pant. So Drusilla must have spoken twice before I heard her and turned and saw in the instant Aunt Jenny and Louvinia watching us, hearing Drusilla now, the unsentient bell quality gone now, her voice whispering into that quiet death-filled room with a passionate and dying fall: "Bayard." She faced me, she was quite near; again the scent of the verbena in her hair seemed to have increased a hundred times as she stood holding out to me, one in either hand, the two duelling pistols. "Take them, Bayard," she said, in the same tone in which she had said "Kiss me" last summer, already pressing them into my hands, watching me

1051

with that passionate and voracious exaltation, speaking in a voice fainting and passionate with promise: "Take them. I have kept them for you. I give them to you. Oh you will thank me, you will remember me who put into your hands what they say is an attribute only of God's, who took what belongs to heaven and gave it to you. Do you feel them? the long true barrels true as justice, the triggers (you have fired them) quick as retribution, the two of them slender and invincible and fatal as the physical shape of love?" Again I watched her arms angle out and upward as she removed the two verbena sprigs from her hair in two motions faster than the eye could follow, already putting one of them into my lapel and crushing the other in her other hand while she still spoke in that rapid passionate voice not much louder than a whisper: "There. One I give to you to wear tomorrow (it will not fade), the other I cast away, like this—" dropping the crushed bloom at her feet. "I abjure it. I abjure verbena forever more; I have smelled it above the odor of courage; that was all I wanted. Now let me look at you." She stood back, staring at me—the face tearless and exalted, the feverish eyes brilliant and voracious. "How beautiful you are: do you know it? How beautiful: young, to be permitted to kill, to be permitted vengeance, to take into your bare hands the fire of heaven that cast down Lucifer. No; I. I gave it to you; I put it into your hands; Oh you will thank me, you will remember me when I am dead and you are an old man saying to himself, 'I have tasted all things.'—It will be the right hand, won't it?" She moved; she had taken my right hand which still held one of the pistols before I knew what she was about to do; she had bent and kissed it before I comprehended why she took it. Then she stopped dead still, still stooping in that attitude of fierce exultant humility, her hot lips and her hot hands still touching my flesh, light on my flesh as dead leaves yet communicating to it that battery charge dark, passionate and damned forever of all peace. Because they are wise, women are—a touch, lips or fingers, and the knowledge, even clairvoyance, goes straight to the heart without bothering the laggard brain at all. She stood erect now, staring at me with intolerable and amazed incredulity which occupied her face alone for a whole minute while her eyes were completely empty; it seemed to me that I stood there for a full minute while Aunt Jenny and Louvinia watched us, waiting for her eyes to fill. There was no blood in her face at all, her mouth open a little and pale as one of those rubber rings women seal fruit jars with. Then her eyes filled with an expression of bitter and passionate betrayal. "Why, he's not—" she said. "He's not—And I kissed his hand," she said in an aghast whisper; "*I kissed his hand!*" beginning to laugh, the laughter rising, becoming a scream yet still remaining laughter, screaming with laughter, trying herself to deaden the sound by putting her hand over her mouth, the laughter spilling between her fingers like vomit, the incredulous betrayed eyes still watching me across the hand.

"Louvinia!" Aunt Jenny said. They both came to her. Louvinia touched and held her and Drusilla turned her face to Louvinia.

"I kissed his hand, Louvinia!" she cried. "Did you see it? *I kissed his hand!*" the laughter rising again, becoming the scream again yet still remaining laughter, she still trying to hold it back with her hand like a small child who has filled its mouth too full.

"Take her upstairs," Aunt Jenny said. But they were already moving toward the door, Louvinia half-carrying Drusilla, the laughter diminishing as they neared the door as though it waited for the larger space of the empty and brilliant hall to rise again. Then it was gone; Aunt Jenny and I stood there and I knew soon that I would begin to pant. I could feel it beginning like you feel regurgitation beginning, as though there were not enough air in the room, the house, not enough air anywhere under the heavy hot low sky where the equinox couldn't seem to accomplish, nothing in the air for breathing, for the lungs. Now it was Aunt Jenny who said "Bayard" twice before I heard her. "You are not going to try to kill him. All right."

"All right?" I said.

"Yes. All right. Don't let it be Drusilla, a poor hysterical young woman. And don't let it be him, Bayard, because he's dead now. And don't let it be George Wyatt and those others who will be waiting for you tomorrow morning. I know you are not afraid."

"But what good will that do?" I said. "What good will that do?" It almost began then; I stopped it just in time. "I must live with myself, you see."

"Then it's not just Drusilla? Not just him? Not just George Wyatt and Jefferson?"

"No," I said.

"Will you promise to let me see you before you go to town tomorrow?" I looked at her; we looked at one another for a moment. Then she put her hands on my shoulders and kissed me and released me, all in one motion. "Goodnight, son," she said. Then she was gone too and now it could begin. I knew that in a minute I would look at him and it would begin and I did look at him, feeling the long-held breath, the hiatus before it started, thinking how maybe I should have said, "Goodbye, Father" but did not. Instead I crossed to the piano and laid the pistols carefully on it, still keeping the panting from getting too loud too soon. Then I was outside on the porch and (I don't know how long it had been) I looked in the window and saw Simon squatting on a stool beside him. Simon had been his body servant during the War and when they came home Simon had a uniform too—a Confederate private's coat with a Yankee brigadier's star on it and he had put it on now too, like they had dressed Father, squatting on the stool beside him, not crying, not weeping the facile tears which are the white man's futile trait and which Negroes know nothing about but just sitting there, motionless, his lower lip slacked down a little; he raised his hand and touched the coffin, the black hand rigid and fragile-looking as a clutch of dead twigs, then dropped the hand; once he turned his head and I saw his eyes roll red and unwinking in his skull like those of a cornered fox. It had begun by that time; I panted, standing there, and this was it—the regret and grief, the despair out of which the tragic mute insensitive bones stand up that can bear anything, anything.

IV

After a while the whippoorwills stopped and I heard the first day bird, a mockingbird. It had sung all night too but now it was the day song, no longer the drowsy moony fluting. Then they all began—the sparrows from the stable, the thrush that lived in Aunt Jenny's garden, and I heard a quail too from the pasture and now there was light in the room. But I didn't move at once. I still lay on the bed (I hadn't undressed) with my hands under my head and the scent of Drusilla's verbena faint from where my coat lay on a chair, watching the light

1053

glow, watching it turn rosy with the sun. After a while I heard Louvinia come up across the back yard and go into the kitchen; I heard the door and then the long crash of her armful of stovewood into the box. Soon they would begin to arrive—the carriages and buggies in the drive—but not for a while yet because they too would wait first to see what I was going to do. So the house was quiet when I went down to the diningroom, no sound in it except Simon snoring in the parlor, probably still sitting on the stool though I didn't look in to see. Instead I stood at the diningroom window and drank the coffee which Louvinia brought me, then I went to the stable; I saw Joby watching me from the kitchen door as I crossed the yard and in the stable Loosh looked up at me across Betsy's head, a curry comb in his hand, though Ringo didn't look at me at all. We curried Jupiter then. I didn't know if we would be able to without trouble or not, since always Father would come in first and touch him and tell him to stand and he would stand like a marble horse (or pale bronze rather) while Loosh curried him. But he stood for me too, a little restive but he stood, then that was done and now it was almost nine o'clock and soon they would begin to arrive and I told Ringo to bring Betsy on to the house.

I went on to the house and into the hall. I had not had to pant in some time now but it was there, waiting, a part of the alteration, as though by being dead and no longer needing air he had taken all of it, all that he had compassed and claimed and postulated between the walls which he had built, along with him. Aunt Jenny must have been waiting; she came out of the diningroom at once, without a sound, dressed, the hair that was like Father's combed and smooth above the eyes that were different from Father's eyes because they were not intolerant but just intent and grave and (she was wise too) without pity. "Are you going now?" she said.

"Yes." I looked at her. Yes, thank God, without pity. "You see, I want to be be thought well of."

"I do," she said. "Even if you spend the day hidden in the stable loft, I still do."

"Maybe if she knew that I was going. Was going to town anyway."

"No," she said. "No, Bayard." We looked at one another. Then she said quietly, "All right. She's awake." So I mounted the stairs. I mounted steadily, not fast because if I had gone fast the panting would have started again or I might have had to slow for a second at the turn or at the top and I would not have gone on. So I went slowly and steadily, across the hall to her door and knocked and opened it. She was sitting at the window, in something soft and loose for morning in her bedroom only she never did look like morning in a bedroom because here was no hair to fall about her shoulders. She looked up, she sat there looking at me with her feverish brilliant eyes and I remembered I still had the verbena sprig in my lapel and suddenly she began to laugh again. It seemed to come not from her mouth but to burst out all over her face like sweat does and with a dreadful and painful convulsion as when you have vomited until it hurts you yet still you must vomit again—burst out all over her face except her eyes, the brilliant incredulous eyes looking at me out of the laughter as if they belonged to somebody else, as if they were two inert fragments of tar or coal lying on the bottom of a receptacle filled with turmoil: "I kissed his hand! *I kissed his hand!*" Louvinia entered, Aunt Jenny must have sent her directly after me; again I walked slowly and steadily so it would not start yet, down the stairs where Aunt Jenny stood beneath the chandelier in the hall as Mrs. Wilkins had stood yesterday at the University. She had my hat in her hand. "Even if you hid all day in the stable, Bayard," she said. I took the hat; she said quietly, pleasantly, as if she were talking to a stranger, a guest: "I used to see a lot of blockade runners in Charleston. They were heroes in a way, you see—not heroes because they were helping to prolong the Confederacy but heroes in the sense that David Crockett or John Sevier would have been to small boys or fool young women. There was one of them, an Englishman. He had no business there; it was the money of course, as with all of them. But he was the Davy Crockett to us because by that time we had all forgot what money was, what you could do with it. He must have been a gentleman once or associated with gentlemen before he changed his name, and he had a vocabulary of seven words, though I must admit he got along quite well with them. The first four were, 'I'll have rum, thanks,' and then, when he had the rum, he would use the other three—across the champagne, to whatever ruffled bosom or low gown: 'No bloody moon.' No bloody moon, Bayard."

Ringo was waiting with Betsy at the front steps. Again he did not look at me, his face sullen, downcast even while he handed me the reins. But he said nothing, nor did I look back. And sure enough I was just in time; I passed the Compson carriage at the gates, General Compson lifted his hat as I did mine as we passed. It was four miles to town but I had not gone two of them when I heard the horse coming up behind me and I did not look back because I knew it was Ringo. I did not look back; he came up on one of the carriage horses, he rode up beside me and looked me full in the face for one moment, the sullen determined face, the eyes rolling at me defiant and momentary and red; we rode on. Now we were in town—the long shady street leading to the square, the new courthouse at the end of it; it was eleven o'clock now: long past breakfast and not yet noon so there were only women on the street, not to recognise me perhaps or at least not the walking stopped sudden and dead in midwalking as if the legs contained the sudden eyes, the caught breath, that not to begin until we reached the square and I thinking *if I could only be invisible until I reach the stairs to his office and begin to mount.* But I could not, I was not; we rode up to the Holston House and I saw the row of feet along the gallery rail come suddenly and quietly down and I did not look at them, I stopped Betsy and waited until Ringo was down then I dismounted and gave him the reins. "Wait for me here," I said.

"I'm going with you," he said, not loud; we stood there under the still circumspect eyes and spoke quietly to one another like two conspirators. Then I saw the pistol, the outline of it inside his shirt, probably the one we had taken from Grumby that day we killed him.

"No you ain't," I said.

"Yes I am."

"No you ain't." So I walked on, along the street in the hot sun. It was almost noon now and I could smell nothing except the verbena in my coat, as if it had gathered all the sun, all the suspended fierce heat in which the equinox could not seem to occur and were distilling it so that I moved in a cloud of verbena as I might have moved in a cloud of smoke from a cigar. Then George Wyatt was beside me (I don't know where he came from) and five or six others of Father's

1055

old troop a few yards behind, George's hand on my arm, drawing me into a doorway out of the avid eyes like caught breaths.

"Have you got that derringer?" George said.

"No," I said.

"Good," George said. "They are tricky things to fool with. Couldn't nobody but Colonel ever handle one right; I never could. So you take this. I tried it this morning and I know it's right. Here." He was already fumbling the pistol into my pocket, then the same thing seemed to happen to him that happened to Drusilla last night when she kissed my hand—something communicated by touch straight to the simple code by which he lived, without going through the brain at all: so that he too stood suddenly back, the pistol in his hand, staring at me with his pale outraged eyes and speaking in a whisper thin with fury: "Who are you? Is your name Sartoris? By God, if you don't kill him, I'm going to." Now it was not panting, it was a terrible desire to laugh, to laugh as Drusilla had, and say, "That's what Drusilla said." But I didn't. I said,

"I'm tending to this. You stay out of it. I don't need any help." Then his fierce eyes faded gradually, exactly as you turn a lamp down.

"Well," he said, putting the pistol back into his pocket. "You'll have to excuse me, son. I should have knowed you wouldn't do anything that would keep John from laying quiet. We'll follow you and wait at the foot of the steps. And remember: he's a brave man, but he's been sitting in that office by himself since yesterday morning waiting for you and his nerves are on edge."

"I'll remember," I said. "I don't need any help." I had started on when suddenly I said it without having any warning that I was going to: "No bloody moon."

"What?" he said. I didn't answer. I went on across the square itself now, in the hot sun, they following though not close so that I never saw them again until afterward, surrounded by the remote still eyes not following me yet either, just stopped where they were before the stores and about the door to the courthouse, waiting. I walked steadily on enclosed in the now fierce odor of the verbena sprig. Then shadow fell upon me; I did not pause, I looked once at the small faded sign nailed to the brick *B. J. Redmond. Atty at Law* and began to mount the stairs, the wooden steps scuffed by the heavy bewildered boots of countrymen approaching litigation and stained by tobacco spit, on down the dim corridor to the door which bore the name again, *B. J. Redmond* and knocked once and opened it. He sat behind the desk, not much taller than Father but thicker as a man gets who spends most of his time sitting and listening to people, freshly shaven and with fresh linen; a lawyer yet it was not a lawyer's face—a face much thinner than the body would indicate, strained (and yes, tragic; I know that now) and exhausted beneath the neat recent steady strokes of the razor, holding a pistol flat on the desk before him, loose beneath his hand and aimed at nothing. There was no smell of drink, not even of tobacco in the neat clean dingy room although I knew he smoked. I didn't pause. I walked steadily toward him. It was not twenty feet from door to desk yet I seemed to walk in a dreamlike state in which there was neither time nor distance, as though the mere act of walking was no more intended to encompass space than was his sitting. We didn't speak. It was as if we both knew what the passage of words would be and the futility of it; how he might have said, "Go out, Bayard. Go away, boy" and then, "Draw then. I

1056

will allow you to draw" and it would have been the same as if he had never said it. So we did not speak; I just walked steadily toward him as the pistol rose from the desk. I watched it, I could see the foreshortened slant of the barrel and I knew it would miss me though his hand did not tremble. I walked toward him, toward the pistol in the rocklike hand, I heard no bullet. Maybe I didn't even hear the explosion though I remember the sudden orange bloom and smoke as they appeared against his white shirt as they had appeared against Grumby's greasy Confederate coat; I still watched that foreshortened slant of barrel which I knew was not aimed at me and saw the second orange flash and smoke and heard no bullet that time either. Then I stopped; it was done then. I watched the pistol descend to the desk in short jerks; I saw him release it and sit back, both hands on the desk, I looked at his face and I knew too what it was to want air when there was nothing in the circumambience for the lungs. He rose, shoved the chair back with a convulsive motion and rose, with a queer ducking motion of his head; with his head still ducked aside and one arm extended as though he couldn't see and the other hand resting on the desk as if he couldn't stand alone, he turned and crossed to the wall and took his hat from the rack and with his head still ducked aside and one hand extended he blundered along the wall and passed me and reached the door and went through it. He was brave; no one denied that. He walked down those stairs and out onto the street where George Wyatt and the other six of Father's old troop waited and where the other men had begun to run now; he walked through the middle of them with his hat on and his head up (they told me how someone shouted at him: "Have you killed that boy too?"), saying no word, staring straight ahead and with his back to them, on to the station where the south-bound train was just in and got on it with no baggage, nothing, and went away from Jefferson and from Mississippi and never came back.

I heard their feet on the stairs then in the corridor then in the room, but for a while yet (it wasn't that long, of course) I still sat behind the desk as he had sat, the flat of the pistol still warm under my hand, my hand growing slowly numb between the pistol and my forehead. Then I raised my head; the little room was full of men. "My God!" George Wyatt cried. "You took the pistol away from him and then missed him, missed him *twice?*" Then he answered himself—that same rapport for violence which Drusilla had and which in George's case was actual character judgment: "No; wait. You walked in here without even a pocket knife and let him miss you twice. My God in heaven." He turned, shouting: "Get to hell out of here! You, White, ride out to Sartoris and tell his folks it's all over and he's all right. Ride!" So they departed, went away; presently only George was left, watching me with that pale bleak stare which was speculative yet not at all ratiocinative. "Well by God," he said. "—Do you want a drink?"

"No," I said. "I'm hungry. I didn't eat any breakfast."

"I reckon not, if you got up this morning aiming to do what you did. Come on. We'll go to the Holston House."

"No," I said. "No. Not there."

"Why not? You ain't done anything to be ashamed of. I wouldn't have done it that way, myself. I'd a shot at him once, anyway. But that's your way or you wouldn't have done it."

"Yes," I said. "I would do it again."

"Be damned if I would.—You want to come home with me? We'll have time to eat and then ride out there in time for the——" But I couldn't do that either.

"No," I said. "I'm not hungry after all. I think I'll go home."

"Don't you want to wait and ride out with me?"

"No. I'll go on."

"You don't want to stay here, anyway." He looked around the room again, where the smell of powder smoke still lingered a little, still lay somewhere on the hot dead air though invisible now, blinking a little with his fierce pale unintroverted eyes. "Well by God," he said again. "Maybe you're right, maybe there has been enough killing in your family without—Come on." We left the office. I waited at the foot of the stairs and soon Ringo came up with the horses. We crossed the square again. There were no feet on the Holston House railing now (it was twelve o'clock) but a group of men stood before the door who raised their hats and I raised mine and Ringo and I rode on.

We did not go fast. Soon it was one, maybe after; the carriages and buggies would begin to leave the square soon, so I turned from the road at the end of the pasture and I sat the mare, trying to open the gate without dismounting, until Ringo dismounted and opened it. We crossed the pasture in the hard fierce sun; I could have seen the house now but I didn't look. Then we were in the shade, the close thick airless shade of the creek bottom; the old rails still lay in the undergrowth where we had built the pen to hide the Yankee mules. Presently I heard the water, then I could see the sunny glints. We dismounted. I lay on my back, I thought *Now it can begin again if it wants to.* But it did not. I went to sleep. I went to sleep almost before I had stopped thinking. I slept for almost five hours and I didn't dream anything at all yet I waked myself up crying, crying too hard to stop it. Ringo was squatting beside me and the sun was gone though there was a bird of some sort still singing somewhere and the whistle of the north-bound evening train sounded and the short broken puffs of starting where it had evidently stopped at our flag station. After a while I began to stop and Ringo brought his hat full of water from the creek but instead I went down to the water myself and bathed my face.

There was still a good deal of light in the pasture, though the whippoorwills had begun, and when we reached the house there was a mockingbird singing in the magnolia, the night song now, the drowsy moony one, and again the moon like the rim print of a heel in wet sand. There was just one light in the hall now and so it was all over though I could still smell the flowers even above the verbena in my coat. I had not looked at him again. I had started to before I left the house but I did not, I did not see him again and all the pictures we had of him were bad ones because a picture could no more have held him dead than the house could have kept his body. But I didn't need to see him again because he was there, he would always be there; maybe what Drusilla meant by his dream was not something which he possessed but something which he had bequeathed us which we could never forget, which would even assume the corporeal shape of him whenever any of us, black or white, closed our eyes. I went into the house. There was no light in the drawing room except the last of the afterglow which came through the western window where Aunt Jenny's colored glass was; I was about to go on up stairs when I saw her sitting there beside the window.

1058

She didn't call me and I didn't speak Drusilla's name, I just went to the door and stood there. "She's gone," Aunt Jenny said. "She took the evening train. She has gone to Montgomery, to Dennison." Denny had been married about a year now; he was living in Montgomery, reading law.

"I see," I said. "Then she didn't——" But there wasn't any use in that either; Jed White must have got there before one o'clock and told them. And besides, Aunt Jenny didn't answer. She could have lied to me but she didn't, she said, "Come here." I went to her chair. "Kneel down. I can't see you."

"Don't you want the lamp?"

"No. Kneel down." So I knelt beside the chair. "So you had a perfectly splendid Saturday afternoon, didn't you? Tell me about it." Then she put her hands on my shoulders. I watched them come up as though she were trying to stop them; I felt them on my shoulders as if they had a separate life of their own and were trying to do something which for my sake she was trying to restrain, prevent. Then she gave up or she was not strong enough because they came up and took my face between them, hard, and suddenly the tears sprang and streamed down her face like Drusilla's laughing had. "Oh, damn you Sartorises!" she said. "Damn you! Damn you!"

As I passed down the hall the light came up in the diningroom and I could hear Louvinia laying the table for supper. So the stairs were lighted quite well. But the upper hall was dark. I saw her open door (that unmistakable way in which an open door stands open when nobody lives in the room any more) and I realised I had not believed that she was really gone. So I didn't look into the room. I went on to mine and entered. And then for a long moment I thought it was the verbena in my lapel which I still smelled. I thought that until I had crossed the room and looked down at the pillow on which it lay—the single sprig of it (without looking she would pinch off a half dozen of them and they would be all of a size, almost all of a shape, as if a machine had stamped them out) filling the room, the dusk, the evening with that odor which she said you could smell alone above the smell of horses. (*1938*)

Nobel Prize Award Speech

Stockholm, Sweden
Dec. 10, 1950

I feel that this award was not made to me as a man but to my work—a life's work in the agony and sweat of the human spirit, not for glory and least of all for profit, but to create out of the materials of the human spirit something which did not exist before. So this award is only mine in trust. It will not be difficult to find a dedication for the money part of it commensurate with the purpose and significance of its origin. But I would like to do the same with the acclaim too, by using this moment as a pinnacle from which I might be listened to by the young men and women already dedicated to the same anguish and travail, among whom is already that one who will some day stand here where I am standing.

Reprinted by courtesy of Random House, Inc.

1059

Our tragedy today is a general and universal physical fear so long sustained by now that we can even bear it. There are no longer problems of the spirit. There is only the question: when will I be blown up? Because of this, the young man or woman writing today has forgotten the problems of the human heart in conflict with itself which alone can make good writing because only that is worth writing about, worth the agony and the sweat.

He must learn them again. He must teach himself that the basest of all things is to be afraid; and, teaching himself that, forget it forever, leaving no room in his workshop for anything but the old verities and truths of the heart, the old universal truths lacking which any story is ephemeral and doomed—love and honor and pity and pride and compassion and sacrifice. Until he does so he labors under a curse. He writes not of love but of lust, of defeats in which nobody loses anything of value, of victories without hope and worst of all without pity or compassion. His griefs grieve on no universal bones, leaving no scars. He writes not of the heart but of the glands.

Until he relearns these things he will write as though he stood among and watched the end of man. I decline to accept the end of man. It is easy enough to say that man is immortal simply because he will endure; that when the last ding-dong of doom has clanged and faded from the last worthless rock hanging tideless in the last red and dying evening, that even then there will still be one more sound: that of his puny inexhaustible voice, still talking. I refuse to accept this. I believe that man will not merely endure: he will prevail. He is immortal, not because he alone among creatures has an inexhaustible voice, but because he has a soul, a spirit capable of compassion and sacrifice and endurance. The poet's, the writer's, duty is to write about these things. It is his privilege to help man endure by lifting his heart, by reminding him of the courage and honor and hope and pride and compassion and pity and sacrifice which have been the glory of his past. The poet's voice need not merely be the record of man, it can be one of the props, the pillars to help him endure and prevail.

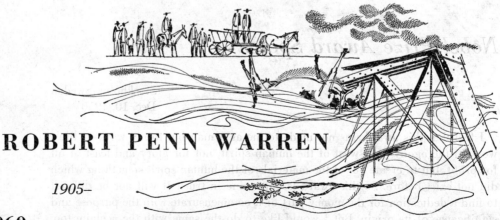

ROBERT PENN WARREN

1905–

Robert Penn Warren was born in Guthrie, Kentucky, April 24, 1905. He graduated in 1925 from Vanderbilt University, where he became closely associated with John Crowe Ransom and Donald Davidson. Warren received his M.A. degree from the University of California in 1927, spent a year doing further work at Yale, and from 1928 to 1930 studied at Oxford as a Rhodes Scholar. Since that time he has taught English at Southwestern College, Vanderbilt University, Louisiana State University, and the University of Minnesota. In 1951 he was appointed Professor of Drama at Yale.

A member of the Fugitive and Agrarian movements, Warren contributed to both *I'll Take My Stand* (1930) and *Who Owns America?* (1936). He was one of the founders of the influential *Southern Review* and with Cleanth Brooks served as managing editor of that magazine until its demise in 1942. He then became an advisory editor of *The Kenyon Review*. From 1944–1945 Warren served as Consultant in Poetry at the Library of Congress.

Warren has been active in nearly every field of literature—as critic, novelist, short-story writer, poet, and editor. He has received many awards and recognitions for both poetry and fiction, including the Pulitzer Prize for fiction in 1947. His most generally known work has been in the field of the novel, of which he has thus far published four: *Night Rider* (1939), *At Heaven's Gate* (1943), *All the King's Men* (1946), and *World Enough and Time* (1950). In addition to these he has published several volumes of poetry, most notably his *Selected Poems* (1944); a collection of short stories, *The Circus in the Attic* (1947); and a biography, *John Brown: the Making of a Martyr* (1929). With Cleanth Brooks he was co-author of two college texts, *Understanding Poetry* (1938) and *Understanding Fiction* (1943).

Terror

"I Volontari Americani Presso Eserciti Stranieri Non Perdono La Cittadinanza." [1]
—*Il Messaggero*, Roma, Sabato, 27 Gennaio, 1940

Not picnics or pageants or the improbable
Powers of air whose tongues exclaim dominion
And gull the great man to follow his terrible
Star, suffice; not the window-box, or the bird on
The ledge, which mean so much to the invalid,
Nor the joy you leaned after, as by the tracks the grass
In the emptiness after the lighted Pullmans fled,
Suffices; nor faces, which, like distraction, pass

Under the street-lamps, teasing to faith or pleasure,
Suffice you, born to no adequate definition of terror.
For yours, like a puppy, is darling and inept,
Though his cold nose brush your hand while you laugh at his clowning;
Or the kitten you sleep with, though once or twice while you slept
It tried to suck your breath, and you dreamed of drowning,
Perjured like Clarence, sluiced from the perilous hatches;

1061

[1] *American volunteer soldiers in foreign wars do not lose their citizenship.*

But never of lunar wolf-waste or the aboreal
Malignancy, with the privy breath, which watches
And humps in the dark; but only a dream, after all.
At the worst, you think, with a little twinge of distress,
That contagion may nook in the comforting fur you love to caress.

Though some, unsatisfied and sick, have brought
That immitigable face, whose smile is ice,
And fired their hearts like pitch-pine, for they thought
Better flame than the damp worm-tooth of compromise:
So Harry L. I knew, whose whores and gin
Had dwindled to a slick smile in the drug store
But for the absurd contraption of a plane,
Which flung on air the unformulable endeavor
While heart bled to lave the applauded name.
The crash was in an old cornfield; not even flame.

So some, whose passionate emptiness and tidal
Lust swayed toward the debris of Madrid,
And left New York to loll in their fierce idyll
Among the olives, where the snipers hid;
And now the North, to see that visioned face
And polarize their iron of despair,
Who praise no beauty like the boreal grace
Which greens the dead eye under the rocket's flare.
They fight old friends, for their obsession knows
Only the immaculate itch, not human friends or foes.

They sought a secret which, perhaps, the Moor,
Hieratic, white-robed, pitiless, might teach,
Who duped and dying but for pride, therefore
Hugged truth which cause or conscience scarcely reach.
As Jacob all night with the angelic foe,
They wrestle now, by frozen fen and floe,
New Courier, in fury sanctified;
And seek that face which, greasy, frost-breathed, in furs,
Bends to the bomb-sight over bitter Helsingfors.

Blood splashed on the terrorless intellect creates
Corrosive fizzle like the splattered lime,
And its enseamed stew but satiates
Itself, in that lewd and faceless pantomime.
You know, by radio, how hotly the world repeats,
When the brute crowd roars or the blunt boot-heels resound
In the Piazza or the Wilhelmplatz,
The crime of Onan, spilled upon the ground;
You know, whose dear hope Alexis Carrel kept
Alive in a test tube, where it monstrously grew, and slept.

But it is dead, and you now, guiltless, sink
To rest in lobbies, or pace gardens where
The slow god crumbles and the fountains prink,
Nor heed the criminal king, who paints the air
With discoursed madness and protruding eye,
Nor give the alarm, nor ask tonight where sleeps
That head which hooped the jewel Fidelity,
But like an old melon now, in the dank ditch, seeps;
But you crack nuts, while the conscience-stricken stare
Kisses the terror; for you see an empty chair.

(1944)

Pursuit

The hunchback on the corner, with gum and shoelaces,
Has his own wisdom and pleasures, and may not be lured
To divulge them to you, for he has merely endured
Your appeal for his sympathy and your kind purchases;
And wears infirmity but as the general who turns
Apart, in his famous old greatcoat there on the hill
At dusk when the rapture and cannonade are still,
To muse withdrawn from the dead, from his gorgeous subalterns;
Or stares from the thicket of his familiar pain, like a fawn
That meets you a moment, wheels, in imperious innocence is gone.

Go to the clinic. Wait in the outer room,
Where like an old possum the snag-nailed hand will hump
On its knee in murderous patience, and the pomp
Of pain swells like the Indies, or a plum.
And there you will stand, as on the Roman hill,
Stunned by each withdrawn gaze and severe shape,
The first barbarian victor stood to gape
At the sacrificial fathers, white-robed, still;
And even the feverish old Jew regards you with authority
Till you feel like one who has come too late, or improperly clothed, to a party.

The doctor will take you now. He is burly and clean;
Listening, like lover or worshiper, bends at your heart;
But cannot make out just what it tries to impart;
So smiles; says you simply need a change of scene.
Of scene, of solace: Therefore Florida,
Where Ponce de Leon clanked among the lilies,
Where white sails skit on blue and cavort like fillies,
And the shoulder gleams in the moonlight corridor.

1063

A change of love: if love is a groping Godward, though blind,
No matter what crevice, cranny, chink, bright in dark, the pale tentacle find.

In Florida consider the flamingo,
Its color passion but its neck a question;
Consider even that girl the other guests shun
On beach at bar, in bed, for she may know
The secret you are seeking, after all;
Or the child you humbly sit by, excited and curly,
That screams on the shore at the sea's sunlit hurlyburly.
Till the mother calls its name, toward nightfall.
Till you sit alone: in the dire meridians, off Ireland, in fury
Of spume-tooth and dawnless sea-heave, salt rimes the lookout's devout eye.

Till you sit alone—which is the beginning of error—
Behind you the music and lights of the great hotel:
Solution, perhaps, is public, despair personal,
But history held to your breath clouds like a mirror.
There are many states, and towns in them, and faces,
But meanwhile, the little old lady in black, by the wall,
Who admires all the dancers, and tells you how just last fall
Her husband died in Ohio, and damp mists her glasses;
She blinks and croaks, like a toad or a Norn, in the horrible light,
And rattles her crutch, which may put forth a small bloom, perhaps white.

(1944)

Original Sin: A Short Story

Nodding, its great head rattling like a gourd,
And locks like seaweed strung on the stinking stone,
The nightmare stumbles past, and you have heard
It fumble your door before it whimpers and is gone:
It acts like the old hound that used to snuffle your door and moan.

You thought you had lost it when you left Omaha,
For it seemed connected then with your grandpa, who
Had a wen on his forehead and sat on the veranda
To finger the precious protuberance, as was his habit to do,
Which glinted in sun like rough garnet or the rich old brain bulging through.

But you met it in Harvard Yard as the historic steeple
Was confirming the midnight with its hideous racket,
And you wondered how it had come, for it stood so imbecile,

1064

With empty hands, humble, and surely nothing in pocket:
Riding the rods, perhaps—or grandpa's will paid the ticket.

You were almost kindly then, in your first homesickness,
As it tortured its still face to speak, but scarcely mewed;
Since then you have outlived all your homesickness,
But have met it in many another distempered latitude:
Oh, nothing is lost, ever lost! at last you understood.

But it never came in the quantum glare of sun
To shame you before your friends, and had nothing to do
With your public experience or private reformation:
But it thought no bed too narrow—it stood with lips askew
And shook its great head sadly like the abstract Jew.

Never met you in the lyric arsenical meadows
When children call and your heart goes stone in the bosom;
At the orchard anguish never, nor ovoid horrow,
Which is furred like a peach or avid like the delicious plum.
It takes no part in your classic prudence or fondled axiom.

Not there when you exclaimed: "Hope is betrayed by
Disastrous glory of sea-capes, sun-torment of whitecaps
—There must be a new innocence for us to be stayed by."
But there it stood, after all the timetables, all the maps,
In the crepuscular clatter of *always, always, or perhaps.*

You have moved often and rarely left an address,
And hear of the deaths of friends with sly pleasure,
A sense of cleansing and hope, which blooms from distress;
But it has not died, it comes, its hand childish, unsure,
Clutching the bribe of chocolate or a toy you used to treasure.

It tries the lock; you hear, but simply drowse:
There is nothing remarkable in that sound at the door.
Later you may hear it wander the dark house
Like a mother who rises at night to seek a childhood picture;
Or it goes to the backyard and stands like an old horse cold in the pasture.

(*1944*)

The Ballad of Billie Potts

(When I was a child I heard this story from an old lady who was a relative
of mine. The scene, according to her version, was in the section of Western Ken-

tucky known as "Between the Rivers," the region between the Cumberland and the Tennessee. Years later, I came across another version in a book on the history of the outlaws of the Cave Inn Rock, or the Cave-In-Rock. The name of Bards-town in the present account refers to Bardstown, Kentucky, where the first race track west of the mountains was laid out late in the eighteenth century.)

Big Billie Potts was big and stout
In the land between the rivers.
His shoulders were wide and his gut stuck out
Like a croker of nubbins and his holler and shout
Made the bob-cat shiver and the black-jack leaves shake
In the section between the rivers.
He would slap you on your back and laugh.

Big Billie had a wife, she was dark and little
In the land between the rivers,
And clever with her wheel and clever with her kettle,
But she never said a word and when she sat
By the fire her eyes worked slow and narrow like a cat
In the land between the rivers.
Nobody knew what was in her head.

They had a big boy with fuzz on his chin
So tall he ducked the door when he came in,
In the land between the rivers,
A clabber-headed bastard with snot in his nose
And big red wrists hanging out of his clothes
And a whicker when he laughed where his father had a beller
In the section between the rivers.
They called him Little Billie.
He was their darling.

(It was not hard to see the land, what it was.
Low hills, and oak. The fetid bottoms where
The slough uncoiled and in the tangled cane,
Where no sun comes, the muskrat's astute face
Was lifted to the yammering jay; then dropped.
Some cabin where the shag-bark stood and the
Magnificent tulip-tree; both now are gone.
But the land is there, and as you top a rise,
Beyond you all the landscape steams and simmers
—The hills, now gutted, red, cane-brake and black-jack yet.
The oak leaf steams under the powerful sun.
"Mister, is this the right road to Paducah?"
The red face, seamed and gutted like the hill,
Slow under time, and with the innocent savagery

1066

Of Time, the bleared eyes rolling, answers from
Your dream: "They names hit so, but I ain't bin.")

Big Billie was the kind who laughed but could spy
The place for a ferry where folks would come by
In the land between the rivers.
He built an inn and folks bound West
Hitched their horses there to take their rest
And grease the gall and grease the belly
And jaw and spit under the trees
In the section between the rivers.
Big Billie said: "Git down, friend, and take yore ease!"
He would slap you on your back and set you at his table.

(Leaning and slow, you see them move
In massive passion colder than any love:
Their lips move but you do not hear the words
Nor trodden twig nor fluted irony of birds
Nor hear the rustle of the heart
That, heave and settle, gasp and start,
Heaves like a fish in the ribs' dark basket borne
West from the great water's depth whence it was torn.

Their names are like the leaves, but are forgot
—The slush and swill of the world's great pot
That foamed at the range's lip, and spilled
Like quicksilver across green baize, the unfulfilled
Disparate glitter, gleam, wild symptom, seed
Flung in the long wind: silent, proceed
Past meadow, salt-lick, and the lyric swale;
Enter the arbor, shadow of trees, fade, fail.)

Big Billie was sharp at swap and trade
And could smell the nest where the egg was laid,
He could read and cipher and they called him squire
In the land between the rivers.
And he added up his money while he sat by the fire
And sat in the shade while folks sweated and strove,
For he was the one who fatted and throve,
In the section between the rivers.
"Thank you kindly, sir," Big Billie would say
When the man in the black coat paid him at streak of day
And swung to the saddle and was ready to go
And rode away and didn't know
That he was already as good as dead
In the section between the rivers.
For at midnight the message had been sent ahead:
"Man in black coat, riding bay mare with star."

1067

(There was a beginning but you cannot see it.
There will be an end but you cannot see it.
They will not turn their faces to you though you call,
Who pace a logic merciless as light,
Whose law is their long shadow on the grass,
Sun at the back; pace, pass,
And passing nod in that glacial delirium
While the tight sky shudders like a drum
And speculation rasps its idiot nails
Across the dry slate where you did the sum.

The answer is in the back of the book but the page is gone.
And grandma told you to tell the truth but she is dead.
And heedless, their hairy faces fixed
Beyond your call or question now, they move
Under the infatuate weight of their wisdom,
Precious but for the preciousness of their burden,
Sainted and sad and sage as the hairy ass, who bear
History like bound faggots, with stiff knees;
And breathe the immaculate climate where
The lucent leaf is lifted, lank beard fingered, by no breeze,
Rapt in the fabulous complacency of fresco, vase, or frieze:

And the testicles of the fathers hang down like old lace.)

Little Billie was full of steam and vinegar
And full of sap as a maple tree
And full of tricks as a lop-eared pup,
In the land between the rivers.
So one night when the runner didn't show up,
Big Billie called Little and said, "Saddle up,"
And nodded toward the man who was taking his sup
With his belt unlatched and his feet to the fire.
Big Billie said, "Give Amos a try,
Fer this feller takes the South Fork and Amos'll be nigher
Than Baldy or Buster, and Amos is sly
And slick as a varmint, and I don't deny
I lak bizness with Amos fer he's one you kin trust
In the section between the rivers,
And hit looks lak they's mighty few.
Amos will split up fair and square."

Little Billie had something in his clabber-head
In addition to snot, and he reckoned he knew
How to skin a cat or add two and two.
So long before the sky got red
Over the land between the rivers,

1068

He hobbled his horse back in the swamp
And squatted on his hams in the morning dew and damp
And scratched his stomach and grinned to think
How his Pap would be proud and his Mammy glad
To know what a thriving boy they had
In the section between the rivers.
He always was a good boy to his darling Mammy.

(Think of yourself riding away from the dawn,
Think of yourself and the unnamed ones who had gone
Before, riding, who rode away from *goodbye, goodbye,*
And toward *hello,* toward Time's unwinking eye;
And like the cicada had left, at cross-roads or square,
The old shell of self, thin, ghostly, translucent, light as air;
At dawn riding into the curtain of unwhispering green,
Away from the vigils and voices into the green
World, land of the innocent bough, land of the leaf.
Think of your face green in the submarine light of the leaf.

Or think of yourself couched at the swamp-edge,
Dawn-silence past last owl-hoot and not yet at day-verge
First bird-stir, titmouse or drowsy warbler not yet.
You touch the grass in the dark and your hand is wet.
Then light: you wait for the stranger's hoofs on the soft trace,
And under the green leaf's translucence the light bathes your face.

Think of yourself at dawn: Which are you? What?)

Little Billie heard hoofs on the soft grass,
But he squatted and let the rider pass,
For he didn't want to waste good lead and powder
Just to make the slough-fish and swamp-buzzard prouder
In the land between the rivers.
But he saw the feller's face and thanked his luck
It was the one Pap said was fit to pluck.
So he got on his horse and cantered up the trace.
Called, "Hi thar!" and the stranger watched him coming,
And sat his mare with a smile on his face,
Just watching Little Billie and smiling and humming
In the section between the rivers.
Little Billie rode up and the stranger said,
"Why bless my heart, if it ain't Little Billie!"

"Good mornen," said Billie, and said, "My Pap
Found somethin you left and knowed you'd be missen,
And he ain't wanten nuthin not proper his'n."
But the stranger didn't do a thing but smile and listen

1069

Polite as could be to what Billie said.
But he must have had eyes in the side of his head
As they rode along beside the slough
In the land between the rivers,
Or known what Billie was out to do,
For when Billie said, "Mister, I've brung hit to you,"
And reached his hand for it down in his britches,
The stranger just reached his own hand, too.

"Boom!" Billie's gun said, and the derringer, "Bang!"
"Oh, I'm shot!" Billie howled and grabbed his shoulder.
"Nor bad," said the stranger, "for you're born to hang,
But I'll save some rope 'fore you're a minute older
If you don't high-tail to your honest Pap
In the section between the rivers."
Oh, Billie didn't tarry and Billie didn't linger,
For Billie didn't trust the stranger's finger
And didn't admire the stranger's face
And didn't like the climate of the place,
So he turned and high-tailed up the trace,
With blood on his shirt and snot in his nose
And the stranger just sits and admires how he goes
In the section between the rivers,
And says, "Why, that boy would do right well back on the Bardstown track!"

"You fool!" said his Pap, but his Mammy cried
To see the place where the gore-blood dried
Round the little hole in her darling's hide.
She wiped his nose and patted his head,
But Pappy barred the door and Pappy said,
"That bastard has maybe got some friends
In the section between the rivers,
And you can't say how sich bizness ends
And a man ain't sure he kin trust his neighbors,
For thar's a mortal spite fer him sweats and labors
Even here between the rivers."
He didn't ask Little how he felt,
But said, "Two hundred in gold's in my money belt,
And take the roan and the brand-new saddle
And stop yore blubberen and skeedaddle,
And the next time you try and pull a trick
Fer God's sake don't talk but do hit quick."
So Little Billie took his leave
And left his Mammy there to grieve
And left his Pappy in Old Kaintuck
And headed West to try his luck
And left the land between the rivers,

1070

For it was Roll, Missouri,
It was Roll, roll, Missouri.
And he was gone nigh ten long year
And never sent word to give his Pappy cheer
Nor wet pen in ink for his Mammy dear.
For Little Billie never was much of a hand with pen-staff.
(There is always another country and always another place.
There is always another name and another face.
And the name and the face are you, and you
The name and the face, and the stream you gaze into
Will show the adoring face, show the lips that lift to you
As you lean with the implacable thirst of self,
As you lean to the image which is yourself,
To set the lip to lip, fix eye on bulging eye,
To drink not of the stream but of your deep identity.
But water is water and it flows,
Under the image on the water the water coils and goes
And its own beginning and its end only the water knows.
There are many countries and the rivers in them
—Cumberland, Tennessee, Ohio, Colorado, Pecos, Little Big Horn,
And Roll, Missouri, roll.
But there is only water in them.

And in the new country and in the new place
The eyes of the new friend will reflect the new face
And his mouth will speak to frame
The syllables of the new name
And the name is you and is the agitation of the air
And is the wind and the wind runs and the wind is everywhere.

The name and the face are you.
The name and the face are always new
And they are you.
Are new.

For they have been dipped in the healing flood.
For they have been dipped in the redeeming blood.
For they have been dipped in Time
And Time is only beginnings
Time is only and always beginnings
And is the redemption of our crime
And is our Saviour's priceless blood.

For Time is always the new place,   **1071**
And no-place.
For Time is always the new name and the new face,
And no-name and no-face.

For Time is motion
For Time is innocence
For Time is West.)

Oh, who is coming along the trace,
Whistling along in the late sunshine,
With a big black hat above his big red face
And a long black coat that swings so fine?
Oh, who is riding along the trace
Back to the land between the rivers,
With a big black beard growing down to his guts
And silver mountings on his pistol-butts
And a belt as broad as a saddle-girth
And a look in his eyes like he owned the earth?
And meets a man riding up the trace
And looks right sharp and scans his face
And says, "Durn if'n hit ain't Joe Drew!"
"I reckin hit's me," says Joe and gives a spit,
"But whupped if'n I figger how you knows hit,
Fer if'n I'm Joe, then who air you?"
And the man with the black beard says: "Why, I'm Little Billie!"
And Joe Drew says: "Wal, I'll be whupped."

"Be whupped," Joe said, "and whar you goen?"
"Oh, I'm just visiten back whar I done my growen
In the section between the rivers,
Fer I bin out West and taken my share
And I reckin my luck helt out fer fair,
So I done come home," Little Billie said,
"To see my folks if'n they ain't dead."
"Ain't dead," Joe answered, and shook his head,
"But that's the best a man kin say,
Fer it looked lak when you went away
You taken West your Pappy's luck
And maybe now you kin bring hit back
To the section between the rivers."
Little Billie laughed and jangled his pockets and said: "Ain't nuthen wrong with
    my luck."

And said: "Wal, I'll be gitten on home
But after yore supper why don't you come
And we'll open a jug and you tell me the news
In the section between the rivers.
1072   But not too early fer hit's my aim
To git me some fun 'fore they know my name,
And tease 'em and fun 'em fer you never guessed
I was Little Billie what went out West."
And Joe Drew said: "Durn if'n you always wuzn't a hand to git yore fun."

(Over the plain, over mountain and river, drawn,
Wanderer with slit-eyes adjusted to distance,
Drawn out of distance, drawn from the great plateau
Where the sky heeled in the unsagging wind and the cheek burned,
Who stood beneath the white peak that glimmered like a dream,
And spat, and it was morning and it was morning.
You lay among the wild plums and the kildees cried.
You lay in the thicket under the new leaves and the kildees cried,
For all your luck, for all the astuteness of your heart,
And would not stop and would not stop
And the clock ticked all night long in the furnished room
And would not stop
And the *El*-train passed on the quarters with a whish like a terrible broom
And would not stop
And there is always the sound of breathing in the next room
And it will not stop
And the waitress says, "Will that be all, sir, will that be all?"
And will not stop
And the valet says, "Will that be all, sir, will that be all?"
And will not stop
For nothing is ever all and nothing is ever all,
For all your experience and your expertness of human vices and of valor
At the hour when the ways are darkened.

Though your luck held and the market was always satisfactory,
Though the letter always came and your lovers were always true,
Though you always received the respect due to your position,
Though your hand never failed of its cunning and your glands always thoroughly
    knew their business,
Though your conscience was easy and you were assured of your innocence,
You became gradually aware that something was missing from the picture,
And upon closer inspection exclaimed: "Why, I'm not in it at all!"
Which was perfectly true.

Therefore you tried to remember when you had last had whatever it was you
    had lost,
But it was a long time back.
And you decided to retrace your steps from that point,
But it was a long way back.
It was, nevertheless, absolutely essential to make the effort,
And since you had never been a man to be deterred by difficult circumstances,
You came back.
For there is no place like home.)

1073

He joked them and he teased them and he had his fun
And they never guessed that he was the one
Had been Mammy's darling and Pappy's joy
When he was a great big whickering boy

In the land between the rivers,
And he jingled his pockets and he took his sop
And patted his belly which was full nigh to pop
And wiped the buttermilk out of his beard
And took his belch and up he reared
Back from the table and cocked his chair
And said: "Old man, ain't you got any fresh drinken water, this here ain't
    fresherer'n a hoss-puddle?"
And the old woman said: "Pappy, why don't you take the young gentleman down
    to the spring so he kin git hit good and fresh?"
And the old woman gave the old man a straight look.
She gave him the bucket, but it was not empty, but it was not water.

Oh, the stars are shining and the meadow is bright
But under the trees is dark and night
In the land between the rivers.
Oh, on the trace the fireflies spark
But under the trees is night and dark,
And way off yonder is the whippoorwill
And the owl off yonder hoots on the hill
But under the trees is dark and still
In the section between the rivers.
And the leaves hang down in the dark of the trees
And there is the spring in the dark of the trees
And there is the spring as black as ink
And one star in it caught through a chink
Of the leaves that hang down in the dark of the trees,
And the star is there but it does not wink.
And Little Billie gets down on his knees
And props his hands in the same old place
To sup the water at his ease;
And the star is gone but there is his face.
"Just help yoreself," Big Billie said;
Then set the hatchet in his head.

They went through his pockets and they buried him in the dark of the trees.
"I figgered he was a ripe 'un," the old man said.
"Yeah, but you wouldn't done nuthen hadn't bin fer me," the old woman said.

(The reflection is shadowy and the form not clear,
For the hour is late, is late, and scarcely a glimmer comes here
Under the leaf, the bough, in its innocence dark;
And under your straining face you can scarcely mark
The darkling gleam of your face little less than the water dark.

1074

But perhaps what you lost was lost in the pool long ago
When childlike you lost it and then in your innocence rose to go
After kneeling, as now, with your thirst beneath the leaves:

And years it lies here and dreams in the depth and grieves,
More faithful than mother or father in the light or dark of the leaves.
But after, after the irrefutable modes and marches,
After waters that never quench the thirst in the throat that parches,
After the sleep that sieves the long day's dubieties
And the cricket's corrosive wisdom under the trees,
After the rumor of wind and the bright anonymities,

You come, weary of greetings and the new friend's smile,
Weary in art of the stranger, worn with your wanderer's wile,
Weary of innocence and the husks of Time,
Prodigal, back to the homeland of no-Time,
To ask forgiveness and the patrimony of your crime;

And kneel in the untutored night as to demand
What gift—Oh, father, father—from that dissevering hand?)

"And whar's Little Billie?" Joe Drew said.
"Air you crazy," said Big, "and plum outa yore head,
Fer you knows he went West nigh ten long year?"
"Went West," Joe said, "but I seen him here
In the section between the rivers,
Riden up the trace as big as you please
With a long black coat comen down to his knees
And a big black beard comen down to his guts
And silver mountens on his pistol-butts.
And he said out West how he done struck
It rich and wuz bringen back yore luck
To the land between the rivers."
"I shore-God could use some luck," Big Billie said,
But his woman wet her lips and craned her head
And said: "Come riden with a big black beard, you say?"
And Joe: "Oh, hit wuz Billie as big as day."
And the old man's eyes bugged out of a sudden and he croaked like a sick
    bull-frog and said: "Come riden with a long black coat?"

Oh, the night is still and the grease-lamp low
And the old man's breath comes wheeze and slow.
Oh, the blue flame sucks on the old rag wick
And the old woman's breath comes sharp and quick,
And there isn't a sound under the roof
But her breath's hiss and his breath's puff,
And there isn't a sound outside the door
As they hearken but cannot hear any more
The creak of the saddle or the plop of the hoof,
For a long time now Joe Drew's been gone
And left them sitting there alone

1075

While the dark outside gets big and still,
For the owl doesn't hoot off there on the hill
Any more and is quiet, and the whippoorwill
Is quiet in the dark of the trees and still
In the land between the rivers.
And so they sit and breathe and wait
And breathe while the night gets big and late,
And neither of them gives move or stir
And she won't look at him and he won't look at her.
He doesn't look at her but he says: "Git me the spade."
She grabbled with her hands and he dug with the spade
Where the leaves let down the dark and shade
In the land between the rivers.
She grabbled like a dog in the hole they made,
But stopped of a sudden and then she said,
"I kin put my hand on his face."
They light up a pine-knot and lean at the place
Where the man in the black coat slumbers and lies
With trash in his beard and dirt on his face;
And the torch-flame shines in his wide-open eyes.
Down the old man leans with the flickering flame
And moves his lips, says: "Tell me his name."
"Ain't Billie, ain't Billie," the old woman cries,
"Oh, hit ain't my Billie, fer he wuz little
And helt to my skirt while I stirred the kittle
And called me Mammy and hugged me tight
And come in the house when hit fell night."
But the old man leans down with the flickering flame
And croaks: "But tell me his name."
"Oh, he ain't got none, fer he just come riden
From some fer place whar he'd bin biden,
And ain't got a name and never had none,
But Billie, my Billie, he had one,
And hit wuz Billie, hit wuz his name."
But the old man croaked: "Tell me his name";
"Oh, he ain't got none and hit's all the same,
But Billie had one, and he wuz little
And offen his chin I would wipe the spittle
And wiped the drool and kissed him thar
And counted his toes and kissed him whar
The little black mark wuz under his tit,
Shaped lak a clover under his left tit,
With a shape fer luck and I'd kiss hit—"
And the old man blinks in the pine-knot flare
And his mouth comes open like a fish for air,
Then he says right low, "I had nigh fergot."
"Oh, I kissed him on his little luck-spot

1076

And I kissed and he'd laff as lak as not—"
The old man said: "Git his shirt open."
The old woman opened the shirt and there was the birthmark under the left tit.
It was shaped for luck.

(The bee knows, and the eel's cold ganglia burn,
And the sad head lifting to the long return,
Through brumal deeps, in the great unsolsticed coil,
Carries its knowledge, nagivator without star,
And under the stars, pure in its clamorous toil,
The goose hoots north where the starlit marshes are.
The salmon heaves at the fall, and wanderer, you
Heave at the great fall of Time, and gorgeous, gleam
In the powerful arc, and anger and outrage like dew,
In your plunge, fling, and plunge to the thunderous stream:
Back to the silence, back to the pool, back
To the high pool, motionless, and the unmurmuring dream.
And you, wanderer, back,
Brother to pinion and the pious fin that cleave
Their innocence of air and the disinfectant flood
And wing and welter and weave
The long compulsion and the circuit hope
Back,
And bear through that limitless and devouring fluidity
The itch and humble promise which is home.
And you, wanderer, back,
For the beginning is death and the end may be life,
For the beginning was definition and the end may be definition,
And our innocence needs, perhaps, new definition,
And the wick needs the flame
And the father waits for the son.
The hour is late,
The scene familiar even in shadow,
The transaction brief,
And you, wanderer, back,
After the striving and the wind's word,
To kneel
Here in the evening empty of wind or bird,
Or kneel in the sacramental silence of evening
And the feet of the old man
And the evil and ignorant and old,
But her
And there little black mark under your heart,
Which is your name,
Which is shaped for luck,
Which is your luck.)

1077

(1944)

Blackberry Winter

It was getting into June and past eight o'clock in the morning, but there was a fire—even if it wasn't a big fire, just a fire of chunks—on the hearth of the big stone fireplace in the living room. I was standing on the hearth, almost into the chimney, hunched over the fire, working my bare toes slowly on the warm stone. I relished the heat which made the skin of my bare legs warp and creep and tingle, even as I called to my mother, who was somewhere back in the dining room or kitchen, and said: "But it's June, I don't have to put them on!"

"You put them on if you are going out," she called.

I tried to assess the degree of authority and conviction in the tone, but at that distance it was hard to decide. I tried to analyze the tone, and then I thought what a fool I had been to start out the back door and let her see that I was barefoot. If I had gone out the front door or the side door she would never have known, not till dinner time anyway, and by then the day would have been half-gone and I would have been all over the farm to see what the storm had done and down to the creek to see the flood. But it had never crossed my mind that they would try to stop you from going barefoot in June, no matter if there had been a gully-washer and a cold spell.

Nobody had ever tried to stop me in June as long as I could remember, and when you are nine years old, what you remember seems forever; for you remember everything and everything is important and stands big and full and fills up Time and is so solid that you can walk around and around it like a tree and look at it. You are aware that time passes, that there is a movement in time, but that is not what Time is. Time is not a movement, a flowing, a wind then, but is, rather, a kind of climate in which things are, and when a thing happens it begins to live and keeps on living and stands solid in Time like the tree that you can walk around. And if there is a movement, the movement is not Time itself, any more than a breeze is climate, and all the breeze does is to shake a little the leaves on the tree which is alive and solid. When you are nine, you know that there are things that you don't know, but you know that when you know something you know it. You know how a thing has been and you know that you can go barefoot in June. You do not understand that voice from back in the kitchen which says that you cannot go barefoot outdoors and run to see what has happened and rub your feet over the wet shivery grass and make the perfect mark of your foot in the smooth, creamy, red mud and then muse upon it as though you had suddenly come upon that single mark on the glistening auroral beach of the world. You have never seen a beach, but you have read the book and how the footprint was there.

The voice had said what it had said, and I looked savagely at the black stockings and the strong, scuffed brown shoes which I had brought from my closet as far as the hearth rug. I called once more, "But it's June," and waited.

"It's June," the voice replied from far away, "but it's blackberry winter."

I had lifted my head to reply to that, to make one more test of what was in that tone, when I happened to see the man.

The fireplace in the living room was at the end; for the stone chimney was built, as in so many of the farmhouses in Tennessee, at the end of a gable, and there was a window on each side of the chimney. Out of the window on the north side of the fireplace I could see the man. When I saw the man I did not call out what I had intended, but, engrossed by the strangeness of the sight, watched him, still far off, come along the path by the edge of the woods.

What was strange was that there should be a man there at all. That path went along the yard fence, between the fence and the woods which came right down to the yard, and then on back past the chicken runs and on by the woods until it was lost to sight where the woods bulged out and cut off the back field. There the path disappeared into the woods. It led on back, I knew, through the woods and to the swamp, skirted the swamp where the big trees gave way to sycamores and water oaks and willows and tangled cane, and then led on to the river. Nobody ever went back there except people who wanted to gig frogs in the swamp or to fish in the river or to hunt in the woods, and those people, if they didn't have a standing permission from my father, always stopped to ask permission to cross the farm. But the man whom I now saw wasn't, I could tell even at that distance, a sportsman. And what would a sportsman have been doing down there after a storm? Besides, he was coming from the river, and nobody had gone down there that morning. I knew that for a fact, because if anybody had passed, certainly if a stranger had passed, the dogs would have made a racket and would have been out on him. But this man was coming up from the river and had come up through the woods. I suddenly had a vision of him moving up the grassy path in the woods, in the green twilight under the big trees, not making any sound on the path, while now and then, like drops off the eaves, a big drop of water would fall from a leaf or bough and strike a stiff oak leaf lower down with a small, hollow sound like a drop of water hitting tin. That sound, in the silence of the woods, would be very significant.

When you are a boy and stand in the stillness of woods, which can be so still that your heart almost stops beating and makes you want to stand there in the green twilight until you feel your very feet sinking into and clutching the earth like roots and your body breathing slow through its pores like the leaves—when you stand there and wait for the next drop to drop with its small, flat sound to a lower leaf, that sound seems to measure out something, to put an end to something, to begin something, and you cannot wait for it to happen and are afraid it will not happen, and then when it has happened, you are waiting again, almost afraid.

But the man whom I saw coming through the woods in my mind's eye did not pause and wait, growing into the ground and breathing with the enormous, soundless breathing of the leaves. Instead, I saw him moving in the green twilight inside my head as he was moving at that very moment along the path by the edge of the woods, coming toward the house. He was moving steadily, but not fast, with his shoulders hunched a little and his head thrust forward, like a man who has come a long way and has a long way to go. I shut my eyes for a couple of seconds, thinking that when I opened them he would not be there at all. There was no place for him to have come from, and there was no reason for him to come where he was coming, toward our house. But I opened my

1079

eyes, and there he was, and he was coming steadily along the side of the woods. He was not yet even with the back chicken yard.

"Mama," I called.

"You put them on," the voice said.

"There's a man coming," I called, "out back."

She did not reply to that, and I guessed that she had gone to the kitchen window to look. She would be looking at the man and wondering who he was and what he wanted, the way you always do in the country, and if I went back there now she would not notice right off whether or not I was barefoot. So I went back to the kitchen.

She was standing by the window. "I don't recognize him," she said, not looking around at me.

"Where could he be coming from?" I asked.

"I don't know," she said.

"What would he be doing down at the river? At night? In the storm?"

She studied the figure out the window, then said, "Oh, I reckon maybe he cut across from the Dunbar place."

That was, I realized, a perfectly rational explanation. He had not been down at the river in the storm, at night. He had come over this morning. You could cut across from the Dunbar place if you didn't mind breaking through a lot of elder and sassafras and blackberry bushes which had about taken over the old cross path, which nobody ever used any more. That satisfied me for a moment, but only for a moment. "Mama," I asked, "what would he be doing over at the Dunbar place last night?"

Then she looked at me, and I knew I had made a mistake, for she was looking at my bare feet. "You haven't got your shoes on," she said.

But I was saved by the dogs. That instant there was a bark which I recognized as Sam, the collie, and then a heavier, churning kind of bark which was Bully, and I saw a streak of white as Bully tore round the corner of the back porch and headed out for the man. Bully was a big, bone-white bull dog, the kind of dog that they used to call a farm bull dog but that you don't see any more, heavy chested and heavy headed, but with pretty long legs. He could take a fence as light as a hound. He had just cleared the white paling fence toward the woods when my mother ran out to the back porch and began calling, "Here you, Bully! Here you!"

Bully stopped in the path, waiting for the man, but he gave a few more of those deep, gargling, savage barks that reminded you of something down a stone-lined well. The red clay mud, I saw, was splashed up over his white chest and looked exciting, like blood.

The man, however, had not stopped walking even when Bully took the fence and started at him. He had kept right on coming. All he had done was to switch a little paper parcel which he carried from the right hand to the left, and then reach into his pants pocket to get something. Then I saw the glitter and knew that he had a knife in his hand, probably the kind of mean knife just made for devilment and nothing else, with a blade as long as the blade of a frog-sticker, which will snap out ready when you press a button in the handle. That knife must have had a button in the handle, or else how could he have had the blade out glittering so quick and with just one hand?

Pulling his knife against the dogs was a funny thing to do, for Bully was a big, powerful brute and fast, and Sam was all right. If those dogs had meant business, they might have knocked him down and ripped him before he got a stroke in. He ought to have picked up a heavy stick, something to take a swipe at them with and something which they could see and respect when they came at him. But he apparently did not know much about dogs. He just held the knife blade close against the right leg, low down, and kept on moving down the path.

Then my mother had called, and Bully had stopped. So the man let the blade of the knife snap back into the handle, and dropped it into his pocket, and kept on coming. Many women would have been afraid with the strange man who they knew had that knife in his pocket. That is, if they were alone in the house with nobody but a nine-year-old boy. And my mother was alone, for my father had gone off, and Dellie, the cook, was down at her cabin because she wasn't feeling well. But my mother wasn't afraid. She wasn't a big woman, but she was clear and brisk about everything she did and looked everybody and everything right in the eye from her own blue eyes in her tanned face. She had been the first woman in the county to ride a horse astride (that was back when she was a girl and long before I was born), and I have seen her snatch up a pump gun and go out and knock a chicken hawk out of the air like a busted skeet when he came over her chicken yard. She was a steady and self-reliant woman, and when I think of her now after all the years she has been dead, I think of her brown hands, not big, but somewhat square for a woman's hands, with square-cut nails. They looked, as a matter of fact, more like a young boy's hands than a grown woman's. But back then it never crossed my mind that she would ever be dead.

She stood on the back porch and watched the man enter the back gate, where the dogs (Bully had leaped back into the yard) were dancing and muttering and giving sidelong glances back to my mother to see if she meant what she had said. The man walked right by the dogs, almost brushing them, and didn't pay them any attention. I could see now that he wore old khaki pants, and a dark wool coat with stripes in it, and a gray felt hat. He had on a gray shirt with blue stripes in it, and no tie. But I could see a tie, blue and reddish, sticking in his side coat-pocket. Everything was wrong about what he wore. He ought to have been wearing blue jeans or overalls, and a straw hat or an old black felt hat, and the coat, granting that he might have been wearing a wool coat and not a jumper, ought not to have had those stripes. Those clothes, despite the fact that they were old enough and dirty enough for any tramp, didn't belong there in our back yard, coming down the path, in Middle Tennessee, miles away from any big town, and even a mile off the pike.

When he got almost to the steps, without having said anything, my mother, very matter-of-factly, said, "Good morning."

"Good morning," he said, and stopped and looked her over. He did not take off his hat, and under the brim you could see the perfectly unmemorable face, which wasn't old and wasn't young, or thick or thin. It was grayish and covered with about three days of stubble. The eyes were a kind of nondescript, muddy hazel, or something like that, rather bloodshot. His teeth, when he opened his mouth, showed yellow and uneven. A couple of them had been knocked out.

1081

You knew that they had been knocked out, because there was a scar, not very old, there on the lower lip just beneath the gap.

"Are you hunting work?" my mother asked him.

"Yes," he said—not "yes, mam"—and still did not take off his hat.

"I don't know about my husband, for he isn't here," she said, and didn't mind a bit telling the tramp, or whoever he was, with the mean knife in his pocket, that no man was around, "but I can give you a few things to do. The storm has drowned a lot of my chicks. Three coops of them. You can gather them up and bury them. Bury them deep so the dogs won't get at them. In the woods. And fix the coops the wind blew over. And down yonder beyond that pen by the edge of the woods are some drowned poults. They got out and I couldn't get them in. Even after it started to rain hard. Poults haven't got any sense."

"What are them things—poults?" he demanded, and spat on the brick walk. He rubbed his foot over the spot, and I saw that he wore a black, pointed-toe low shoe, all cracked and broken. It was a crazy kind of shoe to be wearing in the country.

"Oh, they're young turkeys," my mother was saying. "And they haven't got any sense. I oughtn't to try to raise them around here with so many chickens, anyway. They don't thrive near chickens, even in separate pens. And I won't give up my chickens." Then she stopped herself and resumed briskly on the note of business. "When you finish that, you can fix my flower beds. A lot of trash and mud and gravel has washed down. Maybe you can save some of my flowers if you are careful."

"Flowers," the man said, in a low, impersonal voice which seemed to have a wealth of meaning, but a meaning which I could not fathom. As I think back on it, it probably was not pure contempt. Rather, it was a kind of impersonal and distant marveling that he should be on the verge of grubbing in a flower bed. He said the word, and then looked off across the yard.

"Yes, flowers," my mother replied with some asperity, as though she would have nothing said or implied against flowers. "And they were very fine this year." Then she stopped and looked at the man. "Are you hungry?" she demanded.

"Yeah," he said.

"I'll fix you something," she said, "before you get started." She turned to me. "Show him where he can wash up," she commanded, and went into the house.

I took the man to the end of the porch where a pump was and where a couple of wash pans sat on a low shelf for people to use before they went into the house. I stood there while he laid down his little parcel wrapped in newspaper and took off his hat and looked around for a nail to hang it on. He poured the water and plunged his hands into it. They were big hands, and strong looking, but they did not have the creases and the earth-color of the hands of men who work outdoors. But they were dirty, with black dirt ground into the skin and under the nails. After he had washed his hands, he poured another basin of water and washed his face. He dried his face, and with the towel still dangling in his grasp, stepped over to the mirror on the house wall. He rubbed one hand over the stubble on his face. Then he carefully inspected his face, turning first

1082

one side and then the other, and stepped back and settled his striped coat down on his shoulders. He had the movements of a man who had just dressed up to go to church or a party—the way he settled his coat and smoothed it and scanned himself in the mirror.

Then he caught my glance on him. He glared at me for an instant out of the bloodshot eyes, then demanded in a low, harsh voice, "What you looking at?"

"Nothing," I managed to say, and stepped back a step from him.

He flung the towel down, crumpled, on the shelf, and went toward the kitchen door and entered without knocking.

My mother said something to him which I could not catch. I started to go in again, then thought about my bare feet, and decided to go back of the chicken yard, where the man would have to come to pick up the dead chicks. I hung around behind the chicken house until he came out.

He moved across the chicken yard with a fastidious, not quite finicking motion, looking down at the curdled mud flecked with bits of chicken-droppings. The mud curled up over the soles of his black shoes. I stood back from him some six feet and watched him pick up the first of the drowned chicks. He held it up by one foot and inspected it.

There is nothing deader looking than a drowned chick. The feet curl in that feeble, empty way which back when I was a boy, even if I was a country boy who did not mind hog-killing or frog-gigging, made me feel hollow in the stomach. Instead of looking plump and fluffy, the body is stringy and limp with the fluff plastered to it, and the neck is long and loose like a little string of rag. And the eyes have that bluish membrane over them which makes you think of a very old man who is sick about to die.

The man stood there and inspected the chick. Then he looked all around as though he didn't know what to do with it.

"There's a great big old basket in the shed," I said, and pointed to the shed attached to the chicken house.

He inspected me as though he had just discovered my presence, and moved toward the shed.

"There's a spade there, too," I added.

He got the basket and began to pick up the other chicks, picking each one up slowly by a foot and then flinging it into the basket with a nasty, snapping motion. Now and then he would look at me out of the bloodshot eyes. Every time he seemed on the verge of saying something, but he did not. Perhaps he was building up to say something to me, but I did not wait that long. His way of looking at me made me so uncomfortable that I left the chicken yard.

Besides, I had just remembered that the creek was in flood, over the bridge, and that people were down there watching it. So I cut across the farm toward the creek. When I got to the big tobacco field I saw that it had not suffered much. The land lay right and not many tobacco plants had washed out of the ground. But I knew that a lot of tobacco round the country had been washed right out. My father had said so at breakfast.

My father was down at the bridge. When I came out of the gap in the osage hedge into the road, I saw him sitting on his mare over the heads of the other men who were standing around, admiring the flood. The creek was big here, even in low water; for only a couple of miles away it ran into the river, and

1083

when a real flood came, the red water got over the pike where it dipped down to the bridge, which was an iron bridge, and high over the floor and even the side railings of the bridge. Only the upper iron work would show, with the water boiling and frothing red and white around it. That creek rose so fast and so heavy because a few miles back it came down out of the hills, where the gorges filled up with water in no time when a rain came. The creek ran in a deep bed with limestone bluffs along both sides until it got within three quarters of a mile of the bridge, and when it came out from between those bluffs in flood it was boiling and hissing and steaming like water from a fire hose.

Whenever there was a flood, people from half the county would come down to see the sight. After a gully-washer there would not be any work to do anyway. If it didn't ruin your crop, you couldn't plow and you felt like taking a holiday to celebrate. If it did ruin your crop, there wasn't anything to do except to try to take your mind off the mortgage, if you were rich enough to have a mortgage, and if you couldn't afford a mortgage you needed something to take your mind off how hungry you would be by Christmas. So people would come down to the bridge and look at the flood. It made something different from the run of days.

There would not be much talking after the first few minutes of trying to guess how high the water was this time. The men and kids just stood around, or sat their horses or mules, as the case might be, or stood up in the wagon beds. They looked at the strangeness of the flood for an hour or two, and then somebody would say that he had better be getting on home to dinner and would start walking down the gray, puddled limestone pike, or would touch heel to his mount and start off. Everybody always knew what it would be like when he got down to the bridge, but people always came. It was like church or a funeral. They always came, that is, if it was summer and the flood unexpected. Nobody ever came down in winter to see high water.

When I came out of the gap in the bodock hedge, I saw the crowd, perhaps fifteen or twenty men and a lot of kids, and saw my father sitting his mare, Nellie Gray. He was a tall, limber man and carried himself well. I was always proud to see him sit a horse, he was so quiet and straight, and when I stepped through the gap of the hedge that morning, the first thing that happened was, I remember, the warm feeling I always had when I saw him up on a horse, just sitting. I did not go toward him, but skirted the crowd on the far side, to get a look at the creek. For one thing, I was not sure what he would say about the fact that I was barefoot. But the first thing I knew, I heard his voice calling, "Seth!"

I went toward him, moving apologetically past the men, who bent their large, red or thin, sallow faces above me. I knew some of the men, and knew their names, but because those I knew were there in a crowd, mixed with the strange faces, they seemed foreign to me, and not friendly. I did not look up at my father until I was almost within touching distance of his heel. Then I looked up and tried to read his face, to see if he was angry about my being barefoot. Before I could decide anything from that impassive, high-boned face, he had leaned over and reached a hand to me. "Grab on," he commanded.

I grabbed on and gave a little jump, and he said, "Up-see-daisy!" and whisked me, light as a feather, up to the pommel of his McClellan saddle.

"You can see better up here," he said, slid back on the cantle a little to make me more comfortable, and then, looking over my head at the swollen, tumbling water, seemed to forget all about me. But his right hand was laid on my side, just above my thigh, to steady me.

I was sitting there as quiet as I could, feeling the faint stir of my father's chest against my shoulders as it rose and fell with his breath, when I saw the cow. At first, looking up the creek, I thought it was just another big piece of driftwood steaming down the creek in the ruck of water, but all at once a pretty good-size boy who had climbed part way up a telephone pole by the pike so that he could see better yelled out, "Golly-damn, look at that-air cow!"

Everybody looked. It was a cow all right, but it might just as well have been driftwood; for it was dead as a chunk, rolling and roiling down the creek, appearing and disappearing, feet up or head up, it didn't matter which.

The cow started up the talk again. Somebody wondered whether it would hit one of the clear places under the top girder of the bridge and get through or whether it would get tangled in the drift and trash that had piled against the upright girders and braces. Somebody remembered how about ten years before so much driftwood had piled up on the bridge that it was knocked off its foundations. Then the cow hit. It hit the edge of the drift against one of the girders, and hung there. For a few seconds it seemed as though it might tear loose, but then we saw that it was really caught. It bobbed and heaved on its side there in a slow, grinding, uneasy fashion. It had a yoke around its neck, the kind made out of a forked limb to keep a jumper behind fence.

"She shore jumped one fence," one of the men said.

And another: "Well, she done jumped her last one, fer a fack."

Then they began to wonder about whose cow it might be. They decided it must belong to Milt Alley. They said that he had a cow that was a jumper, and kept her in a fenced-in piece of ground up the creek. I had never seen Milt Alley, but I knew who he was. He was a squatter and lived up the hills a way, on a shirt-tail patch of set-on-edge land, in a cabin. He was pore white trash. He had lots of children. I had seen the children at school, when they came. They were thin-faced, with straight, sticky-looking, dough-colored hair, and they smelled something like old sour buttermilk, not because they drank so much buttermilk but because that is the sort of smell which children out of those cabins tend to have. The big Alley boy drew dirty pictures and showed them to the little boys at school.

That was Milt Alley's cow. It looked like the kind of cow he would have, a scrawny, old, sway-backed cow, with a yoke around her neck. I wondered if Milt Alley had another cow.

"Poppa," I said, "do you think Milt Alley has got another cow?"

"You say 'Mr. Alley,'" my father said quietly.

"Do you think he has?"

"No telling," my father said.

Then a big gangly boy, about fifteen, who was sitting on a scraggly little old mule with a piece of croker sack thrown across the saw-tooth spine, and who had been staring at the cow, suddenly said to nobody in particular, "Reckin anybody ever et drownt cow?"

He was the kind of boy who might just as well as not have been the son of Milt Alley, with his faded and patched overalls ragged at the bottom of the pants and the mud-stiff brogans hanging off his skinny, bare ankles at the level of the mule's belly. He had said what he did, and then looked embarrassed and sullen when all the eyes swung at him. He hadn't meant to say it, I am pretty sure now. He would have been too proud to say it, just as Milt Alley would have been too proud. He had just been thinking out loud, and the words had popped out.

There was an old man standing there on the pike, an old man with a white beard. "Son," he said to the embarrassed and sullen boy on the mule, "you live long enough and you'll find a man will eat anything when the time comes."

"Time gonna come fer some folks this year," another man said.

"Son," the old man said, "in my time I et things a man don't like to think on. I was a sojer and I rode with Gin'l Forrest, and them things we et when the time come. I tell you. I et meat what got up and run when you taken out yore knife to cut a slice to put on the fire. You had to knock it down with a carbeen butt, it was so active. That-air meat would jump like a bullfrog, it was so full of skippers."

But nobody was listening to the old man. The boy on the mule turned his sullen sharp face from him, dug a heel into the side of the mule and went off up the pike with a motion which made you think that any second you would hear mule bones clashing inside that lank and scrofulous hide.

"Cy Dundee's boy," a man said, and nodded toward the figure going up the pike on the mule.

"Reckin Cy Dundee's young-uns seen times they'd settle fer drownt cow," another man said.

The old man with the beard peered at them both from his weak, slow eyes, first at one and then at the other. "Live long enough," he said, "and a man will settle fer what he kin git."

Then there was silence again, with the people looking at the red, foam-flecked water.

My father lifted the bridle rein in his left hand, and the mare turned and walked around the group and up the pike. We rode on up to our big gate, where my father dismounted to open it and let me myself ride Nellie Gray through. When he got to the lane that led off from the drive about two hundred yards from our house, my father said, "Grab on." I grabbed on, and he let me down to the ground. "I'm going to ride down and look at my corn," he said. "You go on." He took the lane, and I stood there on the drive and watched him ride off. He was wearing cowhide boots and an old hunting coat, and I thought that that made him look very military, like a picture. That and the way he rode.

I did not go to the house. Instead, I went by the vegetable garden and crossed behind the stables, and headed down for Dellie's cabin. I wanted to go down and play with Jebb, who was Dellie's little boy about two years older than I was. Besides, I was cold. I shivered as I walked, and I had goose-flesh. The mud which crawled up between my toes with every step I took was like ice. Dellie would have a fire, but she wouldn't make me put on shoes and stockings. Dellie's cabin was of logs, with one side, because it was on a slope, set on limestone chunks, with a little porch attached to it, and had a little whitewashed fence around it and a gate with plow-points on a wire to clink when somebody came in, and had two big white oaks in the yard and some flowers and a nice privy in the back with some honeysuckle growing over it. Dellie and Old Jebb, who was Jebb's father and who lived with Dellie and had lived with her for twenty-five years even if they never had got married, were careful to keep everything nice around their cabin. They had the name all over the community for being clean and clever Negroes. Dellie and Jebb were what they used to call "white-folks' niggers." There was a big difference between their cabin and the other two cabins farther down where the other tenants lived. My father kept the other cabins weatherproof, but he couldn't undertake to go down and pick up after the litter they strewed. They didn't take the trouble to have a vegetable patch like Dellie and Jebb or to make preserves from wild plum, and jelly from crab apple the way Dellie did. They were shiftless, and my father was always threatening to get shed of them. But he never did. When they finally left, they just up and left on their own, for no reason, to go and be shiftless somewhere else. Then some more came. But meanwhile they lived down there, Matt Rawson and his family, and Sid Turner and his, and I played with their children all over the farm when they weren't working. But when I wasn't around they were mean sometimes to Little Jebb. That was because the other tenants down there were jealous of Dellie and Jebb.

I was so cold that I ran the last fifty yards to Dellie's gate. As soon as I had entered the yard, I saw that the storm had been hard on Dellie's flowers. The yard was, as I have said, on a slight slope, and the water running across had gutted the flower beds and washed out all the good black woods-earth which Dellie had brought in. What little grass there was in the yard was plastered sparsely down on the ground, the way the drainage water had left it. It reminded me of the way the fluff was plastered down on the skin of the drowned chicks that the strange man had been picking up, up in my mother's chicken yard.

I took a few steps up the path to the cabin, and then I saw that the drainage water had washed a lot of trash and filth out from under Dellie's house. Up toward the porch, the ground was not clean any more. Old pieces of rag, two or three rusted cans, pieces of rotten rope, some hunks of old dog dung, broken glass, old paper, and all sorts of things like that had washed out from under Dellie's house to foul her clean yard. It looked just as bad as the yards of the other cabins, or worse. It was worse, as a matter of fact, because it was a surprise. I had never thought of all that filth being under Dellie's house. It was not anything against Dellie that the stuff had been under the cabin. Trash will get under any house. But I did not think of that when I saw the foulness which had washed out on the ground which Dellie sometimes used to sweep with a twig broom to make nice and clean.

I picked my way past the filth, being careful not to get my bare feet on it, and mounted to Dellie's door. When I knocked, I heard her voice telling me to come in.

It was dark inside the cabin, after the daylight, but I could make out Dellie piled up in bed under a quilt, and Little Jebb crouched by the hearth, where a low fire simmered. "Howdy," I said to Dellie, "how you feeling?"

Her big eyes, the whites surprising and glaring in the black face, fixed on

1087

me as I stood there, but she did not reply. It did not look like Dellie, or act like Dellie, who would grumble and bustle around our kitchen, talking to herself, scolding me or Little Jebb, clanking pans, making all sorts of unnecessary noises and mutterings like an old-fashioned black steam thrasher engine when it has got up an extra head of steam and keeps popping the governor and rumbling and shaking on its wheels. But now Dellie just lay up there on the bed, under the patch-work quilt, and turned the black face, which I scarcely recognized, and the glaring white eyes to me.

"How you feeling?" I repeated.

"I'se sick," the voice said croakingly out of the strange black face which was not attached to Dellie's big, squat body, but stuck out from under a pile of tangled bedclothes. Then the voice added: "Mighty sick."

"I'm sorry," I managed to say.

The eyes remained fixed on me for a moment, then they left me and the head rolled back on the pillow. "Sorry," the voice said, in a flat way which wasn't question or statement of anything. It was just the empty word put into the air with no meaning or expression, to float off like a feather or a puff of smoke, while the big eyes, with the whites like the peeled white of hard-boiled eggs, stared at the ceiling.

"Dellie," I said after a minute, "there's a tramp up at the house. He's got a knife."

She was not listening. She closed her eyes.

I tiptoed over to the hearth where Jebb was and crouched beside him. We began to talk in low voices. I was asking him to get out his train and play train. Old Jebb had put spool wheels on three cigar boxes and put wire links between the boxes to make a train for Jebb. The box that was the locomotive had the top closed and a length of broom stick for a smoke stack. Jebb didn't want to get the train out, but I told him I would go home if he didn't. So he got out the train, and the colored rocks, and fossils of crinoid stems, and other junk he used for the load, and we began to push it around, talking the way we thought trainmen talked, making a chuck-chucking sound under the breath for the noise of the locomotive and now and then uttering low, cautious toots for the whistle. We got so interested in playing train that the toots got louder. Then, before he thought, Jebb gave a good, loud *toot-toot*, blowing for a crossing.

"Come here," the voice said from the bed.

Jebb got up slow from his hands and knees, giving me a sudden, naked, inimical look.

"Come here!" the voice said.

Jebb went to the bed. Dellie propped herself weakly up on one arm, muttering, "Come closer."

Jebb stood closer.

"Last thing I do, I'm gonna do it," Dellie said. "Done tole you to be quiet."

Then she slapped him. It was an awful slap, more awful for the kind of weakness which it came from and brought to focus. I had seen her slap Jebb before, but the slapping had always been the kind of easy slap you would expect from a good-natured, grumbling Negro woman like Dellie. But this was different. It was awful. It was so awful that Jebb didn't make a sound. The

1088

tears just popped out and ran down his face, and his breath came sharp, like gasps.

Dellie fell back. "Cain't even be sick," she said to the ceiling. "Git sick and they won't even let you lay. They tromp all over you. Cain't even be sick." Then she closed her eyes.

I went out of the room. I almost ran getting to the door, and I did run across the porch and down the steps and across the yard, not caring whether or not I stepped on the filth which had washed out from under the cabin. I ran almost all the way home. Then I thought about my mother catching me with the bare feet. So I went down to the stables.

I heard a noise in the crib, and opened the door. There was Big Jebb, sitting on an old nail keg, shelling corn into a bushel basket. I went in, pulling the door shut behind me, and crouched on the floor near him. I crouched there for a couple of minutes before either of us spoke, and watched him shelling the corn.

He had very big hands, knotted and grayish at the joints, with calloused palms which seemed to be streaked with rust with the rust coming up between the fingers to show from the back. His hands were so strong and tough that he could take a big ear of corn and rip the grains right off the cob with the palm of his hand, all in one motion, like a machine. "Work long as me," he would say, "and the good Lawd'll give you a hand lak cass-ion won't nuthin' hurt." And his hands did look like cast iron, old cast iron streaked with rust.

He was an old man, up in his seventies, thirty years or more older than Dellie, but he was strong as a bull. He was a squat sort of man, heavy in the shoulders, with remarkably long arms, the kind of build they say the river natives have on the Congo from paddling so much in their boats. He had a round bullet-head, set on powerful shoulders. His skin was very black, and the thin hair on his head was now grizzled like tufts of old cotton batting. He had small eyes and a flat nose, not big, and the kindest and wisest old face in the world, the blunt, sad, wise face of an old animal peering tolerantly out on the goings-on of the merely human creatures before him. He was a good man, and I loved him next to my mother and father. I crouched there on the floor of the crib and watched him shell corn with the rusty cast-iron hands, while he looked down at me out of the little eyes set in the blunt face.

"Dellie says she's mighty sick," I said.

"Yeah," he said.

"What's she sick from?"

"Woman-mizry," he said.

"What's woman-mizry?"

"Hit comes on 'em," he said. "Hit just comes on 'em when the time comes."

"What is it?"

"Hit is the change," he said. "Hit is the change of life and time."

"What changes?"

"You too young to know."

"Tell me."

"Time come and you find out everthing."

I knew that there was no use in asking him any more. When I asked him things and he said that, I always knew that he would not tell me. So I continued to crouch there and watch him. Now that I had sat there a little while, I was cold again.

"What you shiver fer?" he asked me.

"I'm cold. I'm cold because it's blackberry winter," I said.

"Maybe 'tis and maybe 'tain't," he said.

"My mother says it is."

"Ain't sayen Miss Sallie doan know and ain't sayen she do. But folks doan know everthing."

"Why isn't it blackberry winter?"

"Too late fer blackberry winter. Blackberries done bloomed."

"She said it was."

"Blackberry winter just a leetle cold spell. Hit come and then hit go away, and hit is growed summer of a sudden lak a gunshot. Ain't no tellen hit will go way this time."

"It's June," I said.

"June," he replied with great contempt. "That what folks say. What June mean? Maybe hit is come cold to stay."

"Why?"

"Cause this-here old yearth is tahrd. Hit is tahrd and ain't gonna perduce. Lawd let hit come rain one time forty days and forty nights, 'cause He wus tahrd of sinful folks. Maybe this-here old yearth say to the Lawd, Lawd, I done plum tahrd, Lawd, lemme rest. And Lawd say, Yearth, you done yore best, you give 'em cawn and you give 'em taters, and all they think on is they gut, and, Yearth, you kin take a rest."

"What will happen?"

"Folks will eat up everthing. The yearth won't perduce no more. Folks cut down all the trees and burn 'em cause they cold, and the yearth won't grow no more. I been tellen 'em. I been tellen folks. Sayen, maybe this year, hit is the time. But they doan listen to me, how the yearth is tahrd. Maybe this year they find out."

"Will everything die?"

"Everthing and everbody, hit will be so."

"This year?"

"Ain't no tellen. Maybe this year."

"My mother said it is blackberry winter," I said confidently, and got up.

"Ain't sayen nuthin' agin Miss Sallie," he said.

I went to the door of the crib. I was really cold now. Running, I had got up a sweat and now I was worse.

I hung on the door, looking at Jebb, who was shelling corn again.

"There's a tramp came to the house," I said. I had almost forgotten the tramp.

"Yeah."

"He came by the back way. What was he doing down there in the storm?"

"They comes and they goes," he said, "and ain't no tellen."

"He had a mean knife."

"The good ones and the bad ones, they comes and they goes. Storm or sun, light or dark. They is folks and they comes and they goes lak folks."

I hung on the door, shivering.

He studied me a moment, then said, "You git on to the house. You ketch yore death. Then what yore mammy say?"

I hesitated.

"You git," he said.

When I came to the back yard, I saw that my father was standing by the back porch and the tramp was walking toward him. They began talking before I reached them, but I got there just as my father was saying, "I'm sorry, but I haven't got any work. I got all the hands on the place I need now. I won't need any extra until wheat thrashing."

The stranger made no reply, just looked at my father.

My father took out his leather coin purse, and got out a half-dollar. He held it toward the man. "This is for half a day," he said.

The man looked at the coin, and then at my father, making no motion to take the money. But that was the right amount. A dollar a day was what you paid them back in 1910. And the man hadn't even worked half a day.

Then the man reached out and took the coin. He dropped it into the right side pocket of his coat. Then he said, very slowly and without feeling: "I didn't want to work on your ——— farm."

He used the word which they would have frailed me to death for using.

I looked at my father's face and it was streaked white under the sunburn. Then he said, "Get off this place. Get off this place or I won't be responsible."

The man dropped his right hand into his pants pocket. It was the pocket where he kept the knife. I was just about to yell to my father about the knife when the hand came back out with nothing in it. The man gave a kind of twisted grin, showing where the teeth had been knocked out above the new scar. I thought that instant how maybe he had tried before to pull a knife on somebody else and had got his teeth knocked out.

So now he just gave that twisted, sickish grin out of the unmemorable, grayish face, and then spat on the brick path. The glob landed just about six inches from the toe of my father's right boot. My father looked down at it, and so did I. I thought that if the glob had hit my father's boot something would have happened. I looked down and saw the bright glob, and on one side of it my father's strong cowhide boots, with the brass eyelets and the leather thongs, heavy boots splashed with good red mud and set solid on the bricks, and on the other side the pointed-toe, broken, black shoes, on which the mud looked so sad and out of place. Then I saw one of the black shoes move a little, just a twitch first, then a real step backward.

The man moved in a quarter circle to the end of the porch, with my father's steady gaze upon him all the while. At the end of the porch, the man reached up to the shelf where the wash pans were to get his little newspaper-wrapped parcel. Then he disappeared around the corner of the house and my father mounted the porch and went into the kitchen without a word.

I followed around the house to see what the man would do. I wasn't afraid of him now, no matter if he did have the knife. When I got around in front, I saw him going out the yard gate and starting up the drive toward the pike. So I ran to catch up with him. He was sixty yards or so up the drive before I caught up.

I did not walk right up even with him at first, but trailed him, the way a kid

1091

will, about seven or eight feet behind, now and then running two or three steps in order to hold my place against his longer stride. When I first came up behind him, he turned to give me a look, just a meaningless look, and then fixed his eyes up the drive and kept on walking.

When we had got around the bend in the drive which cut the house from sight, and were going along by the edge of the woods, I decided to come up even with him. I ran a few steps, and was by his side, or almost, but some feet off to the right. I walked along in this position for a while, and he never noticed me. I walked along until we got within sight of the big gate that let on the pike.

Then I said: "Where did you come from?"

He looked at me then with a look which seemed almost surprised that I was there. Then he said, "It ain't none of yore business."

We went on another fifty feet.

Then I said, "Where are you going?"

He stopped, studied me dispassionately for a moment, then suddenly took a step toward me and leaned his face down at me. The lips jerked back, but not in any grin, to show where the teeth were knocked out and to make the scar on the lower lip come white with the tension.

He said: "Stop following me. You don't stop following me and I cut yore throat, you little son-of-a-bitch."

Then he went on to the gate, and up the pike.

That was thirty-five years ago. Since that time my father and mother have died. I was still a boy, but a big boy, when my father got cut on the blade of a mowing machine and died of lockjaw. My mother sold the place and went to town to live with her sister. But she never took hold after my father's death, and she died within three years, right in middle life. My aunt always said, "Sallie just died of a broken heart, she was so devoted." Dellie is dead, too, but she died, I heard, quite a long time after we sold the farm.

As for Little Jebb, he grew up to be a mean and ficey Negro. He killed another Negro in a fight and got sent to the penitentiary, where he is yet, the last I heard tell. He probably grew up to be mean and ficey from just being picked on so much by the children of the other tenants, who were jealous of Jebb and Dellie for being thrifty and clever and being white-folks' niggers.

Old Jebb lived forever. I saw him ten years ago and he was about a hundred then, and not looking much different. He was living in town then, on relief—that was back in the Depression—when I went to see him. He said to me: "Too strong to die. When I was a young feller just comen on and seen how things wuz, I prayed the Lawd. I said, Oh, Lawd, gimme strength and meke me strong fer to do and to in-dure. The Lawd hearkened to my prayer. He give me strength. I was in-duren proud fer being strong and me much man. The Lawd give me my prayer and my strength. But now He done gone off and fergot me and left me alone with my strength. A man doan know what to pray fer, and him mortal."

1092   Jebb is probably living yet, as far as I know.

That is what has happened since the morning when the tramp leaned his face down at me and showed his teeth and said: "Stop following me. You don't stop following me and I cut yore throat, you little son-of-a-bitch." That was what he said, for me not to follow him. But I did follow him, all the years. (1947)

The names of those authors represented by selections appear in **boldface;** the numerals in boldface following the name of the author refer to the pages on which his biographical sketch and selections appear.

Selections which are reprinted in this book are listed in ***boldface italics;*** the numerals in boldface following a title refer to the pages on which the selection itself may be found.

1095

1097

1099

1103

1105